D1645528

WEST HAM UNITED
THE ELITE ERA
– A Complete Record –

DESERT ISLAND FOOTBALL HISTORIES	ISBN
Aberdeen: A Centenary History 1903-2003	978-1-874287-57-5
Aberdeen: Champions of Scotland 1954-55	978-1-874287-65-0
Aberdeen: The European Era	978-1-905328-32-1
Bristol City: The Modern Era – A Complete Record	978-1-905328-27-7
Bristol City: The Early Years 1894-1915	978-1-874287-74-2
Bristol Rovers: The Bert Tann Era	978-1-905328-37-6
Cambridge United: The League Era – A Complete Record	978-1-905328-06-2
Cambridge United: 101 Golden Greats	978-1-874287-58-2
Carlisle United: A Season in the Sun 1974-75	978-1-905328-21-5
The Story of the Celtic 1888-1938	978-1-874287-15-5
Chelsea: Champions of England 1954-55	978-1-874287-94-0
Colchester United: Graham to Whitton – A Complete Record	978-1-905328-35-2
Colchester United: From Conference to Championship	978-1-905328-28-4
Coventry City at Highfield Road 1899-2005	978-1-905328-11-6
Coventry City: The Elite Era – A Complete Record	978-1-874287-83-4
Coventry City: An Illustrated History	978-1-874287-59-9
Derby County: Champions of England 1971-72, 1974-75	978-1-874287-98-8
Dundee: Champions of Scotland 1961-62	978-1-874287-86-5
Dundee United: Champions of Scotland 1982-83	978-1-874287-99-5
History of the Everton Football Club 1878-1928	978-1-874287-14-8
Halifax Town: From Ball to Lillis – A Complete Record	978-1-874287-26-1
Hereford United: The League Era – A Complete Record	978-1-874287-91-9
Hereford United: The Wilderness Years 1997-2006	978-1-905328-22-2
Huddersfield Town: Champions of England 1923-1926	978-1-874287-88-9
Ipswich Town: The Modern Era – A Complete Record	978-1-905328-24-6
Ipswich Town: Champions of England 1961-62	978-1-874287-63-6
The Old Farm: Ipswich Town v Norwich City	978-1-905328-12-3
Kilmarnock: Champions of Scotland 1964-65	978-1-874287-87-2
Leyton Orient: A Season in the Sun 1962-63	978-1-905328-05-5
Luton Town at Kenilworth Road: A Century of Memories	978-1-905328-10-9
Luton Town: The Modern Era – A Complete Record	978-1-874287-90-2
Luton Town: An Illustrated History	978-1-874287-79-7
Manchester United's Golden Age 1903-1914: Dick Duckworth	978-1-874287-92-6
The Matt Busby Chronicles: Manchester United 1946-69	978-1-874287-96-4
Motherwell: Champions of Scotland 1931-32	978-1-874287-73-5
Northampton Town: A Season in the Sun 1965-66	978-1-905328-01-7
Norwich City: The Modern Era – A Complete Record	978-1-874287-67-4
Peterborough United: The Modern Era – A Complete Record	978-1-874287-33-9
Peterborough United: Who's Who?	978-1-874287-48-3
Plymouth Argyle: The Modern Era – A Complete Record	978-1-874287-54-4
Plymouth Argyle: 101 Golden Greats	978-1-874287-64-3
Plymouth Argyle: Snakes & Ladders – Promotions and Relegations	978-1-905328-34-5
Portsmouth: The Modern Era	978-1-905328-08-7
Portsmouth: From Tindall to Ball – A Complete Record	978-1-874287-25-4
Portsmouth: Champions of England – 1948-49 & 1949-50	978-1-874287-50-6
The Story of the Rangers 1873-1923	978-1-874287-95-7
The Romance of the Wednesday 1867-1926	978-1-874287-17-9
Seventeen Miles from Paradise: Saints v Pompey	978-1-874287-89-6
The Southend United Chronicles 1906-2006	978-1-905328-18-5
Stoke City: The Modern Era – A Complete Record	978-1-874287-76-6
Stoke City: 101 Golden Greats	978-1-874287-55-1
Potters at War: Stoke City 1939-47	978-1-874287-78-0
Swansea City: Seasons in the Sun	978-1-905328-02-4
Third Lanark: Champions of Scotland 1903-04	978-1-905328-03-1
Tottenham Hotspur: Champions of England 1950-51, 1960-61	978-1-874287-93-3
West Bromwich Albion: Champions of England 1919-1920	978-1-905328-04-8
West Ham: From Greenwood to Redknapp	978-1-874287-19-3
West Ham: The Elite Era – A Complete Record	978-1-905328-33-8
Hammers Through the Looking Glass	978-1-905328-23-9
Wimbledon: From Southern League to Premiership	978-1-874287-09-4
Wimbledon: From Wembley to Selhurst	978-1-874287-20-9
Wimbledon: The Premiership Years	978-1-874287-40-7
Wrexham: The European Era – A Complete Record	978-1-874287-52-0
England's Quest for the World Cup – A Complete Record	978-1-905328-16-1
Scotland: The Quest for the World Cup – A Complete Record	978-1-897850-50-3
Ireland: The Quest for the World Cup – A Complete Record	978-1-897850-80-0
Blinded by the Lights: A History of Night Football in England	978-1-905328-13-0
Red Dragons in Europe – A Complete Record	978-1-874287-01-8
The Book of Football: A History to 1905-06	978-1-905328-00-4
Football's Twelve Apostles: The Making of the League 1886-1889	978-1-905328-09-3
Football's War & Peace: The Tumultuous Season of 1946-47	978-1-874287-70-4
Freestaters: Republic of Ireland 1921-39	978-1-905328-36-9

WEST HAM UNITED

THE ELITE ERA

— A Complete Record —

(3rd Edition)

Series Editor: Clive Leatherdale

Text by

John Helliar

OFFICIAL HISTORIAN TO WEST HAM UNITED

Statistics by

Clive Leatherdale

DESERT ISLAND BOOKS LIMITED

Third Edition published in 2007
Second Edition published in 2005
First Edition published in 2000

DESERT ISLAND BOOKS LIMITED
7 Clarence Road, Southend-on-Sea, Essex SS1 1AN
United Kingdom
www.desertislandbooks.com

British Library Cataloguing-in-Publication Data
A catalogue record for this book is available from the British Library

ISBN: 978-1-905328-33-8

Printed in Great Britain
by
Biddles Ltd, King's Lynn

John Helliar wishes to thank the following for the use of various photographs reproduced in this book:
Steve Bacon, Arthur Edwards, Arthur Smith, Peter Hampshire, Arthur Wilson, M Press, West Ham United FC.
Particular thanks to Steve Bacon for photographs from 2005-06 and 2006-07

CONTENTS

			Page
Author's Note			viii
Introduction			10
1. FROM FENTON TO GREENWOOD – 1958-1961			
1958-59			13
MATCH OF THE SEASON	v	Wolves	15
1959-60			17
MATCH OF THE SEASON	v	Huddersfield (FAC)	19
1960-61			21
MATCH OF THE SEASON	v	Arsenal	23
2. THE GLORY YEARS – 1961-1966			
1961-62			25
MATCH OF THE SEASON	v	Manchester United	27
1962-63			29
MATCH OF THE SEASON	v	Tottenham	31
1963-64			33
MATCH OF THE SEASON	v	Manchester United (FAC)	36
1964-65			38
MATCH OF THE SEASON	v	TSV Munich (ECWC)	41
1965-66			43
MATCH OF THE SEASON	v	West Brom (LC)	45
3. THE WILDERNESS YEARS – 1966-1974			
1966-67			47
MATCH OF THE SEASON	v	Leeds (LC)	49
1967-68			51
MATCH OF THE SEASON	v	Tottenham	53
1968-69			55
MATCH OF THE SEASON	v	Sunderland	57
1969-70			59
MATCH OF THE SEASON	v	Manchester City	61
1970-71			63
MATCH OF THE SEASON	v	Blackpool (FAC)	67
1971-72			68
MATCH OF THE SEASON	v	Stoke (LC)	71
1972-73			73
MATCH OF THE SEASON	v	Stockport (LC)	75
1973-74			77
MATCH OF THE SEASON	v	Hereford (FAC)	79

4. FROM WEMBLEY TO WEMBLEY – 1974-1980

1974-75			81
Match of the Season	v	Fulham (FAC)	83
1975-76			85
Match of the Season	v	Anderlecht (ECWC)	88
1976-77			90
Match of the Season	v	Manchester United	92
1977-78			94
Match of the Season	v	Bristol City	97
1978-79			98
Match of the Season	v	Wrexham	100
1979-80			102
Match of the Season	v	Arsenal (FAC)	104

5. LET THE GOOD TIMES ROLL – 1980-1986

1980-81			107
Match of the Season	v	Liverpool (LC)	110
1981-82			112
Match of the Season	v	Tottenham	114
1982-83			116
Match of the Season	v	Tottenham	119
1983-84			120
Match of the Season	v	Bury (LC)	122
1984-85			124
Match of the Season	v	Ipswich	127
1985-86			128
Match of the Season	v	Newcastle	131

6. TURMOIL AT THE BOLEYN – 1986-1990

1986-87			133
Match of the Season	v	Arsenal	136
1987-88			138
Match of the Season	v	Chelsea	140
1988-89			142
Match of the Season	v	Liverpool (LC)	145
1989-90			147
Match of the Season	v	Oldham (LC)	151

7. 'BONDS' AND 'BONDS' – 1990-1994

1990-91			152
Match of the Season	v	Notts County	155
1991-92			157
Match of the Season	v	Manchester United	160
1992-93			162
Match of the Season	v	Wolves	165
1993-94			166
Match of the Season	v	Ipswich	169

8. REDKNAPP'S FOREIGN LEGION – 1994-2001

1994-95			170
Match of the Season	v	Blackburn	174
1995-96			175
Match of the Season	v	Sheffield Wednesday	178
1996-97			179
Match of the Season	v	Tottenham	183

1997-98 184
MATCH OF THE SEASON v Arsenal (FAC) 187
1998-99 189
MATCH OF THE SEASON v Liverpool 193
1999-00 194
MATCH OF THE SEASON v Bradford City 197
2000-01 199
MATCH OF THE SEASON v Manchester United (FAC) 203

9. TO THE DEPTHS AND BACK – 2001-2007
2001-02 204
MATCH OF THE SEASON v Manchester United 207
2002-03 209
MATCH OF THE SEASON v Bolton 213
2003-04 215
MATCH OF THE SEASON v West Brom 220
2004-05 222
MATCH OF THE SEASON v Preston (P/O) 257
2005-06 259
MATCH OF THE SEASON v Liverpool (FAC) 267
2006-07 269
MATCH OF THE SEASON v Tottenham 278

SEASONAL SUMMARIES 279

AUTHOR'S NOTE

In the first edition of this book (2000) I wrote: 'They say that "everybody has a book in them". Well, if that is true, this is mine.'

The fact that my thoughts about, and perceptions of, the events associated with West Ham United over almost five decades have been published at all is due entirely to Clive Leatherdale of Desert Island Books. Although I have contributed various items on a regular basis to the Hammers' club programme and other publications issued since 1992, I would never have presumed that I was capable of writing such a history. I arrived on the football press scene somewhat by default, owing to my family's involvement with what was simply our local soccer team. That involvement dates back to my great grandfather, who, as a brassfounder, worked for the Thames Ironworks at Canning Town when they formed a soccer team around 1895. With the birth of West Ham United FC in 1900 that association continued. A few years later when my great grandfather started the family printing firm, the connection deepened further when he began working for the club on a commercial basis, supplying many of their printing requirements. Our family's involvement with the Hammers has endured ever since.

Some years after World War II, my father Jack began writing match reports and other items for the club programme. With the Hammers' promotion to the First Division in 1958 my father was asked to develop the concept of a new-style programme. From then until 1983 he was its editor, writer, compiler, designer, as well as printer via the family business. Over the years he had become an ardent follower of the team, travelling not only around this country and continental Europe but also to America. He also undertook the duties of press-room steward on match days. When in 1983 the club decided that new printers should undertake the production of the matchday programme, my father, although no longer editor, continued to write for the new publication. Even before I joined the family business I had helped him to run the press-room at Upton Park and upon his death in 1992 I was asked by the then club secretary, Tom Finn, if I would take over the duties he had performed.

I first met Clive Leatherdale in the press-room at Upton Park, largely through his work on the statistical predecessor to this book – *From Greenwood to Redknapp* (1997) – which he has updated for this publication. He then massaged my ego by suggesting that I should write a season by season history to compliment those bare match details. It has been a seemingly endless journey of reminiscences and recollections as I have delved through the comprehensive press-cuttings books that my father compiled since the Hammers returned to the old First Division and from which this book takes it's title – 'The Elite Era'.

I was perhaps naive when accepting Clive's challenge as the complexity and magnitude of all that has happened during the last 49 years at Upton Park only became apparent the further I delved into the archives. Many times I felt as if I could not continue as the sheer volume of facts flowed onto my blank computer screen. Through it all Clive, as my editor and publisher, has been a constant source of inspiration as he has boosted my confidence by praising my meagre efforts, gently bullied and chided me as I missed every deadline he set, and finally put into a sensible format my often over-elaborate descriptions and thoughts. His patience has verged on the saintly for what must have been for him many frustrating months.

Finally, once again and as always, thanks to my wife Betty who has been extremely understanding during the time it has taken to finish what for me became a marathon undertaking. During the 1970s and early 80s she also made the pilgrimage to Upton Park on matchdays as she developed a keen interest in football whilst watching the Hammers.

NB. The narrative for the 2006-07 season was written by my co-author Clive Leatherdale.

DEDICATION

I would like to dedicate this third edition to the two people who have been the most influential in my life – my wife Betty and my father Jack. I can only sum up his effect on my life with the following: 'He cast a giant shadow that was at times all-enveloping and for many years after his death I felt his influence directing me in the path I was pursuing through life.' If that sentiment sounds morbid or ungrateful it is not meant to be, as I loved him dearly and in completing this book he has been my constant inspiration as I have re-read so many of his own words written in the four decades between the 1950s up until his death in 1992. Since then, he has been constantly in my thoughts, as well as my inspiration in much of what I have achieved in life. To my wife I can only express my constant gratitude 'just being there and supporting both myself and our three children in all we do'.

JOHN HELLIAR

INTRODUCTION

West Ham United FC arose in July 1900 not so much from the demise of its predecessor, Thames Ironworks FC, as from the realisation by those associated with the shipbuilding conglomerate that professionalism in the world of football was here to stay.

The dawning of the twentieth century proved, in retrospect, a watershed for many of the ideals associated with the 'golden age' of British history, which had seen many wealthy Victorians attempt to improve the lot of their fellow citizens.

Those ideals of helping one's fellow man had been personified in London's East End – especially the West Ham, Canning Town, Custom House and Silvertown area – by Arnold F Hills, the owner of the family business from which the original club had taken its name. Hills was a wealthy Victorian, the product of a family with inherited money, and had been educated at Harrow and Oxford. A university blue in athletics, he had been the English mile champion as well as playing top quality football before joining the family business. During his early years in industry, Hills lived in a small house a short distance from the company's shipyards, situated on the River Lea. Thus he saw at first hand the deprivation that blighted the lives of his employees and their families. The environs in which they lived contained many of the problems – overcrowding, filth, poor sanitation and lack of open play areas – that were the scourge of other similar areas of London, in what was considered the hub of the world's greatest and richest empire.

Arnold Hills was a militant advocate of temperance as well as being a vegetarian and a crusader for 'good causes'. He introduced these ideals into the lives of his employees by forming societies and clubs for the improvement of his fellow workers. To this end, leisure activities such as a string band, brass band, choral society, drama club, temperance society – as well as clubs associated with sporting pursuits such as rowing, cycling, athletics, cricket and football – were formed under his patronage. All were linked with another of his personal tenets – 'amateur' – not for monetary gain.

The football club flourished in its first couple of years to such an extent that more famous and longer established soccer clubs within the metropolitan area fell victim to the Ironworkers, who did more than merely hold their own in a number of friendly matches against all-comers.

Such was the team's progress – allied with a move to Hills' purpose-built sporting stadium, the Memorial Grounds – that by the turn of the century the committee running the club talked of turning professional. They had, after all, reinforced their ranks with what their President, Hills himself, described as 'mercenaries'.

This prospect was contrary to all of Hills' ideals, not to mention the sound reasons why he had originally set up the various clubs for the recreational needs of his staff. However, he conceded that such was the broad following that the football club had achieved since its formation, that its days of 'shamateurism' were at an end. Combined with other changes in the business format of the parent company, he proposed that a limited company be formed to run the football club – hence the birth of West Ham United. He did not distance himself entirely from the 'foundling' as he gave financial support to ensure that its future was safeguarded.

Having spent fifteen seasons in the Southern League, in 1919 the club attained League status in an expanded Second Division. Its reputation quickly grew: an appearance in the first Wembley FA Cup final, in 1923, and promotion to the First Division thrust its name across not only the sports sections but also the front pages of the national press. Within a decade the Hammers became victims of the depression and in 1931-32 they finished bottom of the League and were sent back to the Second Division.

The squad of players that Charlie Paynter had assembled by 1939 was in his opinion good enough to return to the First Division – as was demonstrated by their winning of the League War Cup final of 1940. However, by the time League football resumed in 1946 the potential of seven years previously had withered on the vine. Many of the players from that era were elsewhere, or past their peak.

In 1950, the retirement of Charlie Paynter after 50 years' service necessitated the appointment of a successor. Although it was only the third time since the club's inception that the directors had found it necessary to appoint a manager, the return of the prodigal son, Ted Fenton, to Upton Park a year previously meant that the take-over was harmonious. The new man was already in place, as well as being an 'old boy' already acquainted with the atmosphere and traditions of the Boleyn Ground.

Fenton's appointment, however, marked the dawning of a new era at the club. He realised that for many years West Ham United had suffered from its inability to plunge into the transfer market to make big-name signings. The answer, he decided, was to produce home-grown players. Within a short space of time he initiated a youth policy which meant that talented boys from the East London and Essex areas soon found their way to the doors of Upton Park. Although this policy soon proved its worth – with success in local junior leagues, the FA Youth Cup, the Southern Junior Floodlit Cup, and the winning of international youth caps by a number of his young protégés – Fenton knew that this was a long-term policy that would only bear fruit five or ten years into the future. In the meantime, he had to contend with the perennial problem of getting the Hammers back to the top flight of English football. To this end, he had to look to older and more experienced players.

The first seven seasons of Fenton's tenure saw the Hammers finish no higher than eighth, and in five of those campaigns they ended up in the bottom half of the table. And when one takes into account monetary considerations, few at the club saw any reason to expect promotion in 1957-58. For over 25 years, since relegation in 1932, West Ham supporters had dreamt of a return to the First Division, but those dreams (like the 'bubbles' sung about in their anthem) had always faded and died.

The 1957-58 season started in similar vein and it was not until October, coupled with the arrival of centre-forward Vic Keeble, that the team hit promotion form. A run of thirteen games undefeated was only surrendered on Boxing Day, away to Ipswich. Just two more defeats in the next eighteen League games, coupled with a fifth-round exit in the FA Cup (a blessing in disguise), resulted in West Ham United being crowned champions on the final Saturday of the season. They took the title by just one point from Blackburn Rovers.

The success of the first team was mirrored that season by the achievements of the youth team, which not only won the Southern Junior Floodlit Cup for the second successive year – having also reached the final of the FA Youth Cup in 1957 – but likewise earned recognition on the Continent. The youngsters' cultured displays in Belgium against wide-ranging opposition saw them finish joint holders of a tournament trophy.

It had taken many years to come to fruition, but with the depth of experience of the senior players and the aspirations and developing talents of the younger members of the staff, the new season was anticipated with no misplaced optimism.

1

FROM FENTON TO GREENWOOD 1958-1961

LEAGUE DIVISION 1	**1958-59**
Division 1	6th
FA Cup	3rd Round

On winning promotion Ted Fenton, the Hammers' manager, was asked if he would be seeking any new players during the close season. After all, only Vic Keeble had experience of First Division football. Fenton replied that: 'If we didn't get any new players it's probable that we would hold our own.'

When the season actually began his words proved prophetic. His opening line-up contained ten of the team that had played in the championship clinching match four months previously. The eleventh, Bill Lansdowne, had played in seventeen of that season's fixtures. Some 7,000 fans travelled to Portsmouth for the curtain-raiser and were cock-a-hoop as a goal apiece from the prolific strike-force, Keeble and Dick, earned a 2-1 victory. If that served notice of West Ham's credentials, the next two matches emphatically gave warning to the other sides that here was a force to be reckoned with. Two home games the following week saw the current champions, Wolves, and fellow Midland giants Aston Villa beaten. When Ted Fenton took his team back to Molineux, the draw left the Hammers joint top of the table after just four games.

Despite a slip-up at Luton two days later, an emotionally charged Boleyn Ground erupted as the might of Manchester United were taught a footballing lesson. West Ham raced into a three-goal lead with half an hour to go. Although Matt Busby's post-Munich Red Devils pulled two goals back, the win ensured that West Ham looked down from the dizzy heights of the top of the table, having mustered nine points from a possible twelve.

It had been a remarkable return to the First Division in that the Hammers had taken on the cream of English soccer and not been found wanting. Another feature of the Hammers' initial success was that Fenton fielded an unchanged team for the first five games.

An injury to left-half Lansdowne necessitated a forced alteration to Fenton's regular line-up against Manchester United. With two of his other senior wing-halves incapacitated, the choice for the No 6 shirt lay between Malcolm Allison and an untried youngster. Former club skipper Allison had just returned from a long illness that had seen him miss virtually all of the previous season. The fact that Fenton, after consulting with team captain Noel Cantwell, opted instead for young Bobby Moore – who had come through the Youth Section development programme – marked a watershed in the history and development of the club.

Although he had gained international honours at youth level, along with a number of other youngsters at the club, 17-year-old Moore was the first significant product of the youth policy – instigated by Fenton – to break into the first team. He had signed as a professional during the summer, after making seventeen appearances (a record for any one player) for England, whom he had skippered the previous season when they finished runners-up to Italy in the European Youth tournament. Although Moore was to make only five first-team appearances this season, it was obvious to all that he was more than just a player of promise. For Allison it was the beginning of the end of his playing career, as within a few months the tuberculosis that had sidelined him for almost a year finally forced him to hang up his boots.

Like most newly promoted sides, West Ham found it difficult to maintain such an explosive start. In the ensuing months losses outnumbered victories, with six wins, two draws and nine defeats being recorded up to the New Year. Nevertheless, extravagant home wins over Blackburn (6-3) and Portsmouth (6-0), not to mention a Christmas double over Spurs, kept the faithful happy.

A second significant milestone arrived in early November with the signing of Phil Woosnam from neighbours Leyton Orient. At £30,000, the Welsh international was the costliest addition the Hammers had ever made to their ranks. The outlay put to rest the old chestnut that had dogged the club for most of its existence, that West Ham United was a 'selling club'.

Not only was Woosnam an artistic inside-forward, he was also one of the games 'thinking' players. A 26-year-old qualified schoolteacher and graduate, he proved in his time at Upton Park and afterwards that he had a deep understanding of soccer, as well as a profound perception of how the game should be played.

An early FA Cup dismissal at White Hart Lane continued the Hammers' unhappy string of failures in this competition. They had now failed to progress beyond the third or fourth rounds for the eleventh time in thirteen attempts since the end of the War.

DID YOU KNOW?

Although West Ham finished 6th in 1958-59, they had the joint best home record in the division – identical to that of champions Wolverhampton Wanderers.

Just four losses in the final eighteen league fixtures from January onwards resulted in the Hammers hauling themselves back up the table. So much so that with one game to go they were in third place. That 0-1 defeat at Elland Road dumped them back to sixth. That position was, however, much higher than most pundits had predicted at the start of the campaign. To the fans, who had seen a continuance of the electrifying football of the previous season, that first campaign in the higher echelons instilled a belief that their favourites could live with the so called 'big clubs' of English football.

In the week following the completion of the League season the Youth team contested the final of the FA Youth Challenge Cup against Blackburn. Although they drew 1-1 at Upton Park a solitary goal defeat at Ewood Park meant that the Young Hammers were denied for a second time in three years the opportunity of winning what had become the biggest prize in English youth soccer. However, the club's decision to develop its own talent was proving a winner, and was destined to bear fruit in the coming years.

Match of the Season 1958-59

West Ham 2 Wolves 0

Division 1, 25 August 1958

This match stands out for a host of reasons. Primarily, it was the Hammers' first home game played in the First Division after a wait of 26 years, and as such was a momentous occasion in the history of West Ham United. Secondly, the visit of the defending League champions would provide an early test of West Ham's ability to live with the best. Wolves fielded their strongest team, having contemptuously brushed aside Nottingham Forest 5-1 two days earlier. Thirdly, it was for the majority of fans the first occasion they had to salute their heroes since gaining promotion. Fourthly, very few of those in attendance could remember the last time the club had played in the First Division, whilst for ten of the team, apart from the opening day win at Fratton Park, this was only their second experience of soccer in the top grade. Doubtless, if asked, anyone present that evening could elicit any of the above reasons to explain why this fixture was special.

However, with hindsight, perhaps the underlying significance of the Wolves visit can be summed up in the light of what has happened since – namely the enigma that is West Ham United FC. All those who have followed the club or studied its history cannot be but confounded and bewildered by its ability to compete with the best teams in England and Europe, yet on other occasions plumb the depths with heartbreaking performances. The words of its Blowing Bubbles anthem never reflected so aptly the fluctuations in a club's fortunes.

A 37,500 crowd packed into the tight, homely enclosure known as Upton Park. Some had been queuing for five hours for the 7pm kick-off. Up to 7,000 fans were locked out when the game started, many of whom stayed outside to follow the match from the cheers of those inside. One match report the following morning read: 'The unlucky ones missed one of football's great games.'

Time after time the Hammers unleashed rapier thrusts that tore holes in the famed Wolves defence. They were the sort of moves that Wolves themselves had used to scale the peaks of British soccer and carried them into European competition.

For 44 tense minutes the crowd kept up a constant roar of encouragement, the Hammers having on several occasions come within inches of a goal. The right side of the visitors' defence then got into a tangle on the halfway line. In a flash Malcolm Musgrove darted through the gap. Down the left flank he went before passing to Vic Keeble, who crossed into the middle. John Dick collected the ball, evaded a tackle and fired home from six yards. It was the second goal in three days from the lanky Scot.

The Midlanders showed their class as they fought back at the start of the second half, but defending in depth the Hammers weathered the storm before once again cracking open their opponents. Andy Malcolm regained possession before streaking forward and sliding a low pass through to his inside forward, John Smith, who whipped a shot past goalkeeper Malcolm Finlayson.

The final score did not do justice to the richness and merit of the Hammers' win, for as one commentator said afterwards: 'Make no mistake! West Ham will be a power in the land of football if they retain this mood.' Viewed from today, it was perhaps a somewhat prophetic observation.

For the visitors, defeat was but a momentary hiccup. Come May they retained their league title.

LEAGUE DIVISION 1	**1959-60**
Division 1	14th
FA Cup	3rd Round

The close season heralded a change to Upton Park's facilities, with a new entrance leading from Green Street to the main West Stand. Not only was there new access to the seating accommodation in the upper tier, but also to the club offices, situated under the stand. Other parts of the Boleyn Ground, such as the terraces, had more turnstiles installed to alleviate congestion problems the fans had suffered the previous season. There were also new entrances for the players, directors and visiting officials. All this provided proof that chairman Reg Pratt and his co-directors would spare no expense to consolidate West Ham United's position in the top flight.

There was less enterprise with regard to buying players. Ted Fenton made only one excursion into the transfer market, having offloaded several players he had 'listed' in May. It was obvious that the manager had confidence in the squad that had served him well during their initial taste of First Division football.

For the start of the new campaign Fenton was able to field his strongest side, something denied him since the previous January. Vic Keeble and Phil Woosnam returned after cartilage operations whilst keeper Noel Dwyer, signed the previous winter to succeed the ageing Ernie Gregory, was showing the form that in November was to lead to a full international cap for the Republic of Ireland. The two wingers, Grice and Musgrove, had not lost any of their speed whilst the half-back line of Malcolm, Brown and John Smith were as sound as ever. In fact, the form of the 20-year-old Smith would shortly lead him to the verge of England honours.

The hopes and aspirations generated by the Hammers' top-six finish the previous spring were once more in evidence, and such was the team's start to the new campaign that the fans believed this could be the season the championship arrived. Although defeats were sustained against Leeds and Spurs at home and Bolton and Fulham away, by the second Saturday in November, after seventeen fixtures, the Hammers were once again top of the table. Preston, with the same number of points (23), were second because of their inferior goal-average.

The following Saturday, a 3-2 home win, courtesy of a Dick hat-trick, against the champions Wolves – before the largest home attendance (38,000) so far of the season – consolidated West Ham's position. Ken Brown also celebrated being the first Hammer to win an England cap in twenty years after playing in the 2-1 win over Northern Ireland at Wembley the previous Wednesday.

DID YOU KNOW?

West Ham's collapse in 1959-60 was spectacular. Top of the table on 21 November, they kept just one more clean-sheet and avoided relegation by just 4 points.

Nobody was prepared for the events of the last Saturday of November, when a trip to Hillsborough brought a 0-7 thrashing. The Hammers were three goals down in the opening eight minutes and the game was a personal nightmare for Dwyer who looked anything but an international goalkeeper.

Cantwell and his colleagues bounced back with a 4-1 home win, but a sequence of three away defeats was only halted by a victory over Birmingham at Upton Park three days before the New Year.

The loss of Keeble, through a back injury sustained in October, and Dick's inconsistency in front of goal, was beginning to tell. January finished with three League defeats and a replay cup exit, following a draw at Huddersfield. By early February the Hammers were down to tenth, and it was around this time that the popular joke of West Ham being like the Christmas decorations – coming down in January – first entered football folklore.

To alleviate his striker problem, Fenton drafted John Bond into the No 9 shirt and to the delight of the fans 'Muffin' responded with a hat-trick against Chelsea. Two weeks later the Hammers lost 3-5 at home to Newcastle. Newspaper reports suggested that the result had been 'fixed', and although the rumours were proved unfounded Dwyer never played for the first team again.

Just before the transfer deadline, the manager swapped John Smith for the Tottenham striker Dave Dunmore. Many considered the transfer of Smith a great loss but his departure was necessitated by the needs of the rest of the team and in Bobby Moore there was a ready replacement. Dunmore's arrival sparked a home win over Blackburn – who seven days later sought FA Cup glory in a semi-final tie – but the Hammers would win only one more game (against Manchester United) in the nine that remained.

The pre-Christmas promise of an improvement on the previous season was undoubtedly affected by long-term injuries to key players at crucial times and the inexperience of their replacements. With hindsight, the lengthy absences of Dick and Keeble were the main factors in the bubble being burst. They had missed only a handful of games over the previous two seasons, but Dick, with just 24 appearances (eleven goals) and Keeble with fifteen (six goals) were sorely missed. Coupled with only 26 appearances from Dwyer, before his demotion to the reserves, it could be seen that three key areas in the team lacked experience. Left-winger Malcolm Musgrove was top scorer with fifteen goals in 41 appearances, and he was named 'Hammer of the Year'.

During the season the Hammers revived the practice of playing friendlies against foreign opposition. FC Austria of Vienna, UDA Dukla (Prague) and Fluminense of Brazil all came to East London to demonstrate their widely differing skills. In the final weeks of the campaign Ernie Gregory announced he would be retiring at the end of the season after 24 years on the Upton Park staff. Little did he or anyone else realise that it would be another two and a half decades before he actually finally finished serving the Hammers. His new career in coaching and management was about to begin.

Match of the Season 1959-60

West Ham 1 Huddersfield 5

FA Cup, 3rd Round replay, 13 January 1960

The previous Saturday West Ham led at Leeds Road with less than twenty minutes to go. Dick netted four minutes after half-time in a game dominated by defences. Though Noel Dwyer, the Hammers' goalkeeper, had pulled off some good saves, he could do little about Denis Law's equaliser. When the final whistle sounded the home fans were still grumbling about the 80th-minute 'winner' disallowed by the referee, who ruled that Dwyer had been fouled as the ball was dislodged from his grasp before it was netted. Not only the Terriers, but a number of neutral sports reporters also thought the Londoners lucky to still be in the competition.

The replay kicked off at 2pm on a bitter afternoon on a surface that was nearer to an ice-rink than a football pitch. Heavy snow had fallen in the past few days and it had to be heavily sanded to help the players keep their feet. In the event, the game was to all intents won 30 minutes before the start. It was then that the visitors' acting manager, the unknown Eddie Boot, decided that his side should play in rubber-soled boots instead of the conventional leather variety. The West Ham players were allowed to make up their own minds, and most chose wrongly.

For the unfancied, unquoted, homespun Second Division club, the player who caused all the problems was Law. As a 19-year-old inside-forward, he was already a full Scottish international and was rated as a £40,000+ transfer target. Although he never actually scored in this replay, Law gave a performance that was described as 'lethal, bewildering, arrogant and tireless'. It was one of the finest seen for many years in its sheer majesty, as Law massacred a First Division club on its own territory.

Two goals down in the first 25 minutes, the Hammers clawed their way back in the 39th minute. But goals either side of half-time in a three-minute spell put the visitors back in command. A fifth goal from an incredible angle with twenty minutes to go was the icing on the cake for Huddersfield.

If Law's performance had the visiting fans dreaming of Wembley and a promotion challenge, the home supporters could only mutter of the nightmare that described Noel Dwyer's afternoon. As one match reporter commented: 'For Noel – the goalkeeper hailed as Britain's best recently – must take the blame for two and possibly three of the goals that made this a great day for talented Huddersfield.'

I was at school so could not attend the game. But I well remember that afternoon as a 14-year-old walking with some schoolfriends towards Upton Park station to catch the Underground on our way home from our school in Forest Gate. As we turned into Green Street we encountered the thousands streaming down from the opposite direction as they made their way home after the final whistle. They conveyed the news of the score to my eager ears. At first I could not believe what I had heard and so enquired again, only to have my doubts confirmed from another source. One can imagine the ribbing I got from my 'friends' who knew of our family connections with the Hammers, which were as old as the club itself.

When one considers that the West Ham defence was packed with internationally honoured stars, the defeat was a humiliation. The Hammers' rearguard had appeared to offer little resistance and capitulated in front of the horror-struck fans. For a club that had forged its reputation during the first three decades of its existence on a cup-fighting spirit – which had seen it defeat teams from higher divisions, especially during the Hammers' non-league days – the wheel had turned full circle. West Ham now found themselves victims of 'giant-killers' from a lower division. Unfortunately, it was a story that would be repeated time and again in different cup competitions during the next four decades of the club's history. It became a characteristic jinx that would haunt the club even in some of the golden periods of the 60s, 70s and 80s, as well as the Premiership days of the 1990s.

LEAGUE DIVISION 1	**1960-61**
Division 1	16th
League Cup	2nd Round
FA Cup	3rd Round

The death of one of the club's directors saw the appointment of Roland (Ron) Brandon to the board. It was only the third time in a decade that it had seen a new member, sustaining the close-knit family atmosphere for which West Ham were famous. During that period the only vacancies had arisen through natural selection – the demise of a director. As such, once elected it became a 'job for life': it also continued the traditional values of service to the local community, epitomised by the long connections with the club of both the Cearns and Pratt families.

Longevity of service was not confined to directors, as instanced over the past six decades by the likes of Syd King and Charlie Paynter. Now, after 38 years as a player and trainer, Billy Moore retired. Although born in the north-east, Moore had been transferred to Upton Park in 1922 and was the last surviving link between the Cup final and promotion side of 1923 and the championship team of 1958, which he had helped to train. That other long-serving Hammers stalwart, Ernie Gregory, hung up his goalkeeping jersey to join the training staff and continue an association with the club that would endure over half a century.

Two other senior players were also absent for the new season. Medical advice curtailed Vic Keeble's playing career at the age of 29, following a succession of injuries. He was granted a free transfer. Goalkeeper Noel Dwyer's role in the infamous 3-5 home defeat by Newcastle the previous February meant that he never played for the first team again. Although the rumours were never substantiated, such was the cloud hanging over Dwyer that his departure was inevitable. The reasons were summed up in the Hammers' first match programme of the new season: 'We became of the opinion that a change of club would be the fairest way of ensuring Noel's future in soccer, and are certain that he will attain new successes with Swansea Town.'

A visit to Molineux for the opening fixture unveiled yet another shock. The Hammers made soccer history by playing with an experimental 4-2-4 formation. A goal up inside seven minutes against the mighty Wolves – runners-up after two successive championships – West Ham held the upper hand before Ron Flowers headed an equaliser. Three second-half Wolves goals, before a late Phil Woosnam consolation, resulted in a chastening defeat, although watching pundits praised the visitors' new tactics.

DID YOU KNOW?

Contrary to popular belief, Ron Greenwood was not the architect of West Ham's 4-2-4 tactics in 1960-61. He only took charge for the last 4 matches, drawing 3, losing 1.

Manager Fenton, described by some newspaper reports as the 'originator of the plan' afterwards claimed not to be disheartened because 'we know it will take a month or so to sort everything out, but I'm sure it will pay dividends.' Welsh wizard Woosnam, in his analysis, reflected that he, too, was satisfied: Wolves' first two goals were things which happen only once a season, he said, whilst their last two were too soft for words – a broad hint that goalkeeping blunders were to blame. For many years afterwards West Ham followers speculated as to whether it was Fenton or his players who instigated 4-2-4. One rumour suggested that when the manager proposed a try-out of the new continental formation, he was told by his senior pros, 'but we've been playing that way in practice matches for weeks now.'

Once again it was the Hammers' home form that kept them afloat, as on their travels they stumbled from defeat to defeat. It was not until mid-November that a 2-1 win at Maine Road ended a run of twenty away games in twelve months with only one point to show – and that had come in the previous match at Fulham.

In late September, Charlton had played under Upton Park's floodlights on a Monday evening to inaugurate the new League Cup competition. A month later, in the second round, the Hammers tumbled red-faced from the tournament at Fourth Division Darlington. Sadly, it would be a saga repeated too often for comfort over the next 40 years – losing in humiliating fashion to lower division clubs in the various domestic cups.

Dave Dunmore proved to be an able replacement for Keeble – notching fourteen goals before Christmas in 21 League games. These, allied to eleven from winger Malcolm Musgrove and nine from the ever reliable Dick, helped to keep the side in the top half of the table. Two defeats in two days over Christmas against the formidable Spurs, however, highlighted the chasm between the good and the great.

These setbacks were capped by an FA Cup third round replay defeat at Stoke. The ill-tempered affair left West Ham furious that the tie ever went ahead in such icy conditions. But once again it was a side from a lower division who progressed to the next round.

The rot now blighted West Ham's League form. Apart from home wins over Chelsea (3-1), when debutant Harry Obeney scored, and Everton (4-0), when he notched two more, the first three months of 1961 were barren – capped by five successive defeats. The run of losses was not helped by the turmoil caused by Fenton's sudden resignation, the circumstances of which have never been satisfactorily explained.

Dunmore's short stay of just over twelve months at Upton Park ended on transfer deadline day – 16 March – when he moved to Leyton Orient with Alan Sealey arriving in a straight swap. That day a local newspaper ran a banner headline: 'What's Going On?' The accompanying article featured a photo of Ted Fenton but queried his absence. The Hammers' board issued a statement to the effect that Fenton had been suffering from strain and been granted sick leave. His resignation finally ended the saga.

Now desperate for points as they cascaded down the table, rudderless West Ham were grateful for a goalless draw at Highbury on 25 March. Easter brought further respite, a narrow home win over Leicester and a squeaky home draw against bottom-of-the-table Newcastle. Despite the distraction of the coming FA Cup final, Leicester exacted handsome revenge – a 5-1 win at Filbert Street which put the skids under West Ham yet again.

On Tuesday, 11 April 1961 it was announced that Arsenal's head coach Ron Greenwood had been appointed West Ham's manager-coach and would take sole charge of the playing staff. To provide him with full scope in that direction he would be freed of administrative duties, which would be shouldered by the club secretary, Eddie Chapman.

Greenwood's initial bounty was three successive draws, which clawed the team to safety. He tasted defeat for the first time on the last Saturday of the season, when at Upton Park Burnley scored two goals in the closing minutes. The Hammers thus finished sixteenth, just four points clear of relegation.

Match of the Season 1960-61

West Ham 6 Arsenal 0

Division 1, 5 November 1960

This game epitomised the Hammers' early-season form. They were virtually invincible at home – this being their seventh victory out of eight (the other being a 3-3 draw with Blackpool), scoring 30 goals and conceding fourteen – whilst their dismal away form had produced just one point from eight trips – a return matched only by lowly Manchester United.

It was just ten days since Darlington of the Fourth Division had humbled West Ham in the League Cup, so Arsenal arrived at the

Boleyn with justified hopes of some reward. But Guy Fawkes Day saw the Gunners exploded in a goal-rush that finished just one goal short of West Ham's record First Division victory against Arsenal, established in 1927. But for Arsenal's best player – goalkeeper Jack Kelsey – that record would surely have been broken. Although he had no chance with the six that beat him, the Welsh international made a string of saves and cut out numerous cross-balls which might have led to double figures in the final count.

The crowd of 29,375 – the best of the season so far – had hardly settled before Dunmore was gifted a goal in the third minute, thanks to a defensive mistake. Although the Hammers' centre-forward added a second, with a twenty-yard left-foot drive, and rounded off his day with the sixth goal of the afternoon to complete his hat-trick in the last minute, it was Phil Woosnam who grabbed the headlines in the newspaper reports of the match. Despite the quagmire conditions, the Welsh wizard inspired his team-mates with an individual performance that was described by one reporter as 'the best he had ever seen from an inside-forward'. Other than Dunmore's opener, Woosnam engineered openings for four of the remaining five goals – the exception being when he netted himself with twelve minutes to go.

Outstanding displays from the half-back line of Andy Malcolm (who scored his only First Division goal), Ken Brown and Bobby Moore – not to mention a fine handling performance from much-criticised goalkeeper Brian Rhodes – blunted the menace of the Arsenal attack, which boasted the likes of David Herd, Mel Charles and John Barnwell.

For many weeks before and after the match newspaper speculation insisted that Woosnam was for sale, in order that the club might sign a new goalkeeper and a striker. Various reports linked his name with Juventus – where he would have joined his Welsh international colleague John Charles – Wolves, and the Gunners themselves. As Woosnam trudged poker-faced from the pitch, splattered with mud, the fans roared their appreciation of his genius, hoping against hope that he would stay. For the time being they had their wish. Woosnam stayed another two years before finally decamping for Aston Villa. But the seeds of doubt as to whether his transfer value made him expendable, irrespective of his supreme scheming skills, were undoubtedly sown by the rumours that once raised never died.

2

THE GLORY YEARS 1961-1966

LEAGUE DIVISION 1	**1961-62**
Division 1	8th
League Cup	2nd Round
FA Cup	3rd Round

The appointment of Ron Greenwood as manager-coach marked a radical departure by the club. Almost since its birth it had recruited managers and officials from the ranks of former players steeped in the traditions of a club that prided itself on its family connections and which took care of players after their sell-by date. A number of these, such as Ted Fenton, had learnt the trade of coaching and management elsewhere before returning to the Boleyn Ground to resume their association with the Hammers.

Although known throughout the soccer scene because of his position as chief coach at Highbury – which he combined with looking after the England Under-23 team in which Bobby Moore had shone over the last couple of years – Greenwood was to many in East London, especially the fans, an unknown quantity.

Having assessed his players during the closing games of the previous campaign, Greenwood promptly axed eight of them. The most senior of these was winger Mike Grice, who in six years at Upton Park had made 150 appearances (eighteen goals) and had been a regular in the 1958 promotion side.

Grice's departure was offset by the arrival of Ian Crawford from Hearts. He had won every possible club honour north of the border as well as being capped at Under-23 level. Equally at home on either wing, he had scored 30 goals in the past two seasons. Greenwood's other major signing was another Scot, Lawrie Leslie, who solved the club's goalkeeping problem. The 26-year-old arrived from Airdrie for £14,000. He was courageous and fearless and an established Scottish international. As a child, Leslie had been run over by a lorry but had confounded medical opinion that he might never walk again by reaching the top of his profession.

DID YOU KNOW?

The first match in which Bobby Moore, Geoff Hurst and Martin Peters all played together was at Cardiff City on 23 April 1962. West Ham lost 0-3.

As in every close season since the Hammers returned to the First Division, money was injected into ground improvements. In addition to covering the North Bank (now the site of the Centenary Stand) at a cost of £20,000, new floodlights had been installed at a further cost of over £15,000.

Professional football in England in 1961 underwent one of the most momentous and fundamental changes that it had ever experienced when the 'maximum wage' was abolished. Like every other professional football club in England, West Ham had to adjust to the new-found players' power that marked the dawn of a new era in the game.

Another important change was the FA's decision to permit pre-season friendlies against other clubs. For those fans turning up for the public practice match against Charlton, the decision to sign Leslie was viewed with mixed emotions. Although the Hammers triumphed 4-3, the flying Scot's debut was marred by defensive mix-ups that cost his side three goals.

Fears were dispelled five days later when Leslie inspired his team-mates to fight back and share the points with Manchester United in a fast and exhilarating game. Amongst the visitors was Noel Cantwell, making his first playing appearance at Upton Park since his departure for £30,000 the previous November. It was not until the fourth game that Ron Greenwood earned his first victory as Hammers' manager. But it was worth waiting for, as he plotted a 2-1 home win over the reigning champions, Tottenham Hotspur, before a crowd of over 36,000. The stars of that night, in addition to the new floodlights, were Leslie, captain Woosnam, and 19-year-old Alan Sealey, who made amends for previous misses by scoring the winner.

The following month Chelsea were beaten by the same score, also at home, despite the Hammers finishing the game with ten men when Leslie was stretchered off with a head wound. An ill-tempered match was exacerbated by poor refereeing. Some fans invaded the pitch, prompting one newspaper to demand the introduction of fences or moats to prevent re-occurrences.

Although knocked out of the League Cup at home by Aston Villa, by the turn of the year the Hammers were fifth in the League. Two veterans – Dick with seventeen goals and Musgrove ten – were ably assisted by youngster Sealey's ten. The team had rediscovered the goalscoring touch that had eluded them in the latter months of the previous season.

A third round exit from the FA Cup at Plymouth, and a spell of arctic weather were forgotten as League 'doubles' were completed over Villa and Chelsea. But a run of seven games without a win was finally ended only on the last day of March by a solitary goal at West Brom. Mixed fortunes in April resulted in the Hammers finishing eighth, their best position for three years.

During the season Crawford and several younger players enjoyed extended runs in the first team. Tony Scott shared the right-wing spot with Crawford whilst Geoff Hurst emerged at wing-half, as did Martin Peters for the final five games.

The signing of Johnny Byrne in March 1962 proved to be one of the most important that Greenwood was ever to make. The fee, £65,000, with Crystal Palace broke several records, and demonstrated that the directors were not afraid to pay record sums in pursuing the best.

As for young Bobby Moore, he had accumulated a record number of England Youth caps and captained the Under-23 team, and speculation had been rife for a year that he would make his full England debut. It finally arrived during England's South American tour prior to the World Cup finals of 1962.

Match of the Season 1961-62

Manchester United 1 West Ham 2

Division 1, 16 December 1961

Over the decades, every club in England has used Manchester United as the benchmark against which to judge themselves. Often a win against the Mancunians, especially during a poor season, will temporarily serve to gloss over their own team's shortcomings.

This victory over United, however, was important for a number of other reasons. West Ham had once again started strongly, with a top-six place by the end of November, but since their return to the First Division they had suffered a trio of heavy defeats at Old Trafford – 1-4, 3-5 and 1-6. Pre-match forecasts predicted another drubbing, even though Matt Busby's team had got off to a sluggish start to the season. Home wins over Fulham (3-0) and Real Madrid (3-1) suggested Busby's team were on the mend. Those pundits looked likely to be rewarded as West Ham had a twelfth-minute 'goal' disallowed for offside, followed by the home side taking the lead six minutes later with the Hammers defence appealing for a similar decision.

Where previously the Hammers had been prone to crumple when going a goal behind in such circumstances, this particular contest witnessed a new team-spirit and composure under pressure. Leslie pulled off a string of saves in the opening period, including one back-breaking effort after half an hour. The defence was further inspired by Bobby Moore, just back from suspension. Phil Woosnam, although closely marked, initiated many of West Ham's moves from his deep-lying schemer role, combining expertly with centre-forward Ron Tindall. The crowning glory to a true team performance was the explosive goalscoring of the lanky Scotsman, John Dick, who fired home two goals to snatch the points and take his tally to sixteen for the season. But for home keeper Gaskell, Dick might have had another three on a mist-shrouded afternoon that saw him back to the form that had so terrorised defences two and three years previously.

It is perhaps inappropriate to view this win in the context of a solitary victory or just one match in a season. More importantly this success has to be seen in relation to the general position of the Hammers in the League table at that time and the fixtures that were played in the period around it. West Ham had ended the previous month with a 3-1 home win over Everton. A 2-2 draw at Highbury on the first Saturday of December was followed seven days later by a single-goal home victory over Bolton. A week later came the Man U game. This fine run was capped by a 4-2 home trouncing of Wolves on an ice-rink of a pitch two days later. Two goals from Moore, and one each from Musgrove and wing-half Geoff Hurst (his first in League soccer) put the Hammers in second place in the table. It looked as though under Ron Greenwood the team had found the steely underbelly that they had previously lacked.

Unfortunately, in their next match, at home on Boxing Day, the bubble was burst by a 17-year-old virtually unknown visitor. A two-goal West Ham lead melted away on the icy surface as Blackburn Rovers' John Byrom grabbed a fifteen-minute hat-trick. Rovers had conceded twenty goals in their ten previous away games and were rooted in the bottom four. As one newspaper commented: 'Hammers revived all too vividly the memory of recent seasons' bitter experiences when the brilliance of pre-Christmas has soured into New Year despondency.'

LEAGUE DIVISION 1	**1962-63**
Division 1	12th
League Cup	2nd Round
FA Cup	Quarter-finals

June 1962 saw the majority of the Hammers' senior professionals take part in a tour of Southern Rhodesia (what is now Zimbabwe) and Ghana. Favourable press comments included the following: 'The best touring side seen in recent years ... with so much to admire in their ball control, quick short passes and general timing ... a happy, high-spirited bunch; they dress and act like true ambassadors of professional soccer.'

Absentees included Bobby Moore (on World Cup duty with England), Phil Woosnam, who stayed behind for domestic reasons, and Joe Kirkup, who was getting married. Two other notable stay-at-homes were Geoff Hurst and Ron Tindall. They were playing county cricket, which at the time was seen by many pro footballers as a means of supplementing their wages during the close season; not to mention keeping fit.

In September, Alan Hardaker, then Secretary of the Football League, offered his thoughts on the consequences of freeing the maximum wage twelve months previously. 'Another improvement I would like to see this season is in the attitude to the game of a few of the players. Once again the players as a whole have to suffer for the attitude of the few who seem to think there is an unlimited amount of financial gain to be taken from the game for the minimum amount of effort. It is hoped that those few players will realise that in return for those unlimited earnings the clubs and public expect an unlimited return. We have heard so often the phrase "public entertainer". The New Deal has now given the image of the public entertainer to all spectators, and they will expect – whatever the result of any particular game – 90 minutes of entertainment from 22 players on the field every match.'

Although a new name was added to the West Ham board when Brian Cearns joined his two elder brothers, Greenwood imported no new faces into his senior squad – although a certain local boy from Poplar, Harry Redknapp, signed up as an apprentice professional. The season started off with an away defeat at Aston Villa (1-3) followed by two at Upton Park by Wolves (1-4) and Cup holders Spurs (1-6). A goalless draw at League leaders Wolves was followed by another away defeat, against newly promoted Leyton Orient, for whom former Hammer Dave Dunmore scored. One point from five matches plunged West Ham to the foot of the table, in what was one of their worst starts to a season in living memory.

Two days later Liverpool were beaten 1-0. The Hammers' line-up was not decided until shortly before the kick-off as Greenwood rang the changes. Wingers Tony Scott and Malcolm Musgrove were recalled, as was right-back John Bond. It was the fourth player to be reinstated that evening who would have perhaps the greatest impact on, not only the future of the Hammers, but on world soccer in general. By moving Geoff Hurst into the forward line Greenwood sparked one of the most significant role conversions ever achieved in English football. Hurst progressed in the next few years to being one of the most feared and deadly strikers in the world. Although he did not score that evening – Scott netted from Musgrove's free-kick – Hurst looked a natural. His weight, height and strength caused untold problems for the opposing defence and his unselfish running, agility and distribution gave the side much needed power and mobility in attack.

The following Saturday at Maine Road Hurst opened his account in the 6-1 annihilation of fellow strugglers Manchester City. At 4-1 the game was interrupted by a bizarre incident. The City defence stood still, expecting an offside decision, but Musgrove ran on to head in Scott's centre. This so incensed City keeper Bert Trautmann that he dashed after the referee and following an angry exchange of words picked up the ball and booted it into the official's back. Knowing what was coming, the blond-haired German took off his green jersey and threw it on the ground as he walked off.

Two days previously John Dick had been transferred to Brentford. He had been a Hammer for nine seasons, and the £17,500 fee was a then record for a Fourth Division club. After protracted negotiations, in mid-October Greenwood signed Peter Brabrook from Chelsea for £35,000.

In November, fearless Lawrie Leslie broke his left leg against Bolton. In seeking a replacement, Greenwood turned to Luton keeper Jim Standen, whom he had known at Highbury. Another change saw the transfer, finally, of Phil Woosnam, who decided on a move to Aston Villa. His departure opened the door for Ron Boyce, and such were his performances that the media were soon talking of him winning an England Under-23 cap. Malcolm Musgrove, despite being one of West Ham's leading goalscorers, departed for Leyton Orient just before Christmas.

These comings and goings, coupled with the promotion of many younger players – Hurst, Peters, Boyce, Jack Burkett, Eddie Bovington – marked a watershed in Ron Greenwood's management of West Ham. After nearly two years in charge he had by early 1963 assembled the core of the squad which over the next four years would bring trophies to Upton Park.

DID YOU KNOW?

A legend is born. Geoff Hurst began the 1962-63 season at right-half. He finished it as an established centre-forward and as the Hammers' top scorer.

January's fixture-list was lost to the weather but when play resumed the Hammers marched to the quarter-finals of the FA Cup for the first time in seven seasons. The dream ended at Anfield, where commentators agreed that Moore had been inspirational in an eye-catching tactical battle that frustrated the home team and deserved a replay. It had been a different story in the League Cup, where the Hammers surrendered once again on their travels to a team from a lower division – Rotherham, 1-3.

A dozen matches in the final six weeks of the season left West Ham twelfth. Despite playing in less than two thirds of matches, Hurst finished as leading scorer with thirteen League goals. The Youth Section policy, begun some ten years previously, and which had produced over two dozen of the current seniors at the club, was rewarded with its first piece of silverware. At the third attempt, having lost in the finals of 1957 and 59, the Colts won the FA Youth Cup, overcoming a 1-3 deficit from the first leg on Merseyside to beat Liverpool 6-5 on aggregate. Two days later, Harry Redknapp – a member of the team – collected his second winners medal as Chelsea Colts were beaten in the London Minor Cup final.

Match of the Season 1962-63

Tottenham 4 West Ham 4

Division 1, 22 December 1962

This match was the high-point of a number of London derbies in which the Hammers participated during the 1960s. Whether at Upton Park, White Hart Lane, Highbury or Stamford Bridge, the multitudes were often treated to a footballing extravaganza.

A crowd of 44,000, many of them Hammers supporters, forfeited their last-minute Christmas shopping to watch a game that pre-match commentators predicted would result in a comfortable home win. Spurs were second in the table; West Ham fourteenth.

With twenty minutes gone the home side led 2-0; former Hammer John Smith, a last-minute inclusion at right-half, netted in his first appearance of the season, and Dave Mackay slammed home a twenty-yarder with his left foot. Many in the crowd were speculating 'how many' when Martin Peters struck after 30 minutes with a shot from close-range, following a pass from Bobby Moore.

The second half saw an immediate transformation as West Ham abandoned their vain attempt to play defensively and hurled everything into attack. Spurs' hitherto solid defence began to look fragile and within nine minutes Joe Kirkup equalised. Peters' fine effort had been parried to Tony Scott, who saw his drive similarly turned away before Kirkup forced the rebound home. Immediately from the kick-off Tottenham struck again. Jimmy Greaves crossed the ball, which fell awkwardly at Jack Burkett's feet before rebounding into the path of Mackay, who netted. It was bad luck on Burkett, who otherwise had a fine game. Curiously, all five goals so far had been scored by non-forwards.

West Ham drew level again in the 65th minute. An Alan Sealey throw was coolly hooked over his head by Johnny Byrne into the path of Ronnie Boyce, who slid the ball past Spurs keeper Bill Brown. Eight minutes later the turnaround looked complete as Boyce fed the overlapping Burkett. His deep curling cross was hammered home by Scott to give West Ham the lead for the first time in the game.

Now it was Spurs who were out-thought, out-paced and out-manoeuvred. Brown made two improbable saves from Scott and Sealey, whilst Moore netted again, only to be ruled offside. The skills of 'Budgie' Byrne and 'Ticker' Boyce orchestrated West Ham's every move.

One man on the Lilywhites' side, however, had not given up, showing why he was such a dominant force in the game. With just 30 seconds to go, up popped Dave Mackay in the middle of the Hammers penalty area to complete his hat-trick, driving the ball in from ten yards with that famous left foot.

The Hammers doubtless felt they deserved to win but although the spoils were shared they did at least claim the benefit of a moral victory, having stunned Spurs by their fightback. The result helped to eclipse the memory of the home 1-6 thrashing they had received in early August at the hands of Bill Nicholson's Cup holders.

LEAGUE DIVISION 1	**1963-64**
Division 1	14th
League Cup	Semi-finals
FA Cup	Winners

Before May was out West Ham were competing as English representatives in the American International Soccer League. The New York tournament comprised two groups of seven teams, West Ham's being completed by teams from Scotland, Italy, France, West Germany, Mexico and Brazil. The arrival in the Big Apple halfway through of Bobby Moore and Johnny Byrne, who had been on an England tour of Europe, helped the Hammers to top their group. That meant they returned to New York in late July to meet the Poles of Gornik, the other section winners in a two-leg decider in the Randall Islands Stadium – a baseball arena. The first game was played midweek under floodlights before a 10,000 crowd containing many ex-patriot Poles, and finished 1-1. The second was contested on a steamy Sunday afternoon. Geoff Hurst's first-half goal (his ninth of the tournament), coupled with two disallowed Gornik goals in the second, caused tempers among the watching Poles to boil over. A pitch invasion caused injury to the referee and a hold-up of 30 minutes. When the match was finally completed, with no further scoring, Moore was voted the Most Valuable Player of the tournament and received the Dwight D Eisenhower Trophy.

West Ham were now scheduled to meet Dukla Prague in another two-leg tie for the American Challenge Cup, which the Czechs had won for the previous two years. The Dukla team contained six of the Czech national side that had reached the 1962 World Cup final. The first leg was played under floodlights at Soldiers Field, Chicago, before an 11,000 crowd, and was won 1-0 by Dukla. A crowd of 15,000 – the largest of the tournament – turned up the following Sunday afternoon at Randalls Island Stadium for the second leg. Tony Scott's goal was cancelled out by the legendary Josef Masopust, to enable Dukla to retain the trophy.

Ron Greenwood declared: 'Our second game against Dukla was the most perfect technical display I have seen from any British team I have been connected with ... The team gained more experience in ten matches against teams from other nations than the average League player at home gains in 15 years.'

Once the League started, two wins and two draws in their first four games meant the Hammers topped the table, but successive home defeats told a different tale. A 2-1 victory at Anfield – Liverpool's third consecutive home reverse – brought only a fleeting change of fortune, as Shankly's men finished champions.

DID YOU KNOW?

In just five seasons – 1961-62 to 1965-66 – Blackburn Rovers' striker John Byrom scored 12 goals against West Ham. These included three hat-tricks!

A 6-0 home romp against Fourth Division Workington directed the Hammers into the League Cup semi-finals for the first time, but nothing could prepare players or supporters for the events of Boxing Day. Table-toppers Blackburn came to London and inflicted an 8-2 thrashing on Greenwood's men. It entered the record books as the Hammers' worst home defeat and Rovers' best away win.

In those days it was customary to play the same team twice over the holiday period, and at Ewood Park two days later Greenwood proved what a master tactician he was. Bovington replaced Peters with orders to 'put Bryan Douglas out of the game'. This he did in a manner worthy of the man-marking skills of ex-Hammer Andy Malcolm. With Douglas shackled, Rovers fired blanks and West Ham won 3-1.

The victory provided the springboard for a barnstorming FA Cup run. Within a few months West Ham had recovered from their darkest hour to claim Wembley's biggest prize. In the early rounds the Hammers overcame three Second Division teams – Charlton, Leyton Orient, and Swindon to earn a quarter-final home tie against Burnley, who were twelfth in the League, two places above the Hammers at the time. A crowd of 36,651, including England manager Alf Ramsey, saw a thriller that had everybody on their toes as play ebbed and flowed. The Burnley defence thwarted the home forwards during the first half, in which John Connelly's 35-yard dribble had given the visitors a fifteenth-minute lead. After the interval, teenager Sissons grabbed an equaliser from an improbable angle, assisted by an opposing defender who could only help the ball over the line. With the Upton Park roar reverberating around the ground, Johnny Byrne grabbed two goals in a twelve-minute spell that sent the home fans crazy. Ten minutes before the end Burnley pulled a goal back to produce a nail-biting finish.

With hindsight, this match is often taken to mark the moment when the Hammers came of age, exhibiting a ruthless determination that had often been lacking in their make-up. That new-found confidence can be best summed up in the following post-match press comment: 'In football mere ability, alone and unsupported, seldom wins anything. In recent years West Ham, never short of talent, have generally lacked the character to go with it; travelling hopefully they have never really arrived. This year at last it may, one hopes, be different.'

Three days later the two teams met again, this time in a re-arranged league fixture at Turf Moor, and not unsurprisingly the home side gained their revenge against a below par Hammers side missing three of their heroes from the previous Saturday. Since the New Year, League form had been topsy-turvy, with home wins against the eventual champions Liverpool (1-0), Spurs (4-0), who finished fourth, and Sheffield Wednesday (4-3), who finished sixth. Away from home, the story was not quite so good, with defeats registered at Sheffield United, Burnley, Manchester United, Stoke, Bolton, Fulham and Everton. League form was not helped by West Ham's involvement in two cup competitions, which saw them playing an average of a game every four days.

It was in the midst of this hectic period that the Hammers travelled to Leicester for the first leg of the League Cup semi-final. Although losing by the odd goal in seven, West Ham looked good value to progress to the final. The second leg was not played for six weeks, when West Ham were denied a first League Cup final appearance by Gordon Banks and his defenders, who provided the bedrock for Leicester's 2-0 victory.

In the League, the Hammers lost 0-2 at home to a Manchester United side aiming for a League and FA Cup double. Matt Busby's team had qualified for the semis with a win over Sunderland and were now paired with West Ham. As a pre cup-tie indicator, the 0-2 reverse was a non-event. Busby fielded five reserves and therefore won the psychological battle. But the Hammers' performance was so dire that it reminded spectators of the Boxing Day massacre. Seven days later it was a different story as the Hammers defeated the Cup holders to reach their first Wembley appearance since 1940, and their first FA Cup final since the famous 'White Horse' epic of 1923 (Match of the Season covers the Man U semi-final).

Having announced in January that he had no choice but to retire through a persistent leg injury, John Lyall was given a testimonial match on the Monday before the Wembley final with Preston North End. A crowd of 18,000 took the opportunity to turn up, not only to salute their heroes, but also to acknowledge Lyall's contribution since joining the Upton Park groundstaff after leaving school. Little did those fans, or even the affable Lyall himself, realise what a profound effect he would have on the club's fortunes over the next quarter of a century.

Five days later Bobby Moore, who had just won the Football Writers Association nomination as Footballer of the Year, led out his team onto the Wembley turf as the bookies' Cup favourites. Preston had finished third in Division Two, missing out on promotion by five points, and despite their status as underdogs were determined to rescue their season. They twice took the lead and had to suffer the heartache of losing when Ron Boyce hit the winner deep into injury-time, in what many commentators concurred was the most entertaining and dramatic final in a decade.

The following day the East End of London virtually came to a standstill as the Hammers brought home the Cup for the first time in the club's history. For many of the tens of thousands applauding as the team coach slowly edged its way down the Barking Road, the Wembley triumph was the realisation and culmination of all their hopes and dreams. But for Ron Greenwood, it had a greater significance. The FA Cup was but a stepping stone to what he considered would lead to even greater opportunities and prizes for his team – a place in European competition.

Match of the Season 1963-64

Manchester United 1 West Ham 3

FA Cup, semi-final, 14 March 1964

The 1963-64 season has no consensus over its Match of the Season. Of 56 competitive fixtures, any number might have earned that accolade. The FA Cup-tie against Burnley and the final against Preston, not to mention two League Cup semi-finals with Leicester, could all have a case argued for them. In the League, away wins at Anfield, Old Trafford and Ewood Park all made headlines, while – for the masochistic – the shattering home defeat by Blackburn merits pride of place.

The epic quarter-final with Burnley had shown West Ham to possess previously unseen grit, and the semi-final with Manchester United exhibited further steely qualities, belying the reputation of a team that many considered could only play football on the firm, flat pitches of autumn and spring. When West Ham came out of the hat with the Cup holders, many pundits considered the result to be a foregone conclusion, especially when it was decided to stage the match at Hillsborough, much nearer Manchester than London. Travelling northwards by train, car and coach on the morning of the match, Hammers supporters were greeted by rain, rain and more nagging rain. A deluge seemed to be cascading off the Pennines, creating a vista that to the eye was just a giant sea of water. The sight of so much rain – given West Ham's renowned preference for dry pitches – shortened the odds yet further in Manchester's favour. In fact, it was a wonder that the game even started. It was still pouring when the two teams lined up and continued much the same for the next two hours or more.

The first half witnessed narrow escapes at both ends, but showed that against all the forecasts the Hammers were adapting better to the heavy conditions. They had two early scares after the interval but took the lead eleven minutes into the half when Ronnie Boyce fired a 25-yarder into the net. It was now that the Hammers began to show their footballing prowess. Full-back Jack Burkett's curling centre was met by Boyce's expertly timed run, which resulted in a glancing header beyond Gaskell. Twelve minutes from time Manchester hit back via Denis Law, and many held that Man U's tremendous rallying spirit would again prevail. One player, above all, had other ideas. Bobby Moore capped one of his greatest performances by snuffing out an attack and carrying the ball into the opposing half. Fending off two challenges, he somehow kept the ball in play before hitting a perfect pass into the gap vacated by the Manchester pivot, Bill Foulkes, who had moved wide to cover Moore's surge upfield. Hurst tore through the gap vacated by Foulkes to strike the ball wide of Gaskell. For Hurst it was fitting reward for his unceasing efforts in near impossible conditions.

At the final whistle, fists punched the air in delight. West Ham had done what few believed they were equipped to do. The tactical battles in curtailing the genius of Best and Law, the power of Crerand and Setters, and the infinite skills of Bobby Charlton, were all won by Moore, his ten colleagues and the ultimate architect of the triumph – Ron Greenwood.

In the post-match hysteria it was Greenwood who made perhaps the most telling comments when he proclaimed: 'Look at them – this is the greatest day in their lives. I have been proud to be associated with this bunch of youngsters. Now the world and his friend will claim them. I accept that this must happen, but I will not let the leeches, hangers-on, glad-handers destroy what they have built for themselves. I will do everything I can to protect them from the wrong sort of reaction to this success.'

The glories that were to follow over the next few years did not stem from that isolated success at quagmire Hillsborough. They were rooted in the preparations and planning of the previous two years and the visionary ideals that Greenwood had instilled in his players. The win over Manchester United, important in itself, was merely the springboard that catapulted his side into a wider arena than they had previously known from their East London base.

LEAGUE DIVISION 1	**1964-65**
Division 1	9th
League Cup	2nd Round
FA Cup	4th Round
FA Charity Shield	Joint holders
European Cup-Winners' Cup	Winners

Victory over Preston meant that the Hammers now qualified for European competition for the first time. No strangers to playing Continental opposition – having toured Europe on and off since the early 1920s under Syd King, Charlie Paynter and Ted Fenton – West Ham found that this season their travels would provide a different dimension. No longer would the word 'friendly' designate their Continental matches. The European stage, Greenwood hoped, would provide the perfect arena to showcase to the rest of English football just how good his side was, as well as to exhibit his own philosophy on how he believed the game should be played.

Greenwood promoted John Lyall to take charge of the youth team. Amongst those he coached were two newcomers to the apprentice professional ranks – Frank Lampard and Roger Cross – who would themselves serve the club in a coaching capacity some 30 odd years later.

During the close season Bobby Moore and Johnny Byrne had taken part in the full England side's six internationals, including a tournament in Brazil, whilst Geoff Hurst had played in the Under-23 tour. Pre-season training was rounded off by a three-match tour of Austria and Germany, followed by the Charity Shield fixture against champions Liverpool at Anfield. West Ham twice came from behind, the match ended 2-2, and the trophy was shared.

The League campaign opened with a win at Fulham and another at home to Manchester United before a 37,000 crowd as the FA Cup was paraded in front of an uproarious full house. Once again a dream start was spoiled by three consecutive losses before two home wins put Moore and his team back on course.

The first round of the European Cup-Winners' Cup paired the Hammers with La Gantoise of Belgium. West Ham went into the ties with no sort of form, fourteenth in the League, scoring freely but shipping goals equally so. The Hammers' baptism in Europe proved somewhat unsettling. The part-timers from Ghent adopted tactics that stood normal cup football on its head, defending in depth at home, even after Boyce's header had broken the deadlock. Nor was the second leg any easier: the Belgians snatched a shock lead after half an hour before Budgie Byrne levelled just before the interval. The Upton Park crowd of 22,000 vented their displeasure in the second half, slow-handclapping and jeering their favourites, who limped unconvincingly into the next round.

The disappointment of an early exit from the League Cup at Sunderland was offset by a stirring run in the League – one defeat in twelve – that lifted the Hammers to fourth by mid-December. Towards the end of that run the Czech side Spartak Prague came to Upton Park with a mission: to defend in depth with ruthless determination. For 58 minutes they frustrated the Hammers with a white-shirted wall, until John Bond blasted a left-foot volley from 25 yards into the roof of their net. With eight minutes left, Alan Sealey crashed home a rebound, after hitting a post, to give his side a vital second goal. The crowd of 27,590 (paying new record receipts of £10,600) relished the performance of their heroes, all the more so considering that skipper Moore, out for one month, would not return for another two.

Just 120 Hammers supporters made the 1,800-mile round trip to Prague for the return leg. With fourteen minutes gone, they rose as one when Sissons lashed Byrne's pass high into the net. A 35th-minute penalty save from Jim Standen kept the Czechs at bay until late in the game, when Standen pushed a shot onto his crossbar and Mraz knocked it in. Mraz's second goal came too late to change the outcome, and with the refrain of 'Bubbles' ringing round the national stadium, West Ham held on.

His team's display was described by the normally reticent and press-wary Greenwood as 'simply fantastic'. Such was the savagery of the Czech tackling that Sealey required seven stitches in his shin, opened up by a stud, whilst Sissons was manhandled from the field by the referee as he requested treatment. If any player could be singled out as the man of the match it had to be 21-year-old Ron Boyce, who played the sweeper's role in a manner worthy of its greatest exponent – the absent Moore. Once again Boyce's name was talked of in England terms, while Greenwood was handed the accolade of 'master tactician'.

With the European quarter-finals not scheduled till March, minds returned to domestic affairs. By the turn of the year Byrne had scored twenty goals in just 23 League games whilst the ever-present Hurst had netted ten. But January proved to be a barren month – two defeats out of three in the League and an FA Cup exit at home to Chelsea, courtesy of Bobby Tambling's goal. February turned out even worse. Three losses were only halted with a win on the last Saturday at home against Liverpool. The losing sequence was repeated in March, but two wins in four days over Arsenal (home) and Aston Villa (away) pushed Greenwood's team back into the top half of the standings.

DID YOU KNOW?

In the mid-1960s Real Zaragoza beat Dundee, Cardiff, Shamrock Rov, Hearts, Leeds, Dunfermline, Everton and Aberdeen in European games. Only West Ham beat them.

Mid-February had seen the return of Moore, after a run-out in the reserves watched by a crowd of 6,600 at Upton Park. His return was timely, to say the least, as injuries since Christmas had forced Greenwood to shuffle his pack. That injury crisis resulted in young Brian Dear being given an unexpected chance. His robust performances confounded not only the opposition but also his critics. He scored West Ham's first goal, on his European debut, in the 2-1 away win against the Swiss team, Lausanne, and a week later in the second leg a 32,000 crowd saw him go one better. The Hammers eased into the semi-finals with a 4-3 win that was a credit to both teams.

Two weeks later it was Brian Dear, once again, who bagged the opening goal, added to by Byrne, which earned a 2-1 first-leg lead to take back to the Spanish team Real Zaragoza. It seemed that Dear could do no wrong, for he netted ten goals in ten starts in the League. An extraordinary five-goal burst in a twenty-minute spell during the 6-1 annihilation of West Brom on Good Friday morning earned Dear a place in the record books for fastest goalscoring. Come season's end, his tally would be fourteen goals from fifteen senior games.

The League campaign had concluded, with the Hammers ninth in the table, by the time they stepped out onto Spanish soil for the second leg in Zaragoza. Their opponents held both the UEFA and Spanish Cups, had already disposed of Dundee and Cardiff en route to meeting West Ham, and over the years would prove to be the *bête noire* of British clubs in Europe. Midway through the first half Real levelled the aggregate scores, 2-2, at which point the Hammers' captain once again showed his qualities, marshalling his colleagues against the Zaragoza forward line that had been dubbed the 'Magnificent Five' because they were reputed to be the finest club attack in the world.

Playing without a recognised No 9, in the absence of the injured Byrne, the Hammers pulled Hurst and Boyce back into a defensive formation that blocked the opposition's full-backs from surging down the flanks. These tactics had been conceived by Greenwood and perfected on the training ground at Chadwell Heath.

As half-time approached, the Spanish players in their exasperation were resorting to thumping high balls up the middle. Nine minutes into the second half the cacophony of noise within the stadium was silenced as Dear chested the ball down, then stroked a pass to Sissons – at nineteen the youngest player on the field. Sissons drew the goalkeeper before putting a right-foot shot deep into the corner of the net. The 400 travelling fans were ecstatic, despite their celebrations at the final whistle being interrupted by a volley of cushions hurtled by disgruntled home supporters.

Three weeks later a 100,000 crowd witnessed one of the greatest club matches ever to take place in Europe. At its conclusion, Bobby Moore lifted a trophy for the second time in twelve months within Wembley's hallowed arena, to the delight of not only his colleagues and nearly 40,000 Hammers' fans, but also to a television audience across Europe estimated at 30 million.

Match of the Season 1964-65

West Ham 2 TSV Munich 0

Cup-Winners' Cup, final, 19 May 1965

In a campaign that saw so many superb performances and thrilling encounters, only one deserves the ultimate accolade of Match of the Season. From the Charity Shield, closely followed by the home win over Matt Busby's champions-to-be Manchester United, through five London derby wins before Christmas, an Easter special against West Brom, memorable matches in Europe against Spartak Prague, Lausanne and Real Zaragoza, the Cup-Winners' Cup final dwarfed them all. Greenwood summed it up succinctly: 'This was West Ham's greatest win.'

As such, all that had happened in the past twelve months, or perhaps since he had taken over at Upton Park, just four years previously, was of little consequence compared to what was achieved on that balmy May evening at Wembley. Many would say that nothing the three former West Ham managers had accomplished in seven decades could compete with Ron Greenwood's achievement in bringing to a small, homely and friendly East End club one of the greatest prizes in European football.

Such a point of view would, in fairness, be disrespectful not only to the aforementioned trio, but to Greenwood himself. He was a different type and breed of manager to the likes of King, Paynter and Fenton, who in their eras were as far-seeing as Greenwood was in his. The difference in his outlook was his ability to focus on the tactics that were necessary in the modern era during each individual game, and to appreciate that the various strengths and weaknesses of each opposing side had to be overcome in contrasting ways. Literally he was the master tactician.

The Hammers' opponents at Wembley, TSV Munich 1860, were one of West Germany's lesser lights. Their domestic Cup success in 1964 was their first trophy of any kind, though they would become German champions in 1966. They had overcome US Luxembourg, Porto, Legia Warsaw, and Torino (in a third-match replay) to reach the final, and were understandably aggrieved to have to play in the host city of their opponents – Wembley having been designated for the final at the commencement of the season.

Although West Ham had their chances in the opening half, they found a black-garbed barrier in Munich's Yugoslav goalkeeper, Peter Radenkovic. He stood defiant until he was beaten twice in a two-minute spell midway through the second period of the game by the unlikeliest of goalscoring heroes – Alan Sealey.

But it takes two teams to make a great spectacle, and the Munich players contributed to the occasion by their industrious and mobile play, linked to sharp, penetrating raids combined with a hard yet fair and spirited defensive attitude.

The final margin might have been wider, as Sissons twice hit the woodwork, whilst Dear had a goal disallowed and on three occasions players missed chances that were in the 'free gift' category. As had come to be expected, Moore was again magnificent in all he did, such was his anticipation and ability to read the game that at times he even appeared to know what the Germans were going to do before they themselves did. Nevertheless, the win was achieved by eleven superb performances in which tactics, teamwork and collective skills all proved why the Hammers were later to be voted 'Team of the Year' in the BBC's Sportsview awards the following December.

There was something special about the victory, and the manner of it, that was best summed up many years later by Bobby Moore who, when asked to select the greatest game of his career, picked not the 1966 World Cup final but this particular match. 'We had all come through the ranks together,' he said, 'it was like winning the cup with your school team.'

Little did all those associated with West Ham United realise that night, and in the ensuing weeks – cocooned in the euphoria of the victory whilst dreaming of greater glories to come – that this would stand as the pinnacle of the club's achievements for the next ten years. Once again those immortal words within the Hammers' theme tune would ring true: 'just like my dreams they ...'

LEAGUE DIVISION 1	**1965-66**
Division 1	12th
League Cup	Finalists
FA Cup	4th Round
European Cup-Winners' Cup	Semi-finalists

Success in 1965 was not restricted to West Ham's seniors. The club's youngsters had themselves achieved a notable triumph. At Whitsun, for the third year running, they won the Augsberg International Youth Tournament in West Germany. A record crowd of 8,000 saw a repeat of the previous year's final against Bologna, the Young Hammers winning 1-0. Over the three years they had won ten and drawn two of their dozen games, and on winning the trophy for the third time it was presented to them to be retained. Three of the team would link up many years later – Harry Redknapp, voted Player of the Tournament, Frank Lampard, and Roger Cross.

In June, Greenwood and his squad returned to New York – for a second time in three years – to compete in the American International League. This time they finished bottom of their group, their only victory coming against their old Wembley rivals TSV Munich. Greenwood admitted his team's performances had been 'disgraceful', adding, 'Still, the beatings we have taken over here should have cut us down to size. After this we will not start the new season with any pre-conceived notions of our own greatness, and that is a good thing.'

A pre-season tour of West Germany ended with a loss, a win and a draw. The draw, watched by a crowd of 40,000, was against TSV once again. These exertions took their toll. The new League season commenced with Byrne, Alan Sealey and Brian Dear all on the long-term injured list. Ninety seconds into the new campaign, the Hammers were trailing at West Brom, who added two further goals without reply. Yet more injuries forced Greenwood to pitch young Redknapp into the fray, at home to Sunderland, and he sparkled in a 1-1 draw before a crowd of almost 35,000. A win over Leeds, far from settling a rocking ship, ushered in four straight defeats. In the last three of these Standen was beaten five times, first by Sheffield United, then by Liverpool, finally by Leicester, at which point West Ham were third from bottom. By the end of September they had recorded five losses and just two wins in the opening ten games, although Hurst with seven goals and Peters with five were keeping opposing defences busy.

The next nine League games brought another five losses, interspersed by three wins and a draw. Although all the reverses were away from Upton Park, the sixteen goals conceded pinpointed a major frailty. One such defeat was at First Division newcomers Northampton, who gained their first win in fourteen attempts.

It was in the League Cup and in the defence of their Cup-Winners' Cup crown that the Hammers' Jekyll and Hyde characteristics came to the fore. Whilst struggling in the League, their cup football encouraged the fans to dream of further glories. Where in previous seasons they had often exited the domestic cups at the hands of teams from lower divisions, this time they progressed to the semi-final with wins over Bristol Rovers, Mansfield, Rotherham and Grimsby, each of whom – other than Rotherham – was in the soccer basement. Meanwhile, in Europe, West Ham (as defending champions) enjoyed a bye in the first round and effortlessly cleared the hurdle presented by Olympiakos of Greece in the second. By mid-December the Hammers' balance sheet made curious reading: through to the semi-finals of the League Cup, the quarter-finals of the Cup-Winners' Cup, and yet seventeenth in Division One.

A 5-2 home win over Second Division Cardiff in the first leg of the League Cup semi-final raised hopes of making the final, but Christmas fixtures in the League were iced off and West Ham welcomed in the New Year by being crushed at home, 0-3 by Nottingham Forest. It was not until late January that the Hammers enjoyed another taste of victory, 4-0 over West Brom, and it took two attempts to get past Third Division Oldham in the FA Cup. There was no time for back-slapping, following a 5-1 win at Cardiff to secure their place in the two-leg League Cup final, for five days later West Ham were thrashed 0-5 at Leeds in the League.

But the Hammers appeared to be over the worst. They logged four consecutive League victories, plus a 2-1 home win in the first leg of the League Cup final against West Brom, and a 2-1 aggregate win over the East Germans of Magdeburg in the Cup-Winners' Cup. The only blip appeared to be losing at Blackburn in the FA Cup, after a replay.

But a further chaotic string of results saw West Ham lose in the League to strugglers Blackpool and Fulham, and go down 1-4 at the Hawthorns as West Brom took the League Cup 5-3 on aggregate to secure their place in next season's European Fairs Cup. The only route into Europe now open to the Hammers was to retain the Cup-Winners' Cup. To achieve that end they needed to get past the West German side Borussia Dortmund in the semi-final. Those hopes foundered in sixty sickening seconds of the first leg at Upton Park. West Ham led 1-0 with four minutes to play when Dortmund left-winger Lothar Emmerich – shortly to face Bobby Moore in the World Cup final – netted twice to turn the tie on its head.

DID YOU KNOW?

In the 1965-66 season West Ham created an unwelcome record. In the space of eight days in September 1965 they conceded 5 goals in three successive matches.

That clinical finishing by Emmerich in the first leg proved not to be a fluke, as he scored in the first minute in the return leg and added a second goal within half an hour. At 1-4 down overall, the Hammers were down and out, though both sides netted a further goal. West Ham's morale could not have been helped by a behind-the-scenes dispute between Greenwood and Moore, who was refusing to sign a new contract except under greatly improved terms. Moore apparently asked for a transfer, as a result of which he was temporarily stripped of the captaincy, which passed to Budgie Byrne.

Amongst the junior players at Upton Park, Frank Lampard, Trevor Brooking and Roger Cross collected losers' medals from the Southern Junior Floodlit Cup final. Lampard also celebrated his first England Youth cap and a place in the 16-strong squad for the forthcoming European Youth Tournament in Yugoslavia in May.

With the World Cup finals just weeks away two more Hammers – Hurst and Peters – joined Moore and Byrne in Alf Ramsey's 28-man England squad which on 6 June assembled at Lilleshall for further training. Only a month previously Peters had earned his first full cap and Hurst just his third in an international against Yugoslavia. Before the summer was over, three Hammers would become famous beyond their wildest dreams.

Match of the Season 1965-66

West Brom 4 West Ham 1

League Cup final, 2nd leg, 23 March 1966

After three years of success as the architects and exponents of an enviable style of cup football, West Ham found to their cost that their opponents in the League Cup final had learnt well the lessons they had been taught. West Brom were past the stage of being mere students at the knee of their more sophisticated London rivals, who had pioneered the theory of play that required a tight and disciplined defence and free-running play that encouraged forwards who drew opposing defences out of position.

This was the last occasion that the final of such a prestigious competition would be staged over two legs. The following season, and thereafter, the League Cup final would be staged at Wembley.

This denied West Ham the chance to grace the national stadium for the finals of three different cup competitions in three successive years. As it was, Byrne's last-minute goal at Upton Park gave the Hammers a 2-1 lead to take to the Hawthorns, where a crowd of nearly 32,000 witnessed a thriller. The Albion players never stopped running, chasing and shooting, overwhelming a defence that European opposition had found almost impenetrable over the past two seasons.

John Kaye quickly levelled the aggregate scores and an injury to centre-half Ken Brown left him, and the Hammers' defence, severely handicapped. A mistake by Johnny Byrne, when he misplaced a header back to his goalkeeper, led to Albion's second, and before half an hour had been played the Hammers were three down on the night. A fourth before the interval, when the West Brom skipper Graham Williams fired in from 30 yards via an upright, completed Albion's storming start. Two long-range efforts from Byrne that flew over the bar and a Brabrook header that hit a post were the nearest the Hammers had come.

Martin Peters wore No 3 and played at left-back, and with hindsight this proved to be a tactical mistake. It was hoped that he would provide an extra weapon with his overlapping, attacking as an extra forward by ghosting in from deep positions. But he was forced to stay in defence to allow Bobby Moore to police Albion's deep-lying centre-forward, John Kaye, who dragged Moore into midfield. By the time the roles were reversed at the start of the second half it was too late. Despite attacking incessantly after the interval, hopes soon faded, and although Peters headed a goal with fifteen minutes to go it was all too late.

The significance of this match is that it was the first of three cup defeats – together with those to come against Borussia Dortmund – that halted the sequence of cup successes that had taken the club from being also-rans to winners. Moreover, they had been winners with style, allied to a steely core, and that had pushed the name 'West Ham' to the forefront, not only on the domestic, but also the international scene. In less than twelve months they had slipped back to being just another First Division side which promised much but failed to deliver – especially away from Upton Park.

It would be another decade before the fans of West Ham United could once again taste the delights of supporting a cup-winning side headed for Europe. In between there would be a great deal of frustration, angst and soul-searching for all connected with the club as they sought explanations for what had gone wrong.

3

THE WILDERNESS YEARS 1966-1974

LEAGUE DIVISION 1	**1966-67**
Division 1	16th
League Cup	Semi-finalists
FA Cup	3rd Round

As far as the West Ham fans were concerned, their team had won the World Cup. For Bobby Moore, as England captain, much praise was heaped upon his shoulders, not only for his leadership but also for his own personal performances, which earned him the title of Player of the Tournament. To many who had observed his development since debuting for West Ham back in September 1958 it had been obvious that Moore was destined for great things. For Geoff Hurst and Martin Peters, their rise to international stardom was to say the least unexpected and was worthy of inclusion in a Boy's Own Annual. Both had only recently broken into the national team, but their impact once there had been exceptional. Their goals in the final, as well as their general team play throughout the tournament, confirmed them to be world-class internationals.

Having seen their team win the World Cup – as endlessly parroted by Alf Garnett – expectations for the new campaign throughout the rapidly expanding fan-base of West Ham were, predictably, sky-high. During the close season Greenwood had attempted to sign Millwall keeper Alex Stepney, but Chelsea lured him for a record £55,000 fee. Insult was added to injury when Chelsea then refused to sell Peter Bonetti, whom Stepney had been bought to replace. West Ham's policy of refusing to pay 'signing-on' fees also meant that Terry Venables refused to sign. Better news concerned Bobby Moore, who agreed a new contract and was reappointed captain. As for the stadium, the Main Stand had been extended and facilities for fans, players and the media upgraded.

An undefeated pre-season tour of West Germany, undertaken just six days after the World Cup final, gave little hint of what the new campaign held in store. A home defeat by Chelsea on the opening day was followed by two losses away from home. Despite the excellent form of Moore, Hurst, Peters and Byrne, points were hard to find, but by early October West Ham had gone seven games unbeaten in the League, and with victories over Spurs and Arsenal in the League Cup it looked as though the corner had been turned. Tactically, the return of Ken Brown after injury released Moore from his role as a stand-in central defender to bolster the midfield. This illustrated Moore's versatility, equally at home at the back or in midfield. Later, of course, he concentrated on being sweeper.

In November, West Ham hit top form with home wins over Fulham (6-1) and Newcastle (3-0), a buccaneering 4-3 win at White Hart Lane, and an extraordinary 7-0 crushing of Don Revie's Leeds in the League Cup. Victory in the quarter-finals at Blackpool in early December took the Hammers to the semi-finals for the second year running. They featured in a knockabout 5-5 League draw at Stamford Bridge, and when Leicester came to Upton Park on New Year's Eve Greenwood's men boasted the unique distinction of having scored in every English League game. Gordon Banks' defiance in goal put paid to that record, but Bobby Moore's anguish was tempered that day when it was announced that he was to be honoured by the Queen with an OBE.

That oft-quoted jibe of West Ham being like the Christmas decorations that come down in January was voiced again when they mustered just one League victory in the first two months of 1967. Moreover, their League Cup challenge was once again savaged by West Brom, who for the second year running blitzed the Hammers with a four-goal first-half burst at the Hawthorns. In the FA Cup, Greenwood's men suffered humiliation. Hurst's hat-trick could not prevent Third Division Swindon forcing a 3-3 draw at a packed Upton Park. Three days later, on 31 January, the little Wiltshire club, inspired by winger Don Rogers, avenged their defeat of three years previously and won 3-1. No wonder Greenwood described January 1967 as 'the blackest month we have known'.

While Easter was kind – with three wins out of three – it was followed by seven straight defeats, the most painful of which was the 1-6 home thrashing by Manchester United, who clinched the championship in style. The Hammers' final position of sixteenth was embarrassing for a team that had won the World Cup!

Before Christmas the Hammers had scored virtually at will, but afterwards the goals had dried up. Even so, in the final analysis, only champions Man U had scored more League goals. In all competitions, Hurst had netted 41, Peters sixteen, and Byrne thirteen before his sudden transfer to Palace in February. On the downside, only two clubs had conceded more than West Ham's 84 goals.

DID YOU KNOW?

When Bobby Moore lifted the World Cup at Wembley in 1966, his registration with West Ham United had lapsed. Professionally speaking, he had ceased to exist.

Nor must it be forgotten that a team that had played virtually without a break for the past four years still managed to cram into their schedule six friendly fixtures, including a November trip to Egypt and a five-day trip to the United States in April. They played in the Houston Astrodome against Real Madrid, in an exhibition match that was the first soccer game ever to take place on a full-size pitch completely under cover. Moore, Hurst, Peters and Boyce were also four of the team that won the indoor London Five-a-Side Championship in early May at the Wembley Pool.

Greenwood had announced after the cup defeats that changes were necessary. To that end Budgie Byrne returned to his former club after five years and Ken Brown enjoyed a testimonial before leaving for Torquay. For the second year running, England Youth internationals Frank Lampard and Trevor Brooking, together with leading scorer Roger Cross, were part of the Hammers Youth Team that reached the final of the Southern Junior Floodlit Cup.

Match of the Season 1966-67

West Ham 7 Leeds 0

League Cup, 4th Round, 7 November 1966

In the space of fourteen days in November 1966 the Hammers scored twenty goals in winning four matches. Three of those victories were in the League, but the most startling was the 7-0 execution of Leeds in the League Cup. Humiliation is not too strong a word to use in this context, as Don Revie's side at that time were by any standards at the pinnacle of English football.

Having won the Second Division title in 1963-64, Leeds had been First Division runners-up in the following two seasons and FA Cup finalists in 1965. For a decade, few could match them. Amongst their team was England World Cup hero Jack Charlton, buttressed by the fiery Scot Billy Bremner and the uncompromising Norman Hunter. Nicknamed 'bite your legs', in honour of his fearsome tackling, Hunter might have played in Alf Ramsey's World Cup-winning team, were it not for the imperious Moore. Johnny Giles and Paul Madeley played in midfield, with Jimmy Greenhoff an emerging force at centre-forward. Although missing regular keeper Gary Sprake, his deputy, David Harvey, did not disgrace himself.

The tone of the contest was set in the opening minutes as Bremner was uncompromisingly challenged by Moore and ended up in a crumpled heap against the Chicken Run fencing on the halfway line. Byrne and Brown thundered in shots that Harvey somehow kept out. It was Byrne at his mercurial best who fashioned the opening goal as he baffled the opposing defenders before slipping the ball to Sissons on the left, who curled a cross-shot into the far corner. Just 90 seconds had elapsed.

Left-winger Sissons had previously scored only once that season, but before half-time he had completed a hat-trick. Byrne, again, then Brabrook, provided the openings. The onslaught continued and with four minutes to go to the interval Byrne lashed in a shot which appeared to hit Hurst on the back of his legs as it flew into the net.

The fifth goal was delayed till the hour. Byrne lured Jack Charlton to the by-line, survived his reckless lunge, juggled the ball three times, and sent Hurst racing through to unleash a left-foot piledriver. Ten minutes later Peters collected a pass from Boyce, dribbled past two defenders on the left, then fired an equally fine right-footer past Harvey for the sixth. The crowd could hardly believe it. Three minutes later Byrne crossed for Hurst to slam home the seventh.

Leeds had not been disgraced by the margin of their defeat, for they came close on a number of occasions to scoring. But West Ham were in one of those moods and on a winning run when not even the best in Europe could have lived with them. Byrne was described in the next day's papers as 'the nearest thing we have in English football to a Di Stefano'.

It is a sobering postscript, but Leeds recovered to defeat West Ham twice in the League that season.

LEAGUE DIVISION 1	**1967-68**
Division 1	12th
League Cup	4th Round
FA Cup	5th Round

The first of Greenwood's new intake was completed on the last Saturday of the 1966-67 season. The signing of Billy Bonds from Charlton for around £50,000 was viewed by many as a change of direction on the part of Greenwood. A swashbuckling right-back aged 21, Bonds had played nearly a hundred games for Charlton. During his time at Upton Park he was to become a legend, admired and respected by all he came into contact with. The purchase of 'Bonzo', by the time he finally retired 21 years later, proved to be one of the shrewdest bargains in West Ham's history.

In the summer Greenwood acquired a further two defenders, both Scots. Bobby Ferguson cost £65,000, a record fee for a British goalkeeper. He had played in a friendly at Upton Park the previous season for Kilmarnock and impressed. His CV showed a Scottish championship medal and seven full caps. John Cushley came from Celtic, where he was understudy to Scotland's international centre-half Billy McNeill. A former Scottish Youth cap, he had won League and League Cup runners-up medals.

A pre-season tour of West Germany highlighted West Ham's continued defensive weakness in the air. Just one win in the opening six League games – which included a 1-5 thrashing at White Hart Lane – showed that little had been gained from the outlay of £140,000. An 18-year-old emerging talent by the name of Trevor Brooking made an impressive debut at Burnley, but otherwise there was little to cheer. Defeat at Everton might have been followed by another at Sunderland, where the home side led for an hour, courtesy of Moore's own-goal, before a burst of five West Ham goals in sixteen minutes produced a first away win of the season. Ironically, the victory was achieved without Bonds, injured, and with Ferguson dropped in favour of Jim Standen, who was shortly contracted to go to Detroit to finish his career in the newly emerging American leagues.

Despite being Division One's joint highest scorers away from home, and netting twenty goals overall, West Ham had nevertheless conceded 21 in their first eight fixtures. Fortunately Hurst and Peters had a keen eye for goal and Hurst had joined that select band of Hammers to have scored a century of League goals. He had accomplished that feat in just over four seasons, since his conversion to a striker, and from only 221 starts, including those when he played at half-back.

DID YOU KNOW?

Wembley hosted the League Cup final from 1967. Had it done so in 1966, West Ham would have played there in the finals of three different cups in three successive years.

West Ham's defensive frailties were never more apparent than against Stoke at home, when a 3-0 interval lead was transformed into a 3-4 defeat. By now, Greenwood's team were just one point clear of the bottom two and he rang the changes. Both wingers – Redknapp and Sissons – were dropped, paving the way for a switch to a 4-3-3 formation which, among other changes, paired Bonds and Cushley as double centre-halves. Following a frank Friday team-talk, Greenwood sent out his new-look side at Stamford Bridge against an equally poor Chelsea and saw his team win 3-1.

The opening three months of the season, although full of anxiety in the League, had been brightened by progress in the League Cup. Walsall had been trounced away, 5–1, and Second Division Bolton were given a goal start at Upton Park before being routed by a Hurst foursome. If Greenwood thought he had discovered a winning formula at Chelsea, he was to be quickly disillusioned. An unchanged team quickly found themselves a goal down at Second Division Huddersfield in the fourth round of the League Cup, thanks to Ferguson completely missing the ball when coming out to collect a cross. His humiliation was compounded in the second half when he jumped too late to intercept Chris Cattlin's 35-yarder. For the Hammers, the ghost of cup defeats against lower division clubs had reared its ugly head again.

West Ham had a good Christmas with three wins out of three, including back-to-back 4-2 wins over Leicester. Much of the credit was down to the reinstated Brian Dear – who responded with a burst of goalscoring – and young Brooking, who was now holding down a regular place in the team. It was Dear and Brooking whose goals paved the way for the 7-2 demolition of bottom club Fulham – West Ham's biggest League win since they had swamped the Cottagers 6-1 fifteen months previously. It was symptomatic of the Hammers' problems that attention focussed not on their seven goals, but on Fulham's two, for they presented as feeble an attack as anyone could remember.

The New Year also brought new interest – the FA Cup. Ferguson saved his side at Burnley with four outstanding saves in a 3-1 win. Three weeks later, another trio of goals at Stoke meant further progress, and many were of the opinion that the watching Alf Ramsey had seen in Billy Bonds a natural successor to his attack-minded England right-back, George Cohen.

Hopes of a Cup run were dashed by Sheffield United, who shrugged off the fact that they had failed to win any of their last *fifteen* away League games by winning 2-1 at Upton Park. Slow handclapped by a post-war record crowd of 38,440 (paying likewise record receipts of £9,240), Greenwood's post-match comments summed it up: 'We didn't deserve a replay. We played badly as a team and never got on top of them. We created no chances. Even our goal was handed on a plate.' The Blades won despite fielding five reserves and they would be relegated in May.

Greenwood could delay team-strengthening no longer, hoping to solve his central defensive problem by signing Alan Stephenson from Crystal Palace. Capped at Under-23 level, Stephenson, at six feet plus, was a more traditional No 5 than the shorter Cushley. The defence had also introduced some home-grown talent since Christmas, and 19-year-old Frank Lampard produced some rave performances. Sadly, in late April he broke his right leg at Bramall Lane and would be out for a year. Substitute Brian Dear took his place and exacted retribution on anyone playing in red and white stripes. He was eventually booked, but would undoubtedly have been sent off in today's stricter climate.

The arrival of Stephenson appeared to ease the team's defensive problems. In the twelve matches he played that season the Hammers conceded only nine goals, and three of those were in the away defeat by eventual champions Manchester City. Nowhere was this keener defence more noticeable than at home to Liverpool, who – under the eyes of Alf Ramsey – were unable to peg back Martin Peters' goal.

Everton's visit on the final day of the season was nostalgic in the sense that Upton Park bade farewell to the East Terrace, popularly known as the Chicken Run. A new modern stand would replace it, seating 3,500. This, together with covered standing terrace accommodation – holding some 4,000 (the same as the old wooden structure) – would be the next phase of ground development. In the matchday programme it was stated that the top price of a season ticket for the following year would be £15.

Match of the Season 1967-68

West Ham 2 Tottenham 1

Division 1, 23 December 1967

The programme notes welcoming Spurs to this first local derby of the season said: 'The North Londoners received a double setback last week; in the space of four days, they were dismissed from the

European Cup-Winners Cup by Olympique Lyonnais, and then defeated 0-1 by Leicester City in a League game that terminated their record of 29 successive undefeated games at home.'

Seventh in the table, as against West Ham's nineteenth, Spurs looked the likely winners. But in the Match Review section in the programme for the next home match, these sentences put the Spurs result into context: 'Our League position prior to Christmas could aptly be described as precarious, and the prospects of a local derby followed by a double-header against a vastly-improved Leicester City side, were not conducive to over-optimism. But soccer being the game it is, nothing can be taken for granted, and although many commentators have said that the Hammers are too good a side to be so low in the table we still have to give proof of our proficiency. Certainly one swallow doesn't make a summer, and three successive League victories did not mean that we have eluded the threat of relegation, but at least those six points ... have given our supporters, players and officials encouragement to hope that the darker days of the 1967-68 season are of the past.'

West Ham built their 2-1 victory around first-rate performances from Moore, Peters and Hurst. The whole performance, however, served only to emphasise how ridiculous was their lowly position. It was fast and furious stuff, with Moore lobbing Pat Jennings in the Spurs goal from 35 yards, only for the ball to nestle on the top netting. But a home goal was not long delayed. Bonds won possession on the halfway line, inter-passed with Brooking, and strode unchallenged to let fly from 30 yards, the ball brushing Jennings' fingers. It was Bonds' first goal for the Hammers. Young Lampard, at left-back, was more than equal to the visitors' Scottish international winger, Jimmy Robertson, but could do nothing to prevent him equalising. Keeper Ferguson and centre-half Cushley got in a tangle and ended up in a heap.

After the interval, the Hammers raised their game and Moore, Sissons, Dear, Peters and Bonds all went close. In the 73rd minute they were finally rewarded for their efforts, when Bonds raced at full tilt upfield to run onto a Hurst throw-in, and crossed accurately into the centre. Peters miscued in front of goal, but his sliced shot rolled kindly to Dear, who happily hooked it home.

LEAGUE DIVISION 1	**1968-69**
Division 1	8th
League Cup	3rd Round
FA Cup	5th Round

There were no summer additions to Ron Greenwood's squad, but he lost the services of Peter Brabrook, who left for Orient, and Jack Burkett, to Charlton. As usual, the players undertook a pre-season tour of West Germany.

The new campaign began with two League wins and a draw, West Ham's best start for eight years. The 31,000 fans attending the first home match, against Nottingham Forest, had to cram into three sides of the ground because of building work on the new East Stand and Terrace. The match programme was extended to twenty pages, included a coloured section, and the price increased to one shilling (5p). No advertising was included, other than that related to club matters. Curiously, the five London clubs were the only ones in the First Division not to carry commercial advertising.

The team's strong opening was no flash in the pan. At the final whistle on the first Saturday in October, West Ham had lost only once and were sixth in the table, just two points off the top. Martin Peters with nine goals, Hurst (six) and Brooking (three) had provided the main thrust, while the speed and crosses of Harry Redknapp had earned him an extended run in the side.

A League Cup run also looked likely after Bolton were swept aside 7-2 at Upton Park, but a dour, negative display in the next round by Coventry, masterminded by their manager, ex-Hammer Noel Cantwell, resulted in a scoreless draw. West Ham succumbed in the replay, 2-3: the referee gifted the home side their first two goals by ignoring fouls in the build-up to both.

The death of Billy Moore – a member of the 1923 Cup final team who had been associated with the club for 46 years – saddened those who knew him and may have preyed on the minds of the players, whose defeat at Burnley in October was their first away from home all season. Worse was to follow at Leeds, where a 0-2 defeat was compounded by the expulsion of Redknapp, who back-chatted the referee while being booked for a retaliatory foul on Billy Bremner. Redknapp thus became only the second West Ham player to be sent off during Greenwood's reign – the first having been Bobby Moore at Manchester City back in November 1961. Ron Greenwood's post-match comments summed up his feelings: 'Obviously the club are upset about it. We have a proud record for behaviour on the field. You cannot go seven years without a player being sent off unless discipline is of a high standard. I am not forgiving Redknapp, but a young player does not kick out like that unless something has happened to him.'

The Bremner-Redknapp run-in, compared with a later incident in the same match, graphically illustrated a major problem with English soccer at that time. Stephenson fouled Johnny Giles from behind. The referee blew for a foul, as expected. Giles got up and launched himself at Stephenson, fists flying. Leeds had a free-kick but Giles was not even cautioned. Redknapp and Giles had both indulged in retaliation but received contrasting punishments. A newspaper commented: 'In actual fact there was one major – and perhaps all important – difference in the circumstances surrounding both these fouls. In the case of Redknapp the crowd were chanting "Off, Off, Off." In the case of Giles there was a sympathetic silence from 40,786 spectators who have been educated at Elland Road that treachery is part of soccer success.' The revolution in outlawing foul play that finally dawned in the enlightened 1990s could not come soon enough for all true lovers of our beautiful game.

Sunderland bore the brunt of West Ham's backlash seven days later. Playing 3-3-4, with both Redknapp and Sissons out wide, the Hammers won 8-0. For Hurst it marked a personal milestone, as he scored a double hat-trick to equal Vic Watson's record of nearly four decades earlier. On the same day, Burnley dented ruthless Leeds' title ambitions, winning 5-1 at Turf Moor.

The last Saturday of the year, and the visit of Arsenal, was to have marked the opening of the seating accommodation in the East Stand. The weather decreed otherwise and the game was postponed. It was, therefore, the visit of Bristol City a week later, in the third round of the FA Cup, that christened the new facility, which had cost less than £200,000 and increased Upton Park's capacity to 42,000. The official opening was performed ten days later by 'Mr West Ham United', Charles Paynter, who unveiled a plaque.

Inclement weather was playing havoc with the fixture list. Having overcome Bristol City and Huddersfield, West Ham's fifth round-tie at Mansfield only took place at the sixth attempt. The relegation-threatened Third Division side ploughed through the mud with determination, confidence and passion to dump the pussy-footing Hammers out of the competition. It was a major Cup shock and provided another instance in West Ham's long history of cup defeats against lowly opponents.

Bouncing back with four wins in their next five League games, the Hammers then ran out of goals. In their final nine fixtures – none of which they won – they found the net only four times. Geoff Hurst and Martin Peters were ever-presents this season, netting 25 and nineteen League goals respectively. A final position of eighth, although the highest since Greenwood's first season, proved anti-climactic when set against the team's sparkling form during the first two months of the season.

Match of the Season 1968-69

West Ham 8 Sunderland 0

Division 1, 19 October 1968

Having been eliminated from the League Cup in early October, then lost their undefeated away League record a week later at Burnley, and endured an ill-tempered defeat at Leeds, West Ham's early season form looked to have evaporated.

Typical of Ron Greenwood's sides of the 1960s and early 70s was the way they habitually answered their critics. The players could go from a performance bereft of commitment and passion to one that in the very next match touched the heights. But for that elusive 'will-o'-the-wisp' consistency, the trophy cabinets would have groaned under the weight of silverware during Ron Greenwood's stewardship.

Sunderland had come off worst in matches against West Ham over the past two seasons, losing both matches at Roker Park (2-4 and 1-5) and drawing both at Upton Park. On the morning of the game Sunderland lay tenth in the table with four wins, six draws, and four losses from the fourteen fixtures they had played. The Hammers were four places ahead of them, but had not won any of their previous seven League games.

In some ways it was surprising that the visitors survived until the eighteenth minute, when Geoff Hurst scored the first goal. Harry Redknapp might have put his side into the lead as early as the opening seconds and three further shots followed from different players that whistled wide of their mark before the deadlock was finally broken. That first goal came via a Martin Peters cross, with Hurst diving full length to score. It was only after the game that Hurst admitted the ball had hit his outstretched hand, and not his head, but whether it would have averted the final one-sided outcome – had it been ruled out – is doubtful. The second goal, some five minutes later, was pure class. Bobby Moore thundered a 35-yard free-kick into the net with the outside of his right foot. In the 34th minute Billy Bonds and Trevor Brooking combined to set up a far-post header for Hurst. A minute before the interval Bonds took a short corner to Redknapp, whose centre was volleyed home by Hurst to complete his first hat-trick of the afternoon, and his first for twelve months.

DID YOU KNOW?

Geoff Hurst scored six goals in West Ham's 8-0 home win over Sunderland in October 1968. After the match he admitted he had fisted, not headed, his first goal.

There was little respite for the visitors in the second half, as within three minutes of the re-start Hurst scored again. Sissons, Brooking and Peters combined before the England striker chested the ball down and shot home. Another thirteen minutes elapsed before the Hammers added number six, and it was Hurst who claimed it, lashing home a rebound from 25 yards that left Jim Montgomery, in the Sunderland goal, clutching at straws.

Sloppy marking allowed Brooking to get in on the goalscoring act with an angled shot. Hurst then completed his double hat-trick, when Brooking released Redknapp down the right flank and he crossed low into the goalmouth. Eight goals, but those who saw them – ironically this was West Ham's smallest home crowd of the season – agreed that but for goalkeeper Montgomery it might well have been double figures.

As one report emphasised only too clearly: 'West Ham played no better than when I saw them draw with Tottenham and Sheffield Wednesday. There is genius in their play, but they are balanced on such a nice edge that they can as easily fall one way as the other. Yesterday they fell the right way.'

As ever the manager was philosophical about it all, commenting: 'We could have done this sort of thing before. Martin Peters could have scored six goals against Sheffield Wednesday but didn't get one!'

For the fans waiting outside to salute Hurst after the match they had never seen anything remotely like it before. Nor had virtually anybody else in East London, as it had taken nearly four decades for a West Ham player to equal Vic Watson's previous feat. His double hat-trick had accounted for Leeds, 8-2 at Upton Park.

LEAGUE DIVISION 1	**1969-70**
Division 1	17th
League Cup	3rd Round
FA Cup	3rd Round

The previous season had concluded with another trip to the United States, where the Hammers represented Baltimore in the North American Soccer League International Cup. Wolves represented Kansas City, Aston Villa (Atlanta), Dundee United (Dallas) and Kilmarnock (St. Louis). Hoped-for large attendances failed to materialise. As one reporter said: 'My first reaction was that I had never seen so many people wearing hearing aids in my life. Then I began to get a clue of what was happening. The Orioles (the local baseball team) were playing in Minnesota at the same time and even the Oriole executives, who are backing the soccer experiment, were watching the game in front of them with one ear tuned to baseball.' Greenwood's team played ten matches, criss-crossing the continent twice, then playing a friendly with Southampton in Bermuda. The youth team, captained by Pat Holland, toured Zambia and Malawi, then Switzerland and Italy. The team included future stars John McDowell, Tony Carr, Peter Grotier, and Clive Charles.

Pre-season training again concluded with a three-match tour of West Germany. The new season kicked off early to take account of next summer's World Cup finals in Mexico. Two quick home wins provided a false dawn: five defeats and two draws in the next seven games left the Hammers two places off the bottom by mid-September. Although beating Halifax in the League Cup, West Ham could not repeat the feat at Nottingham Forest, losing by the only goal. By the turn of the year the Hammers were still in the bottom six. The team struggled to find consistency, with both Hurst and Peters missing games through injury. Although Frank Lampard and Trevor Brooking had missed the early part of the campaign, both had returned. But injury struck again in the last match of 1969, at home to Forest, side-lining Lampard until March and Brooking until the new season.

All hopes of salvaging the season were shattered on the first Saturday of the New Year, following an FA Cup exit at Second Division Middlesbrough. With nothing to occupy the mind except the fight against relegation, Greenwood signed Peter Eustace from Sheffield Wednesday for £90,000 – yet another record fee for the Hammers. Eustace was a creative midfielder and was earmarked as a replacement for Martin Peters, rumours of whose impending departure intensified by the month. The reasons for his wanting away appeared to be psychological as much as anything else. Being labelled in the public mind as West Ham's 'third World Cup hero' – obliging him to play in the shadow of Moore and Hurst – may have had something to do with his discontent.

The injury woes that had plagued Greenwood since August, coupled with the team's poor results, gave unexpected opportunities to youth and fringe players. Amongst these were Peter Bennett, Jimmy Lindsay, Roger Cross, Bobby Howe, Pat Holland and Peter Grotier, but only the versatile Howe and goalkeeper Grotier did enough to merit an extended run in the first team. With rumblings among the fans and protest banners appearing on the terraces, Greenwood responded by dropping keeper Ferguson for youngster Grotier. The final straw had been the 2-3 away defeat at Turf Moor, where the Scot had been blamed for Burnley's opening two goals.

The other young prospect who made an impact – by his sheer presence as much as anything else – was a tall, gangly, robust but deceptively fast Bermudian called Clyde Best, who possessed a venomous shot as well as fearsome heading ability. Best had signed professional forms at the end of the previous season after only a short time at Upton Park, where he had turned up one morning, unannounced, with just a pair of boots. He had apparently travelled to London from the Caribbean with no other object in mind than to obtain a trial with the Hammers. In his time at the Boleyn Ground the amiable giant became something of a cult hero, as much for his unpredictability as for his unrealised potential.

The 'Peters situation' was finally resolved on transfer deadline day, when a British record fee of £200,000 took the 26-year-old player – once dubbed by England manager Alf Ramsey as 'ten years ahead of his time', to which critics replied that Peters would not start playing well for another ten years – to White Hart Lane. As part of the deal Jimmy Greaves moved in the opposite direction for £50,000. Although past his prime, Greaves, now 30, was hailed by the Upton Park faithful as the Messiah coming home – he had been born in nearby Dagenham – and would provide the missing link to bring back the glory days. His debut at Maine Road maintained his personal record of scoring on every debut he had ever made. Earlier in the season, Manchester City had trounced West Ham 4-0 at Upton Park. Now the tables were turned, and two goals apiece from Greaves and Hurst, plus a 50-yarder from Ron Boyce, produced a 5-1 win.

In fact, of West Ham's final six games – in which Greaves was ever-present – only one was lost. The Hammers ended the season seventeenth, ten points ahead of relegated Sunderland and eleven ahead of bottom club Sheffield Wednesday. However, nothing could disguise the fact that this had been a depressing season, which for the first time in memory saw supporters protesting within the confines of the ground at the fare they had endured. It was the team's inconsistency that so frustrated them. Top-seven teams like Chelsea, Derby, Liverpool and Newcastle were all beaten at Upton Park, whilst home points had been dropped against struggling Southampton, Ipswich, Nottingham Forest, Sunderland and West Brom. The Hammers' final points tally of 36 was their joint-lowest since the club returned to the top division. Before the arrival of Greaves, Greenwood's team had just 28 points, whereupon three wins, two draws, and just one defeat had allowed the team to claw their way to 36. Without Greaves, it would undoubtedly have been worse, while Bobby Moore was just Bobby Moore – being voted Hammer of the Year for a record fourth time.

The gloom was somewhat dissipated in the following weeks as Billy Bonds led the unfancied Hammers to victory in the London Five-a-Side Championships, sponsored by the *Evening Standard*. Alongside Bonds and Johnny Sissons – who had missed more than half the League season because of injury – were a trio of newer names, Grotier, Howe and Clive Charles, brother of the famous John. Geoff Hurst sat out the competition, a permanent substitute, so successful were the other five.

Match of the Season 1969-70

Manchester City 1 West Ham 5

Division 1, 21 March 1970

A day of which fairy-tales are made is the only way to describe the outcome of this match and the events leading up to it.

Since their early dismissal from the FA Cup, the Hammers had slipped from bad to worse. The first rumblings amongst supporters had been heard during goalless home draws with lowly Southampton and Ipswich. Away from home, the team had crashed to heavy defeats at Newcastle (1-4) and Derby (0-3). The unsettled Martin Peters seemed symptomatic of a club that was massively under-achieving. Given the calibre of players on their books, West Ham should have been title-challengers, not relegation contenders. But now Peters had gone, Greaves had arrived, and the new cocktail would be unleashed on an unsuspecting Manchester City.

Much had been made in the preceding months of Greaves' waning career and dwindling appetite for goals. Even his manager at Spurs, Bill Nicholson, suggested he might be fading a little. Greaves had last scored on 10 January, ten weeks earlier – ironically the same day that Peters had last netted for West Ham.

DID YOU KNOW?

One of the joys of English football in the late 1960s was the refereeing of bald, tubby Roger Kirkpatrick, who sprinted around as fast as his short legs would carry him.

It took Greaves just ten minutes to get off the mark. Young winger Pat Holland ignored appeals for offside to cross the ball, which fell for Greaves to evade a tackle and score from almost point-blank range. That strike enabled him to continue his record of scoring on his debut for Chelsea, England, AC Milan, Spurs, and now West Ham.

Although Francis Lee equalised three minutes later with a long-range effort that slipped through Grotier's grasp, Greaves was determined to have fun. After twice going close, he netted again in the 37th minute. Bonds' cross led to a mighty scramble, which saw the ball bounce off goalkeeper Corrigan's chest to Greaves. Whilst all around him panicked, he simply stooped, looked up and slid the ball home. On the stroke of half-time, Hurst dived to head West Ham's third goal.

The score remained unchanged until the last few minutes. It was then that the Hammers scored a goal so bizarre, that had it been televised it might grace our screens to this day. Corrigan drop-kicked a clearance downfield from the right edge of his penalty area and foolishly turned away to saunter back into his goalmouth. The ball dropped into the centre-circle, where Ron Boyce, seeing the unguarded net, tried his luck. His volley was perfection, the ball flying like an arrow towards the centre of Corrigan's goal. A roar of disbelief erupted from the crowd. Corrigan looked up, just in time to see the ball swishing around in the back of the net. There was time before the final whistle for Hurst to lash a fifth goal, thereby sealing the Hammers' biggest win of the season.

Though Greaves's two goals were not sensational in themselves – and for impact they were dwarfed by Boyce's effort – their effect on his new team-mates is impossible to exaggerate. They appeared to offer ample proof that here was a man who could do the most difficult job in football, score goals, effortlessly and consistently. West Ham no doubt believed that in the blink of an eye they would become a winning side – and such misplaced optimism would shortly be crushingly dispelled.

As for Martin Peters, his debut for Spurs was rather less memorable. Though he scored, Spurs lost at home, 1-2 to Coventry.

LEAGUE DIVISION 1	**1970-71**
Division 1	20th
League Cup	3rd Round
FA Cup	3rd Round

The previous season concluded as early as 4 April, to allow some respite before the Mexico World Cup finals. This meant that when Ron Greenwood assembled his squad for pre-season training in mid-July most had not played a competitive match for three and a half months, the longest break many of them had ever experienced. The exceptions were Bobby Moore and Geoff Hurst, on England duty. For these two, apart from one month off each summer, and rare periods of injury, football had become a year-round profession. This was partly because of England call-ups, but also partly because of the burgeoning reputation of the Hammers under Greenwood, which regularly saw the club invited during the close season to play in the United States and elsewhere.

For Greenwood too it had been a busy summer. He had been in Mexico as a member of the FIFA Technical Committee, which prepared reports on the tactics, preparations, etc, of the sixteen competing finalists. He had attended the 1966 World Cup finals in England in the same capacity.

One other West Ham player travelled to Mexico that summer, but for other reasons and under his own steam. He took part as a member of the Ford team in the World Cup Car Rally that preceded the football competition. With co-driver Tony Fall, Jimmy Greaves travelled some 16,000 miles in various stages, completing a European section before the cars were transported by sea to South America. From there the rally continued over rough terrain before the closing stage in Mexico City. The mere fact that Greaves' car was placed sixth out of only 26 cars that eventually finished, bearing in mind the far greater total which started the rally, bore testimony to his abilities behind the steering wheel.

At home during the summer recess the club had spent large sums on ground improvements. The floodlighting system had been updated, at a cost of £30,000, to make them ten times brighter than previously, whilst a new permanent gantry for TV cameras had been installed. Improvements to the West Stand were completed. It was re-roofed for £11,000, and what at the time were called C and E Blocks were re-seated with new tip-up seats.

Greenwood transferred John Sissons to Sheffield Wednesday but made no new signings, despite speculation that he was after Mordechai Spiegler, captain of the Israeli national team in Mexico. Spiegler, a midfielder, had been in pre-season training with the

Hammers and excelled in friendlies at Portsmouth and Orient. Although expressing how much he loved training for West Ham, Spiegler signed for French club Nantes, on account of obscure contractual difficulties with the Israeli authorities should he sign for an English club. West Ham completed their preparations against Bournemouth under their new manager, ex-Hammer, John Bond, who had recruited as his assistant another Upton Park favourite, Ken Brown, together with former team-mates Tony Scott, Keith Miller and Trevor Hartley.

The opening five games on the fixture list looked tough, with London derbies against Spurs, Arsenal and Chelsea, followed by trips to Leeds and Manchester United. The Hammers drew four, lost at Elland Road, and found themselves fifteenth with a long season ahead of them. The first of those matches, at White Hart Lane, had promised much, as Greaves scored an ecstatically greeted equaliser against his old team-mates, before Peter Bennett headed a second leveller to earn West Ham a point. That day, however, belonged to Moore. Despite the traumas he had suffered with the Bogota jewellery affair, threats of blackmail, the need of police protection, as well as pre-match sniping from a lunatic element in the crowd, he played as well as ever, rallying his team when they were 1-2 down. As Alan Stephenson remarked afterwards 'Bobby is fantastic. After all he's gone through, with all the worries on his mind, he just goes out and plays like the man he always is.' Moore was voted the *Evening Standard* player of the month.

But September was to prove even tougher than August. A draw at newly promoted Huddersfield was all the Hammers had to show from four League outings. The month ended with West Ham still winless after ten games and twentieth in the table. It was not until the eleventh game of the campaign that a Hurst hat-trick finally earned victory, at home to bottom-placed Burnley.

The only bright spots of September had been a League Cup home win over Hull and a 2-2 draw against Pele-inspired Santos in an exhibition game at Randalls Island Stadium, New York. That win over Terry Neill's Second Division Hull had been a close call, Eustace scoring the only goal five minutes from time. The game was marred shortly before the end when Billy Bonds was sent off. Nor was there any light at the end of the League Cup tunnel. In the next round the Hammers were knocked out at Coventry. Behind the scenes, John Lyall was promoted from his job of supervising the third team and the Colts to become Greenwood's assistant. From now on he travelled with the League side.

With his defence struggling, Stephenson facing a long lay-off following a cartilage operation, and John Cushley having already returned to Scotland, Greenwood had to buy. He signed 19-year-old Tommy Taylor from Orient for £78,000, Peter Bennett moving in the opposite direction as makeweight.

Results hardly improved at all, and the Hammers became almost permanently mired in twentieth position, with only Blackpool and Burnley beneath them. Greenwood's predicament was not eased by injuries and suspensions that prevented him fielding his preferred eleven each week. Thus it was that a number of young reserves were blooded, such as John McDowell and John Ayris, whilst Jimmy Lindsay, Brian Dear and Pat Holland also made a limited number of appearances.

In November the club had rewarded Bobby Moore for his loyal service with a testimonial, and a crowd of 24,448 turned up to see the England captain help his side to a 3-3 draw with Celtic. It was estimated that there were 5,000 Scots in the crowd. This provoked the suggestion that the hardcore of Hammers' fans had snubbed the occasion, admission prices having been hiked by match-sponsors Esso Petroleum. Only twenty per cent of season ticket holders had taken their normal seats, with many preferring to stand on the terraces. The price for that privilege had been increased from six shillings (30p) to ten shillings (50p), whilst stand seats had also been nearly doubled in price. The cost of a programme was three shillings (15p), instead of the usual one shilling. It was estimated that Moore would clear somewhere in the region of £15,000, a similar amount to that he earned each year, directly and indirectly, from soccer. It was noted that that same evening in Glasgow 50,000 had turned out to see Rangers play Moscow Dynamo.

If West Ham's precarious position in the League was worrying, their exit from the FA Cup at Blackpool hit the club like an earthquake. The score, 0-4, was bad enough, but it soon emerged that up to eight players had been revelling in a Blackpool nightclub until the early hours of Saturday morning. Four of the miscreants admitted their participation. Had they been fringe players the incident might have been glossed over. But the names included Bobby Moore and Jimmy Greaves, along with Brian Dear and Clyde Best. Each was fined and censored for 'irresponsible behaviour', as well as dropped while their futures were discussed. Moore's ban lasted two games, Greaves' three, Best's rather longer. Brian Dear never played for West Ham again.

Although Moore's image as the golden boy of English football was tarnished by the affair, there were those who thought the axe should fall on Greenwood – who had apparently been unaware of the incident until several days later – on account of the team's dreadful performances. In Greenwood's defence, chairman Reg

Pratt came out firmly in support. 'We have hit a bad patch but we have every confidence in the manager.' There was speculation that Moore would be sold, largely on account of his occasionally frosty relationship with Greenwood, and the latter's public criticism of Moore's widening interests outside the game. Media pundits suggested the England captain was now surplus to requirements at Upton Park. Stephenson was regaining fitness and Tommy Taylor could slot in beside him. John McDowell was doing well at right-back, which freed Billy Bonds to play in midfield.

Moore returned to action as a half-time substitute at home to Derby, who were already three goals up. Banners in the crowd called for Greenwood's sacking. Three days later, at Coventry, Moore and Greaves lined up at the start, alongside Ron Boyce, who had been out for four months through injury. Greaves scored the vital goal, whilst Moore's performance was described as 'majestic'. Greenwood again tried to buy his way out of trouble, paying a new club record £120,000 to Newcastle for their top scorer, Bryan 'Pop' Robson, who had scored both goals in the Magpies' 2-0 win at Upton Park in September. Robson was an instant success, scoring on his debut in the 2-0 home win over Nottingham Forest. In the fourteen matches he played for the Hammers that season, he was on the losing side only four times. But the club's League position did not improve. They finished twentieth, and their 34 points was the fewest so far since promotion in 1958.

The European Footballer of the Year award, voted on by football journalists from around the continent, saw Bobby Moore runner-up to Gerd Muller, the West German striker, who polled 77 votes to Moore's 69. Hurst finished joint eighteenth. Billy Bonds polled most votes for Hammer of the Year, having been runner-up last time. Jimmy Greaves quit the game 'while I am a First Division player. I only wanted to stay in football while I was enjoying it.' Greenwood may have had no more use for Greaves in any case. He indulged in a mini-purge, transfer-listing Peter Eustace, Trevor Brooking, Jimmy Lindsay and Dave Llewelyn, and giving free-transfers to another seven, among them Brian Dear and John Charles. The reason that some junior players departed was due to the decision to scrap the third team, which played in the Metropolitan League. In the London Five-a-Side Championships, the Hammers again reached the final, but lost to QPR and their wonder keeper, Phil Parkes.

In June the Hammers undertook a 20,000-mile trip around North America. One reporter wrote: 'This was one journey that wasn't really necessary. Time will prove me right or wrong but one thing is certain. Right now West Ham are a very tired side and with pre-season training looming ... that's not a good sign.'

DID YOU KNOW?

While warming up for a home FA Cup-tie with Bristol City in January 1969, Bobby Moore accidentally belted a ball into the face of a trombonist in the band.

Moore and Hurst, in addition, had four England internationals to play. All of which prompted Moore to note in his newspaper column: 'I had to laugh when I read those reports last week about making the season an eleven-month affair. For Geoff and myself it has been virtually that for the last seven years.'

Match of the Season 1970-71

Blackpool 4 West Ham 0

FA Cup, 3rd Round, 3 January 1971

The Cup was all West Ham had left to look forward to. Blackpool had won only three out of 23 matches in the First Division and only two cup-ties in the past ten seasons. Two days prior to this match the Seasiders had appointed Bob Stokoe manager, following the dismissal of Les Shannon. Stokoe left pre-match preparations in the hands of Jimmy Meadows and Harry Johnston. West Ham were missing Hurst and Brooking through injury.

On a hard, slippery pitch, Blackpool took a half-hour lead with a fine solo effort from Tony Green. Eight minutes later he added a second, firing back a half-clearance from the edge of the area. Two minutes into the second half Bobby Howe was dispossessed and the ball broke to Craven for 3-0. It was academic now, but Moore went into midfield, Eustace pushed forward, and Dear came on for Ayris with Clyde Best going out wide. With ten minutes to go, Mowbray, the home side's left-back, hit a cross-shot past Ferguson from just inside the penalty area.

Some 370 fans travelling back on a British Rail 'special' organised a petition demanding Greenwood's sacking, and there was talk of a mass boycott at the next home game. The press headlines for the moment concentrated on the match and how easily West Ham had capitulated. But word was already spreading about the shenanigans at a Blackpool nightclub owned by local ex-boxer Brian London. By Monday the press were saying players did not return to their hotel rooms until 3am and were ordering breakfast at 11.

Dropping players as punishment hardly helped, as the Hammers lost all three games that Moore and Greaves missed. In many ways, Upton Park would never be quite the same again, despite the veneer that appeared to gloss over the sorry saga.

LEAGUE DIVISION 1	**1971-72**
Division 1	14th
League Cup	Semi-finals
FA Cup	3rd Round

After the relegation scare of the previous season, Ron Greenwood, in a pre-season newspaper interview, outlined his reasons for optimism. The purchase of Tommy Taylor and Bryan Robson had given his squad more options, particularly as both were adaptable players. Taylor, not yet twenty, could play either in defence or in the midfield pushing forward, whilst Robson, who had played behind the front runners when first signed, would now play – because of Greaves's retirement – alongside Hurst. This took some of the weight off Hurst, who was set a target of twenty goals. Another plus was the form of Bobby Ferguson. Greenwood noted that since returning to the side in November, the country's most expensive goalkeeper 'had fulfilled all my hopes. At long last, he had arrived, and I think Taylor helped.' Billy Bonds had switched to midfield, where his competitive edge was so valuable. The emergence of John McDowell at right-back and Clyde Best up front were other positive factors. So too was the return from injury of Alan Stephenson and Ron Boyce. Transfer-listed Trevor Brooking and Peter Eustace were on the fringes of the team, Greenwood having received no bids that matched his valuation of the players.

If the start to the previous season had been bad, this one was worse. Three matches, no goals, no points. For the third of these defeats, at Nottingham Forest, Brooking was reinstated in the team, where he remained for the rest of season, and Taylor reverted to centre-half at the expense of Stephenson, who in November was loaned to Fulham before being finally transferred to Portsmouth.

At last, Greenwood appeared to have got it right. By the end of October, eleven more matches having been played, West Ham had won six, drawn four, lost only one, and lay ninth in the table. Much of the success was down to the nine goals accredited to Best, as well as the side more or less picking itself. The resurgence sparked a run in the League Cup that saw Cardiff, Leeds and Liverpool pushed aside to propel the Hammers into the quarter-finals. November illustrated, however, yet again the fickle nature of Greenwood's team. They lost all four League matches played, but once they put on their cup boots crushed Sheffield United (newly promoted to the top division) 5-0 – Robson netting his first hat-trick. Eleven days beforehand the Blades had visited Upton Park in the League and won 1-0, ending their own sequence of five winless games and also West Ham's run of ten matches without defeat.

DID YOU KNOW?

When West Ham played at Chelsea in August 1969, the new floodlights had not been properly installed and the beams danced giddily across the pitch like in a storm.

Two bright spots in November were Geoff Hurst's testimonial – when West Ham drew 4-4 with a European XI before a crowd of 29,000, who paid up to £1 for a seat or half that to stand – and first Under-23 caps for Brooking (who also scored) and Lampard in the draw with Switzerland. Moore and Hurst, meanwhile, played for the England side in the European Nations Cup-tie in Greece.

The League Cup semi-final was the first occasion that West Ham had reached the last four of a major tournament for five years. Against mid-table Stoke in the first leg, the Hammers got off to a flying start with a 2-1 win at the Victoria Ground, secured by Hurst's penalty and Best's volley. In the second leg a week later, John Ritchie scored for Stoke to level the scores overall. Away goals at that time had no place in the rules, otherwise West Ham would have booked their place in the final. If extra-time did not produce a decisive goal, a replay would be required. In fact, though extra-time saw no goals it did produce an incident sufficiently dramatic to be regularly shown on television. With the tie just four minutes from a replay, Gordon Banks, Stoke's World Cup goalkeeper, fumbled a shot and in his desperation to regain possession took the legs from under Harry Redknapp. All Hurst had to do was convert the penalty to send West Ham to Wembley. On England get-togethers Hurst and Banks must have got to know each other's strengths and weaknesses as intimately as if they had been team-mates, and over the years Banks must have faced any number of Hurst penalties on the practice ground. This should have counted for little in the hurly-burly of a cup semi-final, particularly as Hurst, as was his custom, opted for power instead of placement. In Hurst's favour was the fact that the ball was struck with power. Against him was the fact that it flew at mid-height, not too far to Banks' right. The keeper guessed correctly, plunging to his right to fist away Hurst's rocket over the bar. Emerging from a scrum of grateful team-mates, Banks busily focussed their minds on the impending corner-kick. Later, he would describe his save as on a par with that against Pele's header in 1970. In truth, the Pele save had called upon far more than simple reflexes. But for Hurst the burden would be heavy should West Ham fail in the replay.

Back in the League, Moore & Co suffered a home defeat against Newcastle, who scored after five minutes and spent the remainder of the game with ten men behind the ball. West Ham had now gone seven games and two months without a League win, so it was perhaps inevitable that two days after Christmas, before a crowd of 54,000, they ended Spurs' unbeaten home record. Best's header did the damage. On New Year's Day, table-topping Manchester United were brushed aside, 3-0 at Upton Park.

The players were therefore on a high when, four days later, they turned out at Hillsborough for the Stoke replay. Both keepers were unbeatable, even during extra-time, necessitating yet another replay, this time at Old Trafford three weeks later. By then, the Hammers had overcome the first hurdle in the FA Cup, defeating Second Division Luton 2-1 at home in a tie that saw Bobby Moore stretchered off with what was feared to be a broken leg. Mercifully, the injury was diagnosed as no more serious than a damaged nerve. Moore was back in his usual place the following week for the 3-3 draw against title-chasing Derby.

Stoke had won the toss to decide the venue for the second replay – the fourth episode of this protracted tie. As Match of the Season describes, the fates conspired against West Ham, enabling Stoke to contest their first Wembley final in the 108 years of their existence. Inevitably, the psychological effect on the Hammers was immense. They found wins hard to come by in the League, and needed two games even to squeeze past non-league Hereford in the FA Cup. Hereford, of course, had just eliminated Newcastle, and endless re-runs of Ronnie Radford's famous goal must have eaten away at West Ham's confidence. A fifth-round tie at Huddersfield, destined to finish bottom of the First Division on account of their dreadful home record, offered realistic hopes of a place in the last eight. But Huddersfield, who would muster just twelve home League goals all season, conjured up four in 90 minutes to leave Greenwood close to despair. League form likewise fell away: West Ham won just four (all at home) of their final sixteen fixtures to leave them a disappointing fourteenth.

To confirm his own personal improvement, Trevor Brooking was voted Hammer of the Year, whilst Bobby Ferguson's exploits and performances between the posts, which had materially improved the team's defensive record, earned him runner-up spot in the poll. It was announced at the season's end that Harry Redknapp had been transfer listed after ten years at Upton Park, during which he had made 150 appearances. He joined on that list Peter Eustace who, since his listing a year earlier, had played in just four further games. Behind the scenes, the board took the decision to permit from the following season commercial advertising around the pitch and in the match programme. The extra revenue to be generated was reckoned to be around £20,000 per annum.

Match of the Season 1971-72

Stoke City 3 West Ham 2

League Cup, semi-final, 2nd replay, 26 January 1972

It had been eight long years since West Ham last graced Wembley, and only Moore and Hurst were still around from the team that overcame Preston in the FA Cup final of 1964. For the rest of the current Hammers team, cup finals were things that happened only in dreams. At the end of 90 chaotic minutes in the Old Trafford mud, any thoughts of cup finals were tantamount to nightmares. Both teams had been averaging two games a week since the start of the season, and on top of their natural fatigue they were now asked to perform in ankle-deep mud on a bone-shakingly cold night in blinding rain and swirling wind. What ensued was a cup-tie of the kind often described as 'typically British', namely blood and guts, end-to-end action, spills galore, and a large dollop of controversy. Needless to say, one team had to lose, and on this occasion that team was West Ham.

Much hinged on a thirteenth-minute incident, when Ferguson dived at the feet of Stoke winger Terry Conroy, whose sliding leg landed the goalkeeper's head a sickening blow. The motionless Ferguson was clearly in a bad way. It took seven long minutes before the concussed Scot was able to rise to his feet and endeavour to resume his position. Plainly dizzy, he was seen reeling around his goal like a drunk. This prompted Moore to signal for further attention from the trainer, upon which Ferguson was led groggily to the dressing room for treatment. Moore pulled on Ferguson's green jersey, temporarily, he hoped, while efforts were made to see if Ferguson could continue.

For the moment down to ten men, West Ham tried hard to conceal their handicap, as well as protect their captain from a now rampant Stoke attack. Twelve minutes after Moore went in goal, a wretched back-pass resulted in Stoke's John Ritchie being upended as the ball slowed in the mud. Penalty to Stoke, the last thing ten-man West Ham needed. Despair turned to delight and back to despair as Moore beat away Mike Bernard's spot-kick, only to see the ball rebound to the same player, who swept it in.

Against the odds, Billy Bonds thumped an equaliser from twenty yards, at which point Ferguson returned to the fray, defying the advice of the Manchester United doctor to take no further part. Level once more in numbers and in goals, the tide was unmistakably with West Ham, and it came as no surprise when Bonds crossed for Brooking to drive a left-foot volley past Banks. At that stage few would have wagered money on a Stoke recovery, but George Eastham's wizardry set up an equaliser for Peter Dobing and the dynamics of the game changed yet again. A Stoke cross from the right was cleared by Tommy Taylor to the edge of the area, only for Conroy to hit the ball first-time and see it skid under Ferguson and squeeze into net by the far post.

It is a truism that many Northerners thought, and think, that the Hammers were a soft touch when facing adversity. Not on this day, they weren't. Yet again they stormed into attack. Redknapp hit a post, Moore fired inches over, Best saw a header expertly saved by Banks, whilst Robson had a 'goal' ruled offside. But perhaps the cruellest twist occurred when Hurst appeared to be clearly fouled in the box, but West Ham's strident appeals for a penalty were brushed away by referee Pat Partridge.

In the end the Hammers could not quite close the gap; but my goodness how they had tried, as Stoke's veteran inside-forwards, Eastham and Dobing, calmed and eased the pressure on their teammates by slowing the game in midfield. While Greenwood praised the courage and spirit of all his players, his opposite number, Tony Waddington ruefully commented: 'It is a shame that any side had to lose. It sounds ridiculous but after this Wembley could be something of an anti-climax.' Perhaps he had momentarily forgotten that it would be his club's first appearance on that hallowed turf since they had been founded.

LEAGUE DIVISION 1	**1972-73**
Division 1	6th
League Cup	3rd Round
FA Cup	4th Round

In the summer of 1972 the cinder track in front of the West Stand was widened by erecting a new retaining wall. Not only did this allow advertising hoardings around the perimeter of the pitch, it also eliminated the likelihood of the players 'going over the top' into the crowd. This had been the regular fate of flying wingers when faced with robust shoulder charges.

On the playing side, the one prominent newcomer, Dudley Tyler – who had impressed for Hereford in the FA Cup – was eclipsed by the identities of those leaving Upton Park. The departures of Alan Stephenson to Portsmouth, Harry Redknapp to Bournemouth and Peter Eustace to Sheffield Wednesday were expected. The sale of Geoff Hurst to Stoke for £80,000 came as a bolt from the blue. Now 30, and a Hammer for fourteen years – during which time he had played nearly 500 games and scored 248 goals – Hurst had learned from Greenwood that an earlier bid from QPR had been seriously considered. That fact alone made Hurst realise that his days at Upton Park were numbered, and he had put in a written transfer request. Contractual wrangles with other players carried on after the season had started. After five matches, pay-rebel Bobby Ferguson was dropped and transfer-listed by Greenwood just hours before the game at Arsenal. It would be another eleven games before Ferguson was recalled.

The team got off to their best start for four years, winning two and drawing one of their first three games. Three away losses interrupted the momentum, but by the end of November – following a win at Everton in Bobby Moore's 500th League game – West Ham were eighth. Earlier that month Moore had earned his 98th cap in a 1-0 win over Wales in Cardiff. He was therefore unavailable to play in Ronnie 'Ticker' Boyce's testimonial, in which Manchester United were beaten 5-2 before a crowd of 19,000.

The most obvious factor in West Ham's modest resurgence was the goalscoring of Bryan 'Pop' Robson – he topped the division's scoring charts by the New Year with seventeen goals in 25 League games. With Brooking netting eight and Best six, the team looked to have solved the threat of a goal-drought posed by the sale of Hurst. But transfer talk was rife. Ted MacDougall was supposed to be coming, and Robson going, when he protested about being played in midfield during the 0-1 home loss to leaders Liverpool. McDowell and Taylor were selected for the England Under-23s.

DID YOU KNOW?

At home to Liverpool in January 1973, Ron Greenwood played Pop Robson – the division's leading scorer – in midfield. West Ham lost and failed to score.

It went without saying that West Ham needed a good cup run to revitalise their season. Apart from the previous campaign's semi-final of the League Cup, in recent years cup tournaments had not been happy hunting grounds for Greenwood's teams, and too often for comfort they had been knocked out by lower-division sides. But this season would be no different. Participation in the League Cup had ended with a humiliating defeat at Fourth Division Stockport. In the FA Cup, following a squeaky 1-0 win at Third Division Port Vale, the Hammers then travelled to Hull. On a foggy afternoon on Humberside, the mid-table Second Division side outpaced, out-played and out-thought their more illustrious opponents, and fully merited their one-goal victory.

How different it had been seven days previously in the League, when the Hammers blitzed Chelsea at Upton Park 3-1, with Robson scoring twice and Brooking showing the class that would lead to international honours. The performance had commentators purring that this was the sharpest the Hammers had looked for some time. And one week after the Hull debacle, the Hammers once again showed their other side, winning at League Cup finalists Norwich. Life was not easy, being a Hammers supporter.

February 1973 brought more headlines. Bobby Moore overtook Jimmy Ruffell's record number of League appearances for the club, with his 509th game in the First Division. Ruffell's record had gone unchallenged since 1936. The England captain was also presented with a silver tray, inscribed with the flags of the nations he had played against, to mark his 100th full international. On the transfer front, Ted MacDougall finally signed from Manchester United for £150,000, though the ongoing rail-strike delayed his registration, and hence his debut, until March. 'Supermac' mouthed off about his miserable 150 days at Old Trafford, in ways that would ring a bell when he finally left Upton Park.

MacDougall made a super start, four goals in his first five games, helping the team to a nine-game unbeaten run which carried them up to fifth. Though defeat by Arsenal in the final fixture meant they slipped back to sixth, it nevertheless constituted West Ham's highest position in Greenwood's twelve years at the club. The ever-present Pop Robson, with his 28 goals, was voted Hammer of the Year (Brooking was runner-up), though contractual problems linked Robson with a possible move to Cup-winners Sunderland.

The youth section also had their moments. Although they did not progress far in the two major competitions – the FA Youth Cup and the Southern Junior Floodlit Cup – they reached the final of the London Youth Cup (Senior Section) and won the Junior Section, as well as the South East Counties League Division Two Cup.

Match of the Season 1972-73

Stockport 2 West Ham 1

League Cup, 3rd Round, 4 October 1972

There cannot be much doubt that this result ranked as one of the greatest upsets to befall not only West Ham, but any First Division team, since the inception of the League Cup over a decade previously. The Hammers had proved on countless occasions their inability to overcome teams, not only from lower divisions, but also First Division clubs inferior in technical ability and skill but superior in other ways.

No strangers to giant-killing in this competition, Fourth Division County had already put paid to First Division Crystal Palace in the previous round, and the visit of 'upper crust' Hammers to Edgeley Park generated tremendous pre-match publicity. A crowd of 13,410, packed into the tight stadium, saw West Ham start the game smoothly and full of composure, forcing two corners in the opening three minutes. Stockport had barely taken meaningful aim themselves when, to everyone's surprise, they snatched a lead after nineteen minutes. Inside-forward Russell collected the ball 30 yards out and hit a dipper under Peter Grotier's crossbar.

West Ham dismissed the affront with an equaliser eight minutes later. Robson's fierce drive created the opening, the ball being parried by keeper Ogley and finding its way to Clyde Best, whose drive wriggled inside a post. Moments later a bewitching run by Dudley Tyler left Robson with an easy header which he planted against a post. That miss was to have heavy overtones. Shortly before the interval, County winger Garbett hoisted a centre beyond the far post and for no apparent reason McDowell bundled Hugh Ryden off his feet as Grotier caught the ball. Tommy Spratt, Stockport's captain, took responsibility from the spot.

West Ham came out for the second period with quickened tread. Moore thrust forward, whilst Bonds made prudent use of the right flank. Best headed over the bar, Robson twice broke clear, only to have Ogley stretch full-length to thwart goal-bound shots. It was virtually one-way traffic for the whole of the half. Unfortunately, it was to no avail. Time and again County regrouped to defend in depth, playing their way out of tight corners to frustrate their visitors.

With just seconds to go, Best latched onto a bad back-pass and with the arrogance and menace of a man who seemed certain to score bore down on goal. The big Bermudian striker drew Ogley to one side, before ghosting past him to unleash a shot towards the inviting net. In any other game, it would have been a goal. But somehow the Stockport goalkeeper hauled himself off the floor, flung up an arm and deflected the ball over the crossbar. Best's somersault of disgust and despair, which ended with him sprawled in a crumpled heap, summed up the anguish of his team.

The next day's papers carried a banner headline – 'Shockport County'. For Greenwood and his players it was another episode in a long-running saga of self-inflicted misery. Stockport's winning side had been pieced together and assembled for all of £2,000. Nor were they the first team from Division Four to k.o. First Division West Ham in the League Cup. Darlington had done the same in 1960. Bobby Moore was part of that Hammers' side too!

LEAGUE DIVISION 1	**1973-74**
Division 1	18th
League Cup	2nd Round
FA Cup	3rd Round

The Hammers embarked on a series of end-of-season friendlies, which saw them visit Israel, Norway and lastly Spain, where, in the City of Zaragoza Trophy tournament, a number of regulars were unavailable through international calls or injuries. On the transfer front, the close season saw no major ins or outs.

But the Football League was in the throes of revolution. No longer were only two clubs to be relegated to the Second Division. From 1973-74 three down and three up would be introduced, the rationale being to generate interest in what had hitherto been tame end-of-season affairs. The same logic would eventually lead to the introduction of play-offs in the late 1980s. For clubs like West Ham, in recent years more often to be found in the lower, rather than the higher, reaches of the division, the new rule spelled instant peril. Indeed, had it been in place in 1970-71, the Hammers would have gone down then.

Other off-field changes included the introduction of VAT, which at a stroke increased ticket prices for football supporters across the country. Curiously, the number of applications to renew season tickets at Upton Park remained constant, with a waiting list of 2,000. Perhaps they were attracted by the coming Watney Cup, a new pre-season trophy designed to reward the two highest scoring teams in each division which had failed to win promotion or qualify for Europe. West Ham had finished third top scorers in the First Division – behind champions Liverpool and third-placed Leeds, who entered the UEFA Cup – and were drawn to play the winners of the previous year's Watney Cup, Third Division Bristol Rovers at Eastville. The match was played in the midst of the Hammers' pre-season training, but that was no excuse for the team's lame showing. 'A fragile and wan West Ham' wrote one sports reporter afterwards, even though Rovers needed a penalty shoot-out to claim the tie. West Ham had been short-priced favourites to win the trophy, but that journalist's words damned them: 'The Hammers will not start favourites to win any other soccer competition this season.'

He was right. West Ham's League start exceeded all others in its awfulness. By late October, when the players travelled to Coventry, they were winless after eleven games and had only four draws and ten goals to their credit. At kick-off, Coventry sat fourth, West Ham were bottom, yet John McDowell's second-half volley was enough to upset the form-book.

DID YOU KNOW?

An era draws to a close. The great Bobby Moore finally bowed out of Upton Park after half an hour of the FA Cup-tie with Hereford on 5 January 1974. He went off injured.

The wretched start left Upton Park in turmoil. Team selection had caused headaches from the start. McDowell was injured and Ferguson had domestic problems, opening the door to 18-year-old Mervyn Day. Ferguson was transfer-listed after describing Upton Park as a 'morgue' and accusing his team-mates of being 'gutless and spineless'. Injury meant Best was in and out of the side, and wayward shooting meant MacDougall shared the same fate – he was then sent off for butting Burnley's Doug Collins. Dudley Tyler found the chasm between Southern League and First Division too wide to bridge, and there was also talk of Frank Lampard's future at the club being under threat.

But perhaps the most traumatic event of all was the dropping of the team captain, Moore, who was omitted from the side at Manchester United, in Greenwood's words, because of 'unexpected adverse publicity that was bad for morale'. This fuelled speculation that Moore's career at West Ham was over and that Brian Clough's Derby were about to sign him. Some months earlier, Clough had reputedly bid £400,000 for both Moore and Trevor Brooking. Both players, meanwhile, were selected for Ramsey's England squad to play Austria. In the event, Brooking would not win his first cap until April, whereas Moore had already overtaken Bobby Charlton's record with his 107th.

Three weeks after losing in Manchester the Hammers crashed at home to Burnley. This time the knives were out for the manager – in the press, on radio, and on Match of the Day. Greenwood replied 'I'm certainly not quitting and I have no intentions of resigning.' Despite his chairman's public backing, press gossip insisted that it was only a matter of time before Greenwood moved up to general manager, relinquishing his involvement in the day-to-day running of the side.

It was to be another seven games after that first win before the second arrived. In the interim, Greenwood signed the experienced striker Bobby Gould for £70,000, midfielder Graham Paddon for £170,000, and defender Mick McGiven on loan. The Paddon deal took Ted MacDougall in the opposite direction, to Norwich, while Dudley Tyler was sold back to Hereford. Day, meantime, had made the goalkeeper's jersey his own.

West Ham were still rooted to the foot of the table at Christmas, and home gates had slipped to just 16,500. But the new intake of players finally paid dividends. Starting at Chelsea on Boxing Day – when they overhauled a 0-2 half-time deficit to win 4-2 – the Hammers lost just once in twelve League fixtures, to leave them in the comparative luxury of sixteenth place.

This did not mean that all was rosy once more in the West Ham garden. Far from it, for while the team were picking up points they were suffering yet more ignominy in the FA Cup. This time their conquerors were Hereford, no longer non-league but, following two promotions in two years, now in the Third Division. The Hammers were just two minutes from elimination at Upton Park on 5 January, when Pat Holland's equaliser got them (temporarily) off the hook. Of greater significance was the injury Moore sustained half an hour into the tie which took him from the pitch. Although he returned in late February to the reserves, he never again graced the first team. Instead, in early March, Robert Frederick Chelsea Moore quit the club by 'mutual agreement' to sign for Second Division Fulham. His fee was £25,000. Moore was just short of his 33rd birthday and had been a first-teamer for West Ham for sixteen seasons. With hindsight, his England career was over too. He had earned what turned out to be his final cap in November, against Italy.

Prior to West Ham's home game with Coventry on 16 March, Moore waved an emotional farewell to his countless admirers, who responded in kind. Moore shook hands publicly with Greenwood on the pitch. Both men had reasons to smile: Moore received a handsome bonus as a signing-on fee, while Greenwood had been named Manager of the Month for February. All was smiles, but few knew the feelings that lay beneath the friendly facade. No matter, it was the end of an era. Ninety minutes later West Ham lost their first game in thirteen and were plunged back into the relegation dogfight. They eventually crossed the finishing line one point clear of third-from-bottom Southampton, who were relegated.

As the campaign closed, transfer talk again surrounded Pop Robson, who had missed half the season through injury and scored just eight goals, and Brooking, for whom a rival London club had apparently bid £400,000.

Match of the Season 1973-74

Hereford 2 West Ham 1

FA Cup, 3rd Round, replay, 9 January 1974

1973-74 saw many potential candidates for Match of the Season – a first ever win at Coventry; the victory at Chelsea after being two goals down; wins over bottom-placed Norwich, over champions-elect Leeds and Southampton, which, had the result been reversed, would have seen the Hammers relegated. A case could also be made for the 2-2 draw with Liverpool on the final Saturday of the campaign. But the Cup-ties with Hereford stand out, partly because they witnessed the last time Bobby Moore ever pulled on the claret and blue, and partly because the Hammers *twice* failed to beat their lowly opponents. In the past, it had generally been in away cup-ties that West Ham had proved vulnerable. But against Hereford they almost came a cropper at home, the visitors hitting a post after they had taken the lead and holding out until seconds from time.

Britain had for some time been in the grip of industrial disputes that obliged Ted Heath's Tory Government to impose a 'three-day working week'. To conserve energy and avert the need for floodlights, the matches with Hereford kicked off at 1.45pm, including the midweek replay, which invited much absenteeism from work in Herefordshire.

The maxim for small clubs drawn against bigger ones in the Cup is simple: win at the first attempt, for you will be found out at the second. This was not the case for Hereford who, having felt cruelly deprived by Pat Holland's late equaliser at Upton Park, brooked no argument about their replay win at Edgar Street. West Ham even drew first blood – Clyde Best heading in Frank Lampard's cross – but within two minutes Keith Coleman tripped Brian Evans in the area and the two teams were suddenly on level terms. In the second half, Hereford's longest-serving player, centre-half Alan Jones, ventured upfield for a corner. Dudley Tyler miscued a shot into his path and Jones scored inside a post.

That defeat drew a line, at least for a few years, under the sequence of terrible results against lowly teams in the cup that had plagued the Hammers since the glory days of the mid-1960s. The departure of Moore severed the link between the Greenwood era and that of John Lyall, whose growing influence on team selection and tactics overhauled the club from the mid-1970s onwards.

4

FROM WEMBLEY TO WEMBLEY 1974-1980

LEAGUE DIVISION 1	**1974-75**
Division 1	13th
League Cup	3rd Round
FA Cup	Winners

Having missed half the season through injury, been forced to play in midfield instead of up front, and finally been named as twelfth man in the final match of the season, Pop Robson demanded to leave. He returned to his native north-east, signing for Sunderland. Greenwood was in no hurry to sign a replacement, confident that his forward line was potent enough even without Robson.

Pre-season consisted of a tour of Norway and participation in the Texaco Cup, which was entered by invitation. West Ham's interest did not last long: they lost to Luton and Southampton in the group stage, showing that the problems of the previous season were still manifest. And when they collapsed 0-4 at Manchester City in the League opener, pessimism hung heavy in the air. Seven games into the season West Ham were once again bottom of the pile, but by that time the players had a new boss.

Following a home defeat by Everton, a London paper reported that John Lyall was taking control of team affairs for the rest of the season whilst Ron Greenwood would be scouting for new players. The press 'leak' resulted in club chairman Reg Pratt calling a hastily arranged press conference and going on TV to explain the changes. Greenwood had apparently suggested the change himself, and Pratt insisted that there was no question of Greenwood being demoted – 'He is still manager.' Lyall took a different slant: 'It is now my team and I'm going to stamp my personality on the side. Ron and I have disagreed on a couple of matters, but now the team will reflect my ideas.' Indeed, it was not long before Lyall was confirmed as 'team manager'.

Lyall's initial impact was little less than sensational. The players shrugged off a defeat at Spurs, which left them bottom, to hit

Leicester for six and launch a seventeen-match run with only one defeat. In the space of just over three months they soared from last to fifth, just two points behind leaders Ipswich and Middlesbrough. It was ironic, but somehow predictable, that it should be their former star striker Geoff Hurst, now at Stoke, who burst the bubble by scoring the winning goal in a 1-2 reverse at the Victoria Ground in the last match of 1974.

Lyall had not been slow to buy, signing Watford striker Billy Jennings for £110,000 and Keith Robson, a no-nonsense if temperamental left-winger, for £45,000 from Newcastle. Both in their early twenties, both scored on their League debuts, and in tandem they gave Lyall's side the attacking punch that had been lacking. With Bobby Gould also finding his goalscoring touch, a defence that was tighter and meaner than had been seen for many years, and the clenched-fist captaincy of Billy Bonds, the new-look Hammers began to play with a style that was a throw-back to the best of the Greenwood era.

Fulham, and their new recruit, Bobby Moore, were destined to play a big part in West Ham's fortunes this season. The teams were paired in the League Cup at Craven Cottage, and at half-time the Hammers led by a Trevor Brooking goal and were seemingly on course for the next round. Moore had been made Fulham captain for the night and did his noble best for his new club. Shortly after the interval Alan Mullery equalised, then one of the four floodlights failed, at the end West Ham were defending. The game was held up for some 25 minutes, with the crowd of nearly 30,000 – Fulham's biggest for ten years – still inside the ground. At length the referee allowed play to resume, having obtained the agreement of keeper Mervyn Day, though the lights had not been fully repaired. Five minutes after the resumption, whilst still adjusting to the dimmed vision, Day was deceived by a half-hit shot that trickled into the far corner of his net. Moore's new team had beaten his old.

The FA Cup was a more cheerful story. Relegated Southampton fell at the Dell at the first stage, and Third Division Swindon at the second – though not before West Ham had nearly committed cup suicide. Swindon scored a late equaliser at Upton Park, then, at a packed County Ground, snatched a first-half lead in the replay. Brooking's brilliance and Day's defiance turned the tables and set up a home tie with QPR in the fifth round. Once again West Ham came from behind, earning a place in the quarter-finals for the first time since they had won the trophy eleven years earlier. Arsenal at Highbury, where the Hammers had already lost 0-3 in the League, was the next obstacle. Lyall now introduced his secret weapon, a slightly built 21-year-old called Alan Taylor, known by his team-mates as 'Sparrow.' In late November Taylor had signed from Fourth Division Rochdale for £45,000 and he now shot to fame in a manner worthy of any 'Boy's Own' Annual. Taylor had made just three appearances, two of them as substitute, when Lyall threw him in at the deep end at Highbury. Taylor responded by scoring both goals in the north London mud.

The Cup run proved costly for the Hammers. A number of key regulars – Bonds, Holland and Keith Robson – all missed games through injury, added to which the distractions of a possible visit to Wembley caused the team to take their eye off the ball in the League. They slid down the table as quickly as they had risen up it. The second half of the season brought just two wins, dumping the Hammers down to sixteenth, before a final day victory over Arsenal enabled them to finish three places higher.

Two of those defeats preceded the semi-final at Villa Park against Ipswich. The Suffolk side, managed by Bobby Robson, had no such League problems. They came into the semi-final on a high, having knocked Liverpool off the top of the table at Easter, but now looked disorganised and leg weary as the Hammers stumbled to a goalless draw. The replay four days later at Stamford Bridge might have been a different story. Ipswich put Bonds and his colleagues on the rack as they dominated for long periods. But their only joy came when Jennings sliced an attempted clearance into his own net. Fortunately for his team-mates, Alan Taylor netted twice yet again, the second in extra-time, to save the day.

Three more League defeats ensued, including one at Portman Road as Ipswich gained token revenge, before the Hammers signed off the campaign with a fortuitous win over Arsenal on the Monday prior to the final. There they faced Fulham, who had dumped the Hammers out of the League Cup some seven months before. Wembley would provide an emotional reunion between Moore and his former colleagues, and make a superstar out of Alan Taylor.

West Ham's youngsters also made it to the final of the FA Youth Cup, where they lost 1-5 to Ipswich. It was the one trophy claimed by Bobby Robson's club, whose seniors missed out on the League title by two points. Derby claimed the championship.

Match of the Season 1974-75

Fulham 0 West Ham 2

FA Cup final, 3 May 1975

The most poignant newspaper photo to appear after this emotional all-London final was not one of the obvious ones. It did not feature

DID YOU KNOW?

In 1974-75, helter-skelter Hammers soared from bottom (in September) to 5th (on Boxing Day), then slid all the way back to 16th with one match to play.

Alan Taylor's goal, or skipper Bonds lifting the Cup, or the joyous Hammers' players skipping round Wembley on their lap of honour, or the ecstatic fans celebrating their team's success. No, the arresting photo was of Bobby Moore, who in other circumstances might have climbed those 39 steps as West Ham captain to hoist the Cup, but who now trudged almost unnoticed from the pitch – unnoticed, that is, except for one alert cameraman. Moore, a man who had lived his life in the spotlight, now found himself ignored, but he never won a medal in braver company. Moore, his friend and team-mate Alan Mullery, and Fulham's wily manager Alec Stock, had taken the Second Division club so close. As Moore raised his left arm to his cheek, in a gesture that had become his own over the years, one could speculate on whether or not he was wiping away the sweat of his afternoon's labours or perhaps a tear. It was perhaps ironic that the man of the match for each side, scoring nine marks out of ten, were Moore for Fulham and the young Hammer who had worn the No 6 shirt since the maestro's departure – Kevin Lock – of whom many were tipping a full cap.

When all is said and done, the final was decided in West Ham's favour by the team's youth, their swifter pace in the second period, and their domination of midfield. For all the efforts of Mullery and the skill and anticipation of Moore, these were not enough to revive Fulham after Taylor had scored twice in a four-minute period after an hour's play. Both goals stemmed from Fulham keeper Peter Mellor's failure to cleanly gather the ball.

If there were any doubts at the beginning of the season, when Lyall took over as team manager, about whether his position would be made permanent at the end of it, these were now dispelled. The team's victories en route to the Cup had in many critics' eyes been tentative, even lucky, but as far as the fans were concerned the end result was all that mattered. For Lyall, it was the start of a period that would see him become the most successful manager in the club's history.

LEAGUE DIVISION 1	**1975-76**
Division 1	18th
League Cup	4th Round
FA Cup	3rd Round
European Cup-Winners' Cup	Finalists

Like true gentlemen, Greenwood and Lyall each gave credit for the Cup triumph to the other. They, it appeared, were as much a team themselves, in the continental two-tier tradition of general overlord (Greenwood) and track-suited manager (Lyall). Both believed that the Hammers' return to European competition after a decade's absence would be just the start. The squad was young enough, and good enough – they maintained – to keep winning trophies for another four or five years.

A pre-season tour of Norway was capped by another visit to Wembley, this time to play Derby in the FA Charity Shield. The League champions proved superior in the sauna conditions, with West Ham missing the driving force of their captain, Billy Bonds, recuperating from surgery on a groin injury that had plagued him for months. The absence of their charismatic leader did not seem to worry his colleagues, who got off to a flyer in the League. By the end of September the Hammers had won six and drawn three of their first nine fixtures and were kept off the top of the table only on goal-difference by QPR. Bonds made his comeback in the midst of that winning run, helping to sustain the momentum. These were happy weeks for all concerned with the club. Chairman Reg Pratt was the recipient of a surprise presentation from his fellow directors to mark his quarter-century in that office.

A mistake by keeper Day resulted in a 0-1 defeat in Fiorentina in the first leg of the revived Anglo-Italian Cup. Lyall's team faired better in the opening shots of the European Cup-Winners' Cup, comfortably disposing of the Finnish part-timers of Reipas Lahden. Progress was also made in the early stages of the League Cup at the expense of Bristol City and Darlington.

October and November were also good months. The Hammers kept up the pressure in their quest for a first League title by beating Newcastle and leaders Manchester United at Upton Park. In the latter game, Man U fans invaded the pitch, causing the referee to take the teams off the field and the match to be halted for nineteen minutes until order was restored by the police. The ref afterwards admitted that he had set a time limit of twenty minutes on any delay before abandoning the match. West Ham's victory meant that QPR, Man U and Lyall's men were all locked on nineteen points at the top. The win over Tommy Docherty's Manchester was all the more remarkable as the Hammers had only returned home two days earlier following a 6,400-mile round-trip to Armenia (via Moscow) in the next stage of their quest for the Cup-Winners' Cup. The second leg was played on Bonfire Night, when Bonds & Co set East London alight with a scintillating exhibition of attacking football that swept them into the last eight.

The only dark spots in November were a 1-2 defeat at Derby, who thereby went top of the League, and by Spurs in the League Cup at Upton Park, after West Ham thought they had done the hard part in drawing at White Hart Lane. A cause of concern for Lyall during this time was the absence of Bonds, now suffering from a tear in the scar tissue of his troublesome groin. He would be missing from the side for four crucial months, and not return until the European campaign resumed after its winter break.

Ron Greenwood was reported to have turned down the chance of a new career in the North American Soccer League. The offer, which he described as 'the best I've ever had', was reportedly worth £35,000, but Greenwood added 'there are some things more important than money'. One departure from the Boleyn Ground was super-sub Bobby Gould who returned to one of his former clubs, Wolves.

December was a let-down. Fiorentina, after taking an early lead in the second leg of the Anglo-Italian Cup, frustrated Upton Park with a superbly organised defence. Worse, five League fixtures brought four defeats. In one of them, at home to Ipswich, Keith Robson was sent off for throwing a punch in a bad-tempered and petulant televised game that would land him a four-match ban. Come the New Year, West Ham were down to sixth, and nor did matters improve. Bob Paisley's Liverpool ended any interest in the FA Cup with a controlled display against a weakened Hammers at Upton Park. Four weeks later they returned in the League to inflict a crushing four-goal defeat and show why they were headed for the championship. They would pip Dave Sexton's QPR for that honour, and ironically it was Rangers who had been the visitors to Upton Park immediately prior to Liverpool's 4-0 demolition. West Ham beat QPR 1-0, a result that not only, in retrospect, denied Rangers the title, but also provided the Hammers with their last League win of 1975-76. Sixteen games harvested just five draws to plunge West Ham down to a finishing position of eighteenth, two above the relegation line.

In these circumstances it was extraordinary that West Ham did as well as they did in the Cup-Winners' Cup, which was now their only remaining chance of silverware. The quarter-final, first leg, was staged in early March, with the Hammers making the short trip across the North Sea to Dutch club Den Haag. With Lyall down with flu, Greenwood took charge. Brooking was also out with the virus, while Holland and McDowell were injured. At half-time it looked as though the game was up. Abetted by some strange decisions from the East German referee, the home side led 4-0. A change of tactics and a spirited second-half display resulted in two goals for Billy Jennings and a glimmer of hope for the second leg. An unforgettable night at Upton Park two weeks later saw West Ham sweep into a three-goal lead by half-time to lead 5-4 on aggregate. With just over half an hour to play Den Haag levelled the overall scores and proceeded to frustrate opponents and spectators alike with their offside trap. It was a close run thing, but Lyall's side progressed on the away-goals rule.

Fourteen days later West Ham travelled to West Germany to meet Eintracht Frankfurt in the first leg of the semi-final. The Germans had won every tie so far, but were shocked by Paddon's early 30-yarder. They recovered to score twice and keep their record intact. The Hammers, however, were handicapped by the absence of leading scorer Alan Taylor, on account of damaged knee ligaments sustained in a testimonial match at Chelsea. Taylor was still missing two weeks later when, on a rain-swept night, Brooking turned on the style to destroy the German defensive blockade. After a scoreless opening half, a three-goal salvo looked to have given the Hammers a comfortable cushion, but the dogged visitors hit back to score with three minutes left to make the final margin appear closer than it should have.

If their League form had lacked commitment and been generally inept, the lure of European success showed the other side of this West Ham team. Like their predecessors of a decade earlier, they knew how to rise to the occasion when matched against the best that Europe could offer. Those Jekyll and Hyde characteristics, so prominent throughout the 1960s, were just as conspicuous to the discerning watcher in the mid-1970s.

The Hammers' European dream burned brightly for 42 minutes in the final, as Brooking's elegant control, Bonds' willingness to drive forward, and Holland's goal gave them a deserved lead. It all turned sour, of course, as is retold in Match of the Season. But with hindsight it could be said that Greenwood and Lyall had worked wonders in getting the Hammers so far. Injuries had ravaged the squad and greatly reduced the options from August right through until the end of the season. There was seldom a time when they were able to field the same eleven two games running. But for those prosperous early months, the Hammers might have had the threat of relegation looming over them instead of a European final.

Match of the Season 1975-76

Anderlecht 4 West Ham 2

Cup-Winners' Cup final, 5 May 1976

West Ham's Cup run began at the Dell in January 1975, paused at Wembley against Fulham in May, and now climaxed a year later in the Heysel Stadium, Brussels. That the Belgian capital was also home to the Hammers' opponents, Anderlecht, only evened things up. West Ham, of course, had won this very cup in 1965, not on neutral territory, but in London, at Wembley. But history was now against them. No team of European finalists had ever been beaten in their own back yard.

Anderlecht's had been a gentle path to the final, though they were made to sweat against Wrexham in the quarter-finals. Their team boasted not only Belgian but also Dutch internationals, a number of whom had played at the highest level around the world. As a club, Anderlecht were highly experienced, having competed in the various European competitions in sixteen of the last twenty seasons, and all of the last twelve. West Ham took something like 10,000 supporters to Brussels, among a crowd of 58,000.

Wearing a new team strip especially commissioned for the final, the Hammers began brightly on a fine evening, scoring through Pat Holland after Paddon's cross had been headed down to him. It was no more than West Ham deserved, as Brooking had earlier hit the bar from 25 yards.

It required a twist of fate for Anderlecht to draw level: out wide near the touchline, Frank Lampard endeavoured to put the ball back to his keeper, who had advanced off his line in anticipation. But Lampard caught his studs in the longer than normal grass and underhit his back-pass. Mervyn Day was stranded as Peter Ressel stole in and flicked the ball square to Rob Rensenbrink. The Dutch World Cup star scored easily. There were just three minutes until half-time, and one sensed that the destiny of the final had shifted. As for poor Lampard, in attempting the pass he tore a stomach muscle and aggravated the groin injury that had plagued him for months. He limped immediately from the fray, his final over.

At half-time, rather than simply replace left-back Lampard with the naturally left-sided substitute Kevin Lock, Lyall made a tactical gamble. He switched McDowell into Lampard's position, moved Holland into midfield, and sent on Alan Taylor to play up front. But hardly had play recommenced than Van Der Elst – who six years later would be signed by Lyall – scored with a chip over Day's head after Rensenbrink had found him with a telling pass.

DID YOU KNOW?

Having defeated West Ham in the Cup-Winners' Cup final of 1976, Anderlecht reached the final in 1977 too. This time they lost to Hamburg, 0-2.

Now having to chase the game, West Ham showed character in adversity, never abandoning their attacking traditions. Brooking roamed and probed down the left, Paddon, Holland and Keith Robson covered every inch of ground, and the Hammers' reward was an equalising goal. Brooking curled over a centre to Robson, who bent low to head home off a post. For a few minutes the bubbles burst forth with renewed vigour from West Ham's exuberant fans, but their songs were silenced when Pat Holland robbed Resenbrink, who sprawled spectacularly in the penalty area. The French referee awarded a penalty which to West Ham's eyes looked highly dubious, and Rensenbrink rose from the turf to hammer the ball past Day.

As the Hammers stretched forward once more, the Belgian side exploited the gaps. With time running out, Rensenbrink propelled a long pass to Van Der Elst, who streaked through before popping the ball into the net.

Notwithstanding the result, it had been a marvellous match, full of skill and passion, and a fitting climax to a season that had promised much for so long.

LEAGUE DIVISION	**1976-77**
Division 1	17th
League Cup	4th Round
FA Cup	4th Round

The 'new look' strip first worn against Anderlecht in May was not the only change at Upton Park for the new season. Club director Ronnie Brandon died in July, having served on the board for sixteen years. Born within earshot of the Boleyn Ground, he had first seen the Hammers play there in 1904, when they moved from the Memorial Grounds. On the playing front, Clyde Best had transferred to Tampa Bay Rowdies after 'guesting' for the Florida club the previous season. Another well-known member of the backroom staff had also decided to leave after 47 years as a player, scout and finally as the chief representative in charge of developing the youth policy. As such, Wally St Pier had been instrumental, since the founding of the youth section 25 years previously, in signing all the major young players; from Moore, Hurst, Peters, Boyce, Sissons, Redknapp, Brooking, Lampard, Day, to latest discovery Alan Curbishley; who had progressed through the ranks to senior status. After a year among the backroom staff, Bill Nicholson returned to Tottenham, which had been his previous home for 38 years.

The intake included Bill Green, a 25-year-old, 6ft 4in centre-half bought from Carlisle for £90,000. Eddie Baily, formerly Nicholson's assistant at White Hart Lane, was appointed as club representative in succession to St Pier. As for the much-criticised pitch, it and the surrounding track had undergone a facelift by relaying the top six inches of soil and improving the drainage.

Frank Lampard resumed training after surgery on a groin injury in time for the pre-season tour to Scandinavia, but stayed behind with Curbishley (hamstring) and Alan Taylor (knee) for further treatment when the rest of the squad competed in a tournament in Spain. There, keeper Ferguson came on as an outfield substitute and scored the late goal that won the trophy in Santander.

In the League, an opening-day 0-4 hammering at Villa Park extended the team's winless sequence to seven months, but two days later QPR were vanquished by a dipping 30-yarder by Paddon. The irony was that Rangers had provided West Ham's last win, too, back on 24 January. But this would be no fresh dawn. Lyall's men picked up no further win bonuses in their first dozen fixtures and plunged to the foot of the table. A second League win was delayed until November, when fellow strugglers Spurs were overcome 5-3. West Ham were so edgy that at 5-1 up they let their opponents score twice and threaten to equalise in the closing minutes.

On the evening before the Spurs game Chairman Reg Pratt had made a surprise statement, denying press gossip of a rift between Greenwood and Lyall. Shortly afterwards Pratt also quashed rumours that Bobby Moore was being offered the managership. The situation was exacerbated by comments Moore had made about his former manager in his recently published biography.

Part of Lyall's problems during this period – which saw Dave Sexton's QPR avenge their League defeat with a win at Upton Park in the League Cup – was a worrying injury list. Pat Holland had broken his leg and McDowell would miss the entire season, following a cartilage operation. Lock, Keith Robson, Geoff Pike, Curbishley, Jennings and John Ayris were also long-term absentees, as was Lampard, who missed half-a-dozen games with a hip problem. So bad was the want of strikers that Pop Robson was re-signed from Sunderland for £80,000. The evergreen Robson, now 30, proved his worth, ending up top scorer with fourteen goals in 30 League games. To further boost the front line, Greenwood was rumoured to have enquired about Ray Hankin (Burnley), Paul Mariner (Plymouth), Derek Hales and Mike Flanagan (Charlton), Alan Warboys and Bruce Bannister (Bristol Rovers) and finally David Cross (Coventry). All, it seemed, were less than keen on joining West Ham and a number transferred to other clubs shortly afterwards, though Cross and Hales ended up at Upton Park a year or so later. The Hammers' two immediate signings were Anton Otulakowski from Barnsley, who had played in the League Cup-tie at the Boleyn in September, and the veteran Arsenal striker John Radford. The arrival of midfielder Otulakowski permitted Paddon to return to Norwich. One further addition to the staff was Alan Devonshire, who soon made his mark as a bright prospect and forced his way into the first team.

Following the Spurs win, only two others – over Manchester United and Liverpool – arrived before the end of January. Although Bolton had been beaten in the FA Cup, the joy was short lived: on successive Saturdays Aston Villa put paid to the Hammers in both League and Cup. To offset talk of Brooking being lured to the Continent, West Ham slapped a £450,000 price tag on their England star, whose contract would expire in the summer.

February was unexpectedly prosperous. Three wins on the trot moved the Hammers up to eighteenth. A week later, however, a 0-6 roasting at Roker by fellow relegation candidates Sunderland tossed them back into the drop zone. The price for beating title chasers Manchester City was losing centre-half Green for the rest of the season with a broken leg. Fortunately, Tommy Taylor – who had played in defence, midfield and up front – was able to return to his favourite position. Defeat at championship contenders Ipswich resulted in West Ham sinking again to the foot of the table, but then, Lazarus-like, they began to rise from the dead. Three wins, nine draws and only one loss in their last thirteen games pushed them up the standings. It had once again been a close call. Within the space of three days the two last fixtures of the campaign – a goalless draw at Anfield and a 4-2 home win over Manchester United – harvested the necessary points to avert relegation.

Match of the Season 1976-77

West Ham 4 Manchester United 2

Division 1, 16 May 1977

'We're staying up ... Hammers put on a super escape show.'

The headlines in the next morning's newspapers summed it up, putting into a few words all the pent-up feelings of thousands of Hammers fans who had suffered for the past ten long months with the dread of relegation, but who now celebrated the joyous release of seeing their team survive.

This match had been postponed twice as a result of Manchester United's involvement in the FA Cup semi-finals. Originally rearranged for Monday, 9 May, the Football League then pushed the game back a further week – to the Monday before the Cup final. On grounds of fairness, this meant that both finalists, United and Liverpool, would play outstanding fixtures on the same evening.

Two days previously the Hammers had gone to Anfield and drawn 0-0. That point was enough for Liverpool to secure a second successive championship. But now West Ham required at least one point, preferably two, to have a chance of survival. In their favour was the obvious fact that Tommy Docherty's players had nothing to play for, and would not wish to incur unnecessary injuries. Against the Hammers was the equally obvious fact that no team likes to turn out at Wembley fresh from a recent defeat.

Indeed, the men from Manchester opened the scoring after just 25 seconds when left-winger Gordon Hill stole in behind the home defence. Within a minute Alan Taylor had headed against the bar, as if to confirm that the fates were against West Ham.

Their Wembley date appeared to be the last thing on Manchester's mind as they racked the Hammers with attacking play that threatened further goals by the minute. But if the visitors glittered they had no one to rival the brilliance of Trevor Brooking who, in this furious opening spell appeared to be taking on the opposition single-handed.

DID YOU KNOW?

In 1976-77, West Ham faced both FA Cup finalists in their last two matches. The draw at Anfield was only the third point Liverpool had dropped at home all season.

In the 29th minute Brooking's corner fell to Lampard, who lashed a ferocious shot in off the post from 30 yards. A minute before the interval the referee adjudged that Brooking was fouled in the box, only for Geoff Pike to blaze his spot-kick high and wide. It took Pike only eight minutes of the second half to make amends, as he galloped onto a loose ball and ran from almost the centre-circle before firing home from long range. It was not long before West Ham's lead was extended to 3-1, sending a chorus of 'Bubbles' ringing round the ground, as Alan Taylor nodded the ball to Pop Robson, who hammered it past United keeper Paddy Roche.

But almost before the cheers subsided Tommy Taylor cleared off his goal-line from Gordon Hill, and Stuart Pearson dipped a volley over the head of Mervyn Day. Day then turned a Lou Macari shot round a post as the Red Devils came again.

It was Robson who settled the nerves with his second goal of the game, outjumping Pearson to glance in Brooking's corner. It was Robson's eleventh goal in the last fifteen games. Each had been vital in winning the battle against relegation. Lyall revealed afterwards that Robson had been unable to train for much of that time, on account of a stomach strain for which he was having daily treatment. Rest was the only real cure but the ever-willing Robson refused to consider that option. 'I'm all right, I'll play,' he said, game after game.

There were corner-kicks and anxious moments at both ends in the closing minutes before captain Bonds and his colleagues could enjoy their First Division survival with a champagne celebration in the team bath. As it transpired, had West Ham lost they would have gone down.

A few days later Lyall issued a warning. His team would face another tough survival battle the following campaign if they failed to learn the lessons of this season's struggle. 'Adversity is always a useful experience, providing you learn from it,' he declared. Little did he realise that in twelve months his words would come back to haunt him.

LEAGUE DIVISION 1	**1977-78**
Division 1	20th (relegated)
League Cup	3rd Round
FA Cup	4th Round

After it was announced at the end of the previous season that ticket prices would rise, some season-ticket holders reported the club to the Government's Price Commission. Their complaints were turned down. The hike in prices ranged from £8 to £12, making the cost of the most expensive season ticket £45. On a match-by-match basis the cost of seat tickets ranged from £1.70p to a maximum of £2.50p for the best, with the cost of standing on the terraces up to £1 in the North and South Banks and £1.20-30p for the West and East Enclosures. The cost of a programme increased by half to 15p.

New safety regulations imposed by the Greater London Council meant that the granting of a ground safety licence was delayed while work was completed to comply with the new standards.

Perhaps the most worrying aspect pre-season was the fact that Brooking was in talks with Ron Greenwood over a new contract. It was reported that the demands of the England midfielder had not been met. Mervyn Day and left-back Frank Lampard were also holding out for better terms. The most serious injury problem to arise before the warm-up tours to Norway and Majorca concerned Billy Bonds' calf, as a result of which he missed the opening ten League fixtures plus the League Cup exit at Nottingham Forest. Brian Clough's newly promoted side brushed aside the injury-ridden Hammers 5-0.

If it seemed that West Ham United had its problems during the summer of 1977, they could in retrospect be seen as just part of the underlying problems affecting soccer in general. In 1974 Leeds' boss Don Revie had been appointed manager of England. Now, in mid-1977, Revie's sudden departure to take up a lucrative post in the United Arab Emirates sent shock waves through the sport. A few days before the new season kicked off it was announced that Ron Greenwood had been released by the club to become acting national team manager for the next three internationals. His immediate task was to pick up the pieces left by the unlamented Revie's departure and try to squeeze England into the 1978 World Cup finals. A drawn friendly and two World Cup qualifying wins were not enough to take England to Argentina, but earned enough respect for Greenwood to be offered the England job permanently. There was something strange about this. His sixteen-year association with the Hammers had seen them finish above halfway in Division One just four times, yet that record was considered just fine for England.

The editorial for the first home programme of the new season began thus: 'The birth of a new soccer season is the starting-point from which all 92 League clubs set out in search of new honours to add to past triumphs. In theory all commence equal, but – to use a familiar expression – some are more equal than others!'

Relegation clouds hung over West Ham from the off, with three League defeats and just one goal. A surprise away win against fellow strugglers Newcastle slightly eased the problem, but in the next home programme Chairman Reg Pratt felt compelled to issue a statement to the supporters. Recalling the injury problems that had decimated the Hammers a year earlier, he pointed out that the club's current sick-list included a dozen of the first-team squad. In short, it was not hard to see why the team was struggling. The search for new players would continue but with the implementation of the 'Safety of Sports Ground Act' some £200,000 had to be spent to comply with its directives. Never having been a wealthy club, the costs were a body-blow to the finances of West Ham. Pratt's message ended with a plea for everybody connected with the club to keep faith through the difficult times.

A home win over doomed Leicester on New Year's Eve was only the fifth League success in the opening 23 fixtures, but it could not lift the Hammers above nineteenth place. It had taken until 10 December to notch a first home win. Derek Hales had signed in September from Derby to help solve the goals problem but he failed to recapture the form that had made him so prolific for Charlton.

Following Ron Greenwood's appointment as England boss, John Lyall was confirmed as West Ham manager on 13 December. Lyall had just signed David Cross from West Brom. The tall, lean, six-foot plus Cross had become a Hammers target a year previously, when on Coventry's books, and over the next five years 'Psycho', as he became known, would become a firm favourite at Upton Park. In goal, Bobby Ferguson – the forgotten man with just one appearance in nearly four years – was suddenly recalled. Mervyn Day's form had gone to pieces. Three months later, following a spell in the reserves and clear-the-air talks with Lyall, 22-year-old Day was rumoured to be up for sale for £200,000, although he had neither sought a move nor been transfer-listed.

The New Year brought little respite. The satisfaction of knocking Graham Taylor's Fourth Division Watford out of the FA Cup, 1-0, was undone in Round 4 by a 1-6 replay thrashing at QPR. After just fourteen months at Upton Park, Arsenal misfit John Radford left to join Blackburn. In 30 senior appearances for West Ham he had failed to score – surely a record for an international striker – but he soon regained his goalscoring touch, netting on his Rovers debut.

DID YOU KNOW?

England managers Ramsey and Revie had both managed League champions. But Greenwood's Hammers seldom finished in the top half and never higher than sixth.

The Hammers tore at their fans' emotions in March and early April, winning five matches out of six. The introduction of home-grown young Alvin Martin looked to have stiffened the backbone of the side. The team were now up to seventeenth, but only one point above the drop zone. Newspaper pundits were asking if West Ham could repeat their Houdini act and extend their twenty-year stay in the First Division.

Strikers Robson and Hales missed vital matches through injury, whilst long-term absentees Jennings and Alan Taylor made only a dozen appearances between them all season. In defence, McDowell returned for a few games, only to be sidelined again, and Bill Green had returned in February, only to suffer the same fate. Paul Brush, who had made his debut at the start of the campaign, missed most of the action after Christmas, as did Devonshire after March.

Equally worrying was the epidemic of hooliganism that invited the first murmurs from the media for the erection of crowd barriers to prevent the pitch invasions and fisticuffs that were now a regular occurrence at certain grounds. Sadly, some so-called fans earned West Ham the worst kind of headlines.

The Hammers now had just three matches in which to pick up enough points to ensure safety. Following a second-half collapse at Old Trafford, which brought a 0-3 defeat, the team travelled to Middlesbrough for a midweek fixture. Two goals from David Cross were enough to win the game, but now only a visit from Liverpool remained. The European Cup holders and finalists for a second year running, Bob Paisley's men were in no mood for charity. Before a best of the season crowd of 37,400, Liverpool cruised to victory 2-0. The final whistle brought the curtain down on West Ham's season with their fate still unclear. They were outside the bottom three, but one of those beneath them, Wolves, still had games to play. In fact it was not until Wolves beat Aston Villa three days later that West Ham's relegation was confirmed. Understandably, there was little relief in the Hammers reserves winning the Football Combination.

Much was made of rumours that Brooking, who had enjoyed a £27,000 testimonial some six months earlier, intended quitting Upton Park if the club were relegated. Instead, he quickly pledged his loyalty: 'I will be happy to do whatever the club requires. I don't want to rock the boat. It would be a terrible wrench to leave.' One who did leave was Kevin Lock, in a £60,000 move to Fulham.

Match of the Season 1977-78

Bristol City 3 West Ham 2

Division 1, 17 September 1977

'We flattered to deceive in last Saturday's match at Ashton Gate, for after taking a quick lead we conceded the advantage and ended 3-2 losers.' That match review in the following week's programme summed up the feelings of those who had watched the clash with newly promoted City who, like West Ham, were strong candidates for relegation.

The West Country team had mustered just two draws from their opening five matches, and Trevor Brooking's post-match comment said it all: 'After winning at Newcastle and drawing with QPR, we expected to get something out of this one.'

West Ham started with the kind of football that had enthralled so many soccer-lovers over the years. Finding space and rhythm, they had their opponents on the ropes. Pop Robson rattled the bar from 25 yards, then went one better, lashing a 30-yarder into the net following a pass from Alan Taylor.

Sixty seconds later City equalised with a close-in header from a long cross. Both sides then created and muffed chances, with the Hammers' Alan Taylor proving to be the biggest culprit. City winger Clive Whitehead slowly emerged as the game's dominant figure, burrowing down either flank with ease and tormenting West Ham's full-backs with his old-fashioned wing-play. Midway through the first half Whitehead set up City's second goal, driven home from the edge of the area.

It was the sort of game where goals were expected at either end. Day denied the City forwards by pulling off a number of saves. But after the interval he could only block a shot – as once again his defensive colleagues were exposed – and watch as Ritchie pounced on the rebound. Bristol City led 3-1.

Robson was denied by John Shaw's save of the match, clawing the ball away one-handed for a corner. With a few minutes left, substitute Geoff Pike headed home to reduce the arrears and add to the drama, but it was too little, too late and made little difference to City's second-half domination.

Yet again West Ham had lost to a team which, on paper, should have stood little chance, but whose wholehearted, earthy performance had overcome the Hammers' superior yet brittle talents.

LEAGUE DIVISION 2	**1978-79**
Division 2	5th
League Cup	2nd Round
FA Cup	3rd Round

In addition to Kevin Lock, the summer recess saw the departure of Bill Green to Peterborough and Derek Hales back to his original roots at Charlton. Frank Lampard, hoping to finish his career in the top division, almost signed for Norwich, but could not agree personal terms. Frank would remain at Upton Park for another seven years, adding further honours to his collection as well as reappearing on the First Division stage. Despite interest from other clubs, Pop Robson and Tommy Taylor also stayed.

Behind the scenes, two new directors joined the board, one of whom was Martin Cearns, son of the vice-chairman. Improvements had been carried out to the pitch as well as the training ground at Chadwell Heath, which was also to have an all-weather surface and indoor ball-court.

With a renewal rate of 94 percent on season tickets, and over 2,000 names on the waiting list, support remained strong amongst the fans. This was confirmed when a crowd of 25,387 turned up for the first fixture in Division 2. Five goals up in the first hour had many supporters thinking of an immediate return to the First Division but the gloss wore off as Notts County rallied to claw back two goals. Two home defeats in four days finally dispelled thoughts of an easy return to the top flight. First, Third Division Swindon dumped the Hammers from the League Cup, then Fulham hung on to Margerrison's goal in the League. The following week West Ham threw away a two-goal lead to lose at Burnley.

The absence of Brooking through injury was proving costly, and on his return results improved. By mid-November the Hammers were up to third, two points behind leaders Crystal Palace. Robson and Cross were rediscovering their goalscoring touch, while Billy Bonds, now wearing No 6 and ten years a Hammer, was rewarded with a testimonial to which 21,000 turned up.

John Lyall's main problem, as it had been for some years, was that of injuries. Once again he was rarely able to field his preferred XI two games running. A shoulder injury to Ferguson meant Day once again returning between the posts, whilst others sidelined included Brooking, Lampard, Curbishley, Alan Taylor, McDowell, Jennings, Holland, Alvin Martin and Pike. Despite the list of war-wounded, the Hammers entered the New Year in fourth position.

Once again, as the Christmas decorations came down so did hopes of an FA Cup run. This time it was Fourth Division Newport who exposed all the Hammers' frailties against clubs from lower divisions. West Ham were hanging on at 1-1 when the luckless Mervyn Day missed a cross to the far post.

The weather caused havoc in January as games fell victim to icy spells. But in early February it was Day, not the weather, who was blamed for conceding two goals in the 3-3 home draw against fellow promotion hopefuls Sunderland. His crisis in confidence was not helped by a section of the home crowd who taunted him mercilessly. Although Lyall had been linked with several outfield players, he staggered the football world when plucking Phil Parkes from First Division QPR for a world record fee for a goalkeeper of £565,000. Insisting that Day would be staying at Upton Park, Lyall now boasted three keepers who had all made banner headlines. Bobby Ferguson had himself cost a British record fee for a goalkeeper, Mervyn Day had prompted the normally reticent Ron Greenwood to declare, 'this is the West Ham goalkeeper for the next ten years' – a tag that six years later weighed around Day's head like a millstone. Now there was the most expensive signing in the club's history, the fair-haired giant Parkes.

Parkes' impact was immediate: he conceded just one goal in his first two games, whilst his forwards knocked in seven at the other end. Indeed, much of the success the Hammers would achieve over the next few years would stem from the rapport that developed between Parkes and Alvin Martin, the youngster now installed at centre-half. But promotion in 1978-79 remained an elusive dream. Though the defence was more secure, at the other end goals dried up like a puddle in the desert. The main strike-force of Cross (who failed to score after February) and Robson (with just four goals in that period) were unable to rekindle the goal-power that had brought them a combined total of 37 goals in the first 26 games.

The Hammers were locked in fifth place till the season's end and vital points were dropped in goalless draws against Brighton, Preston, Cambridge, Charlton and Cardiff. West Ham's cause was not helped by a fresh injury to Brooking. The England midfielder sprained his ankle at home to Newcastle, missed the next eleven games, and returned only for the season's last, meaningless fixture. When the curtain came down, the Hammers were six points adrift of third-placed Stoke.

As if to question the club's over-reliance on Brooking's undoubted talents, Alan Curbishley, the club's Under-21 midfielder, launched a bitter attack, claiming that he had made no progress in the last three years and would not be signing a new contract. He added: 'It's keep ball and give it to Trevor Brooking. He's a great player, I don't dispute that – but everything at West Ham seems to be centred around his ability and getting the ball to him. What has happened since his injury seems to underline that. Right now I believe I could stay here another ten years without getting any recognition. I've asked for a move on four occasions and been turned down.' His outburst cost Curbishley a fine of two weeks wages and a transfer to Birmingham City the following month.

Match of the Season 1978-79

West Ham 1 Wrexham 1

Division 2, 28 April 1979

In a successful League season – as 1978-79 must be considered, as it brought many more wins (eighteen) than losses (ten) – there are likely to be many candidates for Match of the Season. A reasoned review of this season must also take into account the failings that turned a possible promotion team into also-rans. It would be churlish in such circumstances to be forever critical of a failing that has appeared deeply rooted in the psyche of the Hammers for many decades – their death-wish against clubs from lower divisions in cup competitions. Yet during 1978-79 this failing manifested itself against Swindon, and, more embarrassingly, Newport.

Before a ball had been kicked in earnest the Hammers were one of the favourites for an automatic return to the First Division. That belief seemed justified, though in the event the injury crisis proved insurmountable. Only seven players made 30 or more League appearances.

On the morning of this final home fixture, against Wrexham, the Hammers were sitting in fifth spot with three further matches to play, all away. They had one or more games in hand over all the clubs above them. Wrexham were in the bottom third of the table and as if in expectation of an easy victory an Upton Park crowd of nearly 29,000 turned up to cheer their heroes. But it was Wrexham who made all the early running.

The game would be marred by a number of controversial decisions that were given or not, dependent on whether you were a Hammers or a Wrexham fan, by the experienced referee Ken Baker. His first ruling came as the Wrexham winger, Fox, crossed. Alvin Martin was unable to get his head to the ball, so sneakily fisted it away from Dixie McNeil, the visiting centre-forward. The linesman's flag went up, only to come down again. Wrexham were naturally outraged, but their protests were in vain. Visiting keeper Dai Davies' claims were soon similarly ignored when he demanded a free-kick after taking a knock in the back from David Cross.

DID YOU KNOW?

In 1978-79 West Ham used three goalkeepers – Ferguson, Day, Parkes – two of whom were record buys, while Day would be the Hammers' keeper 'for 10 years'.

Thus the scene was set for the 28th-minute drama when West Ham took the lead. Alan Devonshire crossed from the left and it looked as though a claret and blue arm helped the ball over Davies to Billy Bonds, who headed home at close range. Astonishingly, Mr Baker permitted the goal to stand. An irate Davies pursued him to the touchline, urging him to consult his linesman. Since the latter had already retreated to the halfway line, Davies' actions appeared to constitute assault and he was red-carded. Pop Robson later admitted that he had been the culprit, instinctively flicking the ball on with his hand when he realised he was not going to get his head to it. He apologised to Davies afterwards.

In a post-match interview the referee said he had seen Martin's earlier handball, but as his linesman was signalling for a previous Wrexham foul he had let play proceed. Mr Baker insisted he had not seen the handling offence by Robson, but had no option but to send Davies off after the keeper had laid hands on him.

West Ham, it might be said, could not have scripted it better. They were now a goal up against ten men, with the most irreplaceable member of the opposition missing. However, stand-in keeper Wayne Cegielski promptly showed he had other ideas. The longer the game went on, the more defiant Wrexham became. Though creating little themselves, they were frustrating the Hammers with increasing ease.

It looked as if the Hammers had settled for a 1-0 win when, with two minutes left, McDowell lost possession in midfield to what he clearly considered to be a foul tackle. This time the referee sided with the visitors, allowing play to proceed. Seconds later a centre was headed past Phil Parkes to stun the home supporters, who vented their frustration by chanting 'What a load of rubbish.'

Lyall kept his players in a locked dressing room for a half-hour verbal roasting. His terse comment to the press summed up his feelings: 'I told them what I thought. It just wasn't good enough. They have not only let themselves down but also the fans. This I am not prepared to allow.' According to one of his players, 'We got the biggest rucking we've ever had.' The dropped point was the final nail in West Ham's season. They proceeded to lose at Blackburn and Millwall, both of whom went down in any case.

LEAGUE DIVISION 2	**1979-80**
Division 2	7th
League Cup	Quarter-finals
FA Cup	Winners

The summer of 1979 saw another exodus from Upton Park, with the departure of Alan Curbishley to Birmingham and a return to Sunderland for Pop Robson. Tommy Taylor and Mervyn Day moved across East London to Brisbane Road, where they joined up with former Hammers' midfielder Jimmy Bloomfield, now the Orient manager. Day's transfer fee, £100,000, was a club record for the O's at the time. In the two weeks before the new season kicked off, John Lyall lured Stuart Pearson from Manchester United for around £220,000, then offloaded three players who had stalled over new contracts. John McDowell and Alan Taylor moved to Norwich, while Billy Jennings followed the trail to Orient.

Behind the scenes at the Boleyn Ground other changes were taking place. Reg Pratt had been on the board for 38 years, all but nine of them as chairman, but now stood down. He was succeeded by Len Cearns, who had been his deputy since 1950. It was, in many respects, the end of an era. With the Pratt-Cearns partnership at the helm the club had prospered both on and off the field by their good husbandry and wise council. Their unbounded efforts for the good of West Ham United had made the club's name not only well known on the domestic front but internationally as well. Stability in the boardroom was reflected in stability with mangers, of whom there had only been three in the last 30 years. Mr Pratt's appointment as President meant that he retained his links with the club that his family had served for six decades. After 23 years as club secretary, and a further twenty as a player and administrator, Eddie Chapman became chief executive in charge of the day-to-day running of the club, whilst Brian Blower was appointed commercial manager. The Government's doubling of VAT resulted in admission prices being increased for the second time in three months as the club was forced to adjust the previously announced rises to accommodate the change.

For the first time in memory the Hammers did not go abroad for their pre-season tour, but competed in the Tennant-Caledonian Cup tournament in Glasgow. They fared badly, and their poor form carried over to the League, where they lost their first two matches 0-1. The 3-1 home win over Barnsley in the League Cup was a milestone, in that it was the first occasion that a West Ham match had been sponsored. The club's printers, who had family links dating back to the Thames Ironworks days, enjoyed the honour.

The faltering start in the League, coupled with an injury to Stuart Pearson, prompted Lyall to sign Ray Stewart, a defender, from Dundee United and Jimmy Neighbour from Norwich. Further injuries forced Lyall to blood 17-year-old Paul Allen at the end of September. Captain of the England Youth team, Allen had only signed as a professional the previous month, but he and Stewart became the catalyst that would transform the season.

The need to juggle between newcomers, youngsters, and players returning from injury did little to improve consistency. The Hammers entered November still in the bottom half of the table and their makeshift look was largely responsible for the three games needed to dispose of Third Division Southend in the League Cup. Southend led in two of those matches, before being sunk 5-1, courtesy of a Billy Lansdowne hat-trick.

But at least the team was on the up. Sunderland were the next to fall in the League Cup and by the time the Hammers faced Nottingham Forest in the December quarter-finals they were up to seventh in the League. Brian Clough's Forest were defending the trophy, which they won in March. They had won the European Cup in May and were now riding high in the First Division. The tie and the replay ended goalless, and it was only in extra-time at the City Ground that Forest scored the three goals that put an unkind gloss on West Ham's efforts.

On the Friday before Christmas, amid a snowstorm, the smallest home crowd for 25 years witnessed the start of a remarkable run. In the next eight League games Lyall's team only dropped two points, climbing to fifth. They were now just two points adrift of leaders Chelsea and Birmingham City, where Alan Curbishley was making his presence felt. The team also progressed to the quarter-finals of the FA Cup. There, with seconds remaining of an enthralling home tie against First Division Aston Villa, the referee awarded West Ham a penalty. Villa disputed it vehemently. After the pandemonium had subsided, the coolest man on the field stepped up to bang the ball home. In defender Ray Stewart, Lyall had found a marksman with ice-cool nerve and velocity of shooting that had not been seen at Upton Park since the days of Geoff Hurst. As the ball flew past keeper Jimmy Rimmer, Stewart was mobbed by his colleagues for converting his eighth successful penalty that season.

Three days later, anticlimactically, West Ham's winning streak was ended at home to lowly Notts County, who stunned Upton Park with two goals in four minutes. It was the start of a losing run that saw just one point earned in five games, pitching the team down to eighth, but more importantly nine points behind the leaders. The Hammers needed to steady themselves before facing

Everton in the semi-finals, and did so by beating Orient and drawing 0-0 at leaders Birmingham.

The semi-final was a ding-dong affair, with drama, a hotly-disputed penalty for Everton, the sending-off of Everton's Brian Kidd, three bookings and a final frenzied half-hour when West Ham ought to have sewn it up against Everton's ten men. They didn't and the game ended 1-1.

Four days later the replay at Elland Road was still undecided at the end of normal time. In extra-time Devonshire netted, but with just seven minutes left Bob Latchford glanced in a cross at Parkes' near post. A third match, this time at Coventry, beckoned when Brooking's centre was flicked on by Cross and Lampard dived full stretch to head the winner. What was Lampard, who had missed the previous game, doing in Everton's box? Who knew, who cared! It was the full-back's first goal of the season, his first ever headed goal, and a fitting celebration for his 501st senior appearance.

It was perhaps not surprising – although Lyall insisted that promotion was the ultimate aim – that the players had tunnel-vision on Wembley. But first they had to cram in six League games in three weeks. The Hammers had to win them all to re-set their sights on promotion, but back-to-back home losses to Birmingham (in a fiery context in which Bonds was dismissed) and Shrewsbury soon made that academic.

The final League match, at Roker Park, had to be delayed until the Monday after the Cup final. Sunderland's win before a 47,000 capacity crowd took them up at the expense of Chelsea, managed by Geoff Hurst, leaving West Ham seventh. Sunderland's Pop Robson would once again be playing in the First Division, but West Ham had their hands on the Cup.

Match of the Season 1979-80

Arsenal 0 West Ham 1

FA Cup final, 10 May 1980

If one aspect of football summed up West Ham throughout the first 80 years of their history it would be contained in the simple yet emotive phrase of 'cup-tie soccer'. From the earliest days Hammers teams had shown how they could turn it on as underdogs, firstly in the FA Cup, then the European Cup-Winners' Cup. The downside, as every supporter knew, was seeing the team plumb the depths of ineptitude when pitted against teams of lesser ability.

The FA Cup final of 1980 typified this conundrum. As in 1975, West Ham were participating in an all-London final. But this time they wore all white, not claret and blue, and this time their opponents were not from a division below but from a division above. No longer favourites, the Hammers were now underdogs, reduced in some eyes to just a walk-on part against mighty Arsenal, who had finished fourth in Division One by conceding just 36 goals in 42 games. One newspaper observed: 'Most folk have a soft spot for the Hammers. They always try to play attractively. They never shout the odds. Their supporters are among the most loyal in the country and Wembley is the kind of arena they deserve.'

But Terry Neill's battle-hardened Gunners had survived a four-match semi-final marathon against champions Liverpool, which spoke volumes for Arsenal's strength of character and tactical nous. Four days after Wembley they would head off to contest the final of the European Cup-Winners' Cup. Although Neill warned his players to guard against over-confidence, Lyall knew that the FA Cup final would be a cat and mouse affair, a game of patience with neither side prepared to take risks.

As it turned out, Lyall, a shrewd tactician in his own right who had learnt so much from his predecessor and mentor, got it spot-on. He left David Cross alone up front to compete against Arsenal's back four and withdrew Pearson into midfield to provide an extra man. In Billy Bonds, his socks around his boots and sweat staining his shirt, Lyall had the driving force and indomitable spirit that embodied his team. The manager could also count upon the cultured head of another vital cog in his side – Trevor Brooking. On this occasion it was not only Brooking's intelligent play and accurate passing that took the eye; it was the use of his head in a way not often seen.

When Devonshire's thirteenth-minute cross rebounded off a defender it caught Pearson off-balance but his mis-hit shot allowed Brooking to claim, in this his 500th senior performance, one of the few headed goals of his career. If the Arsenal players and supporters looked dumfounded, West Ham's were equally so.

It could not be classed as a classic final but for the remainder of the match the Hammers sat back, playing disciplined and sensible football that tied down their opponents in midfield and up front, while leaving open opportunities for counter-attack. Although Lyall had the proverbial eleven heroes on the pitch that day, in young Paul Allen he had unearthed a jewel from the youth policy that had already produced so many famous names. At seventeen, Allen was the youngest player ever to appear in an FA Cup final, but he displayed maturity beyond his years as he set about stifling the threat posed by Liam Brady. But to the millions of watching neutrals, Allen was the victim of an altogether sadder moment.

DID YOU KNOW?

Despite challenging for promotion from Division Two in 1979-80, West Ham scored only 17 goals away from home. Only three other teams in the division scored fewer!

With just three minutes left, Allen burst through on a precocious run that looked likely to reward his side with a second goal. In what was branded one of the most cynical tackles ever to disgrace the national stadium, the youngster was cynically chopped down from behind as he approached the edge of the area. Rising to his feet he merely exchanged a handshake with Willie Young, his transgressor, and continued to beam that infectious smile that had not left his baby-faced features all day. Young's punishment – a yellow card – seemed scant punishment, given the enormity of the professional foul. No one doubts that in today's climate Young would have been off.

Prior to the game, Brooking had been scathingly dismissed by Brian Clough with the put-down 'he floated like a butterfly ... and stung like one.' Amid the jubilant after-match celebrations, the jovial England midfielder must surely have felt he had put one over on Cloughie.

As for Arsenal, four days later they lost to Valencia on penalties in the final of the Cup-Winners' Cup. It wasn't their week.

5

LET THE GOOD TIMES ROLL 1980-1986

LEAGUE DIVISION 2	**1980-81**
Division 2	Champions
League Cup	Finalists
FA Cup	3rd Round
European Cup-Winners' Cup	Quarter-finals

John Lyall had completed five eventful years as manager and his contract was up for renewal. There was little doubt that he would be offered a new one, especially after the tactics that had destroyed Arsenal had proved him to be one of the best brains in football. It is said that Chairman Cearns simply asked him 'How long and how much?'

The accolades bestowed upon Lyall came no higher than those from his own players. Billy Bonds summed up their feelings: 'There is no doubt in my mind that John won the Cup for West Ham.' David Cross added: 'They talk about top coaches like Don Howe, Terry Venables and Dave Sexton. Well, John Lyall is right up there now.' As for the terms of his new contract, Lyall ever the gentleman, would only admit: 'I have always had a strong belief in my ability. I suppose it is not a bad time to negotiate a new deal.'

With his sights on the coming season Lyall said: 'We naturally have the First Division as our goal ... European competition, which I always consider is invaluable to both the club and supporters, will enable everyone involved to reach new horizons.' To give substance to his words, Lyall paid QPR £800,000 for 20-year-old striker Paul Goddard on the eve of the new season.

The cost of season tickets rose from £64 to £86 for the best, with others up from £59 to £74 and £49 to £62, with match-day admission similarly increased. A short tour in Scotland preceded a return to Wembley for the Charity Shield, which Liverpool retained 1-0 in a dreary game amid complaints that the football season was too long and so was the grass. Paisley's men played well enough, and by the end of the season would lift the European Cup and League Cup.

Any thoughts that promotion was a formality looked foolish on the opening Saturday at Upton Park, when Luton came from behind to win a match of three penalty-kicks. Two away draws followed, to leave the Hammers seventeenth after three games, but the shock of defeat would be a long time repeating itself. At Upton Park it would not happen again all season. Ironically, it was the Hatters again who next pulled the rug from under the Hammers. By then it was mid-November and the goals of Cross and Goddard had already taken West Ham to the top of the table, from where they never looked back.

If in the past there had been doubts about the Hammers' ability to sustain an assault on more than one front, Lyall's blend of experience and youth did their best to dispel them. Three Third Division teams, which might in the past have proved stumbling blocks, were brushed aside in the League Cup, whilst progress in the European competition was made at the expense of Castilla of Spain and the Romanians of Politecnica Timisoara.

The first leg in Madrid against Castilla saw a slick performance by the Hammers and a one-goal lead until crowd trouble disturbed their concentration and led to a three-goal response from the home side. Lyall had earlier opined: 'it would indeed be a great club success if next year we proved to be the most disciplined team and supporters in this country and in Europe.' Although he had control over his players, the antics of hooligans were beyond his authority. UEFA, however, reacted by fining West Ham for the mayhem they incited, as well as ordering the second leg to be played at least 300 miles from Upton Park. On appeal this was changed to the game being played at home but behind closed gates. Just 250 people, including players, team officials, observers and press, were allowed inside the Boleyn Ground in what is one of the weirdest games ever to take place in England. The eerie silence was pierced only by the shouts of the players, but Cross's hat-trick, completed in extra-time, carried the Hammers through 6-4 on aggregate.

By the New Year West Ham had opened up a four-point lead at the top of the table. With the Cup-Winners Cup' in winter hibernation, it was the domestic cups that took centre stage. The Hammers' next victims in the League Cup were First Division Tottenham. It was a maelstrom of a match played before a home crowd of 36,000, and settled by Cross's 21st goal of the season with nine minutes to go. That score looked likely to be repeated on the first Saturday of the New Year, when the Hammers took on the defence of the FA Cup at home to Wrexham, mid-table in the same division as themselves. With three minutes to go, the visitors equalised Stewart's earlier penalty, and with no goals in the first replay the tie went to a second, also at the Racecourse Ground. Normal time failed to separate the sides, but extra-time did, the all-important goal falling to Wrexham's veteran marksman Dixie McNeil.

It is a truism that elimination from the Cup enhances efforts in the League. But in this instance there is little doubt that Wrexham did the Hammers a mighty favour. They were still chasing two other cups, never mind the week-to-week grind of trying to pick up promotion points. In fact, following defeat at QPR on Boxing Day the Hammers embarked upon one of their greatest unbeaten League sequences. The remaining eighteen fixtures of the campaign saw fourteen wins and four draws. As the Hammers were top of the table when that run begun, it comes as no surprise to find that they stayed there, or that promotion was secured with six matches left to play. Bottom-of-the-League Bristol Rovers were the sacrificial lambs. The date was 4 April and the League season still had more than a month to run. David Cross celebrated by running in four goals at Grimsby in the very next match.

The icing on the cake came in a 1-0 win at Hillsborough in West Ham's final fixture of a famous season in which they had played 61 games. That victory gave them a total of 66 points, a Division Two record (in the era of two points for a win), overtaking Middlesbrough's tally of 65 established seven years earlier. The man least pleased by West Ham's achievement was Jack Charlton – manager of that Boro side, now boss of Sheffield Wednesday – who had to endure the sight of his record torn up before his eyes. It was no surprise that Lyall was named Division Two Manager of the Year.

But there was more to 1980-81 than a divisional championship. In the first leg of the League Cup semi-final at Highfield Road, Coventry's young side fought back from a 0-2 first-half deficit to win with virtually the last kick of the match. That result set up a cracker of a second leg. Despite playing in the first half what Lyall described as 'some of the best football I've ever seen from a West Ham team', it was not until the hour that Goddard scored his sixteenth and probably best goal of the season to level the aggregate scores. Then, with extra-time looming, up popped an unlikeliest hero in Jimmy Neighbour, who was only playing because of Pat Holland's injury. Ten years previously the little winger had helped Tottenham win the same trophy. Now, his mis-hit winner ensured that for the third time in ten months the Hammers would grace Wembley, and following their Charity Shield encounter, the opposition would again be Liverpool.

Beforehand, the Hammers had an important date with Dinamo Tbilisi in the Cup-Winners' Cup. At Upton Park, the Soviet side put on one of the most formidable performances ever seen, and were not flattered by their 4-1 first-leg advantage. A philosophical Lyall remarked: 'Seeing players like that stimulates you. Their game is a whole new dimension in space. When you start thinking you're the best, that's when you start destroying yourself. The credit we have been getting this season, while warranted, wasn't making us any better players. We're going to watch the video tapes, over and over, and work out training practices round their game.'

A fortnight later West Ham recovered some pride, winning 1-0 before 80,000 cheering Georgians, whose hospitality was in marked contrast to the obstructive bureaucracy of Moscow.

Sandwiched between those two games was the League Cup final with Liverpool, whom, ironically, Tbilisi had beaten the previous year in the European Cup. The final was roundly condemned for its tedium until it flared up in the closing minutes of extra-time. First, referee Clive Thomas allowed Alan Kennedy's goal to stand despite his linesman flagging for offside against another Liverpool player. Thomas shrugged off furious West Ham demands that he consult the linesman. But with the final kick of the game, justice appeared to be done as Ray Stewart crashed home a penalty, awarded against Terry McDermott for 'saving' Alvin Martin's goal-bound header. Upon the concluding whistle words were exchanged between Lyall and Thomas, as a consequence of which the Hammers' manager was reported to the FA. The replay at Villa Park seventeen days later saw Liverpool at their irresistible best, and the painful lessons meted out are relived in Match of the Season.

Come May, as the senior members of West Ham's various teams celebrated with the silverware on display in the trophy cabinet, so too did the club's would-be future stars. The previous August Lyall had stressed the importance of the youth policy. By winning the FA Youth Cup, the South-East Counties League Division One Cup, the Division Two title and a youth tournament in Holland, the young Hammers under his direction were demonstrating once again that the policy introduced three decades earlier was the way to success.

Match of the Season 1980-81

Liverpool 2 West Ham 1

League Cup final, replay, 1 April 1981

What a change from the first match. Liverpool had to fare without Souness and Heighway, but included young Ian Rush, in only his second game since his transfer from Chester. Rush's pace repeatedly troubled Alvin Martin, who had barely survived a fitness test, and Parkes was forced to make three early saves from Dalglish.

Yet just as Paisley's men were settling into their murderous stride West Ham plundered a goal. Jimmy Neighbour evaded Alan Hansen's lunge on the right and crossed to the near post. Paul Goddard – recently named in the England Under-21 squad – headed the ball so hard that England's Ray Clemence could only help it over the line. Undaunted, Liverpool simply came on stronger than ever. Afterwards, Goddard commented: 'When I scored it was like pulling the pin on a hand-grenade, the way they came at us.'

Parkes was thankful to the crossbar for keeping out Rush's drive but the equaliser was only delayed. Dalglish met Terry McDermott's chip by flicking the ball across his own body beyond the reach of Parkes. Wasting no time on self-congratulation, Liverpool resumed their assault and four minutes later breached the Hammers' defence a second time, this time fortuitously. Jimmy Case's corner was met by Hansen, whose header was deflected in off Bonds' knee. 'I just stuck my leg out to clear it. It's one of those things,' Bonds explained. Parkes added: 'I dived to cover the header and I'm sure I would have got it but the ball struck Bill and flicked up six inches over my hands and went in off the post.'

Only half an hour had been played, but once in front the Liverpool of those days were almost unbeatable. Ray Stewart buried a shot into the side-netting. David Cross's aggression earned him a booking, and Alvin Martin emerged upfield to test Clemence with a low drive. In the second half, Lampard and Stewart overlapped down the flanks, but the chances created were not as clear as those Liverpool contrived on the break. Parkes saved sharply twice from Dalglish and Phil Neal, drawing praise from his opposite number. When Clive Thomas – who officiated despite an inquiry into his TV comments after the first game – blew the final whistle Lyall's team still had hopes of forcing another bout of extra-time.

Although their second League Cup final had ended like the first (against West Brom) in defeat, the Hammers had the consolation of turning what at one stage threatened to be a mauling into a gripping encounter. The performance proved that Lyall had rebuilt the Hammers from the ashes of the side that had struggled for three years prior to relegation into a new unit capable of holding its own in the top flight. For Liverpool, this was the first time they had claimed the League Cup, ensuring their participation in European competition for the eighteenth consecutive year.

The most disappointing aspect of the evening was the size of the Villa Park crowd, just 37,000, reduced no doubt by the occasion being screened live on TV for the first time in the competition's 21-year history. An audience of nearly seventeen million watched the match, for which ITV had paid £120,000 for the privilege.

LEAGUE DIVISION 1	**1981-82**
Division 1	9th
League Cup	3rd Round
FA Cup	4th Round

After an absence of three years the Hammers had regained their First Division status, but John Lyall had no illusions about the task ahead: 'The main aim must be to re-establish ourselves back in our old tradition as a long-standing First Division club.' In the Second Division wilderness he had paid out big fees for Parkes, Stewart and Goddard, and he was now linked with further big names. In the event, the only new arrival was goalkeeper Tom McAlister, signed on a free-transfer as back-up for Parkes – Bobby Ferguson having moved to Australia. Of the new crop of youngsters to sign apprenticeship forms, the most notable future stars were Alan Dickens and Tony Cottee.

Pre-season games took in a tournament in Scotland plus a one-match trip to Holland and the usual encounters with local teams. The biggest injury worries concerned Brooking, who was to miss the first seven fixtures, Pat Holland, suffering from a broken arm and Achilles problems, and the injury-prone Stuart Pearson. Fans turning up for the opening home fixture were greeted by the sight of the former West Enclosure standing area re-designed for seats, increasing the number of season-ticket holders to some 12,000.

West Ham's winning ways in the League continued where they had left off. They extended their run of eighteen unbeaten games in Division Two with nine more in Division One. This meant that their first League defeat of 1981 did not come until mid-October, when they lost 2-3 at Aston Villa. For some weeks West Ham had even been top – helped by the introduction of three points for a win – with Goddard and Cross causing defences all kinds of problems. Lyall was named Manager of the Month for September and was almost a darling of the football media, who increasingly appreciated the transformation he had worked at Upton Park. Lyall had somehow injected the necessary steel into the tender spine of the team he had inherited, without sacrificing the verve for which the Hammers had always been noted.

The new-look Hammers also drew the attention of the England manager. Ron Greenwood selected four of Lyall's team – Goddard, Devonshire, Brooking and Martin – for his squad for the World Cup qualifier against Hungary at Wembley. Only Brooking and Martin actually played in that critical win and it was thought that Brooking, now 33, would more likely go to the finals in Spain as a pundit rather than as a player.

DID YOU KNOW?

In 1980 and 1981 West Ham went 16 months unbeaten at home in the League. After losing 2-3 to Luton on 16 Aug 80 they next lost at Upton Park to Arsenal on 5 Dec 81.

League Cup progress had been made at the expense of Derby, but after both legs against West Brom were drawn, Cyrille Regis's goal took Albion through. Two players were sent off in that ill-tempered replay, which inflicted West Ham's first home defeat in any competition for sixteen months.

That defeat on 1 December triggered a disastrous League run of four straight defeats that extended until late January, when it was ended by a home victory over ... West Brom! It was a bleak period for the country and football at large, as well as for the Hammers, with snow blanketing much of England. West Ham were out of the FA Cup, too. A penalty save by Parkes had denied Everton a replay in the third round, only for the Hammers to succumb meekly at Graham Taylor's Second Division Watford in the fourth. The nature of the surrender put supporters in mind of the bad old days.

Lyall had taken advantage of the weather-induced inactivity to sign two players. François van der Elst and Neil Orr cost around £400,000 apiece. Now aged 27, the Belgian international was playing for New York Cosmos, but having scored twice for Anderlecht against West Ham in the 1976 Cup-Winners' Cup final, he needed little introduction. Five years younger, Orr signed from Morton. Capped by Scotland Under-21s, he was at home anywhere in the back four, but preferred to play sweeper.

There was little to lighten the gloom during February, by the end of which West Ham had slipped to fourteenth. Considering they had been top in late September, the Hammers' current form made them serious relegation material. Devonshire's two-month absence with a foot injury had not helped matters, but his return against Ipswich in early March sparked a nine-match run that saw only one defeat. The team were now back up to eighth, though they would put their fans through another helter-skelter ride by winning only one of their final nine games. In losing 2-3 at high-flying Ipswich, Neighbour was stretchered off with ligament damage. He joined captain Bonds, who would miss the remainder of the season with jaundice, and other absentees Lampard, Brush and Pearson. By late April Alvin Martin's season was in ruins, as were his chances of playing in the World Cup finals, when he broke his collarbone for a second time in three weeks.

Faint hopes of qualifying for the UEFA Cup were dashed in the crowd-troubled defeat at windswept Highbury on May Day. A smoke bomb produced a sickly yellow cloud that drove some spectators onto the pitch to escape its effects. Coins were thrown at the players and after the match a youth was fatally stabbed.

The season ended with defeat at Wolves, who were relegated despite their win. John Lyall missed the game, slipping up to Scotland to sign Airdrie striker Sandy Clark. David Cross would be a hard act to follow for Clark, having finished the season as the Hammers' top scorer with nineteen League and cup goals. But Cross had declined to sign the new contract offered to him.

For Lyall it had been a highly satisfactory campaign, the more so given the injuries which decimated his options for long periods. The team had finished in the top half of Division One for the first time in nine years. The youth policy was again bearing fruit. His protégés had won the Southern Junior Floodlit Cup, plus the South East Counties Senior and Junior League Cups. With 39 goals to his name, Tony Cottee had broken scoring records in the junior leagues and, like Alan Dickens, was poised to break into the big-time.

Match of the Season 1981-82

Tottenham 0 West Ham 4

Division 1, 2 September 1981

This was the second match of the season. After their respective results on the opening day – Spurs winning 3-1 at Middlesbrough, West Ham held to a home draw by Brighton – FA Cup-holders Tottenham were clear favourites in this London derby.

All roads around White Hart Lane had been jammed for two hours before kick-off. With Brooking still unfit and Spurs' Argentinian hero Ossie Ardiles sick, the game was deprived of two players who might have lifted it to the heights. But it exhibited enough endeavour, excitement and goals to keep the Hammers contingent in the sell-out crowd of 41,000 happy.

After West Ham had weathered Spurs' initial assaults, it was a former Tottenham favourite, Jimmy Neighbour – returning to White Hart Lane for the first time in three seasons – who made his presence felt. Seemingly boxed in by defenders out on the right, the little winger lifted a centre into the goalmouth. The ball was flicked on by Goddard to the far post, where David Cross drove it past Spurs' goalkeeper, Ray Clemence – newly signed from Liverpool – the ball brushing his fingers on its way in.

An injury to Spurs' central defender – Welsh international Paul Price – sustained when tackling Paul Allan on the half-hour, resulted in a Tottenham substitution at half-time. Their reshaped defence was still getting to grips when Cross hit them twice more. A low cross from Stewart stretched the home defence. Perryman and Miller got in a tangle and Cross escaped to shoot past Clemence's left hand.

Cross described the 57th-minute strike that completed his hat-trick as 'special and probably the best I've ever scored'. Geoff Pike raced onto Goddard's pass to deliver a knee-high centre which the lanky, bearded striker met with a flying, full-blooded volley. At 3-0, there was no way back for Spurs, although Hoddle and Ricky Villa tried to rally their team-mates.

With a few minutes left Clemence spilled Devonshire's shot, failed to recover the ball, and in the confusion Cross whipped in his fourth goal. Clemence would not quickly forget his baptism before the hyper-critical White Hart Lane fans.

For those who said that 30-year-old Cross would struggle against top-class defenders, following his 27 goals the previous season in a lower division, his four-goal burst provided the perfect riposte. A late developer as a prolific goalscorer, Cross described the occasion as 'a special night for me, for the team and the fans'. It was also a special night for Phil Parkes, as Cross presented the Hammers' goalkeeper with the match ball. Cross explained: 'The last time I got the match ball, following my previous four-goal haul against Grimsby, when we clinched the Second Division title at the end of last season, Phil said that it was all right for forwards, but goalkeepers never seem to get mementoes. So I decided to give him the ball tonight.'

The drubbing of Spurs injected sufficient confidence into West Ham to carry them unbeaten into October.

LEAGUE DIVISION 1	**1982-83**
Division 1	8th
Milk Cup	Quarter-finals
FA Cup	3rd Round

The previous season the Hammers had aimed at re-establishing themselves in the First Division, and by finishing ninth they had done so. Now their task was to use that consolidation as a springboard for better things. It is often the case that teams find life more difficult the second season following promotion, when the adrenaline has worn off, when opponents become wise to their tactics, and when supporters with short memories start demanding cup finals and championships.

Lyall was under no illusions: 'You have to go into every season with a target. Last season ours was to consolidate. Now we must go forward from there, build upon what was achieved ... so the target must be to get into European competition.'

Yet again his pre-season preparations were disrupted by injuries. Orr and Holland were nursing hamstrings, while Brooking was still dogged by the groin injury which had blighted his World Cup finals with England. For long-serving Holland, it had been a miserable eighteen months, as one injury followed another. Pre-season friendlies had commenced with trips to Scotland, Belgium, Holland and Finland. The League kick-off was put back to the last Saturday of the month, on account of the World Cup finals. Brian Clough's Nottingham Forest took advantage of Brooking's absence and Sandy Clark's sluggish debut to win 2-1 at Upton Park and extend their unbeaten run against the Hammers to nine games. The next day it was reported that Brooking would be back in full training the following morning. It was a forlorn hope. After a few reserve games pelvic surgery was recommended and he was destined not to return to first-team action until May.

In the fourth game of the season Billy Bonds rewrote Upton Park history when he passed Bobby Moore's record of 544 League games for the Hammers. It had taken the 35-year-old Bonds fifteen years to reach the target. Ipswich threatened to spoil the occasion by capitalising on a rare penalty miss by Ray Stewart, but an equally rare goal from Lampard salvaged a draw.

At that stage Clark had yet to break his goalscoring duck. Lyall admitted 'what Sandy needs more than anything at the moment is a goal.' As if on cue, the Scot netted five times in five games, all of which were won. With four goals from Van der Elst and three from Goddard, the Hammers netted seventeen times during that purple patch. The first of those wins saw Frank Lampard become only the fourth Hammer to make 500 League appearances; the fifth and last was at home to the defending champions Liverpool, a result that pushed the Hammers up into second place.

If West Ham had serious intents on the championship, the next two games would show. Points at lowly Southampton and Brighton ought to have been theirs for the taking, and might take them top. Alas, the Hammers conceded six goals on the south coast, picked up no points, and at Brighton Lampard became one of nine players that Saturday to be sent off. The veteran defender had committed a sliding tackle from behind (on Mick Robinson), which the FA now deemed to be 'serious foul play', meriting automatic expulsion. Though it was the first time Lampard had been sent off, he was reduced to a mere statistic, joining the 82 other miscreants to have received marching orders so far during the FA clampdown.

Just to prove their contrariness the Hammers responded to these setbacks by overwhelming Manchester United 3-1. Ron Atkinson's team had previously conceded just eight goals and lost just once in eleven matches, and arrived at Upton Park topping the League. West Ham's performance made Man U appear pedestrian, so that at 5pm that afternoon Atkinson's men were dumped down to third, with the Hammers filling the sandwich between them and new leaders Liverpool.

Commercialism was taking a front seat in the running of soccer clubs and West Ham found themselves castigated in the media when it was discovered that the mascot who led the team out was being charged for the privilege. The club's commercial manager replied that with a two-year waiting list for matchday mascots, many parents obviously did not object to the cost. Further afield, Manchester United's chairman, Martin Edwards, proposed the re-structuring of English football and the creation of a Super League.

The last weeks of 1982 brought three away League defeats. That at Stoke, 2-5, was galling as a month earlier Lyall's team had drawn there in the Milk (formerly the League) Cup. A home win in the second leg set up an away tie at Third Division Lincoln, the Imps' late equaliser forcing a replay that was settled by Sandy Clark late in extra-time. In the next round the Hammers were two down at First Division Notts County, when Van der Elst's hat-trick put them in sight of victory. County salvaged a draw but had no answers in the replay. West Ham were now in the last eight, so a tie at League leaders Liverpool was the last thing they wanted. A depleted Hammers were four minutes from a replay when Graeme Souness's twenty-yarder skidded off the snow under Parkes. Bob Paisley's team would go on to claim the Cup for the third successive year, having overcome West Ham in the first and third of these.

DID YOU KNOW?

West Ham finished 9th in 1981-82 and 8th the following season. This was the first time they had ever finished in the top half of Division 1 two seasons running.

Reliable home form enabled the Hammers to enter 1983 in fifth position, ten points adrift of pace-setters Liverpool. On New Year's day, at home to Spurs, injuries forced Lyall to give a debut to 17-year-old Tony Cottee, who was given two hours' notice of his inclusion. It was to be a dream debut. In the 25th minute the lad was fouled. From the ensuing free-kick the ball was headed against the bar and rebounded for Cottee to head back in, setting the Hammers on the path to victory. Cottee netted three days later, too, in a home defeat by Luton, but Lyall was not going to get carried away, using him sparingly, mostly on the bench, for the rest of the season. Nevertheless, everyone knew that a star was born.

It had been nineteen years since West Ham and Manchester United last met in the FA Cup, when the Hammers triumphed in the semi-final en route to Wembley. This time they were paired at Old Trafford in the third round, Manchester United winning 2-0 on their way to lifting the trophy in May.

The defeats by Luton and Manchester United heralded an awful three months which brought only one win and pitched West Ham down from fifth to fourteenth. Once again lack of goals was mainly to blame. Lyall duly sold Clark to Glasgow Rangers and signed David Swindlehurst from Derby. Press reports had linked Lyall with any number of strikers, so when he swooped for Swindlehurst it took everyone by surprise. The newcomer made an immediate impact, as did 18-year-old Alan Dickens, helping to secure three wins over Easter. Dickens was soon being spoken of as the new Trevor Brooking, his creativity in midfield allied to a keen eye for goal, which brought six strikes in his first ten appearances.

Following three straight wins in early April, Lyall began thinking again of finishing high enough to qualify for the UEFA Cup. Defeats at Manchester City and Everton put paid to those flickering hopes. The season ended with victory at managerless Coventry, who had sacked ex-Hammer Dave Sexton hours before the game. Coventry stayed up anyway. As for the Hammers, in the circumstances eighth was a satisfactory finishing position, particularly as it enabled Lyall the unprecedented achievement of guiding West Ham to a position in the top ten of the top division for two seasons running. Trevor Brooking made one belated appearance. Of all the 'if onlys' of this frustrating season, the biggest was 'if only Brooking had been fit'.

Match of the Season 1982-83

West Ham 3 Tottenham 0

Division 1, 1 January 1983

Local derbies over Christmas or New Year have a tradition of producing a feast of soccer. Those between West Ham and Tottenham are no exception. Bank holidays are not holidays for professional footballers: they are working days on which they play or train. Lyall's practice on New Year's Eve was to lock his squad in an Essex motel and impose a curfew.

Both teams had been plagued by injuries. Lyall was without Brooking, Bonds, Lampard, Neil Orr and Paul Brush, and Goddard, who was a late call-off with ankle ligament damage sustained at Watford two days' previously. Less than two hours before kick-off Lyall notified two of his junior stars that they were playing. Alan Dickens probably anticipated his elevation, for what would be the biggest home gate of the season. Tony Cottee, however, undoubtedly did not.

Tottenham had not scored away from home since September but started off bossing the midfield. Perryman, Archibald, Brooke and Hoddle all had useful efforts on goal as Spurs sought to end their famine. Instead the crucial first goal fell to West Ham. Geoff Pike, captain for the day, floated over a free-kick and Joe Gallagher – released by Wolves and on a second monthly contract at Upton Park – headed against the crossbar. Cottee nodded the rebound into the net. As Lyall said afterwards: 'Anticipation, that's what all the great goalscorers have had. He really is a sharp little fellow. He has that natural goal touch and reminds me of Pop Robson. The goal was simple, I'll agree, but did you notice that there was no one within ten yards of him except the goalkeeper. You can't teach someone to react like that, it's natural.'

Midway through the second half Devonshire sped away, only to be upended by a clumsy challenge in the penalty area. Stewart claimed his ninth successful conversion of the season. That goal gave the Hammers a cushion, and Pike crowned an excellent display by sweeping home Devonshire's pass.

Lyall summed up his thoughts on the match: 'New Year is always a time for looking ahead, for seeking out the good things. The fans now know these are players to watch and when you see young Paul Allen performing so well in the unfamiliar position of right back, you can look to the future of the club with confidence.' Less happy was Spurs boss Keith Burkinshaw, who behind locked doors vented his feelings for almost an hour on his team's showing.

LEAGUE DIVISION 1	**1983-84**
Canon Division 1	9th
Milk Cup	4th Round
FA Cup	5th Round

In the summer Van der Elst returned to Belgium for family reasons. Pat Holland and Jimmy Neighbour also left the club. New arrivals included Steve Walford, a left-sided defender from Norwich, and Steve Whitton, who had top scored for Coventry the previous season. The fees were around £170,000 each. Neither was a stranger to East London: Walford had once been at Upton Park as a junior, before signing for Spurs, whilst Whitton had played for Newham Boys. Amongst the new intake of apprentices were Steve Potts and Kevin Keen. The Upton Park pitch had been dug up so that a new drainage system could be installed. The cost was £30,000, money well spent if the improved playing surface produced better results – especially during severe winters.

The Football League was in the first throes of commercial revolution, designed to enrich all its members. The League would be sponsored by Canon, new television deals were being struck, and it was agreed that each club would no longer give a percentage of gate receipts to the visitors, but would keep them all. It was clear that the principal beneficiaries would be bigger clubs, who would get still richer, to the detriment of the smaller. It was the start of a trend that today shows no sign of abating.

West Ham had always counted upon the loyalty of supporters, but now for the first time in memory some season tickets went unsold. Fans complained to the local press about how mercenary the club had become over recent years. Attendances had fallen the previous season by nearly 4,000 per match, despite the team having a relatively successful campaign. They needed another one to stop more supporters drifting away.

This season saw a new-style match programme. Having used the same local family printing company for over 60 years, the directors switched to a 'financially more lucrative' deal with another printer which already produced many clubs' programmes. The accounts for the last financial year showed that West Ham had increased its profits from programme sales to £82,000. The cost of the new format issue would be increased by 10p to 50p. Other new commercial ventures saw the club take over catering services and an offer to season-ticket holders to pay £10 for their seat to bear a personalised plate. A Junior Hammers Club was also introduced, sponsored by a local company, the giant Tate & Lyle Sugar Refiners of Canning Town.

Admitting that the last two campaigns had left him dissatisfied, Lyall said his aim was to finish 'higher than sixth and thus win a place in Europe. The key to a more successful campaign this season is consistency. The aim is to make sure we beat sides who, on paper, we *should* beat.' He could not have asked for a better start, the best since election to the League in 1919. The first five games yielded five wins and fifteen goals, shared around the new strike-force of Swindlehurst, Cottee and Whitton. Cottee played only because Goddard – Lyall's most expensive signing – was injured, but Goddard had to sit out almost the entire season.

The next six games brought only one win, but it was not until 15 October that the Hammers were deposed from the top of the League, when Liverpool won handsomely at Upton Park, and not until 17 December that they relinquished second spot. By then West Ham were also out of the Milk Cup, but not before they had rewritten the record books, crushing Fourth Division Bury 10-0 in the second leg to record their biggest ever victory. Bury recouped some cash, if not pride, the following February when Lyall bought their centre-half, Paul Hilton, for £100,000. It is curious to think that a defender could stand out in a 0-10 thrashing. If he was so good, what did that say about his fellow defenders? A late Swindlehurst header carried West Ham past Brighton, but thoughts of Wembley were extinguished in extra-time in a replay at Everton.

Mid-season saw another injury crisis. Bonds, Goddard and Paul Allen were all encased in plaster, Martin had six broken ribs, Whitton a dislocated shoulder from a car crash, Devonshire cartilage trouble, and Brooking suffering the effects of old age! All told, nine first-team players were lost to Lyall. Somehow, his patched-up side collected enough points to stay third until late February, when a 2-4 home loss to Watford, inspired by John Barnes, pushed them down to fourth. Even so, leaders Liverpool were not yet out of sight over the horizon. West Ham were free to concentrate on catching them, having gone out of the FA Cup in the fifth round. Birmingham were heading for relegation but had already beaten Lyall's team 3-0 at St Andrews in the League before repeating the score in the Cup. The tie is remembered for the mud that disfigured the football and the violence that saw 'fans' rampaging across the pitch. Play was halted twice before mounted police restored order. FA Secretary Ted Croker claimed it was the worst violence he had seen: 32 were arrested and many more, including women and children, were injured. Shamefully, it was fans in claret and blue who were mainly responsible, attempting to have the game abandoned after their team fell three goals behind. They certainly earned no sympathy from Lyall for dragging the club's name through the mud.

Brooking returned from injury to inspire a 3-0 win at Ipswich. With 37-year-old Bonds also firing on all cylinders, Lyall's wished-for top-six finish seemed attainable. By now the FA five-man commission had reported on the mayhem at St Andrews. Both clubs were found guilty of spectator misconduct and banned from entering the next two FA Cup competitions. At long last it seemed that football had decided to clamp down hard on the hooligan problem, but the FA had in fact chickened out. Sentence was suspended, depending on the good conduct of players, officials and spectators. Even so, the two clubs felt the sentence harsh, claiming they had no jurisdiction over rogue fans wearing their colours.

Vital points were dropped at home to struggling Wolves and QPR, while at Leicester it was hard to know which hurt most, the 1-4 drubbing ('our worst performance of the season' – Lyall) or the crowd trouble which undermined West Ham's appeal against their Cup ban. In late March Reg Pratt died at the age of 79. He had been at the heart of the club since first becoming a director in 1941 and introduced many of the innovations which carried the club onwards as well as instilling much-needed stability. The sadness at his passing was not eased by the team's 0-6 capitulation at Liverpool. In fact, the Hammers won only one of their last twelve, finishing ninth, when with four more points they would have managed the top-six finish Lyall had set his sights on.

There had been much speculation that Trevor Brooking would bow out this season. And the speculation proved correct. The 35-year-old was still the timeless master of his craft, and the fans' final tribute was to vote him Hammer of the Year for a record fifth time.

Speculation about the manager proved incorrect. Lyall's name was linked with the vacant jobs at QPR and Tottenham. His reputation as a coach and tactician had never been higher and he admitted that he considered Spurs, with all their financial resources, to be a club of enormous potential. He had one year left on his contract and after talks with chairman Len Cearns decided to stay. His loyalty to West Ham, to a club that had given him his chance, was one factor in his decision. Five years later, after he had been sacked, some questioned whether that loyalty had been misplaced.

Match of the Season 1983-84

West Ham 10 Bury 0

Milk Cup, 2nd Round, 2nd leg, 25 October 1983

Yes, Bury were Fourth Division and West Ham were in the First. Yes, the Hammers had won the away leg 2-1. Yes, the second leg

DID YOU KNOW?

Trevor Brooking's final game was the 0-1 home defeat by Everton in May 1984. Afterwards, Lyall roasted his players in the dressing room. Did he spare Trevor?

looked a formality. What was not expected was that the Hammers would expose the gulf between the First and Fourth Divisions, particularly given their historic vulnerability against the underdog. What made this Milk Cup-tie special was that it rewrote the record books. It was fifteen years since West Ham had thrashed Sunderland 8-0, and this blitz of lowly-rated opponents exhibited a ruthlessness that some thought would for ever lay the ghost of past failings against cup minnows.

The Hammers scored as early as the second minute and barely stopped until the massacre was over. They scored five goals in each half on a night none present will ever forget. The irony was that the 10,896 crowd was West Ham's lowest ever for a cup-tie and the smallest at a first-team game since the early 1950s. The sparse attendance could be attributed partly to the result of the first leg and partly to the fact that it was the third home game in eleven days.

Tony Cottee led the way with a four-goal haul which included a first ever senior hat-trick before half-time. Three of his goals were headers, remarkable for a small man. Yet the key moment came at 1-0 when Bonds fouled Entwhistle in the box, only for Bramhall's penalty to hit a post. The rebound was blazed wide. Whether West Ham would have scored ten had that penalty gone in is a big 'if'. But when Ray Stewart's free-kick was headed home by Martin the floodgates opened. Brooking dummied past three defenders before scoring. Cottee got his second, then completed his hat-trick with the goal of the game, reward for a flowing move involving Steve Walford and Paul Allen.

After the interval Orr replaced Bonds, Cottee made it six, and Devonshire fired in the seventh from 25 yards. Number eight came from the penalty spot when Devonshire was bundled over, number nine was a deflected shot from Brooking, and the final nail, driven in by Devonshire, followed a neat interchange with Brooking.

Bury's shell-shocked manager, Jim Iley, declared afterwards: 'We've had a hell of a hiding, what else can one say about it. West Ham were far, far superior, but while we are only a Fourth Division side, we feel we are a good one at that level. And what we can take away from this game are some very useful lessons.' John Lyall commiserated with the routed visitors: 'I told Jim Iley at the end that they had been unlucky to meet us on such a night.'

LEAGUE DIVISION 1	**1984-85**
Canon Division 1	16th
Milk Cup	3rd Round
FA Cup	Quarter-finals

The new season found West Ham at a crossroads in almost every sense, with new challenges to be overcome both on and off the field. Manager John Lyall was not released to take over at QPR and was obliged to see out the final year of his contract. He needed to take stock of his squad. Of the old-timers, Brooking had gone, while Bonds and Lampard were no longer regulars. Two other key men, Parkes and Devonshire, were both out with long-term injuries and Swindlehurst would be missing until December. Despite his problems, Lyall remained upbeat: 'The game is all about tomorrows not yesterdays. You can't replace a Trevor Brooking. Talent of that kind is just not available. If it were you would not be able to buy it. We enter a new era with the emphasis firmly on youth.' To this end he made only one major signing, defender Tony Gale. Along with Paul Allen, Alvin Martin, Tony Cottee and Alan Dickens, this meant one of the youngest Hammers sides in ages.

The Hammers youth policy had long produced outstanding talent, but for that to continue the club needed an FA license to provide one of the new 'schools of excellence'. With its Chadwell Heath training facilities, which were second to none, and with Tony Carr – who had a fine record developing young talent – as director of coaching, it was felt that 'the Academy would at last be officially recognised by the FA'.

Admission prices were raised for standing accommodation but seat prices would be pegged, apart from the six biggest games – Manchester United, Liverpool and the four London derbies, for which there would be a surcharge of £1. This was reasoned to increase revenue without alienating supporters. After 47 years with the club, popular chief executive Eddie Chapman was awarded the Canon League Loyalty Award.

Pre-season training included tours to France and Germany. Once again they made a good start to the League, standing second after five games. But that was as good as it got. Whitton and Goddard were now added to the list of walking wounded, forcing 37-year-old Bonds to come off the subs' bench and teach his younger colleagues a thing or two with his all-action displays. At Chelsea, where the Hammers lost 0-3, police fought running battles with armed thugs and made over 90 arrests. One officer said: 'You half expect this kind of thing when these teams play. But it always shocks you. Football didn't use to be like this, did it?' No, was the answer.

As stand-in keeper for the injured Parkes, Tom McAlister proved to be an unsung hero, emerging from two years in the shadows to earn rave reviews. This was especially so in the first leg of the Milk Cup at Bristol City, where the Hammers twice had to come from behind to spare themselves the indignity of losing to the Third Division side. A goal-avalanche in the second leg then carried the Hammers through to meet Second Division Manchester City. After seemingly having done the hard work by drawing 0-0 at Maine Road, West Ham fell at home to a winning goal scored just 60 seconds after they had equalised.

City merely rubbed salt into the wound inflicted by Ron Atkinson's United, who had trounced West Ham 5-1 at Old Trafford. Notwithstanding their shortcomings, Lyall's men were still a creditable fifth in November when table-topping Everton survived West Ham's second-half barrage at Upton Park to steal the points. Worse was to follow when Bonds and Stewart were added to the casualty list, while Walford's loss of form saw him replaced by Brush. The Hammers plunged down the table. They had slipped eight places in December when two Cottee goals at Coventry in the last fixture of 1984 brought a first win in seven games.

New Year's Day brought a home defeat by QPR and the loss of Tony Gale with ligament damage. In the circumstances, the visit of Fourth Division Port Vale in the FA Cup spelled danger, but Paul Goddard, who had never scored an FA Cup goal, broke his duck with a hat-trick. Help for Lyall's beleaguered forces now came from an unlikely source. Lyall needed time to get his crocks fit again, and Arctic weather duly obliged, cancelling all West Ham's fixtures for the rest of January.

Sadly, the enforced lay-off did little to help – at least in the League, where the Hammers went another two months without winning. By 30 March, when they triumphed at Nottingham Forest, they had sunk to sixteenth, relegation was now a palpable threat, and Upton Park was so inhospitable to its hosts that six months elapsed between one League win and the next. The only ray of light came in the FA Cup, by which time the fixture backlog meant playing two, three and even four games a week. For example, on the first Saturday in March West Ham lost at Arsenal in the League. On the Monday, they drew with Second Division Wimbledon in the FA Cup. On the Wednesday, Cottee's hat-trick helped overcome the Dons in an Upton Park replay, and three days later, on the Saturday, West Ham fell 2-4 at Old Trafford in the quarter-finals. This time, it was flu that was largely to blame, affecting six players. There was even talk of postponement, but the tie went ahead and Manchester's Norman Whiteside bagged his first ever hat-trick.

DID YOU KNOW?

Between 15 November 1984 and 6 May 1985, West Ham played ten League games at Upton Park – and failed to win any of them. Relegation threatened but was averted.

In March, after protracted negotiations, John Lyall signed a new long-term contract. Still only 45, he declined to reveal how long, but commented: 'Naturally, I am delighted ... Everybody involved with West Ham United sticks with you through thick and thin – and these are the sort of things that you have to consider.'

The abject home form continued into May. After a 1-5 mauling at West Brom, it looked as though the Hammers' fate hinged on their last six games, to be crammed into the final fourteen days of the season. The first of those games welcomed back Norwich, whom West Ham had beaten 2-1 in the fourth round of the FA Cup. Four minutes from time it was still 0-0, at which point Bobby Barnes, a recent substitute for Dickens, turned in a rebound for 'the most important of the not many goals I've scored in my nine years here.' Norwich were at the time only three points better off and the defeat would ultimately help to send them down. It was West Ham's first home League win in eleven attempts.

Two days later the Hammers lost at Everton – who received the championship trophy before kick-off – and three days after that went down 1-2 at Sheffield Wednesday, where Stewart missed a rare penalty. West Ham were locked in nineteenth place; they dared go no lower; and they had only three games left to save themselves. Cometh the hour, cometh the man, they say, and it was at this point that Billy Bonds made his mark. Having recently returned to the side, following five months out with knee trouble, he now turned out against Stoke at home to play his fifth game in ten days. Captain Marvel demonstrated what pride and honest endeavour can achieve, admittedly against a woeful side that, statistically speaking, is still the worst ever to play in the English top division. Bonds scored the first and fourth goals in a 5-1 win. As he waded through the mud he seemed to roll back the years, cajoling players, some of whom were young enough to be his sons. His manager, just seven years older, summed up the thoughts of the lowest crowd of the season, 13,362: 'He was incredible.'

West Ham looked safe only because Coventry looked doomed. But things are never so simple where Coventry are concerned and by winning their last three matches they pulled off another Houdini act. This meant that had West Ham lost at Ipswich they would have gone down. In the event they won. This was just as well as their last game was at home to Liverpool who needed to win to ensure they finished runners-up to Everton. As it happened, Liverpool won in a canter. With no 'ever-presents' this season and eight players out for two months or more, Lyall pinpointed injuries and poor form at home as the key factors behind the relegation struggle.

Match of the Season 1984-85

Ipswich 0 West Ham 1

Division 1, 17 May 1985

After the unprecedented comfort of a top-half finish in the previous three seasons, the Hammers went from bad to worse in 1984-85. Their existing 49 points would in all probability be enough, barring a Coventry revival, but safety could be guaranteed by one more win, either at Ipswich or at home to Liverpool.

In West Ham's favour at injury-hit Ipswich was their away form, which had already earned five wins against teams in the top half of the table. Nor could the Hammers have wished for a better start, when Cottee headed home Goddard's cross in the eleventh minute. The goal was disputed by Ipswich, who complained that Goddard was offside and, to boot, had allowed the ball to cross the by-line before pulling it back. Either way, the goal took Cottee's tally to 24 in all competitions.

Hilton headed over, Goddard shot narrowly wide, and Cottee's swerver dropped onto the roof of the net as West Ham pressed throughout the first half, with the home team committing a series of fouls as their frustration grew. Early in the second half Goddard was knocked over without winning a penalty and Pike came close to a second goal, but inevitably the tide began to turn. Parkes pulled off a couple of vital saves before Stewart broke free to blast the ball into the side-netting.

The remaining minutes seemed endless, but the Hammers hung on for their third successive win at Portman Road. Its importance was underlined afterwards when news came in that Coventry, seven points behind, had won at Stoke and still had two games to play. The Sky Blues won both, avoiding relegation by one point for the third year in a row. Norwich, managed by former Hammer Ken Brown, were relegated instead. But had West Ham lost at Ipswich (then lost to Liverpool) they would have fallen below Norwich on goal-difference and gone down in their place. That is why it merits the accolade of Match of the Season.

LEAGUE DIVISION 1	**1985-86**
Canon Division 1	3rd
Milk Cup	3rd Round
FA Cup	Quarter-finals

Having refused a new contract, Paul Allen signed for Tottenham for £400,000, the fee being set by a Football League tribunal. Other departures included Dave Swindlehurst to Sunderland and Frank Lampard, who became player-coach with his former skipper, Bobby Moore, at Southend.

In a bid to find replacements John Lyall scoured the Continent. He thought he had signed 20-year-old winger Danny Hoekman from Nijmegen but the two-year deal foundered when Hoekman's mother vetoed it, preferring a maximum of twelve months. Under Dutch law a player under 21 needed parental consent before signing for another club, so Hoekman stayed in Holland. Lyall's response was to pay £250,000 for a winger from Oldham whom some labelled 'the next Alan Ball'. Mark Ward was not dissimilar to Paul Allen in height (5ft 5in) and age (22). Ward teamed up with Scottish Under-21 international Frank McAvennie. The 24-year-old Scot, who could operate in midfield or up front, had been admired by Lyall for some time, and was snapped up from St Mirren for £340,000. With Devonshire, Gale and Orr back to full fitness, Lyall's squad was now virtually full strength. The only notable absentees were Geoff Pike (groin) and Billy Bonds (toe). Although Bonds, at 39, was no longer officially a first-team player, few were rash enough to write his footballing obituaries.

In the wider context, English soccer had experienced two horrific years, culminating with football-related tragedies at Birmingham, Brussels and Bradford City. The Government accepted that violence in football stadia was spiralling out of control and sought measures to ban alcohol from inside grounds. In the opening programme for the new season Chairman Len Cearns made an impassioned plea to West Ham supporters to set a good example. For many years the slogan 'Keep the fences away from Upton Park' had been intended to deter troublemakers. He now spoke out against foul language, citing the 'family section' in the stands in what had always been a 'family club'. CCTV had been installed throughout Upton Park to monitor violence and enable perpetrators to be prosecuted.

National TV fanned the flames with a documentary entitled 'Hooligan', portraying 'a group of West Ham United supporters who are known and feared around the country'. In fact, those featured had no connection with the club, but had merely used its name as a banner under which to travel unofficially to away games.

Given West Ham fans' own part in troubles at Birmingham in recent years, there were misgivings when the fixture computer invited them back to the newly promoted club for the curtain raiser, which on police instructions kicked off at 11.30am. A heavy police presence and a low gate enabled the game to pass off without incident. But St Andrews continued to be a graveyard for West Ham sides, who lost there for the fourth time in a row. Perhaps the bigger worry for Lyall was the loss of Goddard before half-time with a shoulder injury. By the time he was fit again there would be no room for him. Goddard would not start another game this season.

Goddard's loss was McAvennie's gain. For the visit of QPR Lyall switched him from midfield to partner Cottee. The Scot responded with two goals in the 3-1 win, flicking home a Cottee cross and netting with a solo effort. With the other new boy, Mark Ward, supplying the cross for West Ham's other goal, Lyall had reason to be pleased with his new signings.

It was a different story at home to unbeaten Luton the next Saturday, when West Ham lost 0-1. One paper reported: 'The new season already has the makings of being another difficult one for the Hammers, despite their injection of half a million quidsworth of new talent.' Defeat at Old Trafford in match No 4 pitched West Ham down to seventeenth and allowed Ron Atkinson's United to extend their 100 percent start. They would not taste defeat until their sixteenth match, in November. When one considers that West Ham had to wait until their eighth game to record their second win, the odds on their overhauling Manchester United must have been astronomical. But that, of course, is exactly what happened.

In fact, West Ham might have slipped even lower in the table. Although Liverpool had to come from behind to draw at Upton Park, Lyall's men needed late equalisers at Southampton and Sheffield Wednesday to avert a slide into the bottom three.

Then something remarkable happened. Starting with those three draws, West Ham went eighteen League games undefeated. This equalled the run in 1980-81, which secured promotion from the Second Division, but far exceeded anything they had achieved in the top flight. The high point of the run was nine successive wins from mid-October to mid-December, which was halted by a goalless draw on the Saturday before Christmas. Luton's plastic pitch, it must be said, caused trouble to all visiting sides, added to which a high wind ruled out constructive football.

Such a run of results catapulted the Hammers from seventeenth to third in three months, by which time Manchester United's lead had been cut to just four points. Injuries – or rather the lack of them – played a big part, for Lyall was able to field an unchanged team for match after match. Indeed, only Stewart, Devonshire, McAvennie (playing for Scotland in Australia) and Dickens had not played in every game. In George Parris, Lyall had unearthed a player who could cover for absentees either in defence or midfield. McAvennie (eighteen goals by Christmas) and Cottee (ten) had terrorised opposing defences. The defence was conceding on average under a goal a game – a rare statistic for any West Ham side – and the 0-0 draw at Luton was Parkes' fifth clean sheet in a row.

Absence of injuries had spill-over effects, too. By avoiding the loss of players to a disrupted first team, West Ham's reserves were riding high in their own league. John Lyall was named as Bell's Whisky Manager of the Month for November, his eleventh award in eight years. Others with cause to celebrate that month were Ernie Gregory, who had now been with the club for 50 years since signing on as a 14-year-old, and goalkeeper Phil Parkes, who made his 250th League appearance.

The Hammers' only reverse between September and late December arrived in the Milk Cup. Having comfortably overcome John Bond's Swansea, they went out at Old Trafford in the next round. That 0-1 defeat is remembered for Mark Ward's indirect free-kick that appeared to brush keeper Gary Bailey's fingers on its way into the net, but the 'goal' was ruled out.

In the League, West Ham were within five minutes of extending their unbeaten run into 1986. Tottenham skipper Steve Perryman then turned in a near-post cross, his first goal for fifteen months.

Wintry weather forced a clutch of postponements as West Ham set off on their latest FA Cup campaign. Charlton were beaten in the last seconds of a televised tie at Selhurst Park; Ipswich put up stubborn resistance before finally bowing out after five and a half hours of defiance; and Manchester United came out of the hat in the fifth round. The two clubs had been paired in last season's FA Cup and this season's Milk Cup, both games going against the Hammers. This time a replay was required at Old Trafford, where West Ham had failed to win in League or cup for ten years, and this time they came up trumps. Lyall's team had no time to come down off cloud nine for, three days later, they were pitched into a quarter-final at Hillsborough. Sheffield Wednesday were going well in the League, and did better in the first half than West Ham did in the second, fully meriting their 2-1 win.

For once, the cliché that being out of the Cup benefited League form was wide of the mark, for the Hammers slumped at Arsenal and Aston Villa and slipped to seventh. But now they got their second wind, closing the gap on the joint leaders from Merseyside, and with games in hand.

At one stage Lyall's men had to play three home games in a week. It was the third of these – against a Chelsea side recently humbled 4-0 at Stamford Bridge – that brought West Ham's second home defeat of the season. Chelsea came from behind to snatch a win that, with hindsight, might have denied West Ham the championship. Games came thick and fast, but the Hammers won six out six – including an extraordinary 8-1 win over Newcastle – with just the trip to Everton to come.

West Ham began that match in second place. Kenny Dalglish's Liverpool, sadly, could not be caught and had secured the first part of their League and Cup double. But with Everton one point behind Lyall's team, the runners-up position was up for grabs. This did not make for a do-or-die finale. The fact of Everton being deposed as champions by their bitterest rivals lent an air of anticlimax to the occasion. Added to which, West Ham, after a gruelling season, ran out of puff. Everton won 3-1, without being unduly extended. Gary Lineker's two goals took his tally to 30 and paved the way for his Golden Boot award in the coming World Cup finals. Cottee's last-minute reply took his own League total to twenty, six short of his partner, McAvennie. It was the first time since the Hammers returned to the First Division in 1958 that two players claimed twenty goals in one season.

Inevitably, there was a sense of disappointment at missing out and failing to break the northern grip on the championship trophy. 'If only' the Hammers had beaten Chelsea and Everton. 'If only' they had picked up more points in the early, barren weeks of the season. Nevertheless, third place was the highest in the club's history, and the team had done it with style. Looking back, Lyall said: 'To sustain a challenge over 42 games, as it was then, against the best teams in the country, is the pinnacle of achievement in the game. It is a prize only a few have lifted. Most managers can spend a lifetime in the game and not get close. At least I got close.' He had proved again that in the modern era his name ranked amongst the elite of English managers. Oh yes, and the reserves won the Football Combination, scoring 141 goals.

Match of the Season 1985-86

West Ham 8 Newcastle 1

Division 1, 21 April 1986

In a season when so many records were set it is asking much to single out any particular match. Therefore one can only look for the unusual and in that respect this game has all the qualifications.

DID YOU KNOW?

When West Ham beat Newcastle 8-1 in April 1986, keeper Martin Thomas conceded the first four goals, Chris Hedworth let in one, and Peter Beardsley the last three.

West Ham hosted mid-table Newcastle two days after winning at Watford, and two days after Newcastle had drawn at fourth-placed Chelsea. Of the 90 minutes that followed, one reporter wrote: 'The record books will be unable to do justice to the breathtaking fluidity of the attacking football which signalled the potency of their [West Ham's] challenge to the Merseyside monopoly.'

The visitors were eventually overwhelmed by a combination of enthralling football and wretched misfortune. They were handicapped from the start by goalkeeper Martin Thomas's suspect shoulder, but had no choice but to play him as both other keepers on their books also had disabling knocks.

A fully fit keeper might have prevented two of West Ham's four first-half goals – long-range efforts by Stewart and Orr that flew into the net through Thomas's hands. The keeper revealed afterwards that he had aggravated his shoulder early on, but he could not be faulted for Alvin Martin's thunderous volley or Glenn Roeder's headed own-goal just before the break.

At half-time Thomas was replaced by midfielder Chris Hedworth who then got hurt saving from Cottee. He did not know it yet, but he had broken his collar-bone. After Martin headed the Hammers' fifth goal, England's Peter Beardsley went in goal and Hedworth returned to the outfield, until his pain eventually took him from the field. Newcastle were now five goals down and a man short, at which point they scored themselves. West Ham replied with three in as many minutes: sub Goddard heading in with his first touch, McAvennie heading his 27th goal of the season, and Alvin Martin completing his first senior hat-trick from the spot after Roeder had handled. Cottee then hit the bar in injury-time.

Newcastle manager Willie McFaul observed, 'It was one of those nights', but one of his players, David McCreery, quipped, 'When our one went in I thought – we're on for a draw here.'

West Ham's biggest League win since Sunderland (8-0) in 1968 contained a statistical oddity. Prior to the game, the strike-force of McAvennie and Cottee had netted 41 League goals between them. Yet against stricken Newcastle, McAvennie scored just once and Cottee none.

6

TURMOIL AT THE BOLEYN 1986-1990

LEAGUE DIVISION 1	**1986-87**
Today Division 1	15th
Littlewoods Cup	Quarter-finals
FA Cup	5th Round

Following West Ham's best ever finish, Lyall warned everyone at the club: 'In football you gain respect for what you have done. The greatest compliment ... is to have opponents playing against us with a sweeper ... Obviously this will be even more the case next season. They say it is tough at the top, and everyone will be anxious to prove something when they play West Ham ... I also believe that we have yet to see the best of this side.' Famous last words!

The biggest sadness was West Ham's exclusion from Europe. Ordinarily, third place would have entitled them to a shot at the UEFA Cup, but they now found themselves paying the price for the horrors of Heysel in 1985, and the consequent ban on English clubs which lasted until 1990.

There were no major comings and goings during the summer. Behind the scenes, however, the retirement of chief executive Eddie Chapman after nearly 50 years service as player and administrator meant that new secretary Keith Godbee took the helm for the day-to-day running of the club. Another missing face, or rather voice, was that of DJ and match-day announcer Bill Remfry, who hung up his microphone after 24 years and 1,100 matches.

A pre-season tour in Holland saw the Hammers win a four-team tournament. In the League, they carried on as they had left off in May, beating Coventry at home and then – notably – Manchester United away. Following a goalless draw at Oxford, West Ham stood third, behind Liverpool and Tottenham. But that was as good as it got. In the space of four days Brian Clough's Forest and Liverpool both won at Upton Park, the latter by the humiliating margin of 5-2. Tony Cottee, weighed down by the awards of 'Young Footballer of the Year' and 'Hammer of the Year', had started the season sluggishly, but on a drizzly afternoon at QPR rediscovered his scoring knack, bagging a hat-trick. His return to form lifted the team, who went five League games unbeaten until promoted Charlton inflicted a third home defeat. Worryingly, West Ham's defence had now leaked thirteen goals in just six home games.

When the going gets tough, the tough get going. Billy Bonds had not played in the first team for sixteen months. By the turn of the year he was back in the side, which, unlike the previous season, was once again beset with injuries. At one time or other Lyall lost Martin, Devonshire, Stewart, Gale, Parkes, McAvennie, Dickens and Orr, often for long spells. This meant that youngsters Keen, Potts and Ince had to be drafted in to plug the gaps, but sooner or later Lyall knew he would have to buy his way out of trouble. His funds came from the sale of Paul Goddard. The emergence of Cottee and McAvennie as the Hammers' main strike-force was hard on the club's record signing, who had to rely on injuries to others to get a game. In November, bottom placed Newcastle paid a club record fee to resurrect his career.

After beating Southampton at home in early December, West Ham bounced back to fifth, but thereafter wins became increasingly hard to come by. Christmas was wretched – losing 0-4 at Tottenham, then seeing new-boys Wimbledon twice come from behind to win at Upton Park, a result that dumped the Hammers into the bottom half of the table. A grim-faced Lyall explained: 'We made all our own problems today by not doing the right things defensively.' In fact, the problem was deep-seated: only three other teams had conceded more goals.

Tottenham seemed to have it in for the Hammers this season. Progress had been made in the League Cup (now sponsored by Littlewoods) at the expense of Preston and two First Division clubs, Watford and Oxford, when in the quarter-finals Lyall's men were paired with a third – Spurs. A 1-1 draw took the teams to White Hart Lane for the replay. There, Tottenham bettered their 4-0 win in the League with a 5-0 rout, spearheaded by a hat-trick from Clive Allen which took his season's tally to 33 goals in 31 matches.

To compensate clubs for the European ban, various 'filler' cups had been introduced with the lure of a Wembley final. West Ham went out of the Full Members' Cup to Chelsea at the first hurdle.

A New Year's Day win against bottom placed Leicester was as predictable as was the pointless excursion to Anfield two days later. It was then that John Lyall gambled £700,000 on Arsenal midfielder Stewart Robson, who had undergone surgery two months earlier to repair a torn stomach muscle and double hernia. The table-topping Gunners apparently did not want to lose Robson, who had asked for a transfer back in September, but manager George Graham was unable to sway his mind.

The big freeze did its best to obliterate football for much of January. Orient and West Ham had to wait three weeks to settle their FA Cup-tie after Orient – five places off the bottom of the Fourth Division – had forced a replay with a last-minute penalty. The Hammers pulled through in the second match and survived a flu scare to account for Second Division Sheffield United. This set them up for a fifth round meeting with the other Sheffield side, Wednesday, who had ended their Wembley dreams the previous season. Once West Ham had drawn at Hillsborough they must have felt confident about reaching the last eight, especially as Wednesday arrived in London for the replay with the weight of five consecutive away defeats on their shoulders. But history repeated itself, Wednesday scoring twice to march on at West Ham's expense.

The slump continued with five consecutive League defeats. The only bright spot in March was the signing of Liam Brady for a give-away fee of some £100,000 from Ascoli, after seven productive years in Italy. His new manager said that it was one of the easiest transfer deals he had ever done as Brady just told Lyall to 'pay me what you think I am worth without upsetting the pay structure at the club.' Shortly before the transfer deadline centre-half Gary Strodder was signed from Lincoln, as both Martin and his cover, Hilton, would miss the rest of the season. Left-back Tommy McQueen came from Aberdeen in another £100,000+ deal.

Play-offs had been introduced this season not only to determine promotion but relegation too, and by late March the Hammers were plummeting towards the play-off zone. Their depressing sequence was halted fifteen seconds from time at home to Watford, George Parris hammering in from twenty yards. As he said afterwards, 'It's the best goal I've ever scored.' Although it was only the fourth time he had scored in his career, it was surely the most vital. Brady's influence on the team gradually began to tell, particularly in view of the injured Devonshire. The indomitable Bonds donned the captain's armband from the injured Martin as the vice-captain, Stewart, was also out for the rest of the season.

Those who suspected that Brady would be content to see out his playing days were quickly proved wrong. His goal that sealed a 3-1 win over his old club Arsenal sparked an Italian-style celebration in front of the Hammers fans that was not appreciated by the referee, who booked him. Cottee's two goals in that game ended a five-game drought that had marooned him on 99 career goals.

All four final away fixtures proved pointless. Everton were about to retain their championship, while the defeats at Leicester and

Aston Villa would not save either side from relegation. And when West Ham slumped at Southampton it was their seventh away loss running. What a turnaround: Lyall's team had started the season unbeaten away from home in eight, and had been the last side in the division to surrender their unbeaten away record. Fortunately, a couple of wins and draws at home was enough to keep West Ham clear of the play-off slot that would be occupied by Charlton.

Though injury kept him out of the final home game, veteran Billy Bonds got the loudest cheers when he stepped up to receive the Hammer of the Year award for the fourth time in his nineteen years at Upton Park. What was remarkable was that the 40-year-old had only played in seventeen League and seven cup games, but such had been his impact that there was only one possible recipient of the honour. The season ended with rumours that Tony Cottee wanted to leave as 'he was unhappy and felt in need of a change'.

Match of the Season 1986-87

West Ham 3 Arsenal 1

Division 1, 8 April 1987

In the previous match the Hammers had beaten Watford to record their first win in eight games. It halted a slide from ninth to fifteenth and terrors lurked. The Arsenal game had been postponed until Wednesday because of the Gunners' successful battle in the Littlewoods Cup final three days previously. Buoyed up by the Cup, and fifth in the League, George Graham's side would present a mighty test.

Aside than the quest for points, the game was charged for other reasons. Two former Highbury favourites, Liam Brady and Stewart Robson, lined up for the Hammers, whilst Tony Cottee wanted just one goal for his 'ton'. Lyall was also compelled to field what might be best described as a makeshift team. Phil Parkes, who had kept goal in the previous 33 League games, was out with an infected elbow, joining long-term fellow injured regulars Alvin Martin, Ray Stewart and Alan Devonshire. As for Frank McAvennie, he was starting a two-match suspension. Lyall had drafted into his line-up in the past few games new signings Brady, Strodder and McQueen, whilst recalling the old campaigner Bonds and moving Parris from his normal position of left-back into midfield, with fit again Dickens supporting Cottee in attack. McAlister took over in goal for his first game in two years. In sum, Arsenal were riding the crest of a wave, whilst West Ham were suffering any number of woes – injuries, suspensions, lack of confidence, you name it.

DID YOU KNOW?

Do West Ham fade and die like the Christmas decorations? Yes! In their first 14 years in Division 1, only 4 times did they finish higher than they had been at Christmas!

As sometimes happens in football, the underdogs made a dream start when Cottee scored after four minutes. An error by an Arsenal player allowed Mark Ward to cross and Bonds headed down for Cottee to sweep the ball on the turn. Cottee's broad smile showed what a weight had been lifted off his shoulders by scoring this, his 100th senior goal.

The visitors fought back with spirit to equalise ten minutes later. Parris floored the creative Rocastle in the penalty area and although McAlister saved Hayes' first penalty, the referee ordered a retake for multiple encroachment on West Ham's part. This time McAlister had no answer.

Crowd trouble erupted at half-time and the referee was forced to take the players off the field until the police could restore order. In consequence the second half kicked off ten minutes late. But the pace was unrelenting. One visiting Dutch journalist summarised what he saw: 'This is a typical English League game where no bone in the body is spared.' Wilmot, deputising between Arsenal's posts for the rested Lukic, distinguished himself with sharp saves from Cottee, Ward and then Cottee again. In pursuit of the ball after the last of those efforts the Arsenal keeper brought down Parris and up stepped Cottee to drive home the resulting penalty to restore his side's lead.

The fairy-tale atmosphere had another magic moment to be savoured. With ten minutes to go the scene was set for Brady to become the focus of the party mood, amongst Hammers' fans that is. The slightly built Irishman scooted 30 yards down the left before unleashing a low cross-shot on the run. The ball sped past Wilmot to ensure the defeat of Brady's former colleagues and the delight of his new ones. The crowd of 26,174 rose as one to salute their new hero who, in celebrating his goal Italian-style – being engulfed in their midst – was booked for the 'inflammatory gesture'.

The little maestro's goal set the seal on a tremendous Hammers' performance in a tremendous local derby, full of excitement and incident. More importantly it gave Lyall's team their second home win in ten days and another vital three points.

LEAGUE DIVISION 1	**1987-88**
Barclays Division 1	16th
Littlewoods Cup	2nd Round
FA Cup	4th Round

The coming season would see the First Division reduced to 21 clubs – with the next down to twenty – under the re-structuring proposed by the League, with the Second correspondingly increased to 23. John Lyall as usual was outwardly confident, but he had a number of problems to sort out. The previous season had been traumatic for the club, particularly in terms of injuries, forcing Lyall to introduce new faces. Now, newspapers were reporting that Frank McAvennie wanted to leave Upton Park and that following an enquiry from Celtic a £1.5 million price tag had been slapped on the Scottish striker. Both manager and player described themselves as baffled by the report which Lyall said had 'no substance'. It was simply the latest in a line of so-called 'exclusives' that had linked Martin, Ward, Cottee and Stewart with transfers.

Pre-season had taken the squad to Finland, Holland (against Sparta Prague and PSV Eindhoven) and Switzerland, but a number of senior players missed all or part of the three trips. Returning to England there were games against Leyton Orient and Plymouth before a final friendly in a testimonial for the club's former player and long-serving official Eddie Chapman.

Behind the scenes the club had a new secretary in the likeable and capable Tom Finn, who had held a similar post with Oldham. The chairman was once again urging the fans 'to keep the fences away from Upton Park', reminding them that the Boleyn was one of only two London grounds which did not have fenced-in compounds. With hindsight, it is noteworthy that both society and the Football League considered that fences around the perimeters of pitches 'protected' those they enclosed. It would not be long before events radically changed that opinion.

The injury list of Gale, Walford and Parkes was extended by the addition of Alan Devonshire, following a recurrence of his Achilles tendon injury. Equally worrying was the ease with which QPR won, 3-0, at Upton Park on the opening day, and by late September the Hammers were in the bottom three.

The emergence of home-grown talent in Paul Ince and Kevin Keen looked promising, but rumours of a festering feud between McAvennie and Cottee suggested that that summer 'exclusive' had had substance – particularly as Lyall accepted an offer from Celtic, enabling McAvennie to return to Scotland to play for the team he had supported as a boy. It was the second deal that Lyall had done with a Scottish club in the past six weeks, as Neil Orr had signed for Hibernian for £100,000. Further speculation suggested Everton had their sights on Cottee, who had come off the transfer list, and Terry Venables hankered after a return to England from Barcelona to buy a stake in West Ham. Before long the sports pages insisted that Lyall was looking at Kerry Dixon of Chelsea, Mick Harford of Luton, John Fashanu of Wimbledon, and was even pondering a return to London for Paul Goddard.

Despite staying undefeated in five League games in October, there were calls for Lyall's head following a humiliating home defeat by Second Division Barnsley in the Littlewoods Cup. Two goals up at the interval, West Ham were overwhelmed 2-5 after extra-time. As ever, his chairman backed Lyall: 'There was a lot of fuss made about our board meeting last week, but it was a routine meeting with a perfectly normal agenda. There was no talk about Mr Lyall's position and certainly no mention of Terry Venables.' Lyall was also publicly backed by the Hammers' three former World Cup stars. Hurst considered that he was 'one of the top bosses', Peters noted that the team 'need two or three more class players', while Moore, now a journalist, felt that the side 'no longer produce the classy football for which they are renowned'.

Another Second Division side, Millwall, heaped further problems on Lyall, knocking the Hammers out of the Simod Cup at Upton Park. The bigger worry, however, was the loss of skipper Alvin Martin, whose foot operation would keep him out for the rest of the season. In such circumstances West Ham knew they had someone they could count upon, so at 41 Billy Bonds was drafted back into harness, and his inspiration fired his colleagues to three wins and two draws in their next five fixtures. The sight of Bonds, head swathed in a bandage after receiving a nasty cut above his eye, battling against title-chasing Forest with a midfield performance that would have done credit to a man half his age, recalled memories of days gone by. Bonds had become quite literally the heart and soul of the club in its hour of need.

If deeds merit rewards, the announcement that Bonds was to receive an MBE in the Queen's New Year's honours list was greeted with delight by all who knew him. For the man himself his pleasure was tinged with regret, for Christmas and New Year yielded no points for his team. But after beating Charlton in the FA Cup and winning at QPR in the League, it seemed that a fourth round tie at QPR's tight little ground would not be such a hardship. However, in a game delayed for an hour by a crowd overspill that displayed the best aspects of both sets of fans, the West London side got their revenge for the earlier defeat.

DID YOU KNOW?

In season 1987-88 there were an odd number of clubs in Division One – 21. This meant that each week one team found itself without a game.

Typical of the Hammers, they then defied the odds at Anfield to become the first team this season to escape with a (0-0) draw. It was to be a different story in the remaining seven away fixtures, as apart from a scoreless draw at Nottingham Forest, defeat followed defeat. How strange, Liverpool finished top and Forest third, but four of those away defeats were at the hands of teams who finished in the bottom half of the table.

If West Ham were finding life tough on the road, the situation at home was almost as grim. Four relegation-haunted teams had to visit the Boleyn in the final months of the season. Portsmouth stretched their unbeaten run to nine matches when they equalised late on, and Oxford likewise grabbed a point. But Watford were beaten, narrowly, and Chelsea, emphatically. At the season's end Portsmouth, Watford and Oxford were all relegated, whilst Chelsea joined them after losing in the play-offs. It was fortunate for the Hammers that Chelsea had to play Charlton on the final Saturday. The game was drawn, all three teams ended up on 42 points, with West Ham topping the trio by virtue of a better goal-difference. But whatever the result at Stamford Bridge, either Chelsea or Charlton would have finished beneath the Hammers, whose last-day defeat at Newcastle was therefore immaterial.

West Ham were indebted to the £275,000 signing from Fulham of Leroy Rosenoir, whose goals against Watford and Chelsea earned six precious points. Lyall also paid £300,000 for a 19-year-old left-back from Birmingham, Julian Dicks. A star was born as another was poised to go. Cottee was attracting covetous eyes from Arsenal, Everton and Italy. As for Bonds, he got a standing ovation when presented with a special merit award at the PFA annual dinner.

Match of the Season 1987-88

West Ham 4 Chelsea 1

Division 1, 2 May 1988

Following defeat at Southampton the previous Saturday, the table showed West Ham with a solid rule line beneath their name and a dotted one above it. That meant they occupied the relegation play-off position. Chelsea were two places and two points ahead of the Hammers, with another London club, Charlton, separating them.

The editorial in the match programme bore the heading 'Don't Fence Us In' and carried a picture of fans watching a soccer match from behind a metal perimeter fence. It appealed to fans to avoid trouble and pitch invasions, and noted: 'This morning sees us embroiled with Chelsea in what is probably our most important game of the season, a game which is of the utmost importance to both clubs, a game which is going to involve the fans passionately.' Perhaps only a few who read behind the lines could see another meaning, but it was there for all to ponder.

As this was a morning kick-off, by lunch-time both sets of players knew their likely fate. West Ham had won and climbed one point above Chelsea, who had to play Charlton in their final fixture. Provided the Hammers did not lose by a landslide at Newcastle, either Chelsea or Charlton or both would stay below them and cushion them from the dreaded play-off spot.

A local match report summed up not only the game, but also the season and the enigma that West Ham had become once more. 'Why didn't they play like this all season. Just when Hammers had reached the bottom line, with everything stacked against them and the trapdoor to Division Two gaping wide, they turn season-long struggling form upside down with a total eclipse of rivals whose own problems were equally urgent. It defies rational explanation. Maybe they were just kidding all along, leaving it to the last possible moment simply to wind us up. And it did that all right.'

Before a crowd of 28,521, Leroy Rosenoir had struck twice in the first half as Chelsea shrank under the pressure. Stewart Robson, Dickens and Ward all returned to peak form. As for Paul Hilton, the announcement of his name in the No 5 shirt was greeted with groans, but he responded to his recall with a magnificent performance that completely shut out Chelsea's Kerry Dixon, who had rejected a move to Upton Park before Rosenoir was signed. It was the lanky 'Hilts' who, eleven minutes after the break, moved up at a corner and smashed home an attempted clearance. By his endeavours at either end of the pitch, the affable northerner won over fans who previously had given him stick.

Within five minutes of going 3-0 up, Rosenoir was sent off for retaliation, grabbing Clarke's jaw. Clarke, who had already been booked, went unpunished, clutching at his face in supposed agony. It was the type of ham acting that made lovers of the game wonder what some so-called 'sportsmen' were doing in soccer.

The ten men held out until near the end, when Chelsea's West pulled a goal back. But there was still time for Ward to get away down the right and cross for Cottee to head home. It would be Cottee's last Hammers goal for many years.

LEAGUE DIVISION 1	**1988-89**
Barclays Division 1	19th (Relegated)
Littlewoods Cup	Semi-finals
FA Cup	Quarter-finals

The close season was hectic. The biggest deal was the sale of Tony Cottee to Everton for a sum in excess of £2 million, making the 23-year-old striker the most expensive player in British football. After being linked with several big-name replacements – Arsenal's Niall Quinn and Everton's Wayne Clarke – Lyall settled on 22-year-old Republic of Ireland international David Kelly from Third Division Walsall. Another Irish signing was goalkeeper Allen McKnight from Celtic, for whom he had won Scottish championship and cup medals despite making less than twenty appearances for the Glasgow giants. There would be no more Bonds. With his 42nd birthday approaching, he said 'That's it. I won't be playing again and this time I mean it.' After 665 League games for the Hammers, Bonzo was given responsibility for coaching the youth team.

The pre-season warm-up schedule ended with a testimonial for Alvin Martin against Tottenham, but although West Ham won 2-0, the new campaign opened as badly as the previous one had closed. A trip to The Dell saw Stuart Slater concussed in the opening minute, Tony Gale limp off at the interval, and Kelly have a blank afternoon which ended in a 0-4 defeat. It was no better when Charlton won 3-1 at Upton Park to dump the Hammers at the foot of the table. Although Bonds had said his beloved club would need to be 'in dire straits' to tempt him back, many thought his recall to be only a matter of time.

By mid-October, another four consecutive losses meant West Ham were staring relegation in the face. One newspaper spoke of Lyall having sleepless nights at the prospect of the sack, while another insisted his job was safe because with four members of the Cearns family on the five-man board the stability that characterised the club would not be rashly changed. Within a few weeks the club was reputedly resisting a take-over bid designed to wrest control from the Cearns family. In a move to strengthen the board, a new director was appointed, Charles Warner, whose great grandfather, Arnold Hills, had owned the Thames Ironworks Company from which West Ham United FC had been formed in 1900. A solicitor, the new director spoke on behalf of the Hills family, who still controlled 25 percent of the club shares.

This had the appearance of being a strange season, with unfashionable clubs like Norwich, Millwall and Coventry leading the table in October. By the turn of the year West Ham were still bottom, three points adrift. Of their three League wins so far, only one had been at home, and the goal count registered 15-33. Lyall's injury-ravaged side was chopped and changed from week to week.

If League form was disastrous, the cups provided welcome relief as well as a bucketful of goals. In the Littlewoods Cup, Sunderland of the Second Division, then Derby, Liverpool and Aston Villa from the First were swept aside as the Hammers in the opening four rounds scored sixteen goals and conceded only three. The Liverpool tie was the highlight of the run. Having just lost at home to Everton in the League, the Hammers four days later roasted Dalglish's team 4-1. It was as if midweek floodlit cup-ties brought out a different team from the harsh reality of Saturday afternoons.

The first four months of 1989 effectively sealed West Ham's fate. Of their nine home League fixtures, the only victory came in the ninth, against Millwall, a week after the Hillsborough tragedy, when the minute's silence was punctuated by obscenities from a section of visiting fans. The score, 3-0, was West Ham's biggest in the League since September 1985. But such was the Hammers' plight that the Millwall win helped their position only to the extent of closing the gap with Newcastle to four points.

During the same period the Hammers played just four away League fixtures. In two of those, against high-flying Derby and lowly Aston Villa, they pulled off victories.

Since early in the year protest banners had declared 'Lyall Out', but the manager remained philosophical. More worrying for him was the growing injury list. Ray Stewart joined Stewart Robson as being out for the rest of the season, and no sooner did Stuart Slater return to fitness than he was crocked again. The performances of two players – new signings McKnight and Kelly – earned abuse from the crowd. David Kelly's meagre return of six goals had the crowd chanting for the return of McAvennie, while McKnight's goalkeeping blunders had shattered his confidence so much that 38-year-old Phil Parkes was recalled in February. McKnight's calamities had put paid to the Hammers' interest in the League Cup semi-final against fellow strugglers Luton.

As in the Littlewoods Cup, West Ham found respite from their League woes in the FA Cup, though they needed replays to beat both table-toppers Arsenal and Second Division Swindon, managed by Lou Macari, who six months later would be installed as Lyall's successor. Parkes' heroics then defied Charlton and some fans began dreaming of Wembley. Alas, in a Carrow Road replay, Norwich powered their way to the semi-finals for the first time in 30 years.

After being thwarted by the inflated asking prices for a number of strikers, Lyall made a last desperate throw of the dice, re-signing

Frank McAvennie. Celtic accepted West Ham's offer of £1.25 million (£400,000 more than they had bought him for) after the player had clashed once too often with manager Billy McNeill.

The arrival of the blond-haired extrovert provided a welcome Easter present. McAvennie lifted the Hammers to win at Villa Park, but as he failed to score in any of the eight matches he played in, prior to getting injured, his signing was only a qualified success. Three of those eight fixtures were crucial. In the space of a week Lyall's men played three home games, earning only one point and losing to fellow paupers Middlesbrough and Southampton. Against Boro, West Ham were leading with six minutes to go but lost. That was not the way to defy relegation.

McAvennie's injury coincided with Leroy Rosenior's return from cartilage surgery and a welcome upturn in form. West Ham won five games out of six, three of them on their travels in a distorted climax that left them to play their final four matches away from home. In theory they could still save themselves in their last game, except that it was at Liverpool who were neck and neck with Arsenal in the race for the title. Kenny Dalglish's team did not mess about, demolishing West Ham 5-1 to propel them into the Second Division. Three days later Arsenal dashed Liverpool's hopes of another League and Cup double, winning 2-0 at Anfield to take the title on the number of goals scored, both teams having finished with identical points and goal-difference. As for the Hammers, in the final analysis they went down because of the worst home record in their history – just three wins out of nineteen fixtures. On their travels they had won seven games and drawn two. But despite everything, West Ham were just one win from safety.

In the closing weeks of the season there was much talk of players quitting Upton Park in the event of relegation. Lyall's contract, too, expired in the summer, but the consensus was that a club like West Ham were unlikely to sack someone who had served it for 34 years – indeed he was the League's longest serving manager. Many thought he would be offered another position within the club, such as general manager, where his great knowledge of football, players, contracts and the like, would be of use.

But Lyall was sacked. He was informed during a meeting with his chairman arranged over a week previously, ostensibly to discuss more routine matters. The board's decision not to renew his contract was apparently reached by majority: it was not unanimous. Many supporters thought the decision marked not only the ending of an era at Upton Park, but the defining moment when the way of doing things at West Ham United changed irrevocably. Whether that was for better or worse remained to be seen.

DID YOU KNOW?

Although 1988-89 saw West Ham's worst ever home record, they did not finish bottom. Newcastle's home record was equally bad and their away form was worse.

The club advertised for applications to fill the vacant position. A number of names were canvassed. It was said that Bournemouth refused permission for their manager, Harry Redknapp, to speak to his former club after an 'illegal approach' had been made to him. After much guessing, Swindon boss Lou Macari was offered the job, becoming just the sixth West Ham manager in the club's history. The appointment surprised many in that Macari had no past link with the Hammers. His arrival was a leap into the unknown.

He did not land upon a happy ship. He inherited a mutinous crew, with certain out-of-contract players determined to get away. But nor did Macari's new bosses realise that the former Manchester United and Scotland star had created waves at Swindon, or that over the coming months a trickle of conjecture would transform into a flood of accusations.

Match of the Season 1988-89

West Ham 4 Liverpool 1

Littlewoods Cup, 30 November 1988

At the conclusion of this masterful tactical triumph, Lyall summed up his thoughts: 'Obviously a magnificent performance and as good as any cup win we have had for many, many years. I don't think it is too often that Liverpool lose in a cup-tie and when you have got four against them of course it is a marvellous performance for us.'

If the score, as it flashed through the news agencies and across television screens, raised eyebrows it was because West Ham were just one off the bottom while Liverpool were sturdily defending their championship. The Hammers had not beaten the Merseysiders in their last thirteen meetings spread over six years, and just a month previously had lost 0-2 to Dalglish's side at Upton Park in the League. The margin of victory – 4-1 – constituted Liverpool's heaviest cup defeat since World War II.

As had been demonstrated so many times before, cup-ties under the lights of Upton Park brought out the best in the Hammers. This particular display, like the result, was a throwback to a more golden era. From the start the Hammers were confident in everything they did and were unrecognisable from the side of the previous Saturday who had capitulated at home so easily to Everton.

Sharp in their passing, the Hammers launched wave after wave of attacks at the Liverpool defence. Victory was secured on the strength of West Ham's midfield, where Paul Ince, Liam Brady and Alan Devonshire enjoyed one of those nights. In the 21st minute Brady curled over a cross which Ince met with a spectacular volley. If that stunned the visitors his second goal three minutes later left them dumbfounded, as he dashed in to head home Devonshire's corner. The home fans' joy was curtailed in the 34th minute when Alvin Martin fouled John Aldridge in the box. Aldridge took the kick himself and suddenly Liverpool were back in contention.

The outcome hung on a knife-edge until the 56th minute. There appeared to be little danger when David Kelly's cross dropped into the Liverpool penalty area, only for Steve Staunton to stoop to guide the ball back to his goalkeeper. Unfortunately for him, Staunton misdirected his header against a post and into the net. For once, Liverpool heads appeared to drop.

With fourteen minutes to go the Hammers' victory was complete. Julian Dicks was fouled 25 yards out. Tony Gale curled the free-kick over the Liverpool wall and beyond the grasping fingers of keeper Mike Hooper. It was a suitably classy finish to a classic evening, and revived hopes for a climb away from the relegation zone.

For Ince especially, it was a night to remember. The 21-year-old's performance suggested that he would one day become a very fine player. Liam Brady certainly thought so: 'This lad will surely play for England by the end of this season.' Not this season, as it turned out, but certainly before too long.

LEAGUE DIVISION 2	**1989-90**
Barclays Division 2	7th
Littlewoods Cup	Semi-finals
FA Cup	3rd Round

Upton Park saw numerous changes in the summer. Alan Dickens moved to Chelsea for £600,000, the fee determined by a League tribunal. The sum was twice their chairman's valuation but only three-quarters of what the Hammers had originally demanded.

The major new presence was the arrival of a local replacement window, door and conservatory company as the club's new sponsors. After signing a two-year deal, described as the best in the division, the new playing strip – once again supplied by Bukta – and all club publicity would be emblazoned with the logo of BAC Windows. Even the footballs used in matches and for training came from a new supplier, Mitre.

But within weeks of Macari's arrival there was newspaper talk of rumblings amongst players over new training routines. The tough little Scot explained: 'The first thing I expect from players is fitness and dedication. The game is littered with players who had above average ability but failed to fulfil their potential because they lacked the required fitness ... Their attitude was wrong. Our attitude has to be right when the new season opens next month, and our fitness has to be spot on.' Macari then outlined what was expected of him: 'I will be judged on results. The reason I was offered this job was because West Ham were in trouble – if they don't improve, my neck will ultimately be on the chopping block. I have got no magic wand ... It is an input from everyone that gets achievement. I knew this job would present immediate problems, but I took it because I believed in myself.' When challenged about his robust and direct approach at Swindon, and its effect on the West Ham philosophy, Macari replied: 'I'm not going to close down the Academy.'

The 'immediate problems' he referred to concerned Mark Ward's third transfer request and rumours of squabbles with McAvennie. The biggest worry, however, was the disgruntled Paul Ince who, according to his agent, had been refused a wage increase by his new boss, who insisted he honour his existing contract. The emergence of player's agents and their role in English football was summed up by Ince's representative, who stated: 'I shall pursue my efforts to get Paul away from West Ham before the start of the season, particularly bearing in mind the attitude of the management.' Determined to get away, Ince pulled out of a pre-season tour to Sweden only to be pictured two days later wearing a Manchester United shirt. But the £2 million deal dramatically collapsed when pelvic problems were disclosed during his medical. The transfer was off, then on again a few weeks later when West Ham agreed a down-payment of £800,000 plus extra payments for each appearance made. The actions of Ince in parading himself in a red United shirt while still a West Ham player would see him vilified by Hammers supporters. Their torrent of abuse whenever he appeared at Upton Park in subsequent years showed they would neither forget nor forgive his betrayal.

Though Macari had been linked with various new players he preferred to bide his time. He was robbed of a winning start only by a late equaliser at Stoke. What did force his hand was a nasty tackle on McAvennie that broke his left leg and kept him out of football for the next six months.

Macari's first signings were midfielder Martin Allen from QPR for £650,000, and shortly afterwards Colin Foster, a £750,000 central defender from Nottingham Forest. In late December he signed Ian Bishop (midfield) and Trevor Morley (striker) from Manchester City, in exchange for Mark Ward in a £1 million package deal, and Jimmy Quinn, another striker, who signed for £320,000 from Bradford City. In February Ludek Miklosko, after a delay of more than a month, was given a work permit that permitted the Czech international goalkeeper to play in England.

In the opening fifteen League fixtures Macari's new-look team suffered just three defeats, despite nineteen different players having to be used on account of injuries. By early November they lay fifth, combining physical presence with traditional flare.

The Littlewoods Cup was proving fruitful, as in the previous season. Both Birmingham clubs, City and Aston Villa, were ousted before a pitched battle of a game with Wimbledon at Upton Park saw a 17-man brawl, a sending-off and six bookings, and both clubs let off with the trifling punishment of a £20,000 fine. Many thought the FA's leniency was tantamount to condoning the actions of clubs that were dragging the game through the gutter. West Ham's reward for Martin Allen's late winner against the Dons was a three-match marathon against Derby, which carried them to the semi-finals for the second year running, this time against Oldham.

If Lou Macari thought that his first few months in East London had been eventful, nothing could have prepared him for the explosions set to blow up around him and West Ham in the next few months. The first problems came on the pitch. The last six games of 1989 earned the Hammers just one point and they slid down to eleventh, seventeen points behind leaders Leeds. A third round FA Cup-tie at struggling Torquay, who had not won for eight games against Fourth Division opponents, promised easy access to round four, except that a goal by an 18-year-old Torquay substitute sent West Ham spinning out.

The slump in form was undoubtedly linked to events that had been building up since Macari's arrival. To rumblings of disharmony between manager, players and coaches were now added accusations of an altogether more serious nature. Macari and his former Swindon chairman were charged by the FA with a breach of rules over unauthorised betting on an FA Cup-tie two years earlier. Just two days before the Torquay debacle coach Mick McGiven had quit after sixteen years as a player and coach under John Lyall. McGiven had felt upset by Lyall's sacking and had to be dissuaded by chairman Len Cearns from leaving in the summer. This time there was no stopping him and McGiven became Chelsea's youth team manager. A further shock came with the news that Cearns himself was ready to stand down after 42 years as a director, of which the last eleven had been spent as chairman. One newspaper suggested that he had become dismayed at the way the Hammers' image had been tarnished by recent events. The same paper reported that Frank McAvennie had struck the club's commercial manager at a party. A writ was about to be served upon the Scottish striker if an apology was not forthcoming. In yet another damaging revelation, four players had been fined by Macari for their involvement in wild behaviour in the early hours at an Essex hotel on New Year's Eve.

Veteran goalkeeper Parkes, although critical of his style, said: 'We are all behind Lou Macari and we wanted to win the Torquay match for him. We hoped it would take some of the pressure off.' Former star Trevor Brooking, speaking on the Upton Park 'Clubcall' was more forthright: 'The last week has been the blackest in the club's history, an unprecedented catalogue of disasters. This kind of thing never happened during my days and I'm shocked by it all.' As was the custom at Upton Park, no official statement was issued and everyone from directors to coaching and playing staff closed ranks around the manager to protect him from his 'trial by media'. Some close to the club wryly reflected that the scandals had undermined years of carefully nurtured and jealously guarded image-making and felt that whatever his faults Lyall would never have allowed the club to descend into such squalor.

John Lyall, since his dismissal, had published his autobiography, joined England manager Bobby Robson's 'think-tank' to help assess likely rivals for the World Cup in Italy, and taken up the post of technical co-ordinator at Tottenham. Spurs' manager Terry Venables said: 'John is too good at his job to be out of the game.' By the end of the season Lyall would be back as a manager with Ipswich.

The only sunshine at West Ham came in the Littlewoods Cup. The three-match, five-hour marathon with First Division Derby saw Stewart Robson play his first game in sixteen months, Martin Allen red-carded and banned for five games, and the Hammers paired with Second Division rivals Oldham in the last four.

By then, however, Peter Storrie had been appointed as a new director amid talk of a boardroom shake-up. As for Macari, it looked as if his career at Upton Park was safe. Although found guilty, he was fined just £1,000 and censured for his part in the breaching of FA rules regarding betting on matches. If some thought Macari had enjoyed the luck of the devil, his world was shattered a few days later on the plastic pitch of Boundary Park, where Oldham handed his team an unimaginable 6-0 thrashing in the first leg of the Littlewoods Cup semi-final. Four days later the little Scot failed to turn up for the League game at his former club, Swindon, and the next day Hammers secretary Tom Finn announced that the board had accepted his resignation. The reason given was that Macari had decided to appeal against the FA decision in an attempt to clear his name and prove his innocence. The press speculated that the club had wanted Macari to accept the fine and let the matter drop. Macari had refused to do so and resigned in order to fight without his hands being tied. His had been a controversial eight-month reign, the most turbulent period in the club's history, and at 229 days the shortest tenure by any of its managers.

In turning to Ron Boyce as caretaker boss, the club put in charge a stalwart with 30 years experience in the ways of Upton Park. Within days it was confirmed that Len Cearns had handed over the chairmanship to his son Martin, but would remain as a director. One of the new chairman's first tasks was to appoint Billy Bonds as the new manager. Bonds promptly installed Boyce as his No 2. If Bonds was the popular choice of the 20,000 crowd who turned up to salute him at his first game in charge, it was understandable, for they felt that the 'West Ham family' was once more intact. The rousing ovation Bonds received as a manager, following 23 years as a player, helped to exorcise the pain of the past months.

Wembley was, of course, a pipe-dream unless West Ham could muster a result of astronomical proportions in the home leg against Oldham, which did not happen. But good form in the League drove the Hammers ever nearer a play-off position. In the end they were denied by two points. Sunderland were indebted to their 4-3 home win over West Ham for their place in the play-offs, when a draw would have handed that prize to Bonzo's men.

The 34-year-old Liam Brady bade farewell in the final game of the season, against Wolves, with a jinking run and memorable goal.

Match of the Season 1989-90

West Ham 3 Oldham 0

Littlewoods Cup, semi-final, 2nd leg, 7 March 1990

The turmoil building up at Upton Park had exploded in the first leg on the notorious plastic pitch at Boundary Park, where Oldham had gone 32 games unbeaten. The 0-6 scoreline was not only their heaviest, but also West Ham's most humiliating cup defeat in their history. For those who like such things, the date was also that of the St Valentine's Day Massacre – 14 February.

Three weeks later it was a different story. Even if Bonds was the Messiah, it was asking much even for him to conjure the six goals needed to stay alive, particularly as his prodigious energies would be directed not on the pitch but from the dug-out. It says much for the man and his players that not for one moment did they consider this to be a 'nothing match'.

With four players cup-tied, Bonds paired Leroy Rosenoir – back after five months out with injury – and David Kelly as his strike-force, whilst Miklosko replaced Parkes in goal. With Brady at the heart of everything, the Hammers laid siege to the visitors' goal. Two penalty appeals were rejected before Keen's corner was headed on by Gale at the near post for Martin to nod home at the far.

Shortly after the turnaround Miklosko launched a huge clearance downfield, Rosenoir headed on and Keen was brought down by Hallworth in the Oldham goal. Julian Dicks made it 2-0 from the spot. When the Czech keeper repeated the feat, a poor defensive header allowed David Kelly to drive home from fifteen yards. With 25 minutes still to play the impossible was suddenly possible. Dicks, Rosenoir, Keen and Kelly all went close. If Dicks' rasping twenty-yarder, that nearly lifted the crossbar off its moorings, had been a few inches lower, who knows what might have happened. Signs of tension even affected the boisterous travelling Oldham supporters, who fell quieter than one would expect, given that their team had been leading 6-0.

In the end Oldham held out without further damage, leaving both sets of fans with reasons to celebrate. Oldham had reached a Wembley final for the first time in their 91-year history. They would be seconds from winning the trophy when Mark Hughes equalised for Manchester United, who comfortably took the replay. For their part, West Ham received a standing ovation from their fans for repairing their damaged pride and in inflicting on Oldham their first defeat in thirteen games. Honour had been satisfied all round.

7

'BONDS' AND 'BONDS' 1990-1994

LEAGUE DIVISION 2	**1990-91**
Barclays Division 2	2nd (Promoted)
Rumbelows Cup	3rd Round
FA Cup	Semi-finalists

Several familiar faces from the Lyall era departed in the summer of 1990. Phil Parkes, having agreed to stay as goalkeeping coach, then joined Lyall at Ipswich instead. Another old boy, Mick McGiven, then joined Lyall as his No 2. Alan Devonshire left on a 'free' and joined Watford, whilst Gary Strodder agreed a move to West Brom. What with Brady's retirement, Kelly's transfer to Leicester in the spring, the impending sale of McQueen to Falkirk and the loan of Rosenoir to Fulham and Charlton, the dressing-room at the Boleyn looked decidedly different.

Everyone at Upton Park was aware that the team were fancied for promotion, but Bonds reckoned a dozen teams were capable of doing well and would not be drawn into rash predictions. His impact since his arrival encouraged record receipts from season ticket sales. The protest by supporters who frequented the East Terrace standing area following the last game of the previous season was heeded by the board, who postponed for twelve months the decision to install seats in the area. Extensive work, however, had been done on the pitch, which saw a new carpet of grass.

Preferring not to venture abroad for the usual pre-season warm-ups, Bonds used testimonials for Ray Clemence (of Spurs) and Phil Parkes, now of course at Ipswich, to test his squad. But with Gale, Foster, Stewart, Robson, Potts and Rosenoir all out injured, Bonds could have learned little.

After twelve years as a director, Jack Petchey switched allegiance to Elton John's Watford, buying the singer's stake for £6 million to take control of the Hertfordshire club. As a locally born business-man, many felt that his leaving was the result of frustration born out of being unable to gain control at Upton Park.

If the Hammers' opening to the new campaign was considered low-key, it was nevertheless steady and productive. Goals were scarce at both ends of the pitch, but West Ham's outnumbered the opposition's and this ensured that week after week, month after month, points were stacked away. It seemed that the good times were once again returning to East London as Bonds got the club and its supporters bubbling again. On 24 November a McAvennie goal earned a win at Plymouth that took the Hammers to the top of the table. Another victory seven days later over West Brom created a new club record of nineteen League games unbeaten. The figure of just twelve goals conceded was music to those who doubted that kamikaze tactics were the way to gain promotion. That unbeaten run eventually extended to 21 games and only came to an end, at Barnsley, on the Saturday before Christmas. His team's exploits earned Bonds the 'Barclays League Second Division Manager of the Month' award two months running.

It had not been quite such smooth-sailing in the cups, however. Having overcome Stoke in the League Cup (now sponsored by Rumbelows), West Ham succumbed at Oxford, 30 seconds into injury-time. It was their first loss of the season in any competition. In the Zenith Data Systems Cup, Bonds fielded six reserves against First Division Luton on their plastic pitch. One of those was transfer-listed reserve keeper Allen McKnight, who had not played in the first team for nineteen months. Sadly, he was at fault for at least three of the Hatters' five goals.

Two months previously Bonzo had made his first buy, paying £600,000 for the Luton right-back Tim Breacker, who was prepared to step down a division. In November Bonds became the first ever Hammer to have a second testimonial match staged in his honour. A crowd of over 10,000 turned up on a rainswept Monday evening to pay tribute and salute him once again.

Other new faces at the club included that of Terence Brown as a director, full-back Chris Hughton, as cover for the injured Julian Dicks, and a new physio, John Green, when Rob Jenkins took early retirement after 25 years service. One notable departure was that of the club's DJ and announcer, Ian Crocker, who took up a position with Capital Gold.

If the senior side were 'on song', so was the youth team, who created fireworks on Guy Fawkes Night at Upton Park, establishing a new club record by beating Horndean FC from Hampshire 21-1 in a first round FA Youth Cup-tie. The young Hammers eventually lost in the semi-finals.

After being temporarily dislodged from the top of the table by the loss at Barnsley, Bonds' side regained the No 1 spot on Boxing

Day with a 2-0 victory over their usurpers, Oldham. The win went some way to eradicating the memory of Joe Royle's side's dismissal of West Ham from the Littlewoods Cup earlier that year.

The triumphs of the Old Year continued into the New as in both the League and the FA Cup further successes were recorded until the first Saturday in February. It was a League trip to Molineux that ended the run. By then, the Hammers had repaid Luton for the five-goal hiding inflicted in the Zenith Data. This time, in the FA Cup, they came away from the Kenilworth Road plastic pitch with a 1-1 draw, and warmed up Upton Park on one of the coldest nights of the year with a 5-0 demolition of the Hatters in the replay.

Much of February was lost to the weather, but a home win over Crewe put Bonds' team into the quarter-finals of the Cup, and another over Millwall kept them in front of Oldham in the League. March was to prove a testing month as the Hammers had to play seven League games and an FA Cup quarter-final. A fine performance by Stuart Slater destroyed First Division Everton in the Cup to put West Ham in the semi-finals for the first time in eleven years. In the League, though the team went off the boil, the loss to Sheffield Wednesday was Bonds' first at home in any competition in his fourteen months in charge. A cliff-hanging draw at Oldham might have been a win, but for conceding a late penalty. An incident earlier that month, when leading scorer Trevor Morley was stabbed during a domestic dispute, clearly affected the harmony within Upton Park.

April was to prove just as busy, with another eight fixtures crammed in. West Ham were back on top again, and stayed there despite going down 0-1 at Brighton. Four days later the Hammers stepped out at Villa Park for their FA Cup semi-final with Brian Clough's Nottingham Forest. McAvennie's earlier dismissal against Bristol City meant he was suspended, but Morley's quick recovery enabled him to start the game. The tie, however, made news for weeks afterwards on account of a 25th-minute incident, when at 0-0 Tony Gale was sent off by referee Keith Hackett for a professional foul on Forest's Gary Crosby. TV pundits argued the ins and outs, but the fact that the Forest player was heading away from goal towards the corner flag left West Ham incensed by the injustice. Forest ran in four second-half goals, and despite later appeals for Hackett to reconsider, Gale was banned for the last three vital fixtures of the season.

West Ham responded to their Cup exit by winning their next two games to secure their return to the big time with five fixtures still to play. An Iain Dowie goal against Swindon removed all doubt. Dowie had been signed in March from Luton for £480,000 and would become something of a cult figure over the next few years. He scored again in the next game to salvage a home point against Newcastle, and again at lowly Blackburn, who had found themselves three goals up after just fourteen minutes. With West Ham focused on the Second Division championship these were stupid points to drop. Bonds warned: 'If we continue to play like that the title isn't a possibility. When I made a double substitution in the second half I could have pulled anybody off.' Oldham's win at Ipswich meant the gap had closed to one point. In Bonds' defence it could be argued that one or more of his three recognised centre-backs – Foster, Martin and Gale – had been missing for long stretches. Martin had not played since December, and Foster only in spells, like the patched-up Gale.

With just one game to play the destination of the title was firmly in West Ham's hands. All they had to do was beat Notts County.

Match of the Season 1990-91

West Ham 1 Notts County 2

Division 2, 11 May 1991

Billy Bonds wrote in the match programme for this match: 'It's funny how the fixtures have worked out on this, the last day of the season. The top four teams in the Second Division meet today and whilst we are aiming to beat fourth-placed Notts County, we know that Oldham Athletic will be just as determined to win at home against third-placed Sheffield Wednesday.'

West Ham had put themselves in pole position by beating Bristol Rovers at home on the Wednesday, a result which gave them a two-point margin over Joe Royle's Oldham going into the final game. As Oldham's goal-difference was better, only a Hammers win could make the Oldham result an irrelevance, but no one could have foreseen the twists and turns that would unfold – minute by nail-biting minute, before, during and even after the match – before the destination of the championship was decided.

What complicated matters was the attitude of the opposition. Neither Sheffield Wednesday nor Notts County had anything to play for, other than the pleasure of party-pooping. Wednesday had finished third and would therefore join West Ham and Oldham in Division One. County had finished fourth, missing out on automatic promotion but assured of their play-off place. But County came to Upton Park as the form side of the division with six successive wins. West Ham had not looked so lively: victory over Bristol Rovers had been their first win in four.

DID YOU KNOW?

In 1990-91, West Ham were denied the Division Two championship by seconds. Their final match against Notts County also saw both No 3s named Par(r)is.

From the off County adopted a 'no prisoners' policy and Craig Short was booked for scything Stuart Slater, but Upton Park was stilled after seventeen minutes when Mark Draper fired County in front from the edge of the area. Ten minutes later a sloppy Colin Foster clearance was fired back by Draper from twenty yards for the little midfielder's second goal. Goalkeeper Miklosko looked dumbfounded: before the start he had celebrated winning the 'Hammer of the Year' trophy.

At half-time Bonds made a tactical change by introducing both substitutes, McAvennie and Keen. To their niggling time-wasting, County now added the ploy of going down like ninepins. On 64 minutes Foster was led from the pitch with a gash that needed six stitches. Having used both subs, the Hammers had to fight on with just ten men. All was not lost, however. News came through that Oldham were likewise two goals down, and barring their recovery the title was West Ham's.

With eleven minutes left Keen set up George Parris, who lashed in his eighth goal of the season. Then came the news that Oldham were also back to 1-2. Nerves were shredded. Ian Bishop's free header bounced behind off the bar, Parris's effort was turned for a corner, and now Oldham scored again to equalise. But they had to win. Surely there wasn't time.

Suddenly, two minutes early, referee Brian Hill blew for full-time, grabbing the ball off Miklosko and legging it for the tunnel, gesturing as he went for the astonished players to accompany him. Underneath the main stand amazing scenes ensued as Barclays League officials prepared their presentation tableau to be set up on the pitch – a claret-and-blue bedecked table for the championship trophy and presentation medals. Champagne corks were popped and backs slapped. Suddenly it was learned that Oldham were still playing and, horror of horrors, two minutes into injury-time had been awarded a penalty. Neil Redfearn took the kick and scored, whereupon red-faced League officials packed up their bags and beat an embarrassed retreat from Upton Park. The despair was palpable. Bonds said: 'I am shattered. In the dressing-room we were shaking hands and patting each other on the back. Then we heard the news. It was cruel.' Although the perfect day had turned sour, Billy Bonds' record in his first fourteen months had been astonishing.

LEAGUE DIVISION 1	**1991-92**
Barclays Division 1	22nd (Relegated)
Rumbelows Cup	4th Round
FA Cup	5th Round

Having been thrust with little experience into the cauldron of football management, Billy Bonds had done remarkably well. But getting the Hammers into the top division was easy compared with keeping them there. If all seemed calm on the surface at Upton Park, things looked murkier underneath. In guiding West Ham to promotion Bonds had spent a little over £1 million – peanuts by contemporary standards. He had acquired Chris Hughton on a free transfer, but had generated nearly half the club's outlay by selling four players he had inherited.

The implementation of the Taylor Report – which decreed that every football stadium must be all-seater within two years – meant that money earmarked for new players had to be diverted to ground safety. The new legislation crippled several small and medium-sized clubs as they endeavoured to comply with the law. In West Ham's case, in order to implement the crowd safety proposals in the wake of the Heysel, Bradford and Hillsborough disasters, the club had appointed a former police superintendent, John Ball, as Stadium Manager and Safety Officer.

These circumstances restricted Bonds' spending money to just £1 million. To trim the wage bill he also gave Stewart Robson, Ray Stewart, Allen McKnight and Paul Kelly free transfers. Bonds hoped to raise £200-£300,000 from the sale of Jimmy Quinn, but eventually settled for just £40,000 when Quinn joined Bournemouth. Bonds had to wheel and deal, which must have been frustrating when he recalled the large sums available to John Lyall, especially as £1 million pound players were now commonplace in the English game. In all, a record sum of £50 million was spent on player transfers that summer, with the likes of Teddy Sheringham going for £2 million and Keith Curle for £2.5 million.

Bonds had to make do with Dean Martin, an 18-year-old striker from non-league football for a small fee, Mitchell Thomas, a defender from Tottenham for £500,000, and Mike Small, a striker, for slightly less from Brighton. Full-back Kenny Brown, son of the former 1950s and 60s centre-half Ken senior, arrived from Plymouth on a loan which eventually became a permanent move, and Tony Parks joined as understudy to Miklosko.

The pre-season build-up produced few smiles, partly because of injuries, partly because of strong opposition in the Makita Tournament at Highbury and the visit of Brazilian side Botafogo to Upton

Park. Even in that gentle friendly, McAvennie managed to get sent off, and was thus banned for the opening three games.

Bonds wrote in his opening programme notes about the size of the hurdles ahead, and supporters were soon in no doubt as to how the club's meagre resources would be stretched. The fixture list had been kind in the opening weeks, but in the fifth match a 0-2 home defeat by Notts County – who had denied West Ham the title four months previously, and come up via the play-offs – showed once again how vulnerable the Hammers were to such spoiling antics. The departure of Iain Dowie to Southampton after just a dozen games gave Bonds some much-needed cash, though a £2 million bid from Celtic for Stuart Slater was rejected. Not for long, as it turned out. Slater signed for new Celtic manager Liam Brady the following summer.

Though the Hammers spluttered, the form of Mike Small helped placate those fans chanting 'what a lot of rubbish' and 'sack the board'. In his first nineteen games Small had hit thirteen goals out of the 26 the Hammers had scored in all competitions. Minor cartilage surgery seemed to unsettle him, however, and his goals dried up. By the end of October the sorry tale was that West Ham had only won twice at home in the League and lay seventeenth.

In November, Peter Storrie, on the board less than two years, became the club's first managing director, having responsibility for the day to day running of the club. It was also announced that the club would not relocate but would remain at the Boleyn Ground. The redevelopment at Upton Park would cost a projected £15.5 million and take some three years to transform into a 25,000 capacity all-seater stadium. To help finance all this the 'Hammers Bond' scheme would be launched with supporters buying a stake that would guarantee their seats for payments of £500 upwards. With hindsight it was a terrible move, driving a schism between club and supporters that would take years to heal. It also meant that in the West Ham context the word 'bonds' would induce a shiver, whereas 'Bonds' – as in Bonzo – at that time evoked only awe.

In a further bid to placate irate fans who – in the wake of lucrative cup runs and the sale of players – had been demanding 'Where's the money gone?' the board broke with tradition to reveal financial figures showing a net deficit of over £2 million. Operating costs had increased by far more than income from ticket sales.

Meanwhile, Billy Bonds had signed a two-year extension to his contract that would take him to July 1994. Unsung defender Steve Potts, back in the first team after a combination of injury and competition from Breacker, Gale and Foster, also committed himself for the same duration.

Having shocked everyone by winning at champions Arsenal, the Hammers hit the depths, taking just three draws from the next nine League games and losing to Norwich in the Rumbelows Cup. By mid-January they were 21st and the writing was on the wall. The only team beneath them, Southampton, knocked the Hammers out of the Zenith Data Systems Cup, a result which kick-started the Saints' season and saw them climb out of the relegation places.

Just before Christmas the charismatic Julian Dicks had returned, following fourteen months out with a serious knee injury. It was his goal that earned a replay in the third round of the FA Cup against non-League Farnborough, who had forfeited home advantage for the benefit of a big pay day at Upton Park. That replay, also staged at the Boleyn, was seconds from extra-time before Morley's winner spared the Hammers' blushes.

One notable absentee at those games was Jack Helliar, who since the war had missed just a handful of games at Upton Park. He had become an authority on the Hammers as an historian and archivist, as well as being editor and printer of the matchday programme for much of the period. In the past eight seasons Jack had contributed to the new matchday magazine and ministered to the press room on match days. His close association with the club went back, like those of the Cearns family, via his father and grandfather (who had worked as a brass founder and was a member of the football committee which in 1895 formed the Thames Ironworks FC) to the earliest days of the formation of West Ham United in July 1900. On the morning of the first Farnborough game he was taken ill, and shortly before the replay Jack Helliar – my father – passed away.

Round four paired West Ham with Fourth Division strugglers Wrexham, who had just toppled Arsenal. The Welsh team equalised twice at Upton Park, to leave their 3,000 singing fans dreaming of another famous scalp in the replay. In the event West Ham scored the only goal. Round five took the Hammers to Second Division Sunderland, who earned a replay with a miskicked equaliser. In the replay, though West Ham recovered from 0-2 down, Sunderland scored again to march on to Wembley.

Cup elimination by a lesser-division team sparked even greater unrest. Bizarre scenes were observed as seated fans stood up and those standing sat down. Small wonder that the players had little confidence in themselves or anyone else. The manager alone stood above reproach, but he was forced to admit that his entire squad was up for sale. The board, far from abandoning the bonds scheme, decided to re-launch it but with new incentives. The implications of the Taylor Report sparked protests nationwide, with red balloons being released up and down the country. At Upton Park 10,000 were set free before the home match with Everton. When the Hammers went 0-2 down hundreds of fans invaded the pitch in a separate protest over the bond scheme. Mercifully, fears that the ground would be closed or points deducted proved unfounded. Former players came out to denounce the bond scheme, which had clearly become a bridge too far for those expected to bear the costs.

Another nine-game losing run through to early April saw the Hammers sink to the bottom. Clive Allen was signed from Chelsea for £275,000 in a vain bid to avert the inevitable. It was his eighth move in a fourteen-year career that had chalked up £6.3 million in transfer fees. Clive became the third member of the Allen clan – added to Paul and Martin – to don the claret and blue.

Apart from a 4-0 win over Norwich, and a headline-grabbing win over Manchester United, which cost Alex Ferguson's men their first title under his reign, those last weeks brought little but gloom. Frank McAvennie ended his West Ham career in the final match as a substitute against Nottingham Forest, and duly recorded a hat-trick. Some argued that he was needed for a promotion push, but he no longer had the legs, was increasingly injury-prone, and had scored only three other League goals all season.

All things considered, the headline 'An all-time low' in a local paper aptly summed up West Ham's predicament. Worse, there was no quick-fix answer, and short-term measures might even hinder long-term solutions. Peter Storrie and Billy Bonds planned a major restructuring of the club, for whom 'lows' would be a mid-table position in the new Premier League, and 'highs' a top-six placing. Storrie concluded: 'We may, in years ahead, look back on this as being the season that West Ham United changed its way, changed its ambitions and restructured to become a major force in the future of the game.' Viewed today, Storrie's words in those darkest days of 1992 have an unexpected ring of truth.

As the Hammers contemplated life outside the big time, the star of former manager John Lyall was in the ascendant. As West Ham went down, Ipswich came up.

Match of the Season 1991-92

West Ham 1 Manchester United 0

Division 1, 22 April 1992

The great enigma – once again! How was it possible to play so bad so often, and achieve a result that totally confused the critics and pundits? Three days after this momentous win, the Hammers went down 0-1 at Coventry to confirm relegation.

DID YOU KNOW?

In 1991-92 West Ham finished bottom of Division One with 38 points. That was the most points for any wooden-spoonists since Brighton's 40 nine years previously.

In his programme notes for the final home match, against Forest, Bonds wrote: 'There is no in between – we've either been good or bloody awful. People ask me to explain how we can play so well to beat a side of United's quality and then lose to the likes of Coventry and Notts County, and I'm not sure of the answer. I've got my own thoughts on the problems that exist but this isn't the place for me to air those views.'

Ferguson's team arrived at Upton Park having squandered their games in hand over Leeds to such an extent that the Yorkshire club were now in the driving seat. Having spent £13 million on building his side, Ferguson could only watch in despair as his team fell apart against a Hammers side virtually resigned to relegation. Manchester were missing their influential captain Bryan Robson in midfield, as well as other key players, but, against a West Ham side that had failed to score in nine of their previous twelve matches, they too suddenly found the opposing goal too small.

After a hectic first half in which Alvin Martin and Tony Gale subdued Mark Hughes and Ryan Giggs, it became evident that West Ham's midfield was starting to dominate the opposition. The flair of Ian Bishop and drive of Mitchell Thomas enabled West Ham to break quickly and ensure that Peter Schmeichel was the busier of the two goalkeepers. A right-wing cross from Stuart Slater fell to the feet of England defender Gary Pallister, whose clearance flew back into the net off the onrushing Kenny Brown. Although something of a fluke, the goal lifted Bonds' side. Admittedly, too, it seemed that Miklosko's goal led a charmed life thereafter, but Schmeichel's was also threatened by Mike Small and the powerful overlaps of Julian Dicks.

The final whistle blew to deny United their first title for 25 years. There was some irony in this, for Ferguson's men could reflect that their own bubble had 'faded and died' on the very ground where their forebears – Charlton, Best, and Law – had clinched their own championship a quarter of a century earlier.

DIVISION 1 (New Style)	**1992-93**
Barclays Division 1	2nd (Promoted)
Coca-Cola Cup	2nd Round
FA Cup	4th Round

English football was ushering in the metamorphosis that would make it the multi-million pound media business that we see today. The Premiership had been born, West Ham were not part of it, and just to confuse everybody were now in a renamed First Division. By one of those quirks of English logic the Hammers were still playing in the division from which they had just been relegated. West Ham, as departing members of the old First Division, had the consolation of sharing the money from TV coverage in an arrangement that threatened complications with the rump of the Football League.

After rumours that he would be leaving, Miklosko signed an extension to his contract, whilst Alvin Martin, 33, also negotiated a new one-year stay. Martin Allen, Trevor Morley, Colin Foster and George Parris also signed new contracts. Rumours suggested 'Pop' Robson would return to Upton Park as No 2 to Billy Bonds – with incumbent Ron Boyce taking on scouting duties. But in July, Harry Redknapp, who had quit Bournemouth saying he 'needed a break from the game', was confirmed as Bonds' assistant. Tony Carr took over the development of the youth section, on which there was to be a new emphasis, whilst Paul Hilton succeeded him as reserve team coach. That same month Ted Fenton, the manager who had taken the Hammers back into the First Division in 1958, died aged 77, following a road accident.

In May Terry Brown and Martin Cearns had swapped positions. The holiday camp tycoon became chairman, and Martin – the fourth generation of the Cearns family to be a director – was named as his deputy. The club's new sponsors were local car dealers Dagenham Motors. Commercial manager Brian Blower lost his job, the biggest casualty in the club's huge cost-cutting exercise implemented by managing director Peter Storrie.

With big money signings out of the question – in line with most clubs – Bonds focused on value-for-money imports who would not cost a fortune. The departure of Stuart Slater to Celtic for £1.5 million helped fund the capture of Peter Butler (£170,000) from Southend and Matt Holmes (£40,000) from Bournemouth. Yugoslavian international Budimir Vujacic failed to get a work permit, but winger Mark Robson joined as a free signing from Tottenham.

Bonds warned that with eight or more good teams competing for three promotion places, getting into the Premier League would be hard. West Ham also had the fixture computer to contend with, for nine of their first fourteen fixtures were away from home. In addition to the 46-game League schedule and an unknown number of domestic cup-ties, they were also committed to participate in a revamped Anglo-Italian Cup. It would be a long season.

A televised win at Barnsley was the perfect start, but defeats by Charlton and Newcastle left West Ham nineteenth and underlined Bonds' warnings about there being no easy games. He was, moreover, unhappy with certain players' commitment and collective spirit. Despairing of captain Julian Dicks' bad-boy image, following his red card for elbowing an opponent, Bonds 'had a go' at the fiery full-back, who responded by hitting two goals against Bristol Rovers in the opening game of the Anglo-Italian competition.

Dicks' colleagues responded in like manner with six wins and two draws in the League, plus a win at Southend in the Anglo-Italian Cup. The one blemish on their copybook was the Coca-Cola Cup replay defeat by Third Division Crewe. By now up to second, though still ten points behind Kevin Keegan's runaway Newcastle, the Hammers suffered back-to-back losses to halt their progress.

Criticised for hiking tickets prices, which prompted a drop in season ticket renewals, the board were now faced with plummeting attendances. Where gates had averaged 21,000 the previous season, after the first five League games of the new campaign the average was down to under 14,000. The fact that the country was suffering an economic recession did not help, so the board decided to slash admission prices from between 15-25 percent, and offer incentives to watch the poorly attended Anglo-Italian games. The board issued this apology: 'We want to acknowledge to the club's supporters that by increasing ticket prices at the start of this season, the club misread the economic situation and were asking the supporters to purchase tickets at prices they could simply not afford.'

Progress in the Anglo-Italian Cup had required the toss of a coin, and a big win was required in the final Group B game at home to Pisa to guarantee a semi-final spot. The match ended goalless, and Derby's win in Italy secured them the coveted semi-final place. In the League, by the turn of the year West Ham were third, fourteen points behind rampant Newcastle. Bonds had signed two more strikers – 24-year-old Canadian Alex Bunbury for £200,000, and the speedy Steve Jones, two years younger, who cost one tenth of that sum, from non-league Billericay. Both made their senior debuts as suspensions and injuries played their part in depleting the number of players available to the manager.

The downside of signing new players was the need to sell others. Gale, Bishop and Small therefore joined Mitchell Thomas and Colin Foster on the transfer list. Younger fringe players were loaned out to save on wages and help them gain first-team experience elsewhere. By February none of his transfer-listed players had attracted worthwhile bids, which pleased Bonds as much as it displeased the board. Less pleasing to the manager was the Hammers' disciplinary record. Seven players had been sent off by mid-January, including Dicks three times, whilst 29 yellow cards had been shown. Martin Allen led the list of offenders with eight, while Dicks had a more modest three. Such was his concern that Bonds, no shrinking violet himself in his playing days, lambasted the worst offenders for letting themselves down, not to mention the team, the fans and the image of the club itself.

On a stormy windswept Sunday the Hammers' interest in the FA Cup was blown away at Barnsley, 1-4, permitting the Oakwell side to avenge their opening-day defeat and put an end to West Ham's seven-game unbeaten run. Bouncing back, the Hammers reeled off another undefeated run, extending to nine League games, that saw them reduce the gap with leaders Newcastle to just five points.

The new-found team spirit had beneficial effects in other ways. Those disillusioned fans who had protested so vehemently against the bond scheme and ticket pricing structure began to return to the fold. Attendances increased through November, December and January. Whereas only 10,000 had turned out for the visit of Sunderland in October, 24,000 were enticed to see north-east neighbours Newcastle in February.

Nothing could have prepared the club for the news that Bobby Moore had died from cancer at the age of 51. The death of the golden boy of West Ham and England unleashed a tide of emotion that enveloped the Boleyn Ground in a sea of flowers and swept away the last vestiges of conflict between the club and supporters. Men, women and children, babes in arms and grannies, poured to the ground to pay their respects. Many had never seen the great man play, but his legend had been passed down the generations, so that none were unaware of the giant taken from their midst. The extent of the grief seemed to have taken club officials by surprise. The death of its greatest son had reminded West Ham of its proud reputation as a family club. That delicate bond, so disastrously ripped apart in previous months, was now restored.

A tide of emotion carried the Hammers through home games with Wolves and Grimsby, both of which were won to intensify their challenge for promotion. Those doubts that lingered concerned scoring goals away from Upton Park. Three vital away fixtures against teams in the bottom half of the table were lost 0-1 and another 0-2 between mid-March and mid-April.

With two automatic promotion places, plus another via the play-offs, attention focused on Portsmouth, who had come up on the blind side with an astonishing run of eleven wins in twelve games, the other being drawn. The destiny of the promotion places took a possibly decisive turn on the first weekend of May. On Saturday Portsmouth lost 1-4 at Sunderland and had two men sent off in the process. On Sunday West Ham won 2-1 at Swindon to reclaim second spot from Portsmouth on goals scored, which had replaced goal-difference in the Football League. Bonds must have envied Keegan's resources at Newcastle; Bonds had to make do with on-loan David Speedie from Southampton to strengthen his team. Now, in the last game, promotion depended on beating Cambridge, who had to win themselves to avoid relegation.

In the event, West Ham won 2-0, the second goal in injury-time, to secure their prize. Though beating Grimsby, Portsmouth had to settle for the play-offs, which they lost. For David Speedie it was the end of his brief Hammers' career, but his four goals in eleven appearances played their part in the promotion surge.

Match of the Season 1992-93

West Ham 3 Wolves 1

Division 1, 6 March 1993

The outpouring of grief following the death of Bobby Moore reached its crescendo with the visit of Wolves. The actual match was almost incidental. The atmosphere inside Upton Park was one of the most emotional ever experienced. It became almost a point of honour to have been able to say of Moore: 'I was there to see him play.' The biggest crowd of the season rose as Geoff Hurst and Martin Peters, who had shared in many of his triumphs – accompanied by former manager Ron Greenwood – came out with a huge floral tribute in the shape of Moore's famous No 6 shirt. The five-foot high shirt was the focus of attention as the two teams gathered around the centre circle. The public address system replayed Kenneth Wolstenholme's commentary when Moore lifted the Cup-Winners' Cup at Wembley in 1965. Lips trembled and tears flowed during an eerie silence produced by nearly 25,000 people packed into the Boleyn Ground.

On this day, no player wore the No 6 shirt: Ian Bishop wore No 12 instead. When play began, West Ham came from behind to score three goals which gave them their biggest win in three months. It was a credit to the whole team that they were able to concentrate on the task in hand. The King was dead but his legend would endure.

FA CARLING PREMIERSHIP	**1993-94**
Premiership	13th
Coca-Cola Cup	3rd Round
FA Cup	Quarter-finals

No sooner had West Ham been promoted than they were bookies' tips as relegation favourites. With the club committed to spending a fortune on a new South Stand – which in the interim reduced the Boleyn to three sides – plus other improvements to comply with the Taylor Report, Billy Bonds' hands were tied in the transfer stakes. Although paying Rangers £750,000 for Dale Gordon, £600,000 of that fee had been financed by the sale of Kevin Keen to Wolves. Bonds had signed central defender Simon Webster from Charlton for £525,000, a fee determined by a transfer tribunal. Sadly, both imports would have their careers terminated by injury. Two weeks after signing, Webster broke his ankle in a pre-season training clash with Dicks. Five appearances as sub two years later was all Webster achieved. Winger Gordon was hit by an ankle injury, a mystery virus, and persistent knee problems which required surgery.

Two other arrivals were from the lower echelons of the League. Keith Rowland and Paul Mitchell came from Harry Redknapp's former charges, Bournemouth. Rowland, a 21-year-old Irishman, initially cost £150,000 and could play left-back or on the flank. His good performances soon came to the notice of the Northern Ireland selectors. Mitchell played right-back or right-half. His fee was £40,000 and his opportunities limited.

Bonds' aim, of course, was to establish the Hammers back in the top flight and put an end to the yo-yo years of the recent past. The season got off to a controversial start at home to Wimbledon, whose owner, Sam Hammam, admitted to being personally responsible for daubing the visitors' dressing room with what he described as 'fun notes' to incite his players. The graffiti, which contained four-letter words and which thankfully had not been seen by kiddies on a pre-match tour of the ground, was more aptly described by managing director Storrie as 'foul and filthy words'. Bonds added: 'I don't know what the game is coming to when the boss of a club sneaks into a dressing room and writes a lot of filth all over the walls. It's an absolute disgrace. He was obviously hoping his team would think it was someone from West Ham who had done it and that would stoke them up for the game.' The furore was only settled once the club received a written apology. As for the game, West Ham lost 0-2, both goals scored in the wasteland of the south end.

It was not until the third game that the Hammers recorded their first goal and first point – at Coventry. The honour of scoring West

Ham's first Premiership goal fell to new-boy Gordon. Two Clive Allen goals at home to Sheffield Wednesday earned the first win, but three days later QPR brought Bonds' team back to earth, scoring four goals without reply. A 0-3 reverse at defending champions Manchester United saw the Hammers slip down to nineteenth. With winless Swindon next to visit Upton Park, three points looked on the cards, but the Wiltshire team emerged with a 0-0 draw.

Though publicly denying it, Julian Dicks was thought to want to try his luck with a better team. Liverpool were certainly that, and in mid-September he moved to Anfield, with David Burrows and Mike Marsh coming to Upton Park in part-exchange. In another deal that cost Bonds less than the reported £250,000 quoted, the once-feared striker, Lee Chapman, having turned down West Ham in favour of Portsmouth, signed after all. Bonds justified the deals by saying that although he had lost one quality player, he had gained three. The immediate results backed his judgment. Chapman scored in a 2-0 win at Blackburn, Burrows seamlessly fitted into Dicks' left-back slot, whilst Marsh did not look out of place in midfield.

Another new face was that of Jeroen Boere who had signed for £165,000 from Go Ahead Eagles. Though the Dutchman made his mark at Upton Park, it was usually for the wrong reasons. Coming on as a substitute at Newcastle he was red carded and thus became the first Hammer to be sent off on his debut. His notoriety increased over the months: though signing for three years, he was loaned out to Portsmouth and West Brom, drifted back to Holland, and West Ham were not sad to see him go.

Bonds was furious at his side's 1-2 exit from the Coca-Cola Cup at First Division strugglers Nottingham Forest, notwithstanding the colossal impact of Forest's new signing, Stan Collymore. But this was an isolated setback in the dying months of 1993. League wins outnumbered losses to nudge the Hammers into the top half by Christmas, with a comfortable points cushion as insurance against any collapse in form.

The first months of 1994 were equally satisfactory. A spate of draws kept the Hammers clear of danger, though Sheffield United, Swindon and Manchester City were at the wrong end of the table and ought to have been ripe for picking. These were points lost, not won. It was the FA Cup, however, that promised most cheer. West Ham squeezed unconvincingly past two First Division teams – Watford and Notts County. A fifth-round tie at Kidderminster from the Vauxhall Conference offered the prospect of further progress, except in the minds of bookies, who were quick to spot a potential upset. In the event, Kidderminster seldom threatened and their 0-1 defeat was perhaps kinder than they deserved. Nearly 7,000 fans turned up at Upton Park to watch the game beamed back live. When the quarter-finals pitched Bonds' men at home to lowly First Division Luton, the Hammers must have set their sights on the semi-finals. No Premiership opponents had darkened their path, but Luton burst the bubble, coming from behind to win 3-2 in a replay.

In January manager Bonds and assistant Redknapp had signed new three-and-a-half-year extensions to their contracts, reward for what the pair had achieved since Harry's arrival eighteen months previously. Bonds remarked: 'Harry coming here gave me a lift. He gave everyone a lift. He has really helped me. We have always been very good friends and we have a good working relationship.' Redknapp agreed: 'I've enjoyed it here. I wanted to help Bill and the club get back into the Premier League and we have done that.' Just six months later everything turned pear-shaped and Bonds quit the club in circumstances no less murky today than they were then.

March was tough. Cup defeat at Luton was sandwiched between a string of losses that extended West Ham's winless League run to nine games, since New Year's Day. All of a sudden the club was looking over its shoulder. Two Easter wins in early April banished those terrors once and for all, and a final position of thirteenth, ten points clear of the drop-zone, would have been grabbed with both hands back in August.

Throughout the season the former South Bank had loomed eerily over the ground, first as a demolition site, then as an awesome new stand. When first commissioned it had not been named, but in the wake of Bobby Moore's death a groundswell of feeling had linked the great player of the past with the great edifice of the future. In October 1993, Stephanie, Bobby's widow, sealed a time capsule full of memorabilia into the foundations of the new stand. The lower tier of the £4.9 million project was opened in late January and six weeks later the whole was officially opened when an FA Premier Select XI played the Hammers in a memorial match to the great man's memory. It attracted a crowd of 20,000, with the proceeds donated to the Bobby Moore Family Trust and Imperial Cancer Research.

As the season closed it was announced that the North Bank was also to be redeveloped, whilst the East Stand lower tier area would be converted from terraces to seats. The outcome would be the transformation of Upton Park into an all-seater stadium. Tony Gale was rewarded with a testimonial after ten years service and over 350 games for the club. To the surprise of many, Gale was not offered a new contract and moved to Blackburn. Clive Allen joined Millwall, his seventh London club, and Mitchell Thomas went to Luton.

DID YOU KNOW?

In 1993-94 Swindon became the first club in modern times to concede 100 league goals in the top division. West Ham contributed just one goal to that total.

Match of the Season 1993-94

West Ham 2 Ipswich 1

Premiership, 2 April 1994

This game was vital to West Ham's survival, as in the previous two weeks they had suffered three League defeats and been dumped from the FA Cup by Luton. In his programme notes Bonds stated: 'Ipswich Town are in a similar position to us. We are both being sucked into the fringe area of the relegation issue and have to be careful we don't slip up.' Ipswich lay thirteenth with 40 points; West Ham were fifteenth with 38 points, with a game in hand.

This win was the Hammers' first at home in the League since New Year's Day, and also their last at Upton Park that season. Of perhaps greater significance was that, following the victory over Ipswich, Bonds' men won at Tottenham, Oldham, and Arsenal, giving West Ham the unusual distinction of picking up more points away than at home that season.

In order to stir things up against Ipswich, Bonds dropped joint top scorer Lee Chapman (after a 35-game run) and drafted Matthew Rush into a five-man midfield. Trevor Morley foraged alone up front. It was Rush's first start of the season, having been recalled on transfer deadline day from a loan spell at Swansea.

Both sides were edgy. West Ham's need to win was matched by Ipswich's urgency not to lose, but the Hammers got the start they wanted. Rowland's seventeenth-minute cross was headed out to Rush, who responded with a dipping 25-yard volley. All Ipswich achieved in the first half was three bookings. Their best chance arrived after an hour, when an overhead kick flew just over the bar. With fifteen minutes to go they made a double substitution, and seconds later fouled Rush. Matt Holmes' centre was glanced in by Morley. Rush rounded off an eventful afternoon by having to be stretchered off with a trapped nerve in his knee. Shortly before the end ex-Hammer Stuart Slater robbed Peter Butler before whipping in a cross that was headed in by Paul Mason.

Bonds said: 'It was an important win, especially when we came off and saw today's other results.' Lowly Chelsea, Spurs, Manchester City, Oldham and Sheffield United all won, while last-placed Swindon drew at Arsenal. Ipswich finally stayed up by one point.

8

REDKNAPP'S FOREIGN LEGION 1994-2001

FA CARLING PREMIERSHIP	**1994-95**
Premiership	14th
Coca-Cola Cup	4th Round
FA Cup	4th Round

'It's been a traumatic pre-season but now we've got to look to the future.' With those words Harry Redknapp began his programme notes for the opening home fixture of the new season. Ten days earlier Redknapp had been Billy Bonds' assistant, but following a volcanic upheaval Bonzo had gone and Harry had been installed as the club's eighth manager. Redknapp had signed a five-year contract and brought in his brother-in-law, Frank Lampard, as his No 2. The official line was that Bonds had 'decided to call it a day'.

Piecing together the gaps in the story, it appears that Redknapp had been approached to return to his former club Bournemouth. A new consortium was taking over at Dean Court and made him a handsome offer. Redknapp had kept West Ham informed, but as the club were reluctant to lose him they felt they had no alternative but to reappraise the whole managerial set-up at Upton Park. All options were considered, including that of the relationship between Bonds and his assistant.

Defending the club's handling of the crisis, managing director Peter Storrie said: 'We were in a no-win situation ... There were no ultimatums ... We didn't ask Bill to stand down as manager, but he indicated that if Harry went, he might not want to continue here on his own. So we were then faced with the possibility of not only losing one part of the managerial duo, but two! And where would that have left us? One of the options mentioned – and I stress it was only one – was Bill becoming a paid director [no ex-players have ever joined the West Ham board]. The job, a sort of Director of Football role, could have evolved. But Bill said he was quitting. We tried to persuade him to reconsider but he'd made up his mind. No one has put the knife in, and Bill hasn't said that happened either.'

Following Storrie's press-statement, Bonds – who had been with the club for 27 years – said that his impression was that the board preferred Redknapp to lead the team. He had declined the offer of a paid directorship because he felt that he still had something to offer as a manager. This raised the question of whether Bonds had in fact resigned or been pushed aside.

The next day the club was plunged into deeper crisis when a distressed Redknapp denied suggestions that he had played a part in the downfall of his colleague and friend, at whose wedding in 1967 he had been best man. Redknapp warned 'I can't go on in this job knowing people might think I stitched Bill up. How am I going to take training? How can I look players in the eye? I want the truth to be told because I've never felt as bad in my life. If people think I've stabbed my best friend in the back then I can't stay. My friendship with Bill is worth more than anything to me. I'm Bill's best mate and I want to be his best mate in twenty years time.' With the flames threatening to consume the club, Storrie insisted that Bonds had resigned *before* they offered him the job as Director of Football, that at no time was he told they preferred Redknapp as manager, and that only after he quit did they appoint Harry.

It was left to another Hammers' legend, Trevor Brooking – a close friend of Bonzo – to sum up the feelings of many. 'I was stunned when I heard the news. To have treated a man like Billy in this way is not good. It could have been handled much, much better. I feel very sad about the whole thing. It is a sad day for the club, but right back to the resignation of John Lyall, they have never been good at handling these things.'

After mulling the situation over, Redknapp decided to stay. Though the club hoped publicly that Bonds' association with West Ham might at some time be renewed, it was several years before Bonds returned to the Boleyn Ground and then only in the capacity as a match-day summariser for a London radio station. Eight weeks after leaving the club Bonds did once again don the famous claret and blue. This time it was as a guest player for Brooking's Havering NALGO team. The Brentwood Sunday League side played in a replica West Ham strip.

The Bonds-Redknapp fiasco climaxed a close season of bizarre proportions. In June the club had signed John Moncur for about £1 million from relegated Swindon and Joey Beauchamp from Oxford for £850,000. The Hammers had tried to capture Beauchamp back in March, but he chose to stay. Oxford, in fact, were so resigned to losing their talented winger that they had secured the loan of a replacement. This led to Beauchamp being left out of the Oxford team for a period when he decided he was going nowhere.

No sooner had he changed his mind and signed for West Ham than 23-year-old Beauchamp protested about the 140-mile daily round trip by car from his parents' home in Oxford to the Chadwell Heath training ground, not least because of traffic congestion on the M40 and M25 motorways. He was not prepared to move nearer his new club because his girlfriend was studying at Oxford University. So ill-at-ease did he appear that Beauchamp was left on the bench for a pre-season friendly at Portsmouth. He publicly lamented his decision to join West Ham in preference to nearby Swindon, who had also sought his signature. Bonds initially took a hard line: 'He has signed a three-year contract and he's got to settle down here. I was shy when I first came to the club ... but you have to grow up.'

Gordon Taylor, head of the PFA (Professional Footballers' Association) was called upon to make Beauchamp see sense, but by this time the fans wanted nothing whatever to do with him. In the next friendly, at Southend, he endured torrents of abuse at their hands, which intensified when he came off the bench for the final minutes. Clearly he had to go, and within days Swindon took him in a part-exchange deal that brought Adrian Whitbread to Upton Park, plus a cash adjustment in West Ham's favour.

What with the Beauchamp saga and the painful circumstances of Redknapp's appointment, the new campaign was clearly going to present tough challenges, not least because reducing the size of the Premiership from 22 to twenty clubs next season meant an extra, fourth, club would be relegated in May. And so it proved. West Ham failed to win any of their first five games, drew only two, lost Trevor Morley for most of the season through cartilage problems, and scored only one goal. That was a penalty against Newcastle, netted by Don Hutchison, who had signed the day before from Liverpool for a club record £1.5 million.

Desperate for reinforcements, Redknapp re-signed Tony Cottee from Everton, where he had been for six years, with David Burrows and a cash adjustment going to Goodison. It was the first instance of Redknapp's supreme talent for wheeling and dealing, one of several reasons he had come to Upton Park in the first place. Cottee marked his second Hammers debut by getting sent off in a goalless draw at Anfield, then scoring the only goal to defeat Aston Villa and lift the club out of the bottom four.

By mid-October Julian Dicks was also back on board, after 399 miserable days at Liverpool. He marked his homecoming with a yellow card in a 2-0 home win over Southampton. In the next home match, against Leicester, Dicks resumed his penalty-taking duties to ensure another win, but bad-boy Don Hutchison was sent off and started an immediate four-match ban.

DID YOU KNOW?

In 1995, TV pundit Alan Hansen predicted an FA Cup upset at Wycombe. When West Ham went 2-0 in front, supporters chanted 'There's only one Trevor Brooking'.

That victory over Leicester, on Guy Fawkes' Day, set in train a wretched patch that by February had dumped the Hammers down to twentieth place. Ipswich and Leicester were already so far adrift as to accept their fate, but any two of ten teams might accompany them into the darkness of the Football League. One of the few bright spots that winter was the 3-1 home win over high-flying Nottingham Forest. One of West Ham's goals that day was scored by recent arrival Michael Hughes, a Northern Ireland international winger cum midfielder. He had been signed on loan from French club Strasbourg, Danish international defender Marc Rieper joined from Brondby, and Redknapp continued his wheeler dealing by selling Steve Jones to Bournemouth for £150,000, at a good profit. Mike Marsh was sold to Coventry for £500,000 and Lee Chapman, after a couple of loan spells here and there, joined Ipswich, who ended up with the wooden spoon.

The cups did not detain the Hammers long. Though accounting for Chelsea in the Coca-Cola Cup, they went out at home to First Division Bolton under a hail of penalties and own-goals. Nor did they get far in the FA Cup, although at least their conquerors, QPR, were from the same division as themselves.

Injuries did their best to disrupt Redknapp's team-planning, but March and April were profitable months. Eight unbeaten games into early May might have helped morale, but they were not enough to put clear water between West Ham and the other drowning sides beneath them. In his programme notes for the visit of Blackburn on 30 April, Redknapp said he had set a target of 50 points. In the event, he erred on the side of caution. West Ham reached that number but would have been safe with five fewer. Survival was ensured in the penultimate fixture with a 3-0 home success over Coca-Cola Cup winners Liverpool. A 1-1 draw at home to Manchester United on the final day was enough to deny Alex Ferguson's side the championship, as they failed to capitalise on Blackburn's defeat at Anfield. Had West Ham needed points, who knows how the tension would have affected the players.

It had been a stressful season but Harry Redknapp had achieved what all the pundits had said was essential – avoid relegation at all costs. In his new position of manager he had also done much to consolidate the club's position by laying the foundations for what was to be accomplished in the coming years.

Match of the Season 1994-95

West Ham 2 Blackburn 0

Premiership, 30 April 1995

The Hammers went into this match by stringing together six games without defeat. Even so, only goal-difference kept them above the drop zone. Kenny Dalglish's Rovers held an eight-point lead over defending champions Manchester United. With their SAS strike-force of Shearer (33 goals) and Sutton (fifteen), few gave West Ham much chance of holding out against the Premiership's top scorers and away specialists. On their travels Rovers had lost only three times and failed to score in the same number.

With Tony Cottee ruled out with a calf strain, Don Hutchison was recalled to play alongside Jeroen Boere. The game started at a fast pace with Colin Hendry marshalling Rovers' massed defence. The first half was noted more for flying tackles than neat play, which resulted in nineteen fouls, the worst of which was a lunge at Ian Bishop's groin by David Batty. The referee was perhaps lenient in showing Batty only a yellow card.

Five minutes after half-time, Rieper, who had blunted Shearer and Sutton in the first half, met Moncur's corner with a downward header that went in off a post. The goal had been made by Boere's dart to the near post, which dragged big Colin Hendry with him. It was the Dane's first goal for the Hammers and rubbed salt into Dalglish's wounds. Earlier in the season Blackburn's boss could have signed Rieper himself.

Matthew Rush replaced Boere, who had broken his nose, and the substitution was responsible for West Ham's second goal. Rush skinned Hendry for pace, then cut back a cross into the path of Moncur, whose shot was deflected against goalkeeper Tim Flowers. Hutchison swept in the rebound. With only seven minutes to go, it was too high a hurdle for Rovers to overcome and the strains of 'Bubbles' reverberated around the ground.

There was an irony about the result. Rovers now looked likely to be overhauled on the finishing line, just as Manchester United had been three years previously. Then Alex Ferguson had described the Hammers' performance as 'obscene'. On hearing of this score his comments were doubtless more complimentary, as his team had games in hand on Blackburn. Unfortunately they had to visit Upton Park on the final day. Manchester United needed to win, but West Ham made sure they didn't, denying United the title by one point.

FA CARLING PREMIERSHIP	**1995-96**
Premiership	10th
Coca-Cola Cup	3rd Round
FA Cup	4th Round

One day after denying Manchester United the title the Hammers jetted off to Australia for an end of season tour. It was also a PR trip, laying the foundations for the club's Soccer Academies 'down under', which would see the arrival of a number of 'socceroos' over the next few years.

Marc Rieper had already signed permanently for £1.1 million, and when the players returned from Oz their ranks were expanded by Dutchman Marco Boogers from Sparta Rotterdam (£800,000), plus the first two Australians – Robbie Slater and Stan Lazaridis – wingers who had both won international caps. Boogers had been rated the third best player in Holland the previous season. He was coveted by English and Italian clubs but chose West Ham because they impressed him the most. But no sooner had he signed than he was red-carded at Old Trafford. He was then reported as wanting to return to Holland, all of which made Boogers one of the costliest disasters ever associated with the club.

The arrival of 30-year-old Slater from new champions Blackburn, however, was good business by Redknapp, who collected £600,000 in a cash adjustment when Mattie Holmes went to Ewood Park as part of a £1.2 million deal. Although Redknapp said 'I've known [Holmes] since he was a 15-year-old kid with me at Bournemouth,' one could not fault the manager's logic as the little midfielder had originally cost just £40,000. Holmes was popular with the fans and his departure caused disquiet in some quarters. As for Lazaridis, few in England had ever heard of him, but although raw in the soccer sense, he had impressed so much in West Ham's friendly against Western Australia that after further trials in England he was soon signed for £300,000. Holding a Greek passport, on account of his parentage, Lazaridis was also able to sidestep the hassles of obtaining a work permit under EEC regulations. Despite turning 37, Alvin Martin accepted Redknapp's offer of a one-year contract, and although Moncur and Bishop were linked with moves both stayed to fight their corner for the Hammers.

Two familiar faces were, however, missing for the new season. Trevor Morley had signed for Reading whilst Matthew Rush moved to Norwich for £330,000 and shortly after suffered knee ligament damage. In September, Redknapp signed ex-Hammer Iain Dowie from Crystal Palace, with Boere soon headed in the other direction, whilst in October Michael Hughes returned for a second loan spell.

With Cottee and Dicks fit, pre-season talk was that the club had its strongest squad in years, but once again the Hammers botched the start, not winning in the League till late September, when Dicks slammed home two penalties against Everton in an ugly match. Dicks had grabbed the headlines the previous week at Highbury when red-carded for the fifth time in his Hammers career. He was then banned for 'bringing the game into disrepute', his crime being to stamp on a Chelsea player's head.

In October Frank Burrows joined the coaching staff. Paul Hilton departed, to be followed by chief scout Ronnie Boyce, who severed his connections after 37 years' service at Upton Park. That month West Ham's fortunes took an upturn: Cottee scored his first goal for six months and Dowie celebrated his return with two goals in as many games. His header against Blackburn looked enough to secure all three points until Alan Shearer netted at the death. By now up to twelfth, the Hammers' only black mark for October was the exit from the Coca-Cola Cup at the Dell.

Having excelled in the youth team for some years, Rio Ferdinand marked his seventeenth birthday by signing as a full professional in November. Redknapp was surely understating when he noted: 'I'm sure we're going to hear a lot more about him in the future.' Ever mindful of the need to capitalise on the marketability of his players, Redknapp sold reserve goalkeeper Ian Feuer to Luton for £600,000 in December. The giant American had cost just £70,000 three years earlier. Redknapp loaned out fringe players such as Kenny Brown to reduce the wage bill and to enable younger players such as Frank Lampard Jnr to gain experience.

The loss of Feuer proved expensive in points terms when Ludo Miklosko was sent off at Everton when conceding a penalty. Dicks took over in goal as there was no other goalie amongst the subs. When the Czech served his one-game ban, which broke a run of 162 consecutive League games, Redknapp was forced to play 17-year-old Neil Finn at Manchester City on New Year's Day – regular reserve Les Sealey having been injured in training. The goalkeeping crisis had been exacerbated by the FA's refusal to waive their '48-hour' rule, thwarting Redknapp's attempts to sign a loan replacement. Finn, who also had a slight injury, could not be faulted for City scoring twice in 90 minutes for the first time that season, though he never played for the Hammers again.

That 1-2 defeat at Maine Road was exacerbated by the fact that Upton Park had just had two games frozen off, prompting renewed demands for under-soil heating to be installed. The anger generated by frustrated fans raised temperatures everywhere around Upton Park except where it was most needed – on the pitch.

During the first week of 1996 Harry Redknapp broke the club's outgoing transfer record, paying £1.65 million to the German club Karlsruhe for Croatian international defender Slaven Bilic. These were busy times for West Ham's boss, who failed to lure Romanian superstar Gheorghe Hagi on loan, but fixed up goalkeeping cover in the form of veteran Peter Shilton and Australian Steve Mautone. Redknapp sold out-of-favour Don Hutchison to Sheffield United and the following month Martin Allen to Portsmouth. Ilie Dumitrescu was signed from Tottenham in another £1.5 million deal, though work-permit problems delayed his debut for two months. The farcical situation regarding work permits was highlighted when two Russian players made instant debuts for Millwall. They had acquired Portuguese passports, having played there the previous year. In February Dani joined the Upton Park 'Foreign Legion', on loan from Sporting Lisbon, but looking to the future Redknapp also blooded two of his youngsters, Lampard and Ferdinand.

On the field, January was a testing month. Defeat at Maine Road was followed by defeat at Leeds, where Lee Chapman (via West Ham and Ipswich) was dismissed for elbowing Rieper, and defeat at home to Manchester United. Dicks was immersed in further controversy as he went unpunished for a two-footed lunge on Andy Cole but seconds later became the victim when upended by a vengeful Nicky Butt, who was sent off. It was not until the last day of the month that Redknapp's side registered the first win of 1996, against Coventry.

Hopes of squeezing into the top ten looked feasible in February as the Hammers reeled off four more wins, including one over table toppers Newcastle United, and climbed to eleventh. The winning run was halted at home to Arsenal, who scored from a messy back-pass and survived when a concussed Dicks wasted a penalty. The other low point that month was defeat in an FA Cup replay by First Division Grimsby.

March and April continued the positive trend. Defeats at title hopefuls Newcastle and Liverpool were excusable, at struggling QPR less so, but enough points were gathered to keep West Ham locked in eleventh place for months on end. In the final game, at home to Sheffield Wednesday, Julian Dicks celebrated being voted 'Hammer of the Year' by heading West Ham in front, only for the relegation-haunted visitors to grab a point with a last-gasp goal. The point earned left the Hammers tenth, their highest position in the top flight since they finished third in 1986. The youth team won the South East Counties League and reached the final of the FA Youth Cup. The policy of developing home-grown talent, under the guidance of Tony Carr, was beginning to harvest the fruits of success.

Match of the Season 1995-96

West Ham 1 Sheffield Wednesday 1

Premiership, 5 May 1996

Twelve months previously the Hammers had clinched four valuable points in their final two home games against Liverpool and Manchester United to guarantee their Premiership status. Now they needed only a draw against Wednesday to mark another milestone – their highest ever placing in the Premiership. For the first time in ten years West Ham would finish in the top half of the top division in English football.

It could be said that there were any number of other games that merited the title of Match of the Season, not least the 2-0 home win over Kevin Keegan's leaders Newcastle. The curtain-fall against Wednesday was not one of the best games to grace Upton Park that season, but it did result in its most significant outcome – a top-ten finish. And that engendered in the fans the belief that Redknapp could accomplish even greater feats in the coming years.

West Ham created a number of chances in the first half with the best efforts coming from Dowie and Rowland. The second period began in similar vein but it was not until the 72nd minute that a Michael Hughes free-kick was headed home by Dicks. The goal meant that 'Hammer of the Year' Dicks ended up as joint top scorer with Tony Cottee on ten Premiership goals.

With minutes remaining, chants for substitute Alvin Martin to make a farewell appearance were answered, but with seconds left Wednesday turned party-poopers, equalising through Newsome's header. That goal proved academic as far as the visitors were concerned, who began play needing a point to ensure survival, but as the results of other teams at the nether end of the table came in it was already clear that they were safe.

Afterwards, Redknapp's reading of the situation was accurate: 'We must strengthen the squad to maintain our progress and I'm looking to bring in three, maybe four, during the summer.' Doubtless amongst those would be a couple of strikers, as on only three occasions had his side scored more than two goals in a League game. Those teams on the receiving end were all at the bottom.

FA CARLING PREMIERSHIP	**1996-97**
Premiership	14th
Coca-Cola Cup	4th Round
FA Cup	3rd Round

The attention of Hammers fans was focused not only on the fortunes of England during that summer's Euro 96 – despite there being no West Ham contingent in the England squad – but also on games involving Denmark and Croatia, for whom Rieper and Bilic were engaged. The unfortunate Dumitrescu, however, had been ruled out of Romania's squad by the same injury that had plagued him since finally being granted his work permit.

Redknapp had said in June: 'I've had to wheel and deal, people have come and gone, and at times I made moves that I didn't really want to make.' Although he would shortly break the club's record transfer fee for the third time in under two years, he was still bound by monetary constraints. His ability to 'wheel and deal' would be one of the focal points of his managership right through to the new millennium, as the club struggled to balance its books whilst undertaking the biggest redevelopment ever seen at Upton Park, both on and off the field.

In May, Alvin Martin and Les Sealey had joined Leyton Orient, but in a surprise £200,000 deal Steve Jones returned to Upton Park after eighteen months at Bournemouth. Three years and just eleven first-team games after signing for £750,000, Dale Gordon was given a free transfer. Rio Ferdinand and Frank Lampard Jnr, two of the outstanding stars of an outstanding youth team, confirmed their immediate future with the club by signing new three-year contracts.

Early July saw one of the most intense periods of transfer activity since Redknapp's appointment. No fewer than five recruits were paraded in the space of three days. The first was no stranger to Upton Park: Michael Hughes had arrived at the club on loan in December 1994 but now signed permanently under the Bosman ruling. A second free-transfer Bosman signing was also an international, Portugal's Paulo Futre, who had been released by AC Milan. The legendary Futre had in his time accounted for transfer fees amounting to £20 million! England Under-21 central defender Richard Hall joined from Southampton with the fee (later set at £1.9 million) decided by a transfer tribunal as he was out of contract at the Dell. Redknapp 'put the icing on the cake' with the record signing of Romanian international Florin Raducioiu at £2.4 million from Espanol, who had finished fourth in the Spanish League. Raducioiu had played for Romania in Euro 96. Redknapp's final capture was Welsh utility defender Mark Bowen from Norwich.

These purchases, the extra salaries, plus the delayed payments in respect of Boogers, Dumitrescu and Bilic, meant that West Ham had committed something like £7 million to their current season's budget. The manager put the state of English football into context in his first programme notes: 'I've spent something in the region of £4 million and everyone got excited – then Newcastle paid £15 million for Alan Shearer, which puts everything into perspective.'

Optimism was high amongst the Hammers fraternity, for it was felt that the playing squad was the strongest for many years. Redknapp, however, struck a cautious note: 'Something tells me it's going to be even harder.' Not for the first time, he was to be proved a canny judge of the situation.

Injuries sustained in pre-season warm-ups meant that for the curtain-raiser at Arsenal eight first-team players were sidelined – including Raducioiu and Hall, whilst Futre reportedly stormed out after being named only as substitute – as the managerless Gunners won 2-0. Redknapp denied the Futre reports in typical East End language. By the end of September West Ham were entrenched in the bottom half of the table. Although Redknapp occasionally saw Futre display his range of skills, he quickly realised that some of his foreign imports did not have the heart for a scrap.

Undeterred, Redknapp brought in Hugo Porfirio on loan from Sporting Lisbon. He had already sold Robbie Slater to Southampton for £250,000 and then offloaded Cottee at £775,000 to a Malaysian club and Whitbread (£225,000) to Portsmouth, to trim a squad of nearly 40 professionals. In the New Year, Steve Jones (£400,000) joined Charlton, Kenny Brown moved to Birmingham (£75,000), and goalkeeper Steve Mautone (£250,000) signed for Reading. Although linked with other clubs, Bilic signed a new contract that was said to bind him to the Hammers until June 2000. It later appeared there was a get-out clause.

By the end of November the Hammers were still in the bottom half, but had daylight between themselves and the bottom three. It was a different story following the visit of bottom club Nottingham Forest on New Year's Day, as woeful defending allowed the visitors to win by a solitary goal. December had been a miserable month. Futre's dodgy knee had finally forced him to retire, whilst Second Division Stockport had burst the Coca-Cola Cup bubble in an away replay in which Iain Dowie's contribution was an own-goal and a broken ankle. On the eve of that match rumours circulated that an ex-bookmaker wanted to buy the club, proposing that shareholders should oppose the re-election of Chairman Terence Brown. Worst was to follow when it was learned that Raducioiu on the morning of the Stockport replay had not turned up for the coach trip north. He had gone shopping with his in-laws in London. Originally, the official reason for his absence had been flu.

In mid-January, after much mutual recrimination, the Romanian rejoined Espanol for £1.7 million. Redknapp admitted that so many foreign imports had been unwise, for it now left West Ham fighting relegation. Dumitrescu had already been sold to a Mexican club for £1 million. He had played so infrequently that there were doubts about his eligibility for a new work permit: he could therefore have walked away without the club recouping anything.

Apart from grabbing a Cup equaliser at snowy Wrexham and playing above themselves to draw at top-of-the-table Liverpool, the rest of January was bleak for West Ham. Following a home defeat by Leeds a fickle section of fans called for Redknapp's resignation. This intensified when Wrexham won the replay at Upton Park. In the aftermath Redknapp was reported to have offered to resign, but this was rejected. At the next home game, four days later, some supporters mounted a red-card protest against Redknapp.

MP and radio pundit David Mellor – who had previously upset Redknapp with his forthright views on Julian Dicks – stirred the waters by moaning about Redknapp's treatment of foreign players. Then the Barbados-based ex-bookie, a friend of Redknapp's, turned up the heat by offering to invest £30 million on players and facilities, promising to steer clear of the day to day running of the club if accepted. Managing director Peter Storrie retorted that the buy-in offer of the so-called 'White Knight' (some £8 million up front) was not the simple gift it appeared. As for Redknapp, he could not express an opinion as he could not afford to alienate the current directors. In late-January he emerged from a crisis board meeting to declare: 'The West Ham's manager's job has become mission impossible. There is not a manager or coach in the world who could come in here with the situation we have and not find it difficult to win games. We don't have a fit striker at the club and we need to buy two new ones. It's up to me to find players within my budget, but I also want to make sure I get the right pair.'

Not surprisingly, every available striker, and a few who were not, was now linked with West Ham. These included Dean Holdsworth (Wimbledon), Pierre van Hooijdonk (Celtic), Mike Sheron (Stoke), Clive Mendonca (Grimsby), Paul Kitson (Newcastle), Daniele Dichio (QPR), Dion Dublin (Coventry), *et al.*

When asked if he felt under pressure, Redknapp replied: 'I have had a special relationship for too long with this club to stick around if they don't want me. It's breaking my heart to be in this situation. I'm not a quitter by nature, but there are times when you have to accept what's going on. If the chairman decides I have to go, then

I'll accept it. I'm working like a lunatic to turn this around, yet I don't know where our next goal is coming from. But this is not pressure. Pressure is being in the situation I was in not so long ago, on a life-support machine, wondering if someone was going to give up on me and turn it off. This is not pressure because I've been in worse scrapes than this in my life. At least only my pride has been hurt this time.' Redknapp was alluding to a road accident during the 1990 World Cup in Italy in which his friend, the Bournemouth director Brian Tiler, had been killed. Redknapp had been flown home where he spent two months in intensive care. He also added wryly: 'It wasn't long ago that I was the best thing since sliced bread when we finished tenth in the Premiership and now, bosh, everything has gone boss-eyed.'

In a desperate gamble Redknapp signed Paul Kitson for £2.3 million and 21-year-old John Hartson from Arsenal in an attempt to solve the team's chronic goalscoring problems. On transfer deadline day he pounced for Manchester City's 23-year-old Northern Ireland international Steve Lomas for £1.6 million. The red-haired Lomas would prove to be one of Redknapp's most influential signings in the coming years, as the toiling midfielder brought a grittiness to the side often lacking in the past. The Hartson deal involved another club record outlay. If all the clauses in the complex deal were invoked, the sum involved would exceed £5 million. It was only three years since Hartson had become Britain's most expensive teenager when transferred from Luton to Arsenal for £2.5 million.

Hartson and Kitson made their debuts at Derby on 15 February. Although West Ham lost 0-1, the new strike-force quickly became a feared and fearsome double act. Between them they scored thirteen goals in the following thirteen games. Five of those were won, five drawn, and only three lost – all three being away from Upton Park. By the time of the last of those, on the final day at Old Trafford, a result that confirmed Manchester United as champions, West Ham had ensured their survival. The astute signing of the three newcomers, plus the emergence of new young heroes Ferdinand and Lampard, had transformed the atmosphere around Upton Park. The Hammers had once again done Houdini proud.

The fickle fans who back in August had expected so much could once again look forward to a new dawn – until the one foreigner they had taken to their hearts announced he was leaving. Three days after the final fixture Slaven Bilic confirmed his £4.5 million move to Everton, which he described as 'a bigger club' even though they had finished below West Ham. If Redknapp had been guilty of making some bad deals when it came to overseas players, it was still the case that his successes far outweighed his failures.

DID YOU KNOW?

In 1996-97, Paul Kitson only made 14 League appearances for West Ham, but that was enough for him to be the Hammers' top League scorer with 8 goals.

Match of the Season 1996-97

West Ham 4 Tottenham 3

Premiership, 24 February 1997

If there was a turning point in West Ham's season it surely started on this filthy wet night at Upton Park. Thereafter, hope breathed anew that survival was possible. It was cold, with aquatic conditions that most foreign players were not accustomed to. Of the eleven Hammers that took the field, only one had not been born in the UK, but Czech goalkeeper Ludo Miklosko had been at Upton Park since 1989 and was the first and longest lasting of the current crop of continentals to come to Upton Park.

In the final analysis it is always difficult to say which points are the most critical over the course of a season. Wins at Coventry and Leicester towards the end of the campaign were no less crucial, but the launch pad for those victories was this home win over Spurs.

The game kicked off in near hurricane conditions, with rain, sleet and swirling wind. When Sheringham headed Spurs in front after eight minutes it looked odds on that West Ham would end the match as they had begun it – in the bottom three. It was inspirational captain Dicks who levelled, heading home from Michael Hughes. Seconds later, from a corner, Kitson darted in at the near post for his first goal on his home debut.

Tottenham grabbed a 29th-minute leveller when Anderton deftly lobbed Miklosko. Before half-time West Ham's other home debutant also marked his card. Dicks swung over a free-kick to the far post which Hartson headed home. After the interval Spurs came back once more, Howells making it 3-3 with a low twenty-yarder. The game could have gone either way, but Dicks urged his men forward, into the icy wind that stung their faces. Hartson's physical presence was something West Ham had not seen since the days of Geoff Hurst. Now, holding the ball up in the box, the Welsh firebrand was recklessly brought down.

It was a situation made for Dicks, who having placed the ball on the penalty spot struck it with such brutal force that Walker in the Tottenham goal was motivated more by self-preservation than futile heroics. West Ham had scored four League goals for the first time this season, needing all four to earn their first win in two months.

FA CARLING PREMIERSHIP	**1997-98**
Premiership	8th
Coca-Cola Cup	Quarter-finals
FA Cup	Quarter-finals

Harry Redknapp's unhappy experiences with some of his foreign buys did not deter him from signing Eyal Berkovic in June for £1.75 million from Maccabi Haifa. The 25-year-old Israeli international, an attacking, goalscoring midfielder, was not unknown to the Premiership, having spent most of the previous season on loan at Southampton. Berkovic's signing, in the circumstances, was quite a coup as he was coveted by various clubs. It also showed that Redknapp had learnt from his mistakes with foreign players. The little playmaker was the right age and approaching his peak, whereas Raducioiu and Futre, with hindsight, were either past it or ill-suited to the English game.

A day after signing Berkovic, Redknapp bought Andy Impey from QPR for £1.2 million. The right-winger was another known quantity – a former Under-21 international who always seemed to cause West Ham problems when wearing a Rangers shirt. Impey's transfer was, however, put on hold pending the outcome of foot surgery, and he did not finally arrive until late September. Realising he did not have enough goalkeeping cover for Miklosko, Redknapp paid £500,000 to Ipswich for Canadian Craig Forrest. One player who almost signed (under the Bosman ruling) but didn't, preferring to stay on the continent to advance his international career, was the Portuguese Hugo Porfirio. Dicks and Hall were both sidelined with expected long-term injuries, but press gossip concerning the departure of Rio Ferdinand were quickly denied. Steve Potts was granted a testimonial to celebrate twelve years as a Hammer.

Plans for further redevelopment of Upton Park included construction of a new West Stand, accommodating 17,500 seats, thus raising the ground capacity to around 36,000, as well as having hospitality suites, new dressing rooms and other facilities. Although Dagenham Motors had ended their five-year deal as club sponsors – their bid for a new deal was considered insufficient – they were still involved on a match-to-match basis as discussions with other major sponsors failed to materialise.

The problems that had beset the Hammers at the start of each of the past four seasons were forgotten as they won their first two fixtures – at promoted Barnsley and at home to Tottenham. Hartson provided the goal-power up front, whilst Berkovic's silky midfield skills added an extra dimension to the team. Such was to be the Israeli's impact on Upton Park that the fans were soon marvelling at his abilities, not seen by a wearer of claret and blue since the days of Brooking. The brand of soccer played was equal to anything ever previously produced at the 'academy'.

After apparently agreeing to join West Ham, John Barnes – given a free transfer by Liverpool – signed for Newcastle. Redknapp then pulled off one of his best transfer deals, selling Danny Williamson to Everton in mid-August. The gifted youth product had found it difficult to secure a midfield place in the first team since making his debut in 1994. In obtaining £1 million, plus David Unsworth, for the youngster, Redknapp harvested another generous profit as well as solving one of his positional problems. The England defender was naturally left-sided and fitted into that part of the manager's defensive formation. It was ironic that the debuts of both Unsworth and Williamson were made against their former clubs – at Goodison in the next game. Unsworth's value as a solid defender, good in the air, powerful in the tackle and with a fierce left-foot shot, gave the Hammers better balance.

By now, the new-look Hammers were becoming the focus for international managers. Players such as Lomas, Berkovic, Rieper, Hughes, Dowie, and – to a lesser extent – Hartson, Rowland and Lazaridis, were already established on the international scene. But for the first time since Cottee in 1989, an English-born Hammer was picked for a full England squad. Rio Ferdinand was called up by coach Glenn Hoddle for a World Cup qualifier against Moldova, but was omitted after being convicted of drink-driving. It was to be another two months before Rio made his full England debut as a substitute in a friendly against Cameroon. He thereby became the youngest player, at nineteen, since 1955 to represent the full side. Frank Lampard was also making his mark and was drafted into the Under-21 side, amid reports that Italian giants Internazionale of Milan were eyeing him up.

Redknapp now had an additional problem to the usual one of injuries. So many of his first-team squad were missing on international duty that training and tactical talks between games was severely hampered. Added to which, there was always the risk of players picking up injuries while away, playing for their countries.

With Julian Dicks' troublesome knee requiring yet more surgery, various defenders were linked with the club. Work permit problems scuppered a deal for Australian international Steve Horvat, though Redknapp signed Blackburn's Ian Pearce for around £2.3 million. The linking of Pearce with Ferdinand and Unsworth gave the Hammers' defence its most solid look since the club's return to the Premiership. As Paul Kitson required a groin operation, the arrival in late October of Frenchman Samassi Abou for £250,000 soon gave the crowd a new favourite. Abou's unfamiliar style of play and his antics made him a cult hero, in the mode of Iain Dowie. 'Abooooo' sang the crowd whenever he touched the ball.

There were high-profile departures as well as arrivals. Marc Rieper, who would have been entitled to a Bosman move at the end of the season, was sold to Celtic for £1.5 million, whilst Michael Hughes, unsettled at being passed over in favour of Berkovic, was sold to Wimbledon for rather more. Once again Redknapp had sold two players at a handsome profit, as well as extracting the best from them during their time at Upton Park. English football had been transformed from the days when managers were allowed a number of years over which to build a team.

By late October the Hammers were eleventh and had progressed to the fourth round of the Coca-Cola Cup. Hartson was top scorer in all competitions amongst Premiership players, while Berkovic had contributed five goals in eleven League appearances. By the New Year, West Ham were up to eighth. Ferdinand and Lampard were regulars in the side, Kitson was back after injury and scoring goals, and Impey and Lazaridis had their share of good moments on the flanks. The only blemish had been a much publicised on-field fracas between Berkovic and Moncur during the defeat at Chelsea, which Redknapp insisted would be settled 'internally'.

One of the strangest incidents in Upton Park's long history had occurred in early November, when a Monday evening game against Crystal Palace – being screened on Sky TV – had to be abandoned. In the 65th minute, seconds after Frank Lampard's goal made it 2-2, the floodlights failed. West Ham had been two goals down but had staged a stirring fightback. When electricians failed to restore the lights after half an hour, the game was called off. There was much speculation, reinforced by later developments, that Far East gambling syndicates were behind this and similar power failures at other Premiership grounds. The one thing all these abandoned fixtures had in common was that the scores were level at the time the lights failed! In any case, Redknapp had forgotten his frustration a month later when the re-staged fixture saw his team cruise home 4-1.

Injury to Miklosko resulted in an extended run for Craig Forrest, but for added cover Redknapp took French international Bernard Lama on loan for the rest of the season. Lama had been released by Paris Saint-Germain following a drugs ban. Forrest kept him out of the side until late February, when he too succumbed to injury, allowing Lama to keep goal for the final fourteen fixtures. His good form saw him named in the French World Cup squad, and despite an offer to stay at West Ham, he returned to play in France.

DID YOU KNOW?

In 1997-98, West Ham reached the quarter-finals of both the Coca-Cola and FA Cups. They were beaten in both Cups at Upton Park by Arsene Wenger's Arsenal.

In early January Arsenal ended West Ham's interest in the Coca-Cola Cup at the quarter-final stage, and it was the Gunners again who, two months later, repeated the punishment at the same stage of the FA Cup – this time following a penalty shoot-out – as they marched on to complete the 'double'.

Redknapp bought QPR's midfielder-cum-striker Trevor Sinclair in a player-plus-cash deal. Dowie, Rowland and £1.6 million went to Loftus Road. Redknapp was immediately repaid for his faith in resurrecting the 24-year-old's flagging career, as the former Under-21 international scored twice on his debut. In February, Redknapp signed Rochdale's England youth goalkeeper – 16-year-old Stephen Bywater. With a further eye to the future, managing director Peter Storrie and youth section boss Tony Carr travelled to Australia, consolidating the club's links 'down under' by opening two soccer schools of excellence, in Sydney and Perth. Although Lazaridis was the most senior Aussie to have made his mark at Upton Park, other youngsters, such as the Coyne brothers and Richard Garcia, were impressing in the club's youth section. More would soon arrive. As Storrie said: 'You only need to find one or two players and the investment will pay for itself.' Lazaridis, a winger, was a bargain £300,000 when bought in 1995, but was reportedly the target of a seven-figure bid. The departure of coach Frank Burrows saw Roger Cross as his replacement, enabling Cross to renew his acquaintance with former team-mates Redknapp and Lampard.

Sinclair's seven goals in fourteen appearances and the team's all-round improvement had everyone thinking of a UEFA Cup berth. Although the Hammers touched sixth place, bad defeats dumped them back to eighth – too low for Europe, but their highest finish in the Premiership. Added to which, the team had lost at home just twice in the League all season. As for the youth team, they won the South East Counties League for the second time in three years.

Match of the Season 1997-98

West Ham 1 Arsenal 1

FA Cup, quarter-final, replay, 17 March 1998

The Gunners presented one hurdle too many in both domestic cups in the first weeks of 1998. Arsene Wenger's multi-national side had already ended West Ham's Coca-Cola Cup hopes to move into the last four, where they were beaten by eventual winners Chelsea.

It looked like the Hammers would ride their luck in the FA Cup, having reached this stage by winning on penalties at Blackburn. Drawn away to Arsenal, they had battled to a richly deserved draw. Redknapp said of his walking wounded, 'Four of 'em shouldn't even have played.' Nine days later the odds appeared to have tilted in West Ham's favour. Upton Park had become a fortress this season, witnessing just one defeat in the League and one in the cups – to Arsenal, in the Coca-Cola.

The match was beset with controversy and high drama. Dennis Bergkamp had netted a penalty in the first game, but now, nearing half-time, responded to Lomas's tug at his shirt by elbowing him in the face. Bergkamp was immediately red-carded. With Arsenal reduced to ten men, the Hammers should have been on track for a semi-final clash with Wolves, but the Gunners now showed their famous resolve. Bang on half-time Anelka curled home a shot from twenty yards to put the visitors ahead.

Upon the change of ends West Ham set up camp in the Arsenal half, but Adams and Keown were indomitable and young Austrian goalkeeper Alex Manninger was equal to everything that Hartson, Abou, and Lampard threw at him. But as the minutes ticked away Hartson cut in from the flank, muscled past Keown, Dixon and Petit, and drove a low shot from fifteen yards into the net. Extra-time arrived and Manninger this time was equal to Hartson's effort, which he tipped onto the angle of bar and post. From the corner, the Hammers' striker headed just over. Other efforts from Moncur, Unsworth and Hodges came close to ending the tie, but a penalty shoot-out could not be averted, and with it Arsenal's best chance of progress in the circumstances.

Arsenal's Stephen Hughes converted his side's first kick, as did Unsworth for the Hammers. Arsenal missed their next, but were relieved to see Hartson's crash against a post to keep it at 1-1. The Gunners made it 2-1 before Lampard levelled once more. The next Arsenal effort screwed wide, only for Manninger to magnificently save from Berkovic. Patrick Vieira put his side in front again, but up stepped skipper Steve Lomas to keep the scores all-square. Having had five kicks apiece, it was now sudden death. Arsenal captain Tony Adams made it 4-3 with one of the worst penalties ever to beat a goalkeeper, let alone Lama, as he sidefooted weakly down the middle but still found the net. Abou had to score to keep West Ham alive, but his attempt struck a post and the Hammers were out. Arsenal marched on, in Arsene Wenger's first full season, to a famous League and Cup double.

FA CARLING PREMIERSHIP	**1998-99**
Premiership	5th
Worthington Cup	2nd Round
FA Cup	3rd Round

The club was busy with transfers before and after the World Cup finals in France. Chilean Javier Margas arrived for £2.2 million. The 29-year-old defender, capped 55 times by his country, had come to Redknapp's notice during Chile's 2-0 Wembley win over England in February and during the summer when he represented his country in World Cup 98 with his hair dyed red. Liverpool's 30-year-old Neil 'Razor' Ruddock was also signed to provide central defensive cover. French midfielder Marc Keller arrived from Karlsruhe on a free transfer. Prodigious striker Ian Wright, no longer guaranteed first-team football by Arsenal, was signed for an undisclosed fee, thought to involve an initial down-payment of some £750,000. Ironically, 34-year-old Wright linked up with former team-mate Hartson, whom he had kept out of the side at Arsenal. Not least of West Ham's imports was Newcastle keeper Shaka Hislop, signed under the Bosman ruling. Six months previously the Toons claimed to have rejected £1.7 million for him, though presumably not from West Ham, who stated 'We're been watching him over the last couple of years and were aware that he was going to be out of contract at the end of June.' Once again Redknapp had proved his dexterity at wheeling and dealing, bringing in five new players at a net outlay of around £3 million.

The major departure was the homesick Unsworth, sold initially to Aston Villa for £3 million, in the hope of being nearer his family in Merseyside, but within days of being sold on to his original club, Everton. His departure – notwithstanding West Ham's handsome profit – was sorely felt as his contribution to the left of defence had been a highlight of the previous campaign. But with the return to fitness of Julian Dicks and Ian Pearce, and Lampard committed to a new five-year deal, it looked as though Redknapp had a squad capable of winning a trophy. In a lighter frame of mind Dicks (with a handicap of three) announced that when he retired from football he fancied becoming a professional golfer.

Off the field, West Ham signed a three-year sponsorship deal with Dr Martens Boots. After a season without a sponsor's name appearing on the club's shirts, the new deal was said to be the biggest in the club's history.

The first fixture saw Wright score the only goal at Hillsborough, but he was missing from the home draw with Manchester United a week later. Wright was named, along with Ferdinand, in the squad for the Euro 2000 qualifier with Sweden. Lampard was named in the Under-21 team and made the first goal before firing home a penalty in his side's 2-0 victory. Lomas and Hartson were also in their respective international squads.

A draw at Coventry continued the team's useful start, and when Wimbledon conceded three goals in half an hour at Upton Park the bubbles were being blown in earnest. Somehow, the 'Crazy Gang' came back from the dead to score four times and burst those lovely bubbles. Three days later the Hammers put that nightmare behind them to knock leaders Liverpool off top spot.

In late September the club was rocked by reports of a training ground spat at Chadwell Heath involving Berkovic and Hartson. It was soon apparent that the flair-up was serious; video film showed Hartson kick Berkovic, who was on the ground, in the head. Hartson was fined, and Redknapp urged him to seek counselling to curb his temper. The FA, bizarrely, charged Hartson with misconduct on the same day it was announced that he had been named 'Welsh Player of the Year'.

In November another crisis hit the club, involving Redknapp and chief executive Peter Storrie. The cause was the sale of Andy Impey to Leicester for £1.5 million, allegedly without the manager's say-so. Redknapp was told to omit the player for the clash at Derby in case he was injured and his transfer jeopardised. Redknapp threatened to resign, but Storrie hit back: 'The books had to be balanced and Harry knew that. If he doesn't like things, he has got to lump it. If the fans want the truth, it is me who has done all the deals, yet I don't get any praise. If we are winning, the manager's a hero – if we are losing, it's sack the board. But that is life and I accept it.'

Redknapp apologised, but before his diplomatic climbdown he snapped: 'I'm not a mug and I don't need a job that badly that I'll let people walk all over me. If someone walks in and says they are selling Rio Ferdinand without telling me, then I'll resign. They probably thought maybe it's all right to sell Andy because the fans don't like him too much and no one will really care. I feel I have been undermined in front of my players and everyone else. The day I stop choosing who I buy and who I sell is the day I am not managing a football club anymore.' Storrie had the final word: 'Harry wears his heart on his sleeve and you have to put up with that at times, but it is disappointing.'

Perhaps sensing that other players might be available, Tottenham's new boss George Graham launched an audacious £4.3 million bid for Frank Lampard, who by now was captaining the England Under-21s. That was fended off, but by the New Year, Aston Villa were reportedly bidding £6 million for the young midfielder.

DID YOU KNOW?

The last time West Ham scored more goals than they conceded in the top division was when finishing third in 1985-86. They have had negative goal figures ever since.

The net result of all these traumas, together with the monetary needs generated by the challenges of football in the 1990s, was to portray a club that had shed its image of being largely a family concern. West Ham United FC was now run first and foremost as a business.

On the pitch, the team played ten more League games by the end of November, losing only twice despite another crippling list of injuries. One of those defeats was at Charlton, where West Ham led 2-1 with seventeen minutes left but lost 2-4. Shades of Wimbledon. Yet victory over Tottenham on the final Saturday of the month saw West Ham go second. Redknapp was named Carling Manager of the Month but then received less welcome publicity as Billy Bonds blasted his former colleague when giving his version of events surrounding Bonds' 1994 departure from Upton Park.

Nor did a winning team in the League mean a winning team in the cups. Defeat by Second Division Northampton in the Worthington Cup must have given Redknapp nightmares. Having conceded two late goals in the away leg, the Hammers – despite 27 goal attempts, seventeen corners and the return of Dicks after an eighteen-month absence – had only Lampard's injury-time goal to show for their second-leg efforts.

It was a similar story in the FA Cup. Dicks' equaliser four minutes from time salvaged a replay against Swansea, but in the mud-splattered replay at Vetch Field the Welsh team grabbed the only goal. The sole consolation from the first game was the long-awaited debut of another player from the youth production line – one Joe Cole – whom Redknapp and others believed would be a bigger star than even Ferdinand and Lampard. With Dicks having a stinker, Redknapp signed Scott Minto for £1 million from Benfica.

Shortly before Christmas, Sinclair and Ruddock's 'high spirits' brought more unwanted publicity, and Miklosko, aggrieved at not being given a free transfer after nine years at Upton Park, finally severed his connections with East London, by moving to the West, making permanent his previous loan transfer to QPR. In February he was joined by Tim Breacker, freed under the Bosman ruling.

All this was nothing compared to the shock news of Hartson's departure to Wimbledon for a mind-boggling £7.5 million. The Dons had made an offer for the out-of-form, out-of-condition striker that was impossible to refuse. It was Redknapp's finest sale, unloading a player who, from being heralded less than two years earlier as the saviour of West Ham's Premiership status, had become an overweight liability. Lack of fitness would later deny Hartson multi-million pound transfers to Tottenham and Rangers.

With such funds at the club's disposal, Redknapp became linked with all and sundry, in this country and on the continent. He might have landed Newcastle's Robert Lee, but their £2 million valuation for a 32-year-old exceeded his. He did land Marc-Vivien Foe for £4.5 million from French champions Lens, and Paolo Di Canio for £2 million. Foe had been a target of Manchester United until being injured. As for Di Canio, the arrival of the disgraced player from Sheffield Wednesday ranks as perhaps Redknapp's shrewdest deal, as the maverick Italian quickly became the darling of the West Ham fans, as he had those at Celtic and Hillsborough beforehand. He brought a degree of footballing skill and showmanship to Upton Park that in all honestly eclipses everything the club had ever seen, mesmerising and enthralling in equal measure. His questionable temperament and infamous eleven-match ban for pushing a referee were forgotten as soon as he demonstrated his awesome talent.

The first months of 1999 brought its share of problems. Margas went AWOL in Chile, whilst Ian Wright was in France recuperating from a cartilage operation. After a two-and-a-half year fitness battle, Richard Hall announced that the foot injury sustained soon after his arrival had forced him to quit.

By early April the Hammers were fifth and admitting that they had applied to take part in the summer's InterToto Cup – a back-door entry into the UEFA Cup. Redknapp had changed his mind on this matter when it was announced that with regard to the last UEFA Cup spot, FA Cup semi-finalists Newcastle, in mid-table, had priority over whoever finished fifth in the Premiership. Redknapp's mood worsened when it was revealed that another place would go to the winners of the Premiership Fair Play League. 'It's farcical,' he raged. 'Next year we'll finish fourth from bottom and have no tacklers in the side.'

It was also announced that managing director Peter Storrie was leaving at the end of the season, and that Graham Mackrell from Sheffield Wednesday would take over as new company secretary. It seemed to outsiders that Storrie had lost out in a boardroom power struggle with Chairman Brown, whose shareholding – when added to that of the Hills and Cearns families – made him by far the most powerful voice at West Ham United.

Despite being thrashed at home by Leeds 1-5 and at Everton 0-6, a 4-0 win over Middlesbrough on the last afternoon of the campaign ensured that the Hammers finished fifth, their highest position in the Premiership and their second highest ever – despite the quirk of conceding more goals than they scored. Manager, players, officials and supporters looked forward to the return of European action as the Hammers prepared for the InterToto Cup.

The youth section proved that there were more young jewels coming through. The Under-19s won their group in the FA Premier Academy League and also the play-off championship trophy, and Tony Carr saw his protégés cap their memorable year by winning the FA Youth Cup by a record breaking 9-0 aggregate.

Match of the Season 1998-99

West Ham 2 Liverpool 1

Premiership, 12 September 1998

Three days after the debacle at home to Wimbledon, when a 3-0 lead transformed into a 3-4 defeat, the Hammers had to pick themselves up for the visit of leaders Liverpool. Which was the real West Ham, the team unbeaten in its first three games without conceding a goal, or the shambles who caved in against the Dons?

Once again Redknapp's side roared out of the starting stalls. The sell-out crowd saluted John Hartson's quick headed opener. The goal arrived from the game's first corner, the ball deflected past American keeper Brad Friedel off the shoulder of Carragher. Liverpool struggled, with Michael Owen a lone force up front as they packed their midfield in a bid to quell the threat posed by Berkovic, Lampard and Moncur, together with the forward runs of wing-backs Sinclair and Lazaridis. Friedel's uncertainty became infectious and the impetus that had pushed Liverpool to the top of the table was suddenly missing. Owen found Steve Potts, playing his first game of the season, in superb form.

Shortly after the change-round Berkovic played a one-two with Hartson, received a square pass back, and struck a rasping twenty-yard low shot past Friedel, the ball again being deflected, this time off the legs of ex-Hammer Paul Ince.

Liverpool boss Gerard Houllier made substitutions, one of which was to introduce Karlheinz Riedle, who had partnered Owen effectively in Liverpool's opening fixtures. With time running out the German lost his marker at the far post to head in. The referee then allowed five minutes of injury-time, adding to frayed nerves.

It would not be until the second week of the New Year that the Hammers were again beaten at home.

FA CARLING PREMIERSHIP	**1999-2000**
Premiership	9th
Worthington Cup	Quarter-finals
FA Cup	3rd Round
UEFA Cup	2nd Round

The main departures were Eyal Berkovic, who was sold to Celtic for £5.75 million, and Stan Lazaridis, who moved to Birmingham for £1.9 million. The Australian winger had cost just £300,000 four years earlier. Julian 'The Terminator' Dicks, 31, finally swapped the soccer ball for the golf ball, and Ian Wright was loaned to Nottingham Forest before signing for Celtic on a free.

Stay-away defender Javier Margas was discovered playing for Chile against Brazil and eventually returned to Upton Park. Harry Redknapp signed striker Paolo Wanchope for £3.5 million and, later, central defender Igor Stimac for £600,000 – both from Derby. Another £1.2 million later secured Gary Charles from Benfica. The manager was not so lucky with an attempt to bring back Slaven Bilic. Everton's out-of-favour defender failed a medical. Newcastle left-back Stuart Pearce, 37, arrived on a free transfer and impressed everyone with his commitment and professionalism. In his first season at the Boleyn he broke the same leg twice yet still fought his way back into the first team.

In his five years in charge at Upton Park, Redknapp had turned over around £80 million in transfer fees. He returned a profit of some £10 million, yet still had a squad valued in excess of £50 million. He knew that a ground capacity of 26,000 imposed limits on his spending power and made it hard to attract the kind of players who would help the club consistently finish in the top six. Nevertheless he had achieved much. Now European competition beckoned after a gap of eighteen years.

Football had become a year-round activity and the Hammers' involvement in the InterToto Cup meant their campaign kicked off in mid-July. It had been the shortest close season in memory – just 62 days – before West Ham took the field against Jokerit of Finland. When the Premiership season kicked off on the first Saturday of August – itself starting early because of Euro 2000 the following summer – the Hammers had already played four InterToto games. Although losing at home in the first leg, a fine performance against FC Metz in France in the second secured a place in the UEFA Cup and a return to senior European competition. Two victories over the Croatians of NK Osijek in September saw Redknapp's team face Steaua Bucharest of Romania, who proved too strong in the away tie, and profited from West Ham's profligacy at Upton Park.

For one player tragedy struck in the opening Premiership match. Ian Pearce collided with namesake Stuart and tore cruciate ligaments in his right knee. The injury would keep him out all season.

Four wins and a draw in their opening five games meant that by mid-September West Ham were joint second with Chelsea, both teams having two games in hand on the rest. Back-to-back away losses marred that fine opening, but it was not until the Saturday before Christmas that Manchester United inflicted the Hammers' first home defeat. A three-goal opening burst, as Beckham and Giggs worked their magic on the flanks, threatened an avalanche, but two goals from Di Canio galvanised the home supporters into believing the impossible was possible. Giggs crossed for Yorke to put the result beyond doubt, but Alex Ferguson admitted: 'Di Canio gave them life and I feared the worst.'

Doubtless the Hammers were still traumatised by the events of the previous seven days. They had once again fallen from the FA Cup to a side from a lower division. Their inept performance in losing 0-1 at Tranmere was described by one paper as 'spineless and wretched, and one of which the team should be ashamed'. The manager told the press: 'For the first time this season I've had a real go at them in the dressing room. It had to be done.'

Four days later Redknapp's side beat Aston Villa in a marathon quarter-final home tie in the Worthington Cup. With the score 2-2 after extra-time, the Hammers squeezed through 5-4 on penalties, only to learn that one of their substitutes, Manny Omoyinmi – who had been on the field just six minutes and hardly touched the ball – was cup-tied. He had played for Gillingham on loan in an earlier round. The League could have disqualified the Hammers. Instead it ruled that the tie should be replayed. When it was, a month later, it again went to extra-time, when Villa got the vital goals.

The ramifications of the sad affair were far-reaching, not only in costing the Hammers a lucrative semi-final and a possible place in Europe. Club Secretary Graham Mackrell and his assistant, Football Secretary Alison O'Dowd, were held responsible for the fiasco and resigned. Redknapp was so incensed by Omoyinmi's failure to tell anyone he was cup-tied that the Nigerian youngster was quickly loaned out again and later released on a free transfer.

Returning to the Cup demise at Tranmere, it is noteworthy that over the past four decades – commencing with the FA Cup defeat by Huddersfield in 1960 – West Ham have been knocked out of one or other of the two domestic cups by lesser division teams on 23 occasions! Redknapp, who in his Bournemouth years basked in giant-killing triumphs, struggled to pinpoint the reasons why the Hammers had been afflicted by such a problem for so long.

DID YOU KNOW?

In the period covered by this book, West Ham have been knocked out of the FA Cup or League Cup by lower-division opponents 27 times.

A long injury list meant that as the new millennium dawned Redknapp was forced to fill the substitutes' bench with youngsters. In January an FA tribunal ordered the club to pay Arsenal £400,000 compensation – with the possibility of it reaching £2 million with add-ons – for signing 17-year-old Leon Britton. The lad had been at Highbury since his schooldays but suddenly moved to Upton Park when he became a 'senior'. It was the second time that West Ham had fallen foul of the authorities on this question. The previous summer Charlton had accused the club of illegally procuring Jermain Defoe, who had been on their books as a schoolboy. Both the player and West Ham refuted the allegations, but the Hammers were ordered to pay their neighbours an initial £400,000, which might rise to £1.65 million.

The fans had contrasting views of the talents of West Ham's two main strikers. They revered Di Canio, who apart from his extraordinary skill was also leading scorer, but were less convinced by the other Paulo – Wanchope. Redknapp was quick to defend his Costa Rican striker, claiming that the admittedly ungainly player was an important foil for Di Canio. Wanchope was only 23, it was almost impossible to knock him off the ball, and he scored goals (as well as missing them). Although he would be sold the following summer to Manchester City, it must be said in Wanchope's favour that his 46 appearances for the Hammers brought fifteen goals (twelve in 35 Premiership games) which is a commendable return in today's football environment. Redknapp wanted to keep him, but the books had to be balanced.

Recovering from a 0-4 home defeat by Everton in February, West Ham won their next two games to climb to sixth, with their sights on qualifying for the UEFA Cup. By the end of March they were still eighth, following a televised home victory over Wimbledon. The match was all the more remarkable because of two memorable moments, so far as home fans were concerned. Nine minutes into the game Sinclair sent over a deep centre from the right. The ball fell to Di Canio who was already airborne but somehow adjusted to volley an angled right-footer past the Dons goalkeeper. The Italian had scored some remarkable goals in the claret and blue, but none could compare with this one, which earned the accolade 'goal of the season'. If anyone had any doubts that Di Canio would be denied the 'Hammer of the Year' award, that goal surely settled the matter.

The second moment concerned new arrival Freddie Kanoute, on loan from Olympique Lyonnais, who scored on his debut. Such was his impact that the fans demanded that Redknapp sign him immediately, but although Kanoute played out the season for West Ham his move did not become permanent until later. His fee matched that which Manchester City shortly paid for Wanchope.

With Hislop injured in January, Redknapp called upon four different goalkeepers during the rest of the campaign. With second choice Forrest away on Canadian international duty, the problem became so acute that Sasa Ilic and Ian Feuer were signed on loan and even young Stephen Bywater had to step in.

Perhaps the fixture computer had a sense of humour when on Saturday, 1 April it sent West Ham to play at Old Trafford. That match would be burned into the memories of Hammers fans, for before a crowd of over 61,600 West Ham were swamped 1-7 by the champions-elect. Surprisingly, it spurred or shocked the Hammers into three straight wins, though three consecutive losses followed. On the final Sunday a 0-0 draw with Leeds confirmed West Ham's final position of ninth, whilst also ensuring that Leeds would be in the Champions League.

Once again Harry Redknapp had endured a season beset with controversy, injury problems and incident, coupled with a crowd that expected more and more of him and his players. Through it all he had remained his usual wisecracking self, if only on the surface, but doubtless somewhat frustrated within himself as the club and its players could not achieve another top-five finish, or claim some silverware via the cups. Nevertheless, only John Lyall has likewise led the club to three top-ten placings in successive seasons.

Match of the Season 1999-2000

West Ham 5 Bradford City 4

Premiership, 12 February 2000

There have been some amazing matches played at Upton Park since West Ham returned to the First Division in 1958, but perhaps none to compare with this nine-goal thriller. As one newspaper reported the following day: 'This game will take some beating for breathless excitement, unexpected drama and thrill-a-minute entertainment.' Another summed it up in the performance of one man: 'Paolo Di Canio's crazy, mixed up world of brilliance and Latin histrionics erupted at Upton Park when he exploded like Vesuvius.'

If anyone thought that the relegation-haunted visitors would be an easy target they were quickly reminded that although Bradford were down they certainly were not out. The Yorkshire team hassled and hurried from the start, chasing any half-chance as though their lives depended on it – their soccer future certainly depended on it. Dean Saunders' desire to chase a Lomas back-pass undoubtedly had a profound effect on the rest of the proceedings. In clearing upfield, Hislop accidentally kicked the striker's boot, an impact which saw the keeper stretchered off with a broken leg.

With second choice keeper Forrest on international duty, 18-year-old Stephen Bywater warmed the bench and was now pitched into the fray for his Premiership debut. For the youngster it was a baptism of fire as the visitors sensed his nerves and played on them – which was only to be expected.

Indecision in the Hammers defence – with the young keeper uncertain whether to come off his line and his colleagues unsure as to whether he would or not – was exploited by a close-range Bradford header. Sinclair quickly levelled. On half-time Moncur became hero then villain in the space of sixty seconds. First he received a free-kick and his deflected shot put West Ham ahead. Then in his own penalty area he nudged the theatrical Saunders and Peter Beagrie fired home from the spot. 2-2.

Within five minutes of the turnaround the Hammers had conceded two more goals. Bywater failed to hold a long-range shot, allowing a simple tap-in for the orange-haired Lawrence, who then compounded West Ham's misery by twisting past Stimac and floating the ball over the head of the embarrassed Bywater. West Ham almost conceded a fifth but Saunders' angled drive hit a post.

Di Canio, frustrated at having three appeals for penalties fall on deaf ears, lost the plot and demanded to be substituted. Redknapp took a leaf out of the referee's book and likewise cocked a deaf ear. When substitute Kitson was impeded in the act of shooting, the ref did at last give a penalty and Di Canio and Lampard wrestled each other for the ball and the honour of taking the kick. The Italian won the argument, drove home his kick and retrieved the ball from the net in his haste to resume the match.

Joe Cole played a one-two with Sinclair before netting a low shot to level at 4-4. With seven minutes remaining Di Canio centred for Lampard to drive into the top corner. Their previous altercation was forgotten as Di Canio launched himself upon an even more ecstatic Lampard. With thrills, spills, drama, great attacking football, some amazing 'faux-pas', coupled with nine goals, it could be said that the fans went home satisfied – well at least the West Ham ones did. Redknapp said: 'I don't care where you go, you won't see more exciting football than you see here at Upton Park.' But then that's always been the way for supporters of the Hammers.

FA CARLING PREMIERSHIP	**2000-01**
Premiership	15th
Worthington Cup	4th Round
FA Cup	Quarter-finals

Leeds were reported to have made an audacious £10 million bid for Rio Ferdinand as the previous season had drawn to a close – in time for their 2000-01 European campaign – whilst Glasgow Rangers were hoping to snatch the on-loan Freddie Kanoute. Harry Redknapp's chances of taking the Hammers back into Europe had been thwarted by the referee failing to spot Petit's handball at Highbury, and Arsenal's last-gasp winner. Points dropped at Sunderland and at home to Leeds had brought a miserable end to the season.

Under Redknapp there was always much press speculation about summer transfers, and this year was no exception. With Lampard and Carrick in the England Under-21 squad for the European Championship finals, and Ferdinand in the preliminary 28-man full international squad for Euro 2000, the Hammers' youth were making their mark on the wider stage. Although the Under-21s captained by Lampard crashed out in Slovakia, Leeds were mulling over an £8 million bid for him. He was then put on standby for the full England squad, although his friend Rio Ferdinand was left out of Kevin Keegan's plans.

£3.7 million secured Kanoute from Olympique Lyonnais, but the same club's £6 million bid for Marc-Vivien Foe was too good to refuse, so the Cameroon international moved in the opposite direction. Trevor Sinclair, although failing to win an England place, signed a one-year contract extension intended to keep him at Upton Park until 2005. Nigel Winterburn signed for £250,000 from Arsenal and Croatian Davor Sukor followed him on a free. Redknapp said of the France '98 Golden Boot winner: 'I believe that Davor will prove a terrific signing.' Also arriving on a free was 23-year-old Australian international defender Hayden Foxe, from the Japanese J-League club Sanfrecce Hiroshima, but Foxe's work permit was blocked. It would be another eight months – which saw a number of failed appeals and a broken foot – before he finally played. Only by wedding his French girlfriend did he acquire the necessary work permit.

Leaving the Boleyn was Costa Rican striker Paulo Wanchope, who went to Manchester City for £3.65 million. The player wanted to stay but according to Redknapp could not be guaranteed a starting place. Neil Ruddock left on a free to Crystal Palace; American giant goalkeeper Ian Feuer to Wimbledon; Samassi Abou back to France; the ill-fated Manny Omoyinmi to Oxford United; and Stephen Purches to Bournemouth.

DID YOU KNOW?

In Redknapp's last season, 2000-01, West Ham were bottom after 6 games, 6th after 16, but 15th at the close. Their 42 points would see them relegated two years later.

Whilst holidaying in Cyprus, Ferdinand and Lampard made headlines for the wrong reasons after a video allegedly surfaced. When the tabloids said Leeds were set to clinch the £10 million capture of Ferdinand, Redknapp was furious: 'We turned down £15 million for Rio three months ago, so we're not going to accept £10 million for him now. He's not for sale anyway.' Barcelona's supremo was also willing to bid £16.5 million, commenting 'We need him and we'll do everything to get him'.

The priceless collection of Bobby Moore's memorabilia was bought by the club for £2 million, where it would take pride of place in the proposed Museum. There was also talk that Sir Geoff Hurst's collection, but not his World Cup medal, was up for sale.

Fans turning up for the new season were greeted by a complete change of vista. The area in front of the West Stand and on the site of the old Primary school and playground was now a huge building site. The £35 million redevelopment of the Boleyn was underway. A new school had been built, funded by the club, to the north to facilitate this, and a new West Stand named after club sponsors Dr Martens would take shape with the construction of the framework behind the existing structure. It would be a mammoth task but would bring the club into the new millennium as far as stadia were concerned and increase capacity to 35,000. The pitch would be shifted 40 yards. In time a new East Stand would complete the redevelopment to raise the capacity to 40,000 seats.

After an ill-tempered pre-season testimonial against Athletic Bilbao, in which he played a cameo second-half role, Julian Dicks hung up his boots to become a golfer.

With three defeats and three draws in their opening six games, the Hammers made their worst start since relegation in 1992, but a defiant Redknapp insisted he had the best Hammers team for 20 years. A win at Coventry finally broke the duck and sparked a run of a dozen games in which the 1-2 home reversal to Arsenal was the only defeat. The Hammers climbed from bottom to eighth, and Cole and Carrick were both selected for the Under-21s, together with Ferdinand and Lampard for the seniors.

Another to emerge was 17-year-old Jermain Defoe, who had controversially joined a year previously from Charlton. He came off the bench to pounce for the only goal at Walsall in the Worthington Cup. Before the start of the season the youngster had scored twice after coming on as a substitute in England Under-21s' 4-0 win over Holland. He was then loaned to Bournemouth, where he became one of the hottest properties in football by setting a League record of scoring in eleven consecutive matches.

In November, after Ferdinand gave an immaculate display at Elland Road – where the Hammers won for the first time since 1978 – Leeds upped the stakes by bidding £18 million, a world record fee for a defender. The board reluctantly accepted, but left the decision to the player. An unhappy Redknapp conceded that in an uncertain transfer market – the European Union were expected to confirm a massive shake-up – the offer was too good to refuse. The money would help to strengthen the squad and, of course, the cost of the new West Stand was also to be considered.

Fans' reactions were divided. Realists saw the logic behind the sale, and the need for the youngster to progress to a larger stage on which to improve. Others felt betrayed, believing that Ferdinand should not be sold at any price. The realities of football finances, as well as the ever increasing wage-bill on a club the size of West Ham, finally won the day. Furthermore, no other club had actually tabled an offer. Leeds had effectively out-bid themselves.

With other clubs hovering for Kanoute, Di Canio and Lampard, Redknapp slapped a 'Not for Sale' sign on his prize assets. Instead he bought Rigobert Song (£2.5 million), Titi Camara (£1.7 million), Ragnvald Soma (£800,000), Christian Dailly (£1.75 million), Svetoslav Todorov (£500,000), and took Sebastian Schemmel on loan. Paul Kitson, Marc Keller and Gary Charles, together with several reserves, were loaned out or freed. Steve Lomas opted to stay.

Ever since his arrival in Britain, Di Canio's exploits on and off the pitch have always grabbed headlines. With West Ham it was no different, whether it be differences of opinion with his manager, scoring audacious goals, transfer talk, or spurning a last-minute match-winning scoring attempt by catching the ball so that the injured Everton goalkeeper Paul Gerrard could receive treatment. The spontaneous applause by the Goodison faithful was echoed not only by the press but also with a Carling Number One award and a letter from the FIFA President, who wrote: 'Gestures like this are all too rare in football.' Redknapp philosophically remarked: 'Obviously you'd like to get three points and what you never know in football, or in life, is whether anyone would do the same thing for you. In fairness the lad's missed the ball and would've got treatment just as quickly if Paolo had scored. Paolo's done what he's done and that's it.'

Progress in both cups was halted at the Boleyn Ground – in the Worthington Cup by a resurgent Sheffield Wednesday of Division

One and, after three away wins in the FA Cup, at the quarter-final stage by Spurs.

The 5-0 Boxing Day home rout of Charlton was the highlight of the Premiership campaign, but the New Year was ushered in by a thrashing from the champions-elect at Old Trafford. It was the start of a grim decline that saw the Hammers win just three and draw four of their next seventeen League games. The slide was exacerbated by a worsening injury list. Only the progress of Lampard, Cole and Carrick in Eriksson's plans provided any real highlights in a campaign that most fans simply wanted to see the back of.

It needed victory in the final home game to mathematically ensure safety in fifteenth place, after which the fans quit the West Stand for the last time – after 75 years. When they returned next season, a new edifice would welcome them. It had gradually taken shape over the past year, becoming the new dominant feature of the Upton Park skyline.

There was a two-week gap (to accommodate the FA Cup final) before the visit to the Riverside Stadium for the final fixture. Middlesbrough's victory confirmed their salvation and took them above their visitors in the final table.

However, it was the days prior to that last match which had the biggest impact upon the Hammers. Nothing could upstage the shock news that the Redknapp era, which had lasted seven years, was over. Together with his assistant, Frank Lampard Senior – who is also his brother-in-law, Redknapp parted company with the club he first joined as an apprentice in 1964. It was generally considered that Redknapp's job was safe for as long as he wanted it, and it is unclear whether he had jumped or was pushed. Diplomatically, he would only say: 'The last eight weeks or so haven't been particularly enjoyable and I feel that, maybe, it's time for a change.'

The real reasons for his departure have never been made public, but by his own admission a meeting with his chairman had 'gotten out of hand'. He later confessed that 'leaving the club was the last thing on my mind when I went over this morning. I never dreamed it would happen.' Rumours spread about an alleged row with the board over the size of the summer's transfer fund, and also about more deep-rooted reasons.

Glenn Roeder was appointed caretaker-manager, leaving Harry to remark 'I'm very pleased with the way the club have handled the situation'. Some took this to mean that he was bound by a vow of silence, as part of his severance package.

For the younger Lampard, who missed the last three fixtures due to a hernia operation, it was a difficult time. He had overcome the prejudice of many fans when first introduced into the team by his uncle Harry and father Frank (Senior). His determination and burgeoning talent was now apparent for all to see. But now he reportedly told friends he would never play for the club again. With hindsight, the repercussions from the saga would reverberate around Upton Park for many months, perhaps even years, to come.

Match of the Season 2000-01

Manchester United 0 West Ham 1

FA Cup, 4th Round, 28 January 2001

This was the steal of the season, so far as Sir Alex Ferguson was concerned. Earlier in January his side had swept the Hammers aside 3-1, though the score flattered West Ham. The previous April the Hammers had also been annihilated 1-7.

This was a thrilling Cup-tie which United should have put under lock and key in the first half. Ferguson later lamented: 'If you keep missing your chances, you run the risk of defeat.' How true that was proved to be.

A crowd of 67,000, and millions watching on TV, saw a patched up Hammers side take the field with two foreigners on loan (Finnish central defender Hannu Tihinen) and right-back (Schemmel), plus a half-fit goalkeeper (Hislop) and centre-forward (Kanoute), and the youngest ever Premiership midfield. Ferguson's team were only missing midfielder Paul Scholes.

The efforts of Carrick – who revealed a rare maturity for one so young, of Lampard – with his diligent running and ceaseless work-rate, and of Cole who, after a quiet first period, revealed a tactical wisdom that his admirers had yearned to see, outshone David Beckham, England's newest captain.

After West Ham were fortunate to escape two possible penalties, it was a peach of a goal from the audacious Di Canio that settled the issue in the 76th minute. Some thought him offside, but the video recording proved otherwise when Kanoute slid the ball forward. The Italian beat the offside trap, drew a wildy gesticulating Barthez, who appealed vainly to the referee, before tweaking the ball past him to the delight of 9,000 travelling fans. It was West Ham's first success in eleven visits to Old Trafford, since a fifth-round replay victory fifteen years earlier.

The win was especially sweet as, despite squandering their numerous chances, Manchester had played well. Some said the win equalled, if not surpassed, in tactical terms, an earlier most surprising victory at Old Trafford during Redknapp's managerial career – by his former team Bournemouth in the FA Cup in 1984.

9

TO THE DEPTHS AND BACK 2001-2007

FA PREMIERSHIP	**2001-02**
Barclaycard Premiership	7th
Worthington Cup	2nd Round
FA Cup	4th Round

As would be expected of a Premiership club seeking a new manager, the tabloids had a field day, although the directors tended to favour former players schooled in the ways of the club. The favourite was Alan Curbishley who had proved himself at Charlton on a tight budget and always got the best out of his players. The ex-Hammer declared himself 'flattered' to be linked with the job. Stuart Pearce, who had ended the previous campaign as 'Hammer of the Year' when hanging up his playing boots, also threw his hat in the ring: 'If West Ham fancy a gamble, they know my number.' It presumably never rang, for a few weeks later he joined the Kevin Keegan revolution at Manchester City as a coach.

With Charlton unlikely to release Curbishley, other names outside the closed circle of former players emerged, including Ruud Gullit and George Graham. The prospect of Graham, associated with functional rather than pretty football at Arsenal, Leeds and Spurs, sent shivers down the spines of some fans, while others thought his discipline was exactly that the Hammers needed. All eyes then turned to Steve McClaren, who had impressed as No 2 at Manchester United, but he was quickly installed at Middlesbrough. Preston's David Moyes and Hibernian's Alex McLeish were the next names to be canvassed.

There was player unrest too, with bids supposedly coming in for Lampard (from Leeds, Aston Villa, Chelsea, Liverpool) and Kanoute (Juventus, Aston Villa, Fulham). Di Canio, recovering from a sinus operation in Italy, lashed out at the Hammers' failure to lure a big-name manager and Sinclair's wanting to leave.

Better news concerned Cole and Carrick, who made their full England debuts, as did Defoe for the Under-21s. He scored too.

DID YOU KNOW?

In 2001-02, no other club conceded fewer goals at home than West Ham's 14. But no other club exceeded the number they conceded away – 43. Bizarre!

Chelsea's £11 million bid for Frank Lampard was accepted, and 36 days after Redknapp's departure, to everyone's surprise, Glenn Roeder was promoted from coach to manager. Having seen Curbishley, and McClaren turn down the job, the 45-year-old said 'I feel a bit like Foinavon in the 1967 Grand National. I'm the only one left standing.' Only the ninth manager in the club's history, Roeder had joined the coaching staff two years earlier after spells with the England national side – as a coach under Glenn Hoddle, as player-manager at Gillingham, and manager of Watford.

It could be said the directors went for the 'known quantity' or the 'easy option' as they had seen Roeder at first hand and admired his work. His credentials as a Hammer went back to the age of nine, when watching the team from the Chicken Run. He appointed Paul Goddard as his first-team coach, Ludek Miklosko as his goalkeeping coach, and kept on Roger Cross with responsibility for the reserves. All three were steeped in West Ham's ways, as was Hammers' legend Trevor Brooking, who joined the board as a non-executive director.

Meanwhile, Sir Geoff Hurst accepted a 'substantial' offer from the club for his 1966 medal, which now joined the other exhibits, such as the Johnny Byrne Collection, in the new Museum.

Roeder immediately quelled stories of a swap between Di Canio and Manchester United's Dwight Yorke, and Arsenal's reputed bid of £15 million for Carrick as Patrick Vieira's replacement. Instead, the new manager signed loanee Sebastian Schemmel for £465,000 before capturing England goalkeeper David James from Aston Villa for £3.25 million. Roeder and James had been team-mates at Watford in the early 1990s.

Having demonstrated his willingness to buy, Roeder was suddenly linked with all and sundry, notably Ray Parlour (Arsenal) and ex-Hammer Don Hutchison (Sunderland). Yet disaster struck when David James damaged knee ligaments, colliding with Martin Keown when appearing as a substitute in England's defeat by Holland. He would be out until November.

The first home game heralded the opening of the Upper Tier and Executive Boxes of the new West Stand, named after club sponsors Dr Martens. In late November the Lower Tier also opened, and for the first time since the Taylor Report (1990) gates of 32,000-plus became the norm once more at Upton Park. The new-look stadium was now one of the finest in the country, but one newspaper reported that the club had held talks about quitting Upton Park and moving to a new Olympic Stadium at Stratford, should London's bid for the 2012 Games be successful.

With the season underway, Hutchison broke the club's transfer payment record in a £5 million deal, only for that to be upstaged two weeks later when Czech central defender Tomas Repka completed a £5.5 million move from near-bankrupt Fiorentina of Italy. Repka marked his debut with a red card at Middlesbrough.

It was not until the fifth game, at home to Newcastle, that Roeder's team got their first win, after two defeats and two draws, plus elimination from the Worthington Cup on penalties by Second Division Reading. Worse was to follow. Successive trips to Everton and Blackburn brought 0-5 and 1-7 defeats. The latter result equalled West Ham's worst ever in the Premiership, with Repka again seeing red.

The club announced: 'We support him [Roeder] 100 per cent. There is no question of us giving Glenn anything other than our complete backing.' Brooking added: 'There is a view that the present squad is not good enough. Glenn has been let down. Too many players went missing during games.'

The situation was not helped by Harry Redknapp, now at Portsmouth, publicly airing his views on his successor and the Upton Park situation. A dignified Roeder replied: 'I think the world of Harry, he gave me a job when I was out of work.'

Just three losses in their next thirteen games lifted the Hammers to mid-table, but defeat at table-topping Leeds on New Year's Day began a sequence of five away losses that was not ended until a 1-0 win at Fulham. Apart from the FA Cup fourth round replay defeat to Chelsea and the League loss to Manchester United (the footballing highlight of the season) no team avoided leaving Upton Park unbeaten. Those home wins were enough to ensure that Roeder's Hammers finished a creditable seventh. In what had been a difficult baptism, with most of his players injured at one time or another – only Dailly was ever present – and other off-pitch problems, Roeder had acquitted himself well with a dignity that was a credit to him.

As this topsy-turvy campaign drew to its conclusion, the non-footballing highlight of the new millennium, if not in the history of West Ham United Football Club, was a visit in her Golden Jubilee Year to the East End of London by Her Majesty The Queen. She was accompanied by The Duke of Edinburgh. The Queen officially opened the Dr Martens West Stand in early May 2002 to the delight of cheering crowds that thronged Green Street and the surrounding area.

Match of the Season 2001-02

West Ham 3 Manchester United 5

Premiership, 16 March 2002

If many ask why Manchester United feature so often in Match of the Season polls with the Hammers, it is easy to explain. Both clubs have an attitude to football that is a credit to their teams and to their players, who seem to raise their game.

The knowledgeable David Miller reported on this match: 'For as long as I can remember, two of the best places to watch football have been Upton Park and Old Trafford: 45 years of continual entertainment. Unsurprising, therefore, that these two clubs should produce the match of the season ... I hear the murmur of some cynical professionals that bad defending makes attractive matches. Maybe, but what Sir Alex Ferguson, Glenn Roeder and their players give to the game is a commitment to go forward.'

For the crowd of 35,281, the simple fact was that league leaders Manchester United defended better than West Ham who, though tenth, mathematically could still be relegated. Roeder's team had conceded more goals overall – although only seven at home – than any other team except the bottom four.

The match started at a breathless pace and simply got faster. So fluent was West Ham's passing in the first half-hour that the visitors were obliged to withdraw nine men behind the ball. Carrick, returning after a hernia operation, and Joe Cole in central midfield, played one-touch football, with Vladimir Labant – the Slovakian acquired two months earlier – and Lomas on the flanks. Di Canio and Kanoute constantly pulled the defence wide. It was classic Hammers. When Lomas converted after seven minutes with a leaping header from Labant's diagonal cross, it seemed the 'double' was on. The lead lasted but nine minutes, as Scholes intercepted a loose pass from Cole, found Beckham with a diagonal pass, and the England man, from the edge of the penalty area, floated the ball over James.

The Hammers regained the lead when a perfect pass from Carrick down the right sent Schemmel racing clear on the overlap. His early low cross was swept home by Kanoute. The response was instant as, from a disputed free-kick for shirt pulling, Beckham flighted a subtle swerving ball to Nicky Butt who equalised with a bicycle-kick at the far post in a crowded area.

The pace did not slacken but it was not until ten minutes after the interval, as the rain came down, that a fifth goal arrived to give the visitors the lead for the first time. It was Scholes, restored to the side at the expense of Veron, after the midweek draw with Bayern Munich, who netted after the mercurial Ole Gunnar Solskjaer had held off two defenders before pulling the ball back to his late-arriving colleague. The Norwegian then got in on the act as, from another Beckham cross, he netted from an acute angle after Van Nistelrooy's effort was foiled by James.

At 2-4, with the game seemingly lost, Roeder gambled by sending on Defoe. Within four minutes the youngster got in front of his marker to sweep home Kanoute's cross. The Hammers surged forward to grab an equaliser but became vulnerable at the back. Thus it was Scholes, crowning an impressive personal performance, who broke into the area with two minutes remaining, only to be scythed down by Repka. The penalty was converted by Beckham, snuffing out any hope of a late point.

Perhaps Sir Alex summed up the feelings of all with one of his after-match comments: 'It was a privilege to be involved in such a marvellous game.' All except Glenn Roeder that is, whose philosophical but melancholy riposte was: 'It might have been a terrific game for the spectators but we're very disappointed to score three at home and lose. We contributed to our own downfall by giving away five sloppy ones.'

Personally speaking, up until this moment in his career, I had considered David Beckham to be overrated as a footballing entity – being, I felt, a product of media, personal, and Mancunian hype, not to mention the Spice Girls' image via his wife. His performance in this match, whereby his skills and talent came to the fore as he sprayed 60-yard passes from one wing to the other into the path of a colleague, who did not have to check his run as he received the ball, coupled with his dead-ball skills, shooting abilities, and determination, marked him out as something unique in English football, thus changing my opinion in one short afternoon. His manager, who had left him out for a long spell earlier in the season, best summed up his performance: 'Beckham was magnificent. He's been really brilliant lately but today he was just outstanding.' Unfortunately the honeymoon for both the manager, as well as myself, would not stand the test of time.

FA PREMIERSHIP	**2002-03**
Barclaycard Premiership	18th (Relegated)
Worthington Cup	3rd Round
FA Cup	4th Round

With high hopes following such an excellent finish, there was a buoyant mood around the Boleyn Ground, as shown by an all-time record 20,000 season ticket sales. This amazing statistic was helped by the board imposing a price freeze on match and season tickets for the second year running. Twelve months previously, before Roeder's appointment, the board had offered to refund the cost of season tickets to unhappy buyers. Now everyone was optimistic. Such was the fickle nature of soccer fans.

With football becoming a family social leisure activity, the club ensured as many youngsters as possible could attend games and grow up supporting the Hammers. There had been a large increase in families buying season tickets and 'The Kids for a Quid' scheme had proved popular since being introduced a couple of years earlier. As Ticket Office manager Steve Kitcher commented: 'To my knowledge no other Premiership club has offered a similar deal to their young fans.' Likewise, the club made strenuous efforts to assist physically handicapped supporters, to boost the aims of 'Football in the Community'. The ideals of a family orientated club, nurtured for over a century, were still being accomplished by the current board in the more materialistic environment of the new millennium.

For once, the close season was relatively quiet, the biggest job being to move the pitch sideways some 16 yards towards the Dr Martens West Stand. The pitch had also been raised to comply with the Football Licensing Authority's legislation on sightlines, so that all supporters could have an uninterrupted view from their seats. A new TV gantry and studio were housed in the West Stand to enhance the viewing for armchair spectators at home for live or recorded broadcasts. The new focus was on introducing state of the art technology and the reconstruction of the Chadwell Heath training ground, where a £2 million renovation began.

Much of the club's rich heritage was now on display at the Museum – medals, caps, jerseys and memorabilia – which was officially opened in October by Bobby Moore's daughter Roberta. Six months later, in February, the unveiling of 'The Champions' sculpture by Prince Andrew, HRH The Duke of York, on a newly landscaped site at the junction of the Barking Road (opposite the Boleyn Pub), further captured the part that Moore, Hurst and Peters had played in that moment after the triumph of 1966, as the England captain was carried aloft by his team-mates.

DID YOU KNOW?

Do West Ham play better against top teams? Between 1994-2003 they beat Liverpool just four times (in 20 league games), Arsenal three times, and Man Utd only once.

The close season witnessed the departure of long-serving former skipper Steve Potts (after a 19-year association), Paul Kitson, Shaka Hislop, Gary Charles and Craig Forrest. The latter two were released due to medical reasons, the others on free transfers. After just a handful of appearances, Aussie Hayden Foxe ended his protracted saga by joining Portsmouth for a fee of around £450,000. Thus, like Hislop, he once again linked up with Harry Redknapp who had taken over the reins at Fratton Park.

With a squad left thin by a restricted budget and so many departures, Roeder opted to sign replacements on free transfers or on loan. After impressing for the Republic of Ireland in the summer's World Cup finals, central defender Gary Breen was signed for free after failing to agree a new contract with cash-strapped Coventry. Ex-Manchester United goalkeeper Raimond Van Der Gouw likewise came on a free as cover for James, as did French Under-18 international striker Youssef Sofiane, who was considered one to watch. Edouard Cisse had made over 100 appearances for Paris St Germain: the French Under-21 international arrived on a one-year loan. A fourth international arrival was Trinidad and Tobago forward Brent Rahim.

Having thought they were leaving, Nigel Winterburn and John Moncur were given new one-year contracts. Peter Brabrook, a 1964 FA Cup winner, retired after a successful career as a coach with the Hammers Youth Academy, to be replaced by another former player, Kevin Keen. The death from cancer of 1960s full-back John Charles, aged 57, was a shock to all, but it was followed in October by the loss of former secretary/chief executive Eddie Chapman, aged 79, who had served the club for 49 years.

During the summer, James, Cole, Sinclair, and Carrick had all been on international duty at one level or another for England, as well as Dailly (Scotland) and Breen, and many others at Upton Park. Yet the team made the worst possible start, earning just two points from their opening six games. It was not until late September that the first win was recorded, at Chelsea, thanks in part to two goals from Di Canio, one with just minutes to go. It was only on the road that the pressure of winning was lifted, as further victories arrived at Sunderland and Fulham. In the Worthington Cup, a penalty shoot-out win at Chesterfield only led to a home defeat by Second Division Oldham, managed by ex-Hammer Ian Dowie.

Those three away wins pushed Roeder's side up to 14th with a quarter of the season gone, but by Christmas they were bottom and the critics were out in force, not only in the tabloids but also at the AGM earlier in December. The adage that no Premiership team bottom on Christmas Day has ever escaped relegation was relentlessly repeated. Whilst his agent reportedly gave West Ham until the end of the month to open new contract negotiations, press speculation linked Di Canio with Manchester United. Sir Alex Ferguson insisted: 'Last season? Yes, but a bid would not be justified now.' West Ham refused to open contract discussions until they are in 'safer waters'. One tabloid believed James would be going to Old Trafford for £3 million, whilst another claimed Cole would join Liverpool for £8 million. The only actual business saw Labant rejoining Sparta Prague less than a year after his arrival.

The injury list included Hutchison, Lomas, Breen, Kanoute (who went to America to see a re-hab specialist for a groin strain), Di Canio (back in Italy to clear up a knee injury), Carrick and others. Roeder was forced to play Ian Pearce up front as a makeshift striker until the winter transfer window opened, when he signed controversial Leeds midfielder Lee Bowyer, long-term target Les Ferdinand (both for nominal fees until the end of the season) and 33-year-old Fulham defender Rufus Brevett on a free to replace Winterburn, who required an operation on a wrist injury. Leaving were Rahim for Luton, Laurent Courtois to France, and Titi Camara to Saudi Arabia on loan until the end of the season.

It was not until January, in the FA Cup – after twice trailing to Nottingham Forest – that the first home win was recorded, and later that month in the League. The thirteenth home League game proved to be unlucky for visiting Blackburn who, after taking the lead, conceded Di Canio's penalty before Defoe dramatically won the game in the last minute. Sandwiched between these two victories were a home draw and two away defeats (against London rivals), but nothing could prepare anyone, including the 9,000 travelling fans, for the six-goal televised fourth round battering at Old Trafford – the Hammers' worst ever FA Cup defeat.

In February, on the tenth anniversary of Bobby Moore's death, it was revealed that the England captain had been gagged by the Foreign Office when questioned about the Bogota bracelet incident in the Colombian capital prior to the 1970 World Cup in Mexico. Although obviously the victim of a Latin American plot, staged to undermine England's World Cup campaign, Bobby was naturally anxious to be officially cleared of any involvement, but was told not to protest too much as it might provoke a diplomatic incident. Suppressed for 33 years by the British Government's Public Records

Office, it seemed Bobby had been warned to 'lay very low indeed' as the courts debated whether or not he would face proceedings following his release from 'house arrest' to rejoin his team-mates in Mexico. Now, with the Hammers facing a desperate fight against the drop, it was no surprise that the legacy of the great man – who many fans never actually saw play – was in everyone's thoughts. Many posed the question 'What has gone wrong?'

With the demise of Wembley – which had for so long been like the maestro's second home during his 108 caps – England played international fixtures around the country. Eriksson's travelling circus came to Upton Park for a friendly against Australia. David James was West Ham's sole representative, with Joe Cole confined to the bench. It was only Cole, Defoe, newly blooded Glen Johnson, and at times the charismatic Di Canio who earned the fans' approval for their club performances. Carrick's skills were sadly missed, repeated injuries contributing to his loss of form.

Matters were not helped, however, by Hutchison's talk of a possible return to Sunderland, or by Breen's remarks after Ireland's victory over Christian Dailly's Scotland: 'I love being in a team that's organised as opposed to what's at home. Ireland are a well-drilled team, we all know what we're supposed to be doing. At times, it's difficult at West Ham because there's a lot of things going on and I don't know if everyone there knows what they're supposed to be doing!' Likewise, a fuming Di Canio, substituted in the win at West Brom, blasted his boss. The Italian returned to his homeland for a fitness assessment in early March and only returned for the last two fixtures, when he came off the substitutes' bench to score each time.

The win at the Hawthorns sparked a stirring run in which the Hammers were defeated only once in their final eleven fixtures – at fellow strugglers Bolton. Those six wins and four draws was form that should have ensured safety if it had come earlier, but it was the 0-1 defeat at Bolton that was the crucial result in a troubled season. Although the Hammers' late results could not be faulted, their fate was always out of their own hands. Aston Villa, Fulham, Leeds and Bolton were also in the dogfight to avoid the final relegation spot – Sunderland and West Brom having been doomed for some time – and all of them kept picking up enough points to keep them above West Ham.

The pressure was intense on everyone at the club. Following the Easter Monday home victory over Middlesbrough, Roeder collapsed in his office and was rushed to hospital. The next day it was confirmed that he had suffered a blockage of a blood vessel in his brain. He was now out of intensive care but would take no further part in club matters. He required neurosurgery on a lesion in his brain, but was expected to make a complete recovery.

For the final three matches Trevor Brooking agreed to stand in as caretaker manager. In his first of these, a late Kanoute goal earned victory at Manchester City. In the second, it was like a story from a *Boys Own* comic as Di Canio, in an emotional but glorious goodbye, came off the bench to bag the winner against fourth-placed Chelsea. The normally phlegmatic Brooking was delighted, but gave due credit to Roeder after the first win: 'Glenn already had everything mapped out for the week so the players and the staff deserve a pat on the back.' After the second he added: 'This result means a lot to everyone. I always felt we had a chance today but for many weeks now I've always thought that the trip to Birmingham City will be the hardest game of the lot.'

The last Sunday of the season at a nervy St Andrews saw long-suffering supporters glued to their radios and mobiles for news from elsewhere. They were boosted when Les Ferdinand nodded in Cole's left-wing cross after 65 minutes, but depressed when City scored twice near the end. Di Canio crowned his final appearance with a far-post header to salvage a point. It was not enough, as Bolton had beaten Middlesbrough 2-1, sealing the fate of the Hammers, who became the first Premiership team ever to be relegated with 42 points since it was reduced to twenty clubs in 1995-96. Had West Ham beaten Birmingham they would have gone down on 44!

Ever the diplomat, Brooking said: 'It's been a three-week burst for me and I'm pleased with the quality and character shown by the lads during my time. It's certainly a strange situation to go down with 42 points.' Others were more scathing. One tabloid said: 'West Ham are not the third worst team in the Premiership. Therein lies the embarrassment, the despair and the shame.' Another wrote: 'The list of star names is the most damming indictment of where West Ham find themselves now – the most talented squad to be relegated in the Premiership's 11 seasons.' Those thoughts, and others, summed up the feelings of all Hammers supporters as the inquest began. But at that moment, few fully realised the ramifications of life in the lower division.

Match of the Season 2002-03

Bolton 1 West Ham 0

Premiership, 19 April 2003

The root cause of West Ham's relegation in 2003 was their abysmal home form before Christmas. Losses against fellow likely strugglers

Charlton, West Brom, Birmingham, Leeds, and 1-1 draws against Bolton and Fulham, put great strain on the team and the manager. Some, with hindsight, said the writing was on the wall in the first home game, against Arsenal, following Kanoute's dire penalty miss which would have wrapped things up, surely, with the Hammers already leading 2-1 and only minutes to play.

From early November, seventeenth was the highest the side achieved. In late February a sequence of good results started which raised hopes. Yet it was the loss at The Reebok on Easter Saturday that said the tide of ill-fortune could not be stemmed. If instead of a 1-0 Bolton victory the Hammers could have drawn, their final points total would have been 43 and the Trotters' 42. Consequently, Sam Allardyce's team would have been relegated.

Apart from a stunning Jay-Jay Okocha run from inside his own half, which he finished off with a swerving 20-yarder in the 38th minute, there was perhaps little to choose between the two sides in some ways. But in others, in the view of non-partisan observers, there were fundamental differences. Bolton seemed to have more spirit and passion – until the Hammers raised themselves in the second half – as well as more verve and power in midfield. The loss of Carrick for the last few matches due to injury had proved crucial. Things might have been different if Kanoute had converted an early chance, or even one of the other opportunities presented to him, or finally if Defoe's twelve-yard snapshot had not flown agonisingly wide towards the end.

The end result, however, was that it was yet another six-pointer that had slipped away. With just four matches to go it gave Bolton a six-point advantage. The situation was compounded by victories on the same day for Birmingham, Fulham and Aston Villa, who also had a six-point cushion.

In many ways as worrying for the Hammers was the rumpus that ensued following the dismissal of Ian Pearce for a straight red card offence, and the virtual open warfare between players from both sides after the final whistle. Hammers captain Cole squared up to a Bolton player and a punch appeared to be thrown. Cole's anger continued out of sight, and he was alleged to have 'kicked out and damaged the tunnel'. Brevett was seen in altercation with a police officer as he left the field.

If there had been any positives to be taken from the defeat, they were lost in the final pandemonium. The long journey back home was made worse by it being 'a bad day at the office'.

NATIONWIDE DIVISION 1	**2003-04**
Division 1	4th (Play-offs)
Carling Cup	3rd Round
FA Cup	5th Round

West Ham United had been relegated. That was a fact of life that the club would have to live with for at least twelve months.

Within 24 hours of relegation being confirmed, Jermain Defoe's agent advised him to demand a transfer, which endeared him to no one and was rejected. Relegation meant financial cutbacks to a club needing to service debts incurred by the building of the Dr Martens West Stand and facing a wage bill in the top ten in the Premiership. The club released out of contract Di Canio, Bowyer, Breen, Moncur, Winterburn, Minto, Cisse, and Van Der Gouw. Les Ferdinand signed for Leicester, and Schemmel for Portsmouth.

It was not only the players who felt the squeeze. At an Extraordinary General Meeting to pass amendments to ensure that financial limits under Company law were not breached, three directors announced they would take a 50 per cent wage cut until promotion was achieved. Despite assurances that the club could survive within the constraints of the Nationwide League, a vociferous minority of shareholders demanded that the board resign or take on new members prepared to invest, or inject more of their own money to ensure no key players were sold. These mystery backers, often domiciled offshore for tax purposes, eventually disappeared. Nobody came forward with an offer remotely realistic to the actual value of the club. There was talk of issuing more shares, but that would obviously dilute the value of those already in existence. Some views expressed on fanzine-style websites and in correspondence to shareholders provoked writs for defamation.

James, Sinclair, Cole, Bywater and Johnson were all on England duty for the seniors or Under-21s over the summer. Cole, a sub, scored his first England goal, a match-winning 25-yard free-kick in a 2-1 friendly win at Leicester over Serbia-Montenegro, but was then confined to the bench for a Euro 2004 qualifier.

In June, Glenn Roeder declared: 'I've never thought of packing it in. There's unfinished business and I expect to be up and running by the time we return to pre-season training.' A month later his doctors gave him the all-clear, but ex-Hammers' midfielder Marc-Vivien Foe collapsed and died on the pitch during Cameroon's Confederation Cup semi-final against Colombia.

In July the first of West Ham's stars departed. A £6 million deal took Under-21 defender Glen Johnson to Chelsea, following Roman Abramovich's takeover. It was amazing business for the Hammers, as this latest breakthrough from the Academy was only eighteen, had made his debut six months earlier, and made just sixteen first-team appearances. Although Trevor Sinclair pledged his future to West Ham – 'Just because it hasn't worked out this season doesn't mean I'm going to be spitting my dummy out and submitting another transfer request' – he then signed for Manchester City for £2.5 million.

Roeder was forced to seek bargain-basement deals. Robert Lee signed a one-year contract, and Wimbledon's David Connolly – 36 caps for the Republic of Ireland – signed for a modest £285,000.

In August Kanoute went to Tottenham in a swap deal that saw winger Matthew Etherington, plus a £3.5 million cash adjustment, arrive at Upton Park. Joe Cole became the latest Chelsea import. He cost £6.6 million, saying he would not have signed a new contract once his present one expired a year later: 'I felt I'd gone as far as I could at West Ham as a player.'

Over the previous fifteen years or so, although producing great players through the Academy – Ince, Ferdinand, Lampard, Johnson, Cole – it was usually after they had left Upton Park that their talents truly blossomed. It was a timely reminder to those who had watched the Hammers over the decades that West Ham were once again 'a selling club'. However, on this occasion it was dictated by financial necessity. Had the club hung on to Cole, he could have left in 2004 under a Bosman (as Sol Campbell had done from Spurs).

Neil Mellor signed on a season-long loan from Liverpool, and his inclusion in the starting eleven for the first League fixture at Preston upset Connolly, who replaced Mellor and scored the winner after Defoe had equalised Preston's two-minute opener. The next day Connolly vented his anger in the Sunday papers, claiming Mellor had been 'promised' a starting place.

West Ham struggled to overcome Rushden & Diamonds in the Carling Cup, then drew 0-0 against Sheffield United in their first home League match. Making his debut was Kevin Horlock, signed for £300,000 from Manchester City. Horlock had been a youth-team player at Upton Park a decade earlier.

Two pages in the Sheffield United programme were taken by Chairman Terence Brown to explain the background to the summer exodus. The club needed to repay £8 million in loans, while relegation had reduced its income by £20 million. That meant £28 million had to be recouped in savings and transfers: the wage-bill had been reduced by £10 million and £18 million netted in player sales. Weeks earlier, prior to Johnson's sale, Brown had been offered £500,000 for Sinclair, £1.5 million each for Defoe and Johnson, and £2 million for Cole, on the basis that the club would 'save the wages'. The

Abramovich deal for Johnson was the turning point, and in Brown's words 'I received no further frivolous telephone calls after Glen signed for Chelsea'. Stressing the club's family traditions, Brown added that to put the club into administration would have hurt many local suppliers who have supported it for generations.

The £18 million received for departing players had undoubtedly helped in paying off creditors who might otherwise have forced the club into administration or receivership. In which case the Boleyn Ground would probably have been sold, to house a supermarket or retail outlet, and requiring the Hammers to ground-share.

The chairman's logic could not be faulted, but once again the familiar chants of 'Sack the Board' resounded inside and outside the stadium. Eighteen thousand season ticket holders showed their commitment to the club, and a gate of 28,972 had turned up for the Blades' visit. But the ramifications following the trip to Millmoor for the third League game were far reaching. Roeder's team lost 0-1 to a side that would struggle all season. Three days earlier, in England's friendly against Croatia, James kept a clean sheet (in his 45 minutes' action) and former Hammers Lampard, Cole, Sinclair and Ferdinand were all picked. In November Johnson would win his first full cap.

West Ham's fall from grace could not be starker. Roeder's contract was terminated. Once again Trevor Brooking was asked to temporarily fill the void. Among the names canvassed to replace Roeder were Oldham boss Iain Dowie, Stuart Pearce, Steve Cotterill, Steve Coppell, Nigel Winterburn, and former Middlesbrough boss Bryan Robson. There were 50 applications for the job.

Brooking's second reign began with wins over Bradford City and at Ipswich. With the players reportedly responding to Brooking's style, 'the legend' became the fans' favourite to take on the job, but his other commitments and television work, coupled with the long-term pressure of being a football manager, meant that the required lifestyle was not something Brooking would contemplate.

The board asked Reading if they could approach manager Alan Pardew, but got a firm no. Pardew promptly resigned, but that too was rejected. Royals' chairman John Madejski said: 'We've got a contract with the manager and I believe it should be honoured. While he would be allowed to talk to a Premiership club, we certainly won't give him permission to talk to one of our main Division One rivals.' Pardew responded by walking out on Reading, who were due at Upton Park the following Saturday. Brooking made it three out of three with a 1-0 win over the managerless Royals, and a 3-0 win at Crewe lifted the Hammers to second.

Despite defeat at Gillingham, the Brooking bandwagon rolled on unbeaten until mid-October, when Pardew, after serving six weeks' 'gardening leave' – the price extracted by Madejski, in addition to £380,000 and an undertaking that no other Reading staff would leave – took charge. Brooking's caretaker role, which he expected to last for ten days, had extended to eight weeks.

Pardew did not enjoy a happy honeymoon, with three draws against mid-table opposition and a loss at White Hart Lane in the Carling Cup. The fans had expected something more, having witnessed the Brooking factor. Hayden Mullins was Pardew's first signing, from Crystal Palace for £600,000, followed by striker Brian Deane on a free from Leicester City.

Five straight draws meant the loss of ten points, but that was nothing compared with the visit of West Brom, who were three down in twenty minutes yet fought back to claim a 4-3 victory that was compounded by the dismissal of Defoe, who received a five-match ban. Even beforehand, West Ham had amassed fewer home points than any other team in the top nine and it was only the away form that kept them in the top six.

In mid-November Pardew signed Nottingham Forest's Marlon Harewood for £500,000, knowing he needed more firepower with the likely departure of Defoe in January's transfer window. Injuries were another worry. Of the twenty League and League Cup games played, Carrick had appeared in just twelve, Hutchison fourteen (including six as a substitute), Brevett (broken ankle) in three, and Lomas (after ankle surgery) none. Yellow and red cards had also brought suspensions, which meant the same XI was never picked in consecutive matches.

One of the plusses was the emergence of Anton Ferdinand (Rio's younger brother) from the Academy. The contribution of Tony Carr, Youth Academy Director, in unearthing local talent was immense, as was that of Jimmy Hampson, Director of Youth Development.

Trevor Brooking was appointed by the FA as Director of Football. At last the powers in Soho Square had the vision to select a 'football man' to such a vital post. His work at Sport England, his spells as a caretaker manager, his playing record for West Ham and England, his analytical brain and the fact that in all his years in football he won friends, never enemies, made him the right person for the job. In the Queen's Birthday Honours of June 2004 Brooking was knighted, joining Sir Geoff Hurst, which meant the Hammers were the first club to have two former players so honoured.

It was not until his eighth match that Pardew enjoyed his first win, 4-0 against high-flying Wigan. The elation was tempered by the visitors being a goal down after four minutes, then conceding an own-goal and having a man dismissed either side of the interval. Only then did Harewood net twice to open his scoring account.

DID YOU KNOW?

In 1998-99, West Ham led Wimbledon 3-0 at home after 27 minutes – but lost 3-4.
In 2003-04, West Ham led West Brom 3-0 at home after 18 minutes – but lost 3-4.

An away point at table-topping West Brom suggested Pardew's side had turned the corner, only for Stoke – with the worst away record in the division – to inflict another home defeat.

A stormy AGM in early December saw Chairman Brown deny that the sale of Defoe (probably to Old Trafford), Carrick (to Spurs) and James (to Celtic) was inevitable. Defoe's contribution was to get a third red card and yet another ban. Although normally adopting a low-key profile, in the New Year the chairman gave an interview with *Hammers News*. He candidly spoke of his early life, his boyhood support of the Hammers, but more importantly of the events and decisions of recent years, in respect of relegation, finances, Redknapp, other managers, fan abuse, as well as the future.

When David Seaman retired, Manchester City signed James for around £1.5 million, giving Stephen Bywater his chance. Defender Ian Pearce joined Fulham, with Andy Melville and a cash adjustment coming in the opposite direction. Pardew used some of the money to sign the Wimbledon midfield pair of Nigel Reo-Coker (an Under-21 international) and Adam Nowland for undisclosed fees. They were soon joined by team-mate Jobi McAnuff, although Neil Mellor returned to Anfield through injury.

Deciding to 'change the chemistry', in January Pardew replaced Paul Goddard as his assistant with Peter Grant, coach at Bournemouth. Having played over 500 games for Celtic, Grant won Scottish League and FA Cup medals, as well as two international caps, and was known to Pardew when at Reading.

With the transfer window closing, Defoe joined Tottenham for £7 million, with Bobby Zamora moving to Upton Park. The former Brighton striker had scored the only goal against West Ham in the Carling Cup two months earlier. Zamora had once been a youth-team player at Upton Park, and thus realised his dream of playing for the club he had supported as a boy.

Despite indifferent form in the League after Christmas, the Hammers progressed to the fifth round of the FA Cup with wins at Wigan and doomed Premiership strugglers Wolves. They then drew at Fulham, who were lucky to survive, but in the replay the Cottagers scored twice in a three-minute spell, adding a last-minute third, to claim a plum tie at Old Trafford.

These Cup exploits spurred the Hammers to an eight-match unbeaten League run, although four draws meant more lost points.

Only the play-off places were now attainable, but four successive away defeats – the last to Iain Dowie's revitalised Crystal Palace, where Connolly received two yellow cards – looked to have put even this beyond reach. Three wins in the final four games, followed by Deane's last-minute headed equaliser at Wigan, cemented fourth spot, while denying the last play-off slot to Wigan. It went to Palace instead.

In the semi-final first leg, Joe Royle's Ipswich seized a one-goal advantage. The second leg saw Etherington level the tie soon after the interval, before skipper Dailly sealed the trip to the Millennium Stadium, although he was fortunate not to concede a penalty. Five months earlier nobody could have forecast that it would be Dowie's Eagles against Pardew's Hammers at Cardiff, but that was the scenario as Palace overcame Sunderland after a penalty shoot-out. Ex-Hammer Michael Hughes converted the vital penalty.

For the loyal and vociferous Hammers contingent who made the pilgrimage to the superb Millennium Stadium the match turned out to be an anticlimax. Chances were few but the Hammers seemed to get stage fright on the big occasion and lost 0-1. Palace were hardly world-beaters, but they knuckled down to the task with an honesty reminiscent of their manager, whilst the Hammers on the day proved they just weren't good enough, lacking the passion and will to win that marks out the extraordinary from the rest, whatever the division. As one fan remarked: 'There was an air of inevitability about it, and we've seen that a few times this season.'

Match of the Season 2003-04

West Ham 3 West Brom 4

Division 1, 8 November 2003

Although unbeaten at home, a run of five draws (three at home, two away) had dropped the Hammers to sixth. Of those five draws, only opponents Norwich were in the leading pack, the rest in mid-table. Now, having seen his team take a three-goal lead against second-placed West Brom, Pardew must have thought that he would be rewarded with his first win. Defoe had cut in to fire home from an acute angle, and two goals from Brian Deane – one a tap in and the other a header from Defoe's quickly taken free-kick – had the home fans buzzing.

But as has been proved on many previous occasions, being a supporter of the Hammers is not always good for one's health. As Pardew said afterwards: 'I felt that at 3-0 we took our foot off the gas a bit and I don't expect that. We will either look back on this day as a negative or a positive one. I know how I will look back on it and I know what I want to see as a reaction to it.'

He was speaking after his team had somehow lost 3-4. Albion, who had conceded just thirteen goals in their previous sixteen games, had been 'pathetic at the start and defended worse than schoolboys' according to their manager Gary Megson. He had been apoplectic at three down, but could only pinch himself at the end, after his team had gone top of the table.

Dailly and James hesitated over a through pass, allowing Hulse to poke the ball home. The same player then blasted in from 30 yards as Dailly once again failed to clear. Just before the interval Defoe lunged high at an opponent, and having earlier been booked for diving, now received his second yellow – harshly according to his manager. With the Hammers down to ten men, Albion attacked with venom after the break. From a corner, Deane turned from hero to villain, slicing an own-goal whilst attempting to clear. And when James failed to punch cleanly from yet another corner, substitute Hughes volleyed home. For Deane it was re-living hell. Just before his transfer from Leicester two weeks earlier, he had watched a three-goal Foxes lead surrendered to Wolves.

Pardew perhaps summed up the turn of events: 'There are players here who are very well paid, on Premiership money, and I expected a lot better from them than that. I expected leadership out there, not the signs you saw today from a team who were relegated last season. I thought the senior players should have shown more than they did after a junior member of the team was sent off. I'm not going to get myself in a position where I lose faith in my ability in terms of what I can give this team. I certainly won't do that. The players will either come with me, or I will get rid of them.'

This would prove to be one of the low points of the season, but fortunately the defeat would not prove fatal. Instead, the season's nadir would be saved for the capitulation at Cardiff's Millennium Stadium months later.

Newer Hammers supporters might not have endured the identical transformation when Wimbledon were the visitors in 1998. But for older fans, further examples can be found within the elite era covered by this book. Home games against Stoke in 1967 and 1969 spring to mind and are still impressed on my memory. The adage 'a leopard can't change his spots' might spring to mind, but could the same be said of football clubs?

COCA-COLA CHAMPIONSHIP 2004-05

Championship	6th (Play-off winners; Promoted)
Carling Cup	3rd Round
FA Cup	4th Round

Just 71 days after losing at Cardiff, the Hammers kicked off the new season at The Walkers Stadium, Leicester, on the first Saturday in August. The pressure was on Alan Pardew and his players, as well as everybody else at Upton Park, because this was the second and final season of 'parachute' payments from the Premiership paymasters. Failure this time would result in further cut-backs.

Although once again among the favourites to gain automatic promotion, the grim realities of life outside the top flight were perhaps even more apparent. No longer were the likes of Carrick, Defoe, James and Pearce – regular members of the team for so long – now available, but even lesser-lights David Connolly and Kevin Horlock had left after yet another pruning session.

Much was thus expected of Etherington, Harewood, Mullins and Brevett, who had arrived during 2003, as well as of Reo-Coker, Zamora, Nowland and Melville, who had joined since the beginning of the year, and especially the experienced Dailly, Lomas, Hutchison and Repka, the last of the high-earning stalwarts from Premiership days. Youth was represented in the form of Bywater and Anton Ferdinand, of whom much was now expected. The squad had been further strengthened by the arrival of Luke Chadwick, Sergei Rebrov, Jimmy Walker and the 'jewel in the crown' Teddy Sheringham. All had been signed on free transfers, except Carl Fletcher (£280,000). Despite the parlous state of the club's finances, the Hammers' wage bill was reported as being the highest outside the Premiership and three or four times larger than any of their rivals. Within the budgetary restraints imposed upon him, the playing staff could now be deemed the choice of Alan Pardew.

After an undefeated pre-season, the Hammers got off to a reasonably good start. A draw at Leicester, who for all but seventeen minutes played with ten men, was a foretaste of what was to come – an inability to finish off the opposition. Home wins over Reading, Burnley, and Rotherham, plus a draw against promotion rivals Ipswich, and away wins at Crewe and Sheffield United, together with a draw at Derby, ensured a top-six place with a quarter of the season played. In the same period a home reverse to Wigan, coupled with 1-2 losses at financially stricken Coventry and winless Nottingham Forest, showed that promotion was far from automatic.

Worryingly, an injury to Dailly would endure all season, in spite of optimistic announcements that he would be back in action by

Christmas. Nor did Lomas, Melville, Brevett, Rebrov and Zamora stamp their authority by playing regularly, either through loss of form or injuries.

Hard-won progress had been made in the Carling Cup with home wins over Southend and Notts County, both two divisions lower, but was halted by a solitary goal at under-strength Chelsea. The frustration of Hammers fans was heightened, not only by seeing Lampard's penalty saved and a late header thumping the Blues' woodwork, but by former heroes Lampard, Cole and Johnson about to power Chelsea to their first title in 50 years. Realists were reluctant to point out that but for Abramovich's millions West Ham United might have gone bust.

The defence seemed to be in a constant state of flux. Although Walker had acquitted himself well in the Carling Cup, Bywater was first choice in the League. Yet by Christmas Repka was the only other ever-present defender. The introduction of Malky MacKay, for £300,000, and Callum Davenport, on loan from Tottenham, looked to have solved the central defensive problem. MacKay had been captain of Norwich the previous season and in the absence of Daily had the experience to guide the younger players through, whilst the talented Davenport showed why his former club, Nottingham Forest, had extracted such a large fee from Spurs. The honeymoon did not last long, however, as first Davenport was injured, on international duty, before being recalled to White Hart Lane, and MacKay missed ten games through injury.

To fill the gaps Pardew was forced once more to take players on loan. Darren Powell (Crystal Palace) and Chris Powell (Charlton) made temporary moves across London. Tottenham's Mauricio Taricco signed on a free but his career at Upton Park was the shortest on record: 27 minutes into his debut at Millwall a hamstring injury forced his retirement. His offer to tear up his contract and quit was accepted. The 0-1 defeat against the old enemy was a bitter pill to swallow. Midfielder Gavin Williams cost £250,000 from Yeovil and was heralded as one for the future.

Wheeling and dealing was the order of the day for outgoing transfers too. In August Jobi McAnuff left for Cardiff in a £500,000 deal, and in November Adam Nowland (£250,000) to Nottingham Forest. Both players were sacrificed for the sake of Pardew's team-building. Loan deals involving Hutchison, to Nottingham Forest and later Leeds, did not materialise. It was reported that the out-of-favour and injury-prone midfielder continued to earn £30,000 per week at Upton Park.

In late October the board announced that the PLC company had made a pre-tax profit of £11.8 million for the year ended 31 May

2004. Chairman Terence Brown stated: 'Following the devastating financial effects of relegation, the group's financial results are a little short of extraordinary. We shall continue to contend with the financial consequence of relegation.' He added that net bank borrowings stood at £33.8 million. Although learning that the club was solvent, the AGM in December was once again a stormy affair with raised tempers from a number of shareholders who demanded that money be spent on bringing in new players during the forthcoming transfer window. The tabloids linked several businessmen and consortiums with takeover ambitions, but these were usually prompted by hopes of buying the club for a knockdown price on account of its fragile financial situation.

By New Year's Day the Hammers had never been higher than fourth. They languished in sixth spot, some dozen points behind leaders Ipswich and Wigan. Although beating teams in the top half of the table, it was their failure away from home against struggling sides – Cardiff City (1-4), Plymouth (1-1), Preston (1-2) and bottom of the table Rotherham (2-2) that infuriated many supporters. This was compounded by the home loss to Brighton (0–1), who rode their luck, and Leeds (1-1), whose controversial injury-time penalty equaliser was hard to swallow.

Pardew was under mounting pressure, with stories of his being replaced and others speculating about his deteriorating relationship with his players. There was talk of bids for strikers Harewood and Zamora, but the form of the injury-prone Etherington and Sheringham had the crowds enthralled. The team took on a new perspective when the winger was on song, whilst the 38-year-old, who was expected to support the main strike-force of Harewood (thirteen goals) and Zamora (five), was by early April the leading scorer with nineteen League goals from 22 starts and seven as a substitute. The veteran had been a revelation, despite being injured at times, and his enthusiasm was an inspiration to all.

Although disposing of Premiership strugglers Norwich in the FA Cup, the Hammers in the next round lost out on penalties after a replay at Sheffield United, who thus added to their January League win at the same venue.

Three straight defeats, followed by home draws against Crewe and Leicester, meant the Hammers slipped to eighth, thereby heaping more pressure on the manager. The club vehemently denied rumours that the FA's Sir Trevor Brooking was set to return as caretaker boss. 'To suggest I could cope with two jobs is ludicrous,' said the Upton Park legend. Other stories circulated, such as the only reason Pardew was not fired was that the club could not afford to pay up his contract.

West Ham's favourite son, Bobby Moore, kisses the World Cup at Wembley in 1966

Alan Taylor scores his second FA Cup final goal against Fulham, 1975

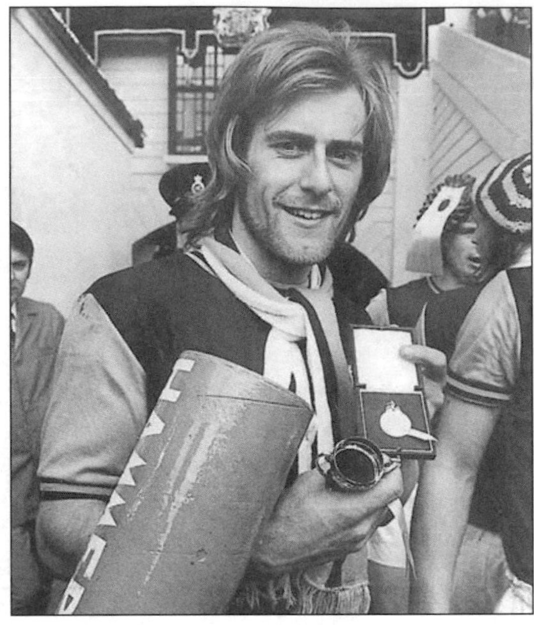

Graham Paddon shows off his FA Cup winners medal

Crowds celebrate with the players after the 1975 FA Cup final win

Billy Jennings lunges for the ball against Sheffield United

Frank Lampard shoots against QPR at Loftus Road

Mervyn Day saves against Arsenal at Highbury. Brian Kidd lurks for spills

Clyde Best (hidden by Tommy Taylor) has just scored against Sheffield United

Keith Robson celebrates his goal against Liverpool at Anfield

Keith Coleman takes a long-distance view of this pitch invasion

Alan Taylor is congratulated by Trevor Brooking

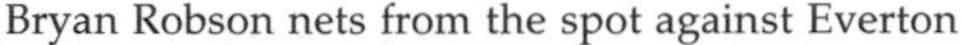
Bryan Robson nets from the spot against Everton

Alan Curbishley and Frank Lampard (Snr) lead this training run

The late John Lyall gives a pep talk to the troops

Bryan Robson receives an award from Chairman Reg Pratt

The West Ham golf team – Taylor, Day, Ferguson, Robson and Brooking

Manchester United's Stepney watches as Martin Buchan clobbers Bobby Gould

Billy Jennings rests his head during the Charity Shield with Derby in a heatwave

Bryan 'Pop' Robson has just scored against Charlton

John McDowell scores the Hammers' fourth goal against Newcastle in March 1979

Ray Stewart scores from the spot against Aston Villa in March 1980

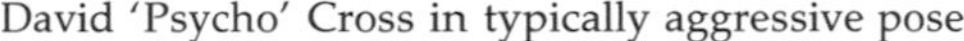
David 'Psycho' Cross in typically aggressive pose

Bloodied but unbowed – the inspirational Billy Bonds

The West Ham squad pose with the 1980 FA Cup

The joyous Hammers show off the 1980 FA Cup from the balcony

Van der Elst celebrates his goal against Aston Villa in March 1982

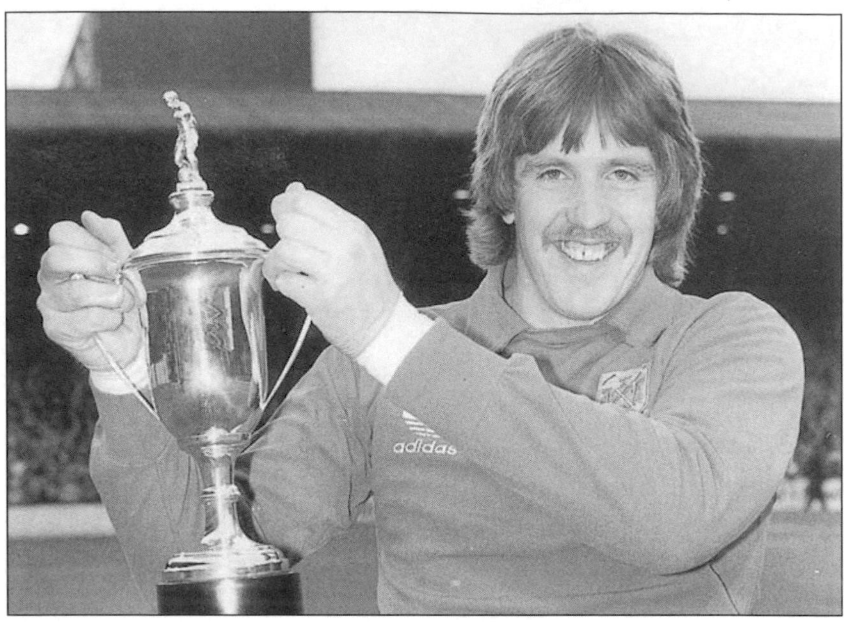

Phil Parkes and his Hammer of the Year Trophy 1980-81

Alan Devonshire scores goal No 4 against Chelsea in February 1981

Geoff Pike on the Chadwell Heath 'assault course'

More police than spectators at the home match with Castilla

Training under the East Stand

Referee Clive Thomas forces the West Ham wall back against Newcastle

Phil Parkes, Billy Bonds and Jimmy Neighbour in Christmas hats

Billy Bonds unmasks Santa as Ray Stewart

Geoff Pike celebrates his goal at home to Liverpool

Alvin Martin with his Hammer of the Year award 1982-83

Julian Dicks heads clear against Watford at Upton Park

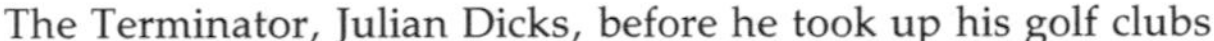

The Terminator, Julian Dicks, before he took up his golf clubs

John Hartson fires past Arsenal's Petit and Keown

Trevor Sinclair in action against Middlesbrough

Harry Redknapp welcomes Ian Wright to Upton Park

Arguably the most skilful Hammer ever – Paolo di Canio

England international defender Rio Ferdinand

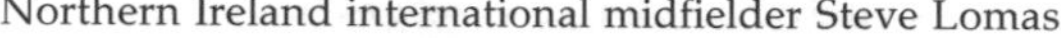
Northern Ireland international midfielder Steve Lomas

Bobby Zamora's second goal at Ipswich (2004-05 play-off semi-final)

West Ham fans at Ipswich show their delight at the 2-0 win (2004-05 play-off)

Chris Powell clears from Ipswich's Shefki Kuqi (2004-05 play-off semi-final)

Steve Bywater, a late sub, saves as Preston's Agyemang lurks (play-off final)

Matthew Etherington against Preston in the play-off final, May 2005

Bobby Zamora (left) scores the promotion-winning goal at Cardiff, May 2005

Entering Upton Park after the 2004-05 play-off victory parade

Bobby Zamora, Nigel Reo-Coker and the 2004-05 play-off trophy

Dean Ashton and Liverpool's Steven Gerrard (FA Cup final 2006)

Paul Konchesky's cross puts West Ham 3-2 ahead (FA Cup final 2006)

Hammers' Teddy Sheringham nets in the penalty shoot-out (FA Cup final 2006)

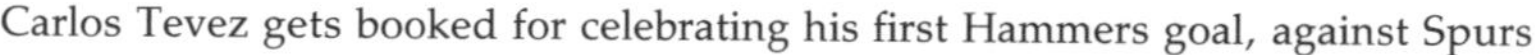
Carlos Tevez gets booked for celebrating his first Hammers goal, against Spurs

Tevez nets from the spot at Blackburn to start West Ham's revival (March 2007)

Zamora's lob inflicts Arsenal's first defeat at the Emirates Stadium (April 2007)

Mark Noble during West Ham's 0-3 defeat at Sheffield United (April 2007)

Luis Boa Morte opens the scoring against Wigan (April 2007)

Yossi Benayoun fires the second goal at Wigan (April 2007)

Tevez in the thick of it against Bolton at Upton Park (May 2007)

Lucas Neill in the vital match at Old Trafford (May 2007)

Carlos Tevez scores the winning goal at Manchester United (May 2007)

DID YOU KNOW?

They say the final League table never lies. In 2003-04, West Ham finished 12 points off automatic promotion. A year later they were 14 points short. Hooray for play-offs!

It was during this period that MacKay was once again injured, virtually forcing Pardew into pairing two of his youngest players, Ferdinand and Ward, in central defence. Both were just twenty, but proved to be the answer to the problem that had beset the team for most of the season. The experienced Repka and dependable Chris Powell now played either side of the Academy graduates. Another vital change Pardew made was to install Jimmy Walker in goal. He also signed from Wolves, for an initial £10,000, Shaun Newton – no stranger to promotion challenges. The new-look Hammers now had a purpose about them. With just one defeat (against Sunderland – the champions) in their final ten matches, and with other results going their way, they scraped into sixth place and into the play-offs.

With Sheringham again injured, the play-offs saw Zamora paired up front with Harewood. The former Spurs man came into his own and finally made the sceptics eat their words, scoring four vital goals in the three games that would secure promotion.

Match of the Season 2004-05

West Ham 1 Preston 0

Championship, Play-off final, 30 May 2005

Some might say the Hammers were lucky to be back at the Millennium Stadium for a second time, as their League record of 21 wins, ten draws and perhaps more pertinent fifteen defeats, was not the form of Premiership hopefuls. But the nature of the play-off system makes such statistics irrelevant, providing a team finishes in the top six and then triumphs in the semis. Ipswich, this time a dozen points better off than Pardew's men, knew what it was like to fall at the final hurdle for a second time in two years. To be at Cardiff was everything in the bitter end, as it was the only way to get back to the Premiership after finishing outside the top two.

Twelve months previously, Crystal Palace had exactly the same set of wins, draws and losses as West Ham to earn their place in the play-offs, and had overcome the then form team – Sunderland – to book their place in the final. Would history repeat itself two years in a row? Could the Hammers be that lucky and defy the odds?

The tens of thousands of supporters who travelled to Cardiff to see their team face Preston showed once again what it meant to them to be a follower of the claret and blue. Even before the two teams entered the stadium, there was a cacophony of sound that seemed to cleanse the air of all the disappointments of the last two years.

Although Preston rarely threatened, their earthy, direct football was always a worrying feature, as the Hammers, despite a number of chances, failed to get the breakthrough their flowing football deserved. From the fifth minute, when a post denied Repka, followed by the palming away by Nash of Etherington's shot, and the two instinctive blocks that denied Harewood, until finally Zamora clipped home Etherington's cross in the 57th minute, the tension was almost unbearable.

It was further heightened when Walker was stretchered off, with a few minutes to go, after falling awkwardly and damaging knee ligaments as he rose to collect a high cross on the edge of his area. Bywater substituted and was immediately in the thick of the action as he saved on the goal-line, only for the referee to then announce seven minutes of injury-time. The final whistle was greeted not only by cheers of jubilation but with sighs of relief from the thousands who knew what the result really meant to a club that had been to the brink and looked into the abyss.

In that moment, Pardew – who had endured eighteen months of constant criticism, nail-biting tension and at times a torrent of abuse from fans over his tactics, his choice of players and virtually everything else he had done or was supposed to do since his arrival – knew he had been vindicated.

All was forgiven, well at least for the time being. West Ham United had won the lottery – some pundits estimated it was worth £30 million to be back in the Premiership – and nobody could take that away from Pardew and his chairman. Both in their own worthy way had played their part in the return to the promised land.

BARCLAYCARD PREMIERSHIP 2005-06

Barclays Premiership	9th
Carling Cup	3rd Round
FA Cup	Finalists

Two years away from the bright lights and headline grabbing newspaper columns of top flight English football had been rectified the previous May. The ecstatic celebrations that had followed the play-off victory at the Millennium Stadium continued for many weeks afterwards. But just 75 days after Alan Pardew and his team had left the pitch a new era began when a new Premiership season opened with Blackburn as the Hammers' first opponents.

Over the summer Pardew had been busy, signing the experienced goalkeeper Roy Carroll on a free from Manchester United, the promising central defensive duo of Danny Gabbidon and James Collins from Cardiff City for undisclosed fees, and then left-back Paul Konchesky for £1.5 million from neighbours and soon to be rivals Charlton. The Welsh international duo from Ninian Park had impressed many, besides their new manager, with their growing reputations earned in the cauldron that was the Championship over several campaigns. For Konchesky it was like a return home, as he had spent several years as a schoolboy prospect at Upton Park, as well as being like the rest of his family a lifelong Hammers fan, before heading south of the river.

At £2.5 million, the 25-year-old Israeli international Yossi Benayoun – an attacking midfielder – was undoubtedly Pardew's biggest capture. Although unknown to the majority of English fans, his signing was considered a coup by those in the know after his impressive displays for previous clubs Hapoel Beer Sheva, Maccabi Haifa and latterly Racing Santander of Spain, where he had finished top scorer the previous season. Although many other clubs sought his services, Benayoun had sought the advice of fellow countryman Eyal Berkovic, who had been such a favourite at the Boleyn Ground in the late 1990s. Berkovic had 'sold' the club to his young friend with his praise of both it and its supporters.

Two final pieces in Pardew's squad jigsaw saw the return of the ever-popular Shaka Hislop, as goalkeeping cover, on a free from Portsmouth, and Stoke City captain and Republic of Ireland international left-sided defender Clive Clarke for £275,000. Days before kick-off Petr Mikolanda, a Czech Republic Under-21 striker, also signed. Amongst the departures was the injury-prone and hugely disappointing – for what had been at the time a £5 million club record signing – Don Hutchison; Chris Powell to Charlton Athletic; and Sergei Rebrov to Dynamo Kiev – all on free-transfers, as were

Rufus Brevett and youngster Greg Pearson. A week after the new term began Malky Mackay also left, for Watford, when his contract was terminated by mutual consent.

A rigorous pre-season went well. Pardew's men remained undefeated in normal play during eight warm-up games, only losing on penalties to CA Osasuna of Spain, in what was becoming a now-traditional final friendly against foreign opposition, on the last Saturday before the new season kicked-off.

The fixture list had been kind in many ways, for it was not until the sixth game that the Hammers were pitted against any of the so called 'big four' clubs. An opening day home win, after falling a goal behind, against the new-look and highly organised Blackburn – motivated by their forceful manager Mark Hughes – was followed by a draw at St James' Park. West Ham had to play for 35 minutes a man short, following Konchesky's red card for what many – including later the FA Disciplinary Commission who rescinded it – considered an excellent tackle.

The bubble burst on the last Saturday of August at home, when an uncompromising Bolton side gained a narrow victory against a West Ham side that produced much flowing forward football in the opening stages but squandered fine opportunities in front of goal, with Marlon Harewood being the chief culprit. The gritty determination that was becoming the hallmark of manager Sam Allardyce's team illustrated one attribute needed to succeed at the highest level. If life in the Championship had been difficult, the vicissitudes of life in the Premiership were even more unforgiving when opportunities were not taken. It was a lesson that if not taken on board would cause problems later.

Like many clubs following promotion, the Hammers did experience something of a honeymoon period as the next few matches resulted in victories at home to Aston Villa, followed by away wins at Fulham and the expected defeat of Sheffield Wednesday (in the Carling Cup), as well as a draw at home to Arsenal and one at the Stadium of Light.

October and November bought mixed fortunes. Although there were defeats against the two Manchester clubs – City away and United at home – as well as Liverpool at Anfield, these were with all due respects expected for a newly promoted club, as was the exit from the Carling Cup at the Reebok Stadium.

However, it must be said in fairness to Pardew and his squad that the differences between the Hammers and their opponents were a lot closer than the results perhaps implied. It had been a sharp learning curve for the manager's mostly young and at times naïve squad, but there were many impartial pundits who were impressed by the style of play and commitment. Much credit was due to the experienced heads of Carroll and Hislop between the posts and Sheringham up front, as well as the emerging defensive talents of Ferdinand and Gabbidon and the stylist and creative play of Benayoun – three of the younger players who, week in and week out, produced many excellent performances. The same could be also said of Gabbidon's substitute Collins, who ably deputised for him when his Welsh colleague was injured.

Although December produced just two victories and a draw from seven fixtures played, the seven points earned were against teams who were below the Hammers in the table and once more emphasised the fact that to succeed or, more importantly survive, in the Premiership it was essential that you did not lose to teams who were below you. The overall picture that greeted Hammers supporters as they welcomed in the New Year was that – despite the defeat that afternoon at The Valley – their team had acquitted themselves well in the opening twenty League fixtures and two cup-ties so far played, and the team's position of tenth was better than perhaps might have been expected by many. Likewise, being some twelve points above the relegation places also gave a feeling of comfort.

It was perhaps not unexpected that the New Year got off on a wrong footing as the all-conquering 'blue army' from the King's Road, west London arrived at Upton Park on the second day of January. The Roman Abramovich cash-fuelled and Jose Mourinho-managed champions were literally cantering away with the title once again, having dropped just four points to the turn of the year. They were a comfortable dozen or so points clear of nearest rivals and only possible challengers, Manchester United.

Hammers old boy Frank Lampard was of course the villain of the piece in more ways than one, having never been forgiven – and doubtless he never will by those who did not know all of the facts surrounding his inevitable transfer – by the infuriated Upton Park crowd for the circumstances of his departure. Apparently unfazed by the booing that greeted his every touch, Lampard showed what a class player he had become over the last four and a half years, and why he had stamped his mark on the international scene. Scoring the opening goal, Lampard continued as he had begun, running tirelessly and probing continually to prise openings for his colleagues.

Although Harewood evened things up 60 seconds after the interval with his tenth goal of the campaign, the relentless pressure and superior skills of the visiting superstars eventually saw them home with another two goals in the final half-hour.

DID YOU KNOW?

West Ham played at the Millennium Stadium in three consecutive years 2004-06. They only players to start in all three games were Harewood and Etherington.

Perhaps two match facts succinctly illustrated the gap between the two teams. For every goal-attempt (six) that Pardew's team had, Chelsea had three times as many (seventeen), but more importantly perhaps the efforts on target were likewise in the same ratio (three for West Ham, ten for Chelsea). The difference between the heady heights of title contenders and mid-table finishers?

There is an old saying that out of adversity not only hope but likewise success springs. Such was the case with Pardew's team as five days later a visit to Carrow Road in the FA Cup resulted in a narrow but significant victory. Norwich City were perhaps the ideal candidates at this precise moment in helping the Hammers bounce back after three disappointing defeats, especially those against Wigan and Charlton, if not so much against Chelsea.

The Hammers over the decades had often fallen foul of teams from lower divisions at this stage of different cups. Not so this year, as a goal after just six minutes settled their nerves and a second twelve minutes into the second half put the meat on a workmanlike display. The manager summed it up with his post-match comments: 'our work rate was tremendous today ... After the second goal, it looked like it was going to be comfortable, but we don't do things comfortably at West Ham. We gifted them a goal and then there was a spell of ten minutes we had to see out.' The victory would prove to be a springboard to even greater glory that few would have thought possible just five months before.

Pardew's words: 'Having a good cup run and getting back up there in the League is a realistic target for us' were to come true over the next four months. The win at Norwich was followed seven days later with yet another away win at Villa Park, and then one at home against Fulham.

That against the Cottagers was also special in two other aspects. Firstly it marked the end of the Hammers' career of full-back Tomas Repka. A record £5 million signing some five years before, the Czech international had endeared himself to many supporters with his wholehearted performances in which he neither gave nor expected any quarter. From his first two yellows, resulting in a red, on his debut his disciplinary record was perhaps the worst ever recorded in the Premiership – 59 yellow cards and four reds in 188 club appearances. That spoke volumes, although in the latter part of his stay he did become a more controlled professional. His return to his native land was because of the love of his family, especially his two children, who lived there. They, like his wife, were homesick and also needed to be educated. Secondly, Anton Ferdinand scored what could only be described as 'the goal of the season'. With his back to goal he swivelled to unleash an unstoppable right-footed volley from eighteen yards into the top corner.

On the day Repka made his farewell appearance, a new name was introduced to the Upton Park faithful. Pardew had berated his strikers earlier in the season for their low return. His remedy, with the backing of his chairman, was to make yet another club record signing – this time around £7 million for Dean Ashton, a 22-year-old striker from Norwich. There had been much speculation about Ashton leaving Carrow Road, especially as he had been left out of the Canaries v West Ham FA Cup-tie. That was apparently to enhance his transfer value by not-being Cup-tied – although he also claimed to be injured.

As it happened, the striker – a product of the Dario Gradi/ Crewe Alexandra soccer academy and considered by many to be in the Alan Shearer mould – did not make his full West Ham debut until the first Saturday in February, having come on as a substitute for the final fifteen minutes the previous Wednesday.

Many clubs, according to the media, were keen to sign Ashton but only West Ham it seemed were willing to meet the asking price for a player whose raw talent and early deeds promised much. Ex-Hammer Julian Dicks' believed Ashton would have a similar impact following his arrival as John Hartson had nine years previously. Both were of a similar mould, being big strong lads with a knack of knowing where the goal was and capable of leading the line in the traditional style. They were also of similar age when moving to the Boleyn Ground.

If this coup were not enough, before the transfer window closed the manager also added Lionel Scaloni, an Argentinian international right-back, on loan for the rest of the season from Deportivo La Coruna, and Yaniv Katan, an Israeli striker. Pardew had approached his board prior to the transfer window with a proposal; that he described as a 'statement of intent', which 'if fulfilled would let the supporters and his players know that we are serious about taking the club back to the level where they belong'. In signing the three he said he 'was overjoyed to report that we've achieved just that and he wanted to thank his chairman and board for their support and faith'.

The last Saturday in January saw the fourth round of the FA Cup and all knew that the visit of Blackburn would be a severe test. The northerners had avenged their opening-day Upton Park defeat on their own midden the previous month, whilst holding a place in the top half of the table over recent months. When the visitors scored in the first seconds everyone realised what a mammoth task the Hammers faced. Responding in fine style Pardew's men equalised through a Sheringham penalty and shortly afterwards took the lead. An own-goal provided a cushion but Hislop was called upon to deny the visitors until their captain Neill scored with a delightful shot. Zamora finally killed off Rovers' revival, following up to slot home after Harewood had been denied. Within the next two weeks wins at Highbury and at home to Sunderland and Birmingham extended the winning run to seven and consolidated the team's place in mid-table.

Sandwiched between the last two wins came the news that Ron Greenwood had died on 9 February at his Suffolk home after a long illness. Not only those who had known Ron during his time at Upton Park, but the football world in general, were saddened. If one man was personally responsible for the birth of 'The Elite Era', that man was Greenwood. His influence on those who followed him as managers or coaches – such as John Lyall, Billy Bonds, Ron Boyce, Harry Redknapp, Trevor Brooking, Frank Lampard senior *et al* – plus all those who had been players during his time and had moved on to other clubs, was immeasurable. Everybody seemed to love football played 'the West Ham way'.

Like one of his predecessors as England manager, Walter Winterbottom, Greenwood had seen the annihilation of the England team by the Hungarians in 1953 at Wembley and six months later in Budapest, and knew things had to change. His arrival at West Ham allowed him to put his theories into practice and thus propelled the Hammers into Europe. His style of play put the club on the map and saw it grow into what has become – an internationally recognised and sought-after major football entity.

Always thinking to the future, Greenwood's foresight in expanding what was to become the West Ham Academy was a legacy that he left for latter generations to build on. His appointment as a Technical Advisor to FIFA during the 1966 and 1970 World Cups said much about his stature amongst his peers, whilst his pleasure in seeing the part played by three of his protégées – Moore, Hurst and Peters – in 1966 and beyond made him immensely proud.

When called to higher office, his tenure as England manager carried the international side through a difficult period but he always acquitted himself with dignity and led England to both the European and World Cup finals. His induction into the FA's Hall of Fame, like his appointment as a CBE by the Queen, said much about how Greenwood was viewed by the country as a whole.

Being drawn at the Reebok in the fifth round of the FA Cup did not seem such a daunting task to some, even though Bolton were themselves pushing towards the top six in the Premiership. A hard-fought yet frustrating goalless draw, with Shaka Hislop earning the plaudits as Man of the Match, earned a return to Upton Park. It was a month before the tie could be settled as a two-week international break was followed by a trip to Goodison, where goals from Harewood and the impressive Ashton earned another valuable League point.

The undefeated run finally ended with a return to the Reebok the following Saturday, but four days later that 1-4 League reverse was replaced by a 2-1 extra-time win, courtesy of an own-goal and Harewood's 96th-minute winner. The result meant progress to the quarter-finals for the first time in five seasons.

It was perhaps not so surprising that, three days later, the return of Harry Redknapp to Upton Park resulted in a humiliating defeat by Portsmouth that left Pardew berating his players: 'I am bitterly disappointed about some of the performances today. I'm not making any excuses for that performance. It's not good enough and I said that to the players afterwards.' For Redknapp it was a valuable back-to-back win on his competitive return to the Boleyn that would eventually help steer Portsmouth to safety after what had seemed an impossible task.

Two days later, two goals from Ashton capped a superb personal display at the City of Manchester Stadium to fire the Hammers into the semi-finals of the FA Cup. Pardew's comment, 'That performance was for the fans, we owed them that,' summed up the bond between him, his players and the supporters. Pardew realised that the fans were important in adding an extra dimension and edge that urged his young players onwards. The aim was to make West Ham a meaningful force not only in the Premiership but the cups as well.

West Ham's progress had surprised many upon their return to the Premiership, and although defeats were perhaps to be expected at Old Trafford, Stamford Bridge and at home to Liverpool, it was the away wins at Wigan and West Bromwich that helped maintain the mid-table comfort zone that all newly promoted teams crave in their first season back in the top flight. Although forced to ride their luck at times, Pardew's squad had one vital thing in their favour: they were all working together and when changes were forced on his team selection those players drafted in seemed to blend in effortlessly. The loss of Ferdinand or Gabbidon at various times was covered by the inclusion of Collins, who proved what many had felt – he was a very good player who was unlucky not to have been a more permanent fixture over the season.

The League fixture compilers, by a quirk of fate, pitched the Hammers against Middlesbrough at the Riverside Stadium six days before their FA Cup semi-final. Although not much could be read into Boro's comfortable home win, both managers made changes for the second meeting at neutral Villa Park. Pardew urged his players; after a lacklustre first-half performance, to a momentous single-goal victory that took the Hammers into an FA Cup final for the first time in 26 years. As the manager said: 'Perhaps it was destiny,' because earlier that week once again not only West Ham fans but the whole footballing world had been rocked by the sudden death – at the age of just 66 – of the most successful manager the club had during its whole history, John Lyall.

Lyall's dismissal and departure from Upton Park had come in acrimonious circumstances in 1989, but it was a colossal shock to many. By the time of his death, only the older generation amongst the supporters and those of the coaching, backroom and administrative staff who had been at the club for more than two decades could remember him as the driving force who developed and blossomed under his mentor – Greenwood – before directing team affairs in his own right for fifteen years.

Although relegated twice during Lyall's tenure, the Hammers also enjoyed one of their most successful periods – winning the FA Cup twice, reaching the final of the European Cup-Winners' Cup and the League Cup, a Second Division Championship, their highest position (third) in the old First Division, and a number of quarter finals in the domestic cup tourneys.

Equally significant in many people's opinion were the FA Youth Cup win, South-East Counties League championships, and a Youth Academy that was the envy of many other managers, plus the development of a host of players brought up in the West Ham way through the junior ranks. After leaving Upton Park Lyall had spells with Spurs and England, where his great knowledge was sought and valued, before taking charge at Ipswich Town whom he guided to promotion for the inaugural season of the Premier League in 1992.

Lyall's place in the annals of West Ham's history over some 34 years at the Boleyn Ground is in the top bracket, and his stature in the world of football was legendary. Admired by all who knew him, John Lyall was a 'gentleman', always fair but hard at times when circumstances dictated. He was blessed with humility as well as great loyalty. As a coach and manager he became a father-figure to players and staff alike, who by his actions continued the 'family tradition and ethos' that was unique to West Ham United in modern-day football. This was seen by the packed St Mary le Tower

Church in Ipswich at which his memorial service was held, as not only many of his former players and fellow managers but a plethora of press men and dignitaries from the governing bodies within soccer, as well as many who had the privilege of knowing him throughout his life, gathered to mourn his passing.

The 2005-06 season's final League game saw the visit of Spurs in what became rather strange circumstances. Many of their players were hit by what was thought to be food poisoning after an overnight stay at a Docklands hotel. Tottenham asked that the game be postponed for 24 or 48 hours to help their recovery, but Premiership officials denied them their request, insisting that all the fixtures had to be completed on the final Sunday of the campaign. The match was finally played after a delayed start. West Ham's narrow victory denied their north London rivals a place in the Champions League, but it seemed that their manager, Martin Jol, whenever speaking about the incident, believed that it was a conspiracy by the Hammers, as well as others, which was responsible for denying him and his team a place among Europe's elite.

Six days later Pardew and his players' season was capped by a return to the Millennium Stadium for what was to be the highlight of their endeavours. It could truly be said that the manager and his squad had proved themselves worthy of their place in the Premiership. They had finished above not only the other two teams who had joined them at the start of the campaign following promotion from the Championship, but other more experienced outfits.

Match of the Season 2005-06

Liverpool 3 West Ham 3 (Liverpool win on penalties)

FA Cup final, 13 May 2006

It was a record that was unlikely to be ever broken as the Hammers returned to The Millennium Stadium for a third successive appearance. The first two had been in the Championship Play-Off finals, but this was something extra special for Hammers fans, with the club's great traditions in FA Cup finals over a period of some nine decades.

To finally lose out in the most heartbreaking fashion, after extra-time and then through a penalty shoot-out was cruel in most pundits' opinions, not to mention the millions of neutrals around the world who watched one of the greatest FA Cup finals ever. It was a match of many great moments and showed that although the Hammers might have a soft underbelly in some departments, their free-flowing and open play was pure West Ham United and harked back to the days of Greenwood and Lyall. The two recently deceased former managers must have been looking down from above with pride as their philosophy of pure football was displayed by the new generation who wore the claret and blue – albeit their away strip of white with blue trimmings. As one banner proclaimed: 'Lyall Style Pardew's Cockney Kings.'

Twelve months earlier the two protagonists had been not just a division apart: Liverpool had been preparing for a European Cup final against AC Milan in Istanbul, which they won on penalty kicks after recovering from a 0-3 half-time deficit.

Now, after taking a two-goal lead – through a deflected own-goal and a spilled rebound which Ashton poked home – the Hammers were pulled back, but within ten minutes they had once again gone ahead as Konchesky's deep cross sailed into the top corner of the net over the head of a surprised goalkeeper.

With seconds to go and all Hammers supporters screaming at the referee to blow for time, the fourth official signalled there would be four extra minutes of injury-time. As it turned out, one special – perhaps exceptional – player would prove the difference on the day, and in Steven Gerrard the Reds had such a man. After scoring the equaliser to make it 2-2, the England international, struggling with cramp, latched onto a Gabbidon header out of defence and flashed home an astonishing 30-yarder past the otherwise excellent Hislop.

As Gerrard later admitted, it was a last-ditch effort as he was unable to run any more and just 'hit and hoped'. It was the last cruel throw of the dice that would deny Pardew, his assistant Peter Grant, and his players the reward their efforts over the last nine months deserved. Reo-Coker was denied a winner, thwarted by a fabulous Reina save. Extra-time came and went, and then the drawn-out spectacle of a penalty shoot out, where Liverpool showed their superiority.

Pardew's words spoke for all: 'Obviously, I'm very disappointed with the outcome of the game but nothing can hide the pride and respect I have for my players after the way they represented West Ham United.'

BARCLAYCARD PREMIERSHIP 2006-07 *(by Clive Leatherdale)*

Barclays Premiership	15th
Carling Cup	3rd Round
FA Cup	4th Round
UEFA Cup	1st Round

The line that separates footballing triumph from disaster had never been thinner, so far as Alan Pardew was concerned. As the 2006 FA Cup final entered its final moments of normal time – with West Ham clinging on to their 3-2 advantage secured by Konchesky's fluke goal – Pardew was seconds away from being acclaimed as one of the Hammers' finest masterminds, a manager who seemingly could do no wrong. Modern managers are given little time to prove themselves, but Pardew was set to crown the promotion earned at the Millennium Stadium in 2005 with the FA Cup just twelve months later.

Alas, Steven Gerrard's piledriver pulled the rug from under West Ham and from under Pardew. With hindsight, perhaps Lionel Scaloni should have done better than hoof the ball aimlessly away in those fateful moments before Gerrard's lethal strike. The blame game pointed here and there, but the pain could only be exorcised on the pitch, which was why the new 2006-07 season could not come quickly enough for Pardew and his players.

The summer of 2006 saw England limp only as far as the quarter-finals of the World Cup in Germany, in which almost every player under-performed. No current West Ham players were involved, though former Hammers Joe Cole and Frank Lampard took the eye for different reasons. Joe Cole was probably the pick of a poor bunch, and at least had a super goal against Sweden to remember. Poor Lampard looked constantly out of sorts, yet recorded more shots on goal than any other player in the tournament. He failed to score with any of them.

The need to recharge World Cup players' batteries pushed the opening of the new Premiership season back to 19 August. For West Ham the summer transfer market was quieter than most, so that the team which lined up for the visit of Charlton in the League opener was not radically different from that deflated by Liverpool in Cardiff. Only two of the defeated Cup final starters had departed – goalkeeper Shaka Hislop, for a second time, and full-back Scaloni had also played his last for West Ham

Two others changes were inescapable. Hayden Mullins might have expected to play in Cardiff but for suspension, and Dean Ashton would certainly have played against Charlton had his ankle not been broken by Shaun Wright-Phillips in a training-ground accident. Ashton had been celebrating his call-up to the full England squad. Now, instead of pulling on England's white shirt and steering West Ham to another famous season, Ashton would sit out the whole campaign. No player is genuinely indispensable to a club, but it is probably fair to say that Ashton's absence proved insurmountable in the troubled months ahead.

Bobby Zamora, a substitute in Cardiff, started against Charlton, and Scaloni's place was fleetingly filled by Tyrone Mears. The other newcomer was not really a newcomer at all. Eyebrows were raised when Pardew recruited Lee Bowyer from Newcastle. Bowyer had turned out ten times on loan for West Ham during Glenn Roeder's futile attempts to escape relegation in 2003. Bowyer was then at the height of his Leeds bad-boy image, failed to make his mark at the Boleyn Ground, and went to Newcastle instead. When signed by Pardew, Bowyer was 29 and had mellowed to some extent, but was clearly not the force he once was. Otherwise, presumably Newcastle would not have let him go.

The opener against Charlton was rich in portents. Just like the first game against Blackburn twelve months previously, West Ham overturned a half-time deficit to win 3-1. If the rest of the season panned out as a carbon-copy, few were likely to complain. But the 2006-07 campaign did not turn out remotely like its predecessor, and the seeds of that were evident from the start against Charlton. The Addicks did not arrive at Upton Park under the familiar charge of Alan Curbishley, whose presence at The Valley was second only to that of Sir Alex Ferguson at Old Trafford. Curbishley evidently felt he could do no more for the club he had guided since 1991. Some restless Addicks fans demanded more success than Curbishley felt he could offer, not appreciating that the club's likely direction after he left was more likely to be down than up. Charlton appointed another former Hammer, Iain Dowie, as his successor. Crucially, Curbs was not snapped up by another club, which meant he was ready and waiting in the wings when the call came ...

West Ham's second game was at promoted Watford, which on paper they expected to win, but in reality were perhaps fortunate to draw. Four points from two games replicated results from 2005-06, and when Bobby Zamora put the Hammers ahead at Anfield the League table hinted at a rosy look by 5pm. Sadly, Benitez's team were ahead by half-time and stayed there.

When Zamora equalised at home to Martin O'Neill's Aston Villa it meant the striker had scored in each of West Ham's opening four games, the team had come from behind in three, defeats had been restricted to one, and West Ham stood eighth. It would never get better than that. In fact it was about to get a whole lot worse.

One of the advantages of playing Liverpool in the 2006 Cup final was that whatever the outcome West Ham would qualify for the coming UEFA Cup campaign – their first European excursion since 1999. Liverpool's place in the Champions League had freed a UEFA Cup slot for the other FA Cup finalists.

West Ham's initial opponents were Palermo. Sicilian football was on a high, with no fewer than three of the island's clubs – Palermo, Catania and Messina – enjoying the riches of Serie 'A'. The Italian game might be mired in corruption and violence – a policeman was killed when Palermo visited Catania; Juventus had been relegated and other clubs deducted points for bribery allegations – but Italian clubs were still unequalled in snatching goals when pinned against the ropes. West Ham appeared to be getting the upper hand at home in the first leg, but Palermo – whose first booking arrived in the opening seconds – snatched a goal in the closing moments of the first half, and that was that.

The second leg started brightly but ended embarrassingly for all connected with West Ham. The players conceded three more goals without reply, and a few inebriated fans treated the Sicilian capital to the excesses everyone hoped had vanished from English football.

Sandwiched between the Palermo games, West Ham lost 0-2 to Newcastle and Manchester City. They were down to fifteenth and hadn't scored for four games.

Off the pitch, dramatic initiatives had been implemented that would scar West Ham United and the whole season. Footballers are normally contracted to football clubs, but in the cloudy world of modern finance even that simple truth is no longer straightforward. Enter Iranian-born Kia Joorabchian and Media Sports Investments. It was they, rather than the Brazilian club Corinthians, who owned the playing contracts of Argentinian international World Cup stars Carlos Tevez and Javier Mascherano. Although the players were known to be available to English clubs, none had been tempted to meddle with the tortuous contractual implications until the pair were unveiled as West Ham players on transfer deadline day, 31 August. Whether or not Alan Pardew was involved, or approved their arrival, has never been clarified. All that appeared clear was that the Hammers hadn't paid a penny for the players in transfer fees, and wouldn't get a penny for them if and when they moved on.

None of this was conducive to building team spirit. Nor could the newcomers' halting command of English. Tevez was introduced from the bench against Aston Villa, and both players started both games against Palermo. Having two Argentines, both new to the passions of the Premiership, in the side quickly appeared a luxury.

It wasn't long before Tevez was back on the bench and Mascherano was back in the stands.

By the last Saturday in October the Hammers were in free-fall. Chesterfield had added to Pardew's woes, overturning Harewood's goal to expel the Hammers from the Carling Cup at the first hurdle. The records show West Ham lasted until the third round, but that obscures the fact that all Premiership clubs are exempt from the first round and those competing in Europe were shooed straight through to the third. In the Premiership, defeats by Reading, Portsmouth and Tottenham left West Ham one off the bottom, propped up (temporarily) by Watford. Eight straight losses in three competitions had brought just that one goal, from Harewood. Other than Zamora (four) and Carlton Cole (one), no other player had scored at all, and no one remotely looked like filling the boots of the absent Ashton. Noises emanating from the dressing room made depressing listening. Team-spirit had apparently fractured, Pardew had become a figure of fun to certain players, and on and off the pitch a sense of crisis hung in the air.

If footballers 'owned' – as opposed to 'represented' – by agents sounded unfamiliar, the idea of Icelandic businessmen taking over a Premiership football club sounded so outlandish as to be dismissed as fantasy. True, a Russian billionaire owned Chelsea and an American business family had seized control of Manchester United. But tiny Iceland – whose population of 300,000 is the same as that of Coventry, and whose most famous non-footballing export is a musical pixie called Bjork – seemed the least likely source to take control at Upton Park.

The group holding Tevez and Mascherano's contracts were the first to go public with their wish to buy West Ham United, but that would have made muddy waters yet muddier. Instead, an Icelandic consortium headed by Eggert Magnusson was ready to buy for a reported £85 million, and on 21 November the deal was announced to the world. As bald as an egg, which rhymed with his name, the 'Egg Man' was not slow in pledging a fabulous future for the club. Instead, his animated despairing features soon cropped up regularly on *Match of the Day* whenever a goal flew into the Hammers net, which was often. Behind the scenes, the Icelandic invasion would provide a culture shock to everyone at Upton Park. Wherever one went, on stairs and in corridors the air was thick with unintelligible consonants, which to secretaries and office staff must have felt rather like landing on Mars.

Although the team's losing run had been terminated by back-to-back wins over Blackburn and Arsenal – the latter provoking some touchline argy-bargy between Pardew and Arsene Wenger following

Harewood's last-gasp winner – the next six matches produced just one goal and West Ham slid back into the drop-zone again.

Matters came to a head on 9 December at Bolton. Previously, Magnusson had been full of public support for Pardew, insisting what a good manager he was, and that his job was safe. Then West Ham capsized at the Reebok. Four goals confirmed the Hammers' tenth successive away defeat, by opponents who had recently lost the art of winning themselves. As the TV cameras panned the directors box, only the top of Magnusson's head was visible as he squirmed ever lower in his seat.

That spelled the end for Alan Pardew and his three and a half years at the Boleyn Ground. In May he had been on the cusp of becoming one of the club's most successful managers, and now he was gone with the sound of silence ringing in his ears.

The following Sunday rampant leaders Manchester United were due at Upton Park, and perhaps fear of another embarrassing defeat prompted Magnusson to sack Pardew when he did. Everyone he asked apparently advised him that the man to go for was Alan Curbishley, who some years before had turned down West Ham to stay at The Valley. Curbishley had the inestimable advantage of being out of work, so that by the time of Manchester United's visit he was in place and preparing to do what he had never done as manager of Charlton – defeat the Red Devils.

Considering the traumas that lay in wait, Curbs' first decisive act invited controversy. Tevez had finally persuaded Pardew of his worth and had started the last five matches. Weighing up the situation and taken soundings from the dressing room, the new manager appeared unpersuaded. Tevez would not take the field at all in the first two matches under Curbishley, would not start a Premiership game in the first five, and would not play a full 90 minutes in the first ten!

By then it was late February. Mascherano had been offloaded in the January transfer window to Liverpool, for whom – come May – he would grace a Champions League final. Having a player capable of such heights languishing in West Ham's reserves seemed to speak volumes for Rafa Benitez's shrewder appreciation of the Argentinian midfielder.

Initially, however, Curbs' gut instinct seemed to be paying off. Against the odds West Ham beat Manchester United, and then drew at Fulham, four precious points earned with no contribution from either of the Argentines. But then the defeats started to stack up and Curbishley had to return to the drawing board.

2007 began grimly with a 0-6 debacle at Steve Coppell's Reading, who chalked up their first win in six games. Pardew's team had never posted a result as bad as that. He had been sacked after his team conceded four goals at Bolton. So what now for Curbishley? He responded by uncharacteristic outbursts against both his players and the media. The players he described as living a 'Baby-Bentley' culture, a problem which was immediately obvious to him as soon as he walked into Upton Park. Their attitude would have to change. Certain players were certainly off their game compared with the previous season – Anton Ferdinand, Marlon Harewood and skipper Nigel Reo-Coker to name but three – but on being asked searching questions by the press about team spirit, specifically that skipper Reo-Coker had been instrumental in getting Pardew the sack, Curbs responded testily and left the room.

Curbishley is a multi-faceted manager. Through his many TV appearances, whether giving post-match summaries off the cuff, or more relaxed match analyses in the studio, he comes across as calm, measured, articulate, and a gracious loser, qualities that endear him to millions of football fans across the country. Point a camera at him and clip a microphone to his collar and Curbs is seen at his best. One cannot imagine him hurling tea-cups across the dressing room at half-time. In short, he talks a good game.

But alone with his players Curbishley clearly has a sharper edge. This is evident from the reactions of those he transferred from Charlton, some of whom, for whatever reason, showed no great enthusiasm for being reunited with him. One such player was England international full-back Paul Konchesky, quickly dropped from the West Ham team and then sold to Fulham in the summer. Konchesky was not slow to fire a parting broadside at the man who showed him the door from Upton Park.

If West Ham were relegated, as seemed increasingly inevitable, it was rumoured to be touch and go whether Magnusson would keep faith with his under-fire manager. Pardew's seventeen games in charge this season had yielded four League wins and fourteen points. Curbishley's first twelve Premiership games produced that solitary opening victory over Man U and six points. Watford did the unthinkable and won 1-0 at the Boleyn *twice*, two weeks apart, first in the FA Cup, then in the Premiership. By any candid assessment, after eleven League games without a victory, West Ham appeared worse off under Curbishley than under Pardew.

Competing assessments of the two men set tongues wagging, particularly as Pardew had been snapped up by Charlton – their third manager of the season – and set about bringing some much needed points to The Valley. Charlton seemed to be clawing their way to safety, while West Ham were simply going from bad to worse. When Charlton crushed the Hammers 4-0 in late February, the margin of performance was so great that Addicks fans chanted 'thank you for Pardew' at their miserable Hammers counterparts, and *Match of the Day*'s pundits condemned the performance of Curbishley's team as insipid and spineless – and not for the first time either.

Many fans started to question Magnusson's judgment, first in firing Pardew so precipitously, rather than giving him the time he requested to get things right, then in hiring Curbishley who, his critics argued, might be good as keeping modest Charlton in the Premiership year after year, but was not likely to cut the mustard with a more ambitious club like West Ham. Curbishley's proven talents lay with ensuring survival. He did not arrive with a track record of winning things, and were West Ham now to be relegated there were some who thought he would be shown the door.

And West Ham certainly appeared doomed. Publicly, Curbs did not dish out any fighting talk, which many interpreted as throwing in the towel. In this they were clearly mistaken, as was clear from the performance that followed the Charlton debacle. The Hammers' 3-4 home defeat by Tottenham receives fuller discussion in Match of the Season, but the consequence of that Sunday's shattering reverse convinced even the last remaining optimists that the Hammers were down.

Watford's draw with Charlton the previous day had lifted the Hornets above West Ham, leaving them bottom of the table on goal-difference. Defeat by Spurs left them there. There were just nine matches left, five of them away from home, where West Ham had gathered just three draws all season. They were ten points adrift of Manchester City in seventeenth place, the last safe position. Stuart Pearce's men also had two games in hand and an uncatchable goal-difference. However you performed the arithmetic the situation was irredeemable. Had West Ham taken eighteen points from those nine games, history shows it would not have been enough to save them. In fact, incredibly, they won seven of them.

At least, that is what the records say. But the first of those seven wins was a gift from the gods. Trailing at Blackburn, West Ham were given a soft penalty and then a second goal when the ball clearly did not cross the line, with or without goal-line technology. Instead of having relegation all but confirmed, they had a first away win. Playing with the freedom of no-hopers, West Ham then beat Middlesbrough before becoming the first opponents ever to win at Arsenal's new Emirates stadium. Arsenal had 25 shots, fourteen corners, and hit bar and post, yet West Ham somehow won 1-0. Nine points from three games had slashed the safety gap to two points. Was the impossible possible?

DID YOU KNOW?

West Ham like to claim they are a powerful club. Yet the last time they scored more goals than they conceded in the top division was back in 1985-86, over 20 years ago.

The next match was a six-pointer at Sheffield United, one place above them in the table. The Blades won 3-0 at a canter, and when Chelsea swept in four at Upton Park it left West Ham five points below the cut-off line with just four games left to play.

As if that prospect was not daunting enough, the ramifications of what was becoming known as 'The Tevez Affair' threatened to derail faint hopes of safety. A Premier League investigation into abnormalities in the Argentinians' contracts delivered its judgment. West Ham had admitted to not being entirely honest in their submissions – though it should be stressed that this related to the previous regime, and that the Icelandic consortium were blameless. In fact, that change of ownership is probably what saved West Ham United. Had the *ancien regime* still been in charge, the club would probably have been docked points they could not afford to lose, hastening relegation which seemed inescapable – in other words a meaningless punishment. Instead, the club were hit by a record fine, £5.5 million, but, crucially, were not deducted any points.

To the wider football world this verdict seemed extraordinarily generous to West Ham. Over the years points had been deducted from other clubs for what appeared lesser transgressions that those for which the Hammers had been condemned. And the fact that West Ham were publicly accused of dishonesty seemed to many onlookers justification for a points deduction in itself.

The Premier League's judgment was delivered on Friday, 27 April. The previous Saturday West Ham had fended off Everton to grab another three points, leaving them three from safety with three games to play. The Hammers were still in with a chance. And that invited another problem. Other clubs in the relegation dogfight – principally Fulham, Sheffield United and Wigan – were threatening legal challenges over The Tevez Affair, whether or not any of those three clubs went down. In effect, it was like a 'class action' lawsuit directed at what was viewed as improper leniency shown to West Ham. Such action, if it came about, would be messy, protracted, divisive and costly. Many observers suspected the Premier League hierarchy of keeping their fingers crossed that West Ham would go down, if only to avoid the legal nightmare that loomed if they stayed up.

Either way, the issue might have been settled at Wigan the next day. Wigan were three points better off than the Hammers, for whom defeat was unthinkable. Yet West Ham's 3-0 win was their biggest of the season. Only goal-difference kept West Ham below the trap door and Lady Luck now smiled on them again. The last home match was against Bolton, obdurate opponents under Sam Allardyce, who quit just in time for Sammy Lee to take charge at Upton Park. This was, in short, the perfect time to face Bolton, and West Ham went three goals up inside half an hour. The win hoisted them three points clear of the drop with one match to play.

One match to play! But what a finale – at Old Trafford. This fixture had always looked likely to scupper any Hammers revival, and in most circumstances it probably would have. But two facts gave reason for hope. Manchester United had already secured the Premiership crown from Chelsea. They were champions whatever the outcome against West Ham, and with a looming FA Cup final the following Saturday – Manchester United v Chelsea at the new Wembley – Ferguson would be tempted to rest key players.

To add spice to this already intriguing last day, Sheffield United would host Wigan. Watford and Charlton were already down. The club joining them would be West Ham, Wigan or Sheffield United. The Hammers' safety would be guaranteed either if they drew at Old Trafford or Wigan failed to win at Bramall Lane.

Tevez's winning goal, scored on the stroke of half-time, will live for ever in West Ham mythology. What Sir Alex had to say to Wes Brown, whose flimsy challenge on the Argentinian preceded the goal, we can only guess. The final whistle confirmed West Ham were safe, following the most dramatic escape from relegation they had ever experienced. The arguments and legal threats, however, continued for months. Sheffield United, relegated by a one-goal goal-difference, carried their grievance as far as they could, but could not overturn the Premier League's decision not to deduct points from West Ham

Carlos Tevez's Old Trafford goal inscribed a place for himself in the list of West Ham giants. Despite failing to score in his first nineteen Hammers appearances, it was clear to almost everyone – Pardew and Curbishley perhaps excepted – that his special talent demanded inclusion in the side. Before the coming 2007-08 season started he had signed for Manchester United. Sir Alex Ferguson had seen Tevez at close quarters and rarely signs indifferent players. Small, strong, skilful, mobile, brave, tackling back when necessary, he was the sort of player that fans adore. At West Ham, everything might be sinking around him, but Tevez gave his all, and his seven goals in those final ten games did more than anything to snatch survival from the jaws of defeat. He won the Hammers Player of the Year award with 84 per cent of the supporters' votes!

Match of the Season 2006-07

West Ham 3 Tottenham 4

Premiership, 4 March 2007

This fixture had a recent sour history. Martin Jol's team certainly had no love for West Ham. Tottenham had also been the visitors on the last day of the 2005-06 season, when a fuss about alleged food poisoning, allied to Spurs' 1-2 defeat, knocked them out of the top four places for the first time in months. It had been a critical match for Spurs but a meaningless one for West Ham. Now the situation was almost reversed, although Spurs were still chasing a European place. If one was able to predict these things, West Ham might willingly have traded that earlier win for victory now, when they needed it most.

One might think that losing 3-4 at home is, at most, a once-in-a-decade experience. For most clubs perhaps it is, but West Ham have made rather a habit of it. Four times in recent seasons they have posted such a score – against Wimbledon in 1998-99, Leeds in 2002-03, West Brom in 2003-04, and now. Against the Dons and the Baggies, West Ham had led 3-0, and they also led Spurs by two goals at half-time. A first strike for his club by young Mark Noble was followed by an exquisite free-kick by Tevez that flew in off the crossbar. It was his first West Ham goal and you could see how much it meant by his galloping shirt-twirling leap into the fans which earned him a mandatory booking.

Managers are fond of saying it's the result that matters, not the performance, but here was a case of West Ham playing well, deserving their lead, and threatening Spurs with more goals in the second half. The seeds of their destruction were sowed when Lee Bowyer brought down Aaron Lennon early in the second half. Ex-Hammer Defoe scored with the penalty, and when Lennon back-heeled the ball Tainio levelled the scores with a low strike.

One point was of no use to West Ham. Curbishley sent on leading scorer Bobby Zamora and with five minutes left Zamora's first contact with the ball – a looping header – restored West Ham's lead. Surely they could hang on, but no. Berbatov made it 3-3 with a free-kick which flew in over the defensive wall. Once again West Ham charged forward, leaving themselves exposed to the killer punch, which arrived in the fifth minute of injury time. Defoe shot, Robert Green parried, and Spurs substitute Stalteri rolled the ball into the empty net.

Guide to Seasonal Summaries

Col 1: Match number (for league fixtures); Round (for cup-ties).
e.g. 2:1 means 'Second round; first leg.'
e.g. 4R means 'Fourth round replay.'

Col 2: Date of the fixture and whether Home (H), Away (A), or Neutral (N).

Col 3: Opposition.

Col 4: Attendances. Home gates appear in roman; Away gates in *italics*.
Figures in **bold** indicate the largest and smallest gates, at home and away.
Average home and away attendances appear after the final league match.

Col 5: Respective league positions of West Ham and their opponents after the match.
West Ham's position appears on the top line in roman.
Their opponents' position appears on the second line in *italics*.
For cup-ties, the division and position of opponents is provided.
e.g. *2:12* means the opposition are twelfth in Division 2.

Col 6: The top line shows the result: W(in), D(raw), or L(ose).
The second line shows West Ham's cumulative points total.

Col 7: The match score, West Ham's given first.
Scores in **bold** indicate West Ham's biggest league win and heaviest defeat.

Col 8: The half-time score, West Ham's given first.

Col 9: The top line shows West Ham's scorers and times of goals in roman.
The second line shows opponents' scorers and times of goals in *italics*.
A 'p' after the time of a goal denotes a penalty; 'og' an own-goal.
The third line gives the name of the match referee.

Team line-ups: West Ham line-ups appear on the top line, irrespective of whether they are home or away. Opposition teams appear on the second line in *italics*.
Players of either side who are sent off are marked !
West Ham players making their league debuts are displayed in **bold**.

Substitutes: Names of substitutes appear only if they actually took the field.
A player substituted is marked *
A second player substituted is marked ^
A third player substituted is marked "
These marks do not indicate the sequence of substitutions.

N.B. For clarity, all information appearing in *italics* relates to opposing teams.

No	Date	Att	Pos	Pt	F-A	H-T	Scorers, Times, and Referees	1	2	3	4	5	6	7	8	9	10	11
1	A PORTSMOUTH			W	2-1	1-0	Keeble 37, Dick 50	Gregory	Bond	Cantwell	Malcolm	Brown	Lansdowne	Grice	Smith	Keeble	Dick	Musgrove
	23/8	*40,470*		2			*Harris P 52*	*Uprichard*	*McGhee*	*Hayward*	*Phillips*	*Dickinson*	*Casey*	*Harris P*	*Gordon*	*Dougan*	*Harris H*	*Newman*
							Ref: W Clements	After 26 years West Ham return to the elite against opponents who missed relegation on goal-average and who will now, under new manager Freddie Cox, finish bottom. Keeble pounces on a rebound and Dick fires in from Grice's centre. Derek Dougan then sends Peter Harris clear.										
2	H WOLVES			W	2-0	1-0	Dick 45, Smith 72	Gregory	Bond	Cantwell	Malcolm	Brown	Lansdowne	Grice	Smith	Keeble	Dick	Musgrove
	25/8	37,485		4				*Finlayson*	*Stuart*	*Harris*	*Slater*	*Wright*	*Flowers*	*Deeley*	*Broadbent*	*Henderson*	*Mason*	*Horne*
							Ref: F Gerrard	Wolves are defending champs, so theirs is a huge scalp. These dropped points will not deny them a second title. Dick evaded Harris' tackle and wrong-footed Finlayson, and when a linesman half-raised his flag Smith settled Wolves' fate. 'We want six' sang the rain-soaked crowd.										
3	H ASTON VILLA			W	7-2	4-0	Musg' 15, 19, Lans' 30, Keeble 36, 73,	Gregory	Bond	Cantwell	Malcolm	Brown	Lansdowne	Grice	Smith	Keeble	Dick	Musgrove
	30/8	30,506		6			*Sewell 76, Smith 88* [Dick 75, 89]	*Sims*	*Lynn*	*Aldis*	*Crowe*	*Dugdale*	*Saward*	*Smith*	*Hitchens*	*Sewell*	*Myerscough*	*McPartland*
							Ref: M Dixon	This is not a shock when one realises that Villa are going down. Fenton's Furies squander many chances, in addition to the seven taken. Villa start well but Musgrove beats three men for the opener and it was 6-0 before Villa got another look-in. Andy Malcolm was man of the match.										
4	A WOLVES		2	D	1-1	1-0	Grice 19	Gregory	Bond	Cantwell	Malcolm	Brown	Lansdowne	Grice	Smith	Keeble	Dick	Musgrove
	3/9	*52,317*	*13*	7			*Broadbent 62*	*Finlayson*	*Stuart*	*Harris*	*Slater*	*Wright*	*Flowers*	*Deeley*	*Broadbent*	*Henderson*	*Booth*	*Mullen*
							Ref: H Haworth	It was the habit to play one team twice early on, and Wolves once again fall short, though Peter Broadbent missed five good chances. Gregory defied everything thrown at him until Henderson dummied Deeley's cross. Grice foxed Gerry Harris with a first-timer from the outside the box.										
5	A LUTON			L	1-4	1-0	Keeble 12	Gregory	Bond	Cantwell	Malcolm	Brown	Lansdowne	Grice	Smith	Keeble	Dick	Musgrove
	6/9	*25,715*		7			*Brown 57, Turner 71, 83, Pacey 86*	*Baynham*	*Dunne*	*Hawkes*	*Morton*	*Owen*	*Pacey*	*Bingham*	*Turner*	*Brown*	*Groves*	*Adam*
							Ref: N Taylor	Both teams began unbeaten, but Luton triumph after a second-half turnaround. Just before half-time, tubby referee Taylor went off after taking Musgrove's shot in the kidneys. He returned to allow Luton's second goal: seeing an offside flag, Brown handled, but Turner netted anyway.										
6	H MANCHESTER U		1	W	3-2	2-0	Dick 8, Smith 36, Musgrove 59	Gregory	Bond	Cantwell	Malcolm	Brown	**Moore**	Grice	Smith	Keeble	Dick	Musgrove
	8/9	35,672		9			*Webster 69, McGuinness 82*	*Gregg*	*Foulkes*	*Greaves*	*Goodwin*	*Cope*	*McGuinness*	*Webster*	*Taylor*	*Viollet*	*Charlton*	*Scanlon*
							Ref: J Hunt	Hammers top the league after this nail-biter. Even after Man U fought back to 3-2, West Ham refused to indulge in time-wasting tactics. Bobby Moore's debut was rewarded by warm words from Matt Busby. The hobbling McGuinness crossed for Man U's first, and floated the second.										
7	A NOTT'M FOREST			L	**0-4**	0-1		Gregory	Bond	Cantwell	Malcolm	Brown	Moore	Grice	Smith	Keeble	Dick	Musgrove
	13/9	*30,518*		9			*Dwight 25, 89, Wilson 78, Quigley 87*	*Thomson*	*Whare*	*McDonald*	*Whitefoot*	*McKinlay*	*Burkitt*	*Dwight*	*Quigley*	*Wilson*	*Gray*	*Imlach*
							Ref: D Martin	West Ham's short-passing game came unstuck against Forest's young tigers, and despite sporting a 'Brazilian look' have still failed to win at the County Ground since the War. Keeble was unable to shake off McKinlay. Quigley's cheeky 87th-min backheeler was the goal of the game.										
8	A MANCHESTER U			L	1-4	1-3	Bond 36	Gregory	Bond	Cantwell	Malcolm	Brown	Lansdowne	Wragg	Smith	Keeble	Dick	Grice
	17/9	***53,276***		9			*Webster 7, Scanlon 26, 40, 65*	*Gregg*	*Foulkes*	*Greaves*	*Goodwin*	*Cope*	*McGuinness*	*Webster*	*Taylor*	*Dawson*	*Charlton*	*Scanlon*
							Ref: A Holland	Another four-goal drubbing, as Man U toyed with West Ham in the second half. Their one consolation came when Foulkes handled, and Bond netted at the second attempt. Man U's first two goals went in off a post. Albert Scanlon enjoys his England Under-23 call-up with a hat-trick.										
9	H CHELSEA			W	4-2	3-1	Grice 6, Smith 8, Keeble 37, Dick 80	Gregory	Bond	Cantwell	Malcolm	Brown	Nelson	Wragg	Smith	Keeble	Dick	Grice
	20/9	31,127		11			*Greaves 2, Brabrook 65*	*Robertson*	*Sillett P*	*Sillett J*	*Mortimore*	*Scott*	*Saunders*	*Brabrook*	*Greaves*	*Tindall*	*Nicholas*	*Harrison*
							Ref: R Mann	Chelsea condemned West Ham to relegation on the closing day of the 1931-32 season, so revenge was sweet. Chelsea have shipped 26 goals in nine matches and Greaves' early poach, when Nicholas hit the post, could not save them. Grice smote a leveller and crossed for Smith's goal.										
10	A BLACKPOOL			L	0-2	0-1		Gregory	Bond	Cantwell	Malcolm	Brown	Nelson	Grice	Smith	Keeble	Dick	Musgrove
	27/9	*32,662*		11			*Snowdon 30, Mudie 80*	*Farm*	*Armfield*	*Garrett*	*Kelly J*	*Gratrix*	*Kelly H*	*Matthews*	*Mudie*	*Snowdon*	*Durie*	*Perry*
							Ref: C Sant	West Ham are wobbling on their travels. Out-of-form Cantwell's weak back-pass allowed man-of-the-match Stanley Matthews to steal the ball and set up Brian Snowdon for his first league goal. South African Bill Perry then crossed for Jackie Mudie in the clear, and he lobbed Gregory.										

No	Venue	Opponent / Date	Att	Res / Pos	F-A	H-T	Scorers, Times, and Referees	1	2	3	4	5	6	7	8	9	10	11
11	H	BLACKBURN		W	6-3	2-1	Keeble 17, 44, 53, 76, Cantwell 69,	Gregory	Bond	Cantwell	Malcolm	Brown	Nelson	Grice	Smith	Keeble	Dick	Musgrove
		4/10	25,280	13			*Vernon 14, D'bing 80* [W'ds 46 (og)]	*Leyland*	*Whelan*	*Eckersley*	*Smith*	*Woods*	*McGrath*	*Douglas*	*Dobing*	*Johnston*	*Vernon*	*McLeod*
							Ref: G McCabe	Keeble's four goals earned him a £6 bonus and the orange ball as a prize. His first was a spinning volley, his second a flying header. Yet ball-juggling Rovers had all the early play. The game was decided seconds after half-time when Matt Woods side-footed a back-pass past Leyland.										
12	H	BIRMINGHAM		L	1-2	1-0	Musgrove 15	Gregory	Bond	Cantwell	Malcolm	Brown	Nelson	Grice	Smith	Keeble	Dick	Musgrove
		11/10	29,500	13			*Neal 50, Hooper 77*	*Merrick*	*Hall*	*Green*	*Watts*	*Sissons*	*Neal*	*Hooper*	*Gordon*	*Brown*	*Orritt*	*Murphy*
							Ref: C Kingston	Hammers' first home defeat since September 1957. Their fans even slow-handclapped when Brum's Peter Murphy collapsed when kicked in the chest. Musgrove netted a deflected goal off Watts on a glue-pot pitch. Ex-Hammer Harry Hooper, skipper for the day, volleyed the winner.										
13	A	WEST BROM		L	1-2	0-1	Keeble 62	Gregory	Bond	Cantwell	Malcolm	Brown	Nelson	Grice	Smith	Keeble	Dick	Musgrove
		18/10	*36,991*	13			*Campbell 21, Howe 84p*	*Potter*	*Howe*	*Williams G*	*Setters*	*Barlow*	*Dudley*	*Campbell*	*Robson*	*Kevan*	*Burnside*	*Hogg*
							Ref: R Jordan	Albion's Derek Hogg fell under Smith's challenge and Don Howe converted to give struggling Albion a first home win of the season. West Ham protested, but had enjoyed the luck earlier when Derek Kevan shrugged off Cantwell to score, only for the ref to give Kevan a free-kick.										
14	H	BURNLEY		W	1-0	1-0	Nelson 30	Gregory	Bond	Cantwell	Malcolm	Brown	Nelson	Grice	Smith	Keeble	Dick	Musgrove
		25/10	29,387	15				*McDonald*	*Angus*	*Smith*	*Seith*	*Cummings*	*Adamson*	*Connolly*	*McIlroy*	*Robson*	*Cheeseboro'*	*Pilkington*
							Ref: L Callaghan	A messy game was settled by a messy goal. Burnley's defence had conceded only three goals in the last five games, but now paid for their one mistake. Nelson's cross from the left led to a flurry under the bar, and England keeper Colin McDonald scooped the ball out from over the line.										
15	A	BOLTON		W	2-0	1-0	Grice 1, Dick 50	Gregory	Bond	Cantwell	Malcolm	Brown	Nelson	Grice	Smith	Keeble	Dick	Musgrove
		15/11	*31,067*	17				*Hopkinson*	*Hartie*	*Edwards B*	*Hennin*	*Higgins*	*Edwards M*	*Bannister*	*Stevens*	*Lofthouse*	*Hill*	*Holden*
							Ref: H Webb	Inside 45 seconds, Dick's shot is blocked and Grice follows up. The ball came back off Hopkinson's body, but the ref said it was over the line. When Grice broke down the right, Dick turned in his cross for 2-0. Holden's shot was cleared off the line and Hennin hit the post for Bolton.										
16	H	ARSENAL		D	0-0	0-0		Gregory	Bond	Cantwell	Malcolm	Brown	Nelson	Grice	**Woosnam**	Keeble	Dick	Musgrove
		8/11	**38,250** *1*	18				*Kelsey*	*Wills*	*Evans*	*Ward*	*Dodgin*	*Docherty*	*Clapton*	*Groves*	*Herd*	*Bloomfield*	*Henderson*
							Ref: R Warnke	Crew-cutted £30,000 debutant Phil Woosnam was seldom on the same wavelength as his partners. The visit of table-topping Arsenal meant the gates were shut half an hour before kick-off. The last match between these sides, at Easter 1932, finished 1-1 – it was the Hammers' last point.										
17	A	EVERTON		D	2-2	2-1	Dick 8, Bond 44p	Gregory	Bond	Cantwell	Malcolm	Brown	Nelson	Grice	Woosnam	Keeble	Dick	Musgrove
		15/11	*40,549*	19			*Thomas 23, Harris J 62*	*Dunlop*	*Parker*	*Bramwell*	*King*	*Jones*	*Harris B*	*Harris J*	*Thomas*	*Hickson*	*Collins*	*O'Hara*
							Ref: A Ellis	On a gluey pitch, Hammers played it long, and Woosnam headed down for Dick's opener. Thomas equalised at the second attempt before Alex Parker handled on the line for Bond's penalty. In the second half Gregory fisted out from Thomas, but Jimmy Harris netted from a tight angle.										
18	H	LEICESTER		L	0-3	0-3		Gregory	Bond	Cantwell	Malcolm	Brown	Nelson	Grice	Woosnam	Keeble	Dick	Musgrove
		22/11	23,500	19			*Kelly 9, Keyworth 33, Hines 43*	*McLaren*	*Cunningham*	*Baillie*	*Newman*	*King*	*Keyworth*	*McDonald*	*Kelly*	*Hines*	*Walsh*	*Leek*
							Ref: J Mitchell	Lowly Leicester pull off one of the shocks of the season. Bernard Kelly beat Nelson in the tackle the blast their first goal; Ken Keyworth added another from 35 yards; and Hines took a pass from Walsh to slide No 3 past the unsighted Gregory. In the second half City protected their lead.										
19	A	PRESTON		L	1-2	1-0	Dick 14	Gregory	Bond	Cantwell	Malcolm	Brown	Nelson	Grice	Woosnam	Keeble	Dick	Musgrove
		29/11	*19,436*	19			*Hatsell 49p, 87*	*Else*	*Cunningham*	*Walton*	*Milne*	*Dunn*	*O'Farrell*	*Mayers*	*Hatsell*	*Finney*	*Baxter*	*Taylor*
							Ref: R Windle	Micky Grice had the chances to win this for West Ham, but he missed them. They were hanging on to Dick's goal when Bond handled. The ref didn't see it, but the linesman did. Dennis Hatsell's second goal was equally controversial, shoving off Brown near the end to head the winner.										
20	H	LEEDS		L	2-3	0-2	Dick 76, Keeble 90	Gregory	Bond	Cantwell	Malcolm	Brown	Nelson	Grice	Woosnam	Keeble	Dick	Musgrove
		6/12	22,022	19			*Overfield 7, Bond 10 (og), Crowe 55p*	*Wood*	*Ashall*	*Hair*	*Cush*	*Charlton*	*Gibson*	*Humphries*	*Crowe*	*Shackleton*	*Revie*	*Overfield*
								Leeds had never previously won at Upton Park in 20 previous visits, but winger Overfield outpaced Bond for the first goal and Bond then sent a 20-yard back-pass wide of Gregory. Predictably, it was the luckless Bond who fouled Overfield for the penalty. A nightmare game for Bond.										
21	A	MANCHESTER C		L	1-3	0-0	Dick 87	Gregory	**Kirkup**	Bond	Malcolm	Brown	Cantwell	Grice	Woosnam	Keeble	Dick	Musgrove
		13/12	*22,500*	19			*Barlow 52, 57, 69*	*Trautmann*	*Leivers*	*Sear*	*Cheetham*	*Ewing*	*Barnes*	*Hayes*	*Barlow*	*Hannah*	*McAdams*	*Fagan*
								18-year-old Joe Kirkup endures a sad debut, as Hammers lose to Colin Barlow's hat-trick. Musgrove had missed a sitter. City were better in the second half, helped by a new ball after the original got stuck in the roof. Barlow kicked the ball out of Gregory's hands for his first goal.										

No	Date	Att	Pos	Pt	F-A	H-T	Scorers, Times, and Referees	1	2	3	4	5	6	7	8	9	10	11
22	H PORTSMOUTH			W	**6-0**	4-0	W'snam 8, Keeble 37, 43, M'grove 44,	Gregory	Bond	Cantwell	Malcolm	Brown	Smith	Grice	Woosnam	Keeble	Dick	Musgrove
	20/12	31,500		21			[Dick 73, Smith 81]	*Uprichard*	*McGhee*	*Wilson*	*Dickinson*	*Hayward*	*Casey*	*Barnard*	*Newman*	*Saunders*	*Harris H*	*Cutler*
								This is West Ham's first win since signing Phil Woosnam six weeks ago. He scored from 20 yards, then he set up Hammers' next two goals. Johnny Smith, who scored, is the sixth left-half Hammers have tried so far. Pompey boss Freddie Cox was away scouting, with good cause.										
23	H TOTTENHAM			W	2-1		Dick, Keeble	Gregory	Bond	Cantwell	Malcolm	Brown	Smith	Grice	Woosnam	Keeble	Dick	Musgrove
	25/12	26,178		23			*Smith*	*Hollowbread*	*Baker*	*Henry*	*Blanchflower*	*Norman*	*Iley*	*Medwin*	*Harmer*	*Smith*	*Stokes*	*Jones*
								Once upon a time teams played on Christmas Day, and Boxing Day too. A welcome victory is marred by a right-knee injury sustained by Phil Woosnam at a quagmire Upton Park. The result sends Spurs perilously near the relegation zone. They haven't won a match since 15 November.										
24	A TOTTENHAM			W	4-1	2-0	Dick 23, Bond 39, Henry 47 (og),	Gregory	Bond	Cantwell	Malcolm	Brown	Smith	Grice	**Smillie**	Keeble	Dick	Musgrove
	26/12	*43,817*		25			*Stokes 56* [Keeble 88]	*Hollowbread*	*Baker*	*Henry*	*Blanchflower*	*Norman*	*Iley*	*Brooks*	*Harmer*	*Smith*	*Stokes*	*Jones*
							Ref: J Baxter	Andy Smillie comes in for the injured Woosnam. Hollowbread and Norman got mixed up, allowing Dick to hook the first goal. Bond found himself unmarked for No 2. But the goal of the game belonged to Ron Henry, who pivoted on one foot and with the other swept an own-goal.										
25	A ASTON VILLA			W	2-1	0-0	Cantwell 68, Dugdale 74 (og)	Gregory	Bond	Cantwell	Malcolm	Brown	Smith	Grice	Smillie	Keeble	Dick	Musgrove
	3/1	*33,360*		27			*McParland 48*	*Sims*	*Jackson*	*Aldis*	*Dixon*	*Dugdale*	*Crowe*	*Smith*	*Hitchens*	*Myerscough*	*Wylie*	*McParland*
							Ref: J Pickles	This match kicked-off in a snowstorm and finished in a mud-bath. The attendance of 33,000 was described as 'thin'. Peter McParland's header from Wylie's knock-back looked offside but Cantwell headed in Bond's free-kick to level. Grice's winner was deflected by Dugdale past Sims.										
26	H NOTT'M FOREST			W	5-3	2-2	Dick 18, 29, W'snam 62, K'ble 70, 84	Gregory	Bond	Cantwell	Malcolm	Brown	Smith	Grice	Woosnam	Keeble	Dick	Musgrove
	31/1	26,676		29			*Quigley 10, Wilson 36, Dwight 68*	*Thomson*	*Whare*	*McDonald*	*Morley*	*McKinlay*	*Burkitt*	*Dwight*	*Quigley*	*Wilson*	*Gray*	*Imlach*
								Forest boss Billy Walker missed this thriller with a chill. Almost all the goals were special. Dick struck two with his much-maligned right foot. Following Roy Dwight's fantastic solo effort for 3-3, Keeble struck Hammers' fourth, then dashed through the middle onto Malcolm's pass.										
27	A CHELSEA			L	2-3	2-2	Keeble 14, 33	Gregory	Bond	Cantwell	Malcolm	Brown	Smith	Grice	Woosnam	Keeble	Dick	Musgrove
	7/2	*52,968*		29			*Tambling 15, Bridges 22, Greaves 84*	*Matthews*	*Sillett P*	*Sillett J*	*Mortimore*	*Scott*	*Crowther*	*Brabrook*	*Cliss*	*Bridges*	*Greaves*	*Tambling*
							Ref: C Sant	Ted Drake's kindergarten Chelsea – for whom 17-year-old debutants Bridges and Tambling both scored – snatched an unlikely late win when 18-year-old Jimmy Greaves netted from David Cliss's pass. Old man Keeble had netted from Woosnam's pass, then headed in Grice's lob.										
28	H BLACKPOOL			W	1-0		Dick	Gregory	Bond	Cantwell	Malcolm	Brown	Smith	Grice	Woosnam	Keeble	Dick	Musgrove
	16/2	28,500		31				*Farm*	*Armfield*	*Garrett*	*Hauser*	*Gratrix*	*Kelly H*	*Mudie*	*Kelly J*	*Charnley*	*Durie*	*Perry*
								Dick's goal wipes the smiles from the faces of Ron Stuart's Seasiders, who have just beaten West Brom 3-1 to go into the quarter-finals of the FA Cup. That's just about as far as they progress in that competition though, as they bow out 0-1 in the replay to Luton Town a month later.										
29	A BLACKBURN			W	2-1	1-0	Keeble 6, Musgrove 55	Gregory	Bond	Cantwell	Malcolm	Brown	Smith	Grice	Woosnam	Keeble	Dick	Musgrove
	21/2	*17,163*		33			*McLeod 63*	*Leyland*	*Taylor*	*Whelan*	*Clayton*	*Woods*	*McGrath*	*Douglas*	*Dobing*	*Swindells*	*Vernon*	*McLeod*
								West Ham do the double over last year's promotion partners on what is normally a bogey ground for them. Keeble headed in Musgrove's cross and Musgrove robbed Taylor before hooking the ball past Leyland, who got a hand to it. Bryan Douglas set up McLeod's goal for Rovers.										
30	A BIRMINGHAM		6	L	0-3	0-1		Gregory	Bond	Cantwell	Malcolm	Brown	Smith	Grice	Smillie	Keeble	Dick	Musgrove
	28/2	*21,001*	*8*	33			*Larkin 7, 49, Neal 46*	*Merrick*	*Hall*	*Allen*	*Watts*	*Sissons*	*Neal*	*Astell*	*Gordon*	*Stubbs*	*Larkin*	*Hooper*
							Ref: A Jobling	Fenton is furious at his team's showing. Bernard Larkin picked his spot for both his goals. The other stemmed from Gordon Astall, who was in acres of space before crossing to Neal. One newspaper said 'West Ham looked like a team that had strayed into the First Division by mistake'.										
31	H WEST BROM		6	W	3-1	2-1	Dick 9, 37, 79	Gregory	Bond	Cantwell	Malcolm	Brown	Smith	Grice	Woosnam	Keeble	Dick	Musgrove
	7/3	30,157	*7*	35			*Robson 20*	*Potter*	*Howe*	*Williams*	*Setters*	*Barlow*	*Drury*	*Allen*	*Jackson*	*Robson*	*Kevan*	*Hogg*
							Ref: F Collinge	Future England manager Bobby Robson outpaced Brown to hit a bullet equaliser from 15 yards. But that proved to be rough-house Albion's only interruption to West Ham's control. Dick's second was lucky, a wicked deflection off Don Howe. Keeble limped through the second half.										

No	Date	H/A	Opponent	Att	Pos	Res	Pts	F-A	H-T	Scorers, Times, and Referees	1	2	3	4	5	6	7	8	9	10	11
32		A	BURNLEY			L		0-1	0-0		Gregory	Bond	Cantwell	Malcolm	Brown	Moore	Grice	Smith	Dare	Dick	Musgrove
	14/3			*17,311*			35			*Connelly 89*	*McDonald*	*Cummings*	*Smith*	*Seith*	*Miller*	*Adamson*	*Connelly*	*McIlroy*	*Pointer*	*Robson*	*Harris*
										Ref: J Cook	Turf Moor barracked John Connelly throughout, but he had the last laugh, pouncing on Cantwell's fluffed clearance from Jimmy Adamson's cross. West Ham's best chance came when Malcolm hit the bar, but they deserved little for keeping nine men in defence for most of the match.										
33		H	BOLTON			W		4-3	1-1	Obeney 38, Bond 46, 70, Dick 57	**Dwyer**	Kirkup	Cantwell	Malcolm	Brown	Smith	Grice	**Obeney**	Bond	Dick	Musgrove
	21/3			27,722			37			*Stevens 44, Parry 65, Hill 73*	*Hopkinson*	*Hartle*	*Banks*	*Hennin*	*Higgins*	*Edwards*	*Holden*	*Stevens*	*Lofthouse*	*Hill*	*Parry*
											Cup-holders Bolton will finish fourth, so this is a fine win for new-look Hammers, though Hartle claimed to have cleared Dick's shot for 3-1 off the line. Debutant Harry Obeney lobbed the first goal. Bond plays centre-forward for the first time, netting twice, the second from 25 yards.										
34		H	NEWCASTLE		7	W		3-0	2-0	Dick 16, Musgrove 35, Obeney 51	Dwyer	Kirkup	Cantwell	Malcolm	Brown	Smith	Grice	Obeney	Bond	Dick	Musgrove
	27/3			35,000	*13*		39				*Harvey*	*Keith*	*McMichael*	*Franks*	*Scoular*	*Mitchell*	*Hughes*	*Allchurch*	*Marshall*	*Eastham*	*Taylor*
										Ref: J Barradell	Mid-table Magpies are well beaten. Makeshift centre-forward John Bond did not score, but his pass set up Dick for the first goal, and his cross was whacked home by Obeney for the third. Musgrove headed the second from Grice's cross. Hammers' half-back line takes all the plaudits.										
35		A	ARSENAL		6	W		2-1	1-1	Dick 15, 47	Dwyer	Kirkup	Cantwell	Malcolm	Brown	Smith	Grice	Obeney	Bond	Dick	Musgrove
	28/3			*52,452*	*3*		41			*Henderson 39*	*Standen*	*Evans*	*McCullough*	*Ward*	*Dodgin*	*Docherty*	*Clapton*	*Groves*	*Henderson*	*Julians*	*Nutt*
										Ref: J Pickles	24 hours after beating Newcastle, Hammers overcome George Swindin's Arsenal to insist they are London's top club. This was a turgid match to which Arsenal contributed little. Hammers used the offside trap to good effect, and won through Dick's long hop, in off a post, and a volley.										
36		A	NEWCASTLE		7	L		1-3	0-2	Obeney 89	Dwyer	Kirkup	Cantwell	Malcolm	Brown	Smith	Grice	Obeney	Bond	Dick	Musgrove
	30/3			*20,911*	*13*		41			*Taylor 6, Keith 28, Allchurch 84*	*Harvey*	*Keith*	*McMichael*	*Franks*	*Scoular*	*Mitchell*	*Taylor*	*Allchurch*	*Gibson*	*Eastham*	*McGuigan*
										Ref: T Cooper	Newcastle avenge their recent defeat before a tiny crowd. West Ham had no answer to the runs of England's George Eastham or the wizardry of Bobby Mitchell. Kirkup replaced the injured Dwyer in goal in the last minute, and with the last kick Obeney side-footed in Grice's pass.										
37		H	EVERTON			W		3-2	1-1	Bond 24, Dick 77, Grice 85	Dwyer	Kirkup	Cantwell	Malcolm	Brown	Smith	Grice	Obeney	Bond	Dick	Musgrove
	4/4			28,500	*15*		43			*Hickson 38, Laverick 87*	*Dunlop*	*Parker*	*Bramwell*	*Harris B*	*Labone*	*Meagan*	*Harris J*	*Thomas*	*Hickson*	*Collins*	*Laverick*
										Ref: W Clements	John Dick celebrates being the first Hammer to be selected for Scotland by captaining the side against lowly Everton and restoring West Ham's lead from Bond's pass. Scotland's other inside-forward, Everton's Bobby Collins, looked good but was thwarted by West Ham's offside game.										
38		A	LEICESTER			D		1-1	0-1	Bond 63	Dwyer	Kirkup	Cantwell	Malcolm	Brown	Smith	Grice	Bond	Keeble	Smillie	Musgrove
	11/4			*23,825*			44			*McDonald 35*	*Maclaren*	*Chalmers*	*Baillie*	*Newman*	*Knapp*	*Appleton*	*McDonald*	*Stephenson*	*Walsh*	*Leek*	*Wills*
										Ref: A Moore	Leicester are hauling themselves off the bottom and will escape the drop by two points. Tommy McDonald looked like giving them a priceless win by belting Wills' cross past Dwyer. But Bond, this time playing at inside-right, shot from 20 yards and deceived Dave Maclaren in goal.										
39		H	LUTON			D		0-0	0-0		Dwyer	Kirkup	Cantwell	Malcolm	Brown	Smith	Grice	Obeney	Bond	Dick	Musgrove
	13/4			27,000			45				*Baynham*	*McNally*	*Hawkes*	*Groves*	*Owen*	*Pacey*	*Bingham*	*Brown*	*Morton*	*Cummins*	*Adam*
											Lowly Luton have just reached the FA Cup Final, and apart from Adam this will be their Wembley team. The Hatters have won away once all season, but this point enables them to stay clear of the drop zone. It is the first time the Hammers have failed to score at home since November.										
40		H	PRESTON			D		1-1	1-1	Dare 13	Dwyer	Kirkup	Cantwell	Malcolm	Brown	Smith	Grice	Bond	Dare	Dick	Musgrove
	18/4			**21,500**			46			*Baxter 8*	*Else*	*Cunningham*	*Walton*	*O'Farrell*	*Mattison*	*Smith*	*Mayers*	*Thompson*	*Hatsell*	*Baxter*	*Taylor*
										Ref: G Pullin	The last time Preston played at Upton Park was in 1956, when they lost 2-5 in the Cup. Billy Dare played centre-forward for West Ham then, and now, with Keeble failing a fitness test. Musgrave's cross flew in off Dare's leg for the leveller, after Baxter had side-footed Preston ahead.										
41		H	MANCHESTER C			W		5-1	2-0	Cantwell 23, Dick 40, 68, Grice 66	Dwyer	Kirkup	Bond	Malcolm	Brown	Moore	Grice	Smith	Cantwell	Dick	Musgrove
	20/4			23,500			48			*Barlow 48*	*Trautmann*	*Leivers*	*Brannigan*	*Cheetham*	*Ewing*	*Shawcross*	*Barlow*	*Johnstone*	*McAdams*	*Hayes*	*Sambrook*
											City will escape relegation by one point. Dick's two goals take his season's total to 27, a Hammers post-war record. Trautmann was to blame for at least two goals, and centre-half Ewing played with strapped ribs for most of the game. City also had four goals ruled out through offside.										
42		A	LEEDS			L		0-1	0-0		Dwyer	Kirkup	Bond	Malcolm	Brown	Moore	Grice	Smith	Cantwell	Dick	Musgrove
	24/4			*11,257*			48			*Shackleton 72*	*Burgin*	*Dunn*	*Hair*	*McConne*	*Charlton*	*Cush*	*Crowe*	*Revie*	*Shackleton*	*Peyton*	*Meek*
		Home		Away						Ref: J Swain	Leeds end the season with seven points out of eight. Star of the game was Alan Shackleton, who scored after Crowe's centre was pushed on by Noel Peyton. Jack Charlton subdued Cantwell. Out-of-touch Dick had West Ham's best chance, but his header down was cleared off the line.										
Average	28,998			32,360																	

FA Cup				F-A	H-T	Scorers, Times, and Referees	1	2	3	4	5	6	7	8	9	10	11
3	A	TOTTENHAM	L	0-2	0-0		Gregory	Bond	Cantwell	Malcolm	Brown	Smith	Grice	Smillie	Keeble	Dick	Musgrove
	10/1	*56,252*				*Jones 48, Smith 52*	*Hollowbread*	*Baker*	*Hopkins*	*Dodge*	*Norman*	*Iley*	*Brooks*	*Harmer*	*Smith*	*Dunmore*	*Jones*
						Ref: B Griffiths	West Ham did a Christmas double over struggling Spurs in the League. In icy conditions, which caused players to wear rubber studs, Hammers pressed hard in the first half. Gregory punched out Brooks' cross, but only to Cliff Jones. Bobby Smith then headed in David Dunmore's cross.										

		Home					Away					
	P	W	D	L	F	A	W	D	L	F	A	Pts
1 Wolves	42	15	3	3	68	19	13	2	6	42	30	61
2 Manchester U	42	14	4	3	58	27	10	3	8	45	39	55
3 Arsenal	42	14	3	4	53	29	7	5	9	35	39	50
4 Bolton	42	14	3	4	56	30	6	7	8	23	36	50
5 West Brom	42	8	7	6	41	33	10	6	5	47	35	49
6 WEST HAM	42	15	3	3	59	29	6	3	12	26	41	48
7 Burnley	42	11	4	6	41	29	8	6	7	40	41	48
8 Blackpool	42	12	7	2	39	13	6	4	11	27	36	47
9 Birmingham	42	14	1	6	54	35	6	5	10	30	33	46
10 Blackburn	42	12	3	6	48	28	5	7	9	28	42	44
11 Newcastle	42	11	3	7	40	29	6	4	11	40	51	41
12 Preston	42	9	3	9	40	39	8	4	9	30	38	41
13 Nott'm Forest	42	9	4	8	37	32	8	2	11	34	42	40
14 Chelsea	42	13	2	6	52	37	5	2	14	25	61	40
15 Leeds	42	8	7	6	28	27	7	2	12	29	47	39
16 Everton	42	11	3	7	39	38	6	1	14	32	49	38
17 Luton	42	11	6	4	50	26	1	7	13	18	45	37
18 Tottenham	42	10	3	8	56	42	3	7	11	29	53	36
19 Leicester	42	7	6	8	34	36	4	4	13	33	62	32
20 Manchester C	42	8	7	6	40	32	3	2	16	24	63	31
21 Aston Villa	42	8	5	8	31	33	3	3	15	27	54	30
22 Portsmouth	42	5	4	12	38	47	1	5	15	26	65	21
	924	239	91	132	1002	690	132	91	239	690	1002	924

Odds & ends

Double wins: (5) Portsmouth, Villa, Blackburn, Bolton, Tottenham.
Double losses: (2) Birmingham, Leeds.

Won from behind: (3) Chelsea (h), Blackburn (h), Forest (h).
Lost from in front: (3) Luton (a), Birmingham (h), Preston (a).

High spots: Beating champions Wolves in first home match.
Going top of the table in September when beating Manchester U.
Finishing sixth in first season back in Division One.
Completing the double over five clubs, including Spurs.
Winning five games on the trot in December and January.
Having two players score 20 League goals or more.

Low spots: Losing 0-4 at Forest immediately after going top.
Losing four games in a row in November and December.
Losing to Spurs in the FA Cup after beating them twice in the League.

Ever-presents: (5) Bond, Cantwell, Malcolm, Brown, Grice.
Hat-tricks: (2): Vic Keeble (1), John Dick (1).
Leading scorer: (27) John Dick.

	Appearances		Goals		
	Lge	FAC	Lge	FAC	Tot
Bond, John	42	1	7		7
Brown, Ken	42	1			
Cantwell, Noel	42	1	3		3
Dare, Billy	2		1		1
Dick, John	41	1	27		27
Dwyer, Noel	10				
Gregory, Harry	32	1			
Grice, Harry	42	1	6		6
Keeble, Vic	32	1	20		20
Kirkup, Joe	11				
Lansdowne, Billy	6		1		1
Malcolm, Andy	42	1			
Moore, Bobby	5				
Musgrove, Malcolm	40	1	7		7
Nelson, Andy	12		1		1
Obeney, Harry	6		3		3
Smillie, Andy	4	1			
Smith, John	36	1	4		4
Woosnam, Phil	13		2		2
Wragg, Douglas	2				
(own-goals)			3		3
20 players used	**462**	**11**	**85**		**85**

No	Date		Att	Pos	Pt	F-A	H-T	Scorers, Times, and Referees	1	2	3	4	5	6	7	8	9	10	11
1	H	LEICESTER			W	3-0	1-0	Smith 24, Keeble 71, Grice 85	Dwyer	Bond	Cantwell	Malcolm	Brown	Smith	Grice	Woosnam	Keeble	Dick	Musgrove
	22/8		28,000		2				*MacLaren*	*Chalmers*	*Baillie*	*Newman*	*Knapp*	*Appleton*	*Riley*	*Cheesebrough*	*Hines*	*Leek*	*Wills*
								Ref: W Clements	Fenton fields his preferred 11 for the first time since January, and avenges last season's home defeat. Mind you, Keeble and Woosnam both struggled to shake off the effects of cartilage surgery. Musgrove set up Smith, Keeble headed in Bond's cross, and Grice, Dick's free-kick.										
2	A	PRESTON			D	1-1	1-1	Musgrove 32	Dwyer	Bond	Cantwell	Malcolm	Brown	Smith	Grice	Woosnam	Keeble	Dick	Musgrove
	25/8		*29,433*		3			*Thompson 35*	*Else*	*Cunningham*	*Walton*	*O'Farrell*	*Dunn*	*Smith*	*Mayers*	*Thompson P*	*Finney*	*Sneddon*	*Taylor*
								Ref: N Hough	19-year-old John Smith created both goals, passing for Musgrove's opener from 25 yards, then slipping to let in Derek Mayers, who was about to shoot when Tommy Thompson whipped the ball off his toes. Hammers' tactics of 10 attackers and 10 defenders deserved more than a draw.										
3	A	BURNLEY		2	W	3-1	1-1	Woosnam 8, Smillie 63, Grice 77	Dwyer	Bond	Cantwell	Malcolm	Brown	Smith	Grice	Woosnam	Keeble	Smillie	Musgrove
	29/8		*26,783*	*5*	5			*Connelly 3*	*Blacklaw*	*Angus*	*Cummings*	*Seith*	*Miller*	*Adamson*	*Connelly*	*McIlroy*	*Pointer*	*Robson*	*Pilkington*
								Ref: M McCoy	Burnley had won their first two games, and when John Connelly pounced on a blocked save by the heroic Dwyer, it looked like a third win. Woosnam belted an equaliser from 25 yards, and when John Angus fell on his backside Smillie poked the ball under the advancing Blacklaw.										
4	H	PRESTON			W	2-1	0-0	Smillie 52, Keeble 65	Dwyer	Bond	Cantwell	Malcolm	Brown	Smith	Grice	Woosnam	Keeble	Smillie	Musgrove
	31/8		32,000		7			*Smith 79*	*Else*	*Cunningham*	*Walton*	*O'Farrell*	*Dunn*	*Smith*	*Finney*	*Milne*	*Hatsell*	*Sneddon*	*Taylor*
								Ref: W Pullin	Preston had drawn their first three, but looked unlikely to continue that sequence when young Andy Smillie crowned his first home game with a sharp turn and shot inside the near post. Preston were pressing for an equaliser when Grice crossed: Keeble charged Fred Else over the line.										
5	H	LEEDS			L	1-2	1-1	Keeble 14	Gregory	Bond	Cantwell	Malcolm	Brown	Smith	Grice	Woosnam	Keeble	Smillie	Musgrove
	5/9		28,000		7			*Crowe 42p, 50*	*Burgin*	*Ashall*	*Hair*	*McConnell*	*Charlton*	*Cush*	*Meek*	*Cameron*	*Revie*	*Crowe*	*Overfield*
								Ref: R Smith	West Ham played like fairies against lowly Leeds, inspired by 32-year-old skipper Don Revie. When Peter McConnell limped off on 29 mins, Revie dropped back in defence. Keeble had headed in Grice's cross but Malcolm fouled Meek in the box. Soldier Chris Crowe headed No 2.										
6	A	TOTTENHAM		3	D	2-2	1-1	Keeble 43, Musgrove 73	Dwyer	Bond	Cantwell	Malcolm	Brown	Smith	Grice	Woosnam	Keeble	Smillie	Musgrove
	9/9		***58,909***	*2*	8			*Smith 22, Jones 66*	*Brown*	*Baker*	*Hopkins*	*Marchi*	*Norman*	*Mackay*	*Medwin*	*Harmer*	*Smith*	*Dunmore*	*Jones*
								Ref: J Hunt	A huge crowd sees this table-topping contest. Blanchflower, captain, of Bill Nicholson's Spurs, was out with a knee injury. Both sides carved a memorable goal apiece – West Ham, when Bond overlapped to cross for Keeble; Spurs, when Harmer sent Jones clear to dribble round Dwyer.										
7	A	BOLTON			L	1-5	1-1	Keeble 43 *[Stevens 82]*	Dwyer	Bond	Cantwell	Malcolm	Brown	Smith	Grice	Woosnam	Keeble	Smillie	Musgrove
	12/9		*24,191*		8			*Hill 36, Banks 52, Bannister 75, 89,*	*Hopkinson*	*Hennin*	*Banks*	*Stanley*	*Higgins*	*Edwards B*	*Bannister*	*Hill*	*Stevens*	*Parry*	*Holden*
								Ref: M Dixon	21st plays 3rd, with this amazing outcome. Reserve winger Neville Bannister made the difference, capitalising on two blunders by Cantwell. The other winger, Doug Holden, tortured Bond throughout. It might have been worse. Parry fired a penalty wide for the second time in a week.										
8	H	TOTTENHAM			L	1-2	0-1	Bond 80p	Dwyer	Bond	Cantwell	Malcolm	Brown	Smith	**Wragg**	Woosnam	Keeble	**Brett**	Grice
	14/9		37,500		8			*Marchi 25, Smith 54*	*Brown*	*Baker*	*Hopkins*	*Blanchflower*	*Norman*	*Mackay*	*Medwin*	*Marchi*	*Smith*	*Dunmore*	*Dyson*
								Ref: R Warnke	Two handling errors by Dwyer presented Spurs with their fourth away win out of five. Terry Medwin's fierce cross-shot slipped through his hands and fell to Tony Marchi, and Dwyer then misjudged Bobby Smith's long-range header. Mel Hopkins felled Grice for a disputed penalty.										
9	A	CHELSEA		7	W	4-2	2-0	Musgrove 6, Dick 19, 87, Woosnam 61	Dwyer	Bond	Cantwell	Malcolm	Brown	Smith	Grice	Woosnam	Keeble	Dick	Musgrove
	19/9		*54,349*	*15*	10			*Blunstone 59, Livesey 62*	*Matthews*	*Sillett P*	*Whittaker*	*McMillan*	*Scott*	*Compton*	*Brabrook*	*Greaves*	*Livesey*	*Tambling*	*Blunstone*
								Ref: J Williams	Ted Drake's young Chelsea score many and concede more, typified by this game. Musgrove netted off a post and Keeble set up Dick in a one-sided first half when Greaves was shackled. But Brabrook got the better of Cantwell in the second, though Woosnam's super chip settled it.										
10	H	WEST BROM		6	W	**4-1**	1-0	Musgrove 1, 50, W'snam 53, Grice 70	Dwyer	Bond	Cantwell	Malcolm	Brown	Smith	Grice	Woosnam	Keeble	Dick	Musgrove
	26/9		30,570	*9*	12			*Burnside 52*	*Potter*	*Howe*	*Williams*	*Setters*	*Kennedy*	*Robson*	*Dixon*	*Burnside*	*Allen*	*Kevan*	*Hogg*
								Ref: J Mitchell	Hammers climb above Albion after another four-goal haul, seen by England boss Walter Winterbottom. Bond outplayed his opposite number, Don Howe, an England regular but harassed by Musgrove throughout. Inter-passing between Woosnam, Grice and Dick forged the opener.										

11	A	NEWCASTLE		5	D	0-0	0-0		Dwyer	Bond	Cantwell	Malcolm	Brown	Smith	Grice	Woosnam	Keeble	Dick	Musgrove
	3/10		*41,890*	*18*	13				*Mitchell S*	*Whitehead*	*Ferguson*	*Scoular*	*Stokoe*	*Bell*	*White*	*Allchurch*	*Scott*	*Eastham*	*Mitchell R*
								Ref: G McCabe	Seconds before half-time Woosnam brought down Allchurch, but Dwyer saved George Eastham's penalty. Fenton made ex-Newcastle Keeble skipper for the day, but he was chained by Bob Stokoe. Outplayed in the first half, West Ham twice hit a post through Dick early in the second.										
12	H	LUTON		5	W	3-1	0-0	Woodley 48, 59, Keeble 72	Dwyer	Bond	Cantwell	Malcolm	Brown	Smith	**Woodley**	Woosnam	Keeble	Dick	Musgrove
	10/10		23,500	*22*	15			*Turner 86*	*Baynham*	*Dunne*	*Hawkes*	*Morton*	*Kelly*	*Groves*	*Bingham*	*Turner*	*Pacey*	*Brown*	*Cummins*
								Ref: J Carr	Syd Owen's Luton are bottom and going down. 17-year-old schoolboy cap Derek Woodley sinks them with a walk-in first goal and a poached rebound for No 2. Keeper Ron Baynham was stretchered off for ten minutes in the first half, returning to face Bond's penalty, which hit a post.										
13	A	EVERTON		3	W	1-0	0-0	Musgrove 85	Dwyer	Bond	Cantwell	Malcolm	Brown	Moore	Grice	**Cartwright**	Keeble	Smillie	Musgrove
	17/10		*30,563*	*21*	17				*Dunlop*	*Parker*	*Bramwell*	*King*	*Jones*	*Harris B*	*Harris J*	*Thomas*	*Hickson*	*Collins*	*Shackleton*
								Ref: A Ellis	Hammers owed a debt to Dwyer, who saved from 40 yards from Johnny King and what would have been a neat own-goal from Brown. Moore, playing because John Smith was England's reserve, surged up the right before releasing Musgrove, who shot left-footed under Albert Dunlop.										
14	H	BLACKPOOL		2	W	1-0	0-0	Musgrove 86	Dwyer	Bond	Kirkup	Malcolm	Brown	Smith	Grice	Woosnam	Cantwell	Dick	Musgrove
	24/10		32,500	*14*	19				*Farm*	*Armfield*	*Martin*	*Kelly J*	*Gratrix*	*Kelly H*	*Hill*	*Peterson*	*Mudie*	*Durie*	*Kaye*
								Ref: Hackney	Dwyer has been capped by Eire. West Ham barely deserved one point from this awful game. Yet again they are indebted to a late Musgrove winner, this time a header from Brown's lofted 40-yarder into the box. Pool were without Stanley Matthews and had Jim Kelly a passenger.										
15	A	FULHAM		3	L	0-1	0-0		Dwyer	Kirkup	Cantwell	Malcolm	Brown	Smith	Grice	Woosnam	Keeble	Dick	Musgrove
	31/10		*44,695*	*6*	19			*Stokes 69*	*Macedo*	*Cohen*	*Langley*	*Mullery*	*Bentley*	*Lowe*	*Key*	*Stokes*	*Cook*	*Haynes*	*Chamberlain*
								Ref L Hamer	Craven Cottage's biggest gate of the season sees Fulham's fifth straight win and West Ham's first defeat in seven. Ex-Spur Alf Stokes hit the outside of a post before scoring the all-important goal. Johnny Haynes dummied Key's cross, leaving Stokes in the clear, just three yards out.										
16	H	MANCHESTER C		2	W	**4-1**	2-0	Cantwell 5p, McTavish 39 (og), [Obeney 59, M'grove 76]	Dwyer	Kirkup	Cantwell	Malcolm	Brown	Smith	Grice	Woosnam	Obeney	Dick	Musgrove
	7/11		25,500	*12*	21			*Hayes 80*	*Trautmann*	*Leivers*	*Sear*	*Cheetham*	*McTavish*	*Shawcross*	*Barlow*	*Hannah*	*Kerr*	*Hayes*	*Colbridge*
								Ref: S Yates	Brown has been capped by England. Recalled Obeney had three glaring misses before beating Trautmann, who had parried from Dick. Roy Cheetham allegedly fouled Dick for the penalty, but it looked harsh. Then John McTavish, pressured by Dick, turned the ball past his keeper.										
17	A	ARSENAL		1	W	3-1	1-1	Dick 31, Obeney 50, Musgrove 84	Dwyer	Kirkup	Cantwell	Malcolm	Brown	Smith	Grice	Woosnam	Obeney	Dick	Musgrove
	14/11		*49,760*	*12*	23			*Bloomfield 5*	*Kelsey*	*Wills*	*McCullough*	*Charles*	*Dodgin*	*Petts*	*Clapton*	*Herd*	*Groves*	*Bloomfield*	*Haverty*
								Ref: J Kelly	Defeat for Spurs, coupled with this famous win, takes West Ham top. Clapton and Groves conjured Bloomfield's goal, and Arsenal might have had more until Herd's injury turned the tide. Dick slid a angled equaliser, Musgrove carved a goal for Obeney, and Grice made Musgrove's.										
18	H	WOLVES		1	W	3-2	2-0	Dick 3, 15, 55	**Rhodes**	Bond	Cantwell	Malcolm	Brown	Smith	Grice	Woosnam	Obeney	Dick	Musgrove
	21/11		**38,000**	*5*	25			*Mason 70, Broadbent 73*	*Finlayson*	*Stuart*	*Harris*	*Clamp*	*Showell*	*Flowers*	*Deeley*	*Mason*	*Murray*	*Broadbent*	*Horne*
								Ref: J Williams	Champions Wolves would have overtaken Hammers had they won. Instead they trailed 0-3 to Dick's wonder hat-trick, the first two with his feet, the third with a flying header. What a debut for Canvey's Brian Rhodes in goal. West Ham will gather only 13 more points all season.										
19	A	SHEFFIELD WED		3	L	**0-7**	0-4	*F'tham 3, 7, W'kinson 8, Finney 22, 75, [Craig 68, Ellis 71]*	Dwyer	Bond	Cantwell	Malcolm	Brown	Smith	Grice	Woosnam	Obeney	Dick	Musgrove
	28/11		*38,367*	*9*	25				*Springett*	*Johnson*	*Megson*	*McAnearney*	*Swan*	*Kay*	*Wilkinson*	*Craig*	*Ellis*	*Fantham*	*Finney*
								Ref: T Cooper	The rot sets in for cocky West Ham. Three goals in the first eight minutes will ruin their season. Free-kicks brought the first two goals, which West Ham were unable to clear. Noel Dwyer takes the blame, clueless at dealing with crosses and being transfixed by the Owls' fourth goal.										
20	H	NOTT'M FOREST		3	W	**4-1**	0-0	Obeney 59, 83, Woosnam 80, 88	Dwyer	Bond	Cantwell	Malcolm	Brown	Smith	Grice	Woosnam	Obeney	Dick	Musgrove
	5/12		26,000	*16*	27			*Imlach 84*	*Thomson*	*McDonald*	*Patrick*	*Whitefoot*	*McKinlay*	*Iley*	*Barton*	*Booth*	*Wilson*	*Gray*	*Imlach*
								Ref: K Howley	Preston and Spurs are still above unchanged West Ham, who labour before turning over the Cup-holders in the closing minutes. Musgrove hit a post, Obeney pounced and everyone expected a 1-0 win. Musgrove also set up No 2. But for Dwyer, Forest could have been ahead at half-time.										
21	A	BLACKBURN		4	L	2-6	2-4	Woosnam 9, Dick 29	Dwyer	Bond	Cantwell	Malcolm	Brown	Smith	Grice	Woosnam	Obeney	Dick	Musgrove
	12/12		*22,400*	*7*	27			*Dougan 11, 18, 36, 42, Dobing 53, 63*	*Jones*	*Bray*	*Whelan*	*Clayton*	*Woods*	*McGrath*	*Bimpson*	*Dobing*	*Dougan*	*Vernon*	*McLeod*
								Ref: R Windle	Brown had played for England instead of Billy Wright, but he came unstuck against Dougan, who scored four first-half goals, two headers and one after a 40-yard sprint. West Ham did the double over Rovers last season and Woosnam's bullet opener suggested another comfortable win.										

No	Date		Att	Pos	Pt	F-A	H-T	Scorers, Times, and Referees	1	2	3	4	5	6	7	8	9	10	11
22	A	LEICESTER		5	L	1-2	1-2	Obeney 3	Dwyer	Bond	Cantwell	Malcolm	Brown	Smith	Grice	Woosnam	Obeney	Dick	Musgrove
	19/12		*20,000*	*18*	27			*White 18, Cheesebrough 33*	*Banks*	*Chalmers*	*Cunningham*	*White*	*Knapp*	*Appleton*	*McDonald*	*Cheesebrough*	*Keyworth*	*Leek*	*Wills*
								Ref: H Callaghan	Struggling Leicester tamed mighty Wolves and now West Ham. They overcome Obeney's early goal from Musgrove's pass by playing long, low passes on the greasy pitch. Dwyer feebly punched Wills' cross to White, and Keyworth pushed the ball through to Albert Cheesebrough.										
23	A	BIRMINGHAM		5	L	0-2	0-2		Dwyer	Kirkup	Cantwell	Malcolm	Brown	Smith	Woodley	Woosnam	Brett	Dick	Musgrove
	26/12		*29,745*	*20*	27			*Hooper 34, Astall 35*	*Schofield*	*Farmer*	*Allen*	*Watts*	*Smith*	*Larkin*	*Astall*	*Barrett*	*Stubbs*	*Gordon*	*Hooper*
								Ref: R Leafe	The ref made Dwyer change his black jersey, first to a dark green one, then to a light green one. Not that it helped West Ham, who got bogged in the St Andrews mud. Bond was dropped. Hooper scored from a rebound; then the recalled Gordon Astall blasted a second from the wing.										
24	H	BIRMINGHAM		5	W	3-1	1-1	Musgrove 14, 81, Brett 58	Dwyer	Kirkup	Cantwell	Malcolm	Brown	Smith	Woodley	Smillie	Brett	Dick	Musgrove
	28/12		26,000	*21*	29			*Astall 11*	*Schofield*	*Farmer*	*Allen*	*Watts*	*Smith*	*Neal*	*Astall*	*Gordon*	*Stubbs*	*Larkin*	*Hooper*
								Ref: J Parkinson	Woosnam is dropped for the first time. England's Trevor Smith dominated Ron Brett, but the two occasions he got away brought goals. He netted with a 15-yard drive and began the move which led to Musgrove's second. Hooper and Dick were booked on the hour in this hard game.										
25	H	BURNLEY		6	L	2-5	1-3	Woosnam 13, Cantwell 77p	Dwyer	Kirkup	Cantwell	Malcolm	Brown	Smith	Grice	Woosnam	Obeney	Dick	Musgrove
	2/1		26,000	*2*	29			*Law'n 10, 74, P'kton 33, Con'ly 44, 89*	*Blacklaw*	*Angus*	*Elder*	*Seith*	*Miller*	*Adamson*	*Connelly*	*Lawson*	*Pointer*	*Robson*	*Pilkington*
								Ref: K Stokes	Another pasting, this time from the champions-to-be. This mudbath has seen Hammers concede 24 goals in seven games. Young Ian Lawson replaced Jimmy McIlroy and scored when standing still, removing some mud from his eye. No one knew why West Ham were given a penalty.										
26	A	LEEDS		8	L	0-3	0-1		Rhodes	Bond	Cantwell	Malcolm	Brown	Moore	Musgrove	Smith	Keeble	Obeney	Woosnam
	16/1		*15,000*	*18*	29			*McCole 36, Crowe 80, Meek 88*	*Wood*	*Ashall*	*Hair*	*Cush*	*Charlton*	*Gibson*	*Crowe*	*Revie*	*McCole*	*Peyton*	*Meek*
								Ref: K Collinge	West Ham compound their Huddersfield FA Cup debacle by presenting lowly Leeds with their first home win since November, and their first 'double' of the season. Dwyer's replacement, Brian Rhodes, had an unhappy time. John McCole capitalised on Ken Brown's bad clearance.										
27	H	BOLTON		10	L	1-2	1-2	Dick 16	Dwyer	Kirkup	Bond	Moore	Brown	Smith	Grice	Woosnam	Cantwell	Dick	Musgrove
	23/1		**21,600**	*6*	29			*Parry 8, Stevens 13*	*Hopkinson*	*Hartle*	*Farrimond*	*Hennin*	*Higgins*	*Stanley*	*Birch*	*Hill*	*Stevens*	*Parry*	*Holden*
								Ref: R Mann	Fenton makes nine changes before Upton Park's smallest crowd. Parry netted from close in from Holden's pass. Parry then made the opening for Stephens. Dick passed a late fitness test and scored with a rising shot. The winter mud is widely held to blame for West Ham's malaise.										
28	H	CHELSEA		8	W	4-2	1-2	Bond 44, 55p, 57, Dick 65	Dwyer	Kirkup	**Lyall**	Malcolm	Brown	Moore	Scott	Woosnam	Bond	Dick	Musgrove
	6/2		29,500	*16*	31			*Brabrook 5, Tindall 37*	*Matthews*	*Sillett J*	*Sillett P*	*Venables*	*Mortimore*	*Anderton*	*Brabrook*	*Brooks*	*Tindall*	*Greaves*	*Blunstone*
								Ref: T Dawes	John Lyall enjoys a better debut than Chelsea's Terry Venables. Brabrook's solo goal and Tindall's header make it 0-2. Bond, skipper for the day, has a blinder at No 9, netting from a free-kick, a penalty (John Sillett fouling Musgrove), and a header – and crossed for Dick's header.										
29	H	NEWCASTLE		11	L	3-5	2-3	Dick 38, W'snam 39, 48 *[Eastham 60]*	Dwyer	Kirkup	Cantwell	Malcolm	Brown	Smith	Scott	Woosnam	Bond	Dick	Musgrove
	20/2		25,000	*10*	31			*Hughes 2, Allchurch 20, White 27, 63,*	*Harvey*	*Keith*	*McMichael*	*Scoular*	*Stokoe*	*Bell*	*Hughes*	*Eastham*	*White*	*Allchurch*	*Luke*
									In ankle-deep mud, West Ham go three down, recover to 3-3, then allow George Eastham to square-dance past four defenders for a sensational goal. Dwyer goes from bad to worse, pushing Hughes' shot over his head into the net, then diving too late for Ivor Allchurch's trickled shot.										
30	A	NOTT'M FOREST		11	L	1-3	0-2	Musgrove 89	Rhodes	Kirkup	Lyall	Malcolm	Brown	**Hurst**	Scott	Woosnam	Bond	Cantwell	Musgrove
	27/2		*26,317*	*17*	31			*Wilson 27, Booth 34, 60*	*Armstrong*	*Patrick*	*McDonald*	*Whitefoot*	*McKinlay*	*Burkitt*	*Barton*	*Booth*	*Wilson*	*Bowden*	*Gray*
								Ref: D Martin	Forest's Billy Walker, 62, is the game's longest serving manager. Fenton plays both full-backs, Bond and Cantwell, in attack. Bond hit the bar but Cantwell reverted to defence when injures a knee. Both of Forest's early goals stemmed from free-kicks. Forest's win-bonus was all of £4.										
31	H	EVERTON		10	D	2-2	1-0	Bond 39, Dick 86	Rhodes	Kirkup	Cantwell	Malcolm	Brown	Moore	Grice	Woosnam	Bond	Dick	Musgrove
	5/3		25,000	*19*	32			*Vernon 68, 70*	*Dunlop*	*Parker*	*Bramwell*	*Gabriel*	*Labone*	*Meagan*	*Lill*	*Collins*	*Harris*	*Vernon*	*Ring*
								Ref: P Carr	Everton won't win away all season, but were within four minutes of doing so here. Then Musgrove, who wove through on his own to force Albert Dunlop to block. The ball fell to Dick. After Vernon had scored direct from a free-kick, Brown and Rhodes left the ball to each other.										

No		Opponents	Pos	Res	F-A	H-T	Scorers, Times, and Referees	1	2	3	4	5	6	7	8	9	10	11
32	A	WEST BROM	11	L	2-3	1-1	Grice 9, Bond 67p	Rhodes	Kirkup	Cantwell	Malcolm	Brown	Moore	Grice	Woosnam	Bond	Dick	Musgrove
	9/3	*11,980*	*5*	32			*Kevan 3, 47, Allen 68p*	*Wallace*	*Howe*	*Williams*	*Drury*	*Kennedy*	*Robson*	*Jackson*	*Burnside*	*Allen*	*Kevan*	*Aitken*
							Ref: L Hamer	This game, played on slushy snow, came to life with two second-half penalties in a minute. First, Albion's Chuck Drury handled a cross. Then Kirkup made a diving save from Derek Kevan – denied his hat-trick when Ronnie Allen took the kick. Woosnam put Grice away for his goal.										
33	A	BLACKPOOL	11	L	2-3	1-2	Bond 40, Brett 54	Rhodes	Kirkup	Cantwell	Malcolm	Brown	Smith	Grice	Woosnam	Bond	Brett	Musgrove
	12/3	*14,515*	*10*	32			*Perry 14, 81, Charnley 16*	*Waiters*	*Armfield*	*Martin*	*Kelly J*	*Gratrix*	*Durie*	*Matthews*	*Kaye*	*Charnley*	*Green*	*Perry*
							Ref: N Hough	West Ham were two down when Rhodes injured a shoulder, whereupon open-to-offers Young England John Smith went in goal. 10-man West Ham fought back. Tony Waiters fumbled Bond's shot into goal and Brett headed a fine equaliser. Perry escaped Kirkup to fire in a cross-shot.										
34	H	BLACKBURN	11	W	2-1	2-0	Woosnam 21, Musgrove 25	Rhodes	Bond	Cantwell	Malcolm	Brown	Hurst	Grice	Woosnam	**Dunmore**	Brett	Musgrove
	19/3	26,000	*15*	34			*Bimpson 60*	*Leyland*	*Bray*	*Whelan*	*Clayton*	*Woods*	*England*	*Bimpson*	*Crowe*	*Dobing*	*Douglas*	*Ratcliffe*
								Rovers face an FA Cup semi-final on Saturday. They gave a debut to Chris Crowe, who did nothing. West Ham's Dave Dunmore from Spurs did better, playing his part in Woosnam's opener, and making an overhead kick which Musgrove headed in. Louis Bimpson burst past Brown.										
35	A	MANCHESTER C		L	1-3	1-0	Musgrove 9	Rhodes	Kirkup	Bond	Malcolm	Brown	Hurst	Grice	Woosnam	Dunmore	Brett	Musgrove
	30/3	*29,572*		34			*Law 55, Barlow 56, McAdams 61*	*Trautmann*	*Leivers*	*Branagan*	*Barnes*	*McTavish*	*Oakes*	*Barlow*	*Law*	*McAdams*	*Hayes*	*Colbridge*
							Ref: J Taylor	Trautmann failed to hold a greasy ball and Musgrove rammed it in. Then Malcolm flattened Denis Law. With the ball on the spot, Ken Barnes jumped over it and Billy McAdams netted. Ref Jack Taylor awarded a goal, then changed his mind, whereupon Rhodes saved Barnes' re-take.										
36	H	ARSENAL	13	D	0-0	0-0		Rhodes	Bond	Cantwell	Malcolm	Brown	Moore	Grice	Woosnam	Dunmore	Dick	Musgrove
	2/4	29,000	*12*	35				*Kelsey*	*Magill*	*McCullough*	*Charles*	*Docherty*	*Groves*	*Henderson*	*Herd*	*Julians*	*Bloomfield*	*Haverty*
							Ref: G McCabe	Arsenal played two centre-halves – Mel Charles and Tommy Docherty – as defence smothered attack. On 72 mins McCullough brought down Musgrove but Bond drove the penalty straight at Jack Kelsey. Rhodes tipped over Herd's header for Hammers' first clean sheet since October.										
37	A	WOLVES	13	L	0-5	0-1	*[Mannion 63]*	Rhodes	Bond	Cantwell	Malcolm	Brown	Moore	Grice	Woosnam	Dunmore	Smillie	Musgrove
	11/4	*48,086*	*1*	35			*Murray 17, 77, Clamp 49, Horne 52,*	*Finlayson*	*Showell*	*Harris*	*Clamp*	*Slater*	*Flowers*	*Mannion*	*Mason*	*Murray*	*Broadbent*	*Horne*
							Ref: W Crossley	This game was postponed from Saturday because England called up three Wolves players v Scotland. Now, under floodlights, Wolves soar to the top with a first win over West Ham in four games. Jim Murray's diving header paved the way. Eddie Clamp volleyed No 2 from 25 yards.										
38	H	MANCHESTER U	12	W	2-1	2-1	Musgrove 6, Grice 7	Rhodes	Bond	Cantwell	Malcolm	Brown	Moore	Grice	Woosnam	Dunmore	Smillie	Musgrove
	15/4	35,000	*8*	37			*Dawson 25*	*Gregg*	*Foulkes*	*Carolan*	*Setters*	*Cope*	*Brennan*	*Bradley*	*Giles*	*Dawson*	*Lawton*	*Charlton*
							Ref: J Cooke	A Good Friday for Hammers who gain a rare win. Thousands were locked out. Two goals from pinpoint crosses gave Hammers a healthy lead. Alex Dawson pulled one back from 20 yards and Lawton's snapshot hit a post. Man U skipper Maurice Setters is jeered for repeated handling.										
39	H	FULHAM	12	L	1-2	1-1	Smillie 37	Rhodes	Bond	Cantwell	Malcolm	Brown	Moore	Grice	Woosnam	Dunmore	Smillie	Musgrove
	16/4	24,085	*10*	37			*Chamberlain 31, O'Connell 68*	*Macedo*	*Cohen*	*Langley*	*Mullery*	*Lampe*	*Lawler*	*Key*	*O'Connell*	*Bentley*	*Haynes*	*Chamberlain*
								Alan Mullery lights up Fulham's midfield, while their wingers – John Key and Tosh Chamberlain had a field day. Key crossed for Chamberlain's volley. Key hit a post before Smillie levelled when Tony Macedo missed the ball. Brian O'Connell headed the winner from Key's corner.										
40	A	MANCHESTER U	16	L	3-5	3-2	Dunmore 5, Cantwell 30p, Scott 37	Rhodes	Kirkup	Cantwell	**Bovington**	Moore	Smillie	Scott	Cartwright	Dunmore	Brett	Musgrove
	18/4	*34,676*	*8*	37			*D'son 25, 62, Ch'rlton 34, 49, Q'xall 84*	*Gregg*	*Foulkes*	*Carolan*	*Setters*	*Cope*	*Brennan*	*Giles*	*Quixall*	*Dawson*	*Viollet*	*Charlton*
							Ref: L Howarth	With nine changes, West Ham led three times but still lost. Dunmore's 25-yard rocket was his first goal for the club. Cartwright was felled for Cantwell's penalty and Scott played a one-two with Cartwright for the third, disputed as offside. Johnny Giles laid on three of Man U's goals.										
41	A	LUTON	16	L	1-3	0-3	Dunmore 69 *[Cummins 32]*	Rhodes	Bond	Cantwell	Malcolm	Lansdowne	Moore	Grice	Cartwright	Dunmore	Smillie	Musgrove
	23/4	***11,404***	*22*	37			*Lansdowne 3 (og), McBride 24,*	*Baynham*	*Dunne*	*Daniel*	*Morton*	*Kelly*	*Pacey*	*Tracey*	*Turner*	*McBride*	*Groves*	*Cummins*
							Ref: R Reddaway	Basement club Luton have it all too easy. All three goals could be traced to bad covering and hesitancy. Billy Lansdowne, a last-minute deputy for Brown, lobbed his pass-back over Rhodes. Moore was at fault for McBride's goal, and everyone stood still as Cummins chipped Rhodes.										
42	H	SHEFFIELD WED	14	D	1-1	1-1	Woosnam 11	Rhodes	Bond	Cantwell	Malcolm	Brown	Moore	Grice	Woosnam	Dunmore	Smillie	Musgrove
	30/4	22,000	*5*	38			*Fantham 32*	*Springett*	*Johnson*	*Megson*	*McAnearney*	*Swan*	*Kay*	*Wilkinson*	*Craig*	*Froggatt*	*Fantham*	*Finney*
	Home	Away					Ref: R Mann	Hammers avert relegation by just four points. They had lost 0-7 to the Owls earlier. Woosnam's header was followed by Fantham capitalising on Rhodes' block from Craig. Had Redfern Froggatt not blazed over from five yards, Wednesday would have earned £250 more talent money.										
Average	28,131	31,554																

FA Cup					F-A	H-T	Scorers, Times, and Referees	1	2	3	4	5	6	7	8	9	10	11
3	A	HUDDERSFIELD	6	D	1-1	0-0	Dick 49	Dwyer	Bond	Cantwell	Malcolm	Brown	Smith	Grice	Woosnam	Obeney	Dick	Musgrove
	9/1	*40,526*	*2:*				*Law 72*	*Wood*	*Gibson*	*Wilson*	*Taylor*	*Coddington*	*McGarry*	*McHale*	*Law*	*Dinsdale*	*Massie*	*Hawksworth*
							Ref: K Collinge	Dick collided with Munich survivor Ray Wood in scoring and went off, returning with a strapped leg. Scottish cap Denis Law levelled after McHale tore open West Ham's defence. When Ken Taylor (Yorkshire cricketer) dislodged the ball from Dwyer's grasp to net, it was ruled out.										
3R	H	HUDDERSFIELD	6	L	1-5	1-3	Musgrove 39 *[Connor 47, 69]*	Dwyer	Bond	Cantwell	Malcolm	Brown	Smith	Grice	Woosnam	Obeney	Smillie	Musgrove
	13/1	22,605	*2:*				*Massie 16, 44, McGarry 25,*	*Wood*	*Gibson*	*Wilson*	*Taylor*	*Coddington*	*McGarry*	*Ledger*	*Law*	*Connor*	*Massie*	*Hawksworth*
							Ref: K Collinge	Dwyer is blamed for three goals on an icy pitch. He misjudged Ledger's corner, which Bill McGarry shot home; he was out of position when Massie put Town 3-1 up; and allowed Connor to score from an impossible angle. Caretaker boss Eddie Boot made Town wear rubber boots.										

		Home					Away					
	P	W	D	L	F	A	W	D	L	F	A	Pts
1 Burnley	42	15	2	4	52	28	9	5	7	33	33	55
2 Wolves	42	15	3	3	63	28	9	3	9	43	39	54
3 Tottenham	42	10	6	5	43	24	11	5	5	43	26	53
4 West Brom	42	12	4	5	48	25	7	7	7	35	32	49
5 Sheffield Wed	42	12	7	2	48	20	7	4	10	32	39	49
6 Bolton	42	12	5	4	37	27	8	3	10	22	24	48
7 Manchester U	42	13	3	5	53	30	6	4	11	49	50	45
8 Newcastle	42	10	5	6	42	32	8	3	10	40	46	44
9 Preston	42	10	6	5	43	34	6	6	9	36	42	44
10 Fulham	42	12	4	5	42	28	5	6	10	31	52	44
11 Blackpool	42	9	6	6	32	32	6	4	11	27	39	40
12 Leicester	42	8	6	7	38	32	5	7	9	28	43	39
13 Arsenal	42	9	5	7	39	38	6	4	11	29	42	39
14 WEST HAM	42	12	3	6	47	33	4	3	14	28	58	38
15 Everton	42	13	3	5	50	20	0	8	13	23	58	37
16 Manchester C	42	11	2	8	47	34	6	1	14	31	50	37
17 Blackburn	42	12	3	6	38	29	4	2	15	22	41	37
18 Chelsea	42	7	5	9	44	50	7	4	10	32	41	37
19 Birmingham	42	9	5	7	37	36	4	5	12	26	44	36
20 Nott'm Forest	42	8	6	7	30	28	5	3	13	20	46	35
21 Leeds	42	7	5	9	37	46	5	5	11	28	46	34
22 Luton	42	6	5	10	25	29	3	7	11	25	44	30
	924	232	99	131	935	683	131	99	232	683	935	924

Odds & ends

Double wins: (1) Chelsea.
Double losses: (3) Leeds, Bolton, Fulham.

Won from behind: (4) Burnley (a), Arsenal (a), Birmingham (h), Chelsea (h).
Lost from in front: (5) Leeds (h), Blackburn (a), Leicester (a), Manchester C (a), Manchester U (a).

High spots: Being top in November after beating Arsenal and Wolves.

Low spots: A dreadful collapse, avoiding relegation by just four points.
After going top, losing 0-7 at Sheffield Wed.
Keeping just one clean sheet after October.
Last season two Hammers scored 20 goals: this season only one exceeds eleven.
A defence which conceded 7 goals once, 6 goals once, and 5 *six* times.

Hammer of the Year: Malcolm Musgrove.
Ever-presents: (0).
Hat-tricks: (2) John Dick (1), John Bond (1).
Leading scorer: (16) Malcolm Musgrove.

	Appearances		Goals		
	Lge	FAC	**Lge**	FAC	**Tot**
Bond, John	**35**	2	**7**		**7**
Bovington, Edward	**1**				
Brett, Ronald	**7**		**2**		**2**
Brown, Ken	**40**	2	**3**		**3**
Cantwell, Noel	**40**	2			
Cartwright, John	**3**				
Dick, John	**24**	1	**11**	1	**12**
Dunmore, David	**9**		**2**		**2**
Dwyer, Noel	**26**	2			
Gregory, Harry	**1**				
Grice, Harry	**34**	2	**5**		**5**
Hurst, Geoff	**3**				
Keeble, Vic	**15**		**6**		**6**
Kirkup, Joe	**16**				
Lansdowne, Billy	**1**				
Lyall, John	**2**				
Malcolm, Andy	**40**	2			
Moore, Bobby	**13**				
Musgrove, Malcolm	**41**	2	**15**	1	**16**
Obeney, Harry	**9**	2	**5**		**5**
Rhodes, Brian	**15**				
Scott, Anthony	**4**		**1**		**1**
Smillie, Andy	**13**	1	**3**		**3**
Smith, John	**28**	2	**1**		**1**
Woodley, Derek	**3**		**2**		**2**
Woosnam, Phil	**38**	2	**11**		**11**
Wragg, Douglas	**1**				
(own-goals)			**1**		**1**
27 players used	**462**	**22**	**75**	**2**	**77**

No	Date		Att	Pos	Pt	F-A	H-T	Scorers, Times, and Referees	1	2	3	4	5	6	7	8	9	10	11
1	A	WOLVES			L	2-4	1-1	Dick 7, Woosnam 89	Rhodes	Bond	Cantwell	Malcolm	Brown	Moore	Grice	Woosnam	Dunmore	Dick	Musgrove
	20/8		*37,266*		0			*Fl'wers 34, 47, Br'dbent 68, Murray 72*	*Sidebottom*	*Showell*	*Harris*	*Clamp*	*Stuart*	*Flowers*	*Deeley*	*Mason*	*Murray*	*Broadbent*	*Horne*
								Ref: K Collinge	Wolves lost the title by just one point. West Ham have sponsored the 4-2-4 system. Dick scored from Woosnam's pass, but England man Ron Flowers turned the tide with a header, followed by a 25-yarder. Peter Broadbent trapped the ball before scoring. Murray netted from a rebound.										
2	H	ASTON VILLA			W	5-2	3-2	Woos' 15, Dun' 37, Dick 39, Bond 58,	Rhodes	Bond	Cantwell	Malcolm	Brown	Moore	Grice	Woosnam	Dunmore	Dick	Musgrove
	22/8		28,959		2			*Thomson 17, Hitchens 42* [M'grove 88]	*Sims*	*Lynn*	*Neal*	*Crowe*	*Dugdale*	*Saward*	*MacEwan*	*Thomson*	*Hitchens*	*Wylie*	*McParland*
								Ref: C Kingston	Woosnam lobbed the first; Bobby Thomson levelled at the second attempt. The outcome was put beyond Villa's grasp by John Bond's 25-yard belter. In all, West Ham's 4-2-4 'Brazil' system mustered 27 shots, more than sufficient to justify the extra shilling on the admission charge.										
3	H	BOLTON			W	2-1	1-1	Musgrove 13, Dick 89	Rhodes	Bond	Cantwell	Malcolm	Brown	Moore	Grice	Woosnam	Dunmore	Dick	Musgrove
	27/8		24,283		4			*Deakin 25*	*Hopkinson*	*Hartle*	*Banks*	*Stanley*	*Higgins*	*Edwards*	*Birch*	*Deakin*	*Parry*	*Hill*	*Holden*
								Ref: P Brandwood	The fans slow-handclapped Hammers' 4-2-4 until the final minute, when a flowing move from one goalmouth to the other produced Dick's lobbed winner. The jeers turned to cheers. Bolton boss Bill Ridding was unimpressed. Midfield duo Woosnam and Moore have to work hard.										
4	A	ASTON VILLA			L	1-2	1-0	Dunmore 18	Rhodes	Bond	Cantwell	Hurst	Brown	Moore	Grice	Woosnam	Dunmore	Smillie	Musgrove
	29/8		*30,000*		4			*Hitchens 59, Thomson 88*	*Sims*	*Lynn*	*Neal*	*Crowe*	*Dugdale*	*Saward*	*MacEwan*	*Thomson*	*Hitchens*	*Wylie*	*McParland*
									Dunmore netted after Sims dropped Andy Smillie's effort. But in the second half Villa overpowered Woosnam and Hurst – the two link-men. Rhodes parried from Peter McParland and Gerry Hitchens rammed the equaliser. Bobby Thomson headed the winner from Wylie's free-kick.										
5	A	SHEFFIELD WED			L	0-1	0-0		**Shearing**	Bond	Cantwell	Malcolm	Brown	Moore	Grice	Woosnam	Dunmore	Dick	Musgrove
	3/9		*28,359*		4			*Fantham 50*	*Springett*	*Johnson*	*Megson*	*McAnearney*	*Swan*	*Kay*	*Wilkinson*	*Craig*	*Quinn*	*Fantham*	*Finney*
								Ref: K Howley	22-year-old Peter Shearing, ex-Hendon amateur, was beaten once, when Wilkinson fed John Fantham, who pivoted and shot low and hard. It was 7-0 last season so this was better, though the 4-2-4 which had four defenders line up on the edge of the penalty box was boring to watch.										
6	H	MANCHESTER U			W	2-1	1-1	Brett 18, Musgrove 54	Shearing	Bond	Cantwell	Malcolm	Brown	Moore	Grice	Woosnam	Dunmore	Brett	Musgrove
	5/9		30,000		6			*Quixall 44*	*Gregg*	*Foulkes*	*Brennan*	*Setters*	*Cope*	*Nicholson*	*Quixall*	*Giles*	*Dawson*	*Viollet*	*Charlton*
								Ref: L Callaghan	The daftest goal sunk Man U. Bond fired low and hard but wide. The ball hit Woosnam's bum, bounced into the goalmouth, where Musgrove pounced. Four backs retreating before every attack baffled Man U in the first half but in the second Brown performed two goal-line clearances.										
7	A	CHELSEA			L	2-3	1-2	Dunmore 27, Grice 76	Shearing	Bond	Cantwell	Malcolm	Brown	Moore	Grice	Woosnam	Dunmore	Brett	Musgrove
	10/9		*37,873*		6			*Blunstone 3, Greaves 32, Livesey 73*	*Bonetti*	*Sillett J*	*Sillett P*	*Venables*	*Evans*	*Bradbury*	*Brabrook*	*Greaves*	*Livesey*	*Brooks*	*Blunstone*
								Ref: K Stokes	Despite conceding two goals, 18-year-old keeper Peter Bonetti is man of the match. Musgrove and Bond had goalbound shots clawed away and at the end joined in the applause for Bonetti. Livesey beat Shearing at his near post, Woosnam hit the bar, and it was not West Ham's day.										
8	A	MANCHESTER U		14	L	1-6	1-2	Brett 44 *[Scanlon 75, Quixall 87p]*	Shearing	Bond	Cantwell	Malcolm	Brown	Moore	Woodley	Woosnam	Dunmore	Brett	Musgrove
	14/9		*33,695*	*18*	6			*Viollet 19, 39, Charlton 46, 60,*	*Gregg*	*Foulkes*	*Brennan*	*Setters*	*Cope*	*Nicholson*	*Quixall*	*Giles*	*Viollet*	*Charlton*	*Scanlon*
								Ref: R Leafe	This is only Man U's second win of the season. Matt Busby's shoot-on-sight strugglers rampage throughout the second half. It all went wrong when Brown spooned Viollet's shot over Shearing's head. Brett linked with Musgrove for West Ham's goal, and hit the underside of the bar.										
9	H	BLACKPOOL		14	D	3-3	2-1	Bond 9, Musgrove 38, Woodley 77	Shearing	Kirkup	Cantwell	Malcolm	Brown	Moore	Woodley	Woosnam	Bond	Dunmore	Musgrove
	17/9		23,521	*21*	7			*Charnley 19, 62, Mudie 87*	*Waiters*	*Armfield*	*Martin*	*Kelly J*	*Gratrix*	*Salt*	*Matthews*	*Kaye*	*Charnley*	*Mudie*	*Campbell*
								Ref: A Sparling	The first break in Hammers' 'win at home; lose away' sequence. Blackpool have only won once. The most eye-catching duel was that between Moore and Stanley Matthews, who was no doubt motivated by the Upton Park programme: he 'has decided to go into semi-retirement!' it said.										
10	A	EVERTON		16	L	1-4	1-2	Beesley 10	Shearing	Bond	Cantwell	Malcolm	Brown	Moore	Woodley	Woosnam	Dunmore	**Beesley**	Musgrove
	24/9		*46,291*	*3*	7			*Lill 5, Ring 13, Vernon 66, 76*	*Dunlop*	*Parker*	*Jones*	*Gabriel*	*Labone*	*Harris B*	*Lill*	*Collins*	*Harris J*	*Vernon*	*Ring*
								Ref: H Horner	Hammers have gone 16 away games without a win. 18-year-old debutant Mike Beesley's header equalised Mick Lill's left-footed belter from 18 yards. Beesley faded after a head knock. The stranded Shearing palmed Tommy Ring's shot over his head, after which it all slipped away.										

No	Venue	Opponent / Date	Att	Pos	Pts	F-A	H-T	Scorers, Times, and Referees	1	2	3	4	5	6	7	8	9	10	11
11	H	BLACKBURN		15	W	3-2	2-1	Dick 22, 82, Woosnam 28	Rhodes	Bond	Lyall	Malcolm	Brown	Moore	Grice	Woosnam	Dunmore	Dick	Musgrove
		1/10	17,519	*5*	9			*McLeod 7, Thomas 67*	*Jones*	*England*	*Pickering*	*Clayton*	*Woods*	*McGrath*	*Douglas*	*Thomas*	*Dougan*	*Crowe*	*McLeod*
								Ref: S Yates	Blackburn boss Jack Marshall felt his team lacked fight. McLeod headed them in front, Bond cleared Thomas's effort off the line, and Derek Dougan posed many problems. The tide turned when Dick headed in Woosnam's chip. Pickering then 'saved' Woosnam's shot over the line.										
12	H	BIRMINGHAM		13	W	4-3	2-1	Grice 14, 51, M'grove 23, Dunmore 60	Rhodes	Bond	Lyall	Malcolm	Brown	Moore	Grice	Woosnam	Dunmore	Dick	Musgrove
		8/10	16,000	*14*	11			*Hellawell 29, 83, Rudd 74*	*Schofield*	*Farmer*	*Allen*	*Watts*	*Sissons*	*Neal*	*Hellawell*	*Gordon*	*Stubbs*	*Rudd*	*Astall*
								Ref: N Hough	Woosnam, who is expected to join Wolves next week, shone through this match. Keeper Schofield appealed for offside when Grice headed the first. Woosnam's shot then rebounded for Musgrove. Red-headed Hellawell's volley was answered by two further Woosnam-inspired goals.										
13	A	WEST BROM		12	L	0-1	0-0		Rhodes	Bond	Lyall	Malcolm	Brown	Moore	Grice	Woosnam	Dunmore	Dick	Musgrove
		15/10	*21,300*	*15*	11			*Robson 51*	*Potter*	*Howe*	*Williams G*	*Billingham*	*Kennedy*	*Robson*	*Smith*	*Burnside*	*Allen*	*Jackson*	*Hogg*
								Ref: J Catlin	Albion skipper Bobby Robson decides this otherwise grim match with a screaming daisy-cutter that beats Rhodes to his right. Grice shot wide with only Potter to beat; Dick headed over the bar; and Woosnam missed from long range. The question is, will Ted Fenton abandon 4-2-4?										
14	H	PRESTON		12	W	5-2	2-2	M'grove 5, 81, 82, Bond 20p, Dick 69	Rhodes	Bond	Lyall	Malcolm	Brown	Moore	Grice	**Boyce**	Dunmore	Dick	Musgrove
		22/10	16,287	*14*	13			*Thompson T 10, 30*	*Else*	*Cunningham*	*O'Neill*	*Fullam*	*Singleton*	*Wylie*	*Alston*	*Thompson T*	*Thompson P*	*Sneddon*	*Taylor*
								Ref: R Windle	Preston have only won away once, yet twice pulled back to level. Musgrove's hat-trick comprised a 30-yarder, an interception of O'Neill's bad pass-back, and a conversion of Grice's cross. Musgrove was also felled by Alston for the penalty. Moore's arrogance is blotting his copy-book.										
15	A	FULHAM		12	D	1-1	1-1	Dunmore 10	Rhodes	Bond	Lyall	Malcolm	Brown	Moore	Woodley	Woosnam	Dunmore	Dick	Grice
		29/10	*20,809*	*6*	14			*Leggat 44*	*Macedo*	*Cohen*	*Langley*	*Mullery*	*Bentley*	*Edwards*	*Key*	*Hill R*	*Brown*	*Haynes*	*Leggat*
								Ref: H New	Having just lost to Darlington in the League Cup, West Ham earn their first away point of the season. Moore's through ball enabled Dunmore to shoot past the advancing Tony Macedo. Graham Leggatt levelled with a low shot from the edge of the box, after a pass from Alan Mullery.										
16	H	ARSENAL		10	W	**6-0**	2-0	Dunmore 4, 32, 89, Dick 70, [Woosnam 78, Malcolm 83]	Rhodes	Bond	Lyall	Malcolm	Brown	Moore	Woodley	Woosnam	Dunmore	Dick	Grice
		5/11	29,375	*9*	16				*Kelsey*	*Wills*	*McCullough*	*Docherty*	*Sneddon*	*Groves*	*Strong*	*Barnwell*	*Charles*	*Herd*	*Haverty*
								Ref: L Hamer	This bizarre score over George Swindin's Gunners is highlighted by Dunmore's hat-trick. Billy McCullough presented him with the first, an exchange of passes with Woosnam and Dick with No 2, and Woosnam's pass – taken on the run – his third. But Woosnam was the destroyer.										
17	A	MANCHESTER C		9	W	2-1	2-1	Dunmore 37, Grice 44	Rhodes	Bond	Lyall	Malcolm	Brown	Moore	Grice	Woosnam	Dunmore	Dick	Musgrove
		12/11	*33,721*	*8*	18			*Barlow 7*	*Trautmann*	*Betts*	*Sear*	*Barnes*	*Plenderleith*	*Shawcross*	*Barlow*	*Law*	*Hannah*	*Baker*	*Colbridge*
								Ref: J Bellwood	Fenton's 4-2-4 became 11-0-0 as his team hung on for their first away win in 20 matches. Ken Barnes' cross had been tucked away by Colin Barlow, but Dunmore headed in Malcolm's cross and when Barry Betts blocked Grice's first effort, the winger followed up. Denis Law shone.										
18	H	NOTT'M FOREST		11	L	2-4	2-2	Palmer 19 (og), Dunmore 32	Rhodes	Kirkup	Bond	Malcolm	Brown	Moore	Grice	Woosnam	Dunmore	Dick	Musgrove
		19/11	21,047	*22*	18			*Vowden 21, 62, Gray 44, Le Flem 47*	*Grummitt*	*Patrick*	*McDonald*	*Palmer*	*McKinlay*	*Burkitt*	*Gray*	*Booth*	*Vowden*	*Quigley*	*Le Flem*
								Ref: J Parkinson	Andy Beattie's basement club – with four teenagers, including a 17-year-old goalie – shatter Hammers' unbeaten home record, despite leading twice. Woosnam never plays well against Forest. Rhodes' gaffes were mostly responsible for this defeat. Gray's shot slipped under his body.										
19	H	CARDIFF		10	W	2-0	1-0	Musgrove 35, Dunmore 48	Rhodes	Bond	Lyall	Malcolm	Brown	Moore	Grice	Woosnam	Dunmore	Dick	Musgrove
		3/12	**14,000**	*17*	20				*Vearncombe*	*Harrington*	*Stitfall*	*Gammon*	*Malloy*	*Baker*	*Walsh*	*Edgley*	*Tapscott*	*Watkins*	*Hogg*
								Ref: P Brandwood	A dour battle in driving rain with promoted Cardiff. Dick found Musgrove, who sent a swerver round Graham Vearncombe. The ref then gave an iffy free-kick to West Ham, which was taken far from the right place, and while Cardiff protested Grice sped away to cross for Dunmore.										
20	A	NEWCASTLE		8	D	5-5	2-1	Mus' 4, McMichael 20 (og), Dun' 55,	Rhodes	Bond	Lyall	Malcolm	Brown	Moore	Grice	Woosnam	Dunmore	Dick	Musgrove
		10/12	*20,100*	*17*	21			*White 5, 64, Mc G' 79, Bell 84, Mit' 88*	*Garrow*	*McKinney*	*McMichael*	*Neale*	*Stokoe*	*Bell*	*Hughes*	*McGuigan*	*White*	*Mitchell*	*Scanlon*
								Ref: J Bullough [Bond 63p, Dick 72]	West Ham led 5-2 with 11 minutes left. Then Lyall headed out to John McGuigan. Len White passed three defenders to make it 4-5. And when McGuigan hit a post, Bob Mitchell equalised. Musgrove's shot had been deflected in by McMichael. Stokoe fouled Woosnam for the penalty.										
21	H	WOLVES		7	W	5-0	2-0	Musgrove 5, Dunmore 39, 74, Dick 85, [Moore 49]	Rhodes	Bond	Lyall	Malcolm	Brown	Moore	Grice	Woosnam	Dunmore	Dick	Musgrove
		17/12	22,336	*3*	23				*Sidebottom*	*Stuart*	*Harris*	*Clamp*	*Slater*	*Kirkham*	*Deeley*	*Stobbart*	*Farmer*	*Broadbent*	*Durandt*
								Ref: K Seddon	This win lifts Hammers – unbeaten at home to Wolves – to 7th, the high point of the season. Sidebottom injured his leg trying to save Moore's goal and was stretchered off, which killed the contest. Kirkham went in goal. Goal No 1 was the best, end to end, topped by a diving header.										

No	Date	Att	Pos	Pt	F-A	H-T	Scorers, Times, and Referees	1	2	3	4	5	6	7	8	9	10	11
22	A TOTTENHAM		8	L	0-2	0-1		Rhodes	Bond	Lyall	Malcolm	Brown	Moore	Grice	Woosnam	Dunmore	Dick	Musgrove
	24/12	***54,930***	*1*	23			*White 25, Dyson 88*	*Brown*	*Baker*	*Henry*	*Blanchflower*	*Norman*	*MacKay*	*Jones*	*White*	*Smith*	*Allen*	*Dyson*
							Ref: R Leafe	An 11.15 kick-off against super Spurs, defeated just once all season. John White's header that went in off Lyall and Terry Dyson's soft header that crept past Rhodes tell only half the story. The mud and sand was unplayable and injury to Cliff Jones reduced Spurs to 10 men at half-time.										
23	H TOTTENHAM		9	L	0-3	0-2		Rhodes	Bond	Lyall	Malcolm	Brown	Moore	Grice	Woosnam	Dunmore	Dick	Musgrove
	26/12	**34,481**	*1*	23			*Brown 24 (og), Allen 43, White 82*	*Hollowbread*	*Baker*	*Henry*	*Blanchflower*	*Norman*	*MacKay*	*Medwin*	*White*	*Smith*	*Allen*	*Dyson*
							Ref: R Mann	West Ham, beaten at home just once, were expected to provide rampant Spurs with a tough test. The test became tougher when Brown turned Bobby Smith's shot past Rhodes, and tougher still when Les Allen chested down a misplaced pass to pick his spot. White netted No 3 off a post.										
24	A BOLTON		10	L	1-3	1-2	Musgrove 20	Rhodes	Bond	Lyall	Malcolm	Brown	Hurst	Smillie	Woosnam	Dunmore	Dick	Musgrove
	31/12	*15,931*	*18*	23			*Stevens 38, McAdams 42, Birch 57*	*Hopkinson*	*Hartle*	*Farrimond*	*Stanley*	*Edwards B*	*Cunliffe*	*Birch*	*Stevens*	*McAdams*	*Deakin*	*Holden*
							Ref: J Hemmingway	Burnden Park roared on their heroes – a rare experience this season. Woosnam set up Musgrove to net close in and Hurst hit a post but then the tide turned. Hammers' defence stood appealing for offside and Dennis Stevens rounded Rhodes. Billy McAdams was left unmarked for No 2.										
25	H SHEFFIELD WED		11	D	1-1	0-1	Dick 86	Rhodes	Kirkup	Lyall	Malcolm	Brown	Moore	Scott	Woosnam	Dunmore	Dick	Musgrove
	14/1	20,620	*3*	24			*Ellis 24*	*Springett*	*Johnson*	*Megson*	*McAnearney*	*O'Donnell*	*Kay*	*Wilkinson*	*Quinn*	*Ellis*	*Fantham*	*Finney*
							Ref: F Stringer	Tony Scott plays his first game of the season, and it was his chip that enables Dick to equalise. Keith Ellis had hooked in a corner by the future England boss Howard Wilkinson. Between times, England goalie Ron Springett, aided by the post which denied Musgrove – kept Owls intact.										
26	H CHELSEA		9	W	3-1	2-1	Obeney 11, Woosnam 13, Dick 65	Rhodes	Kirkup	Lyall	Malcolm	Brown	Moore	Scott	Woosnam	Obeney	Dick	Musgrove
	21/1	21,829	*17*	26			*Blunstone 4*	*Bonetti*	*Sillett P*	*Harris*	*Venables*	*Evans*	*Anderton*	*Brabrook*	*Greaves*	*Livesey*	*Tindall*	*Blunstone*
							Ref: J Taylor	Frank Blunstone dribbled round three defenders to put Ted Drake's team in front. Greaves hasn't scored in six games, missing a penalty after being felled by limpet Malcolm. Scott laid on Obeney's goal, Woosman let fly from 20 yards, and man-of the-match Muzzie walloped No 3.										
27	A BLACKPOOL		10	L	0-3	0-2		Rhodes	Kirkup	Lyall	Malcolm	Brown	Moore	Scott	Woosnam	Obeney	Dunmore	Musgrove
	4/2	***9,947***	*21*	26			*Crawford 21, Parry 41, Charnley 89*	*West*	*Armfield*	*Garrett*	*Hauser*	*Gratrix*	*Durie*	*Campbell*	*Kelly*	*Charnley*	*Crawford*	*Parry*
							Ref: A Holland	Next-to-bottom Blackpool can't believe their luck. West Ham created chances and missed 'em, giving 17-year-old Gordon West a clean sheet; Blackpool created little, but took the lot. Ray Parry's cross brought Bruce Crawford's header and Parry angled a second goal after a solo run.										
28	H EVERTON		9	W	4-0	1-0	Obeney 6, 53, Dick 84, Musgrove 89	Rhodes	Kirkup	Lyall	Malcolm	Brown	Moore	Scott	Woosnam	Obeney	Dick	Musgrove
	11/2	22,322	*5*	28				*Dunlop*	*Parker*	*Thomson*	*Gabriel*	*Labone*	*Sharples*	*Bingham*	*Young*	*Wignall*	*Vernon*	*Harris*
								A dire game, ruined by a blustery wind, which took Obeney's header from Scott's corner over Albert Dunlop's head. It was Obeney's day: his second came when Woosnam's shot flew off Brian Labone's back, onto the bar, and dropped at his feet. West Ham won't win again for ages.										
29	A BIRMINGHAM		13	L	2-4	2-2	Musgrove 3, Scott 10	Rhodes	Kirkup	Lyall	Malcolm	Brown	Moore	Scott	Woosnam	Obeney	Dick	Musgrove
	25/2	*16,850*	*14*	28			*Neal 18, Harris 28p, 53, Bloomfield 66*	*Withers*	*Famer*	*Allen*	*Watts*	*Sissons*	*Neal*	*Astall*	*Gordon*	*Harris*	*Bloomfield*	*Taylor*
							Ref: Pickles	Unbearable! Scott cut in to score left-footed from 25 yards to make it 2-0 after just ten minutes but then West Ham fell apart. Dick Neal headed in Jimmy Harris's cross, and when Lyall fouled Astall in the box it was 2-2. Harris outwitted Brown again, 3-2, and Bloomfield netted a curler.										
30	H WEST BROM		13	L	1-2	1-1	Dick 8	Rhodes	Kirkup	Bond	Malcolm	Brown	Moore	Scott	Woosnam	Dunmore	Dick	Musgrove
	4/3	21,607	*17*	28			*Lovatt 43, Hope 68*	*Wallace*	*Howe*	*Williams S*	*Robson*	*Jones*	*Drury*	*Jackson*	*Burnside*	*Lovatt*	*Hope*	*Clark*
							Ref: T Dawes	Albion's defence stood with arms raised when Dick lobbed Wallace. Jack Lovatt – who had hit the underside of bar – capped his WBA debut by rounding Brown to equalise. Clark finished off a neat run by freeing Bobby Hope to score. Bobby Robson shackled Woosnam completely.										
31	A PRESTON		14	L	0-4	0-1		Rhodes	Kirkup	Bond	Malcolm	Brown	Moore	Brett	Woosnam	Obeney	Dick	Musgrove
	11/3	*12,084*	*21*	28			*Th'mpson 36, Fullam 46, 68, Alston 66*	*Else*	*Cunningham*	*O'Neill*	*Wylie*	*Singleton*	*O'Farrell*	*Mayers*	*Fullam*	*Alston*	*Sneddon*	*Thompson P*
							Ref: A Murdoch	Next-to-bottom Preston win their fourth game out of five. Other than Rhodes, no other Hammer passed muster. After an abject opening period, Thompson converted Sneddon's low cross. Alston nodded back Mayers' centre for Fullam to head the first of three second-half headed goals.										

No	Venue	Opponent / Date	Att	Pos	Pts	F-A	H-T	Scorers, Times, Referees	1	2	3	4	5	6	7	8	9	10	11
32	H	FULHAM		14	L	1-2	1-1	Obeney 21	Rhodes	Kirkup	Bond	Malcolm	Brown	Moore	Grice	Woosnam	Obeney	Dick	Musgrove
		18/3	18,742	*16*	28			*Cook 43, Langley 60p*	*Macedo*	*Cohen*	*Langley*	*Mullery*	*Dodgin*	*Lowe*	*Watson*	*Leggat*	*Cook*	*Haynes*	*Johnson*
								Ref: G Thorpe	Hammers should have won, but lost when Moore handled in the box. Grice's cross had found Obeney's head to give Hammers a deserved lead, but against the run of play Rhodes parried Mullery's effort to Graham Leggat, whose angled shot bounced off Rhodes' chest to Maurice Cook.										
33	A	BLACKBURN		14	L	1-4	0-1	Woods 63 (og)	Rhodes	Kirkup	Bond	Malcolm	Brown	Moore	Grice	Woosnam	Beesley	Smillie	Musgrove
		20/3	*14,000*	*6*	28			*MacL'd 35, 82, Dobing 73, McEvoy 88*	*Reeves*	*Taylor*	*Bray*	*McEvoy*	*Woods*	*Clayton*	*Douglas*	*Dobing*	*Pickering*	*Thomas*	*MacLeod*
									Fenton has gone. 7th in December, West Ham are now just four points clear of the relegation line. Rhodes is blamed for this defeat, dropping the ball for Rovers' first goal and dispossessed by Pickering for their second. At the other end, Reeves pushed a corner onto Matt Woods' head.										
34	A	ARSENAL		15	D	0-0	0-0		Rhodes	Kirkup	Bond	Hurst	Brown	Moore	Grice	Woosnam	Obeney	Dick	Musgrove
		25/3	*27,663*	*8*	29				*Kelsey*	*Bacuzzi*	*McCullough*	*Charles*	*Neill*	*Groves*	*Henderson*	*Eastham*	*Herd*	*Barnwell*	*Haverty*
								Ref: A Moore	West Ham end a run of eight away defeats, though most of their worrying moments stemmed not from Arsenal's forwards but from trying to be super-subtle in their penalty area. Hurst was almost caught in possession. Rhodes later made the save of the day from Bond's 'clearance'.										
35	H	LEICESTER		14	W	1-0	1-0	Dick 9	Rhodes	Kirkup	Bond	Malcolm	Brown	Moore	Grice	Woosnam	Obeney	Dick	Musgrove
		31/3	22,010	*9*	31				*Banks*	*Sjoberg*	*Norman*	*McLintock*	*King*	*Appleton*	*Riley*	*Cheesebr'gh*	*Leek*	*Keyworth*	*Meek*
								Ref: L Callaghan	Matt Gillies' Leicester are preparing for the FA Cup final and are suitably distracted. They fail to create a chance whereas West Ham carve out six. But the goal comes from good old Route One. Bond belts the ball upfield, Frank McLintock mis-heads it, and Dick judges the bounce.										
36	H	NEWCASTLE		13	D	1-1	1-1	Musgrove 2	Rhodes	Kirkup	Bond	Malcolm	Brown	Hurst	Brett	Cartwright	Obeney	Dick	Musgrove
		1/4	17,103	*20*	32			*Scanlon 8*	*Hollins*	*McKinney*	*McMichael*	*Neale*	*McGrath*	*Bell*	*Hughes*	*Harrower*	*McGuigan*	*Allchurch*	*Scanlon*
								Ref: H New	Newcastle need both points, and their failure will get them relegated. Cartwright trapped a throw-in, crossed, and Musgrove headed in. When Rhodes, Allchurch and Albert Scanlon converged on a cross, Scanlon judged it best. The second half brought slow handclaps ringing round.										
37	A	LEICESTER		15	L	1-5	1-3	Kirkup 19 *[McIlmoyle 76]*	Rhodes	Kirkup	Bond	Malcolm	Brown	Hurst	Scott	Boyce	**Sealey**	Dick	Musgrove
		3/4	*23,776*	*10*	32			*Cheesebrough 2, 43, 88, Riley 44,*	*Banks*	*Sjoberg*	*Norman*	*White*	*Knapp*	*McLintock*	*Riley*	*Walsh*	*McIlmoyle*	*Cheesebr'gh*	*Meek*
									Leicester are playing for their Wembley places. Two 19-year-old centre-forwards make their debuts. Alan Sealey was an anonymous as his team, but Hugh McIlmoyle engineered City's first goal and scored the fourth. Joe Kirkup, advancing upfield, took Bond's pass to equalise.										
38	A	NOTT'M FOREST		15	D	1-1	1-0	Dick 14	Rhodes	Kirkup	Bond	Malcolm	Brown	Moore	Scott	Woosnam	Sealey	Dick	Musgrove
		8/4	*26,081*	*12*	33			*Vowden 81*	*Grummitt*	*Wealthhall*	*McDonald*	*Palmer*	*McInley*	*Iley*	*Cobb*	*Addison*	*Vowden*	*Quigley*	*Le Flem*
								Ref: P Brandwood	Tony Scott pinged over any number of threatening crosses, and from one of them Dick headed a fine goal. It would have earned a second away win for Hammers, but for Rhodes' late clanger. He got both hands to Billy Cobb's corner, but dropped the ball at the feet of Jeff Vowden.										
39	H	MANCHESTER C		15	D	1-1	0-0	Sealey 64	Rhodes	Kirkup	Bond	Malcolm	Brown	Moore	Scott	Woosnam	Sealey	Dick	Musgrove
		15/4	17,982	*18*	34			*Barlow 85*	*Trautmann*	*Betts*	*Sear*	*Cheetham*	*Ewing*	*Oakes*	*Barlow*	*Hannah*	*Baker*	*Hayes*	*Wagstaffe*
								Ref: D Smith	A new era begins with the arrival of Ron Greenwood. Struggling City missed Denis Law, and 38-year-old Bert Trautmann had a jittery game. Sealey, exchanged for Dunmore at Orient, nets his first goal when Dick's cross bounces off Ewing to him. Hannah's pass sets up Colin Barlow.										
40	A	BURNLEY		15	D	2-2	0-0	Musgrove 73, 77	Rhodes	Kirkup	Lyall	Malcolm	Brown	Moore	Scott	Boyce	Sealey	Dick	Musgrove
		18/4	*12,409*	*5*	35			*Moore 51 (og), Pointer 70*	*Blacklaw*	*Angus*	*Elder*	*Joyce*	*Cummings*	*Miller*	*Connelly*	*McIlroy*	*Pointer*	*Robson*	*Harris*
									Burnley are chasing fourth-place 'talent money'. When Moore stuck out a foot to deflect Connelly's shot past Rhodes, and Pointer headed in Connelly's cross, they looked on course. But Scott's low crosses brought two goals for Musgrove. Brian Robson hit Rhodes' post at the death.										
41	A	CARDIFF		15	D	1-1	0-1	Dick 72	Rhodes	Kirkup	Lyall	Malcolm	Brown	Moore	Scott	Woosnam	Sealey	Dick	Musgrove
		22/4	*10,000*	*16*	36			*Donnelly 37*	*Vearncombe*	*Harrington*	*Milne*	*Hole*	*Malloy*	*Baker*	*Walsh*	*Moore*	*Tapscott*	*Donnelly*	*Hogg*
								Ref: Mitchell	It's now eight games without a win for Bill Jones' Cardiff. They complain hard after Colin Baker's shot bounced down off the bar, behind the line, but the ref was unsighted. That would have made it 2-0. Scott's cross brought Dick's equaliser. West Ham don't often come from behind.										
42	H	BURNLEY		16	L	1-2	1-0	Woosnam 12	Rhodes	Kirkup	Lyall	Malcolm	Brown	Hurst	Scott	Woosnam	Sealey	Dick	Musgrove
		29/4	18,761	*4*	36			*Lawson 77, Harris 87*	*Blacklaw*	*Angus*	*Cummings*	*Joyce*	*Talbut*	*Adamson*	*Connelly*	*Lawson*	*Pointer*	*Robson*	*Harris*
		Home	Away						Burnley end the season unbeaten by any of London's five clubs. Ron Greenwood's first defeat looked unlikely when Woosnam took a return pass from Musgrove to score from 20 yards. Rhodes foolishly rushed from his goal for Lawson's equaliser, then failed to gather from Harris.										
	Average	21,847	25,385																

League Cup							F-A	H-T	Scorers, Times, and Referees	1	2	3	4	5	6	7	8	9	10	11
1	H	CHARLTON		16	W		3-1	1-1	Dick 23, Musgrove 48, Moore 64	Rhodes	Bond	Lyall	Malcolm	Brown	Moore	Woodley	Cartwright	Dunmore	Dick	Musgrove
	26/9		12,496	2:					*Leary 16*	*Duff*	*Sewell*	*Townsend*	*Hinton*	*Tocknell*	*Lucas*	*Lawrie*	*Edwards*	*Leary*	*Werge*	*Summers*
									Ref: F Clarke	The Football League's new competition has the impact of a damp squib. Woosnam and Cantwell were away on international duty. Charlton are mid-table in Div 2. When Bond lost possession Stuart Leary put them ahead. Dick's left foot levelled; Hinton let in Musgrove; Moore volleyed.										
2	A	DARLINGTON		12	L		2-3	1-1	Dunmore 21, Dick 68	Rhodes	Bond	Lyall	Malcolm	Brown	Moore	Grice	Woosnam	Dunmore	Dick	Musgrove
	24/10		*16,911*	*4:*					*Spencer 1, Rayment 53, Robson 64*	*Tinsley*	*Henderson*	*Mulholland*	*Furphy*	*Greener*	*Spencer*	*Rayment*	*Milner*	*Robson*	*Baxter*	*Morton*
									Ref: M Dixon	Fourth Division Darlington spring the shock of shocks. Their five forwards rocked West Ham from the off, when Baxter's pass set up Spencer from 25 yards. Dunmore chased a long kick to level, but Rayment pounced when Rhodes spilled his effort. Bond's short back-pass led to No 3.										

FA Cup							F-A	H-T	Scorers, Times, and Referees	1	2	3	4	5	6	7	8	9	10	11
3	H	STOKE		10	D		2-2	1-1	Dunmore 35, Dick 59	Rhodes	Bond	Lyall	Malcolm	Brown	Moore	Smillie	Woosnam	Dunmore	Dick	Musgrove
	7/1		21,545	2:					*Ratcliffe 44, Andrew 85*	*O'Neill*	*Wilson D*	*Allen*	*Howitt*	*Andrew*	*Skeels*	*Bentley*	*Ratcliffe*	*King*	*Wilshaw*	*Ward D*
									Ref: K Seddon	Tony Waddington's Div 2 Stoke are ultra-defensive. West Ham play in their blue, with two hoops, away strip. Dick's diving header looked to have put West Ham through, but after Bentley's 'equaliser' was given then ruled out, Brown fluffed a clearance and big Ron Andrew pounced.										
3R	A	STOKE		10	L		0-1	0-0		Rhodes	Kirkup	Lyall	Malcolm	Brown	Moore	Grice	Woosnam	Brett	Dick	Musgrove
	11/1		*28,914*	*2:*			*aet*		*Wilshaw 91*	*O'Neill*	*Ward T*	*Allen*	*Howitt*	*Andrew*	*Skeels*	*Bentley*	*Ratcliffe*	*King*	*Wilshaw*	*Ward D*
									Ref: K Seddon	35-year-old Dennis Wilshaw played for England in the 1954 World Cup. On an icy pitch Hammers somehow survived 90 minutes, but seconds into extra-time Kirkup and Brown miskicked in trying to clear King's centre and Wilshaw netted from close in. Musgrove then missed a sitter.										

		Home					Away					
	P	W	D	L	F	A	W	D	L	F	A	Pts
1 Tottenham	42	15	3	3	65	28	16	1	4	50	27	66
2 Sheffield Wed	42	15	4	2	45	17	8	8	5	33	30	58
3 Wolves	42	17	2	2	61	32	8	5	8	42	43	57
4 Burnley	42	11	4	6	58	40	11	3	7	44	37	51
5 Everton	42	13	4	4	47	23	9	2	10	40	46	50
6 Leicester	42	12	4	5	54	31	6	5	10	33	39	45
7 Manchester U	42	14	5	2	58	20	4	4	13	30	56	45
8 Blackburn	42	12	3	6	48	34	3	10	8	29	42	43
9 Aston Villa	42	13	3	5	48	28	4	6	11	30	49	43
10 West Brom	42	10	3	8	43	32	8	2	11	24	39	41
11 Arsenal	42	12	3	6	44	35	3	8	10	33	50	41
12 Chelsea	42	10	5	6	61	48	5	2	14	37	52	37
13 Manchester C	42	10	5	6	41	30	3	6	12	38	60	37
14 Nott'm Forest	42	8	7	6	34	33	6	2	13	28	45	37
15 Cardiff	42	11	5	5	34	26	2	6	13	26	59	37
16 WEST HAM	42	12	4	5	53	31	1	6	14	24	57	36
17 Fulham	42	8	8	5	39	39	6	0	15	33	56	36
18 Bolton	42	9	5	7	38	29	3	6	12	20	44	35
19 Birmingham	42	10	4	7	35	31	4	2	15	27	53	34
20 Blackpool	42	9	3	9	44	34	3	6	12	24	39	33
21 Newcastle	42	7	7	7	51	49	4	3	14	35	60	32
22 Preston	42	7	6	8	28	25	3	4	14	15	46	30
		245	97	120	1029	695	120	97	245	695	1029	924

Odds & ends

Double wins: (0).

Double losses: (2) West Brom, Tottenham.

Won from behind: (4) Blackburn (h), Manchester C (a), Chelsea (h), Charlton FAC (h).

Lost from in front: (8) Wolves (a), Aston Villa (a), Nott'm Forest (h), Bolton (a), Birmingham (a), West Brom (h), Fulham (h), Burnley (h).

High spots: Beating Arsenal 6-0.

Good form at home during the start of the season.

This lifted the Hammers to 7th.

Low spots: The subsequent slide from 7th in December to being just four points clear of relegation in March.

Losing to Fourth Division Darlington in the League Cup.

Losing 1-6 To Manchester U.

Hammer of the Year: Bobby Moore.

Ever-presents: (1) Ken Brown.

Hat-tricks: (2) Malcolm Musgrove, John Dick.

Leading scorer: (19) John Dick.

	Appearances			Goals			
	Lge	LC	FAC	Lge	LC	FAC	Tot
Beesley, Michael	2			1			1
Bond, John	34	1	2	4			4
Boyce, Ronald	3						
Brett, Ronald	5	1		2			2
Brown, Ken	42	2	2				
Cantwell, Noel	10						
Cartwright, John	1		1				
Dick, John	34	2	2	16	2	1	19
Dunmore, David	27	1	2	14	1	1	16
Grice, Harry	24	1	1	4			4
Hurst, Geoff	6						
Kirkup, Joe	20	1		1			1
Lyall, John	21	2	2				
Malcolm, Andy	40	2	2	1			1
Moore, Brian	38	2	2	1	1		2
Musgrove, Malcolm	40	2	2	17	1		18
Obeney, Harry	9			4			4
Rhodes, Brian	36	2	2				
Scott, Anthony	12			1			1
Sealey, Alan	6			1			1
Shearing, Peter	6						
Smillie, Andy	3	1					
Woodley, Derek	5		1	1			1
Woosnam, Phil	38	2	1	6			6
(own-goals)				3			3
24 players used	**462**	22	22	**77**	5	2	**84**

LEAGUE DIVISION 1   Manager: Ron Greenwood   SEASON 1961-62

No	Date	Att	Pos	Pt	F-A	H-T	Scorers, Times, and Referees	1	2	3	4	5	6	7	8	9	10	11
1	H MANCHESTER U			D	1-1	1-1	Dick 37	**Leslie**	Kirkup	Bond	Malcolm	Brown	Moore	Scott	Woosnam	Sealey	Dick	Musgrove
	19/8	32,628		1			*Stiles 18*	*Gregg*	*Brennan*	*Cantwell*	*Stiles*	*Foulkes*	*Setters*	*Quixall*	*Viollet*	*Herd*	*Pearson*	*Charlton*
							Ref: M Fussey	Ron Greenwood misses the season's opening game because of a terrible head cold. Both sides entertained the crowd with fast, neat play. Man U also welcomed David Herd, a £30,000 signing from Arsenal. Viollet's lob was turned in by Stiles, then Sealey squared for Dick to tap in.										
2	A TOTTENHAM			D	2-2	1-1	Woosnam 40, Musgrove 54	Leslie	Kirkup	Bond	Malcolm	Brown	Moore	Scott	Woosnam	Sealey	Dick	Musgrove
	23/8	***50,214***		2			*Dyson 7, 80*	*Brown*	*Baker*	*Henry*	*Blanchflower*	*Norman*	*Marchi*	*Jones*	*Collins*	*Smith*	*Allen*	*Dyson*
							Ref: E Jennings	A Wednesday night game. Double-winning Spurs' new floodlights draw gasps from the crowd when they are switched on. Phil Woosnam signs a new contract seven hours before kick-off. Both Scottish goalies played blinders. Both Terry Dyson's goals went in off a goal-post.										
3	A WOLVES		14	L	2-3	1-1	Musgrove 19, Sealey 87	Leslie	Kirkup	Bond	Malcolm	Brown	Moore	Scott	Woosnam	Sealey	Dick	Musgrove
	26/8	*25,471*	*11*	2			*Murray 33, 63, Deeley 57*	*Finlayson*	*Stuart*	*Harris*	*Clamp*	*Slater*	*Flowers*	*Deeley*	*Mason*	*Murray*	*Broadbent*	*Hinton*
							Ref: J Cattlin	Wolves' debutants Alan Hinton and John Harris inspired the home side to their first win aided by a fluke goal. Hinton's corner was completely miskicked by Norman Deeley, the ball spinning in an arc past Leslie, leaving the keeper beating his fists into the ground and muttering darkly.										
4	H TOTTENHAM			W	2-1	1-0	Scott 40, Sealey 77	Leslie	Kirkup	Bond	Malcolm	Brown	Moore	Scott	Woosnam	Sealey	Dick	Musgrove
	28/8	**36,348**		4			*Allen 64*	*Brown*	*Baker*	*Henry*	*Blanchflower*	*Norman*	*Marchi*	*Jones*	*Smith J*	*Smith R*	*Allen*	*Dyson*
							Ref: R Smith	Upton Park's £30,000 new floodlights are switched on. The hot, humid conditions made many fans faint and the St John's Ambulance men were kept busy. Following 19-year-old Alan Sealey's super goal the crowd chanted 'We want six'. Sealey had previously missed two sitters.										
5	H NOTT'M FOREST		7	W	3-2	1-1	Scott 42, Sealey 46, Musgrove 65	Leslie	Kirkup	Bond	Malcolm	Brown	Moore	Scott	Woosnam	Sealey	Dick	Musgrove
	2/9	23,000	*6*	6			*Addison 45, 69*	*Grummitt*	*Palmer*	*Gray*	*Whitefoot*	*McKinlay*	*Iley*	*Burton*	*Addison*	*Vowden*	*Quigley*	*Le Flem*
							Ref: L Callaghan	Forest's first league defeat was not an occasion to savour. Compared to the Spurs fiesta, this was an error-strewn game. Musgrove made it 3-1, going past two defenders before scoring in off a post. After Addison replied with a swirling 35-yarder, Forest pressed hard for an equaliser.										
6	A BLACKPOOL			L	0-2	0-1		Leslie	Kirkup	Bond	Hurst	Brown	Moore	Woosnam	**Boyce**	Sealey	Dick	Scott
	4/9	*19,838*		6			*Horne 38, Hill 54*	*West*	*Armfield*	*Martin*	*Hauser*	*Gratrix*	*Durie*	*Hill*	*Peterson*	*Charnley*	*Parry*	*Horne*
							Ref: K Collinge	West Ham had no punch near goal, but nevertheless looked in little danger themselves until they were undone by a freak goal. Des Horne threaded a pass forward. No one moved and it trundled past Lawrie Leslie into the net. Andy Hill's 20-yarder secured Blackpool's second win.										
7	A ASTON VILLA		6	W	4-2	0-0	Dick 47, 64, Scott 62, Sealey 74	Leslie	Kirkup	Bond	Hurst	Brown	Moore	Scott	Woosnam	Sealey	Dick	**Crawford**
	9/9	*32,000*	*17*	8			*Crowe 46, McParland 58*	*Sidebottom*	*Neal*	*Lee*	*Crowe*	*Dugdale*	*Deakin*	*McEwan*	*Baker*	*McParland*	*O'Neill*	*Burrows*
							Ref: G Hartley	Villa were desperately unlucky to lose this. They led 2-1 through McParland, the best goal of the game, when keeper Geoff Sidebottom handed Hammers two goals on a plate. First he lost Moore's high lob to let Dick equalise. Then he let Dick's shot bounce out of his hands into the net.										
8	H CHELSEA		5	W	2-1	2-0	Dick 7, Musgrove 24	Leslie	Kirkup	Bond	Hurst	Brown	Moore	Scott	Woosnam	Sealey	Dick	Musgrove
	16/9	27,000	*15*	10			*Bridges 58*	*Bonetti*	*Sillett J*	*Harris*	*Docherty*	*Scott*	*Mortimore*	*Brabrook*	*Blunstone*	*Bridges*	*Tambling*	*Harrison*
							Ref: L Hamer	Violence on the pitch and in the crowd. Woosnam had already gone off for treatment following Docherty's concrete tackle, then Tambling's boot opened up Leslie's head. The ball broke to Bridges. Irate fans invaded the pitch as Leslie was carried off. Bobby Moore went into goal.										
9	H BLACKPOOL			D	2-2	0-0	Musgrove 49, Boyce 65	Rhodes	Kirkup	Bond	Hurst	Brown	Moore	Scott	Boyce	Sealey	Dick	Musgrove
	18/9	26,000		11			*Hauser 86, Parry 88*	*West*	*Armfield*	*Martin*	*Hauser*	*Gratrix*	*Durie*	*Hill*	*Crawford*	*Charnley*	*Parry*	*Perry*
							Ref: J Taylor	West Ham might have been three goals up had not the referee disallowed acting skipper, John Bond's, 40-yarder for a foul on the keeper. Blackpool's South African Peter Hauser sparked a heart-breaking finish, heading Pool's first goal, then crossing for Parry's equalising header.										
10	A SHEFFIELD UTD		3	W	**4-1**	2-0	Dick 13, 88, Musgrove 41, Sealey 87	Rhodes	Kirkup	Bond	Hurst	Brown	Moore	Scott	Woosnam	Sealey	Dick	Musgrove
	23/9	*21,034*	*17*	13			*Pace 90*	*Hodgkinson*	*Coldwell*	*Shaw G*	*Richardson*	*Shaw L*	*Summers*	*Allchurch*	*Russell*	*Pace*	*Kettleborough*	*Simpson*
							Ref: A Jobling	The Bramall Lane crowd were entertained beforehand by the Regimental Band of the Coldstream Guards, then tormented by West Ham once play began, then infuriated when the ref disallowed Kettleborough's effort which would have made it 2-1. Three goals in the last three minutes.										

No	Venue	Opponents / Date	Att	Pos	Res	F-A	H-T	Scorers, Times, and Referees	1	2	3	4	5	6	7	8	9	10	11
11	H	LEICESTER		2	W	**4-1**	4-0	Sealey 4, Dick 14, 37, Woosnam 38	Leslie	Kirkup	Bond	Hurst	Brown	Moore	Scott	Woosnam	Sealey	Dick	Musgrove
		30/9	26,746	*16*	15			*McLintock 80*	*Banks*	*Chalmers*	*Norman*	*McLintock*	*King*	*Appleton*	*Riley*	*Keyworth*	*McIlmoyle*	*Wills*	*Mitten*
								Ref: P Bye	Matt Gillies' Leicester are sunk under a torrent of first-half goals. Woosnam scored one and made three. The first goal came when Woosnam's shot hit Banks' legs and Sealey crashed home the rebound. This was John Dick's 300th league game, and only Burnley are above West Ham.										
12	A	IPSWICH		3	L	2-4	0-0	Sealey 71, Musgrove 87	Leslie	Kirkup	Bond	Hurst	Brown	Moore	Scott	Woosnam	Sealey	Dick	Musgrove
		7/10	*28,051*	*4*	15			*Crawford 57, 67, Phillips 66, 73*	*Bailey*	*Carberry*	*Compson*	*Baxter*	*Nelson*	*Elsworthy*	*Stephenson*	*Moran*	*Crawford*	*Phillips*	*Leadbetter*
								Ref: P Brandwood	Almost an hour passed without a goal, then six came in a rush. Alf Ramsey's Ipswich are the only team to have beaten leaders Burnley. Lawrie Leslie, wearing a jockey's cap against the sun, dived over Ted Phillips' first goal. West Ham had tried to sign the burly Phillips last season.										
13	H	BURNLEY		2	W	2-1	2-1	Crawford 3, Dick 6	Leslie	Kirkup	Bond	Malcolm	Brown	Moore	Crawford	Boyce	Sealey	Dick	Musgrove
		14/10	32,234	*1*	17			*Harris 27*	*Blacklaw*	*Angus*	*Elder*	*Adamson*	*Cummings*	*Miller*	*Towers*	*McIlroy*	*Lochhead*	*Robson*	*Harris*
								Ref: E Jennings	West Ham win this clash of the titans without Woosnam, playing for Wales. Burnley were minus Pointer and Connelly, playing for England. Ian Crawford, appearing for the first time on the right wing, scored first. Dick hit a 20-yarder. Harris scored off a post; Towers then hit the bar.										
14	A	FULHAM		2	L	0-2	0-1		Leslie	Kirkup	Bond	Malcolm	Brown	Moore	Crawford	Woosnam	Sealey	Dick	Musgrove
		21/10	*32,275*	*5*	17			*Mullery 14, Leggat 63*	*Macedo*	*Cohen*	*Langley*	*Mullery*	*Dodgin*	*Lowe*	*Leggat*	*Metchick*	*Cook*	*Haynes*	*Chamberlain*
								Ref: H Richards	A local derby played in a commendable spirit. The Fulham midfield of Johnny Haynes, Lowe, and young Alan Mullery destroyed West Ham. Mullery headed in George Cohen's cross and Haynes then chipped a free-kick onto Graham Leggat's head. This result lifts Fulham up to fifth.										
15	H	SHEFFIELD WED		6	L	2-3	1-2	Bond 29p, Dick 89	Leslie	Kirkup	Bond	Malcolm	Brown	Moore	Crawford	Woosnam	Sealey	Dick	Musgrove
		28/10	26,463	*7*	17			*Griffin 19, 84, Megson 38*	*Springett*	*Johnson*	*Megson*	*McAnearney*	*Swan*	*Kay*	*Finney*	*Griffin*	*Ellis*	*Fantham*	*Dobson*
								Ref: J Kelly	Monsoon conditions help Vic Buckingham's Owls inflict West Ham's first home defeat. Wednesday's Ron Springett and Swan both played for England in midweek. Griffin thumped in Kay's free-kick for the first goal which was soon cancelled out when Kay felled Musgrove in the box.										
16	A	MANCHESTER C		4	W	5-3	1-3	Dick 20, 75, Musgrove 54,	Leslie	Kirkup	Bond	Hurst	Brown	Moore !	Crawford	Woosnam	Sealey	Dick	Musgrove
		4/11	*18,839*	*12*	19			*Dobing 6, 15, 25* [Sealey 55, 58]	*Trautmann*	*Betts*	*Sear*	*Kennedy*	*Ewing*	*Oakes*	*Baker*	*Dobing*	*Barlow*	*Hayes*	*Wagstaffe*
								Ref: K Tuck	City's Peter Dobing, signed from Blackburn, scored a first-half hat-trick that few will remember in view of the second-half transformation. Seconds from time Bobby Moore fouled Dave Wagstaffe and was sent off, though no one knew it until the ref confirmed it after the match.										
17	H	WEST BROM		3	D	3-3	3-1	Musgrove 16, Sealey 17, Bond 25p	Leslie	Kirkup	Bond	Hurst	Brown	Moore	Crawford	Woosnam	Sealey	Dick	Musgrove
		11/11	**18,000**	*14*	20			*Jackson 32, Howe 54p, Kevan 70*	*Millington*	*Howe*	*Williams*	*Robson*	*Jones*	*Drury*	*Jackson*	*Burnside*	*Smith*	*Kevan*	*Clark*
								Ref: W Crossley	The exact opposite of last week's turnaround, as this time West Ham squander a three-goal lead. Albion boss Archie Macaulay can't believe his eyes. England's Don Howe conceded one penalty, fouling Musgrove, which made it 3-0, then scored from the spot after Smith was fouled.										
18	A	BIRMINGHAM		5	L	0-4	0-0	*[Bloomfield 89]*	Leslie	Kirkup	Bond	Hurst	Brown	Moore	Crawford	Woosnam	Sealey	Dick	Musgrove
		18/11	*20,645*	*18*	20			*Auld 58, Orritt 59, Harris 69p,*	*Schofield*	*Lynn*	*Sissons*	*Hennessey*	*Smith*	*Beard*	*Hellawell*	*Bloomfield*	*Harris*	*Orritt*	*Auld*
								Ref: J Finney	Bertie Auld, so often barracked at St Andrews, masterminded this surprise thrashing, heading in Hellawell's cross for the first goal. Orritt's goal was also a header, while Harris's penalty was awarded for a push by Bond. Strange to say, West Ham had started the match in fine fettle.										
19	H	EVERTON		4	W	3-1	0-1	Dick 57, 62, Crawford 88	Leslie	Kirkup	Bond	Hurst	Brown	Moore	Crawford	Woosnam	**Tindall**	Dick	Musgrove
		25/11	27,100	*3*	22			*Vernon 28*	*Dunlop*	*Parker*	*Thomson*	*Gabriel*	*Labone*	*Harris*	*Bingham*	*Collins*	*Young*	*Vernon*	*Fell*
								Ref: D Howell	Tindall has a quiet debut, closely marshalled by Brian Labone. Leslie was stranded in no man's land when Vernon put Everton ahead, but West Ham levelled when Dunlop fisted out Musgrove's cross to Dick. For once it was not the Hammers who lacked bite, but fancy-boys Everton.										
20	A	ARSENAL		6	D	2-2	1-2	Tindall 2, 90	Leslie	Kirkup	Bond	Hurst	Brown	Moore	Crawford	Woosnam	Tindall	Dick	Musgrove
		2/12	*47,206*	*7*	23			*Strong 36, Skirton 40*	*Kelsey*	*Bacuzzi*	*McCullough*	*Clamp*	*Brown*	*Groves*	*MacLeod*	*Ward*	*Strong*	*Eastham*	*Skirton*
								Ref: K Burns	Ron Tindall's last-minute header from Bond's cross cruelly denied Arsenal their first win over West Ham since World War II. It would have been academic had man-of-the-match George Eastham shot under rather than over the bar from close in. He had made both Arsenal goals.										
21	H	BOLTON		5	W	1-0	0-0	Woosnam 72	Leslie	Kirkup	Bond	Hurst	Brown	Bovington	Crawford	Woosnam	Sealey	Dick	Musgrove
		9/12	19,472	*12*	25				*Hopkinson*	*Harris*	*Farrimond*	*Threlfall*	*Edwards*	*Rimmer*	*Holden*	*Stevens*	*McAdams*	*Hill*	*Pilkington*
								Ref: J Loynton	A maul in the mud. This best-forgotten game was rescued by Woosnam who somehow kept his balance when shoved in the back by Threlfall. He accepted a return pass from Sealey and dribbled round two defenders to score the winner. Moore missed the match through suspension.										

No	Date			Att	Pos	Pt	F-A	H-T	Scorers, Times, and Referees	1	2	3	4	5	6	7	8	9	10	11
22		A	MANCHESTER U		4	W	2-1	0-1	Dick 75, 85	Leslie	Kirkup	Bond	Hurst	Brown	Moore	Crawford	Woosnam	Tindall	Dick	Musgrove
	16/12			*29,472*	*20*	27			*Herd 18*	*Gaskell*	*Brennan*	*Dunne*	*Nicholson*	*Foulkes*	*Setters*	*Chisnall*	*Giles*	*Herd*	*Lawton*	*Charlton*
									Ref: L Callaghan	Moore returns after his one-match suspension and helps to heap more trouble on lowly Man U. Herd put them ahead with defenders appealing for offside. Poor visibility caused the floodlights to be switched on early. John Dick thundered the equaliser, then converted Musgrove's pass.										
23		H	WOLVES			W	4-2	2-1	Musgrove 1, Hurst 4, 78, 81	Leslie	Kirkup	Bond	Hurst	Brown	Moore	Crawford	Woosnam	Tindall	Dick	Musgrove
	18/12			21,261		29			*Murray 9, 53*	*Finlayson*	*Stuart*	*Kelly*	*Kirkham*	*Slater*	*Flowers*	*Wharton*	*Durandt*	*Murray*	*Broadbent*	*Hinton*
									Ref: D Smith	Wrote Norman Giller afterwards: 'I have always been a Moore fan. Now I rate him with the late, great Duncan Edwards.' Wolves were sent spinning to their seventh straight defeat at Upton Park by a goal inside 14 seconds. Musgrove's cross-shot was the quickest goal of the season.										
24		H	BLACKBURN		5	L	2-3	2-3	Tindall 10, Dick 12	Leslie	Kirkup	Bond	Hurst	Brown	Moore	Crawford	Woosnam	Tindall	Dick	Musgrove
	26/12			22,250	*16*	29			*Byrom 19, 21, 35,*	*Else*	*Taylor*	*Newton*	*Clayton*	*Woods*	*McEvoy*	*Douglas*	*Lawther*	*Pickering*	*Byrom*	*Ratcliffe*
									Ref: W Clements	An icy morning frolic that ends with Blackburn notching their second away win of the season. They owe a huge debt to John Byrom, who bags his first ever league hat-trick. He fittingly had the last kick of the game. Had Hammers won they would have been top of the table till tea-time.										
25		A	NOTT'M FOREST		5	L	0-3	0-2		Leslie	Kirkup	Bond	Hurst	Brown	Moore	Crawford	Woosnam	Tindall	Dick	Musgrove
	13/1			*20,359*	*16*	29			*Gray 16, Julians 44, 88*	*Grummitt*	*Palmer*	*Gray*	*Iley*	*McKinlay*	*Quigley*	*Hockey*	*Booth*	*Julians*	*Addison*	*Le Flem*
									Ref: L Tirebuck	At 36, Billy Gray is the oldest player on view, yet his shot from 25 yards beats Leslie all ends up. The keeper later moaned: 'I've never seen anything like it. I had the shot covered but the wind caught the ball and it seemed to go all ways.' West Ham haven't won here in 26 visits.										
26		H	ASTON VILLA		5	W	2-0	2-0	Woosnam 2, Dick 18	Leslie	Kirkup	Bond	Bovington	Brown	Moore	Scott	Woosnam	Sealey	Dick	Musgrove
	20/1			20,000	*12*	31				*Sims*	*Lee*	*Aitken*	*Crowe*	*Sleeuwenhoek*	*Deakin*	*McEwan*	*McMorran*	*Dougan*	*Wylie*	*Burrows*
									Ref: P Rhodes	Alan Deakin commits a quick foul, Tony Scott flights the free-kick, and Woosnam heads West Ham in front. The lead was doubled when Sims came out for Musgrove's centre but missed it. Villa look completely clueless in attack, which enables West Ham to hang on comfortably.										
27		A	CHELSEA		4	W	1-0	1-0	Moore 34	Leslie	Kirkup	Bond	Bovington	Brown	Moore	Scott	Woosnam	Sealey	Tindall	Musgrove
	3/2			*34,258*	*21*	33				*Bonetti*	*Shellito*	*Butler*	*Malcolm*	*Scott*	*Bradbury*	*Brabrook*	*Shaw*	*Moore*	*Tambling*	*Blunstone*
									Ref: E Crawford	Chelsea will finish bottom, and won't thank Moore for his peach of a goal that inflicts yet another defeat. When Moore shaped to collect from Woosnam, everyone expected him to pass. Instead he let fly on the volley. When Chelsea's Scott fouled Tindall, Bond fired the penalty wide.										
28		H	SHEFFIELD UTD		5	L	1-2	0-1	Woosnam 88	Leslie	Kirkup	Bond	Bovington	Brown	Moore	Scott	Woosnam	Sealey	Dick	Musgrove
	10/2			21,829	*6*	33			*Pace 41, 74*	*Hodgkinson*	*Coldwell*	*Shaw G*	*Richardson*	*Shaw J*	*Summers*	*Allchurch*	*Kettleborough*	*Pace*	*Russell*	*Simpson*
									Ref: R Mann	All West Ham's early season gloss has disappeared. The Blades have gone 13 games without defeat and in Derek Pace have one of the stars of the moment. Walter Winterbottom must have admired his volley which opened the scoring. At the death, Woosnam scored, then hit the bar.										
29		A	LEICESTER		4	D	2-2	1-1	Woosnam 36, Dick 88	Leslie	Kirkup	Bond	Bovington	Brown	Moore	Scott	Woosnam	Sealey	Dick	Musgrove
	17/2			*21,312*	*9*	34			*Keyworth 1, 51*	*Banks*	*Chalmers*	*Norman*	*White*	*King*	*Appleton*	*Riley*	*Walsh*	*Keyworth*	*Gibson*	*Stringfellow*
									Ref: J Parkinson	Stringfellow centres in the first minute and Keyworth heads in. Leicester are pegged back by Woosnam's thumping 20-yard volley. Another Keyworth header, this time from Gibson's cross, restores the lead. Moore then heads down to Dick lurking near the goal-line to make it 2-2.										
30		H	IPSWICH		4	D	2-2	1-1	Dick 6, Kirkup 46	Leslie	Kirkup	Bond	Bovington	Brown	Moore	Scott	Boyce	Sealey	Dick	Musgrove
	24/2			27,760	*3*	35			*Leadbetter 20, Phillips 78p*	*Bailey*	*Carberry*	*Compton*	*Baxter*	*Nelson*	*Elsworthy*	*Stephenson*	*Moran*	*Crawford*	*Phillips*	*Leadbetter*
									Ref: P Brandwood	West Ham needed to win to overtake Alf Ramsey's high-flying Ipswich. Woosnam missed the game with a twisted knee sustained in training. Just after half-time Kirkup's 30-yard effort spun through Bailey's hands over the line. Musgrove then handled in the box to concede a penalty.										
31		A	BURNLEY		5	L	**0-6**	0-3	*[Pointer 44, Elder 85]*	Leslie	Kirkup	Lyall	Bovington	Brown	Moore	Scott	Woosnam	Sealey	Dick	Musgrove
	3/3			*24,279*	*1*	35			*Robson 1, 76, Towers 24, 73,*	*Blacklaw*	*Angus*	*Elder*	*Adamson*	*Cummings*	*Miller*	*Connelly*	*McIlroy*	*Pointer*	*Robson*	*Towers*
									Ref: J Powell	This massacre by the league leaders widens the gap between them to seven points. Burnley have now scored 51 goals in 13 home games, an average of almost four a game. 'We want eight' roared the crowd. Lyall made his comeback and Moore kept up a running battle with the ref.										

No	Venue	Opponent	Att	Pos	Res	F-A	H-T	Scorers, Times, and Referees	1	2	3	4	5	6	7	8	9	10	11
32	A	SHEFFIELD WED		5	D	0-0	0-0		Leslie	Kirkup	Bond	Hurst	Brown	Moore	Sealey	Woosnam	**Byrne**	Tindall	Musgrove
	17/3		*31,403*	*8*	36				*Springett*	*Johnson*	*Megson*	*Hardy*	*Swan*	*Kay*	*Finney*	*Dobson*	*Young*	*Fantham*	*Holliday*
								Ref: H Richards	Johnnie Byrne makes his debut after signing from Crystal Palace for £65,000. His impact is negligible as Springett enjoys a 90-minute holiday. The action was all at the other end, where Leslie's acrobatics, two goal-line clearances by Joe Kirkup, and a post from Dobson, earned a point.										
33	H	MANCHESTER C		6	L	0-4	0-2		Leslie	Kirkup	Bond	Hurst	Brown	Moore	Woodley	Woosnam	Byrne	Tindall	Musgrove
	24/3		25,808	*11*	36			*Hayes 17, Dobing 36, 56, 81*	*Trautmann*	*Kennedy*	*Sear*	*Benson*	*Leivers*	*Oakes*	*Young*	*Dobing*	*Barlow*	*Hayes*	*Wagstaffe*
								Ref: A Sparling	Peter Dobing scores a simple hat-trick as West Ham's slide continues. It is his third of the season and second against the Hammers. Not the ideal match for Derek Woodley to come in on the wing. The result might have been different had Woosnam's 5th-minute effort not hit a post.										
34	A	BLACKBURN		6	L	0-1	0-1		Leslie	Kirkup	Bond	Hurst	Brown	Moore	Woodley	Woosnam	Byrne	Tindall	Musgrove
	28/3		*8,800*	*10*	36			*Byrom 13*	*Else*	*Taylor*	*Newton*	*Clayton*	*England*	*McGrath*	*Douglas*	*Lawther*	*Pickering*	*Byrom*	*Haverty*
								Ref: D Carr	John Byrom, Rovers' 17-year-old starlet who sunk West Ham with a Boxing Day hat-trick, scores the crucial goal in yet another defeat. In driving sleet and snow, Leslie fumbles Clayton's 20-yard effort and Byrom pounces. Centre-half Mike England marks Byrne out of the game.										
35	A	WEST BROM		6	W	1-0	1-0	Musgrove 23	Leslie	Kirkup	Bond	Hurst	Brown	Moore	Woodley	Woosnam	Byrne	Tindall	Musgrove
	31/3		*18,000*	*13*	38				*Millington*	*Howe*	*Williams G*	*Robson*	*Jones*	*Drury*	*Jackson*	*Hope*	*Smith*	*Kevan*	*Clark*
								Ref: W Crossley	Greenwood's team adopt hit and run tactics, with nine Hammers defending for most of this one-sided match, and constantly after they scored. The only goal came when Jones miscued in attempting to clear Kirkup's through ball, which runs to Musgrove. Drury hit the bar for Albion.										
36	H	BIRMINGHAM		6	D	2-2	0-0	Musgrove 55, 75	Leslie	Kirkup	Bond	Hurst	Brown	Moore	Woodley	Byrne	Sealey	Tindall	Musgrove
	6/4		22,548	*10*	39			*Bloomfield 59, Lynn 60*	*Schofield*	*Lynn*	*Sissons*	*Hennessey*	*Smith*	*Beard*	*Hellawell*	*Bloomfield*	*Harris*	*Leek*	*Auld*
								Ref: K Collinge	A Friday night match. Musgrove's two goals temporarily silence the Upton Park boo-boys. All Johnnie Byrne achieved was to be lectured by the ref after a flare-up with Bloomfield. Considering Stan Lynn limped out on the wing for 88 minutes, City were effectively playing with 10.										
37	A	EVERTON		7	L	0-3	0-1		Leslie	Kirkup	Bond	Hurst	Brown	Moore	Woosnam	Tindall	Byrne	Dick	Musgrove
	14/4		*45,171*	*3*	39			*Stevens 41, Vernon 47, Temple 73*	*Dunlop*	*Meagan*	*Thomson*	*Gabriel*	*Labone*	*Harris*	*Bingham*	*Stevens*	*Young*	*Vernon*	*Temple*
								Ref: H Wilson	Everton extend their unbeaten home record to 15 games. New boy Stevens had squandered three simple chances before lobbing Leslie from the edge of the box. At 2-0 Thompson handled, but John Bond fired his penalty straight at Dunlop, the ball wedging between the keeper's ankles.										
38	H	CARDIFF		6	W	**4-1**	1-0	Baker 15 (og), Sealey 53, Crawford 68,	Leslie	Kirkup	Lyall	**Peters**	Lansdowne	Moore	Scott	Byrne	Sealey	Dick	Crawford
	20/4		25,459	*21*	41			*Pickerell 58* [Byrne 83]	*John*	*Stitfall*	*Milne*	*Baker*	*Rankmore*	*Hole*	*McCarthy*	*King*	*Charles*	*Durban*	*Pickerell*
								Ref: H Horner	Greenwood drops six players, among them Woosnam, Bond, and Hurst. Moore is made captain. Cardiff were dreadful, typified by Baker's hilarious own-goal. Byrne almost scored when hitting the bar, from which Sealey netted, then from a tight angle scored his first for West Ham.										
39	H	ARSENAL		6	D	3-3	1-1	Scott 16, Dick 75, Lansdowne 84	Leslie	Kirkup	Lyall	Peters	Lansdowne	Moore	Scott	Byrne	Sealey	Dick	Crawford
	21/4		31,912	*8*	42			*MacLeod 42, Clapton 60, Strong 70*	*Kelsey*	*Magill*	*McCullough*	*Brown*	*Neill*	*Petts*	*Clapton*	*Griffiths*	*Strong*	*Eastham*	*MacLeod*
								Ref: J Mitchell	Had Arsenal won it would have lifted them above West Ham. Early in the second half Lawrie Leslie's hand was stamped on. John Lyall went in goal while Leslie played out time on the right wing. Leslie sped past two men to force a corner from which Billy Lansdowne equalised.										
40	A	CARDIFF		7	L	0-3	0-2		**Rhodes**	Bond	Peters	Hurst	Brown	Moore	Musgrove	Woosnam	Sealey	Byrne	Crawford
	23/4		*11,200*	*21*	42			*Ward 5, 37, Tapscott 73*	*Vearncombe*	*Stitfall*	*Milne*	*Hole*	*Rankmore*	*Baker*	*King P*	*Tapscott*	*Ward*	*Durban*	*Pickerell*
								Ref: E Norman	Stand-in keeper Rhodes dislocates a shoulder. This time it is Peters who goes in goal. There is almost half an hour still to play, yet Peters saves three powerful shots before being beaten by Tapscott. The loudest cheer came at half-time when Cardiff fans heard that Fulham were losing.										
41	A	BOLTON		10	L	0-1	0-0		**Dickie**	Kirkup	Lyall	Peters	Lansdowne	Moore	Scott	Byrne	Sealey	Dick	Crawford
	28/4		*17,333*	*11*	42			*Holden 89*	*Hopkinson*	*Hartle*	*Farrimond*	*Hatton*	*Edwards*	*Rimmer*	*Holden*	*Hill*	*Davies*	*McGarry*	*Pilkington*
								Ref: E Jennings	West Ham play three different keepers in three games. Alan Dickie is only 17 and he is denied a clean-sheet in the last minute when Wyn Davies harasses Peters into an error and Holden's 25-yard effort flies in off a post. That at least gave spectators something to talk about.										
42	H	FULHAM		8	W	4-2	2-1	Dick 32, 39, Crawford 46, 68	Dickie	Kirkup	**Burkett**	Peters	Lansdowne	Moore	Scott	Byrne	Sealey	Dick	Crawford
	30/4		22,000	*20*	44			*Langley 36p, Henderson 65*	*Macedo*	*Cohen*	*Langley*	*Mullery*	*Dodgin*	*Lowe*	*Leggat*	*Henderson*	*Cook*	*Haynes*	*O'Connell*
	Home		Away					Ref: R Mann	Fulham are already assured of another season in the top division. Although Cardiff are only two points behind, their goal-average is far inferior. The left-footed Dick put West Ham ahead when shooting with his right. Moore fisted out Henderson's drive to concede the penalty.										
Average	25,515		26,531																

League Cup									Scorers, Times, and Referees	1	2	3	4	5	6	7	8	9	10	11
							F-A	H-T												
1	H	PLYMOUTH		6		W	3-2	1-1	Crawford 31, 83, Woosnam 65	Rhodes	Kirkup	Bond	Hurst	Brown	Moore	Scott	Woosnam	Sealey	Dick	Crawford
	11/9		12,170	*2:5*					*Maloy 39, Williams 68*	*MacLaren*	*Robertson*	*Fulton*	*Williams*	*Newman*	*Casey*	*Anderson*	*Carter*	*Kirby*	*McAnearney*	*Maloy*
									Ref: K Burns	Lucky West Ham. Ian Crawford, a £7,000 signing from Hearts, scores first and last in this five-goal fiesta. His first, a fierce shot, was hardly merited by his team-mates on the balance of play. His last, sparing West Ham the indignity of a replay, was set up by a cross from Tony Scott.										
2	H	ASTON VILLA		3		L	1-3	1-2	Musgrove 26	Leslie	Kirkup	Bond	Hurst	Brown	Moore	Scott	Woosnam	Sealey	Dick	Musgrove
	9/10		17,775	*14*					*McParl'd 35, Burrows 44, Bond 83 (og)*	*Sidebottom*	*Neal*	*Aitken*	*Tindall*	*Sleeuwenhoek*	*McMorran*	*McEwan*	*Baker*	*McParland*	*Wylie*	*Burrows*
									Ref: G Roper	Villa are defending the League Cup with the youngest side in their history. Six of their players are under 21. The crucial moments came when Villa were hanging on to a 2-1 lead. Both Dick and Sealey hit Sidebottom's crossbar before John Bond turned Burrows' cross into his own net.										

FA Cup										1	2	3	4	5	6	7	8	9	10	11
3	A	PLYMOUTH		5		L	0-3	0-1		Leslie	Kirkup	Bond	Hurst	Brown	Moore	Crawford	Woosnam	Tindall	Dick	Musgrove
	3/1		*26,915*	*2:5*					*Carter 13, Williams 56, Maloy 85*	*MacLaren*	*Robertson*	*Fulton*	*Williams*	*Fincham*	*Newman*	*Anderson*	*Carter*	*Kirby*	*McAnearney*	*Maloy*
									Ref: D Smith	Second Division Plymouth gain revenge for their League Cup defeat. Early on they were indebted to their huge keeper MacLaren, but once Carter headed in Maloy's corner West Ham struggled. Williams had another Plymouth 'goal' disallowed before scoring No 2 from 25 yards.										

		Home					Away					
	P	W	D	L	F	A	W	D	L	F	A	Pts
1 Ipswich	42	17	2	2	58	28	7	6	8	35	39	56
2 Burnley	42	14	4	3	57	26	7	7	7	44	41	53
3 Tottenham	42	14	4	3	59	34	7	6	8	29	35	52
4 Everton	42	17	2	2	64	21	3	9	9	24	33	51
5 Sheffield Utd	42	13	5	3	37	23	6	4	11	24	46	47
6 Sheffield Wed	42	14	4	3	47	23	6	2	13	25	35	46
7 Aston Villa	42	13	5	3	45	20	5	3	13	20	36	44
8 WEST HAM	42	11	6	4	49	37	6	4	11	27	45	44
9 West Brom	42	10	7	4	50	23	5	6	10	33	44	43
10 Arsenal	42	9	6	6	39	31	7	5	9	32	41	43
11 Bolton	42	11	7	3	35	22	5	3	13	27	44	42
12 Manchester C	42	11	3	7	46	38	6	4	11	32	43	41
13 Blackpool	42	10	4	7	41	30	5	7	9	29	45	41
14 Leicester	42	12	2	7	38	27	5	4	12	34	44	40
15 Manchester U	42	10	3	8	44	31	5	6	10	28	44	39
16 Blackburn	42	10	6	5	33	22	4	5	12	17	36	39
17 Birmingham	42	9	6	6	37	35	5	4	12	28	46	38
18 Wolves	42	8	7	6	38	34	5	3	13	35	52	36
19 Nott'm Forest	42	12	4	5	39	23	1	6	14	24	56	36
20 Fulham	42	8	3	10	38	34	5	4	12	28	40	33
21 Cardiff	42	6	9	6	30	33	3	5	13	20	48	32
22 Chelsea	42	7	7	7	34	29	2	3	16	29	65	28
	924	246	106	110	958	624	110	106	246	624	958	924

Odds & ends

Double wins: (2) Aston Villa, Chelsea.
Double losses: (1) Blackburn.

Won from behind: (3) Villa (a), Man C (a), Man U (a).
Lost from in front: (3) Wolves (a), Blackburn (h), Villa LC (h).

High spots: Three straight wins in December leaving the Hammers 4th.

Low spots: Seven games without a win in February and March.
Losing to Second Division Plymouth Argyle in the FA Cup.
Losing 0-6 at Burnley.

West Ham faced Plymouth in both domestic cups.

Hammer of the Year: Lawrie Leslie.
Ever-presents: (0).
Hat-tricks: (0).
Leading scorer: (23) John Dick.

	Appearances			Goals			
	Lge	LC	FAC	Lge	LC	FAC	Tot
Bond, John	37	2	1	2			2
Bovington, Eddie	7						
Boyce, Ronnie	4			1			1
Brown, Ken	38	2	1				
Burkett, Jackie	1						
Byrne, Johnny	11			1			1
Crawford, Ian	19	1	1	5	2		7
Dick, John	35	2	1	23			23
Dickie, Alan	2						
Hurst, Geoff	24	2	1	1			1
Kirkup, Joe	41	2	1	1			1
Lansdowne, Billy	4			1			1
Leslie, Lawrie	37	1	1				
Lyall, John	4						
Malcolm, Andy	8						
Moore, Bobby	41	2	1	3			3
Musgrove, Malcolm	36	1	1	13	1		14
Peters, Martin	5						
Rhodes, Brian	3	1					
Scott, Tony	22	2		4			4
Sealey, Alan	32	2		11			11
Tindall, Ron	13		1	3			3
Woodley, Derek	4						
Woosnam, Phil	34	2	1	6	1		7
(own-goals)				1			1
24 players used	**462**	**22**	**11**	**76**	**4**		**80**

No	Date	Att	Pos	Pt	F-A	H-T	Scorers, Times, and Referees	1	2	3	4	5	6	7	8	9	10	11
1	A	ASTON VILLA		L	1-3	0-2	Byrne 78	Leslie	Kirkup	Peters	Hurst	Lansdowne	Moore	Crawford	Boyce	Byrne	Dick	Musgrove
	18/8	*37,000*		0			*Dougan 1, McEwan 3, Thomson 46*	*Sims*	*Lee*	*Aitken*	*Crowe*	*Sleeuwenhoek*	*Deakin*	*McEwan*	*Baker*	*Dougan*	*Thomson*	*Burrows*
							Ref: R Windle	Hammers did the double over Villa last season, but three minutes into this they are 0-2 down. Baker, Dougan and McEwan all hit Leslie's post in the second half. When West Ham delayed their reappearance, Dougan entertained the crowd by playing with claret and blue balloons.										
2	H	WOLVES		L	1-4	0-1	Musgrove 86	Leslie	Kirkup	Lyall	Peters	Brown	Moore	Crawford	Woosnam	Byrne	Dick	Musgrove
	20/8	30,020		0			*Crowe 37, Wharton 61, Farmer 62, 85*	*Davies*	*Showell*	*Thomson*	*Goodwin*	*Woodfield*	*Flowers*	*Wharton*	*Crowe*	*Farmer*	*Murray*	*Hinton*
							Ref: J Cooke	Stan Cullis's Wolves – average age 21 – scored eight in their first match and four in this, their second. Their pace and power brush West Ham aside like gossamer. Wolves' first three goals were all driven in from 25 yards or more, securing their first win at Upton Park in four years.										
3	H	TOTTENHAM	22	L	**1-6**	0-2	Woosnam 83 *[Jones 62, White 74]*	Leslie	Kirkup	Lyall	Peters	Brown	Moore	Crawford	Woosnam	Sealey	Byrne	Musgrove
	25/8	30,517	*4*	0			*Ly'll 10 (og), M'dwin 14, Gr'ves 54, 58,*	*Brown*	*Baker*	*Henry*	*Blanchflower*	*Norman*	*Mackay*	*Medwin*	*White*	*Allen*	*Greaves*	*Jones*
							Ref: K Burns	The FA Cup-holders inflict yet more misery on West Ham, yet manager Bill Nicholson winced as his team squandered another half-dozen easy chances. Goal of the match was Spurs' third, finished by Greaves after bewildering interplay. Lyall began the rout, turning in Allen's cross.										
4	A	WOLVES	22	D	0-0	0-0		Leslie	Kirkup	Burkett	Peters	Brown	Moore	**Dear**	Woosnam	Sealey	Byrne	Crawford
	29/8	*32,000*	*1*	1				*Davies*	*Showell*	*Thomson*	*Goodwin*	*Woodfield*	*Flowers*	*Wharton*	*Crowe*	*Farmer*	*Murray*	*Hinton*
							Ref: R Johnson	This looked a home-banker for top v bottom. Wolves had scored 14 in three matches, West Ham had conceded 13. Only once was Leslie beaten, but Moore flung himself to jab Crowe's effort away. After the break Hammers even pressed forward and Davies saved from Woosnam.										
5	A	LEYTON ORIENT	22	L	0-2	0-2		Leslie	Kirkup	Burkett	Peters	Brown	Moore	Dear	Woosnam	Sealey	Byrne	Crawford
	1/9	*23,918*	*18*	1			*Dunmore 6, Graham 40*	*Robertson*	*Charlton*	*Lewis*	*Lucas*	*Bishop*	*Lea*	*Deeley*	*Bolland*	*Dunmore*	*Graham*	*McDonald*
							Ref: J Pickles	West Ham need to beat winless, promoted Orient, but quickly fall behind to Dunmore's header from Deeley's corner. Graham ran 20 yards before firing the second goal. Several fans fainted in the heat. Off the field Upton Park is disrupted by pay squabbles, now apparently settled.										
6	H	LIVERPOOL	20	W	1-0	1-0	Scott 5	Leslie	Bond	Burkett	Peters	Brown	Moore	Scott	Woosnam	Byrne	Hurst	Musgrove
	3/9	22,262	*9*	3				*Furnell*	*Byrne*	*Moran*	*Milne*	*Yeats*	*Ferns*	*Callaghan*	*Hunt*	*St John*	*Melia*	*A'Court*
							Ref: H Hackney	The unexpected always happens. Bill Shankly's promoted Liverpool are going well, but are undone by a team determined to restore its pride. Roger Hunt hit Leslie's post in the third minute. Had it gone in, who knows what would have happened. Within minutes Scott volleyed home.										
7	A	MANCHESTER C	19	W	**6-1**	4-1	Musgrove 27, 70, Scott 37, Byrne 40,	Leslie	Bond	Burkett	Peters	Brown	Moore	Scott	Woosnam	Byrne	Hurst	Musgrove
	8/1	*25,000*	22	5			*Barlow 28* [Peters 43, Hurst 80]	*Trautmann !*	*Betts*	*Kennedy*	*Benson*	*Leivers*	*Oakes*	*Barlow*	*Dobing*	*Harley*	*Young*	*Hayes*
							Ref: K Stokes	Another bizarre result, this time against the team which replaces West Ham at the bottom. When Musgrove put Hammers 5-1 up, City keeper Trautmann insisted he was offside. He booted the ball into the ref's back and was sent off for the second time in his career. Oakes went in goal.										
8	A	LIVERPOOL	19	L	1-2	0-1	Byrne 50	Leslie	Bond	Burkett	Peters	Brown	Moore	Scott	Woosnam	Byrne	Hurst	Musgrove
	12/9	*39,261*	*10*	5			*St John 39, 86*	*Furnell*	*Byrne*	*Moran*	*Milne*	*Yeats*	*Leishman*	*Callaghan*	*Hunt*	*St John*	*Melia*	*A'Court*
							Ref: R Smith	Revenge for Shankly, but it was barely merited. Liverpool keeper Furnell's long throw-out set up Ian St John's first goal. Furnell then allowed deep-lying Byrne's shot to slip through his hands for the equaliser. Near the end Yeats headed against the bar and St John forced the ball in.										
9	H	BLACKPOOL	18	D	2-2	1-2	Musgrove 32, Scott 84	Leslie	Bond	Burkett	Peters	Brown	Moore	Scott	Woosnam	Byrne	Hurst	Musgrove
	14/9	24,000	*13*	6			*McPhee 20, 33*	*Waiters*	*Armfield*	*Martin*	*Crawford*	*James*	*Durie*	*Watt*	*Green*	*Charnley*	*McPhee*	*Horne*
								Ronnie Stuart's Blackpool enjoyed two gift goals in the Friday night fixture. Peters and Brown made a mess of a clearance for the first goal, and Brown's clearance bounced off Charnley for the second. Musgrove's 25-yarder was followed by Tony Scott bagging the second equaliser.										
10	A	BLACKBURN	15	W	4-0	1-0	Hurst 35, Musgrove 62, Byrne 88,	Leslie	Bond	Burkett	Peters	Brown	Moore	Scott	Woosnam	Byrne	Hurst	Musgrove
	22/9	*15,400*	*20*	8			[Peters 90]	*Else*	*Taylor*	*Bray*	*Clayton*	*Woods*	*Newton*	*Douglas*	*Ferguson*	*Pickering*	*Byrom*	*Harrison*
							Ref: W Downey	At start of play, both teams had identical records. 90 minutes later West Ham's revival had pitched Rovers to the bottom. Blackburn pressed strongly at first and Pickering came close, but the tide had turned by the time Hurst headed in. Two late goals distorted the balance of play.										

No	Venue	Opponent / Date	Att	Pos	Res / Pts	F-A	H-T	Scorers, Times, and Referees	1	2	3	4	5	6	7	8	9	10	11
11	H	SHEFFIELD UTD		13	D	1-1	0-1	Scott 64	Leslie	Bond	Burkett	Peters	Brown	Moore	Scott	Woosnam	Byrne	Hurst	Musgrove
		29/9	22,707	*8*	9			*Shaw G 22p*	*Hodgkinson*	*Coldwell*	*Shaw G*	*Richardson*	*Shaw J*	*Summers*	*Allchurch*	*Kettleborough*	*Pace*	*Hodgson*	*Hartle*
								Ref: R Spittle	Blades' manager John Harris was aggrieved about Scott's equaliser, from Bond's booming cross, which might have been offside. West Ham had gone behind when Moore toppled Allchurch, and Graham Shaw fired the penalty in off the bar. Thereafter Alan Hodgkinson stood defiant.										
12	H	BIRMINGHAM		11	W	5-0	2-0	Hurst 3, Byrne 18, 49, Musgrove 52, [Brown 87]	Leslie	Bond	Burkett	Peters	Brown	Moore	Scott	Woosnam	Byrne	Hurst	Musgrove
		6/10	21,039	*22*	11				*Withers*	*Foster*	*Lynn*	*Hennessey*	*Smith*	*Beard*	*Hellawell*	*Bullock*	*Harris*	*Leek*	*Auld*
								Ref: H New	Hammers squeeze into the top half after this demolition. Birmingham have now lost all seven away games, conceded 21 goals and scored none. Walter Winterbottom watched Hurst, enjoying the switch to centre-forward, and Byrne grab important goals. Brown hit his first league goal.										
13	A	ARSENAL		10	D	1-1	0-1	Scott 58	Leslie	Bond	Burkett	Peters	Brown	Moore	Scott	Woosnam	Byrne	Hurst	Musgrove
		13/10	***49,597***	*15*	12			*Baker 20*	*McClelland*	*Magill*	*McCullough*	*Neill*	*Brown*	*Snedden*	*MacLeod*	*Strong*	*Baker*	*Eastham*	*Skirton*
								Ref: A Sparling	Billy Wright's Arsenal have adopted Wolves' up-and-under tactics. They score first through £70,000 signing Joe Baker, after Leslie spilled McLeod's effort, but are denied their first post-war win over West Ham when Byrne's pass set up Scott's leveller. A petty, niggling match.										
14	H	BURNLEY			D	1-1	1-1	Hurst 1	Leslie	Bond	Burkett	Peters	Brown	Moore	**Brabrook**	Woosnam	Byrne	Hurst	Musgrove
		22/10	**34,612**		13			*Robson 40*	*Blacklaw*	*Angus*	*Elder*	*Adamson*	*Talbut*	*Miller*	*Connelly*	*Lochhead*	*Towers*	*Robson*	*Harris*
								Ref: J Osborne	Peter Brabrook, a £35,000 signing from Chelsea, took 40 seconds to project the cross from which Hurst netted. Burnley had flown down, but got caught in traffic, arriving 10 minutes before kick-off. Jimmy Adamson's 400th league game was rewarded by Jimmy Robson's equaliser.										
15	A	MANCHESTER U		14	L	1-3	1-2	Musgrove 29	Leslie	Burkett	Lyall	Peters	Brown	Moore	Brabrook	Woosnam	Sealey	Byrne	Musgrove
		27/10	*29,204*	*20*	13			*Quixall 17p, 41, Law 79*	*Gregg*	*Brennan*	*Cantwell*	*Stiles*	*Foulkes*	*Setters*	*Giles*	*Quixall*	*Herd*	*Law*	*Charlton*
								Ref: D Howell	Man U climb off the bottom with this important win. Leslie sent Nobby Stiles spinning inside the box and Albert Quixall netted the penalty. Following Musgrove's equaliser, Sealey missed an open goal and Brabrook hit the bar. Leslie pushed out Giles' centre to the lurking Quixall.										
16	H	BOLTON		16	L	1-2	1-1	Moore 45	Leslie	Bond	Burkett	Peters	Brown	Moore	Brabrook	Woosnam	Byrne	Hurst	Musgrove
		3/11	19,866	*14*	13			*McGarry 10, 62*	*Hopkinson*	*Hartle*	*Farrimond*	*Stanley*	*Edwards*	*Rimmer*	*Lee*	*Hill*	*Davies*	*McGarry*	*Pilkington*
								Ref: G Pullin	Bolton's first away win enables them to leapfrog over West Ham, who played as though 20 lateral passes were better than one forward one. Just after he fumbled a cross to enable McGarry to restore Bolton's lead, Leslie collided with Rimmer and broke his left leg. Peters deputised.										
17	A	LEICESTER		17	L	0-2	0-1		Dickie	Bond	Burkett	Peters	Brown	Moore	Brabrook	Boyce	Byrne	Hurst	Musgrove
		10/11	*21,064*	*4*	13			*Stringfellow 25, McLintock 58*	*Banks*	*Chalmers*	*Norman*	*McLintock*	*King*	*Appleton*	*Cheesebrough*	*Heath*	*Keyworth*	*Gibson*	*Stringfellow*
								Ref: H Richards	On a murky day high-flying Leicester maintain their unbeaten home record. Scottish signing David Gibson looked a class apart. Young keeper Dickie was beaten by Stringfellow's header and McLintock's thumping volley from 25 yards. Hurst and Byrne missed inviting chances.										
18	H	FULHAM		17	D	2-2	0-0	Hurst 57, Peters 85p	Dickie	Kirkup	Burkett	Peters	Brown	Moore	Brabrook	Boyce	Sealey	Hurst	Scott
		17/11	17,668	*21*	14			*Leggat 55, Langley 78*	*Macedo*	*Cohen*	*Langley*	*Robson*	*Lampe*	*Lowe*	*Leggat*	*Metchick*	*Brown*	*Henderson*	*O'Connell*
								Ref: J Finney	A wretched first half was followed by a stirring second. Henderson's cheeky back-pass set up a goal for Leggat. Brabrook's cross gave a tap-in equaliser for Hurst. Fulham skipper Langley thumped a shot into the corner before Leggat's arm kept out Ronnie Boyce's goal-bound effort.										
19	A	SHEFFIELD WED		18	W	3-1	3-1	Brabrook 2, Peters 27p, Scott 40	**Standen**	Kirkup	Burkett	Peters	Brown	Moore	Brabrook	Boyce	Sealey	Hurst	Scott
		24/11	*23,764*	*8*	16			*Fantham 24*	*Springett*	*Johnson*	*Birks*	*McAnearney*	*Swan*	*Kay*	*Finney*	*Wilkinson*	*Layne*	*Fantham*	*Holliday*
								Ref: J Cattlin	Jim Standen, signed for £7,000, helps inflict Wednesday's second home defeat. Hurst dummies Brabrook's cross, which beats Ron Springett. The Owls' keeper brought down Sealey for Peters to restore the lead from the spot. Tony Scott's left-footer sealed the win before half-time.										
20	H	WEST BROM		16	D	2-2	0-0	Moore 52, Hurst 85	Standen	Kirkup	Burkett	Peters	Brown	Moore	Brabrook	Boyce	Sealey	Hurst	Scott
		1/12	20,680	*13*	17			*Smith 56, 79*	*Potter*	*Howe*	*Williams*	*Cram*	*Jones*	*Drury*	*Jackson*	*Fenton*	*Smith*	*Kevan*	*Clark*
								Ref: K Dagnall	A replica of the last home game, with Fulham – a drab first half, followed by four shared goals in the second. Moore's header from Boyce's free-kick was overturned by Keith Smith's two close-range goals. A miscued defensive header enabled Hurst to volley the late point-saver.										
21	A	EVERTON		17	D	1-1	1-1	Brabrook 17	Standen	Kirkup	Burkett	Peters	Brown	Moore	Brabrook	Boyce	Sealey	Byrne	Scott
		8/12	*38,701*	*1*	18			*Stevens 5*	*West*	*Parker*	*Meagan*	*Gabriel*	*Labone*	*Harris*	*Bingham*	*Stevens*	*Young*	*Vernon*	*Veall*
								Ref: A Luty	Harry Catterick's Everton pace-setters, unbeaten at home, would have won as expected but for an incredible last-minute miss by Alex Young, who blazed over an empty net from two yards. Young was booed by the Goodison crowd at the final whistle. Both early goals were messy.										

No		Date	Att	Pos	Pt	F-A	H-T	Scorers, Times, and Referees	1	2	3	4	5	6	7	8	9	10	11
22	H	ASTON VILLA		14	D	1-1	1-0	Peters 43	Standen	Kirkup	Burkett	Peters	Brown	Moore	Brabrook	Boyce	Sealey	Byrne	Scott
		15/12	21,532	*5*	19			*Thomson 63*	*Sidebottom*	*Fraser*	*Aitken*	*Crowe*	*Sleeuwenhoek*	*Deakin*	*McEwan*	*Thomson*	*Dougan*	*Woosnam*	*Burrows*
								Ref: T Dawes	Phil Woosnam returns to Upton Park as a Villa player and is marked tightly. In heavy conditions Peters drives a spot-kick over the bar after Aitken handles, but makes amends when converting Brabrook's pass. Bobby Thomson's first-timer earned Villa's fourth away draw in a row.										
23	A	TOTTENHAM		14	D	4-4	1-2	Pet'rs 30, Kirkup 54, B'yce 66,Sc'tt 73	Standen	Kirkup	Burkett	Peters	Brown	Moore	Brabrook	Boyce	Sealey	Byrne	Scott
		22/12	*44,106*	*2*	20			*Smith J 8, Mackay 20, 55, 89*	*Brown*	*Baker*	*Henry*	*Smith J*	*Marchi*	*Mackay*	*Medwin*	*White*	*Smith R*	*Greaves*	*Jones*
								Ref: E Norman	John Smith, ex-Hammer, scores for Spurs in his first game of the season. Inspired by Peters, West Ham turn a 0-2 deficit into a 4-3 lead, only to be pegged back in the last moments when pocket battleship Dave Mackay secured his hat-trick with Jim Standen frozen to his goal-line.										
24	A	NOTT'M FOREST		11	W	4-3	1-2	McK'lay 7 (og), Byrne 50, B'br'k 54, 84	Standen	Kirkup	Burkett	Peters	Brown	Moore	Brabrook	Boyce	Sealey	Byrne	Scott
		29/12	*18,587*	*8*	22			*Vowden 24, Addison 30, Palmer 49*	*Grummitt*	*Baird*	*Gray*	*Whitefoot*	*McKinlay*	*Palmer*	*Hockey*	*Quigley*	*Addison*	*Vowden*	*Le Flem*
								Ref: A Atherton	A snow-covered pitch was barely fit to play on. Not even the tonic of Bob McKinlay turning Scott's cross into his own net could prevent West Ham stumbling to what appeared to be a crushing defeat. Byrne's switch to centre-forward turned the tide. Boyce made both Brabrook's goals.										
25	A	SHEFFIELD UTD		10	W	2-0	1-0	Boyce 34, Sealey 77	Standen	Kirkup	Burkett	Bovington	Brown	Moore	Brabrook	Boyce	Sealey	Byrne	Scott
		16/2	*18,176*	*12*	24				*Hodgkinson*	*Coldwell*	*Shaw G*	*Richardson*	*Shaw J*	*Summers*	*Allchurch*	*Kettleborough*	*Pace*	*Hodgson*	*Simpson*
								Ref: C Duxbury	Six weeks have been frozen off. The icy pitch causes Standen and others to come out after half-time wearing canvas boots with rubber soles. The change helped earn West Ham's fifth away win, bettered only by Everton and Wolves. Boyce scored off a post; Sealey headed the second.										
26	H	ARSENAL		12	L	0-4	0-2	*[Strong 78]*	Standen	Kirkup	Burkett	Bovington	Brown	Moore	Brabrook	Boyce	Sealey	Byrne	Scott
		2/3	31,967	*8*	24			*McCullough 27, Baker 38, 55,*	*McClelland*	*Magill*	*McCullough*	*Barnwell*	*Brown*	*Sneddon*	*McLeod*	*Strong*	*Baker*	*Eastham*	*Anderson*
								Ref: D Smith	West Ham's dreadful home form continues. Billy McCullough was allowed to run 40 yards before hitting a shot that bounced, skidded and long-hopped past Standen. Joe Baker volleyed the best goal of the game, which saw as many chances created by the hosts as by the Gunners.										
27	A	BURNLEY		10	D	1-1	0-0	Byrne 86	Standen	Kirkup	Burkett	Bovington	Brown	Moore	Brabrook	Boyce	Sealey	Byrne	Scott
		9/3	*17,287*	*5*	25			*Pointer 59*	*Blacklaw*	*Angus*	*Elder*	*Adamson*	*Talbot*	*Miller*	*Connelly*	*Pointer*	*Lochhead*	*Robson*	*Harris*
								Ref: A Luty	Burnley have lost at home just once, but supporters are so angry at the sale of McIlroy to Stoke that they stay away in droves. Greenwood adopts ultra-defensive tactics and is perhaps fortunate to escape with a point when Alan Sealey's cross hits Byrne and deflects into the net.										
28	H	MANCHESTER U		11	W	3-1	1-0	Brown 36, Sealey 78, Brennan 89 (og)	Rhodes	Kirkup	Burkett	Bovington	Brown	Moore	Brabrook	Boyce	Sealey	Hurst	Scott
		18/3	28,950	*15*	27			*Herd 76*	*Gregg*	*Brennan*	*Cantwell*	*Crerand*	*Foulkes*	*Setters*	*Giles*	*Stiles*	*Herd*	*Law*	*Charlton*
								Ref: A Moore	West Ham's first home league win in five months comes against wealthy Man U, whose team cost a huge £250,000. Ken Brown bundled in Sealey's free-kick. Herd hit the bar before heading the equaliser, but Bovington then passed over Foulkes' head for Hurst to restore the lead.										
29	A	BOLTON		11	L	0-3	0-0		Rhodes	Kirkup	Burkett	Bovington	Brown	Moore	Brabrook	Boyce	Sealey	Hurst	Scott
		23/3	*19,071*	*16*	27			*Russell 50, Lee 62, Butler 67*	*Hopkinson*	*Hartle*	*Farrimond*	*Stanley*	*Edwards*	*Rimmer*	*Lee*	*Russell*	*Davies*	*Hill*	*Butler*
								Ref: J Finney	Bolton's Billy Russell, just 18, outjumped Brian Rhodes to score on his debut and send West Ham spinning to defeat. Two other 18-year-olds, Francis Lee and Dennis Butler, added further goals. The Hammers seemed preoccupied by the looming FA Cup quarter-final with Liverpool.										
30	H	SHEFFIELD WED			W	2-0	1-0	Hurst 14, Byrne 66p	Standen	Kirkup	Burkett	Peters	Brown	Moore	Brabrook	Boyce	Hurst	Byrne	Scott
		30/3	22,408		29				*Springett*	*Johnson*	*Megson*	*McAnearney*	*Swan*	*Young*	*Finney*	*Quinn*	*Wilkinson*	*Fantham*	*Dobson*
								Ref: H New	Alf Ramsey watched this mediocre match, in which West Ham looked to have a 'Liverpool' hangover. Wednesday's defence was so bad that they gave the Hammers every encouragement. England's Peter Swan fluffed a clearance to let in Hurst, then handled for Byrne's penalty.										
31	A	FULHAM		13	L	0-2	0-0		Standen	Kirkup	Burkett	Bovington	Brown	Peters	Brabrook	Boyce	Sealey	Byrne	Scott
		6/4	*26,861*	*10*	29			*Cook 47, Key 88*	*Macedo*	*Cohen*	*Langley*	*Mullery*	*Lowe*	*Robson*	*Key*	*Leggat*	*Cook*	*Brown*	*O'Connell*
								Ref: P Brandwood	Fulham soar into the top half with their eighth win in a row. Ken Brown deputised as West Ham captain in the absence of Moore, on England duty against Scotland. Leggat squared to Cook for the first goal, whereupon Tony Scott missed a hat-trick of inviting chances to equalise.										

No	Venue/Date	Opponent/Att	Pos	Res/Pts	F-A	H-T	Scorers, Times, Referees	1	2	3	4	5	6	7	8	9	10	11
32	H	IPSWICH	13	L	1-3	1-1	Scott 8	Standen	Kirkup	Burkett	Peters	Brown	Moore	Brabrook	Boyce	Hurst	Byrne	Scott
	12/4	23,170	*18*	29			*Moran 44, Phillips 50, Crawford 75*	*Bailey*	*Carberry*	*Compton*	*Baxter*	*Nelson*	*Elsworthy*	*Stephenson*	*Moran*	*Crawford*	*Phillips*	*Leadbetter*
							Ref: P Bye	Lowly Ipswich have waved goodbye to their league title, but they pick up two vital points. Hammers fell behind following a bizarre blunder by Standen, who caught Phillips' header from Stephenson's cross, then dropped it over the line. 'It's a disgrace,' yelled angry fans at directors.										
33	H	LEICESTER	13	W	2-0	1-0	Sealey 19, 62	Standen	Kirkup	Burkett	Bovington	Brown	Moore	Sealey	Boyce	Hurst	Peters	Brabrook
	13/4	25,689	*2*	31				*Banks*	*Sjoberg*	*Norman*	*McLintock*	*King*	*Appleton*	*Riley*	*Cross*	*Keyworth*	*Gibson*	*Stringfellow*
							Ref: G Hartley	Leicester are knocked off the top after an unbeaten run of 16 games, as West Ham do a good turn to London rivals Spurs, who lead the pack. Greenwood reshuffled his team and was rewarded by Sealey doubling his goal tally for the season. Standen did not have one hard shot to save.										
34	A	IPSWICH	11	W	3-2	1-1	Brabrook 41, Peters 54, Hurst 75	Standen	Kirkup	Burkett	Bovington	Brown	Moore	Sealey	Boyce	Hurst	Peters	Brabrook
	15/4	*21,971*	*18*	33			*Crawford 20, Stephenson 53*	*Bailey*	*Carberry*	*Compton*	*Baxter*	*Nelson*	*Elsworthy*	*Stephenson*	*Moran*	*Crawford*	*Phillips*	*Leadbetter*
							Ref: K Stokes	Ipswich have not won at home since December, though they twice took the lead in this topsy-turvy match. First, Standen dropped a free-kick for Crawford to pounce, then Moore miskicked to let in Stephenson. Emergency centre-forward Hurst hit the winner from Moore's cross.										
35	A	WEST BROM	11	L	0-1	0-1		Standen	Kirkup	Burkett	Bovington	Brown	Moore	Sealey	Boyce	Hurst	Peters	Brabrook
	20/4	***11,600***	*16*	33			*Jackson 17*	*Potter*	*Howe*	*Williams*	*Cram*	*Jones*	*Bradley*	*Foggo*	*Jackson*	*Fenton*	*Hope*	*Carter*
							Ref: J Cattlin	Albion's new manager Jimmy Hagan smiles as Alec Jackson latched on to Hope's through pass to lash the ball past Standen from 25 yards. West Brom had lost their last four and relegation looms. They are grateful that Hurst is off form and Hammers manage just one shot on target.										
36	H	NOTT'M FOREST		W	4-1	1-1	Hurst 12, 61p, Peters 66, Moore 79	Standen	Kirkup	Burkett	Peters	Brown	Moore	Scott	Boyce	Sealey	Hurst	Brabrook
	22/4	18,179		35			*Julians 38*	*Grummitt*	*Grant*	*Wilson*	*Baird*	*McKinlay*	*Winfield*	*Hockey*	*Cobb*	*Julians*	*Addison*	*Quigley*
							Ref: C Woan	Geoff Hurst scrambled his first goal, after Grummitt spilled his first effort, then in the absence of the injured Byrne took two penalties in two minutes. The first, after McKinlay fouled Sealey, he put away; the second, after Baird handled, Hurst drove wide, spurning his hat-trick.										
37	H	EVERTON	11	L	1-2	1-2	Meagan 18 (og)	Standen	Kirkup	Burkett	Peters	Brown	Moore	Sealey	Boyce	Byrne	Hurst	Brabrook
	27/4	28,461	*1*	35			*Vernon 31, Temple 44*	*Dunlop*	*Parker*	*Meagan*	*Gabriel*	*Labone*	*Kay*	*Scott*	*Stevens*	*Young*	*Vernon*	*Temple*
							Ref: N Matthews	Harry Catterick's pace-setters recovered after full-back Meagan inexplicably prodded Brabrook's cross into his own goal and go on to their first victory in London this season. They also claim revenge for their FA Cup defeat, playing negative possession tactics after half-time.										
38	A	BIRMINGHAM	11	L	2-3	2-1	Scott 23, Hurst 34	Standen	Kirkup	Burkett	Peters	Brown	Moore	Scott	Boyce	Sealey	Hurst	Brabrook
	1/5	*14,392*	*21*	35			*Auld 40, Hennessey 60, Harris 75*	*Withers*	*Lynn*	*Green*	*Hennessey*	*Smith*	*Beard*	*Hellawell*	*Bloomfield*	*Harris*	*Leek*	*Auld*
							Ref: J Thacker	Gil Merrick's relegation-haunted Birmingham win their first home fixture since October, and do it the hard way, coming back from two goals down. Greenwood had reverted to the team which dumped Forest 4-1, which meant the axe for Byrne. Hennessey inspired City's fight-back.										
39	H	BLACKBURN	14	L	0-1	0-1		Leslie	Kirkup	Lyall	Peters	Moore	**Charles**	Scott	Boyce	**Britt**	**Sissons**	Brabrook
	4/5	18,898	*11*	35			*Pickering 44*	*Else*	*Bray*	*Newton*	*Clayton*	*Woods*	*England*	*Douglas*	*McEvoy*	*Pickering*	*Byrom*	*Harrison*
							Ref: E Jennings	The time is right to throw in the kids, and Greenwood throws in three of them. It did not produce a winning formula. Bryan Douglas fed Fred Pickering, who dribbled round Leslie, returning after his broken leg. In the second half Bobby Moore switched to the forward line, to no avail.										
40	H	LEYTON ORIENT	14	W	2-0	1-0	Brabrook 17, Scott 84	Leslie	Bond	Burkett	Peters	Brown	Moore	Brabrook	Boyce	Sealey	Byrne	Scott
	11/5	16,745	*22*	37				*Pinner*	*Charlton*	*Taylor*	*Lucas*	*Bishop*	*Lea*	*Mason*	*Gibbs*	*Musgrove*	*Bolland*	*Elwood*
							Ref: G McCabe	Orient will make a speedy return to Division 2. Greenwood dumps his kids as quickly as he had introduced them. Malcolm Musgrove, who left Upton Park for Orient, missed the chances that could have earned an away win. Brabrook's header and Scott's overhead kick win the points.										
41	A	BLACKPOOL		D	0-0	0-0		Leslie	Bond	Burkett	Peters	Brown	Moore	Brabrook	Boyce	Sealey	Hurst	Byrne
	13/5	*12,434*		38				*Waiters*	*Thompson*	*Martin*	*McPhee*	*Gratrix*	*Cranston*	*Lea*	*Quinn*	*Charnley*	*Crawford*	*Parry*
							Ref: K Tuck	Both sides are locked together in mid-table. Blackpool, minus skipper Jim Armfield, bring down the curtain on their season with this lifeless, goalless draw. When Byrne did beat Waiters, Barry Martin was on hand to clear off the line. Leslie saved well from Charnley and Crawford.										
42	H	MANCHESTER C	12	W	**6-1**	4-0	Hurst 4, 8, Sealey 28, 82, Boyce 33, [Brabrook 53]	Leslie	Bond	Burkett	Bovington	Brown	Moore	Brabrook	Boyce	Sealey	Hurst	Dear
	18/5	**16,600**	*21*	40			*Oakes 83*	*Dowd*	*Kennedy*	*Sear*	*Oakes*	*Leivers*	*Gray*	*Young*	*Dobing*	*Harley*	*Hayes*	*Wagstaffe*
Average	Home 23,593	Away 25,657					Ref: S Yates	To stay up, City need to win massively and hope Birmingham lose massively. Instead, West Ham repeat the score by which they won at Maine Road, and in the process City concede their 100th goal. Moore's errant back-pass led to Oakes' consolation. West Ham now play in New York.										

League Cup						F-A	H-T	Scorers, Times, and Referees	1	2	3	4	5	6	7	8	9	10	11
1	H	PLYMOUTH		15	W	6-0	4-0	Peters 3, Byrne 18, 30, 38p,	Leslie	Bond	Burkett	Peters	Brown	Moore	Scott	Boyce	Byrne	Hurst	Musgrove
		26/9	9,714	*2:12*				[Musgrove 51, Hurst 58]	*MacLaren*	*Roberts*	*Fulton*	*Williams*	*Wyatt*	*Newman*	*Corbett*	*Jackson*	*Garden*	*Thorne*	*Anderson*
								Ref: E Jennings	These teams also met in both last season's cups with one 'rubber' apiece. But Plymouth are sunk by Byrne's 20-minute hat-trick – two headers and a penalty after Fulton had fisted over Scott's lob. Injury-ravaged Plymouth were finished from the moment Peters headed in Scott's corner.										
2	A	ROTHERHAM		10	L	1-3	0-1	Hurst 52	Leslie	Bond	Burkett	Bovington	Brown	Peters	Scott	Woosnam	Byrne	Hurst	Musgrove
		16/10	*11,581*	*2:14*				*Kirkman 44, Waterh'se, 64, Weston 80*	*Ironside*	*Jackson*	*Morgan*	*Lambert*	*Madden*	*Waterhouse*	*Weston*	*Kirkman*	*Bennett*	*Houghton*	*Taylor*
								Ref: F Cowan	The last time these teams met was in Division 2 in 1958, when West Ham won 8-0. Rotherham have a fine record in the League Cup, and went ahead when Kirkman beat Burkett in the air and evaded Leslie. Hurst's header was followed by a missed penalty, when Houghton shot wide.										

FA Cup																			
3	H	FULHAM		12	D	0-0	0-0		Standen	Kirkup	Burkett	Bovington	Brown	Moore	Brabrook	Boyce	Sealey	Byrne	Scott
		4/2	21,000	*21*					*Macedo*	*Cohen*	*Langley*	*Mullery*	*Lowe*	*Robson*	*Leggat*	*Cook*	*Brown*	*Henderson*	*Stratton*
								Ref: A Holland	The weather postponed the original tie, but the pitch is still snow-bound as the worst winter in memory tightens its grip. Fulham chairman Tommy Trinder was delighted with a draw, though Byrne might have sealed a home win when he broke through but was thwarted by Macedo.										
3R	A	FULHAM		10	W	2-1	1-0	Boyce 14, Byrne 72p	Standen	Kirkup	Burkett	Bovington	Brown	Moore	Brabrook	Boyce	Sealey	Byrne	Scott
		20/2	*20,000*	*21*				*Robson 86*	*Macedo*	*Cohen*	*Langley*	*Mullery*	*Lowe*	*Robson*	*Key*	*Cook*	*Brown*	*Haynes*	*Metchick*
								Ref: A Holland	A replay in a snowstorm. Boyce fired in off a post from 25 yards. In the second half Boyce was fouled taking the ball round Lowe and Byrne sent Macedo the wrong way from the spot. Future England boss Bobby Robson set up a frantic climax, then Standen saved well from Haynes.										
4	H	SWANSEA		10	W	1-0	1-0	Boyce 36	Standen	Kirkup	Burkett	Bovington	Brown	Moore	Brabrook	Boyce	Sealey	Byrne	Scott
		4/3	25,924	*2:15*					*Dwyer*	*Evans*	*Griffiths*	*Hughes*	*Johnson*	*Saunders*	*Jones*	*Thomas*	*Todd*	*Reynolds*	*Morgan*
								Ref: A Moore	Only in the corners is there any grass. Otherwise the pitch is mud, mud, glorious mud. Byrne back-heeled man-of-the-match Brabrook's near-post cross and Ron Boyce netted to give Hammers their first home win since early October. Byrne later hit a post and the ball stuck in the mud.										
5	H	EVERTON		10	W	1-0	0-0	Byrne 60p	Standen	Kirkup	Burkett	Bovington	Brown	Moore	Brabrook	Boyce	Sealey	Byrne	Scott
		16/3	31,770	*3*					*West*	*Parker*	*Meagan*	*Gabriel*	*Labone*	*Kay*	*Bingham*	*Stevens*	*Young*	*Vernon*	*Morrissey*
								Ref: J Finney	Everton had won three previous cup-ties with West Ham by the same score, 2-1. Hammers were outplayed in the first half, but the tie turned when Stevens tried to check Moore and handled. Four policemen were called upon to eject an irate Everton fan who dashed onto the pitch.										
QF	A	LIVERPOOL		11	L	0-1	0-0		Standen	Kirkup	Burkett	Peters	Brown	Moore	Brabrook	Boyce	Sealey	Byrne	Scott
		30/3	*49,036*	*4*				*Hunt 81*	*Lawrence*	*Byrne*	*Moran*	*Milne*	*Yeats*	*Stevenson*	*Callaghan*	*Hunt*	*St John*	*Melia*	*Lewis*
								Ref: W Clements	Unlucky West Ham silenced the Kop for long stretches of this match. West Ham's adventurous 4-2-4 had Shankly's team at sixes and sevens, but Hunt, who had earlier hit the post, slid in Melia's pass from a tight angle. Sealey ought to have scored when heading straight at Lawrence.										

		Home					Away					
	P	W	D	L	F	A	W	D	L	F	A	Pts
1 Everton	42	14	7	0	48	17	11	4	6	36	25	61
2 Tottenham	42	14	6	1	72	28	9	3	9	39	34	55
3 Burnley	42	14	4	3	41	17	8	6	7	37	40	54
4 Leicester	42	14	6	1	53	23	6	6	9	26	30	52
5 Wolves	42	11	6	4	51	25	9	4	8	42	40	50
6 Sheffield Wed	42	10	5	6	38	26	9	5	7	39	37	48
7 Arsenal	42	11	4	6	44	33	7	6	8	42	44	46
8 Liverpool	42	13	3	5	45	22	4	7	10	26	37	44
9 Nott'm Forest	42	12	4	5	39	28	5	6	10	28	41	44
10 Sheffield Utd	42	11	7	3	33	20	5	5	11	25	40	44
11 Blackburn	42	11	4	6	55	34	4	8	9	24	37	42
12 WEST HAM	42	8	6	7	39	34	6	6	9	34	35	40
13 Blackpool	42	8	7	6	34	27	5	7	9	24	37	40
14 West Brom	42	11	1	9	40	37	5	6	10	31	42	39
15 Aston Villa	42	12	2	7	38	23	3	6	12	24	45	38
16 Fulham	42	8	6	7	28	30	6	4	11	22	41	38
17 Ipswich	42	5	8	8	34	39	7	3	11	25	39	35
18 Bolton	42	13	3	5	35	18	2	2	17	20	57	35
19 Manchester U	42	6	6	9	36	38	6	4	11	31	43	34
20 Birmingham	42	6	8	7	40	40	4	5	12	23	50	33
21 Manchester C	42	7	5	9	30	45	3	6	12	28	57	31
22 Leyton Orient	42	4	5	12	22	37	2	4	15	15	44	21
	924	223	113	126	895	641	126	113	223	641	895	924

Odds & ends

Double wins: (3) Manchester C, Sheffield Wed, Nott'm Forest.
Double losses: (1) Bolton.

Won from behind: (2) Nott'm Forest (a), Ipswich (a).
Lost from in front: (2) Everton (h), Birmingham (h).

High spots: Beating Manchester City 6-1 home and away.
Six unbeaten games in September and October, climbing up to 10th.

Low spots: Losing three league games in a row *three* times, in August, in October-November, and April-May.
Losing to Second Division Rotherham in the League Cup.

West Ham faced Plymouth in three successive cup competitions – in League Cup and FA Cup in 1961-62 and the League Cup in 1962-63.

Hammer of the Year: Bobby Moore.
Ever-presents: (0).
Hat-tricks: (1) Johnny Byrne.
Leading scorer: (15) Geoff Hurst.

	Appearances			Goals			
	Lge	LC	FAC	Lge	LC	FAC	Tot
Bond, John	**14**	2					
Bovington, Eddie	**10**	1	4				
Boyce, Ronnie	**27**	1	5	**3**		2	**5**
Brabrook, Peter	**29**		5	**7**			**7**
Britt, Martin	**1**						
Brown, Ken	**40**	2	5	**2**			**2**
Burkett, Jackie	**38**	2	5				
Byrne, Johnny	**30**	2	5	**9**	3	2	**14**
Charles, John	**1**						
Crawford, Ian	**5**						
Dear, Brian	**3**						
Dick, John	**2**						
Dickie, Alan	**2**						
Hurst, Geoff	**27**	2		**13**	2		**15**
Kirkup, Joe	**27**		5	**1**			**1**
Lansdowne, Billy	**1**						
Leslie, Lawrie	**20**	2					
Lyall, John	**4**						
Moore, Bobby	**41**	1	5	**3**			**3**
Musgrove, Malcolm	**15**	2		**7**	1		**8**
Peters, Martin	**36**	2	1	**8**	1		**9**
Rhodes, Brian	**2**						
Scott, Tony	**27**	2	5	**10**			**10**
Sealey, Alan	**26**		5	**6**			**6**
Sissons, John	**1**						
Standen, Jim	**18**		5				
Woosnam, Phil	**15**	1		**1**			**1**
(own-goals)				**3**			**3**
27 players used	**462**	**22**	**55**	**73**	**7**	**4**	**84**

No	Date		Att	Pos	Pt	F-A	H-T	Scorers, Times, and Referees	1	2	3	4	5	6	7	8	9	10	11
1	A	CHELSEA			D	0-0	0-0		Standen	Kirkup	Burkett	Peters	Brown	Moore	Brabrook	Boyce	Byrne	Hurst	Scott
	24/8		*46,298*		1				*Bonetti*	*Shellito*	*McCreadie*	*Venables*	*Mortimore*	*Harris*	*Murray*	*Tambling*	*Mulholland*	*Moore G*	*Blunstone*
								Ref: K Seddon	West Ham's summer tournament in New York, which they won, has robbed them of new-season freshness. Harris curtailed Byrne by fair means or foul, but otherwise there was little of note. Promoted Chelsea were delighted with a draw. The ref's father played in three Cup finals.										
2	H	BLACKPOOL			W	3-1	2-0	Peters 22, Boyce 35, Brabook 72	Standen	Kirkup	Burkett	Peters	Brown	Moore	Brabrook	Boyce	Byrne	Hurst	Scott
	26/8		25,533		3			*Charnley 87*	*Waiters*	*Armfield*	*Martin*	*McPhee*	*Gratrix*	*Cranston*	*Lea*	*Quinn*	*Charnley*	*Parry*	*Horne*
								Ref: D Howell	The score might not suggest it, but this was a rout. Byrne was unstoppable, and had two shots cleared off the line. Moore earned rave reviews. Boyce and Scott played a one-two to set up Peters' opener; Boyce ghosted past four defenders to add a second; and Brabrook curled the third.										
3	H	IPSWICH			D	2-2	1-0	Byrne 41, Boyce 61	Standen	Kirkup	Burkett	Peters	Brown	Moore	Brabrook	Boyce	Byrne	Hurst	Scott
	30/8		27,599		4			*Baxter 55, Phillips 73*	*Bailey*	*Bolton*	*Compton*	*Baxter*	*Nelson*	*Elsworthy*	*Stephenson*	*Moran*	*Crawford*	*Phillips*	*Blackwood*
								Ref: G Roper	Twice West Ham led. If they had hung on they would have gone top. But they were undone by Ted Phillips, whose shooting had been timed at 67 mph with his right foot, 64 with his left. First he pulled an indirect free-kick back to Baxter; then blasted a shot that stuck in the stanchion.										
4	A	BLACKPOOL		1	W	1-0	0-0	Byrne 57p	Standen	Kirkup	Burkett	Peters	Brown	Moore	Brabrook	Boyce	Byrne	Hurst	Scott
	2/9		*18,407*	*18*	6				*Waiters*	*Armfield*	*Martin*	*McPhee*	*Gratrix*	*Durie*	*Lea*	*Quinn*	*Charnley*	*Parry*	*Horne*
								Ref: R Harper	This game serves as a reminder of how negative and defensive West Ham could be in these years. They scored with their only chance of the match, from the spot, after Horne had brought Byrne down, and provoked the home crowd to boos and slow-handclaps. Leslie Lea hit the bar.										
5	H	SHEFFIELD UTD		5	L	2-3	2-2	Byrne 34, Boyce 42	Standen	Kirkup	Burkett	Peters	Brown	Moore	Brabrook	Boyce	Byrne	Hurst	Scott
	7/9		23,837	*13*	6			*Wagstaff 4, Allchurch 8, 63*	*Hodgkinson*	*Coldwell*	*Shaw B*	*Richardson*	*Shaw J*	*Summers*	*Allchurch*	*Kettleborough*	*Pace*	*Wagstaff*	*Simpson*
								Ref: S Yates	Hammers are toppled off their perch by Blades' first win of the season. When Allchurch let fly from 20 yards to make it 0-2 few would have bet on Hammers' revival. Byrne's header and Boyce's speed of foot made it 2-2. Jim Standen flapped at a cross to gift Allchurch the winner.										
6	H	NOTT'M FOREST			L	0-2	0-2		Standen	Kirkup	Burkett	Peters	Brown	Moore	Brabrook	Boyce	Byrne	Sealey	Hurst
	9/9		26,200		6			*Addison 34, Palmer 44*	*Grummitt*	*Wilson*	*Mochan*	*Palmer*	*McKinlay*	*Winfield*	*Hockey*	*Addison*	*Wignall*	*Quigley*	*Le Flem*
								Ref: J Osborne	Forest boss Johnny Carey suspended Calvin Palmer, then restored him, and Palmer plays a leading role in putting dreadful West Ham to the sword. Colin Addison was unmarked when hooking in Trevor Hockey's cross, and Palmer outjumped the limping Brown for the killer goal.										
7	A	LIVERPOOL		9	W	2-1	2-0	Peters 11, Hurst 34	Standen	Kirkup	Burkett	Peters	**Bickles**	Moore	Brabrook	Boyce	Byrne	Hurst	Dear
	14/9		*45,495*	*11*	8			*Hunt 64*	*Furnell*	*Byrne G*	*Moran*	*Milne*	*Yeats*	*Ferns*	*Callaghan*	*Hunt*	*St John*	*Melia*	*Thompson*
								Ref: V James	Shankly's Liverpool have now lost all three home games. Peters' cool finish, from Moore's pass, and Hurst's lob established what ought to have been an unassailable lead. On the hour Moore handled, but Standen saved from Ron Moran. Roger Hunt beat three players to make it 2-1.										
8	A	NOTT'M FOREST		11	L	1-3	0-1	Byrne 80	Standen	Kirkup	Burkett	Peters	Bickles	Moore	Brabrook	Boyce	Byrne	Hurst	Dear
	17/9		*25,369*	*2*	8			*Le Flem 26, Wignall 60, Addison 67*	*Grummitt*	*Wilson*	*Mochan*	*Whitefoot*	*McKinlay*	*Winfield*	*Hockey*	*Addison*	*Wignall*	*Quigley*	*Le Flem*
								Ref: J Mitchell	Forest's fourth successive win leaves Jim Standen with the cheers of the home crowd ringing in his ears. He alone prevented a rout. Byrne was forced to play deep to help out. Le Flem shot into the roof of the net and Wignall headed in Mochan's free-kick to leave West Ham in disarray.										
9	H	ASTON VILLA		13	L	0-1	0-1		Standen	Kirkup	Burkett	Bovington	Moore	Peters	Brabrook	Boyce	Byrne	Hurst	Dear
	21/9		20,346	*12*	8			*Burrows 11*	*Sims*	*Wright*	*Lee*	*Crowe*	*Sleeuwenhoek*	*Deakin*	*McEwan*	*Baker*	*Hateley*	*Woosnam*	*Burrows*
								Ref: T Dawes	Joe Mercer's Villa, watched by Alf Ramsey, leap-frog over West Ham with this win. Moore looked wasted at centre-half and was given the runaround by big Tony Hateley, who also teed-up Harry Burrows' winner. Ex-Hammer Phil Woosnam came in for some rough treatment.										
10	A	TOTTENHAM		15	L	0-3	0-2		Standen	Kirkup	Burkett	Bovington	Brown	Moore	Sealey	Boyce	Peters	Byrne	Scott
	28/9		***50,886***	*4*	8			*Jones 27, Mackay 39, Brown 61 (og)*	*Brown*	*Hopkins*	*Henry*	*Blanchflower*	*Norman*	*Mackay*	*Jones*	*White*	*Smith*	*Greaves*	*Dyson*
								Ref: E Crawford	Spurs maintain their 100% home record with ease, orchestrated by 37-year-old Danny Blanchflower. West Ham looked in dire need of a striker. Cliff Jones' header and Mackay's dipping drive – both set up by John White – were followed by Brown's blunder from Dyson's cross.										

No	Venue	Opponent / Date	Att	Pos	Res / Pts	F-A	H-T	Scorers, Times, and Referees	1	2	3	4	5	6	7	8	9	10	11
11	H	WOLVES		18	D	1-1	0-0	Byrne 76	Standen	Kirkup	Burkett	Bovington	Brown	Moore	Sealey	Boyce	Peters	Byrne	Scott
		5/10	21,409	*15*	9			*Hinton 50*	*Davies*	*Thomson*	*Harris*	*Goodwin*	*Woodfield*	*Flowers*	*Wharton*	*Crowe*	*Crawford*	*Broadbent*	*Hinton*
								Ref: R Tinkler	After a disjointed start this match livened up. By the close it might have finished five goals apiece. Greenwood experimented by playing Peters at centre-forward, which failed dismally. Stan Cullis's team went in front with Hinton's 18-yarder, but were pegged back by Byrne's header.										
12	H	BURNLEY		18	D	1-1	0-1	Sealey 62	Standen	Kirkup	Burkett	Bovington	Brown	Moore	Sealey	Boyce	Peters	Byrne	Scott
		7/10	21,372	*10*	10			*Harris 17*	*Blacklaw*	*Angus*	*Joyce*	*Adamson*	*Talbut*	*Miller*	*Price*	*Bellamy*	*Lochhead*	*Harris*	*Connelly*
								Ref: H New	Hammers found themselves trailing for the fifth home game in a row when Gordon Harris lashed Lochhead's pass beyond Standen from 18 yards. Alan Sealey, the man the crowd love to hate, crowned a marvellous personal performance by smashing the equaliser from similar range.										
13	A	SHEFFIELD WED		16	L	0-3	0-0		Standen	Kirkup	Burkett	Bovington	Brown	Peters	Brabrook	Boyce	Sealey	Sissons	Scott
		12/10	*23,503*	*12*	10			*Dobson 57, Pearson 62, Holliday 81*	*Springett*	*Hill*	*Megson*	*McAnearney*	*Swan*	*Young*	*Finney*	*Pearson*	*Layne*	*Dobson*	*Holliday*
								Ref: W Downey	Byrne is recovering from a car crash. West Ham had the edge when they fell behind, although Wednesday had gone closest when Layne hit the angle. Dobson turned Young's pass beyond Standen, then Man U import Mark Pearson fired a second from 18 yards for his first home goal.										
14	H	EVERTON		14	W	4-2	2-2	Boyce 27, Hurst 42, Brabrook 76, 84	Standen	Bond	Burkett	Peters	Brown	Moore	Sealey	Boyce	Britt	Hurst	Brabrook
		19/10	25,163	*9*	12			*Kay 5, Rees 31*	*West*	*Parker*	*Harris*	*Gabriel*	*Labone*	*Kay*	*Scott*	*Stevens*	*Rees*	*Vernon*	*Temple*
								Ref: K Burns	West Ham's second home win was a long time coming. It was unexpected too, as they went 1-2 down to the defending champions to a goal by debutant Barry Rees. The goal that put West Ham in front was struck by Peter Brabrook but flew off Gabriel and over Gordon West's hands.										
15	A	MANCHESTER U		13	W	1-0	1-0	Britt 36	Standen	Bond	Burkett	Peters	Brown	Moore	Sealey	Boyce	Britt	Hurst	Brabrook
		26/10	*42,120*	*2*	14				*Gregg*	*Dunne*	*Cantwell*	*Crerand*	*Foulkes*	*Setters*	*Moir*	*Chisnall*	*Herd*	*Law*	*Charlton*
								Ref: J Thacker	Man U were welcomed onto the pitch by the majorettes, but lost their league leadership and their 100% home record to Martin Britt's goal. Hurst had hit the bar, only for the ball to bounce into Gregg's arms. West Ham were down to 10 after an hour when Sealey went off injured.										
16	H	WEST BROM		13	W	4-2	1-2	Simpson 2 (og), Hurst 65p, 70, [Brabrook 88]	Standen	Bond	Burkett	Peters	Brown	Moore	Sealey	Boyce	Britt	Hurst	Brabrook
		2/11	22,888	*11*	16			*Foggo 5, Cram 12*	*Potter*	*Howe*	*Williams*	*Fraser*	*Jones*	*Simpson*	*Foggo*	*Macready*	*Cram*	*Jackson*	*Clark*
								Ref: J Cooke	Albion's coach broke down on the M1 and they had to finish their journey crammed into a van. Their mood was not helped when Simpson ran Hurst's shot into his own net after it came back off a post. Geoff Hurst made it 2-2 from the spot after the ball bounced against Cram's hand.										
17	A	ARSENAL		13	D	3-3	1-2	Byrne 1, 53, Peters 75	Standen	Bond	Burkett	Peters	Brown	Moore	Sealey	Boyce	Byrne	Hurst	Brabrook
		9/11	*52,742*	*2*	17			*McLeod 5, Eastham 31, Anderson 55*	*Wilson*	*Magill*	*McCullough*	*Brown L*	*Ure*	*Barnwell*	*McLeod*	*Strong*	*Baker*	*Eastham*	*Anderson*
								Ref: A Jobling	It takes Byrne 12 seconds of his come-back match to head past flat-footed Bob Wilson. Arsenal have not beaten West Ham at home since the war, when whisky was 12s 6d a bottle, but they stormed back to lead twice. Peters' 25-yard screamer ensures that the proud record continues.										
18	H	LEICESTER		13	D	2-2	2-1	Britt 24, Hurst 41	Standen	Bond	Burkett	Peters	Brown	Moore	Sealey	Boyce	Britt	Hurst	Brabrook
		16/11	23,073	*11*	18			*Stringfellow 20, Keyworth 56*	*Banks*	*Chalmers*	*Norman*	*McLintock*	*King*	*Appleton*	*Riley*	*Cross*	*Keyworth*	*Gibson*	*Stringfellow*
								Ref: J Mitchell	Mike Stringfellow's cross-cum-shot was deflected into his own net by Standen. Britt flicked an equaliser, and Hurst bulleted Sealey's corner past Banks. Leicester had lost on their last four visits to Upton Park, but bucked the trend when Keyworth hooked in Gibson's knock-down.										
19	A	BOLTON		12	D	1-1	0-0	Hurst 52	Standen	Bond	Burkett	Peters	Brown	Moore	Sealey	Boyce	Britt	Hurst	Brabrook
		23/11	***10,864***	*21*	19			*Lee 89p*	*Hopkinson*	*Hartle*	*Farrimond*	*Hatton*	*Hulme*	*Lennard*	*Davison*	*Bromley*	*Davies*	*Deakin*	*Lee*
								Ref: A Sparling	Bolton have won only once at home; their gates have plummeted. West Ham lost Sealey after five minutes with a fractured ankle and thereafter erected an eight-man barricade. Brabrook set up Hurst's breakaway goal, but Francis Lee netted from the spot after Peters tripped Deakin.										
20	H	FULHAM		13	D	1-1	0-1	Moore 71	Standen	Bond	Burkett	Peters	Brown	Moore	Byrne	Boyce	Britt	Hurst	Brabrook
		30/11	23,715	*18*	20			*Leggat 10*	*Macedo*	*Cohen*	*Drake*	*Mullery*	*Keetch*	*Robson*	*Key*	*Cook*	*Leggat*	*Haynes*	*Howfield*
								Ref: J Bullough	Fulham had only scored three goals in 10 away games, so Leggat's shot from a tight angle, under the eyes of Alf Ramsey, provoked ecstatic celebrations among the white shirts. Moore levelled following a half-cleared corner. Hurst hit the bar twice. Byrne looked lost out on the wing.										
21	A	BIRMINGHAM		14	L	1-2	0-1	Britt 64	Standen	Bond	Burkett	Peters	Brown	Moore	Brabrook	Boyce	Britt	Hurst	Byrne
		7/12	*15,357*	*20*	20			*Auld 28, Lynn 75p*	*Withers*	*Lynn*	*Green*	*Hennessey*	*Smith*	*Beard*	*Hellawell*	*Bloomfield*	*Thomson*	*Leek*	*Auld*
								Ref: F Cowan	Birmingham inflict West Ham's first defeat in 10 games in league and cup. Standen half-saved Bertie Auld's shot, which climaxed a spell of intense City pressure. Britt headed in Peters' cross at the far post, but Brown then flattened Mike Hellawell. Stan Lynn netted from the spot.										

No	Date		Att	Pos	Pt	F-A	H-T	Scorers, Times, and Referees	1	2	3	4	5	6	7	8	9	10	11
22	H	CHELSEA		13	D	2-2	0-2	Byrne 65, 67	Standen	Bond	Burkett	Peters	Brown	Moore	Scott	Boyce	Byrne	Hurst	Brabrook
	14/12		21,950	*11*	21			*Blunstone 15, Tambling 40*	*Bonetti*	*Hinton*	*McCreadie*	*Harris R*	*Mortimore*	*Upton*	*Murray*	*Tambling*	*Bridges*	*Venables*	*Blunstone*
								Ref: J Taylor	Tommy Docherty's Chelsea extend their unbeaten sequence to six. A headed goal by tiny Blunstone, followed by a 30-yarder by Tambling, looks like earning a win, but Tambling's withdrawal on a stretcher – torn ligaments – reduces Chelsea to 10 men and Byrne takes advantage.										
23	A	IPSWICH		13	L	2-3	1-0	Byrne 22p, Brabrook 57	Standen	Bond	Burkett	Peters	Brown	Moore	Brabrook	Boyce	Byrne	Hurst	Sissons
	20/12		*11,765*	*22*	21			*Blackwood 62, Moran 67, Baker 75*	*Bailey*	*Davin*	*Compton*	*Baxter*	*Bolton*	*Dougan*	*Broadfoot*	*Moran*	*Baker*	*Hegan*	*Blackwood*
								Ref: R Spittle	Ipswich's second win of the season cannot lift them off the bottom. West Ham had led 2-0, courtesy of an iffy penalty awarded when the ball struck Joe Davin on the arm, and Brabrook's cross deceiving Bailey. Then the Hammers fell apart, and worse will follow in their next match.										
24	H	BLACKBURN		16	L	**2-8**	1-4	Byrne 10, 60 *[McEvoy 35, 65, 78,]*	Standen	Bond	Burkett	Peters	Brown	Moore	Brabrook	Boyce	Byrne	Hurst	Sissons
	26/12		20,500	*1*	21			*Pickering 5, 55, 89, Douglas 29,*	*Else*	*Bray*	*Newton*	*Clayton*	*England*	*McGrath*	*Ferguson*	*McEvoy*	*Pickering*	*Douglas*	*Harrison*
								Ref: J Osborne *[Ferguson 40]*	Days don't come blacker than this. West Ham lose back-to-back matches against the bottom and top clubs. This marks the biggest away win in Division 1 for eight years, it was Rovers' biggest ever away win. Star of the show was Bryan Douglas. Byrne was denied a hat-trick by the bar.										
25	A	BLACKBURN		16	W	3-1	1-1	Hurst 16, Byrne 58, 65	Standen	Bond	Burkett	Bovington	Brown	Moore	Brabrook	Boyce	Byrne	Hurst	Sissons
	28/12		*28,990*	*1*	23			*McEvoy 31*	*Else*	*Bray*	*Newton*	*Clayton*	*England*	*McGrath*	*Ferguson*	*McEvoy*	*Pickering*	*Douglas*	*Harrison*
								Ref: J Carr	Who would have bet on this extraordinary result? On a sodden pitch Rovers' first defeat in 11 games is a tactical triumph for Greenwood, who brings in tough-tackling Bovington for Peters, to man-mark Douglas, plus Sissons out wide. Byrne, with two more goals, likes playing Rovers.										
26	A	SHEFFIELD UTD		17	L	1-2	0-1	Sissons 82	Standen	Bond	Burkett	Bovington	Brown	Moore	Brabrook	Boyce	Byrne	Hurst	Sissons
	11/1		*18,733*	*10*	23			*Pace 25, Wagstaff 54*	*Hodgkinson*	*Coldwell*	*Shaw B*	*Richardson*	*Shaw J*	*Summers*	*Allchurch*	*Jones*	*Pace*	*Wagstaff*	*Hartle*
								Ref: Dagnall	The only reason lowly Hammers are not terrified of relegation is because Bolton and Ipswich are so far adrift. The Blades complete the double over the Hammers; indeed, they let them off lightly. In addition to the goals, Jones struck Standen's crossbar. Pace might have had a hat-trick.										
27	H	LIVERPOOL		15	W	1-0	1-0	Byrne 28	Standen	Bond	Burkett	Bovington	Brown	Moore	Brabrook	Boyce	Byrne	Hurst	Sissons
	18/1		25,546	*3*	25				*Lawrence*	*Thomson*	*Byrne G*	*Milne*	*Lawler*	*Stevenson*	*Callaghan*	*Hunt*	*Arrowsmith*	*St John*	*Thompson*
								Ref: J Finney	West Ham's second league win 11 games is a tribute to Byrne, who pivoted to score a sweet goal, and the defence, who withstood continuous bombardment throughout the second half. Callaghan hit a post, and in the final seconds Standen pulled off the save of the match from Hunt.										
28	A	ASTON VILLA		15	D	2-2	1-1	Hurst 25, 66	Standen	Bond	Burkett	Bovington	Brown	Moore	Brabrook	Boyce	Byrne	Hurst	Sissons
	1/2		*16,850*	*17*	26			*Burrows 10, Woosnam 49*	*Sidebottom*	*Wright*	*Aitken*	*Tindall*	*Sleeuwenhoek*	*Deakin*	*McEwan*	*Wylie*	*Hateley*	*Woosnam*	*Burrows*
								Ref: Crossley	Early in the second half, with Villa leading 2-1, Moore crash-tackled Tony Hateley, forcing his withdrawal. Though no foul was given, Moore was booed thereafter. Villa couldn't hang on with 10 men and it was not long before Hurst sprinted 30 yards to head in Brabrook's centre.										
29	H	TOTTENHAM		14	W	4-0	2-0	Hurst 20, Sissons 31, Boyce 70,	Standen	Bond	Burkett	Bovington	Brown	Moore	Brabrook	Boyce	Byrne	Hurst	Sissons
	8/2		**36,934**	*1*	28			[Byrne 84]	*Hollowbread*	*Baker*	*Hopkins*	*Beal*	*Norman*	*Marchi*	*Jones*	*White*	*Smith*	*Greaves*	*Dyson*
								Ref: P Brandwood	Successive defeats by Chelsea and West Ham have dampened Spurs' title chances. It is rare for Bill Nicholson's team to be given such a runaround. Geoff Hurst almost scored in the second minute, soon hit a post, and then tucked away Peter Brabrook's cross for the first goal.										
30	A	WOLVES		14	W	2-0	1-0	Hurst 25, Byrne 67	Standen	Kirkup	Bond	Bovington	Peters	Moore	Brabrook	Boyce	Byrne	Hurst	Sissons
	17/2		*14,000*	*15*	30				*Davies*	*Showell*	*Thomson*	*Broadbent*	*Woodfield*	*Flowers*	*Wharton*	*Knowles*	*Crawford*	*Crowe*	*Le Flem*
								Ref: P Bye	This Monday night fixture sees hot-shot Hurst take his recent tally to 10 goals in six games, scoring at the second attempt after the keeper had parried the first. Sissons set up the second goal, smashed in by Byrne. Wolves' sorties were soaked up by Hammers' 'funnel' defensive system.										
31	H	SHEFFIELD WED		14	W	4-3	2-1	Byrne 17, 45, 65p, Hurst 51	Standen	Bond	Burkett	Bovington	Brown	Moore	Brabrook	Boyce	Byrne	Hurst	Sissons
	22/2		24,578	*7*	32			*Finney 26, Dobson 75, Fantham 87*	*Springett*	*Hill*	*Megson*	*McAnearney*	*Swan*	*Young*	*Finney*	*Pearson*	*Layne*	*Fantham*	*Dobson*
								Ref: D Smith	Not quite the ding-dong struggle the score suggests, as West Ham led 4-1 until the closing stages. Byrne had completed his hat-trick from the spot after Megson brought down Brabrook. West Ham still can't climb the table, being the lowest on goal-average of five clubs on 32 points.										

No	Venue	Opponent / Date	Att	Pos	Pts	Res	HT	Scorers, Times, and Referees	1	2	3	4	5	6	7	8	9	10	11
32	A	BURNLEY			L	1-3	0-2	Byrne 85	Standen	Kirkup	Burkett	Bovington	Peters	Moore	Sealey	Boyce	Byrne	Hurst	Brabrook
		3/3	*14,328*		32			*Harris 5, Robson 39, 46*	*Blacklaw*	*Angus*	*Elder*	*O'Neil*	*Talbut*	*Miller*	*Morgan*	*Robson*	*Lochhead*	*Harris*	*Connelly*
								Ref: V James	Burnley gain quick revenge for their Cup exit. Greenwood left out key players, but that could not prevent cup vendettas being played out. Gordon Harris treated John Bond to a left hook on Saturday, and Bobby Moore to a vicious foul today. Hurst twice drove against a goal-post.										
33	H	MANCHESTER U		14	L	0-2	0-0		Standen	Bond	Burkett	Bovington	Brown	Moore	Brabrook	Boyce	Byrne	Hurst	Sissons
		7/3	27,177	*5*	32			*Sadler 72, Herd 86*	*Gaskell*	*Brennan*	*Dunne*	*Crerand*	*Tranter*	*Stiles*	*Anderson*	*Chisnall*	*Sadler*	*Herd*	*Moir*
								Ref: W Clements	These teams meet soon in the FA Cup semi-finals and West Ham are all at sea. Nevertheless they might have escaped with a draw but for John Bond's silly back-pass that let in David Sadler. West Ham pressed forward, leaving gaps that David Herd exploited when racing clear for No 2.										
34	A	LEICESTER		15	D	2-2	1-2	Hugo 31, Burkett 81	Standen	Bond	Burkett	Bovington	Brown	Peters	Sealey	Boyce	Hurst	**Hugo**	Brabrook
		18/3	*11,980*	*9*	33			*Gibson 6, Keyworth 37*	*Heyes*	*Sjoberg*	*Appleton*	*McLintock*	*King*	*Cross*	*Hodgson*	*Heath*	*Keyworth*	*Gibson*	*Stringfellow*
								Ref: L Hamer	West Ham have reached one final, and shortly face Leicester with the chance of another. Greenwood rests key players for this unimportant league fixture. Roger Hugo scores on his debut and nearly bags a late winner. Burkett also scores his first ever league goal in a late flourish.										
35	H	ARSENAL		15	D	1-1	0-1	Hurst 74	Standen	Bond	Burkett	Bovington	Brown	Moore	Brabrook	Boyce	Byrne	Hurst	Sissons
		21/3	28,170	*8*	34			*Skirton 35*	*Furnell*	*Magill*	*McCullough*	*Neill*	*Ure*	*Simpson*	*Skirton*	*Court*	*Radford*	*Eastham*	*Anderson*
								Ref: R Spittle	With an eye on Wembley, Hammers fans don't take kindly to the rough treatment meted out to Byrne by Ian Ure – once nudging Budgie over a barrier. Skirton headed in Eastham's free-kick. It might have become 0-2 when Burkett fouled Skirton, but Standen saved Eastham's penalty.										
36	H	STOKE		14	W	4-1	2-1	Moore 4, Byrne 14, Boyce 69,	Dickie	Bond	Burkett	Bovington	Brown	Moore	Brabrook	Boyce	Byrne	Hurst	Sealey
		27/3	29,484	*19*	36			*Dobing 29* [Brabrook 71]	*Leslie*	*Asprey*	*Allen*	*Palmer*	*Kinnell*	*Skeels*	*Dobing*	*Viollet*	*Ritchie*	*McIlroy*	*Bebbington*
								Ref: T Dawes	Stoke beat Ipswich 9-1 in their previous match. Ex-Hammer Lawrie Leslie is made skipper for the day, but is quickly caught out of position as Moore heads in Bond's free-kick. A mesmerising four-man move was climaxed by Byrne's goal. Dobing beat Alan Dickie from 30 yards.										
37	A	WEST BROM		12	W	1-0	0-0	Hugo 72	Dickie	Kirkup	Burkett	Peters	Brown	Moore	Brabrook	Boyce	Byrne	Hugo	Sealey
		28/3	*16,000*	*10*	38				*Potter*	*Howe*	*Williams G*	*Fraser*	*Jones*	*Simpson*	*Foggo*	*Fenton*	*Kaye*	*Jackson*	*Clark*
								Ref: V Batty	Both teams appeared to be going through the motions, so much so that it came as a surprise that either team should score. Happiest player was ex-ground staff lad Roger Hugo, who took Hurst's place and grabbed his second goal in two games. Hugo wouldn't mind the slight deflection.										
38	A	STOKE		12	L	0-3	0-0		Dickie	Kirkup	Bond	Bovington	Brown	Peters	Sealey	Boyce	Byrne	Hurst	Hugo
		31/3	*24,900*	*19*	38			*Palmer 46, McIlroy 61, Dobing 85*	*Leslie*	*Stuart*	*Allen*	*Palmer*	*Kinnell*	*Skeels*	*Dobing*	*Viollet*	*Ritchie*	*McIlroy*	*Bebbington*
								Ref: N Matthews	Tony Waddington's Stoke desperately needed these points, and this is as good a time as any to face West Ham. Preston boss Jimmy Milne must have gone away scratching his head. The nearest Hammers came to scoring was when Skeels headed out Byrne's lob after 75 minutes.										
39	H	BOLTON		14	L	2-3	2-2	Sealey 25, Byrne 38	Standen	Bond	Burkett	Bovington	Peters	Moore	Brabrook	**Bennett**	Byrne	Hurst	Sealey
		4/4	**19,398**	*21*	38			*Taylor 36, Lee 40, Bromley 77*	*Hopkinson*	*Hartle*	*Farrimond*	*Rimmer*	*Edwards*	*Lennard*	*Davison*	*Bromley*	*Lee*	*Hill*	*Taylor*
								Ref: K Burns	Desperate Bolton resort to time-wasting, jeered by the fans, but it paid off. Mistakes by Moore and Bond, both irritatingly casual, cost two goals. Moore, of all people, was dispossessed in the box by Taylor. Bromley looked offside when receiving Francis Lee's pass for the winner.										
40	A	FULHAM		15	L	0-2	0-1		Standen	Bond	Burkett	Bovington	Brown	Peters	Brabrook	Boyce	Britt	Hurst	Sissons
		11/4	*22,020*	*14*	38			*Keetch 30, Haynes 73*	*Macedo*	*Mealand*	*Langley*	*Robson*	*Keetch*	*Callaghan*	*Earle*	*Metchick*	*Leggat*	*Haynes*	*O'Connell*
								Ref: J Lowry	Fulham climb above West Ham with this win. Three losses in a row is hardly the way to prepare for Wembley. Bond headed off the line, only for Keetch to head it back in. Haynes clinched matters with a belter from 25 yards. Metchick was offside but deemed not interfering with play.										
41	H	BIRMINGHAM		14	W	**5-0**	2-0	Brabrook 4, 53, Hurst 35, Sissons 58,	Standen	Kirkup	Burkett	Bovington	Brown	Moore	Brabrook	Boyce	Byrne	Hurst	Sissons
		17/4	22,106	*21*	40			[Byrne 63]	*Schofield*	*Lynn*	*Martin*	*Hennessey*	*Smith*	*Thomson*	*Hellawell*	*Bloomfield*	*Leek*	*Thwaites*	*Auld*
								Ref: R Tinkler	This result leaves Birmingham three points behind Bolton with two to play. They were down to 10 men for most of the match when Hennessey smashed a clearance into the face of team-mate Smith, who departed with concussion. It was only 1-0 at the time. City will survive, yet again.										
42	A	EVERTON		14	L	0-2	0-1		Standen	Bond	Burkett	Bovington	Brown	Peters	Brabrook	Boyce	Britt	Hurst	Sealey
		25/4	*33,090*	*3*	40			*Pickering 35, 75*	*Rankin*	*Brown*	*Meagan*	*Gabriel*	*Labone*	*Harris*	*Scott*	*Stevens*	*Pickering*	*Vernon*	*Temple*
		Home	Away					Ref: D Corbett	Fred Pickering cheekily yells 'leave it' to Martin Peters, who, thinking it is a team-mate, does so. Pickering scored. Everton were in no mood for kid gloves, and Pickering missed the chance for the simplest of hat-tricks. Moore and Byrne were omitted so they could spy on Preston.										
Average		24,618	25,890																

League Cup

League Cup					F-A	H-T	Scorers, Times, and Referees	1	2	3	4	5	6	7	8	9	10	11
2	H	LEYTON ORIENT	13	W	2-1	2-1	Scott 23, Byrne 43	Standen	Kirkup	Burkett	Bovington	Bickles	Moore	Sealey	Boyce	Peters	Byrne	Scott
25/9		11,800	*2:16*				*Bolland 9*	*Davies*	*Charlton*	*Lewis*	*Lucas*	*Bishop*	*Lea*	*Deeley*	*Mason*	*Bolland*	*Ward*	*Musgrove*
							Ref: J Cooke	Orient deserved better than to lose. They controlled the midfield and Gordon Bolland tortured Dave Bickles throughout, as when taking the ball round Standen for the first goal. Scott headed the equaliser and Byrne netted the winner at the fourth attempt after rounding Reg Davies.										
3	A	ASTON VILLA	16	W	2-0	0-0	Bond 68, Britt 75	Standen	Bond	Burkett	Peters	Brown	Moore	Sealey	Boyce	Britt	Hurst	Brabrook
16/10		*11,194*	*19*					*Sims*	*Wright*	*Aitken*	*Crowe*	*Sleeuwenhoek*	*Tindall*	*Baker*	*Wylie*	*Hateley*	*Woosnam*	*Burrows*
							Ref: V O'Callaghan	Struggling Villa have lost five out of six home fixtures, so this result is no great shock, though Villa had won at Upton Park in the league. Villa were the first winners of the League Cup in 1961, and were finalists again in 1963. Ex-Hammer Phil Woosnam does his bit to inspire victory.										
4	A	SWINDON	13	D	3-3	2-2	Hurst 20, Brabrook 27, Boyce 47	Standen	Bond	Burkett	Peters	Brown	Charles	Sealey	Boyce	Britt	Hurst	Brabrook
4/11		*12,050*	*2:14*				*Rogers 36, Smith 39, McPherson 83*	*Turner*	*Dawson*	*Trollope*	*Morgan*	*McPherson*	*Woodruff*	*French*	*Hunt*	*Smith*	*Summerbee*	*Rogers*
							Ref: E Jennings	Division 2 Swindon boast an up-and-coming star in 17-year-old Don Rogers, and he begins Swindon's fight-back in the Wiltshire mud. Centre-half McPherson came close to scoring before he finally did so in a late melee. Moore had been left out as he plays for England the next day.										
4R	H	SWINDON	12	W	4-1	1-0	Hurst 1, Brabrook 50, Byrne 67, [Scott 84]	Standen	Bond	Burkett	Charles	Brown	Moore	Scott	Boyce	Byrne	Hurst	Brabrook
25/11		15,778	*2:14*				*Rogers 62*	*Turner*	*Morgan*	*Trollope*	*Sproates*	*Hallett*	*Woodruff*	*French*	*Summerbee*	*Smith*	*Smart*	*Rogers*
							Ref: J Taylor	Bert Head's Swindon babes saw their plans wrecked inside 40 seconds when Bobby Woodruff's mis-kick allowed Hurst to smash the opener. The tie stayed alive until Byrne headed against the bar and Brabrook flung himself to convert the rebound. Spies again looked at Don Rogers.										
QF	H	WORKINGTON	13	W	6-0	4-0	Byrne 12, 41, 52, Boyce 20, Hurst 38, [Scott 50]	Standen	Bond	Burkett	Bovington	Brown	Moore	Brabrook	Boyce	Byrne	Hurst	Scott
16/12		10,160	*4:3*					*Ower*	*Johnston*	*Lumsden*	*Furphy*	*Brown*	*Burkinshaw*	*Middlemass*	*Timmins*	*Carr*	*Moran*	*Martin*
							Ref: R Tinkler	Fourth Division versus First produces a predictable outcome. The show began to roll once Byrne put away Hurst's cross, at which point Workington player-manager Ken Furphy's tactical masterplan became redundant. The crowd ended up cheering Workington's few attacks.										
SF 1	A	LEICESTER	15	L	3-4	1-3	Hurst 30, 70, Sealey 82 *[McLint'k 50]*	Standen	Bond	Burkett	Peters	Brown	Moore	Sealey	Boyce	Byrne	Hurst	Brabrook
5/2		*14,087*	*9*				*Keyw'rth 5, R'berts 13, Stringf'low 19,*	*Banks*	*Sjoberg*	*Norman*	*McLintock*	*King*	*Appleton*	*Hodgson*	*Roberts*	*Keyworth*	*Gibson*	*Stringfellow*
							Ref: E Crawford	Three goals down after 19 minutes of this first-leg semi-final, and 1-4 after 69 minutes, West Ham seemed doomed to miss out on a final with Stoke. But Hurst's sixth goal in three games, shrugging off King's tackle, followed by Sealey scoring on his come-back, keeps the dream alive.										
SF 2	H	LEICESTER	15	L	0-2	0-1		Standen	Bond	Burkett	Bovington	Brown	Moore	Brabrook	Boyce	Byrne	Hurst	Sissons
23/3		27,393	*9*				*McLintock 33, Gibson 71*	*Banks*	*Sjoberg*	*Norman*	*McLintock*	*King*	*Appleton*	*Hodgson*	*Cross*	*Roberts*	*Gibson*	*Stringfellow*
							Ref: J Finney (Hammers lose 3-6 on aggregate)	Leicester deny West Ham the chance of being the first club to claim both domestic cups in one season. This was a stirring cup-tie, with Banks inspired on his come-back after a five-week injury. When Roberts swung over a free-kick for McLintock to belt into the net, it looked all over.										

FA Cup

FA Cup					F-A	H-T	Scorers, Times, and Referees	1	2	3	4	5	6	7	8	9	10	11
3	H	CHARLTON	16	W	3-0	2-0	Hurst 10, Brabrook 25, Sissons 89	Standen	Bond	Burkett	Bovington	Brown	Moore	Brabrook	Boyce	Byrne	Hurst	Sissons
4/1		34,155	*2:4*					*Rose*	*Stocks*	*Kinsey*	*Bailey*	*Haydock*	*Tocknell*	*Kenning*	*Matthews*	*Firmani*	*Edwards*	*Glover*
							Ref: J Osborne	The last match at the Boleyn ended 2-8, but memories are erased by this all-so-easy win over Division 2 Charlton. Byrne's dummy set up Hurst's opener, and man-of-the-match Byrne made the second goal too. Eddie Firmani missed what few opportunities came Charlton's way.										
4	A	LEYTON ORIENT	17	D	1-1	1-1	Brabrook 43	Standen	Bond	Burkett	Bovington	Brown	Moore	Brabrook	Boyce	Byrne	Hurst	Sissons
25/1		*34,345*	*2:16*				*Deeley 2*	*Pinner*	*Charlton*	*Lewis*	*Lucas*	*Bishop*	*Lea*	*Deeley*	*Dunmore*	*Gregory*	*Bolland*	*Musgrove*
							Ref: T Dawes	Norman Deeley headed Gregory's corner past Standen for a quick-fire opening, and Orient might have scored more goals during their early dominance. Sissons dummied his way past Charlton to lay on the equaliser for Brabrook. Near the end both sides seemed to settle for the draw.										
4R	H	LEYTON ORIENT	17	W	3-0	3-0	Hurst 6, 8, Byrne 15	Standen	Bond	Burkett	Bovington	Brown	Moore	Brabrook	Boyce	Byrne	Hurst	Sissons
29/1		35,383	*2:16*					*Pinner*	*Charlton*	*Lewis*	*Lucas*	*Bishop*	*Lea*	*Deeley*	*Bolland*	*Gregory*	*Dunmore*	*Musgrove*
							Ref: T Dawes	Late-comers entering the ground were astonished to find the game wrapped up. Thereafter the 22 players seemed happy to indulge in a friendly kick-about. On 51 minutes Pinner felled Hurst in the box and helped him to his feet. Hurst repaid the gesture by having his spot-kick saved.										

Rd		Opponent		Res		H-T	Scorers, Times, and Referees											
5	A	SWINDON	14	W	3-1	1-1	Hurst 11, 77, Byrne 73	Standen	Bond	Burkett	Bovington	Brown	Moore	Brabrook	Boyce	Byrne	Hurst	Sissons
15/2		28,582	*2:14*				*McPherson 34*	*Turner*	*Wollen*	*Trollope*	*Morgan*	*McPherson*	*Woodruff*	*Summerbee*	*Atkins*	*Stevens*	*D'arcy*	*Rogers*
							Ref: J Mitchell	West Ham face Orient and Swindon in both cups in the same season. Hammers drew 3-3 here in the League Cup, but this time are prepared for Don Rogers' magic. With a replay looking increasingly likely, Brabrook fires in two crosses and Byrne and Hurst connect with them both.										
QF	H	BURNLEY	14	W	3-2	0-1	Sissons 57, Byrne 60, 68	Standen	Bond	Burkett	Bovington	Brown	Moore	Brabrook	Boyce	Byrne	Hurst	Sissons
29/2		36,651	*11*				*Connelly 13, Pointer 80*	*Blacklaw*	*Angus*	*Elder*	*O'Neil*	*Talbut*	*Miller*	*Morgan*	*Pointer*	*Lochhead*	*Harris*	*Connelly*
							Ref: E Jennings	John Connelly skips past three tackles to put Burnley in front. Sissons screwed the ball goalwards from the by-line and Elder helped it over the line for the equaliser. Byrne's awesome volley, under the eyes of Alf Ramsey, put West Ham ahead. Byrne's next goal was hotly contested.										
SF	N	MANCHESTER U	14	W	3-1	0-0	Boyce 56, 63, Hurst 80	Standen	Bond	Burkett	Bovington	Brown	Moore	Brabrook	Boyce	Byrne	Hurst	Sissons
14/3		*65,000*	*5*				*Law 78*	*Gaskell*	*Brennan*	*Dunne*	*Crerand*	*Foulkes*	*Setters*	*Herd*	*Chisnall*	*Charlton*	*Law*	*Best*
		(at Hillsborough)					Ref: K Stokes	West Ham reach their first FA Cup final since 1923, overturning last week's league defeat on a mud-heap of a pitch. Ron Boyce let rip from 25 yards past the stranded Gaskell, then added another from a short-corner. Law lunged feet-first into Standen. Moore was a Trojan in defence.										
F	N	PRESTON	14	W	3-2	1-2	Sissons 12, Hurst 52, Boyce 90	Standen	Bond	Burkett	Bovington	Brown	Moore	Brabrook	Boyce	Byrne	Hurst	Sissons
2/5		*100,000*	*2:3*				*Holden 10, Dawson 40*	*Kelly*	*Ross*	*Smith*	*Lawton*	*Singleton*	*Kendall*	*Wilson*	*Ashworth*	*Dawson*	*Spavin*	*Holden*
		(at Wembley)					Ref: A Holland	The facts show Second Division Preston had 23 goal attempts to West Ham's 16. Outplayed in the first half, Hammers dug deep and were rewarded, first, when Kelly prods Hurst's header over the line, and then in injury-time when Boyce heads the winner from Brabrook's cross.										

		Home					Away					
	P	W	D	L	F	A	W	D	L	F	A	Pts
1 Liverpool	42	16	0	5	60	18	10	5	6	32	27	57
2 Manchester U	42	15	3	3	54	19	8	4	9	36	43	53
3 Everton	42	14	4	3	53	26	7	6	8	31	38	52
4 Tottenham	42	13	3	5	54	31	9	4	8	43	50	51
5 Chelsea	42	12	3	6	36	24	8	7	6	36	32	50
6 Sheffield Wed	42	15	3	3	50	24	4	8	9	34	43	49
7 Blackburn	42	10	4	7	44	28	8	6	7	45	37	46
8 Arsenal	42	10	7	4	56	37	7	4	10	34	45	45
9 Burnley	42	14	3	4	46	23	3	7	11	25	41	44
10 West Brom	42	9	6	6	43	35	7	5	9	27	26	43
11 Leicester	42	9	4	8	33	27	7	7	7	28	31	43
12 Sheffield Utd	42	10	6	5	35	22	6	5	10	26	42	43
13 Nott'm Forest	42	9	5	7	34	24	7	4	10	30	44	41
14 WEST HAM	42	8	7	6	45	38	6	5	10	24	36	40
15 Fulham	42	11	8	2	45	23	2	5	14	13	42	39
16 Wolves	42	6	9	6	36	34	6	6	9	34	46	39
17 Stoke	42	9	6	6	49	33	5	4	12	28	45	38
18 Blackpool	42	8	6	7	26	29	5	3	13	26	44	35
19 Aston Villa	42	8	6	7	35	29	3	6	12	27	42	34
20 Birmingham	42	7	7	7	33	32	4	0	17	21	60	29
21 Bolton	42	6	5	10	30	35	4	3	14	18	45	28
22 Ipswich	42	9	3	9	38	45	0	4	17	18	76	25
	924	228	108	126	935	636	126	108	228	636	935	924

Odds & ends

Double wins: (3) Blackpool, Liverpool, WBA.
Double losses: (2) Sheffield Utd, Nott'm Forest.

Won from behind: (5) Everton (h), WBA (h), Orient LC (h), Burnley FAC (h), Preston FAC (n).
Lost from in front: (2) Ipswich (a), Bolton (h).

High spots: Winning FA Cup.
Reaching semi-final of League Cup.
Seven unbeaten league games in October and November.

Low spots: Losing 2-8 at home to Blackburn.
Eight successive league games without a win in November-December.

Two days after losing 2-8 at home to Blackburn, West Ham won 3-1 at Ewood Park.
West Ham faced both Leyton O and Swindon in *both* domestic cups.
The Hammers scored 39 goals in the two cup competitions.

Hammer of the Year: Johnny Byrne.
Ever-presents: (0).
Hat-tricks: (2) Johnny Byrne (2).
Leading scorer: (33) Johnny Byrne.

	Appearances			Goals			
	Lge	LC	FAC	Lge	LC	FAC	Tot
Bennett, Peter	1						
Bickles, Dave	2	1					
Bond, John	26	6	7		1		1
Bovington, Eddie	22	3	7				
Boyce, Ronnie	41	7	7	6	2	3	11
Brabrook, Peter	38	6	7	8	2	2	12
Britt, Martin	9	2		3	1		4
Brown, Ken	36	6	7				
Burkett, Jackie	40	7	7	1			1
Byrne, Johnny	33	5	7	24	5	4	33
Charles, John		2					
Dear, Brian	3						
Dickie, Alan	3						
Hugo, Roger	3			2			2
Hurst, Geoff	37	6	7	14	5	7	26
Kirkup, Joe	18	1					
Moore, Bobby	37	6	7	2			2
Peters, Martin	32	4		3			3
Scott, Tony	10	3			3		3
Sealey, Alan	18	4		2	1		3
Sissons, John	14	1	7	3		3	6
Standen, Jim	39	7	7				
(own-goals)				1			1
22 players used	**462**	**77**	**77**	**69**	**20**	**19**	**108**

No	Date		Att	Pos	Pt	F-A	H-T	Scorers, Times, and Referees	1	2	3	4	5	6	7	8	9	10	11
1	A	FULHAM			W	2-1	1-0	Byrne 18, Sissons 65	Standen	Bond	Burkett	Bovington	Brown	Moore	Brabrook	Boyce	Byrne	Hurst	Sissons
	22/8		*31,200*		2			*Metchick 60*	*Macedo*	*Cohen*	*Langley*	*Robson*	*Keetch*	*Callaghan*	*Earle*	*Metchick*	*Leggat*	*Haynes*	*O'Connell*
								Ref: P Rhodes	Johnny Byrne and Johnny Haynes were the respective men of the match. Byrne started and finished Hammers' first league goal of the season. Metchick levelled when swinging an aimless boot to send the ball in off a post. Tony Macedo then parried Hurst's shot out to John Sissons.										
2	H	MANCHESTER U			W	3-1	2-0	Byrne 4, Sissons 19, Hurst 85	Standen	Bond	Burkett	Bovington	Brown	Moore	Brabrook	Boyce	Byrne	Hurst	Sissons
	24/8		**37,070**		4			*Law 79*	*Gaskell*	*Brennan*	*Dunne*	*Setters*	*Foulkes*	*Stiles*	*Connelly*	*Charlton*	*Herd*	*Law*	*Best*
								Ref: K Burns	A full house on this Monday evening. Man U play the last half-hour with 10 men after Maurice Setters is carried off after Boyce's studs sliced through his boot. Byrne scored after Sissons' shot was blocked. Sissons then lobbed a second. Dennis Law's header set up a furious climax.										
3	H	NOTT'M FOREST			L	2-3	1-1	Byrne 14p, Sissons 71	Standen	Bond	Burkett	Bovington	Brown	Moore	Brabrook	Boyce	Byrne	Hurst	Sissons
	28/8		26,760		4			*Barnwell 36, 58, Hinton 73*	*Grummitt*	*Wilson*	*Grant*	*Newton*	*McKinlay*	*Whitefoot*	*Crowe*	*Addison*	*Wignall*	*Barnwell*	*Hinton*
								Ref: N Burtenshaw	Hammers' bogey team do it again. This Friday night cracker saw a harsh penalty given against McKinlay, whereupon broken glass rained onto the pitch from Forest fans. John Barnwell scored twice but was lucky to be still on the pitch, having shoved the referee during the penalty row.										
4	A	MANCHESTER U		14	L	1-3	1-2	Stiles 6 (og)	Standen	Bond	Burkett	Bovington	Brown	Moore	Brabrook	Boyce	Byrne	Hurst	Sissons
	2/9		*45,123*	*12*	4			*Connelly 1, Law 28, Best 53*	*Gaskell*	*Brennan*	*Dunne*	*Crerand*	*Foulkes*	*Stiles*	*Connelly*	*Charlton*	*Sadler*	*Law*	*Best*
								Ref: H Wilson	Man U chalk up their first win of the season, helped by a 45-second goal by Connelly after Best had dummied Bond, not once but twice. Stiles then turned Byrne's cross past Gaskell, but that only made Man U turn up the heat. They created chances galore but only took two of them.										
5	A	STOKE		17	L	1-3	1-1	Byrne 14	Standen	Bond	Burkett	Bovington	Brown	Moore	Brabrook	Boyce	Byrne	Hurst	Sissons
	5/9		*26,420*	*9*	4			*Viollet 38, Dobing 46, Bebbington 63*	*Leslie*	*Asprey*	*Allen*	*Palmer*	*Kinnell*	*Skeels*	*Dobing*	*Viollet*	*Ritchie*	*McIlroy*	*Bebbington*
								Ref: K Seddon	Tony Waddington's Stoke had lost their previous two home games, trailed to Byrne's shot in off the bar, and finished this match with nine fit men. Moore had a poor game. Standen was at fault with at least one goal. Dobing scored from a tight angle; Bebbington had an easy header.										
6	H	WOLVES			W	5-0	3-0	Hurst 27, 80, Byrne 33, Sissons 43,	Standen	Bond	Burkett	Bovington	Peters	Moore	Sealey	Boyce	Byrne	Hurst	Sissons
	7/9		26,879	*21*	6			[Moore 47]	*Davies*	*Thomson*	*Harris*	*Goodwin*	*Flowers*	*Woodruff*	*Broadbent*	*Kirkham*	*Crawford*	*Melia*	*Wharton*
								Ref: N Matthews	Greenwood drops Brown and Brabrook. Wolves' boss Stan Cullis is absent through illness, which was probably made worse when he heard the score. So casual did West Ham become at 4-0 that the crowd jeered and slow-handclapped them. Greenwood defended the fans' right to do so.										
7	H	TOTTENHAM			W	3-2	1-0	Byrne 23, 78, 87	Standen	Bond	Burkett	Bovington	Peters	Moore	Sealey	Boyce	Byrne	Hurst	Sissons
	12/9		36,730		8			*Greaves 57, 71p*	*Jennings*	*Knowles*	*Henry*	*Mullery*	*Norman*	*Beal*	*Robertson*	*Jones*	*Saul*	*Greaves*	*Dyson*
								Ref: G McCabe	Two penalties within a minute shape the destiny of this match. Greaves put Spurs ahead after Standen brought down Cliff Jones, then Knowles shoved Sealey at the other end, only for Jennings to catch Byrne's spot-kick. Even that could not deny Byrne a hat-trick, juggling a late winner.										
8	A	WOLVES		12	L	3-4	1-2	Brabrook 39, Harris 51 (og), Byrne 61p	Standen	Bond	Burkett	Bovington	Peters	Moore	Sealey	Boyce	Byrne	Hurst	Brabrook
	14/9		*16,000*	*22*	8			*Crawford 3, 77, Knowles 34, Harris 87*	*Davies*	*Thomson*	*Harris*	*Goodwin*	*Showell*	*Woodruff*	*Thompson*	*Knowles*	*Crawford*	*Broadbent*	*Wharton*
								Ref: F Schofield	Wolves' first win can't lift them off the bottom but it can exact revenge for the thrashing at Upton Park. Standen, who in the summer helped Worcestershire win the cricket county championship, spilled two 'googlie' crosses by Harris. Woodruff pushed Hurst to concede the penalty.										
9	A	BURNLEY		13	L	2-3	1-2	Byrne 21, Boyce 79	Standen	Bond	Burkett	Bovington	Peters	Moore	Sealey	Boyce	Byrne	Hurst	Sissons
	19/9		*13,541*	*19*	8			*Pointer 16, Lochhead 34, Towers 77*	*Blacklaw*	*Angus*	*Elder*	*Walker*	*Miller*	*O'Neil*	*Morgan*	*Pointer*	*Lochhead*	*Robson*	*Towers*
								Ref: H Hackney	Burnley, like Wolves before them, win their first game of the season at West Ham's expense. Alf Ramsey watches as Ray Pointer, returning after a seven-month lay-off, shot the first goal and crossed for the second. Boyce made it 2-3, then squandered an easy chance to make it 3-3.										
10	H	SHEFFIELD UTD		12	W	3-1	3-1	Byrne 11, 40p, Sissons 34	Standen	Bond	Peters	Bovington	Brown	Moore	Brabrook	Boyce	Byrne	Hurst	Sissons
	26/9		22,526	*5*	10			*Docherty 3*	*Hodgkinson*	*Badger*	*Shaw G*	*Richardson*	*Shaw J*	*Matthewson*	*Docherty*	*Kettleborough*	*Jones*	*Birchenall*	*Hartle*
								Ref: L Callaghan	High-flying Blades go in front through John Docherty's neat dummy and shot. Byrne celebrates fathering a daughter by scoring twice, one of them from the spot after being brought down by Richardson. Key to the overall outcome was three astonishing misses by Blades' Birchenall.										

No	Venue	Opponent / Date	Att	Pos	Res	Pts	F-A	H-T	Scorers, Times, and Referees	1	2	3	4	5	6	7	8	9	10	11
11	A	EVERTON		12	D		1-1	0-0	Byrne 52	Standen	Bond	Burkett	Bovington	Brown	Peters	Brabrook	Boyce	Byrne	Hurst	Sissons
		3/10	*45,430*	*4*		11			*Harris 89*	*Rankin*	*Parker*	*Brown*	*Stevens*	*Labone*	*Harris*	*Scott*	*Harvey*	*Gabriel*	*Temple*	*Morrissey*
									Ref: J Taylor	Only seconds separate West Ham from their first win at Goodison for five years, and Everton from their first home defeat of the season, when Temple's pass sets up Harris's equaliser. Rankin had got both hands to Byrne's rocket, but couldn't keep it out. Then Hammers shut up shop.										
12	H	ASTON VILLA		8	W		3-0	1-0	Byrne 39, Boyce 67, Peters 89	Standen	Bond	Peters	Bovington	Brown	Moore	Brabrook	Boyce	Byrne	Hurst	Sissons
		10/10	20,600	*21*		13				*Sidebottom*	*Wright*	*Aitken*	*Tindall*	*Sleeuwenhoek*	*Lee*	*McLeod*	*Pountney*	*Hateley*	*Wylie*	*Burrows*
									Ref: J Cattlin	Villa never look like adding to their solitary away point, though it took Hammers a while to shrug off their Gantoise hangover. Villa are under acting manager Dick Taylor, but he is as helpless as his players as Hurst sets up a goal on a plate for Byrne. Boyce hooked in the second goal.										
13	A	LIVERPOOL		11	D		2-2	1-2	Hurst 23, 64	Standen	Bond	Peters	Bovington	Brown	Moore	Brabrook	Boyce	Byrne	Hurst	Sissons
		17/10	*36,029*	*17*		14			*St John 7, Hunt 27*	*Lawrence*	*Byrne G*	*Moran*	*Milne*	*Lawler*	*Stevenson*	*Callaghan*	*Hunt*	*St John*	*Graham*	*Thompson*
									Ref: K Burns	A repeat of the Charity Shield score. The champions can't get their act together in the league, and can't even hang on despite twice going in front. Hurst's close-in header levelled the first goal, a scramble on the line preceded the second, with Lawrence claiming Hurst had fouled him.										
14	H	SHEFFIELD WED		14	L		1-2	0-1	Brabrook 84	Standen	Bond	Peters	Bovington	Brown	Moore	Brabrook	Boyce	Byrne	Hurst	Sissons
		24/10	22,800	*7*		14			*Fantham 14, Quinn 85*	*Springett*	*Hill*	*Megson*	*Eustace*	*Mobley*	*Young*	*Finney*	*Quinn*	*Wilkinson*	*Fantham*	*Dobson*
									Ref: W Handley	Alan Brown's Owls arrived still looking for their first away win, having scored fewer away goals – three – than any other team. Yet they were leading in this match for 70 minutes until Brabrook unleashed a swirler from 30 yards. Straight from the kick-off Quinn netted from 10 yards.										
15	A	BLACKPOOL		12	W		2-1	1-0	Hurst 25, Brabrook 81	Standen	Bond	Peters	Bovington	Brown	Moore	Brabrook	Boyce	Hurst	Sissons	Scott
		31/10	*14,383*	*9*		16			*Green 83*	*Waiters*	*Armfield*	*Thompson*	*Rowe*	*James*	*Green*	*Oates*	*Ball*	*Charnley*	*Fisher*	*Horne*
									Ref: M Fussey	Blackpool's first home defeat was harsh, given the pressure they had exerted. Sissons prised open the defence for Hurst's goal, with Hammers thereafter defending in growing numbers. Alan Ball bored his way through many times and almost won a penalty before Brabrook's header.										
16	H	BLACKBURN		12	D		1-1	0-1	Sissons 63	Standen	Bond	Burkett	Bovington	Brown	Peters	Brabrook	Boyce	Byrne	Hurst	Sissons
		7/11	22,725	*5*		17			*Byrom 23*	*Else*	*Newton*	*Joyce*	*Clayton*	*England*	*McGrath*	*Ferguson*	*McEvoy*	*Byrom*	*Douglas*	*Harrison*
									Ref: D Smith	Rovers had won on their previous three visits to Upton Park, the last of which by 8-2. John Byrom, in particular, can't stop scoring against the Hammers and Alf Ramsey watches as he slams home Douglas's square pass. Sissons' left foot brought the equaliser from Boyce's nod-down.										
17	A	ARSENAL		7	W		3-0	1-0	Hurst 37, Byrne 60, Peters 64	Standen	Bond	Burkett	Bovington	Brown	Peters	Sealey	Boyce	Byrne	Hurst	Sissons
		14/11	*36,026*	*12*		19				*Burns*	*Howe*	*McCullough*	*McLintock*	*Neill*	*Court*	*Skirton*	*Radford*	*Baker*	*Eastham*	*Armstrong*
									Ref: K Dagnall	Seventh is the highest so far for West Ham, though they remain nine points behind leaders Man U. Arsenal missed the injured Ure, and Hurst took advantage with a flick that was turned into his own net by David Court. Peters played so well that the injured Moore wasn't missed at all.										
18	H	LEEDS		6	W		3-1	3-0	Kirkup 16, Byrne 20, Peters 35	Standen	Kirkup	Burkett	Bovington	Brown	Peters	Sealey	Boyce	Byrne	Hurst	Sissons
		21/11	28,150	*3*		21			*Belfitt 52*	*Sprake*	*Reaney*	*Bell*	*Bremner*	*Charlton*	*Hunter*	*Giles*	*Storrie*	*Belfitt*	*Collins*	*Henderson*
									Ref: J Lowry	Leeds had won their last seven, so crash to earth with a mighty bump. Kirkup, playing his first league game of the season, raced up to net from Boyce's centre. Byrne walked the ball in for No 2 after beating Sprake to Sissons' pass. Bremner hit the bar before Belfitt pulled a goal back.										
19	A	CHELSEA		6	W		3-0	3-0	Sealey 8, Peters 24, Hurst 38	Standen	Bond	Burkett	Bovington	Brown	Peters	Sealey	Boyce	Byrne	Hurst	Sissons
		28/11	*44,204*	*2*		23				*Bonetti*	*Hinton*	*McCreadie*	*Hollins*	*Mortimore*	*Harris*	*Murray*	*Graham*	*Bridges*	*Venables*	*Tambling*
									Ref: P Brandwood	Chelsea boss Tommy Docherty offered no excuses for his high-flyers' heaviest defeat so far, not even the fact that they hit the woodwork three times, or the fact that Hollins was carried off 10 minutes from time. West Ham are the only team to have scored in every match they've played.										
20	H	LEICESTER		6	D		0-0	0-0		Standen	Bond	Burkett	Bovington	Brown	Peters	Sealey	Boyce	Byrne	Hurst	Sissons
		5/12	**20,515**	*8*		24				*Banks*	*Sjoberg*	*Norman*	*Roberts*	*King*	*McDermott*	*Hodgson*	*Cross*	*Goodfellow*	*Gibson*	*Stringfellow*
									Ref: J Osborne	Here is an irony. Leicester have one of the worst defences in the division, conceding 44 goals in 20 games, but they become the first team to defy Hurst, Byrne *et al*. A wet, miserable afternoon was enjoyed mostly by Gordon Banks. Sissons and Byrne hit the bar in the same move.										
21	H	FULHAM		4	W		2-0	1-0	Byrne 10, 60	Standen	Bond	Burkett	Bovington	Brown	Peters	Brabrook	Boyce	Byrne	Hurst	Sissons
		12/12	21,985	*17*		26				*Macedo*	*Mealand*	*Langley*	*Robson*	*Keetch*	*Brown*	*Howfield*	*Callaghan*	*Marsh*	*Haynes*	*Chamberlain*
									Ref: D Lyden	Fourth place is the highest West Ham will reach this season. Matches like this, following a tiring European journey, are often lost, and Fulham had two 'goals' disallowed. Byrne, however, takes his tally to 19. Hammers are now just seven points behind the leaders with a game in hand.										

No	Date		Att	Pos	Pt	F-A	H-T	Scorers, Times, and Referees	1	2	3	4	5	6	7	8	9	10	11
22	A	NOTT'M FOREST		4	L	2-3	1-2	Byrne 33, Hurst 68	Standen	Bond	Burkett	Bovington	Brown	Peters	Brabrook	Boyce	Byrne	Hurst	Sissons
	19/12		*20,009*	*5*	26			*Hindkley 39, Quigley 42, Chapman 60*	*Grummitt*	*Hindley*	*Mochan*	*Newton*	*McKinlay*	*Whitefoot*	*Crowe*	*Quigley*	*Chapman*	*Barnwell*	*Storey-Moore*
								Ref: E Crawford	John Carey's Forest, without two international forwards – Wignall and Hinton – overtake West Ham, who placed too much of a burden on the overworked Johnnie Byrne. Hurst's 20-yarder to make it 2-3 did not spark a ferocious finale. In fact Hammers failed to create another chance.										
23	A	BIRMINGHAM		7	L	1-2	0-1	Hurst 90	Standen	Bond	Burkett	Bovington	Brown	Peters	Brabrook	Boyce	Byrne	Hurst	Sissons
	26/12		*23,324*	*19*	26			*Lynn 36, Thwaites 74*	*Schofield*	*Lynn*	*Green*	*Hennessey*	*Foster*	*Beard*	*Jackson*	*Sharples*	*Thomson*	*Vowden*	*Thwaites*
								Ref: K Stokes	The score flattered West Ham in this dress-rehearsal for the first defence of the FA Cup. City coach Joe Mallett came up with perfect tactics, pushing his full-backs up. Stan Lynn's goal, skidding through Standen's frozen fingers, confirmed him as the league's top scoring full-back.										
24	H	BIRMINGHAM		5	W	2-1	1-1	Byrne 30p, Kirkup 71	Standen	Kirkup	Peters	Bovington	Brown	Boyce	Sealey	Hurst	Byrne	Sissons	Scott
	28/12		23,800	*19*	28			*Sharples 10*	*Schofield*	*Lynn*	*Martin*	*Hennessey*	*Foster*	*Beard*	*Jackson*	*Sharples*	*Vowden*	*Auld*	*Thwaites*
								Ref: R Tinkler	City's five-game unbeaten run ends, despite Sharples' glancing header from Jackson's free-kick. Hammers looked ill at ease in rubber boots and gloves, and needed a penalty to square things when Auld stopped Hurst's header with his arm. Kirkup scored the winner at the near post.										
25	H	STOKE		7	L	0-1	0-1		Standen	Kirkup	Bond	Bovington	Brown	Peters	Brabrook	Boyce	Byrne	Hurst	Sissons
	2/1		23,913	*15*	28			*Viollet 39*	*Leslie*	*Asprey*	*Allen*	*Setters*	*Kinnell*	*Skeels*	*Palmer*	*Viollet*	*Ritchie*	*McIlroy*	*Dobing*
								Ref: E Jennings	Byrne couldn't shake off his markers, Hurst's best effort came back off a post, and big, strong John Ritchie charged Brown out of the way to nod down to Viollet, who scored. That summed up this match. West Ham resorted to long balls down the middle and hardly created a chance.										
26	A	TOTTENHAM		7	L	2-3	1-1	Byrne 17, Sissons 48	Standen	Bond	Peters	Bovington	Brown	Boyce	Sealey	Hurst	Byrne	Sissons	Scott
	16/1		***50,000***	*4*	28			*Greaves 7, 49, Dyson 62*	*Brown*	*Knowles*	*Henry*	*Mullery*	*Norman*	*Clayton*	*Robertson*	*Greaves*	*Gilzean*	*Jones*	*Dyson*
								Ref: W Clements	West Ham have won at Arsenal, Chelsea and Fulham, but were denied on a ground where only two teams have escaped with so much as a draw. When Byrne set up a goal for Sissons, an away win looked likely. But within seconds, Alan Mullery's shot flew in off Greaves' knee.										
27	H	BURNLEY		5	W	3-2	2-2	Boyce 18, Bond 44, Byrne 61	Standen	Bond	Peters	Bovington	Brown	Boyce	Sealey	Hurst	Byrne	Sissons	Scott
	23/1		25,490	*15*	30			*Lochhead 31, Irvine 38*	*Blacklaw*	*Smith*	*Angus*	*O'Neil*	*Talbut*	*Miller*	*Morgan*	*Lochhead*	*Irvine*	*Harris*	*Towers*
								Ref: N Burtenshaw	Four of the five goals were directly attributable to unforced defensive errors. The exception was the first, thumped in by Boyce from 20 yards. Bond was at fault for both Burnley goals, and was much relieved when Blacklaw dropped Sissons' drive, which fell to Byrne to win the game.										
28	A	SHEFFIELD UTD			L	1-2	1-1	Sealey 4	Standen	Kirkup	Bond	Bovington	Brown	Peters	Sealey	Boyce	Byrne	Hurst	Sissons
	6/2		*16,265*		30			*Jones 2, Birchenall 72*	*Hodgkinson*	*Badger*	*Shaw G*	*Richardson*	*Shaw J*	*Matthewson*	*Woodward*	*Kettleborough*	*Jones*	*Birchenall*	*Hartle*
								Ref: K Walker	West Ham applauded Blades' Joe Shaw on to the pitch for this, his 600th league appearance, and then played so aimlessly that he was given no one to mark. Mick Jones' header was cancelled out by Sealey scoring from Sissons' pass. Birchenall headed the winner from Hartle's corner.										
29	H	EVERTON		10	L	0-1	0-0		Standen	Bond	Peters	Bovington	Brown	Moore	Sealey	Boyce	Byrne	Hurst	Sissons
	13/2		25,163	*9*	30			*Temple 82*	*West*	*Wright*	*Wilson*	*Gabriel*	*Labone*	*Stevens*	*Scott*	*Harvey*	*Pickering*	*Vernon*	*Temple*
								Ref: G Roper	Moore returned for his first match since October but cannot prevent yet another defeat. That, however, is the fault of the forwards, who missed chances galore before Derek Temple took Harvey's pass to sprint away down the left, outstrip a bare defence and slide the ball past Standen.										
30	A	SUNDERLAND		11	L	2-3	0-1	Byrne 70, Hurst 78	Standen	Bond	Peters	Bovington	Brown	Moore	Sealey	Boyce	Byrne	Hurst	Sissons
	20/2		*32,885*	*20*	30			*Hood 34, Sharkey 84, 89*	*McLaughlan*	*Parke*	*Ashurst*	*Harvey*	*Hurley*	*McNab*	*Usher*	*Herd*	*Hood*	*Sharkey*	*Mulhall*
								Ref: J Bullough	West Ham stumble to their fifth successive away defeat, a result which lifts Sunderland out of the relegation places. Byrne's hook, followed by Hurst's rifling 20-yarder, the best goal of the game, had silenced the Roker faithful. Then Parke centred and Nick Sharkey scored on the turn.										
31	H	LIVERPOOL		10	W	2-1	0-1	Presland 48, Hurst 53	Standen	Kirkup	**Presland**	Bovington	Moore	Peters	Brabrook	Boyce	Byrne	Hurst	Sissons
	27/2		25,750	*6*	32			*Hunt 22*	*Lawrence*	*Lawler*	*Byrne G*	*Milne*	*Smith*	*Stevenson*	*Graham*	*Hunt*	*St John*	*Arrowsmith*	*Wallace*
								Ref: H New	Liverpool's 21-match unbeaten run comes to an end, and so does Hammers' run of defeats. West Ham have become something of a bogey team for Bill Shankly's outfit. Eddie Presland will always remember his debut: his shot from 30 yards brushed Smith and deceived Lawrence.										

No	Venue	Opponent	Pos	Res	F-A	H-T	Scorers, Times, and Referees	1	2	3	4	5	6	7	8	9	10	11
32	A	SHEFFIELD WED	10	L	0-2	0-0		Standen	Kirkup	Presland	Bovington	Moore	Peters	Brabrook	Boyce	Byrne	Hurst	Sissons
6/3		14,931	8	32			Mobley 48, Hickton 72	Springett	Hill	Megson	Eustace	Mobley	Smith	Finney	Quinn	Hickton	Fantham	Dobson
							Ref: F Schofield	A poor game, and Wednesday's opening goal was both poor and dubious. Mobley's header from Finney's corner was stopped on the line by Kirkup. Standen picked it up to find the ref signalling that it had crossed the line. Hickton's later header couldn't assuage West Ham's anger.										
33	H	SUNDERLAND	12	L	2-3	1-2	Dear 10, 59	Standen	Kirkup	Presland	Bovington	Moore	Peters	Brabrook	Boyce	Hurst	Dear	Sissons
13/3		23,360	18	32			Harvey 38, Herd 44, 61	McLaughlan	Parke	Ashurst	Harvey	Hurley	McNab	Hellawell	Herd	Hood	Sharkey	Mulhall
							Ref: L Hamer	George Hardwick's lowly Sunderland secure the double over West Ham with their second away win of the season. With Lausanne looming, Greenwood left out Byrne, then lost Bovington in the third minute with an injured knee. Dear's first game of the season earned him two goals.										
34	A	BLACKBURN	13	L	**0-4**	0-2		Standen	Kirkup	Bovington	Charles	Brown	Moore	Sealey	Boyce	Hurst	Dear	Scott
20/3		**8,990**	9	32			Byrom 33, 58, 62, Douglas 43p	Jones	Wilson	Joyce	Clayton	England	Sharples	Ferguson	Newton	Byrom	Douglas	Bradshaw
							Ref: J Carr	Rovers' smallest gate for years watched this emphatic win. Byrom bagged his second recent hat-trick against Hammers, below par following their trip to Lausanne. It might have been different: Sealey and Scott both hit the woodwork at 0-0. Presland tripped Ferguson for the penalty.										
35	H	ARSENAL	11	W	2-1	0-0	Hurst 82, Byrne 87p	Standen	Kirkup	Peters	Boyce	Brown	Moore	Sealey	Hurst	Byrne	Dear	Sissons
27/3		24,000	10	34			Baker 72	Burns	Howe	McCullough	McLintock	Ure	Neill	Tawse	Radford	Baker	Eastham	Armstrong
							Ref: J Finney	Arsenal boss Billy Wright moaned afterwards about the cruelty of football. With time running out, Sissons fired against the bar and Hurst leapt to head past Burns. Then Ian Ure, booed roundly by those with memories of his rough handling of Byrne last season, under-hit a back-pass.										
36	A	ASTON VILLA	10	W	3-2	0-2	Hurst 50, Byrne 58, Dear 63	Standen	Kirkup	Burkett	Peters	Bickles	Moore	Sealey	Hurst	Byrne	Dear	Sissons
31/3		19,900	20	36			Hateley 29, Aitken 30	Withers	Lee	Aitken	Wylie	Pountney	Deakin	Baker	Chatterley	Hateley	Woosnam	MacLeod
							Ref: M Fussey	This famous fightback doesn't do Villa's relegation worries any good. Ex-Hammer Phil Woosnam engineered two Villa goals inside a minute, moments after Byrne had hit a post. Hurst's 25-yarder dipped under the bar, Byrne headed the equaliser, and Dear turned in Byrne's cross.										
37	A	LEEDS	10	L	1-2	0-0	Dear 66	Standen	Kirkup	Burkett	Peters	Brown	Moore	Sealey	Hurst	Byrne	Dear	Boyce
3/4		41,918	2	36			Peacock 64, Bremner 80	Sprake	Reaney	Bell	Bremner	Charlton	Hunter	Giles	Storrie	Peacock	Collins	Cooper
							Ref: E Norman	Wembley-bound Leeds are pressing hard for the double, yet they should have been turned over by West Ham who seemed determined to fluff all the chances they created. Peacock's header was answered by Sprake, who dropped Byrne's cross. Bremner scrambled home Hunter's cross.										
38	H	CHELSEA		W	3-2	3-0	Hurst 4, 25, Sissons 19	Standen	Kirkup	Burkett	Peters	Brown	Moore	Sealey	Boyce	Hurst	Dear	Sissons
12/4		33,288		38			Venables 54, Bridges 69	Bonetti	Hinton	Harris	Hollins	Mortimore	Boyle	Murray	Graham	Bridges	Venables	Tambling
							Ref: R Tinkler	Title-chasing Chelsea do a Zaragoza and nearly come back from the dead. Bonetti was partly to blame for Hammers' first two goals, failing to hold shots by Peters and Sealey respectively. Bonetti also got a touch to Hurst's second goal, from 25 yards. Revenge for the FA Cup defeat.										
39	H	WEST BROM	7	W	**6-1**	2-1	Peters 30, Dear 44, 53, 56, 59, 64	Standen	Kirkup	Burkett	Peters	Bickles	Moore	Brabrook	Boyce	Hurst	Dear	Sissons
16/4		27,706	14	40			Astle 45	Potter	Cram	Williams	Howshall	Jones	Fraser	Foggo	Astle	Kaye	Hope	Clarke
							Ref: D Smith	Brian Dear's five-goal haul in 20 minutes is unequalled in First Division football. He only played because Byrne was injured, and though he overtook John Dick's four against Rotherham, he only equalled the feat of Torquay's Robin Stubbs, who hit five against Newport in 1963.										
40	A	LEICESTER	8	L	0-1	0-1		Standen	Bond	Burkett	Peters	Brown	Moore	Sealey	Boyce	Hurst	Dear	Scott
17/4		15,880	16	40			Gibson 40	Banks	Walker	Norman	Cross	Sjoberg	Appleton	Hodgson	Sweenie	Roberts	Gibson	Goodfellow
							Ref: C Cooke	Standen palmed Gibson's shot into the net, whereupon Boyce hit a post. There was little else to report upon in the first half. After 77 minutes Boyce turned Scott's cross past Banks, but when the ref gave offside Moore was booked for dissent. Boyce also hit the underside of the bar.										
41	A	WEST BROM		L	2-4	0-3	Hurst 49, Boyce 85	Standen	Kirkup	Peters	**Dawkins**	Brown	Moore	Bennett	Boyce	Hurst	Dear	Sissons
19/4		14,000		40			Foggo 8, Astle 14, Brown 33, 60	Potter	Cram	Williams G	Howshall	Jones	Fraser	Foggo	Astle	Crawford	Hope	Brown
							Ref: Seddon	Unfazed by an Arctic blizzard, Albion gain revenge for the 6-1 blitz inflicted on them on Friday. Two quick goals, both from corners, and both of which were wind-assisted, gave West Ham a mountain to climb. The crucial period came at 1-3 when Dear and Boyce had goals disallowed.										
42	H	BLACKPOOL		W	2-1	0-1	Brown 47, Dear 79	Standen	Kirkup	Burkett	Boyce	Brown	Moore	Sealey	Brabrook	Hurst	Dear	Sissons
23/4		22,762		42			Moir 6	Waiters	Armfield	Rowe	McPhee	James	Green	Lea	Ball	Charnley	Robson	Moir
	Home	Away					Ref: G Martin	Ken Brown headed his second goal in a 13-year Hammers career. That Brian Dear should score was rather more predictable: his conversion of Sissons' cross was his 14th goal in 13 games. The game had started badly, Moir dispossessing Boyce and scoring. Now for Zaragoza in Spain.										
Average	25,808	26,974																

Charity Shield			F-A	H-T	Scorers, Times, and Referees	1	2	3	4	5	6	7	8	9	10	11
A LIVERPOOL		D	2-2	1-1	Byrne 41, Hurst 84	Standen	Bond	Burkett	Bovington	Brown	Moore	Brabrook	Boyce	Byrne	Hurst	Sissons
15/8 *40,000*					*Wallace 28, Byrne 49*	*Lawrence*	*Byrne G*	*Moran*	*Milne*	*Yeats*	*Stevenson*	*Callaghan*	*Hunt*	*Arrowsmith**	*Wallace*	*Thompson*
					Ref: K Stokes	The Charity Shield is played at Anfield, not Wembley. Though substitutes have not yet been introduced in the league, Liverpool bring on Phil Chisnall for the injured Arrowsmith after 10 minutes. When Lawrence spilled Brabrook's cross to Hurst, it was totally against the run of play.										

League Cup			F-A	H-T	Scorers, Times, and Referees	1	2	3	4	5	6	7	8	9	10	11
2 A SUNDERLAND	12	L	1-4	0-4	Brabrook 55 *[Usher 38]*	Standen	Bond	Burkett	Bovington	Brown	Peters	Brabrook	Boyce	Byrne	Hurst	Sissons
30/9 *22,382*	*15*				*Mulhall 3, Mitchinson 9, Sharkey 12,*	*McLaughlan*	*Irwin*	*Ashurst*	*Harvey*	*Hurley*	*McNab*	*Usher*	*Herd*	*Sharkey*	*Mitchinson*	*Mulhall*
					Ref: P Rhodes	Accusations are made after this flop that West Ham aren't interested in the League Cup, and the sooner they are out of it the better. Moore was rested in preparation for Saturday's England game. Sunderland won despite playing with 10 men for 43 minutes, McNab's knee taking him off.										

FA Cup			F-A	H-T	Scorers, Times, and Referees	1	2	3	4	5	6	7	8	9	10	11
3 H BIRMINGHAM	7	W	4-2	1-2	Byrne 41, Hurst 52, 70, Sissons 89	Standen	Bond	Peters	Bovington	Brown	Boyce	Sealey	Hurst	Byrne	Sissons	Scott
9/1 31,056	*19*				*Thwaites 7, Jackson 27*	*Schofield*	*Lynn*	*Green*	*Hennessey*	*Foster*	*Beard*	*Jackson*	*Sharples*	*Vowden*	*Auld*	*Thwaites*
					Ref: L Callaghan	The third meeting between these sides in two weeks looks to have turned decisively City's way when Jackson scores direct from a corner to make it 0-2. The turning point came when Sissons drew Schofield from his goal and chipped to Byrne. Sealey squared for Hurst's equaliser.										
4 H CHELSEA	5	L	0-1	0-1		Standen	Kirkup	Bond	Bovington	Brown	Peters	Sealey	Boyce	Byrne	Sissons	Scott
30/1 37,000	*2*				*Tambling 10*	*Bonetti*	*Hinton*	*Harris*	*Hollins*	*Mortimore*	*Boyle*	*Murray*	*Graham*	*Bridges*	*Venables*	*Tambling*
					Ref: D Smith	A minute's silence for the death of Sir Winston Churchill. West Ham's grip on the Cup is prised open when Standen parries Venables' effort, the ball running loose. The longer the match went on the more players Chelsea pulled back. West Ham hadn't the wit to find a way through.										

European Cup-Winners' Cup			F-A	H-T	Scorers, Times, and Referees	1	2	3	4	5	6	7	8	9	10	11
1:1 A LA GANTOISE	13	W	1-0	0-0	Boyce 52	Standen	Bond	Peters	Bovington	Brown	Moore	Sealey	Boyce	Byrne	Hurst	Sissons
23/9 (Belgium) *18,000*	*10*					*Seghers A*	*Devreese*	*De Nayer*	*Delmulle*	*De Baets*	*Mahieu*	*Ghellynck*	*Seghers U*	*Lambert*	*Mayama*	*Storme*
						The Buffaloes of Ghent, the first Belgian team to compete in this competition, are undone when their 40-year-old keeper dithered at Sealey's corner and was beaten by Boyce's slow-motion header. The hosts defended in numbers, reversing the normal pattern for European games.										
1:2 H LA GANTOISE	12	D	1-1	1-1	Byrne 43	Dickie	Bond	Peters	Bovington	Brown	Moore	Brabrook	Boyce	Byrne	Hurst	Sissons
7/10 24,000					*Peters 32 (og)*	*Seghers A*	*Van de Velde*	*Devreese*	*Mahieu*	*Denayer*	*Mayama*	*Ghellynck*	*Seghers U*	*Lambert*	*Bula*	*Storme*
					Ref: E Olsen (Norway) (Hammers win 2-1 on aggregate)	Hammers fans pay record receipts to see this decrepit performance that drives them to jeers and slow-handclaps. Though needing to score, the part-timers sat back as in the first leg. Peters jabbed a back-pass beyond the advancing Dickie. John Sissons' cross set up Byrne's life-saver.										
2:1 H SPARTAK PRAGUE	6	W	2-0	0-0	Bond 58, Sealey 82	Standen	Bond	Burkett	Bovington	Brown	Peters	Sealey	Boyce	Byrne	Hurst	Sissons
25/11 (Czech) 27,590						*Kramerius*	*Gura*	*Taborsky*	*Vojta*	*Kos*	*Steiningel*	*Dyba*	*Mraz*	*Kvasnak*	*Kraus*	*Masek*
					Ref: J de Mendibil (Spain)	The white-clad Czechs survived a tepid first-half only to be roasted in the second. John Bond hit a scorcher from 25 yards for his first goal in three years. Four times the Czechs booted the ball out of the ground to waste time. Alan Sealey hit the far post before poaching the rebound.										
2:2 A SPARTAK PRAGUE	6	L	1-2	1-0	Sissons 14	Standen	Bond	Burkett	Bovington	Brown	Peters	Sealey	Boyce	Byrne	Hurst	Sissons
9/12 *45,000*					*Mraz 73, 88*	*Kramerius*	*Gura*	*Kos*	*Taborsky*	*Tichy*	*Vojta*	*Dyba*	*Mraz*	*Kvasnak*	*Kraus*	*Masek*
					Ref: Dinov (Bulgaria) (Hammers win 3-2 on aggregate)	When 19-year-old Sissons side-stepped Taborsky to make it 3-0 overall, that should have been that. But Bond's handball concedes a penalty for Masek, which Standen saves. It was Standen who let the Czechs back in, pushing Taborsky's shot on to the bar then losing his footing.										

Rd		Opponent	Att	Pos	Res	F-A	H-T	Scorers, Times, and Referees	1	2	3	4	5	6	7	8	9	10	11
QF	A	LAUSANNE		12	W	2-1	1-0	Dear 21, Byrne 53	Standen	Kirkup	Peters	Boyce	Brown	Moore	Sealey	Hurst	Byrne	Dear	Sissons
1	16/3	(Switz)	*20,000*					*Hosp 80*	*Kunzi*	*Grobety*	*Hunziker*	*Duerr*	*Tacchella*	*Schneiter*	*Eschmann*	*Kerkhoffs*	*Armbruster*	*Hosp*	*Hertig*
								Ref: Schiller (Austria)	Hammers survived when Armbruster struck the bar to go ahead through Dear – on his European baptism – when Kunzi failed to hold Ronnie Boyce's free-kick. Johnny Byrne's solo goal further deflated Karl Rappan's Lausanne, who had seven Swiss internationals in their ranks.										
QF	H	LAUSANNE		13	W	4-3	2-1	T'cch'lla 42 (og), Dear 43, 89, Pet'rs 59	Standen	Kirkup	Peters	Boyce	Brown	Moore	Sealey	Hurst	Byrne	Dear	Sissons
2	23/3		31,780					*Kerkhoffs 37, Hertig 48, Eschmann 80*	*Kunzi*	*Grobety*	*Hunziker*	*Schneiter*	*Tacchella*	*Durr*	*Eschmann*	*Kerkhoffs*	*Armbruster*	*Hosp*	*Hertig*
								Ref: P Roomer (Hammers win 6-4 on aggregate)	This thrilling cup-tie only swung decisively West Ham's way in the final minute, when Dear smashed the goal which finally sunk Lausanne. Kerkhoff's header put the cat among the pigeons until Tacchella turned Sealey's cross into his own net. Eschmann's overhead kick was a gem.										
SF	H	REAL ZARAGOZA		10	W	2-1	2-0	Dear 9, Byrne 24	Standen	Kirkup	Burkett	Peters	Brown	Moore	Boyce	Dear	Byrne	Hurst	Sissons
1	7/4	(Spain)	35,000	*3*				*Canario 55*	*Yarza*	*Cortizo*	*Reija*	*Isasi*	*Santamaria*	*Violeta*	*Canario*	*Santos*	*Marcelino*	*Enderiz*	*Lapetra*
								Ref: R Lacoste (France)	Brian Dear heads his eighth goal in eight games. When Byrne takes a pass on his chest and volleys in from 18 yards the Boleyn is in raptures. But for the second half West Ham line up with nine defenders and Zaragoza twist them this way and that. Boos rained down on the Hammers.										
SF	A	REAL ZARAGOZA		9	D	1-1	0-1	Sissons 54	Standen	Kirkup	Burkett	Peters	Brown	Moore	Boyce	Sealey	Hurst	Dear	Sissons
2	28/4		*28,000*					*Lapetra 24*	*Yarza*	*Cortizo*	*Reija*	*Enderiz*	*Santamaria*	*Violeta*	*Canario*	*Santos*	*Marcelino*	*Villa*	*Lapetra*
								Ref: L Horn (Holland) (Hammers win 3-2 on aggregate)	Zaragoza are convinced the ref cost them a place in the final by denying them three penalties. West Ham conceded 19 fouls in the first half alone. Lapetra pounced when Standen blocked Marcelino's header. Sissons converted Dear's pass. Now for Turin or TSV Munich in the final.										
F	N	TSV MUNICH 1860		9	W	2-0	0-0	Sealey 69, 71	Standen	Kirkup	Burkett	Peters	Brown	Moore	Sealey	Boyce	Hurst	Dear	Sissons
	19/5	(W Germ)	*100,000*						*Radenkovic*	*Wagner*	*Kohlars*	*Bena*	*Reich*	*Luttrop*	*Heiss*	*Kuppers*	*Brunnenmeier*	*Grosser*	*Rebele*
		(At Wembley)						Ref: I Zsolt (Hungary)	West Ham's greatest moment. Sealey celebrates his marriage last week by firing his first goal from an impossible angle and his second when Moore's free-kick wasn't cleared. Luckless Sissons struck the post and the bar. Even the ref said it was a wonderfully clean game to control.										

		Home					Away					
	P	W	D	L	F	A	W	D	L	F	A	Pts
1 Manchester U	42	16	4	1	52	13	10	5	6	37	26	61
2 Leeds	42	16	3	2	53	23	10	6	5	30	29	61
3 Chelsea	42	15	2	4	48	19	9	6	6	41	35	56
4 Everton	42	9	10	2	37	22	8	5	8	32	38	49
5 Nott'm Forest	42	10	7	4	45	33	7	6	8	26	34	47
6 Tottenham	42	18	3	0	65	20	1	4	16	22	51	45
7 Liverpool	42	12	5	4	42	33	5	5	11	25	40	44
8 Sheffield Wed	42	13	5	3	37	15	3	6	12	20	40	43
9 WEST HAM	42	14	2	5	48	25	5	2	14	34	46	42
10 Blackburn	42	12	2	7	46	33	4	8	9	37	46	42
11 Stoke	42	11	4	6	40	27	5	6	10	27	39	42
12 Burnley	42	9	9	3	39	26	7	1	13	31	44	42
13 Arsenal	42	11	5	5	42	31	6	2	13	27	44	41
14 West Brom	42	10	5	6	45	25	3	8	10	25	40	39
15 Sunderland	42	12	6	3	45	26	2	3	16	19	48	37
16 Aston Villa	42	14	1	6	36	24	2	4	15	21	58	37
17 Blackpool	42	9	7	5	41	28	3	4	14	26	50	35
18 Leicester	42	9	6	6	43	36	2	7	12	26	49	35
19 Sheffield Utd	42	7	5	9	30	29	5	6	10	20	35	35
20 Fulham	42	10	5	6	44	32	1	7	13	16	46	34
21 Wolves	42	8	2	11	33	36	5	2	14	26	53	30
22 Birmingham	42	6	8	7	36	40	2	3	16	28	56	27
	924	251	106	105	947	596	105	106	251	596	947	924

Odds & ends

Double wins: (5) Fulham, Aston Villa, Blackpool, Arsenal, Chelsea.
Double losses: (4) Nott'm Forest, Stoke, Sheff Wed, Sunderland.

Won from behind: (10) Spurs (h), Sheff U (h), Birmingham (h), Burnley (h), Liverpool (h), Arsenal (h), Villa (a), Blackpool (h), Birmingham FAC (h), Zaragoza (CWC).
Lost from in front: (6) Nott'm F (h&a), Stoke (a), Wolves (a), Spurs (a), Sunderland (h).

High spots: Winning the European Cup-Winners' Cup.
West Ham did the league double over *three* London clubs.
Run of seven unbeaten league games, October to December, up to 4th.

Low spots: Early exits from both domestic cups.
Terrible league sequence of 10 defeats in 13 games, Dec to March.

Hammer of the Year: Martin Peters.
Ever-presents: (0) (Standen and Hurst missed one European game).
Hat-tricks: (1) Brian Dear.
Leading scorer: (29) Johnny Byrne.

	Appearances				Goals				
	Lge	LC	FAC	Eur	Lge	LC	FAC	Eur	Tot
Bennett, Peter	1								
Bickles, Dave	2								
Bond, John	29	1	2	4	1			1	2
Bovington, Eddie	33	1	2	4					
Boyce, Ronnie	41	1	2	9	4			1	5
Brabrook, Peter	22	1		1	3	1			4
Brown, Ken	33	1	2	9	1				1
Burkett, Jackie	24	1		5					
Byrne, Johnny	34	1	2	7	25		1	3	29
Charles, John	1								
Dawkins, Trevor	1								
Dear, Brian	10			5	10			4	14
Dickie, Alan				1					
Hurst, Geoff	42	1	1	9	17		2		19
Kirkup, Joe	15		1	5	2				2
Moore, Bobby	28			7	1				1
Peters, Martin	35	1	2	9	5			1	6
Presland, Eddie	4				1				1
Scott, Tony	6		2						
Sealey, Alan	21		2	7	2			1	3
Sissons, John	38	1	2	9	8		1	4	13
Standen, Jim	42	1	2	8					
(own-goals)					2			1	3
22 players used	**462**	**11**	**22**	**99**	**82**	**1**	**4**	**16**	**103**

LEAGUE DIVISION 1 — Manager: Ron Greenwood — SEASON 1965-66

No	Date	Att	Pos	Pt	F-A	H-T	Scorers, Times, and Referees	1	2	3	4	5	6	7	8	9	10	11	12 sub used
1	A WEST BROM			L	0-3	0-2		Standen	Kirkup	Burkett	Peters	Bovington	Moore	Brabrook	Boyce	Hurst	Bennett	Sissons	
	21/8	*19,900*		0			*Clark 2, 89, Astle 37*	*Potter*	*Cram*	*Williams G*	*Lovett*	*Jones*	*Fraser*	*Foggo*	*Astle*	*Kaye*	*Hope*	*Clark*	
							Ref: I Callaghan	West Ham won't live on past glories, even if they are only a few weeks old. Clive Clark brought them down to earth in 90 seconds, capitalising on a rebound. WBA needed no luck with their second goal, Fraser feeding a perfect pass to Astle. Kay hit a post, the ball bouncing to Standen.											
2	H SUNDERLAND			D	1-1	1-1	Peters 4	Dickie	Kirkup	Burkett	Peters	Bickles	Moore	**Redknapp**	Boyce	Byrne	Hurst	Sissons	
	23/8	34,700		1			*Herd 29*	*McLaughlan*	*Irwin*	*Ashurst*	*Harvey*	*Hurley*	*Baxter*	*Hellawell*	*Herd*	*O'Hare*	*McNab*	*Mulhall*	
							Ref: T Dawes	All eyes are on Sunderland's 'Slim' Jim Baxter, signed from Rangers, and he is instrumental in forging the equaliser. Martin Peters had headed in Redknapp's corner, having already headed over another corner. Little was seen of Baxter after half-time as Sunderland funnelled back.											
3	H LEEDS		14	W	2-1	1-1	Peters 44, Hurst 83	Standen	Kirkup	Burkett*	Bovington	Bickles	Moore	Redknapp	Peters	Byrne	Hurst	Sissons	Bennett
	28/8	27,900	*4*	3			*Peacock 13*	*Sprake*	*Reaney*	*Bell*	*Bremner*	*Charlton*	*Hunter*	*Weston*	*Lorimer*	*Peacock*	*Giles*	*Cooper*	
							Ref: R Aldous	Leeds drop their first points, West Ham notch their first win, and Peter Bennett comes on after 53 minutes as their first ever league substitute. The woodwork was hit twice, first when Sprake allowed Redknapps's cross to pass through his hands; then from Lorimer's ballistic drive.											
4	A SUNDERLAND		17	L	1-2	1-0		Standen	Kirkup	Presland	Bovington	Bickles	Moore	Redknapp	Peters	Byrne	Hurst	Sissons	
	1/9	*48,626*	*6*	3			*Mulhall 52, McNab 73*	*McLaughlan*	*Irwin*	*Ashurst*	*Harvey*	*Hurley*	*Baxter*	*Hellawell*	*Herd*	*O'Hare*	*McNab*	*Mulhall*	
							Ref: S Kayley	Charlie Hurley mistimed an interception to let in Hurst, but then it all started to go wrong. Hurley redeemed himself with a 30-yarder that was blocked and fell to Mulhall. Jim McNab then sprinted 30 yards to head the winner from Hellawell's cross. Hammers hit the woodwork twice.											
5	A SHEFFIELD UTD		18	L	3-5	1-3	Hurst 29, Kirkup 53, Byrne 60	Standen	Kirkup	Presland	Bovington	Bickles	Moore	Brabrook	Peters	Byrne	Hurst	Sissons	
	4/9	*15,796*	*4*	3			*Birch' 9, Docherty 15, K'borough 40,*	*Hodgkinson*	*Badger*	*Mallender*	*Munks*	*Shaw J*	*Matthewson*	*Docherty*	*Kettleb'rough*	*Jones*	*Birchenall*	*Reece*	
							Ref: K Seddon *[Jones 77, 85]*	Blades had only scored three goals before today, yet bag their biggest total since returning to Division 1 in 1961. Byrne's exquisite touch to make it 3-3 looked to have sealed a famous fight-back, but a header, followed by a hooked goal from Mick Jones, condemned West Ham.											
6	H LIVERPOOL			L	1-5	0-4	Peters 53	Standen	Kirkup	Burkett	Peters	Bickles	Moore	Brabrook	Boyce	Byrne	Hurst	Scott	
	6/9	32,144		3			*Milne 11, C'llaghan 25, Hunt 43, 45,46*	*Lawrence*	*Lawler*	*Byrne*	*Milne*	*Yeats*	*Stevenson*	*Callaghan*	*Hunt*	*St John*	*Smith*	*Thompson*	
							Ref: N Burtenshaw	A three-minute hat-trick, straddling half-time, by Roger Hunt put the nail in West Ham's coffin. Liverpool had come to regard the Hammers as a bogey side, but Milne was somehow left unmarked to drive in St John's pull-back. Upton Park rose to applaud Shankly's marvels at the end.											
7	H LEICESTER		20	L	2-5	2-2	Hurst 24, 28p *[Goodfellow 83]*	Standen	Kirkup	Burkett	Bovington	Brown	Moore	Redknapp	Peters	Hurst	Sissons	Scott	
	11/9	21,400	*15*	3			*Dougan 31, 74, Sinclair 34, 47,*	*Hayes*	*Walker*	*Norman*	*Roberts*	*Sjoberg*	*Cross*	*Sinclair*	*Gibson*	*Dougan*	*Goodfellow*	*Stringfellow*	
							Ref: J Osborne	Leicester's first away win brings a hat-trick of five-goal thrashings. This was unexpected, since when Norman handled, Hurst's penalty made it 2-0. 'We want five!' the crowd chanted, not knowing they were to get them. Hammers have the worst defensive record in the Football League.											
8	A LIVERPOOL		20	D	1-1	1-0	Hurst 37	Dickie	Kirkup	Burkett	Bovington	Charles	Moore	Bennett	Peters	Hurst	Boyce	Sissons	
	15/9	*44,397*	*6*	4			*Strong 63*	*Lawrence*	*Lawler**	*Byrne G*	*Milne*	*Yeats*	*Stevenson*	*Callaghan*	*Hunt*	*St John*	*Smith*	*Thompson*	*Strong*
							Ref: R Windle	On a filthy night it was odds-on another five-goal thrashing, which Greenwood counters by playing almost his whole team in their own penalty box. Hurst rammed in Peters' cross in a rare attacking sortie, but Liverpool's first ever league substitute, Geoff Strong, headed the equaliser.											
9	A BLACKBURN		18	W	2-1	1-1	Peters 33, 88	Dickie	Kirkup	Burkett	Bovington	Charles	Moore	Bennett	Peters	Hurst	Boyce	Sissons	
	18/9	***10,178***	*22*	6			*Jones 36*	*Else*	*Newton*	*Wilson*	*Clayton*	*Mulvaney*	*Sharples*	*Ferguson*	*McEvoy*	*Jones*	*Byrom*	*Horrey*	
							Ref: N Callender	If Hammers are going to beat anyone, it would have to be Rovers, whom they send to the bottom. West Ham again packed their defence and won unworthily when Peters headed Kirkup's corner past Else. The public address system announced Hammers' substitute as Harry 'Redcap'.											
10	H BLACKPOOL		18	D	1-1	0-0	Hurst 89	Dickie	Kirkup	Burkett	Bovington	Charles	Moore	Bennett	Peters	Byrne	Hurst	Sissons	
	25/9	21,000	*19*	7			*Charnley 77*	*Waiters*	*Thompson*	*Craven*	*Fisher*	*James*	*Green*	*Moir*	*Ball*	*Charnley*	*Lea*	*Horne*	
							Ref: P Rhodes	No one can say the ball isn't running kindly for West Ham. Yet again they salvage the game in the last seconds, when Waiters saved thrillingly from Byrne, only to deflect the ball to Hurst. The players looked so embarrassed they don't celebrate. Ray Charnley had scored off a post.											

No	Venue	Opponent / Date	Att	Pos	Pts	F-A	H-T	Scorers, Times, and Referees	1	2	3	4	5	6	7	8	9	10	11	12 sub used
11	A	FULHAM		19	L	0-3	0-0		Dickie	**Burnett**	Charles	Peters	Brown	Bovington	Bennett	**Bloomfield**	Byrne	Hurst	Sissons	
		2/10	*22,310*	*18*	7			*Charles 53 (og), Haynes 77, Leggat 86*	*Macedo*	*Nicholls*	*Mealand*	*Robson*	*Dempsey*	*Keetch*	*Key*	*O'Connell*	*Leggat*	*Haynes*	*Dyson*	
								Ref: D Smith	Before kick-off the announcer sought a spare linesman. Dickie shaped to collect O'Connell's cross, only for Charles to intervene and lob it in. Haynes added a fierce shot to set up a bizarre finale. With the ref looking elsewhere, Dickie hit a goal-kick to Leggat, who thumped it back in.											
12	A	NOTT'M FOREST		20	L	**0-5**	0-3	*[Addison 50, Wilson 88]*	Standen	Kirkup	Charles*	Peters	Bovington	Moore	Redknapp	Bloomfield	Hurst	Bennett	Brabrook	Bickles
		9/10	*19,262*	*15*	7			*Hinton 32, Wignall 44, Moore 45,*	*Grummitt*	*Hindley*	*Mochan*	*Newton*	*McKinlay*	*Whitefoot*	*Storey-Moore*	*Addison*	*Wignall*	*Barnwell*	*Hinton*	
								Ref: J Mitchell	Hammers' fourth five-goal drubbing in 12 games. Forest had unleashed 14 shots before going in front, a 25-yarder from Hinton. Although Charles was injured, Greenwood delayed critically in sending on a sub. Kirkup's back-pass landed at the feet of Wignall, who hit the second.											
13	H	SHEFFIELD WED		20	W	4-2	1-2	Sissons 35, Britt 53, 70, Peters 78	Standen	Burnett	Charles	Bovington	Brown	Moore	Brabrook	Peters	Britt	Hurst	Sissons	
		16/10	20,690	*19*	9			*Brown 16 (og), Wilkinson 44*	*Springett*	*Smith*	*Megson*	*Eustace*	*Mobley*	*Young*	*Wilkinson*	*Quinn*	*Hickson*	*Fantham*	*Dobson*	
								Ref: J Lowry	Howard Wilkinson did his best to defeat the Hammers. Standen saved his header, but Brown ran the ball into the net. After Sissons hit back from a rebound, Wilkinson chipped a fine goal. Britt, in his first league game of the season, netted a rebound, then headed in to make it 2-3.											
14	A	NORTHAMPTON		20	L	1-2	0-1	Brown 49	Standen	Burnett	Charles	Peters	Brown	Moore	Brabrook	Bloomfield	Britt	Hurst	Sissons	
		23/10	*15,367*	*21*	9			*Foley 29p, Leek 80*	*Harvey*	*Foley*	*Cockcroft*	*Leck*	*Carr*	*Kiernan*	*Best*	*Leek*	*Hunt*	*Lines*	*Robson*	
								Ref: D Payne	Promoted Cobblers win their first match at the 14th attempt. Burnett fouled Hunt and skipper Theo Foley scored from the spot. Moore refused to shake Foley's hand at the final whistle. Brown headed an equaliser, but Leek's back-heeled winner provoked pitch celebrations at the end.											
15	H	STOKE		19	D	0-0	0-0		Standen	Burnett	Charles	Bovington	Brown	Moore	Brabrook	Peters	Britt	Hurst	Sissons	
		30/10	21,545	*10*	10				*Irvine*	*Palmer*	*Skeels*	*Kinnell*	*Setters*	*Bloor*	*Bridgwood*	*Viollet*	*Dobing*	*Vernon**	*Burrows*	*McIlroy*
								Ref: G Powell	West Ham's first league clean-sheet wasn't difficult, considering Stoke had little wish to score after Vernon went off after six minutes. The nearest the crowd came to seeing a goal came in the seventh minute. Moore's pass found Brabrook, whose header hit the inside of a post.											
16	A	BURNLEY		21	L	1-3	1-1	Britt 40	Standen	Burnett	Charles	Bovington	Brown	Moore	Brabrook	Peters	Britt	Hurst	Sissons	
		6/11	*16,802*	*1*	10			*Irvine 37, 86, Lochhead 76*	*Blacklaw*	*Angus*	*Elder*	*O'Neill*	*Merrington*	*Miller*	*Morgan*	*Lochhead*	*Irvine*	*Harris*	*Coates*	
								Ref: H Hackney	Burnley replace Leeds at the top. Bob Lord's team cost just £1,500 to assemble. For a long time it looked as if Martin Britt's header, allied to sterling defence, would be enough for West Ham to earn a draw, but Lochhead, back from suspension, seized on rebound to fire the killer goal.											
17	H	CHELSEA		20	W	2-1	1-0	Brabrook 32, Peters 49	Standen	Burnett	Charles	Bovington	Brown	Moore	Brabrook	Peters	Britt	Hurst	Sissons	
		13/11	31,540	*10*	12			*Tambling 61*	*Bonetti*	*Shellito*	*Hinton*	*Hollins*	*Young*	*Boyle*	*Fascione*	*Graham*	*Osgood*	*Murray*	*Tambling*	
								Ref: K Walker	Chelsea had lost just once in seven away games, so this is an upset to set before Alf Ramsey. Martin Peters must be giving up hope of being called up for England, and he plays a blinder. Both Hammers goals were headers. Tambling forced the ball home to spark a frantic last period.											
18	A	ARSENAL		20	L	2-3	1-1	Hurst 41, Peters 89	Standen	Burnett*	Charles	Bovington	Brown	Moore	Brabrook	Peters	Britt	Hurst	Sissons	Bloomfield
		20/11	*35,855*	*7*	12			*Skirton 24, 80, Baker 46*	*Burns*	*Howe*	*Storey*	*McLintock*	*Neill*	*Court*	*Skirton*	*Sammels**	*Baker*	*Eastham*	*Armstrong*	*Walley*
								Ref: E Wallace	Swampy Highbury sees Arsenal finally wreck West Ham's 32-year jinx over them. If only the Hammers had been more alert at the start of the second half. Sub Walley sent Joe Baker clear and he netted despite running away from goal. Skirton fired the killer goal off Standen's hands.											
19	H	EVERTON		19	W	3-0	1-0	Sissons 36, 82, Brabrook 88	Standen	Kirkup	Charles	Bovington	Brown	Moore	Brabrook	Peters	Byrne	Hurst	Sissons	
		27/11	21,920	*12*	14				*Rankin*	*Wright*	*Wilson*	*Harvey*	*Labone*	*Harris*	*Temple*	*Young*	*Pickering*	*Stevens*	*Morrissey*	
								Ref: G Roper	Everton have scored just once in five games. Byrne returned for his first league game in two months and was roughly treated by Labone. Byrne crossed for Sissons to head the first goal. Kirkup handled in the box without the ref seeing, then Sissons hit his second from Brabrook's cross.											
20	A	MANCHESTER U		17	D	0-0	0-0		Standen	Kirkup	Charles	Bovington	Brown	Moore	Brabrook	Peters	Byrne	Hurst	Sissons	
		4/12	*32,924*	*8*	15				*Dunne P*	*Dunne A*	*Cantwell*	*Crerand*	*Foulkes*	*Stiles*	*Best*	*Law*	*Charlton*	*Herd*	*Connelly*	
								Ref: K Burns	Man U are still unbeaten at home, but had either of Byrne's shots that struck the woodwork in the 7th and 77th minutes gone in, that might have changed. Former Hammer Noel Cantwell was playing his 100th league game for Man U. West Ham's tactics were 'blanket defence'.											
21	H	NEWCASTLE		17	W	4-3	3-0	Hurst 5, 18, 72, Brabrook 16	Standen	Kirkup	Charles	Bovington	Brown	Moore	Brabrook	Peters	Byrne	Hurst	Sissons	
		11/12	23,758	*20*	17			*Bennett 61, Iley 67, Robson 84*	*Marshall*	*Craig*	*Clark*	*Moncur*	*McGrath*	*Iley*	*Napier*	*Bennett*	*Thompson*	*Hilley*	*Robson*	
								Ref: F Nicholson	West Ham were coasting at half-time; hanging on desperately by the end. Geoff Hurst, having scored early with his left foot and with his head, was called upon to settle nerves with a crashing shot, after Bennett's header and Iley's 30-yarder, in off the bar, threatened the unthinkable.											

No	Date	Att	Pos	Pt	F-A	H-T	Scorers, Times, and Referees	1	2	3	4	5	6	7	8	9	10	11	12 sub used
22	A SHEFFIELD WED		17	D	0-0	0-0		Standen	Kirkup	Charles	Bovington	Brown	Moore	Brabrook	Peters	Byrne	Hurst	Sissons	
	18/12	*12,996*	*15*	18				*Springett*	*Hill*	*Smith*	*Eustace*	*Mobley*	*Young*	*Usher*	*Fantham*	*McCalliog*	*Hickton*	*Dobson*	
							Ref: J Cattlin	Wednesday have the meanest home defence in the division, which partly explains why West Ham fail to score. Thick mud and a greasy ball help neither side, especially the Owls, whose nimble wingers were too easily brushed off the ball. The Owls did get the ball into the net twice.											
23	H NOTT'M FOREST		17	L	0-3	0-2		Standen	Kirkup	Charles	Bovington	Brown	Moore	Brabrook	Peters	Byrne	Hurst	Sissons	
	1/1	*25,131*	*12*	18			*Addis'n 15, Hint'n 34, Bovingt'n 75 (og)*	*Grummitt*	*Hindley*	*Newton*	*Hennessey*	*McKinlay*	*Whitefoot*	*Crowe*	*Addison*	*Wignall*	*Barnwell*	*Hinton*	
							Ref: G Martin	West Ham's game at Villa Park was abandoned after half an hour. Against Forest, Hammers were hit by Colin Addison's fierce shot from Wignall's pass. The result brings Forest their first away win of the season, and under Johnny Carey their sixth straight win over West Ham.											
24	A NEWCASTLE		17	L	1-2	0-1	Byrne 90	Standen	Kirkup	Charles	Bovington	Brown	Moore	Brabrook	Peters	Byrne	Hurst	Sissons	
	8/1	*31,600*	*19*	18			*Bennett 42, Suddick 63*	*Marshall*	*Craig*	*Burton*	*Moncur*	*McGrath*	*Iley*	*Hilley*	*Suddick*	*Bennett*	*Kettleb'rough*	*Robson*	
							Ref: E Norman	Newcastle's first win in nine games is down to new signing Keith Kettleborough from Sheffield United, who supplied the passes from which Bennett headed the first goal and Suddick the second. Though West Ham are without five of the CWC team, this was a doddle for Newcastle.											
25	A EVERTON		17	D	2-2	1-0	Hurst 10, Peters 78	Standen	Burnett	Burkett	Bovington	Brown	Moore	Brabrook	Peters	Britt	Hurst	Dear	
	11/1	*29,915*	*13*	19			*Scott 51, Pickering 85*	*Barnett*	*Wright*	*Wilson*	*Harvey*	*Labone*	*Harris*	*Scott*	*Hurst*	*Pickering*	*Young*	*Temple*	
							Ref: R Harper	Allowing Everton to come back twice was bad enough, but it could have been worse had Fred Pickering not fired over from the spot in the 70th minute, after Burkett fouled Wright. Controversy surrounded West Ham's second goal, scored by Peters after Britt had clattered into Barnett.											
26	H NORTHAMPTON		17	D	1-1	1-1	Hurst 37p	Standen	Burnett	Burkett	Bovington	Brown	Moore	Brabrook	Peters	Britt	Hurst	Dear	
	15/1	21,000	*20*	20			*Brown 14*	*Coe*	*Foley*	*Everitt*	*Carr*	*Branston*	*Kiernan*	*Broadfoot*	*Moore G*	*Brown*	*Hall*	*Lines*	
							Ref: P Walters	West Ham have now dropped three points to Dave Bowen's Northampton and not many teams do that. Bowen complained that his team had hit 15 goal-posts so far. Jim Hall made it 16 early in this match. Brown's angled header for the Cobblers was cancelled out when Everitt handled.											
27	H WEST BROM		17	W	4-0	3-0	Sissons 18, Peters 31, Hurst 35, 68p	Standen	Burnett	Burkett	Bovington	Brown	Moore	Brabrook	Peters	Britt	Hurst	Sissons	
	29/1	25,500	*9*	22				*Potter*	*Crawford*	*Williams*	*Lovett*	*Jones*	*Fraser*	*Kryzwicki*	*Brown*	*Kaye*	*Hope*	*Clark*	
							Ref: H Davies	A dress rehearsal for the League Cup final, if West Ham get past Cardiff. Albion's forwards average more than two goals a game, so keeping them quiet was some feat. Sissons got the crucial first goal with WBA defenders appealing for offside. Britt was fouled for Hurst's penalty.											
28	A LEEDS		18	L	**0-5**	0-2	*[Lorimer 73]*	Standen	Burnett	Burkett	Bovington	Brown	Moore	Brabrook	Peters	Britt	Hurst	Sissons	
	5/2	*33,312*	*4*	22			*Hunter 18, 77, Storrie 42, Bremner 72,*	*Sprake*	*Reaney**	*Bell*	*Bremner*	*Charlton*	*Hunter*	*Storrie*	*Lorimer*	*Belfitt*	*Giles*	*O'Grady*	*Madeley*
							Ref: J Parkinson	It isn't often that Norman Hunter scores twice in one game, but he found West Ham at their most obliging. Leeds showed fewer adverse affects from a rough match with Valencia than Hammers did from their Cardiff fiesta. When Hunter hit the fifth in the mud, the crowd chanted 'easy'.											
29	A ASTON VILLA			W	2-1	1-0	Hurst 40, Sissons 63	Standen	Burnett	Burkett	Bovington	Brown	Moore	Brabrook	Peters	Hurst	Bloomfield	Sissons	
	7/2	*13,440*		24			*Hateley 75p*	*Withers*	*Wright*	*Aitken*	*Tindall*	*Sleeuw'hoek*	*Pountney*	*MacLeod*	*Hamilton**	*Hateley*	*Woosnam*	*Scott*	*Chatterley*
								Geoff Hurst's 31st of the season keeps him as England's leading goal-getter. Not even the driving rain or the ever-present black dog could deny West Ham this win. Tony Hateley's penalty after Brown had handled hardly ruffled Hammers' feathers. Villa were jeered by their supporters.											
30	H SHEFFIELD UTD		14	W	**4-0**	3-0	Matthewson 8 (og), Brabrook 23, [Hurst 33, Peters 73]	Standen	Burnett	Burkett	Peters	Brown	Moore	Brabrook	Boyce	Byrne	Hurst	Sissons	
	19/2	21,220	*10*	26				*Hodgkinson*	*Badger*	*Mallender*	*Matthewson*	*Shaw*	*Wagstaff B*	*Woodward*	*Wagstaff A*	*Jones*	*Birchenall*	*Reece*	
							Ref: N Burtenshaw	Greenwood is spying in Germany and misses Reg Matthewson's bizarre own-goal, shepherding the ball back towards his keeper, who slipped and fell flat on his face. Moore sent Brabrook away for the second. Alan Birchenall and Mick Jones missed countless chances for the Blades.											
31	H ASTON VILLA		14	W	4-2	2-0	Burkett 4, Byrne 9, Brabrook 74, [Hurst 84]	Standen	Burnett	Burkett	Peters	Brown	Bovington	Brabrook	Boyce	Byrne	Hurst	Dear	
	5/3	22,058	*13*	28			*MacLeod 51, Hateley 87*	*Withers*	*Wright*	*Aitken*	*Tindall*	*Sleeuw'hoek*	*Deakin*	*MacLeod*	*Hamilton*	*Hateley*	*Woosnam*	*Scott*	
							Ref: D Wells	This win lifts West Ham 10 points clear of Blackburn in 21st position. The contest was effectively over once Villa missed two early chances and Hammers took two of theirs. Withers was at fault for the first, letting Burkett's wild shot from near the touchline squirm through his arms.											

No	Venue / Date	Opponent	Att	Pos	Res / Pts	F-A	H-T	Scorers, Times, and Referees	1	2	3	4	5	6	7	8	9	10	11	12 sub used
32	H	BLACKBURN		13	W	4-1	0-1	Dear 65, Brabrook 66, Hurst 69,	Standen	Charles	Burkett	Bovington	Brown	Moore	Brabrook	Bloomfield	Hurst	Dear	Sissons	
	12/3		18,566	*22*	30			*McEvoy 25* [Burkett 83]	*Else*	*Wilson*	*Joyce*	*Newton*	*England*	*Sharples*	*Ferguson*	*Jones*	*McEvoy*	*Byrom*	*Harrison*	
								Ref: P Baldwin	How doomed Rovers knocked Hammers out of the FA Cup is, on this evidence, a mystery. But the jeers turned to cheers as three goals in four minutes sends Rovers to the bottom. Dear headed the first. The second came instantly, when Brabrook's shot was cleared from behind the line.											
33	A	BLACKPOOL		13	L	1-2	0-2	Boyce 52	Standen	Burnett	Burkett	Peters	Brown	Moore	Dear	Bloomfield	Byrne	Boyce	Sissons	
	19/3		*10,559*	*19*	30			*Charnley 29, Ball 42*	*Waiters*	*Prentis*	*Thompson*	*Fisher*	*James*	*Green**	*Lea*	*Ball*	*Charnley*	*Waddell*	*Oates*	*McPhee*
								Ref: D Corbett	A precious win for struggling Blackpool, which has schoolboys dancing on the pitch at the final whistle. Alan Ball set up Charnley's goal, then scored himself when racing through a spread-eagled defence. Moore led the fight-back by moving up into attack, setting up Boyce's riposte.											
34	H	FULHAM		13	L	1-3	0-1	Hurst 76	Standen	Burnett	Burkett	Peters	Bovington	Moore	Brabrook	Bloomfield	Hurst	Boyce	Sissons	
	26/3		18,977	*21*	30			*Earle 43, Barrett 46, Leggat 64*	*McClelland*	*Cohen*	*Nicholls*	*Robson*	*Dempsey*	*Brown*	*Earle*	*Leggat*	*Haynes*	*Pearson*	*Barrett*	
								Ref: E Wallace	Vic Buckingham's Fulham have now won their last four and leave out new signing Allan Clarke. 'Easy, easy,' chant their fans at the end, rubbing salt into West Ham's League Cup wounds. Standen saved, then spilled Earle's shot; Haynes sent Barrett away for Fulham's second.											
35	H	BURNLEY		12	D	1-1	0-0	Brabrook 60	Standen	Burnett	Charles	Dawkins	Boyce	Peters	Redknapp	Bloomfield	Byrne	Dear	Brabrook	
	2/4		**17,635**	*2*	31			*Irvine 75*	*Blacklaw*	*Angus*	*Elder*	*O'Neil*	*Miller*	*Todd*	*Morgan*	*Lochhead*	*Irvine*	*Harris*	*Coates*	
								Ref: R Tinkler	This draw leaves Burnley seven points behind leaders Liverpool with just seven games left. Without Moore, Brown and Hurst, Hammers play cautiously, shutting up shop after Brabrook netted, Redknapp's corner having been only partially cleared. Irvine heads in off Standen's arm.											
36	A	TOTTENHAM		12	W	4-1	2-1	Byrne 22, Hurst 24, Redknapp 47,	Standen	Burnett	Charles	Bovington	Bickles	Peters	Redknapp	Boyce	Byrne	Hurst	Sissons	
	8/4		***50,188***	*6*	33			*Gilzean 16* [Boyce 75]	*Brown*	*Kinnear*	*Knowles*	*Mullery*	*Hoy*	*Mackay*	*Robertson*	*Greaves*	*Saul*	*Gilzean*	*Possee*	
								Ref: M Fussey	Moore watches disgruntled from the stand. Mullery stamps on Byrne as he lies on the ground. Gilzean headed Spurs' 54th home goal, the most in Division 1. Peters set up Byrne's leveller, then keeper Brown makes three howlers, spilling a long ball and being beaten by two distant shots.											
37	A	CHELSEA		12	L	2-6	0-4	Harris 81 (og), Bennett 88 *[Harris 80]*	Standen	Burnett	Burkett	Dawkins	Bickles	Moore	Brabrook	Bloomfield	Bennett	Dear	Sissons	
	9/4		*35,958*	*4*	33			*Gr'h'm 5, 48, V'ables 7p, T'bling 14,27,*	*Bonetti*	*Kirkup*	*McCreadie*	*Hollins*	*Hinton*	*Harris*	*Bridges*	*Graham*	*Osgood*	*Venables*	*Tambling*	
								Ref: R Spittle	Two goals in a minute, one at either end, by Harris was just one of many oddities. It was Chelsea's first home win over Hammers in five years. Chelsea signed Joe Kirkup from Hammers last month and make him captain. Brabrook skippered West Ham. Dawkins handled for the penalty.											
38	H	ARSENAL		12	W	2-1	2-1	Byrne 13p, Brabrook 41	Standen	Burnett	Charles	Peters	Bickles	Moore	Brabrook	Boyce	Byrne	Hurst	Sissons	
	16/4		26,022	*16*	35			*Baldwin 19*	*Furnell*	*Court*	*Storey*	*McLintock*	*Ure*	*Neill*	*Skirton*	*Radford*	*Baldwin*	*Eastham*	*Armstrong*	
								Ref: P Brandwood	Twice in the first 80 seconds West Ham hit the bar. They must have thought their luck was out, but Terry Neill tripped Hurst in full flight and Byrne netted the penalty. Tommy Baldwin beat Standen in a race to the ball to equalise, before Brabrook headed in Dennis Burnett's free-kick.											
39	H	TOTTENHAM		12	W	2-0	1-0	Byrne 4p, 82p	Standen	Burnett	Charles	Peters	Bickles	Moore	Brabrook	Boyce	Byrne	Hurst	Sissons	
	25/4		32,321	*9*	37				*Jennings*	*Kinnear*	*Knowles*	*Mullery*	*Brown*	*Beal*	*Greaves*	*Clayton*	*Gilzean*	*Mackay*	*Possee*	
								Ref: J Osborne	Two Byrne penalties topped and tailed this convincing win. Beal rugby-tackled Byrne for the first offence, Joe Kinnear punched out from under the bar for the second. Hammer of the Year Hurst hit the inside of a post, while England rival Greaves missed a sitter from two yards.											
40	H	MANCHESTER U		12	W	3-2	2-0	Hurst 28, 73, Byrne 42p	Standen	Burnett	Charles	Peters	Bickles	Moore	Brabrook	Boyce	Byrne	Hurst	Sissons	
	30/4		**36,416**	*7*	39			*Cantwell 63, Aston 78*	*Gregg*	*Brennan*	*Dunne**	*Crerand*	*Cantwell*	*Stiles*	*Connelly*	*Law*	*Sadler*	*Charlton*	*Aston*	*Herd*
								Ref: P Bye	Alf Ramsey casts his eye over six players contesting places for England's match with Yugoslavia. Cantwell was hissed by the Chicken Run for writing an article slagging off West Ham. Brennan brought down Peters for Byrne's third penalty in five days. Bottles were thrown by 'fans'.											
41	A	STOKE		12	L	0-1	0-1		Standen	Burnett	Charles	Peters	Bickles	Moore	Brabrook	Boyce	Byrne	Hurst	Sissons	
	7/5		*15,670*	*10*	39			*Bridgwood 21*	*Farmer*	*Skeels*	*Bentley*	*Palmer*	*Kinnell*	*Bloor*	*Bernard*	*Bridgwood*	*Ritchie*	*Dobing*	*Bebbington*	
								Ref: H Richards	Gerry Bridgwood capitalised on Standen's mistake for the only goal. Otherwise Standen played well. Peters came nearest for Hammers, firing a free-kick against the bar. Bobby Moore looks very ordinary, and at a giveaway asking price of £80,000 seems certain to be on the move soon.											
42	A	LEICESTER		12	L	1-2	1-2	Byrne 13	Standen	Burnett	Charles	Bovington	Bickles	Peters	Brabrook	Boyce	Byrne	Hurst	Sissons	
	9/5		*16,066*	*6*	39			*Sinclair 8, Dougan 20*	*Banks*	*Walker*	*Norman*	*Roberts*	*Cross*	*Appleton*	*Sinclair*	*Goodfellow*	*Douglas*	*Gibson*	*Stringfellow*	
	Home		Away					Ref: C Cooke	Jackie Sinclair's left-foot bags his 24th goal of the season for Leicester. It came out from the stanchion so fast that some players thought it had hit the bar. Byrne headed in off a post, but Dougan replied with his 20th of the season. The following week John Bond enjoyed a testimonial.											
Average	24,831		25,291																	

League Cup					F-A	H-T	Scorers, Times, and Referees	1	2	3	4	5	6	7	8	9	10	11	12 sub used
2	A	BRISTOL ROV	18	D	3-3	3-2	Hurst 2, 26, Byrne 30	Dickie	Kirkup	Burkett	Bovington	Charles	Moore	Bennett	Peters	Hurst	Byrne	Sissons	
21/9		*18,354*	*3:6*				*Brown 19, Petts 42, Jarman 59*	*Hall*	*Hillard*	*Jones G*	*Petts*	*Stone*	*Mabbutt*	*Jarman*	*Brown*	*Biggs*	*Jones R*	*Munro*	
							Ref: E Jennings	3-1 up after half an hour, West Ham looked set for Round 3 at the expense of their Third Division opponents. Petts' long-range drive closed the gap, and Jarman whipped in Jones' cross to erase it. From then on it could have gone either way. Martin Peters inadvertently hit his own post.											
2R	H	BRISTOL ROV	18	W	3-2	2-0	Byrne 29, 80, Hurst 43	Dickie	Kirkup	Burkett	Bovington	Brown	Charles	Bennett	Peters	Hurst	Byrne	Sissons	
29/9		13,160	*3:6*				*Petts 52, Jones 55*	*Hall*	*Hillard*	*Jones*	*Petts*	*Stone*	*Mabbutt*	*Jarman*	*Brown*	*Biggs*	*Jones*	*Munro*	
							Ref: G Roper	As in the first game, West Ham had only to hang on to a two-goal lead to progress, but as at Eastville, this proved beyond them. Bovington's miscued free-kick was cut out to bring the scores level. Biggs and Brown might have put Rovers in front before Hurst set up Byrne's second.											
3	H	MANSFIELD	20	W	4-0	1-0	Hurst 19, 89, Brabrook 54, Burnett 82	Standen	Burnett	Charles	Bovington	Brown	Moore	Brabrook	Peters	Britt	Hurst	Sissons	
13/10		11,590	*3:3*					*Treharne*	*Nelson*	*Humble*	*Hall*	*Gill*	*Morris*	*Gregson*	*Macready*	*Middleton*	*Cheesebr'gh*	*Scanlon*	
							Ref: N Burtenshaw	Third Division Mansfield never threatened the Hammers, but for too long there was only one goal in it – Geoff Hurst heading in Peters' cross. West Ham were content to play walking-pace football, and were relieved to see Peter Brabrook's shot hit the bar and the post before going in.											
4	A	ROTHERHAM	21	W	2-1	1-0	Moore 23, Hurst 65	Standen	Burnett	Charles	Bovington	Brown	Moore	Brabrook	Peters	Britt	Hurst	Sissons	
3/11		*13,902*	*2:7*				*Galley 70*	*Jones*	*Wilcockson*	*Clish*	*Casper*	*Madden*	*Tiler*	*Lyons*	*Chappel*	*Galley*	*Williams*	*Pring*	
							Ref: J Pickles	As always, the underdogs claimed misfortune. Clish hit a post just after Hurst scored, and in the last minute Brown headed Galley's header off the line. Rotherham are unbeaten at home in Division 2, and enjoy this competition so much that only once have they failed to reach Round 4.											
QF	A	GRIMSBY	20	D	2-2	1-1	Charles 32, Hurst 71	Standen	Burnett	Charles	Bovington	Brown	Moore	Brabrook	Peters	Hurst	Britt	Sissons	
17/11		*16,281*	*3:2*				*Tees 11, Green 65*	*Wright*	*Dobson*	*Taylor*	*Davidson*	*Jobling*	*Clifton*	*Collins*	*Tees*	*Green*	*Foster*	*Hill*	
							Ref: P Rhodes	The Division 3 pacesetters have already accounted for Crystal Palace, Bolton and Preston, and Matt Tees is the leading scorer in the Football League. Grimsby led twice, but were pegged back first by Charles' flukey lob, then by Hurst's scrambled shot. When to squeeze in the replay?											
QF	H	GRIMSBY	17	W	1-0	0-0	Hurst 79	Standen	Kirkup	Charles	Bovington	Brown	Moore	Brabrook	Peters	Byrne	Hurst	Sissons	
R 15/12		17,500	*3:2*					*Wright*	*Thompson*	*Taylor*	*Davidson*	*Jobling*	*Clifton*	*Collins*	*Tees*	*Green*	*Foster*	*Hill*	
							Ref: W Clements	The ref's advantage rule decided this protracted cup-tie. Future England boss Graham Taylor tried to crash-tackle Brabrook as the winger broke down the touchline. Brabrook wriggled free, his limbs in one piece, and crossed for Hurst to maintain his record of scoring in every round.											
SF	H	CARDIFF	17	W	5-2	2-0	Bovington 6, Byrne 42, Brabrook 65,	Standen	Kirkup	Charles	Bovington	Brown	Moore	Brabrook	Peters	Byrne	Hurst	Sissons	
1 20/12		19,980	*2:13*				*Andrews 86, 88* [Sissons 75, Hurst 89]	*Wilson*	*Harrington*	*Rodrigues*	*Hole*	*Murray*	*Houston*	*Farrell*	*Harkin*	*Andrews*	*Williams*	*King*	
							Ref: R Tinkler	Four goals down, Cardiff hadn't a prayer for the second leg. Two quick goals changed all that, but Hurst took advantage of a kind bounce to restore what should be an unassailable lead. Worst of the countless misses was by Brabrook, who faced with an empty goal passed to Peters.											
SF	A	CARDIFF	17	W	5-1	2-0	Hurst 5, 47, Peters 28, 64, Burnett 82	Standen	Burnett	Burkett	Bovington	Brown	Moore	Brabrook	Peters	Britt	Hurst	Sissons	
2 2/2		*14,315*	*2:13*				*Johnston 68*	*Davies*	*Coldrick*	*Yorath*	*Hole*	*Murray*	*Williams*	*Lewis*	*Johnston*	*Andrews*	*King*	*Farrell*	
							Ref: W Clements (Hammers win 10-3 on aggregate)	Cardiff boss Jimmy Scoular was up-beat before the start, but when Hurst quickly rammed in Brabrook's corner the tie was dead and West Ham can look forward to their third consecutive cup final. Shortly after Johnston scored for Cardiff he missed a penalty after Brown had fouled him.											
F:1	H	WEST BROM	14	W	2-1	0-0	Moore 72, Byrne 90	Standen	Burnett	Burkett	Peters	Brown	Moore	Brabrook	Boyce	Byrne	Hurst	Dear	
9/3		28,323	*7*				*Astle 59*	*Potter*	*Cram*	*Fairfax*	*Fraser*	*Campbell*	*Williams*	*Brown*	*Astle*	*Kaye*	*Lovett*	*Clark*	
							Ref: D Smith	Two freak goals rescue West Ham, leaving Albion players forlorn. Astle scored on his comeback after injury. Moore's goal was a cross, not a shot, while out of form Johnny Byrne had his name booed when it was announced. WBA players insisted Byrne fouled Potter before scoring.											
F:2	A	WEST BROM	13	L	1-4	0-4	Peters 75 *[Williams 34]*	Standen	Burnett	Peters	Bovington	Brown	Moore	Brabrook	Boyce	Byrne	Hurst	Sissons	
23/3		31,925	*8*				*Kaye 10, Brown 17, Clark 27,*	*Potter*	*Cram*	*Fairfax*	*Fraser*	*Campbell*	*Williams*	*Brown*	*Astle*	*Kaye*	*Hope*	*Clark*	
							Ref: J Mitchell (Hammers lose 3-5 on aggregate)	West Ham won't be in next season's Fairs Cup, though they may retain the Cup-Winners' Cup. They were swept aside on a night when all they could offer was high balls to Hurst and Byrne. Kaye netted on the half-volley, Brown with a lob, Clark with a header, Williams from 30 yards.											

FA Cup

Rd	Venue	Opponent	Pos	Res	F-A	H-T	Scorers	1	2	3	4	5	6	7	8	9	10	11
3	A	OLDHAM	17	D	2-2	1-1	Burnett 10, Hurst 70	Standen	Burnett	Burkett	Bovington	Brown	Moore	Brabrook	Peters	Byrne	Hurst	Dear
22/1		*25,035 3:20*					*Bloor 36, Quixall 77*	*Bollands*	*Frizzell*	*Ledger*	*Stevens*	*Asprey*	*Lawson*	*Towers*	*Blore*	*Large*	*Quixall*	*Dearden*
							Ref: H Davey	Fans of the Third Division strugglers pointed to a penalty miss which cost their team dear. It came in 14 minutes when Burkett fouled Towers. Standen saved Quixall's kick. West Ham's first goal was a freak, an 80-yard hurried clearance by Burkett that bounced over Bollands' head.										
3R	H	OLDHAM	17	W	2-1	1-1	Hurst 20, Brabrook 70	Standen	Burnett	Burkett	Bovington	Brown	Moore	Brabrook	Peters	Byrne	Hurst	Sissons
24/1		35,330 *3:20*					*Pennington 3*	*Bollands*	*Frizzell*	*Ledger*	*Stevens*	*Asprey*	*Bowie*	*Pennington*	*Blore*	*Large*	*Towers*	*Dearden*
							Ref: H Davey	Greenwood was livid after this win, which was hard on gutsy Grimbsy. The biggest home crowd of the season was mortified by what they saw from Euro champs. Pennington's free-kick sailed over Standen's head. Hurst equalised on the turn and Peter Brabrook headed the winner.										
4	H	BLACKBURN	18	D	3-3	1-2	Bloomfield 25, Sissons 58, Hurst 83	Standen	Burnett	Burkett	Bovington	Brown	Moore	Brabrook	Peters	Hurst	Bloomfield	Sissons
12/2		32,350 *21*					*Byrom 8, 37, 71*	*Else*	*Wilson*	*Newton*	*Clayton*	*England*	*Joyce*	*Ferguson*	*Byrom*	*McEvoy*	*Douglas*	*Harrison*
							Ref: E Crawford	After just 12 minutes Douglas is crocked by Bovington and reduced to a virtual passenger, but even against 10 fit men West Ham struggle to impose themselves. They are also up against John Byrom, who bags his third hat-trick against the Hammers. Peters sets up Hurst's late goal.										
4R	A	BLACKBURN	18	L	1-4	1-4	Hurst 15	Standen	Burnett	Burkett	Bovington	Boyce	Moore	Brabrook	Peters	Hurst	Bloomfield	Byrne
16/2		*25,547 21*					*McEvoy 14, 41, 44, Byrom 34*	*Else*	*Wilson*	*Newton*	*Clayton*	*England*	*Joyce*	*Darling*	*Byrom*	*McEvoy*	*Ferguson*	*Harrison*
							Ref: E Crawford	Tonsillitis causes the withdrawal of Ken Brown, and for some reason Greenwood hands the No 5 shirt to Ron Boyce, for his first game in five months. Moore had a stinker, and Rovers' superiority was etched in the fact that in addition to their goals they hit the woodwork four times.										

European Cup-Winners' Cup			F-A	H-T	Scorers, Times, and Referees	1	2	3	4	5	6	7	8	9	10	11	12 sub used
2:1 H OLYMPIAKOS	20	W	4-0	2-0	Hurst 24, 43, Byrne 56, Brabrook 72	Standen	Kirkup	Charles	Bovington	Brown	Moore	Brabrook	Peters	Byrne	Hurst	Sissons	
24/11 (Greece) 27,250						*Fronimidis*	*Plessas*	*Pavlidis*	*Polychronou*	*Stefanakos*	*Zanderoglou*	*Vassiliou*	*Sideris*	*Gaitantzis*	*Yuysos*	*Botinos*	
					Ref: K Keller (Switzerland)	Long before the end, the graceless Greeks were kicking and hacking anything in claret and blue. Hurst latched onto Moore's pass to crack the first goal, and further goals followed at regular intervals. Hurst and Brabrook added headers, while Byrne capitalised on the keeper's mistake.											
2:2 A OLYMPIAKOS	19	D	2-2	1-0	Peters 28, 53	Standen	Kirkup	Charles	Bovington	Brown	Moore	Brabrook	Peters	Byrne	Hurst	Sissons	
1/12 *40,000*					*Bovington 56 (og), Polychroniou 80p*	*Fronimidis*	*Plessas*	*Milisis*	*Polychroniou*	*Stefanakos*	*Gaitantzis*	*Vassiliou*	*Aganian*	*Yuysos*	*Papazoglou*	*Botinos*	
					Ref: Bachramov (Russia) (Hammers win 6-2 on aggregate)	The Soviet ref is the linesman who will flag Hurst's goal okay in the World Cup final. Injuries diverted Peters to centre-forward, in which position he scored twice, first with a deflection, then a header. Bovington lobbed an own-goal, and Brown's foul was punished by a penalty.											
QF H MAGDEBURG	14	W	1-0	0-0	Byrne 46	Standen	Burnett	Burkett	Peters	Brown	Moore	Brabrook	Boyce	Byrne	Hurst	Sissons	
1 2/3 (E Germ) 30,620						*Blochwitz*	*Wiedemann*	*Busch*	*Zapf*	*Kubisch*	*Fronzeck*	*Klingbiel*	*Segger*	*Geschke*	*Seguin*	*Stocker*	
					Ref: J Tricot (France)	Ernst Kuemmel's team predictably defended in depth; what was less predictable was the array of chances wasted by the Hammers, who have it all to do in the away leg. The one goal came when Hurst back-headed to Byrne, who flashed a shot under the bar. No 'Bubbles' song this time.											
QF A MAGDEBURG	14	D	1-1	0-0	Sissons 79	Standen	Burnett	Burkett	Bovington	Brown	Moore	Brabrook	Boyce	Hurst	Peters	Sissons	
2 16/3 *35,000*					*Walter 78*	*Blochwitz*	*Wiedemann*	*Zapf*	*Kubisch*	*Fronzeck*	*Hirshmann*	*Klingbiel*	*Sparwasser*	*Walter*	*Seguin*	*Stocker*	
					Ref: Lauraux (Belgium) (Hammers win 2-1 on aggregate)	Sissons' instant equaliser in the Ernst Grube stadium silenced the home roars in their throats. Hirshmann had hit Standen's post in the opening minute and Sparwasser blasted over from two yards. West Ham ventured into Magdeburg's penalty area only three times in the whole match.											
SF H BOR DORTMUND	12	L	1-2	0-0	Peters 53	Standen	Brown	Charles	Peters	Boyce	Moore	Brabrook	Bloomfield	Byrne	Hurst	Dear	
1 5/4 (W Germ) 28,130					*Emmerich 86, 87*	*Tilkowski*	*Cyliax*	*Redder*	*Kurrat*	*Paul*	*Assauer*	*Libuda*	*Schmidt*	*Held*	*Sturm*	*Emmerich*	
					Ref: J de Mendibil (Spain)	West Ham avoid Liverpool and Celtic, the other semi-finalists. Byrne replaces Moore, who wants away, as captain. Hurst will encounter Hans Tilkowski in the World Cup final, and Emmerich too, who takes his Cup-Winners' Cup tally to 12, but these are his first with his right foot.											
SF A BOR DORTMUND	12	L	1-3	1-2	Byrne 43	Standen	Bovington	Charles	Peters	Brown	Moore	Brabrook	Boyce	Byrne	Hurst	Bloomfield	
2 13/4 *35,000*					*Emmerich 1, 29, Cyliax 87*	*Tilkowski*	*Cyliax*	*Redder*	*Kurrat*	*Paul*	*Assauer*	*Libuda*	*Schmidt*	*Held*	*Sturm*	*Emmerich*	
					Ref: Campanai (Italy) (Hammers lose 2-5 on aggregate)	The away-goals rule means West Ham must win 2-0 or 3-1. Having lost 2-6 on Saturday, this is unlikely, especially once Emmerich scores within 20 seconds, hitting the bar with his first effort, the net with his second. Emmerich scored again from a free-kick. Byrne headed a goal.											

		Home					Away					
	P	W	D	L	F	A	W	D	L	F	A	Pts
1 Liverpool	42	17	2	2	52	15	9	7	5	27	19	61
2 Leeds	42	14	4	3	49	15	9	5	7	30	23	55
3 Burnley	42	15	3	3	45	20	9	4	8	34	27	55
4 Manchester U	42	12	8	1	50	20	6	7	8	34	39	51
5 Chelsea	42	11	4	6	30	21	11	3	7	35	32	51
6 West Brom	42	11	6	4	58	34	8	6	7	33	35	50
7 Leicester	42	12	4	5	40	28	9	3	9	40	37	49
8 Tottenham	42	11	6	4	55	37	5	6	10	20	29	44
9 Sheffield Utd	42	11	6	4	37	25	5	5	11	19	34	43
10 Stoke	42	12	6	3	42	22	3	6	12	23	42	42
11 Everton	42	12	6	3	39	19	3	5	13	17	43	41
12 WEST HAM	42	12	5	4	46	33	3	4	14	24	50	39
13 Blackpool	42	9	5	7	36	29	5	4	12	19	36	37
14 Arsenal	42	8	8	5	36	31	4	5	12	26	44	37
15 Newcastle	42	10	5	6	26	20	4	4	13	24	43	37
16 Aston Villa	42	10	3	8	39	34	5	3	13	30	46	36
17 Sheffield Wed	42	11	6	4	35	18	3	2	16	21	48	36
18 Nott'm Forest	42	11	3	7	31	26	3	5	13	25	46	36
19 Sunderland	42	13	2	6	36	28	1	6	14	15	44	36
20 Fulham	42	9	4	8	34	37	5	3	13	33	48	35
21 Northampton	42	8	6	7	31	32	2	7	12	24	60	33
22 Blackburn	42	6	1	14	30	36	2	3	16	27	52	20
	924	245	103	114	877	580	114	103	245	580	877	924

Odds & ends

Double wins: (3) Blackburn, Aston Villa, Spurs.
Double losses: (3) Leicester, Fulham, Nott'm Forest.

Won from behind: (5) Leeds (h), Sheff W (h), Blackburn (h), Spurs (a), Oldham FAC (h).
Lost from in front: (4) Sunderland (a), Leicester (h), WBA LC, Dortmund (CWC).

High spots: Reaching semi-final of League Cup.
Reaching semi-final of Cup-Winners' Cup.
Scoring four goals in three games in a row.
Winning four league games in a row in February and March.

Low spots: Coming so close, but not winning anything.
Conceding five goals in three games in a row, dropping to 20th.

Hammer of the Year: Geoff Hurst.
Ever-presents: (0).
Hat-tricks: (1) Geoff Hurst.
Leading scorer: (40) Geoff Hurst.

	Appearances								Goals				
	Lge	*Sub*	LC	*Sub*	FAC	*Sub*	Eur	Sub	**Lge**	LC	FAC	Eur	**Tot**
Bennett, Peter	**7**	*1*	2						**1**				**1**
Bickles, Dave	**12**	*1*											
Bloomfield, Jimmy	**9**	*1*			2		2				1		**1**
Bovington, Eddie	**31**		9		4		4			1			**1**
Boyce, Ronnie	**16**		2		1		4		**2**				**2**
Brabrook, Peter	**32**		8		4		6		**8**	2	1	1	**12**
Britt, Martin	**10**		4						**3**				**3**
Brown, Ken	**23**		9		3		6		**1**				**1**
Burkett, Jackie	**19**		4		4		2		**2**				**2**
Burnett, Dennis	**24**		6		4		2			2	1		**3**
Byrne, Johnny	**23**		6		3		5		**9**	5		3	**17**
Charles, John	**25**		7				4			1			**1**
Dawkins, Trevor	**2**												
Dear, Brian	**7**		1		1		1		**1**				**1**
Dickie, Alan	**5**		2										
Hurst, Geoff	**39**		10		4		6		**23**	11	4	2	**40**
Kirkup, Joe	**17**		4				2		**1**				**1**
Moore, Bobby	**37**		9		4		6			2			**2**
Peters, Martin	**40**		10		4		6		**11**	3		3	**17**
Presland, Eddie	**2**												
Redknapp, Harry	**7**								**1**				**1**
Scott, Tony	**2**												
Sissons, John	**36**		9		2		4		**5**	1	1	1	**8**
Standen, Jim	**37**		8		4		6						
(own-goals)									**2**				**2**
24 players used	**462**	*3*	**110**		**44**		**66**		**70**	**28**	**8**	**10**	**116**

No	Date			Att	Pos	Pt	F-A	H-T	Scorers, Times, and Referees	1	2	3	4	5	6	7	8	9	10	11	12 sub used
1		H	CHELSEA			L	1-2	0-1	Boyce 57	Standen	Burnett	Charles	Peters	Moore	Bovington	Brabrook	Boyce	Byrne	Hurst	Sissons	
	20/8			36,126		0			*Hollins 38, Cooke 72*	*Bonetti*	*Kirkup*	*McCreadie*	*Hollins*	*Hinton*	*Harris*	*Boyle*	*Graham*	*Osgood*	*Cooke*	*Tambling*	
									Ref: K Dagnall	West Ham's World Cup-winning trio take the field ahead of the rest and receive a tumultuous reception. This match was a tale of two keepers. Jim Standen was out of position, letting Cooke score into an empty goal. Bonetti was so brilliant, Greenwood is rumoured to be making a bid.											
2		A	ARSENAL			L	1-2	1-2	Byrne 42	Standen	Burnett	Charles	Peters	Moore	Bovington	Brabrook	Boyce	Byrne	Hurst	Sissons	
	23/8			*40,533*		0			*Baldwin 4, Radford 37*	*Furnell*	*Court*	*Storey*	*McLintock*	*Ure*	*Neill*	*Skirton**	*Baldwin*	*Radford*	*Sammels*	*Armstrong*	*Simpson*
									Ref: R Prichard	Arsenal's coach Dave Sexton ordered an early blitz of high balls into the box. He is rewarded when Baldwin follows up after Radford had hit the bar. Eyes were cast on Standen who had already missed one cross. West Ham had chances, notably when Hurst hit the underside of the bar.											
3		A	LEICESTER		20	L	4-5	0-2	Brabrook 48, 56, Hurst 62, 89	Standen	Burnett	Charles	Peters	Moore	Bovington	Brabrook	Boyce	Byrne	Hurst	Sissons	
	27/8			*26,850*	*11*	0			*D'gan 18, Sinclair 30, 49, 79, Good' 61*	*Banks*	*Rodrigues*	*Norman*	*Roberts*	*Sjoberg*	*Cross*	*Sinclair*	*Goodfellow*	*Dougan*	*Gibson*	*Stringfellow*	
									Ref: R Egan	Believe it or not, Hammers are playing well, and might have been three up before Derek Dougan netted from close range. The second half saw seven goals, three by Scotsman Jackie Sinclair. A great run by Roberts set up Sinclair's third goal. Banks couldn't hold Brabrook's first goal.											
4		H	ARSENAL		20	D	2-2	1-1	Moore 34, Brabrook 61	Standen	Burnett	Charles	Peters	Moore	Bovington	Brabrook	Boyce	Byrne	Hurst	Sissons	
	29/8			34,964	2	1			*McLintock 30, Sammels 89*	*Furnell*	*Simpson*	*Storey*	*McLintock*	*Ure*	*Neill*	*Coakley*	*McGill*	*Baldwin*	*Sammels*	*Armstrong*	
									Ref: E Jennings	West Ham's cockiness at the end denied them their first win. On a rain-swept night they had recovered from Standen - rooted to his line - being beaten by Frank McLintock. West Ham replied with Moore's 30-yard dipper and Brabrook's glancing header. Sammels netted from 20 yards.											
5		H	LIVERPOOL		19	D	1-1	1-0	Hurst 6	Standen	Burnett	Charles	Peters	Bickles*	Moore	Brabrook	Boyce	Byrne	Hurst	Sissons	Bennett
	3/9			33,000	*10*	2			*Strong 89*	*Lawrence*	*Lawler*	*Smith*	*Yeats*	*Milne*	*St John*	*Stevenson*	*Callaghan*	*Strong*	*Hunt*	*Thompson*	
									Ref: D Corbett	Play was held up in the second half so that broken glass flung by Liverpool fans could be swept from the goalmouth. Shankly's offside tactics did not go down well. Hurst's close-range header looked like bringing West Ham their first win until Geoff Strong headed in a late corner-kick.											
6		A	MANCHESTER C		17	W	4-1	3-0	Hurst 20, 63, Boyce 33, Sissons 43	Standen	Burnett	Charles	Peters	Brown	Moore	Brabrook	Boyce	Byrne	Hurst	Sissons	
	7/9			*31,989*	*15*	4			*Bell 64*	*Dowd*	*Book*	*Kennedy*	*Pardoe*	*Heslop*	*Oakes*	*Connor*	*Bell*	*Summerbee*	*Crossan*	*Young*	
									Ref: K Burns	City's first home defeat was as comprehensive as the score suggests. 'West Ham, with three World Cup men in their side, often played as if they had 11,' wrote one paper. Hurst and Boyce made a goal for each other, and Sissons sealed the points when thumping home Peters' cross.											
7		H	STOKE			D	1-1	1-0	Hurst 21	Standen	Burnett	Burkett	Peters	Brown	Moore	Brabrook	Bovington	Byrne	Hurst	Sissons	
	10/9			33,293		5			*Dobing 72*	*Farmer*	*Palmer*	*Skeels*	*Viollet*	*Setters*	*Philpott*	*Bridgwood*	*Dobing*	*Ritchie*	*Eastham*	*Burrows*	
									Ref: D Brady	West Ham take their first point off Stoke since City returned to Division 1. Stoke had just beaten Man U 3-0, but under the gaze of Alf Ramsey looked to be heading for defeat once Hurst's effort ricocheted in off both Farmer and Skeels. Peter Dobing levelled from Bridgwood's cross.											
8		A	SHEFFIELD WED		14	W	2-0	1-0	Boyce 26, Byrne 60	Standen	Burnett	Charles	Peters	Brown	Moore	Brabrook	Boyce	Byrne	Hurst	Sissons	
	17/9			*29,171*	*5*	7				*Springett*	*Smith*	*Megson*	*Eustace*	*Ellis*	*Young*	*Pugh*	*Fantham*	*McCalliog*	*Ford*	*Quinn*	
									Ref: R Bickerstaffe	The Owls' first defeat is down to Jim Standen and maybe to the angry West Ham team. Wednesday boss Allan Brown protested about a colour clash, and West Ham played in the second half in all white. Boyce dribbled round Ellis and Springett for his goal. Byrne's was a diving header.											
9		H	SOUTHAMPTON		14	D	2-2	1-2	Hurst 27, Peters 46	Standen	Burnett	Charles	Peters	Brown	Moore	Brabrook*	Boyce	Byrne	Hurst	Sissons	**Howe**
	24/9			32,301	*13*	8			*Chivers 17, Davies 44*	*MacLaren*	*Webb*	*Hollywood*	*Wimshurst*	*Knapp*	*Walker*	*Paine*	*Chivers*	*Davies*	*Melia*	*Sydenham*	
									Ref: R Johnson	Ted Bates' newly promoted Saints have only lost once away from home, and Ron Davies is a handful in the air for any defence. His goal followed a huge punt downfield by keeper MacLaren. Peters levelled through a packed goalmouth. Brabrook was subbed because of a cut eye.											
10		A	SUNDERLAND		12	W	4-2	2-1	Byrne 18p, 79, Hurst 35, Peters 86	Standen	Burnett	Charles	Peters	Brown	Moore	Brabrook	Boyce	Byrne	Hurst	Sissons	
	1/10			*29,227*	*19*	10			*Martin 6, Sharkey 78*	*Montgomery*	*Irwin*	*Ashurst*	*Herd*	*Harvey*	*McNab*	*Gauden*	*Sharkey*	*Martin*	*Baxter*	*Mulhall*	
									Ref: K Walker	West Ham's third away win leaves them in the bottom half. Byrne levelled Martin's early header with a twice-taken penalty when Montgomery flattened Hurst. The keeper saved Byrne's first attempt. Sharkey's lobbed equaliser was immediately countered by Byrne, from Hurst's pass.											

No	Venue / Date	Opponent / Att	Pos	Res / Pts	F-A	H-T	Scorers, Times, and Referees	1	2	3	4	5	6	7	8	9	10	11	12 sub used
11	H	EVERTON	14	L	2-3	1-1	Peters 29, Hurst 63	Standen	Burnett	Charles	Peters	Brown	Moore	Brabrook	Boyce	Byrne	Hurst	Sissons	
	8/10	32,784	*10*	10			*Young 25, Temple 49, 69*	*West*	*Wright*	*Wilson*	*Gabriel*	*Labone*	*Harvey*	*Scott**	*Ball*	*Young*	*Temple*	*Morrissey*	*Brown*
							Ref: M Fussey	Hammers' first defeat since August is watched by Alf Ramsey. The winning goal was a triumph for man-of-the-match Alan Ball, who actually made a mug of Moore when setting up Derek Temple. Minutes earlier Hurst had made it 2-2, reacting first when West saved from Peters.											
12	A	FULHAM	15	L	2-4	1-2	Byrne 19, Hurst 82	Standen	Burnett	Charles	Peters	Bickles	Moore	Brabrook	Boyce	Byrne	Hurst	Sissons	
	15/10	*34,826*	*18*	10			*Earle 10, Burnett 43 (og), Clarke 53, 62*	*McClelland*	*Cohen*	*Dempsey*	*Robson*	*Callaghan*	*Conway*	*Haynes*	*Brown*	*Earle*	*Clarke*	*Barrett*	
							Ref: R Baldwin	Fulham's first home win makes a mockery of West Ham's imposing away form. Last season Charles's own-goal sunk the Hammers at Craven Cottage; this time it's Burnett, deflecting Haynes' wayward shot past Standen. Allan Clarke takes his Fulham tally to 11 goals from five games.											
13	H	NOTT'M FOREST		W	3-1	2-0	Hurst 17, 28, Bovington 73	Standen	Burnett	Burkett	Bovington	Brown	Moore	Brabrook	Boyce	Bennett	Hurst	Peters	
	26/10	23,000		12			*Moore 87*	*Grummitt*	*Hindley*	*Winfield*	*Hennessey*	*McKinlay*	*Newton*	*Crowe*	*Barnwell*	*Storey-Moore*	*Wignall*	*Hinton*	
							Ref: H New	It's late October and at last West Ham win at home. They do it without Byrne and Sissons, both dropped. Without Baker, ill with tonsillitis, Forest looked light in attack. They still wove their pretty patterns but were cut to shreds by Hurst's diving header. His 15th goal soon followed.											
14	A	SHEFFIELD UTD	14	L	1-3	0-2	Peters 48 *[Burnett 60 (og)]*	Standen	Burnett	Burkett*	Bovington	Brown	Moore	Brabrook	Boyce	Bennett	Hurst	Peters	Sissons
	29/10	*20,579*	*10*	12			*Wagstaff T 41, Woodward 42,*	*Hodgkinson*	*Coldwell*	*Mallender*	*Munks*	*Matthewson*	*Wagstaff B*	*Woodward*	*Wagstaff T*	*Bell*	*Fenoughty*	*Reece*	
							Ref: C Cooke	Alan Hodgkinson is skipper on his 400th appearance for the Blades. It was a black day for two Hammers in particular. Jackie Burkett clashed heads with 6ft 3in Bell and suffered concussion. With Hammers pushing forward, Bell then pressured Burnett to turn the ball into his own net.											
15	H	FULHAM	13	W	**6-1**	1-1	Hurst 29, 67, 71, 87, Peters 61, 80	Standen	Bovington	Charles	Peters	Brown	Moore	Brabrook	Boyce	Byrne	Hurst	Sissons	
	5/11	22,260	*21*	14			*Callaghan 19*	*McClelland*	*Cohen*	*Dempsey*	*Robson*	*Callaghan*	*Conway*	*Haynes*	*Brown*	*Earle*	*Clarke*	*Barrett*	
							Ref: D Wells	When Johnny Haynes squared to Callaghan for Fulham's goal, the thousands who stayed away seemed vindicated. West Ham's response was sparked by the recalled Byrne, though he did not score. Hurst completed his hat-trick from 20 yards, and added a fourth from Brabrook's cross.											
16	A	TOTTENHAM	11	W	4-3	3-2	Byrne 7, Brab'k 29, Siss'ns 32, H'st 78	Standen	Bovington	Charles	Peters	Brown	Moore	Brabrook	Boyce	Byrne	Hurst	Sissons	
	12/11	*51,157*	*8*	16			*Greaves 24p, Venables 33, Gilzean 61*	*Jennings*	*Beal*	*Knowles*	*Mullery*	*England*	*Mackay*	*Robertson*	*Greaves*	*Gilzean*	*Venables*	*Jones*	
							Ref: R Tinkler	17 goals in a week for fantastic Hammers. The final outcome owed much to Jimmy Greaves, who hit the bar in the first minute, netted from the spot when brought down by Bovington, then missed his first ever penalty for Spurs when Moore handled. Spurs hit the woodwork three times.											
17	H	NEWCASTLE	8	W	3-0	1-0	Peters 11, Byrne 59p, Hurst 85	Standen	Bovington	Charles	Peters	Brown*	Moore	Brabrook	Boyce	Byrne	Hurst	Sissons	Burnett
	19/11	31,285	*21*	18				*McFaul*	*Clark*	*Guthrie*	*Burton*	*Moncur*	*Iley*	*Robson*	*Bennett*	*Davies*	*Suddick*	*Allen*	
							Ref: E Wallace	Lowly Newcastle have scored just 12 goals all season. Within 30 seconds they were within a whisker of their 13th, but Wyn Davies headed narrowly wide. Peters scored No 1 from an acute angle, and Byrne No 2 from the spot after Bobby Moncur toppled man-of-the-match Boyce.											
18	A	LEEDS	11	L	1-2	1-1	Hurst 4	Standen	Bovington	Charles	Peters	Bickles	Moore	Brabrook	Boyce	Byrne	Hurst	Sissons	
	26/11	*37,382*	*10*	18			*Johanneson 11, Giles 81*	*Sprake*	*Reaney*	*Charlton*	*Hunter*	*Bell*	*Bremner*	*Giles*	*O'Grady*	*Lorimer*	*Greenhoff*	*Johanneson*	
							Ref: J Taylor	Leeds gain revenge for the seven-goal League Cup massacre, though Hurst's shot – deflected in off Bell – had given Hammers the perfect start. Albert Johanneson headed in Peter Lorimer's cross and Giles blasted a late winner. Byrne shaved Gary Sprake's crossbar in the dying seconds.											
19	H	WEST BROM	10	W	3-0	2-0	Redknapp 14, Peters 35p, Dear 85	Standen	Burnett	Charles	Bovington	Bickles	Moore	Redknapp	Boyce	Dear	Peters	Sealey	
	3/12	22,961	*20*	20				*Sheppard*	*Cram*	*Fairfax*	*Lovett*	*Jones*	*Fraser*	*Foggo*	*Brown*	*Kaye*	*Hope*	*Clark*	
							Ref: P Bye	A £25,000 price tag has been placed on Brian Dear, who crowns his recall by blasting a spectacular goal from 25 yards. He also provided the cross from which Harry Redknapp drove in the first goal. The penalty was the result of Clive Clark whipping Burnett's legs from under him.											
20	A	BURNLEY	11	L	2-4	2-2	Hurst 21, 42	Standen	Burnett	Charles	Bovington	Bickles	Moore	Peters	Boyce	Byrne	Hurst	Sissons	
	10/12	***19,509***	*6*	20			*Irvine 8, 77, O'Neill 11, Lochhead 58*	*Blacklaw*	*Angus*	*Miller*	*Todd*	*Elder*	*O'Neil*	*Harris*	*Morgan*	*Lochhead*	*Irvine*	*Latcham*	
							Ref: V James	Burnley are the most prolific home side in Division 1, West Ham the most prolific away, so this thriller was always on the cards. Standen was at fault for the second goal, missing a cross, but in the last minute saved Irvine's penalty after Charles had fouled man-of-the match Morgan.											
21	A	CHELSEA	11	D	5-5	2-1	Brab' 24, P't'rs 29, Sis' 55, 58, Byrne 60p	Standen	Bovington	Charles*	Peters	Brown	Moore	Brabrook	Boyce	Byrne	Hurst	Sissons	Burnett
	17/12	*47,805*	2	21			*Baldwin 40, Hateley 51, Cooke 54*	*Bonetti*	*Kirkup*	*McCreadie*	*Hollins*	*Hinton*	*Harris*	*Boyle*	*Baldwin*	*Hateley*	*Cooke*	*Tambling*	
							Ref: H Richards *[Tambling 80p, 89]*	Chelsea have won only three times at home. West Ham led 2-0 and 5-3, but are pegged back by two goals by Tambling, which gives him a new Chelsea record of 129. Moore fouled Hateley for the penalty, then Tambling put away Cooke's cross. Best of the goals was Cooke's volley.											

No	Date		Att	Pos	Pt	F-A	H-T	Scorers, Times, and Referees	1	2	3	4	5	6	7	8	9	10	11	12 sub used
22	A	BLACKPOOL		10	W	4-1	2-0	Hurst 8, Dear 18, Byrne 80, Sissons 87	Standen	Bovington	Burnett	Peters	Brown	Moore	Dear	Boyce	Byrne	Hurst	Sissons	
	26/12		*26,901*	*22*	23			*Charnley 66p*	*Waiters*	*Armfield*	*Hughes*	*McPhee*	*James*	*Green*	*Skirton*	*Robsosn*	*Charnley*	*Suddick*	*Moir*	
								Ref: K Stokes	Hammers flew up to Blackpool, with Dear taking the place of Brabrook, who had stomach trouble. Not even a debut for Alan Suddick can conceal the gulf between the sides. Peters made early goals for Hurst and Dear, but Brown's foul on Charnley in the box rekindled the contest.											
23	H	BLACKPOOL		7	W	4-0	1-0	Byrne 14, M're 80, H'rst 87, Peters 89	**M'cklew'rth**	Bovington	Burnett	Peters	Brown	Moore	Brabrook	Dear	Byrne	Hurst	Sissons	
	27/12		29,300	*22*	25				*Waiters*	*Thompson*	*Hughes*	*Fisher*	*James*	*McPhee*	*Skirton*	*Robson*	*Charnley*	*Suddick*	*Lea*	
								Ref: J Yates	Harry Redknapp is given the day off for his engagement party. Three late goals distorted the balance of play. For over an hour only Byrne's shot on the turn separated the sides. Blackpool were pressing hard when Moore fired in from 30 yards, a candidate for goal of the season.											
24	H	LEICESTER		10	L	0-1	0-0		Standen	Burnett	Charles*	Peters	Brown	Moore	Brabrook	Bovington	Byrne	Hurst	Sissons	Burkett
	31/12		34,168	*9*	25			*Sinclair 74*	*Banks*	*Rodrigues*	*Norman*	*Roberts*	*Sjoberg*	*Nish*	*Sinclair*	*Sweenie*	*Dougan*	*Gibson*	*Stringfellow*	
								Ref: P Walters	West Ham were the last Division 1 side to have scored in every match, but after 28 matches Gordon Banks has the final word. John Charles' error presented the chance for Jackie Sinclair. Hurst played deeper than usual. When Banks was beaten, defenders twice cleared off the line.											
25	A	LIVERPOOL		11	L	0-2	0-2		Standen	Burnett	Burkett	Peters	Brown	Moore	Brabrook	Bovington	Byrne	Hurst	Sissons	
	7/1		*48,518*	*1*	25			*Thompson 34, 40*	*Lawrence*	*Lawler*	*Milne*	*Smith*	*Yeats*	*Stevenson*	*Callaghan*	*Hunt*	*St John*	*Strong*	*Thompson*	
								Ref: J Carr	Bobby Moore OBE cannot prevent leaders Liverpool maintaining their unbeaten home record. In fact this was a totally one-sided affair, and but for Standen's agility the margin of defeat would have been greater. Peter Thompson fired in the first from 20 yards, then added a solo goal.											
26	A	STOKE		12	D	1-1	1-0	Hurst 7	Standen	Burnett	Charles	Peters*	Brown	Moore	Brabrook	Boyce	Byrne	Hurst	Sissons	Dear
	14/1		*27,274*	*4*	26			*Burrows 59*	*Farmer*	*Palmer*	*Skeels*	*Viollet**	*Bloor*	*Allen*	*Bridgwood*	*Philpott*	*Vernon*	*Eastham*	*Burrows*	*Bernard*
								Ref G Hill	Stoke confirm their reputation as one of West Ham's bogey-sides. Hurst wrong-footed Bloor to convert John Sissons' cross, but when Harry Burrows got on the end of Eastham's pass, this ageing Stoke side began to pose most of the questions. Substitute Bernard missed a sitter.											
27	H	SHEFFIELD WED		9	W	3-0	0-0	Dear 65, Hurst 75p, Sissons 84	Standen	Bovington	Charles*	Peters	Bickles	Moore	Brabrook	Sealey	Dear	Hurst	Sissons	Dawkins
	21/1		29,220	*13*	28				*Springett*	*Branfoot*	*Megson*	*Mobley*	*Ellis*	*Young*	*Pugh*	*McCalliog*	*Quinn*	*Ford*	*Eustace*	
								Ref: C Nicholls	Greenwood plays five strikers, but the breakthrough was a long time coming. Brabrook then headed back across goal to Dear. Young gave away the penalty when fouling Sissons. At the time West Ham were down to 10, Trevor Dawkins having come on as sub without permission.											
28	A	SOUTHAMPTON		11	L	2-6	0-4	Hurst 59, Burkett 76 *[Chivers 31, 75]*	Standen	Bovington	Burkett	Peters	Brown	Moore	Brabrook	Boyce	Byrne	Hurst	Sissons	
	4/2		*30,123*	*17*	28			*Hollyw'd 3, Davies 18, Paine 26p, 57p,*	*MacLaren*	*Webb*	*Hollywood*	*Wimshurst*	*Knapp*	*Walker*	*Paine*	*Chivers*	*Davies*	*Melia*	*Sydenham*	
								Ref: K Wynn	The Dell's biggest crowd for 18 years enjoys more misery being heaped upon Hammers. Davies fouled Brown before scoring No 2. Davies took an early knock from Moore, who was booed thereafter. Paine's penalties came after two fouls on him, first by Moore, then by Bovington.											
29	H	SUNDERLAND		11	D	2-2	1-1	Byrne 17, Hurst 89	Standen	Burnett	Burkett	Dawkins	**Andrew**	Bovington	Redknapp	Boyce	Byrne	Hurst	Peters	
	11/2		27,965	*15*	29			*Mulhall 16, Martin 73*	*Montgomery*	*Irwin*	*Harvey*	*Todd*	*Kinnell*	*Baxter*	*Kerr*	*O'Hare*	*Martin*	*Herd*	*Mulhall*	
								Ref: R Windle	Greenwood starts to rebuild. Johnny Byrne is expected to sign for Stoke, and signs off with a goal. Peters and Hurst were anonymous. Hurst missed from the spot after Byrne was tripped, but redeemed himself in the closing seconds when heading in Byrne's cross from a tight angle.											
30	A	EVERTON		13	L	0-4	0-3	*[Husband 46]*	Standen	Burnett	Bovington	Dawkins	Andrew	Boyce	Redknapp	Bennett	Brabrook	Hurst	Sissons	
	25/2		*42,504*	*7*	29			*Temple 10, Young 14, Morrissey 37,*	*West*	*Wright*	*Wilson*	*Hurst*	*Labone*	*Harvey*	*Young*	*Ball*	*Temple**	*Husband*	*Morrissey*	*Brown*
								Ref: K Burns	Everton's Alan Ball masterminded this feast of attacking football. Temple netted from Husband's pull-back. Young chipped Standen for the second. Morrissey added a third when running from the halfway line. The nearest Hammers came was when Labone headed onto his own bar.											
31	A	NOTT'M FOREST		14	L	0-1	0-0		Standen	Burkett	**Kitchener**	Peters	**Heffer**	Moore	Brabrook	Boyce	Bennett*	Hurst	Sissons	Redknapp
	18/3		*31,426*	*3*	29			*Baker 79*	*Grummitt*	*Hindley*	*Winfield*	*Hennessey*	*McKinlay*	*Newton*	*Lyons*	*Barnwell*	*Baker*	*Wignall*	*Storey-Moore*	
								Ref: R Prichard	The highest scorers in Division 1 take on the meanest defenders, and the latter win. Mind you, it took a freakish goal from Joe Baker – the ball looping over Standen after bouncing off Moore – to separate the sides. Greenwood bloodied two more youngsters in this transitional team.											

No	Date	Opponent / Att	Pos	Pts	Res	H-T	Scorers, Times, and Referees	1	2	3	4	5	6	7	8	9	10	11	12 sub used
32	H	ASTON VILLA	14	W	2-1	1-1	Boyce 37, Peters 48	Standen	Burkett	Kitchener	Peters	Heffer	Moore	Redknapp	Boyce	Hurst	Sissons	Brabrook	
	24/3	28,716	*18*	31			*Anderson 13*	*Withers*	*Wright*	*Aitken*	*Tindall*	*Sleeu'nhoek*	*Pountney*	*Anderson*	*Chatterley*	*Stobart*	*Broadbent*	*MacLeod*	
							Ref: D Counsell	Bobby Moore played a part in all three goals. First, his mistimed clearance bounced kindly for Willie Anderson to put Villa ahead. Then his free-kick paved the way for Boyce's header. Yet another Moore free-kick was finished off by Peters for the winner. Villa are going down.											
33	H	BURNLEY	11	W	3-2	1-1	Peters 13, 64, Sissons 68	Standen	Charles	Kitchener	Bovington	Heffer	Moore	Redknapp	Boyce	Peters	Hurst	Sissons	
	25/3	24,428	*12*	33			*Morgan 11, O'Neil 59*	*Thomson*	*Smith*	*Latcham*	*O'Neil*	*Miller*	*Merrington*	*Morgan*	*Todd*	*Blant*	*Harris*	*Coates*	
							Ref: N Burtenshaw	Hurst failed to score but made all three goals for his team-mates. He also laid out Fred Smith, who was foolish enough to get in the way of a belter. Sissons claimed the winner after a blunder by Dave Merrington, who had cleared straight to Sissons' feet. Hammers go above Burnley.											
34	A	ASTON VILLA	10	W	2-0	1-0	Hurst 4, 62	Standen	Charles	Kitchener	Bovington	Heffer	Moore	Brabrook	Boyce	Peters	Hurst	Sissons*	Redknapp
	28/3	*22,033*	*19*	35				*Withers*	*Wright*	*Aitken*	*Tindall*	*Sleeu'nhoek*	*Pountney*	*Anderson*	*Chatterley*	*Stobart*	*Broadbent*	*MacLeod*	
							Ref: D Laing	An unexceptional match, except for Geoff Hurst, who takes his season's tally to 41. West Ham's Easter double over Villa is something from which Villa never recover. They appeared to know their fate as early as the fourth minute when Hurst nipped in to convert Brabrook's pass.											
35	A	MANCHESTER U	11	L	0-3	0-1		Standen	Charles	Kitchener	Bovington	Heffer	Moore	Redknapp	Boyce	Peters	Hurst	Brabrook	
	1/4	***61,380***	*1*	35			*Charlton 3, Best 86, Law 89*	*Stepney*	*Dunne*	*Noble*	*Crerand*	*Foulkes*	*Stiles*	*Best*	*Law*	*Sadler*	*Charlton*	*Aston*	
							Ref: W Handley	The magic threesome score the goals that keep Man U two points ahead of Forest. In a one-sided affair, West Ham trailed through Hurst's wayward pass till the closing minutes. Charles fouled Best but Law hit the post from the spot. Best's volley and Law's hook seal an easy win.											
36	H	SHEFFIELD UTD		L	0-2	0-0		Mackleworth	Charles	Kitchener	Bovington	Heffer	Moore	Redknapp	Boyce	Peters	Hurst	Sissons	
	4/4	22,006		35			*Jones 56, Munks 73*	*Hodgkinson*	*Badger*	*Shaw*	*Munks*	*Matthewson*	*Wagstaff*	*Woodward*	*Mallender*	*Jones*	*Barlow*	*Cliff*	
							Ref: R Johnson	Upton Park at the end resembled a morgue. Norman Giller described the Hammers as 'tigers suddenly transformed into tortoises.' The Blades were little better, but were sparked into life by Mick Jones' bullet from 15 yards. Munks then netted a rebound after Woodward had hit the bar.											
37	H	LEEDS	14	L	0-1	0-1		Standen	Charles	Kitchener	Peters	Moore	Bovington	Brabrook	Boyce	Bennett	Hurst	Sissons	
	22/4	25,429	*4*	35			*Lorimer 34*	*Sprake*	*Reaney*	*Cooper*	*Bremner*	*Madeley*	*Hunter*	*Lorimer*	*Belfitt*	*Greenhoff*	*Gray*	*Johanneson**	*Bates*
							Ref: H Davies	West Ham return from playing Real Madrid in the Houston Astrodome. Leeds are distracted by their looming FA Cup semi-final, but win with ease. Lorimer's angled 30-yarder squeezed inside the far post. Near the end Eddie Gray started mickey-taking West Ham's feeble efforts.											
38	A	NEWCASTLE	14	L	0-1	0-1		Standen	Charles	Burkett	Peters	Heffer	Moore	Redknapp	Boyce	Hurst	Sissons	Brabrook	
	26/4	*38,870*	*19*	35			*Burkett 14 (og)*	*Marshall*	*Craig*	*Clark*	*Elliott*	*McNamee*	*Iley*	*Bennett*	*Noble*	*Davies*	*Hilley*	*Robson*	
							Ref: K Dagnall	Newcastle haul themselves out of the relegation places, courtesy of Burkett's own-goal. Attempting to intercept from Pop Robson, Burkett steered the ball into his own net. And Burkett was only playing because Bill Kitchener had flu. Wyn Davies later headed against an upright.											
39	A	WEST BROM		L	1-3	0-2	Bennett 89	Standen	Charles	Burkett	Peters	Heffer	Moore	Redknapp	Bennett	**Hartley**	Hurst	Boyce	
	28/4	*23,219*		35			*Brown 24p, 32p, Astle 79*	*Osborne*	*Fairfax*	*Williams*	*Talbut*	*Colquhoun*	*Brown*	*Foggo*	*Astle*	*Kaye*	*Hope*	*Clark*	
							Ref: R Darlington	Debutant Trevor Hartley is blameless as the Hammers crash to their fifth straight defeat. Albion were helped on their way by two controversial penalties, for pushes by Heffer and Charles on Astle and Clark respectively. Charles' foul on Clark also led to a free-kick, headed in by Astle.											
40	H	MANCHESTER U	17	L	**1-6**	0-4	Charles 46 *[Best 25, Law 63p, 79]*	Mackleworth	Burkett	Charles	Peters	Heffer	Moore	Redknapp	Bennett	Boyce	Hurst	Sissons	
	6/5	**38,424**	*1*	35			*Charlton 2, Crerand 7, Foulkes 10,*	*Stepney*	*Brennan*	*Dunne*	*Crerand*	*Foulkes*	*Stiles*	*Best*	*Law*	*Sadler*	*Charlton*	*Aston*	
							Ref: R Spittle	Upton Park's biggest gate since the war sees Man U clinch the championship. Burkett made a hash of a clearance and Charlton netted. It was soon 0-4. Charles conceded a penalty for No 5, pushing Law after he had been slapped round the face. Crowd trouble erupted at the end.											
41	H	TOTTENHAM	17	L	0-2	0-0		Standen	Burnett	Charles	Bovington	Bickles	Moore	Peters	Boyce	Hurst	Sealey	**Eadie**	
	9/5	35,750	*3*	35			*Greaves 70, Gilzean 89*	*Jennings*	*Kinnear*	*Knowles*	*Mullery*	*England*	*Mackay*	*Robertson*	*Greaves*	*Gilzean*	*Venables*	*Saul*	
							Ref: J Taylor	Spurs' G-men – Greaves and Gilzean – clinched a place in Europe with two smart goals. They extend Spurs unbeaten run to 22 matches, and also inflict a seventh straight loss on the Hammers. Cyril Knowles pushed Hurst over the barrier into the crowd. Spurs have an FA Cup final.											
42	H	MANCHESTER C	16	D	1-1	1-0	Peters 42	Standen	Charles	Kitchener	Peters	Bickles	Moore	Sealey	Boyce	Hartley	Hurst	Eadie	
	13/5	**17,186**	*15*	36			*Bell 75*	*Dowd*	*Book*	*Pardoe*	*Connor*	*Heslop*	*Oakes*	*Summerbee*	*Bell*	*Crossan*	*Young*	*Coleman*	
	Home	Away																	
Average	29,265	33,302					Ref: T Dawes	Doug Eadie crossed low and hard for Martin Peters to net. But West Ham fell to pieces trying to protect their lead and Colin Bell rounded Kitchener to equalise. West Ham earn their first point since 28 March. Standen plays his last game. Ken Brown shortly receives a testimonial.											

League Cup						F-A	H-T	Scorers, Times, and Referees	1	2	3	4	5	6	7	8	9	10	11	12 sub used
2	H	TOTTENHAM		17	W	1-0	1-0	Hurst 8	Standen	Burnett	Charles	Peters	Brown	Moore	Brabrook	Boyce	Bennett	Hurst	Sissons	
		14/9	34,000	4					*Jennings*	*Kinnear*	*Knowles*	*Mullery*	*Beal*	*Clayton*	*Robertson*	*Greaves*	*Gilzean !*	*Venables*	*Saul*	
								Ref: H New	Alan Gilzean is sent off after 65 minutes for verbally abusing a linesman. That did not help Spurs' cause, already trailing to Hurst's seventh goal of the season – thumping home Moore's cross after Beal had failed to clear. Fisticuffs enlivened the North Bank during the interval.											
3	A	ARSENAL		12	W	3-1	1-1	Peters 26, Hurst 52, 55	Standen	Burnett	Charles	Peters	Brown	Moore	Brabrook	Boyce	Byrne	Hurst	Sissons	
		5/10	*33,647*	*14*				*Jenkins 29*	*Furnell*	*Simpson*	*Storey*	*Woodward*	*Ure*	*Boot*	*Coakley*	*Jenkins*	*Walley*	*Sammels*	*Armstrong*	
								Ref: G Roper	West Ham extend their unbeaten run to nine games, but owe a debt to Hurst for a bullet header and a rasping left-foot drive which put the game beyond Arsenal's reach. Earlier Peters had run 25 yards before heading the first goal. Jenkins levelled with an overhead that deceived Standen.											
4	H	LEEDS		14	W	7-0	4-0	Sissons 2, 28, 34, Hurst 41, 60, 73, [Peters 70]	Standen	Bovington	Charles	Peters	Brown	Moore	Brabrook	Boyce	Byrne	Hurst	Sissons	
		7/11	27,474	9					*Harvey*	*Reaney*	*Bell*	*Bremner*	*Charlton*	*Hunter*	*Madeley*	*Belfitt*	*Greenhoff*	*Giles*	*O'Grady*	
								Ref: E Jennings	Six against Fulham on Saturday. Seven v Leeds on Monday. Leeds had won away just once all season. Sissons' hat-trick all came with his left foot. Hurst's hat-trick was of the ballistic sort, but it was only afterwards that it was confirmed that his first goal would not go down to Byrne.											
QF	A	BLACKPOOL		10	W	3-1	2-0	Hurst 2, 25, Byrne 52	Standen	Burnett	Charles	Bovington	Brown	Moore	Boyce	Hurst	Byrne	Peters	Sissons	
		7/12	*15,831*	*22*				*Charnley 59*	*Waiters*	*Armfield*	*Hughes*	*Fisher*	*James*	*McPhee*	*Skirton*	*Robson*	*Charnley*	*Moir*	*Lea*	
								Ref: K Stokes	Hurst's 25th and 26th goals of this prolific season put this tie beyond poor Blackpool. His first is a belter from 18 yards, his second a close-range knock in from Sissons' cross. Blackpool had little luck – Hughes hit the bar from 30 yards – forcing Hammers into desperate defence.											
SF 1	A	WEST BROM		11	L	0-4	0-4		Standen	Burnett	Burkett	Bovington	Brown	Moore	Brabrook	Peters	Byrne	Hurst	Sissons	
		18/1	*29,796*	*20*				*Astle 1, 23, 45, Collard 14*	*Sheppard*	*Cram*	*Williams*	*Collard*	*Jones*	*Fraser*	*Brown*	*Astle*	*Kaye*	*Hope*	*Clark*	
								Ref: J Cattlin	Ken Brown has a stinker, and knows he is partially to blame for the first three goals. Astle headed in after 50 seconds. By half-time it is clear that West Ham won't be contesting an all-London final with QPR and that Moore won't be lifting his fourth trophy at Wembley in four years.											
SF 2	H	WEST BROM		11	D	2-2	2-1	Byrne 13, Hurst 35	Standen	Bovington	Burkett	Peters	Brown	Moore	Brabrook	Boyce	Byrne	Hurst	Sissons	
		8/2	35,790	*20*				*Hope 22, Clark 63*	*Sheppard*	*Cram*	*Williams*	*Collard*	*Jones*	*Fraser*	*Foggo*	*Brown*	*Kaye*	*Hope*	*Clark*	
								Ref: T Dawes (Hammers lose 2-6 on aggregate)	Jimmy Hagan's Albion have to withstand an electric atmosphere inside Upton Park. West Ham set out to retrieve their huge deficit with pride and passion. Hurst was marked by two or three defenders, but escaped to score from Brabrook's cross. Then Clark broke clear down the left.											

FA Cup																				
3	H	SWINDON		9	D	3-3	2-1	Hurst 20, 30, 76	Standen	Bovington	Burkett	Peters	Bickles	Moore	Brabrook	Sealey	Dear	Hurst	Sissons	
		28/1	37,400	*3:8*				*Rogers 26, 71, Brown 59*	*Hicks*	*Thomas*	*Trollope*	*Morgan*	*Nurse*	*Harland*	*Brown*	*Penman*	*Skeen*	*Smart*	*Rogers*	
								Ref: J Osborne	West Ham's biggest gate for seven years looks forward to a contest between Hurst and Swindon's rising superstar Don Rogers. Rogers scores two and makes one for the Division 3 outfit. In the middle of the second half Swindon are on top, but then Peters chips onto Hurst's head.											
3R	A	SWINDON		9	L	1-3	0-1	Sissons 78	Standen	Bovington	Burkett	Peters	Bickles	Moore	Dear	Boyce	Byrne	Hurst	Sissons	
		31/1	*25,789*	*3:8*				*Penman 18, Rogers 84, Skeen 88*	*Hicks*	*Thomas*	*Trollope*	*Morgan*	*Nurse*	*Harland*	*Brown*	*Penman*	*Skeen*	*Smart*	*Rogers*	
								Ref: J Osborne	'This is the blackest month we have known,' admitted Greenwood afterwards. Moore backed off to permit Willie Penman's rocket. Sissons hit the equaliser from a corner taken by the recalled Byrne. Rogers set the stadium alight when diving between Bovington and Standen to score.											

		P	W	D	L	Home F	Home A	W	D	L	Away F	Away A	Pts
1	Manchester U	42	17	4	0	51	13	7	8	6	33	32	60
2	Nott'm Forest	42	16	4	1	41	13	7	6	8	23	28	56
3	Tottenham	42	15	3	3	44	21	9	5	7	27	27	56
4	Leeds	42	15	4	2	41	17	7	7	7	21	25	55
5	Liverpool	42	12	7	2	36	17	7	6	8	28	30	51
6	Everton	42	11	4	6	39	22	8	6	7	26	24	48
7	Arsenal	42	11	6	4	32	20	5	8	8	26	27	46
8	Leicester	42	12	4	5	47	28	6	4	11	31	43	44
9	Chelsea	42	7	9	5	33	29	8	5	8	34	33	44
10	Sheffield Utd	42	11	5	5	34	22	5	5	11	18	37	42
11	Sheffield Wed	42	9	7	5	39	19	5	6	10	17	28	41
12	Stoke	42	11	5	5	40	21	6	2	13	23	37	41
13	West Brom	42	11	1	9	40	28	5	6	10	37	45	39
14	Burnley	42	11	4	6	43	28	4	5	12	23	48	39
15	Manchester C	42	8	9	4	27	25	4	6	11	16	27	39
16	WEST HAM	42	8	6	7	40	31	6	2	13	40	53	36
17	Sunderland	42	12	3	6	39	26	2	5	14	19	46	36
18	Fulham	42	8	7	6	49	34	3	5	13	22	49	34
19	Southampton	42	10	3	8	49	41	4	3	14	25	51	34
20	Newcastle	42	9	5	7	24	27	3	4	14	15	54	33
21	Aston Villa	42	7	5	9	30	33	4	2	15	24	52	29
22	Blackpool	42	1	5	15	18	36	5	4	12	23	40	21
		924	232	110	120	836	551	120	110	232	551	836	924

Odds & ends

Double wins: (3) Sheffield Wed, Blackpool, Aston Villa.
Double losses: (5) Leicester, Everton, Sheff Utd, Leeds, Manchester U.

Won from behind: (4) Sunderland (a), Fulham (h), Villa (h), Burnley (h).
Lost from in front: (1) Leeds (a).

High spots: Reaching semi-final of League Cup.
Beating Leeds 7-0 in League Cup.
Beating Fulham 6-1 in the league.
Scoring 32 goals in just nine league games in November and December.
Only champions Manchester U scored more than Hammers' 80 goals.

Low spots: Losing to Third Division Swindon in FA Cup.
Losing seven league games in a row in April and May.
Conceding six goals at Southampton and at home to Manchester U.
Conceding more league goals than everyone except Southampton and Aston Villa.

Hammer of the Year: Geoff Hurst.
Ever-presents: (0).
Hat-tricks: (4) Geoff Hurst (3), John Sissons (1).
Leading scorer: (41) Geoff Hurst.

	Appearances Lge	*Sub*	LC	*Sub*	FAC	*Sub*	Goals Lge	LC	FAC	Tot
Andrew, George	**2**									
Bennett, Peter	**7**	*1*	1				**1**			**1**
Bickles, Dave	**8**				2					
Bovington, Eddie	**28**		4		2		**1**			**1**
Boyce, Ronnie	**37**		5		2		**4**			**4**
Brabrook, Peter	**32**		5				**5**			**5**
Brown, Ken	**18**		6							
Burkett, Jackie	**11**	*1*	2		2		**1**			**1**
Burnett, Dennis	**24**	*2*	4							
Byrne, Johnny	**25**		5		2		**11**	2		**13**
Charles, John	**31**		4				**1**			**1**
Dawkins, Trevor	**2**	*1*								
Dear, Brian	**4**	*1*			2		**3**			**3**
Eadie, Doug	**2**									
Hartley, Trevor	**2**									
Heffer, Paul	**9**									
Howe, Bobby		*1*								
Hurst, Geoff	**41**		6		2		**29**	9	3	**41**
Kitchener, Bill	**8**									
Mackleworth, Colin	**3**									
Moore, Bobby	**40**		6		2		**2**			**2**
Peters, Martin	**41**		6		2		**14**	2		**16**
Redknapp, Harry	**10**	*2*					**1**			**1**
Sealey, Alan	**4**									
Sissons, John	**34**	*1*	6		2		**7**	3	1	**11**
Standen, Jim	**39**		6		2					
26 players used	**462**	***10***	**66**		**22**		**80**	**16**	**4**	**100**

No	Date	Att	Pos	Pt	F-A	H-T	Scorers, Times, and Referees	1	2	3	4	5	6	7	8	9	10	11	12 sub used
1	H SHEFFIELD WED			L	2-3	0-1	Hurst 58, Peters 60	**Ferguson**	**Bonds**	Charles	Bovington	**Cushley**	Moore	Redknapp	Peters	Hurst	Boyce	Sissons	
	19/8	29,603		0			*Fantham 16, Ritchie 70, McCalliog 88*	*Springett*	*Smith*	*Megson*	*Mobley*	*Ellis*	*Young*	*Fantham*	*McCalliog*	*Ritchie*	*Usher*	*Quinn**	*Eustace*
							Ref: G Roper	Greenwood has splashed out £65,000 on Ferguson and £55,000 on Bonds. Together with other new boy, John Cushley, the defence has been remodelled. West Ham were 2-1 up when the ball came off Cushley's knee to Ritchie. Ferguson then let McCalliog's dolly shot over his head.											
2	H BURNLEY			W	4-2	0-1	Peters 53, Hurst 54, 63, Redknapp 79	Ferguson	Bonds	Charles	Peters	Cushley	Moore	Redknapp	Dear	Hurst	Boyce	Sissons	
	21/8	30,420		2			*Irvine 25, Casper 58*	*Thomson*	*Angus*	*Latcham*	*O'Neil*	*Merrington*	*Todd*	*Morgan*	*Bellamy*	*Irvine*	*Harris*	*Casper*	
							Ref: R Spittle	Great entertainment for the fans, dreadful blunders by both defences. Irvine headed Burnley ahead when Ferguson missed a cross. Peters' 35-yard rocket put West Ham level, before Hurst converted crosses by Redknapp and Sissons. Managerless Coventry are after Ron Greenwood.											
3	A TOTTENHAM		19	L	**1-5**	0-2	Sissons 80 *[Saul 77]*	Ferguson	Bonds	Charles	Peters	Cushley	Moore	Redknapp	Boyce	Hurst	Dear	Sissons	
	26/8	*55,831*	*4*	2			*Greaves 36, 76p, Jones 39, Mullery 68*	*Jennings*	*Kinnear*	*Knowles*	*Mullery*	*England*	*Mackay**	*Robertson*	*Greaves*	*Saul*	*Venables*	*Jones*	*Beal*
							Ref: K Dagnall	Greenwood adopts back to the wall away tactics, with Peters as an auxiliary full-back. But West Ham are blown away from the moment Greaves escapes his marker, John Charles. When Jones headed the second, school-kids invaded the pitch. Bonds felled Greaves for the penalty.											
4	A BURNLEY			D	3-3		Moore 10, Peters 60, Hurst 77	Ferguson	Bonds	Charles	Peters	Cushley	Moore	Redknapp	**Brooking**	Hurst	Boyce	Sissons	
	29/8	*16,620*		3			*Lochead 45, Bellamy 46, Harris 70p*	*Thomson*	*Latcham*	*Buxton*	*O'Neil*	*Angus*	*Bellamy*	*Morgan*	*Lochhead*	*Irvine*	*Harris*	*Casper*	
							Ref: N Callender	Bobby Moore was at the heart of everything, scoring a sweet goal at one end and twice kicking off the line at the other. Volleys by Lochhead and Bellamy, seconds before and seconds after the interval, changed the complexion of the game. Redknapp fouled Latcham for the penalty.											
5	H MANCHESTER U		20	L	1-3	0-0	Peters 78	Ferguson	Bonds*	Charles	Peters	Cushley	Moore	Redknapp	Dear	Hurst	Boyce	Sissons	Brooking
	2/9	**36,562**	*9*	3			*Kidd 53, Sadler 54, Ryan 80*	*Stepney*	*Dunne*	*Burns*	*Crerand*	*Foulkes*	*Stiles*	*Ryan*	*Sadler*	*Charlton*	*Kidd*	*Best*	
							Ref: E Jennings	West Ham had the better of the first half against the defending champions, but Hurst and Dear missed good chances. When Bobby Charlton hooked the ball over Cushley's head to Kidd, the die was cast. Peters headed in Redknapp's corner. 18-year-old sub Brooking caught the eye.											
6	A EVERTON			L	0-2	0-1		Ferguson	Charles	Kitchener	Peters	Cushley	Moore	Redknapp	Brooking	Hurst	Boyce	Sissons	
	5/9	*46,762*		3			*Kendall 35, Young 52*	*West*	*Wright*	*Brown*	*Kendall*	*Labone*	*Harvey*	*Young*	*Ball*	*Royle*	*Hurst*	*Temple*	
							Ref: R Harper	Only Everton's profligacy in front of goal saved Hammers from a hammering. £60,000 signing Howard Kendall scored with a fine header, then hit the post twice. Young dispossessed Peters and shot from 30 yards. Ferguson appeared to have saved it, but appearances can be deceptive.											
7	A SUNDERLAND		16	W	5-1	0-1	Peters 60, Hurst 61, 75, Redknapp 63,	Standen	Charles	Kitchener	Peters	Cushley	Moore	Redknapp	Brooking	Hurst	Boyce	Brabrook	
	9/9	*39,772*	*7*	5			*Moore 12 (og)* [Moore 76]	*Montgomery*	*Parke*	*Ashurst*	*Todd*	*Kinnell*	*Baxter*	*Herd*	*Suggett*	*Martin*	*Heslop*	*Mulhall*	
							Ref: G McCabe	When Moore turned Martin's cross past Ferguson, it seemed Sunderland's unbeaten home record was safe. None could have predicted the second-half turnaround. Peters' scorcher was the first of three goals in three minutes. Both Redknapp and Moore scored with 30-yard bullets.											
8	H WOLVES		20	L	1-2	1-1	Hurst 36	Standen	Charles	Kitchener	Peters	Cushley	Moore	Redknapp	Boyce	Brooking	Hurst	Sissons	
	16/9	30,780	*14*	5			*Dougan 35, 88*	*Parkes*	*Taylor*	*Thomson*	*Bailey*	*Woodfield*	*Holsgrove*	*Wharton*	*Knowles*	*Dougan*	*Evans*	*Wagstaffe*	
							Ref: R Johnson	Derek Dougan spent the match ankle-tapping defenders, in between scoring the goals that brought Wolves only their second win at Upton Park in 12 seasons. The first goal came when Standen missed a cross from 17-year-old Alun Evans; the winner when Dougan sidestepped Cushley.											
9	A FULHAM		16	W	3-0	2-0	Hurst 7, Moore 39, Sissons 89	Ferguson	Bovington	Charles	Peters	Cushley	Moore	Redknapp	Boyce	Brabrook	Hurst	Sissons	
	23/9	*29,234*	*18*	7				*McClelland*	*Cohen**	*Dempsey*	*Ryan*	*Callaghan*	*Conway*	*Brown*	*Moss*	*Clarke*	*Haynes*	*Barrett*	*Earle*
							Ref: R Weedon	Fulham are struggling once again. Only Haynes looks to have any ideas and Craven Cottage starts emptying long before the end. Ferguson did not help his confidence by letting Alan Clarke outjump him twice near the end, but headers by Hurst and Moore had long sealed the result.											
10	H LEEDS		15	D	0-0	0-0		Ferguson	Bonds	Charles	Bovington	Cushley	Moore	Redknapp	Boyce	Hurst	Peters	Brabrook	
	30/9	29,740	*9*	8				*Sprake*	*Reaney*	*Madeley*	*Bremner*	*Charlton*	*Hunter*	*Greenhoff*	*Lorimer*	*Jones*	*Gray*	*Cooper*	
							Ref: R Kirkpatrick	England boss Alf Ramsey watches a match policed exuberantly by referee Roger Kirkpatrick, whose high-stepping Tiller Girl antics have the crowd in stitches. Leeds were in almost total control by the end, but somehow could not force the goal their abundant possession merited.											

11	H	STOKE		17	L	3-4	3-0	Hurst 24, 40, Peters 35	Ferguson	Bonds	Charles	Peters	Cushley	Moore	Redknapp	Bovington	Brabrook	Hurst	Sissons	
		7/10	24,471	*8*	8			*Burrows 65, 72, Dobing 67, 72*	*Banks*	*Skeels*	*Bentley*	*Palmer*	*Bloor**	*Allen*	*Bridgwood*	*Eastham*	*Dobing*	*Vernon*	*Burrows*	*Bernard*
								Ref: C Nicholls	A catastrophic collapse. Upton Park echoed to the chants of 'easy, easy' in the first half, as Hurst's side-foot and header and Peters' hook made it 3-0. But Stoke plundered four goals in seven minutes, with Hammers' defence standing like statues pointing accusing fingers at each other.											
12	A	LIVERPOOL		19	L	1-3	0-2	Peters 75	Ferguson	Bonds	Charles	Peters	Cushley	Moore	Redknapp	Boyce	Brabrook	Hurst	Sissons	
		14/10	*46,951*	*1*	8			*St John 14, 37, Smith 68*	*Lawrence*	*Lawler*	*Byrne*	*Smith*	*Yeats*	*Hughes*	*Callaghan*	*Hunt*	*Hateley*	*St John*	*Thompson*	
								Ref: I Thacker	West Ham set out with a safety-first approach, which was rendered useless once Ian St John was left unmarked to poach an easy goal. Worse was to come when Tommy Smith robbed Sissons and sent a 40-yard cross over Ferguson's head. Hammers only came to life when 0-3 down.											
13	H	SOUTHAMPTON		19	L	0-1	0-1		Ferguson	Bonds	Charles	Peters	Cushley	Moore	Redknapp	Bovington	Brabrook	Hurst	Sissons	
		23/10	32,550	*10*	8			*Paine 11*	*Martin*	*Jones*	*Hollywood*	*Fisher*	*Webb*	*Walker*	*Paine*	*Chivers*	*Davies*	*Melia*	*Gabriel*	
								Ref: K Walker	Both sides set their sights on mutual destruction in this Monday night match. West Ham were no angels, kicking Ron Davies over the wall into the crowd. The goal came when Ferguson pushed Gabriel's shot out to Paine, who scored from a tight angle. Saints conceded corners a-plenty.											
14	A	CHELSEA		18	W	3-1	1-1	Dear 9, Hurst 53, Peters 69	Ferguson	Bonds	Charles	Peters	Cushley	Moore	Burkett	Boyce	Brabrook	Hurst	Dear	
		28/10	*40,303*	*19*	10			*Osgood 17*	*Bonetti*	*Butler*	*McCreadie*	*Hollins*	*Hinton*	*Harris*	*Fascione*	*Baldwin*	*Osgood*	*Boyle*	*Cook*	
								Ref: J Finney	Greenwood rings the changes and switches to 4-3-3, pushing Bobby Moore into midfield. Dave Sexton's Chelsea are sunk by the power of Hurst, who made two goals and headed the other from Moore's cross. Peter Osgood's fantastic solo goal brought Stamford Bridge to its feet.											
15	A	NEWCASTLE		19	L	0-1	0-0		Ferguson	Bonds	Burkett	Charles	Cushley	Peters	Brabrook	Brooking	Hurst	Boyce	Sissons	
		11/11	*32,850*	*9*	10			*Davies 69*	*Marshall*	*Burton*	*Clarke*	*Elliott*	*McNamee*	*Moncur*	*Scott*	*Bennett*	*Davies*	*Iley*	*Robson*	
								Ref: F Nicholson	Newcastle extend their unbeaten run to 16 games thanks to Wyn Davies' towering header. Brooking conceded a needless free-kick. Iley took it, Ferguson didn't get to it and Wyn Davies did. Brabrook missed two easy chances in the first half. Newcastle have dropped just one home point.											
16	H	MANCHESTER C		20	L	2-3	1-2	Peters 29, Hurst 78	Ferguson	**Lampard**	Burkett	Peters	Cushley	Moore	Redknapp	Boyce	Brabrook	Hurst	Sissons	
		18/11	25,425	*3*	10			*Lee 24, 60, Summerbee 28*	*Mulhearn*	*Book*	*Pardoe*	*Doyle*	*Heslop*	*Oakes*	*Lee*	*Bell*	*Summerbee*	*Young*	*Coleman*	
								Ref: W Gow	This defeat leaves West Ham with the worst home record in all four divisions. Not the sort of match in which to give 19-year-old Frank Lampard his debut. Francis Lee and Tony Coleman gave him a baptism of fire. Star of the show was undoubtedly Lee, with two super goals.											
17	A	ARSENAL		20	D	0-0	0-0		Ferguson	Bonds	Burkett	Peters	Cushley	Moore	Redknapp	Brabrook	Hurst	Boyce	Sissons	
		25/11	*42,029*	*8*	11				*Furnell*	*Storey*	*McNab*	*McLintock*	*Neill*	*Simpson*	*Radford*	*Johnston*	*Graham*	*Sammels*	*Armstrong*	
								Ref: N Burtenshaw	Hurst played in midfield to disguise a painful foot injury and also to reinforce a packed defence. Arsenal spent the entire match battering the Hammers goal and late on Ferguson saved from McLintock from point-blank range. Arsenal, unbeaten at home, fail to score for the first time.											
18	H	SHEFFIELD UTD		20	W	3-0	2-0	Sissons 5, 62, Brabrook 33	Standen	Bonds	Burkett	Peters	Heffer	Moore	Redknapp	Boyce	Brabrook	Hurst	Sissons	
		2/12	22,510	*22*	13				*Hodgkinson*	*Badger*	*Shaw*	*Munks*	*Mallender*	*Barlow**	*Woodward*	*Carlin*	*Hill*	*Addison*	*Reece*	*Wagstaff*
								Ref: D Corbett	Sissons scored both his goals with his right foot, a rarity. Detroit-bound Jim Standen steps in for the flu-stricken Ferguson. The Blades go bottom as a result of this defeat, which was hard on them. Colin Addison twice hit the woodwork. West Ham's first home win since August.											
19	A	COVENTRY		20	D	1-1	1-1	Hurst 30	Ferguson	Charles	Burkett	Peters	Bonds	Moore	Redknapp	Boyce	Brabrook	Hurst	Sissons	
		8/12	*28,393*	*22*	14			*Baker 8*	*Glazier*	*Kearns*	*Bruck*	*Coop*	*Setters*	*Clements*	*Hannigan*	*Gibson*	*Baker*	*Machin*	*Rees*	
								Ref: J Osborne	Jimmy Hill's promoted Coventry have won only twice all season. Both managers, Greenwood and Cantwell, wanted this Friday night match postponed on account of the thick snow. Baker headed in Gibson's corner. Sissons hit the bar before Hurst chested down Peters' free-kick.											
20	H	WEST BROM			L	2-3	1-0	Hurst 7p, Brabrook 85	Ferguson	Charles	Burkett	Peters	Bonds	Moore	Redknapp	Boyce	Brabrook	Hurst*	Sissons	Bennett
		11/12	**18,340**		14			*Kryzwicki 50, Astle 78, Hope 87p*	*Osborne*	*Colquhoun*	*Williams*	*Brown*	*Talbut*	*Fraser*	*Kryzwicki*	*Kaye*	*Astle*	*Hope*	*Clark*	
								Ref: H New	West Ham's seventh home defeat was watched by their smallest crowd. They ended up making their own entertainment, booing or cheering, whoever was in possession. Brown shoved Sissons for Hurst's penalty. Albion's spot-kick came when Peter Bennett impeded Kryzwicki.											
21	A	SHEFFIELD WED		19	L	1-4	1-3	Dear 24	Ferguson	Charles	Burkett	Bonds	Cushley	Bovington	Dear	Boyce	Brooking	Hurst	Sissons	
		16/12	*24,003*	*5*	14			*Ritchie 22, 43, F'ntham 32, Whit'm 59*	*Springett*	*Smith*	*Megson*	*Mobley*	*Ellis*	*Young*	*Whitham*	*Fantham*	*Ritchie*	*McCalliog*	*Branfoot*	
								Ref: P Baldwin	Wednesday forced Hammers to change kit, lending them body-hugging white shirts that squeezed the life out of the players. The Owls are now unbeaten at home in 19 games. West Ham's only consolation was to score the best goal of the match – Brian Dear's swerving left-footer.											

No Date	Att	Pos	Pt	F-A	H-T	Scorers, Times, and Referees	1	2	3	4	5	6	7	8	9	10	11	12 sub used
22 H TOTTENHAM		19	W	2-1	1-1	Bonds 26, Dear 75	Ferguson	Bonds	Lampard	Peters	Cushley	Moore	Dear	Boyce	Brooking	Hurst	Sissons	
23/12	32,116	*10*	16			*Robertson 39*	*Jennings*	*Kinnear*	*Knowles*	*Mullery*	*Beal*	*Mackay*	*Robertson*	*Greaves**	*Saul*	*Bond*	*Jones*	*Venables*
						Ref: P Walters	West Ham avenge August's 1-5 thrashing in a hot-tempered affair. Jennings' helped Bonds' 25-yarder into the net. Ferguson and Cushley collided with each other going for Mackay's free-kick, and Robertson equalised. Dear's was a messy winner. Greaves went off with a cut eye.											
23 H LEICESTER		17	W	4-2	2-2	Dear 32, 61, 74, Brooking 40	Ferguson	Bonds	Lampard	Peters	Cushley	Moore	Dear	Boyce	Brooking	Hurst	Sissons	
26/12	26,520	*18*	18			*Large 8, Sinclair 12*	*Shilton*	*Rodrigues*	*Bell*	*Roberts*	*Sjoberg*	*Nish*	*Tewley*	*Large*	*Stringfellow*	*Gibson*	*Sinclair*	
						Ref: R Pritchard	For half an hour West Ham looked a defensive shambles. Large's header and Sinclair's chip gave Leicester a two-goal lead, but when Dear rounded Shilton it sparked an epic fight-back. Hurst squared for Brooking to equalise with his first ever league goal. Dear back-heeled No 3.											
24 A LEICESTER		14	W	4-2	1-2	Brooking 8, Dear 55, 87, Sissons 64	Ferguson	Bonds	Lampard	Peters	Cushley	Moore	Dear	Boyce	Brooking	Hurst	Sissons	
30/12	*24,589*	*18*	20			*Svarc 21, Large 42*	*Shilton*	*Rodrigues*	*Bell*	*Roberts*	*Sjoberg*	*Nish*	*Tewley*	*Large*	*Svarc*	*Gibson*	*Glover*	
						Ref: R Harper	A repeat score, once again after West Ham had trailed. Youth internationals Lampard and Brooking are behind the 4-3-3 revival of Hammers' fortunes, plus the scoring feats of overweight Dear. Sissons scores direct from a corner. West Ham's first win at Filbert Street since 1948.											
25 A MANCHESTER U		15	L	1-3	1-1	Brooking 22	Ferguson	Bonds	Lampard	Peters	Cushley	Moore	Dear	Boyce	Brooking	Hurst	Brabrook	
6/1	***58,598***	*1*	20			*Charlton 11, Best 50, Aston 75*	*Stepney*	*Dunne*	*Burns*	*Crerand*	*Sadler*	*Fitzpatrick*	*Best*	*Kidd*	*Charlton*	*Law*	*Aston*	
						Ref: K Howley	Bobby Charlton celebrates his 400th league game for Man U with a 20-yarder. Dear's cross set up Trevor Brooking's equaliser. George Best somehow got in a scoring header despite being surrounded by defenders. The defending champions are now unbeaten at home in 36 games.											
26 A WOLVES		18	W	2-1	0-0	Dear 47, Hurst 52	Ferguson	Bonds	Lampard	Peters	Cushley	Moore	Dear	Boyce	Brooking	Hurst	Sissons	
20/1	*32,273*	*17*	22			*Dougan 88*	*Williams*	*Taylor*	*Wilson*	*Bailey*	*Woodfield*	*Holsgrove*	*Kenning*	*Knowles*	*Dougan*	*Munro*	*Farrington*	
						Ref: G McCabe	Wolves crash to their sixth successive defeat. Two quick-fire headers early in the second half reduce the Molineux crowd to numbed silence. Hurst's was his first goal in two months. The result was signed and sealed long before Derek Dougan turned in a low centre as a consolation.											
27 H FULHAM		16	W	**7-2**	3-1	Dear 30, Brooking 42, 43, Moore 49, [Hurst 54, 78,]	Ferguson	Bonds	Lampard	Peters	Cushley	Moore	Dear	Boyce	Brooking	Hurst	Sissons	
3/2	31,248	*22*	24			*Earle 18, Clarke 69*	*Macedo*	*Drake*	*Dempsey*	*Brown*	*Ryan*	*Conway*	*Haynes*	*Earle*	*Gilroy*	*Clarke*	*Barrett*	
						Ref: D Lyden [Peters 63]	Fulham had the cheek to score first – Haynes setting up Steve Earle. There seemed little chance of West Ham matching last season's 6-1 win. When Peters made it 6-1 this time there was still nearly half an hour to play. Fulham's new boss, Bobby Robson, knows his team are doomed.											
28 A LEEDS		16	L	1-2	1-1	Dear 43	Ferguson	Bonds	Lampard	Peters	Cushley	Moore	Dear	Bennett	Brooking	Hurst	Sissons	
10/2	*41,814*	*2*	24			*Lorimer 4, 49*	*Sprake*	*Reaney*	*Cooper*	*Bremner*	*Madeley*	*Hunter*	*Greenhoff*	*Lorimer*	*Belfitt*	*Giles*	*Gray*	
						Ref: W Handley	Moore's early slip not only presents a goal for Peter Lorimer, it also sets up a refrain of 'Hunter for England' from the crowd. When Lorimer restored the lead from a fortunate rebound, Leeds exhibited all that was worst about Revie's team. Time-wasting at the corner flag by Giles.											
29 A STOKE		16	L	0-2	0-0		Ferguson	Bonds	Lampard	Peters	Cushley	Moore	Dear	Bennett	Brooking	Hurst	Sissons	
26/2	***16,092***	*15*	24			*Dobing 50, Mahoney 51*	*Banks*	*Elder*	*Bentley*	*Moore*	*Bloor*	*Stevenson*	*Conroy*	*Eastham*	*Dobing*	*Mahoney*	*Burrows*	
						Ref: R Pritchard	Stoke enjoy swift revenge for their FA Cup loss. When Terry Conroy reached up and grabbed the ball inside the box the ref gave a free-kick outside it. Two quick goals sealed West Ham's fate. First, Cushley's miscued pass fell to Eastham, who fed Dobing. Mahoney volleyed No 2.											
30 A SOUTHAMPTON		19	D	0-0	0-0		Ferguson	Bonds	Lampard	Peters	**Stephenson**	Moore	Dear	Boyce	Brooking	Hurst	Sissons	
16/3	*27,734*	*15*	25				*Martin*	*Kirkup*	*Jones*	*Walker*	*McGrath*	*Gabriel*	*Channon*	*Saul*	*Davies*	*Paine*	*Sydenham*	
						Ref: L Callaghan	On a bone hard pitch, Hurst and Dear missed so many chances that Saints fans jeered and applauded them. One of Hurst's misses was so bad – skying over – that no one could believe it. Max Marquis wrote : 'Southampton were so bad they couldn't have won with an Act of Parliament.'											
31 H CHELSEA		19	L	0-1	0-1		Ferguson	Bonds	Lampard	Peters	Stephenson	Moore	Dear	Boyce	Brooking	Hurst	Sissons	
23/3	36,301	*9*	25			*Osgood 4*	*Bonetti*	*Harris*	*McCreadie*	*Boyle*	*Hinton*	*Hollins*	*Cooke*	*Tambling*	*Osgood*	*Birchenall*	*Houseman*	
						Ref: J Finney	Even though they are struggling, only two teams have scored more goals than West Ham. You would not have guessed it, from the way Ron Harris snuffed out Hurst. Hinton also kept Dear in his pocket. Alf Ramsey admired Osgood's sweet turn and shot. Ferguson dived over the top.											

No	Date	Opponent / Att	Pos	Res	Pts	F-A	H-T	Scorers, Times, and Referees	1	2	3	4	5	6	7	8	9	10	11	subs used
32	H	ARSENAL	19	D		1-1	1-1	Brooking 13	Ferguson	Bonds	Lampard	Peters	Stephenson	Moore	Redknapp	Boyce	Brooking	Dear	Sissons	
	29/3	33,942	*11*	26				*Armstrong 3*	*Wilson*	*McNab*	*Storey*	*McLintock*	*Neill*	*Simpson*	*Radford*	*Gould*	*Graham*	*Court*	*Armstrong*	
								Ref: H Davey	Arsenal's ferocious tackling threatened a shortage of stretchers. Not to be intimidated, West Ham gave as good as they got in the second half. The Gunners' goal was a joke, Armstrong's cross squeezing past Ferguson, who was deceived by Graham's dummy. Lampard set up Brocking.											
33	H	NEWCASTLE	17	W		5-0	1-0	Brooking 25, 64, 75, Sissons 58, 89	Ferguson	Bonds	Lampard	Peters	Stephenson	Moore	Redknapp	Boyce	Brooking	Dear	Sissons	
	6/4	27,780	*7*	28					*Marshall*	*Burton*	*Clark*	*Iley*	*McNamee*	*Moncur*	*Sinclair*	*Scott*	*Davies*	*Robson B*	*Robson T*	
								Ref: T Dawes	On a sun-drenched pitch, high-flying Newcastle are put to the sword. The result is even more surprising as Hammers were without the injured Hurst. Marshall 'lost' Redknapp's free-kick and Brooking pounced. Sissons' header made it 2-0. Brooking's volley completed his hat-trick.											
34	H	NOTT'M FOREST	15	W		3-0	1-0	Sissons 4, Dear 46, 55	Ferguson	Bonds	Lampard	Peters	Stephenson	Moore	Redknapp	Boyce	Brooking	Dear	Sissons	
	12/4	36,589	*10*	30					*Williamson*	*Hindley*	*Winfield*	*Baxter**	*McKinlay*	*Newton*	*Lyons*	*Barnwell*	*Baker*	*Storey-Moore*	*Hall*	*Hilley*
								Ref: K Dagnall	A Good Friday thriller. Hurst was fit enough to be named substitute, which meant the strikers played out of their skins to stop him coming on. John Sissons played in the middle and volleyed in Brooking's cross. The third goal came when Williamson's goal-kick went straight to Dear.											
35	A	MANCHESTER C	15	L		0-3	0-1		Ferguson	Bonds	Lampard	Peters	Stephenson	Moore	Redknapp	Boyce	Brooking*	Dear	Hurst	Charles
	13/4	*38,754*	*3*	30				*Young 12, 58, Doyle 82*	*Mulhearn*	*Book*	*Pardoe*	*Kennedy*	*Heslop*	*Oakes*	*Lee*	*Doyle*	*Summerbee*	*Young*	*Coleman*	
								Ref: W Handley	Joe Mercer's City are third now, but will finish champions. Hurst only got his place back because John Sissons was conveniently injured. Tony Coleman's cross was turned in by Young, whose second goal was set up by a pass from Francis Lee, who was lying on his back at the time.											
36	A	NOTT'M FOREST		D		1-1	0-1	Peters 51	Ferguson	Bonds	Lampard	Peters	Stephenson	Moore	Redknapp	Boyce	Hurst	Dear	Sissons	
	16/4	*22,198*		31				*Baker 32*	*Williamson*	*Brindley*	*Winfield*	*Hindley*	*McKinlay*	*Newton*	*Lyons*	*Baxter*	*Baker*	*Storey-Moore*	*Hilley*	
								Ref: R Spittle	Baker's goal came totally against the run of play, when Lyons' cross somehow bypassed the whole West Ham defence. Peters levelled in a goal-mouth scramble following a corner. Williamson had a great game in goal for Forest. The recuperating Hurst managed to hit the crossbar.											
37	H	LIVERPOOL	15	W		1-0	1-0	Peters 40	Ferguson	Bonds	Lampard	Peters	Stephenson	Moore	Redknapp	Boyce	Dear	Hurst	Sissons	
	20/4	33,060	*4*	33					*Lawrence*	*Lawler*	*Hughes*	*Smith*	*Yeats*	*Wall*	*Callaghan*	*Hunt*	*Hateley**	*St John*	*Thompson*	*Livermore*
								Ref: P Bye	Alf Ramsey watches Moore and Peters at their best. Hurst's lack of fitness saw him play in midfield, but he still forced Tommy Lawrence to pull off the save of the match. Peters ran in on the blind side to head in Redknapp's cross. This defeat puts the nail in Liverpool's title hopes.											
38	H	SUNDERLAND	14	D		1-1	0-1	Dear 72	Ferguson	Bonds	Lampard	Brooking	Stephenson	Moore	Redknapp	Boyce	Dear	Hurst	Sissons	
	24/4	29,153	*17*	34				*Mulhall 10*	*Montgomery*	*Harvey*	*Ashurst*	*Hurley*	*Kinnell*	*Todd*	*Harris*	*Herd*	*Brand*	*Suggett*	*Mulhall*	
								Ref: I Jones	Ferguson stretched for Herd's cross, missed it, and Mulhall netted from three yards. White-shirted Sunderland then stood back and watched West Ham demonstrate their ability to miss chances by the dozen. Brian Dear glanced home the equaliser from Bobby Moore's corner-kick.											
39	A	SHEFFIELD UTD	11	W		2-1	1-0	Hurst 9, 74	Ferguson	Bonds	Lampard*	Peters	Stephenson	Moore	Redknapp	Boyce	Brooking	Hurst	Sissons	Dear
	27/4	*19,530*	*20*	36				*Reece 67*	*Hodgkinson*	*Badger*	*Shaw*	*Munks*	*Wagstaff*	*Barlow*	*Woodward*	*Carlin*	*Currie*	*Fenoughty*	*Reece*	
								Ref: E Jennings	Four minutes from time Frank Lampard emerges from a collision with Willie Carlin with a broken right leg. The crack could be heard all around the ground. The good news is that Hurst is back to form, volleying his first goal, hooking the second over Alan Hodgkinson's head.											
40	A	WEST BROM	12	L		1-3	1-2	Peters 3	Ferguson	Bonds	Charles	Peters	Cushley	Moore	Dear	Boyce	Brooking	Hurst	Sissons	
	1/5	*25,009*	*7*	36				*Astle 21, 29, 53*	*Osborne*	*Clark*	*Fairfax*	*Lovett*	*Talbut*	*Kaye*	*Rees*	*Collard*	*Astle*	*Hope*	*Hartford*	
								Ref: K Dagnall	The uncapped Jeff Astle scores his second hat-trick in three days. WBA's supporters don't like the fact that Hurst, who had a poor game, is the incumbent England No 9. Martin Peters' early header only served to light the touch-paper under Astle, whose first two goals were headers.											
41	H	COVENTRY	12	D		0-0	0-0		Ferguson	Bonds	Howe	Peters	Stephenson	Moore	Redknapp	Boyce	Dear	Hurst	Sissons	
	4/5	30,180	*19*	37					*Glazier*	*Bruck*	*Cattlin*	*Hill*	*Setters*	*Clements*	*Hannigan*	*Machin*	*Martin*	*Tudor*	*Carr*	
								Ref: W Gow	It's nip and tuck for Coventry down at the bottom. They man the barricades, determined only to keep West Ham out, and this point gained will ultimately keep them up. They might have won had they not wasted two early headers. At the death Ernie Machin hit the bar from 30 yards.											
42	H	EVERTON	12	D		1-1	0-1	Peters 63	Ferguson	Bonds	Howe	Peters	Stephenson	Moore	Redknapp	Boyce	Brooking	Dear	Sissons	
	11/5	28,880	*5*	38				*Husband 23*	*Barnett*	*Wright*	*Brown*	*Kendall*	*Kenyon*	*Harvey*	*Humphries*	*Husband*	*Young*	*Hurst*	*Morrissey*	
	Home	Away						Ref: M Fussey	Everton, headed for the FA Cup final, leave out West, Ball, Royle, Labone, and Wilson. But West Ham showed few signs of superiority and Bonds has a stinker. Peters' volley, which went in off a defender, averted defeat. Had Hammers won they would have finished in the top half.											
Average	29,818	33,778																		

League Cup			F-A	H-T	Scorers, Times, and Referees	1	2	3	4	5	6	7	8	9	10	11	12 sub used
2 A WALSALL	16	W	5-1	3-0	Brabrook 2, Peters 22, 83, Hurst 44p,	Standen	Charles	Kichener	Peters	Cushley	Moore	Redknapp	Boyce	Brabrook	Hurst	Sissons	
13/9 *17,752*	*3:7*				*Jackson 73p* [Evans 86 (og)]	*Ball*	*Gregg*	*Evans*	*Simpson*	*Bennett*	*Atthey*	*Middleton**	*Baker*	*Murray*	*McMorran*	*Taylor*	*Jackson*
					Ref: R Egan	Third Division Walsall had 12 shots to West Ham's four in the first half, but Hammers led 3-0. Both sides scored a penalty. Boyce fouled Baker for Walsall's; Evans tripped Peters from behind for West Ham's. The luckless Evans also put through his own goal. It wasn't his night.											
3 H BOLTON	17	W	4-1	3-1	Hurst 11, 14, 38p, 65	Ferguson	Bonds	Charles	Peters	Cushley	Moore	Redknapp	Boyce	Brabrook	Hurst	Sissons	
11/10 20,510	*2:12*				*Byrom 6*	*Hopkinson*	*Hatton*	*Farrimond*	*Ritson*	*Hulme*	*Greaves*	*Rimmer*	*Bromley*	*Byrom*	*Hill*	*Taylor*	
					Ref: G Roper	Hurst takes his tally in this competition over the past three years to 25. He was unmarked for his first two headers, extraordinarily generous of Bolton, who led after Gordon Taylor's shot came back off the bar. Handball on the line gave Hurst his hat-trick, admired by Alf Ramsey.											
4 A HUDDERSFIELD	18	L	0-2	0-1		Ferguson	Bonds	Charles	Peters	Cushley	Moore	Burkett	Boyce*	Brabrook	Hurst	Dear	Redknapp
1/11 *17,729*	*2:17*				*Worthington 2, Cattlin 70*	*Oldfield*	*Parkin*	*Cattlin*	*Nicholson*	*Ellam*	*Meagan*	*Hellawell*	*Dobson*	*Worthington*	*McGill*	*Hill*	
					Ref: Lyden	Lowly Second Division side Huddersfield expel Hammers from the League Cup. 19-year-old Frank Worthington couldn't believe his luck when Ferguson missed Cattlin's early cross. Ferguson was also at fault with Chris Cattlin's 25-yarder which many keepers would have saved.											

FA Cup																	
3 A BURNLEY	16	W	3-1	1-1	Dear 23, Peters 50, 55	Ferguson	Bonds	Lampard	Peters	Cushley	Moore	Dear	Boyce	Brooking	Hurst	Sissons	
27/1 *23,452*	*12*				*Casper 15*	*Thomson*	*Ternent*	*Latcham*	*O'Neil*	*Waldron*	*Merrington*	*Morgan*	*Lochhead*	*Casper*	*Bellamy**	*Coates*	*Irvine*
					Ref: K Howley	Burnley might have been more than one goal ahead by the time West Ham got going. Ferguson made save after save from shoot-on-sight full-back Latcham. The referee pulled a muscle in the opening seconds. Yet Latcham helped Peters' free-kick on its way to put West Ham in front.											
4 A STOKE	16	W	3-0	1-0	Sissons 2, 77, Hurst 86	Ferguson	Bonds	Lampard	Peters	Cushley	Moore	Dear	Bennett	Brooking	Hurst	Sissons	
17/2 *36,704*	*15*					*Banks*	*Skeels*	*Bloor*	*Allen*	*Elder*	*Mahoney**	*Dobing*	*Stevenson*	*Palmer*	*Vernon*	*Burrows*	*Eastham*
					Ref: J Carr	Alf Ramsey must have been impressed with Bonds, who rampaged down the right flank throughout the match. Sissons scored his first goal at the second attempt, after Banks had parried. Hurst was then brought down but drove the penalty against the bar. He atoned with a 30-yarder.											
5 H SHEFFIELD UTD	18	L	1-2	1-1	Dear 43	Ferguson	Bonds	Lampard	Peters	Cushley	Moore	Dear	Bennett	Brooking	Hurst	Sissons	
9/3 38,440	*19*				*Cliff 33, 84*	*Hodgkinson*	*Badger*	*Shaw*	*Munks*	*Mallender*	*Barlow*	*Cliff*	*Carlin*	*Hill*	*Wagstaff T*	*Reece*	
					Ref: L Hamer	Blades boss John Harris admits: 'We love playing West Ham'. The Hammers were so dire that Greenwood left his seat in the directors' box to come down to the dug-out. Moore found himself playing centre-forward. To no avail. Cliff scored No 1 with a long-range looping header.											

		Home					Away					
	P	W	D	L	F	A	W	D	L	F	A	Pts
1 Manchester C	42	17	2	2	52	16	9	4	8	34	27	58
2 Manchester U	42	15	2	4	49	21	9	6	6	40	34	56
3 Liverpool	42	17	2	2	51	17	5	9	7	20	23	55
4 Leeds	42	17	3	1	49	14	5	6	10	22	27	53
5 Everton	42	18	1	2	43	13	5	5	11	24	27	52
6 Chelsea	42	11	7	3	34	25	7	5	9	28	43	48
7 Tottenham	42	11	7	3	44	20	8	2	11	26	39	47
8 West Brom	42	12	4	5	45	25	5	8	8	30	37	46
9 Arsenal	42	12	6	3	37	23	5	4	12	23	33	44
10 Newcastle	42	12	7	2	38	20	1	8	12	16	47	41
11 Nott'm Forest	42	11	6	4	34	22	3	5	13	18	42	39
12 WEST HAM	42	8	5	8	43	30	6	5	10	30	39	38
13 Leicester	42	7	7	7	37	34	6	5	10	27	35	38
14 Burnley	42	12	7	2	38	16	2	3	16	26	55	38
15 Sunderland	42	8	7	6	28	28	5	4	12	23	33	37
16 Southampton	42	9	8	4	37	31	4	3	14	29	52	37
17 Wolves	42	10	4	7	45	36	4	4	13	21	39	36
18 Stoke	42	10	3	8	30	29	4	4	13	20	44	35
19 Sheffield Wed	42	6	10	5	32	24	5	2	14	19	39	34
20 Coventry	42	8	5	8	32	32	1	10	10	19	39	33
21 Sheffield Utd	42	7	4	10	25	31	4	6	11	24	39	32
22 Fulham	42	6	4	11	27	41	4	3	14	29	57	27
	924	244	111	107	850	548	107	111	244	548	850	924

Odds & ends

Double wins: (3) Fulham, Sheffield Utd, Leicester.
Double losses: (5) Sheff Wed, Man U, Man C, Stoke, WBA.

Won from behind: (7) Burnley (h), Sunderland (a), Leicester (h&a), Fulham (h), Bolton LC (h), Burnley FAC (a).
Lost from in front: (4) Sheff W (h), Stoke (h), WBA (h&a).

High spots: Five league wins out of six, December to February.
Beating Fulham 7-2.

Low spots: West Ham lost four times to the two Manchester clubs.
Following the 7-2 win over Fulham by failing to win any of their next five games
Losing in the FA Cup to Second Division Huddersfield.

West Ham did the double over Sheff Utd but lost to them in the FA Cup.

Hammer of the Year: Bobby Moore.
Ever-presents: (0).
Hat-tricks: (3) Brian Dear, Trevor Brooking, Geoff Hurst.
Leading scorer: (25) Geoff Hurst.

	Appearances						Goals			
	Lge	*Sub*	LC	*Sub*	FAC	*Sub*	Lge	LC	FAC	Tot
Bennett, Peter	2	*1*			2					
Bonds, Billy	37		2		3		1			1
Bovington, Eddie	6									
Boyce, Ronnie	38		3		1					
Brabrook, Peter	14		3				2	1		3
Brooking, Trevor	24	*1*			3		9			9
Burkett, Jackie	8		1							
Charles, John	19	*1*	3							
Cushley, John	27		3		3					
Dear, Brian	25	*1*	1		3		14		2	16
Ferguson, Bobby	39		2		3					
Heffer, Paul	1									
Howe, Bobby	2									
Hurst, Geoff	38		3		3		19	5	1	25
Kitchener, Bill	3		1							
Lampard, Frank	19				3					
Moore, Bobby	40		3		3		4			4
Peters, Martin	40		3		3		14	2	2	18
Redknapp, Harry	28		2	*1*			2			2
Sissons, John	37		2		3		8		2	10
Standen, Jim	3		1							
Stephenson, Alan	12									
(own-goals)								1		1
22 players used	**462**	***4***	**33**	***1***	**33**		**73**	**9**	**7**	**89**

LEAGUE DIVISION 1

Manager: Ron Greenwood

SEASON 1968-69

No	Date	Opponent	Att	Pos	Pt	F-A	H-T	Scorers, Times, and Referees	1	2	3	4	5	6	7	8	9	10	11	12 sub used
1	A	NEWCASTLE			D	1-1	0-0	Dear 90	Ferguson	Bonds	Charles*	Peters	Stephenson	Moore	Redknapp	Boyce	Dear	Hurst	Brooking	Sissons
	10/8		*36,830*		1			*Robson 50*	*McFaul*	*Craig*	*Clark*	*Elliott*	*McNamee*	*Burton*	*Robson B*	*Bennett**	*Davies*	*Ross*	*Sinclair*	*Robson T*
								Ref: R Harper	There is great expectation attending the Hammers this season, but they have only won at Newcastle once in 36 attempts. Dave Elliott turned the ball back for Pop Robson to score. In injury-time Peters miscued Redknapp's low cross against a post and Brian Dear pounced on the rebound.											
2	A	STOKE			W	2-0	0-0	Peters 59, Sissons 86	Ferguson	Bonds	Charles	Peters	Stephenson	Moore	Redknapp	Boyce	Dear	Hurst	Sissons	
	14/8		*22,131*		3				*Banks*	*Skeels*	*Elder*	*Allen*	*Bloor*	*Stevenson*	*Conroy*	*Dobing*	*Herd*	*Eastham*	*Burrows*	
								Ref: L Callaghan	Two of Division 1's lightweights collide, and Stoke prove to be featherweights. Peters strolled through their defence to collect Sissons' shrewd pass. Sissons skated away on his own to seal the win, though David Herd narrowly missed two late chances. Bonds and Dobing were booked.											
3	H	NOTT'M FOREST		2	W	1-0	1-0	Hurst 13	Ferguson	Bonds	Charles	Peters	Stephenson	Moore	Redknapp	Boyce	Dear	Hurst	Sissons	
	17/8		31,114	*16*	5				*Williamson*	*Hindley*	*Winfield*	*Hennessey*	*McKinlay*	*Newton*	*Lyons*	*Richardson*	*Baker*	*Baxter*	*Moore*	
								Ref: T Lockett	West Ham opened with a roar, finished with a whimper. Johnny Carey's Forest could have been swept away by half-time, but lost to a messy goal. Peters' shot flew off Newton's leg onto the bar and rebounded to Hurst. Another Hurst shot hit the keeper in the face and k.o.'d him.											
4	H	EVERTON			L	1-4	0-1	Peters 51	Ferguson	Bonds	Charles	Peters	Stephenson	Moore	Redknapp	Boyce	Dear*	Hurst	Sissons	Brooking
	19/8		34,895		5			*Husband 14, Royle 63, Ball 70, [Harvey 88]*	*West*	*Wright*	*Brown*	*Kendall*	*Labone*	*Harvey*	*Husband*	*Ball*	*Royle*	*Hurst*	*Morrissey*	
								Ref: I Jones	The Hammers would have gone top had they won. They looked good going forward but dreadful in defence. Every high cross spelled danger. Ferguson flapped at Morrissey's cross for the first goal. Peters' reply was erased by Royle's free header. The best goal was Colin Harvey's.											
5	A	COVENTRY		5	W	2-1	1-1	Peters 3, Brooking 58	Ferguson	Bonds	Charles	Peters	Stephenson	Moore	Redknapp	Boyce	Brooking	Hurst	Sissons	
	24/8		*33,716*	*22*	7			*Setters 32*	*Glazier*	*Bruck*	*Cattlin*	*Machin*	*Setters*	*Hill*	*Hannigan*	*Tudor*	*Baker*	*Gibson*	*Clements*	
								Ref: A Jones	Ex-Hammer Noel Cantwell's Coventry have still to earn their first point, but would have deserved one here. Peters' header from Redknapp's cross put West Ham in front. Maurice Setters then hit Hannigan's corner inside a post, but Boyce's through ball set up Brooking's winner.											
6	H	BURNLEY		1	W	5-0	4-0	Peters 18, Hurst 21, 31, Br'king 40, 58	Ferguson	Bonds	Charles	Peters	Stephenson	Moore	Redknapp	Boyce	Brooking	Hurst	Sissons*	**Cross**
	26/8		28,430	*12*	9				*Thomson*	*Smith*	*Latcham*	*O'Neil*	*Waldron*	*Bellamy*	*Coates*	*Lochhead*	*Casper*	*Kindon*	*Thomas*	
								Ref: E Wallace	West Ham go top amid a flurry of goals, controversy, and a slice of luck. This came at the end of the first half when the ref, having been hit on the head by the ball, was replaced by a linesman plucked from the crowd, who ignored Brooking being yards offside to permit the fourth goal.											
7	H	WEST BROM		3	W	4-0	1-0	Peters 19, 68, 80, Redknapp 77	Ferguson	Bonds	Charles	Peters	Stephenson	Moore	Redknapp	Boyce	Brooking	Hurst	Sissons	
	31/8		29,908	*14*	11				*Sheppard*	*Clarke*	*Williams*	*Lovett*	*Talbut*	*Kaye*	*Rees*	*Brown*	*Astle*	*Hope*	*Clark*	
								Ref: C Thomas	Martin Peters' hat-trick against the FA Cup-holders takes his tally to seven. Geoff Hurst also caught the eye, looking far more menacing than his England rival Jeff Astle. Hurst made the third goal, crossing for Redknapp, then rounded off the scoring by heading in Redknapp's centre.											
8	A	MANCHESTER U		3	D	1-1	0-0	Hurst 67	Ferguson	Bonds	Charles	Peters	Stephenson	Moore	Redknapp	Boyce	Brooking	Hurst	Sissons	
	7/9		***63,274***	*9*	12			*Law 59*	*Stepney*	*Dunne*	*Burns*	*Fitzpatrick*	*Foulkes*	*Stiles*	*Morgan*	*Sadler*	*Charlton*	*Law*	*Best*	
								Ref: E Jennings	West Ham laboured under a transparent inferiority complex for more than an hour. George Best chipped a gem of a pass to the far post where Law headed in, but Redknapp loaded the gun for the impressive Hurst's equaliser. Charlton, Law and Best were not at their best. Fortunately.											
9	H	TOTTENHAM		4	D	2-2	0-0	Peters 59, Hurst 61	Ferguson	Bonds	Charles	Peters	Stephenson	Moore	Redknapp	Boyce	Brooking	Hurst	Sissons	
	14/9		35,802	*12*	13			*Gilzean 62, Greaves 88*	*Jennings*	*Kinnear*	*Knowles*	*Mullery*	*England*	*Beal*	*Robertson*	*Greaves*	*Chivers*	*Venables*	*Gilzean*	
								Ref: M Fussey	Driving rain, quagmire pitch, insufferable Hammers arrogance as they stroll about playing out time before Mike England sends Greaves away to steal a point. Peters' volley and Hurst's cheeky lob had put West Ham firmly in charge, but Gilzean hit back within seconds with a header.											
10	A	CHELSEA		5	D	1-1	0-1	Peters 81	Ferguson	Bonds	Howe	Peters	Stephenson	Moore	Redknapp	Boyce	Brooking	Hurst	Sissons	
	21/9		*58,062*	*4*	14			*Tambling 2*	*Bonetti*	*Harris*	*McCreadie*	*Hollins*	*Webb*	*Boyle*	*Baldwin*	*Cooke*	*Osgood*	*Birchenall*	*Tambling*	
								Ref: N Burtenshaw	West Ham's pulling power lures an extra 10,000 to Chelsea's previous highest gate. Chelsea looked dangerous in breakaways, but otherwise stubbornly defended Tambling's early goal. Peters' header hits the bar and comes down over the line. Bonetti claws it out but the goal is given.											

No	Venue	Opponent / Date	Att	Pos	Pts	Res	F-A	H-T	Scorers, Times, Referees	1	2	3	4	5	6	7	8	9	10	11	12 sub used
11	H	SHEFFIELD WED		4		D	1-1	1-1	Hurst 4	Ferguson	Bonds	Charles	Peters	Stephenson	Moore	Redknapp	Boyce	Brooking	Hurst	Sissons	
		28/9	31,182	*7*	15				*Witham 29*	*Springett*	*Young*	*Megson*	*Ellis*	*Mobley*	*Eustace*	*Witham*	*McCalliog*	*Warboys*	*Ford*	*Fantham*	
									Ref: D Counsell	The Owls did the double over West Ham last season and are becoming one of their bogey sides. The Hammers' run of draws continues even though they put Springett's goal under siege. Hurst's early header was cancelled by Witham, with Hammers' defenders appealing for offside.											
12	H	SOUTHAMPTON		6		D	0-0	0-0		Ferguson	Bonds	Charles	Peters	Stephenson	Moore	Redknapp	Boyce	Brooking	Hurst	Sissons	
		5/10	29,558	*14*	16					*Gurr*	*Kirkup*	*Hollywood**	*Kemp*	*McGrath*	*Gabriel*	*Payne*	*Channon*	*Davies*	*Fisher*	*Walker*	*Saul*
									Ref: V Batty	Saints have an unsavoury reputation for thuggery and are happy to pack eight players in defence. Denis Hollywood fouled everything that moved before limping off after 25 minutes. On the hour Saints broke away and Ron Davies hit the post. West Ham never came that close.											
13	A	BURNLEY				L	1-3	0-2	Brooking 60	Ferguson	Bonds	Charles	Peters	Stephenson	Moore	Redknapp	Boyce	Brooking*	Hurst	Sissons	Lindsay
		8/10	**13,869**		16				*Murray 8, Kindon 27, Dobson 59*	*Thomson*	*Smith*	*Latcham*	*Todd*	*Waldron*	*Blant*	*Thomas*	*Murray*	*Casper*	*Dobson*	*Kindon*	
									Ref: D Corbett	Injury-hit Burnley field their youngest ever side, including a debut for former rugby wing three-quarter Steve Kindon. Burnley's kids inflict a first away defeat on full-strength Hammers. John Murray's header was his first league goal. Kindon's burst of speed earned him a goal too.											
14	A	LEEDS		6		L	0-2	0-1		Ferguson	Bonds	Charles	Peters	Stephenson	Moore	Redknapp !	Boyce	Brooking	Hurst	Sissons	
		12/10	*40,786*	*1*	16				*Lorimer 13, Giles 62p*	*Sprake*	*Reaney*	*Cooper*	*Bremner*	*Charlton*	*Hunter*	*O'Grady*	*Giles*	*Jones*	*Madeley*	*Lorimer*	
									Ref: T Pallister	After 30 minutes Harry Redknapp lashes out at Bremner's shins in retaliation and becomes only the second Hammer to be sent off under Ron Greenwood's reign. Ferguson was still lining up the wall when the first goal flashed past him. Bremner's swallow dive earned Leeds a penalty.											
15	H	SUNDERLAND		6		W	**8-0**	4-0	Hurst 18, 34, 44, 48, 61, 71, [Moore 26, Brooking 62]	Ferguson	Bonds	Charles	Peters	Stephenson	Moore	Redknapp	Boyce	Brooking	Hurst	Sissons	
		19/10	**24,718**	*13*	18					*Montgomery*	*Irwin*	*Palmer*	*Hurley*	*Harvey*	*Porterfield*	*Herd*	*Harris*	*Brand*	*Suggett*	*Hughes*	
									Ref: K Burns	The season's lowest crowd witness Hammers' biggest win and Geoff Hurst's record-breaking feat of scoring a hat-trick in each half. The post-match atmosphere was soured by Hurst's frank admission that he had punched in his first goal with a left hook. Sunderland were not amused.											
16	A	ARSENAL		6		D	0-0	0-0		Ferguson	Bonds	Charles	Peters	Stephenson	Moore	Redknapp	Boyce	Brooking	Hurst	Sissons*	**Hartley**
		26/10	*59,533*	*4*	19					*Wilson*	*Storey*	*McNab*	*McLintock*	*Neill*	*Ure*	*Robertson*	*Radford*	*Graham*	*Simpson*	*Armstrong*	
									Ref: K Howley	This is the fourth successive draw between the sides, though had it been a boxing match Arsenal would have won on points. Arsenal won on corners 11-4. Long diagonal balls into the Hammers' box caused Ferguson no end of trouble. Twice his defenders had to clear off the line.											
17	H	QP RANGERS		6		W	4-3	3-1	Moore 30, Peters 39, Hurst 42,	Ferguson	Bonds	Charles	Peters	Stephenson	Moore	Redknapp	Boyce	Brooking	Hurst	Hartley	
		2/11	36,008	*22*	21				*Bridges 19, Leach 56,66* [R'dknapp 69]	*Springett*	*Watson*	*Harris*	*Keen*	*Hunt*	*Hazell*	*Bridges*	*Leach*	*Allen*	*Wilks*	*Morgan*	
									Ref: Finney	This was the right match to televise, since the other Division 1 matches produced only nine goals between them. QPR fought back gamely from 1-3 down but were sunk by Redknapp's volley, the best goal of the match. QPR veteran Les Allen was a constant thorn in Hammers' defence.											
18	A	WOLVES		7		L	0-2	0-2		Ferguson	Bonds	Charles	Peters	Stephenson	Moore	Redknapp	Boyce	Brooking	Hurst	Hartley	
		9/11	*29,704*	*15*	21				*Farrington 4, Bailey 14*	*Parkes*	*Parkin*	*Thomson*	*Bailey*	*Woodfield*	*Holsgrove*	*Farrington*	*Knowles*	*Dougan*	*Wilson*	*Wagstaffe*	
									Ref: F Nicholson	Hammers' England trio are exhausted after their midweek game in Romania, and none of their team-mates seem able to assume the baton of responsibility. John Farrington netted after Derek Dougan's shot rebounded off Ferguson, and Wolves' skipper Mike Bailey volleyed a second.											
19	H	LEICESTER		6		W	4-0	2-0	Woollett 20(og), Dear 43, 89, Pet'rs 64	Ferguson	Bonds	Charles	Cushley	Stephenson	Moore	Peters	Boyce	Dear	Hurst	Sissons	
		16/11	26,328	*20*	23					*Shilton*	*Potts*	*Woollett*	*Cross*	*Manley*	*Nish*	*Glover*	*Clarke*	*Lochhead**	*Fern*	*Hutchins*	*Sjoberg*
									Ref: T Dawes	Brian Dear celebrates his eighth anniversary as a West Ham pro by scoring twice on his recall. Dear has the Indian sign on 20-year-old Peter Shilton, having scored seven times against him in three matches. Woollett's own-goal from Geoff Hurst's cross opened the flood-gates.											
20	A	IPSWICH		5		D	2-2	2-0	Hurst 35, 43p	Ferguson	Bonds	Charles	Cushley	Stephenson	Moore	Peters	Boyce	Dear	Hurst	Sissons*	**Miller**
		23/11	*28,964*	*17*	24				*Morris 60, Viljoen 78*	*Hancock*	*Mills*	*Houghton*	*Morris*	*Baxter*	*Jefferson*	*Hegan*	*Viljoen*	*Crawford*	*O'Rourke*	*Brogan*	
									Ref: J Hunting5	Two days earlier Ipswich manager Bill McGarry resigned. West Ham looked razor sharp for an hour, but once Bobby Ferguson was beaten by Peter Morris's absurdly optimistic effort from 35 yards, they lost their nerve. Jefferson had fouled Hurst for the penalty, which looked harsh.											
21	H	MANCHESTER C		5		W	2-1	2-0	Hurst 3, Peters 15	Ferguson	Bonds	Charles	Cushley	Stephenson	Moore	Redknapp	Boyce	Dear	Hurst	Peters	
		30/11	33,082	*16*	26				*Lee 78p*	*Dowd*	*Pardoe*	*Mann*	*Doyle*	*Book*	*Oakes*	*Lee*	*Bell*	*Summerbee*	*Young*	*Connor*	
									Ref: W Gow	Another Jekyll and Hyde performance, so good early on, so bad once the pitch cut up badly. Peters and Hurst each crossed for the other to head a goal. Bonds fell on the ball and handled it. He was so incensed by the penalty decision that he belted the ball into the crowd and was booked.											

No	Date		Att	Pos	Pt	F-A	H-T	Scorers, Times, and Referees	1	2	3	4	5	6	7	8	9	10	11	12 sub used
22	A	LIVERPOOL		5	L	0-2	0-1		Ferguson	Bonds	Charles	Cushley	Stephenson	Moore	Redknapp	Boyce	Dear	Hurst	Peters	
	7/12		*48,632*	*1*	26			*Hughes 45, Thompson 47*	*Lawrence*	*Lawler*	*Strong*	*Smith*	*Yeats*	*Hughes*	*Callaghan*	*Hunt*	*Evans*	*St John*	*Thompson*	
								Ref: W Handley	West Ham are the last London side to have won at Anfield, five years ago, and wasted early chances to have taken the lead this time. Seconds before half-time Emlyn Hughes drives through a forest of legs for his first goal of the season. West Ham are now 10 points adrift from the top.											
23	H	LEEDS		5	D	1-1	0-1	Peters 88	Ferguson	Bonds	Charles	Cushley	Stephenson	Moore	Redknapp	Boyce	Dear	Hurst	Peters	
	14/12		**24,718**	*2*	27			*Gray 19*	*Sprake*	*Reaney*	*Madeley*	*Bremner*	*Charlton*	*Hunter*	*O'Grady*	*Lorimer*	*Jones*	*Giles*	*Gray*	
								Ref: P Walters	The pitch is icy and Leeds are at their cynical worst. When Cushley lost his footing, Eddie Gray took advantage to score. Hurst then chipped a free-kick over Sprake's head and Peters outjumped Charlton. Had not Brian Dear missed from a couple of yards, West Ham might have won.											
24	A	SUNDERLAND		6	L	1-2	1-2	Hurst 27	Ferguson	Bonds	Charles	Cushley	Stephenson	Moore	Redknapp	Boyce	Hurst	**Lindsay**	Peters	
	21/12		*23,094*	*13*	27			*Palmer 6, Harris 13*	*Montgomery*	*Irwin*	*Harvey*	*Hurley*	*Todd*	*Palmer*	*Kerr*	*Harris*	*Hughes*	*Suggett*	*Mulhall**	*Porterfield*
								Ref: A Robinson	Jimmy Lindsay makes his debut as Sunderland take quick revenge for their 0-8 drubbing. Ferguson was partly at fault for both goals, first when Palmer scored at the second attempt from a free-kick, then when Hurley headed on to Harris. Montgomery blundered for West Ham's goal.											
25	A	SOUTHAMPTON		6	D	2-2	1-0	Hurst 45p, 55	Ferguson	Bonds	Charles	Cushley	Stephenson	Moore	Redknapp	Boyce	Hurst	Lindsay	Peters	
	26/12		*27,465*	*11*	28			*Davies 49, 84*	*Gurr*	*Kirkup*	*Hollywood*	*Gabriel*	*McGrath*	*Kemp*	*Paine*	*Channon*	*Davies*	*Walker*	*Saul*	
								Ref: J Taylor	Yet again Hammers fail to cling on to a lead. In this case twice. On the stroke of half-time ex-Hammer Joe Kirkup felled Redknapp in the box. Walker's deep cross over Stephenson's head brought Ron Davies' 100th Saints goal. Paine's cross was bulleted in by Davies for the second.											
26	A	QP RANGERS		6	D	1-1	1-1	Dear 36	Ferguson	Bonds	Charles*	Peters	Stephenson	Cushley	Redknapp	Lindsay	Brooking	Hurst	Dear	Boyce
	11/1		*28,645*	*22*	29			*Clarke 33*	*Spratley*	*Watson*	*Clement*	*Sibley*	*Hunt*	*Keetch*	*Morgan I*	*Leach*	*Clarke*	*Marsh*	*Morgan R*	
								Ref: H New	QPR are in deep relegation trouble, yet few Hammers fans want them to go down. The last 11 meetings have yielded 42 goals. Rodney Marsh returned to the QPR side and chipped audaciously onto the bar. Clarke turned in Roger Morgan's low cross and Dear headed in at the far post.											
27	A	LEICESTER		6	D	1-1	0-0	Dear 57	Ferguson	Bonds	Charles	Peters	Stephenson	Moore	Redknapp	Lindsay	Brooking	Hurst	Dear	
	1/2		*31,002*	*19*	30			*Clarke 89*	*Shilton*	*Rodrigues*	*Nish*	*Roberts*	*Woollet*	*Cross*	*Fern*	*Gibson*	*Lochhead*	*Clarke*	*Glover*	
								Ref: F Cowen	West Ham have not won away in the league since August, though they were seconds away from doing so here. When Dear scored off a post it was his eighth goal in four matches against Leicester. But Allan Clarke eluded Moore for the only time to convert Lochhead's knock-down.											
28	H	LIVERPOOL		7	D	1-1	1-0	Sissons 31	Ferguson	Bonds	Charles*	Peters	Stephenson	Moore	Redknapp	Lindsay	Brooking	Hurst	Sissons	Boyce
	22/2		36,498	*2*	31			*Hunt 51*	*Lawrence*	*Lawler*	*Strong*	*Smith*	*Yeats*	*Hughes*	*Callaghan*	*Hunt*	*Evans*	*St John*	*Thompson*	
								Ref: D Smith	Liverpool's heavyweight keeper Tommy Lawrence is much maligned. But he enjoys a distinguished match, keeping out everything West Ham throw at him apart from Sissons' goal, from Hurst's cross, and even getting his hand to that. Roger Hunt levelled from Callaghan's cross.											
29	H	NEWCASTLE		5	W	3-1	2-0	Brooking 2, Peters 14, Hurst 72	Ferguson	Bonds	Howe	Peters	Stephenson	Moore	Redknapp	Boyce	Brooking	Hurst	Sissons	
	1/3		26,336	*15*	33			*Davies 70*	*McFaul*	*Craggs*	*Clark*	*Gibb*	*Burton*	*Moncur*	*Scott*	*Horsfield*	*Davies*	*Robson*	*Hindson*	
								Ref: M Fussey	West Ham must pick themselves up after the Cup debacle at Mansfield. Brooking turned Moncur to ease the nerves, and Peters' half-volley from Redknapp's cross had the crowd roaring. When Ron Davies floated over a 45-yard cross it sailed over Ferguson's head for a farcical goal.											
30	A	NOTT'M FOREST		6	W	1-0	0-0	Hurst 71	Ferguson	Bonds	Howe	Peters	Stephenson	Moore	Redknapp	Boyce	Brooking	Hurst	Sissons	
	8/3		*24,303*	*19*	35				*Marshall*	*Hindley*	*Winfield*	*Hennessey*	*McKinlay*	*Newton*	*Lyons*	*Barnwell*	*Baker*	*Chapman*	*Rees*	
								Ref: P Baldwin	This is the weakest Forest side of recent years and they get off lightly. Three times West Ham hit the woodwork, though their winner had a touch of luck. Boyce's chip sent Hurst away, but he mis-hit his shot which bobbled in at the far post. West Ham's first double of the season.											
31	H	COVENTRY		6	W	5-2	2-0	Sissons 2, Peters 12, Hurst 59p, 81p	Ferguson	Bonds	Howe	Peters	Stephenson	Moore	Redknapp	Boyce	Brooking	Hurst	Sissons	
	14/3		29,053	*21*	37			*Machin 47, Hunt 73* [Bonds 86]	*Glazier*	*Coop*	*Cattlin*	*Machin*	*Curtis*	*Blockley*	*Hannigan*	*Hunt*	*Martin*	*Carr*	*Clements*	
								Ref: R Johnson	Coventry played their part in this Friday night thriller and were not finally despatched till the final minutes. They got off to a bad start, Sissons' shot turned in by Curtis, and Peters' header going through Glazier's hands. Machin felled Sissons for one penalty, Coop handled for the other.											

No	Venue	Opponent / Date	Att	Pos	Res / Pts	F-A	H-T	Scorers, Times, and Referees	1	2	3	4	5	6	7	8	9	10	11	12 sub used
32	H	IPSWICH		6	L	1-3	1-1	Hurst 29	Ferguson	Bonds	Howe	Peters	Stephenson	Moore	Redknapp	Boyce	Brooking	Hurst	Sissons	
		21/3	32,574	*11*	37			*Woods 11, Wigg 47, O'Rourke 50*	*Best*	*Mills*	*Houghton*	*Morris*	*McNeill*	*Jefferson*	*Hegan*	*Viljoen*	*Wigg*	*O'Rourke*	*Woods*	
								Ref: E Jennings	West Ham forced five corners in the first six minutes but were hit by three classic counter-attacks. Wigg nodded down for Woods to volley in before Hurst levelled with a glancing header. Wigg then brushed off Stephenson's challenge to restore the lead. Viljoen crossed for O'Rourke.											
33	H	WOLVES		6	W	3-1	1-0	Peters 32, 63, Brooking 55	Ferguson	Charles	Howe	Peters	Stephenson	Moore	Bonds	Boyce	Brooking	Hurst	Sissons	
		24/3	25,221	*12*	39			*Wilson 80*	*Parkes*	*Taylor*	*Parkin*	*Bailey*	*Holsgrove*	*McAlle*	*Wilson*	*Knowles*	*Dougan*	*Seal*	*Farrington*	
								Ref: C Nicholls	Wolves arrive at Upton Park with an unenviable reputation for uncompromising play. They concede 24 free-kicks, two of which produce goals. Peters headed the first from Moore's chipped free-kick. Keeper Parkes blundered for the second goal, spilling Brooking's volley over the line.											
34	H	MANCHESTER U		6	D	0-0	0-0		Ferguson	Charles	Howe	Peters	Stephenson	Moore	Bonds	Boyce	Brooking	Hurst	Sissons	
		29/3	**41,546**	*11*	40				*Stepney*	*Fitzpatrick*	*Dunne*	*Crerand*	*James*	*Stiles*	*Ryan*	*Kidd*	*Aston*	*Law*	*Best*	
								Ref: I Jones	This was an all-action goalless draw under the eyes of England boss Alf Ramsey. Young Stephen James handled the experienced Hurst as well as anyone. A game of few fouls but plenty of injuries. Dunne fractured his jaw when colliding with Stephenson, and Crerand broke his nose.											
35	A	EVERTON		6	L	0-1	0-0		Ferguson	Howe	Charles	Peters	Stephenson	Moore	Redknapp	Bonds*	Boyce	Hurst	Sissons	Brooking
		1/4	*37,212*	*4*	40			*Husband 51*	*West*	*Wright*	*Brown*	*Jackson*	*Labone*	*Harvey*	*Husband*	*Ball*	*Royle*	*Hurst*	*Morrissey*	
								Ref: G Kew	Everton achieve their sixth double of the season. Both sides went into the match chasing a place in next season's Fairs Cup, but West Ham's chances have gone. West Ham played their usual 4-3-3 'away' formation, but it merely extended their winless run at Goodison to seven years.											
36	A	SHEFFIELD WED		6	D	1-1	1-1	Hurst 31	Ferguson	Bonds	Charles	Peters	Stephenson	Moore	Redknapp	Boyce	Brooking	Hurst	Sissons	
		5/4	*24,268*	*14*	41			*Warboys 25*	*Springett*	*Smith*	*Megson*	*Eustace*	*Mobley*	*Young*	*Irvine*	*McCalliog*	*Ritchie*	*Warboys*	*Fantham*	
								Ref: W Handley	The Owls favour the big welly, the ball living in the sky. For all that, they deserved to win this match. Moore handled unseen by the ref, and both Warboys and Eustace hit Ferguson's crossbar. Owls' forwards hadn't scored for 11 games. A local bus-strike kept down the attendance.											
37	H	STOKE		6	D	0-0	0-0		Ferguson	Howe	Charles	Peters	Stephenson	Moore	Redknapp	Bonds	Brooking	Hurst	Sissons	
		8/4	26,577	*17*	42				*Banks*	*Marsh*	*Pejic*	*Lacey*	*Smith*	*Stevenson*	*Eastham*	*Dobing*	*Herd*	*Vernon*	*Burrows*	
								Ref: T Reynolds	Stoke have now not won in 19 away games. They created little themselves. Not that Gordon Banks was overstretched. He spent the 90 minutes watching West Ham's forwards shoot high, wide and handsome. Everyone lost count of the number of times Denis Smith fouled Geoff Hurst.											
38	H	CHELSEA		6	D	0-0	0-0		Ferguson	Bonds	Charles	Howe	Stephenson	Moore	Bennett	Boyce	Hurst	Peters	Sissons	
		12/4	32,332	*5*	43				*Bonetti*	*Webb*	*McCreadie*	*Hollins*	*Dempsey*	*Osgood*	*Boyle**	*Birchenall*	*Hutchinson*	*Harris*	*Houseman*	*Tambling*
								Ref: R Spittle	A Fairs Cup place may still be open to the winners, but neither side can raise a sweat. Bobby Moore's 28th birthday brings West Ham's third successive home 0-0 draw. Chelsea erected an eight-man defence and Hurst wasted the best chance of the match, firing over from four yards.											
39	A	WEST BROM		6	L	1-3	0-0	Peters 80	Ferguson	Bonds	Charles	Howe	Stephenson	Moore	Redknapp	Boyce	Brooking	Hurst	Peters	
		14/4	*20,092*	*13*	43			*Astle 65, 70, Brown 81*	*Osborne*	*Fraser*	*Williams*	*Brown*	*Talbut*	*Kaye*	*Martin*	*Lovett*	*Astle*	*Hope*	*Clark*	
								Ref: V James	Ferguson gives away another bizarre goal, directing a goal-kick straight to Jeff Astle who put it away with Ferugson's arms raised in surrender. When Astle shortly headed in Hope's cross, the Hawthorns gave vent to a chorus of 'Geoff Hurst out, Astle in!' Alf Ramsey was in the stand.											
40	A	TOTTENHAM		7	L	0-1	0-0		**Grotier**	Bonds	Charles*	Howe	Stephenson	Moore	Redknapp	Boyce	Hurst	Peters	Sissons	Brooking
		19/4	*50,970*	*8*	43			*Greaves 47*	*Jennings*	*Beal*	*Knowles*	*Mullery*	*England*	*Pratt*	*Johnson*	*Greaves*	*Gilzean*	*Pearce*	*Morgan*	
								Ref: K Walker	Alan Gilzean's flick bounces off Bobby Moore's chest and Greaves pokes the ball through debutant Grotier's legs. Grotier let another shot rebound off his legs to Greaves, who frivolously shot over. This result means Spurs become the first London club to beat Hammers this season.											
41	H	ARSENAL		7	L	1-2	1-2	Sissons 15	Grotier	Bonds	Howe	Cushley	Stephenson	Moore	**Holland**	Brooking	Hurst	Peters	Sissons	
		21/4	34,941	*3*	43			*Graham 30, Sammels 43*	*Wilson*	*Storey*	*McNab*	*McLintock*	*Simpson**	*Graham*	*Robertson*	*Sammels*	*Court*	*Radford*	*Armstrong*	*Gould*
								Ref: R Castle	A frighteningly physical match which showed that West Ham, in the mood, need no lessons in thuggery. Sissons beat the stranded Wilson from 25 yards. Grotier got a hand to Graham's equaliser. Sammels chested down the ball to fire the winner. With the goal open, Brooking hit a post.											
42	A	MANCHESTER C		8	D	1-1	0-0	Peters 52	**Death**	Bonds	Lampard	Peters	Stephenson	Moore	Redknapp	Boyce	Brooking	Hurst	Sissons	
		30/4	*31,846*	*13*	44			*Pardoe 66*	*Dowd*	*Book*	*Pardoe*	*Doyle*	*Booth*	*Oakes*	*Summerbee*	*Bell*	*Lee*	*Young*	*Coleman*	
		Home / Away						Ref: J Finney	West Ham applaud Man C onto the pitch with their FA Cup. Lampard plays his first game since breaking his leg last season. Stephenson kept ruffling Death's hair, presumably to give him encouragement. West Ham haven't won in nine games. A win would have lifted them to sixth.											
Average		30,991	34,971																	

League Cup					F-A	H-T	Scorers, Times, and Referees	1	2	3	4	5	6	7	8	9	10	11	12 sub used
2	H	BOLTON	3	W	7-2	4-1	Hurst 4p, 28, 32, Peters 7, Sissons 69,	Ferguson	Bonds	Charles	Peters	Stephenson	Moore	Redknapp	Boyce	Brooking	Hurst	Sissons	
		4/9	24,937 *2:17*				*Wharton 40p, Taylor 78,* [Brooking 79]	*Hopkinson*	*Ritson*	*Farrimond*	*Williams*	*Hulme*	*Hatton*	*Wharton*	*Hill*	*Greaves*	*Bromley*	*Taylor*	
							Ref: R Spittle [Redknapp 89]	Hurst scored all four against Bolton in the League Cup last season. Now he adds three more. Bolton's caretaker boss Nat Lofthouse describes the Hammers as 'magnificent'. Hatton handled for Hurst's early penalty; Stephenson fouled Roy Greaves for Wharton's twice-taken spot-kick.											
3	H	COVENTRY	5	D	0-0	0-0		Ferguson	Bonds	Charles	Peters	Stephenson	Moore	Redknapp	Boyce	Brooking	Hurst	Sissons	
		25/9	27,594 *19*					*Glazier*	*Coop*	*Cattlin*	*Curtis*	*Setters*	*Hill*	*Hannigan*	*Machin*	*Hunt*	*Carr*	*Clements*	
							Ref: R Johnson	Coventry lined up with a defensive 4-2-4 in their quest for a draw. Bill Glazier was man of the match, if only for his save from Redknapp's half-volley. Bobby Moore lent his skills to the Hammers front line in the second half, but he too was thwarted by Glazier – three times.											
3R	A	COVENTRY	4	L	2-3	1-2	Hurst 45, Peters 86	Ferguson	Howe	Charles	Peters	Cushley	Moore	Redknapp	Boyce	Brooking	Hurst	Dear	
		1/10	*25,988 17*				*Hunt 43, Tudor 44, Clements 53*	*Glazier*	*Coop*	*Bruck*	*Machin*	*Curtis*	*Hill*	*Hunt*	*Carr*	*Tudor*	*Gibson**	*Clements*	*Hannigan*
							Ref: I Jones	A riotous end to the first half. Ernie Hunt shoves Charles in the back and scores in the confusion. Seconds later Tudor raced through to score an 'offside' goal. Hurst's instant volley set up a keen second half. Tudor hit a post and Clements turned the ball in. Coventry now meet Swindon.											

FA Cup																			
3	H	BRISTOL CITY	6	W	3-2	1-1	Peters 14, 65, Hurst 53	Ferguson	Bonds	Charles	Cushley	Stephenson	Moore	Redknapp	Boyce	Hurst	Lindsay	Peters	
		4/1	32,526 *2:20*				*Galley 10, Skirton 89*	*Gibson*	*Jacobs*	*Briggs*	*Wimshurst*	*Connor*	*Parr*	*Skirton*	*Garland*	*Galley*	*Kellard*	*Sharpe*	
							Ref: E Jennings	When Moore trotted out he belted a ball into the face of a trombonist in the band. City are 20th in Division 2, so put up more of a fight than they had a right to. Martin Peters equalised Galley's goal with a fierce downward header in a crowded box that went through a defender's legs.											
4	A	HUDDERSFIELD	6	W	2-0	0-0	Peters 51, Hurst 62	Ferguson	Heffer	Bonds	Peters	Stephenson	Moore	Redknapp	Lindsay	Brooking	Hurst	Boyce	
		25/1	*30,992 2:6*					*Poole*	*Smith*	*Hutt*	*Nicholson*	*Ellam*	*Cherry*	*Dobson*	*Lawson*	*Aimson*	*McGill*	*Hill*	
							Ref: D Corbett	The Hammers lost on this ground last year in the League Cup and Division 2 Huddersfield gave West Ham a first-half pounding. A sweet counter-attack climaxed with Hurst crossing low to Peters. Harry Redknapp then flighted West Ham's first corner of the match to Hurst.											
5	A	MANSFIELD	7	L	0-3	0-2		Ferguson	Bonds	Howe	Peters	Stephenson	Moore	Redknapp	Lindsay*	Brooking	Hurst	Sissons	Boyce
		26/2	*21,117 3:15*				*Roberts 23, Keeley 38, Sharkey 51*	*Hollins*	*Pate*	*Hopkinson*	*Quigley*	*Boam*	*Waller*	*Keeley*	*Sharkey*	*Ledger*	*Roberts*	*Goodfellow*	
							Ref: W Gow	Division 3 Mansfield enjoy the greatest night in their history. And yet West Ham could not have asked for better chances to come their way. But Redknapp and Hurst missed them, and Dudley Roberts netted neatly from Goodfellow's cross. Ray Keeley thumped in a volley for No 2.											

		Home						Away					
	P	W	D	L	F	A	W	D	L	F	A	Pts
1 Leeds	42	18	3	0	41	9	9	10	2	25	17	67
2 Liverpool	42	16	4	1	36	10	9	7	5	27	14	61
3 Everton	42	14	5	2	43	10	7	10	4	34	26	57
4 Arsenal	42	12	6	3	31	12	10	6	5	25	15	56
5 Chelsea	42	11	7	3	40	24	9	3	9	33	29	50
6 Tottenham	42	10	8	3	39	22	4	9	8	22	29	45
7 Southampton	42	13	5	3	41	21	3	8	10	16	27	45
8 WEST HAM	42	10	8	3	47	22	3	10	8	19	28	44
9 Newcastle	42	12	7	2	40	20	3	7	11	21	35	44
10 West Brom	42	11	7	3	43	26	5	4	12	21	41	43
11 Manchester U	42	13	5	3	38	18	2	7	12	19	35	42
12 Ipswich	42	10	4	7	32	26	5	7	9	27	34	41
13 Manchester C	42	13	6	2	49	20	2	4	15	15	35	40
14 Burnley	42	11	6	4	36	25	4	3	14	19	57	39
15 Sheffield Wed	42	7	9	5	27	26	3	7	11	14	28	36
16 Wolves	42	7	10	4	26	22	3	5	13	15	36	35
17 Sunderland	42	10	6	5	28	18	1	6	14	15	49	34
18 Nott'm Forest	42	6	6	9	17	22	4	7	10	28	35	33
19 Stoke	42	9	7	5	24	24	0	8	13	16	39	33
20 Coventry	42	8	6	7	32	22	2	5	14	14	42	31
21 Leicester	42	8	8	5	27	24	1	4	16	12	44	30
22 QP Rangers	42	4	7	10	20	33	0	3	18	19	62	18
	924	233	140	89	757	456	89	140	233	456	757	924

Odds & ends

Double wins: (2) Nott'm Forest, Coventry.
Double losses: (1) Everton.

Won from behind: (2) QPR (h), Bristol C FAC (h).
Lost from in front: (1) Arsenal (h).

High spots: A record league win, 8-0 over Sunderland.
Briefly going top of the league at the end of August.

Low spots: Losing to Third Division Mansfield in FA Cup.
Failing to win any of the last nine league games, dropping to 8th.

West Ham drew 5 games in a row, and later drew 4 games in a row.

Hammer of the Year: Geoff Hurst.
Ever-presents: (2) Martin Peters, Geoff Hurst.
Hat-tricks: (3) Geoff Hurst (2), Martin Peters (1).
Leading scorer: (31) Geoff Hurst.

	Appearances						Goals			
	Lge	*Sub*	LC	*Sub*	FAC	*Sub*	Lge	LC	FAC	Tot
Bennett, Peter	**1**									
Bonds, Billy	**42**		2		3		**1**			**1**
Boyce, Ronnie	**37**	*2*	3		2	*1*				
Brooking, Trevor	**29**	*3*	3		2		**7**	1		**8**
Charles, John	**35**		3		1					
Cross, Roger		*1*								
Cushley, John	**9**		1		1					
Dear, Brian	**11**		1				**5**			**5**
Death, Steve	**1**									
Ferguson, Bobby	**39**		3		3					
Grotier, Peter	**2**									
Hartley, Trevor	**2**	*1*								
Heffer, Paul					1					
Holland, Pat	**1**									
Howe, Bobby	**13**		1		1					
Hurst, Geoff	**42**		3		3		**25**	4	2	**31**
Lampard, Frank	**1**									
Lindsay, Jimmy	**5**	*1*			3					
Miller, Keith		*1*								
Moore, Bobby	**41**		3		3		**2**			**2**
Peters, Martin	**42**		3		3		**19**	2	3	**24**
Redknapp, Harry	**36**		3		3		**2**	1		**3**
Sissons, John	**31**	*1*	2		1		**4**	1		**5**
Stephenson, John	**42**		2		3					
(own-goals)							**1**			**1**
24 players used	**462**	***10***	**33**		**33**	***1***	**66**	**9**	**5**	**80**

No	Date	Att	Pos	Pt	F-A	H-T	Scorers, Times, and Referees	1	2	3	4	5	6	7	8	9	10	11	12 sub used
1	H NEWCASTLE			W	1-0	0-0	Hurst 67	Ferguson	Bonds	Charles	Peters	Stephenson	Moore	Redknapp	Boyce	Bennett	Hurst	Sissons	
	9/8	33,323		2				*McFaul*	*Craig**	*Clark*	*Gibb*	*Burton*	*Moncur*	*Sinclair*	*Robson*	*Davies*	*Arentoft,*	*Foggon*	*Duffy*
							Ref: L Callaghan	Newcastle have just won the Fairs Cup. Geoff Hurst conceded five free-kicks, the most of any player on the field, as he refused to be reduced to a Geordie punch-bag. It was his 301st league game, played in high humidity, settled in West Ham's favour from Harry Redknapp's corner.											
2	H CHELSEA			W	2-0	0-0	Peters 65, Hurst 85	Ferguson	Bonds	Charles	Peters	Moore	Boyce	Redknapp	Lindsay	Bennett	Hurst	Sissons	
	11/8	39,003		4				*Bonetti*	*Harris*	*McCreadie*	*Hollins*	*Dempsey*	*Osgood*	*Cooke*	*Hinton*	*Hutchinson**	*Houseman*	*Tambling*	*Baldwin*
							Ref: J Finney	More crowd trouble, this time under a herringbone sky. On the pitch, Martin Peters snatches the ball off Peter Osgood for the first goal, then plays a one-two with Hurst to crash through the Chelsea defence like a tank for the second. Chelsea have now lost two games and six goals.											
3	A STOKE		11	L	1-2	1-1	Lindsay 29	Ferguson	Bonds	Charles	Peters	Moore	Boyce	Redknapp	Lindsay	Bennett	Hurst	Sissons	
	16/8	*23,361*	*8*	4			*Ritchie 37, Dobing 88*	*Banks*	*Marsh*	*Elder*	*Skeels*	*Smith*	*Allen*	*Conroy**	*Dobing*	*Ritchie*	*Greenhoff*	*Burrows*	*Eastham*
							Ref: I Jones	John Ritchie's power in the air gives Moore a testing time. Ritchie scored when the ball rebounded off Ferguson to his feet, then set up the winner with a cross that Dobing headed in. At the other end, Denis Smith had the measure of Geoff Hurst, leaving the Hammers lightweight.											
4	A CHELSEA		7	D	0-0	0-0		Ferguson	Bonds	Lampard	Peters	Moore	Boyce	Cross	Lindsay	Bennett	Hurst	Sissons	
	20/8	*43,347*	*15*	5				*Bonetti*	*McCreadie*	*Houston*	*Hollins*	*Dempsey*	*Hinton*	*Osgood*	*Tambling**	*Hutchinson*	*Houseman*	*Cooke*	*Birchenall*
							Ref: K Walker	Stamford Bridge's new floodlights are not yet securely mounted, and the beams dance giddily across the pitch. Chelsea ended the game with 11 walking wounded. Hinton had a strapped thigh, Hutchinson and Dempsey facial injuries. West Ham did nothing more than pump high crosses.											
5	H WEST BROM		10	L	1-3	1-2	Peters 44	Ferguson	Bonds	Charles	Peters	Stephenson	Moore	Lindsay	Boyce	Bennett	Hurst	Sissons	
	23/8	32,867	*12*	5			*Suggett 21, Brown 37, Krzywicki 83*	*Cumbes*	*Fraser*	*Williams*	*Brown*	*Talbut*	*Merrick*	*Hegan*	*Suggett*	*Krzywicki*	*Hughes*	*Hartford*	
							Ref: P Walters	This deplorable performance provoked a slow-handclap from the crowd. West Ham had opened brightly but got steadily worse. Alan Ashman's Albion went in front through Suggett's hook, from Kryzwicki's corner, then extended their lead when Brown raced through to beat Ferguson.											
6	H ARSENAL		10	D	1-1	1-0	Cross 10	Ferguson	Bonds	Lampard*	Peters	Stephenson	Moore	**Best**	Boyce	Brooking	Hurst	Cross	Howe
	25/8	39,590	*8*	6			*Lampard 52 (og)*	*Wilson*	*Storey*	*McNab*	*McLintock*	*Neill*	*Simpson*	*Robertson*	*George*	*Court*	*Graham*	*Radford*	
							Ref: G Hill	Bermudan Clyde Best makes his debut. Roger Cross headed in Bonds' free-kick, only for Lampard to turn George's cross into his own net. West Ham twice hit the bar, Arsenal once. At the start of the second half Arsenal's Court and Graham both emerged wearing No 9 shirts.											
7	A NOTT'M FOREST		13	L	0-1	0-0		Ferguson	Bonds	Lampard	Peters	Stephenson	Moore	Best	Boyce	Brooking	Hurst	Cross*	Miller
	30/8	*29,097*	*11*	6			*Hilley 75*	*Hill*	*Hindley*	*Winfield*	*Chapman*	*Hennessey*	*Newton*	*Rees*	*Lyons*	*Hilley*	*Barnwell*	*Moore*	
							Ref: W Gow	The City Ground's main stand was destroyed by fire last year. West Ham sacrificed flair in order to try to secure a 0-0 draw against Matt Gillies' Forest, but Hilley netted from Storey-Moore's centre. The home crowd sang 'Saved by the bell' as they trooped away at the end.											
8	H TOTTENHAM		17	L	0-1	0-0		Ferguson	Bonds	Lampard	Howe	Stephenson	Moore	Best*	Peters	Brooking	Hurst	Sissons	Boyce
	6/9	40,561	*4*	6			*Pearce 75*	*Jennings*	*Beal*	*Knowles*	*Mullery**	*England*	*Collins*	*Pearce*	*Greaves*	*Gilzean*	*Pratt*	*Morgan*	*Want*
							Ref: D Smith	Few observers could genuinely say Spurs were the better side, but West Ham's defence stood staring at a linesman as Pearce sprinted through to score. Though the flag went up, the referee ignored it. Clyde Best limped off after 33 minutes and Spurs' Alan Mullery was carried off.											
9	A EVERTON		20	L	0-2	0-0		Ferguson	Bonds	Lampard	Peters	Stephenson	Moore	Howe	Boyce	Brooking	Hurst	Cross	
	13/9	*49,052*	*3*	6			*Ball 73, Husband 77*	*West*	*Wright*	*Brown*	*Kendall*	*Labone*	*Harvey*	*Husband*	*Ball*	*Royle*	*Hurst*	*Morrissey*	
							Ref: W Gow	With Brian Labone having the upper hand over Hurst, this game was largely one-way traffic. West saved superbly from Roger Cross's header, but Hammers were defending in numbers when Ball snapped up Kendall's miscued shot. Husband scored when Ferguson parried from Wright.											
10	H SHEFFIELD WED		15	W	3-0	1-0	Redknapp 7, Branfoot 62 (og), Hurst 67	Ferguson	Bonds	Lampard	Boyce	Stephenson	Moore	Redknapp	Brooking	Hurst	Cross	Peters	
	20/9	23,487	*20*	8				*Wicks*	*Smith*	*Megson*	*young*	*Ellis*	*Craig*	*Branfoot*	*Pugh*	*Prendergast*	*Ford*	*Fantham**	*Prophett*
							Ref: T Dawes	West Ham's incessant barrage of attacks would have deflated better teams than Wednesday, who played in a strange strip of orange shirts and blue shorts. Redknapp scored off a post, then Branfoot inadvertently steered Hurst's cross past his own keeper. Hurst's header rounded it off.											

No	H/A	Opponent	Pos	Res	FT	HT	Scorers, Times, and Referees	1	2	3	4	5	6	7	8	9	10	11	12 sub used
11	A	MANCHESTER U	17	L	2-5	1-2	Hurst 25, 77 *[Kidd 85]*	Ferguson	Bonds	Lampard	Howe	Stephenson	Moore	Redknapp	Lindsay	Best	Hurst	Peters	
27/9		*58,579*	*8*	8			*Burns 5, Best 12, 83, Charlton 66,*	*Stepney*	*Fitzpatrick*	*Dunne*	*Burns*	*Ure*	*Sadler*	*Morgan*	*Kidd*	*Charlton*	*Aston*	*Best*	
							Ref: R Tinkler	Greenwood: 'With one or two reservations, that's the best we have played all season.' Only in the closing minutes did the score look one-sided. Clyde Best constantly beat Ian Ure. Pick of the goals was Best's solo run and cross onto Hurst's head. Peters has gone on the transfer list.											
12	H	BURNLEY	15	W	3-1	2-0	Best 12, 15, Brooking 64	Ferguson	Bonds	Lampard	Howe	Stephenson	Moore	Redknapp	Lindsay	Brooking	Hurst*	Best	Sissons
4/10		26,445	*20*	10			*Kindon 80*	*Mellor*	*Angus*	*Latcham*	*O'Neil*	*Merrington*	*Todd*	*Thomas*	*Coates*	*Casper*	*Dobson*	*Kindon*	
							Ref: D Corbett	This is the first time since the 1966 World Cup final that both Hurst and Peters have been missing together. Mind you, West Ham were leading 2-0 when Hurst went off after 74 minutes with back trouble, having set up both Best goals. Brooking took unsettled Peters' role in midfield.											
13	H	STOKE	15	D	3-3	3-0	Best 3, Brooking 11, Sissons 20	Ferguson	Bonds	Lampard*	Howe	Stephenson	Boyce	Redknapp	Lindsay	Brooking	Sissons	Best	Cross
6/10		26,860	*5*	11			*Smith 67, 87, Burrows 83*	*Banks*	*Marsh*	*Pejic*	*Steels*	*Smith*	*Bloor*	*Conroy**	*Dobing*	*Ritchie*	*Eastham*	*Burrows*	*Herd*
							Ref: R Spittle	All three World Cup stars are missing as West Ham stage an astonishing collapse. 3-0 up after 20 minutes, they are still 3-0 up after 66 Then Smith heads in Eastham's corner. At 3-3 Burrows hit the bar. What is more, the limping, thigh-strained Gordon Banks couldn't take goal-kicks.											
14	A	COVENTRY	15	D	2-2	1-1	Brooking 30, Sissons 46	Ferguson	Bonds	Lampard	Howe	Stephenson	Moore	Redknapp	Lindsay	Brooking	Sissons	Best	
11/10		*34,277*	*6*	12			*Joicey 31, Clements 54*	*Glazier*	*Coop*	*Bruck*	*Setters**	*Curtis*	*Blockley*	*Hunt*	*Joicey*	*Martin*	*Carr*	*Clements*	*Mortimer*
							Ref: H New	Although twice in front, West Ham are left still searching for their first away win. At one point, Best stood nonchalantly by the ball at the corner-flag, like Mohammed Ali, daring opponents to come and get it. Coventry's Brian Joicey, on his debut, had a goal ruled out for offside.											
15	A	WOLVES	16	L	0-1	0-0		Ferguson	Bonds	Lampard	Howe*	Stephenson	Moore	Redknapp	Lindsay	Brooking	Sissons	Best	Hurst
18/10		*28,762*	*4*	12			*McCalliog 81*	*Parkes*	*Taylor*	*Parkin*	*Wilson*	*Holsgrove*	*Munro*	*McCalliog*	*O'Grady*	*Dougan*	*Curran*	*Wagstaffe*	
							Ref: G Kew	Jim McCalliog's goal was late but not undeserved for Wolves, for whom Hugh Curran twice had 'goals' disallowed. A 15th-minute injury to Bobby Howe allowed Hurst to return to the side in the unfamiliar role of substitute. Best and Redknapp's pairing up front was unproductive.											
16	H	SUNDERLAND	16	D	1-1	1-0	Peters 19	Ferguson	Bonds	Lampard	Howe	Stephenson	Moore	Redknapp	Peters	Brooking	Hurst	Best	
25/10		29,171	*22*	13			*Hughes 47*	*Montgomery*	*Irwin*	*Ashurst*	*Todd*	*Heslop*	*McGiven*	*Park*	*Hughes*	*Baker*	*Kerr*	*Tueart*	
							Ref: M Fussey	Transfer-seeking Martin Peters returns to the side, controls Moore's lob and slides the ball past Jim Montgomery. Geoff Hurst misses three sitters, one of them from five yards when he balloons over. Moore is regularly caught in possession and is at fault for Sunderland's equaliser.											
17	A	SOUTHAMPTON	16	D	1-1	1-0	Brooking 32	Ferguson	Bonds	Lampard	Howe	Stephenson	Moore	Best	Peters	Brooking	Hurst	Sissons	
1/11		*26,894*	*20*	14			*Channon 82*	*Martin*	*Kirkup*	*Hollywood*	*Kemp*	*McGrath*	*Gabriel**	*Paine*	*Channon*	*Davies*	*Walker*	*Sydenham*	*Byrne*
							Ref: C Thomas	Lampard retaliates at Terry Paine, and his third booking of the season means he will face an FA disciplinary enquiry. West Ham faded after a bright start and increasingly relied on Alan Stephenson to keep out energetic Saints. Twice in the closing minutes Saints might have clinched it.											
18	H	CRYS PALACE	14	W	2-1	2-0	Best 10, Hurst 26	Ferguson	Bonds	Lampard	Howe	Stephenson	Moore	Redknapp	Peters	Brooking	Hurst	Best	
8/11		31,515	*18*	16			*Bonds 83 (og)*	*Jackson*	*Loughlan*	*Blyth*	*Payne*	*McCormick*	*Hynd*	*Kember*	*Taylor*	*Hoy*	*Queen*	*Dawkins*	
							Ref: K Walker	On the balance of play, Bert Head's Palace should have lost by five or six goals. Instead, West Ham are almost made to pay for their strolling arrogance. Hurst, Peters and Best might each have claimed a hat-trick. Despite having just one forward, Palace are pressing strongly at the end.											
19	A	LIVERPOOL	14	L	0-2	0-1		Ferguson	Bonds	Lampard	Howe	Stephenson	Moore	Redknapp	Boyce	Brooking	Hurst	Best	
15/11		*39,668*	*3*	16			*Lawler 28, Graham 89*	*Lawrence*	*Lawler*	*Strong*	*Smith*	*Yeats*	*Hughes*	*Callaghan*	*Peplow**	*Graham*	*St. John*	*Thompson*	*Hunt*
							Ref: B Lyden	When Peters flew back to attend to his sick baby, 18-year-old Bobby Sutton was named as sub. His mother works in the canteen at Upton Park. Sutton left his boots behind and in any case was considered too risky to play, so Billy Bonds, injured at the start had to play on despite his pain.											
20	H	DERBY	14	W	3-0	1-0	Hurst 20, 70, Peters 57	Ferguson	Bonds	Lampard	Howe	Stephenson	Moore	Redknapp	Peters	Brooking	Hurst	Best	
22/11		32,485	*6*	18				Green	Webster	Robson*	Durban	McFarland	Mackay	McGovern	Carlin	O'Hare	Hector	Hinton	Stewart
							Ref: E Jennings	Derby made the mistake of allowing West Ham to play football. Only stalwart Dave Mackay looked in the mood to resist, as Redknapp and Brooking took control. Full-backs Bonds and Lampard enjoyed the luxury of pushing up to join the attack. On this form, West Ham look great.											
21	A	IPSWICH	15	L	0-1	0-0		Ferguson	Bonds	Lampard	Howe	Stephenson	Moore	Redknapp	Peters	Brooking	Hurst	Best	
29/11		*17,456*	*18*	18			*Mills 64*	*Best*	*Carroll*	*Mills*	*Morris*	*Baxter*	*McNeil*	*Woods*	*Collard*	*Hill*	*Viljoen*	*Lambert*	
							Ref: E Wallace	It was so cold that several Hammers sported gloves. Having squandered chance after chance, West Ham are beaten by a sucker punch out of the blue. Mick Mills' well-directed shot caught Ferguson flat-footed. Clyde Best seldom got involved and Peters was twice just off target.											

No	Date		Att	Pos	Pt	F-A	H-T	Scorers, Times, and Referees	1	2	3	4	5	6	7	8	9	10	11	12 sub used
22	H	MANCHESTER C		16	L	0-4	0-1		Ferguson	Bonds	Lampard	Howe	Stephenson	Moore	Redknapp	Peters	Brooking	Hurst	Best	
	6/12		27,491	*4*	18			*Lee 10, Bowyer 63, 75, Doyle 87*	*Corrigan*	*Book*	*Pardoe*	*Doyle*	*Booth*	*Oakes*	*Summerbee*	*Bell*	*Lee*	*Young**	*Bowyer*	*Connor*
								Ref: M Kerkhof	Alf Ramsey watches as all three of his England Hammers have stinkers. West Ham are run off their feet by Francis Lee and Colin Bell. Poor Bobby Ferguson was at fault to some extent with all four City goals. Whenever Hammers attacked, City packed their goalmouth to good effect.											
23	H	EVERTON		17	L	0-1	0-1		Ferguson	Bonds	Lampard	Howe	Stephenson*	Moore	Sissons	Peters	Boyce	Hurst	Best	Brooking
	13/12		*26,689*	*1*	18			*Whittle 29*	*West*	*Wright**	*Brown*	*Kendall*	*Labone*	*Jackson*	*Whittle*	*Ball*	*Royle*	*Hurst*	*Morrissey*	*D'arcy*
								Ref: A Oliver	Harry Catterick's Everton top the league but West Ham were hard done by. They had 21 direct shots at goal, twice hit the inside of a post, and had two penalty claims turned down. Bobby Moore's blunder let in Alan Whittle. Royle whacked Stephenson so hard that he was hospitalised.											
24	A	LEEDS		17	L	**1-4**	0-2	Hurst 82	Ferguson	Bonds	Lampard	Howe	Peters	Boyce	Redknapp	Bennett	Brooking	Hurst	Sissons	
	17/12		*30,659*	*1*	18			*Lorimer 29, 39, Clarke 50, Giles 73*	*Sprake*	*Reaney*	*Cooper*	*Bremner*	*Charlton*	*Hunter**	*Lorimer*	*Clarke*	*Jones*	*Giles*	*Madeley*	*Yorath*
								Ref: A Jones	Leeds go top, and look far superior to Everton, who they overtake. Moore is missing with a knee injury. Peter Lorimer scored the first goal from Giles' low cross and the second when Terry Cooper's cross was deflected to him. As well as the goals, Leeds hit the wood three times.											
25	A	TOTTENHAM		15	W	2-0	2-0	Hurst 12, Peters 14	Ferguson	Bonds	Lampard	Howe	Moore	Boyce	Redknapp	Peters	Brooking	Hurst	Sissons	
	20/12		*23,375*	*14*	20				*Jennings*	*Kinnear*	*Knowles*	*Mullery*	*Beal*	*Evans*	*Johnson*	*Greaves*	*Pearce*	*Perryman*	*Morgan*	
								Ref: L Callaghan	West Ham's first away win in nine months is so clear-cut that Spurs fans stream away long before the end. Moore's frailty in the air was often exposed. Spurs' last chance came with a penalty which Jimmy Greaves side-footed wide. Greaves was often caught in possession by Howe.											
26	A	WEST BROM		16	L	1-3	1-1	Peters 33	Ferguson	Bonds	Lampard	Howe	Moore	Boyce	Redknapp	Hurst	Bennett	Sissons	Peters	
	26/12		*32,867*	*15*	20			*Suggett 19, 50, Astle 80*	*Osborne*	*Fraser*	*Wilson*	*Brown*	*Potter*	*Kaye*	*Martin*	*Suggett*	*Astle*	*Hartford*	*Hope**	*Hughes*
								Ref: J Finney	Two mistakes by Bobby Ferguson cost West Ham two goals and the match. He drops Asa Hartford's corner for the first goal, and mis-punches a ball he should have held for the third. In the second half Jeff Astle twice brushed off Bobby Moore's presence to head against the crossbar.											
27	H	NOTT'M FOREST		16	D	1-1	1-0	Bonds 28	Ferguson	Bonds	Lampard	Howe	Moore	Boyce	Redknapp	Peters	Hurst	Brooking*	Best	Bennett
	27/12		31,829	*13*	21			*Moore 80*	*Hill*	*Hindley*	*Winfield*	*Chapman*	*O'Kane*	*Newton*	*Rees*	*Lyons**	*Hilley*	*Richardson*	*Moore*	*McCaffrey*
								Ref: R Johnson	Bobby Moore's 387th appearance is a post-war West Ham record. His team should have sealed the points in the first half, but Geoff Hurst's incredible misses and Redknapp's terrible crosses keep Forest alive. Ian Storey-Moore led the fightback which nearly resulted in a Forest win.											
28	A	SHEFFIELD WED		16	W	3-2	1-0	Peters 26, 46, Hurst 61p	Ferguson	Bonds	Howe	Peters	Stephenson	Moore	Holland	Lindsay	Hurst	**Eustace**	Best	
	10/1		*28,135*	*22*	23			*Craig 51, Prophett 73*	*Springett*	*Wilcockson*	*Megson*	*Pugh*	*Prophett*	*Craig*	*Sinclair*	*Whitham**	*Downes*	*Smith*	*Coleman*	*Warboys*
								Ref: D Smith	Peter Eustace has signed from Sheffield Wednesday for £90,000 but has an inconspicuous debut. Owls' Peter Springett is to blame for two goals, though not for Hurst's ballistic penalty. Yet again a match that Hammers should have won comfortably has them hanging on desperately.											
29	H	MANCHESTER U		16	D	0-0	0-0		Ferguson	Bonds	Howe	Peters	Stephenson	Moore	Holland	Lindsay	Hurst	Eustace	Best	
	17/1		**41,643**	*8*	24				*Rimmer*	*Edwards*	*Burns*	*Crerand*	*Ure*	*Sadler*	*Morgan*	*Sartori*	*Charlton*	*Kidd*	*Aston*	
								Ref: W Gow	Man U are without the suspended George Best, so only one Best takes the field. This was an eventful goalless draw, with chances at either end. Peters' header is hooked off the line, while two solo runs by Brian Kidd end up with wayward shots. 19-year-old Pat Holland performs well.											
30	A	BURNLEY		16	L	2-3	0-2	Eustace 50, Lindsay 84	Ferguson	Bonds	Howe	Peters	Stephenson	Moore	Holland*	Lindsay	Hurst	Eustace	Best	Heffer
	31/1		***14,454***	*17*	24			*Thomas 24, Kindon 43, Coates 73*	*Mellor*	*Angus*	*Thomson*	*Merrington*	*Dobson*	*O'Neil*	*Thomas*	*Coates*	*Casper*	*Wilson*	*Kindon*	
								Ref: J Taylor	With West Ham knocked out of the FA Cup by Middlesbrough at the first hurdle, Ron Greenwood remodels his side. Though Eustace plays his best game yet, two first-half blunders by Ferguson prove fatal. This result leaves the Hammers just seven points clear of the relegation places.											
31	H	COVENTRY		17	L	1-2	1-1	Hurst 10p	Grotier	Bonds	Howe	Peters	Stephenson	Moore	Brooking	Lindsay	Eustace	Hurst	Best	
	11/2		22,723	*4*	24			*Martin 23, 52*	*Glazier*	*Coop*	*Cattlin*	*Hunt*	*Barry*	*Clements**	*Hannigan*	*Carr*	*Martin*	*O'Rourke*	*Mortimer*	*Hill*
								Ref: G Hartley	West Ham have drawn 1-1 with Slovan Bratislava in a friendly. Hurst's penalty is his 154th league goal, a post-war Hammers record. But Noel Cantwell's side go fourth with two goals from Martin – the second a strong header. Upton Park echoes to the sound of slow hand-clapping.											

No	H/A	Opponent / Att	Pos	Res	F-A	H-T	Scorers, Times, and Referees	1	2	3	4	5	6	7	8	9	10	11	12
32	A	SUNDERLAND	17	W	1-0	1-0	Hurst 43	Grotier	Bonds	Howe	Peters	Stephenson	Moore	Redknapp	Lindsay	Hurst	Eustace	Sissons	
	21/2	*16,900*	*22*	26				*Montgomery*	*Irwin*	*Ashurts*	*Todd*	*Heslop*	*McGiven*	*Tueart*	*Park*	*Baker**	*Harris*	*Hughes*	*Kerr*
							Ref: K Burns	Clyde Best has been dropped, but recalled wingers Redknapp and Sissons achieved little. Sunderland look dire, good bets for relegation. Jimmy Lindsay missed two good chances and a hat-trick was there for the taking for Peters. Moore was superb and Eustace purposeful and aggressive.											
33	H	SOUTHAMPTON	17	D	0-0	0-0		Grotier	Bonds	Howe	Peters	Stephenson	Moore	Redknapp	Lindsay	Hurst	Eustace	Sissons	
	28/2	27,088	*18*	27				*Martin*	*Kirkup*	*Byrne*	*Fisher*	*McGrath*	*Gabriel*	*Paine*	*Channon*	*Davies*	*Walker*	*Jenkins*	
							Ref: G Lyden	Banners are waved proclaiming 'Greenwood Out!' Ferguson and Boyce have already been axed, but on the evidence of this match more heads need to roll. West Ham failed to create a single opening. Saints' half-fit Ron Davies hit the bar and Channon forced a great save from Grotier.											
34	A	NEWCASTLE	17	L	1-4	1-2	Eustace 28 *[Foggon 81]*	Grotier	Bonds	Howe	Peters	Stephenson	Moore	Redknapp	Lindsay	Hurst	Eustace	Sissons	
	2/3	*27,500*	*10*	27			*Davies 8, Robson 40, Dyson 74,*	*McFaul*	*Craig*	*Craggs*	*Gibb*	*McNamee*	*Moncur*	*Robson*	*Smith*	*Davies*	*Foggon*	*Dyson*	
							Ref: W Castle	West Ham are outfought and out-thought by the Fairs Cup holders. Under the eyes of Alf Ramsey, Wyn Davies out-jumps Stephenson for the first goal, but Eustace's volley squares it. Robson stabbed a low drive inside a post before Robson and Smith combined for Dyson's clincher.											
35	A	DERBY	17	L	0-3	0-0		Grotier	Bonds	Lampard	Cushley	Stephenson	Moore	Best	Peters	Hurst	Eustace	Howe	
	7/3	*35,615*	*4*	27			*Durban 58, Hinton 78p, O'Hare 84*	*Green*	*Webster*	*Robson*	*Hennessey*	*McFarland*	*Mackay*	*Durban*	*Carlin*	*O'Hare*	*Hector*	*Hinton*	
							Ref: V Batty	This result was harsh on West Ham. Martin Peters had a goal disallowed and Clyde Best sliced a chance wide from 10 yards. Derby's second goal, a penalty, was dubious, but the Hammers are so short on confidence that they fell away in the final stages. Seven goals lost in two games.											
36	H	IPSWICH	17	D	0-0	0-0		Grotier	Bonds	Lampard	Cushley	Stephenson	Moore	Best*	Peters	Hurst	Eustace	Howe	Boyce
	14/3	**20,934**	*20*	28				*Best*	*Carroll*	*Harper*	*Morris*	*Baxter*	*Jefferson*	*Woods*	*Collard*	*Whymark*	*Mills*	*Lambert*	
							Ref: R Kirkpatrick	An inept performance against an Ipswich side who look even worse. Keeper David Best hurt an arm in the opening stages but was not put under serious pressure. Best miskicked in front of an open goal. Near the end Lambert chipped onto the bar and Whymark hit the side-netting.											
37	A	MANCHESTER C	17	W	**5-1**	3-1	Greaves 10, 37, H'st 45, 88, Boyce 83	Grotier	Bonds	Lampard	Boyce	Stephenson	Moore	Holland	Eustace*	Hurst	**Greaves**	Howe	**Llewellyn**
	21/3	*28,353*	*11*	30			*Lee 13*	*Corrigan*	*Book*	*Mann*	*Doyle*	*Booth*	*Oakes*	*Towers*	*Lee*	*Bowyer*	*Young*	*Pardoe*	
							Ref: P Baldwin	Peters has signed for Spurs and Jimmy Greaves for West Ham for £200,000. City were without Bell and Summerbee but had few excuses by the end. Greaves supplied two ice-cool finishes and Ronnie Boyce thumped a huge shot past Corrigan from somewhere near the centre-circle.											
38	A	CRYS PALACE	17	D	0-0	0-0		Grotier	Bonds	Lampard	Boyce*	Stephenson	Moore	Holland	Bennett	Hurst	Greaves	Howe	Llewellyn
	24/3	*34,801*	*21*	31				*Jackson J*	*Sewell*	*Hoadley*	*Payne*	*McCormick*	*Blyth*	*Scott*	*Kember*	*Hoy*	*Queen*	*Taylor*	
							Ref: R Nicholson	Palace fight ruthlesssly for every ball in an effort to stave off relegation. They are Greaves' bogey team, for he played them four times while with Spurs without scoring. Boyce went off after colliding with Kember. Palace came nearest to a goal when Payne clipped the top of the bar.											
39	H	LIVERPOOL	17	W	1-0	1-0	Holland 14	Grotier	Bonds	Lampard	Bennett	Stephenson	Moore	Holland	Eustace	Hurst	Greaves	Howe	
	28/3	38,239	*5*	33				*Clemence*	*Lawler*	*Evans R*	*Smith*	*Lloyd*	*Hughes*	*Thompson*	*Livermore*	*Evans A*	*Callaghan*	*Graham*	
							Ref: R Tinkler	Greaves' home debut pulls in a huge crowd for this otherwise meaningless end-of-season fixture. For their part, Liverpool field a team of kids. Greaves did little, other than hit the roof of the stand with a volley. Holland's goal was so classy that Greaves stood open-mouthed to applaud.											
40	H	WOLVES	17	W	3-0	1-0	Greaves 2, Bonds 57, Howe 84	Grotier	Bonds	Lampard	Bennett	Stephenson	Moore	Holland	Eustace	Hurst	Greaves	Howe	
	31/3	26,386	*11*	35				*Parkes*	*Taylor*	*Parkin*	*Wilson*	*Holsgrove*	*Shaw*	*Bailey*	*McCalliog*	*Dougan*	*Curran*	*Wagstaffe*	
							Ref: R Reynolds	Wolves' boss Bill McGarry described his team's defence as the worst in the world after this defeat. Greaves headed in Lampard's cross with Parkes rooted to his line. Parkes failed to cut out a corner for No 2. Curran and Wilson hit the bar and Dougan's diving header was disallowed.											
41	H	LEEDS	16	D	2-2	2-1	Best 33, Bonds 36	Grotier	Bonds	Charles	Eustace	Moore	Miller	Redknapp	Lindsay	Best	Greaves	Sissons	
	2/4	26,140	*2*	36			*Clarke 22, 78*	*Sprake*	*Reaney*	*Davey*	*Yorath*	*Madeley*	*Gray*	*Lorimer*	*Clarke*	*Belfitt**	*Bates*	*Giles*	*Hibbitt*
							Ref: J Finney	Leeds' England full-back Paul Reaney broke his leg in the 48th minute after a collision with Keith Miller, playing his first full game. The crack could be heard all around the ground. West Ham fielded a pack of reserves in protest against Don Revie's broad hint that he might do the same.											
42	A	ARSENAL	16	L	1-2	1-2	Greaves 4	Grotier	Bonds	Lampard	Bennett	Stephenson	Moore	Holland	Eustace	Hurst	Greaves	Sissons	
	4/4	*36,218*	*9*	36			*Kelly 29, Radford 44*	*Wilson*	*Storey*	*McNab*	*Kelly*	*McLintock*	*Simpson*	*Marinello*	*Sammels*	*Radford*	*George*	*Graham*	
	Home	Away					Ref: R Capey	Greaves is a mini-god at the moment. His goals have put paid to fears of relegation and this is West Ham's first defeat since he came. 36 points is West Ham's lowest since returning to Division 1, 10 years earlier. Kelly's soft goal let Arsenal back into a game that West Ham began well.											
Average	30,689	31,399																	

League Cup						F-A	H-T	Scorers, Times, and Referees	1	2	3	4	5	6	7	8	9	10	11	12 sub used
2	H	HALIFAX	13		W	4-2	2-0	Lampard 15, Best 34, Hurst 71, 88	Ferguson	Bonds	Lampard	Peters	Stephenson	Moore	Redknapp	Lindsay	Brooking	Hurst	Best	
	3/9		20,717	*3:18*				*Lawther 50, Wallace 89*	*Smith*	*Burgin*	*Pickering*	*Lennard*	*McCarthy*	*Robertson*	*Shawcross*	*Hill*	*Ryden**	*Lawther*	*Flower*	*Wallace*
								Ref: J Osborne	The eye-catching duel in this untidy cup-tie was between Hurst and his rugged marker, Dave Lennard. Hurst got so angry by his mistreatment that he took the law into his own hands and got booked. He also scored the goal of the match, a perfect run and header from Redknapp's cross.											
3	A	NOTT'M FOREST	15		L	0-1	0-1		Ferguson	Bonds	Lampard	Boyce	Stephenson	Moore	Redknapp	Brooking	Hurst	Cross	Peters	
	23/9		*20,939*	*12*				*Lyons 30*	*Hill*	*Hindley*	*Winfield*	*Chapman*	*Hennessey*	*Newton*	*Rees*	*Lyons*	*Hilley*	*Barnwell*	*Moore*	
								Ref: N Burtenshaw	This is the first season that all 92 league clubs have entered the League Cup. West Ham are beaten by Hilley's through ball to Lyons which flummoxed Bonds. Ian Storey-Moore also hit the bar with a bender free-kick. West Ham had the edge after going behind but couldn't get back.											

FA Cup																				
3	A	MIDDLESBROUGH	16		L	1-2	0-1	Stephenson 86	Ferguson	Bonds	Lampard	Howe	Stephenson	Moore	Boyce	Peters	Best*	Hurst	Sissons	Redknapp
	3/1		*31,295*	*2:4*				*McIlmoyle 29, Downing 83*	*Whigham*	*Smith A*	*Jones*	*Smith G*	*Gates*	*Spraggon*	*Laidlaw*	*Maddren*	*McIlmoyle*	*Hickton*	*Downing*	
								Ref: T Pughe	Three hairline offside decisions went against West Ham, who were up against a team happy to use spoiling tactics. Moore and Bonds were booked in the second half and at the end sarcastically applauded the officials off the pitch. For this West Ham will be reported to the FA.											

		P	W	D	L	Home F	Home A	W	D	L	Away F	Away A	Pts
1	Everton	42	17	3	1	46	19	12	5	4	26	15	66
2	Leeds	42	15	4	2	50	19	6	11	4	34	30	57
3	Chelsea	42	13	7	1	36	18	8	6	7	34	32	55
4	Derby	42	15	3	3	45	14	7	6	8	19	23	53
5	Liverpool	42	10	7	4	34	20	10	4	7	31	22	51
6	Coventry	42	9	6	6	35	28	10	5	6	23	20	49
7	Newcastle	42	14	2	5	42	16	3	11	7	15	19	47
8	Manchester U	42	8	9	4	37	27	6	8	7	29	34	45
9	Stoke	42	10	7	4	31	23	5	8	8	25	29	45
10	Manchester C	42	8	6	7	25	22	8	5	8	30	26	43
11	Tottenham	42	11	2	8	27	21	6	7	8	27	34	43
12	Arsenal	42	7	10	4	29	23	5	8	8	22	26	42
13	Wolves	42	8	8	5	30	23	4	8	9	25	34	40
14	Burnley	42	7	7	7	33	29	5	8	8	23	32	39
15	Nott'm Forest	42	8	9	4	28	28	2	9	10	22	43	38
16	West Brom	42	10	6	5	39	25	4	3	14	19	41	37
17	WEST HAM	42	8	8	5	28	21	4	4	13	23	39	36
18	Ipswich	42	9	5	7	23	20	1	6	14	17	43	31
19	Southampton	42	3	12	6	24	27	3	5	13	22	40	29
20	Crys Palace	42	5	6	10	20	36	1	9	11	14	32	27
21	Sunderland	42	4	11	6	17	24	2	3	16	13	44	26
22	Sheffield Wed	42	6	5	10	23	27	2	4	15	17	44	25
		924	205	143	114	702	510	114	143	205	510	702	924

Odds & ends

Double wins: (1) Sheffield Wed.
Double losses: (2) WBA, Everton.

Won from behind: (0).
Lost from in front: (3) Stoke (a), Coventry (h), Arsenal (a).

High spots: Winning first two league games.
Seven league games with only one defeat from early October.
Winning 5-1 at Manchester City.

Low spots: Losing to Second Division Middlesbrough in League Cup.
Losing four league games on the trot in November and December.

Hammer of the Year: Bobby Moore.
Ever-presents: (1) Billy Bonds.
Hat-tricks: (0).
Leading scorer: (18) Geoff Hurst.

	Appearances Lge	*Sub*	LC	*Sub*	FAC	*Sub*	Goals Lge	LC	FAC	Tot
Bennett, Peter	**11**	*1*								
Best, Clyde	**24**		1		1		**5**	1		**6**
Bonds, Billy	**42**		2		1		**3**			**3**
Boyce, Ronnie	**18**	*2*	1		1		**1**			**1**
Brooking, Trevor	**20**	*1*	2				**4**			**4**
Charles, John	**5**									
Cross, Roger	**5**	*1*	1				**1**			**1**
Cushley, John	**2**									
Eustace, Peter	**14**						**2**			**2**
Ferguson, Bobby	**30**		2		1					
Greaves, Jimmy	**6**						**4**			**4**
Grotier, Peter	**12**									
Heffer, Paul		*1*								
Holland, Pat	**8**						**1**			**1**
Howe, Bobby	**32**	*1*			1		**1**			**1**
Hurst, Geoff	**38**	*1*	2		1		**16**	2		**18**
Lampard, Frank	**30**		2		1			1		**1**
Lindsay, Jimmy	**17**		1				**2**			**2**
Llewellyn, David		*2*								
Miller, Keith	**1**	*1*								
Moore, Bobby	**40**		2		1					
Peters, Martin	**31**		2		1		**7**			**7**
Redknapp, Harry	**23**		2			*1*	**1**			**1**
Sissons, John	**19**	*1*			1		**2**			**2**
Stephenson, John	**34**		2		1				1	**1**
(own-goals)							**1**			**1**
25 players used	**462**	***12***	**22**		**11**	***1***	**51**	**4**	**1**	**56**

LEAGUE DIVISION 1 — Manager: Ron Greenwood — SEASON 1970-71

No	Date		Att	Pos	Pt	F-A	H-T	Scorers, Times, and Referees	1	2	3	4	5	6	7	8	9	10	11	12 sub used
1	A	TOTTENHAM			D	2-2	1-2	Greaves 32, Bennett 59	Grotier	Bonds	Lampard	Bennett	Stephenson	Moore	Best	Brooking	Hurst	Greaves	Howe	
	15/8		*53,640*		1			*Gilzean 31, 39*	*Jennings*	*Evans*	*Knowles*	*Mullery*	*England*	*Bond*	*Gilzean*	*Perryman*	*Chivers*	*Peters*	*Pearce*	
								Ref: R Matthewson	Four of England's World Cup team from Mexico are on show. There is much national head-shaking at England's elimination, but this vibrant match raises spirits. All the goals were special, notably Gilzean's diving header. This is a worthy game for Sunday afternoon's The Big Match.											
2	H	ARSENAL			D	0-0	0-0		Grotier	Bonds	Lampard	Bennett	Stephenson	Moore	Best	Brooking	Hurst	Greaves	Howe	
	17/8		39,004		2				*Wilson*	*Storey*	*McNab*	*Kelly*	*McLintock*	*Roberts*	*Armstrong*	*Kennedy*	*Radford*	*Marinello*	*Graham*	
								Ref: J Finney	'Nought plus nought equals nought' wrote *The Times* scathingly about this 'paupers' ration of football'. The only action was on the terraces, which saw some argy-bargy. Two 'goals' were handled in what would later be called 'Maradona style'. Greaves was hacked mercilessly.											
3	H	CHELSEA			D	2-2	2-0	Howe 11, Hurst 21	Grotier	Bonds	Lampard	Bennett	Stephenson	Moore	Best	Brooking	Hurst	Greaves	Howe	
	22/8		39,240		3			*Weller 60, 74*	*Bonetti*	*Mulligan*	*Harris*	*Hollins*	*Dempsey*	*Hinton*	*Weller*	*Hudson*	*Osgood*	*Hutchinson*	*Houseman*	
								Ref: F Nicholson	Greaves did not score but he was a constant threat to Chelsea in this thriller. The other star was another ex-Spur, Keith Weller, who netted from two half-chances which made his £100,000 fee seem cheap. Bobby Moore was not at his best, nor was young Grotier, particularly at crosses.											
4	A	LEEDS		15	L	0-3	0-1		Grotier	Bonds	Lampard	Bennett	Stephenson	Moore	Best	Brooking	Hurst	Greaves	Howe	
	26/8		*42,677*	1	3			*Giles 43p, Jones 55, Belfitt 89*	*Sprake*	*Madeley*	*Cooper*	*Bates*	*Charlton*	*Hunter*	*Lorimer*	*Clarke*	*Jones*	*Giles**	*Gray*	*Belfitt*
								Ref: J Taylor	West Ham could have been hit for six, their only chance coming when Brooking burst through but shot against Sprake's legs. Lorimer danced round Lampard, who inexplicably handled. In addition to the goals Gray and Lorimer hit the woodwork. Elland Road gave a standing ovation.											
5	A	MANCHESTER U		15	D	1-1	1-1	Hurst 2	Grotier	Bonds	Lampard	Bennett	Stephenson	Moore	Best	Brooking	Hurst	Greaves	Howe	
	29/8		*50,643*	*17*	4			*Fitzpatrick 28*	*Rimmer*	*Edwards*	*Dunne*	*Fitzpatrick*	*Ure*	*Sadler*	*Morgan*	*Law*	*Charlton*	*Stiles*	*Best*	
								Ref: E Wallace	Man U still can't win at home. With Bonds policing George Best as well as anybody could, Old Trafford was uncharacteristically subdued. Sadly for West Ham, Greaves was equally nondescript. Old Trafford has never seen the best of him, though his shrewd pass did set up Hurst.											
6	H	SOUTHAMPTON		18	D	1-1	0-1	Hurst 65p	Grotier	Bonds	Lampard	Bennett*	Stephenson	Moore	Best	Brooking	Hurst	Greaves	Howe	Eustace
	31/8		26,213	*9*	5			*Jenkins 8*	*Martin*	*Kirkup*	*Hollywood*	*Fisher*	*McGrath*	*Walker*	*Paine*	*Channon*	*Davies*	*O'Neill*	*Jenkins*	
								Ref: R Kirkpatrick	This feeble affair was not worth the admission money, other than to see Jenkins' solo goal for Saints. He beat five defenders and sent a soft shot under Grotier. West Ham had given him a 'free': it is his first ever goal for Saints. David Walker 'fouled' Greaves for a laughable penalty.											
7	H	EVERTON		18	L	1-2	0-2	Moore 67	Grotier	Bonds	Lampard	Eustace	Stephenson	Moore	Best*	Brooking	Hurst	Greaves	Howe	Redknapp
	5/9		29.171	*17*	5			*Royle 30, Husband 39*	*West*	*Wright*	*Newton K*	*Kendall*	*Kenyon*	*Harvey*	*Husband*	*Ball*	*Royle*	*Hurst*	*Morrissey**	*Brown*
								Ref: K Howley	The defending champions have yet to win a match, until now. Joe Royle's unchallenged header was followed by Jimmy Husband shooting in off Stephenson. Moore scored from long range and Bonds hit a post. Peter Eustace was cheered at the start but jeered long before the end.											
8	A	WEST BROM		19	L	1-2	1-1	Howe 7	Grotier	Bonds	Lampard	Bennett	Stephenson	Moore	Brooking	Eustace	Best	Greaves	Howe	
	12/9		*24,913*	*15*	5			*Suggett 6, 84*	*Cumbes*	*Hughes*	*Merrick*	*Brown*	*Talbut*	*Kaye*	*McVitie*	*Suggett*	*Astle*	*Hope*	*Cantello*	
								Ref: G Jones	Jimmy Greaves is still searching for the 350th goal of his career. He might have taken a lesson from Colin Suggett, whose late winner was out of the Greaves' handbook. The referee ignored a linesman's raised flag, enabling Bobby Howe to quickly equalise Suggett's shot on the turn.											
9	H	NEWCASTLE		20	L	0-2	0-1		Grotier	Bonds	Lampard	Bennett	Stephenson	Moore	Redknapp*	Eustace	Hurst	Greaves	Best	Brooking
	19/9		25,841	*10*	5			*Robson 21, 55*	*McFaul*	*Craig*	*Clark*	*Gibb*	*Burton*	*Moncur*	*Robson*	*Dyson*	*Davies*	*Arentoft*	*Young*	
								Ref: R Darlington	Redknapp looks to be the only Hammer on form, and his substitution produces howls of boos from the crowd. The player to catch the eye is Newcastle's all-action Pop Robson, who volleyed the first goal and headed the second. West Ham now fly off to USA to play Pele's Santos.											
10	A	HUDDERSFIELD		20	D	1-1	0-1	Hurst 62p	Grotier	Bonds	Lampard	Boyce	Stephenson	Moore	Best	Brooking	Hurst	Eustace	Howe	
	26/9		*20,887*	*18*	6			*Smith 3*	*Poole*	*Jones*	*Hutt*	*Nicholson*	*Ellam*	*Clarke*	*Smith*	*Kryzwicki*	*Worthington*	*McGill*	*Dobson*	
								Ref: W Castle	West Ham drew 2-2 with Santos and return to UK to stage another draw. Bonds' miscued clearance let in Smith to volley past Grotier. Hurst levelled from the spot after he had been fouled by McGill, then Hammers fell back in defence. Greaves missed the game with back trouble.											

No	Venue	Opponent	Att	Pos	Res	F-A	H-T	Scorers, Times, Referees	1	2	3	4	5	6	7	8	9	10	11	12
11	H	BURNLEY		18	W	3-1	2-0	Hurst 27, 38, 80	Grotier	Bonds	Lampard	Boyce*	Eustace	Moore	**Ayris**	Brooking	Hurst	Best	Howe	Heffer
3/10			23,295	*22*	8			*Coates 82*	*Waiters*	*Angus*	*Merrington*	*Docherty*	*Waldron*	*Probert**	*Thomas*	*Coates*	*Casper*	*Wilson*	*West*	*Nulty*
								Ref: R Tinkler	Both teams are seeking their first win, and Jimmy Adamson's abject Burnley must wait awhile longer. Cockney-kid Johnny Ayris enjoys a confident debut, supplying the corner from which Hurst scored his first goal. His hat-trick came with a shot that flew in off Colin Waldron.											
12	A	STOKE		19	L	1-2	1-1	Greaves 22	Grotier	Bonds	Lampard	Lindsay	Stephenson	Moore	Boyce*	Best	Hurst	Brooking	Greaves	Eustace
10/10			*23,035*	*9*	8			*Greenhoff 33, Dobing 89*	*Banks*	*Marsh*	*Pejic*	*Bernard*	*Smith D*	*Bloor*	*Conroy*	*Greenhoff*	*Ritchie*	*Dobing*	*Burrows*	
								Ref: J Thacker	Vintage acrobatics from Greaves, whose overhead kick flies in off a post to leave Banks dumbstruck. Peter Dobing squared to Greenhoff for the equaliser, then collected Conroy's pass for the winner. Stephenson needs a cartilage operation, so a new centre-half must be found quickly.											
13	H	TOTTENHAM		20	D	2-2	1-2	Eustace 21, Hurst 51	Grotier	Bonds	Lampard	Eustace	**Taylor**	Moore	Ayris	Lindsay	Hurst	Greaves	Dear	
17/10			**42,322**	*4*	9			*Mullery 6, England 40*	*Jennings*	*Kinnear*	*Knowles*	*Mullery*	*England*	*Beal*	*Gilzean*	*Perryman*	*Chivers*	*Peters*	*Pearce*	
								Ref: B Homewood	Tommy Taylor, signed from Orient for £78,000, has a daunting debut against England's Martin Chivers. Moore stands tall as West Ham look to be falling apart before half-time, but driven on by Eustace – who had publicly disparaged the club a few hours earlier – they finish strongly.											
14	A	CRYS PALACE		20	D	1-1	1-0	Howe 5	Grotier	Bonds	Lampard	Eustace	Taylor	Moore	Howe	Lindsay	Hurst	Greaves	Dear	
24/10			*41,486*	*4*	10			*Taylor 75*	*Jackson*	*Sewell*	*Wall*	*Payne*	*McCormick*	*Blyth*	*Taylor*	*Kember*	*Queen**	*Birchenall*	*Tambling*	*Headley*
								Ref: R Johnson	Palace's record against London clubs is dreadful, but this season is better than usual for Bert Head's annual strugglers, who point to two strong penalty claims waived away. West Ham might have been three goals up by half-time and only looked shaky after Palace had drawn level.											
15	H	BLACKPOOL		16	W	2-1	1-1	Greaves 27, Eutstace 76	Grotier	**McDowell**	Lampard	Eustace*	Taylor	Moore	Ayris	Lindsay	Hurst	Greaves	Dear	Heffer
31/10			26,239	*21*	12			*Green 26*	*Thomson*	*Armfield*	*Mowbray*	*Craven*	*James*	*Alcock*	*Suddick*	*Green*	*Burns*	*Bentley*	*Hutchison*	
								Ref: J Yates	This was a ridiculously hard-earned win over the team that will finish bottom of the division. Even Bobby Moore had a stinker, as Blackpool found themselves with unexpected space in midfield. Mind you, West Ham wasted chances galore. Johnny Ayris laid on both Hammers' goals											
16	A	IPSWICH		17	L	1-2	1-0	Hurst 25	Grotier	McDowell	Lampard	Heffer*	Taylor	Eustace	Redknapp	Lindsay	Hurst	Best	Howe	Holland
7/11			*22,990*	*15*	12			*Hill 52, Mills 54*	*Sivell*	*Hammond*	*Mills*	*Morris*	*Baxter*	*McNeill**	*Robertson*	*Viljoen*	*Clarke*	*Woods*	*Hill*	*Lambert*
								Ref: W Gow	Max Marquis wrote 'this scrappy game, full of unforced errors, refereed with lamentable lack of authority.' Eustace played in Moore's shirt. Injury-hit Hammers went in front through acting skipper Hurst's 25-yarder. Hill drove in Morris's cross and Mills' winner flew in off Taylor.											
17	H	WOLVES		18	D	3-3	1-1	Best 34, 75, Moore 52	Grotier	McDowell	Lampard	Eustace	Taylor	Moore	Ayris	Lindsay	Best	Hurst	Howe	
14/11			23,978	5	13			*McCalliog 6, 83, Gould 88*	*Parkes*	*Shaw*	*Parkin**	*Bailey*	*Munro*	*McAlle*	*McCalliog*	*Hibbitt*	*Gould*	*Curran*	*Wagstaffe*	*Richards*
								Ref: Lewis	3-1 up with seven minutes to go, and West Ham blow it. Tommy Taylor was partially at fault with both late goals. Injuries to Greaves and Dear allowed Best to grab the limelight. Moore, who blasted a goal with his injured right foot, now looks forward to his testimonial against Celtic.											
18	A	MANCHESTER C		19	L	0-2	0-1		Ferguson	McDowell	Lampard	Eustace	Taylor	Moore	Holland	Lindsay*	Greaves	Hurst	Best	Howe
21/11			*28,485*	5	13			*Lee 9, 84*	*Corrigan*	*Book*	*Pardoe*	*Doyle*	*Heslop*	*Oakes*	*Summerbee*	*Bell*	*Lee*	*Mann*	*Towers*	
								Ref: D Corbett	Bobby Ferguson returns after an eight-month lay-off and plays superbly. Not even his heroics can stunt the skills of Colin Bell and Francis Lee, but one save from Alan Oakes' thunderbolt drew applause from Maine Road. It was the same old story for West Ham. Skill yes, effort no.											
19	H	COVENTRY		19	L	1-2	0-2	Best 57	Ferguson	McDowell	Lampard	Eustace	Taylor	Moore	Holland	Howe	Best	Hurst	Greaves	
28/11			**22,800**	*10*	13			*Clements 36, O'Rourke 38*	*Glazier*	*Coop*	*Smith*	*Mortimer*	*Blockley*	*Parker*	*Hill*	*Carr*	*Martin*	*O'Rourke*	*Clements*	
								Ref: L Callaghan	The first half was so bad the players were treated to bouts of slow-handclapping, and at the end Greenwood locked his players indoors for an ear-wagging. Bobby Moore had ducked under a corner, which was headed in by Dave Clements. Ferguson then failed to come out for a cross.											
20	A	DERBY		19	W	**4-2**	2-2	Greaves 16, Brooking 19, Best 71, 88	Ferguson	Bonds	Lampard	Eustace	Taylor	Moore	Lindsay	Brooking	Best	Hurst	Greaves	
5/12			*30,806*	*16*	15			*Wignall 9, Durban 28*	*Green*	*Webster*	*Robson*	*Durban*	*Hennessey*	*Mackay*	*McGovern*	*Wignall*	*O'Hare*	*Hector*	*Gemmill*	
								Ref: G Hartley	Two main talking points from this match. First, Greaves marking his 500th league match with a typical goal. Second, Ferguson's 81st-minute penalty save after Eustace had blocked Gemmill's run. Ferguson clearly moved early to save from Dave Mackay, denying Derby a 3-3 draw.											
21	H	LIVERPOOL		19	L	1-2	1-2	Greaves 41	Ferguson	Bonds	Lampard	Eustace	Taylor	Moore	Lindsay*	Brooking	Best	Hurst	Greaves	Ayris
12/12			27,459	*5*	15			*Witham 25, Boersma 43*	*Clemence*	*Lawler*	*Boersma**	*Smith*	*Lloyd*	*Hughes*	*Hall*	*McLaughlin*	*Heighway*	*Witham*	*Thompson*	*Ross*
								Ref: D Nippard	Even without towering John Toshack, Liverpool still possess sufficient aerial threat to beat West Ham with two headers. Jack Witham's is his first goal for Liverpool. He, like Boersma, was grateful to Ferguson staying rooted to his line. Greaves scored a gem, but missed two sitters.											

No	Date		Att	Pos	Pt	F-A	H-T	Scorers, Times, and Referees	1	2	3	4	5	6	7	8	9	10	11	12 sub used
22	A	CHELSEA		19	L	1-2	1-2	Lampard 40	Ferguson	Bonds	Lampard*	Eustace	Taylor	Moore	Ayris	Brooking	Dear	Lindsay	Greaves	Best
	19/12		*42,075*	*3*	15			*Osgood 19, 21*	*Bonetti*	*Boyle*	*Harris*	*Hollins*	*Hinton*	*Webb*	*Weller**	*Cooke*	*Osgood*	*Baldwin*	*Houseman*	*Hudson*
								Ref: D Pugh	West Ham's defence was regularly opened up by Chelsea's powerful surges. Peter Osgood's first was splendidly opportunist, though his second bobbled in off Ferguson. Lampard volleyed in from 15 yards. Only when Best came on at half-time did West Ham threaten Chelsea.											
23	A	ARSENAL		19	L	0-2	0-1		Ferguson	McDowell	Lampard	Bonds	Taylor	Howe	Redknapp	Lindsay	Best*	Brooking	Eustace	Llewellyn
	9/1		*49,007*	*2*	15			*Graham 40, Kennedy 80*	*Wilson*	*Rice*	*Nelson*	*Storey*	*McLintock*	*Simpson*	*Armstrong*	*Sammels*	*Radford*	*Kennedy*	*Graham*	
								Ref: A Taylor	Moore, Greaves, Best and Dear have been dropped for nightclubbing before a cup-tie. Bonds is acting skipper. Pat Rice crosses for Graham's stooping header. Ferguson's blunder gave Ray Kennedy a simple goal. The ref later signalled a 'goal' after Sammels' shot hit the side-netting.											
24	H	LEEDS		20	L	2-3	0-1	Eustace 78, Brooking 81	Grotier	McDowell	Lampard	Bonds	Taylor	Howe	Redknapp	Lindsay	Hurst	Brooking	Eustace	
	16/1		34,396	*1*	15			*Giles 32, Hunter 65, Belfitt 84*	*Sprake*	*Reaney*	*Cooper*	*Bates*	*Charlton*	*Hunter*	*Lorimer*	*Clarke*	*Jones**	*Giles*	*Madeley*	*Belfitt*
								Ref: V Batty	Hurst is acting captain. Leeds looked to be winning effortlessly when West Ham hauled themselves back with two headers in three minutes. Leeds immediately reasserted themselves. Jack Charlton said: 'Apart from the last 10 minutes this was the worst West Ham side I have seen.'											
25	H	DERBY		20	L	**1-4**	0-3	Eustace 48	Grotier	McDowell	Lampard	Bonds	Taylor	Howe*	Redknapp	Lindsay	Hurst	Brooking	Eustace	Moore
	6/2		26,606	*15*	15			*Hector 7, 19, Hinton 29, 68*	*Boulton*	*Webster*	*Robson*	*Durban*	*McFarland*	*Mackay*	*McGovern*	*Gemmill*	*O'Hare*	*Hector*	*Hinton*	
								Ref: J Finney	A game of two halves, as they say. Derby ran rampant in the first. For the second, the floodlights and Moore came on. West Ham fought their way back into contention. Grotier's feeble goal-kick cost the Hammers the first goal, then he failed to cut out Hinton's corner for the second.											
26	A	COVENTRY		20	W	1-0	1-0	Greaves 25	Ferguson	McDowell	Lampard	Bonds	Taylor	Moore	Redknapp	Boyce	Hurst	Greaves*	Eustace	Lindsay
	9/2		*25,083*	*12*	17				*Glazier*	*Coop*	*Smith*	*Mortimer*	*Blockley*	*Parker*	*Hunt*	*Carr*	*Martin*	*Joicey*	*Alderson*	
								Ref: G Kew	Moore, reappointed as captain, has seldom played better than now, on his recall from club suspension. Greaves, another of the Blackpool 'bad boys' caps his return with a crucial goal, after Glazier had repulsed Hurst's shot. When Coventry did threaten, they found Ferguson inspired.											
27	A	LIVERPOOL		20	L	0-1	0-0		Ferguson	McDowell	Lampard	Bonds	Taylor	Moore	Redknapp	Boyce	Hurst	Eustace	Greaves	
	16/2		*38,082*	*5*	17			*Toshack 58*	*Clemence*	*Lawler*	*Yeats*	*Smith*	*Lloyd*	*Hughes*	*Boersma*	*McLaughlin*	*Heighway*	*Toshack*	*Hall*	
								Ref: L Callaghan	John Toshack's flying header settled the points. It is the big Welshman's 7th goal in 15 games since his £110,000 signing. But West Ham could have few complaints. Twice Moore appeared to handle without the referee giving a penalty, and Taylor came within inches of an own-goal.											
28	H	MANCHESTER C		20	D	0-0	0-0		Ferguson	McDowell	Lampard	Bonds	Taylor	Moore	Redknapp	Boyce	Hurst	Eustace	Greaves	
	20/2		30,168	*7*	18				*Corrigan*	*Book*	*Towers*	*Doyle*	*Booth*	*Oakes*	*Jeffries*	*Young*	*Lee*	*Hill*	*Bowyer*	
								Ref: E Wallace	City have just lost in the FA Cup to Arsenal. Ron 'Ticker' Boyce is still only 28 and his return to the team is well merited. His superb pass into the path of Peter Eustace almost brought a winner. If West Ham escape the drop it will only be because Blackpool and Burnley are so far adrift.											
29	H	NOTT'M FOREST		20	W	2-0	1-0	Hurst 16, Robson 56	Ferguson	McDowell	Lampard	Bonds	Taylor	Moore	Redknapp	**Robson**	Hurst	Eustace*	Greaves	Lindsay
	24/2		35,601	*19*	20				*Barron*	*Hindley*	*Winfield*	*Chapman*	*O'Kane*	*Jackson*	*Lyons*	*Fraser*	*Martin*	*Cormack*	*Moore*	
								Ref: D Nippard	'Pop' Robson, a £120,000 buy from Newcastle, is an instant hit. His work-rate lifts the spirits of team-mates. His goal, following Redknapp's chip to the near post, was rapturously received. Geoff Hurst's far-post header from Moore's free-kick was his first goal since 7 November.											
30	A	BLACKPOOL		19	D	1-1	0-1	Hurst 73p	Ferguson	McDowell	Lampard	Bonds	Taylor	Moore	Redknapp	Boyce	Hurst	Eustace*	Robson	Greaves
	27/2		***15,639***	*22*	21			*Kemp 1*	*Ramsbottom*	*Armfield*	*Suddaby*	*Kemp*	*James*	*Hatton*	*Burns*	*Mowbray*	*Craven*	*Coleman**	*Hutchison*	*Johnston*
								Ref: G Hill	Blackpool had won only twice at home in 14 games, plus the 4-0 FA Cup debacle. Fred Kemp capitalised on Ferguson's weak punch out after just 26 seconds. Craven and Burns should have extended the lead before Suddaby panicked and handled Moore's cross. Hurst hit the penalty.											
31	H	CRYS PALACE		19	D	0-0	0-0		Ferguson	McDowell	Lampard	Bonds	Taylor	Moore	Redknapp	Boyce	Hurst	Robson	Greaves	
	6/3		26,157	*11*	22				*Jackson*	*Sewell*	*McCormick*	*Payne*	*Hoadley*	*Blyth*	*Wharton*	*Tambling*	*Queen*	*Birchenall*	*Taylor*	
								Ref: H Williams	Billy Bonds has been a revelation since his switch to midfield, in partnership with Boyce. John Jackson's saves earned Palace a point, none better than that from Robson at the death. Motiveless Palace had no thrust, and seemed to be daydreaming of their coming holiday to Jersey.											

No	Venue	Opponent / Date	Att	Pos	Pts	F-A	H-T	Scorers, Times, and Referees	1	2	3	4	5	6	7	8	9	10	11	12
32	A	WOLVES		20	L	0-2	0-0		Ferguson	McDowell	Lampard	Bonds	Taylor	Moore	Redknapp*	Robson	Hurst	Boyce	Eustace	Greaves
		13/3	*25,066*	*4*	22			*Gould 56, 80*	*Parkes*	*Shaw*	*Parkin*	*Bailey*	*Munro*	*McAlle*	*McCalliog*	*Hibbitt*	*Gould*	*Dougan**	*Wagstaffe*	*Walker*
								Ref: P Partridge	A horror-show for Hurst, who has one of those games when nothing goes in. At 0-0 Greaves set up a goal on a plate, but Hurst tries to pass to Robson and the chance is gone. Greaves turns pale in disgust. Gould dived to head a daisy cutter for No 1, then Moore messes up a back-pass.											
33	H	IPSWICH		20	D	2-2	1-0	Greaves 14, 74	Ferguson	McDowell	Lampard	Bonds	Taylor	Moore	Ayris	Boyce	Hurst	Robson*	Greaves	Best
		20/3	25,957	*17*	23			*Bell 59, Robertson 67*	*Sivell*	*Hammond*	*Mills*	*Morris*	*Bell*	*Jefferson*	*Robertson*	*Woods*	*Clarke*	*Collard*	*Hill*	
								Ref: R Mathewson	The spotlight is on Jimmy Greaves, partly for two once-typical, smash-and-grab goals, partly because of mounting rumours that he is set to retire. West Ham looked to Pop Robson for drive and inspiration until he went off injured. Lampard and Boyce both hit the Ipswich woodwork.											
34	A	EVERTON		20	W	1-0	1-0	Kendall 34 (og)	Ferguson	McDowell	Lampard	Bonds	Taylor	Moore	Redknapp	Boyce	Hurst	Robson	Greaves	
		30/3	*28,794*	*12*	25				*Rankin*	*Wright*	*Newton H*	*Kendall*	*Kenyon*	*Harvey*	*Whittle*	*Ball*	*Royle*	*Hurst*	*Morrissey*	
								Ref: V James	Everton are down in the dumps after losing an FA Cup semi-final. Redknapp returns from injury and drives in a low cross that Howard Kendall diverts into his own goal. Thereafter West Ham man the barricades to keep Everton out and register their first win at Goodison for 11 years.											
35	H	MANCHESTER U		20	W	2-1	2-0	Hurst 4, Robson 10	Ferguson	McDowell	Lampard	Bonds	Taylor	Moore	Redknapp	Boyce	Hurst	Robson	Greaves	
		3/4	38,507	*10*	27			*Best 56*	*Stepney*	*Fitzpatrick*	*Dunne*	*Crerand*	*Edwards*	*Sadler**	*Morgan*	*Law*	*Charlton*	*Best*	*Aston*	*Burns*
								Ref: D Lyden	After 10 minutes West Ham led by two and it might have been four. The first half showing is a revelation, as Hurst's fierce shot and Robson's deft placement has Upton Park roaring its approval. Aston's cross deflected off the referee into the path of Best. Then Law headed onto the bar.											
36	H	WEST BROM		19	W	2-1	0-1	Robson 67, Greaves 86	Ferguson	McDowell	Lampard	Bonds	Taylor	Moore	Redknapp	Boyce*	Hurst	Robson	Greaves	Brooking
		9/4	34,981	*16*	29			*Astle 30*	*Osborne*	*Hughes*	*Merrick*	*Cantello*	*Wile*	*Kaye*	*McVitie**	*Brown*	*Astle*	*Hope*	*Hartford*	*Suggett*
								Ref: T Reynolds	This win stretches West Ham's lead over 21st-placed Burnley to eight points, and survival seems assured. Albion have not won away for 16 months, but were a mite unlucky here. Astle missed three easy chances and Greaves hit the winner after the ball bounced kindly off a defender.											
37	A	NOTT'M FOREST		20	L	0-1	0-1		Ferguson	McDowell	Lampard*	Bonds	Taylor	Moore	Redknapp	Lindsay	Hurst	Robson	Greaves	Stephenson
		10/4	*23,032*	*17*	29			*Moore 45*	*Barron*	*Hindley*	*Winfield*	*Chapman*	*O'Kane*	*Fraser*	*Jackson*	*Richardson**	*Martin*	*Cormack*	*Moore*	*Rees*
								Ref: J Finney	Burnley's win over Blackpool cuts West Ham's safety margin at the bottom to six points. Hammers were sunk on half-time when Ian Storey-Moore outpaced the defence and side-stepped Ferguson. Pat Gibson wrote: 'It must have been the most overwhelming 1-0 win of the season.'											
38	A	BURNLEY		20	L	0-1	0-0		Ferguson	McDowell	Howe	Bonds	Taylor	Moore	Redknapp	Eustace	Hurst	Robson	Best	
		13/4	*15,822*	*21*	29			*Nulty 65*	*Waiters*	*Angus*	*Latcham*	*Docherty*	*Dobson*	*Nulty*	*Casper*	*Coates*	*Fletcher*	*Bellamy*	*Collins*	
								Ref: D Smith	The safety gap is now down to four, and Burnley have a game in hand too. When Ralph Coates crossed, three Burnley players were queuing up to head it in. West Ham came unashamedly for a point. They must hope that Burnley's run in – four away games out of five – proves too much.											
39	H	STOKE		20	W	1-0	0-0	Hurst 56	Ferguson	McDowell	Lampard	Stephenson	Taylor	Moore	Redknapp	Bonds	Hurst	Robson	Greaves	
		17/4	26,269	*15*	31				*Banks*	*Skeels*	*Pejic*	*Bernard*	*Smith D*	*Bloor*	*Jump**	*Greenhoff*	*Ritchie*	*Mahoney*	*Haslegrave*	*Lees*
								Ref: E Merchant	Despite the need for points, West Ham failed to display any urgency. Only Billy Bonds and Robson were above criticism. Bonds has just been named Hammer of the Year. Robson initiated the move that was finished off by Hurst. If Arsenal beat Burnley tomorrow, West Ham are safe.											
40	A	NEWCASTLE		20	D	1-1	1-1	Hurst 43	Ferguson	McDowell	Lampard	Stephenson	Taylor	Moore	Redknapp	Bonds	Hurst	Robson	Howe	
		24/4	*22,720*	*11*	32			*Tudor 38*	*McFaul*	*Craggs*	*Clark*	*Gibb*	*McNamee*	*Moncur*	*Foggan*	*Tudor*	*Dyson*	*Smith*	*Young*	
								Ref: F Nicholson	Robson returns to St James' and is booed throughout. John Tudor's half-hit shot deceived Ferguson, who was going the wrong way. Harry Redknapp's centre was then pushed home by Hurst. Because of the high wind, the referee took off his toupee rather than have it blown away.											
41	A	SOUTHAMPTON		17	W	2-1	1-0	Taylor 17, Hurst 65	Ferguson	McDowell	Lampard	Stephenson	Taylor	Moore	Llewellyn	Bonds	Hurst	Robson	Howe	
		27/4	*19,395*	*7*	34			*Davies 73*	*Martin*	*Kirkup*	*Hollywood*	*Fisher*	*McGrath*	*Gabriel*	*Paine*	*Channon*	*Davies*	*O'Neill*	*Jenkins*	
								Ref: Walker	This is Hammers' first win over Southampton in 10 Division 1 matches, and it wrecks the Saints hopes of playing in Europe next season. The home team attacked throughout. Mick Channon volleyed against the bar before Tommy Taylor ambled up unchallenged to score from 30 yards.											
42	H	HUDDERSFIELD		20	L	0-1	0-0		Ferguson	McDowell	Lampard	Stephenson	Taylor	Moore	Redknapp	Bonds	Hurst	Robson	Greaves	
		1/5	24,983	*15*	34			*Lawson J 49*	*Lawson D*	*Clarke*	*Jones*	*Nicholson*	*Ellam*	*Cherry*	*Barry*	*Mahoney*	*Worthington*	*McGill*	*Lawson J*	
		Home	Away					Ref: N Burtenshaw	Greaves' piledriver was kicked off the line and Robson hit the underside of the bar. It was that sort of day for West Ham, who wasted countless other chances, and lost when Mike Barry's shot was deflected in off Jimmy Lawson's hip. Lawson knew nothing about the goal he had scored.											
Average		29,961	30,680																	

League Cup			F-A	H-T	Scorers, Times, and Referees	1	2	3	4	5	6	7	8	9	10	11	12 sub used
2 H HULL	18	W	1-0	0-0	Eustace 85	Grotier	Bonds !	Lampard	Eustace	Stephenson	Moore	Best	Redknapp	Hurst	Greaves	Howe	
9/9	19,116 *2:5*					*McKechnie*	*Beardsley*	*de Vries*	*Wilkinson*	*Neill*	*Simpkin*	*Lord*	*Houghton**	*Chilton*	*Wagstaff*	*Jarvis*	*Greenwood*
					Ref: N Burtenshaw	Three minutes from time Billy Bonds is sent off for spitting at Hull's Chris Simpkin. Bonds already has a three-match suspension hanging over him from last season. The referee needed a police escort from the pitch at the end. Terry Neill's Hull were beaten by Peter Eustace's left-footer.											
3 A COVENTRY	18	L	1-3	0-1	Hurst 85	Grotier	Bonds	Lampard	Lindsay	Stephenson	Moore	Ayris	Best	Hurst	Brooking	Eustace	
6/10	*19,362 14*				*Martin 41p, O'Rourke 71, Carr 90*	*Glazier*	*Coop*	*Bruck*	*Clements*	*Blockley*	*Strong*	*Hunt*	*Carr*	*Martin*	*O'Rourke*	*Alderson*	
					Ref: A Jones	On Saturday Coventry beat champions Everton, courtesy of Ernie Hunt's famous free-kick, and now easily boot West Ham out of the League Cup. Eustace fisted over Alderson's header. Penalty! O'Rourke scored off the bar from 20 yards. Hurst's late bullet breathed life into the game.											

FA Cup																	
3 A BLACKPOOL	19	L	0-4	0-2		Ferguson	Bonds	Lampard	Eustace	Taylor	Moore	Ayris*	Lindsay	Best	Greaves	Howe	Dear
2/1	*21,814 21*				*Green 30, 38, Craven 47, Mowbray 80*	*Taylor*	*Armfield*	*Mowbray*	*Kemp*	*James*	*Hatton*	*Burns*	*Green*	*Craven*	*Coleman*	*Hutchison*	
					Ref: E Wallace	Blackpool's new boss, Bob Stokoe, enjoys this win. Pool have won only two other cup games in the past 10 years. Tony Green capped a mazy run with the first goal and beat Moore with ease for the second. This match has repercussions for Moore and others for off-field 'activities'.											

		Home						Away					
		P	W	D	L	F	A	W	D	L	F	A	Pts
1	Arsenal	42	18	3	0	41	6	11	4	6	30	23	65
2	Leeds	42	16	2	3	40	12	11	8	2	32	18	64
3	Tottenham	42	11	5	5	33	19	8	9	4	21	14	52
4	Wolves	42	13	3	5	33	22	9	5	7	31	32	52
5	Liverpool	42	11	10	0	30	10	6	7	8	12	14	51
6	Chelsea	42	12	6	3	34	21	6	9	6	18	21	51
7	Southampton	42	12	5	4	35	15	5	7	9	21	29	46
8	Manchester U	42	9	6	6	29	24	7	5	9	36	42	43
9	Derby	42	9	5	7	32	26	7	5	9	24	28	42
10	Coventry	42	12	4	5	24	12	4	6	11	13	26	42
11	Manchester C	42	7	9	5	30	22	5	8	8	17	20	41
12	Newcastle	42	9	9	3	27	16	5	4	12	17	30	41
13	Stoke	42	10	7	4	28	11	2	6	13	16	37	37
14	Everton	42	10	7	4	32	16	2	6	13	22	44	37
15	Huddersfield	42	7	8	6	19	16	4	6	11	21	33	36
16	Nott'm Forest	42	9	4	8	29	26	5	4	12	13	35	36
17	West Brom	42	9	8	4	34	25	1	7	13	24	50	35
18	Crys Palace	42	9	5	7	24	24	3	6	12	15	33	35
19	Ipswich	42	9	4	8	28	22	3	6	12	14	26	34
20	WEST HAM	42	6	8	7	28	30	4	6	11	19	30	34
21	Burnley	42	4	8	9	20	31	3	5	13	9	32	27
22	Blackpool	42	3	9	9	22	31	1	6	14	12	35	23
		924	215	135	112	652	437	112	135	215	437	652	924

Odds & ends

Double wins: (0).
Double losses: (2) Leeds, Liverpool.

Won from behind: (3) Blackpool (h), Derby (a), WBA (h).
Lost from in front: (2) Stoke (a), Ipswich (a).

High spots: Three successive league wins in March and April.
Avoiding relegation, but only because Burnley and Blackpool were even worse.

Low spots: Failing to win any of the first 10 league fixtures, dropping to 20th.
Losing five league games on the trot, December to February.
The nature of the capitulation at Blackpool in the FA Cup.

Only two of West Ham's league matches featured four goals by either side. Both were against Derby.

Hammer of the Year: Billy Bonds.
Ever-presents: (0).
Hat-tricks: (1) Geoff Hurst.
Leading scorer: (15) Geoff Hurst.

	Appearances						Goals			
	Lge	*Sub*	LC	*Sub*	FAC	*Sub*	**Lge**	LC	FAC	**Tot**
Ayris, Johnny	**6**	*1*	1		1					
Bennett, Peter	**8**						**1**			**1**
Best, Clyde	**20**	*2*	2		1		**5**			**5**
Bonds, Billy	**37**		2		1					
Boyce, Ronnie	**13**									
Brooking, Trevor	**17**	*2*	1				**2**			**2**
Dear, Brian	**4**					*1*				
Eustace, Peter	**25**	*2*	2		1		**4**	1		**5**
Ferguson, Bobby	**23**				1					
Greaves, Jimmy	**30**	*2*	1		1		**9**			**9**
Grotier, Peter	**19**		2							
Heffer, Paul	**1**	*2*								
Holland, Pat	**2**	*1*								
Howe, Bobby	**20**	*1*	1		1		**3**			**3**
Hurst, Geoff	**39**		2				**14**	1		**15**
Lampard, Frank	**41**		2		1		**1**			**1**
Lindsay, Jimmy	**14**	*2*	1		1					
Llewellyn, David	**1**	*1*								
McDowell, John	**25**									
Moore, Bobby	**38**	*1*	2		1		**2**			**2**
Redknapp, Harry	**20**	*1*	1							
Robson, Bryan	**14**						**3**			**3**
Stephenson, Alan	**15**	*1*	2							
Taylor,Tommy	**30**				1		**1**			**1**
(own-goals)							**2**			**2**
24 players used	**462**	*19*	22		11	*1*	**47**	2		**49**

No	Date	Att	Pos	Pt	F-A	H-T	Scorers, Times, and Referees	1	2	3	4	5	6	7	8	9	10	11	12 sub used
1	H WEST BROM			L	0-1	0-1		Ferguson	McDowell	Lampard	Bonds	Stephenson	Moore	Ayris	Best	Hurst	Taylor	Robson	
	14/8	27,420		0			*Brown 38*	*Cumbes*	*Hughes*	*Wilson*	*Cantello*	*Wile*	*Kaye*	*Hope*	*Suggett*	*Astle*	*Brown*	*Merrick*	
							Ref: T Dawes	Jimmy Greaves has quit. Don Howe's new-look Albion present more threat than West Ham, for whom Pop Robson looks forlorn and wasted wide on the wing. The goal stemmed from a long ball to Tony Brown, with the Hammers' defence spreadeagled. Jim Cumbes did well in goal.											
2	A DERBY			L	0-2	0-2		Ferguson	McDowell	Lampard	Bonds	Stephenson	Moore	Ayris*	Best	Hurst	Taylor	Robson	Howe
	18/8	*30,583*		0			*O'Hare 2, Wignall 8*	*Boulton*	*Webster*	*Robson*	*McGovern*	*Hennessey*	*Todd*	*Gemmill*	*Wignall*	*O'Hare*	*Hector*	*Hinton*	
							Ref: J Hunting	A new FA directive states: 'Referees must issue cautions for dissent.' In which case Moore and several team-mates should have been booked for protesting against a caution for Taylor. In fact, Moore *et al* escaped punishment. Moore had a bad night: his back-header put Derby in front.											
3	A NOTT'M FOREST		22	L	0-1	0-1		Ferguson	McDowell	Lampard	Bonds	Taylor	Moore	Ayris	Robson	Best	Brooking	Howe	
	21/8	*17,185*	*17*	0			*Moore 42p*	*Barron*	*Hindley*	*Chapman*	*O'Kane*	*Winfield*	*Rees*	*Fraser*	*Cormack*	*Moore*	*Martin*	*McKenzie*	
							Ref: W Johnson	Forest pick up their first points, leaving Hammers pointless and goalless. The decisive moment came when Lampard shoved Martin to concede the penalty. West Ham protested vigorously, but no one had their name taken. Martin admitted that Lampard had stumbled. Hurst was dropped!											
4	H IPSWICH		22	D	0-0	0-0		Ferguson	McDowell	Lampard	Bonds	Taylor	Moore	Ayris*	Best	Hurst	Brooking	Robson	Howe
	23/8	25,714	*5*	1				*Best*	*Carroll*	*Harper*	*Morris*	*Bell*	*Jefferson*	*Robertson*	*Mills*	*Clarke*	*Hamilton*	*Miller*	
							Ref: D Pugh	Four games and still no goals. Hurst played the first half on the wing. Only Clyde Best looked capable of besting David Best in the Town goal, though all of his good shots were fired from outside the area. Morris volleyed against a post and Bryan Hamilton missed a sitter at the death.											
5	H EVERTON		21	W	1-0	0-0	Best 54	Ferguson	McDowell	Lampard	Bonds	Taylor	Moore	Ayris	Best	Hurst	Brooking	Robson	
	28/8	26,878	*19*	3				*West*	*Scott*	*Newton*	*Kendall*	*Lyons*	*Harvey**	*Husband*	*Ball*	*Johnson*	*Hurst*	*Morrissey*	*Kenyon*
							Ref: H New	Greenwood bravely sticks with the same team that drew with Ipswich. Guts and endeavour won this game. Clyde Best outjumped keeper West from Bobby Moore's free-kick. Thereafter West Ham funnelled back in numbers, giving way to panic from time to time. Best also hit the bar.											
6	H COVENTRY			W	**4-0**	2-0	Best 17, 51, Hurst 35, Robson 52	Ferguson	McDowell	Lampard	Bonds	Taylor	Moore	Ayris	Best	Hurst	Brooking	Robson	
	30/8	28,176		5				*Glazier*	*Smith*	*Cattlin*	*Mortimer*	*Blackley*	*Barry*	*Young*	*Carr*	*O'Rourke*	*Hurst*	*McGuire*	
							Ref: M Kerkhof	Noel Cantwell's Coventry come unstuck in a fixture that, the previous season, saw Greenwood lambast his players behind closed doors. Once Best had burst through a plodding defence the outcome was clear. Brooking lit the fuses and Geoff Hurst's confidence returned after his goal.											
7	A NEWCASTLE		12	D	2-2	2-1	Hurst 14, Robson 32	Ferguson	McDowell	Lampard	Bonds	Taylor	Moore	Ayris	Best	Hurst	Brooking	Robson	
	4/9	*31,910*	*18*	6			*Tudor 12, Cassidy 66*	*McFaul*	*Craig*	*Clark*	*Gibb*	*Burton*	*Moncur**	*Hindson*	*Tudor*	*Macdonald*	*Guthrie*	*Hibbitt*	*Cassidy*
							Ref: C Fallon	Newcastle lost 1-5 at Leeds in midweek and are so inferior to West Ham that the home team are brutally barracked by their supporters. Robson returns to the ground he left in February and makes one goal and scores one. The man bought to replace him, Malcolm Macdonald, did little.											
8	H CHELSEA		9	W	2-1	0-0	Best 60, 80	Ferguson	McDowell	Lampard	Bonds	Taylor	Moore	Ayris*	Best	Hurst	Brooking	Robson	Howe
	11/9	36,866	*15*	8			*Hollins 74*	*Phillips*	*Mulligan*	*Harris*	*Hollins*	*Dempsey*	*Webb*	*Boyle*	*Garland*	*Osgood*	*Hudson*	*Houseman*	
							Ref: P Walters	Six unbeaten games is West Ham's best run for three years. The much-publicised clampdown by refs on foul play and tackles from behind has played its part. Best is dubbed the new Pele, with his feints and shimmies, and might have had five goals. Ferguson fumbled Hollins' effort.											
9	A MANCHESTER U		12	L	2-4	1-2	Best C 25, Brooking 57	Ferguson	McDowell	Lampard	Bonds	Taylor	Moore	Redknapp	Best	Hurst	Brooking	Robson	
	18/9	*53,334*	*2*	8			*Best G 21, 41, 79, Charlton 62*	*Stepney*	*O'Neil*	*Dunne*	*Gowling*	*James*	*Sadler*	*Morgan*	*Kidd*	*Charlton*	*Law*	*Best*	
							Ref: R Kirkpatrick	West Ham looked good in the first half; Frank O'Farrell's Man U in the second, as Hammers changed tactics and tried to raid down the middle rather than down the flanks. Clyde Best was overshadowed by the limping George Best. Moore dived to head off the line from Law at the end.											
10	H STOKE		10	W	2-1	1-0	Best 26, Moore 79	Ferguson	McDowell	Lampard	Bonds	Taylor	Moore	**Durrell**	Best	Hurst	Brooking	Robson	
	25/9	29,193	*12*	10			*Ritchie 59*	*Banks*	*Marsh*	*Pejic*	*Bernard*	*Smith*	*Bloor*	*Conroy**	*Greenhoff*	*Ritchie*	*Dobing*	*Jump*	*Stevenson*
							Ref: C Thomas	A lenient ref allowed Stoke to go unpunished for crippling tackles. West Ham were so much on top that John Ritchie's equaliser threatened to make a mockery of the game. As is was, West Ham needed a freak winner – Moore's shot looping off Denis Smith's foot and over Banks.											

No / Date	Venue	Opponent	Att	Pos	Res / Pts	FT	HT	Scorers, Times, and Referees	1	2	3	4	5	6	7	8	9	10	11	12
11	A	LEEDS		10	D	0-0	0-0		Ferguson	McDowell	Lampard	Bonds	Taylor	Moore	Redknapp	Best	Hurst	Brooking	Robson	
2/10			*30,942*	*5*	11				*Sprake*	*Reaney*	*Cooper*	*Yorath*	*Charlton*	*Hunter*	*Lorimer*	*Mann**	*Belfitt*	*Giles*	*Madeley*	*Galvin*
								Ref: G Jones	Injury-hit Leeds lack their usual thrust, enabling West Ham a more comfortable draw than they might have hoped for. Had Best's late header gone in instead of bouncing off the bar, it would have ended Leeds' unbeaten home record. Moore escaped a caution for deliberate handball.											
12	H	LEICESTER		12	D	1-1	0-0	Hurst 85	Ferguson	McDowell	Lampard	Bonds	Taylor	Moore	Redknapp	Best	Hurst	Brooking	Robson	
9/10			31,060	*20*	12			*Cross 87*	*Shilton*	*Whitworth*	*Nish*	*Cross*	*Sjoberg*	*Manley*	*Glover*	*Weller*	*Fern*	*Sammels*	*Birchenall*	
								Ref: R Gow	City's Cross presented a goal on a plate for Hurst, only to redeem himself seconds later by moving upfield for an equally scrappy equaliser. A boring, tactical game was enlivened only by Shilton, who pulled off a 'Banks-Pele' save from Pop Robson and also kept out Brooking's volley.											
13	A	WEST BROM		11	D	0-0	0-0		Ferguson	McDowell	Lampard	Bonds	Taylor	Moore	Redknapp	Best	Hurst	Brooking	Robson	
16/10			*20,740*	*16*	13				*Osborne*	*Hughes*	*Wilson*	*Cantello*	*Wile*	*Robertson*	*McLean*	*Brown*	*Astle*	*Gould*	*Hartford*	
								Ref: C Howell	Albion narrowly avoided a fifth successive home defeat, but have still scored only three goals since the end of August. In the latter stages Best, Bonds and Hurst all had chances to secure West Ham's first away win but were thwarted by the excellent Osborne, newly restored in goal.											
14	H	WOLVES		9	W	1-0	1-0	Best 10	Ferguson	McDowell	Lampard	Bonds	Taylor	Moore	Durrell	Best	Hurst	Brooking*	Robson	Howe
23/10			33,883	*11*	15				*Parkes*	*Shaw*	*Parkin*	*Bailey*	*Taylor*	*McAlle*	*Hegan**	*McCalliog*	*Richards*	*Dougan*	*Hibbitt*	*Wilson*
								Ref: K Sweet	Newboy Joe Durrell supplies the pass which Best converts from a tight angle. He also provided the crosses from which Robson and Hurst should have added further goals. Reprieved, Wolves pressed strongly at the close, when Ferguson repulsed Kenny Hibbitt's thunderbolt.											
15	A	CRYS PALACE		9	W	3-0	2-0	Coker 7, Bonds 14, Best 65	Grotier	McDowell	Lampard	Bonds	Taylor	Moore	Redknapp	Best	**Coker**	Brooking	Robson	
30/10			*41,540*	*21*	17				*Jackson*	*Payne*	*Wall*	*Goodman*	*McCormick*	*Blyth*	*Tambling*	*Craven*	*Hughes**	*Kellard*	*Taylor*	*Wallace*
								Ref: K Walker	Ade Coker is the latest youth product to burst through. It takes him just seven minutes to fire West Ham into the lead. Robson won the ball so easily to set up the second goal that Palace boss Bert Head was fuming. October has been a wonderful month for West Ham in league and cup.											
16	H	SHEFFIELD UTD		10	L	1-2	0-1	Robson 48	Ferguson	McDowell*	Lampard	Bonds	Taylor	Moore	Redknapp	Best	Hurst	Brooking	Robson	Ayris
6/11			36,595	*5*	17			*Rees 42, 75*	*Hope*	*Badger*	*Hemsley*	*Flynn*	*Colquhoun*	*Hockey*	*Woodward*	*Salmons*	*Reece*	*Currie*	*Scullion*	
								Ref: R Crabb	Blades overturn the form book to win comfortably in this League Cup rehearsal. Redknapp could not get going and Johnny Ayris was not brought on till the 83rd minute. Two headers by Rees won the game and but for erratic shooting by Scullion the margin could have been wider.											
17	A	HUDDERSFIELD		10	L	0-1	0-0		Ferguson	McDowell	Lampard	Bonds	Taylor	Moore	Redknapp	Best	Coker	Brooking	Robson	
13/11			***14,177***	*18*	17			*Smith D 77*	*Lawson D*	*Clarke*	*Hutt*	*Jones*	*Ellam*	*Cherry*	*Smith D*	*Smith S*	*Worthington*	*Lawson J*		
								Ref: F Nicholson	Wrote Frank Green: 'Having reached the dizzy heights of 10th West Ham relapsed into bad habits, including back-passing to Ferguson at a pace allowing opposing forwards a sporting chance of intervention.' Chapman dispossessed Bonds to set up the goal. Town's first win in nine.											
18	H	MANCHESTER C		13	L	0-2	0-1		Ferguson	Bonds	Lampard	Eustace	Taylor	Moore	Redknapp	Best	Coker*	Brooking	Robson	Durrell
20/11			33,694	*3*	17			*Lee 37p, Davies 60*	*Corrigan*	*Book*	*Donachie*	*Doyle*	*Booth*	*Oates*	*Summerbee*	*Bell*	*Davies*	*Lee*	*Mellor*	
								Ref: W Castle	Tommy Taylor's bitter feud with Wyn Davies, broadcast in detail on TV, cost West Ham a penalty. Davies himself scored City's second, bursting through from the halfway line. Bonds later pushed forward to replace the luckless Eustace, but it was too late. League form is sagging.											
19	A	LIVERPOOL		10	L	0-1	0-0		Ferguson	McDowell	Lampard	Bonds	Taylor	Moore	Redknapp	Best	Hurst	Brooking	Robson	
27/11			*43,399*	*6*	17			*Hughes 69*	*Clemence*	*Lawler*	*Lindsay*	*Smith*	*Ross*	*Hughes*	*Graham*	*Boersma*	*Heighway*	*Whitham*	*Callaghan*	
								Ref: N Burtenshaw	West Ham drew 4-4 with a European XI in Hurst's testimonial. James Mossop now writes: 'Emlyn Hughes cut through the West Ham defence as though its members were obstacles on a training exercise, used Jack Whitham for a quick wall-pass, and rammed in a fierce right-footer.'											
20	H	ARSENAL		13	D	0-0	0-0		Ferguson	McDowell	Lampard	Bonds	Taylor	Moore	Redknapp	Best	Hurst	Brooking	Robson	
4/12			35,155	*8*	18				*Wilson*	*Rice*	*McNab*	*Storey*	*McLintock*	*Simpson*	*Armstrong*	*Kelly*	*Radford*	*Kennedy*	*Graham*	
								Ref: C Nicholls	It is now five years and 11 matches since West Ham defeated Arsenal. They might have ended that sequence had Wilson not saved brilliantly from Robson. Wilson was voted man of the match by most Sunday papers. When Kelly's shot hit Taylor amidships, he appealed for a penalty.											
21	A	SOUTHAMPTON		12	D	3-3	3-2	Bonds 12, Best 21, Brooking 27	Ferguson	McDowell	Lampard	Bonds	Taylor	Moore	Redknapp	Best	Hurst	Brooking*	Robson	Llewellyn
11/12			*20,506*	*18*	19			*Gabriel 28p, Channon 35, Paine 77*	*Martin*	*Kirkup*	*Fry*	*Walker**	*Gabriel*	*Byrne*	*Paine*	*Channon*	*Davies*	*Stokes*	*Jenkins*	*O'Brien*
								Ref: R Tinkler	Hammers fans can hardly believe their eyes as a three-goal lead is casually tossed away. The decisive moment comes seconds after Brooking made it 3-0. Taylor fouled Jenkins and Gabriel clawed a goal back from the spot. Channon rounded Moore to set up Terry Paine's equaliser.											

No	Date		Att	Pos	Pt	F-A	H-T	Scorers, Times, and Referees	1	2	3	4	5	6	7	8	9	10	11	12 sub used
22	H	NEWCASTLE		13	L	0-1	0-1		Ferguson	McDowell	Lampard	Bonds	Taylor	Moore	Ayris	Best	Hurst	Brooking	Robson	
	18/12		21,991	*16*	19			*Busby 5*	*McFaul*	*Clark*	*Guthrie*	*Nattrass*	*Burton*	*Howard*	*Barr'clough**	*Busby*	*Macdonald*	*Reid*	*Hibbitt*	*Gibb*
								Ref: T Reynolds	West Ham's league form is in tatters, and they soon trail to Viv Busby's header from a corner. Newcastle always seemed to win the 50-50 balls. Best hit a post and then faded, and McFaul pulled off two good stops from Robson. At least Taylor handled Malcolm Macdonald well.											
23	A	TOTTENHAM		12	W	1-0	0-0	Best 47	Ferguson	McDowell	Lampard	Bonds	Taylor	Moore	Redknapp	Best	Hurst	Brooking	Robson	
	27/12		***53,888***	*7*	21				*Jennings*	*Evans*	*Knowles*	*Coates*	*England*	*Beal*	*Pratt*	*Perryman*	*Chivers*	*Peters*	*Gilzean*	
								Ref: R Challis	The rub of the green went West Ham's way when Mike England burst clear to miss early on, and when Neighbour shot against a defender's hand with no penalty given. Best nipped between Evans and England to head in Hurst's cross. The teams could meet in the League Cup final.											
24	H	MANCHESTER U		11	W	3-0	1-0	Robson 40, Best 56, Hurst 82p	Ferguson	McDowell	Lampard	Bonds	Taylor	Moore	Redknapp	Best	Hurst	Brooking	Robson	
	1/1		**41,892**	*1*	23				*Stepney*	*Dunne*	*Burns*	*Gowling*	*Edwards*	*Sadler*	*Morgan*	*Kidd*	*Charlton*	*Law*	*Best*	
								Ref: J Taylor	A joyous match with no malicious fouls and neither trainer called upon. Robson, Brooking and Bonds dominated midfield. Man U had lost just twice in 23 matches and were unlucky when Law and Best hit the woodwork. Taylor took fright when his back-pass fell to Law, who missed.											
25	A	EVERTON		14	L	1-2	1-2	Hurst 26p	Ferguson	McDowell	Lampard	Bonds	Taylor	Moore	Redknapp	Best	Hurst	Brooking	Robson	
	8/1		*38,482*	*12*	23			*Johnson 8, Harvey 14*	*West*	*Scott*	*McLaughlin*	*Kendall*	*Kenyon*	*Darracott*	*Johnson*	*Harvey*	*Royle*	*Lyons*	*Whittle*	
								Ref: D Turner	Everton chairman George Watts says: 'West Ham are the best side I have seen for years.' David Johnson whipped the ball off Moore's toe for the first goal, and Everton's second bobbled in after hitting both posts. Peter Scott punched away Geoff Hurst's header to concede the penalty.											
26	H	DERBY		12	D	3-3	1-1	Lampard 42, Robson 49, Brooking 80	Ferguson	McDowell	Lampard	Bonds	Taylor	Moore	Redknapp	Best	Hurst	Brooking	Robson	
	22/1		31,045	*4*	24			*Hinton 4, Durban 65, Hector 87*	*Boulton*	*Webster*	*Robson*	*Durban*	*McFarland*	*Todd*	*McGovern*	*Gemmill*	*O'Hare*	*Hector*	*Hinton*	
								Ref: J Thacker	Taylor's error presents a quick goal to Marvin Hinton. Lampard levelled through a crowded box. Hurst and Best then set up Robson, but Alan Durban stabbed home Hinton's cross. Brooking went past three defenders for 3-1. Derby equalised a third time from yet another Hinton cross.											
27	A	IPSWICH		13	L	0-1	0-0		Grotier	McDowell	Lampard	Bonds	Taylor	Moore	Redknapp	Best	Hurst	Brooking	Robson	
	29/1		*22,766*	*14*	24			*Morris 89*	*Best*	*Mills*	*Hunter*	*Jefferson*	*Harper*	*Morris*	*Viljoen*	*Miller*	*Robertson*	*Belfitt*	*Hill*	
								Ref: H Williams	A last-minute goal by Peter Morris – his first of the season in his 150th first-team game – gave Bobby Robson's Ipswich an ill-deserved win. Mick Hill ducked out of the way and the ball clipped Moore on its way past Grotier. This follows the League Cup disaster with Stoke City.											
28	A	WOLVES		15	L	0-1	0-0		Ferguson	McDowell	Lampard*	Bonds	Taylor	Moore	Ayris	Best	Hurst	Brooking	Robson	Stephenson
	12/2		*26,852*	*6*	24			*Richards 62*	*Parkes*	*Shaw*	*Parkin*	*Taylor*	*Munro*	*McAlle*	*McCalliog*	*Hibbitt*	*Richards*	*Dougan*	*Wagstaffe*	
								Ref: G Hartley	West Ham face a tricky cup replay with Hereford. They have lost their scoring touch and Molineux, where Wolves have yet to lose this season, is hardly the place to find it. Yet Best blazes a great chance at Parkes and West Ham pay the price when Dougan heads down for Richards.											
29	H	CRYS PALACE		13	D	1-1	0-0	Best 70	Ferguson	McDowell*	Lampard	Bonds	Taylor	Moore	Durrell	Best	Hurst	Brooking	Robson	Heffer
	19/2		28,209	*20*	25			*Payne 89*	*Jackson*	*Payne*	*Goodwin*	*Kellard*	*McCormick*	*Blyth*	*Craven*	*Queen*	*Wallace*	*Taylor*	*Tambling*	
								Ref: D Corbett	Both sides wasted chances to win, especially Palace, who looked frustrated when Tambling headed over the bar. Durrell hit a post for West Ham. Payne's late equaliser means West Ham remain just five points ahead of Palace. With just one goal in three games, Hammers lack punch.											
30	A	SHEFFIELD UTD		14	L	**0-3**	0-1		Ferguson	McDowell	Lampard	Bonds	Taylor	Moore	Eustace	Best	Llewellyn*	Brooking	Robson	**Lock**
	29/2		*24,034*	*10*	25			*Dearden 12, 48, 74*	*Hope*	*Badger*	*Hemsley*	*MacKenzie*	*Colquhoun*	*Salmons*	*Woodward*	*Scullion*	*Dearden*	*Currie*	*Ford*	
								Ref: D Laing	Sheffield have not won in seven games and had lost 0-5 to West Ham earlier. Blades' boss John Harris is looking for new strikers, and Billy Dearden, whose place is under threat, responds with three goals – a header sandwiched between two drives. West Ham look in a state of shock.											
31	H	HUDDERSFIELD		12	W	3-0	1-0	Best 37, 64, Robson 82	Ferguson	McDowell	Lampard	Bonds	Taylor	Moore	Redknapp	Best	Hurst	Brooking	Robson	
	4/3		18,521	*21*	27				*Lawson D*	*Clarke*	*Hutt*	*Smith S*	*Ellam*	*Cherry*	*Smith D*	*Dolan*	*Worthington*	*Lawson J*	*Chapman*	
								Ref: C Thomas	Huddersfield have just knocked West Ham out of the cup, though on this showing how they did so is a major mystery. Clyde Best tormented Ellam from first to last, heading in from Redknapp for the first goal, then sprinting past Ellam for the second. A flowing move preceded No 3.											

No / Date		Opponent / Att	Pos	Res / Pts	F-A	H-T	Scorers, Times, and Referees	1	2	3	4	5	6	7	8	9	10	11	12 sub used
32	A	LEICESTER	14	L	0-2	0-0		Ferguson	McDowell	Lampard	Bonds	Taylor	Moore	Redknapp	Best	Hurst	Brooking	Robson	
11/3		*23,345*	*15*	27			*Nish 69, 82*	*Wallington*	*Whitworth*	*Cross*	*Sjoberg*	*Nish*	*Fern*	*Sammels*	*Weller*	*Glover*	*Farrington**	*Birchenall*	*Manley*
							Ref: H Hackney	Windswept Filbert St saw a lesson in artistry by West Ham and a lesson in finishing by full-back David Nish, who was switched to attack after half-time. He scores with a header and a lob. Mark Wallington makes his debut in place of the injured Shilton. Best hit the bar from five yards.											
33	H	NOTT'M FOREST	12	W	4-2	3-0	Robson 2, 30, Hurst 8, Brooking 89	Ferguson	McDowell	Lampard	Bonds	Taylor	Moore	Holland	Best	Hurst	Brooking	Robson	
18/3		20,960	*22*	29			*McKenzie 75, 90*	*Barron*	*Hindley*	*Gemmell*	*Chapman*	*Cottam*	*Fraser*	*Lyons*	*O'Neill*	*Buckley*	*Richardson*	*McKenzie*	
							Ref: D Smith	Three goals up at the break, West Ham went to sleep in the second half. McKenzie's late goal made no difference to Forest's prospects, but even though neither trainer was called upon, the ref allowed plenty of injury-time. This produced two more goals that distort the scoreline.											
34	A	COVENTRY	12	D	1-1	1-1	Best 35	Ferguson	McDowell	**Charles C**	Bonds	Taylor	Moore	Holland	Best	Hurst	Brooking	Robson	
21/3		*18,640*	*18*	30			*Smith 14*	*Glazier*	*Smith*	*Cattlin*	*Machin*	*Blockley*	*Barry*	*McGuire*	*Carr*	*Chilton*	*Graham*	*Hunt*	
							Ref: R Lea	Debutant Clive Charles created the goal that brought Hammers' equaliser, sending over the cross that Holland headed down to Best. Full-back Wilf Smith had fired Sky Blues into the lead. Coventry chief Jimmy Hill had appealed before the start for more vocal backing for the team.											
35	A	CHELSEA	12	L	1-3	0-1	Best 90	Ferguson	McDowell	Lampard	Bonds	Taylor	Moore	Holland	Best	Hurst	Brooking	Robson	
25/3		*45,137*	*10*	30			*Osgood 39, Mulligan 65, Hollins 84*	*Bonetti*	*Mulligan*	*Boyle*	*Hollins*	*Dempsey*	*Harris*	*Kember*	*Webb*	*Osgood*	*Hudson*	*Cooke*	
							Ref: R Matthewson	A meaningless match illuminated only by occasional flashes from Osgood, Hudson or Cooke. Osgood bagged his 30th goal of the season, Paddy Mulligan's 25-yarder somehow eluded a mass of bodies, and West Ham defenders stood by idly as five passes preceded Hollins' goal.											
36	H	LEEDS	12	D	2-2	2-0	Bonds 4, Hurst 35	Grotier	McDowell	Lampard	Bonds	Taylor	Moore	Redknapp	Best	Hurst	Brooking	Robson	
31/3		41,003	*2*	31			*Gray 62, 74*	*Sprake*	*Reaney*	*Cooper*	*Bremner*	*Charlton*	*Hunter*	*Lorimer*	*Clarke*	*Jordan**	*Gray*	*Madeley*	*Bates*
							Ref: H New	A huge crowd comes to see the 'new' Leeds, TV entertainers, but Upton Park was treated to the 'old' Leeds – hard and professional. Robson appeared to handle before crossing for Hammers' second goal. Gray 'bent' Leeds' first goal. Grotier's weak punch preceded Leeds' equaliser.											
37	H	TOTTENHAM	11	W	2-0	1-0	Brooking 40, Coker 89	Grotier	McDowell	Charles	Bonds	Taylor	Moore	Ayris*	Best	Coker	Brooking	Robson	Lock
1/4		30,763	*5*	33				*Jennings*	*Evans*	*Knowles*	*Pratt*	*Collins*	*Naylor*	*Gilzean*	*Perryman*	*Chivers*	*Peters*	*Pearce*	
							Ref: D Nippard	Brooking has been voted Hammer of the Year and he celebrates by scoring one of the goals of the season. He bemused Peter Collins before curling in a 20-yard lob. That strike was against the run of play. Gilzean fell over the ball and Chivers missed a sitter before Lock set up Coker.											
38	A	STOKE	12	D	0-0	0-0		Grotier	McDowell	Lampard	Bonds	Taylor	Moore	Redknapp	Best	Hurst	Brooking	Robson	
4/4		*24,688*	*14*	34				*Banks*	*Marsh*	*Elder*	*Bernard*	*Bloor*	*Skeels*	*Conroy*	*Greenhoff*	*Ritchie*	*Dobing*	*Eastham*	
							Ref: E Wallace	On a rain-soaked pitch Banks once again defies the Hammers in this, the sixth meeting of the sides this season. Hammers missed three chances in the first three minutes, Best missing twice and Hurst once. At the other end Eastham had one effort headed off the line, another hit the post.											
39	A	MANCHESTER C	14	L	1-3	0-1	Hurst 82	Grotier	McDowell	Lampard	Bonds	Taylor	Moore	Redknapp	Best	Hurst	Brooking	Robson	
8/4		*38,491*	*4*	34			*Marsh 11, 68, Bell 49,*	*Healey*	*Book*	*Donachie*	*Towers*	*Booth*	*Oakes*	*Lee*	*Bell*	*Davies*	*Marsh*	*Summerbee*	
							Ref: J Hunting	Rodney Marsh has yet to convince City fans that Malcolm Allison was wise to buy him. Two goals against lifeless Hammers, his first goals for City, helps his cause. Had Redknapp done better than to rattle Healey's crossbar in the sixth minute the outcome might have been different.											
40	H	LIVERPOOL	14	L	0-2	0-1		Ferguson	McDowell	Lampard	Bonds	Taylor	Moore	Redknapp	Best	Hurst	Brooking	Robson	
15/4		32,660	*3*	34			*Toshack 9, Heighway 46*	*Clemence*	*Lawler*	*Lindsay*	*Smith*	*Lloyd*	*Hughes*	*Keegan*	*Hall*	*Heighway*	*Toshack*	*Callaghan*	
							Ref: K Wynn	John McDowell's lamentable attempt to clear Lawler's effort presented an early goal for Toshack. Straight after the turnaround, the previously impeccable Moore was dispossessed by Steve Heighway for the second. Later, the unmarked Clyde Best saw his effort cleared off the line.											
41	A	ARSENAL	15	L	1-2	1-1	Brooking 37	Ferguson	McDowell	Charles	Bonds	Taylor	Lock	Durrell	Best	Coker	Brooking	Robson	
22/4		*42,251*	*6*	34			*Ball 13, 46*	*Barnett*	*Rice*	*McNab*	*Storey*	*McLintock**	*Simpson*	*Armstrong*	*Ball*	*Radford*	*Kennedy*	*Graham*	*Batson*
							Ref: V James	Bertie Mee's Arsenal have their minds on their impending FA Cup final. Despite this, and stand-in keeper Geoff Barnett's tendency to panic, they were still too good for West Ham. Best moment of the game came when Durrell beat two men and crossed for Brooking's classic header.											
42	H	SOUTHAMPTON	14	W	1-0	0-0	Robson 60	Ferguson	Lampard	Charles	Bonds	Stephenson	Taylor	Durrell	Best	Holland	Brooking*	Robson	Boyce
1/5		**18,479**	*19*	36				*Martin*	*McCarthy*	*Hollywood*	*Steele*	*Bennett*	*Talkes*	*Paine*	*Channon*	*Davies*	*O'Brien**	*O'Neill*	*Gabriel*
	Home	Away					Ref: T Spencer	Ron Davies and Mick Channon look knackered from their efforts to stave off relegation for the Saints. Hammers were defied by Eric Martin in goal. He was beaten once, when Robson turned in Lampard's low cross. Bonds and Durrell hit the bar; Steele and Gabriel cleared off the line.											
Average	30,007	31,556																	

League Cup			F-A	H-T	Scorers, Times, and Referees	1	2	3	4	5	6	7	8	9	10	11	12 sub used
2 H CARDIFF	12	D	1-1	1-0	Bonds 32	Ferguson	McDowell	Lampard	Bonds	Taylor	Moore	Ayris	Best	Hurst	Brooking	Robson	
8/9 24,432	*2:19*				*Foggon 63*	*Eadie*	*Jones**	*Bell*	*Sutton*	*Murray*	*Phillips*	*Gibson*	*Clark*	*Woodruff*	*Warboys*	*Foggon*	*Parsons*
					Ref: J Taylor	Pop Robson is being played in midfield rather than up front, which is why he wanted to leave Newcastle. Greenwood placed Brooking on the transfer list last season, but he will have to take him off if he continues playing like this. Five minutes from time Clark hit Ferguson's crossbar.											
2R A CARDIFF	12	W	2-1	0-1	Hurst 83, 84	Ferguson	McDowell	Lampard	Bonds	Taylor	Moore	Redknapp	Best	Hurst	Brooking	Robson	
22/9 *30,100*	*2:19*				*Clark 15*	*Eadie*	*Jones*	*Bell*	*Sutton*	*Murray*	*Phillips*	*Gibson*	*Clark*	*Woodruff*	*Warboys*	*Hoy*	
					Ref: J Taylor	When Warboys headed down to Clark it looked grim for the Hammers. Hurst collected Redknapp's pass to smash a late equaliser, and within seconds Hurst nipped through a stunned defence for the winner. The prize for the winners is a plum home draw against either Derby or Leeds.											
3 H LEEDS	10	D	0-0	0-0		Ferguson	McDowell	Lampard	Bonds	Taylor	Moore	Redknapp	Best	Hurst	Brooking	Robson	
6/10 35,890	*5*					*Sprake*	*Davie*	*Cooper*	*Bremner*	*Charlton*	*Hunter*	*Lorimer*	*Yorath*	*Belfitt*	*Giles*	*Madeley*	
					Ref: R Matthewson	Even without four internationals, Leeds soaked up West Ham pressure. The ref disallowed two West Ham 'goals', Terry Cooper twice cleared off the line, and Hurst hit the bar. After the match a beer can was thrown at the ref and a brick tossed through the Leeds dressing room window.											
3R A LEEDS	11	W	1-0	0-0	Best 98	Ferguson	McDowell	Lampard	Bonds	Taylor	Moore	Redknapp	Best	Hurst	Brooking	Robson	
20/10 *26,504*	*7*		*aet*			*Harvey*	*Reaney*	*Cooper*	*Bremner*	*Charlton*	*Hunter*	*Lorimer*	*Clarke*	*Jones**	*Giles*	*Madeley*	*Gray*
					Ref: R Matthewson	Leeds have now failed to score against West Ham in three quick matches. The home team were undone by a gem of a goal, Redknapp's cross being turned in by a towering Best header. Moore began the move, played brilliantly, and shrugged off the wolf-whistles of the home crowd.											
4 H LIVERPOOL	9	W	2-1	1-1	Hurst 42, Robson 84	Ferguson	McDowell	Lampard	Bonds	Taylor	Moore	Redknapp	Best	Hurst*	Brooking	Robson	Howe
27/10 40,878	*7*				*Graham 30*	*Clemence*	*Lawler*	*Ross*	*Smith*	*Lloyd*	*Hughes*	*Graham*	*Evans*	*Heighway*	*Toshack*	*Callaghan*	
					Ref: D Turner	Geoff Hurst cancelled out Bobby Graham's goal, having been set up by Clyde Best. Hurst, however, had aggravated a thigh injury and failed to reappear after the interval. Redknapp crossed for Robson's winner at the far post. 'I'm forever blowing bubbles' echoed round Upton Park.											
QF H SHEFFIELD UTD	10	W	5-0	3-0	Robson 5, 33, 87, Best 40, 76	Ferguson	McDowell	Lampard	Bonds	Taylor	Moore	Redknapp	Best	Hurst*	Brooking	Robson	Howe
17/11 36,834	*4*					*Hope*	*Badger*	*Goulding*	*Flynn*	*Colquhoun*	*Hockey*	*Woodward*	*Salmons*	*Reece*	*Currie*	*Scullion*	
					Ref: D Smith	11 days earlier the Blades beat West Ham in the league. This is their first defeat in eight games against London opponents. Robson scored the classic hat-trick, one goal with his head, another with his right foot and one with his left. London has three semi-finalists – Chelsea and Spurs.											
SF A STOKE	13	W	2-1	1-1	Hurst 28p, Best 62	Ferguson	McDowell	Lampard	Bonds	Taylor	Moore	Redknapp	Best	Hurst	Brooking	Robson	
1 8/12 *36,400*	*11*				*Dobing 14*	*Banks*	*Marsh*	*Pejic*	*Bernard*	*Bloor*	*Jump*	*Conroy*	*Greenhoff*	*Ritchie*	*Dobing*	*Eastham*	
					Ref: A Morrissey	West Ham failed to withstand Stoke's ferocious early onslaught, but inspired by Bonds they come from behind. They are odds on to reach the final. A four-man move preceded Best's volley in off the bar. Moore's professional foul on Greenhoff earned the second booking of his career.											
SF H STOKE	12	L	0-1	0-0		Ferguson	McDowell	Lampard	Bonds	Taylor	Moore	Redknapp	Best	Hurst	Brooking	Robson	
2 15/12 38,771	*11*		*aet*		*Ritchie 73*	*Banks*	*Marsh*	*Pejic*	*Bernard*	*Bloor*	*Skeels*	*Conroy*	*Greenhoff*	*Ritchie*	*Dobing*	*Eastham**	*Mahoney*
					Ref: K Walker (Hammers draw 2-2 on aggregate)	Only once before has a team which lost the first leg of a League Cup semi-final reached the final. The error by Taylor and McDowell that set up Ritchie would have counted for nothing had not Banks pulled off a super save from Hurst's penalty, after Banks had taken Redknapp's legs.											
SF N STOKE	11	D	0-0	0-0		Ferguson	McDowell	Lampard	Bonds	Taylor	Moore	Redknapp	Best	Hurst	Brooking	Robson	
R 5/1 *49,247*	*12*		*aet*			*Banks*	*Marsh*	*Pejic*	*Bernard*	*Smith*	*Bloor*	*Conroy*	*Dobing*	*Ritchie*	*Greenhoff**	*Eastham*	*Skeels*
(At Hillsborough)					Ref: R Matthewson	Stoke have won nothing in their 108-year history, and had Gordon Banks not saved twice from Best they would still be waiting. Yet Stoke had much of the play, with Conroy and Eastham orchestrating their attacks. Stoke fans gave Moore the bird for an undignified tackle on Greenhoff.											
SF N STOKE	12	L	2-3	1-1	Bonds 39, Brooking 46	Ferguson	McDowell	Lampard	Bonds	Taylor	Moore	Redknapp*	Best	Hurst	Brooking	Robson	Eustace
2R 26/1 *49,247*	*11*				*Bernard 33, Dobing 50, Conroy 55*	*Banks*	*Marsh*	*Pejic*	*Bernard*	*Smith*	*Bloor*	*Conroy*	*Greenhoff*	*Ritchie*	*Dobing*	*Eastham*	
(At Old Trafford)					Ref: P Partridge	Conroy's nasty foul on Ferguson takes the concussed keeper temporarily from the field. Moore saves Bernard's penalty, but not the follow up. Marvellous goals for Bonds and Brooking give West Ham the edge, but Stoke not only scored twice themselves, but missed other chances too.											

FA Cup

No	Venue	Opponent	Att	Pos	Res	F-A	H-T	Scorers, Times, and Referees	1	2	3	4	5	6	7	8	9	10	11	12 sub used
3	H	LUTON		12	W	2-1	2-0	Hurst 2, Best 25	Ferguson	McDowell	Lampard	Bonds	Taylor	Moore*	Redknapp	Best	Hurst	Brooking	Robson	Eustace
	15/1		32,099	*2:13*				*Givens 53*	*Read*	*Ryan*	*Slough*	*Keen*	*Nicholl*	*Moore*	*Anderson*	*Court*	*Halom*	*Givens*	*Hindson*	
								Ref: K Burns	A gripping cup-tie. Brooking set up Hurst in 91 seconds. At 2-0 everything seems settled, but Don Givens' header transformed the match. On 68 minutes Read saved Hurst's penalty. On 78 minutes Gordon Hindson misses one at the other end. Nicholl then shot against Ferguson's legs.											
4	A	HEREFORD		13	D	0-0	0-0		Ferguson	McDowell	Lampard	Bonds	Taylor	Moore	Redknapp	Best	Hurst	Brooking	Robson	
	9/2		*15,000*	*SL*					*Potter*	*Gough*	*Mallender*	*Jones*	*McLaughlin*	*Addison*	*George*	*Tyler*	*Meadows*	*Owen*	*Radford*	
								Ref: R Tinkler	Greenwood sighs with relief as his team avoid the greatest humiliation in their history. The Southern Leaguers, who had beaten Newcastle in Round 3 and launched the career of commentator John Motson, pressed relentlessly. Tyler's shot, deflected by Moore, was cleared by Taylor.											
4R	H	HEREFORD		15	W	3-1	1-0	Hurst 43, 52, 74	Ferguson	McDowell	Lampard	Bonds	Taylor	Moore	Redknapp	Best	Hurst	Brooking	Robson	
	14/2		42,271	*SL*				*Meadows 84*	*Potter*	*Gough*	*Mallender**	*Jones*	*McLaughlin*	*Addison*	*George*	*Tyler*	*Meadows*	*Owens*	*Radford*	*Tucker*
								Ref: R Tinkler	Hereford played their part but never seriously threatened once Best's direct run had carved out Hurst's first goal. But for appalling casualness in front of goal, the score might have been embarrassing. Reg Pratt pledges his support for Hereford's application to join the Football League.											
5	A	HUDDERSFIELD		13	L	2-4	1-1	Robson 45, Best 83 *[Worth'ton 70]*	Ferguson	McDowell	Lampard	Bonds	Taylor	Moore	Redknapp	Best	Hurst*	Brooking	Robson	Heffer
	26/2		*27,080*	*21*				*Lawson J 23, Dolan 51, Smith D 68,*	*Lawson D*	*Clarke*	*Hutt*	*Smith S*	*Ellam*	*Cherry*	*Smith D*	*Dolan*	*Worthington*	*Lawson J*	*Chapman*	
								Ref: N Burtenshaw	The pain of this defeat showed in Ron Greenwood's face. Memories of the capitulation at Blackpool a year earlier came flooding back. West Ham couldn't cope with big Frank Worthington. Five of his blockbuster shots from outside the box almost carried Ferguson into the net.											

		Home						Away					
	P	W	D	L	F	A		W	D	L	F	A	Pts
1 Derby	42	16	4	1	43	10		8	6	7	26	23	58
2 Leeds	42	17	4	0	54	10		7	5	9	19	21	57
3 Liverpool	42	17	3	1	48	16		7	6	8	16	14	57
4 Manchester C	42	16	3	2	48	15		7	8	6	29	30	57
5 Arsenal	42	15	2	4	36	13		7	6	8	22	27	52
6 Tottenham	42	16	3	2	45	13		3	10	8	18	29	51
7 Chelsea	42	12	7	2	41	20		6	5	10	17	29	48
8 Manchester U	42	13	2	6	39	26		6	8	7	30	35	48
9 Wolves	42	10	7	4	35	23		8	4	9	30	34	47
10 Sheffield Utd	42	10	8	3	39	26		7	4	10	22	34	46
11 Newcastle	42	10	6	5	30	18		5	5	11	19	34	41
12 Leicester	42	9	6	6	18	11		4	7	10	23	35	39
13 Ipswich	42	7	8	6	19	19		4	8	9	20	34	38
14 WEST HAM	42	10	6	5	31	19		2	6	13	16	32	36
15 Everton	42	8	9	4	28	17		1	9	11	9	31	36
16 West Brom	42	6	7	8	22	23		6	4	11	20	31	35
17 Stoke	42	6	10	5	26	25		4	5	12	13	31	35
18 Coventry	42	7	10	4	27	23		2	5	14	17	44	33
19 Southampton	42	8	5	8	31	28		4	2	15	21	52	31
20 Crys Palace	42	4	8	9	26	31		4	5	12	13	34	29
21 Nott'm Forest	42	6	4	11	25	29		2	5	14	22	52	25
22 Huddersfield	42	4	7	10	12	22		2	6	13	15	37	25
	924	227	129	106	723	437		106	129	227	437	723	924

Odds & ends

Double wins (1) Spurs.
Doubles losses: (3) Sheffield Utd, Manchester C, Liverpool.

Won from behind: (2) Cardiff LC (a), Liverpool LC (h).
Lost from in front: (1) Stoke LC (n).

High spots: 12 league games with just one defeat from 23 August.
This lifted the Hammers to 9th.
Knocking both Leeds and Liverpool out of the League Cup.

Low spots: Losing the first three league games.
Losing all four league fixtures in November.
Losing to Stoke in dubious circumstances in League Cup semi-final.

Hammer of the Year: Trevor Brooking.
Ever-presents: (4) Bonds, Taylor, Best, and Robson.
Hat-tricks: (2) Geoff Hurst (1), Bryan Robson (1).
Leading scorer: (23) Clyde Best.

	Appearances						Goals			
	Lge	*Sub*	LC	*Sub*	FAC	*Sub*	Lge	LC	FAC	Tot
Ayris, Johnny	**11**	*1*	1							
Best, Clyde	**42**		10		4		**17**	4	2	**23**
Bonds, Billy	**42**		10		4		**3**	2		**5**
Boyce, Ronnie		*1*								
Brooking, Trevor	**40**		10		4		**6**	1		**7**
Charles, Clive	**4**									
Coker, Ade	**5**						**2**			**2**
Durrell, Joe	**5**	*1*								
Eustace, Peter	**2**			*1*		*1*				
Ferguson, Bobby	**36**		10		4					
Grotier, Peter	**6**									
Heffer, Paul		*1*				*1*				
Holland, Pat	**4**									
Howe, Bobby	**1**	*4*		*2*						
Hurst, Geoff	**34**		10		4		**8**	4	4	**16**
Lampard, Frank	**39**		10		4		**1**			**1**
Llewellyn, Dave	**1**	*1*								
Lock, Kevin	**1**	*2*								
McDowell. John	**40**		10		4					
Moore, Bobby	**40**		10		4		**1**			**1**
Redknapp, Harry	**22**		9		4					
Robson, Bryan	**42**		10		4		**9**	4	1	**14**
Stephenson, John	**3**	*1*								
Taylor, Tommy	**42**		10		4					
24 players used	**462**	*12*	**110**	*3*	**44**	*2*	**47**	**15**	**7**	**69**

No	Date		Att	Pos	Pt	F-A	H-T	Scorers, Times, and Referees	1	2	3	4	5	6	7	8	9	10	11	12 sub used
1	A	WEST BROM			D	0-0	0-0		Ferguson	McDowell	Lampard	Bonds	Taylor	Moore	**Tyler**	Best	Coker	Brooking	Robson	
	12/8		*21,509*		1				*Smith*	*Nisbet*	*Wilson*	*Cantello*	*Wile*	*Robertson*	*Brown T*	*Brown A*	*Gould*	*Suggett*	*Hartford*	
								Ref: H Hackney	Geoff Hurst has signed for Stoke and West Ham have bought 27-year-old Dudley Tyler from Hereford for £25,000. Tyler, Robson and Brooking all missed chances that might have earned West Ham two points instead of one. There is talk of signing Bill Garner from Southend.											
2	H	COVENTRY			W	1-0	0-0	Best 53	Ferguson	McDowell	Lampard	Bonds	Taylor	Moore	Tyler	Best	Coker	Brooking	Robson	
	14/8		27,498		3				*Glazier*	*Coop*	*Cattlin*	*Machin*	*Blockley*	*Barry*	*Mortimer*	*Graham*	*Hunt*	*Carr*	*Smith*	
								Ref: J Gow	Coventry erected a 4-4-2 midfield barrage designed to stifle the game and earn them a point. Best hit the bar early on, but the life was being squeezed out of the game when Best headed in. Glazier scooped the ball out but the linesman confirmed a goal. Coventry players were angry.											
3	H	LEICESTER		5	W	5-2	2-2	Moore 17, Coker 38, Robson 53, 78,	Ferguson	McDowell	Lampard	Bonds	Taylor	Moore	Tyler	Best	Coker	Brooking	Robson	
	19/8		25,414	*20*	5			*Stringfellow 3, Glover 32* [Tyler 70]	*Shilton*	*Whitworth*	*Nish*	*Woollett*	*Sjoberg*	*Cross*	*Farrington*	*Sammels*	*Weller*	*Stringfellow*	*Glover*	
								Ref: S Kayley	Dudley Tyler's ability to drift into menacing positions was the source of two Hammers goals. He also netted his first for the club. Leicester manager Jimmy Bloomfield admitted afterwards: 'They destroyed us'. Transfer talk is increasing: Hurst's intended replacement is Bill Garner.											
4	A	WOLVES		5	L	**0-3**	0-0		Ferguson	McDowell	Lampard	Bonds	Taylor	Moore	Tyler	Best	Coker	Brooking	Robson	
	22/8		*21,958*	*8*	5			*McCalliog 74, Richards 88, Dougan 90*	*Parkes*	*Shaw*	*McAlle*	*Sunderland*	*Munro*	*Owen*	*McCalliog*	*Hibbitt*	*Richards*	*Dougan*	*Daley*	
								Ref: E Jolly	Derek Dougan's last-minute header made him the first Irishman to score 200 goals in the Football League. Injury-strapped Wolves had to play their youth-team coach, Brian Owen. McCalliog's cheeky chip broke the deadlock, and as West Ham piled forward they left gaps at the back.											
5	A	LIVERPOOL		12	L	2-3	2-1	Robson 38, 43 *[Hughes 64]*	Ferguson	McDowell	Lampard	Bonds	Taylor	Moore	Tyler	Best	Holland	Brooking	Robson	
	26/8		*50,491*	*1*	5			*Toshack 42, Ferguson 60 (og),*	*Clemence*	*Lawler*	*Lindsay*	*Smith*	*Lloyd*	*Hughes*	*Keegan*	*Hall*	*Heighway*	*Toshack*	*Callaghan*	
								Ref: J Yates	The flash-point comes with Liverpool's second equaliser. Challenged by Keegan, Ferguson drops the ball over his head. Moore earns a four-point caution for dissent. Not many visitors score two at Anfield, and Robson is convinced he was denied a penalty when felled by Lawler.											
6	A	ARSENAL		12	L	0-1	0-1		Grotier	McDowell	Lampard	Bonds	Taylor	Moore	Tyler	Best	Holland	Brooking	Robson*	Lock
	29/8		*43,802*	*2*	5			*Ball 1p*	*Barnett*	*Rice*	*McNab*	*Storey*	*McLintock*	*Simpson*	*Armstrong**	*Ball*	*Radford*	*Kennedy*	*Graham*	*George*
								Ref: J Hunting	Both teams went in search of goals, though the one that mattered came very early. Pat Rice fell at the feet of two defenders and Alan Ball took the penalty. Geoff Barnett made fine saves from Clyde Best and Tommy Taylor. Bobby Moore looks classy, pushed forward into midfield.											
7	H	MANCHESTER U		12	D	2-2	1-1	Robson 31, 78	Grotier	McDowell	Lampard	Bonds	Taylor	Moore	Tyler	Best	Holland	Brooking	Robson	
	2/9		31,939	*21*	6			*Best 10, Moore 77*	*Stepney*	*O'Neil*	*Dunne*	*Buchan*	*James*	*Sadler*	*Morgan*	*Law**	*Charlton*	*Best*	*Moore*	*McIlroy*
								Ref: G Hill	Man U have yet to win. Clyde Best struggled under the burden of being Hurst's replacement. A revitalised George Best fended off Robson for No 1. Robson took Brooking's pass to level. Ian Storey-Moore's first goal of the season was cancelled out by Robson, from McDowell's cross.											
8	A	CHELSEA		11	W	3-1	2-1	Taylor 4, Moore 23, Bonds 82	Grotier	McDowell	Lampard	Bonds	Taylor	Moore	Tyler	Best	Holland	Brooking	Robson	
	9/9		*34,392*	*7*	8			*Garland 15*	*Bonetti*	*Mulligan*	*McCreadie*	*Hollins*	*Webb*	*Harris*	*Garland*	*Kember*	*Osgood*	*Hudson**	*Houseman*	*Garner*
								Ref: K Walker	Chelsea poached Bill Garner from under the noses of West Ham following a League Cup-tie at Roots Hall, when Garner impressed. Injury to Hudson brought Garner off the bench after just nine minutes. Moore sidefooted a free-kick to Taylor, then restored the lead with a corker.											
9	H	NORWICH		9	W	4-0	3-0	Brooking 29, Robson 37, 78p,	Grotier	McDowell	Lampard	Bonds	Taylor	Moore	Tyler	Best	Holland	Brooking	Robson	
	16/9		27,780	*12*	10			[Taylor 41]	*Keelan*	*Payne*	*Butler*	*Anderson*	*Forbes*	*Briggs*	*Livermore*	*Bone*	*Cross*	*Paddon*	*O'Donnell*	
								Ref: A Jones	Moore's incisive passing in midfield is the inspiration for all West Ham's attacking moves. He crosses to Brooking for the first goal, then floats a cross onto Robson's head from 35 yards. Brooking was fouled in the box for the penalty. Will Ramsey play Moore in England's midfield?											
10	A	TOTTENHAM		12	L	0-1	0-0		Grotier	McDowell*	Lampard	Bonds	Taylor	Moore	Tyler	Brooking	Holland	Best	Robson	Charles
	23/9		***51,700***	*2*	10			*Lampard 88 (og)*	*Jennings*	*Evans*	*Knowles*	*Pratt*	*England*	*Beal*	*Gilzean*	*Perryman*	*Chivers*	*Peters**	*Pearce*	*Coates*
								Ref: V James	Just before Spurs' late winner Pop Robson hit Jennings' crossbar. Instead of 1-0 it was shortly 0-1. Mike England's header was going wide until Lampard attempted an awkward clearance and directed the ball into goal off his posterior. A kick on the thigh took Peters off at half-time.											

11	H	BIRMINGHAM	11	W	2-0	1-0	Bonds 3, Best 68	Grotier	Charles	Lampard	Bonds	Taylor	Moore	Tyler	Best	Holland	Brooking	Robson	
	30/9	26,482	*16*	12				*Latchford D*	*Martin*	*Pendrey*	*Campbell**	*Hynd*	*Page*	*Burns*	*Francis*	*Latchford R*	*Hope*	*Taylor*	*Harland*
							Ref: Nicholls	Clyde Best has lost so much confidence that he is delighted with his 12-yard effort that seals victory. Bonds had put West Ham in front with a shot from 18 yards. The ref gave City a penalty when Taylor 'fouled' Gordon Taylor (later of the PFA). Grotier saved Campbell's spot-kick.											
12	A	IPSWICH	10	D	1-1	0-0	Best 65	Grotier	Lampard	Charles	Bonds	Taylor	Moore	Tyler	Best	Holland	Brooking	Robson	
	7/10	*22,377*	*9*	13			*Hamilton 83*	*Best*	*Mills*	*Harper*	*Collard*	*Hunter*	*Beattie*	*Hamilton*	*Viljoen*	*Belfitt*	*Whymark*	*Lambert*	
							Ref: K Wynn	A pleasant autumn afternoon saw West Ham go in front with a picture goal. Brooking crossed to the far post where Clyde Best headed the ball past David Best. Had they hung on, Hammers would have notched their first win at Ipswich in almost a decade. Hamilton headed the equaliser.											
13	H	SHEFFIELD UTD	7	W	3-1	3-0	Brooking 16, Robson 33, 39	Grotier	McDowell	Lampard	Bonds	Taylor	Moore	Tyler	Best	Holland	Brooking	Robson	
	14/10	25,379	*9*	15			*Taylor 50 (og)*	*McAlister*	*Goulding*	*Hemsley**	*Flynn*	*Colquhoun*	*Hockey*	*Woodward*	*Badger*	*Warboys*	*Currie*	*Holmes*	*Mackenzie*
							Ref: D Turner	Alf Ramsey takes in this match. Pop Robson is scoring so frequently that he is rumoured to be Ramsey's target. Robson himself, having at last been pushed from midfield to attack, reckons West Ham need a ball winner, especially away from home, where Robson has scored only twice.											
14	A	MANCHESTER C	10	L	3-4	2-4	Best 16, Ayris 44, Moore 68	Grotier	McDowell	Lampard	Bonds	Taylor	Moore	Ayris	Best	Holland	Brooking	Robson	
	21/10	*30,890*	*17*	15			*T'wers 4, M'rsh 24,34, Summerbee 35*	*Healey*	*Book*	*Donachie*	*Doyle*	*Booth*	*Jeffries*	*Summerbee*	*Bell*	*Marsh*	*Lee*	*Towers*	
							Ref: K Burns	Moore scored with a header, a rarity. It brought the score back to 3-4 and gave West Ham a fighting chance of drawing. Ayris had also scored a peach of a goal, skipping past Doyle and Donachie. Maine Road in recent years has seen 3-5, 1-6, 1-4, 1-5, and now this latest goal-bonanza.											
15	H	CRYS PALACE	8	W	**4-0**	2-0	Brooking 5, 21, McDowell 61, [Robson 65]	Ferguson	Lampard	Charles	McDowell	Taylor	Moore	Ayris	Best	Holland	Brooking	Robson	
	28/10	28,894	*22*	17				*Hammond*	*Payne*	*Taylor*	*Phillip*	*McCormick*	*Blyth*	*Pinkney*	*Cooke*	*Craven*	*Hinshelwood*	*Tambling*	
							Ref: E Wallace	Immediately after the match, which leaves Palace still bottom, Palace boss Bert Head signs Don Rogers from Swindon. Palace could have done with him against West Ham. Bobby Moore set up both Brooking goals with astute passes. John McDowell's was his first ever league goal.											
16	H	WOLVES	6	D	2-2	0-0	Robson 55, Brooking 88	Ferguson	McDowell	Lampard	Lock	Taylor	Moore	Tyler*	Best	Holland	Brooking	Robson	Ayris
	4/11	29,524	*11*	18			*Kindon 64, 75*	*Parkes*	*Shaw*	*McAlle*	*Bailey*	*Munro*	*Jefferson*	*McCalliog*	*Hibbitt*	*Richards*	*Kindon*	*Wagstaffe*	
							Ref: K Styles	This perky game had Wolves' skipper Mike Bailey saying what a pleasure it was to play West Ham. He might have added what a pleasure it was to meet such a generous defence, since Kindon twice took advantage of dithering. Brooking's late header prevented a Wolves' double.											
17	A	COVENTRY	9	L	1-3	0-1	McDowell 64	Ferguson	McDowell	Lampard	Bonds	Taylor	Moore	Tyler	Best	Holland	Brooking	Robson	
	11/11	*27,189*	*13*	18			*Hutchison 25, Stein 58, Alderson 84*	*Glazier*	*Coop*	*Cattlin*	*Smith*	*Barry*	*Parker*	*Mortimer*	*Alderson*	*Stein*	*Carr**	*Hutchison*	*McGuire*
							Ref: I Williams	Coventry general manager Joe Mercer is full of praise for Moore, who played both in defence and midfield. Coventry extend their unbeaten run to six, helped by expensive signings Colin Stein and Tommy Hutchison. West Ham appealed in vain that Coventry's opener was offside.											
18	H	DERBY	11	L	1-2	0-2	Robson 56	Ferguson	Charles	Lampard	Bonds	Taylor	Moore	Tyler	Ayris*	Holland	Brooking	Robson	Best
	18/11	28,154	*15*	18			*Hector 1, 15*	*Boulton*	*Webster*	*Nish*	*Hennessey*	*McFarland*	*Todd*	*McGovern*	*Gemmill*	*O'Hare*	*Hector*	*Hinton*	
							Ref: N Burtenshaw	Coker, Best and Ayris all look disenchanted, and Dudley Tyler is much less effective than when he arrived. Derby spring on West Ham their first home defeat of the season, which looked on the cards from the moment Clive Charles presented the ball to Kevin Hector in 53 seconds.											
19	A	EVERTON	8	W	2-1	1-1	Brooking 44, Best 65	Ferguson	McDowell	Lampard*	Bonds	Taylor	Moore	Tyler	Best	Holland	Brooking	Robson	Lock
	25/11	*27,558*	*14*	20			*Wright B 32*	*Lawson*	*Scott*	*Newton*	*Kendall*	*Kenyon*	*Hurst*	*Wright B*	*Darracott*	*Belfitt*	*Harvey*	*Connolly*	
							Ref: J Taylor	Bobby Moore marks his 500th league game by threading a reverse pass for Brooking's equaliser. Goodison's smallest crowd of the season had welcomed Bernie Wright's earlier header. Clyde Best's 60-yard run climaxed with a dummy round the keeper. A goal of the month contender.											
20	H	NEWCASTLE	7	D	1-1	0-0	Brooking 80	Ferguson	McDowell	Lock	Bonds	Taylor	Moore	Ayris	Best	Holland	Brooking	Robson	
	2/12	23,785	*8*	21			*Craig 81*	*McFaul*	*Craig*	*Clark*	*Nattrass*	*Howard*	*Moncur*	*Barrowclough*	*Smith*	*Macdonald*	*Tudor*	*Hibbitt*	
							Ref: N Paget	It took David Craig just 16 seconds to equalise Brooking's goal, which was his sixth in eight games. Alf Ramsey is watching, but has still to be convinced that Brooking is ready. Robson wasn't sharp either, missing a good chance. With Leeds losing, Hammers could have closed the gap.											
21	A	LEEDS	9	L	0-1	0-1		Ferguson	McDowell	Charles	Bonds	Taylor	Moore	Ayris*	Best	Holland	Brooking	Robson	Boyce
	9/12	*30,270*	*3*	21			*Jones 31*	*Harvey*	*Reaney*	*Cherry*	*Bremner*	*Madeley*	*Hunter*	*Lorimer*	*Clarke*	*Jones*	*Bates*	*Yorath*	
							Ref: A Morrissey	Leeds played all their football before half-time, and West Ham did enough afterwards to feel hard done by at not earning a point. Jones headed the only goal from Lorimer's pin-point centre. Lorimer also hit a post. Best missed a sitter from six yards and Ayris's crosses spelled danger.											

No	Date	Att	Pos	Pt	F-A	H-T	Scorers, Times, and Referees	1	2	3	4	5	6	7	8	9	10	11	12 sub used
22	H STOKE		7	W	3-2	2-1	Robson 32, 36, Best 76	Ferguson	McDowell	Lampard	Bonds	Taylor	Moore	Ayris	Best	Holland	Brooking	Robson	
	16/12	**23,269**	*18*	23			*Hurst 9, Ritchie 89*	*Farmer*	*Lees*	*Elder*	*Mahoney*	*Smith*	*Skeels*	*Conroy*	*Greenhoff*	*Ritchie*	*Hurst*	*Eastham**	*Robertson*
							Ref: R Toseland	Johnny Ayris gets the man-of-the-match vote after this thriller. And this after Geoff Hurst heads in for Stoke within nine minutes of his return to the Boleyn. He cost Stoke £80,000 and this is his 11th goal for them. Robson's two take him to 15. Best of the goals was Best's scorcher.											
23	A SOUTHAMPTON		8	D	0-0	0-0		Ferguson	McDowell*	Lampard	Bonds	Taylor	Moore	Ayris	Best	Holland	Brooking	Robson	Lock
	23/12	*19,429*	*12*	24				*Martin*	*McCarthy*	*Burns*	*Fisher*	*Bennett*	*Steele*	*Paine*	*Channon*	*Gilchrist*	*O'Neil*	*Stokes*	
							Ref: M Sinclair	Niggling overcame skills in this disappointing match. Mick Channon was blatantly 'obstructed' in the box without winning a penalty. The best move of the match was a 50-yard run between Brooking and Robson that split the Saints' defence open, but Brooking's shot was well saved.											
24	H TOTTENHAM		9	D	2-2	0-0	Robson 78, 82p	Ferguson	McDowell	Lampard	Bonds	Taylor	Moore	Lock	Best	Holland	Brooking	Robson	
	26/12	37,397	*7*	25			*Pearce 54, Peters 60*	*Jennings*	*Evans*	*Knowles*	*Pratt*	*Dillon*	*Naylor*	*Coates*	*Perryman*	*Chivers*	*Peters*	*Pearce*	
							Ref: T Reynolds	What a turnaround. After fumbling for 75 minutes West Ham turned into football furies to rescue a point from this Boxing Day morning clash. Ferguson flapped at two crosses to gift Spurs two goals. Robson hit back with a diving header and a penalty, after Terry Naylor had handled.											
25	A LEICESTER		10	L	1-2	1-1	Brooking 4	Ferguson	McDowell	Lampard	Bonds	Taylor	Moore	Ayris	Best	Holland	Brooking*	Robson	Boyce
	30/12	***19,341***	*17*	25			*Farrington 1, Worthington 71*	*Shilton*	*Whitworth*	*Rofe*	*Woollett*	*Manley*	*Tomlin*	*Farrington*	*Birchenall*	*Weller*	*Worthington*	*Glover*	
							Ref: C Howell	It took Leicester 29 seconds for Farrington to put away Tomlin's cross. Brooking equalised with a shot that went in off Manley, but when Brooking limped off after half an hour West Ham lost their rhythm. Farrington headed the ball on for Frank Worthington to nudge the winner.											
26	H LIVERPOOL		12	L	0-1	0-0		Ferguson	McDowell	Lampard	Lock*	Taylor	Moore	Ayris	Best	Holland	Tyler	Robson	Charles
	6/1	34,480	*1*	25			*Keegan 74*	*Clemence*	*Lawler*	*Thompson*	*Smith*	*Lloyd*	*Hughes*	*Keegan*	*Cormack*	*Heighway*	*Boersma*	*Callaghan*	
							Ref: R Tinkler	Shankly's Liverpool are 2-1 on for the title, and against a Hammers team minus both Bonds and Brooking in midfield were not stretched. Once Lock had gone off with a torn hamstring on 38 minutes Liverpool took complete control. Heighway's strong run and cross set up the goal.											
27	A MANCHESTER U		8	D	2-2	2-1	Robson 15, Best 28	Ferguson	McDowell	Charles	Bonds	Taylor	Moore	Tyler	Best	Holland	Ayris	Robson	
	20/1	*50,878*	*22*	26			*Charlton 31p, Macari 80*	*Stepney*	*Young*	*Forsyth*	*Law**	*Holton*	*Buchan*	*Morgan*	*MacDougall*	*Charlton*	*Macari*	*Graham*	*Davies*
							Ref: P Baldwin	Man U, with eight Scots in their team, stay bottom even though Tommy Docherty has spent over £1 million to buy success. Clyde Best set up Robson before scoring the second himself. Taylor handled Morgan's cross for the penalty. Macari's neat equaliser has Old Trafford on its feet.											
28	H CHELSEA		7	W	3-1	1-1	Taylor 13, Robson 68, 81	Ferguson	McDowell	Lampard	Bonds	Taylor	Moore	Tyler	Best	Holland	Brooking	Robson	
	27/1	33,336	*13*	28			*Garner 21*	*Phillips*	*Locke*	*Harris*	*Hollins*	*Dempsey*	*Webb*	*Baldwin*	*Kember*	*Osgood*	*Hudson*	*Garner*	
							Ref: R Matthewson	Trevor Brooking returns after injury and is involved in all three Hammers goals. Pop Robson takes his personal tally to 20, and this is the eighth time this season he has bagged two in a match. Chelsea's goal came when Steve Kember's shot was blocked and fell to Bill Garner.											
29	A NORWICH		7	W	1-0	1-0	Robson 32	Ferguson	McDowell	Lampard	Bonds	Taylor	Moore	Ayris	Best	**Lutton**	Brooking	Robson	
	10/2	*32,597*	*17*	30				*Keelan*	*Payne*	*Butler*	*Stringer*	*Anderson*	*Briggs*	*Livermore*	*Bone**	*Cross*	*Paddon*	*Howard*	*O'Donnell*
							Ref: W Castle	Ron Saunders' Norwich have now gone 11 games without a win, and face Spurs in the League Cup final. Stylish Brooking, industrious Bonds, deadly Robson. The three players combined for Robson's 21st goal of the season – Brooking's corner, Bonds' nod-down, Robson's strike.											
30	H WEST BROM		7	W	2-1	1-0	Bonds 16, Robson 90	Ferguson	McDowell	Lampard	Bonds	Taylor	Moore	Ayris	Best	Holland	Brooking	Robson	
	17/2	26,071	*22*	32			*Brown T 70*	*Latchford*	*Nisbet*	*Wilson*	*Cantello*	*Wile*	*Merrick*	*Woolgar*	*Brown T*	*Robertson*	*Hartford*	*Johnston**	*Glover*
							Ref: M Kherkof	Albion's time-wasting tactics irk the referee to such an extent that he allows seven minutes injury-time. It is well that he did, for the extension permitted Robson to pop in the winner. McDowell's ill-judged back-pass had presented bottom-placed Albion with an ill-deserved equaliser.											
31	A STOKE		7	L	0-2	0-2		Ferguson	McDowell	Lampard	Bonds	Taylor	Moore	Ayris*	Best	Holland	Brooking	Robson	Lock
	24/2	*21,855*	*17*	32			*Greenhoff 3, Robertson 16*	*Farmer*	*Marsh*	*Pejic*	*Mahoney*	*Smith*	*Bloor*	*Robertson*	*Greenhoff*	*Hurst*	*Eastham*	*Conroy*	
							Ref: R Raby	Ted MacDougall has signed from Man U for £170,000, but too late to play. He moans about his 150 days at Old Trafford. Greenhoff's volley from Eastham's free-kick, followed by Robertson's long-range daisy-cutter, leave Hammers with too much to do. Who steps down for Mac?											

No	Date	Opponent	Att	Pos	Res/Pts	FT	HT	Scorers, Times, and Referees	1	2	3	4	5	6	7	8	9	10	11	12 sub used
32	H	IPSWICH		8	L	0-1	0-0		Ferguson	McDowell	Lampard	Bonds	Taylor	Moore	Tyler	Best	Holland	Brooking	Robson	
	2/3		37,004	*4*	32			*Johnson 55*	*Sivell*	*Mills*	*Harper*	*Morris*	*Hunter*	*Beattie*	*Hamilton*	*Viljoen*	*Johnson*	*Whymark*	*Lambert*	
								Ref: H New	This Friday evening fixture was interrupted by a bottle thrown on the pitch. A huge crowd had turned up expecting to see Ted MacDougall's debut, but his forms have not cleared. Ipswich's new buy, Johnson, not only scored but also hit the bar. The North Bank sang 'We want Mac'.											
33	A	SHEFFIELD UTD		9	D	0-0	0-0		Ferguson	McDowell	Lampard	Bonds	Taylor	Moore	Best	Lock	**MacDougall**	Brooking	Robson	
	10/3		*24,024*	*17*	33				*McAlister*	*Badger*	*Hemsley*	*Flynn*	*Colquhoun*	*Eddy*	*Woodward*	*Salmons*	*Dearden*	*Currie*	*Bone*	
								Ref: R Capey	Who will be dropped for Supermac? Will it be Holland or will it be Best? It is Holland. The draw condemns the Blades to a sixth game without a win, and is largely due to Ferguson's two saves from Woodward's twice-taken penalty. Lampard had brought down Woodward in the box.											
34	H	MANCHESTER C		7	W	2-1	0-0	MacDougall 60, Robson 67	Ferguson	McDowell	Lampard*	Bonds	Taylor	Moore	Best	Lock	MacDougall	Brooking	Robson	Holland
	17/3		29,370	*13*	35			*Doyle 85*	*Corrigan*	*Book*	*Donachie*	*Doyle*	*Booth*	*Jeffries**	*Summerbee*	*Bell*	*Whelan*	*Lee*	*Oakes*	*Carrodus*
								Ref: R Crabb	An atmosphere fit for an end-of-season game. Ted MacDougall twists round Tony Book for his first goal for West Ham and his first for anyone since Christmas. A fine run by Holland was then finished off by Robson. Frank Carrodus crossed for Mike Doyle to pull one back for City.											
35	A	CRYS PALACE		7	W	3-1	1-0	R'bson 45, Brooking 55, MacDoug'll 85	Ferguson	McDowell	Holland	Bonds	Taylor	Moore	Best	Lock	MacDougall	Brooking	Robson	
	24/3		*36,915*	*20*	37			*Possee 80*	*Jackson*	*Roffey*	*Taylor*	*Phillip*	*Bell*	*Blyth*	*Possee*	*Hinshelwood*	*Whittle*	*Cooke*	*Rogers*	
								Ref: D Turner	Palace's battle against relegation lends this match an unwelcome violent undercurrent, which culminates with Bobby Bell laying out Ted MacDougall. Jackson failed to hold Best's shot and Robson pounced. Supermac then took Moore's pass and wrong-footed Palace's defence.											
36	H	EVERTON		7	W	2-0	0-0	Robson 67, Lock 89	Ferguson	McDowell	Lampard	Bonds*	Taylor	Moore	Lock	Best	MacDougall	Brooking	Robson	Holland
	31/3		25,531	*17*	39				*Lawson*	*Wright T*	*Styles*	*Kendall*	*Kenyon*	*Hurst*	*Harper*	*Darracott*	*Lyons**	*Buckley*	*Connolly*	*Belfitt*
								Ref: I Jones	The Israeli national team spy on West Ham, whom they shortly play in a testimonial. They fear Brooking, whose run set up Robson's 25th goal of the season. Just before the end Kevin Lock scored his first ever league goal. Bonds and Harper were lucky not to be sent off for fighting.											
37	A	NEWCASTLE		5	W	2-1	1-1	MacDougall 18, 48	Ferguson	McDowell	Lampard	Bonds	Taylor	Moore	Best	Lock	MacDougall	Brooking	Robson	
	7/4		*24,030*	*6*	41			*Tudor 9*	*Burleigh*	*Craig*	*Clark*	*Nattrass*	*Howard*	*Moncur*	*Barrowclough*	*Smith*	*Macdonald*	*Tudor*	*Hibbitt*	
								Ref: K Styles	A gale-force wind ruined the match as a spectacle, but could not prevent Mac bagging two super headed goals, both laid on by Brooking. John Tudor's earlier goal came with Hammers defenders standing still appealing for offside. Later, Ferguson and Taylor squared up to each other.											
38	H	LEEDS		5	D	1-1	0-0	Holland 90	Ferguson	McDowell	Lampard	Bonds	Lock	Moore	Best*	Holland	MacDougall	Brooking	Robson	Lutton
	14/4		**38,804**	*3*	42			*Clarke 83*	*Harvey*	*Reaney*	*Cherry*	*Bremner*	*Yorath*	*Hunter*	*Lorimer*	*Clarke*	*Jones*	*Giles*	*Bates**	*Jordan*
								Ref: N Burtenshaw	When McDowell collides with Ferguson play is held up for 10 minutes and rumours sweep the stadium that the keeper has broken his neck or his back. Ferguson is surrounded by doctors and trainers. He went off suffering from concussion. Allan Clarke then headed past stand-in Best.											
39	H	SOUTHAMPTON		5	W	4-3	2-2	Robson 14, 18, 66, Brooking 84	Grotier	McDowell*	Lampard	Bonds	Lock	Moore	Best	Holland	MacDougall	Brooking	Robson	Lutton
	20/4		33,039	*10*	44			*Gilchrist 28, 42, Channon 89*	*Martin*	*Kirkup*	*Steele**	*Fisher*	*Bennett*	*Walker*	*Paine*	*Channon*	*Gilchrist*	*O'Neil*	*Talkes*	*Beaney*
								Ref: P Walters	Robson had already scored twice in a game eight times. Now at last he gets a hat-trick. His total now stands at 28, compared with 15 for Saints' Channon, who might have had a hat-trick himself in this cracker. Robson might have had five, narrowly missing with two diving headers.											
40	A	DERBY		5	D	1-1	0-0	Lutton 75	Grotier	Charles	Lampard	Bonds	Lock	Moore	Best	Lutton	MacDougall	Brooking	Robson	
	21/4		*28,727*	*9*	45			*Gemmill 87p*	*Moseley*	*Nish*	*Daniel*	*Parry**	*McFarland*	*Todd*	*McGovern*	*Gemmill*	*O'Hare*	*Hector*	*Powell*	*Durban*
								Ref: E Wallace	Greenwood, normally the calmest of managers, storms out of the Baseball Ground following a penalty decision against Moore, for bringing down Hector. Needless to say, Brian Clough said it *was* a penalty. With five regulars injured, Greenwood had to play Pop Robson in defence.											
41	A	BIRMINGHAM		5	D	0-0	0-0		Ferguson	McDowell	Lampard	Bonds	Lock	Moore	Best	Lutton	MacDougall	Brooking	Robson	
	23/4		*36,942*	*11*	46				*Latchford D*	*Martin*	*Pendrey*	*Page*	*Hynd*	*Roberts*	*Campbell*	*Francis*	*Latchford R*	*Burns*	*Taylor*	
								Ref: P Partridge	With City seeking their sixth straight win, and West Ham unbeaten in eight, this match always looked a likely draw. Dreadful weather did not keep the crowd down, though goal chances were at a premium. West Ham penetrated City's penalty box just three times in the whole match.											
42	H	ARSENAL		6	L	1-2	0-2	Rice 73 (og)	Ferguson	McDowell	Lampard	Bonds	Lock	Moore	Best*	Lutton	MacDougall	Brooking	Robson	Ayris
	28/4		37,366	*2*	46			*Kennedy 30, Radford 43*	*Wilson*	*Rice*	*McNab*	*Storey*	*Kelly*	*Simpson*	*Armstrong*	*Ball*	*Radford*	*Kennedy*	*George*	
	Home	Away						Ref: B Homewood	Pop Robson needs one goal to equal Geoff Hurst's post-war Hammers record of 29. He fails to get it, as West Ham slump to their first defeat in 10 games. Robson will later be locked in transfer negotiations. If they fail, Spurs are favourites to sign him as a replacement for Alan Gilzean.											
Average	30,025	31,280																		

League Cup					F-A	H-T	Scorers, Times, and Referees	1	2	3	4	5	6	7	8	9	10	11	12 sub used
2	H	BRISTOL CITY	12	W	2-1	1-0	McDowell 45, Best 77	Groiter	McDowell	Lampard	Bonds	Taylor	Moore	Tyler	Best	Holland	Brooking	Robson	
	6/9	17,688 *2:5*					*Galley 89*	*Cashley*	*Wilson*	*Drysdale*	*Sweeney*	*Rodgers**	*Merrick*	*Tainton*	*Spiring*	*Galley*	*Gow*	*Ritchie*	*Broomfield*
							Ref: N Paget	A forgettable match, other than for two spectacular West Ham goals. Tyler set up the first, for John McDowell to record his first senior goal, and Clyde Best fired in the second from the edge of the area. City's dull second-half pressure was finally rewarded with a late consolation.											
3	A	STOCKPORT	11	L	1-2	1-2	Best 27	Groiter	McDowell	Lampard	Bonds	Taylor	Moore	Tyler	Best	Holland	Brooking	Robson	
	4/10	*13,410 4:11*					*Russell 18, Spratt 42p*	*Ogley*	*Ingle*	*Charter*	*Spratt*	*Hart*	*Ashworth*	*Garbett*	*Ryden*	*Griffiths*	*Russell*	*Davidson*	
							Ref: P Partridge	It happened at Darlington in 1960. Now, for a second time, West Ham lose to a Division 4 team in the League Cup. The critical moment came just before half-time when McDowell felled John Ryden, leaving Tom Spratt to convert the penalty. Near the end Best was thwarted by Ogley.											

FA Cup																			
3	A	PORT VALE	12	W	1-0	0-0	Holland 62	Ferguson	McDowell	Lampard*	Bonds	Taylor	Moore	Tyler	Best	Holland	Brooking	Robson	Charles
	13/1	*20,619 3:6*						*Boswell*	*Brodie*	*Lacey*	*Sum'rscales*	*Cross*	*Mountford*	*Williams*	*Goodwin*	*Morgan*	*Tartt*	*McLaren**	*Gough*
							Ref: A Jones	Vale boss Gordon Lee said: 'To say we deserved a draw is an understatement.' His team had 75% of the play. Mountford's 'goal', early on, was ruled out for pushing and Clive Charles appeared to handle a net-bound shot. Moore's free-kick was headed down by Best to Pat Holland.											
4	A	HULL	7	L	0-1	0-1		Ferguson	McDowell	Lampard	Bonds	Taylor	Moore	Tyler*	Best	Holland	Brooking	Robson	Lock
	3/2	*32,290 2:13*					*Houghton 29*	*McKechnie*	*Banks*	*Beardsley*	*Kaye*	*Neill*	*Knighton*	*McGill*	*Houghton*	*Pearson*	*Holme*	*Greenwood*	
							Ref: N Burtenshaw	West Ham crash to another cup disaster, this time on foggy Humberside. Moore makes the error that lets in Ken Houghton – a bad back-pass that puts Ferguson in trouble. A minute earlier, Clyde Best had hit the post. Hull player-boss Terry Neill now faces an away trip to Coventry.											

		Home					Away					
	P	W	D	L	F	A	W	D	L	F	A	Pts
1 Liverpool	42	17	3	1	45	19	8	7	6	27	23	60
2 Arsenal	42	14	5	2	31	14	9	6	6	26	29	57
3 Leeds	42	15	4	2	45	13	6	7	8	26	32	53
4 Ipswich	42	10	7	4	34	20	7	7	7	21	25	48
5 Wolves	42	13	3	5	43	23	5	8	8	23	31	47
6 WEST HAM	42	12	5	4	45	25	5	7	9	22	28	46
7 Derby	42	15	3	3	43	18	4	5	12	13	36	46
8 Tottenham	42	10	5	6	33	23	6	8	7	25	25	45
9 Newcastle	42	12	6	3	35	19	4	7	10	25	32	45
10 Birmingham	42	11	7	3	39	22	4	5	12	14	32	42
11 Manchester C	42	12	4	5	36	20	3	7	11	21	40	41
12 Chelsea	42	9	6	6	30	22	4	8	9	19	29	40
13 Southampton	42	8	11	2	26	17	3	7	11	21	35	40
14 Sheffield Utd	42	11	4	6	28	18	4	6	11	23	41	40
15 Stoke	42	11	8	2	38	17	3	2	16	23	39	38
16 Leicester	42	7	9	5	23	18	3	8	10	17	28	37
17 Everton	42	9	5	7	27	21	4	6	11	14	28	37
18 Manchester U	42	9	7	5	24	19	3	6	12	20	41	37
19 Coventry	42	9	5	7	27	24	4	4	13	13	31	35
20 Norwich	42	7	9	5	22	19	4	1	16	14	44	32
21 Crys Palace	42	7	7	7	25	21	2	5	14	16	37	30
22 West Brom	42	8	7	6	25	24	1	3	17	13	38	28
	924	236	130	96	724	436	96	130	236	436	724	924

Odds & ends

Double wins: (4) Chelsea, Norwich, Palace, Everton.
Double losses: (2) Liverpool, Arsenal.

Won from behind: (4) Leicester (h), Everton (a), Stoke (h), Newcastle (a).
Lost from in front: (1) Liverpool (a).

High spots: Nine unbeaten league games from 10 March.
Bryan Robson's remarkable scoring exploits.

Low spots: Three successive league defeats in August.
Losing to Second Division Hull in the League Cup and, worst of all, to Fourth Division Stockport in FA Cup.

Hammer of the Year: Bryan Robson.
Ever-presents: (2) Bobby Moore and Bryan Robson.
Hat-tricks: (1) Bryan Robson.
Leading scorer: (28) Bryan Robson.

	Appearances						Goals			
	Lge	*Sub*	LC	*Sub*	FAC	*Sub*	Lge	LC	FAC	Tot
Ayris, Johnny	**13**	*2*					**1**			**1**
Best, Clyde	**41**	*1*	2		2		**7**	2		**9**
Bonds, Billy	**39**		2		2		**3**			**3**
Boyce, Ronnie		*2*								
Brooking, Trevor	**40**		2		2		**11**			**11**
Charles, John	**7**	*2*				*1*				
Coker, Ade	**4**						**1**			**1**
Ferguson, Bobby	**31**				2					
Grotier, Peter	**11**		2							
Holland, Pat	**30**	*2*	2		2		**1**		1	**2**
Lampard, Frank	**38**		2		2					
Lock, Kevin	**14**	*4*				*1*	**1**			**1**
Lutton, Bertie	**4**	*2*					**1**			**1**
McDowell, John	**38**		2		2		**2**	1		**3**
MacDougall, Ted	**10**						**4**			**4**
Moore, Bobby	**42**		2		2		**3**			**3**
Robson, Bryan	**42**		2		2		**28**			**28**
Taylor, Tommy	**37**		2		2		**3**			**3**
Tyler, Dudley	**21**		2		2		**1**			**1**
19 players used	**462**	*15*	**22**		**22**	*2*	**67**	**3**	**1**	**71**

No	Date	Att	Pos	Pt	F-A	H-T	Scorers, Times, and Referees	1	2	3	4	5	6	7	8	9	10	11	12 sub used
1	H NEWCASTLE			L	1-2	1-0	Robson 37	Ferguson	Lampard	Charles	Bonds	Taylor	Moore	Best*	Lutton	MacDougall	Brooking	Robson	Holland
	25/8	28,169		0			*Macdonald 56, 80*	*McFaul*	*Craig*	*Clark*	*Gibb*	*Nattrass*	*Moncur*	*Barrowclough*	*Smith*	*Macdonald*	*Tudor*	*Hibbitt*	
							Ref: G Hill	Bobby Moore is still playing in midfield. Brooking's cross should have been put away by Best and MacDougall before it reached Pop Robson. Malcolm Macdonald headed in Terry Hibbitt's cross and claimed the winner with a shot that slipped through Bobby Ferguson's fingers.											
2	H IPSWICH			D	3-3	2-1	Bonds 5, Brooking 7, Best 80	**Day**	Lampard	Lock	Bonds	Taylor	Moore	Best	Holland	MacDougall	Brooking	Robson	
	27/8	23,335		1			*Whymark 13, Johnson 64, 72*	*Best*	*Mills*	*Harper*	*Morris*	*Keeley*	*Beattie*	*Hamilton*	*Viljoen*	*Johnson*	*Whymark*	*Lambert*	
							Ref: D Biddle	Topsy-turvy Hammers. Ferguson asked to be left out for personal reasons. A Trevor Brooking 'special' made it 2-0 after just seven minutes, but when Mervyn Day punched the air at Harper's free-kick West Ham fell apart. Best rescued a point when Glen Keeley missed a cross.											
3	A NORWICH		14	D	2-2	1-1	Best 12, Robson 71	Ferguson	Lampard	Lock	Bonds	Taylor	Moore	Best	Holland	MacDougall	Brooking	Robson	
	1/9	*25,706*	*16*	2			*Mellor 35, Paddon 80p*	*Keelan*	*Prophett*	*Black*	*Stringer*	*Rollings*	*Briggs*	*Anderson*	*Suggett*	*Cross*	*Paddon*	*Mellor*	
							Ref: J Hunting	Twice West Ham take the lead against Ron Saunders' Norwich. There was nothing fluky about the first goal, Best heading home off the post. But the second, from Brooking's corner, went in off Robson's ear. Lampard then fluffs a clearance and Billy Bonds has to bring down Paddon.											
4	A QP RANGERS			D	0-0	0-0		Ferguson	Lampard	Lock	Bonds	Taylor	Moore	Best	Holland	Ayris	Brooking	Robson	
	4/9	*28,360*		3				*Parkes*	*Clement*	*Watson*	*Venables*	*Mancini*	*Hazell*	*Thomas*	*Francis*	*Leach*	*Bowles*	*Givens*	
							Ref: R Challis	Rangers totally dominated this draw, and West Ham's offside trap was not welcomed by the crowd, who slow-handclapped in frustration. Man-of-the-match Dave Thomas hit a post, had three goals disallowed, and Frank Lampard unwittingly blocked Stan Bowles' header on the line.											
5	H TOTTENHAM		17	L	0-1	0-0		Ferguson	McDowell	Lampard	Bonds	Taylor	Moore	Best	Lock	MacDougall*	Brooking	Robson	Holland
	8/9	30,888	*15*	3			*Chivers 66*	*Jennings*	*Evans*	*Knowles*	*Coates*	*Dillon*	*Beal*	*Gilzean**	*Perryman*	*Chivers*	*Peters*	*Neighbour*	*Kinnear*
							Ref: D Smith	The attendance is 7,000 down on the corresponding fixture last season. The crowd don't like what they see and hundreds leave the ground long before the end. Lock and Best, in particular, rile the fans. Though Ferguson made several fine saves, he was beaten by Chivers' half-hit shot.											
6	H QP RANGERS		17	L	2-3	0-2	Robson 47, Bonds 67p	Ferguson	McDowell	Lampard	Bonds	Taylor	Moore	Tyler	Lock	Lutton	Brooking	Robson	
	10/9	26,042	*10*	3			*Givens 5, 15, Abbott 52*	*Parkes*	*Clement*	*Watson*	*Venables*	*Mancini*	*Hazell*	*Abbott*	*Francis*	*Leach*	*Bowles*	*Givens*	
							Ref: D Turner	Greenwood has now used 17 players in six games. Taylor's error gave Don Givens his first goal and McDowell his second. 19-year-old Ron Abbott headed in Venables' free-kick to make it 1-3. Brooking's corner was handled by Dave Clement for the penalty. QPR deserved to win.											
7	A MANCHESTER U		21	L	1-3	0-1	Bonds 79p	Ferguson	McDowell	Lampard	Bonds	Taylor	Lock	Tyler*	Holland	MacDougall	Brooking	Robson	Lutton
	15/9	***44,757***	*14*	3			*Kidd 7, 62, Moore I 83*	*Stepney*	*Buchan M*	*Young*	*Martin*	*Holton**	*James*	*Morgan*	*Kidd*	*Anderson*	*Graham*	*Moore*	*Buchan G*
							Ref: H Williams	The talk is of Bobby Moore demanding a transfer. Because of this, he is dropped. Brian Kidd's two goals – both thumping, long-range efforts, look to have settled the outcome. Martin Buchan topples Brooking for the penalty, but Ian Storey-Moore's half-hit shot clinches the points.											
8	H LEICESTER		21	D	1-1	1-0	Robson 36	Ferguson	McDowell	Lampard	Bonds	Taylor	Moore	Tyler	Lock	MacDougall*	Brooking	Robson	Coker
	22/9	23,567	*5*	4			*Worthington 87*	*Shilton*	*Whitworth*	*Rofe*	*Farrington*	*Munro*	*Cross*	*Weller*	*Sammels*	*Worthington*	*Birchenall*	*Glover*	
							Ref: P Partridge	Lock failed to clear, leaving Frank Worthington to run through to level the scores for Jimmy Bloomfield's Leicester and leave West Ham still looking for their first win. They only once got the better of the outstanding Shilton, when he miscued a goal-kick to Tyler, who fed Robson.											
9	A STOKE		21	L	0-2	0-1		Ferguson	McDowell	Lampard	Bonds	Taylor	Moore	Tyler	Lock	MacDougall	Brooking	Robson	
	29/9	***16,395***	*17*	4			*Goodwin 40, Hurst 65*	*Farmer*	*Marsh*	*Pejic*	*Dodd*	*Smith*	*Bloor**	*Haslegrave*	*Greenhoff*	*Hurst*	*Goodwin*	*Eastham*	*Ritchie*
							Ref: W Johnson	Stoke's first win of the season dumps West Ham deeper into trouble. Stoke owe their win to an 18-year-old debutant, who nodded Greenhoff's flick over Ferguson, and to ex-Hammer Hurst, who headed in Ritchie's knock-on. MacDougall has a stinker, but Moore and Bonds play well.											
10	H BURNLEY		21	L	0-1	0-0		Day	**Coleman**	Lampard	Bonds	McDowell	Moore	Lutton*	Holland	MacDougall !	Brooking	Robson	Lock
	6/10	23,604	*2*	4			*Waldron 64*	*Stevenson*	*Noble*	*Newton*	*Dobson*	*Waldron*	*Thomson*	*Nulty*	*Hankin*	*Fletcher*	*Collins*	*James*	
							Ref: R Crabb	Ferguson has been dropped for saying: 'There are too many gutless, spineless men in the team.' Day steps in and saves well from Dobson late in the game. Colin Waldron plays a one-two with Nulty to score. Seven minutes later MacDougall is ordered off for head-butting Doug Collins.											

No	Venue	Opponent / Date	Att	Pos	Pts / Res	F-A	H-T	Scorers, Times, and Referees	1	2	3	4	5	6	7	8	9	10	11	12
11	A	EVERTON		22	L	0-1	0-1		Day	Coleman	Lampard	Bonds	Taylor	Moore	Ayris	Best	MacDougall	Brooking	Robson	
		13/10	*34,708*	*5*	4			*Harper 32*	*Lawson*	*Darracott*	*McLaughlin*	*Clements*	*Kenyon*	*Hurst*	*Bernard*	*Buckley*	*Lyons**	*Harper*	*Connolly*	*Irving*
								Ref: P Reeves	Harry Catterick's Everton are going well. McDougall hit a post from one of Brooking's early openings. Coleman's bad back-pass leaves Harper in the clear for the only goal. Day saved a lot, and dropped a lot, too. Clyde Best missed a simple chance to equalise in the closing minutes.											
12	A	COVENTRY		21	W	1-0	0-0	McDowell 68	Day	Coleman	Lampard	Bonds	Taylor	Moore	Tyler	McDowell	Best	Brooking	Robson*	Lock
		20/10	*21,097*	*6*	6				*Glazier*	*Coop*	*Holmes*	*Mortimer*	*Craven**	*Dugdale*	*Smith*	*Alderson*	*Stein*	*Green*	*Hutchison*	*Cartwright*
								Ref: I Jones	Greenwood abandons the safety-first policy that had brought few rewards on opposing grounds and it pays off against a strong Coventry team. McDowell, an England-Under-23 full-back, was switched to midfield but took time off from shadowing Hutchison to volley the winning goal.											
13	H	DERBY		21	D	0-0	0-0		Day	Coleman	Lampard	Bonds	Taylor	Moore	Tyler	McDowell	Best	Brooking	Lock	
		27/10	31,237	*4*	7				*Boulton*	*Webster*	*Nish*	*Newton*	*McFarland*	*Todd*	*McGovern*	*Gemmill*	*Davies*	*Hector*	*Hinton*	
								Ref: A Morrissey	Without both Robson and MacDougall, West Ham's attack was bound to struggle. Greenwood juggled his resources and played McDowell in midfield while pushing Brooking – under protest – into attack. Neither man played well. Now West Ham must focus on the Liverpool replay.											
14	A	LEEDS		21	L	**1-4**	0-2	MacDougall 83	Day	Coleman	Lampard	Bonds	Taylor	Moore	Tyler	McDowell	Best	Brooking	MacDougall	
		3/11	*36,869*	*1*	7			*Bates 19, Jones 21, 51, Clarke 58*	*Harvey*	*Reaney*	*Cherry*	*Bremner*	*McQueen*	*Hunter*	*Lorimer*	*Clarke*	*Jones*	*Bates*	*Madeley*	
								Ref: J Williams	Leeds have dropped just three points all season and extend their lead at the top to six points. Madeley's cross comes back off the bar for Bates to net the first, and Jones collects a return pass from Lorimer to add a second. MacDougall's header from Bonds' cross was too little, too late.											
15	H	SHEFFIELD UTD		21	D	2-2	0-2	Bonds 50, Brooking 51	Ferguson	Coleman	Lampard	Bonds	Taylor	Moore	Tyler	McDowell	Robson	Brooking	MacDougall	
		10/11	21,243	*12*	8			*Woodward 14, 45*	*Connaughton*	*Goulding*	*Ogden*	*Flynn*	*Colquhoun*	*Speight*	*Woodward*	*Salmons*	*Dearden*	*Currie*	*Bone*	
								Ref: A Jones	Greenwood misses his first home match for years, spying on another player. He misses a famous recovery. Teased by Currie in the first half, Hammers trail through two deflections – off Taylor and Moore. Bonds' back-header goes in off a post, whereupon Brooking hits the equaliser.											
16	A	WOLVES		21	D	0-0	0-0		Day	Coleman	Lampard	Bonds	Taylor	Moore	Best	McDowell	MacDougall	Brooking	Robson	
		17/11	*19,587*	*19*	9				*Parkes*	*Palmer*	*Parkin*	*Bailey*	*Munro*	*McAlle*	*Powell*	*Hibbitt*	*Kindon**	*Dougan*	*Wagstaffe*	*McCalliog*
								Ref: H Davy	Robson hates playing in midfield; Brooking hates playing in attack, and Greenwood can't keep upsetting his players like this, especially as Best wants to move on. Greenwood is said to be about to buy two players, Graham Paddon from Norwich and Dennis Tueart from Sunderland.											
17	H	ARSENAL		21	L	1-3	1-1	Bonds 37	Day	Coleman	Lampard	Bonds	Taylor	Moore	**Gould**	McDowell	MacDougall	Brooking	Robson	
		24/11	28,287	*11*	9			*George 29, Ball 55, 87*	*Wilson*	*Rice*	*McNab*	*Storey*	*Simpson*	*Kelly*	*Ball*	*George*	*Hornsby*	*Kennedy*	*Armstrong*	
								Ref: R Capey	Bobby Gould makes his debut in a match where Upton Park resounds to chants of: 'Greenwood out'. Charlie George received a short free-kick and curled the ball into the top corner. Bonds scrambles a goal off his knee, but Ball restores Arsenal's lead with a 'dolly' shot from 20 yards.											
18	A	LIVERPOOL		21	L	0-1	0-1		Day	Coleman	Lampard	Bonds	**McGiven**	Moore	Gould	McDowell	MacDougall	Brooking	Holland	
		1/12	*34,857*	*2*	9			*Cormack 14*	*Clemence*	*Smith*	*Lindsay*	*Thompson*	*Lloyd*	*Hughes*	*Keegan*	*Cormack*	*Heighway*	*Waddle*	*Callaghan*	
								Ref: E Wallace	This was not the tight match the score suggests. Liverpool were always in control after Tommy Smith's cross picked out Cormack, who took the ball round Day. The game was also one to remember for Bobby Moore, playing in midfield, who was booked for back-chatting the ref.											
19	H	MANCHESTER C		20	W	2-1	1-1	Brooking 43, Doyle 60 (og)	Day	McDowell	Lampard	Bonds	Taylor	Moore	Ayris	**Paddon**	Gould	Brooking*	Best	Coleman
		8/12	20,790	*16*	11			*Lee 18*	*MacRae*	*Pardoe*	*Donachie*	*Doyle*	*Booth*	*Towers*	*Summerbee*	*Bell*	*Lee*	*Leman*	*Marsh*	
								Ref: R Toseland	Graham Paddon in, MacDougall out. A first home win of the season, secured against Ron Saunders' City with the aid of an own-goal by Mike Doyle, who headed in Paddon's cross. Francis Lee's earlier header had been answered when Brooking shot through the legs of Keith MacRae.											
20	A	BIRMINGHAM		22	L	1-3	1-1	Gould 4	Day	McDowell	Lampard	Bonds	Taylor	Moore	Ayris	Paddon	Gould	Coleman	Best	
		15/12	*23,787*	*20*	11			*Burns 44, 63, Hatton 76*	*Latchford D*	*Martin*	*Gallagher*	*Pendrey*	*Hynd*	*Roberts*	*Burns*	*Francis*	*Latchford R*	*Hatton*	*Hendrie*	
								Ref: E Jolly	Freddie Goodwin's City overtake West Ham, who slump to the bottom despite Gould's first goal for the club. It was a fine goal, too, a superb volley from Bonds' cross. Trevor Francis and Kenny Burns turned the match around, Burns 'chesting' his first goal and driving in his second.											
21	H	STOKE		22	L	0-2	0-0		Day	McDowell	Lampard	Holland	Taylor	McGiven	Ayris*	Paddon	Gould	Coleman	Best	**Wooler**
		22/12	**16,513**	*18*	11			*Robertson 49, Greenhoff 84*	*McDonald*	*Dodd*	*Pejic*	*Skeels*	*Smith*	*Bloor*	*Robertson*	*Greenhoff*	*Hurst*	*Mahoney*	*Haslegrave*	
								Ref: W Castle	Stoke's first away win is achieved against a team minus the unfit Moore, Brooking, Robson, and the suspended Bonds. Mick McGiven is on loan from Sunderland. Hurst's shot is blocked but runs to Jimmy Robertson. Stoke settle it when Mahoney and Haslegrave set up Greenhoff.											

No	Date		Att	Pos	Pt	F-A	H-T	Scorers, Times, and Referees	1	2	3	4	5	6	7	8	9	10	11	12 sub used
22	A	CHELSEA		21	W	4-2	0-2	Lampard 48, Gould 57, Best 63, 84	Day	Coleman	Lampard	McDowell	Taylor	Moore	McGiven	Paddon	Gould	Brooking	Best	
	26/12		*26,982*	*15*	13			*Britton 10, Hudson 42*	*Bonetti*	*Locke*	*Harris*	*Hollins*	*Webb*	*Kember*	*Britton*	*Baldwin*	*Osgood*	*Hudson*	*Houseman*	
								Ref: R Tinkler	One of the great Hammers fight-backs. Keeper Peter Bonetti was badly positioned when Lampard pulled the first goal back. The turning point came when Peter Osgood volleyed against the bar. Day's huge goal-kick bounced perfectly for Gould. Best won the game with two headers.											
23	A	TOTTENHAM		21	L	0-2	0-0		Day	McDowell	Lampard	Bonds	Taylor	Moore	McGiven	Paddon	Gould	Coleman*	Best	Holland
	29/12		*33,172*	*15*	13			*Pratt 77, Chivers 87*	*Jennings*	*Evans*	*Naylor*	*Pratt*	*England*	*Beal*	*Gilzean*	*Perryman*	*Chivers*	*Peters*	*Coates**	*McGrath*
								Ref: K Styles	West Ham look to be holding out, by hook or by crook. Ralph Coates had hit the post and on 68 minutes McGiven floors Gilzean in the box. Day saves Chivers' penalty after Clyde Best pointed which way to go. But McGrath engineers Pratt's close-range goal and Chivers heads No 2.											
24	H	NORWICH		21	W	4-2	0-2	Gould 23, Paddon 44, 59, Brooking 63	Day	McDowell	Lampard	Bonds	Taylor	Moore	McGiven	Paddon	Gould	Brooking*	Best	Coleman
	1/1		32,259	*22*	15			*McDougall 50, 89*	*Keelan*	*Howard*	*Govier*	*Stringer*	*Rollings*	*Prophett**	*Grapes*	*MacDougall*	*Suggett*	*Briggs*	*Sissons*	*Silvester*
								Ref: K Burns	Paddon and MacDougall each score twice against their former club. Norwich's new manager, John Bond, sees his side stuck to the bottom. Brooking limps off after 70 minutes with a groin strain, but his super goal – bending the ball round Keelan – had assured his team of the win.											
25	H	MANCHESTER U		19	W	2-1	0-0	Bonds 49, Holland 83	Day	Coleman	Lampard	Bonds	Taylor	Wooler	McGiven	Paddon	Lutton	Holland	Best	
	12/1		34,147	*21*	17			*McIlroy 66*	*Stepney*	*Forsyth*	*Houston*	*Greenhoff*	*Holton*	*Buchan M*	*Morgan*	*Macari*	*Kidd**	*Young*	*Graham*	*McIlroy*
								Ref: R Perkin	Just before kick-off the suspended George Best is told he can leave Old Trafford. Clyde Best heads on for Bonds to hit the first goal. A slack pass by Wooler let in McIlroy, after which Man U had two efforts cleared off the line. Holland won the game with a harmless-looking header.											
26	A	NEWCASTLE		19	D	1-1	0-1	Holland 51	Day	Coleman	Lampard	Bonds	Taylor	Brooking	McGiven	Paddon	Gould*	Holland	Best	Lutton
	19/1		*27,216*	*9*	18			*Macdonald 15*	*McFaul*	*Craig*	*Kennedy*	*McDermott*	*Howard*	*Clark*	*Barrowclough*	*Smith*	*Macdonald*	*Tudor*	*Cassidy*	
								Ref: G Hill	Malcolm Macdonald flings himself full length to head Kennedy's cross past Day. With the wind behind them after half-time, West Ham level within six minutes. Holland beat McFaul to Brooking's cross and the ball cannoned in off the keeper. John Tudor blasted a sitter over the bar.											
27	H	BIRMINGHAM		19	D	0-0	0-0		Day	Coleman	Lampard	Bonds	Taylor	McGiven	Holland	Paddon	McDowell	Brooking	Best	
	2/2		27,948	*20*	19				*Sprake*	*Martin*	*Clarke*	*Pendrey*	*Gallagher*	*Hynd*	*Campbell*	*Burns*	*Latchford R*	*Hatton*	*Calderwood*	
								Ref: C Thomas	The critical moment arrives after 52 minutes when Gary Sprake – Britain's most expensive goalkeeper – fells Pat Holland, but Billy Bonds' spot-kick goes wide. Pop Robson has been out for nine weeks now, and without him West Ham still seem far too lightweight up front.											
28	A	IPSWICH		19	W	3-1	2-0	Mills 32 (og), McDowell 37, Best 71	Day	Coleman	Lampard	Bonds	Taylor	McGiven	Holland	Paddon	McDowell	Brooking	Best	
	5/2		*25,747*	*7*	21			*Hamilton 69*	*Sivell*	*Burley*	*Mills*	*Morris*	*Hunter*	*Beattie*	*Hamilton*	*Viljoen**	*Johnson*	*Whymark*	*Lambert*	*Gates*
								Ref: P Reeves	Last Saturday Ipswich beat Southampton 7-0. Hammers borrow Ipswich's all-white strip. In a rain-drenched game Brooking's shot goes in off Mills and a post. McDowell's 30-yarder made it 2-0. Hamilton put in Whymark's header, and Best pounced after Holland's shot was parried.											
29	A	LEICESTER		19	W	1-0	0-0	Best 58	Day	Coleman	Lampard	Bonds	Taylor	McGiven	Holland	Paddon	McDowell	Brooking	Best	
	9/2		*27,032*	*7*	23				*Shilton*	*Whitworth*	*Rofe*	*Earle*	*Munro*	*Cross*	*Weller*	*Sammels*	*Worthington*	*Birchenall*	*Glover*	
								Ref: L Hayes	Two moments won this match for West Ham. The first was when Clyde Best bulleted home a stunning shot. The second came when Day saved Frank Worthington's 75th-minute penalty. The referee had only given the kick on the advice of a linesman, who saw Bonds manhandle Rofe.											
30	H	EVERTON		19	W	4-3	2-2	Paddon 33, Best 41, 49, Bonds 84	Day	Coleman	Lampard	Bonds	Taylor	McGiven	Holland	Paddon	McDowell	Brooking	Best	
	16/2		29,347	*6*	25			*Telfer 5, 20, Harvey 73*	*Lawson*	*Darracott*	*McLaughlin*	*Hurst*	*Kenyon*	*Bernard*	*Harvey*	*Buckley*	*Latchford*	*Jones*	*Telfer*	
								Ref: V James	Clyde Best answers his critics by dominating this thriller. He scored twice, headed down for Graham Paddon's opener, and at one point juggled the ball on his knee and chest and defied any Everton player to take it away. Billy Bonds clinched the victory by heading in Paddon's corner.											
31	A	BURNLEY		19	D	1-1	0-1	Paddon 55	Day	Coleman	Lampard	Bonds	Taylor	McGiven	Holland	Paddon	McDowell	Brooking	Best	
	23/2		*18,216*	*6*	26			*Nulty 33*	*Stevenson*	*Noble*	*Newton*	*Dobson*	*Waldron*	*Thomson*	*Nulty*	*Hankin*	*Fletcher*	*Collins*	*James*	
								Ref: D Smith	A high-class match that might easily have finished 4-4. Jimmy Adamson's Burnley went in front through Nulty's deft header from Thompson's cross. Paddon equalised from outside the box when Holland shielded the ball before laying it into his path. Nulty hit the underside of the bar.											

No		Date / Opponent	Att	Pos	Res	F-A	H-T	Scorers, Times, and Referees												
32	H	CHELSEA		16	W	3-0	2-0	Bonds 5, 37, 57	Day	Coleman	Lampard	Bonds	Taylor	McGiven	Holland	Paddon	McDowell	Brooking	Best	
		2/3	34,043	*19*	28				*Phillips*	*Locke*	*Harris*	*Hollins*	*Droy*	*Webb*	*Britton*	*Garland*	*Kember*	*Garner*	*Cooke*	
								Ref: G Kew	Billy Bonds' first ever hat-trick comprised a header from Paddon's cross, a rebound when Phillips blocked Best's header, and another rebound when Phillips parried Paddon's screamer. Dave Sexton's Chelsea were beaten in midfield, where Bonds, Paddon and McDowell took control.											
33	A	DERBY		16	D	1-1	0-0	Bonds 73	Day	Coleman	Lampard	Bonds	Taylor	McGiven	Holland	Paddon	McDowell	Brooking	Best	
		9/3	*24,684*	*3*	29			*Rioch 63p*	*Boulton*	*Webster*	*Nish*	*Rioch*	*McFarland*	*Todd*	*Powell*	*Newton*	*Davies**	*Hector*	*Bourne*	*Hinton*
								Ref: R Matthewson	Derby boss Dave Mackay is none too impressed by West Ham's packed defence, but it has brought 16 points from 10 unbeaten games, and probably earned survival. West Ham did not like the penalty decision, given for McDowell's foul on Hector. Bonds' header went in off a post.											
34	H	COVENTRY		18	L	2-3	1-2	Bonds 26p, 75	Day	Coleman	Lampard	Bonds	Taylor	McGiven	Holland	Paddon	Robson	Brooking	Best	
		16/3	26,502	*9*	29			*Cross 2, Alderson 38, Carr 86*	*Glazier*	*Smith*	*Holmes*	*Mortimer*	*Craven*	*Dugdale*	*McGuire*	*Alderson*	*Cross*	*Carr*	*Hutchison*	
								Ref: H New	Day drops Alderson's shot to Cross. Taylor's error gives Coventry their second goal. West Ham level when Wilf Smith's weak header is driven back by Bonds. Willie Carr ran the length of the pitch and tricked Lampard for the late winner. Bonds wasted a hat-trick when heading wide.											
35	A	SHEFFIELD UTD		19	L	0-1	0-0		Day	Coleman	Lampard	Bonds	Taylor	McGiven	Holland	Paddon	Robson	Brooking	Best	
		23/3	*19,467*	*9*	29			*Field 82*	*Brown*	*Badger*	*Hemsley*	*Eddy*	*Colquhoun*	*Salmons*	*Woodward*	*Garbett*	*Nicholl*	*Currie*	*Field*	
								Ref: J Hunting	Bobby Moore signed for Fulham before the Coventry game. New skipper Billy Bonds is just eight minutes from leading the team to a precious point when Blades' Tony Field, a new £60,000 signing from Blackburn, headed in a free-kick at the far post. The relegation panic now returns.											
36	H	LEEDS		18	W	3-1	0-1	Best 50, Robson 62, Brooking 84	Day	Coleman	Lampard	Bonds	Taylor	McGiven	McDowell	Paddon	Robson	Brooking	Best	
		30/3	**38,416**	*1*	31			*Clarke 32*	*Harvey*	*Reaney*	*Cherry*	*Bremner*	*McQueen*	*Hunter*	*Giles*	*Clarke*	*Jordan**	*Yorath*	*Madeley*	*Jones*
								Ref: J Yates	This shock win threatens to throw open the championship. Best outpaced McQueen to equalise Allan Clarke's opener. Robson's header was his first goal since September. Paddon's corner was knocked on to Brooking. Liverpool close the gap on Leeds but have still to visit Upton Park.											
37	A	ARSENAL		18	D	0-0	0-0		Day	Coleman	Lampard	Bonds	Taylor	McGiven	McDowell	Paddon	Robson	Brooking	Best	
		6/4	*37,868*	*15*	32				*Wilson*	*Rice*	*Nelson*	*Storey*	*Blockley*	*Kelly*	*Armstrong*	*Ball*	*Radford*	*Kennedy*	*George*	
								Ref: H Hackney	Like West Ham, Arsenal are having a terrible season. Pop Robson wasted Hammers' best chance when failing to convert a cross to the near post. But Arsenal nearly stole both points in the last minute when Charlie George's 25-yard effort bounced off the bar into the North Bank.											
38	H	SOUTHAMPTON		17	W	**4-1**	1-1	Robson 26, 53, Best 49, 82	Day	Coleman	Lampard	Bonds	Taylor	McGiven	McDowell	Paddon	Robson	Brooking	Best	
		12/4	34,163	*19*	34			*Channon 24p*	*Martin*	*McCarthy*	*Mills*	*Fisher**	*Bennett*	*Steele*	*Paine*	*Channon*	*Osgood*	*O'Neil*	*Stokes*	*Gilchrist*
								Ref: W Gow	Saints splashed out £285,000 on Peter Osgood from Chelsea, but he has yet to score in five games for his new club. He was, however, brought down by McGiven for Channon's penalty. Within two minutes Robson headed in Bonds' cross with Saints defenders appealing for offside.											
39	H	WOLVES		17	D	0-0	0-0		Day	Coleman	Lampard	Bonds	Taylor	McGiven	McDowell	Paddon	Robson	Brooking	Best	
		13/4	29,488	*11*	35				*Parkes*	*Palmer*	*Parkin*	*Bailey*	*Munro*	*McAlle*	*Powell**	*Hibbitt*	*Sunderland*	*Kindon*	*Daley*	*Dougan*
								Ref: R Crabb	Struggling Man U beat Newcastle to close the gap with West Ham to six points. Bonds rolled his socks down but not even his all-action game could conjure a goal. Wolves came nearest when Parkin rattled the bar with a 30-yard free-kick. The second half was much ado about nothing.											
40	A	SOUTHAMPTON		17	D	1-1	1-0	Best 44	Day	Coleman	Lampard	Bonds	Taylor	McGiven*	McDowell	Paddon	Robson	Brooking	Best	Gould
		15/4	*26,515*	*19*	36			*Stokes 53*	*Turner*	*McCarthy*	*Peach*	*Fisher*	*Earls*	*Steele*	*Paine*	*Channon*	*Osgood*	*Gilchrist*	*Stokes*	
								Ref: H Davey	McMenemy's Saints need to win more than West Ham, and could be pitched into Division 2 if Man U continue their revival. On 15 December Saints lay 5th, since when they have totally collapsed. Best headed in Paddon's corner. Stokes received a short free-kick to fire the equaliser.											
41	A	MANCHESTER C		18	L	1-2	0-2	Gould 52	Day	Coleman	Lampard	Bonds	Taylor	Holland	McDowell	Paddon	Gould	Brooking	Best	
		20/4	*29,700*	*13*	36			*Booth 3, Bell 17*	*Corrigan*	*Barrett*	*Donachie*	*Doyle*	*Booth*	*Oakes*	*Summerbee*	*Bell*	*Lee*	*Law*	*Tueart*	
								Ref: J Taylor	Two looping headers from Booth and Bell seemed to have put City in command, but the recalled Gould netted from a tight angle to open up the match. West Ham thought they had levelled when Gould 'scored' after Corrigan had dropped the ball but the ref gave a foul against the 'keeper.											
42	H	LIVERPOOL		18	D	2-2	1-0	Lampard 32, Brooking 67	Day	Coleman	Lampard	Bonds	Taylor	McDowell	Holland	Paddon	Gould	Brooking	Best	
		27/4	36,160	*2*	37			*Toshack 58, Keegan 89*	*Clemence*	*Smith*	*Lindsay*	*Thompson*	*Cormack*	*Hughes*	*Keegan*	*Hall*	*Heighway*	*Toshack*	*Callaghan*	
		Home Away Average 28,388 27,749						Ref: T Reynolds	The great escape is complete. There is much talk of how West Ham discovered their form only after they had sold Bobby Moore to Fulham. Bill Shankly agrees that Mervyn Day has been the find of the season, and he proves the point by saving Alec Lindsay's 39th-minute penalty.											

League Cup						F-A	H-T	Scorers, Times, and Referees	1	2	3	4	5	6	7	8	9	10	11	12 sub used
2	H	LIVERPOOL		21	D	2-2	1-1	McDougall 39, Robson 84	Day	McDowell	Lampard	Coleman	Taylor	Lock*	Ayris	Best	MacDougall	Brooking	Robson	Holland
		8/10	25,840	*5*				*Cormack 35, Heighway 55*	*Clemence*	*Lawler*	*Lindsay*	*Smith*	*Lloyd*	*Hughes*	*Keegan*	*Cormack*	*Heighway*	*Hall*	*Callaghan*	
								Ref: J Taylor	Ferguson has been placed on the transfer list. He is no longer the most expensive keeper in Britain, having been overtaken by Lawson and Sprake. West Ham twice come from behind, first when MacDougall heads his first goal of the season, then when heading a pass to Robson.											
2R	A	LIVERPOOL		21	L	0-1	0-1		Day	Coleman	Lampard	Bonds	Taylor	Moore	Tyler	McDowell	Best	Brooking	Lock*	Holland
		29/10	*26,002*	*6*				*Toshack 22*	*Clemence*	*Lawler*	*Lindsay*	*Smith*	*Lloyd*	*Hughes*	*Keegan*	*Cormack*	*Heighway*	*Toshack*	*Callaghan*	
								Ref: J Taylor	A patchy football match is settled by a fine goal. Keegan whips over a low centre and John Toshack dives headlong to nod the ball past Day at the far post. West Ham, as so often on their travels, were too preoccupied with defensive duties to produce much sustained power and skill.											

FA Cup																				
3	H	HEREFORD		21	D	1-1	0-1	Holland 88	Day	McDowell	Lampard	Bonds	Taylor	Moore*	McGiven	Paddon	Gould	Coker	Best	Holland
		5/1	23,087	*3:12*				*Redrobe 21*	*Hughes*	*Radford*	*Naylor*	*McLaughlin*	*Jones*	*Tavener*	*Redrobe**	*Tyler*	*Hinch*	*Evans*	*Rudge*	*Owen*
								Ref: R Challis	Bobby Moore limps off after 30 minutes, never to play for West Ham again. He had earlier been dispossessed by Redrobe for Hereford's goal. Hinch then hit a post. When McDowell went off after 67 minutes Hammers were down to 10 men, but Holland's solo goal kept them alive.											
3R	A	HEREFORD		21	L	1-2	1-1	Best 35	Day	Coleman	Lampard	Bonds	Taylor	Wooler	McGiven	Paddon	Lutton	Holland	Best	
		8/1	*17,423*	*3:12*				*Naylor 37p, Jones 74*	*Hughes*	*Radford*	*Naylor*	*McLaughlin*	*Jones*	*Taverner*	*Redrobe**	*Tyler*	*Hinch*	*Rudge*	*Evans*	*Owen*
								Ref: E Wallace	West Ham must regret voting for Hereford's admission to the Football League. Tyler is back with Hereford. Best headed in Lampard's cross for the perfect start, but when Evans was upended Naylor levelled. Alan Jones then lashed in Evans' cross. Hereford now play Bristol City.											

	Home						Away					
	P	W	D	L	F	A	W	D	L	F	A	Pts
1 Leeds	42	12	8	1	38	18	12	6	3	28	13	62
2 Liverpool	42	18	2	1	34	11	4	11	6	18	20	57
3 Derby	42	13	7	1	40	16	4	7	10	12	26	48
4 Ipswich	42	10	7	4	38	21	8	4	9	29	37	47
5 Stoke	42	13	6	2	39	15	2	10	9	15	27	46
6 Burnley	42	10	9	2	29	16	6	5	10	27	37	46
7 Everton	42	12	7	2	29	14	4	5	12	21	34	44
8 QP Rangers	42	8	10	3	30	17	5	7	9	26	35	43
9 Leicester	42	10	7	4	35	17	3	9	9	16	24	42
10 Arsenal	42	9	7	5	23	16	5	7	9	26	35	42
11 Tottenham	42	9	4	8	26	27	5	10	6	19	23	42
12 Wolves	42	11	6	4	30	18	2	9	10	19	31	41
13 Sheffield Utd	42	7	7	7	25	22	7	5	9	19	27	40
14 Manchester C	42	10	7	4	25	17	4	5	12	14	29	40
15 Newcastle	42	9	6	6	28	21	4	6	11	21	27	38
16 Coventry	42	10	5	6	25	18	4	5	12	18	36	38
17 Chelsea	42	9	4	8	36	29	3	9	9	20	31	37
18 WEST HAM	42	7	7	7	36	32	4	8	9	19	28	37
19 Birmingham	42	10	7	4	30	21	2	6	13	22	43	37
20 Southampton	42	8	10	3	30	20	3	4	14	17	48	36
21 Manchester U	42	7	7	7	23	20	3	5	13	15	28	32
22 Norwich	42	6	9	6	25	27	1	6	14	12	35	29
	924	218	149	95	674	433	95	149	218	433	674	924

Odds & ends

Double wins: (1) Chelsea.

Double losses: (2) Spurs, Stoke.

Won from behind: (5) Man C (h), Chelsea (a), Everton (h), Leeds (h), Southampton (h).

Lost from in front: (3) Newcastle (h), Birmingham (a), Hereford FAC (a).

High spots: 10 unbeaten games, January to March, climbing to 16th.

Beating champions Leeds.

Low spots: Losing to Third Division Hereford in FA Cup.

Failing to win any of the first 11 league games, dropping to last place.

West Ham's average home attendance was higher than the average for the First Division as a whole.

Hammer of the Year: Billy Bonds.

Ever-presents: (1) Frank Lampard.

Hat-tricks: (1) Billy Bonds.

Leading scorer: (13) Clyde Best and Billy Bonds.

	Appearances						Goals			
	Lge	*Sub*	LC	*Sub*	FAC	*Sub*	Lge	LC	FAC	Tot
Ayris, Johnny	**5**		1							
Best, Clyde	**34**		2		2		**12**		1	**13**
Bonds, Billy	**40**		1		2		**13**			**13**
Brooking, Trevor	**38**		2				**6**			**6**
Charles, Clive	**1**									
Coker, Ade		*1*			1					
Coleman, Keith	**31**	*2*	2		1					
Day, Mervyn	**33**		2		2					
Ferguson, Bobby	**9**									
Gould, Bobby	**11**	*1*			1		**4**			**4**
Holland, Pat	**20**	*3*		*2*	1	*1*	**2**		1	**3**
Lampard, Frank	**42**		2		2		**2**			**2**
Lock, Kevin	**9**	*2*	2							
Lutton, Bertie	**4**	*2*			1					
MacDougall, Ted	**14**		1				**1**	1		**2**
McDowell, John	**33**		2		1		**2**			**2**
McGiven, Mike	**21**				2					
Moore, Bobby	**22**		1		1					
Paddon, Graham	**24**				2		**4**			**4**
Robson, Bryan	**22**		1				**7**	1		**8**
Taylor, Tommy	**40**		2		2					
Tyler, Dudley	**8**		1							
Wooler, Alan	**1**	*1*			1					
(own-goals)							**2**			**2**
23 players used	**462**	*12*	**22**	*2*	**22**	*1*	**55**	**2**	**2**	**59**

No	Date			Att	Pos	Pt	F-A	H-T	Scorers, Times, and Referees	1	2	3	4	5	6	7	8	9	10	11	12 sub used
1		A	MANCHESTER C			L	**0-4**	0-1		Day	Coleman*	Lampard	Bonds	Taylor T	McDowell	Holland	Paddon	Gould	Brooking	Best	Lock
	17/8			*30,240*		0			*Tueart 10, Marsh 47, 62, Doyle 77*	*MacRae*	*Barrett*	*Donachie*	*Doyle*	*Clarke*	*Oakes*	*Henson*	*Bell*	*Marsh*	*Hartford*	*Tueart*	
									Ref: J Taylor	John Lyall has taken over team affairs from Ron Greenwood, who is off scouting. City parade several new signings, among them Asa Hartford, who did much to undermine the hapless Hammers. A combination of the woodwork and Mervyn Day's excellence prevented a worse defeat.											
2		H	LUTON			W	2-0	2-0	Lampard 4, Bonds 16	Day	McDowell	Lampard	Bonds	Taylor T	Lock	Holland	Paddon	Ayris	Brooking	Best	
	19/8			23,182		2				*Horn*	*John Ryan*	*Thomson*	*Anderson*	*Litt*	*Garner**	*Aston*	*Husband*	*Butlin*	*West*	*Hindson*	*Shanks*
									Ref: R Kirkpatrick	Luton return to Division 1 after 14 years. They lost their opener 1-2 to Liverpool, and look a poor team now. Greenwood is away watching Alf Wood of Millwall. Lampard scored early with a low volley and Bonds added a second with a header after Horn had punched the ball out.											
3		H	EVERTON		16	L	2-3	0-2	Bonds 71p, McDowell 73	Day	Coleman	Lampard	Bonds	Taylor T	Lock	Holland	Paddon	Gould	McDowell	Best	
	24/8			22,486	*5*	2			*Royle 39p, Latchford 45, Harvey 80*	*Lawson*	*Darracott*	*Seargeant*	*Clements*	*Lyons*	*Hurst*	*Buckley*	*Harvey*	*Royle*	*Latchford*	*Connolly**	*Pearson*
									Ref: K Burns	Again it is West Ham's defenders who get the goals. Buckley was pulled down by McDowell for Everton's penalty; West Ham's was given for handball. The ball came off the bar for Latchford's goal. McDowell dodged Everton's offside trap. Harvey won the game with a rising drive.											
4		A	LUTON			D	0-0	0-0		Day	Coleman	Lampard	Bonds	Taylor T	Lock	Holland	Paddon	Gould	McDowell	Best	
	28/8			*16,931*		3				*Barber*	*Shanks*	*Thomson*	*Anderson*	*Faulkner*	*John Ryan*	*Hindson*	*Husband*	*Butlin*	*West*	*Aston**	*Alston*
									Ref: C Thomas	West Ham's goal-shy forwards also failed to score in three Texaco Cup games. Clyde Best lacked support. His one shot was pushed aside by Barber. Luton are still looking for their first win and did most of the attacking. Elsewhere, Bill Nicholson has resigned at Tottenham.											
5		A	NEWCASTLE		18	L	0-2	0-2		Day	Coleman	Lampard	Bonds	Taylor T	Lock	Holland	Paddon	Gould*	McDowell	Best	Ayris
	31/8			*30,780*	*11*	3			*Tudor 5, Macdonald 24*	*McFaul*	*Craig D*	*Clark*	*McDermott*	*Keeley*	*Howard*	*Burns*	*Nattrass*	*Macdonald*	*Tudor*	*Hibbitt*	
									Ref: H Hackney	Goal-shy Hammers miss Trevor Brooking's midfield guile. Newcastle win so comfortably that after the final whistle they heap salt on the wounds by saying the team they want to play in Round 3 of the FA Cup is West Ham! Little do they know that Hammers are destined to win it.											
6		H	SHEFFIELD UTD		21	L	1-2	1-0	Jennings 18	Day	McDowell	Lampard	Bonds	Taylor T	Lock	Ayris	Paddon	**Jennings**	Holland	Best	
	7/9			**20,977**	*6*	3			*Woodward 76, Dearden 85*	*Brown*	*Badger*	*Hemsley*	*Eddy*	*Colquhoun*	*Franks*	*Woodward*	*Speight*	*Dearden*	*Currie*	*Field*	
									Ref: I Jones	5ft 9in Billy Jennings has signed from Watford for £115,000. He turned in Lampard's long ball and saw another effort superbly saved by Jim Brown. Holland's sloppy square pass let in Alan Woodward. Soon afterwards Dearden scored at the second attempt for Ken Furphy's Blades.											
7		A	TOTTENHAM		22	L	1-2	0-0	Lampard 79	Day	McDowell	Lampard	Bonds	Taylor T	Lock	Holland	Paddon	Jennings	Brooking	Best	
	14/9			*27,959*	*18*	3			*England 56, Chivers 74*	*Jennings*	*Evans*	*Knowles*	*Pratt*	*England*	*Beal*	*Neighbour*	*Perryman*	*Chivers*	*Peters*	*Coates*	
									Ref: R Tinkler	Bill Nicholson resigned two weeks ago. Greenwood watches the Hammers for the first time this season. England outjumped Bonds and Chivers outjumped Taylor for Spurs' goals. Lampard replied with a diving header. Spurs' win hauls them above West Ham, who are now bottom.											
8		H	LEICESTER		19	W	**6-2**	3-1	Jennings 24, 50, B'nds 35, G'ld 40, 56,	Day	McDowell	Lampard	Bonds	Taylor T	Lock	Jennings*	Paddon	Gould	Brooking	**Robson**	Holland
	21/9			21,377	*13*	5			*Worthington 10p, 89* [Robson 68]	*Wallington*	*Whitworth*	*Rofe*	*Sammels*	*Munro*	*Woollett*	*Weller*	*Earle*	*Worthington*	*Birchenall**	*Glover*	*Cross*
									Ref: R Crabb	Keith Robson signs for £60,000 from Newcastle and scores. John Lyall switches to 4-3-3 to accommodate him. Worthington 'dives' to win a penalty. Jennings' looping header makes it 1-1. Bonds' right-footer and Gould's diving header make it 3-1. Brooking is man of the match.											
9		H	BIRMINGHAM		13	W	3-0	1-0	Paddon 44, Jennings 64, Robson 80	Day	McDowell	Lampard	Bonds	Taylor T	Lock	Jennings	Paddon	Gould	Brooking	Robson	
	25/9			29,495	*21*	7				*Latchford*	*Martin*	*Styles*	*Kendall*	*Gallagher*	*Page**	*Campbell*	*Francis*	*Burns*	*Hatton*	*Taylor*	*Hynd*
									Ref: A Lees	Hammers hit the woodwork three times in the opening 20 minutes, but the score was harsh on Freddie Goodwin's City, who had a goal chalked off and live-wire Trevor Francis also hit the bar. Graham Paddon's 30-yarder was followed by Billy Jenning's header from McDowell's cross.											
10		A	BURNLEY		12	W	5-3	1-1	R'bson 18, 55, B'king 65, Jennings 71,	Day	McDowell	Lampard	Bonds	Taylor T	Lock	Jennings	Paddon	Gould	Brooking	Robson	
	28/9			*17,613*	*13*	9			*Fletcher 3, 86, Noble 57* [Bonds 83]	*Stevenson*	*Newton*	*Brennan*	*Ingham*	*Waldron*	*Rodaway*	*Noble*	*Flynn*	*Fletcher*	*Collins*	*James*	
									Ref: G Hill	It is hard to know which is the more remarkable, the thrill-a-minute football match or Trevor Brooking's first ever booking, for a challenge on Leighton James. Jimmy Adamson's Burnley had won at Anfield in midweek but their keeper has one of those matches he would wish to forget.											

No	H/A	Opponent / Date	Att	Pos	Res / Pts	F-A	H-T	Scorers, Times, and Referees	1	2	3	4	5	6	7	8	9	10	11	12 sub used
11	H	DERBY		12	D	2-2	1-1	Robson 8, Bonds 59	Day	McDowell*	Lampard	Bonds	Taylor T	Lock	Jennings	Paddon	Gould	Brooking	Robson	Holland
		5/10	32,900	*9*	10			*Lee 29, Hector 80*	*Boulton*	*Webster*	*Nish*	*Rioch*	*Daniel*	*Todd*	*Newton*	*Gemmill*	*Davies*	*Hector*	*Lee*	
								Ref: P Walters	Brooking is scintillating, despite playing in attack against his wishes. Keith Robson appears to handle before scoring the first goal. After Lee levelled, Lampard crossed for Robson to head on to Bonds. Though Hector equalised, it does not stop talk of Hammers challenging at the top.											
12	A	COVENTRY		12	D	1-1	0-0	Gould 77	Day	Coleman	Lampard	Bonds	Taylor T	Lock	Jennings	Paddon	Gould	Brooking	Robson	
		12/10	*22,519*	*13*	11			*Hutchison 71*	*Ramsbottom*	*Oakey*	*Catlin*	*Mortimer*	*Lloyd*	*Hindley*	*Holmes*	*Alderson*	*Stein*	*Cross*	*Hutchison*	
								Ref: L Hayes	The City match programme devoted three pages to the return of Bobby Gould: the home crowd booed him lethargically and former team-mates playfully kicked him. Gould responded by cracking in a superb volley. That equalised Day's mishap, letting a corner float through his hands.											
13	A	EVERTON		12	D	1-1	1-0	Gould 40	Day	Coleman	Lampard	Bonds	Taylor T	Lock	Jennings	Paddon	Gould	Brooking	Robson	
		15/10	*31,855*	*3*	12			*Lyons 59*	*Davies*	*Bernard*	*Seargeant*	*Lyons*	*Kenyon*	*Clements*	*Buckley*	*Dobson*	*Pearson*	*Royle*	*Connolly*	
								Ref: D Wallace	Never has 19-year-old Day performed better than this, and all under the appreciative eye of England boss Don Revie. Hammers were swamped in midfield, yet took the lead when Gould slid in to connect with Robson's back-header. Lyons ran from half-way to level from a sharp angle.											
14	H	IPSWICH		10	W	1-0	1-0	Jennings 34	Day	Coleman	Lampard	Bonds	Taylor T	Lock	Jennings	Paddon	Gould	Brooking	Robson	
		19/10	33,543	*3*	14				*Sivell*	*Mills*	*Harper*	*Talbot*	*Hunter*	*Beattie*	*Hamilton*	*Collard*	*Johnson*	*Woods*	*Lambert**	*Gates*
								Ref: R Perkin	West Ham extend their unbeaten league record to seven with an uncompromisingly physical performance. Billy Jennings won the game with a super goal, taking a short cross from Robson and slipping past three defenders. The goal had supporters comparing it with Greaves - at his best.											
15	A	ARSENAL		11	L	0-3	0-2		Day	McDowell*	Lampard	Bonds	Taylor T	Lock	Jennings	Paddon	Gould	Brooking	Robson	Coleman
		26/10	*41,004*	*21*	14			*Radford 14, Brady 42, Kidd 50*	*Rimmer*	*Rice**	*McNab*	*Kelly*	*Mancini*	*Simpson*	*Storey*	*Ball*	*Radford*	*Brady*	*Kidd*	*Armstrong*
								Ref: T Reynolds	England boss Don Revie runs his eye over Brooking, but West Ham's midfield is swamped by Arsenal's 4-4-2 formation. Arsenal had so much freedom that Eddie Kelly started taking the mickey. The turning point came when McNab cleared off the line from Gould just after half-time.											
16	H	MIDDLESBROUGH		10	W	3-0	1-0	Robson 29, Boam 84 (og), Paddon 87	Day	Coleman	Lampard	Bonds	Taylor T	Lock	Jennings	Paddon	Gould	Brooking	Robson	
		2/11	28,915	*6*	16				*Platt*	*Craggs*	*Spraggon*	*Souness*	*Boam*	*Maddren*	*Murdoch*	*Mills**	*Hickton*	*Foggon*	*Armstrong*	*Willey*
								Ref: R Mathewson	Kevin Lock plays a stormer alongside Tommy Taylor, locking the door against Hickton and Mills. Gould's cross was unwittingly turned in by Robson. Brooking made the game safe with a goal that went in off Stuart Boam. Paddon's free-kick then flew in from the edge of the box.											
17	A	CARLISLE		9	W	1-0	0-0	Lampard 48	Day	Coleman	Lampard	Bonds	Taylor T	Lock	Jennings	Paddon	Gould	Brooking	Robson	
		9/11	***14,141***	*17*	18				*Clarke T*	*Carr*	*Gorman*	*O'Neill*	*Green*	*Parker*	*Martin*	*Train*	*Clarke F*	*McIlmoyle*	*Balderstone*	
								Ref: K Styles	Lampard's goal leaves West Ham just four points behind the leaders, and even Lyall is foolish enough to start talking about the championship. The bookies are unimpressed, quoting the Hammers at 20-1 for the title. The looming match at Anfield will sort the men from the boys.											
18	H	WOLVES		7	W	5-2	2-0	Bonds 37p, Br'k 44, Lamp' 62, Jen' 78,	Day	Coleman	Lampard	Bonds	Taylor T	Lock	Jennings	Paddon	Gould	Brooking	Robson	
		16/11	31,708	*13*	20			*Richards 70, Kindon 88* [Gould 85]	*Parkes*	*Palmer*	*Parkin*	*Bailey*	*Jefferson*	*McAlle*	*Hibbitt*	*Powell*	*Richards*	*Kindon*	*Farley*	
								Ref: H Davey	'Brooking for England; West Ham for champions' sing the crowd. Wolves had not lost in London on their previous 11 visits, over 27 months. A penalty conceded by Ken Hibbitt – who handled Brooking's cross – lit the touch-paper. Brooking played a part in all but one of the goals.											
19	A	LIVERPOOL		6	D	1-1	1-1	Robson 11	Day	Coleman	Lampard	Bonds	Taylor T	Lock	Jennings	Paddon	Gould	Brooking	Robson	
		23/11	***46,346***	*2*	21			*Smith 12*	*Clemence*	*Smith*	*Lindsay*	*McDermott*	*Lawler*	*Hughes*	*Keegan*	*Cormack*	*Boersma**	*Kennedy*	*Callaghan*	*Heighway*
								Ref: R Capey	West Ham looked full of ideas early on, but were hanging on desperately by the close, when Mervyn Day saved well from Lindsay's point-blank effort. Afterwards Day was hospitalised with tummy pains. X-rays showed his stomach contained gravel. He was told to drink water.											
20	A	QP RANGERS		6	W	2-0	1-0	Jennings 31, Paddon 70	Day	Coleman	Lampard	Bonds*	Taylor T	Lock	Jennings	Paddon	Gould	Brooking	Robson	Holland
		30/11	*28,356*	*17*	23				*Parkes*	*Clement*	*Gillard*	*McLintock*	*Webb*	*Hazell*	*Thomas*	*Francis*	*Rogers*	*Bowles*	*Givens*	
								Ref: M Sinclair	David Webb's error let in Billy Jennings to head the first goal. Man-of-the-match Graham Paddon deserved to score the second, decisive goal, a left-footer from the edge of the box. The chance was set up by Brooking. Kevin Lock padlocked danger-man Stan Bowles out of the game.											
21	H	LEEDS		5	W	2-1	1-0	Gould 29, Jennings 69	Day	Coleman	Lampard	Bonds	Taylor T	Lock	Jennings*	Paddon	Gould	McDowell	Robson	**Taylor A**
		7/12	39,562	*12*	25			*McKenzie 90*	*Harvey*	*Reaney*	*Cherry*	*Bremner*	*McQueen*	*Madeley*	*McKenzie*	*Clarke*	*Jordan*	*Lorimer*	*Yorath*	
								Ref: W Gow	The gates were locked 30 minutes before kick-off. Paddon's corner-kicks brought two goals. The first was headed on by Robson to Gould. The second was headed in by Jennings. Leeds feigned injury and back-chatted the ref throughout, then blamed West Ham for being too physical.											

No	Date		Att	Pos	Pt	F-A	H-T	Scorers, Times, and Referees	1	2	3	4	5	6	7	8	9	10	11	12 sub used
22	H	MANCHESTER C		6	D	0-0	0-0		Day	Coleman	Lampard	Bonds	Taylor T	Lock	Jennings*	Paddon	Gould	Brooking	Robson	McDowell
	14/12		33,908	*4*	26				*MacRae*	*Hammond*	*Donachie*	*Henson*	*Doyle**	*Oakes*	*Horswill*	*Bell*	*Marsh*	*Hartford*	*Tueart*	*Daniels*
								Ref: J Hunting	City skipper Rodney Marsh admits to having agreed during a team-talk to stop rampant West Ham by employing negative tactics. City tried to interrupt Hammers' rhythm with constant time-wasting. Gould missed the best chance, but Day pulled off a super save to prevent a travesty.											
23	A	CHELSEA		5	D	1-1	0-0	Gould 85	Day	Coleman	Lampard	Bonds*	Taylor T	Lock	McDowell	Paddon	Gould	Brooking	Robson	Best
	21/12		*34,969*	*19*	27			*Hutchinson 65*	*Phillips*	*Locke*	*Harris*	*Hollins*	*Droy*	*Hay*	*Kember**	*Wilkins R*	*Garland*	*Hutchinson*	*Cooke*	*Dempsey*
								Ref: R Perkins	Day turned Lock's miscued clearance onto the bar, with Hutchinson waiting for the rebound. Gould, previously marked tight by Droy, chested down and fired the equaliser past Phillips. After 35 matches Best returned to first-team football, but was booked immediately and looked stale.											
24	H	TOTTENHAM		5	D	1-1	1-1	Robson 26	Day	Coleman	Lampard	McDowell	Taylor T	Lock	Jennings*	Paddon	Gould	Brooking	Robson	Taylor A
	26/12		37,682	*18*	28			*Peters 18*	*Jennings*	*Kinnear*	*Knowles*	*Pratt*	*England*	*Naylor*	*Coates*	*Perryman*	*Chivers*	*Peters*	*Duncan*	
								Ref: G Kew	Spurs have lost their last two games. Martin Peters chipped Day from the edge of the box, then Keith Robson headed in Brooking's near-post corner. Robson's fourth booking will bring him an automatic ban. Had West Ham won they would have gone top of the league for four hours.											
25	A	STOKE		6	L	1-2	0-0	Holland 52	Day	Coleman	Lampard	Holland	Taylor T	Lock	Taylor A*	Paddon	Gould	McDowell	Best	Ayris
	28/12		*33,498*	*5*	28			*Salmons 69p, Hurst 79*	*Shilton*	*Marsh*	*Pejic*	*Mahoney*	*Smith*	*Dodd*	*Conroy*	*Greenhoff*	*Hurst*	*Hudson*	*Salmons*	
								Ref: D Richardson	Stoke had lost at home just once, so this was a tough fixture, especially without Brooking, Bonds, Jennings, and Robson. Alan Taylor went off with a twisted knee. Defeat was made worse because Stoke's first goal was a disputed penalty and their second was headed in by Geoff Hurst.											
26	A	LEEDS		9	L	1-2	1-1	Robson 10	Day	Coleman	Lampard	Bonds	McDowell	Lock	Holland	Paddon	Best	Brooking	Robson	
	11/1		*40,099*	*10*	28			*Clarke 37, McKenzie 59*	*Harvey*	*Reaney*	*Gray F*	*Bremner*	*McQueen*	*Madeley*	*McKenzie*	*Clarke*	*Lorimer*	*Giles*	*Gray E*	
								Ref: J Rice	When Keith Robson headed in Bonds' cross it seemed that the Elland Road jinx might be lifted. Hammers had not won here in Division 1 since 1930. Lock's bad back-pass let in Clarke, and Jimmy Armfield's Leeds were on top when McKenzie fired in after Clarke's shot was blocked.											
27	H	QP RANGERS		10	D	2-2	2-1	Jennings15, Bonds 44p	Day	Coleman*	Lampard	Bonds	Taylor T	Lock	Jennings	Paddon	McDowell	Brooking	Robson	Best
	18/1		28,772	*12*	29			*Masson 32, Bowles 73p*	*Parkes*	*Clement*	*Gillard*	*Masson*	*McLintock*	*Webb*	*Thomas*	*Francis*	*Beck*	*Bowles*	*Givens*	
								Ref: P Willis	Jennings side-foots Paddon's cross. Bowles slips a quick free-kick to Masson. Robson signs off before he starts a suspension with a cracking run that earns a penalty. Bowles levelled from another penalty, both of which – against Webb and Lampard – were shown by TV to be correct.											
28	H	CARLISLE		6	W	2-0	2-0	Jennings 18, Holland 38	Day	McDowell	Lampard	Bonds	Taylor T	Lock	Jennings	Paddon	Robson	Brooking*	Holland	Best
	1/2		26,805	*20*	31				*Ross*	*Spearritt*	*Gorman*	*O'Neill*	*Green*	*Parker*	*Martin**	*Train*	*Owen*	*Laidlaw*	*Clarke*	*Barry*
								Ref: R Crabb	Carlisle pressed hard but seldom threatened, not helped by striker Bobby Owen playing deep in midfield. Jennings missed his first shot but scored with his second, with Carlisle defenders standing like statues. Holland snapped up a bad back-pass by Les O'Neill for the second goal.											
29	A	MIDDLESBROUGH		7	D	0-0	0-0		Day	McDowell	Lampard	Bonds*	Taylor T	Lock	Jennings	Paddon	Best	Brooking	Holland	Coleman
	8/2		*29,179*	*8*	32				*Platt*	*Craggs*	*Spraggon*	*Murdoch*	*Boam*	*Maddren*	*Brine*	*Mills*	*Hickton*	*Willey*	*Armstrong**	*Taylor*
								Ref: J Williams	Boro boss Jack Charlton is full of praise for West Ham's football. Boro didn't play any, but still felt they should have won when Day appeared to impede David Mills in the box. Best Hammers' chance fell to Clyde Best, who shimmied through three tackles, then lost control of the ball.											
30	H	LIVERPOOL		6	D	0-0	0-0		Day	McDowell	Lampard	Bonds	Taylor T	Lock	Jennings	Paddon	Robson	Brooking	Holland	
	19/2		**40,256**	*5*	33				*Clemence*	*Neal*	*Smith*	*Thompson*	*McDermott**	*Hughes*	*Keegan*	*Hall*	*Heighway*	*Kennedy*	*Callaghan*	*Waddle*
								Ref: T Reynolds	Tommy Smith is recalled by Liverpool to curtail Robson, and within 36 seconds has kicked him into orbit. The rusty Smith also presents West Ham with their best chance, fluffing a back-pass that Jennings volleyed against a post, with Pat Holland hooking the rebound over the bar.											
31	A	WOLVES		9	L	1-3	0-2	Gould 82	Day	Coleman*	Lampard	McDowell	Taylor T	Lock	Jennings	Paddon	Robson	Brooking	Holland	Gould
	22/2		*24,791*	*14*	33			*Kindon 17, Richards 41, 64*	*Pierce*	*Palmer*	*Parkin*	*Bailey*	*Munro*	*Jefferson*	*Hibbitt*	*Daley*	*Richards*	*Kindon*	*Wagstaffe*	
								Ref: H Hackney	Lyall has no one to do the job of the absent Bonds. West Ham had lost at Molineux, without scoring, for the previous six years, so the result is no surprise, though Gould's goal is. No wonder McGarry's team like playing West Ham, who afterwards retreat to Bournemouth for a break.											

No	Venue	Opponent	Pos	Res	FT	HT	Scorers	1	2	3	4	5	6	7	8	9	10	11	12
32	H	NEWCASTLE	13	L	0-1	0-1		Day	McDowell	Lampard	Robson	Taylor T	Lock	Jennings	Paddon	Gould	Brooking	Holland*	Taylor A
28/2		32,753	*11*	33			*Macdonald 26*	*McFaul*	*Craig D*	*Barker*	*Smith*	*Keeley*	*Nattrass*	*Barrowclough*	*Nulty*	*Macdonald*	*Tudor*	*Craig T*	
							Ref: D Biddle	It's now just one win in 11 games as West Ham's slide continues. Malcolm Macdonald ran 40 yards to beat Hammers' offside-trap for his 16th league goal of the season. Both sides wasted chances. Keith Robson headed against a post and Billy Jennings shot wide from six yards.											
33	H	BURNLEY	12	W	2-1	0-1	Robson 66, Taylor A 76	Day	McDowell	Lampard	Bonds*	Taylor T	Lock	Jennings	Paddon	Taylor A	Brooking	Robson	Gould
15/3		28,830	*2*	35			*Collins 42*	*Stevenson*	*Ingham*	*Newton*	*Noble*	*Waldron*	*Thomson*	*Flynn**	*Hankin*	*Fletcher*	*Collins*	*James*	*Podaway*
							Ref: T Spencer	Bonds is carried off in the first minute with a knee injury. Doug Collins chipped Day, but Keith Robson's cross sailed over Alan Stevenson for the equaliser. Afterwards Bobby Gould claimed he got the faintest of touches and jokingly tried to claim the goal. Lyall awarded it to Robson.											
34	A	BIRMINGHAM		D	1-1	1-0	Taylor A 29	Day	Coleman	Lampard	McDowell	Taylor T	Lock	Gould	Paddon	Taylor A	Brooking	Robson	
18/3		*34,000*		36			*Bryant 67*	*Latchford*	*Calderwood*	*Bryant*	*Kendall**	*Gallagher*	*Roberts*	*Morton*	*Francis*	*Hendrie*	*Hatton*	*Taylor*	*Want*
							Ref: P Partridge	Brooking set up Alan Taylor's fourth goal in three games, but Francis, back after five months out through injury, manufactures City's equaliser through Bryant's first senior goal. After the match Robson suffers from internal bleeding, which together with a leg injury has him on crutches.											
35	A	SHEFFIELD UTD	12	L	2-3	2-1	Gould 7, Jennings 28	Day	Coleman	Lampard	McDowell	Taylor T	Lock	Jennings	Paddon	Taylor A	Brooking	Gould	
22/3		*25,527*	*8*	36			*Currie 8, 78, Woodward 58*	*Brown*	*Badger*	*Bradford*	*Eddy*	*Colquhoun*	*Flynn*	*Woodward*	*Speight*	*Cammack*	*Currie*	*Field*	
							Ref: J Taylor	It is one defeat in 11 for the Blades, who are now only five points behind leaders Everton. The game got off to a furious start, Gould driving in from McDowell's lay-off. Seconds later Cammack hit the post and Currie tapped in the rebound. Man-of-the-match Currie mis-hit the winner.											
36	H	STOKE	12	D	2-2	1-1	Brooking 39, Jennings 69	Day	Coleman	Lampard*	McDowell	Taylor T	Lock	Jennings	Paddon	Taylor A	Brooking	Gould	Ayris
28/3		29,811	*5*	37			*Conroy 40, 49*	*Shilton*	*Bloor*	*Bowers*	*Mahoney*	*Dodd*	*Skeels*	*Conroy*	*Greenhoff*	*Hurst**	*Hudson*	*Salmons*	*Moores*
							Ref: H Davey	Had Tony Waddington's Stoke won they would have been just one point off the top. Carrot-top Conroy scored twice and was at the heart of everything. Brooking had impudently taken the ball around Shilton to put West Ham one up. Jennings side-stepped two defenders to level.											
37	H	CHELSEA	12	L	0-1	0-1		Day	Coleman	McDowell	**Curbishley**	Taylor T	Lock	Jennings*	Paddon	Taylor A	Brooking	Gould	Ayris
29/3		31,025	*18*	37			*Droy 22*	*Phillips*	*Locke*	*Harris*	*Hollins*	*Droy*	*Hinton*	*Kember*	*Hay*	*Langley*	*Houseman*	*Cooke*	
							Ref: A Morrissey	Chelsea are fighting desperately against the drop, and with West Ham's minds on the FA Cup this is the perfect time to play them. Semi-fit giant Mick Droy glanced a header for the only goal. Young Alan Curbishley took the eye on his debut, drafted in for the injured Billy Bonds.											
38	A	LEICESTER	12	L	0-3	0-1		Day	Coleman	McDowell	Holland	Taylor T	Lock	Best	Wooler	Taylor A	Brooking	Gould	
1/4		*30,408*	*18*	37			*Worthington 13p, Garland 86, 87*	*Wallington*	*Whitworth*	*Rofe*	*Lee*	*Blockley*	*Cross*	*Weller*	*Sammels*	*Worthington**	*Birchenall*	*Garland*	*Glover*
							Ref: K McNally	All the bottom clubs are beating West Ham of late. With an FA Cup semi-final looming, Lyall does not relish a punishing Easter schedule, and rests Jennings and Paddon. Pat Holland's foul on Frank Worthington allowed Jimmy Bloomfield's City to go in front. Garland sealed the win.											
39	A	DERBY	13	L	0-1	0-0		Day	McDowell	Lampard	Bonds	Taylor T	Lock	Jennings	Paddon	Taylor A*	Brooking	Gould	Holland
12/4		*31,336*	*1*	37			*Rioch 67*	*Boulton*	*Thomas*	*Nish*	*Rioch*	*McFarland*	*Todd*	*Newton*	*Gemmill*	*Davies**	*Hector*	*Lee*	*Hinton*
							Ref: M Lowe	Bruce Rioch's 20th goal of the season keeps Derby two points out in front with two matches to play. It came when Hinton's corner was only half-cleared, and Rioch slammed the ball in. Sub Hinton had only been on two minutes. Derby boss Dave Mackay: 'I died a death out there'.											
40	H	COVENTRY	14	L	1-2	1-2	Holland 44	Day	Coleman	Lampard	Holland	McDowell	Lock	Jennings	Paddon*	Taylor A	Brooking	Gould	Curbishley
19/4		27,431	*12*	37			*Green 4, Mortimer 45*	*Ramsbottom*	*Oakey*	*Cattlin !*	*Craven*	*Lloyd*	*Dugdale*	*Mortimer*	*Holmes*	*Ferguson*	*Green*	*Hutchison*	
							Ref: R Tinkler	West Ham extend their dismal league run to seven games without a win. Players feared injury against Gordon Milne's Coventry, for whom Chris Cattlin was sent off after just nine minutes. City were leading at the time through Alan Green's effort, when Day and Lampard dithered.											
41	A	IPSWICH	16	L	1-4	1-1	Holland 36 *[Hunter 89]*	Day	Coleman	Lampard	Holland	McDowell	Lock	Jennings	Best	Taylor A	Brooking	Gould	
26/4		*31,592*	*3*	37			*Talbot 27, Whymark 61, Beattie 87,*	*Sivell*	*Burley*	*Mills*	*Talbot*	*Hunter*	*Beattie*	*Hamilton*	*Viljoen*	*Woods*	*Whymark*	*Lambert*	
							Ref: D Turner	In the 86th minute Talbot sends Brooking flying in the box but the referee waves play on. Ipswich immediately broke downfield for Kevin Beattie to make it 1-3. Ipswich's first goal had come when the ref penalised Day for time-wasting and awarded a free-kick on the 18-yard line.											
42	H	ARSENAL	13	W	1-0	1-0	Paddon 3	Day	McDowell	Lampard	Bonds	Taylor T	Lock	Jennings*	Paddon	Taylor A	Brooking	Holland	Gould
28/4		30,195	*16*	39				*Barnett*	*Storey*	*Nelson*	*Kelly*	*Mancini*	*Matthews*	*Ball*	*Brady*	*Hornsby*	*Kidd*	*Rostron*	
Home		Away					Ref: R Matthewson	West Ham's first league win in nine attempts, and only their third in five months. Kelly's mistake gave Paddon the chance of a left-footer over Barnett's shoulder. Taylor missed two good chances, one of which hit the bar. No one can take it easy for fear of being dropped for Wembley.											
Average 30,077		29,673																	

League Cup					F-A	H-T	Scorers, Times, and Referees	1	2	3	4	5	6	7	8	9	10	11	12 sub used
2	A	TRANMERE	21	D	0-0	0-0		Day	McDowell	Lampard	Bonds	Taylor T	Lock	Ayris	Paddon	Holland	Brooking	Best	
11/9			*8,638 3:21*					*Johnson*	*Matthias*	*Flood*	*Moore*	*Philpotts*	*Veitch*	*Coppell*	*Palios*	*Young*	*Tynan*	*Crossley*	
							Ref: A Grey	Hammers' first ever visit to Prenton Park. New signing Billy Jennings is cup-tied. Tranmere knocked out Arsenal last year and had the chances to win this one too. They had Mervyn Day to blame for not taking them. Tranmere 'scored' after 16 minutes, but Ronnie Moore was offside.											
2R	H	TRANMERE	7	W	6-0	2-0	Bonds 23p, 87, Gould 44, 56, 89p,	Day	McDowell	Lampard	Bonds	Taylor T	Lock	Ayris	Paddon	Gould	Brooking	Robson	
18/9			15,854 *3:14*				[Ayris 59]	*Johnson*	*Matthias*	*Flood*	*Moore*	*Philpotts*	*Veitch*	*Coppell*	*Palios**	*Mitchell*	*Tynan*	*Crossley*	*Webb*
							Ref: A Grey	Gould was almost set to join Portsmouth, but takes the place of Jennings to record his first hat-trick in three seasons. That he did so was down to skipper Bonds, who had two goals himself when West Ham were given a last-minute penalty. Bonds selflessly handed the ball to Gould.											
3	A	FULHAM	6	L	1-2	1-0	Brooking 34	Day	Coleman	Lampard	Bonds	Taylor T	Lock	Ayris*	Paddon	Gould	Brooking	Robson	Holland
8/10			*29,611 2:8*				*Mullery 47, Slough 59*	*Mellor*	*Cutbush*	*Strong*	*Mullery*	*Lacy*	*Moore*	*Conway*	*Slough*	*Busby*	*Lloyd*	*Barrett*	
							Ref: H New	Bobby Moore is made Fulham's captain for the day. A floodlight failure interrupted the game at 1-1 for 30 minutes. The ref then asked Day if three pylons were bright enough to continue. Day said yes, and minutes later was beaten by a messy goal by Slough, deflected in by Paddon.											

FA Cup																			
3	A	SOUTHAMPTON	6	W	2-1	2-0	Lampard 25, Gould 40	Day	Coleman	Lampard	Bonds	McDowell	Lock	Jennings	Paddon	Gould*	Brooking	Robson	Holland
4/1			*24,615 2:16*				*Channon 67p*	*Martin*	*Mills*	*Steele*	*Holmes*	*Bennett*	*Blyth*	*Stokes**	*Channon*	*Osgood*	*Crabbe*	*O'Brien*	*Peach*
							Ref: G Hill	Eric Martin fumbles Lampard's free-kick into the net. Southampton never recover. Gould doubles the lead with a header, having received the injury for which he will be substituted. Lampard pushed Bobby Stokes for the penalty. The bookies now make West Ham 9-1 for the Cup.											
4	H	SWINDON	10	D	1-1	0-0	Jennings 75	Day	McDowell	Lampard	Bonds	Taylor T	Lock	Jennings	Paddon	Best	Brooking	Holland	
25/1			35,679 *3:4*				*Eastoe 83*	*Barron*	*Dixon*	*Trollope*	*Jenkins*	*Burrows*	*Prophett*	*Moss*	*McLaughlin*	*Eastoe*	*Butler*	*Anderson*	
							Ref: C Thomas	The last time these teams met in the FA Cup was in 1964. West Ham won 3-1 and went on to win it. Manager Danny Williams was angry that Tommy Taylor's shirt-tugging went unpunished seconds before Jennings fired through Jim Barron's legs. Moss crossed for Eastoe's equaliser.											
4R	A	SWINDON	10	W	2-1	0-1	Brooking 59, Holland 86	Day	McDowell	Lampard	Bonds	Taylor T	Lock	Jennings	Paddon	Best	Brooking	Holland	
28/1			*27,749 3:4*				*Anderson 29*	*Barron*	*Dixon*	*Trollope*	*Jenkins*	*Burrows*	*Prophett*	*Moss*	*McLaughlin*	*Eastoe*	*Butler*	*Anderson*	
							Ref: C Thomas	A thrilling cup-tie. Trevor Anderson heads in Moss's cross. Hammers level when, from a disputed free-kick, Billy Jennings heads down to Brooking. The winner is a messy business. McDowell hits a post, Jennings returns the ball in, and Holland volleys through a ruck of players.											
5	H	QP RANGERS	7	W	2-1	1-1	Holland 34, Robson 46	Day	McDowell	Lampard	Bonds	Taylor T	Lock	Jennings	Paddon	Robson	Brooking	Holland	
15/2			39,193 *12*				*Clement 27*	*Parkes*	*Clement*	*Gillard*	*Masson*	*McLintock*	*Webb*	*Thomas*	*Leach*	*Beck*	*Bowles**	*Givens*	*Rogers*
							Ref: G Kew	Robson's weak back-pass was cut out by Dave Clement, who beat Lampard and Lock before scoring. Pat Holland, playing these days wide on the right, created and executed the equaliser. The brilliant Brooking laid the ball back to Jennings, who crossed for Keith Robson's winner.											
QF	A	ARSENAL	13	W	2-0	1-0	Taylor A 15, 46	Day	McDowell	Lampard	Bonds	Taylor T	Lock	Jennings	Paddon	Taylor A	Brooking	Robson	
8/3			*56,742 18*					*Rimmer*	*Rice*	*McNab*	*Storey*	*Mancini*	*Ssimpson*	*Matthews*	*Ball*	*Radford**	*Kidd*	*Brady*	*Armstrong*
							Ref: K Burns	Alan Taylor is brought in for his first full game, the idea being to discomfort the pedestrian Terry Mancini. The new boy prods in Paddon's chip, then scores the best goal of his life with a fierce right-footer. Just before the break Day rugby-tackled John Radford and got away with it.											
SF	N	IPSWICH	12	D	0-0	0-0		Day	McDowell	Lampard	Bonds	Taylor T	Lock	Jennings	Paddon	Taylor A	Brooking	Gould*	Holland
5/4			*58,000 3*					*Sivell*	*Burley*	*Mills*	*Talbot*	*Hunter**	*Beattie*	*Hamilton*	*Viljoen*	*Woods*	*Whymark*	*Lambert*	*Osborne*
		(At Villa Park)					Ref: C Thomas	Lucky Hammers. Ipswich lose both centre-halves – Beattie and Hunter – and switch centre-forward Trevor Whymark to central defence, where he plays a blinder. Ipswich dominated the game from first to last. In injury-time Billy Jennings cleared off the line with Mervyn Day beaten.											

SF	N	IPSWICH		12	W	2-1	1-1	Taylor A 29, 82	Day	McDowell	Lampard	Bonds	Taylor T	Lock	Jennings*	Paddon	Taylor A	Brooking	Gould	Holland
R	9/4		*45,344*	*3*				*Jennings 44 (og)*	*Sivell*	*Burley*	*Mills*	*Talbot*	*Wark*	*Beattie*	*Hamilton*	*Viljoen*	*Woods*	*Whymark*	*Lambert*
		(At Chelsea)						Ref: C Thomas	Yet again West Ham are outplayed by Bobby Robson's Ipswich, who have two 'goals' disallowed. Alan Taylor's far-post header put West Ham ahead, until Jennings sliced Lambert's corner past Day. Alan Taylor fired Paddon's free-kick in off a post from 25 yards for the winner.										
F	N	FULHAM		13	W	2-0	0-0	Taylor A 61, 64	Day	McDowell	Lampard	Bonds	Taylor T	Lock	Jennings	Paddon	Taylor A	Brooking	Holland
	3/5		*100,000*	*2:9*					*Mellor*	*Cutbush*	*Lacy*	*Moore*	*Fraser*	*Mullery*	*Conway*	*Slough*	*Mitchell*	*Busby*	*Barrett*
		(At Wembley)						Ref: P Partridge	Alec Stock's Fulham knocked West Ham out of the League Cup in October. They might have won this one too, but for Day's two sharp saves from John Mitchell. Fulham had the edge until Peter 'Teflon' Mellor failed to gather two shots, which spilled into the path of Alan Taylor.										

		Home					Away					
	P	W	D	L	F	A	W	D	L	F	A	Pts
1 Derby	42	14	4	3	41	18	7	7	7	26	31	53
2 Liverpool	42	14	5	2	44	17	6	6	9	16	22	51
3 Ipswich	42	17	2	2	47	14	6	3	12	19	30	51
4 Everton	42	10	9	2	33	19	6	9	6	23	23	50
5 Stoke	42	12	7	2	40	18	5	8	8	24	30	49
6 Sheffield Utd	42	12	7	2	35	20	6	6	9	23	31	49
7 Middlesbro	42	11	7	3	33	14	7	5	9	21	26	48
8 Manchester C	42	16	3	2	40	15	2	7	12	14	39	46
9 Leeds	42	10	8	3	34	20	6	5	10	23	29	45
10 Burnley	42	11	6	4	40	29	6	5	10	28	38	45
11 QP Rangers	42	10	4	7	25	17	6	6	9	29	37	42
12 Wolves	42	12	5	4	43	21	2	6	13	14	33	39
13 WEST HAM	42	10	6	5	38	22	3	7	11	20	37	39
14 Coventry	42	8	9	4	31	27	4	6	11	20	35	39
15 Newcastle	42	12	4	5	39	23	3	5	13	20	49	39
16 Arsenal	42	10	6	5	31	16	3	5	13	16	33	37
17 Birmingham	42	10	4	7	34	28	4	5	12	19	33	37
18 Leicester	42	8	7	6	25	17	4	5	12	21	43	36
19 Tottenham	42	8	4	9	29	27	5	4	12	23	36	34
20 Luton	42	8	6	7	27	26	3	5	13	20	39	33
21 Chelsea	42	4	9	8	22	31	5	6	10	20	41	33
22 Carlisle	42	8	2	11	22	21	4	3	14	21	38	29
	924	235	124	103	753	460	103	124	235	460	753	924

Odds & ends

Double wins: (2) Burnley, Carlisle.
Double losses: (2) Newcastle, Sheff U.

Won from behind: (5) Leicester (h), Burnley (h&a), Swindon FAC (a), QPR FAC (h).
Lost from in front: (5) Sheff U (h&a), Stoke (a), Leeds (a), Fulham LC (a).

High spots: Winning the FA Cup.
Only one defeat in 17 league games, September to December, up to 5th.

Low spots: Losing to Second Division Fulham in League Cup.
Terrible start, bottom of the league after seven games.
Terrible finish to league season, winning just once in 13 games from February to April.

Hammer of the Year: Billy Bonds.
Ever-presents: (1) Mervyn Day.
Hat-tricks: (1) Bobby Gould.
Leading scorer: (14) Billy Jennings.

	Appearances						Goals			
	Lge	*Sub*	LC	*Sub*	FAC	*Sub*	Lge	LC	FAC	Tot
Ayris, Johnny	**2**	*4*	3					1		**1**
Best, Clyde	**12**	*3*	1		2					
Bonds, Billy	**31**		3		8		**7**	2		**9**
Brooking, Trevor	**36**		3		8		**3**	1	1	**5**
Coleman, Keith	**27**	*2*	1		1					
Curbishley, Alan	**1**	*1*								
Day, Mervyn	**42**		3		8					
Gould, Bobby	**31**	*3*	2		3		**9**	3	1	**13**
Holland, Pat	**18**	*4*	1	*1*	4	*3*	**4**		2	**6**
Jennings, Billy	**32**				8		**13**		1	**14**
Lampard, Frank	**40**		3		8		**4**		1	**5**
Lock, Kevin	**41**	*1*	3		8					
McDowell, John	**33**	*1*	2		8		**1**			**1**
Paddon, Graham	**40**		3		8		**4**			**4**
Robson, Keith	**25**		2		3		**10**		1	**11**
Taylor, Alan	**11**	*3*			4		**2**		6	**8**
Taylor, Tommy	**39**		3		7					
Wooler, Alan	**1**									
(own-goals)							**1**			**1**
18 players used	**462**	*22*	**33**	*1*	**88**	*3*	**58**	**7**	**13**	**78**

No	Date		Att	Pos	Pt	F-A	H-T	Scorers, Times, and Referees	1	2	3	4	5	6	7	8	9	10	11	12 sub used
1	A	STOKE			W	2-1	2-0	Gould 26, Taylor A 44	Day	McDowell	Lampard	Holland	Taylor T	Lock	Taylor A	Paddon	Gould	Brooking	Robson	
	16/8		*23,744*		2			*Moores 88*	*Shilton*	*Dodd*	*Pejic*	*Mahoney*	*Smith*	*Bloor*	*Skeels**	*Moores*	*Conroy*	*Hudson*	*Salmons*	*Haslegrave*
								Ref: L Hayes	Both teams play open, attacking soccer. Billy Bonds misses the game, owing to a groin operation. Pat Holland played a part in both Hammers goals, the second of which seemed to be turned into his own net by Denis Smith. Alan Taylor claimed he got a touch and Smith did not argue.											
2	A	LIVERPOOL			D	2-2	1-1	Taylor A 35, 63	Day	McDowell	Lampard	Holland	Taylor T	Lock	Taylor A	Paddon	Gould*	Brooking	Robson	Jennings
	19/8		*40,564*		3			*Callaghan 25, Toshack 81*	*Clemence*	*Neal*	*Jones*	*Thompson*	*Cormack*	*Hughes*	*Keegan*	*McDermott*	*Heighway*	*Toshack*	*Callaghan*	
								Ref: H Hackney	Liverpool lost at QPR on Saturday, and seldom do they lose their first two of the season. Yet West Ham were nine minutes from their first win at Anfield in 12 years when Peter Cormack set up Toshack's equaliser. Brooking's inch-perfect pass had paved the way for Hammers' second.											
3	H	BURNLEY		6	W	3-2	0-1	Taylor A 60, 77, Paddon 80	Day	McDowell	Lampard	Holland	Taylor T	Lock	Taylor A	Paddon	Jennings*	Brooking	Robson	Ayris
	23/8		28,048	*15*	5			*James 22, Noble 67*	*Stevenson*	*Docherty*	*Newton*	*Noble*	*Waldron*	*Thomson*	*Flynn*	*Hankin*	*Summerbee*	*Collins**	*James*	*Morgan*
								Ref: K Baker	Burnley boss Jimmy Adamson wanted to buy Alan Taylor when he was at Rochdale, and now pays the price for losing him. James' low shot slipped from Day's grasp for the first goal. Noble and Taylor both headed goals from corners. Paddon side-stepped two players for the winner.											
4	H	TOTTENHAM		1	W	1-0	1-0	Robson 45	Day	McDowell	Lampard	Holland	Taylor T	Lock	Taylor A	Paddon	Jennings	Brooking	Robson	
	25/8		36,567	*11*	7				*Jennings*	*Naylor*	*Knowles*	*Pratt*	*Osgood*	*McAllister*	*Conn*	*Perryman*	*Chivers*	*Jones*	*Duncan**	*McNab*
								Ref: W Gow	Lyall is so impressed with this emphatic win – which takes West Ham top of the table – that he gives his players a day off as a reward. Paddon, Brooking and Holland ruled the midfield. Robson headed in when Pat Jennings came too far out for Holland's cross and exposed an open goal.											
5	A	QP RANGERS		2	D	1-1	0-1	Jennings 82	Day	McDowell	Lampard	Holland	Taylor T	Lock	Taylor A	Paddon	Jennings	Brooking	Robson	
	30/8		*28,408*	*3*	8			*Givens 30*	*Parkes*	*Clement*	*Gillard*	*Leach*	*Abbott*	*Tagg*	*Thomas*	*Francis**	*Masson*	*Bowles*	*Givens*	*Hollins*
								Ref: P Partridge	QPR's opening salvo is rewarded when Day mishandles a Masson free-kick, which falls to Don Givens. Billy Jennings rescues a point late on with a sharp shot from a tight angle. West Ham drop down to second, and in midweek will lose 0-1 to Fiorentina in the Anglo-Italian Cup.											
6	H	MANCHESTER C		2	W	1-0	0-0	Lampard 77	Day	McDowell	Lampard	Holland	Taylor T	Lock	Taylor A*	Paddon	Jennings	Brooking	Robson	Bonds
	6/9		29,752	*13*	10				*Corrigan*	*Clements*	*Donachie*	*Doyle*	*Watson*	*Oakes*	*Hartford*	*Bell*	*Leman*	*Marsh*	*Tueart*	
								Ref: D Nippard	Bonds makes his first appearance of the season. Frank Lampard plays a one-two with Paddon before striking a first-timer that was the least West Ham deserved against fancied City. Alan Taylor limped off with a swollen ankle. Only Man U keep the Hammers off the top of the table.											
7	A	LEICESTER		2	D	3-3	0-3	Bonds 60, Lampard 66, Holland 89	Day	McDowell	Lampard	Bonds	Taylor T	Lock	Holland	Paddon	Jennings	Brooking	Robson	
	13/9		*21,413*	*17*	11			*Worthington 8, Sammels 9, 19*	*Wallington*	*Whitworth*	*Rofe*	*Kember*	*Sims*	*Woollett*	*Weller*	*Alderson*	*Worthington*	*Sammels*	*Lee*	
								Ref: A Morrissey	Three down at half-time, West Ham stage a stirring fight-back. Frank Worthington's header was his first goal since April. In the second half Sammels and Weller are denied the space they relish. In the final seconds Brooking crosses and Pat Holland heads the equaliser at close range.											
8	H	SHEFFIELD UTD		2	W	2-0	0-0	Taylor T 71, Best 87	Day	McDowell	Lampard	Bonds	Taylor T	Lock	Taylor A*	Paddon	Jennings	Brooking	Holland	Best
	20/9		28,744	22	13				*Brown*	*Flynn*	*Calvert*	*Eddy*	*Colquhoun*	*Bradford*	*Woodward*	*Speight*	*Guthrie*	*Currie**	*Field*	*Irving*
								Ref: R Crabb	Ken Furphy's rock-bottom Blades carry little threat, other than from striker Chris Guthrie, who beat Tommy Taylor in the air 18 times out of 21. Yet it is Guthrie's wayward pass that leads to his marker firing the first goal. Clyde Best, on as sub, scores in his first game of the season.											
9	A	WOLVES		2	W	1-0	0-0	Paddon 62	Day	McDowell	Lampard	Bonds	Taylor T	Lock	Taylor A	Paddon	Best	Brooking	Holland	
	27/9		*18,455*	*21*	15				*Pierce*	*Palmer*	*McNab*	*Bailey*	*Munro*	*McAlle*	*Hibbitt*	*Carr*	*Richards*	*Kindon**	*Daley*	*Sunderland*
								Ref: E Garner	Graham Paddon reckons his 40-yard rocket is the best goal of his career. Wolves have taken only five points from six home games and scored just four goals, which is relegation form. Leaders QPR and West Ham, who have a game in hand, are the only unbeaten teams in the division.											
10	H	EVERTON		3	L	0-1	0-0		Day	McDowell	Lampard	Bonds	Taylor T	Lock	Robson	Paddon	Best*	Brooking	Holland	Taylor A
	4/10		31,005	*7*	15			*Jones G 62*	*Davies*	*Seargeant*	*Clements*	*Pearson**	*Kenyon*	*Lyons*	*Buckley*	*Dobson*	*Latchford*	*Telfer*	*Jones G*	*McNaught*
								Ref: T Reynolds	Everton came to defend, yet succeeded in inflicting a first defeat on the Hammers. It might have been averted had Lampard not blazed over a gaping goal after 27 minutes. Jones's header from Buckley's free-kick was deflected in by McDowell. Too many aimless balls from Hammers.											
11	H	NEWCASTLE		3	W	2-1	1-0	Curbishley 2, Taylor A 52	Day	McDowell	Lampard	Bonds	Taylor T	Coleman	Taylor A	Paddon	Best	Curbishley	Holland	
	11/10		30,400	*16*	17			*Howard 47*	*Mahoney*	*Nattrass*	*Kennedy*	*Nulty*	*Bird*	*Howard*	*Barrowclough*	*Burns*	*Macdonald*	*Gowling*	*Craig T*	
								Ref: P Walters	On *Match of the Day* afterwards, Jimmy Hill raves over the performance of 18-year-old Alan Curbishley, who only played because of injury to Brooking. Curbishley netted after two minutes, controlling the ball and shooting in one sweet movement. He then laid on Alan Taylor's header.											

No	Venue / Date	Opponent / Att	Pos	Res	F-A	H-T	Scorers, Times, and Referees												
12	A	MIDDLESBROUGH	3	L	0-3	0-1		Day	McDowell	Lampard*	Bonds	Taylor T	Coleman	Taylor A	Paddon	Best	Brooking	Holland	Curbishley
	18/10	*25,831*	*6*	17			*Souness 42, Armstrong 58, Foggon 72*	*Platt*	*Craggs*	*Cooper*	*Souness*	*Boam*	*Maddren*	*Murdoch*	*Mills*	*Hickton*	*Foggon*	*Armstrong*	
							Ref: R Capey	Unbeaten at home, Middlesbrough look the ultimate professionals. They had two 'goals' disallowed before Graeme Souness sprinted 50 yards to convert a return pass. Only Mervyn Day prevented a complete rout. Frank Lampard had to withdraw at half-time with a thigh strain.											
13	H	MANCHESTER U	3	W	2-1	1-0	Taylor A 6, Gould 70	Day	McDowell	Lampard	Holland	Taylor T	Coleman	Taylor A	Paddon	Gould	Brooking	Robson	
	25/10	**38,528**	*2*	19			*Macari 56*	*Stepney*	*Nicholl*	*Houston*	*Jackson*	*Greenhoff*	*Buchan*	*Coppell*	*McIlroy*	*Pearson*	*Macari*	*Daly**	*McCreery*
							Ref: P Reeves	A shameful match, marred by fighting on the terraces and by fighting between Buchan and Gould. Early in the second half play was held up for 18 minutes when a gate was broken at a corner of the ground. Macari scored on the resumption. Gould then connected with Paddon's cross.											
14	A	BIRMINGHAM	2	W	**5-1**	2-1	Brooking 15, Pendrey 37 (og), Lampard 67, [Taylor A 69, 72]	Day	McDowell	Lampard	Bonds	Taylor T	Coleman	Taylor A	Paddon	Holland	Brooking	Robson	
	1/11	*28,474*	*20*	21			*Francis 5*	*Latchford*	*Martin*	*Pendrey*	*Kendall*	*Gallagher**	*Roberts*	*Campbell*	*Francis*	*Burns*	*Hatton*	*Hibbitt*	*Taylor*
							Ref: J Goggins	John Lyall plays a tactical trump-card which masterminds this crushing victory. He plays an extra man in midfield, which has the effect of giving Brooking, who is pushed into the 'hole' between midfield and attack, more room to wreak havoc. Brooking shines magnificently.											
15	H	COVENTRY	1	D	1-1	0-0	Robson 48	Day	McDowell	Lock	Bonds*	Taylor T	Coleman	Taylor A	Paddon	Holland	Brooking	Robson	Gould
	8/11	29,501	*16*	22			*Powell 67*	*King*	*Coop*	*Brogan*	*Dugdale*	*Lloyd*	*Holmes*	*Powell*	*Mortimer*	*Cross*	*Murphy*	*Hutchison*	
							Ref: K Styles	Lucky Hammers, who struggled to stay afloat once Billy Bonds had limped out of the fray. Pop Robson's blast was cancelled out by Barry Powell's 20-yard rocket. Mortimer and Cross both hit the woodwork for Coventry, although Alan Taylor did the same for West Ham.											
16	A	DERBY	5	L	1-2	1-1	Brooking 42	Day	McDowell	Lampard	Lock	Taylor T	Coleman	Taylor A	Gould*	Holland	Brooking	Robson	Ayris
	15/11	*31,172*	*1*	22			*Rioch 32, George 64*	*Boulton*	*Thomas*	*Nish*	*Rioch*	*McFarland*	*Todd*	*Newton*	*Gemmill*	*Lee*	*Hector*	*George*	
							Ref: R Rice	Though Brooking scores the best goal of the match, West Ham are dumped from the top and plummet to fifth. They are now quoted at 11-1 for the title, with Derby 2-1. Hammers top the Fair Play league, having conceded no penalties, had no players sent off and only three booked.											
17	H	MIDDLESBROUGH	4	W	2-1	1-1	Jennings 35, Holland 70	Day	McDowell	Lock	Holland	Taylor T	Coleman	Taylor A	Paddon	Jennings	Brooking	Robson	
	22/11	26,914	*9*	24			*Mills 12*	*Platt*	*Craggs*	*Spraggon*	*Murdoch*	*Boam*	*Maddren*	*Brine*	*Mills*	*Hickton**	*Cooper*	*Armstrong*	*Foggon*
							Ref: R Newsome	Boro boss Jack Charlton rages against the stand-in ref, taking charge of his first ever game in Division 1. West Ham had been well beaten on Wearside, so revenge is sweet. Billy Jennings' second league goal prompted Trevor Brooking to ignite West Ham's second-half onslaught.											
18	H	ARSENAL	3	W	1-0	1-0	Taylor A 22	Day	McDowell	Lampard	Coleman	Taylor T	Lock	Taylor A	Paddon	Holland	Jennings	Robson	
	29/11	31,012	*18*	26				*Rimmer*	*Rice*	*Nelson*	*Storey*	*O'Leary*	*Powling*	*Ball*	*Armstrong*	*Stapleton*	*Kidd*	*Brady*	
							Ref: G Kew	McDowell plays a stormer, and Graham Paddon marks Alan Ball out of the game. The only goal provoked a storm of controversy. TV replays showed Alan Taylor to be offside when knocking in Jennings' downward header from Lock's cross. Lyall gives his players another holiday.											
19	A	NORWICH	6	L	0-1	0-0		Day	McDowell	Lampard	Coleman	Taylor T	Lock	Taylor A	Paddon	Holland	Brooking	Robson	
	6/12	*27,020*	*16*	26			*MacDougall 78*	*Keelan*	*Jones*	*Sullivan*	*Morris*	*Forbes*	*Stringer*	*Machin*	*MacDougall*	*Boyer*	*Suggett*	*Peters*	
							Ref: H Davey	The tabloids stir up Ted MacDougall's war of words. He is alleged to have said: 'I hate West Ham even more than I hate Manchester United – and that's saying something.' He caps this fine match by heading in Peters' cross, then rugby-tackling an invading fan before officials arrived.											
20	A	BURNLEY	7	L	0-2	0-2		Day	Coleman	Lampard	Curbishley*	Taylor T	Lock	Taylor A	Paddon	Holland	Brooking	Jennings	Ayris
	13/12	***14,907***	*19*	26			*Hankin 19, Kennerley 35*	*Peyton*	*Docherty*	*Newton*	*Ingham*	*Waldron*	*Thomson*	*Summerbee*	*Kennerley*	*Hankin*	*Flynn*	*Bradshaw*	
							Ref: J Taylor	Hammers have gone off the boil, and have lost at home to Fiorentina in the Anglo-Italian Cup. On a frozen pitch at Turf Moor they slither to another defeat. Hankin scored from under Day's nose. Now that Gould has been transferred, Lyall is looking at Southampton's Mick Channon.											
21	H	STOKE	6	W	3-1	2-1	Jennings 28, 35, 61	Day	Coleman	Lampard	McDowell	Taylor T	Lock	Taylor A	Paddon	Holland	Jennings	Robson	
	20/12	21,135	*8*	28			*Bloor 32*	*Shilton*	*Marsh*	*Pejic*	*Mahoney*	*Dodd*	*Bloor*	*Robertson*	*Greenhoff*	*Moores**	*Hudson*	*Salmons*	*Haslegrave*
							Ref: D Nippard	Billy Jennings has got himself fit, at last, and celebrates with a famous hat-trick. He headed into the top corner for the first goal, blasted in Robson's knock-down from a tight angle for No 2, and headed in Coleman's cross for his third. These are Hammers' first goals in three games.											
22	A	ASTON VILLA	6	L	1-4	1-2	Jennings 40	Day	Coleman	Lampard	McDowell	Taylor T	Lock	Taylor A	Paddon	Holland	Jennings	Robson	
	26/12	*51,300*	*12*	28			*Deehan 6, 19, Gray 55, Hamilton 88*	*Burridge*	*Gidman*	*Robson*	*Ross*	*Nicholl*	*Mortimer*	*Graydon*	*Deehan*	*Gray*	*Hamilton*	*Carrodus*	
							Ref: A Jones	Ron Saunders' team leave the field to a standing ovation. Villa have scored 16 goals in their last five home games. Dennis Mortimer makes his debut and sets up John Deehan's first goal. This, and Deehan's second – a volley from Graydon's free-kick – might have been saved by Day.											
23	H	IPSWICH	6	L	1-2	0-0	Taylor T 75p	Day	Coleman*	McDowell	Holland	Taylor T	Lock	Taylor A	Paddon	Brooking	Jennings	Robson !	Curbishley
	27/12	*32,741*	*11*	28			*Lambert 50, Peddelty 84*	*Cooper*	*Burley*	*Beattie*	*Talbot*	*Hunter*	*Peddelty*	*Woods*	*Mills*	*Austin*	*Whymark*	*Lambert*	
							Ref: T Spencer	Keith Robson was booked and sent off in the 67th minute after throwing a punch at George Burley. That completed a disastrous Christmas schedule for the Hammers, who enjoyed an iffy penalty when Paddon appeared to dive. Bobby Robson's Ipswich have lost one game in 13.											

No	Date		Att	Pos	Pt	F-A	H-T	Scorers, Times, and Referees	1	2	3	4	5	6	7	8	9	10	11	12 sub used
24	H	LEICESTER		6	D	1-1	0-0	Taylor A 65	Day	McDowell	Lampard	Holland	Taylor T	Lock	Taylor A	Best	Brooking	Jennings	Curbishley	
	10/1		24,615	*15*	29			*Lee 78*	*Wallington*	*Whitworth*	*Rofe*	*Kember*	*Blockley*	*Woollett*	*Weller*	*Alderson*	*Garland**	*Lee*	*Worthington*	*Sammels*
								Ref: A Lees	Paddon has strained a hamstring and young Alan Curbishley shines until he tires. Alan Taylor 'kneed' in Brooking's curled pass. But Tommy Taylor then stubbed his toe and messed up a back-pass. City boss Jimmy Bloomfield's verdict: 'The wind spoiled it and the pitch was bumpy.'											
25	A	MANCHESTER C		8	L	0-3	0-2		Day	McDowell	Lampard	Holland	Taylor T	Lock	Taylor A*	Paddon	Jennings	Brooking	Curbishley	Best
	17/1		*32,147*	*6*	29			*Royle 11, 58p, Oakes 25*	*Corrigan*	*Barrett*	*Donachie*	*Doyle*	*Clements*	*Oakes*	*Power*	*Keegan*	*Royle*	*Hartford*	*Barnes*	
								Ref: G Courtney	Day's 100th league game is not one to remember fondly. Joe Royle was left unmarked for his first goal, and scored City's third from the spot after Lock had upended Barnes. In between, veteran Alan Oakes seized on Royle's pass to burst through. City have lost Rodney Marsh to USA.											
26	H	QP RANGERS		6	W	1-0	1-0	Taylor A 42	Day	McDowell	Lampard	Holland	Taylor T	Coleman	Taylor A	Paddon	Brooking	Jennings	**Orhan**	
	24/1		26,677	*5*	31				*Parkes*	*Clement*	*Gillard*	*Hollins*	*McLintock**	*Webb*	*Thomas*	*Beck*	*Masson*	*Leach*	*Givens*	*Nutt*
								Ref: A Morrissey	A fast and furious London derby, illuminated by Hammers' Turkish Cypriot debutant, but won by Alan Taylor's 15th goal of the season. QPR were without Bowles (transfer listed), Gerry Francis (injured), and – after half-time – by the concussed McLintock, who sat wrapped in a coat.											
27	H	LIVERPOOL		6	L	0-4	0-0		Day	McDowell	Lampard	Holland	Taylor T	Coleman	Taylor A	Paddon	Jennings*	Brooking	Orhan	Robson
	31/1		26,741	*2*	31			*Toshack 63, 75, 86, Keegan 88*	*Clemence*	*Smith*	*Neal*	*Thompson*	*Kennedy*	*Hughes*	*Keegan*	*Case*	*Heighway*	*Toshack*	*Callaghan*	
								Ref: J Hunting	Liverpool had just lost to Derby in the FA Cup. Ray Clemence said he was glad he wore track-suit bottoms on an icy pitch, otherwise he would have got frostbite. Bob Paisley added: 'I wish we could come here more often.' Toshack completed his hat-trick heading in Heighway's cross.											
28	A	TOTTENHAM		6	D	1-1	0-0	Brooking 77	Day	Coleman	Lampard	Holland	Taylor T	McGiven	Taylor A	Paddon	Jennings	Brooking	Robson	
	7/2		*32,832*	*15*	32			*Duncan 65*	*Jennings*	*Naylor*	*McAllister*	*Pratt*	*Young*	*Osgood*	*Coates*	*Perryman*	*Duncan*	*Jones*	*Neighbour**	*Chivers*
								Ref: R Toseland	Keith Robson returns but after 20 minutes could easily have been sent off for an over-the-top tackle on Keith Osgood that will dominate the sports headlines. John Duncan headed in a cross from man-of-the-match Coates before Lampard's overlap down the left set up the equaliser.											
29	A	COVENTRY		6	L	0-2	0-1		Day	McDowell	Lampard	Holland	Taylor T	McGiven	Taylor A	Paddon	Jennings	Brooking	Robson	
	14/2		*16,173*	*14*	32			*Powell 44, Coop 54*	*Blyth*	*Oakey*	*Cattlin*	*Craven*	*Dugdale*	*Coop*	*Cartwright*	*Powell*	*Cross*	*Murphy*	*Hutchison*	
								Ref: N Ashley	Mervyn Day is showing signs of strain. He helps Mick Coop's sliced cross into his own net for Coventry's second goal. Day was blameless with the first, Barry Powell shooting on the run from 25 yards. West Ham had no answer to the jinking skills of left-winger Tommy Hutchison.											
30	H	DERBY		9	L	1-2	0-0	Brooking 84	Day	Coleman	Lampard	Holland	Taylor T	McGiven	McDowell	Paddon	Orhan*	Brooking	Robson	Jennings
	21/2		24,941	*4*	32			*George 60, Rioch 82*	*Moseley*	*Thomas*	*Nish*	*Rioch*	*McFarland*	*Todd*	*Powell*	*Gemmill*	*Hector*	*George*	*James*	
								Ref: T Reynolds	Derby boss Dave Mackay fanned the flames afterwards when saying he was more worried by Southend United in the FA Cup last week than by West Ham, whose build-up was slow and ponderous. Spies for Den Haag in the Cup-Winners' Cup are equally unimpressed with West Ham.											
31	H	LEEDS			D	1-1	0-0	Taylor A 66	Day	McDowell	Lampard	Holland*	Taylor T	McGiven	Taylor A	Paddon	Curbishley	Brooking	Robson	Jennings
	23/2		28,025		33			*McKenzie 76*	*Harvey*	*Reaney*	*Gray F*	*Bates*	*Madeley*	*Hunter*	*McKenzie*	*Cherry*	*Jordan*	*Yorath*	*Gray E*	
								Ref: R Crabb	Keith Robson missed a sitter at the death that would have given West Ham a deserved win. Under the eyes of the watching England boss Don Revie, Alan Taylor converts Paddon's corner, headed on by Lampard. Joe Jordan's over-the-top lunge at Tommy Taylor inflames the crowd.											
32	A	MANCHESTER U		9	L	0-4	0-0	*[Pearson 86]*	Day	McDowell	Lock	Bonds	Taylor T	McGiven	Taylor A*	Paddon	Curbishley	Brooking	Robson	Jennings
	28/2		***57,240***	*3*	33			*Forsyth 49, Macari 56, McCreery 76,*	*Stepney*	*Forsyth*	*Houston*	*Daly*	*Greenhoff*	*Buchan*	*Coppell*	*McIlroy**	*Pearson*	*Macari*	*Hill*	*McCreery*
								Ref: K Baker	Lyall's five-man defence keeps Tommy Docherty's Man U at bay for the first half. Forsyth then fired a hard shot through a crowded goalmouth and Daly did likewise, the ball glancing off Macari's head as it flew past Day. Coppell and Hill sent over a string of crosses to test Day and Co.											
33	H	BIRMINGHAM		12	L	1-2	0-1	Curbishley 76	Day	Coleman	Lampard	Bonds	Taylor T	Wooler	Taylor A	Paddon	Curbishley	Orhan*	Robson	**Pike**
	6/3		19,868	*19*	33			*Withe 35, Emmanuel 48*	*Latchford*	*Martin*	*Styles*	*Kendall*	*Gallagher*	*Burns*	*Emmanuel*	*Francis*	*Withe*	*Page*	*Hibbitt**	*Calderwood*
								Ref: A Gray	Lyall is in bed with flu, leaving Greenwood to marshal the only 13 fit players available. Terry Hibbitt's free-kick is nodded in by Peter Withe, and Emmanuel converts Trevor Francis' cross. Curbishley's goal went in off Martin. Defeat sends West Ham into the bottom half of the table.											
34	A	LEEDS		12	D	1-1	0-0	Jennings 54	Day	Coleman	Lampard	Bonds	Taylor T	Taylor A	Ayris*	Paddon	Jennings	Curbishley	Robson	Pike
	9/3		*28,453*	*5*	34			*Jordan 68*	*Harvey*	*Reaney**	*Gray F*	*Bates*	*Madeley*	*Hunter*	*McKenzie*	*Clarke*	*Jordan*	*Yorath*	*Cherry*	*Gray E*
								Ref: P Willis	This match had been scheduled for the autumn. Hammers have now won once in 15 games, and taken only six points since Christmas. Without Brooking, Lock and McDowell they seldom looked like subduing Jimmy Armfield's Leeds. Bonds and Clarke were booked for wrestling.											

No	H/A	Opponent	Att	Pos	Res	F-A	H-T	Scorers, Times, and Referees	1	2	3	4	5	6	7	8	9	10	11	12
35	A	NEWCASTLE		11	L	1-2	1-1	Jennings 16	Day	Coleman	Lampard*	Bonds	Taylor T	Taylor A	Ayris	Paddon	Jennings	Curbishley	Robson	McDowell
	13/3		32,842	*14*	34			*Macdonald 20, Craig T 67p*	*Jones*	*Blackhall*	*Kennedy*	*Barrowclough*	*Bird*	*Howard*	*Burns*	*Cassidy*	*Macdonald*	*Gowling*	*Craig T*	
								Ref: K Ridden	Bonds plays his best game since returning form injury. Tommy Taylor is upset about conceding the penalty that cost West Ham the points. He admits that he handled the ball but insists that his arm had been knocked against it and that he should have won a free-kick. Now for Den Haag.											
36	A	ARSENAL		12	L	**1-6**	1-4	Jennings 23	Day	Coleman*	Lampard	Bonds	Taylor T	Lock	Taylor A	Curbishley	Jennings	Brooking	Robson	McGiven
	20/3		*34,011*	*13*	34			*Ball 2, 29p, Armstrong 30, Kidd 44, 55,85*	*Rimmer*	*Rice**	*Nelson*	*Ross*	*Mancini*	*Powling*	*Armstrong*	*Ball*	*Radford*	*Kidd*	*Brady*	*Stapleton*
								Ref: K McNally	Having triumphed over Den Haag, this is a painful let-down. Brian Kidd completed one hat-trick but might have had two. Alan Ball might even have had a hat-trick himself, scoring one penalty and missing another – both were for trips on Kidd. West Ham might have conceded 10.											
37	H	NORWICH		12	L	0-1	0-0		Day	Coleman	Lampard	Bonds	Taylor T	Lock	Paddon	Curbishley	Jennings	McDowell	Robson	
	27/3		20,628	*15*	34			*MacDougall 16*	*Keelan*	*Jones*	*Sullivan*	*McGuire*	*Forbes*	*Powell*	*Miller*	*MacDougall*	*Boyer*	*Suggett*	*Peters*	
								Ref: R Matthewson	Martin Peters, now playing out his days for Norwich, says afterwards: 'They never bothered us'. West Ham showed little fight in a fixture that should have been a full-scale dress rehearsal for Eintracht. Norwich keeper Kevin Keelan never had to make a save. Relegation may yet loom.											
38	H	WOLVES		13	D	0-0			Day	Coleman	Lampard	McDowell	Taylor T	Lock*	Holland	Paddon	Jennings	Brooking	Robson	Ayris
	3/4		**16,769**	*20*	35				*Parkes*	*Sunderland*	*Palmer*	*Parkin*	*Bailey*	*McAlle*	*Daley*	*Carr*	*Kindon*	*Kelly*	*Gould**	*Hibbitt*
								Ref: D Nippard	Wolves are fighting to stay up. They won't make it, but they extend West Ham's winless league sequence to two and half months, in which they have taken just four points from 12 games. Wolves' Bobby Gould was kept quiet, and West Ham frittered away what chances they had.											
39	A	SHEFFIELD UTD		16	L	2-3	1-0	Jennings 16, 60	Day	Coleman	Lampard	Bonds	Taylor T	McDowell	Holland	Paddon	Jennings	Brooking	Robson*	Ayris
	10/4		*18,797*	*22*	35			*Woodward 57, Guthrie 61, Stainrod 63*	*Brown*	*Franks*	*Garner*	*Speight*	*Colquhoun*	*Kenworthy*	*Woodward*	*Bradford*	*Guthrie*	*Currie*	*Stainrod*	
								Ref: D Civil	Blades are so far behind that they are already doomed. West Ham manage more than one goal for the first time in 1976, and lead twice, but still lose. Guthrie's header made it 2-2. 17-year-old Simon Stainrod marked his home debut by scoring off a post. Jennings' goals count for nothing.											
40	H	ASTON VILLA		17	D	2-2	1-2	Robson 14, Brooking 89	Ferguson	Coleman	Lampard	Lock*	Taylor T	McDowell	Holland	Paddon	Jennings	Brooking	Robson	Ayris
	17/4		21,642	*18*	36			*Deehan 4, Hunt 10*	*Findlay*	*Gidman*	*Robson*	*Phillips*	*Nicholl*	*Mortimer*	*Deehan*	*McDonald*	*Gray*	*Hunt*	*Carrodus*	
								Ref: T Bune	Villa are seconds away from their first away win of the season when Brooking lets fly and the ball bounces like a leg-break past Findlay. Two quick Villa headers had silenced Upton Park. Had it not been for Robson's riposte, a header from Brooking's corner, it may have stayed silent.											
41	A	IPSWICH		18	L	0-4	0-2		Day	Bonds	McDowell	Curbishley	Taylor T	McGiven	Ayris	Paddon	Orhan*	Brooking	Robson	Pike
	19/4		*28,217*	*6*	36			*Bertschin 24, Talbot 45, Whymark 70, [Peddelty 89]*	*Cooper*	*Burley*	*Mills*	*Sharkey*	*Hunter*	*Peddelty*	*Talbot*	*Osborne*	*Bertschin*	*Whymark*	*Lambert*	
								Ref: K Styles	West Ham lost 1-4 at Portman Road last season, and 0-4 this, so it is becoming a bogey ground. The Hammers were chasing a lost cause from the moment 19-year-old Keith Bertschin swerved the opening goal from 20 yards. He had also scored on his debut at Highbury on Saturday.											
42	A	EVERTON		18	L	0-2	0-2		Day	Coleman	Lampard	Bonds	Taylor T	McDowell	Holland	Paddon	Jennings	Brooking	Robson*	Taylor A
	24/4		*26,101*	*11*	36			*Bernard 5p, Pearson 23*	*Lawson*	*Bernard*	*Jones D*	*Lyons*	*McNaught*	*King*	*Buckley*	*Dobson*	*Latchford*	*Connolly*	*Pearson*	
		Home	Away					Ref: A Robinson	Hammers conclude the league season without a win in their last 16 games. They were not helped by a disputed penalty when Tommy Taylor tugged Latchford's shirt. Day fumbled a cross which led to Pearson's goal. Skipper Bonds apologises to fans afterwards on behalf of the team.											
Average		27,345	29,433																	

Charity Shield

Date	Opponent	Att	Res	F-A	H-T	Scorers, Times, and Referees	1	2	3	4	5	6	7	8	9	10	11	12
9/8	DERBY		L	0-2	0-2		Day	McDowell	Lampard	Holland	Taylor T	Lock	Taylor A	Paddon	Jennings*	Brooking	Gould^	Robson/Coleman
		59,000				*Hector 20, McFarland 43*	*Boulton*	*Thomas*	*Nish*	*Rioch*	*McFarland*	*Todd*	*Newton*	*Gemmill*	*Lee*	*Hector*	*George*	
	(at Wembley)					Ref: G Kew	Last year was the first Charity Shield to be staged at Wembley, and it was sullied by the dismissal of Liverpool's Keegan and Leeds' Bremner. No such problems this time. Hector won the game with a 20-yard goal followed by a back-heel to McFarland. How West Ham missed Bonds.											

League Cup

Rd	H/A	Opponent	Att		Res	F-A	H-T	Scorers, Times, and Referees	1	2	3	4	5	6	7	8	9	10	11	12
2	H	BRISTOL CITY		2	D	0-0	0-0		Day	McDowell	Lampard	Bonds	Taylor T	Lock	Holland*	Paddon	Jennings	Brooking	Robson	Ayris
	9/9		19,837	*2:5*					*Cashley*	*Sweeney*	*Drysdale*	*Gow*	*Collier*	*Merrick*	*Tainton*	*Ritchie*	*Mann !*	*Cheesley*	*Brolly**	*Gillies*
								Ref: A Robinson	Just after the hour City striker Jimmy Mann was fouled by Jennings, retaliated and was ordered off. Barely was he off the pitch than Merrick handled in the box. Paul Cheesley had played at Norwich with Graham Paddon and pointed to keeper Cashley which way to go. He was right.											
2R	A	BRISTOL CITY		2	W	3-1	0-1	Brooking 75, Best 80, Taylor A 82	Day	McDowell	Lampard	Bonds	Taylor T	Lock	Taylor A	Paddon	Best	Brooking	Holland	
	24/9		*19,643*	*2:4*				*Cheesley 20*	*Cashley*	*Sweeney*	*Drysdale*	*Gow*	*Collier*	*Merrick*	*Tainton*	*Ritchie*	*Mann*	*Cheesley*	*Brolly**	*Gillies*
								Ref: A Robinson	Lyall decides to play Clyde Best – back from America – as an all-muscle striker in the manner of Hurst. The tactic works, though Day – whose boob let in Cheesley – has to save a twice-taken penalty after McDowell fouled Ritchie. Sweeney missed, but Tommy Taylor had encroached.											

League Cup			F-A	H-T	Scorers, Times, and Referees	1	2	3	4	5	6	7	8	9	10	11	12 sub used
3 H DARLINGTON	3	W	3-0	0-0	Paddon 52, Robson 72, Bonds 74p	Day	McDowell	Lampard	Bonds	Taylor T	Lock*	Robson	Paddon	Best	Taylor A	Holland	Jennings
8/10 19,844	*4:17*					*Ogley*	*Nattrass*	*Cochrane*	*Cattrell*	*Noble*	*Blant*	*Holbrook**	*Sinclair*	*Webb*	*Crosson*	*Young*	*Rowles*
					Ref: R Kirkpatrick	Darlington, struggling in the soccer basement, make West Ham sweat for this victory. Webb had a 48th-minute 'goal' disallowed, and Eric Young appeared to equalise with a header that was dubiously annulled. Young later handled in his own area for Bonds to round off the scoring.											
4 A TOTTENHAM	1	D	0-0	0-0		Day	McDowell	Lock	Bonds	Taylor T	Coleman	Taylor A	Paddon	Holland	Brooking	Robson	
12/11 *49,125*	*14*					*Jennings*	*Naylor*	*McAllister*	*Pratt*	*Young*	*Osgood*	*Coates*	*Perryman*	*Duncan**	*Jones*	*Neighbour*	*Conn*
					Ref: M Sinclair	Brooking is again played as a deep-lying centre-forward, though this time without conspicuous success. When he went forward he was marked by Keith Osgood, when he fell back he was picked up by Perryman. Early on Pat Jennings saved when his feet were behind the goal-line.											
4R H TOTTENHAM	4	L	0-2	0-0		Day	McDowell	Lampard	Bonds	Taylor T	Lock	Taylor A	Paddon	Holland	Brooking*	Robson	Jennings
24/11 38,443	*16*		*aet*		*Duncan 101, Young 109*	*Jennings*	*Naylor*	*McAllister*	*Pratt*	*Young*	*Osgood*	*Coates*	*Perryman*	*Duncan*	*Jones*	*Neighbour*	
					Ref: M Sinclair	Fourth Division Doncaster Rovers are the plum awaiting the winners. Terry Neill's Spurs are the lucky ones, but they were distinctly second best until Trevor Brooking went off with a ricked back. Bonds returned after injury but was embarrassingly run off his feet by Ralph Coates.											

FA Cup			F-A	H-T	Scorers, Times, and Referees	1	2	3	4	5	6	7	8	9	10	11	12 sub used
1 H LIVERPOOL	6	L	0-2	0-1		Day	Coleman	Lampard	Holland	McGiven	Lock	Taylor A	Paddon	Brooking	Jennings	Curbishley	
3/1 32,363	*1*				*Keegan 36, Toshack 83*	*Clemence*	*Smith*	*Neal*	*Thompson*	*Kennedy*	*Hughes*	*Keegan*	*Case*	*Heighway*	*Toshack*	*Callaghan*	
					Ref: P Partridge	West Ham are dethroned at the first hurdle. With Bonds, McDowell and Tommy Taylor injured, and Keith Robson suspended, Hammers had their work cut out. Keegan ran the show on his own, scoring the first with Toshack's assistance, then returning the favour for the second goal.											

European Cup-Winners' Cup			F-A	H-T	Scorers, Times, and Referees	1	2	3	4	5	6	7	8	9	10	11	12 sub used
1:1 A LAHDEN REIPAS	2	D	2-2	1-1	Brooking 29, Bonds 76	Day	McDowell	Lampard	Bonds	Taylor T	Lock	Holland	Paddon	Taylor A	Brooking	Robson*	Jennings
17/9 (Finland) *4,587*					*Lindholm 4, Tupasela 55*	*Holli*	*Kosonen*	*Kautonen M*	*Riutto*	*Repo*	*Toivanen*	*Kautonen T*	*Tupasela*	*Jantunen*	*Hamaleinen*	*Lindholm*	
					Ref: U Eriksson	This match was played at Helsinki's Olympic Stadium. The Finns played in red and black stripes that made them look like bees. They scored first when the ball bounced off Day's chest. Brooking's free-kick sailed past everybody and Bonds' goal followed a one-two with Holland.											
1:2 H LAHDEN REIPAS	2	W	3-0	0-0	Robson 60, Holland 77, Jennings 89	Day	McDowell	Lampard	Bonds	Taylor T	Lock	Taylor A*	Paddon	Robson	Brooking	Holland	Jennings
1/10 24,131						*Holli*	*Kosonen*	*Kautonen M*	*Riutto*	*Repo*	*Toivanen**	*Kautonen T*	*Tupasela*	*Jantunen*	*Hamaleinen*	*Lindholm*	*Nordman*
					Ref: A Briguglio (Malta) (Hammers win 5-2 on aggregate)	Clyde Best has returned from USA but is ineligible. The Finns defied predictions and came out to attack, knowing that if they did not score they would go out on the away-goals rule. The tie was effectively settled when Bonds crossed and Robson's shot flew in off post and keeper.											
2:1 A ARARAT EREVAN	3	D	1-1	0-0	Taylor A 56	Day	McDowell	Lampard	Bonds	Taylor T	Coleman	Taylor A	Paddon	Gould	Holland	Robson	
22/10 (USSR) *66,662*					*Petrosian S 66*	*Abramian*	*Gevorkian*	*Sarkissian*	*Martirosian*	*Mesropian*	*Andreassian*	*Azarian**	*Oganesian*	*Markarov*	*Petrosian S*	*Petrosian N^*	*Bondarenko*
					Ref: H Weyland (W Germany) (Ararat's 2nd sub Pogosian)	Mervyn Day stands holding the ball wondering where to kick it, when Petrosian heads it out of his hands and into the net. Day stands aghast, waiting for a foul that is never given. That farcical goal wiped out Alan Taylor's effort, and raised questions about the West German referee.											
2:2 H ARARAT EREVAN	2	W	3-1	2-0	Paddon 16, Robson 27, Taylor A 59	Day	McDowell	Lampard	Bonds	Taylor T	Coleman	Taylor A	Paddon	Holland	Brooking	Robson	
5/11 30,399					*Petrosian N 46*	*Abramian*	*Martirosian*	*Sarkissian*	*Gevorkian*	*Mesropian*	*Andreassian*	*Azarian*	*Oganesian*	*Markarov**	*Petrosian S*	*Petros'n N^*	*Ishtoyan/Bond'*
					Ref: R Helies (France) (Hammers win 4-2 on aggregate)	The experiment of playing Brooking further forward continues, though on this occasion he plays no part in any of the goals. Paddon's spinning left-footer was followed by Robson heading in Alan Taylor's cross, and Taylor himself rounded things off with a disputed offside goal.											
QF A DEN HAAG	9	L	2-4	0-4	Jennings 50, 58	Day	McGiven*	Lampard	Bonds	Taylor T	Lock	Taylor A	Paddon	Jennings	Curbishley	Robson	Coleman
1 3/3 (Holland) *26,000*					*Mansveld 13, 15p, 38p, Schoenmaker 42*	*Thie*	*Mansvelt*	*de Caluwe*	*van Vliet*	*Korevaar*	*Kila*	*Perazic*	*Schoenmaker*	*Ouwenhand*	*van Leeuwen*	*Swanenburg*	
					Ref: R Glockner (E Germany)	Flu keeps Lyall in bed, so Ron Greenwood takes charge. Herr Glockner refereed the 1970 World Cup final between Brazil and Italy. He tells Lock to pull his socks up and awards two disputed penalties when Lock and McGiven handle. Two Paddon crosses yield two Jennings goals.											
QF H DEN HAAG	11	W	3-1	3-0	Taylor A 28, Lampard 33, Bonds 38	Day	Coleman	Lampard	Bonds	Taylor T*	Lock	Taylor A	Paddon^	Jennings	Brooking	Robson	McGiv/Curbishley
2 17/3 29,829					*Schoenmaker 59*	*Thie*	*Mansvelt*	*Ouwehand*	*van Vliet*	*Korevaar*	*Kila**	*Perazic*	*Schoenmaker*	*Bres*	*van Leeuwen*	*Albertsen^*	*Jol/Swanenburg*
					Ref: K Palotai (Hungary) (Hammers win on away goals)	An emotional night, though a frustrating one, with West Ham caught offside 18 times. Thie drops Brooking's shot to make it 3-4 overall. Brooking then curls a pass onto Lampard's boot, before Tommy Taylor goes down in the box. Schoenmaker's goal made Hammers sweat it out.											

SF 1	A	EINTRACHT	12	L	1-2	1-1	Paddon 9	Day	Coleman	Lampard	Bonds	Taylor T	McDowell	Holland	Paddon	Jennings	Brooking	Robson	
31/3		(W Germ) *45,000*					*Neuberger 28, Kraus 47*	*Kunter*	*Reichel*	*Neuberger*	*Simons*	*Beverungen*	*Kraus**	*Korbel*	*Holzenbein*	*Wenzel*	*Grabowski*	*Nickel*	*Weidle*
							Ref: V Rudnev	Eintracht's 35-year-old reserve keeper, Kunter, is a part-time dentist. Paddon's early 30-yarder keeps up West Ham's record of scoring in every away leg. Though they take a 2-1 lead in the Wald Stadium, Eintracht know they need a bigger advantage. They become ragged and frustrated.											
SF 2	H	EINTRACHT	16	W	3-1	0-0	Brooking 49, 78, Robson 67	Day	Coleman	Lampard	Bonds	Taylor T	McDowell	Holland	Paddon	Jennings	Brooking	Robson	
14/4		39,202					*Beverungen 87*	*Kunter*	*Reicehl*	*Neuberger*	*Lorenz*	*Beverungen*	*Weidle*	*Korbel*	*Holzenebin*	*Wanzel*	*Grabowski*	*Nickel*	
							Ref: W Hungerbuhler (Switz) (Hammers win 4-3 on aggregate)	Eintracht were the only team in Europe to have won every tie, home and away. They might have maintained that record but for Mervyn Day's fine early saves from Wanzel and Nickel. Brooking's delicate header put the Hammers ahead on away goals. Robson then curled a 30-yarder.											
F	N	ANDERLECHT	18	L	2-4	1-1	Holland 29, Robson 69	Day	Coleman	Lampard*	Bonds	Taylor T	McDowell	Holland	Paddon	Jennings	Brooking	Robson	Taylor A
5/5		(Belgium) *58,000* (Heysel Stadium)					*Rensenbrink 42, 73p, Van d Elst 48, 85*	*Ruiter*	*Lomme*	*Broos*	*Van Binst*	*Thissen*	*Dockx*	*Coeck**	*Van der Elst*	*Ressel*	*Haan*	*Rensenbrink*	*Vercauteren*
							Ref: R Wurtz (France)	Bonds heads down for Holland's opener. Lampard blames his crazy back-pass that made it 1-1 on the long grass. Van der Elst makes it 1-2 and will later sign for West Ham. Robson levels with a header off a post. Pat Holland concedes the penalty. Rensenbrink was man of the match.											

		Home						Away					
	P	W	D	L	F	A	W	D	L	F	A	Pts
1 Liverpool	42	14	5	2	41	21	9	9	3	25	10	60
2 QP Rangers	42	17	4	0	42	13	7	7	7	25	20	59
3 Manchester U	42	16	4	1	40	13	7	6	8	28	29	56
4 Derby	42	15	3	3	45	30	6	8	7	30	28	53
5 Leeds	42	13	3	5	37	19	8	6	7	28	27	51
6 Ipswich	42	11	6	4	36	23	5	8	8	18	25	46
7 Leicester	42	9	9	3	29	24	4	10	7	19	27	45
8 Manchester C	42	14	5	2	46	18	2	6	13	18	28	43
9 Tottenham	42	6	10	5	33	32	8	5	8	30	31	43
10 Norwich	42	10	5	6	33	26	6	5	10	25	32	42
11 Everton	42	10	7	4	37	24	5	5	11	23	42	42
12 Stoke	42	8	5	8	25	24	7	6	8	23	26	41
13 Middlesbro	42	9	7	5	23	11	6	3	12	23	34	40
14 Coventry	42	6	9	6	22	22	7	5	9	25	35	40
15 Newcastle	42	11	4	6	51	26	4	5	12	20	36	39
16 Aston Villa	42	11	8	2	32	17	0	9	12	19	42	39
17 Arsenal	42	11	4	6	33	19	2	6	13	14	34	36
18 WEST HAM	42	10	5	6	26	23	3	5	13	22	48	36
19 Birmingham	42	11	5	5	36	26	2	2	17	21	49	33
20 Wolves	42	7	6	8	27	25	3	4	14	24	43	30
21 Burnley	42	6	6	9	23	26	3	4	14	20	40	28
22 Sheffield Utd	42	4	7	10	19	32	2	3	16	14	50	22
	924	229	127	106	736	494	106	127	229	494	736	924

Odds & ends

Double wins: (1) Stoke.
Double losses: (4) Everton, Derby, Norwich, Ipswich.

Won from behind: (5) Burnley (h), Birmingham (a), Middlesbrough (h), Bristol C LC (a), Den Haag CWC.
Lost from in front (3) Newcastle (a), Sheff Utd (a), Anderlecht CWC.

High spots: Unbeaten in first nine league games, up to 2nd.
Reaching final of European Cup-Winners' Cup.

Low spots: Terrible end to league season, failing to win any of last 16 games, and only one in 1976.
Relinquishing hold on FA Cup at the first attempt, to Liverpool.
Leading in Cup-Winners' Cup final, and then coming back to equalise, but still losing.

Hammer of the Year: Trevor Brooking.
Ever-presents: (0).
Hat-tricks: (1) Billy Jennings.
Leading scorer: (17) Alan Taylor.

	Appearances								Goals				
	Lge	*Sub*	LC	*Sub*	FAC	*Sub*	Eur	*Sub*	Lge	LC	FAC	Eur	Tot
Ayris, Johnny	3	*6*		*1*									
Best, Clyde	5	*2*	2						1	1			2
Bonds, Billy	17	*1*	5				9		1	1		2	4
Brooking, Trevor	34		4		1		7		5	1		3	9
Coleman, Keith	26		1		1		6	*1*					
Curbishley, Alan	12	*2*			1		1	*1*	1				1
Day, Mervyn	41		5		1		9						
Ferguson, Bobby	1												
Gould, Bobby	4	*1*					1		2				2
Holland, Pat	35		5		1		7		2			2	4
Jennings, Billy	26	*4*	1	*2*	1		5	*2*	11			3	14
Lampard, Frank	37		4		1		9		3			1	4
Lock, Kevin	26		5		1		4						
McDowell, John	36	*1*	5				7						
McGiven, Mike	6	*1*			1		1	*1*					
Orhan, Yilmaz	5												
Paddon, Graham	39		5		1		9		2	1		2	5
Pike, Geoff		*3*											
Robson, Keith	33	*1*	4				9		3	1		4	8
Taylor, Alan	33	*2*	4		1		6	*1*	13	1		3	17
Taylor, Tommy	42		5				9		2				2
Wooler, Alan	1												
(own-goals)									2				2
22 players used	**462**	*24*	**55**	*3*	**11**		**99**	**6**	**48**	**6**		**20**	**74**

No	Date		Att	Pos	Pt	F-A	H-T	Scorers, Times, and Referees	1	2	3	4	5	6	7	8	9	10	11	12 sub used
1	A	ASTON VILLA			L	0-4	0-0		Day	Coleman	Lampard	Taylor T	**Green**	Bonds	Taylor A	Paddon	Holland	Brooking	Curbishley	
	21/8		*39,012*		0			*Gray 49, 75, Graydon 54, 60p*	*Burridge*	*Gidman*	*Smith*	*Phillips*	*Nicholl*	*Mortimer*	*Graydon*	*Little*	*Gray*	*Robson*	*Carrodus*	
								Ref: C Thomas	Bill Green has signed from Carlisle for £100,000, allowing Tommy Taylor to play up front as experimental striker. Green gives away a penalty with a foul on Andy Gray, but Graydon, set for his hat-trick, fired over the bar. Bonds brought down Carrodus for Villa's second penalty.											
2	H	QP RANGERS			W	1-0	0-0	Paddon 76	Day	Coleman	Lampard	Holland	Green	Bonds	Taylor T	Paddon	Taylor A	Brooking	Curbishley	
	23/8		31,668		2				*Parkes*	*Clement*	*Gillard*	*Hollins*	*McLintock*	*Leach*	*Thomas*	*Leach*	*Masson*	*Bowles*	*Givens*	
								Ref: A Glasson	Like West Ham, Dave Sexton's QPR lost their opening match 0-4. Day is the busier keeper and in the space of seconds Bowles and Givens break clear but miss. Paddon's 30-yarder dipped under the bar to give Hammers their first home win in seven months. That was versus QPR.											
3	H	LEICESTER		17	D	0-0	0-0		Day	Coleman	McGiven	Holland	Green	Bonds	Taylor T	Paddon	Taylor A	Brooking	Jennings	
	28/8		24,960	*14*	3				*Wallington*	*Whitworth*	*Rofe*	*Kember**	*Blockley*	*Woollett*	*Weller*	*Alderson*	*Worthington*	*Lee*	*Garland*	*Birchenall*
								Ref: A Grey	Leicester manager Jimmy Bloomfield admitted: 'We were lucky'. His side is full of expensive new signings, but survived only because the woodwork three times came to their assistance. Both matches with Leicester last season were drawn, and both have drawn all matches so far.											
4	A	STOKE		20	L	1-2	0-1	Taylor A 70	Day	Coleman	Lampard	McGiven	Green	Bonds	Taylor T*	Paddon	Taylor A	Brooking	Holland	Jennings
	4/9		*19,131*	*6*	3			*Crooks 32, Conroy 51*	*Shilton*	*Marsh*	*Pejic*	*Mahoney*	*Dodd*	*Bloor*	*Salmons*	*Greenhoff*	*Conroy*	*Hudson*	*Crooks*	
								Ref: W Gow	Stoke are going well and on this evidence deserve to be doing so. 18-year-old Garth Crooks nets his first ever Division 1 goal, and man-of-the-match Terry Conroy fired a screamer. Alan Taylor deflected Brooking's shot past Shilton, and Tommy Taylor hit a post against the run of play.											
5	H	ARSENAL		21	L	0-2	0-1		Day	Coleman*	Lampard	Bonds	Green	McGiven	Taylor T	Paddon	Taylor A	Brooking	Holland	Orhan
	11/9		31,965	*6*	3			*Stapleton 28, Ross 46*	*Rimmer*	*Rice*	*Nelson*	*Ross*	*O'Leary**	*Howard*	*Ball*	*Armstrong*	*Stapleton*	*Cropley*	*Brady*	*Storey*
								Ref: A Robinson	Terry Neill's Arsenal are without £300,000 signing Malcolm Macdonald. Alan Taylor hit a post with one effort and the bar seconds later. Stapleton's header and Trevor Ross's volley earned Arsenal the points. Billy Bonds and Mick McGiven kept feuding between themselves.											
6	A	BRISTOL CITY		20	D	1-1	0-1	Taylor A 69	Day	Coleman	Lampard*	Bonds	Green	Taylor T	Jennings	Paddon	Taylor A	Brooking	Holland	McGiven
	18/9		*28,932*	*5*	4			*Fear 10*	*Cashley*	*Sweeney*	*Drysdale*	*Gow*	*Collier*	*Merrick*	*Tainton*	*Fear*	*Mann*	*Gillies*	*Whitehead*	
								Ref: L Burden	A minute before half-time Pat Holland collides with Jimmy Mann and breaks a shin-bone. With Lampard already off with a strained hip, West Ham must play the second half with 10 men. Strangely, they played better, and deserved their equaliser when Brooking crossed to Alan Taylor.											
7	H	SUNDERLAND		20	D	1-1	0-0	Jennings 52	Day	Coleman	Lock	Bonds	Green	Taylor T	Jennings	Paddon	Taylor A	Brooking	McGiven	
	25/9		24,319	*22*	5			*Bolton 70*	*Montgomery*	*Ashurst*	*Bolton*	*Towers*	*Clarke*	*Holton*	*Train*	*Hughes**	*Greenwood*	*Robson*	*Foggon*	*Rowell*
								Ref: K Baker	Bob Stokoe's Sunderland are searching for their first win. Such is the tension within West Ham's ranks that when Billy Jennings heads in Trevor Brooking's cross he does not celebrate but V-signs the crowd who had baited him. Full-back Bolton levelled from Towers' pass.											
8	A	MANCHESTER C		21	L	2-4	0-1	Taylor A 63, Doyle 84 (og)	Day	Coleman	Lock	Bonds	Green	Taylor T	Jennings	Paddon	Taylor A	Brooking	McGiven*	Ayris
	2/10		*37,795*	*2*	5			*Owen 44, Tueart 50, 89, Hartford 79*	*Corrigan*	*Clements*	*Donachie*	*Doyle*	*Watson*	*Owen*	*Barnes*	*Kidd*	*Royle*	*Hartford*	*Tueart*	
								Ref: J Taylor	Gary Owen's cheeky lob over the stranded Day ignites a second-half goal blitz. When Corrigan punched out Paddon's cross and Doyle headed unwittingly into his own net, West Ham sensed a reprieve. Mick McGiven was carried off. Lyall hopes to sign Plymouth striker Paul Mariner.											
9	H	LEEDS			L	1-3	1-1	Jennings 22	Day	Coleman	Lock	Bonds	Green	Taylor T	Jennings	Paddon	Taylor A	Brooking	Ayris	
	6/10		21,909		5			*Gray E 5, Lorimer 77, Harris 83*	*Harvey*	*Reaney*	*Hampton*	*Madeley*	*McQueen*	*Hunter*	*Cherry*	*Lorimer*	*Jordan*	*Gray F*	*Gray E**	*Harris*
								Ref: R Challis	The crowd is small, morale is low, and Jimmy Armfield's strugglers put the shackles on Brooking by man-marking him with Trevor Cherry. Day is to blame for Eddie Gray's opener. Although Jennings levels with a deflection, by the close Leeds look like scoring with every attack.											
10	H	IPSWICH		21	L	0-2	0-1		Day	Coleman	Lock	Bonds	Green	Taylor T	Jennings	Paddon	Taylor A*	Brooking	Robson B	Ayris
	16/10		24,534	*7*	5			*Woods 10, 87*	*Cooper*	*Burley*	*Mills*	*Talbot*	*Hunter*	*Beattie*	*Osborne*	*Wark*	*Bertschin**	*Whymark*	*Woods*	*Lambert*
								Ref: T Bent	Even though Pop Robson has come back from Sunderland, this is a pathetic showing. Ipswich's Kevin Beattie says: 'They'll be in the Second Division next season.' Man-of-the-match Clive Woods got off the mark following Bertschin's dummy. Ipswich should have scored five or six.											

No	Date	Venue	Opponent	Att	Pos	Res	F-A	H-T	Scorers, Times, and Referees	1	2	3	4	5	6	7	8	9	10	11	12
11		A	EVERTON		21	L	2-3	0-1	McNaught 76 (og), Bonds 87	Day	Bonds	Lampard	Curbishley	Green*	Taylor T	Orhan	Paddon	Robson B	Brooking	Robson K	Lock
	23/10			*23,163*	*4*	5			*Lyons 13, King 54, Latchford 65*	*Davies*	*Darracott*	*Jones*	*Lyons*	*McNaught*	*Hamilton*	*King*	*Dobson**	*Latchford*	*Goodlass*	*Telfer*	*Pearson*
									Ref: R Perkin	When Bob Latchford climaxes a 30-yard run with a 30-yard shot to put Everton three up, West Ham look doomed. But Ken McNaught's own-goal, finishing off a shot from the Cypriot Yilmaz Orhan, breathes life into the Hammers. Bonds' shot went through keeper Dai Davies' hands.											
12		A	WEST BROM		22	L	0-3	0-1		Day	Bonds	Lampard	Curbishley	Lock	Taylor T	**Devonshire**	Paddon	Robson B	Brooking	Robson K*	Orhan
	30/10			*19,856*	*10*	5			*Martin 43, Brown A 76, 86*	*Osborne*	*Mulligan*	*Cantello*	*Brown T*	*Wile*	*Robertson*	*Martin*	*Treacy*	*Edwards**	*Giles*	*Brown A*	*Trewick*
									Ref: G Flint	Six successive defeats, five points from 12 games. That is West Ham's worst run since 1958. Once Johnny Giles' Albion went in front, West Ham failed to create any chances. Day was at fault with both Ally Brown goals, dropping Martin's cross and failing to hold Trewick's shot.											
13		H	TOTTENHAM		21	W	**5-3**	2-1	R'bson 21, Bonds 30, Jen' 69, Br'k 54,	Day	Bonds	Lampard	Curbishley	Lock	Taylor T	Devonshire	Pike	Jennings	Brooking	Robson B	
	6/11			28,997	*19*	7			*Duncan 41, Hoddle 78, Osgood 83p*	*Daines*	*Naylor*	*McAllister*	*Hoddle*	*Young*	*Osgood*	*Pratt*	*Perryman*	*Duncan*	*Conn*	*Taylor**	*Coates*
									Ref: D Lloyd [Goal 5. Curbishley 72]	John Lyall plays four in midfield, most of them kids, and none a natural ball-winner. Spurs have now shipped 24 goals in six away games. Lyall has also signed Anton Otulakowski for £60,000 from Barnsley. He is ineligible, serving a week's notice as a gas board draughtsman.											
14		A	NORWICH		21	L	0-1	0-1		Day	Bonds	Lampard	Curbishley	Lock*	Taylor T	Devonshire	Pike	Jennings	Brooking	Robson B	Coleman
	10/11			*24,762*	*18*	7			*Peters 17*	*Keelan*	*Ryan*	*Sullivan*	*Steele**	*Jones*	*Powell*	*Neighbour*	*Osgood*	*Boyer*	*Suggett*	*Peters*	*Machin*
									Ref: C Maskell	Peter Osgood makes his Norwich debut on loan. Suggett's corner, headed in by Martin Peters, settles a match that West Ham let slip away. They saw enough of the ball, but lacked a cutting edge. Graham Paddon re-signs for Norwich after the game. 'It's great to be back,' he says.											
15		H	NEWCASTLE		22	L	1-2	1-1	Robson B 36	Day	Bonds	Lampard	Curbishley	Lock	Taylor T*	Devonshire	Pike	Jennings	Brooking	Robson B	Robson K
	20/11			21,324	*5*	7			*Nulty 35, Burns 53*	*Mahoney*	*Nattrass*	*Kennedy*	*Cassidy*	*McCaffery*	*Nulty*	*Barrowclough*	*Cannell*	*Burns*	*Gowling*	*Craig T*	
									Ref: H Robinson	Brooking's 300th game for the Hammers is not a happy one. Tommy Craig's free-kick was deflected in by Magpies' skipper Geoff Nulty. Pop Robson's instant equaliser counted for nothing when Mervyn Day hesitated about coming out, leaving Mickey Burns to nip in for the winner.											
16		A	MANCHESTER U		22	W	2-0	2-0	Brooking 19, Jennings 30	Day	Lock	Lampard	**Otulakowski**	Taylor T	Bonds	Devonshire	Pike	Jennings	Brooking	Robson B	
	27/11			*55,366*	*15*	9				*Stepney*	*Forsyth*	*Albiston*	*Daly*	*Greenhoff B*	*Houston*	*Coppell*	*McIlroy*	*Pearson*	*Greenhoff J*	*Hill*	
									Ref: P Reeves	The first away win for a year, against a Man U side who have won just once at home in seven games. 20-year-old, 5ft 6in Anton Otulakowski enjoys a fine debut. Jennings knocked on for Brooking to dash between two defenders for the first. West Ham stay bottom on goal-difference.											
17		H	MIDDLESBROUGH		22	L	0-1	0-1		Day	Lock	Lampard	Otulakowski	Taylor T	Bonds	Devonshire	Pike	Jennings*	Brooking	Robson B	Curbishley
	4/12			20,184	*10*	9			*Boersma 8*	*Platt*	*Craggs*	*Cooper*	*Souness*	*Boam*	*Maddren*	*McAndrew*	*Mills*	*Brine*	*Boersma**	*Armstrong*	*Hickton*
									Ref: C Thomas	Jack Charlton's joyless Boro snatch their first away win of the season with only their third away goal. Charlton is gracious enough to admit the win is undeserved. He did not, however, apologise for his team's stifling, negative tactics as they sought to protect Phil Boersma's early goal.											
18		H	LIVERPOOL		21	W	2-0	0-0	Brooking 59, Jennings 86	Day	Lock	Lampard	Green	Taylor T	Bonds	Robson K	**Radford**	Jennings	Brooking	Robson B	
	18/12			24,175	*2*	11				*Clemence*	*Neal*	*Jones*	*Thompson*	*Kennedy*	*Hughes*	*Keegan*	*McDermott*	*Heighway*	*Toshack**	*Callaghan*	*Case*
									Ref: K Baker	Lyall leaves out most of his youngsters against the defending champions. John Radford, an £80,000 signing from Arsenal, makes his debut. The magnificent Brooking beats the offside trap and side-steps Emlyn Hughes for the first goal. Radford headed down to Jennings for No 2.											
19		A	BIRMINGHAM		21	D	0-0	0-0		Day	Lock	Lampard	Green	Taylor T	Bonds	Robson K	Radford	Jennings	Brooking	Robson B	
	27/12			*39,978*	*8*	12				*Latchford*	*Rathbone*	*Styles*	*Kendall*	*Gallagher*	*Page*	*Jones*	*Francis*	*Burns*	*Hibbitt*	*Connolly*	
									Ref: A Porter	West Ham had the chances in the first half, but Radford and Pop Robson missed them. The defence had to earn their corn after the turnaround, and Mervyn Day enjoyed one of his most defiant displays. Billy Bonds took the eye with the way he controlled the boy-wonder Trevor Francis.											
20		A	TOTTENHAM		21	L	1-2	1-0	Brooking 2	Day	Lock	Lampard	Green	Taylor T	Bonds	Robson K	Radford*	Jennings	Brooking	Robson B	Otulakowski
	1/1			*44,972*	*18*	12			*Osgood 54p, Duncan 61*	*Jennings*	*Naylor*	*Gorman*	*Hoddle*	*Pratt*	*Osgood*	*Conn*	*Perryman*	*Duncan*	*Coates*	*Taylor*	
									Ref: K Burns	Pouring rain, freak goals, bags of controversy. The freak goal was Brooking's, his free-kick aquaplaning through the puddles. The controversy attended Bonds' tackle on Alfie Conn. The linesman's yellow flag signalled a penalty. Then Perryman felled Brooking but this time no penalty.											
21		H	WEST BROM		21	D	0-0	0-0		Day	Lock	Lampard	Green	Taylor T	Bonds	Robson K	Devonshire	Jennings	Brooking	Robson B	
	3/1			25,236	*9*	13				*Osborne*	*Mulligan*	*Robson*	*Brown T*	*Wile*	*Robertson*	*Martin*	*Treacy*	*Cross*	*Trewick*	*Johnston*	
									Ref: L Shapter	Many referees would have postponed this match rather than let it go ahead on a treacherous pitch that made football impossible. Albion stopper John Wile had a comfortable time without the hamstrung John Radford to mark. The best chance fell to Jennings but was acrobatically saved.											

No	Date			Att	Pos	Pt	F-A	H-T	Scorers, Times, and Referees	1	2	3	4	5	6	7	8	9	10	11	12 sub used
22		H	ASTON VILLA		21	L	0-1	0-1		Day	Lock	Lampard	Green	Taylor T	Bonds	Curbishley	Pike*	Jennings	Brooking	Robson B	Devonshire
	22/1			27,577	*4*	13			*Gray 3*	*Burridge*	*Gidman*	*Robson*	*Phillips*	*Nicholl*	*Mortimer*	*Deehan*	*Little*	*Gray*	*Cropley**	*Carrodus*	*Smith*
									Ref: A Grey	Tommy Taylor is so fed up with being told to play in midfield that he gives Lyall an ultimatum: 'Let me play in defence or I quit.' John Deehan fed Andy Gray for his 23rd goal of the season. Ron Saunders' Villa become the 10th side to keep out West Ham's so-called attack.											
23		A	LEICESTER		21	L	0-2	0-1		Day	Bonds	Lampard	Otulakowski	Green	Lock	Taylor A	Radford	Devonshire	Brooking	Robson B	
	5/2			*16,201*	*9*	13			*Worthington 20, Weller 71*	*Wallington*	*Whitworth*	*Rofe*	*Kember*	*Blockley*	*Sims*	*Weller*	*Sammels*	*Worthington*	*Alderson**	*Earle*	*Birchenall*
									Ref: W Gow	This was better than it appears. West Ham held their own against a team beaten at home just twice, but lost to two stupid mistakes. Dennis Rofe's centre was deflected by Bonds to Frank Worthington. When Pop Robson lost possession, Keith Weller made the game safe for City.											
24		H	STOKE		21	W	1-0	1-0	Robson B 8	Day	Bonds	Lampard	Otulakowski	Green	Lock	Taylor A	Radford	Devonshire	Brooking	Robson B*	Robson K
	12/2			**20,160**	*16*	15				*Shilton*	*Dodd*	*Bowers*	*Mahoney*	*Smith*	*Bloor*	*Crooks*	*Suddick**	*Goodwin*	*Conroy*	*Salmons*	*Marsh*
									Ref: A Robinson	Pop Robson's near-post glancing header was oh-so-nearly saved by Shilton. Bonds missed with a 65th-minute penalty and poor Mervyn Day looked increasingly edgy. He saved from Dave Goodwin with his knees and looked as though the final whistle could not come quickly enough.											
25		A	ARSENAL		20	W	3-2	2-1	Taylor A 23, 75, Jennings 34	Day	Bonds	Lampard	Otulakowski	Green	Lock	Taylor A	Radford	Devonshire	Brooking	Jennings	
	19/2			*38,221*	*9*	17			*Brady 13, Stapleton 62*	*Rimmer*	*Rice*	*Nelson*	*Ross*	*Powling*	*Simpson*	*Hudson*	*Brady*	*Macdonald*	*Stapleton*	*Armstrong*	
									Ref: R Challis	This televised match was finally turned West Ham's way when Alan Taylor launched himself at Lampard's low cross and the ball flew into the net. How much Taylor knew of it was debatable. Young Devonshire played a blinder for the Hammers and Lock twice cleared off the line.											
26		H	BRISTOL CITY		18	W	2-0	1-0	Bonds 26p, Jennings 67	Day	Bonds	Lampard	Otulakowski	Green	Lock	Taylor A	Radford	Devonshire	Brooking	Jennings	
	26/2			29,713	*20*	19				*Shaw*	*Gillies*	*Merrick*	*Sweeney*	*Collier*	*Hunter*	*Gow*	*Fear*	*Garland**	*Cormack*	*Whitehead*	*Tainton*
									Ref: A Turvey	The return of Alan Taylor to the side seems to have injected life into a lifeless team. Gerry Gow toppled him for the penalty. Geoff Merrick then deflected Billy Jennings' effort past Shaw. Jennings claimed the goal. Alan Dick's City spent the afternoon running around in circles.											
27		A	SUNDERLAND		20	L	**0-6**	0-3	[Lee 85]	Day	Bonds	Lampard	Otulakowski	Green	Lock	Robson K	Radford	Devonshire	Brooking	Jennings	
	5/3			*35,357*	*18*	19			*Holden 3, 30, Rowell 9, 65, Kerr 53,*	*Siddall*	*Docherty*	*Bolton*	*Arnott*	*Waldron*	*Ashurst*	*Kerr*	*Elliott**	*Holden*	*Lee*	*Rowell*	*Brown*
									Ref: A Jones	West Ham had won their last three. Sunderland had won their last four and had climbed off the bottom by winning 6-1 in their last home game, against WBA. This is Roker's best result for 14 years and ITV's *The Big Match* cameras are there to record it. Rowell set up Holden's opener.											
28		H	MANCHESTER C		18	W	1-0	1-0	Robson B 20	Day	Bonds	Lampard	Otulakowski	Green*	Lock	Pike	Robson B	Devonshire	Brooking	Jennings	Curbishley
	12/3			24,974	*3*	21				*Corrigan*	*Clements*	*Donachie*	*Doyle**	*Watson*	*Conway*	*Barnes*	*Kidd*	*Royle*	*Hartford*	*Tueart*	*Owen*
									Ref: E Read	Disaster for Bill Green as he collides with Joe Royle, cracks a fibula in his right leg and fractures his temple bone too. Just before half-time Bonds misses his second penalty in three weeks. This left the Hammers hanging on to Pop Robson's flick from Trevor Brooking's cross.											
29		A	IPSWICH		22	L	1-4	0-0	Robson B 86p	Day	Bonds	Lampard	Otulakowski	Taylor T	Lock	Pike	Robson B	Devonshire	Brooking	Jennings	
	22/3			*27,315*	*1*	21			*Taylor 56 (og), Mariner 68, 72, 82*	*Cooper*	*Burley*	*Mills*	*Talbot*	*Hunter*	*Roberts*	*Osborne*	*Wark*	*Mariner*	*Whymark**	*Woods*	*Bertschin*
									Ref: B Martin	This fixture was brought forward four days in view of England's World Cup clash with Luxembourg. Tommy Taylor returns after six weeks' absence and heads an own-goal. Talbot felled Devonshire for the penalty. The result sends Ipswich top above Liverpool and West Ham bottom.											
30		H	EVERTON		22	D	2-2	1-1	Robson B 29p, 83	Day	Bonds	Lampard	Otulakowski	Taylor T	Lock	Radford	Robson B	Devonshire	Brooking	Jennings	
	2/4			22,518	*14*	22			*Goodlass 10, Pearson 58*	*Lawson*	*Jones*	*Pejic*	*Lyons*	*McNaught*	*Darracott*	*Hamilton*	*Dobson*	*Latchford*	*Telfer**	*Goodlass*	*Pearson*
									Ref: L Burden	Gordon Lee's Everton extend their unbeaten run to 11. They took the lead twice, despite having come to defend. Mervyn Day, off his line, is catastrophically lobbed by Ronnie Goodlass from near the halfway line. Many supporters identify that goal as the beginning of the end for Day.											
31		A	QP RANGERS		22	D	1-1	0-0	Robson B 62	Day	Bonds	Lampard	Pike	Taylor T	Lock	Radford	Robson B	Devonshire*	Brooking	Jennings	Otulakowski
	4/4			*24,930*	*16*	23			*Eastoe 57*	*Parkes*	*Shanks*	*Gillard*	*Hollins*	*McLintock*	*Abbott*	*Eastoe*	*Leach*	*Masson*	*Webb*	*Givens*	
									Ref: C Biddle	QPR remain three points above West Ham as a result of this draw. Givens headed on to Peter Eastoe, but the lead was cancelled out by Pop Robson, thanks to Brooking's slide-rule pass. It is Robson's fifth goal in four games. Lyall had told him to do less work, and stop chasing back.											

No	Venue / Date	Opponent / Att	Pos	Res / Pts	F-A	H-T	Scorers, Times, and Referees	1	2	3	4	5	6	7	8	9	10	11	12 sub used
32	H	BIRMINGHAM	22	D	2-2	1-2	Jennings 7, Pike 56	Day	Bonds	Coleman	Pike	Taylor T	Lock	Radford	Robson B	Devonshire*	Brooking	Jennings	Taylor A
	8/4	28,167	*12*	24			*Gallagher 22, Francis 23*	*Montgomery*	*Calderwood*	*Pendrey*	*Kendall*	*Gallagher*	*Want*	*Emmanuel*	*Francis*	*Burns*	*Hibbitt*	*Connolly*	
							Ref: R Crabb	The turning point comes in the 48th minute. Pop Robson has taken over responsibility for penalties from Bonds. He is now up against Jim Montgomery, who he knows from their time at Sunderland. Monty guesses right and saves. Day is lobbed by Francis and V-signs the crowd.											
33	A	COVENTRY	21	D	1-1	0-0	Robson B 87	Day	Bonds	Lampard	Pike	Taylor T	McGiven	Taylor A	Robson B	Devonshire	Brooking	Jennings	
	9/4	***15,816***	*19*	25			*Ferguson 76*	*Blyth*	*Roberts*	*McDonald**	*Gooding*	*Yorath*	*Coop*	*Beck*	*Powell*	*Wallace*	*Ferguson*	*Hutchison*	*Green*
							Ref: T Reynolds	Coventry lose their keeper with a knee injury after an hour. Bobby McDonald volunteers to go in goal. Ferguson heads Yorath's free-kick over Day to put City in front. McDonald was all set to celebrate his stint in goal when Robson headed the equaliser from Devonshire's centre.											
34	H	NORWICH	20	W	1-0	0-0	Pike 74	Day	Bonds	Lampard	Pike	Taylor T	McGiven	Radford	Robson B	Devonshire	Brooking	Taylor A	
	11/4	27,084	*13*	27				*Keelan*	*Ryan*	*Sullivan*	*Machin*	*Jones*	*Powell*	*Neighbour*	*Reeves*	*Boyer*	*Steele*	*Peters*	
							Ref: P Reeves	Day looks a bag of nerves and his confidence is not helped by sections of the crowd who are happy to jeer his every touch. At least he has learned his lesson and offers no more V-signs. Geoff Pike's winner was a 25-yarder, capitalising on a half-clearance from Lampard's cross.											
35	A	NEWCASTLE	21	L	0-3	0-1		Day	Bonds	Lampard	Pike	Taylor T	McGiven	Radford	Robson B	Devonshire	Brooking	Taylor A*	Jennings
	16/4	*30,967*	*4*	27			*Gowling 45, Cannell 67, Nulty 78*	*Mahoney*	*Nattrass*	*Kennedy*	*Cassidy**	*McCaffrey*	*Nulty*	*Barrowclough*	*Cannell*	*Burns*	*Gowling*	*Craig T*	*Blackhall*
							Ref: A Morrissey	Pop Robson says: 'We are great at playing but hopeless at scoring.' Newcastle, unbeaten at home, are given a first-half lesson by Brooking and Devonshire and are booed off at half-time. In the second half Gowling nodded in from Nulty, then Day fumbled Burns' cross to Paul Cannell.											
36	A	DERBY	21	D	1-1	0-0	Pike 86p	Day	Bonds*	Lampard	Pike	Taylor T	McGiven	Radford	Robson B	Devonshire	Brooking	Taylor A	Jennings
	20/4	*21,380*	*17*	28			*Daly 59p*	*Boulton*	*Langan*	*Webster*	*Daly*	*McFarland*	*Todd*	*Powell*	*Gemmill*	*Hales*	*Hector*	*James*	
							Ref: R Toseland	Twice Mick McGiven clatters Derek Hales in the box, but only once is a penalty awarded. Two minutes after Daly converts it, Billy Bonds hobbles off. But late in the game Kevin Hector inadvertently handled. Geoff Pike was the only Hammer brave enough to volunteer to take it.											
37	A	LEEDS	21	D	1-1	0-0	Robson B 73	Day	Coleman	Lampard	Pike	Taylor T	McGiven	Radford	Robson B	Devonshire	Brooking	Taylor A	
	26/4	*16,891*	*10*	29			*Jordan 53*	*Stewart*	*Stevenson*	*Hampton*	*Cherry*	*McQueen*	*Madeley*	*Harris*	*McNiven*	*Jordan*	*Currie*	*Gray E*	
							Ref: K Butcher	England manager Don Revie always seems to turn up to watch Leeds play West Ham. Leeds are rebuilding. Tony Currie's corner is volleyed in by Joe Jordan. Brooking then squeezed past three defenders before laying the ball off to Devonshire, who provided Pop Robson's equaliser.											
38	A	MIDDLESBROUGH	19	D	1-1	1-0	Robson B 12	Day	Bonds	Lampard	Pike	Taylor T	McGiven	Jennings	Robson B	Devonshire	Brooking	Taylor A	
	29/4	*16,500*	*11*	30			*Mills 73*	*Platt*	*Craggs*	*Cooper*	*Souness*	*Ramage*	*Maddren*	*McAndrew*	*Mills*	*Wood*	*Brine**	*Armstrong*	*Boersma*
							Ref: K McNally	West Ham squeeze out of the bottom three with this point. When Alan Taylor's shot was blocked it ran to Robson to poke the ball in. Hammers were desperate to hang on to both points, but when Alan Taylor under-hit a back-pass Mills drew Day from his goal to score from a tight angle.											
39	H	COVENTRY	18	W	2-0	1-0	Robson B 20, Pike 51p	Day	Bonds	Lampard	Pike	Taylor T	McGiven	Radford	Robson B	Devonshire	Brooking	Taylor A	
	4/5	25,461	*16*	32				*Sealey*	*Cartwright*	*McDonald*	*Yorath*	*Holton*	*Coop*	*Beck*	*Wallace*	*Ferguson*	*Powell*	*Hutchison*	
							Ref: R Lewis	In the mud and rain, Brooking lights up a fighting performance by the Hammers, feeding Robson, who wriggled round Coop for the first goal. Terry Yorath conceded the second by handling. He angrily claimed the ball had hit him. Sunderland, Spurs and Bristol C are the bottom three.											
40	H	DERBY	19	D	2-2	1-1	Pike 2, Jennings 84	Day	Bonds	Lampard	Pike	Taylor T	McGiven*	Radford	Robson B	Devonshire	Brooking	Taylor A	Jennings
	7/5	**32,079**	*15*	33			*James 44, McGiven 76 (og)*	*Boulton*	*Langan*	*Webster*	*Daly*	*McFarland*	*Todd*	*Powell*	*Gemmill*	*Hector*	*George*	*James*	
							Ref: H Robinson	It takes Pike 98 seconds to bag the first goal. Most unpopular man at Upton Park is Derby's Leighton James, who keeps tumbling whenever a defender gets near. He fired in a free-kick when felled by Taylor and later prompted McGiven's own-goal. The referee needed a police escort.											
41	A	LIVERPOOL	19	D	0-0	0-0		Day	Bonds	Lampard	Pike	Taylor T	McGiven	Jennings	Robson B	Devonshire	Brooking	Taylor A	
	14/5	***55,675***	*1*	34				*Clemence*	*Neal*	*Jones*	*Smith*	*Kennedy*	*Hughes*	*Keegan*	*Case*	*Heighway*	*Johnson**	*McDermott*	*Fairclough*
							Ref: C Seel	West Ham conclude their season by facing both FA Cup finalists, who are bound to be distracted. The magnificent Steve Heighway steals the show and forces a fine save from Day. West Ham have lost once in 14 games, and with Spurs already down have survival in their own hands.											
42	H	MANCHESTER U	19	W	4-2	1-1	Lampard 29, Pike 53, Robson 60, 74	Day	Bonds	Lampard	Pike	Taylor T	McGiven	Radford	Robson B	Devonshire	Brooking	Taylor A	
	16/5	29,311	*6*	36			*Hill 1, Pearson 67*	*Roche*	*Nicholl*	*Albiston*	*McIlroy*	*Greenhoff B*	*Buchan*	*Coppell*	*Greenhoff J**	*Pearson*	*Macari*	*Hill*	*McCreery*
	Home	Away					Ref: C Thomas	A terrace ban on Man U fans means more space for Hammers supporters. Even though the FA Cup final is just five days away, Tommy Docherty's side show great commitment. They take the lead in 25 seconds. Lampard levels off a post from 30 yards and West Ham turn it on.											
Average	26,015	30,106																	

LEAGUE DIVISION 1 (CUP-TIES)

Manager: Lyall & Greenwood

SEASON 1976-77

League Cup						F-A	H-T	Scorers, Times, and Referees	1	2	3	4	5	6	7	8	9	10	11	12 sub used
2	H	BARNSLEY		17	W	3-0	2-0	Holland 21, 60, Paddon 45	Day	Coleman	McGiven	Holland	Green	Bonds	Taylor T	Paddon	Taylor A	Brooking	Jennings	
	1/9		17,889	*4:7*					*Springett*	*Murphy*	*Gorry*	*Otulakowski*	*Burke*	*Pickering*	*Felton*	*Peachey*	*Joicey*	*Brown*	*Millar**	*Price*
								Ref: R Lewis	Barnsley boss Jim Iley admits: 'West Ham have taught us a lot.' He may not have been so generous had Kenny Brown not scooped over Day's crossbar at 0-0. Tommy Taylor is still playing as striker. He is so desperate to score he claimed one of Holland's, though he was yards away.											
3	A	CHARLTON		20	W	1-0	0-0	Taylor A 82	Day	Coleman	McGiven	Bonds	Green	Taylor T	Jennings	Paddon	Taylor A	Brooking	Lock	
	21/9		*32,898*	*2:15*					*Wood*	*Berry*	*Warman*	*Hunt*	*Giles*	*Curtis*	*Powell*	*Hales*	*Flanagan*	*Bowman*	*Peacock*	
								Ref: J Homewood	Charlton's biggest crowd for 14 years are not too impressed by the Hammers, who adopt negative tactics and pass back to Day whenever danger threatens. Nor is manager Andy Nelson impressed with the referee. Alan Taylor won the match after Paddon's shot was blocked.											
4	H	QP RANGERS		21	L	0-2	0-1		Day	Bonds	Lampard	Curbishley	Lock	Taylor T	Orhan	Paddon	Devonshire	Brooking	Robson K	
	27/10		24,565	*13*				*Bowles 38, Clement 87*	*Parkes*	*Clement*	*Gillard*	*Hollins*	*McLintock*	*Webb*	*Thomas**	*Kelly*	*Masson*	*Bowles*	*Givens*	*Leach*
								Ref: R Capey	Alan Devonshire plays his first match after being signed by scout Eddie Baily from Southall for £5,000. Nasty fouls committed by Lampard, Lock and Keith Robson do little for West Ham's nice-guy image. Dave Thomas was carried off after eight minutes, following Lampard's foul.											

FA Cup																				
3	H	BOLTON		21	W	2-1	1-0	Jennings 29, Pike 89	Day	Lock	Lampard	Green	Taylor T	Bonds	Curbishley	Pike	Jennings	Brooking	Robson B	
	8/1		24,147	*2:2*				*Waldron 90*	*McDonagh*	*Nicholson*	*Dunne*	*Greaves*	*Jones**	*Walsh*	*Morgan*	*Whatmore*	*Taylor*	*Reid*	*Smith*	*Waldron*
								Ref: A Hamil	As Ian Greaves' side like to build from the back, Lyall gets his forwards to pressure their defence. When McDonagh scooped out Pike's shot after 50 minutes the ball had crossed the line, though the linesman disagreed. Jennings had already outjumped Jones to put West Ham in front.											
4	A	ASTON VILLA		21	L	0-3	0-0		Day	Lock	Lampard	Green	Taylor T	Bonds	Taylor A	Radford	Jennings	Brooking	Robson B	
	29/1		*46,954*	*4*				*Deehan 58, 66, Mortimer 78*	*Burridge*	*Gidman*	*Robson*	*Phillips*	*Nicholl*	*Mortimer*	*Deehan*	*Little*	*Gray*	*Cowans*	*Carrodus*	
								Ref: P Partridge	West Ham lost to Villa last week in the league. Alan Taylor returns after three months out. Tommy Taylor plays in midfield in the first half but switched with Bonds after the turnaround. Villa's John Deehan made the breakthrough when Day, at a corner, lost his footing on the icy pitch.											

		Home					Away					
	P	W	D	L	F	A	W	D	L	F	A	Pts
1 Liverpool	42	18	3	0	47	11	5	8	8	15	22	57
2 Manchester C	42	15	5	1	38	13	6	9	6	22	21	56
3 Ipswich	42	15	4	2	41	11	7	4	10	25	28	52
4 Aston Villa	42	17	3	1	55	17	5	4	12	21	33	51
5 Newcastle	42	14	6	1	40	15	4	7	10	24	34	49
6 Manchester U	42	12	6	3	41	22	6	5	10	30	40	47
7 West Brom	42	10	6	5	38	22	6	7	8	24	34	45
8 Arsenal	42	11	6	4	37	20	5	5	11	27	39	43
9 Everton	42	9	7	5	35	24	5	7	9	27	40	42
10 Leeds	42	8	8	5	28	26	7	4	10	20	25	42
11 Leicester	42	8	9	4	30	28	4	9	8	17	32	42
12 Middlesbro	42	11	6	4	25	14	3	7	11	15	31	41
13 Birmingham	42	10	6	5	38	25	3	6	12	25	36	38
14 QP Rangers	42	10	7	4	31	21	3	5	13	16	31	38
15 Derby	42	9	9	3	36	18	0	10	11	14	37	37
16 Norwich	42	12	4	5	30	23	2	5	14	17	41	37
17 WEST HAM	42	9	6	6	28	23	2	8	11	18	42	36
18 Bristol City	42	8	7	6	25	19	3	6	12	13	29	35
19 Coventry	42	7	9	5	34	26	3	6	12	14	33	35
20 Sunderland	42	9	5	7	29	16	2	7	12	17	38	34
21 Stoke	42	9	8	4	21	16	1	6	14	7	35	34
22 Tottenham	42	9	7	5	26	20	3	2	16	22	52	33
	924	240	137	85	753	430	85	137	240	430	753	924

Odds & ends

Double wins: (1) Manchester U.
Double losses: (3) Villa, Ipswich, Newcastle.

Won from behind: (1) Arsenal (a).
Lost from in front: (1) Spurs (a).

High spots: Avoiding relegation, after it looked so likely.
Losing only one of the last 13 league games.

Low spots: Five consecutive league defeats in October, down to 22nd.
Being crushed 0-6 at Sunderland.
An anticlimactic season after reaching the Cup-Winners' Cup final the previous year.

Hammer of the Year: Trevor Brooking.
Ever-presents: (2) Mervyn Day and Trevor Brooking.
Hat-tricks: (0).
Leading scorer: (14) Bryan Robson.

	Appearances						Goals			
	Lge	*Sub*	LC	*Sub*	FAC	*Sub*	**Lge**	LC	FAC	**Tot**
Ayris, Johnny	**1**	*2*								
Bonds, Billy	**41**		3		2		**3**			**3**
Brooking, Trevor	**42**		3		2		**4**			**4**
Coleman, Keith	**12**	*1*	2							
Curbishley, Alan	**8**	*2*	1		1		**1**			**1**
Day, Mervyn	**42**		3		2					
Devonshire, Alan	**27**	*1*	1							
Green, Bill	**22**		2		2					
Holland, Pat	**6**		1					2		**2**
Jennings, Billy	**27**	*4*	2		2		**8**		1	**9**
Lampard, Frank	**36**		1		2		**1**			**1**
Lock, Kevin	**25**	*1*	2		2					
McGiven, Mike	**15**	*1*	2							
Orhan, Yilmaz	**1**	*2*	1							
Otulakowski, Anton	**10**	*2*								
Paddon, Graham	**12**		3				**1**	1		**2**
Pike, Geoff	**20**				1		**6**		1	**7**
Radford, John	**18**				1					
Robson, Bryan	**30**				2		**14**			**14**
Robson, Keith	**7**	*2*	1							
Taylor, Alan	**24**	*1*	2		1		**5**	1		**6**
Taylor, Tommy	**36**		3		2					
(own-goals)							**3**			**3**
22 players used	**462**	***19***	**33**		**22**		**46**	**4**	**2**	**52**

No	Date		Att	Pos	Pt	F-A	H-T	Scorers, Times, and Referees	1	2	3	4	5	6	7	8	9	10	11	12 sub used
1	H	NORWICH			L	1-3	0-1	Robson 71p	Day	Lampard	**Brush**	Pike	Taylor T	Lock	Taylor A	Robson	Radford	Brooking	Devonshire	
	20/8		28,178		0			*Ryan 32, Jones 59, 73*	*Keelan*	*Ryan*	*Sullivan*	*Evans*	*Jones*	*Powell*	*Neighbour*	*Busby*	*Reeves*	*Suggett*	*Gibbins*	
								Ref: K Baker	Ron Greenwood is now manager of England. Keith Robson has signed for Cardiff for £30,000. This awful season-opener did not see its first foul for 15 minutes and so lethargic were the players that the crowd was drifting away before the end. Jones felled Alan Taylor for the penalty.											
2	A	LEICESTER			L	0-1	0-0		Day	Brush	Lampard	Pike	Taylor T	Lock	Taylor A	Robson	Radford	Curbishley	Devonshire*	Otulakowski
	24/8		*18,310*		0			*Kember 71*	*Wallington*	*Whitworth*	*Rofe*	*Kember*	*Sims**	*Woollett*	*Alderson*	*Sammels*	*Worthington*	*Kelly*	*Weller*	*Blockley*
								Ref: D Lloyd	Frank Worthington headed down, Day slipped in the mud, and the ball ricocheted off his body and Kember's arm into the net. This cruel goal condemns Hammers to defeat. Brooking was out with a groin strain. Alan Taylor, Pop Robson and Radford missed chances to save the game.											
3	H	MANCHESTER C		21	L	0-1	0-0		Day	Lampard	Brush	Pike	Taylor T	Lock	Taylor A*	Robson	Radford	Curbishley	Devonshire	Otulakowski
	27/8		25,278	*4*	0			*Royle 50*	*Corrigan*	*Clements*	*Donachie*	*Doyle*	*Watson*	*Booth*	*Kidd*	*Channon*	*Royle*	*Hartford*	*Tueart*	
								Ref: A Glasson	John Radford is wondering where his first goal is coming from. He joined the Hammers at Christmas but can't find the net. The club face a worrying fine after a 'fan' rushed onto the pitch to grapple with City's Willie Donachie, who was in the process of being booked by the referee.											
4	A	NEWCASTLE		18	W	3-2	1-2	Jennings 37, Taylor A 49, Robson 80	Day	Lampard	Brush	Holland	Taylor T	Lock	Taylor A	Robson	Jennings	Curbishley	Devonshire	
	3/9		*26,983*	*20*	2			*Burns 8, Cassidy 23*	*Mahoney*	*Blackhall*	*Kennedy*	*Cassidy*	*McCaffrey*	*Bird*	*McLean*	*Mitchell**	*Burns*	*Oates*	*Craig T*	*Nattrass*
								Ref: W Johnson	Newcastle have also made a dreadful start to the season, allowing a two-goal lead to slip through their fingers. Robson's hopeful cross was headed in by Jennings. Three home defenders then failed to clear Holland's cross, which fell to Alan Taylor. Robson headed a simple winner.											
5	H	QP RANGERS		17	D	2-2	1-2	Holland 11, Lock 78	Day	Lampard	Brush	Holland	Taylor T	Lock	Pike	Robson	Jennings*	Curbishley	Devonshire	Otulakowski
	10/9		26,922	*14*	3			*Eastoe 7, Lock 13 (og)*	*Parkes*	*Clement*	*Shanks*	*Hollins*	*Needham*	*Webb*	*Eastoe*	*Francis*	*Masson*	*Bowles*	*Givens**	*Williams*
								Ref: A Robinson	Billy Jennings ruptures an Achilles' tendon; his season is over. Pat Holland is enjoying a rich vein of form, and scores when Tommy Taylor flicks on Lampard's cross to him. Kevin Lock, trying to clear, belted the ball past Day, but made amends with a screamer that rescued a point.											
6	A	BRISTOL CITY		20	L	2-3	1-2	Robson 5, Pike 86	Day	Lampard	Brush	Holland	Taylor T	Lock	Taylor A	Robson	Curbishley	Brooking	Devonshire*	Pike
	17/9		*21,180*	*17*	3			*Mabbutt 6, Ritchie 23, 64*	*Shaw*	*Gillies*	*Sweeney*	*Gow*	*Collier*	*Hunter*	*Tainton*	*Ritchie*	*Mabbutt*	*Cormack*	*Whitehead*	
								Ref: L Burden	City bag their first win of the season, recovering from Robson's 30-yard thunderbolt to equalise within seconds. Clive Whitehead laid on both City's first two goals. Day might have saved the second. Though Hammers' problems lie in defence, Lyall wants Swansea striker Alan Curtis.											
7	H	EVERTON		17	D	1-1	1-0	Dobson 35 (og)	Day	Lampard	Brush	Holland	Taylor T	McGiven	Taylor A	Robson	Curbishley	Brooking	Devonshire	
	24/9		25,296	*6*	4			*McKenzie 52*	*Wood*	*Darracott*	*Pejic*	*Lyons*	*Higgins*	*Rioch*	*King*	*Dobson*	*Latchford*	*McKenzie*	*Thomas**	*Jones*
								Ref: D Nippard	Pop Robson's header flies into the net off Everton's Martin Dobson. The Toffees equalise when Tommy Taylor is caught dithering in his penalty box and is dispossessed by Duncan McKenzie. London Weekend TV pictures confirm that Robson's disallowed header wasn't offside.											
8	A	ARSENAL		20	L	0-3	0-1		Day	Lampard	Brush	Holland	Taylor T	McGiven	Taylor A	Robson	Curbishley*	Brooking	Devonshire	Pike
	1/10		*41,245*	*9*	4			*Stapleton 31, Rice 38, Brady 79p*	*Jennings*	*Rice*	*Nelson*	*Price*	*O'Leary*	*Simpson*	*Brady*	*Ross*	*Macdonald*	*Stapleton*	*Rix*	
								Ref: B Homewood	Hammers' worst display so far. When Jennings saved Devonshire's shot with his feet it amounted to West Ham's one and only serious effort. Stapleton battled past McGiven to score with power; Rice ran from halfway to head in from six yards; and Day toppled Macdonald in the box.											
9	H	MIDDLESBROUGH		20	L	0-2	0-0		Day	Lampard	Brush	Holland	Taylor T	McGiven	Taylor A	Robson	**Hales***	Brooking	Pike	Devonshire
	3/10		26,508	*14*	4			*Mills 70, 81*	*Platt*	*Craggs*	*Cooper*	*Souness*	*Boam*	*Ramage*	*Mahoney*	*Mills*	*Ashcroft*	*McAndrew*	*Armstrong*	
								Ref: A Turvey	Derek Hales, formerly of Charlton, has signed from Derby for £110,000. Two minutes into his debut he collides with Alan Ramage and injures his knee. He is subbed early in the second half. The team will now stay in the Grosvenor Hotel prior to turning out for Brooking's testimonial.											
10	H	NOTT'M FOREST		20	D	0-0	0-0		Day	Lampard	Brush	Curbishley	Taylor T	McGiven	Devonshire	Robson	Radford	Brooking	Pike	
	8/10		26,126	*1*	5				*Shilton*	*Anderson*	*Barrett*	*McGovern*	*Lloyd*	*Burns*	*O'Neill*	*Bowyer**	*Withe*	*Woodcock*	*Robertson*	*Gemmill*
								Ref: C Maskell	Brian Clough's Forest sit top of the league. He praises the Hammers' fighting spirit, though raises an eyebrow at Frank Lampard launching 20-yard tackles at John Robertson. Lampard had been given the runaround last time he faced the Scot and was determined to keep face this time.											

No	Date	Opponent	Att	Pos	Res	F-A	H-T	Scorers, Times, and Referees	1	2	3	4	5	6	7	8	9	10	11	12 sub used
11	A	WOLVES		20	D	2-2	2-1	Pike 28, Robson 38	Day	Lampard	Brush	Bonds	Taylor T	Pike	Devonshire	Robson	Radford	Brooking	Hales	
	15/10		*19,366*	*13*	6			*Richards 43, Hibbitt 84*	*Bradshaw*	*Palmer*	*Daly*	*Patching*	*Brazier*	*Parkin*	*Hibbitt*	*Carr*	*Richards*	*Bell*	*Sunderland*	
								Ref: B Stevens	Billy Bonds returns after his long injury and adds welcome steel to the Hammers. He also lends an arm, for it is that part of his anatomy that turns Geoff Pike's shot into the net for the first goal. Bonds deflected Kenny Hibbitt's equaliser. John Richards scored his 100th league goal.											
12	H	ASTON VILLA		20	D	2-2	1-1	Taylor T 22, Hales 75	Day	Lampard	Brush	Bonds	Taylor T	Pike	Devonshire	Robson	Radford	Brooking	Hales	
	22/10		26,599	*9*	7			*McNaught 27, Gray 78*	*Rimmer*	*Gidman*	*Smith*	*Phillips*	*McNaught*	*Mortimer*	*Deehan**	*Little*	*Gray*	*Cropley*	*Carrodus*	*Cowans*
								Ref: A Gunn	Ron Saunders' Villa have only lost once away. West Ham were winning 2-1 when Day took his eye off the ball to concede a soft equaliser. Back in 1973 Greenwood had said: 'Mervyn will be our first-team goalkeeper for the next 10 years.' It is a heavy burden for the young keeper.											
13	A	IPSWICH		19	W	2-0	1-0	Hales 25, 82	Day	Lampard	Brush	Bonds	Taylor T	Pike	Devonshire	Robson	Radford	Brooking	Hales	
	29/10		*27,308*	*10*	9				*Cooper*	*Mills*	*Tibbott*	*Talbot*	*Hunter*	*Osman*	*Osborne**	*Gates*	*Mariner*	*Whymark*	*Woods*	*Geddis*
								Ref: M Sinclair	Ipswich had dropped just one home point, to Liverpool, so this win is a headline-grabber. Radford headed down for Hales to fire past Paul Cooper. Radford made Hales' second goal too, this time a lob. Hales said later that he had never before played alongside a big target man											
14	A	COVENTRY		19	L	0-1	0-1		Day	Lampard	Brush	Bonds	Taylor T	Pike	Devonshire	Robson	Radford	Brooking	Hales	
	5/11		*23,276*	*4*	9			*Wallace 43*	*Blyth*	*Oakey*	*McDonald*	*Yorath*	*Beck*	*Coop*	*Nardiello*	*Wallace*	*Ferguson**	*Powell*	*Hutchison*	*Graydon*
								Ref: E Hughes	Bonds has been named in the England squad. A minute's silence for the death of City chairman Sir Jack Scamp. Gordon Milne's City have lost at home only once, playing just three at the back. Coop shot wide from the spot when Lampard handled. Ian Wallace back-headed the goal.											
15	H	WEST BROM		20	D	3-3	1-2	Robson 20p, Devonshire 48,	Day	Lampard	Brush	Bonds	Taylor T	Pike	Devonshire	Robson	Curbishley	Brooking	Hales	
	12/11		23,601	*3*	10			*Wile 37, 39, Cunningham 75*	*Godden*	*Mulligan*	*Statham*	*Brown T*	*Wile*	*Robertson*	*Cantello*	*Cunningham*	*Cross*	*Robson*	*Johnston*	
								Ref: E Read	Brooking has had a testimonial against an England XI. Both Devonshire's goals v WBA took deflections, and the penalty given when the ball was driven against Wile's hand seemed harsh. Wile made amends with two headers. Little Laurie Cunningham also found space to head a goal.											
16	A	DERBY		20	L	1-2	0-1	Bonds 52	Day	Lampard	Brush	Bonds	Taylor T	Pike	Devonshire	Robson	Radford	Brooking	Hales	
	19/11		*23,273*	*17*	10			*Nish 11, Rioch 51*	*Middleton*	*Langan*	*Nish*	*Rioch*	*McFarland*	*Todd*	*Curran*	*Hughes*	*Masson*	*George*	*Ryan*	
								Ref: K Walmsley	Derby welcome back Charlie George, who had fractured his cheekbone in a car crash. They need him, having won only one of seven home games. Man-of-the-match Brooking produced a wonderful pass for Bonds to score, but it was not enough to prevent Derby's second home win.											
17	H	LEEDS		20	L	0-1	0-0		Day	Lampard	Brush	Bonds	Taylor T	Pike	Devonshire	Robson	Radford*	Brooking	Hales	Curbishley
	26/11		26,883	*9*	10			*Hankin 53*	*Harvey*	*Cherry*	*Gray F*	*Currie*	*Parkinson*	*Madeley*	*Harris*	*Hankin*	*Jordan*	*Flynn*	*Graham*	
								Ref: W Gow	10 minutes into the game John Radford collides accidentally with Tony Currie and breaks his jaw in two places. The Hammers are beaten by Ray Hankin's fierce header from Frank Gray's cross. Despite their late fight-back they now have the worst home record in the Football League.											
18	A	LIVERPOOL		20	L	0-2	0-1		Day	Lampard	Brush	Bonds	Taylor T*	Pike	Devonshire	Robson	Curbishley	Brooking	Hales	Holland
	3/12		*39,659*	*4*	10			*Dalglish 37, Fairclough 81*	*Clemence*	*Neal*	*Smith*	*Thompson*	*Kennedy*	*Hughes*	*Dalglish*	*McDermott*	*Heighway*	*Fairclough*	*Callaghan*	
								Ref: A Morrissey	Pat Holland returns after a two-month injury. 20 minutes from time Tommy Taylor dislocates his knee. West Ham had created plenty of chances in the first half but Ray Clemence was equal to them. Lyall wanted to buy Roger Davies from Bruges, but he has signed for Leicester.											
19	H	MANCHESTER U		20	W	2-1	1-1	Hales 6, Brooking 81	Day	Lampard*	Brush	Bonds	Taylor T	Pike	Devonshire	Robson	Curbishley	Brooking	Hales	McDowell
	10/12		20,759	*13*	12			*McGrath 19*	*Roche*	*Nicholl*	*Albiston*	*Coppell*	*Greenhoff B*	*Houston*	*McGrath*	*Greenhoff J*	*Pearson*	*Grimes*	*Hill*	
								Ref: A Grey	At last a home win, though Day's fragility in the air almost put paid to it. The continuing ban on Man U's away supporters has the curious effect of making this the lowest gate since February. Ron Greenwood has officially been appointed England manager, so leaves West Ham Utd.											
20	A	WEST BROM		21	L	0-1	0-0		Day	McDowell	Brush	Bonds	Taylor T	Pike	Devonshire	Robson	**Cross**	Brooking	Hales	
	17/12		*18,868*	*4*	12			*Brown A 76*	*Godden*	*Mulligan*	*Statham*	*Brown T*	*Wile*	*Robertson*	*Martin*	*Regis*	*Brown A*	*Robson*	*Johnston*	
								Ref: A Hughes	David Cross cost £200,000 from WBA, whom he faces in his first match. Albion were unbeaten at home, so this was a creditable display. The game was lost to a disputed goal. A linesman flagged Tony Brown offside. The ref consulted the linesman but allowed namesake Ally's goal.											
21	H	BIRMINGHAM		19	W	1-0	0-0	Curbishley 87	Day	McDowell	Lampard	Bonds	Taylor T	Pike	Devonshire	Robson	Cross	Brooking	Curbishley	
	26/12		25,572	*18*	14				*Montgomery*	*Calderwood*	*Pendrey*	*Towers*	*Howard*	*Want*	*Page*	*Francis*	*Bertschin*	*Hibbitt*	*Emmanuel*	
								Ref: R Lewis	A stomach bug lays low Derek Hales. His place goes to Alan Curbishley, who nets the precious winner. It is 'Whizz's' second league goal of his career, struck from 25 yards, and it needed a slight deflection to get the better of Montgomery. Brooking had hit a post after 10 minutes.											

LEAGUE DIVISION 1

Manager: John Lyall

SEASON 1977-78

No	Date		Att	Pos	Pt	F-A	H-T	Scorers, Times, and Referees	1	2	3	4	5	6	7	8	9	10	11	12 sub used
22	A	CHELSEA		19	L	1-2	0-1	Robson 71	Day	McDowell	Lampard	Bonds	Taylor T	Pike	Devonshire	Robson	Cross	Brooking	Curbishley	
	27/12		*44,093*	*14*	14			*Langley 34, Garner 77*	*Bonetti*	*Harris*	*Wilkins G*	*Britton*	*Droy*	*Wicks*	*Garner*	*Lewington**	*Langley*	*Swain*	*Walker*	*Finnieston*
								Ref: T Bune	Poor Day makes two more howlers, which are made all the more glaring in the light of Bonetti's brilliance at the other end. Day flapped at Clive Walker's cross for Chelsea's first, then played silly-beggers with Bonds on the six-yard line, allowing Garner to nip in for the winner.											
23	H	LEICESTER		19	W	3-2	2-0	McDowell 4, Hales 31, Cross 65	Ferguson	McDowell	Lampard	Bonds	Taylor T	Curbishley	Devonshire	Robson	Cross	Brooking	Hales	
	31/12		25,455	*22*	16			*Kember 73, Sims 75*	*Wallington*	*Williams**	*Rofe*	*Kember*	*Sims*	*Webb*	*Sammels*	*Davies*	*Hughes*	*Kelly*	*Armstrong*	*Earle*
								Ref: C Maskell	Mervyn Day has at last been dropped and veteran Bobby Ferguson gets a chance to show what he can do. The result? Ferguson permits Steve Kember's 40-yard cross to float over his head. Hammers had been coasting 3-0, but by the final whistle they are hanging on desperately.											
24	A	NORWICH		19	D	2-2	1-0	Devonshire 7, Hales 85	Ferguson	Brush	Lampard	Bonds	Taylor T	Curbishley	Devonshire	Robson	Cross	Brooking	Hales	
	2/1		*29,480*	*8*	17			*Ryan 66p, Peters 78*	*Keelan*	*Bond*	*Sullivan*	*Ryan*	*Jones*	*Powell*	*Neighbour*	*Suggett*	*Gibbins*	*Reeves*	*Peters*	
								Ref: K Baker	Norwich are unbeaten at home but have to turn to Hammers old-boy Martin Peters to rescue them. Bonds shoved him in the back to give away a penalty, a decision which so incensed Robson that he was booked. West Ham secured their point when Hales back-headed Brooking's cross.											
25	A	MANCHESTER C		19	L	2-3	1-2	Brooking 41, Cross 88	Ferguson	McDowell	Lampard	Bonds	Taylor T	Curbishley	Devonshire	Robson	Cross	Brooking	Hales	
	14/1		*43,627*	*5*	17			*Kidd 20, Booth 30, Barnes 57*	*Corrigan*	*Clements**	*Donachie*	*Booth*	*Watson*	*Owen*	*Barnes*	*Bell*	*Kidd*	*Hartford*	*Tueart*	*Channon*
								Ref: P Partridge	The result may appear close but it condemns West Ham to their eighth successive defeat at Maine Road. Trevor Brooking deserved better, making one goal, scoring another. But the damage had already been done. Kidd's header and Booth's shot were executed without interference.											
26	H	NEWCASTLE		19	W	1-0	1-0	Hales 10	Ferguson	McDowell	Lampard	Bonds	Taylor T	Curbishley	Devonshire*	Pike	Cross	Taylor A	Hales	Holland
	21/1		25,461	*21*	19				*Mahoney*	*Nattrass*	*Barker*	*Cassidy**	*Bird*	*Kennedy*	*Burns*	*Hudson*	*McGhee*	*Larnach*	*Barrowclough*	*Gowling*
								Ref: M Taylor	Both sides desperately need to win this four-pointer. The match had too much at stake to make it pretty. When Newcastle failed to withdraw 10 yards at a free-kick, Bonds bulldozed his way into it to make space. McDowell took aim and the ball flew off a defender and the post to Hales.											
27	H	BRISTOL CITY		19	L	1-2	1-1	Robson 13	Day	McDowell	Lampard	Bonds	Taylor T	Green	Devonshire	Robson	Cross	Brooking	Hales*	Taylor A
	11/2		19,934	*14*	19			*Mann 45, Royle 62*	*Shaw*	*Sweeney*	*Merrick*	*Gow*	*Rodgers*	*Hunter*	*Mann*	*Ritchie*	*Royle*	*Cormack*	*Whitehead*	
								Ref: C Thomas	West Ham paid the price for scoring first then falling back to protect their advantage. Derek Hales is suffering from flu and is pulled off to give Alan Taylor a chance to stretch the City defence. He is the only player on Lyall's books able to pose as a winger. The Hammers have no width.											
28	A	EVERTON		19	L	1-2	1-1	Hales 35	Ferguson	Bonds*	Lampard	Pike	Taylor T	Green	Devonshire	Robson	Cross	Brooking	Hales	McDowell
	18/2		*33,862*	*2*	19			*McKenzie 24, Thomas 60*	*Wood*	*Jones*	*Pejic*	*Lyons*	*Higgins*	*Ross*	*King*	*Dobson*	*Latchford**	*McKenzie*	*Thomas*	*Telfer*
								Ref: T Farley	Dave Thomas always seems to turn it on against West Ham. Once Billy Bonds limped off in the second half with a calf strain Hammers had no one capable of dealing with him or cutting out his crosses. Thomas' winner is his first goal for Everton. Ross missed a penalty for the Toffees.											
29	H	ARSENAL		19	D	2-2	0-2	Taylor A 48, Cross 89	Ferguson	McDowell*	Lampard	Curbishley	Taylor T	Green	Devonshire	Robson	Cross	Brooking	Taylor A	Pike
	25/2		31,675	*5*	20			*Macdonald 25, 28*	*Jennings*	*Rice*	*Nelson*	*Price*	*O'Leary*	*Young*	*Brady*	*Sunderland*	*Macdonald*	*Stapleton*	*Rix**	*Walford*
								Ref: R Crabb	Malcolm Macdonald's second goal sparks trouble in the crowd. Hammers' defence had seen the linesman's raised flag and foolishly not played to the whistle. Full-back Pat Rice also appeared to push Cross before crossing for Macdonald's first goal, a header that went in off a post.											
30	A	NOTT'M FOREST		19	L	0-2	0-0		Ferguson	McDowell	Lampard	Curbishley	Taylor T	Green*	Devonshire	Robson	Cross	Brooking	Hales	Holland
	4/3		*33,924*	*1*	20			*Needham 79, Robertson 81p*	*Shilton*	*Bowyer*	*Clark*	*O'Hare*	*Needham*	*Burns*	*O'Neill*	*Gemmill*	*Withe*	*Woodcock*	*Robertson*	
								Ref: K Hackett	Brian Clough admits that had Derek Hales not committed the miss of the century in the 69th minute, his table toppers would have been sunk. Reprieved, they steal the points through Needham's header and a twice-taken penalty after Trevor Brooking had handled O'Hare's cross.											
31	H	WOLVES		20	L	1-2	0-0	Hales 71	Ferguson	McDowell*	Lampard	Curbishley	Taylor T	Bonds	Devonshire	Holland	Cross	Brooking	Hales !	Otulakowski
	11/3		23,525	*17*	20			*Rafferty 50, Carr 60*	*Parkes*	*Palmer*	*Parkin !*	*Daley*	*Hazell*	*McAlle*	*Brazier*	*Carr*	*Richards*	*Rafferty*	*Patching**	*Daly*
								Ref: A Turvey	10 minutes from time Derek Parkin grabs Hales' shirt, Hales swings a punch, and both are sent off. McDowell and Cross both hit the bar in the first half, and Hammers pay the price when Bill Rafferty netted. He had signed from Carlisle and was thought to be on Lyall's wanted list.											

No	Date	Opponent	Att	Pos	Pts	Res	F-A	H-T	Scorers, Times, and Referees	1	2	3	4	5	6	7	8	9	10	11	subs used
32	A	QP RANGERS		20		L	0-1	0-1		Ferguson	McDowell	Lampard	Bonds	Taylor T	Curbishley	Devonshire	Holland	Cross	Brooking	Pike	
	14/3		*20,394*	*19*	20				*Cunningham 37*	*Parkes*	*Clement*	*Gillard*	*Hollins*	*Howe*	*Cunningham*	*Shanks*	*Busby*	*James**	*Bowles*	*Givens*	*McGee*
									Ref: C Maskell	Six weeks previously QPR had thrashed West Ham 6-1 in the Cup. This time the Hammers were unlucky. They were frustrated by Phil Parkes' save from Devonshire's chip. Tommy Cunningham headed in Leighton James' corner. QPR boss Frank Sibley: 'We played rubbish and won.'											
33	A	ASTON VILLA		20		L	**1-4**	1-2	Brooking 26 *[Mortimer 77]*	Ferguson	McDowell	Lampard	Curbishley	Taylor T	Bonds	Devonshire*	Holland	Cross	Brooking	Hales	**Martin**
	18/3		*28,275*	*10*	20				*Gregory 18, 80, Deehan 34,*	*Rimmer*	*Gidman*	*Smith*	*Phillips*	*McNaught*	*Mortimer*	*Gregory*	*Little*	*Deehan*	*Cowans*	*Carrodus*	
									Ref: D Nippard	It is clutching at straws to suggest this result was worse than West Ham deserved. Frank Lampard hit the bar, Trevor Brooking scored a classic goal, but their fate was sealed when Mortimer headed in Carrodus's corner. West Ham, Newcastle and Leicester are now adrift at the bottom.											
34	H	IPSWICH		20		W	**3-0**	0-0	Cross 51, 44, 59	Ferguson	Bonds	Lampard	Curbishley	Taylor T	Green	Pike	Holland	Cross	Brooking	Hales	
	24/3		23,867	*17*	22					*Cooper*	*Mills*	*Tibbott*	*Talbot*	*Hunter*	*Beattie*	*Osborne**	*Wark*	*Mariner*	*Turner*	*Woods*	*Lambert*
									Ref: H Robinson	'Our worst performance of the season,' complains Ipswich boss Bobby Robson, after emerging from a stormy session with his players. West Ham completed their second double of the season with a tabloid writer's dream headline: 'Hot Cross Fun.' Two headers and an angled shot.											
35	H	CHELSEA		19		W	3-1	0-1	Brooking 79, Green 88, Holland 89	Ferguson	Bonds	Lampard	Curbishley	Taylor T	Green	Pike	Holland	Cross	Brooking	Robson	
	25/3		24,987	*17*	24				*Garner 10*	*Phillips*	*Locke*	*Harris*	*Britton*	*Hay*	*Wicks*	*Finnieston*	*Swain*	*Garner**	*Lewington*	*Walker*	*Langley*
									Ref: J Bent	On 55 minutes Phillips is kicked in the face by Tommy Taylor and is replaced in goal by Langley, leaving Chelsea with 10 men. The incident sparks crowd trouble. Of the game's 36 fouls, 22 were committed by West Ham. Brooking scored from a corner. Bill Green headed the winner.											
36	A	BIRMINGHAM		19		L	0-3	0-2		Ferguson	Bonds	Lampard	Curbishley	Taylor T	Green*	Pike	Holland	Cross	Brooking	Robson	Hales
	28/3		*23,554*	*13*	24				*Francis 31, 43p, Bertschin 89*	*Montgomery*	*Calderwood*	*Pendrey*	*Towers*	*Gallagher*	*Howard*	*Page*	*Francis*	*Bertschin*	*Hibbitt*	*Fox*	
									Ref: S Bates	For half an hour Hammers looked the more positive. But Trevor Francis knocked the ball in after Hibbitt had hit the bar and from that moment West Ham were not at the races. Bobby Ferguson brought down Bertschin for the penalty. Hales has been missing rather than scoring recently.											
37	H	COVENTRY		19		W	2-1	1-0	Taylor T 20, Holland 60	Ferguson	Bonds	Lampard	Curbishley	Taylor T	Green	Pike*	Holland	Hales	Brooking	Robson	Martin
	1/4		**19,260**	*6*	26				*McDonald 62*	*Blyth*	*Roberts*	*McDonald*	*Yorath*	*Holton*	*Osgood*	*Beck*	*Wallace*	*Thompson**	*Powell*	*Hutchison*	*Coop*
									Ref: R Challis	On this evidence, West Ham want First Division survival more than Coventry want a place in the UEFA Cup. 28-year-old Brooking does not relish life in Division 2 and he plays a stormer, supplying the corner for Tommy Taylor's header and the pass from which Holland netted No 2.											
38	A	LEEDS		18		W	2-1	1-1	Martin 44, Hales 53	Ferguson	Bonds	Brush	Martin	Taylor T	Green	Curbishley	Holland	Hales	Brooking	Robson	
	8/4		*22,953*	*7*	28				*Graham 25*	*Harvey*	*Reaney*	*Gray F*	*Flynn*	*Hart*	*Madeley*	*Lorimer*	*Gray E*	*Currie*	*Harris*	*Graham*	
									Ref: K Walmsley	It was 48 years ago that West Ham last won here in Division 1. Alvin Martin, in his first full game, marks Currie out of the match and heads a fine goal. Hales beats the offside trap for the winner. Peter Lorimer misses a 77th-minute penalty, awarded after Currie had run into Robson.											
39	H	DERBY		17		W	**3-0**	2-0	Robson 3, 71, Cross 23	Ferguson	Lampard	Brush	Martin	Taylor T	Green	Curbishley*	Holland	Cross	Brooking	Robson	Otulakowski
	15/4		25,424	*14*	30					*Middleton*	*Langan*	*Buckley*	*Rioch*	*McFarland*	*Todd*	*Powell**	*Daly*	*Masson*	*George*	*Nish*	*Bartlett*
									Ref: T Reynolds	The Indian Summer to West Ham's season has brought five wins out of six and probable survival. Robson played despite a severely bruised instep and is rewarded with his first goals in two months. Cross also scored on his return from suspension. Pat Holland was man of the match.											
40	A	MANCHESTER U		19		L	0-3	0-0		Ferguson	Bonds	Lampard	Martin*	Taylor T	Green	Curbishley	Holland	Cross	Brooking	Robson	Brush
	22/4		***54,089***	*10*	30				*Grimes 68p, McIlroy 75, Pearson 77*	*Stepney*	*Albiston*	*Houston*	*McIlroy*	*McQueen*	*Buchan*	*Coppell*	*Jordan*	*Pearson*	*Grimes*	*Greenhoff B*	
									Ref: T Mills	Alvin Martin's honeymoon is over. Two second-half blunders result in two penalties for Man U. First he handles under pressure from Jordan. Although Ferguson saves Pearson's spot-kick, he then drags Pearson down. But when Martin topples Jordan in the box, the ref looks away.											
41	A	MIDDLESBROUGH				W	2-1	1-1	Cross 42, 80	Ferguson	Bonds	Lampard	Martin	Taylor T	Green	Curbishley	Holland	Cross	Brooking	Robson	
	25/4		***13,247***		32				*Johnston 17*	*Brown*	*Craggs*	*Bailey**	*Johnston*	*Boam*	*Ramage*	*Mills*	*Cummins*	*Ashcroft*	*McAndrew*	*Armstrong*	*Hickton*
									Ref: D Richardson	17-year-old Australian Craig Johnston gives Boro a dream start, but Frank Lampard's chip presents David Cross with an easy equaliser. The winner came from a goalmouth scramble. Keeper David Brown failed to gather a corner cleanly and Cross poked the ball over the goal-line.											
42	H	LIVERPOOL		20		L	0-2	0-1		Ferguson	Bonds	Lampard	Martin	Taylor T*	Green	Curbishley	Holland	Cross	Brooking	Robson	
	29/4		**37,448**	*3*	32				*McDermott 39, Fairclough 67*	*Clemence*	*Neal*	*Hansen*	*Thompson*	*Kennedy*	*Hughes*	*Dalglish*	*Case*	*Fairclough*	*McDermott*	*Souness*	
	Home	Away							Ref: D Reeves	Even if West Ham win they are not safe, since other strugglers have games to play. Hammers wasted early half-chances, and once Case had set up McDermott's goal Liverpool dominated. Wolves must lose their last two games to go down instead, but on 2 May Wolves beat Aston Villa.											
Average	25,655	28,903																			

LEAGUE DIVISION 1 (CUP-TIES) Manager: John Lyall SEASON 1977-78

League Cup					F-A	H-T	Scorers, Times, and Referees	1	2	3	4	5	6	7	8	9	10	11	12 sub used
2	A	NOTT'M FOREST	21	L	0-5	0-2	*[Woodcock 63, Withe 80]*	Day	Lampard	Brush*	Pike	Green	Lock	Taylor A	Robson	Radford	Curbishley	Devonshire	Otulakowski
	30/8	*18,224*	*1*				*O'Neill 10, Bowyer 26, 87,*	*Middleton*	*Anderson*	*Clark*	*McGovern*	*Lloyd*	*Burns*	*O'Neill*	*Bowyer*	*Withe*	*Woodcock*	*Robertson*	
							Ref: D Turner	Clough's Forest inflict West Ham's worst ever defeat in the League Cup. John Robertson handed out the kind of punishment that Lampard will have nightmares over. An early booking was the least of Lampard's worries. Robson and Alan Taylor had missed early chances for Hammers.											

FA Cup																			
3	H	WATFORD	19	W	1-0	0-0	Robson 80	Ferguson	McDowell	Lampard	Bonds	Taylor T	Curbishley*	Devonshire	Robson	Cross	Brooking	Hales	Pike
	7/1	36,745	*4:1*					*Rankin*	*Geidmintis*	*Pritchett*	*Booth*	*Bolton*	*Garner*	*Downes**	*Blissett*	*Jenkins*	*Joslyn*	*Mayes*	*Pollard*
							Ref: J Hunting	BBC planned to show this game on Saturday night, then decided against. Viewers missed a thriller. Elton John's money and Graham Taylor's know-how are building a fine team. Blissett missed early chances. West Ham only won after they started pumping high balls over the defence.											
4	H	QP RANGERS	19	D	1-1	1-0	Bonds 43	Ferguson	McDowell	Lampard	Bonds	Taylor T	Curbishley	Devonshire	Robson	Cross	Brooking	Hales	
	28/1	35,566	*20*				*Howe 75*	*Parkes*	*Clement*	*Gillard*	*Hollins*	*Howe*	*Abbott*	*Shanks*	*Busby*	*James*	*Bowles*	*Givens*	
							Ref: P Reeves	Torrential rain threatens to postpone the match and in Stan Bowles' opinion it should have. The turning point was Phil Parkes' splendid save from Lampard's thunderbolt, when West Ham were already leading 1-0. QPR capitalised when Ernie Howe headed in John Hollins' free-kick.											
4R	A	QP RANGERS	19	L	1-6	1-1	Robson 4 *[Bowles 70p, James 83]*	Ferguson	McDowell	Lampard	Bonds	Taylor T	Curbishley	Devonshire*	Robson	Cross	Holland	Hales	Taylor A
	31/1	*24,057*	*20*				*Givens 38, Hollins 50, Busby 54, 62,*	*Parkes*	*Clement*	*Gillard*	*Hollins*	*Howe*	*Abbott*	*Shanks*	*Busby*	*James*	*Bowles*	*Givens*	
							Ref: P Reeves	Three pitch inspections are necessary. Without Brooking, nursing his ankle, and with Tommy Taylor having a stinker, Hammers are pulverised. Four QPR goals came from set-pieces. Givens equalised Robson's opener from Hollins' free-kick. Tommy Taylor handled for Bowles' penalty.											

		Home					Away					
	P	W	D	L	F	A	W	D	L	F	A	Pts
1 Nott'm Forest	42	15	6	0	37	8	10	8	3	32	16	64
2 Liverpool	42	15	4	2	37	11	9	5	7	28	23	57
3 Everton	42	14	4	3	47	22	8	7	6	29	23	55
4 Manchester C	42	14	4	3	46	21	6	8	7	28	30	52
5 Arsenal	42	14	5	2	38	12	7	5	9	22	25	52
6 West Brom	42	13	5	3	35	18	5	9	7	27	35	50
7 Coventry	42	13	5	3	48	23	5	7	9	27	39	48
8 Aston Villa	42	11	4	6	33	18	7	6	8	24	24	46
9 Leeds	42	12	4	5	39	21	6	6	9	24	32	46
10 Manchester U	42	9	6	6	32	23	7	4	10	35	40	42
11 Birmingham	42	8	5	8	32	30	8	4	9	23	30	41
12 Derby	42	10	7	4	37	24	4	6	11	17	35	41
13 Norwich	42	10	8	3	28	20	1	10	10	24	46	40
14 Middlesbro	42	8	8	5	25	19	4	7	10	17	35	39
15 Wolves	42	7	8	6	30	27	5	4	12	21	37	36
16 Chelsea	42	7	11	3	28	20	4	3	14	18	49	36
17 Bristol City	42	9	6	6	37	26	2	7	12	12	27	35
18 Ipswich	42	10	5	6	32	24	1	8	12	15	37	35
19 QP Rangers	42	8	8	5	27	26	1	7	13	20	38	33
20 WEST HAM	42	8	6	7	31	28	4	2	15	21	41	32
21 Newcastle	42	4	6	11	26	37	2	4	15	16	41	22
22 Leicester	42	4	7	10	16	32	1	5	15	10	38	22
	924	223	132	107	741	490	107	132	223	490	741	924

Odds & ends

Double wins: (2) Newcastle, Ipswich.
Double losses: (3), Manchester C, Bristol C, Liverpool.

Won from behind: (4) Newcastle (a), Chelsea (h), Leeds (a), Midd'bro (a).
Lost from in front: (3) Bristol C (h&a), QPR FAC (a).

High spots: Five league wins out of six in March and April to stand a fair chance of avoiding relegation.

Low spots: Relegation.
Having to wait three days after the last match, v Liverpool, to have that fate confirmed.
Failing to beat any of the top six sides in the league.
Taking just one point from seven games in February and March.
Suffering their heaviest ever defeats in League Cup and FA Cup in the same season (by Forest and QPR respectively).

Hammer of the Year: Trevor Brooking.
Ever-presents: (0).
Hat-tricks: (1) David Cross.
Leading scorer: (11) Bryan Robson.

	Appearances						Goals			
	Lge	*Sub*	LC	*Sub*	FAC	*Sub*	**Lge**	LC	FAC	**Tot**
Bonds, Billy	**29**				3		**1**		1	**2**
Brooking, Trevor	**37**				2		**4**			**4**
Brush, Paul	**23**	*1*	1							
Cross, David	**21**				3		**9**			**9**
Curbishley, Alan	**31**	*1*	1		3		**1**			**1**
Day, Mervyn	**23**		1							
Devonshire, Alan	**32**	*2*	1		3		**3**			**3**
Ferguson, Bobby	**19**				3					
Green, Bill	**13**		1				**1**			**1**
Hales, Derek	**23**	*1*			3		**10**			**10**
Holland, Pat	**18**	*3*			1		**3**			**3**
Jennings, Billy	**2**						**1**			**1**
Lampard, Frank	**40**		1		3					
Lock, Kevin	**6**		1				**1**			**1**
Martin, Alvin	**5**	*2*					**1**			**1**
McDowell, John	**12**	*2*			3		**1**			**1**
McGiven, Mick	**4**									
Otulakowski, Anton		*5*								
Pike, Geoff	**25**	*3*	1			*1*	**2**			**2**
Radford, John	**10**		1							
Robson, Bryan	**37**		1		3		**9**		2	**11**
Taylor, Alan	**10**	*1*	1			*1*	**2**			**2**
Taylor, Tommy	**42**				3		**2**			**2**
(own-goals)							**1**			**1**
23 players used	**462**	*21*	**11**		**33**	*2*	**52**		**3**	**55**

No	Date		Att	Pos	Pt	F-A	H-T	Scorers, Times, and Referees	1	2	3	4	5	6	7	8	9	10	11	12 sub used
1	H	NOTTS CO			W	5-2	4-0	Cross 9, 20, 59, Blockley 11 (og),	Ferguson	Lampard	Brush	Holland	Taylor T	Bonds	Curbishley	Devonshire	Cross	Brooking	Robson	
	19/8		25,387		2			*McCulloch 61, 68* [Devonshire 16]	*McManus*	*Richards*	*O'Brien*	*Benjamin*	*Blockley*	*Stubbs*	*Carter*	*McCulloch*	*Hooks**	*Mann*	*Vinter*	*McVay*
								Ref: H Robinson	This astonishing match sees West Ham 4-0 up after 20 minutes. Frank Lampard made the first three goals with crosses or free-kicks, the most enjoyable of which saw Jeff Blockley bullet an own-goal. But when Ferguson started spilling crosses an unthinkable fightback looked possible.											
2	A	NEWCASTLE			W	3-0	1-0	Devonshire 6, Cross 60, Robson 71	Ferguson	Lampard	Brush	Holland	Taylor T	Bonds	Curbishley	Devonshire	Cross	Brooking*	Robson	Taylor A
	23/8		*27,233*		4				*Mahoney*	*Kelly*	*Barker*	*Cassidy*	*Bird*	*Blackley*	*Walker*	*Suggett*	*Pearson*	*Hibbitt*	*Connolly*	
								Ref: M Peck	Newcastle field six new players since they were relegated, but they are powerless to prevent Brooking's neat pass to Devonshire, who cuts inside two defenders to score. Brooking limped off after 28 minutes, and West Ham were grateful for their second goal, set up by Devonshire.											
3	A	CRYS PALACE		2	D	1-1	1-1	Taylor A 42	Ferguson	Lampard	Brush	Holland	Taylor T	Bonds	Curbishley	Devonshire	Cross	Taylor A	Robson	
	26/8		*32,611*	*6*	5			*Gilbert 45*	*Burridge*	*Hinshelwood*	*Sansom*	*Chatterton*	*Cannon*	*Gilbert*	*Nicholas*	*Murphy*	*Swindlehurst*	*Elwiss*	*Hilaire*	
								Ref: Ref: T Reynolds	This match is best remembered for Billy Gilbert's freak equaliser for Palace on the stroke of half-time. Hit from 35 yards, the ball dipped and swerved and completely bemused Ferguson. His captain, Bonds, exonerates him from blame. Stoke overtake West Ham to go top of the table.											
4	H	FULHAM		4	L	0-1	0-1		Ferguson	Lampard	Brush	Holland	Taylor T	Bonds	Curbishley	Pike	Cross	Taylor A*	Robson	McDowell
	2/9		25,778	*18*	5			*Margerrison 16*	*Peyton*	*Strong*	*Lock*	*Money*	*Banton*	*Gale*	*Bullivant*	*Davies*	*Mahoney*	*Margerrison*	*Evanson*	
								Ref: C Maskell	Minus Brooking and Devonshire, West Ham laboured. Fulham made ex-Hammer Kevin Lock skipper for the day. Evanson's long ball enabled John Margerrison to lob Ferguson, after which Fulham defended in depth. Bonds was pushed into midfield as West Ham grew desperate.											
5	A	BURNLEY		7	L	2-3	2-1	Cross 33, 35	Ferguson	Lampard	Brush	Holland	Taylor T	Bonds	Curbishley	Devonshire	Cross	Martin	Robson	
	9/9		*12,303*	*4*	5			*Brennan 37, Fletcher 50, Thomson 82*	*Stevenson*	*Scott*	*Brennan*	*Noble*	*Thomson*	*Rodaway*	*Cochrane*	*Hall*	*Fletcher*	*Kindon*	*Smith*	
								Ref: A Challinor	Lyall cannot explain how his team can look so good in the first half and so bad in the second. Both Robson and Martin hit the wood. Fletcher levelled with a blind-side goal that might have been averted, and Thomson hit the winner when Bonds and Ferguson left the ball to each other.											
6	H	BRISTOL ROV		4	W	2-0	0-0	Robson 59, Brooking 76	Ferguson	Lampard	Brush	Holland	Taylor T	Bonds	Curbishley	Devonshire	Cross !	Brooking	Robson	
	16/9		22,189	*11*	7				*Thomas*	*Pulis*	*Bater*	*Day*	*Taylor*	*Prince*	*Dennehy**	*Williams*	*Staniforth*	*Randall*	*Barry*	*Hendrie*
								Ref: R Toseland	Ironically, it was the 52nd-minute dismissal of David Cross that changed the course of the game. Cross had been fouling all afternoon, and his expulsion for lunging at Graham Day was inevitable. From that moment West Ham stopped tossing up high balls. Robson netted with a header.											
7	H	SHEFFIELD UTD		3	W	2-0	0-0	Robson 75p, 84p	Ferguson	Lampard*	Brush	Holland	Taylor T	Bonds	Curbishley	Devonshire	Jennings	Brooking	Robson	Pike
	23/9		24,361	*18*	9				*Conroy*	*Cutbush*	*Calvert*	*Kenworthy*	*Matthews*	*Keeley*	*Guy**	*Speight*	*Franks*	*Sabella*	*Hamson*	*Anderson*
								Ref: A Robinson	Two penalties seal the Blades' fate. The first was a result of Chris Calvert fisting out Lampard's effort; the second was given when Brooking's cross smacked against Tony Kenworthy at close range. Blades' boss Harry Haslam set out to defend, which negated Alex Sabella's skills.											
8	A	SUNDERLAND		6	L	1-2	0-1	Cross 59	Ferguson	McDowell	Brush	Holland	Taylor T	Bonds	Curbishley	Devonshire	Cross	Brooking	Robson	
	30/9		*23,676*	*5*	9			*Rowell 27p, 71*	*Siddall*	*Coady*	*Rostron*	*Docherty*	*Clarke*	*Elliott*	*Chisholm*	*Lee*	*Entwhistle*	*Brown*	*Rowell*	
								Ref: C Seel	A mysterious penalty set West Ham on the road to defeat. Brush was alleged to have hauled back Rowell, a decision which led to bookings for Robson and Tommy Taylor. Rowell netted himself, then scored a second with a mis-hit shot that trundled wide of the wrong-footed Ferguson.											
9	H	MILLWALL		4	W	3-0	1-0	Robson 35, 71, 75p	Ferguson	Lampard	Brush	Holland	Taylor T	Bonds	Curbishley	Devonshire	Cross	Brooking	Robson	
	7/10		22,000	*22*	11				*Cuff*	*Hamilton B**	*Gregory*	*Tagg*	*Kitchener*	*Gale*	*Donaldson*	*Seasman*	*Mitchell*	*Pearson*	*Walker*	*Cross*
								Ref: C White	Basement club Millwall have scored just one away goal, so this result goes to form. Devonshire revelled in the space afford by the Lions' obsession with tight-marking Brooking. Leaflets distributed before the game warned of crowd trouble; a police helicopter hovered overhead.											
10	A	OLDHAM		3	D	2-2	1-0	Robson 6, 47	Ferguson	Lampard	Brush	Holland	Taylor T	Bonds	Curbishley*	Devonshire	Cross	Brooking	Robson	McDowell
	14/10		*10,143*	*18*	12			*Taylor 69, 74*	*McDonnell*	*Wood*	*Blair*	*Bell*	*Hicks**	*Hurst*	*Valentine*	*Taylor*	*Young*	*Chapman*	*Gardner*	
								Ref: B Newsome	West Ham took their foot off the throttle after half-time. Brooking could have sealed the win but missed an inviting chance when Hammers were 2-0 ahead. But his miss fired up Oldham, who equalised through two goals from Steve Taylor, following a free-kick and a corner.											

No	Venue	Opponent	Att	Pos	Res	Score	HT	Scorers	1	2	3	4	5	6	7	8	9	10	11	12
11	H	STOKE		5	D	1-1	0-0	Brooking 85	Ferguson	McDowell	Brush	Holland	Taylor T	Bonds	Curbishley	Devonshire	Cross	Brooking	Robson	
21/10			27,859	*2*	13			*Richardson 89*	*Jones*	*Marsh*	*Scott*	*Kendall*	*Smith*	*Doyle*	*Dodd*	*Irvine*	*O'Callaghan*	*Crooks*	*Richardson*	
								Ref: T Bune	Alan Durban's Stoke look a capable team, though when Cross heads down for Brooking to slide a late goal it looked curtains. City are grateful to McDowell's even later error, hooking a clearance against Sammy Irvine to put Stoke in possession. O'Callaghan headed on to Richardson.											
12	A	BRIGHTON		4	W	2-1	2-1	Robson 27, 43	Day	McDowell	Brush	Holland	Taylor T	Bonds	Curbishley	Devonshire	Cross	Brooking	Robson	
28/10			*32,634*	*12*	15			*Sayer 39*	*Moseley*	*Tiler*	*Williams*	*Horton*	*Rollings**	*Lawrenson*	*Ryan*	*Ward*	*Maybank*	*Clark*	*O'Sullivan*	*Sayer*
								Ref: R Lewis	33-year-old Pop Robson has turned down an offer to return north as player-manager of Darlington. Paul Brush laid on both goals with left-wing crosses. Tommy Taylor sports a cut eye following a clash with Maybank. His defiance was typical of Hammers' battling back four.											
13	H	PRESTON		2	W	3-1	1-1	Lampard 19, Devonshire 64, Cross 89	Day	Lampard	Brush	Holland	Taylor T	Bonds	Curbishley	Devonshire	Cross	Brooking	Robson	
4/11			23,579	*21*	17			*Thomson 37*	*Tunks*	*McMahon*	*Cameron*	*Doyle*	*Baxter*	*O'Riordan*	*Coleman*	*Haslegrave*	*Robinson*	*Thomson*	*Bruce*	
								Ref: L Burden	Lyall is away scouting, dampening speculation that he is about to sell Brooking to Coventry. Bonds' continuing vendetta with Alex Bruce costs West Ham a goal. Bonds was out of position when Thomson fired in from 30 yards. In injury-time Taylor handled, but Thomson shot wide.											
14	A	NOTTS CO		4	L	0-1	0-0		Day	Lampard	Brush	Holland	Taylor T	Bonds	Curbishley	Devonshire	Cross	Brooking	Robson	
11/11			*11,002*	*11*	17			*O'Brien 81p*	*McManus*	*Richards*	*O'Brien*	*Benjamin*	*Stubbs*	*Mann*	*McCulloch*	*Masson*	*Hooks*	*Hunt*	*Vinter*	
								Ref: N Ashley	Notts Co are unbelievably negative, playing five men in defence even when at home. Had West Ham come to defend, there wouldn't have been a contest at all. County cannot believe their luck as Robson misses several chances and Brush topples Paul Hooks to concede a late penalty.											
15	H	CRYS PALACE		3	D	1-1	1-0	Bonds 31	Day	Lampard	Brush	Holland*	Taylor T	Bonds	Curbishley	Devonshire	Cross	Brooking	Robson	Taylor A
18/11			31,245	*1*	18			*Elwiss 75*	*Burridge*	*Fenwick*	*Sansom*	*Kember*	*Cannon*	*Gilbert*	*Nicholas*	*Murphy*	*Swindlehurst*	*Walsh*	*Hilaire**	*Elwiss*
								Ref: R Kirkpatrick	Leaders Palace have only lost once away. They trail to Bonds' goal for a long time until Murphy shoots. Day half-saves, but the ball comes off his arm to Elwiss. Day hangs his head. Five minutes from time Alan Taylor comes on in an attempt to inject width. But it is far too late.											
16	A	FULHAM		3	D	0-0	0-0		Day	Lampard	Brush	Holland	Taylor T	Bonds	Curbishley	Devonshire	Cross	Taylor A	Robson	
21/11			*26,556*	*4*	19				*Peyton*	*Evans*	*Strong*	*Lock*	*Money*	*Gale*	*Margerrison*	*Evanson*	*Guthrie*	*Beck*	*Greenaway*	
								Ref: M Baker	West Ham won on points, so to speak, with central defenders Bonds and Taylor giving Fulham barely a sniff at goal. But Bonds' booking – his fifth – for a foul on John Evanson will earn him a three-match ban. Trevor Brooking missed the game, having twisted an ankle in training.											
17	A	LEICESTER		3	W	2-1	1-0	Cross 20, 83	Day	Lampard	Brush	Holland	Taylor T	Bonds	McDowell	Devonshire	Cross	Taylor A	Robson	
25/11			*16,149*	*17*	21			*Christie 56*	*Wallington*	*Whitworth*	*Rofe*	*May*	*Williams*	*Kelly*	*Weller*	*Ridley*	*Christie*	*Henderson**	*Hughes*	*Goodwin*
								Ref: A Morrissey	Lyall admitted afterwards that Jock Wallace's Leicester had been hard done by. City pounded forward after Cross had swept in Alan Taylor's cross, though it took another Day fumble – dropping Weller's free-kick – to let in Christie. Cross's spectacular winner came out of the blue.											
18	H	CAMBRIDGE		3	W	5-0	1-0	Taylor A 3, Robson 69, 88, Bonds 86, [Curbishley 87]	Day	Lampard	Brush	Holland	Taylor T	Bonds	Curbishley	Devonshire	Cross	Taylor A	Robson	
2/12			21,379	*15*	23				*Webster*	*Corbin**	*Smith L*	*Stringer*	*Fallon*	*Leach*	*Christie*	*Spriggs*	*Garner*	*Finney*	*Biley*	*Murray*
								Ref: L Shapter	Bonds staged a 90-minute commercial for his coming testimonial against Spurs with this all-action display. He heads in Holland's corner and bows out for a three-match ban. Alan Taylor's diving header divided the teams for over an hour, during which Alan Biley wasted a free header.											
19	A	WREXHAM		3	L	3-4	1-2	Cross 26, Lampard 84, Robson 89	Day	Lampard	Brush	Holland	Taylor T	Martin	Curbishley	Devonshire	Cross	Taylor A	Robson	
9/12			*15,787*	*6*	23			*Lyons 1, 21p, 49 p, Hill 53*	*Davies*	*Jones J*	*Dwyer*	*Davis*	*Roberts J*	*Cegielski*	*Shinton*	*Sutton*	*McNeil**	*Lyons*	*Hill*	*Evans*
								Ref: K Hackett	A 34-second goal and two penalties. That sums up West Ham's misery at the Racecourse Ground. John Lyons was responsible for all three – netting the quick-fire opener from Bobby Shinton's pass, then netting twice from the spot after Devonshire fouled Shinton and Martin handled.											
20	H	CHARLTON		3	W	2-0	1-0	Robson 37, Cross 63	Day	Lampard	Brush	Holland*	Taylor T	McDowell	Curbishley	Devonshire	Cross	Taylor A	Robson	Pike
16/12			23,833	*11*	25				*Wood*	*Shaw*	*Campbell*	*Gritt*	*Shipperley*	*Berry*	*Brisley*	*Robinson**	*Flanagan*	*Madden*	*Peacock*	*Powell*
								Ref: M Sinclair	Pop Robson nets his 200th league goal – a sweet half-volley from 20 yards. It is his 17th goal of the season. Stand-in skipper Frank Lampard supplied the pass for David Cross to dive waist-high among the flying boots and nod the ball into the net via the keeper's body and the post.											
21	H	ORIENT		4	L	0-2	0-1		Day	Lampard	Brush	Pike	Taylor T	McDowell	Curbishley*	Devonshire	Cross	Taylor A	Robson	Jennings
26/12			29,220	*10*	25			*Mayo 17, Chiedozie 85*	*Jackson*	*Fisher*	*Roffey*	*Grealish*	*Gray N*	*Went*	*Kitchen*	*Moores*	*Mayo*	*Chiedozie*	*Coates**	*Banjo*
								Ref: C Downey	Upton Park's second highest gate of the season saw this Boxing Day upset. Without Bonds and Brooking, West Ham lacked bite and flair. Orient went ahead when Moores nodded the ball over and Joe Mayo tapped it in. Chiedozie's goal was special, running from the halfway line.											

No	Date		Att	Pos	Pt	F-A	H-T	Scorers, Times, and Referees	1	2	3	4	5	6	7	8	9	10	11	12 sub used
22	H	BLACKBURN		4	W	4-0	1-0	Robson 33, Taylor A 60, Cross 64,	Day	Lampard	Brush	Bonds	Martin	McDowell	Taylor A	Devonshire	Cross	Brooking	Robson	
	30/12		21,269	*21*	27			[Curtis 67 (og)]	*Butcher*	*Hird*	*Curtis*	*Metcalfe*	*Keeley*	*Round*	*Fowler*	*Radford*	*Craig**	*Garner*	*Birchenall*	*Morris*
								Ref: P Reeves	Brooking returns to spark three goals. Though they are next to bottom, over the years no team has won at the Boleyn in the league as frequently as Rovers, though they seldom looked likely to add to their 13 wins on this freezing afternoon. Curtis rubbed it in with his headed own-goal.											
23	A	BRISTOL ROV		4	W	1-0	1-0	Robson 34	Day	McDowell	Brush	Curbishley	Martin	Bonds	Taylor A	Devonshire	Cross	Brooking	Robson	
	20/1		*12,418*	*13*	29				*Thomas*	*Day*	*Bater*	*Harding*	*Taylor*	*Aitken*	*Emmanuel*	*Williams**	*White*	*Staniforth*	*Hendrie*	*Dennehy*
								Ref: T Reyolds	Rovers' second home defeat of the season is mostly down to Trevor Brooking, who treats the pitch as if it were his own. Off the pitch, the air is thick with transfer talk. Chelsea's centre-half Steve Wicks is said to be headed for Upton Park. If he comes, is that the end for Tommy Taylor?											
24	H	SUNDERLAND		4	D	3-3	1-2	Cross 22, 58, Robson 50	Day	McDowell	Brush	Curbishley	Taylor T	Bonds	Holland	Devonshire	Cross	Brooking	Robson*	Jennings
	10/2		24,998	*5*	30			*Lee 3, Rostron 35, 63*	*Siddall*	*Henderson*	*Gilbert*	*Arnott*	*Clarke*	*Elliott*	*Chisholm*	*Rostron*	*Entwhistle*	*Lee*	*Rowell*	
								Ref: R Hamil	A match of gladiatorial cruelty. Mervyn Day, Young Footballer of the Year in 1975, makes a hash of Sunderland's second goal and is jeered off the pitch. All this overshadowed Robson's volley, his 20th goal of the season, and Lee's bad back-pass that let in Cross for Hammers' third.											
25	H	OLDHAM		4	W	3-0	1-0	Holland 21, Martin 59, Robson 83	**Parkes**	McDowell	Brush	Curbishley	Martin	Bonds	Holland	Devonshire	Cross	Brooking	Robson	
	24/2		26,052	*19*	32				*McDonnell*	*Wood*	*Blair*	*Bell*	*Hicks**	*Hurst*	*Keegan*	*Halom*	*Young*	*Chapman*	*Gardner*	*Heaton*
								Ref: R Challis	Day is finished. Phil Parkes has signed from QPR for a world record £565,000. He is an instant hit with the Upton park crowd, saving Alan Young's header with aplomb. There is thankfully no animosity between Day and his successor, who both shake hands warmly before kick-off.											
26	A	LUTON		3	W	4-1	1-0	Cross 6, 88, Devonshire 60, Robson 89	Parkes	McDowell	Brush	Curbishley	Martin	Bonds	Holland	Devonshire	Cross	Brooking	Robson	
	26/2		*14,205*	*10*	34			*Turner 75*	*Findlay*	*Stephens*	*Aizlewood*	*West*	*Turner C*	*Price*	*Silkman*	*Carr*	*Taylor*	*Hatton*	*Hill*	
								Ref: D Civil	West Ham's early goal, deflected in off the bar, sparked a sustained spell of Luton pressure. Hatton headed against Phil Parkes' crossbar. A second Hammers goal was followed soon after by Turner's header. Two late clinchers take West Ham above Crystal Palace on goal-difference.											
27	A	STOKE		4	L	0-2	0-1		Parkes	McDowell	Brush	Curbishley	Martin	Bonds	Holland	Devonshire	Cross	Brooking	Robson	
	3/3		*24,912*	*1*	34			*Doyle 9, Randall 85*	*Jones*	*Dodd*	*Scott*	*Kendall*	*Smith*	*Doyle*	*Randall*	*Irvine*	*O'Callaghan*	*Crooks*	*Richardson*	
								Ref: J Bray	On the way to the stadium the windscreen of the team coach shattered, showering glass over all those seated near the front, and especially Phil Parkes. He is lucky to escape serious lacerations. In pouring rain Mike Doyle heads Stoke in front, after which Hammers look impotent.											
28	H	BRIGHTON		5	D	0-0	0-0		Parkes	Lampard	Brush	Curbishley	Martin	Bonds	Holland	Devonshire	Cross	McDowell	Robson	
	10/3		35,802	*1*	35				*Steele*	*Cattlin*	*Williams*	*Horton*	*Rollings*	*Lawrenson*	*Ryan*	*Ward**	*Maybank*	*Clark*	*O'Sullivan*	*Poskett*
								Ref: D Hutchinson	Alan Mullery's Brighton set up an eight-man defensive barricade to face a Hammers team depleted by the late withdrawal of flu-stricken Trevor Brooking. Paul Clark had been designated to mark him. Now he had other duties to perform, including being booked for time-wasting.											
29	A	PRESTON		5	D	0-0	0-0		Parkes	Lampard	Brush	McDowell	Martin	Bonds	Holland	Devonshire	Cross	Brooking	Robson	
	17/3		*15,376*	*12*	36				*Tunks*	*Taylor*	*Cameron*	*Doyle**	*Baxter*	*O'Riordan*	*Coleman*	*Haslegrave*	*Elliott*	*Potts*	*Bruce*	*Wilson*
								Ref: M Peck	This match was billed as the 'High Noon' shoot-out between Division 2's top scorers, Alex Bruce and Pop Robson. In the event it was a dreary match with hardly a shot fired in anger at either end. Preston boss Nobby Stiles was diplomatic enough to say that West Ham were going up.											
30	H	NEWCASTLE		5	W	5-0	4-0	Devonshire 20, Robson 22, Lamp'rd 34,	Parkes	Lampard	Brush	McDowell	Martin	Bonds	Holland	Devonshire	Cross	Brooking*	Robson	Pike
	24/3		24,650	*16*	38			[McDowell 37, 50]	*Hardwick*	*Brownlie*	*Mitchell*	*Martin*	*Bird*	*Nattrass*	*Shoulder*	*Walker**	*Withe*	*Hibbitt*	*Connolly*	*Wharton*
								Ref: D Biddle	Just before half-time Brooking limps off with a twisted ankle. But by then the damage had been done. Oddly, only one of the four goals already scored was manufactured by Brooking. McDowell scored his first 'double' for the Hammers. This game was shown on ITV's *The Big Match*.											
31	H	LEICESTER		5	D	1-1	0-0	Robson 58	Parkes	Lampard	Brush	McDowell*	Martin	Bonds	Holland	Devonshire	Cross	Pike	Robson B	Curbishley
	31/3		23,992	*12*	39			*Henderson 51*	*Wallington*	*Goodwin*	*Rofe*	*Williams*	*May*	*O'Neill*	*Peake*	*Kelly*	*Henderson*	*Buchanan**	*Smith*	*Ridley*
								Ref: L Shapter	Jock Wallace's young Leicester team go in front when Henderson eludes Bonds and heads past Parkes. Robson levelled, heading in a cross from Devonshire. Near the end a post denied Devonshire the winner. After the game Anton Otulakowski was transferred to Southend United.											

No	Venue	Opponent / Date	Att	Pos	Pts	F-A	H-T	Scorers, Times, Referees	1	2	3	4	5	6	7	8	9	10	11	12
32	A	SHEFFIELD UTD		5	L	0-3	0-1		Parkes	Lampard	Brush	McDowell	Martin	Bonds	Holland	Devonshire	Cross	Pike	Robson	
		2/4	*17,720*	*18*	39			*Finnieston 42, Anderson 46, 59*	*Conroy*	*Speight*	*Tibbott*	*Kenworthy*	*MacPhail*	*Matthews*	*Anderson*	*Rioch*	*Finnieston*	*Sabella*	*Hamson*	
								Ref: J Hough	Those who say West Ham are a one-man team find support in this limp showing. Brooking's ankle keeps him out, and no one else provides any spark. Blades' Argentine, Alex Sabella, rules imperiously over the pitch. Steve Finnieston headed in at the near post from Matthews' corner.											
33	A	CAMBRIDGE		5	D	0-0	0-0		Parkes	Lampard*	Brush	Bonds	Martin	Taylor T	Holland	Devonshire	Cross	McDowell	Robson	Pike
		7/4	*11,406*	*12*	40				*Webster*	*Graham*	*Smith L*	*Stringer*	*Fallon*	*Murray*	*Christie**	*Spriggs*	*Buckley*	*Finney*	*Biley*	*Garner*
								Ref: A Jenkins	Cambridge are the division's draw specialists. This is their 10th at home. The home side welcome their biggest ever league crowd, but the game does not deserve them. Hammers came nearest when Robson's header came back off the bar and bounced to the feet of keeper Webster											
34	H	LUTON		5	W	1-0	0-0	Carr 65 (og)	Parkes	McDowell	Brush	Bonds	Martin	Taylor T	Holland	Devonshire	**Morgan**	Pike	Robson	
		9/4	25,498	*6*	42				*Findlay*	*Stephens*	*Aizlewood*	*Donaghy*	*P-Masters*	*Carr*	*Hill*	*West*	*Stein*	*Hatton*	*Moss**	*Taylor*
								Ref: D Reeves	Cross's twisted ankle permits a debut for Nicky Morgan, who was told he was playing one hour before kick-off. The points were won when Pike's low cross was turned in by David Carr. Luton boss David Pleat was angry that McDowell's 'foul' on David Moss wasn't a penalty.											
35	A	ORIENT		5	W	2-0	1-0	Holland 5, Pike 89	Parkes	McDowell	Brush	Bonds	Martin	Taylor T	Holland	Devonshire	Cross	Pike	Robson	
		14/4	*17,517*	*9*	44				*Jackson*	*Hughton*	*Roffey*	*Grealish*	*Gray N*	*Went*	*Chiedozie*	*Moores*	*Mayo**	*Whittle*	*Coates*	*Clarke*
								Ref: R Lewis	Pike's spectacular goal was missed by those who left early. He sprinted 25 yards to fire an explosive shot from a similar range past Jackson. Holland would have been forgiven a sigh, for he had scored a slick goal himself, from a tight angle. Now the headlines would belong to Pike.											
36	H	CARDIFF		5	D	1-1	1-0	Holland 6	Parkes	McDowell	Brush	Bonds	Martin	Taylor T	Holland	Devonshire	Cross	Pike	Robson	
		16/4	29,058	*19*	45			*Bishop 79*	*Healey*	*Jones*	*Sullivan*	*Campbell*	*Roberts*	*Dwyer*	*Bishop*	*Evans*	*Moore*	*Stevens*	*Buchanan*	
								Ref: A Glasson	Both teams are fighting desperate battles, albeit at either end of the division. Holland's brave header might have clinched the points, but Ray Bishop's volley – one of the best goals seen at the Boleyn all season – means both clubs are likely to stay in the Second Division next season.											
37	A	CHARLTON		5	D	0-0	0-0		Parkes	McDowell	Brush	Bonds	Martin	Taylor T	Holland	Devonshire	Cross	Pike	Jennings*	Lampard
		21/4	*22,816*	*17*	46				*Johns*	*Shaw*	*Campbell*	*Tydeman*	*Berry*	*Madden*	*Powell*	*Robinson*	*Gritt*	*Peacock*	*Churchouse**	*Brisley*
								Ref: M Sinclair	Charlton's biggest gate of the season. Robson is out with a groin strain. Billy Jennings is recalled but pulls a hamstring after just 13 minutes. Devonshire's 'goal' was disallowed because Jennings was lying injured in an offside position. Parkes keeps his eighth clean sheet in 13 games.											
38	H	BURNLEY		5	W	3-1	2-1	Bonds 6, Pike 10, Robson 53	Parkes	McDowell	Brush	Bonds	Martin	Taylor T	Holland	Devonshire	Cross	Pike	Robson	
		24/4	24,139	*7*	48			*Noble 1*	*Stevenson*	*Scott*	*Brennan*	*Noble*	*Thomson*	*Rodaway*	*Jakub**	*Ingham*	*Robinson*	*Morley*	*James*	*Hall*
								Ref: C Thomas	Referee Clive Thomas says later that it is a pleasure to officiate at games like this. Noble headed in Morley's cross in the first minute. Cross's low centre was missed by Robson but not by Bonds. Pike's shot goes in off Cross's back. Pike wants Cross to claim it but is not permitted to.											
39	H	WREXHAM		5	D	1-1	1-0	Bonds 28	Parkes	McDowell	Brush	Bonds	Martin	Taylor T	Holland	Devonshire	Cross	Pike*	Robson	**Lansdowne**
		28/4	28,865	*17*	49			*Shinton 88*	*Davies !*	*Cegielski*	*Dwyer*	*Jones J*	*Roberts J*	*Giles*	*Shinton*	*Sutton*	*McNeil*	*Lyons**	*Fox*	*Burton*
								Ref: K Baker	Drama as Bonds gives West Ham the lead. A West Ham player clearly handled moments before, and was gracious (or foolish) enough to admit it later. Dai Davies man-handled the referee and was sent off. 10-man Wrexham felt justice was done when Shinton headed a late equaliser.											
40	A	BLACKBURN		5	L	0-1	0-0		Parkes	Lampard	Brush	Bonds	Martin	Taylor T	Holland	Devonshire	Cross	McDowell*	Robson	Taylor A
		5/5	*7,585*	*21*	49			*McKenzie 49*	*Butcher*	*Rathbone*	*Bailey*	*Garner*	*Round*	*Fazackerley*	*Brotherston*	*Fowler*	*Craig*	*McKenzie*	*Aston*	
								Ref: K Redfern	Much-travelled Duncan McKenzie blazes a shot from 30 yards to finally scupper Hammers' promotion hopes. To make matters worse, Rovers are next to bottom and will finish bottom. Alan Devonshire is voted Hammer of the Year, yet he had wasted the best chance of the match.											
41	A	CARDIFF		5	D	0-0	0-0		Parkes	Lampard	Brush	Bonds	Martin	Taylor T	Holland	Devonshire	Cross	McDowell*	Morgan	**Brignull**
		11/5	*13,140*	*9*	50				*Healey*	*Jones*	*Sullivan*	*Campbell*	*Roberts*	*Dwyer*	*Grapes*	*Evans*	*Moore*	*Stevens*	*Buchanan*	
								Ref: T Spencer	Cardiff's unbeaten run is extended to 10 games. Afterwards, Pat Holland, in the bath, unknowingly poured industrial cleaning fluid down his throat. The club doctor made him drink milk and salt water to try to rinse him out, but Holland had to be rushed to hospital with a police escort.											
42	A	MILLWALL			L	1-2	1-0	Robson 12	Parkes	Lampard	Brush	Bonds	Martin	Taylor T	Holland	Devonshire	Cross	Brooking	Robson	
		14/5	*11,917*		50			*Mehmet 66, Chatterton 81*	*Cuff*	*Donaldson*	*Gregory**	*Chambers*	*Kitchener*	*Coleman*	*Towner*	*Seasman*	*Tagg*	*Walker*	*Chatterton*	*Mehmet*
		Home / Average 25,779	Away / 17,946					Ref: White	Millwall have two games to play after this, so relegation is not yet confirmed. West Ham, on the other hand, have nothing to play for. Brooking returns for his first match in six weeks. Pop Robson's goal is his 24th in the league and his last for West Ham. He shortly signs for Sunderland.											

League Cup					F-A	H-T	Scorers Times, and Referees,	1	2	3	4	5	6	7	8	9	10	11	12 sub used
2	H	SWINDON	2	L	1-2	0-0	Robson 80	Ferguson	Lampard	Brush	Holland	Taylor T	Bonds	Curbishley	Devonshire	Cross	Taylor A*	Robson B	Pike
30/8		19,672	*3:8*				*Miller 58, Guthrie 61*	*Ogden*	*McLaughlin*	*Ford*	*McHale*	*Aizlewood*	*Stroud*	*Miller*	*Carter*	*Guthrie**	*Bates*	*Williams*	*Kamara*
							Ref: M Taylor	West Ham have only themselves to blame for losing to Bobby Smith's 3rd Division side. Alan Taylor's miss was so bad he was pulled off immediately. In the 73rd minute Andy Ford handled Geoff Pike's effort on the goal-line, but David Cross squandered the ensuing penalty.											

FA Cup																			
3	A	NEWPORT	4	L	1-2	1-1	Robson 21	Day	Lampard	Brush	Bonds	Martin	McDowell	Taylor A	Devonshire	Cross	Brooking	Robson B	
9/1		*14,124*	*4:8*				*Goddard 14, Woods 81*	*Plumley*	*Walden*	*Byrne*	*Thompson*	*Davies*	*Bruton*	*Oakes*	*Lowndes*	*Goddard*	*Woods*	*Vaughan*	
							Ref: J Worrall	When Robson equalised – a fantastic effort from 30 yards – the money should have been on West Ham. Howard Goddard's glancing header had put Newport in front, and they regained the lead when Day failed to cut out Goddard's cross, leaving Eddie Woods to head a simple goal.											

		Home					Away					
	P	W	D	L	F	A	W	D	L	F	A	Pts
1 Crys Palace	42	12	7	2	30	11	7	12	2	21	13	57
2 Brighton	42	16	3	2	44	11	7	7	7	28	28	56
3 Stoke	42	11	7	3	35	15	9	9	3	23	16	56
4 Sunderland	42	13	3	5	39	19	9	8	4	31	25	55
5 WEST HAM	42	12	7	2	46	15	6	7	8	24	24	50
6 Notts Co	42	8	10	3	23	15	6	6	9	25	45	44
7 Preston	42	7	11	3	36	23	5	7	9	23	34	42
8 Newcastle	42	13	3	5	35	24	4	5	12	16	31	42
9 Cardiff	42	12	5	4	34	23	4	5	12	22	47	42
10 Fulham	42	10	7	4	35	19	3	8	10	15	28	41
11 Orient	42	11	5	5	32	18	4	5	12	19	33	40
12 Cambridge	42	7	10	4	22	15	5	6	10	22	37	40
13 Burnley	42	11	6	4	31	22	3	6	12	20	40	40
14 Oldham	42	10	7	4	36	23	3	6	12	16	38	39
15 Wrexham	42	10	6	5	31	16	2	8	11	14	26	38
16 Bristol Rov	42	10	6	5	34	23	4	4	13	14	37	38
17 Leicester	42	7	8	6	28	23	3	9	9	15	29	37
18 Luton	42	11	5	5	46	24	2	5	14	14	33	36
19 Charlton	42	6	8	7	28	28	5	5	11	32	41	35
20 Sheffield Utd	42	9	6	6	34	24	2	6	13	18	45	34
21 Millwall	42	7	4	10	22	29	4	6	11	20	32	32
22 Blackburn	42	5	8	8	24	29	5	2	14	17	43	30
	924	218	142	102	725	449	102	142	218	449	725	924

Odds & ends

Double wins: (3) Newcastle, Bristol R, Luton.
Double losses: (0).

Won from behind: (1) Burnley (h).
Lost from in front: (2) Burnley (a), Millwall (a).

High spots: Winning first two league matches.
Four wins and a draw from five matches from 30 December.

Low spots: Slowly slipping out of the promotion race, and failing to win any of the last four games.
Losing to Third Division Swindon in League Cup and, which was worse, to Fourth Division Newport in FA Cup.

Hammer of the Year: Alan Devonshire.
Ever-presents: (1) Paul Brush.
Hat-tricks: (2) David Cross (1), Bryan Robson (1).
Leading scorer: (26) Bryan Robson.

	Appearances						Goals			
	Lge	*Sub*	LC	*Sub*	FAC	*Sub*	Lge	LC	FAC	Tot
Bonds, Billy	**39**		1		1		**4**			**4**
Brignull, Phil	**0**	*1*								
Brooking, Trevor	**21**				1		**2**			**2**
Brush, Paul	**42**		1		1					
Cross, David	**40**		1		1		**18**			**18**
Curbishley, Alan	**26**	*1*	1				**1**			**1**
Day, Mervyn	**13**				1					
Devonshire, Alan	**41**		1		1		**5**			**5**
Ferguson, Bobby	**11**		1							
Holland, Pat	**39**		1				**3**			**3**
Jennings, Billy	**2**	*2*								
Lampard, Frank	**28**	*1*	1		1		**3**			**3**
Lansdowne, Billy	**0**	*1*								
Martin, Alvin	**22**				1		**1**			**1**
McDowell, John	**26**	*2*			1		**2**			**2**
Morgan, Nicky	**2**									
Parkes, Phil	**18**									
Pike, Geoff	**10**	*4*		*1*			**1**			**1**
Robson, Bryan	**40**		1		1		**24**	1	1	**26**
Taylor, Alan	**10**	*3*	1		1		**3**			**3**
Taylor, Tommy	**32**		1							
(own-goals)							**3**			**3**
21 players used	**462**	***15***	**11**	***1***	**11**		**70**	**1**	**1**	**72**

No	Date	Att	Pos	Pt	F-A	H-T	Scorers, Times, and Referees	1	2	3	4	5	6	7	8	9	10	11	12 sub used
1	A WREXHAM			L	0-1	0-0		Parkes	Lampard	Brush	Pike	Martin	Bonds	Holland	Devonshire	Cross	Brooking	**Pearson**	
	18/8	*13,036*		0			*Vinter 60*	*Niedzwiecki*	*Jones J*	*Dwyer*	*Davis*	*Roberts J**	*Giles*	*Sutton*	*Vinter*	*McNeil*	*Whittle*	*Cartwright*	*Fox*
							Ref: D Clarke	Pop Robson has gone for £400,000; Stuart Pearson, with 15 England caps, arrives from Man U for £220,000. Hammers lost at the Racecourse Ground 3-4 last season, so it is becoming an unhappy venue. Parkes and Bonds get in a tizzy over a throw-out and Mick Vinter nips in to score.											
2	H CHELSEA			L	0-1	0-1		Parkes	Lampard	Brush	Bonds	Martin	Holland	Pike	Pearson*	Cross	Brooking	Devonshire	**Banton**
	20/8	31,627		0			*Johnson 6*	*Borota*	*Locke*	*Stride*	*Nutton*	*Droy*	*Harris*	*Britton*	*Bannon*	*Langley*	*Johnson*	*Fillery*	
							Ref: A Robinson	Martin boobed with his clearance to give Danny Blanchflower's Chelsea an early goal. West Ham forced 21 corners but could not equalise. On the hour keeper Borota high-tackled Pearson in the crutch. Pearson had to go off and West Ham were given an indirect free-kick, not a penalty.											
3	H OLDHAM		15	W	1-0	0-0	Holland 59	Parkes	Lampard	Brush	Bonds	Martin	Holland	Pike	Morgan	Cross	Brooking	Devonshire	
	25/8	18,319	*22*	2				*Platt*	*Wood*	*Blair*	*Keegan*	*Hicks*	*Hurst*	*Atkinson*	*Halom*	*Steel*	*Stainrod*	*Heaton*	
							Ref: T Spencer	Two opening defeats mean Upton Park sees its lowest home crowd for almost six years. Oldham had also lost both openers, now they have lost their first three, thanks to Holland's goal. Upon scoring, the barracked player rushes over to the crowd and cups his ear to hear the applause.											
4	A WATFORD		21	L	0-2	0-1		Parkes	Lampard	Brush	Bonds	Martin	Holland	Pike	Pearson*	Cross	Brooking	Devonshire	Lansdowne
	1/9	*23,329*	*12*	2			*Blissett 36, 60*	*Rankin*	*How*	*Harrison*	*Booth*	*Sims*	*Bolton !*	*Joslyn**	*Blissett*	*Jenkins*	*Train*	*Downes*	*Mercer*
							Ref: G Napthine	Luther Blissett wasted two early chances for Watford, but rather than encourage the Hammers they were merely a taster of what was to come. Blissett headed in unchallenged from How's cross. Stuart Pearson was kicked black and blue, and Ian Bolton was sent off for kicking Pike.											
5	A PRESTON		19	D	1-1	0-0	Cross 61	Parkes	Lampard	Brush	Bonds	**Stewart**	Holland	Pike	Banton	Cross	Brooking	Morgan	
	8/9	*10,460*	*6*	3			*Coleman 44*	*Tunks*	*Taylor*	*Cameron*	*Doyle*	*Baxter*	*O'Riordan*	*Coleman*	*Haslegrave*	*Elliott*	*Potts*	*Thomson*	
							Ref: P Willis	19-year-old Ray Stewart has signed from Dundee United for £400,000, and helps West Ham to their first away point of the season. Coleman scored at the second attempt through a packed penalty area. Hammers' equaliser was bizarre – Pike's wayward shot was volleyed in by Cross.											
6	H SUNDERLAND		17	W	2-0	0-0	Cross 57, Pearson 73	Parkes	Lampard	Brush	Bonds	Martin	Stewart	**Neighbour**	Pearson	Cross	Brooking	Devonshire	
	15/9	24,021	*9*	5				*Siddall*	*Whitworth*	*Bolton*	*Clarke*	*Elliott**	*Buckley*	*Ashurst*	*Rostron*	*Brown*	*Robson*	*Arnott*	*Chisholm*
							Ref: A Glasson	A vibrant match. Spectators at Upton Park cast their eyes on two new Hammers, Jimmy Neighbour from Norwich and Ray Stewart. Sunderland boss Ken Knighton watches his new signing Pop Robson blotted out of the game by Billy Bonds. Stuart Pearson bags his 100th league goal.											
7	A QP RANGERS		19	L	0-3	0-1		Parkes	Lampard	Brush	Bonds	Martin	Stewart	Neighbour	Pike*	Cross	Brooking	Devonshire	Holland
	22/9	*24,692*	*4*	5			*Allen 10, 46, Goddard 59*	*Woods*	*Shanks*	*Gillard*	*McCreery*	*Hazell*	*Roeder*	*Bowles*	*Currie*	*Allen*	*Goddard*	*Burke*	
							Ref: M Taylor	QPR's teenage scorers will both end up playing for West Ham, sooner or later. Clive Allen steered in Bowles' quickly taken free-kick and then headed in Bowles' cross. Paul Goddard was sent clear by Bowles for No 3. All in all, a triumph for QPR's new manager, Tommy Docherty.											
8	H BURNLEY		16	W	2-1	0-1	Stewart 66p, Lansdowne 69	Parkes	Stewart	Brush	Bonds	Martin	**Allen**	Neighbour	Lansdowne	Cross	Brooking	Devonshire	
	29/9	18,327	*21*	7			*Scott 42*	*Stevenson*	*Scott*	*Jakub*	*Hall*	*Thomson*	*Rodaway*	*Young**	*Dobson*	*Fletcher*	*Kindon*	*James*	*Brennan*
							Ref: D Hutchinson	Teenager Paul Allen makes his league debut. Poor Burnley have not won a league fixture since Easter. Brooking and Cross both hit the bar early on, but Burnley take the lead. Keeper Alan Stevenson then flattens Brooking and Ray Stewart demonstrates his ferocious penalty-taking.											
9	H NEWCASTLE		16	D	1-1	1-1	Cross 7	Parkes	Stewart	Brush	Bonds	Martin	Allen	Neighbour*	Lansdowne	Cross	Brooking	Devonshire	Holland
	6/10	23,206	*1*	8			*Withe 37*	*Hardwick*	*Brownlie*	*Davies*	*Martin*	*Barton*	*Boam*	*Shoulder*	*Walker*	*Withe*	*Hibbitt*	*Cartwright*	
							Ref: C Thomas	This fixture last season ended 5-0, so Newcastle have stiffened up. Cross opened the scoring by stooping to head in Neighbour's free-kick. When Parkes then claimed a cross with his leg raised, the ref penalised him with an indirect free-kick, taken by Martin and converted by Withe.											
10	A LEICESTER		14	W	2-1	1-1	Martin 29, Cross 51	Parkes	Stewart	Lampard	Bonds	Martin	Holland	Allen	Lansdowne	Cross	Brooking	Neighbour	
	13/10	*22,472*	*6*	10			*Williams 1*	*Wallington*	*Williams*	*Rofe*	*Peake*	*May*	*Welsh*	*Byrne**	*Henderson*	*Young*	*Wilson*	*Smith*	*Lineker*
							Ref: J Worrall	Although falling behind in 15 seconds to a shot deflected in off Lampard, West Ham recover to record their first away win in 11 games. Lyall's tactics of playing two wide men, Neighbour and Holland, to squeeze Newcastle's marauding full-backs paid off. Both goals were low shots.											
11	H LUTON		16	L	1-2	0-2	Allen 64	Parkes	Stewart	Lampard	Bonds	Martin	Holland	Allen	Lansdowne	Cross	Pike	Neighbour	
	20/10	25,049	*1*	10			*Stein 16, Saxby 36*	*Findlay*	*Stephens*	*Donaghy*	*Grealish*	*Saxby*	*Price*	*Hill*	*West*	*Stein*	*Ingram*	*Moss*	
							Ref: W Bombroff	Luton top the league. Both their goals came from set pieces, and Lyall rages against his players at half-time and full-time. Cross did not track Paul Price for Luton's first, and Saxby outjumped Martin for the second. The defeat overshadowed Paul Allen's first league goal for Hammers.											

No	Date	Venue	Opponent	Att	Pos	Res/Pts	F-A	H-T	Scorers, Times, and Referees	1	2	3	4	5	6	7	8	9	10	11	12 sub used
12		A	NOTTS CO		14	W	1-0	0-0	Holland 55	Parkes	Stewart	Lampard	Bonds	Martin	Holland	Allen	Pike	Cross	Brooking	Neighbour	
	27/10			*12,256*	*5*	12				*Avramovic*	*Richards*	*O'Brien*	*Hunt*	*Stubbs*	*Blockley*	*McCulloch*	*Masson*	*Hooks*	*Benjamin*	*Mair**	*Christie*
									Ref: N Midgley	West Ham's poor run of results is making them much more defensive in outlook these days. Out of necessity, some might say. This was a backs-to-the-wall win, County's first home defeat of the season, secured when Holland dived among the flying boots to head Martin's flick-on.											
13		H	WREXHAM		14	W	1-0	0-0	Pike 51	Parkes	Stewart	Lampard	Bonds	Martin	Holland	Allen	Pike	Cross	Devonshire*	Neighbour	Lansdowne
	3/11			20,595	*6*	14				*Davies*	*Hill*	*Dwyer*	*Davis*	*Jones J*	*Giles*	*Fox*	*Cartwright*	*Edwards*	*McNeil*	*Buxton**	*Roberts I*
									Ref: H Robinson	Lyall's more cautious outlook results in just one player up front – Cross. But the tactics work. Holland gets in a shot, Dai Davies blocks, but Pike follows up. High-flying Wrexham looked strangely subdued, and Alvin Martin dealt comfortably with free-scoring striker Dixie McNeil.											
14		A	FULHAM		11	W	2-1	0-0	Stewart 66p, Cross 72	Ferguson	Stewart	Lampard	Bonds	Martin	Holland	Allen	Pike	Cross	Devonshire	Neighbour	
	10/11			*16,476*	*21*	16			*Davies 83*	*Digweed*	*Peters**	*Strong*	*Bullivant*	*Money*	*Gale*	*Marinello*	*Beck*	*Guthrie*	*Lock*	*Davies*	
									Ref: T Bune	The deaths in quick succession of Phil Parkes' father and father-in-law mean that he is given compassionate leave. When John Beck up-ends Pike, it gives Stewart the chance to put away his third penalty. Cross doubles the lead with a looping far-post header from Lampard's cross.											
15		A	CHELSEA		11	L	1-2	1-1	Holland 25	Ferguson	Stewart	Lampard	Bonds	Martin	Holland	Allen*	Devonshire	Cross	Brooking	Neighbour	Lansdowne
	14/11			*30,859*	*5*	16			*Frost 29, Fillery 76*	*Borota*	*Locke*	*Sparrow*	*Bumstead*	*Droy*	*Chivers*	*Britton*	*Fillery*	*Frost*	*Walker*	*Harris*	
									Ref: R Challis	Chelsea are managed by Geoff Hurst. First blood to the Hammers, when Brooking and Stewart set up a chance for Holland. But Martin then headed out to Frost, who drove into the net through a forest of legs. Clive Walker made the winner, turning Stewart inside out before crossing.											
16		H	SWANSEA		8	W	2-0	0-0	Brooking 56, Cross 75	Parkes	Stewart	**Smith**	Bonds	Martin	Holland	Allen	Devonshire	Cross	Brooking	Lansdowne	
	17/11			21,210	*9*	18				*Letheran*	*Evans*	*Rushbury*	*Charles*	*Phillips*	*Stevenson*	*Craig*	*Attley*	*James R*	*Mahoney**	*Callaghan*	*Waddle*
									Ref: J Martin	Lampard's torn hamstring rules him out. Mark Smith is his late replacement. Brooking oozed class throughout, and had Billy Lansdowne's finishing been of equal quality Swansea would have taken a hiding. Brooking made Cross's goal and scored himself. Martin also hit the bar.											
17		H	CARDIFF		7	W	3-0	2-0	Cross 27, Stewart 44p, 85p	Parkes	Stewart	Lampard	Bonds	Martin	Holland	Allen	Pearson	Cross	Brooking	Devonshire	
	24/11			20,242	*13*	20				*Davies J*	*Jones**	*Sullivan*	*Campbell*	*Pontin*	*Thomas*	*Bishop*	*Dwyer*	*Moore*	*Ronson*	*Lewis*	*Stevens*
									Ref: D Reeves	Both penalties were conceded by Rod Thomas, first when tripping Devonshire, then by fisting away Pearson's header. Both penalties were blasted in by Stewart. The FA have introduced random drugs tests. Phil Parkes is chosen but is unable to give a urine sample. He is excused.											
18		A	CHARLTON		7	L	0-1	0-1		Parkes	Stewart	Lampard	Bonds	Martin	Holland*	Allen	Pearson	Cross	Brooking	Devonshire	Neighbour
	1/12			*19,021*	*18*	20			*Gritt 14*	*Wood*	*Hazell*	*Shaw*	*Tydeman*	*Berry*	*Madden*	*Powell*	*Jacobson*	*Hales*	*Walker*	*Gritt*	
									Ref: T Spencer	Players' minds are distracted by the looming cup-tie with Forest, and Lyall loses his rag. Mike Bailey's Charlton won the points through Steve Gritt's far-post header from Powell's cross. That Charlton registered their first clean-sheet so far indicates the flimsiness of West Ham's attack.											
19		H	BRISTOL ROV		7	W	2-1	1-1	Cross 29, 52	Parkes	Stewart	Lampard	Bonds	Martin	Allen	Neighbour	Pearson	Cross	Brooking	Devonshire	
	8/12			17,763	*21*	22			*Barrowclough 2*	*Thomas*	*Bater*	*Williams*	*Mabbutt*	*Taylor*	*Aitken*	*Barrowclough*	*Emmanuel*	*Brown**	*Penny*	*Pulis*	*Jones V*
									Ref: C White	David Cross celebrates his 29th birthday with two goals, taking his total for the season to 14. Rovers' manager Bobby Campbell is not inclined to celebrate, having seen Tony Pulis set Barrowclough clear in the second minute. But Rovers were unable to stem Cross's aerial menace.											
20		A	SHREWSBURY		9	L	0-3	0-0		Parkes	Stewart	Lampard	Bonds	Martin	Pike	Allen	Pearson	Cross	Brooking	Neighbour	
	15/12			*8,513*	*19*	22			*Maguire 59, Chapman 85, Atkins 87*	*Mulhearn*	*King*	*Larkin*	*Lindsay*	*Griffin*	*Keay*	*Tong*	*Atkins*	*Chapman*	*Dungworth*	*Maguire*	
									Ref: L Robinson	For the second time in four days, West Ham fold under late pressure. Parkes comes out, Atkins heads down, and Maguire blasts the ball into the empty net. Pearson might have scored in the opening minutes against Graham Turner's strugglers, but Keay cleared his shot off the line.											
21		H	CAMBRIDGE			W	3-1	0-1	Stewart 47, Pearson 61, Neighbour 70	Parkes	Stewart	Lampard	Bonds	Martin	Devonshire	Allen	Pearson	Cross*	Brooking	Neighbour	Pike
	21/12			11,721		24			*Biley 36*	*Webster*	*Stringer*	*Christie**	*Calderwood*	*Fallon*	*O'Neill*	*Biley*	*Spriggs*	*Reilly*	*Gibbins*	*Murray*	*Turner*
									Ref: C Thomas	A Friday match on a frozen pitch produces a worrying knee injury to Cross, who collides with the keeper after 35 minutes and is stretchered off. Half-time was enlivened briefly by a middle-aged, poorly-endowed streaker. A second-half blizzard almost brought an abandonment.											
22		A	ORIENT			W	4-0	3-0	Pearson 11, 40, Devonshire 24, Pike 54	Parkes	Stewart	Lampard	Bonds	Martin	Devonshire	Allen	Pearson	Pike	Brooking	Neighbour	
	1/1			*23,885*		26				*Day*	*Fisher*	*Smith**	*Taylor*	*Gray N*	*Moores*	*Chiedozie**	*Hughton*	*Mayo*	*Jennings*	*Coates*	*Godfrey*
									Ref: C Downey	A skating rink pitch sees the Hammers scamper about in space-age boots with tiny pimples on the sole. Lyall switched his full-backs so Stewart could mark tricky John Chiedozie. Former West Ham keeper Mervyn Day now plays for Jimmy Bloomfield's Orient and lets in four goals.											
23		H	WATFORD		7	D	1-1	0-0	Bonds 84	Parkes	Stewart	Lampard	Bonds	Martin	Devonshire	Allen	Pearson	Pike	Brooking	Neighbour	
	12/1			*23,553*	*16*	27			*Rostron 48*	*Steele*	*Henderson*	*Harrison*	*Patching*	*Sims*	*Bolton*	*Booth*	*Blissett**	*Ward*	*Train*	*Rostron*	*Poskett*
									Ref: C Maskell	Watford boss Graham Taylor decides to pack the midfield, which forces West Ham to resort to the long ball. These tactics don't impress young Paul Allen, who has lost his way lately. Not the best of games for TV. Not the best advertisement either, when a linesman is hit by something.											

No	Date		Att	Pos	Pt	F-A	H-T	Scorers, Times, and Referees	1	2	3	4	5	6	7	8	9	10	11	12 sub used
24	H	PRESTON		6	W	2-0	0-0	Stewart 55p, Allen 77	Parkes	Lampard	Brush	Bonds*	Martin	Devonshire	Allen	Pearson	Pike	Stewart	Neighbour	Banton
	19/1		17,603	*10*	29				*Tunks*	*Taylor*	*McAteer*	*Doyle*	*Anderson*	*O'Riordan*	*Bell*	*Haslegrave*	*Elliott*	*McGee**	*Bruce*	*Coleman*
								Ref: R Toseland	Preston boss Nobby Stiles can have few complaints as Don O'Riorden barges into Geoff Pike. Stewart's penalty went in off keeper Tunks' fingers and almost removed them. Tunks then dropped Martin's cross to Allen. Bonds gets kicked in the head by Martin and has seven stitches.											
25	H	QP RANGERS		7	W	2-1	1-1	Pearson 39, Hazell 71 (og)	Parkes	Lampard	Brush	Stewart	Martin	Devonshire	Allen	Pearson	Cross	Brooking	Pike	
	9/2		26,037	*9*	31			*Goddard 35*	*Woods*	*Shanks*	*Gillard*	*McCreery*	*Wicks*	*Hazell*	*Goddard*	*Roeder*	*Allen*	*Currie*	*Burke**	*Waddock*
								Ref: B Hill	Clive Allen's shot goes in off Paul Goddard's head to put Rangers in front. Bob Hazell returns from suspension to accomplish an extraordinary own-goal from David Cross's centre. This is Stuart Pearson's best game so far for the Hammers. He hits the crossbar in addition to his goal.											
26	A	BURNLEY		5	W	1-0	1-0	Devonshire 19	Parkes	Lampard	Brush	Stewart	Martin	Devonshire	Allen	Neighbour	Cross	Brooking	Pike	
	19/2		*10,610*	*20*	33				*Stevenson*	*Arins*	*Brennan*	*Burke**	*Overson V*	*Dixon*	*James*	*Dobson*	*Hamilton*	*Young*	*Smith*	*Cavener*
								Ref: G Owen	Alan Devonshire has been under the weather with a bug for some weeks, but shakes it off to dominate the game. The only goal, a delightful scissors movement with Brooking, finished off from 20 yards, is enough to take West Ham to within three points of leaders Luton Town.											
27	H	LEICESTER		6	W	3-1	0-1	Pike 69, Cross 75, Holland 79	Parkes	Lampard	Brush	Stewart	Martin	Devonshire	Allen	Holland	Cross	Brooking	Pike	
	23/2		27,762	*1*	35			*Young 11*	*Wallington*	*Williams*	*Scott*	*Kelly*	*May*	*O'Neill !*	*Goodwin*	*Henderson*	*Young*	*Peake*	*Smith*	
								Ref: B Steven	Leicester top the table but are beaten by a candidate for goal of the season. England boss Ron Greenwood watches as Pike lobs Wallington. O'Neill is sent off for pulling Devonshire's shirt. This is the 14th match of the season in which West Ham recover from being a goal down.											
28	A	LUTON		5	D	1-1	0-1	Stewart 70	Parkes	Lampard	Brush	Stewart	Martin	Devonshire	Allen	Holland*	Cross	Brooking	Pike	Pearson
	1/3		*20,040*	*3*	36			*Hill 3*	*Findlay*	*Stephens*	*Donaghy*	*Grealish*	*Price*	*Price*	*Hill*	*West*	*Stein**	*Hatton*	*Moss*	*White*
								Ref: S Bates	The pre-match entertainment comprised scantily-clad girls, suspended from ropes, wriggling free from straitjackets. The on-field entertainment gave us Hill's volley. Then Stephens dragged down Brooking. Stewart missed his first penalty. Findlay saved, but Stewart got to the loose ball.											
29	H	NOTTS CO		7	L	1-2	0-0	Pike 90	Parkes	Lampard*	Brush	Stewart	Martin	Devonshire	Allen	Pearson	Cross	Brooking	Pike	Holland
	11/3		24,844	*15*	36			*Christie 65, Stubbs 69*	*Avramovic*	*Richards*	*O'Brien*	*Benjamin*	*Stubbs*	*Kilcline*	*McCulloch*	*Masson*	*Christie*	*Hunt*	*Mair*	
								Ref: D Letts	After the Cup win over Villa, this was an anti-climax, West Ham's first defeat in 14 games. Jimmy Sirrel's County employ an offside trap and win the points through Trevor Christie's header, from Richards' cross, and another header from Stubbs, from Don Masson's free-kick.											
30	A	NEWCASTLE		8	D	0-0	0-0		Parkes	Lampard	Brush	Stewart	Martin	Devonshire	Allen	Pearson	Cross	Brooking	Pike*	Holland
	15/3		*25,431*	*7*	37				*Hardwick*	*Brownlie*	*Davies*	*Walker*	*Bird*	*Boam*	*Shoulder*	*Cartwright*	*Rafferty*	*Hibbitt*	*Shinton*	
								Ref: R Bridges	Newcastle boast just one home defeat in 16 games, so this is a point gained rather than a point lost. Paul Allen has found his form again, while Lampard finds the referee's notebook again. He faces a suspension. West Ham are five points behind leaders Chelsea with three games in hand.											
31	H	FULHAM		8	L	2-3	2-2	Devonshire 6, Stewart 16p	Parkes	Lampard	Brush*	Stewart	Martin	Devonshire	Allen	Pearson	Cross	Brooking	Holland	Pike
	22/3		30,030	*21*	37			*Maybank 12, Banton 34, 40*	*Peyton*	*Money*	*Strong*	*Lock*	*Banton*	*Gale*	*Gayle*	*Beck*	*Davies*	*Maybank*	*Lewington*	
								Ref: A Seville	This was the match where dreams of promotion died. Fulham's Geoff Banton scored his first ever league goals, both identical, and both from corners, both the result of Parkes' dislike of having a defender on the far post. Beck flattened Brooking to allow Stewart a twice-taken penalty.											
32	A	SWANSEA		8	L	1-2	0-0	Devonshire 50	Parkes	Stewart	Brush	Bonds	Martin	Devonshire	Allen*	Pearson	Pike	Brooking	Holland	Cross
	29/3		*13,275*	*16*	37			*Craig 56p, 75*	*Stewart*	*Robinson*	*Evans*	*Charles**	*Phillips*	*Stevenson*	*Craig*	*Attley*	*Waddle*	*Giles*	*Mahoney*	*Baker*
								Ref: V Callow	A few weeks earlier bookies had stopped taking bets on West Ham's promotion. Now they are giving odds of 12-1 against their taking the title. Lyall's 4-4-2 formation ensures this match offers little excitement. Martin impeded Waddle for the penalty; Parkes left his line for the winner.											
33	A	CAMBRIDGE		8	L	0-2	0-2		Parkes	Lampard	Brush	Bonds	Martin	Devonshire	Stewart	Pearson	Cross	Brooking	Holland	
	1/4		*8,863*	*15*	37			*Finney 20, 35*	*Webster*	*Donaldson*	*Murray*	*Smith*	*Fallon*	*Gibbins*	*Streete*	*Spriggs*	*Reilly*	*Finney*	*Christie*	
								Ref: M Scott	On the balance of play this result was laughable. Lyall sends out an attacking formation, but a muddy pitch and Malcolm Webster's heroics combine to frustrate the Hammers, who have taken just one point from five games. Tom Finney netted with a header; then from a rebound.											
34	H	ORIENT		9	W	2-0	0-0	Gray 68 (og), Brooking 73	Parkes	Lampard*	Brush	Bonds	Martin	Devonshire	Stewart	Pearson	Cross	Brooking	Holland	Pike
	5/4		22,066	*8*	39				*Day*	*Fisher*	*Roffey*	*Taylor*	*Gray N*	*Hughton*	*Chiedozie*	*Jennings*	*Moores*	*Margerrison*	*Coates*	
								Ref: P Reeves	Nigel Gray's own-goal – turning in Alan Devonshire's cross – means Orient have gifted West Ham an own-goal in all three meetings this season, and Gray has donated two of them – the other being in the FA Cup. This match was Frank Lampard's 500th West Ham appearance.											

No	Venue	Opponent	Att	Pos	Res	F-A	H-T	Scorers, Times, and Referees	1	2	3	4	5	6	7	8	9	10	11	12
35	A	BIRMINGHAM		8	D	0-0	0-0		Parkes	Stewart	Brush	Bonds	Martin	Devonshire	Allen	Pearson	Cross	Brooking	Holland	
7/4			*28,377*	*1*	40				*Wealands*	*Broadhurst*	*Dennis*	*Curbishley*	*Gallagher**	*Towers*	*Todd*	*Ainscow*	*Bertschin*	*Gemmill*	*Dillon*	*Lynex*
								Ref: D Shaw	Jim Smith's Birmingham tackle like demons, and this point will ultimately earn them promotion. Mind you, West Ham hardly deserved their draw. Wealands was untroubled by West Ham's attack. City won 14 corner-kicks. When Parkes dropped Bertschin's header, Holland cleared.											
36	A	CARDIFF		8	W	1-0	1-0	Stewart 29	Parkes	Lampard	Brush	Stewart	Bonds	Devonshire	Allen	Pearson	Cross	Brooking	Pike	
19/4			*12,076*	*13*	42				*Grotier*	*Grapes*	*Lewis*	*Campbell*	*Pontin*	*Thomas*	*Ronson*	*Bishop**	*Stevens*	*Buchanan*	*Harris*	*Sullivan*
								Ref: D Lloyd	Former Hammer Peter Grotier was told he was playing just an hour before kick-off. It is his mistake that keeps West Ham's promotion hopes theoretically alive. He misjudges Brooking's inswinging corner and palms the ball to Cross – who squares to Stewart. It's his ninth league goal.											
37	H	BIRMINGHAM		8	L	1-2	0-1	Martin 53	Parkes	Lampard	Brush	Bonds !	Martin	Devonshire	Allen*	Pearson	Cross	Brooking	Stewart	Pike
22/4			37,167	*1*	42			*Ainscow 37, Bertschin 71*	*Wealands*	*Broadhurst*	*Dennis*	*Curbishley*	*Gallagher*	*Todd !*	*Ainscow*	*Lynex*	*Bertschin*	*Gemmill*	*Dillon*	
								Ref: A Gunn	When Billy Bonds and Colin Todd exchanged kicks on the ground, expulsion was inevitable. It took some effort to keep them apart on their way to the tunnel. Martin's fierce header was followed by Bertschin's easy header, which won the game and hoisted City from fourth to first.											
38	H	SHREWSBURY		9	L	1-3	0-2	Brooking 79	Parkes	Lampard	Brush	Stewart	Martin	Neighbour	Allen	Pearson	Cross*	Brooking	Pike	Morgan
26/4			19,765	*14*	42			*Maguire 17, Keay 40p, Biggins 84*	*Wardle*	*King*	*Leonard*	*Turner*	*Griffin*	*Keay*	*Tong*	*Atkins*	*Biggins*	*Dungworth*	*Maguire*	
								Ref: L Shapter	Even though they are Wembley bound, the Hammers get the bird from their demanding supporters after this shoddy display. Brooking's was an untypical goal, a rasping cross-shot. It briefly brought the game to life, following Maguire's shot and a penalty for Lampard's foul on Maguire.											
39	A	OLDHAM			D	0-0	0-0		Parkes	Lampard	Brush	Bonds	Martin	Allen	Neighbour	Pike*	Cross	Brooking	Stewart	Morgan
29/4			*8,214*		43				*McDonnell*	*Hoolickin*	*Holt*	*Kowenicki*	*Clements*	*Blair*	*Keegan*	*Heaton*	*Steel**	*Stainrod*	*Atkinson*	*Wood*
								Ref: J Haugh	Both teams went through the motions. West Ham bored the crowd by constantly passing back to Parkes. Lyall's players are terrified of picking up injuries before the Cup Final and when Brooking goes off with a dislocated finger one feared the worst. Happily he was soon back in action.											
40	A	BRISTOL ROV		7	W	2-0	0-0	Devonshire 61, Cross 78	Parkes	Lampard	Stewart	Bonds	Martin	Devonshire	Allen	Morgan	Cross	Pike	Neighbour	
3/5			*9,824*	*19*	45				*Thomas*	*Bater*	*Cooper*	*Hughes**	*Mabbutt*	*Griffiths*	*Barrowclough*	*Pulis*	*Penny*	*Bates*	*Barrett*	*Williams*
								Ref: J Lovatt	After 40 seconds Ashley Griffiths' studs shatters Paul Allen's shin pad, but mercifully spares his shin. Allen will be okay for Wembley. Devonshire blasts a great goal from 25 yards and Cross adds another with his head. Rovers were already sure of staying up, so weren't fired up.											
41	H	CHARLTON		7	W	4-1	4-0	Pike 1, Morgan 12, Cross 22, Stewart 45p	Parkes	Stewart	Brush	Bonds	Martin	Banton	Neighbour	Pike	Cross*	Brooking	Morgan	Lampard
5/5			19,314	*22*	47			*Hales 85*	*Johns*	*Hazell !*	*Walker*	*Tydeman*	*Berry*	*Shaw*	*Churchouse*	*Walsh*	*Hales*	*Ostergaard**	*Robinson*	*Smith*
								Ref: E Read	Charlton are so far adrift they have long since given up the ghost. They have not registered an away win for 18 months and were not likely to end that run now. Pike headed the first goal after 20 seconds, and proved such a thorn that on the hour Hazell was sent off for fouling him.											
42	A	SUNDERLAND		7	L	0-2	0-1		Parkes	Stewart	Brush	Bonds	Martin	Devonshire	Neighbour	Pearson*	Cross	Brooking	Pike	Holland
12/5			*47,000*	*2*	47			*Arnott 29, Cummins 67*	*Turner*	*Whitworth*	*Hinnigan*	*Chisholm*	*Hindmarch*	*Elliott*	*Arnott*	*Buckley*	*Hawley*	*Robson*	*Cummins*	
		Home	Away					Ref: J Worrall	Two days after winning the FA Cup Hammers head for Sunderland, who will be promoted at the expense of Chelsea if they win. Hence the electric atmosphere. West Ham lost Pearson and Stewart to injury and finished with 10 men. Cummins' 30-yard clincher ignited a huge party.											
Average		22,868	18,510																	

League Cup																				
2:1	H	BARNSLEY		15	W	3-1	2-0	Brooking 17, Pearson 32, Cross 77	Parkes	Lampard	Brush	Bonds	Martin	Holland	Pike	Pearson	Cross	Brooking	Devonshire	
28/8			12,320	*3:21*				*Glavin 54*	*Pierce*	*Flavell*	*Collins*	*Glavin*	*Dugdale*	*McCarthy*	*Little*	*Riley*	*Pugh*	*Millar*	*Bell*	
								Ref: L Burden	The lowest crowd for 20 years welcomes Allan Clarke's Barnsley to Upton Park. League Cup-ties are now played over two-legs. Lampard's deflected shot was turned in by Pearson, his first Hammers' goal. Sections of the crowd have taken to baiting Geoff Pike, the latest boo-boy.											
2:2	A	BARNSLEY		21	W	2-0	1-0	Cross 19, 76	Parkes	Lampard	Brush	Bonds	Stewart	Holland	Pike	Banton	Cross	Brooking	Morgan	
4/9			*15,898*	*3:23*					*Pierce*	*Flavell**	*Collins*	*Glavin*	*Dugdale*	*McCarthy*	*Little*	*Riley*	*Pugh*	*Banks*	*Bell*	*Millar*
								Ref: K Walmsley (Hammers win 5-1 on aggregate)	When Martin fails a late fitness test, Ray Stewart is pressed into midfield. He became one of four Hammers to be booked, as Barnsley raised the temperature. Though the scoreline does not show it, Phil Parkes had much to do. David Cross's second goal looked to many to be offside.											
3	H	SOUTHEND		19	D	1-1	1-1	Cross 43	Parkes	Stewart	Brush	Bonds	Martin	Holland	Allen	Lansdowne	Cross	Brooking	Devonshire	
25/9			19,658	*3:11*				*Pountney 11*	*Cawston*	*Dudley*	*Moody*	*Cusack*	*Yates*	*Stead*	*Otulakowski*	*Pountney*	*Morris*	*Tuohy*	*Gray*	
								Ref: R Lewis	Southend beat Division 1 Bolton in the 1st Round and set off at a furious pace. Colin Morris's pass was thumped in by Ron Pountney. Phil Dudley missed a sitter and Cross's strong header from Stewart's cross came out of the blue. After the break Southend lived on their nerves.											

League Cup		F-A	H-T	Scorers, Times, and Referees	1	2	3	4	5	6	7	8	9	10	11	12 sub used
3R A SOUTHEND	16 D	0-0	0-0		Parkes	Stewart	Brush	Bonds	Martin	Holland	Allen	Lansdowne	Cross	Brooking	Devonshire	
1/10	*22,497 3:15*	*aet*			*Cawston*	*Dudley*	*Moody*	*Cusack*	*Yates**	*Stead*	*Otulakowski*	*Pountney*	*Morris*	*Tuohy*	*Gray*	*Walker*
				Ref: J Sewell	Despite the lack of goals this replay had its share of thrills. West Ham resorted to brawn rather than brain and Paul Allan and Ray Stewart were booked. Hammers created and wasted most of the chances, the best of which fell to Cross. Blues' boss Dave Smith then lost the toss for venue.											
3 H SOUTHEND	16 W	5-1	2-1	Lansdowne 25, 36, 46, Holland 60,	Parkes	Stewart	Smith	Bonds	Martin	Holland	Allen	Lansdowne	Cross	Brooking	Pike	
RR 8/10	19,718 *3:17*			*Gray 23* [Stewart 79p]	*Cawston*	*Dudley*	*Moody*	*Cusack*	*Walker*	*Stead*	*Otulakowski**	*Morris*	*Pountney*	*Hadley*	*Gray*	*Hull*
				Ref: M Baker	Yet again Southend score first at Upton Park, but this time their lead is erased in seconds by the first instalment of Billy Lansdowne's hat-trick. It is his first hat-trick and came shortly after his father was sacked as Hammers' reserve-team coach. Dudley fouled Paul Allen for the penalty.											
4 A SUNDERLAND	14 D	1-1	0-1	Pike 68	Parkes	Stewart	Lampard	Bonds	Martin	Holland	Allen	Pike	Cross	Brooking*	Devonshire	Lansdowne
31/10	*30,302 11*			*Brown 11*	*Siddall*	*Whitworth*	*Gilbert*	*Clarke*	*Hindmarch*	*Elliott*	*Arnott*	*Lee*	*Brown*	*Robson*	*Rowell*	
				Ref: G Nolan	Alan Brown sprinted through for a fine goal, but not as fine as Geoff Pike's dipping 30-yarder. Trevor Brooking failed to reappear after half-time, and Sunderland's spirits visibly lifted. Pop Robson, playing for Ken Knighton's Sunderland, reckoned that West Ham look a good team.											
4R H SUNDERLAND	14 W	2-1	1-1	Martin 9, Cross 49	Ferguson	Stewart	Lampard	Bonds	Martin	Holland	Allen	Pike	Cross	Devonshire	Lansdowne	
5/11	24,454 *10*			*Brown 6*	*Siddall*	*Whitworth*	*Bolton*	*Clarke*	*Elliott*	*Hindmarch*	*Arnott*	*Gilbert*	*Brown*	*Rowell*	*Dunn*	
				Ref: S Bates	The winners will play European champions Forest, so this is a rare old ding-dong. A bereavement means Phil Parkes is left out. Alan Brown scores another scorcher, but it is soon cancelled out by Martin's header. The winner came from a deflection after Devonshire had hit the post.											
QF H NOTT'M FOREST	7 D	0-0	0-0		Parkes	Stewart	Lampard	Bonds	Martin	Holland	Allen	Pearson	Cross	Brooking	Devonshire	
4/12	35,856 *1:5*				*Shilton*	*Anderson*	*Gray*	*Bowyer*	*Lloyd*	*Burns*	*O'Neill*	*O'Hare*	*Birtles*	*Francis*	*Robertson*	
				Ref: A Grey	A sardine-packed Upton Park welcomes Clough's European champions, who are unbeaten in 21 games but spend the 90 minutes desperately trying to survive. Gary Birtles and Trevor Francis hardly had a kick until the 82nd minute, when Phil Parkes saved superbly at Francis's feet.											
QF A NOTT'M FOREST	7 L	0-3	0-0		Parkes	Stewart	Lampard	Bonds	Martin	Pike	Allen	Pearson	Cross	Brooking	Devonshire	
R 12/12	*25,462 1:7*	*aet*		*O'Hare 99, Birtles 101, O'Neill 108*	*Shilton*	*Anderson*	*Gray*	*Bowyer*	*Lloyd*	*Burns*	*O'Neill*	*O'Hare*	*Birtles*	*Francis*	*Robertson*	
				Ref: N Ashley	Phil Parkes was the main reason this cup-tie stayed goalless throughout normal time. How cruel, then, that it should be his mistake that decides the outcome, when dropping Birtles' cross at John O'Hare's feet. Early in the game Stewart's free-kick had slithered out of Shilton's hands.											

FA Cup		F-A	H-T	Scorers, Times, and Referees	1	2	3	4	5	6	7	8	9	10	11	12 sub used
3 A WEST BROM	9 D	1-1	1-0	Pearson 33	Parkes	Stewart	Lampard	Bonds	Martin	Devonshire	Allen	Pearson	Pike	Brooking	Neighbour	
5/1	*20,572 1:16*			*Regis 90*	*Godden*	*Batson*	*Statham*	*Trewick*	*Wile*	*Robertson*	*Deehan*	*Brown A*	*Regis*	*Owen*	*Barnes*	
				Ref: J Hunting	Ron Atkinson's Albion are left stunned by Phil Parkes' goalkeeping display, which is admired by his family up in the stand. Best of his many saves was when pushing Statham's effort against a post. Pearson's header was cancelled out by Regis's effort, which may have been handled.											
3R H WEST BROM	9 W	2-1	0-0	Pike 53, Brooking 83	Parkes	Stewart	Lampard	Brush	Martin	Devonshire	Allen	Pearson	Pike	Brooking	Neighbour	
8/1	30,689 *1:16*			*Brown T 86*	*Godden*	*Batson*	*Statham*	*Trewick*	*Wile*	*Robertson*	*Deehan*	*Brown A*	*Regis*	*Owen**	*Barnes*	*Brown T*
				Ref: J Hunting	Geoff Pike is drafted in as makeshift striker and plays a blinder, side-footing the first goal. John Deehan contrived an improbable miss for WBA in the first half and paid the price. Albion's goal came from a Parkes mistake. He flapped at Barnes's cross and Tony Brown capitalised.											
4 A ORIENT	6 W	3-2	2-1	Gray 28 (og), Stewart 34p, 81	Parkes	Brush	Lampard	Bonds	Martin	Devonshire	Allen	Pearson	Pike	Stewart	Neighbour	
26/1	*21,521 13*			*Taylor 11p, Chiedozie 61*	*Rafter*	*Fisher*	*Roffey*	*Taylor*	*Gray*	*Moores*	*Chiedozie*	*Hughton*	*Jennings*	*Margerrison*	*Coates*	
				Ref: S Bates	O's Day is injured. Ex-Hammer Tommy Taylor is now Orient's skipper. Bonds handled for the O's early penalty. Nigel Gray headed an own-goal for West Ham before they won a penalty of their own when Moores handled. Stewart saw Taylor point one way, so he aimed the other.											
5 H SWANSEA	6 W	2-0	0-0	Allen 85, Cross 86	Parkes	Lampard	Brush	Stewart	Martin	Devonshire	Neighbour	Pearson*	Cross	Brooking	Pike	Allen
16/2	30,497 *13*				*Letheran*	*Robinson*	*Rushbury*	*Phillips*	*Stevenson*	*Giles*	*Craig*	*James*	*Charles*	*Toshack*	*Callaghan*	
				Ref: K Baker	John Toshack's Swansea felt robbed by this result. They had two 'goals' disallowed for offside. Hammers avoided an uncomfortable replay when Swansea's keeper dropped Cross's volley. West Ham reach the quarter-finals of both domestic cups in the same season for the first time.											

QF	H	ASTON VILLA	5	W	1-0	0-0	Stewart 89p	Parkes	Lampard	Brush	Stewart	Martin	Devonshire	Allen	Pearson	Cross	Brooking	Pike	
	8/3	36,393	*1:6*					*Rimmer*	*Linton*	*Gibson*	*Ormsby*	*McNaught*	*Mortimer*	*Bremner*	*Little*	*Donovan*	*Cowans*	*Bullivant*	
							Ref: D Richardson	Drama in the dying seconds. Villa's Ken McNaught goes up with Alvin Martin with his arm in the air. It makes contact with the ball and a penalty ensues. Villa boss Ron Saunders dismissed it as 'a complete freak'. McNaught's arm had been driven against the ball by Martin's back.											
SF	N	EVERTON	8	D	1-1	0-1	Pearson 70	Parkes	Stewart	Brush	Bonds	Martin	Devonshire	Allen	Pearson*	Cross	Brooking	Holland	Pike
	12/4	47,685	*1:18*				*Kidd 42p*	*Hodge*	*Gidman*	*Bailey*	*Wright*	*Lyons*	*Eastoe*	*Megson**	*King*	*Kidd !*	*Hartford*	*Ross*	*Latchford*
		(at Villa Park)					Ref: C Seel	A highly-charged match sees Devonshire concede a penalty with a challenge on Andy King that seemed fair. Brian Kidd was sent off following a fracas with Stewart. Ross escaped expulsion when scything Brooking. Pearson forced a replay when side-footing home Brooking's cross.											
SF	N	EVERTON	8	W	2-1	0-0	Devonshire 94, Lampard 118	Parkes	Lampard	Brush	Stewart	Bonds	Devonshire	Allen	Pearson	Cross	Brooking	Pike	
R	16/4	40,720	*1:18*		*aet*		*Latchford 113*	*Hodge*	*Gidman*	*Bailey*	*Wright*	*Lyons*	*Ratcliffe*	*King**	*Eastoe*	*Latchford*	*Hartford*	*Ross*	*Varadi*
		(at Elland Road)					Ref: C Seel	Bonds plays out of his skin to take the tie into extra-time, having had a header ruled out for pushing. Latchford's diving header made it 1-1. With two minutes left Lampard, who only played because Martin had tonsillitis, launched himself at Cross's flick-on to earn a Wembley date.											
F	N	ARSENAL	7	W	1-0	1-0	Brooking 13	Parkes	Stewart	Lampard	Bonds	Martin	Devonshire	Allen	Pearson	Cross	Brooking	Pike	
	10/5	100,000	*1:4*					*Jennings*	*Rice*	*Devine**	*Talbot*	*O'Leary*	*Young*	*Brady*	*Sunderland*	*Stapleton*	*Price*	*Rix*	*Nelson*
		(at Wembley)					Ref: G Courtney	Arsenal are holders of the Cup, and needed four matches to get past Liverpool in their semi-final. This is their third successive final, but they are beaten by Brooking's header. Young should have been sent off for tripping Allen. Four days later Arsenal lose the Cup-Winners' Cup final.											

		Home					Away					
	P	W	D	L	F	A	W	D	L	F	A	Pts
1 Leicester	42	12	5	4	32	19	9	8	4	26	19	55
2 Sunderland	42	16	5	0	47	13	5	7	9	22	29	54
3 Birmingham	42	14	5	2	37	16	7	6	8	21	22	53
4 Chelsea	42	14	3	4	34	16	9	4	8	32	36	53
5 QP Rangers	42	10	9	2	46	25	8	4	9	29	28	49
6 Luton	42	9	10	2	36	17	7	7	7	30	28	49
7 WEST HAM	42	13	2	6	37	21	7	5	9	17	22	47
8 Cambridge	42	11	6	4	40	23	3	10	8	21	30	44
9 Newcastle	42	13	6	2	35	19	2	8	11	18	30	44
10 Preston	42	8	10	3	30	23	4	9	8	26	29	43
11 Oldham	42	12	5	4	30	21	4	6	11	19	32	43
12 Swansea	42	13	1	7	31	20	4	8	9	17	33	43
13 Shrewsbury	42	12	3	6	41	23	6	2	13	19	30	41
14 Orient	42	7	9	5	29	31	5	8	8	19	23	41
15 Cardiff	42	11	4	6	21	16	5	4	12	20	32	40
16 Wrexham	42	13	2	6	26	15	3	4	14	14	34	38
17 Notts Co	42	4	11	6	24	22	7	4	10	27	30	37
18 Watford	42	9	6	6	27	18	3	7	11	12	28	37
19 Bristol Rov	42	9	8	4	33	23	2	5	14	17	41	35
20 Fulham	42	6	4	11	19	28	5	3	13	23	46	29
21 Burnley	42	5	9	7	19	23	1	6	14	20	50	27
22 Charlton	42	6	6	9	25	31	0	4	17	14	47	22
	924	227	129	106	699	463	106	129	227	463	699	924

Odds & ends

Double wins: (5) Burnley, Leicester, Cardiff, Bristol R, Orient.
Double losses: (2) Chelsea, Shrewsbury.

Won from behind: (9) Burnley (h), Leicester (h&a), Bristol R (h), Cambridge (h), QPR (h), Southend LC (h), Sunderland LC (h), Orient FAC (a).
Lost from in front: (3) Chelsea (a), Fulham (h), Swansea (a).

High spots: Winning FA Cup.
Dropping just one point in seven league games from 21 December.

Low spots: Bad league run from March, just two points from six games, to spoil chances of promotion.

West Ham played a total of 17 cup-ties, six of them replays.
The gate at Sunderland in the league was 10,000 than the next biggest away gate.

Hammer of the Year: Alvin Martin.
Ever-presents: (0).
Hat-tricks: (1) Billy Lansdowne.
Leading scorer: (18) David Cross.

	Appearances						Goals			
	Lge	*Sub*	LC	*Sub*	FAC	*Sub*	Lge	LC	FAC	Tot
Allen, Paul	31		7		7	*1*	2		1	3
Banton, Dale	2	*2*	1							
Bonds, Billy	34		9		5		1			1
Brooking, Trevor	37		8		7		3	1	2	6
Brush, Paul	27		4		6					
Cross, David	38	*1*	9		5		12	5	1	18
Devonshire, Alan	34		7		8		5		1	6
Ferguson, Bobby	2		1							
Holland, Pat	21	*5*	8		1		4	1		5
Lampard, Frank	35	*1*	6		7				1	1
Lansdowne, Billy	5	*3*	4	*1*			1	3		4
Martin, Alvin	40		8		7		2	1		3
Morgan, Nicky	4	*2*	1				1			1
Neighbour, Jimmy	22	*1*			4		1			1
Parkes, Phil	40		8		8					
Pearson, Stuart	24	*1*	3		8		5	1	2	8
Pike, Geoff	27	*4*	6		7	*1*	5	1	1	7
Smith, Mark	1		1							
Stewart, Ray	38		8		8		10	1	3	14
(own-goals)							2		1	3
19 players used	**462**	***20***	**99**	***1***	**88**	***2***	**54**	**14**	**13**	**81**

No	Date	Att	Pos	Pt	F-A	H-T	Scorers, Times, and Referees	1	2	3	4	5	6	7	8	9	10	11	12 sub used
1	H LUTON			L	1-2	0-0	Stewart 56p	Parkes	Stewart	Brush	Bonds	Martin	Devonshire	Holland	**Goddard***	Cross	Brooking	Pike	Lampard
	16/8	27,933		0			*Moss 64p, 88p*	*Findlay*	*Stephen*	*Donaghy*	*Grealish*	*Saxby*	*Price*	*Hill*	*Stein*	*White**	*Antic*	*Moss*	*West*
							Ref: R Reeves	Paul Goddard signs from QPR for a record £800,000, but is clattered by numerous tackles from behind and goes off with a bruised Achilles tendon. None of the game's three penalties was disputed. Grealish grassed Holland; Martin upended David Moss; and Bonds fouled Stein.											
2	A BRISTOL CITY			D	1-1	1-1	Cross 19	Parkes	Stewart	Brush	Bonds	Martin	Devonshire	Holland	Goddard	Cross	Brooking	Pike	
	19/8	*13,554*		1			*Ritchie 15*	*Cashley*	*Sweeney*	*Baddeley*	*Tainton*	*Rodgers**	*Merrick*	*Fitzpatrick*	*Mabbutt*	*Ritchie*	*Mann*	*Whitehead*	*Garland*
							Ref: D Lloyd	Goddard thought he had scored his first Hammers goal until he saw the linesman's raised flag. Ritchie capitalised when Bonds couldn't repel Fitzpatrick's cross. Cross headed the equaliser from Brooking's centre. David Rodgers was carried off as a result of colliding with the scorer.											
3	A PRESTON		17	D	0-0	0-0		Parkes	Lampard	Brush	Stewart	Martin	Devonshire	Holland	Goddard	Cross	Brooking	Pike	
	23/8	*9,063*	*14*	2				*Tunks*	*Cameron*	*McAteer*	*Burns*	*Baxter*	*Blackley**	*Bell*	*Coleman*	*Elliott*	*Potts*	*McGee*	*Doyle*
							Ref: M Warner	Preston continue their run of early-season draws. There was little to enthuse about from this fixture, which was littered with mistakes from both teams. Lampard returned to the side, with Ray Stewart switched to central defence. At least, two away draws compensate for the home defeat.											
4	H NOTTS CO		7	W	4-0	1-0	Cross 17, Goddard 53, 75, Stewart 67p	Parkes	Stewart	Lampard	Bonds	Martin	Devonshire	Holland	Goddard	Cross	Brooking	Pike	
	30/8	*21,769*	*6*	4				*Avramovic*	*Benjamin*	*O'Brien*	*Kelly*	*Kilcline*	*Richards*	*McCulloch*	*Masson*	*Christie**	*Hunt*	*Hooks*	*Mair*
							Ref: D Hedges	Jimmy Sirrel's County like to mix it. Four of his players were booked, including McCulloch for hurling the ball into the crowd. Cross towered above Kilcline for the first goal, and later won a penalty when fouled by Pedro Richards. Goddard was denied the first hat-trick of his career.											
5	A CHELSEA		4	W	1-0	0-0	Wilkins 88 (og)	Parkes	Stewart	Lampard	Bonds	Martin	Devonshire	Holland	Goddard	Cross	Brooking	Pike	
	6/9	***32,669***	*20*	6				*Borota*	*Wilkins*	*Rofe*	*Bumstead**	*Nutton*	*Pates*	*Britton*	*Fillery*	*Lee*	*Walker*	*Viljoen*	*Chivers*
							Ref: P Reeves	Lyall and scout Eddie Baily are away spying on Castilla in Spain. They miss the sight of Geoff Hurst's Chelsea losing in the dying minutes as a result of a bizarre own-goal by Graham Wilkins. He managed to hook the ball out, but it had already crossed the line. Pike had a good game.											
6	H SHREWSBURY		3	W	3-0	1-0	King 7 (og), Goddard 65, Cross 67	Parkes	Stewart	Lampard	Bonds	Martin	Devonshire	Neighbour*	Goddard	Cross	Brooking	Pike	Morgan
	13/9	22,339	*20*	8				*Wardle*	*King*	*Leonard*	*Lindsay*	*Griffin*	*Keay*	*Tong*	*Atkins*	*Dungworth*	*Edwards*	*Petts*	
							Ref: C Maskell	Shrewsbury beat West Ham twice last season, but John King's own-goal from Brooking's cross ruled out any repetition. David Cross spent the 90 minutes shooting on sight, and was eventually rewarded with his 50th goal for West Ham. Neighbour's comeback lasted just 25 minutes.											
7	H WATFORD		2	W	3-2	0-1	Cross 53, Barnes 67, Brooking 89	Parkes	Stewart	Lampard	Bonds	Martin	Devonshire	**Barnes**	Goddard	Cross	Brooking	Pike	
	20/9	24,288	*15*	10			*Poskett 25, Jackett 55*	*Steele*	*Henderson*	*Jackett*	*Blissett*	*Sims*	*Bolton*	*Callaghan**	*Poskett*	*Jenkins*	*Train*	*Rostron*	*Harrison*
							Ref: A Robinson	The mayhem of Madrid haunts West Ham and Bonds, who, according to the tabloids, labelled certain trouble-makers 'scum'. He was booed onto the pitch, where a wreath was laid for a dead fan. Brooking's late header from Lampard's cross takes Hammers second behind Blackburn.											
8	A CAMBRIDGE		2	W	2-1	1-1	Goddard 10, Cross 71	Parkes	Stewart	Lampard	Bonds	Martin	Devonshire	Holland	Goddard	Cross	Brooking	Pike	
	27/9	*8,591*	*20*	12			*Finney 31*	*Webster*	*Donaldson*	*Buckley**	*Smith*	*Fallon*	*Gibbins*	*Evans*	*Spriggs*	*Reilly*	*Finney*	*Christie*	*O'Neill*
							Ref: P Richardson	A fourth successive league defeat for John Docherty's Cambridge brings a fifth straight win for West Ham. Goddard's low drive was answered by Tom Finney's close-range header. West Ham were in territorial control through the second half and were rewarded by Cross's firm header.											
9	A NEWCASTLE		3	D	0-0	0-0		Parkes	Stewart	Lampard	Bonds	Martin	Devonshire	Holland	Goddard*	Cross	Neighbour	Pike	Brush
	4/10	*24,848*	*10*	13				*Carr*	*Kelly*	*Davies*	*Walker*	*Boam*	*Mitchell*	*Shoulder*	*Hibbitt*	*Shinton*	*Rafferty*	*Koenen*	
							Ref: G Nolan	Newcastle stay unbeaten at home; West Ham stay unbeaten away. The dropped point means the Hammers drop to third behind Notts County. John Lyall has been named Bell's Whisky Manager of the Month for September. A recurrent knee injury forces Paul Goddard's substitution.											
10	H CARDIFF		2	W	1-0	0-0	Neighbour 54	Parkes	Stewart	Lampard	Bonds	Martin	Devonshire	Holland	Morgan	Cross	Neighbour	Pike	
	7/10	**20,402**	*12*	15				*Grotier*	*Grapes*	*Thomas*	*Hughes*	*Pontin*	*Roberts*	*Micallef*	*Kitchen*	*Stevens*	*Ronson*	*Buchanan*	
							Ref: A Gunn	Jimmy Neighbour plays instead of the injured Brooking and bags his second ever goal for the Hammers, turning in Devonshire's cross. The goal came seconds after Peter Kitchen's effort for Cardiff had been ruled out for handball. West Ham go back above Notts Co to second place.											
11	H BLACKBURN		1	W	2-0	1-0	Cross 40, 53	Parkes	Stewart	Lampard	Bonds	Martin	Devonshire	Holland	Goddard	Cross	Neighbour	Pike	
	11/10	32,402	*3*	17				*Butcher*	*Branagan*	*Devries*	*Coughlin*	*Keeley*	*Fazackerley*	*Brotherston**	*Stonehouse*	*Garner*	*Comstive*	*Parkes*	*Rathbone*
							Ref: G Napthine	A titanic battle between the top two. Geoff Pike covers every blade of grass and David Cross takes his season's tally to 14 goals already. The two combined for the second goal. Pike's shot was turned by the keeper out to Cross, who was denied a hat-trick by the width of a goalpost.											

No	Venue	Opponent	Att	Pos	Res/Pts	F-A	H-T	Scorers, Times, and Referees	1	2	3	4	5	6	7	8	9	10	11	12 sub used
12	A	OLDHAM		2	D	0-0	0-0		Parkes	Stewart	Lampard	Bonds	Martin	Devonshire*	Holland	Morgan	Cross	Neighbour	Pike	Barnes
18/10			*8,344*	*11*	18				*McDonnell*	*Sinclair*	*Blair*	*Kowenicki**	*Clements*	*Hurst*	*Keegan*	*Futcher*	*Steel*	*Stainrod*	*Heaton*	*Atkinson*
								Ref: D Civil	A stodgy pitch and a blustery wind combine to reduce the entertainment value. Oldham preserve their unbeaten home record, but with a Cup-Winners tie looming Lyall is more worried about injuries. Brooking is out with a groin strain and Devonshire limps off with the same problem.											
13	H	BOLTON		2	W	2-1	1-0	Walsh 39 (og), Pike 47	Parkes	Stewart	Brush	Bonds	Martin	Devonshire	Holland	Goddard	Cross	Neighbour	Pike	
25/10			25,257	*12*	20			*Kidd 83*	*Poole*	*Graham*	*Burke*	*Cantello*	*Jones*	*Walsh*	*Reid*	*Whatmore*	*Carter*	*Kidd*	*Gowling*	
								Ref: A Grey	West Ham force 22 corners against Stan Anderson's Bolton, which gives a better indication of the balance of play than does the score. Mike Walsh headed an own-goal before Geoff Pike doubled the lead with one of his specials, sprinting from the halfway line to score off a post.											
14	A	BRISTOL ROV		2	W	1-0	1-0	Goddard 26	Parkes	Stewart	Lampard	Bonds	Martin	Devonshire*	Holland	Goddard	Cross	Neighbour	Pike	Brush
1/11			***6,328***	*22*	22				*Thomas*	*Gillies*	*Bater*	*McCaffrey*	*Hughes*	*Cooper*	*Barrowcl'gh**	*Williams G*	*Mabbutt*	*Bates*	*Barrett*	*Emmanuel*
								Ref: L Robinson	Considering Rovers are propping up the table, and are still searching for their first win, this was an unconvincing result. Parkes was the busier keeper and in the second half he was kept on his toes throughout. Paul Goddard's brilliant goal was ideal preparation for the trip to Romania.											
15	H	GRIMSBY		2	W	2-1	1-0	Cross 15, 55	Parkes	Brush	Lampard	Bonds	Martin	Neighbour	Holland	Goddard	Cross	Brooking	Pike	
8/11			25,468	*19*	24			*Stone 89*	*Batch*	*Stone*	*Crosby*	*Waters*	*Wigginton*	*Moore K*	*Brolly*	*Kilmore*	*Drinkell*	*Mitchell*	*Liddell**	*Steeples*
								Ref: L Burden	The players looked knackered after their trip to Romania, and make hard work of beating a side who had scored only six goals all season. Cross headed two typical goals, the first from Brush's cross, the second from Brooking's. Mike Brolly's free-kick raised Grimsby's total to seven.											
16	H	BRISTOL CITY		1	W	**5-0**	2-0	Goddard 11, 89, Martin 16, Brooking 71, [Cross 85]	Parkes	Stewart	Lampard	Bonds	Martin	Devonshire	Holland	Goddard	Cross	Brooking	Pike	
11/11			25,210	*20*	26				*Cashley*	*Sweeney*	*Hay*	*Mann*	*Marshall*	*Whitehead*	*Tainton**	*Fitzpatrick*	*Whitehead*	*Ritchie*	*Pritchard*	*Smith*
								Ref: J Martin	City haven't won away all season and permit West Ham to go top for the first time. Yet what might have happened had City not squandered an easy chance at 0-0? Alvin Martin's shot was deflected in off Merrick, and Cross takes his tally to 19, the same as that for the whole of 1979-80.											
17	A	LUTON		1	L	2-3	1-2	Brooking 44, 49	Parkes	Stewart	Lampard	Bonds	Martin	Devonshire	Holland	Goddard	Cross	Brooking	Pike	
15/11			*17,031*	*10*	26			*Stein 14, 17, Moss 85*	*Findlay*	*Stephens*	*Donaghy*	*Grealish*	*Saxby*	*Price*	*Hill*	*Stein*	*White*	*Aizlewood**	*Moss*	*West*
								Ref: C White	Luton were the last team to beat the Hammers. They now complete the double. The last time Brooking scored twice in one match was against Palace in 1972. He hasn't scored a hat-trick since Newcastle 13 years ago. Having got to 2-2 it was galling to lose; Hill nodded down to Moss.											
18	H	SWANSEA		1	W	2-0	0-0	Cross 66, Goddard 83	Parkes	Stewart	Lampard	Bonds	Martin	Devonshire*	Holland	Goddard	Cross	Brooking	Pike	Neighbour
22/11			27,376	*6*	28				*Stewart*	*Attley*	*Hadziabdic**	*Rushbury*	*Charles*	*Stevenson*	*Craig*	*Waddle*	*James R*	*Mahoney*	*Robinson*	*Loveridge*
								Ref: D Hutchinson	John Toshack's Swansea take no prisoners. He doesn't mince words either, demanding 'Where's the justice?' Goddard was plainly offside as Cross broke the deadlock, and the linesman duly had his flag up. On the run of play Swansea got off lightly. Phillips struck his own crossbar.											
19	A	DERBY		1	L	0-2	0-1		Parkes	Stewart	Lampard	Bonds	Martin	Devonshire	Holland	Goddard	Cross	Brooking	Pike	
26/11			*18,446*	*9*	28			*Biley 19, Clark 88*	*Jones*	*Powell S*	*Richards*	*Clark*	*McFarland*	*Ramage*	*Powell B*	*Swindlehurst*	*Biley*	*Wilson*	*Emson*	
								Ref: D Webb	Keith Burkinshaw, manager of League Cup opponents Spurs, sees West Ham fail to score for only the third time this season. They came close against Colin Addison's Derby when Goddard and Holland hit the bar, but could never get back on terms after Biley headed in Emson's cross.											
20	A	WREXHAM		1	D	2-2	1-1	Devonshire 2, Goddard 51	Parkes	Stewart	Lampard	Bonds	Martin	Devonshire	Holland	Goddard	Cross	Brooking	Pike	
29/11			*8,941*	*17*	29			*Cartwright 35, Edwards 67*	*Davies*	*Sutton*	*Kenworthy*	*Davis*	*Cegielski*	*Carrodus*	*Fox*	*Arkwright*	*Edwards*	*McNeil*	*Cartwright*	
								Ref: C Seel	Devonshire had had a bet with Pat Holland over who would score first this season. Devonshire wins it with a sensational individual goal that saw him waltz through half the Wrexham team. But Holland does not pay up, changing the rules to who scores the most, not who scores first.											
21	H	SHEFFIELD WED		1	W	2-1	2-1	Brooking 40, Holland 42	Parkes	Stewart	Lampard	Bonds	Martin	Devonshire	Holland	Goddard	Cross	Brooking	Pike	
6/12			30,746	*6*	31			*Mirocevic 35*	*Bolder*	*Blackhall*	*Grant*	*Smith*	*Shirtliff*	*Sterland*	*Mirocevic**	*Johnson*	*Leman*	*McCulloch*	*Curran*	*Owen*
								Ref: D Letts	Jack Charlton's Owls provide West Ham with their 10th straight home win. Bookies rate them 8-13 on for promotion. Brooking was booked for the third time in his career for a late tackle. Bolder was only booked for a professional foul and the referee needed a police escort at the end.											
22	A	BLACKBURN		1	D	0-0	0-0		Parkes	Stewart	Lampard	Bonds	Martin	Devonshire	Holland	Goddard	Cross	Brooking	Pike	
13/12			*13,279*	*8*	32				*Butcher*	*Speight*	*Branagan*	*Kendall*	*Keeley*	*Fazackerley*	*Brotherston*	*Stonehouse*	*Lowey*	*McKenzie**	*Parkes*	*Burke*
								Ref: A Saunders	Blackburn have slumped from first to eighth though remain unbeaten at home. West Ham score goals so freely at home that it is surprising to learn they have scored only nine in 11 away games – fewer than nine other sides in the division. In fact, Hammers are away draw specialists.											
23	H	DERBY		1	W	3-1	1-1	Cross 44, Goddard 74, Brooking 85	Parkes	Stewart	Lampard	Bonds	Martin	Devonshire	Holland	Goddard	Cross	Brooking	Pike	
20/12			24,071	*8*	34			*Swindlehurst 42p*	*Jones*	*Emery*	*Richards*	*Clark*	*Osgood*	*Ramage*	*Powell S*	*Hector*	*Biley*	*Swindlehurst*	*Emson*	
								Ref: R Challis	When Pike hauled down Kevin Hector, Colin Addison's Derby must have hoped for an upset. But moments later Lampard's miscued shot fell kindly for Cross to equalise. Brooking dominated the second half, and his solo goal has the crowd on its feet. West Ham go five points clear.											

No	Date		Att	Pos	Pt	F-A	H-T	Scorers, Times, and Referees	1	2	3	4	5	6	7	8	9	10	11	12 sub used
24	A	QP RANGERS		1	L	**0-3**	0-1		Parkes	Stewart	Lampard	Bonds	Martin	Devonshire	Holland	Goddard	Cross*	Brooking	Pike	Neighbour
	26/12		*23,811*	*12*	34			*Silkman 30, Currie 52, Stainrod 84*	*Burridge*	*Shanks*	*Gillard*	*Fenwick*	*Wicks*	*Roeder*	*Flanagan*	*King*	*Stainrod*	*Currie**	*Silkman*	*Waddock*
								Ref: B Hill	Terry Venables' hastily rebuilt Rangers cashed in on the well-travelled Barry Silkman, who scored one goal and made the others. Silkman's bad early back-pass let in Cross, who missed and hurt his ribs. Phil Parkes was responsible for the second goal, fumbling Silkman's cross.											
25	H	ORIENT		1	W	2-1	0-0	Holland 64, Allen 82	Parkes	Stewart	Lampard*	Bonds	Martin	Devonshire	Holland	Goddard	Morgan	Brooking	Pike	Allen
	27/12		34,408	*8*	36			*Chiedozie 71*	*Day*	*Fisher*	*Roffey*	*Taylor T*	*Gray*	*Parsons*	*Chiedozie*	*Moores*	*Mayo*	*Bowles*	*Taylor P*	
								Ref: E Read	A no-holds-barred local derby. Orient boss Jimmy Bloomfield later lambasts Lampard for repeatedly kicking John Chiedozie into orbit. Pat Holland headed in Devonshire's cross; Chiedozie scored a freak equaliser when Parkes fluffed Parson's cross; Allen hit a spectacular winner.											
26	A	SWANSEA		1	W	3-1	2-0	Brooking 24, Pike 34, Cross 58	Parkes	Stewart	Lampard	Bonds	Martin	Devonshire	Holland	Goddard	Cross	Brooking	Pike	
	10/1		*22,110*	*2*	38			*Curtis 54*	*Stewart*	*Attley*	*Hadziabdic*	*Mahoney*	*Stevenson*	*Phillips*	*James R*	*Curtis*	*James L**	*Charles*	*Robinson*	*Giles*
								Ref: M Scott	Hammers win the battle of the top two to go six points clear. Lyall instructed Cross and Goddard to play tight together to frustrate Swansea's sweeper, Phillips, who was pressured into conceding the Hammers' third goal. Paul Goddard's cheeky dummy had set up Brooking's opener.											
27	A	NOTTS CO		1	D	1-1	1-0	Holland 22	Parkes	Stewart	Brush	Bonds	Martin	Devonshire	Holland*	Goddard	Cross	Brooking	Pike	Allen
	17/1		*13,718*	*3*	39			*Hooks 56*	*Avramovic*	*Benjamin*	*O'Brien*	*Kelly*	*Kilcline*	*Richards*	*McCulloch*	*Masson*	*Christie*	*Hunt*	*Hooks*	
								Ref: P Partridge	Holland pays a heavy price for scoring; he collides with Avramovic and goes off with knee ligament damage. Though County have lost just once at home, this was a point lost. Cross incredibly hit the bar from two feet out, Brooking hit a post, and Allen's 'goal' was narrowly offside.											
28	H	PRESTON		1	W	**5-0**	2-0	Goddard 10, Pike 33, Lampard 76, [Devonshire 80, 87]	Parkes	Stewart	Lampard	Bonds	Martin	Devonshire	Neighbour	Goddard	Cross	Brooking	Pike	
	31/1		26,413	*20*	41				*Tunks*	*Westwell*	*McAteer*	*Bell*	*Baxter*	*O'Riorden*	*Coleman*	*Doyle*	*Elliott*	*McGee**	*Houston*	*Sayer*
								Ref: C Thomas	West Ham shrug off defeats by Wrexham and Coventry by serving up five super goals. Pick of the bunch was Lampard's, who drove back a clearance from 30 yards. Preston manager Nobby Stiles admitted: 'They never gave us a look in.' West Ham's lead widens to seven points.											
29	A	SHREWSBURY		1	W	2-0	1-0	Devonshire 33, Cross 90	Parkes	Stewart	Lampard	Bonds	Martin	Devonshire	Neighbour	Goddard*	Cross	Brooking	Pike	Barnes
	7/2		*9,201*	*20*	43				*Wardle*	*King*	*Leonard*	*MacLaren**	*Griffin*	*Keay*	*Tong*	*Atkins*	*Bates*	*Biggins*	*Cross*	*Petts*
								Ref: H King	A statistical quirk. All other 10 games in Division 2 ended in home wins. So casual did West Ham become after half-time that they would have had only themselves to blame had this been a home win. Devonshire's header was followed by Cross connecting with Brooking's free-kick.											
30	H	CHELSEA		1	W	4-0	1-0	Brooking 26, 75, Cross 61, Devonshire 89	Parkes	Stewart	Lampard	Bonds	Martin	Devonshire	Neighbour	Goddard	Cross	Brooking	Pike	
	14/2		35,164	*3*	45				*Borota*	*Locke*	*Rofe*	*Bumstead*	*Droy*	*Chivers*	*Elmes*	*Fillery*	*Lee*	*Mayes*	*Rhr'des-Brown*	
								Ref: S Bates	Thousands are locked out of this top-of-the-table clash. Brooking illuminates it with two classic goals, the first when Cross drags a defender wide to create space; the second with an exquisite chip as Borota strays off his line. West Ham are now 10 points clear of third-placed Chelsea.											
31	H	CAMBRIDGE		1	W	4-2	2-1	Devonshire 33, Stewart 36p, 65, [Goddard 58]	Parkes	Stewart	Lampard	Bonds	Martin	Devonshire	Neighbour	Goddard	Cross	Brooking	Pike	
	21/2		**36,002**	*11*	47			*Reilly 31, Spriggs 82*	*Key*	*Donaldson**	*Murray*	*Smith*	*Fallon*	*Finney*	*Streete*	*Spriggs*	*Reilly*	*Lyons*	*Gibbins*	*O'Neill*
								Ref: T Bune	The ref takes a lenient view of a second-half punch-up between Alvin Martin and George Reilly, sending neither of them off. Reilly's header had opened the scoring for John Docherty's Cambridge. Ray Stewart's penalty was awarded after Fallon had shoved David Cross in the back.											
32	A	WATFORD		1	W	2-1	0-0	Cross 56, 63	Parkes	Stewart	Lampard	Bonds	Martin	Devonshire	Neighbour	Goddard	Cross	Brooking	Pike	
	28/2		*20,786*	*14*	49			*Poskett 85*	*Sherwood*	*Rice*	*Pritchett*	*Taylor*	*Sims*	*Bolton*	*Ward*	*Blissett*	*Armstrong*	*Jackett*	*Poskett*	
								Ref: B Stevens	Watford boss Graham Taylor reckoned the only difference between the sides was Phil Parkes' goalkeeping, especially during Watford's early assaults. Martin needed five stitches in a head wound following a mid-air collision with John Ward. Cross takes his season's goal tally to 27.											
33	H	NEWCASTLE		1	W	1-0	1-0	Cross 3	Parkes	Stewart	Lampard	Bonds	Martin	Allen*	Neighbour	Goddard	Cross	Brooking	Pike	Pearson
	7/3		26,274	*14*	51				*Carr*	*Brownlie*	*Davies*	*Martin*	*Barton*	*Halliday*	*Shoulder*	*Trewick*	*Harford*	*Wharton*	*Waddle**	*Carney*
								Ref: K Baker	West Ham have eaten humble pie after losing to Tbilisi, and this bread and butter game offered little that was memorable. Newcastle had only scored eight away goals all season and carried little threat. Cross's early header takes Hammers 10 points clear of second-placed Notts County.											
34	H	OLDHAM		1	D	1-1	0-0	Goddard 81	Parkes	Stewart	Lampard	Bonds	Martin	Brush*	Pearson	Goddard	Cross	Brooking	Pike	Barnes
	21/3		24,394	*17*	52			*Wylde 49*	*Platt*	*Edwards*	*Blair*	*Keegan*	*McDonough*	*Futcher*	*Wylde*	*Heaton*	*Steel*	*Palmer*	*Atkinson*	
								Ref: J Deakin	Another limp display following European exertions. When Parkes failed to gather a corner-kick the ball fell to Wylde. Martin's dreadful back-pass almost made it 0-2 before Goddard squared things from Barnes' corner. Stewart played in midfield and looked like a fish out of water.											

35	A	BOLTON		1	D	1-1	0-1	Brooking 61	Parkes	Stewart	Lampard	Bonds	Martin*	Devonshire	Neighbour	Goddard	Cross	Brooking	Pike	Pearson
	28/3		*13,271*	*15*	53			*Whatmore 20*	*Poole*	*Nicholson*	*Walsh*	*Reid*	*Jones*	*Cantello*	*Nikolic*	*Whatmore*	*Thomas*	*Hoggan*	*Gowling*	
								Ref: M Heath	Minds are not at Burnden Park but on Liverpool in the League Cup final replay. With promotion a formality, all John Lyall cares about is that his players pick up no injuries. The only doubt is Martin, who was taken off with an ankle injury. Devonshire came through without mishap.											
36	H	BRISTOL ROV		1	W	2-0	1-0	Pike 32, Goddard 50	Parkes	Stewart	Lampard	Bonds	Brush	Devonshire	Neighbour	Goddard	Cross	Brooking	Pike	
	4/4		23,544	*22*	55				*McAlister*	*Gillies*	*Jones*	*McCaffrey*	*Hughes*	*Emmanuel*	*Williams G**	*Williams D*	*Randall*	*Penny*	*Mabbutt*	*Cooper*
								Ref: D Hutchinson	West Ham put defeat by Liverpool out of their minds by celebrating promotion with six matches still to play. Terry Cooper's bottom-placed Rovers have won away only once and were lambs to the slaughter. Pike took Goddard's pass to fire the first goal and launch the celebrations.											
37	A	GRIMSBY		1	W	5-1	1-0	Cross 32, 47, 88, 89, Pike 80	Parkes	Stewart	Lampard	Bonds	Martin	Devonshire	Neighbour	Goddard	Cross	Brooking	Pike	
	11/4		*17,924*	*6*	57			*Waters 70p*	*Batch*	*Stone*	*Crombie**	*Waters*	*Wigginton*	*Moore K*	*Brolly*	*Whymark*	*Drinkell*	*Mitchell*	*Cumming*	*Ford*
								Ref: R Toseland	David Cross had been stuck on 29 goals for five games. He races up to 33 in a magical performance with the first four-goal haul of his career. Grimsby were unlikely victims, having lost only once and conceded just four home goals all season. Stewart tripped Cumming for the penalty.											
38	A	ORIENT		1	W	2-0	2-0	Neighbour 17, Pike 40	Parkes	Stewart	Lampard	Bonds	Martin	Devonshire	Neighbour	Pearson*	Cross	Brooking	Pike	Barnes
	18/4		*14,592*	*15*	59				*Day*	*Fisher*	*Roffey*	*Taylor T**	*Gray*	*Moores*	*Chiedozie*	*Hughton*	*Jennings*	*Bowles*	*Taylor P*	*Mayo*
								Ref: R Lewis	Lyall missed this game, going up to Scotland to try to unearth another nugget like Ray Stewart. A boring match was illuminated only by Jimmy Neighbour bursting between two defenders for the first goal, and Pike rocketing his third in three games. West Ham are still unbeaten in 1981.											
39	H	QP RANGERS		1	W	3-0	2-0	Goddard 8, 28, 81	Parkes	Stewart	Lampard	Bonds	Martin	Devonshire	Neighbour	Goddard	Cross	Brooking*	Pike	Barnes
	21/4		24,599	*10*	61				*Burridge*	*Neill*	*Gillard*	*Fenwick*	*Wicks**	*Roeder*	*Waddock*	*Francis*	*Flanagan*	*Currie*	*Sealy*	*Burke*
								Ref: L Shapter	Terry Venables' QPR were the last league side to beat West Ham, back on Boxing Day. QPR have blown their own promotion hopes in recent weeks. Ex-Ranger Paul Goddard bags the first hat-trick of his career. Parkes saved Gerry Francis' penalty after Bonds had fouled Roeder.											
40	H	WREXHAM		1	W	1-0	1-0	Stewart 43p	Parkes	Stewart	Lampard	Bonds	Martin	Devonshire	Neighbour	Goddard*	Cross	Brooking	Pike	Pearson
	2/5		30,515	*16*	63				*Davies*	*Dowman*	*Dwyer*	*Davis*	*Cegielski*	*Carrodus*	*Fox*	*Buxton**	*Vinter*	*McNeil*	*Hill*	*Edwards*
								Ref: A Grey	West Ham's target is to beat Middlesbrough's Division 2 record of 65 points. Stewart's seventh penalty of the season keeps them on track, and avenges defeat by Wrexham in the FA Cup. Wayne Cegielski conceded the penalty when fouling Cross. Lyall wants to sign Steve Coppell.											
41	A	CARDIFF		1	D	0-0	0-0		Parkes	Stewart	Lampard	Bonds	Martin	Devonshire	Neighbour	Morgan	Cross	Brooking	Pike	
	6/5		*10,558*	*19*	64				*Healey*	*Jones*	*Sullivan*	*Grapes**	*Pontin*	*Dwyer*	*Lewis*	*Kitchen*	*Stevens*	*Ronson*	*Micallef*	*Thomas*
								Ref: P Reeves	Nicky Morgan plays in place of the injured Goddard and does well. This draw averts relegation for Cardiff, and dooms Preston, who won 2-1 at Derby. This is West Ham's ninth away draw in the league. Now they need to win at Hillsborough to break Middlesbrough's points record.											
42	A	SHEFFIELD WED		1	W	1-0	0-0	Morgan 64	Parkes	Stewart	Lampard	Bonds	Martin*	Devonshire	Neighbour	Morgan	Cross	Brooking	Pike	Brush
	8/5		*21,087*	*10*	66				*Bolder*	*Blackhall*	*Grant*	*Smith*	*Shirtliff*	*Johnson*	*Mellor*	*Taylor*	*King**	*McCulloch*	*Curran*	*Pearson*
	Home		Away					Ref: N Midgley	It is ironic that victory over Jack Charlton's Owls enables West Ham to break the 65-points record established by Jack Charlton's Boro. Against all expectations this was an entertaining game, the Hammers 61st of the season. Stuart Pearson is up for sale at a knock-down price.											
Average	27,140		15,625																	
League Cup																				
2:1	A	BURNLEY		17	W	2-0	2-0	Goddard 14, Cross 22	Parkes	Stewart	Lampard	Bonds	Martin	Devonshire	Holland	Goddard	Cross	Brooking	Pike	
	26/8		*6,818*	*3:13*					*Stevenson*	*Wood*	*Thomson*	*Rodaway*	*Laws*	*Scott*	*Dobson*	*Cassidy*	*Cavener*	*Hamilton*	*Taylor*	
								Ref: D Shaw	Goddard is happy to score his first goal – a volley – for West Ham, who might have settled this tie with five or six goals. After David Cross outjumped Jim Thomson to head in Brooking's cross for the second, West Ham took their foot off the gas, and that might prove unwise.											
2:2	H	BURNLEY		7	W	4-0	1-0	Stewart 33p, Goddard 65, Wood 77 (og), [Pike 86]	Parkes	Stewart	Lampard	Bonds	Martin	Devonshire	Holland*	Goddard	Cross	Brooking	Pike	Allen
	2/9		15,216	*3:19*					*Stevenson*	*Laws*	*Holt*	*Scott**	*Dobson*	*Overson*	*Cassidy*	*Young*	*Hamilton*	*Taylor*	*Cavener*	
								Ref: A Seville (Hammers win 6-0 on aggregate)	When Brian Laws brings down Devonshire, Ray Stewart misses his second penalty in 15 attempts since joining West Ham. But as with his other miss, the ball was swept into the net, this time by Goddard. Stewart had already scored one penalty in this match, when Holt handled.											
3	A	CHARLTON		2	W	2-1	1-1	Cross 20, 81	Parkes	Stewart	Lampard	Bonds	Martin	Devonshire	Barnes	Goddard	Cross	Brush	Pike	
	23/9		*17,884*	*3:10*				*Robinson 21*	*Wood*	*Gritt*	*Warman*	*Shaw*	*Berry*	*Tydeman*	*Powell*	*Walsh*	*Hales*	*Smith*	*Robinson*	
								Ref: M Taylor	This vibrant cup-tie saw Phil Parkes make the first goal with a phenomenally long goal-kick, which bounced neatly for Cross to lob Jeff Wood. Charlton's Phil Warman dished out some heavy treatment on Barnes, who had the last laugh when floating over the cross for Cross's winner.											
4	H	BARNSLEY		2	W	2-1	0-0	Martin 69, Cross 71	Parkes	Stewart	Lampard*	Brush	Martin	Devonshire	Holland	Goddard	Cross	Neighbour	Pike	Allen
	28/10		21,548	*3:7*				*Evans 63*	*New*	*Joyce*	*Chambers*	*Glavin*	*Banks*	*McCarthy*	*Evans*	*Riley*	*Aylott*	*Lester*	*Downes*	
								Ref: A Glasson	Lucky Hammers. Barnsley boss Norman Hunter complains that David Cross handled the winning goal into the net while lying on the goal-line. Lyall admitted: 'Barnsley are the best side to come here this season.' Barnsley's bus arrived just 27 minutes before kick-off because of traffic.											

League Cup						F-A	H-T	Scorers, Times, and Referees	1	2	3	4	5	6	7	8	9	10	11	subs used
QF	H	TOTTENHAM		1	W	1-0	0-0	Cross 81	Parkes	Stewart	Lampard	Bonds	Martin	Devonshire	Holland	Goddard	Cross	Neighbour	Pike	
	2/12		36,003	*1:10*					*Daines*	*McAllister*	*Hughton*	*Yorath*	*Lacy*	*Perryman*	*Ardiles*	*Archibald*	*Villa*	*Hoddle*	*Crooks*	
								Ref: J Hunting	The goal was made by Brooking and scored by Cross, yet illness or injury almost ruled out both players. This was not a match for touch-play, and Ardiles, Hoddle and Brooking were largely swamped by flying boots. The win takes West Ham to a first League Cup semi in eight years.											
SF	A	COVENTRY		1	L	2-3	2-0	Bonds 26, Thompson 35 (og)	Parkes	Stewart	Brush	Bonds	Martin	Devonshire	Allen	Goddard	Cross	Brooking	Pike	
1	27/1		*35,468*	*1:15*				*Thompson 71, 90, Daly 76*	*Sealey*	*Thomas*	*Roberts*	*Blair*	*Dyson*	*Gillespie*	*Bodak*	*Daly**	*Thompson*	*Hateley*	*Hunt*	*Jacobs*
								Ref: G Courtney	West Ham stage an incredible collapse after leading 2-0 at half-time to Gordon Milne's Coventry. What's more, West Ham had been handed their two goals on a plate, first when Bonds' weak header squirmed through Sealey's hands, then when Thompson's back-pass eluded Sealey.											
SF	H	COVENTRY		1	W	2-0	0-0	Goddard 60, Neighbour 89	Parkes	Stewart	Lampard	Bonds	Martin	Devonshire	Neighbour	Goddard	Cross	Brooking	Pike	
2	10/2		36,551	*1:15*					*Sealey*	*Thomas*	*Roberts*	*Blair*	*Dyson*	*Gillespie*	*Bodak**	*Daly*	*Thompson*	*Hateley*	*Hunt*	*Jacobs*
								Ref: K Hackett (Hammers win 4-3 on aggregate)	Billy Bonds celebrates his 600th first-team game with this famous victory. Goddard is the only Hammer on the pitch for whom this will be a first appearance to Wembley. So it is fitting that his 20-yard belter paves the way. Earlier, Phil Parkes had saved splendidly from Daly.											
F	N	LIVERPOOL		1	D	1-1	0-0	Stewart 120p	Parkes	Stewart	Lampard	Bonds	Martin	Devonshire	Neighbour	Goddard*	Cross	Brooking	Pike	Pearson
	14/3		*100,000*	*1:4*		*aet*		*Kennedy A 117*	*Clemence*	*Neal*	*Kennedy A*	*Irwin*	*Kennedy R*	*Hansen*	*Dalglish*	*Lee*	*Heighway**	*McDermott*	*Souness*	*Case*
		(at Wembley)						Ref: C Thomas	Controversy rages as the ref allows Alan Kennedy's goal, even though Sammy Lee is lying prostrate in an offside position. In the last seconds McDermott fists Martin's header against the bar, permitting Stewart to force a replay. The 90 minutes normal play had been quite forgettable.											
FR	N	LIVERPOOL		1	L	1-2	1-2	Goddard 10	Parkes	Stewart	Lampard	Bonds	Martin	Devonshire	Neighbour	Goddard	Cross	Brooking	Pike*	Pearson
	1/4		*36,693*	*1:4*				*Dalglish 25, Hansen 29*	*Clemence*	*Neal*	*Kennedy A*	*Thompson*	*Kennedy R*	*Hansen*	*Dalglish*	*Lee*	*Rush*	*McDermott*	*Case*	
		(at Villa Park)						Ref: C Thomas	Live TV coverage dampens the attendance. When Goddard headed in Neighbour's cross, West Ham sensed glory. But McDermott's chip produced an equaliser from Dalglish, whereupon Bonds' knee diverted Hansen's header past Parkes. This was Ian Rush's second full game.											

Charity Shield																				
	N	LIVERPOOL			L	0-1	0-1		Parkes	Stewart	Brush	Bonds	Martin	Devonshire	Allen	Holland	Cross	Brooking	Pike*	Morgan
	9/8		*90,000*					*McDermott 18*	*Clemence*	*Neal*	*Kennedy A*	*Thompson*	*Kennedy R*	*Hansen*	*Dalglish*	*Case*	*Johnson*	*McDermott*	*Souness*	
		(At Wembley)						Ref: J Hunting	Liverpool scored when Alan Kennedy fired in a fierce cross-shot that Parkes couldn't hold. McDermott swept the ball into the net from close range. Bob Paisley's team then wasted many chances, and West Ham might have rescued themselves when Clemence saved at Morgan's feet.											

FA Cup																				
3	H	WREXHAM		1	D	1-1	0-0	Stewart 60p	Parkes	Stewart	Lampard	Bonds	Martin	Devonshire	Holland	Goddard	Cross	Brooking	Pike	
	3/1		30,137	*13*				*Davis 87*	*Davies*	*Hill*	*Jones*	*Davis*	*Cegielski*	*Arkwright*	*Buxton**	*Sutton*	*Edwards*	*McNeil*	*Cartwright*	*Fox*
								Ref: A Hamil	'On my baby's life I never touched him,' protests Wrexham's Joey Jones, as Holland goes down in the penalty area. Ray Stewart was relieved to score, for the Upton Park crowd had been getting at him recently. Wrexham's 33-year-old skipper, Gareth Davis, thumped the equaliser.											
3R	A	WREXHAM		1	D	0-0	0-0		Parkes	Stewart	Lampard	Bonds	Martin	Devonshire	Holland	Goddard	Cross	Brooking	Pike	
	6/1		*13,643*	*13*		*aet*			*Davies*	*Sutton*	*Kenworthy*	*Davis*	*Cegielski*	*Carrodus*	*Fox*	*Arkwright*	*Edwards*	*McNeil*	*Cartwright*	
								Ref: A Hamil	In the second half West Ham thought they had scored. Cross was given offside, although Joey Jones looked to have played him onside. The winners will be at home to Division 4 Wimbledon in Round 4. Wrexham boss Arfon Griffiths called 'heads' correctly for the choice of venue.											
3	A	WREXHAM		1	L	0-1	0-0		Parkes	Stewart	Brush	Bonds	Martin	Devonshire	Allen*	Goddard	Cross	Brooking	Pike	Neighbour
RR	19/1		*14,615*	*15*		*aet*		*McNeil 104*	*Davies*	*Hill*	*Jones*	*Davis**	*Cegielski*	*Arkwright*	*Fox*	*Sutton*	*Edwards*	*McNeil*	*Cartwright*	*Vinter*
								Ref: D Owen	So West Ham relinquish their grip on the FA Cup at the first hurdle. Their interest might have been sustained but for bad misses by Goddard in the 4th and 73rd minutes. A 330-minute cup-tie was finally settled when Cartwright's shot was blocked by Parkes but fell to Dixie McNeil.											

European Cup-Winners' Cup																				
1:1	A	CASTILLA		3	L	1-3	1-0	Cross 17	Parkes	Stewart	Lampard	Bonds	Martin	Devonshire*	Morgana^	Goddard	Cross	Brooking	Pike	Brush/Barnes
	17/9	(Spain)	*40,000*					*Paco 64, Balin 70, Cidon 74*	*Miguel*	*Juanito**	*Casimiro*	*Salguero*	*Espinosa*	*Sanch' Lorenzo*	*Balin*	*Alvarez*	*Paco*	*Bernal*	*Cidon^*	*Chendo/Blanco*
								Ref: Delmer (France)	Castilla are Real Madrid's reserve side. Cross's header gives West Ham the lead in the Bernabeu Stadium, but then they sit back. Hooligans among supporters incite frightening scenes, in which one West Ham fan loses his life. Terrible back-passes by Bonds and Pike cost two goals.											

Rnd	Venue	Opponents		Res	F-A	H-T	Scorers, Times, Referee	1	2	3	4	5	6	7	8	9	10	11	12 sub used
1:2	H	CASTILLA	2	W	5-1	3-0	Pike 19, Cross 30, 103, 119, Goddard 40	Parkes	Stewart	Lampard	Bond	Martin	Devonshire	Holland*	Goddard^	Cross	Brooking	Pike	Brush/Morgan
	1/10	behind closed doors			*aet*		*Bernal 56*	*Miguel*	*Chendo*	*Casimiro*	*Salguero*	*Espinosa*	*Sanch' Lorenzo*	*Balin*	*Alvarez*	*Paco**	*Bernal*	*Cidon^*	*Ramirez/Blanco*
							Ref: J Keizer (Holland) (Hammers win 6-4 on aggregate)	West Ham were originally ordered to play this match 300 kilometres from Upton Park, but the club appealed and were ordered instead to play behind closed doors, with just 70 representatives of each side allowed. The weird atmosphere was evidently to Hammers' liking in extra-time.											
2:1	H	POLI TIMISOARA	2	W	4-0	3-0	Bonds 24, Goddard 25, Stewart 27p, [Cross 75]	Parkes	Stewart	Lampard	Bonds	Martin	Devonshire	Holland	Goddard*	Cross	Neighbour	Pike	Morgan
	22/10	(Romania) 27,257						*Moise*	*Nadu*	*Paltinisanu*	*Visan*	*Sunda*	*Murar*	*Anghel*	*Dembrowsji**	*Nedelcu*	*Dumitru*	*Cotec*	*Titi*
							Ref: H Fahnler (Austria)	Politecnica beat Billy McNeill's Celtic in Round 1, and he obligingly passes on his dossier to Lyall. Bonds' header put West Ham on their way, and two minutes later they lead 3-0 when Visan pushed Goddard in the area. When Moise later fouled Goddard, Stewart's penalty was saved.											
2:2	A	POLI TIMISOARA	2	L	0-1	0-0		Parkes	Stewart*	Lampard	Bonds	Martin	Allen	Holland	Goddard	Cross	Neighbour^	Pike	Brush/Brooking
	5/11	*25,000*					*Paltinisanu 54*	*Moise*	*Sunda*	*Paltinisanu*	*Visan*	*Titi*	*Serbanoiu*	*Anghel*	*Dembrowski**	*Nedelcu*	*Dumitru*	*Cotec*	*Sunda*
							Ref: R Lattanzi (Italy) (Hammers win 4-1 on aggregate)	The Romanians think the tie is winnable, and if not they seem determined to hospitalise as many Hammers as possible. The goal was Parkes' fault, allowing a shot to bounce over his arm. The hosts played their version of Yellow Submarine over the public address system during play.											
3:1	H	DYNAMO TBILISI	1	L	1-4	0-2	Cross 54	Parkes	Stewart	Lampard	Bonds	Martin	Devonshire*	Neighbour	Goddard	Cros	Brooking	Pike	Allen
	4/3	(USSR) 34,957					*Chivadze 23, Gutsaev 31, Shengelia 56,67*	*Gabelia*	*Khisanishvili*	*Chivadze*	*Khinchagashvili*	*Tavadze*	*Daraselia*	*Svanadze*	*Sulakvelidze*	*Gutsayev*	*Kipiani*	*Shengelia*	
							Ref: A Garrido (Portugal)	Had this game also been played behind closed doors West Ham fans would have been denied a sight of the finest performance many of them had seen. Tbilisi were irresistible from the moment Chivadze burst through to score from 25 yards. Lyall had said they were the best team left.											
3:2	A	DYNAMO TBILISI	1	W	1-0	0-0	Pearson 88	Parkes	Stewart	Lampard	Bonds	Martin	Brush	Neighbour	Goddard*	Cross	Brooking	Pike	Pearson
	18/3	*80,000*						*Gabelia*	*Chivadze*	*Khisanishvili*	*Khinchagashvili*	*Tavadze*	*Chilaya**	*Svanadze*	*Sulakvelidze*	*Gutsayev*	*Kipiani*	*Shengelia*	*Muzhir*
							Ref: W Eschweiler (W Germany) (Hammers lose 2-4 on aggregate)	The huge bleak Lenin Stadium sees West Ham salvage their dignity, though they had no hope of progress unless they could conjure up at least four goals. A lifeless match was settled by Pearson's volley, which means they become the third side to win here in Europe in the last six years.											

		Home						Away					
	P	W	D	L	F	A	W	D	L	F	A	Pts
1 WEST HAM	42	19	1	1	53	12	9	9	3	26	17	66
2 Notts Co	42	10	8	3	26	15	8	9	4	23	23	53
3 Swansea	42	12	5	4	39	19	6	9	6	25	25	50
4 Blackburn	42	12	8	1	28	7	4	10	7	14	22	50
5 Luton	42	10	6	5	35	23	8	6	7	26	23	48
6 Derby	42	9	8	4	34	26	6	7	8	23	26	45
7 Grimsby	42	10	8	3	21	10	5	7	9	23	32	45
8 QP Rangers	42	11	7	3	36	12	4	6	11	20	34	43
9 Watford	42	13	5	3	34	18	3	6	12	16	27	43
10 Sheffield Wed	42	14	4	3	38	14	3	4	14	15	37	42
11 Newcastle	42	11	7	3	22	13	3	7	11	8	32	42
12 Chelsea	42	8	6	7	27	15	6	6	9	19	26	40
13 Cambridge	42	13	1	7	36	23	4	5	12	17	42	40
14 Shrewsbury	42	9	7	5	33	22	2	10	9	13	25	39
15 Oldham	42	7	9	5	19	16	5	6	10	20	32	39
16 Wrexham	42	5	8	8	22	24	7	6	8	21	21	38
17 Orient	42	9	8	4	34	20	4	4	13	18	36	38
18 Bolton	42	10	5	6	40	27	4	5	12	21	39	38
19 Cardiff	42	7	7	7	23	24	5	5	11	21	36	36
20 Preston	42	8	7	6	28	26	3	7	11	13	36	36
21 Bristol City	42	6	10	5	19	15	1	6	14	10	36	30
22 Bristol Rov	42	4	9	8	21	24	1	4	16	13	41	23
	924	217	144	101	668	405	101	144	217	405	668	924

Odds & ends

Double wins: (9) Chelsea, Shrewsbury, Watford, Cambridge, Bristol R, Grimsby, Swansea, Sheff Wed, Orient.
Double losses: (1) Luton.

Won from behind: (4) Watford (h), Sheff W (h), Derby (h), Cambridge (h).
Lost from in front: (1) Luton (h).

High spots: Running away with the Second Division championship.
Reaching the League Cup final.
Unbeaten in any competition from 19 August to 15 November, a total of 19 games.

Low spots: Losing League Cup final replay to Liverpool.
Failing to win any of the first three league fixtures.

Hammer of the Year: Phil Parkes.
Ever-presents: (2) Phil Parkes and Geoff Pike.
Hat-tricks: (2) David Cross (1), Paul Goddard (1).
Leading scorer: (27) David Cross.

	Appearances						Goals			
	Lge	*Sub*	LC	*Sub*	FAC	*Sub*	Lge	LC	FAC	Tot
Allen, Paul	1	*2*	1	*2*	1		1			1
Barnes, Bobby	1	*5*	1				1			1
Bonds, Billy	41		8		3			1		1
Brooking, Trevor	36		7		3		10			10
Brush, Paul	8	*3*	3		1					
Cross, David	41		9		3		22	5		27
Devonshire, Alan	39		9		3		6			6
Goddard, Paul	37		9		3		17	4		21
Holland, Pat	25		4		2		3			3
Lampard, Frank	38	*1*	8		2		1			1
Martin, Alvin	41		9		3		1	1		2
Morgan, Nicky	5	*1*					1			1
Neighbour, Jimmy	22	*2*	4			*1*	2	1		3
Parkes, Phil	42		9		3					
Pearson, Stuart	2	*3*		*2*						
Pike, Geoff	42		9		3		6	1		7
Stewart, Ray	41		9		3		5	2	1	8
(own-goals)							3	2		5
17 players used	**462**	***17***	**99**	***4***	**33**	***1***	**79**	**17**	**1**	**97**

LEAGUE DIVISION 1 | Manager: John Lyall | SEASON 1981-82

No	Date		Att	Pos	Pt	F-A	H-T	Scorers, Times, and Referees	1	2	3	4	5	6	7	8	9	10	11	12 sub used
1	H	BRIGHTON			D	1-1	0-0	Stewart 61p	Parkes	Stewart	Lampard	Bonds	Martin	Devonshire	Neighbour	Goddard	Cross	Allen	Pike	
	29/8		30,468		1			*McNab 84p*	*Moseley*	*Shanks*	*Williams*	*Grealish*	*Foster*	*Stevens*	*Case*	*Ritchie**	*Robinson*	*McNab*	*Ryan !*	*Smith*
								Ref: L Shapter	Three points for a win has been introduced. Hammers were heading for their first threesome, courtesy of Foster's push on Cross, when Devon policeman Leslie Shapter penalised Billy Bonds for shoving Michael Robinson. In injury-time Shapter sent off Ryan for a foul on Neighbour.											
2	A	TOTTENHAM			W	**4-0**	1-0	Cross 10, 50, 57, 89	Parkes	Stewart	Lampard	Bonds	Martin	Devonshire	Neighbour	Goddard	Cross	Allen	Pike	
	2/9		*41,200*		4				*Clemence*	*Roberts*	*Miller*	*Price**	*Villa*	*Perryman*	*Hazard*	*Brooke*	*Galvin*	*Hoddle*	*Falco*	*Smith*
								Ref: K Baker	West Ham were determined to keep Spurs' Argentinians, Ardiles and Villa, quiet in midfield. So well did the plan succeed that David Cross was able to demonstrate superb finishing. It is not the first four-goal haul of his career. He performed the same feat versus Grimsby last season.											
3	A	SUNDERLAND		1	W	2-0	1-0	Goddard 39, Cross 54	Parkes	Stewart	Lampard	Bonds	Martin	Devonshire	Neighbour	Goddard*	Cross	Allen	Pike	Pearson
	5/9		*28,347*	*14*	7				*Turner*	*Hinnigan*	*Munro*	*Buckley*	*Clarke*	*Hindmarch*	*Chisholm*	*Ritchie*	*Cooke*	*Rowell*	*Pickering**	*McCoist*
								Ref: A Challinor	Paul Goddard steals the limelight from David Cross. Devonshire laid on the chance, which Goddard stroked into the empty net. When Cross made it 2-0, shaking off his marker at the near post, it made him top scorer in Division 1. Goddard is in England's Under-21 party to Norway.											
4	H	STOKE		1	W	3-2	1-1	Goddard 7, 49, Stewart 69p	Parkes	Stewart	Lampard	Bonds	Martin	Devonshire	Neighbour	Goddard	Cross	Allen	Pike	
	12/9		28,774	*7*	10			*O'Callaghan 28, Maguire 88p*	*Fox*	*Evans*	*Hampton*	*Dodd*	*O'Callaghan*	*Doyle*	*Griffiths*	*Heath*	*Chapman*	*Bracewell*	*Maguire*	
								Ref: J Martin	England have just lost 1-2 to Norway in the World Cup and the nation is in shock. West Ham triumph over Richie Barker's Stoke in a game of two penalties. Stewart scored, when Devonshire was brought down, while Stoke's arrived when Lampard handled. Cross wasted chances.											
5	A	WEST BROM		1	D	0-0	0-0		Parkes	Stewart	Lampard	Bonds	Martin	Devonshire	Neighbour	Goddard	Cross	Allen	Pike	
	19/9		*19,516*	*15*	11				*Godden*	*Batson*	*Statham*	*Brown**	*Wile*	*Robertson*	*Deehan*	*Mills*	*Regis*	*Owen*	*MacKenzie*	*Cross*
								Ref: D Hedges	A rainswept match. Ronnie Allen's WBA indulge in another tough physical game. Cross clashes with Wile and plays on with his face covered in blood. Bryan Robson is out through injury, but will soon sign for Man U. Paul Allen will soon be off to Australia with the FA Youth team.											
6	H	SOUTHAMPTON		1	W	4-2	2-1	Goddard 34, 38, 60, Pike 48	Parkes	Stewart	Lampard	Bonds	Martin	Devonshire	Neighbour	Goddard	Cross	Allen	Pike	
	22/9		**34,026**	*4*	14			*Armstrong 11, Waldron 66*	*Wells*	*Golac*	*Holmes*	*Agboola*	*Watson**	*Waldron*	*Keegan*	*Baker G*	*Puckett*	*Armstrong*	*Ball*	*Rogers*
								Ref: G Napthine	Goddard is violently ill before kick-off but recovers to play a blinder. His best goal is his third, beating three men before chipping Wells. The turning point is when Parkes turns Keegan's effort against a post. Lawrie McMenemy said afterwards: 'Take away the result and I enjoyed it.'											
7	H	LIVERPOOL		2	D	1-1	1-0	Pike 28	Parkes	Stewart	Lampard	Bonds	Martin	Devonshire	Neighbour	Goddard	Cross	Allen	Pike	
	26/9		30,802	*12*	15			*Johnson 79*	*Grobbelaar*	*Neal*	*Kennedy A*	*Thompson*	*Kennedy R*	*Hansen*	*Dalglish*	*Lee*	*Johnson*	*McDermott*	*Souness*	
								Ref: A Robinson	Phil Parkes is struggling with a floating bone in his knee, and he gifts Johnson a simple headed equaliser when dropping Alan Kennedy's cross. The corner count – 17-2 to Liverpool – shows the balance of play. The result knocks West Ham off the top: they are replaced by Ipswich.											
8	A	BIRMINGHAM		2	D	2-2	1-1	Cross 11, 61	**McAlister**	Stewart	Lampard	Bonds	Martin	Devonshire	Neighbour	Goddard	Cross	Brooking	Pike	
	3/10		*22,290*	*15*	16			*Langan 14, Dillon 89*	*Wealands*	*Langan*	*Dennis*	*Dillon*	*Broadhurst*	*Todd*	*Brocken*	*Whatmore*	*Worthington*	*Gemmill*	*Van Mierlo**	*Handysides*
								Ref: D Webb	When 2-1 up, West Ham were denied a penalty when Colin Todd held back Goddard. City boss Jim Smith admitted his player was lucky to get away with it. Trevor Brooking returns to the team but fails to prevent Dillon's late equaliser. A pitch invasion by Hammers fans spells trouble.											
9	H	EVERTON		4	D	1-1	1-1	Martin 39	McAlister	Stewart	Lampard	Bonds	Martin	Devonshire	Neighbour	Goddard	Cross	Brooking	Pike	
	10/10		31,608	*14*	17			*McMahon 1*	*Arnold*	*Stevens*	*Bailey*	*Higgins*	*Lyons*	*Thomas*	*McMahon*	*Biley**	*Ferguson*	*Ross*	*McBride*	*O'Keefe*
								Ref: T Bune	John Lyall celebrates his Bell's Manager of the Month award, but within seconds watches horrified as McMahon's bobbling shot squeezes past McAlister. Martin levelled when heading in Stewart's free-kick. Lyall is reputed to be on the verge of signing Manchester Utd's Steve Coppell.											
10	A	ASTON VILLA		5	L	2-3	1-3	Brooking 2, Cross 49	McAlister	Stewart	Lampard	Bonds	Martin	Devonshire	Neighbour*	Goddard	Cross	Brooking	Pike	Brush
	17/10		*32,064*	*13*	17			*Morley 25, Geddis 26, Mortimer 40*	*Rimmer*	*Williams*	*Gibson*	*Evans*	*Ormsby*	*Mortimer*	*Bremner*	*Shaw*	*Geddis**	*Cowans*	*Morley*	*Blair*
								Ref: N Glover	West Ham's first defeat is largely down to Tom McAlister, who is at fault for Morley's and Geddis's goals. Trevor Brooking scores a vintage goal and the Hammers are denied two strong second-half penalty appeals. Lyall's latest target is said to be Leeds' winger Arthur Graham.											

No	Venue / Date	Opponent / Att	Pos	Res / Pts	F-A	H-T	Scorers, Times, and Referees	1	2	3	4	5	6	7	8	9	10	11	12 sub used
11	A	NOTTS CO	6	D	1-1	0-0	Brooking 50	Parkes	Stewart	Lampard	Bonds	Martin	Devonshire	Brush	Goddard	Cross	Brooking	Pike	
	24/10	*12,505*	*13*	18			*Masson 66*	*Avramovic*	*Goodwin*	*O'Brien*	*Hunt*	*Lahtinen*	*Richards*	*Chiedozie*	*Masson*	*McCulloch*	*Hooks*	*Mair*	
							Ref: Willis	Trevor Brooking's autobiography was launched on this day. He celebrated by directing a trundler that squirmed under Avramovic's body, but otherwise failed to rescue an anaemic match. Parkes returned to the side after knee surgery, but could not keep out former team-mate Masson.											
12	H	MIDDLESBROUGH	6	W	3-2	2-0	Neighbour 32, G'dard 40, Stewart 48p	Parkes	Stewart	Lampard	Bonds	Martin	Devonshire	Neighbour	Goddard	Cross	Brooking	Pike	
	31/10	27,604	*20*	21			*Woof 55, Thomson 79p*	*Platt*	*Nattrass*	*Bolton*	*Angus*	*Baxter*	*McAndrew**	*Cochrane*	*Otto*	*Woof*	*Hodgson*	*Thomson*	*Shearer*
							Ref: L Burden	West Ham were coasting at 3-0 when everything collapsed. Bobby Murdoch's Boro had only scored one away goal so far, but must have thought they could retrieve a point after Jimmy Neighbour's dreadful back-pass let in Woof, and Brooking barged over Cochrane in the box.											
13	A	NOTT'M FOREST	6	D	0-0	0-0		Parkes	Stewart	Lampard	Allen*	Martin	Devonshire	Neighbour	Goddard	Cross	Brooking	Pike	Brush
	7/11	*26,327*	*5*	22				*Shilton*	*Anderson*	*Gunn*	*McGovern*	*Needham*	*Aas**	*Gray*	*Wallace*	*Fashanu*	*Proctor*	*Robertson*	*Walsh*
							Ref: G Tyson	Frank Lampard was once again acting skipper. Brooking earns the sixth booking of his long career when fouling Justin Fashanu. Forest had more of the play but the best chance fell to West Ham in the final minute, when David Cross forced Peter Shilton into a scrambling save.											
14	H	COVENTRY	5	W	5-2	2-1	Brook'g 22, Neighb'r 37, M'rtin 50, 55,	Parkes	Stewart	Lampard	Bonds	Martin	Devonshire	Neighbour	Goddard	Cross	Brooking	Pike	
	21/11	26,065	*17*	25			*Hunt 6, 62* [Stewart 87p]	*Blyth*	*Thomas*	*Roberts*	*Jacobs*	*Dyson*	*Gillespie*	*Bradford*	*Daly*	*Thompson*	*Hateley*	*Hunt*	
							Ref: A Glasson	Brooking's super goal in Hungary, lodging the ball in the stanchion, is the talk of England. This thriller saw a 20-minute delay due to floodlight failure. At 4-2 West Ham were given a penalty. The crowd urged Martin to complete his hat-trick, but an angry Lyall ordered him to leave it.											
15	A	LEEDS	6	D	3-3	0-1	Brooking 55, 86, Cross 77	Parkes	Stewart	Lampard	Bonds	Martin	Devonshire	Neighbour*	Goddard	Cross	Brooking	Pike	Allen
	28/11	*25,637*	*19*	26			*Graham 13, Hird 65p, Cherry 69*	*Lukic*	*Cherry*	*Gray F*	*Stevenson*	*Hart*	*Burns*	*Harris*	*Graham*	*Butterworth*	*Hamson*	*Hird*	
							Ref: P Richardson	West Ham went 1-2 behind to a disputed penalty. Stewart had already been booked for a foul on Graham when he brings him down in the box. The ref waved play on until spotting a linesman's raised flag. Cross pulled a goal back with a toe-ender, before heading down for Brooking.											
16	H	ARSENAL	7	L	1-2	0-2	Pearson 85	Parkes	Stewart	Lampard	Bonds	Martin	Devonshire	Barnes*	Pearson	Cross	Brooking	Allen	Banton
	5/12	33,833	*6*	26			*Whyte 15, Hollins 45p*	*Jennings*	*Robson*	*Sansom*	*Talbot*	*O'Leary*	*Whyte*	*Hollins*	*Sunderland*	*Davis*	*Nicholas*	*Rix*	
							Ref: A Gray	The last time these teams met was in the 1980 FA Cup final. Arsenal's fifth straight win inflicts West Ham's first home league defeat in over a year. Stewart Robson made his Arsenal debut. Pearson is surprisingly recalled in place of Goddard. Stewart fouled Sansom for the penalty.											
17	A	LIVERPOOL	12	L	**0-3**	0-2		Parkes	Stewart	Lampard	Bonds	Martin	Devonshire*	Neighbour	Pearson	Cross	Brooking	Pike	Brush
	5/1	*28,427*	*9*	26			*McDermott 22, Whelan 24, Dalglish 67*	*Grobbelaar*	*Neal*	*Lawrenson*	*Thompson*	*Whelan*	*Hansen*	*Dalglish*	*Kennedy A*	*Rush*	*McDermott*	*Souness*	
							Ref: B Newsome	West Ham did not win their first corner till the final minute. McDermott looked offside when receiving the ball to score at the second attempt. Two minutes later Dalglish set up Whelan's 20-yard scorcher. Whelan then fed Dalglish, who turned and shot in one exquisite movement.											
18	A	BRIGHTON	12	L	0-1	0-0		Parkes	Stewart	Lampard	Bonds	Martin	Devonshire*	Neighbour	Goddard	Cross	Brooking	Pike	**Van der Elst**
	16/1	*22,620*	*8*	26			*Ritchie 77*	*Moseley*	*Shanks*	*Nelson*	*Grealish*	*Foster*	*Gatting*	*Ryan*	*Ritchie*	*Smith*	*McNab*	*Thomas*	
							Ref: G Napthine	These are the two draw specialists of Division 1, with 17 between them. Offside decisions marred the outcome. West Ham claimed Ritchie was offside when taking Nelson's long pass, but TV showed he had been onside. Stewart's 35-yarder was disallowed because Cross was offside.											
19	A	MANCHESTER U	12	L	0-1	0-0		Parkes	Brush	Lampard*	Bonds	Martin	**Orr**	Van der Elst	Stewart	Cross	Brooking	Pike	Goddard
	27/1	***41,291***	*1*	26			*Macari 75*	*Bailey*	*Duxbury*	*Albiston*	*Wilkins*	*Moran*	*McQueen*	*Robson*	*Birtles*	*Stapleton*	*Macari*	*Coppell*	
							Ref: V Callow	Old Trafford jeers West Ham's excessive robustness, but cheer their own new signing from West Brom, Bryan Robson, who played a part in the goal. The hosts won the corner-count 21-1, and go top of the league. Trevor Brooking wasted West Ham's only chance, heading at Bailey.											
20	H	WEST BROM	12	W	3-1	1-0	Goddard 34, Cross 51, 75	Parkes	Stewart	Brush	Bonds	Martin	Orr	Van der Elst	Goddard	Cross	Brooking	Pike	
	30/1	24,423	*14*	29			*King 62*	*Grew*	*Batson*	*Statham*	*King*	*Wile*	*Robertson*	*Jol*	*Whitehead**	*Regis*	*Owen*	*MacKenzie*	*Cross*
							Ref: C Maskell	This time it is WBA who take their own medicine, as Billy Bonds lunges at everything that moves. Ronnie Allen describes the Hammers as the hard men of Division 1. Bonds was also involved in both Cross's goals, the second of which might have been ruled out for a foul on the keeper.											
21	H	MANCHESTER C	12	D	1-1	0-0	Bonds 80	Parkes	Stewart	Brush*	Bonds	Martin	Orr	Van der Elst	Goddard	Cross	Brooking	Pike	Pearson
	2/2	26,552	*4*	30			*Bond 73p*	*Corrigan*	*Ranson*	*McDonald*	*Ryan**	*Bond*	*Caton*	*Kinsey*	*Reeves*	*Francis*	*Hartford*	*Power*	*Hareide*
							Ref: A Gunn	Van der Elst, a £400,000 buy from New York Cosmos, has another anonymous game and the fans are getting at him. Orr brought down Trevor Francis for City's penalty. Bonds' equaliser was a comedy of errors. Orr mis-hit a free-kick and the ball went in off Van der Elst and Goddard.											

No	Date		Att	Pos	Pt	F-A	H-T	Scorers, Times, and Referees	1	2	3	4	5	6	7	8	9	10	11	12 sub used
22	A	STOKE		12	L	1-2	0-1	Van der Elst 71	Parkes	Stewart	Brush	Bonds	Martin	Orr	Van der Elst	Goddard	Cross	Brooking	Pike	
	6/2		*11,987*	*16*	30			*Chapman 10, Maguire 79*	*Fox*	*Kirk*	*Hampton*	*Dodd*	*Watson*	*McAughtrie*	*Griffiths**	*O'Callaghan*	*Chapman*	*Bracewell*	*Maguire*	*Lumsden*
								Ref: J Worrall	Stoke's first home win of 1982 is earned by Maguire's left foot, after Martin failed to cut out a pass to him. West Ham were so bad in the first half that Lyall read the riot act at half-time. He was rewarded by Van der Elst's first goal for the club. But Maguire saw that justice was done.											
23	H	BIRMINGHAM		12	D	2-2	0-1	Orr 46, Stewart 88p	Parkes	Lampard	Brush*	Bonds	Stewart	Orr	Van der Elst	Goddard	Cross	Brooking	Pike	Neighbour
	13/2		22,512	*19*	31			*Whatmore 35, Van Mierlo 55*	*Jones*	*Langan*	*Dennis**	*Curbishley*	*Scott*	*Broadhurst*	*Van Mierlo*	*Whatmore*	*Worthington*	*Phillips*	*Handysides*	*v d Hauwe*
								Ref: I Borrett	Martin is missing with a fractured collarbone. Worthington's rocket was parried by Parkes but fell to Whatmore for the first goal. Jim Smith's City were two minutes from their first away win in 16 months when Geoff Scott handled in the box. Ray Stewart got West Ham off the hook.											
24	A	SOUTHAMPTON		14	L	1-2	1-2	Stewart 15p	Parkes	Stewart	Brush	Bonds	Orr	Van der Elst	Neighbour	Goddard	Cross	Brooking	Pike	
	20/2		*24,026*	*1*	31			*Armstrong 10, Channon 28*	*Katalinic*	*Golac*	*Holmes*	*Baker G*	*Nicholl*	*Waldron*	*Keegan*	*Channon*	*Puckett*	*Armstrong*	*Ball*	
								Ref: E Read	Saints top the table by four points from Man U. Kevin Keegan was superb, and kept winning free-kicks. Two Southampton players looked offside when Armstrong scored. Malcolm Waldron dumped Van der Elst on his backside for the penalty. Mick Channon headed the winner.											
25	A	EVERTON		14	D	0-0	0-0		Parkes	Stewart	Brush	Bonds	Orr	Allen	Neighbour*	Goddard	Van der Elst	Brooking	Pike	Lampard
	27/2		*28,618*	*11*	32				*Southall*	*Borrows*	*Bailey*	*Higgins*	*Wright*	*Richardson*	*Irvine*	*Heath*	*Sharp*	*Biley*	*Ross*	
								Ref: J Key	David Cross is out with a damaged shoulder. John Motson gets into hot water when he tells Howard Kendall before a *Match of the Day* audience that this was the worst game he had seen this season. Everton came nearest to a goal when Graeme Sharp's header hit an upright.											
26	H	IPSWICH		12	W	2-0	1-0	Devonshire 40, Van der Elst 64	Parkes	Stewart	Brush	Bonds	Orr	Devonshire	Allen	Goddard	Van der Elst	Brooking	Pike	
	2/3		24,846	*6*	35				*Cooper*	*Burley*	*McCall*	*Mills*	*Osman*	*Steggles**	*Wark*	*Muhren*	*D'Avray*	*Brazil*	*Gates*	*O'Callaghan*
								Ref: B Hill	Bobby Robson's Ipswich cannot afford defeats like this if they wish to sustain their title challenge. Alan Devonshire is credited with his first goal of the season, even though the ball went in off Steggles. Stewart's astute through ball sets up Van der Elst's first goal at Upton Park.											
27	H	ASTON VILLA		12	D	2-2	1-1	Stewart 39p, Van der Elst 53	Parkes	Stewart	Brush	Bonds	Orr	Devonshire	Allen	Goddard	Van der Elst	Brooking	Pike	
	6/3		26,894	*14*	36			*Cowans 18, Withe 60*	*Rimmer*	*Swain*	*Willams*	*Bremner*	*McNaught*	*Mortimer*	*Blair*	*Shaw*	*Withe*	*Cowans*	*Morley*	
								Ref: J Martin	Villa have just returned from a midweek trip to the Soviet side, Tbilisi, in the European Cup. Brush's error let in Cowan for the first goal. Des Bremner upended Brooking for the penalty. Van der Elst swooped after Rimmer had saved from Goddard, but Shaw then headed on for Withe.											
28	H	NOTTS CO		12	W	1-0	0-0	Stewart 47p	Parkes	Stewart	Lampard	Bonds	Orr	Devonshire	Allen	Goddard	Cross	Van der Elst	Pike	
	13/3		22,145	*14*	39				*Avramovic*	*Benjamin*	*O'Brien*	*Goodwin*	*Kilcline*	*Richards*	*Chiedozie**	*Harkouk*	*McCulloch*	*Hooks !*	*Mair*	*Christie*
								Ref: R Milford	A dreary match, settled by one of many recent penalties. Paul Hooks was the guilty man, fouling Devonshire. Injury-time witnessed a punch-up between the same two players, as a result of which Hooks was sent off. County's Jimmy Sirrel gave a hilarious speech at the press conference.											
29	A	MIDDLESBROUGH		11	W	3-2	2-0	Van der Elst 15, Goddard 29, 89	Parkes	Stewart	Lampard	Bonds	Orr	Devonshire	Allen	Goddard	Van der Elst	Brooking	Pike*	Neighbour
	20/3		*12,134*	*22*	42			*McAndrew 59p, Ashcroft 74*	*Platt*	*Craggs*	*Bailey*	*Ross*	*Baxter*	*McAndrew*	*Cochrane*	*Nattrass*	*Hodgson*	*Ashcroft*	*Thomson*	
								Ref: T Hills	The bottom team provide West Ham with their first away win in 13 attempts. But it was a close thing. West Ham surrendered a two-goal lead before Brooking set up Goddard's late winner. Boro have won only three matches all season. Stewart handled from Ashcroft for the penalty.											
30	H	NOTT'M FOREST		11	L	0-1	0-1		Parkes	Stewart	Lampard	Bonds	Orr	Devonshire	Van der Elst	Goddard	Cross	Brooking	Allen*	Neighbour
	27/3		24,633	*9*	42			*Wallace 30*	*Shilton*	*Anderson*	*Bowyer*	*McGovern*	*Young*	*Gunn*	*Rober*	*Wallace*	*Fashanu*	*Proctor*	*Robertson*	
								Ref: T Bune	Peter Shilton had only one save to make, from Goddard. Paul Allen was at fault for the goal, letting in Wallace, who offered a constant threat. Cross's reward for his endeavour was to get kicked in the face by Willie Young. West Ham have not scored against Forest for 750 minutes.											
31	A	SWANSEA		10	W	1-0	1-0	Van der Elst 10	Parkes	Stewart	Lampard	Orr	Martin	Devonshire	Van der Elst	Goddard	Cross	Brooking	Allen	
	30/3		*20,272*	*4*	45				*Davies*	*Robinson*	*Hadziabdic**	*Irwin*	*Kennedy*	*Rajkovic*	*Curtis*	*James R*	*James L*	*Stevenson*	*Latchford*	*Stanley*
								Ref: B Stevens	The championship hopes of John Toshack's Swansea, damaged by a home defeat by Ipswich on Saturday, are extinguished by the much-maligned Van der Elst, who fires a screamer past Dai Davies. Swansea's subsequent pressure came to nothing, largely thanks to Alvin Martin.											

No	Venue / Date	Opponent / Att	Pos	Res / Pts	F-A	H-T	Scorers, Times, and Referees	1	2	3	4	5	6	7	8	9	10	11	12
32	A	MANCHESTER C	9	W	1-0	0-0	Goddard 80	Parkes	Stewart	Lampard	Orr	Martin	Devonshire	Van der Elst	Goddard	Cross	Brooking	Allen	
	3/4	*30,875*	*8*	48				*Corrigan*	*Ranson*	*McDonald*	*Reid*	*Power*	*Caton*	*Ryan*	*Reeves*	*Hareide*	*Hartford*	*Jackson*	
							Ref: M Scott	West Ham's third successive away win is earned by Paul Goddard's late effort. David Cross's header fell to him and his shot went in off a post. Goddard had come close twice beforehand. Alvin Martin looked much more impressive than City's rival England hopeful, Tommy Caton.											
33	H	WOLVES	8	W	3-1	0-1	Martin 46, Goddard 50, 66	Parkes	Stewart	Lampard	Orr	Martin	Devonshire	Van der Elst	Goddard	Cross	Brooking	Allen	
	6/4	20,651	*20*	51			*Richards 13*	*Bradshaw*	*Humphrey*	*Palmer*	*Matthews*	*Pender*	*Coy*	*Hibbitt*	*Carr*	*Richards*	*Eves*	*Clarke*	
							Ref: D Letts	The players were treated to another Lyall tirade at half-time, and this time it has the desired effect. Martin immediately headed in Devonshire's corner, and Brooking and Martin set up further goals for Paul Goddard. In the first half John Richards had looped a header over Phil Parkes.											
34	H	SWANSEA	8	D	1-1	0-1	Goddard 88	Parkes	Stewart	Lampard*	Orr	Martin	Devonshire	Van der Elst	Goddard	Cross	Brooking	Allen	Neighbour
	10/4	25,566	*3*	52			*James R 34*	*Davies*	*Marustik**	*Hadziabdic*	*Irwin*	*Kennedy*	*Rajkovic*	*Curtis*	*James R*	*Staney*	*Stevenson*	*Latchford*	*Robinson*
							Ref: A Robinson	Belgian manager Guy Thys runs his eye over Van der Elst. Thys sees Brooking and Cross squander chances galore in the first half, before Robbie James fires Swansea ahead with a spectacular 30-yarder. Paul Goddard connects with a late corner to rescue a point. It is his 14th goal.											
35	A	IPSWICH	8	L	2-3	1-2	Cross 42, 80	Parkes	Stewart	Allen	Orr	Martin	Devonshire	Van der Elst	Goddard	Cross	Brooking	Neighbour*	**Cowie**
	13/4	*28,767*	*2*	52			*Brazil 15, Wark 26p, Osman 51*	*Cooper*	*Burley*	*McCall*	*Mills*	*Osman*	*Butcher*	*Wark*	*Muhren*	*Mariner*	*Brazil*	*Gates*	
							Ref: M Taylor	Portman Road's biggest crowd of the season are enticed by an exciting title chase with Liverpool. Mariner and Butcher both return after long absences. Alan Brazil went down for Ipswich's penalty. Osman's free header made it 1-3 before McCall boobs to let in Cross near the end.											
36	A	COVENTRY	8	L	0-1	0-1		Parkes	Stewart	Cowie	Orr	Martin*	Devonshire	Van der Elst	Goddard	Cross	Brooking	Allen	Laronde
	17/4	*13,398*	*15*	52			*Hateley 45*	*Sealey*	*Thomas*	*Roberts*	*Butterworth*	*Dyson*	*Gillespie*	*Whitton**	*Jacobs*	*Hateley*	*Thompson*	*Hunt*	*Hormantsch'k*
							Ref: L Shapter	Martin collides with Parkes, does further damage to his collarbone and is stretchered off. The team coach was returning home when it was flagged down by Martin's father, so that Alvin could climb aboard. With the World Cup finals just weeks away, Martin might not be fit											
37	H	LEEDS	8	W	4-3	0-1	Cross 47, Brooking 52,80, St'wart 88p	Parkes	Stewart	Laronde	Allen	Orr	Devonshire	Van der Elst	Goddard	Cross	Brooking	Pike	
	24/4	24,748	*21*	55			*Connor 20, Graham 56, Flynn 89*	*Lukic*	*Hird*	*Gray F*	*Flynn*	*Hart*	*Cherry*	*Gray E*	*Graham*	*Worthington*	*Butterworth**	*Barnes*	*Connor*
							Ref: J Bray	Allan Clarke's Leeds drop to 21st after this defeat. At 2-2 Leeds looked the likelier team, and they were pressing hard at 2-3 when Frank Gray handled in the box. Brooking's goals – one a far-post header ('Dixie' Brooking) – were his first since playing Leeds back in November.											
38	A	ARSENAL	9	L	0-2	0-2		Parkes	Stewart	Laronde	Allen	Orr	Devonshire	Van der Elst	Cowie*	Cross	Brooking	Pike	Houghton
	1/5	*34,977*	*7*	55			*Rix 16, Sunderland 42*	*Wood*	*Hollins*	*Sansom*	*Talbot*	*O'Leary*	*Whyte*	*Hawley*	*Sunderland*	*Davis*	*Robson*	*Rix*	
							Ref: J Hunting	Arsenal boss Terry Neill is in despair over the dreadful crowd disturbances which disfigured this match. Smoke bombs went off in the North bank and the players were taken off during a 10-minute stoppage. Rix headed in Hawley's cross. Other than Brooking, West Ham looked poor.											
39	H	SUNDERLAND	10	D	1-1	0-1	Stewart 67p	Parkes	Stewart	Laronde	Allen	Orr	Devonshire	Van der Elst	Goddard	Cross	Brooking	Pike	
	4/5	**17,130**	*17*	56			*West 40*	*Turner*	*Hinnigan*	*Munro*	*Hindmarch*	*Chisholm*	*Elliott*	*Buckley*	*West*	*Rowell*	*Pickering*	*Cummins*	
							Ref: J Deakin	Sunderland have lost just one of their last nine. Devonshire won a penalty when wriggling into the box and fouled by Shaun Elliott, who was so incensed he refused to shake hands at the end. At half-time police broadcast a request for information regarding a death at Highbury last week.											
40	H	MANCHESTER U	10	D	1-1	0-0	Cross 48	Parkes	Stewart	Laronde	Allen	Orr	Devonshire	Cowie	Goddard	Cross	Brooking	Pike	
	8/5	26,337	*3*	57			*Moran 62*	*Bailey*	*Gidman*	*Albiston*	*Wilkins*	*Moran*	*Duxbury*	*Moses*	*Birtles**	*Stapleton*	*Grimes*	*Coppell*	*McGarvey*
							Ref: S Bates	Billy Bonds is still out with jaundice and Van der Elst misses the match with bruised toes. The crowd spilled over the wall at the South Bank, putting everyone in fear of yet more crowd disturbances. Gidman's back-pass let in Cross to bring West Ham back on terms with his 18th goal.											
41	H	TOTTENHAM	10	D	2-2	0-1	Brooking 62, Goddard 85	Parkes	Stewart	Laronde	Allen	Orr	Devonshire	Cowie*	Goddard	Cross	Brooking	Pike	Barnes
	10/5	27,667	*4*	58			*Hoddle 10p, Brooke 63*	*Parks*	*Corbett**	*Miller*	*Price*	*Lacy*	*Perryman*	*Hazard*	*Brooke*	*Falco*	*Hoddle*	*Crooks*	*O'Reilly*
							Ref: A Seville	Two Parks in goal, so to speak, as Spurs' 19-year-old Tony Parks makes his debut. Ron Greenwood comes along to watch Brooking and Hoddle, who quickly scored from the spot after Gary Brooke had been flattened. Brooking was not to be outdone, volleying home Pike's chip.											
42	A	WOLVES	9	L	1-2	1-2	Cross 13	Parkes	Stewart	Laronde	Allen	Orr	Devonshire	Cowie	Goddard	Cross*	Brooking	Pike	Barnes
	15/5	*13,283*	*21*	58			*Eves 3, Richards 10*	*Bradshaw*	*Humphrey*	*Atkinson*	*Eves*	*Gallagher*	*Coy*	*Hibbitt*	*Carr*	*Matthews*	*Richards*	*Clarke*	
	Home	Away					Ref: G Owen	Wolves had to win and WBA had to lose if Wolves were to stay up. Albion's win at Notts Co sent Wolves down. David Cross scored his 98th and last West Ham goal and is subbed at half-time. He is refusing to sign a new contract, and Man C manager John Bond is here to watch him.											
Average	26,594	24,694																	

League Cup					F-A	H-T	Scorers, Times, and Referees	1	2	3	4	5	6	7	8	9	10	11	12 sub used
2:1	A	DERBY	2	W	3-2	1-1	Cross 28, Brooking 48, Stewart 82p	McAlister	Stewart	Lampard	Bonds	Martin	Devonshire	Neighbour	Goddard	Cross	Brooking	Pike	
	7/10	13,764	*2:17*				*Stewart 9 (og), Hector 46*	*Cherry*	*Coop*	*Buckley*	*Powell S*	*Ramage*	*Osgood**	*Skivington*	*Powell B*	*Hector*	*Swindlehurst*	*Emson*	*Clayton*
							Ref: R Bridges	Colin Addison's Derby would have been dead and buried, but for Cross and Brooking both hitting the woodwork. Ray Stewart scored at both ends, side-footing into his own net, then netting a penalty after Alan Ramage handled on the line. Kevin Hector scored his 200th Derby goal.											
2:2	H	DERBY	6	W	2-0	1-0	Goddard 36, 70	Parkes	Stewart	Lampard	Bonds	Martin	Devonshire	Neighbour	Goddard	Cross	Brooking	Pike	
	27/10	21,043	*2:16*					*Jones*	*Coop*	*Buckley*	*Powell S*	*Sheridan*	*Powell B*	*Hector**	*Reid*	*Clayton*	*Swindlehurst*	*Emson*	*Gibson*
							Ref: M Taylor (Hammers win 5-2 on aggregate)	Paul Goddard enjoys the nickname 'Sarge'. He was a bit fortunate with his first goal, turning in Frank Lampard's off-target effort, but his second was something special. Trevor Brooking crossed, and Sarge's volley flew in off a post. Derby's Swindlehurst gave Martin a hard time.											
3	H	WEST BROM	6	D	2-2	1-2	Stewart 43p, Cross 64	Parkes	Brush	Lampard	Stewart	Martin	Devonshire	Neighbour	Goddard	Cross	Brooking	Pike	
	10/11	24,168	*17*				*Regis 22, King 40*	*Grew*	*Arthur*	*Statham*	*King*	*Wile*	*Robertson*	*Jol*	*Brown*	*Regis*	*Owen*	*MacKenzie*	
							Ref: T Spencer	England manager Ron Greenwood watches this virtuoso performance by Alan Devonshire. At 0-2, Devonshire won a penalty when tripped by King. Cross then levelled after John Wile had misjudged Alvin Martin's mis-hit shot. Robust Albion might have had two players sent off.											
3R	A	WEST BROM	5	D	1-1	0-0	Stewart 108p	Parkes	Stewart	Lampard	Bonds	Martin	Devonshire	Neighbour	Goddard*	Cross	Brooking	Pike	Allen
	24/11	*15,869*	*16*		*aet*		*Regis 92*	*Grew*	*Batson*	*Statham*	*King*	*Wile*	*Robertson*	*Jol*	*Brown*	*Regis*	*Owen*	*MacKenzie*	
							Ref: H King	Two minutes into extra-time Andy King's long ball enables Cyrille Regis to outpace Martin and put WBA ahead. When Wile is judged to have fouled Brooking in the box, Albion players go demented. Lyall won the post-match toss of the coin for the right of home advantage next time.											
3	H	WEST BROM	6	L	0-1	0-0		Parkes	Stewart	Lampard	Bonds	Martin	Devonshire	Neighbour	Goddard	Cross*	Brooking	Pike	Allen !
RR	1/12	24,760	*17*				*Regis 80*	*Grew*	*Batson*	*Statham*	*King*	*Wile*	*Robertson*	*Jol*	*Brown !*	*Regis*	*Owen*	*MacKenzie*	
							Ref: B Martin	West Ham's first home defeat in 17 months was a tactical triumph for Ronnie Allen, who instructed Jol to stifle Trevor Brooking in midfield. When Paul Allen retaliated after Brown's foul, both were ordered off. MacKenzie put the fleet-footed Cyrille Regis away for the winner.											

FA Cup																			
3	H	EVERTON	10	W	2-1	1-0	Bonds 8, Cross 57	Parkes	Stewart	Lampard	Bonds	Martin	Devonshire	Neighbour	Goddard*	Cross	Brooking	Pike	Pearson
	2/1	24,431	*8*				*Eastoe 65*	*Southall*	*Stevens*	*Ratcliffe*	*Higgins*	*Lyons*	*Kendall*	*Richardson*	*Ross**	*Sharp*	*Eastoe*	*Lodge*	*O'Keefe*
							Ref: K Hackett	Everton player-manager Howard Kendall was incandescent after this defeat against a team who hadn't played for a month. All three goals were headers, but the moment that riled Kendall most was when Sharp was brought down. Ross had missed a penalty last week, and did so again.											
4	A	WATFORD	12	L	0-2	0-0		Parkes	Stewart	Lampard	Bonds	Martin	Van der Elst	Neighbour*	Goddard	Cross	Brooking	Pike	Pearson
	23/1	*27,004*	*2:3*				*Armstrong 47, Callaghan 72*	*Sherwood*	*Rice*	*Pritchett*	*Blissett*	*Terry*	*Bolton*	*Callaghan*	*Armstrong*	*Jenkins**	*Lohman*	*Barnes*	*Rostron*
							Ref: J Martin	Graham Taylor's Watford beat Man U in the previous round, and his promotion chasers do it again. The sight of Elton John leaping around the directors' box was enough to distress West Ham fans, who directed their spleen at debutant Van der Elst. What has he let himself in for?											

		Home					Away					
	P	W	D	L	F	A	W	D	L	F	A	Pts
1 Liverpool	42	14	3	4	39	14	12	6	3	41	18	87
2 Ipswich	42	17	1	3	47	25	9	4	8	28	28	83
3 Manchester U	42	12	6	3	27	9	10	6	5	32	20	78
4 Tottenham	42	12	4	5	41	26	8	7	6	26	22	71
5 Arsenal	42	13	5	3	27	15	7	6	8	21	22	71
6 Swansea	42	13	3	5	34	16	8	3	10	24	35	69
7 Southampton	42	15	2	4	49	30	4	7	10	23	37	66
8 Everton	42	11	7	3	33	21	6	6	9	23	29	64
9 WEST HAM	42	9	10	2	42	29	5	6	10	24	28	58
10 Manchester C	42	9	7	5	32	23	6	6	9	17	27	58
11 Aston Villa	42	9	6	6	28	24	6	6	9	27	29	57
12 Nott'm Forest	42	7	7	7	19	20	8	5	8	23	28	57
13 Brighton	42	8	7	6	30	24	5	6	10	13	28	52
14 Coventry	42	9	4	8	31	24	4	7	10	25	38	50
15 Notts Co	42	8	5	8	32	33	5	3	13	29	36	47
16 Birmingham	42	8	6	7	29	25	2	8	11	24	36	44
17 West Brom	42	6	6	9	24	25	5	5	11	22	32	44
18 Stoke	42	9	2	10	27	28	3	6	12	17	35	44
19 Sunderland	42	6	5	10	19	26	5	6	10	19	32	44
20 Leeds	42	6	11	4	23	20	4	1	16	16	41	42
21 Wolves	42	8	5	8	19	20	2	5	14	13	43	40
22 Middlesbro	42	5	9	7	20	24	3	6	12	14	28	39
	924	214	121	127	672	501	127	121	214	501	672	1265

Odds & ends

Double wins: (1) Middlesbrough.
Double losses: (1) Arsenal.

Won from behind: (4) South'ton, (h), Coventry (h), Wolves (h), Leeds (h).
Lost from in front: (2) Villa (a), Derby LC (a).

High spots: Not losing any of the first nine league games.
Five league wins out of six from 13 March.
David Cross's four goals against Spurs.

Low spots: Four consecutive league defeats from 5 December.
Failing to win any of the last five games.

Hammer of the Year: Alvin Martin.
Ever-presents: (1) Ray Stewart
Hat-tricks: (2) Paul Goddard (1), David Cross (1).
Leading scorer: (19) David Cross.

	Appearances						Goals			
	Lge	*Sub*	LC	*Sub*	FAC	*Sub*	**Lge**	LC	FAC	**Tot**
Allen, Paul	**27**	*1*		*2*						
Banton, Dale		*1*								
Barnes, Bobby	**1**	*2*								
Bonds, Billy	**29**		4		2		**1**		1	**2**
Brooking, Trevor	**34**		5		2		**8**	1		**9**
Brush, Paul	**10**	*3*	1							
Cowie, George	**5**	*1*								
Cross, David	**38**		5		2		**16**	2	1	**19**
Devonshire, Alan	**35**		5		1		**1**			**1**
Goddard, Paul	**38**	*1*	5		2		**15**	2		**17**
Houghton, Ray		*1*								
La Ronde, Everald	**6**	*1*								
Lampard, Frank	**27**	*1*	5		2					
McAlister, Tom	**3**		1							
Martin, Alvin	**28**		5		2		**4**			**4**
Neighbour, Jimmy	**19**	*4*	5		2		**2**			**2**
Orr, Neil	**24**						**1**			**1**
Parkes, Phil	**39**		4		2					
Pearson, Stuart	**2**	*2*				*2*	**1**			**1**
Pike, Geoff	**34**		5		2		**2**			**2**
Stewart, Ray	**42**		5		2		**10**	3		**13**
Van der Elst, François	**21**	*1*			1		**5**			**5**
22 players used	**462**	***19***	**55**	***2***	**22**	***2***	**66**	**8**	**2**	**76**

No	Date		Att	Pos	Pt	F-A	H-T	Scorers, Times, and Referees	1	2	3	4	5	6	7	8	9	10	11	12 sub used
1	H	NOTT'M FOREST			L	1-2	1-1	Stewart 37p	Parkes	Stewart	Lampard	Bonds	Martin	Devonshire	Van der Elst	Goddard	**Clark**	Allen	Pike	
	28/8		23,796		0			*Walsh 10, Robertson 78p*	*Sutton*	*Anderson*	*Bowyer*	*Proctor**	*Young*	*Todd*	*Hodge*	*Wallace*	*Plummer*	*Walsh*	*Robertson*	*Gunn*
								Ref: A Gunn	Only Forest stopped West Ham scoring at home last season and the jinx continues. The new partnership of Goddard and Clark fails to gel and Hammers resort to screaming for penalties. It works when Allen drives the ball against Walsh. Forest got one, too, when Wallace went down.											
2	A	LUTON			W	2-0	0-0	Goddard 49, Bonds 66	Parkes	Stewart	Lampard	Bonds	Martin	Devonshire	Van der Elst	Goddard	Clark	Allen	Neighbour*	Morgan
	31/8		*13,402*		3				*Findlay*	*Stephens*	*Money*	*Horton*	*Goodyear*	*Donaghy*	*Hill*	*Stein*	*Walsh*	*Antic*	*Moss*	
								Ref: A Seville	The music of Chariots of Fire accompanies David Pleat's promoted champions on to the pitch. Billy Bonds heads on Ray Stewart's corner to Goddard. Bonds then heads in from Stewart's free-kick. Jimmy Neighbour lasts 25 minutes before torn knee ligaments takes him from the fray.											
3	A	SUNDERLAND		14	L	0-1	0-1		Parkes	Stewart	Lampard	Bonds	Martin	Devonshire	Van der Elst	Goddard	Clark	Allen	Pike	
	4/9		*19,239*	*4*	3			*Rowell 15*	*Turner*	*Venison*	*Munro*	*Atkins*	*Hindmarch*	*Elliott*	*Buckley*	*Rowell*	*McCoist*	*Pickering*	*Cummins*	
								Ref: R Chadwick	Lyall recalls Geoff Pike and gives Van der Elst a Brooking-like role in midfield. The tactics don't work and the Hammers don't get a whiff of a goal. Parkes is at fault for Sunderland's breakthrough. He tried to smother the ball at Stan Cummins' feet but it ballooned in off his shoulder.											
4	H	IPSWICH			D	1-1	0-1	Lampard 60	Parkes	Stewart	Lampard	Bonds	Martin	Devonshire	Van der Elst	Goddard	Clark	Allen	Pike	
	7/9		21,963		4			*Wark 32*	*Cooper*	*Burley*	*Mills*	*Thijssen*	*Osman*	*Butcher*	*Wark*	*McCall*	*Mariner*	*Brazil*	*Gates*	
								Ref: K Barratt	Billy Bonds' 545th league appearance breaks Bobby Moore's all-time record, and he receives a cut-glass vase beforehand. Stewart let in Wark for Ipswich's goal, then has his penalty saved when Osman fouled Van der Elst. Lampard levelled at the second go from Devonshire's corner.											
5	H	BIRMINGHAM		8	W	**5-0**	2-0	Van Elst 22, Goddard 30, Stewart 60p, [Martin 73, Clark 86]	Parkes	Stewart	Lampard	Bonds	Martin	Devonshire	Van der Elst	Goddard	Clark	Allen	Pike	
	11/9		18,754	*22*	7				*Blyth*	*Hagan*	*Dennis*	*Hawker*	*v d Hauwe**	*Phillips*	*van Mierlo*	*Dillon*	*Harford*	*Curbishley*	*Carrodus*	*Summerfield*
								Ref: M James	Ron Saunders' ragged Birmingham offer little resistance. The penalty is awarded for a foul on Clark, who later nets his first West Ham goal with a neat chip. Goddard managed one goal, a lob, but should have had a hat-trick. The game marked Lampard's 500th league appearance.											
6	A	WEST BROM		6	W	2-1	2-1	Clark 8, Van der Elst 9	Parkes	Stewart	Lampard	Bonds	Martin	Devonshire	Van der Elst	Goddard	Clark	Allen	Pike	
	18/8		*15,321*	*8*	10			*Eastoe 41*	*Grew*	*Batson*	*Whitehead*	*Zondervan*	*Bennett*	*Robertson*	*Jol*	*Brown**	*Regis*	*Owen*	*Eastoe*	*Cross*
								Ref: K Walmsley	Alvin Martin takes advantage of an injury to Liverpool's Phil Thompson to earn an England call-up for the European Championship match against Denmark. Martin keeps a tight grip on Cyrille Regis, Ally Brown and Peter Eastoe. Sandy Clark scores a fine individual goal.											
7	H	MANCHESTER C		4	W	4-1	2-0	Clark 33, 37, Goddard 47, Van Elst 71	Parkes	Stewart*	Lampard	Bonds	Martin	Devonshire	Van der Elst	Goddard	Clark	Allen	Pike	Orr
	25/9		23,883	*9*	13			*Boyer 63*	*Williams*	*Ranson*	*McDonald**	*Baker*	*Bond !*	*Caton*	*Hareide*	*Reeves*	*Boyer*	*Hartford !*	*Power*	*Tueart*
								Ref: D Letts	City end the match with nine men. Kevin Bond was sent off on 59 minutes for kicking Bonds, and Hartford's mouth got him expelled later. Ray Stewart had another penalty saved, this time by the overworked Alex Williams, only playing because England man Corrigan was injured.											
8	A	ARSENAL		4	W	3-2	2-1	Van der Elst 19, Goddard 42, Martin 62	Parkes	Stewart	Lampard	Bonds	Martin	Devonshire	Van der Elst*	Goddard	Clark	Allen	Pike	Orr
	2/10		*30,484*	*18*	16			*Talbot 22, Davis 84*	*Wood*	*Hollins*	*Sansom*	*Talbot*	*O'Leary*	*Whyte*	*Davis*	*Sunderland*	*Chapman*	*Woodcock*	*Rix*	
								Ref: T Bune	Arsenal can't stop leaking goals at home lately. Pin-point Hammers passes set up goals for Van der Elst and Goddard. Martin's goal was a looping header. West Ham had much defending to do after half-time, and Davis' headed goal from Hollins' corner provoked a furious finale.											
9	H	LIVERPOOL		2	W	3-1	1-0	Martin 36, Pike 46, Clark 79	Parkes	Stewart	Lampard	Bonds*	Martin	Devonshire	Neighbour	Goddard	Clark	Allen	Pike	Orr
	9/10		32,500	*5*	19			*Souness 75*	*Grobbelaar*	*Neal*	*Kennedy**	*Thompson*	*Whelan*	*Hansen*	*Dalglish*	*Lee*	*Lawrenson*	*Rush*	*Souness*	*Johnston*
								Ref: A Robinson	Hammers extend their winning league run to five after this exhilarating match. Neighbour and Goddard supplied the crosses for all three West Ham goals. When Liverpool pushed Lawrenson forward, they carried far greater threat. Two defeats on the trot for Liverpool, and that's rare.											
10	A	SOUTHAMPTON		2	L	0-3	0-1		Parkes	Stewart	Lampard	Bonds	Martin	Devonshire	Van der Elst	Goddard	Clark	Allen	Pike	
	16/10		*19,840*	*19*	19			*Williams 15, Ball 60, Moran 89*	*Wells*	*Rofe*	*Holmes*	*Williams*	*Nicholl*	*Wright*	*Ball*	*Moran*	*Fashanu*	*Armstrong*	*Lawrence**	*Puckett*
								Ref: J Hunting	The form book is turned upside down as West Ham's winning run comes to an end. Peter Shilton is missing from McMenemy's Saints, having hurt his shoulder when falling off a log while playing with his child. West Ham's best chance came when Van der Elst hit an upright at 0-2.											

No	Venue	Opponent / Date	Att			F-A	H-T	Scorers, Times, Referees	1	2	3	4	5	6	7	8	9	10	11	subs used
11	A	BRIGHTON		5	L	1-3	0-1	Devonshire 89	Parkes	Stewart	Lampard !	Bonds	Martin	Devonshire	Van der Elst	Goddard	Clark	Allen	Pike	
	23/10		20,490	12	19			Smith 44, Gatting 77, Robinson 84	Moseley	Shanks	Pearce	Stille	Foster	Gatting	Case*	McNab	Robinson	Ward	Smith	Ryan
								Ref: L Burden	After 24 minutes Frank Lampard is sent off for the first time in his career, guilty of a professional foul on Michael Robinson. Brighton are still unbeaten at home, and a huge crowd at the Goldstone Ground turns out to welcome the return of Brighton's prodigal son, Mark Ward.											
12	H	MANCHESTER U		2	W	3-1	1-0	Goddard 32, Stewart 53p, Pike 70	Parkes	Stewart	Lampard	Bonds	Martin	Devonshire	Van der Elst	Goddard	Clark	Allen	Pike	
	30/10		31,684	3	22			Moran 90	Bailey	Duxbury	Albiston	Grimes !	Moran	Buchan	Robson	Muhren	Stapleton	Whiteside	Coppell	
								Ref: D Hedges	Man U's Ashley Grimes is sent off for clipping the ref round the face after a penalty claim goes unheeded. Grimes had earlier conceded the penalty, impeding Clark. Ron Atkinson's team created 17 clear-cut chances. Coppell hit the bar, and Atkinson asks the press 'Am I dreaming?'											
13	A	STOKE		3	L	**2-5**	1-4	Stewart 43p, Pike 77 [McIlroy 45, 76]	Parkes	Stewart	Brush	Bonds	Martin	Devonshire	Van der Elst*	Goddard	Clark	Allen	Pike	Orr
	6/11		17,589	7	22			O'Cal'ghan 15, H'mpton 30, Th'mas 42	Harrison	Parkin D	Hampton	Bracewell	Watson	McAughtrie	Maguire	McIlroy	O'Callaghan*	Thomas	Chamberl'n M	Berry
								Ref: F Roberts	On the day Lyall receives his Bell's Manager of the Month award for October, his team are torn apart, recording their heaviest setback since Sunderland beat them 0-6 in 1967. Devonshire kept trying to beat everyone on his own, and consequently gave the ball away time after time.											
14	H	NORWICH		2	W	1-0	0-0	Clark 53	Parkes	Stewart	Lampard	Bonds	Martin	Devonshire	Van der Elst	Goddard	Clark	Allen	Pike	
	13/11		22,463	22	25				Woods	Haylock	Hareide	Van Wyk	Walford	Watson	Barham*	O'Neill	Deehan	Bertschin	Bennett	Metcalf
								Ref: B Hill	Bobby Robson watched Goddard have a poor game, but he keeps his place in the England squad to play Greece. The pattern was set after two minutes, when Goddard ran from the halfway line, rounded Chris Woods, but pushed the ball too wide. Clark hit the winner from a rebound.											
15	A	TOTTENHAM		4	L	1-2	1-0	Van der Elst 35	Parkes	Stewart	Lampard	Bonds	Martin	Neighbour	Van der Elst	Goddard	Clark	Allen	Pike	
	20/11		**41,960**	8	25			Archibald 55, 88	Clemence	Hughton	Price	Parks	Hazard	Perryman*	Mabbutt	Archibald	Villa	Hoddle	Crooks	Brooke
								Ref: R Lewis	Spurs' boardroom is again in upheaval. Keith Burkinshaw's team have just been knocked out of Europe. Steve Archibald misses several chances for Spurs before seizing on Neighbour's back-pass. Archibald was credited with the late winner, after the ball ricocheted off his chest.											
16	H	EVERTON		5	W	2-0	1-0	Stevens 16 (og), Bonds 85	Parkes	Stewart	Lampard	Bonds	Martin !	Devonshire*	Van der Elst	Goddard	Clark	Allen	Pike	Morgan
	27/11		21,424	15	28				Arnold	Stevens	Ratcliffe	Higgins	Wright	McMahon	Irvine !	Heath*	Sharp	King	Sheedy	Johnston
								Ref: V Callow	Two minutes from time Everton's Alan Irvine kicked the ball at the grounded Van der Elst and all hell was let loose. The outcome was red cards for Irvine and Martin, who had looked the best player on the pitch and just laid on Bonds' goal. Everton's rough play won few admirers.											
17	A	ASTON VILLA		6	L	0-1	0-0		Parkes	Stewart !	Lampard	Orr	Martin	Brush	Van der Elst	Goddard	Clark	Allen	Pike	
	4/12		24,658	3	28			Cowans 83p	Rimmer	Jones	Williams	Evans	McNaught	Mortimer*	Bremner	Shaw	Withe	Cowans	Morley	Walters
								Ref: E Read	This game exploded at the death. Peter Withe dives into Martin, who was running backwards, and wins a penalty. Stewart was then sent off for body-checking Mark Walters, having been booked moments earlier. Lyall refuses to attend the press conference, feeling his team were cheated.											
18	H	COVENTRY		7	L	0-3	0-3		Parkes	Stewart	Lampard	Orr	**Gallagher**	Devonshire*	Van der Elst	Goddard	Brush	Allen	Pike	Morgan
	11/12		19,321	8	28			Hateley 36, Roberts 42, Whitton 45	Sealey	Thomas	Roberts	Butterworth	Dyson	Gillespie	Whitton	Jacobs	Hateley	Melrose	Hunt	
								Ref: A Grey	With half his defence injured or suspended, Lyall signs Wolves' Joe Gallagher on trial, despite his bad-boy reputation. The result is to gift Coventry their first away win of the season. Brian Roberts' goal, a 20-yard volley, was his first in a 10-year career. The third goal was farcical.											
19	A	NOTTS CO		6	W	2-1	2-0	Dickens 6, Hunt 15 (og)	Parkes	Lampard	Brush	Orr	Gallagher	**Dickens**	Van der Elst	Goddard	Clark	Allen	Pike	
	18/12		**8,457**	15	31			Worthington 73	Avramovic	Benjamin	Worthington	Hunt	Kilcline	Richards	Chiedozie	Fashanu	Christie	Hooks	Mair*	Clarke
								Ref: J Worrall	Another debutant, this time 18-year-old Alan Dickens, a Brooking lookalike. He enjoys a fine debut, scoring after Paul Allen's effort had been parried by the keeper. Clark's cross cannoned off David Hunt for the second goal. County debutant Justin Fashanu had a 'goal' disallowed.											
20	H	SWANSEA		4	W	3-2	0-2	Stewart 48p, Van Elst 68, Goddard 86	Parkes	Stewart	Brush	Orr	Martin	Devonshire	Van der Elst	Goddard	Clark	Allen	Pike	
	27/12		23,843	18	34			Latchford 26, 38	Davies	Stanley	Hadziabdic	Robinson	Evans	Rajkovic	James L	James R	Mahoney	Charles	Latchford	
								Ref: I Borrett	At half-time Paul Brush is pushed up from midfield and a lost cause is transformed into an epic win. Gary Stanley toppled Devonshire for the penalty. Devonshire set up Van der Elst's goal. Goddard's late winner, a deflection off the keeper, is his first league goal for two months.											
21	A	WATFORD		5	L	1-2	0-1	Stewart 78p	Parkes	Stewart	Lampard	Gallagher	Martin	Devonshire	Van der Elst	Goddard	Clark	Allen	Pike	
	29/12		24,870	3	34			Jackett 39, Jenkins 58	Sherwood	Rice	Rostron	Taylor	Sims	Bolton	Callaghan	Blissett	Jenkins	Jackett	Barnes	
								Ref: C Thomas	Graham Taylor's Watford are going well. Just before the hour, Gallagher was lucky not to be sent off for deliberate handball. But from John Barnes' free-kick Ross Jenkins headed Watford's second goal. Pat Rice brought West Ham back into contention when fouling Devonshire.											

No	Date		Att	Pos	Pt	F-A	H-T	Scorers, Times, and Referees	1	2	3	4	5	6	7	8	9	10	11	12 sub used
22	H	TOTTENHAM		5	W	3-0	1-0	Cottee 25, Stewart 70p, Pike 80	Parkes	Stewart	Gallagher	Dickens	Martin	Devonshire	Van der Elst	**Cottee**	Clark	Allen	Pike	
	1/1		**33,383**	*12*	37				*Clemence*	*Hughton*	*Mazzon*	*Price*	*Villa*	*Perryman*	*O'Reilly*	*Archibald*	*Brooke*	*Hoddle*	*Crooks*	
								Ref: M Scott	17-year-old Tony Cottee makes his senior debut and scores after Ray Clemence pushes Joe Gallagher's header against the bar. The lead was doubled when Mazzon brought down Devonshire in the area. Spurs' boss Keith Burkinshaw rages at his team, especially the invisible Hoddle.											
23	H	LUTON		5	L	2-3	1-1	Cottee 12, Clark 66	Parkes	Stewart	Gallagher	Dickens	Martin*	Devonshire	Van der Elst	Cottee	Clark	Allen	Pike	Morgan
	4/1		21,435	*17*	37			*Walsh 32, 73, 88*	*Findlay*	*Stephens*	*Thomas*	*Horton*	*Goodyear*	*Donaghy*	*Hill*	*Bunn**	*Walsh*	*Turner*	*Moss*	*Kellock*
								Ref: T Spencer	Luton have a good record at Upton Park and this win takes them out of the bottom three. England manager Bobby Robson watches as Paul Walsh hits the post inside the first minute. Ray Stewart slips to let in Walsh for Luton's very late winner, which completed his hat-trick.											
24	A	NOTT'M FOREST		6	L	0-1	0-0		Parkes	Stewart*	Lampard	Bonds	Martin	Devonshire	Van der Elst	Goddard	Clark	Allen	Pike	Gallagher
	15/1		*17,031*	*3*	37			*Wallace 74*	*Sutton*	*Swain*	*Gunn*	*Todd*	*Young*	*Bowyer*	*Proctor*	*Wallace*	*Birtles*	*Hodge*	*Robertson*	
								Ref: P Tyldesley	It is 11 years since West Ham were successful against Forest at the City Ground. Forest pressed from first to last. Clark volleyed against the bar in the first half, but Hammers would not come so close again. Wallace took Birtles' pass with his back to goal, turned and shot into the corner.											
25	H	WEST BROM		6	L	0-1	0-1		Parkes	Lampard	Gallagher	Bonds	Martin	Devonshire	Van der Elst*	Goddard	Clark	Allen	Pike	Cowie
	22/1		19,887	*13*	37			*Eastoe 10*	*Barron*	*Whitehead*	*Statham*	*Zondervan*	*Wile*	*Robertson*	*Jol*	*Bennett*	*Regis**	*Owen*	*Eastoe*	*Cross*
								Ref: M Taylor	Albion are as physical a team as they come, and Clive Whitehead seemed to foul everyone in sight. But WBA lose Cyrille Regis in the first half with a fractured cheekbone, following a collision with Gallagher. A floodlight failure delayed the start of the second half by 21 minutes.											
26	A	BIRMINGHAM		8	L	0-3	0-1		Parkes	Lampard	Gallagher	Bonds	Martin	Devonshire	Van der Elst	Goddard	Clark	Allen*	Cowie	Dickens
	5/2		*12,539*	*20*	37			*Harford 35, Ferguson 59, Gayle 90*	*Coton*	*Langan*	*Dennis*	*Stevenson*	*Blake*	*Broadhurst*	*Gayle*	*Ferguson*	*Harford*	*Curbishley*	*Dillon*	
								Ref: T Fitzharris	West Ham's sixth successive league defeat leaves veteran Billy Bonds fuming: 'We were absolute rubbish.' It would have been even worse had Kevin Dillon not missed a penalty for City – after Lampard had handled. Birmingham nonetheless win easily enough and climb off the bottom.											
27	H	SOUTHAMPTON		12	D	1-1	1-1	Lampard 44	Parkes	Stewart	Lampard	Bonds	Martin	Devonshire	Van der Elst	Goddard	Clark*	Allen	Pike	Cottee
	26/2		19,626	*10*	38			*Wallace 16*	*Shilton*	*Agboola*	*Mills*	*Williams*	*Nicholl*	*Wright*	*Holmes*	*Baird*	*Moran*	*Armstrong*	*Wallace*	
								Ref: L Robinson	The boo-boys have it in for Sandy Clark, who is barracked throughout. In the 33rd minute Parkes smothered the ball outside his area and is sent off, but a linesman was already flagging for offside. Lampard's deflected shot, through Mick Mills' legs, denies Saints a fourth straight win.											
28	H	BRIGHTON		10	W	2-1	0-0	Dickens 83, Cottee 84	Parkes	Stewart*	Lampard	Gallagher	Martin	Devonshire	Van der Elst	Morgan	Cottee	Allen	Pike	Dickens
	5/3		16,850	*21*	41			*Ryan 82*	*Moseley*	*Ramsey*	*Gatting*	*Grealish*	*Foster*	*Stevens*	*Case*	*Ritchie*	*Robinson*	*Ryan*	*Smillie*	
								Ref: J Deakin	West Ham's first win since New Year's Day looked unlikely after 82 dreadfully tedious minutes. But then the match burst into life. Alan Dickens described his 30-yard goal as the best of his life. Cottee's winner was the first goal scored by a West Ham forward since 4 January.											
29	A	LIVERPOOL		11	L	0-3	0-0		Parkes	Stewart	Lampard	Bonds	Martin	Devonshire	Van der Elst	Morgan	Goddard	Allen	Pike	
	12/3		*28,511*	*1*	41			*Pike 49 (og), Lee 55, Rush 67*	*Grobbelaar*	*Neal*	*Kennedy*	*Lawrenson*	*Whelan*	*Hansen*	*Dalglish*	*Lee*	*Rush*	*Johnston*	*Souness*	
								Ref: K Hackett	Leaders Liverpool remain 14 points clear of second-placed Watford thanks to this emphatic win. West Ham came for a draw and defended in depth. But when Pike dived to head into his own net the floodgates opened. Ian Rush scores his 100th Liverpool goal, his 26th of the season.											
30	H	STOKE		13	D	1-1	0-0	Bould 52 (og)	Parkes	Stewart	Lampard	Bonds	Martin	Devonshire	Van der Elst	Goddard	Morgan	Allen	Pike	
	19/3		**16,466**	*9*	42			*Thomas 70*	*Fox*	*Bould*	*Hampton*	*Bracewell*	*Watson*	*Berry*	*Painter*	*McIlroy*	*O'Callaghan**	*Thomas*	*Chamberl'n*	*MGriffiths*
								Ref: M Bodenham	John Lyall missed this game, taking in another fixture. With the transfer deadline looming he is anxious to make a signing. There are rumours that David Cross might be returning from Man City. Lyall missed an exquisitely scooped own-goal by Steve Bould, later bound for Arsenal.											
31	A	MANCHESTER U		13	L	1-2	0-0	Devonshire 72	Parkes	Stewart	Lampard	Bonds	Martin	Devonshire	Van der Elst	Goddard	Orr*	Allen	Pike	Dickens
	22/3		*30,227*	*3*	42			*Stapleton 46, McGarvey 63*	*Bailey*	*Gidman*	*Albiston*	*Moses*	*McGrath*	*Duxbury*	*Wilkins*	*Muhren*	*Stapleton**	*McGarvey*	*Coppell*	*Macari*
								Ref: A Challinor	Lyall has sold Clark to Glasgow Rangers and Nicky Morgan to Portsmouth, and has signed David Swindlehurst from Derby. Lyall missed the first half of this match, but had taken his seat to see Muhren's corner headed in by Stapleton. McGarvey ran on to Remi Moses' pass for No 2.											

No	H/A	Opponent	Att	Pos	Res/Pts	F-A	H-T	Scorers, Times, and Referees	1	2	3	4	5	6	7	8	9	10	11	subs used
32	A	NORWICH		14	D	1-1	1-0	Dickens 25	Parkes	Stewart	Lampard	Bonds	Martin	Devonshire	Orr	Goddard	**Swindl'urst**	Dickens	Pike	
	26/3		*18,582*	*21*	43			*Deehan 67p*	*Woods*	*Haylock*	*Downs*	*Mendham*	*Walford*	*Watson*	*Barham*	*O'Neill*	*Deehan*	*Bertschin**	*Channon*	*Jack*
								Ref: J Bray	David Swindlehurst makes his debut, his mind troubled by his baby daughter, who has been hospitalised with pneumonia. His team-mates took his mind off her by pumping a stream of high balls at his head. West Ham might even have won, until Martin fouled Mick Channon in the area.											
33	H	WATFORD		12	W	2-1	1-1	Van der Elst 19, Swindlehurst 62	Parkes	Stewart	Lampard	Bonds	Martin	Devonshire	Van der Elst	Goddard	Swindlehurst*	Dickens	Pike	Cottee
	2/4		22,647	*3*	46			*Callaghan 6*	*Sherwood*	*Rice*	*Rostron*	*Taylor*	*Sims*	*Bolton*	*Callaghan*	*Blissett*	*Barnes*	*Lohman**	*Jobson*	*Armstrong*
								Ref: A Robinson	Devonshire played so poorly against Greece that Bobby Robson took the rare step of criticising him publicly. Whether or not by coincidence, Robson watched this match, and Devonshire was stung into playing well. Dickens made the winner, Swindlehurst's first goal for his new club.											
34	A	SWANSEA		10	W	5-1	2-1	Pike 20, 65, D'shire 45, Dickens 82, 88	Parkes	Stewart	Lampard	Bonds	Martin	Devonshire	Van der Elst	Goddard	Orr	Dickens	Pike	
	5/4		*13,303*	*19*	49			*Walsh 2*	*Sander*	*Marustik*	*Richards*	*Stevenson*	*Lewis*	*Rajkovic*	*Loveridge*	*James R*	*Walsh**	*Stanley*	*Latchford*	*Gale*
								Ref: D Civil	Six points out of six over Easter. This win is West Ham's biggest since defeating Grimsby by the same score two years earlier. Swindlehurst misses the game with hamstring trouble. Walsh's shock header was cancelled out by a slovenly half-clearance that fell neatly for Geoff Pike.											
35	H	SUNDERLAND		7	W	2-1	0-0	Dickens 60, Goddard 82	Parkes	Stewart	Lampard	Bonds	Martin	Devonshire	Van der Elst	Goddard	Swindlehurst*	Dickens	Pike	Cottee
	9/4		20,053	*16*	52			*Pickering 70*	*Turner*	*Nicholl*	*Munro*	*Elliott*	*Chisholm*	*Proctor*	*Cummins**	*Rowell*	*Worthington*	*James*	*Pickering*	*McCoist*
								Ref: H Taylor	An hour of tedium and the crowd are getting restless. Alan Dickens' sweet volley – his fourth goal in four games – lifts the tempo, but Nick Pickering replies with a spectacular volley of his own. Paul Goddard shrugs off a heavy challenge to bludgeon his first goal since Christmas.											
36	A	MANCHESTER C		9	L	0-2	0-2		Parkes	Stewart	Lampard	Bonds	Orr	Devonshire	Van der Elst	Goddard*	Allen	Dickens	Pike	Cottee
	16/4		*23,015*	*17*	52			*McDonald 13, Tueart 26p*	*Williams*	*Ranson*	*McDonald*	*Reid*	*Bond*	*Caton*	*Tueart*	*Reeves*	*Kinsey*	*Hartford*	*Power*	
								Ref: A Saunders	City boss John Bond drops leading scorer David Cross and the gamble seems to pay off. Kevin Bond's free-kick was headed in by full-back Bobby McDonald. Then Billy Bonds was ruled to have handled in the area following a City corner. Bonzo thought the decision very harsh.											
37	H	ASTON VILLA		9	W	2-0	0-0	Swindlehurst 59, Bonds 78	Parkes	Stewart	Lampard*	Bonds	Martin	Devonshire	Van der Elst	Goddard	Swindlehurst	Dickens	Pike	Orr
	23/4		21,822	*4*	55				*Spink*	*Williams*	*Gibson*	*Evans*	*McNaught*	*Walker*	*Curbishley*	*Shaw*	*Withe*	*Cowans*	*Morley*	
								Ref: C Thomas	Villa boss Tony Barton has no complaints following this clear-cut defeat. Spink failed to hold Goddard's header, allowing Swindlehurst an easy goal. Devonshire and Dickens set up Bonds' third league goal of the season. Bonds and Withe exchanged blows but escaped punishment.											
38	A	EVERTON		10	L	0-2	0-1		Parkes	Stewart	Brush	Bonds	Martin	Devonshire	Van der Elst	Goddard	Swindlehurst	Dickens	Pike	
	30/4		*16,355*	*7*	55			*Sharp 32, 82*	*Southall*	*Stevens*	*Bailey*	*Ratcliffe*	*Higgins*	*Richardson*	*Ainscow*	*Johnson*	*Sharp*	*Heath*	*Sheedy*	
								Ref: K Holbrook	England international Alvin Martin blunders to present Everton with their first goal. He tackles Graeme Sharp and tries to prod the ball back to Parkes, but Sharp nips in. Sharp side-foots the second goal, from Stevens' cross, as Bonds, Stewart and Parkes all stand staring at each other.											
39	A	IPSWICH			W	2-1	1-1	Goddard 10, Stewart 79p	Parkes	Stewart	Lampard	Bonds	Martin	Devonshire	Van der Elst	Goddard	Swindlehurst	Dickens	Pike	
	3/5		*18,690*		58			*D'Avray 33*	*Cooper*	*Burley*	*Barnes*	*Parkin**	*Gernon*	*Butcher*	*Wark*	*McCall*	*Mariner*	*D'Avray*	*O'Callaghan*	*Turner*
								Ref: G Napthine	This thriller was decided by a late penalty. Back in September Cooper saved a Ray Stewart penalty. This time, after Goddard had been felled by Irvin Gernon, Stewart has his revenge, scoring his 10th penalty of the season. Mich D'Avray had earlier levelled with a superb shot.											
40	H	NOTTS CO		8	W	2-0	1-0	Van der Elst 5, Goddard 70	Parkes	Stewart	Lampard	Bonds	Martin	Devonshire	Van der Elst	Goddard	Swindlehurst	Dickens	Pike	
	7/5		17,534	*16*	61				*Avramovic*	*Benjamin*	*Hunt*	*Goodwin*	*Kilcline*	*Richards*	*Chiedozie*	*Christie*	*McCulloch**	*Lahtinen*	*Worthington*	*Clarke*
								Ref: T Bune	Van der Elst's solo goal does not affect his decision to return to Belgium at the end of the season. Alan Dickens laid on the second goal for Goddard. Poor Notts Co are heartily sick of West Ham, having been beaten by them twice in the league and also knocked out of the Milk Cup.											
41	H	ARSENAL			L	1-3	0-3	Van der Elst 52	Parkes	Stewart	Lampard	Bonds	Martin	Devonshire	Van der Elst	Goddard	Swindlehurst	Brooking	Pike	
	10/5		28,930		61			*Petrovic 9, Whyte 22, McDermott 28*	*Jennings*	*Kay*	*Sansom*	*Whyte*	*O'Leary*	*Nicholas*	*Talbot*	*Davis*	*Petrovic*	*McDermott*	*Hill*	
								Ref: A Gunn	Terry Neill's Arsenal performed a first-half demolition job on West Ham. The Gunners were inspired by Vladimir Petrovic, who turned in Paul Davis' low cross, featured in the build-up to Whyte's goal, then crossed for McDermott's third. Van der Elst's consolation spun off Jennings.											
42	A	COVENTRY		8	W	4-2	1-0	Godd'rd 8, C'tee 54, 88, Swind'h'st 60	Parkes	Stewart	Lampard	Bonds	Orr	Devonshire	Van der Elst	Goddard	Swindlehurst	Allen	Pike	Cottee
	14/5		*10,919*	*19*	64			*Hendrie 55, Whitton 75*	*Sealey*	*Thomas*	*Roberts*	*Hormanschuk*	*Butterworth*	*Gillespie*	*Whitton*	*Singleton*	*Hateley*	*Hendrie*	*Hunt*	
	Home		Away					Ref: B Newsome	A game with no managers. John Lyall was away scouting and Dave Sexton was sacked by Coventry just hours before kick-off. Bobby Gould takes temporary charge. Goddard shot on the run through Sealey's legs. Tony Cottee, a second-half sub, slides home Alan Devonshire's cross.											
Average	22,820		20,265																	

Milk Cup						F-A	H-T	Scorers, Times, and Referees	1	2	3	4	5	6	7	8	9	10	11	12 sub used
2:1	A	STOKE		4	D	1-1	0-0	Stewart 81p	Parkes	Stewart	Lampard	Orr	Martin	Devonshire	Neighbour	Goddard	Clark	Allen	Pike	
6/10			*18,079*	*8*				*Thomas 70*	*Fox*	*Parkin*	*Hampton*	*Bracewell*	*Watson*	*Berry*	*Maguire*	*McIlroy*	*O'Callaghan*	*Thomas*	*Ch'mb'l'n M**	*Griffiths*
								Ref: H King	Lampard assumes the captaincy in the absence of Bonds. An early clash between Alan Devonshire and Mark Chamberlain saw the England winger limp off the pitch. Thomas's goal went in off Phil Parkes' body. Berry's clumsy challenge on Devonshire resulted in Stewart's penalty.											
2:2	H	STOKE		5	W	2-1	0-0	Goddard 80, Clark 82	Parkes	Stewart	Lampard	Bonds	Martin	Devonshire	Van der Elst	Goddard	Clark	Allen	Pike*	Neighbour
26/10			18,270	*8*				*Watson 63*	*Harrison*	*Pike*	*Hampton*	*Bracewell*	*Watson*	*McAughtrie*	*Maguire*	*McIlroy*	*O'Callaghan*	*Thomas*	*Chamberl'n M*	
								Ref: J Martin (Hammers win 3-2 on aggregate)	Bobby Robson watches as England defender Dave Watson heads Paul Maguire's cross beyond Parkes. Goddard's equaliser, after he beat three players to shoot from 20 yards, was special. Stoke were furious over Clark's winner, insisting that Devonshire's pass caught Goddard offside.											
3	A	LINCOLN		3	D	1-1	1-0	Goddard 25	Parkes	Stewart	Brush	Bonds	Martin	Devonshire	Orr*	Goddard	Clark	Allen	Pike	Van der Elst
10/11			*13,899*	*3:1*				*Bell 82*	*Felgate*	*Carr*	*Neale*	*Cockerill*	*Peake*	*Thompson*	*Burke*	*Turner*	*Hobson*	*Bell*	*Shipley*	
								Ref: K Baker	Colin Murphy's Lincoln put West Ham under a second-half siege, forcing corner after corner on a windy night. Peake had hit a post before Bell nodded in Turner's free-kick. The Hammers had been hanging on to Goddard's earlier swerving shot, which was set up by Devonshire.											
3R	H	LINCOLN		5	W	2-1	1-0	Stewart 45, Clark 116	Parkes	Stewart	Lampard	Bonds	Martin	Neighbour*	Van der Elst	Goddard	Clark	Allen	Pike	Barnes
29/11			13,686	*3:1*		*aet*		*Clark 77 (og)*	*Felgate*	*Carr*	*Neale*	*Cockerill*	*Peake*	*Thompson*	*Hibberd*	*Turner*	*Hobson*	*Bell*	*Shipley*	
								Ref: A Glasson	Lyall admits his team were 'very fortunate' after this battle with the Division 3 pace-setters. Turner rugby-tackled Allen to concede a penalty, which Stewart put away only after Felgate saved. George Shipley's cross was dummied by Derek Bell and ricocheted in off Sandy Clark.											
4	A	NOTTS CO		6	D	3-3	0-0	Van der Elst 66, 73, 85	Parkes	Stewart	Lampard	Orr	Martin	Devonshire	Van der Elst	Goddard	Clark*	Allen	Pike	Brush
7/12			*7,525*	*12*				*McCulloch 50, Christie 53p, Hunt 88*	*Avramovic*	*Benjamin*	*Worthington*	*Hunt*	*Kilcline*	*Richards*	*Chiedozie*	*Christie*	*McCulloch*	*Hooks*	*Mair*	
								Ref: G Tyson	Van der Elst celebrates being called into the Belgian national squad with his first Hammers hat-trick. Although Alvin Martin concedes yet another penalty, West Ham recovered and looked to be through – 3-2 winners – until Phil Parkes beat out Chiedozie's cross to David Hunt.											
4R	H	NOTTS CO		6	W	3-0	1-0	Stewart 30p, Clark 62, Allen 88	Parkes	Stewart	Brush	Orr	Martin	Devonshire	Van der Elst	Goddard	Clark	Allen	Pike	
21/12			13,140	*15*					*Avramovic*	*Benjamin*	*Worthington*	*Hunt*	*Kilcline*	*Richards*	*Chiedozie*	*Christie*	*Fashanu*	*Goodwin*	*Clarke**	*Mair*
								Ref: L Shapter	John Lyall is in bed with flu, leaving Ronnie Boyce to take charge. The Hammers have two goals disallowed before Avramovic brings downs Goddard for the penalty. Clark settled the outcome, netting the rebound after Van der Elst had hit a post. Two wins in four days over County.											
QF	A	LIVERPOOL		6	L	1-2	0-0	Allen 75	Parkes	Cowie	Gallagher	Bonds	Martin	Devonshire	Van der Elst	Goddard	Clark	Allen	Pike	
18/1			*23,953*	*1*				*Hodgson 70, Souness 86*	*Grobbelaar*	*Neal*	*Kennedy*	*Lawrenson*	*Johnston**	*Hansen*	*Dalglish*	*Lee*	*Rush*	*Hodgson*	*Souness*	*Whelan*
								Ref: M Heath	Holders Liverpool are unbeaten at Anfield in any cup-tie since 1974. Twice Goddard was through on a snow-bound pitch, but twice he spurned the chances. Time was running out when Parkes allowed Souness's shot to slither under his body. West Ham would have deserved a replay.											

FA Cup									1	2	3	4	5	6	7	8	9	10	11	12 sub used
3	A	MANCHESTER U		5	L	0-2	0-1		Parkes	Stewart	Lampard	Bonds	Gallagher	Devonshire	Van der Elst	Cottee	Clark	Allen	Pike	
8/1			*44,143*	*3*				*Coppell 31, Stapleton 54*	*Bailey*	*Duxbury*	*Albiston*	*Moses*	*Moran*	*McQueen*	*Robson*	*Muhren*	*Stapleton*	*Whiteside*	*Coppell*	
								Ref: D Hutchinson	*The Times* wrote: 'West Ham made no more impact than a man reading the gas meter.' Alan Devonshire, in particular, has a shocker. Arnold Muhren's corner was headed on by Frank Stapleton to Steve Coppell. Man-of-the match Bryan Robson set up Frank Stapleton's clincher.											

	P	W	D	L	F	A	W	D	L	F	A	Pts
		Home					Away					
1 Liverpool	42	16	4	1	55	16	8	6	7	32	21	82
2 Watford	42	16	2	3	49	20	6	3	12	25	37	71
3 Manchester U	42	14	7	0	39	10	5	6	10	17	28	70
4 Tottenham	42	15	4	2	50	15	5	5	11	15	35	69
5 Nott'm Forest	42	12	5	4	34	18	8	4	9	28	32	69
6 Aston Villa	42	17	2	2	47	15	4	3	14	15	35	68
7 Everton	42	13	6	2	43	19	5	4	12	23	29	64
8 WEST HAM	42	13	3	5	41	23	7	1	13	27	39	64
9 Ipswich	42	11	3	7	39	23	4	10	7	25	27	58
10 Arsenal	42	11	6	4	36	19	5	4	12	22	37	58
11 West Brom	42	11	5	5	35	20	4	7	10	16	29	57
12 Southampton	42	11	5	5	36	22	4	7	10	18	36	57
13 Stoke	42	13	4	4	34	21	3	5	13	19	43	57
14 Norwich	42	10	6	5	30	18	4	6	11	22	40	54
15 Notts Co	42	12	4	5	37	25	3	3	15	18	46	52
16 Sunderland	42	7	10	4	30	22	5	4	12	18	39	50
17 Birmingham	42	9	7	5	29	24	3	7	11	11	31	50
18 Luton	42	7	7	7	34	33	5	6	10	31	51	49
19 Coventry	42	10	5	6	29	17	3	4	14	19	42	48
20 Manchester C	42	9	5	7	26	23	4	3	14	21	47	47
21 Swansea	42	10	4	7	32	29	0	7	14	19	40	41
22 Brighton	42	8	7	6	25	22	1	6	14	13	46	40
		255	111	96	810	454	96	111	255	454	810	1275

Odds & ends

Double wins: (2) Notts Co, Swansea.
Double losses: (1) Nott'm Forest.

Won from behind: (4) Swansea (h), Brighton (h), Watford (h), Stoke LC (h).
Lost from in front: (3) Spurs (a), Luton (h), Swansea (a).

High spots: Five successive league wins from 11 September. Up to 2nd.
Finishing the season strongly, with seven wins from the last 10 games.

Low spots: Four consecutive defeats from 4 January.
Going out of the FA Cup at the first hurdle, to Manchester U.

Hammer of the Year: Alvin Martin.
Ever-presents: (1) Phil Parkes.
Hat-tricks: (1) Van der Elst.
Leading scorer: (12) Paul Goddard and Van der Elst.

	Appearances						Goals			
	Lge	*Sub*	LC	*Sub*	FAC	*Sub*	Lge	LC	FAC	Tot
Allen, Paul	**33**		7		1			2		**2**
Barnes, Bobby				*1*						
Bonds, Billy	**34**		4		1		**3**			**3**
Brooking, Trevor	**1**									
Brush, Paul	**6**		2	*1*						
Clark, Sandy	**26**		7		1		**7**	3		**10**
Cottee, Tony	**3**	*5*			1		**5**			**5**
Cowie, George	**1**	*1*	1							
Devonshire, Alan	**39**		6		1		**3**			**3**
Dickens, Alan	**12**	*3*					**6**			**6**
Gallagher, Joe	**8**	*1*	1		1					
Goddard, Paul	**39**		7				**10**	2		**12**
Lampard, Frank	**37**		4		1		**2**			**2**
Martin, Alvin	**38**		7				**3**			**3**
Morgan, Nicky	**3**	*4*								
Neighbour, Jimmy	**3**		2	*1*						
Orr, Neil	**9**	*5*	4							
Parkes, Phil	**42**		7		1					
Pike, Geoff	**40**		7		1		**6**			**6**
Stewart, Ray	**39**		6		1		**8**	3		**11**
Swindlehurst, Dave	**9**						**3**			**3**
Van der Elst, François	**40**		5	*1*	1		**9**	3		**12**
(own-goals)							**3**			**3**
22 players used	**462**	***19***	**77**	***4***	**11**		**68**	**13**		**81**

No	Date		Att	Pos	Pt	F-A	H-T	Scorers, Times, and Referees	1	2	3	4	5	6	7	8	9	10	11	12 sub used
1	H	BIRMINGHAM			W	**4-0**	3-0	Cottee 23, 28, Martin 36,	Parkes	Stewart	**Walford**	Bonds	Martin	Devonshire	**Whitton**	Cottee	Swindlehurst	Brooking*	Pike	Orr
	27/8		19,729		3			[Swindlehurst 52]	*Coton*	*Hagan*	*Stevenson*	*Blake*	*Wright*	*Broadhurst*	*Handysides**	*Phillips*	*Harford*	*v d Hauwe*	*Hopkins*	*Rees*
								Ref: A Robinson	18-year-old Tony Cottee is only playing because of Goddard's damaged knee-ligaments, but now he deserves his place on merit. Brooking's shot was turned in by Cottee, who netted his second when Ray Stewart's free-kick wasn't cleared. Ron Saunders' City looked weak in the air.											
2	A	EVERTON			W	1-0	0-0	Walford 69	Parkes	Stewart	Walford	Bonds	Martin	Devonshire	Whitton	Cottee	Swindlehurst	Orr	Pike	
	29/8		*20,375*		6				*Arnold*	*Harper*	*Bailey*	*Mountfield*	*Higgins*	*Richardson**	*Steven*	*Heath*	*Sharp*	*King*	*Sheedy*	*Johnson*
								Ref: P Tyldesley	Walford's fluke goal, an intended cross that floats over Jim Arnold's head, and the first goal he had ever scored with his right foot, brings West Ham their first win at Goodison since Alvin Martin was an apprentice there. Brooking, in his last season, missed the game with a thigh strain.											
3	A	TOTTENHAM		1	W	2-0	2-0	Whitton 9, Swindlehurst 39	Parkes	Stewart	Walford	Bonds	Martin	Devonshire	Whitton	Cottee	Swindlehurst	Brooking	Pike	
	3/9		*38,042*	*20*	9				*Clemence*	*Hughton*	*Thomas*	*Roberts*	*Stevens*	*Perryman*	*Mabbutt*	*Falco*	*Galvin*	*Hoddle**	*Crooks*	*Miller*
								Ref: J Hunting / D Nevin	The game lost Glenn Hoddle to injury before half-time and the referee, too, during the interval. Whitton put West Ham ahead with a volley on the turn, and Swindlehurst swept in Cottee's cross. Spurs had looked in control, though in the second half their shots were all from long range.											
4	H	LEICESTER		1	W	3-1	1-1	Walford 10, Swind'hurst 48, Cottee 49	Parkes	Stewart	Walford	Bonds	Martin	Devonshire	Whitton	Cottee	Swindlehurst	Brooking	Pike	
	6/9		22,131	*22*	12			*Lineker 8*	*Grew*	*Ramsey*	*Smith B*	*MacDonald*	*Rennie*	*Peake*	*Lynex*	*Lineker*	*Smith A*	*Jones**	*Wilson*	*English*
								Ref: L Burden	Lineker's early goal is the first Leicester have scored – and the first West Ham have conceded – this season. It was quickly cancelled out by Steve Walford's 25-yard effort. Swindlehurst headed No 2 and chipped on to Cottee for the third. West Ham's 'robust' play surprises many.											
5	H	COVENTRY		1	W	5-2	3-2	Swind'hurst 29, 35, 67, Whitton 30,60	Parkes	Stewart	Walford	Bonds	Martin	Devonshire	Whitton	Cottee	Swindlehurst	Brooking	Pike	
	10/9		22,195	*7*	15			*Peake 10, Platnauer 15*	*Suckling*	*Hormantsch'k*	*Roberts*	*Grimes*	*Peake*	*Jacobs*	*Butterworth*	*Withey*	*Platnauer*	*Gibson*	*Adams**	*Singleton*
								Ref: A Crickmore	Bobby Gould's Coventry were unbeaten. This result is one of the great recoveries of the season. At 0-0 Stewart's penalty is saved after Grimes had handled. Before they know it the Hammers are 0-2 down, but Swindlehurst and Whitton turn the tables by half-time. Bonds is magnificent.											
6	A	WEST BROM		1	L	0-1	0-0		Parkes	Stewart	Walford	Bonds	Martin	Devonshire	Orr*	Cottee	Swindlehurst	Brooking	Pike	Goddard
	17/9		*15,161*	*14*	15			*Thompson 87*	*Barron*	*Whitehead*	*Cowdrill*	*Zondervan*	*McNaught*	*Bennett*	*Lewis*	*Thompson*	*Regis*	*Owen*	*Cross**	*Perry*
								Ref: N Wilson	Billy Bonds' 37th birthday. West Ham play for a draw and seldom pose any threat to the Albion defence. They look like surviving until Garry Thompson, the best player on view, heads in Cowdrill's cross. Cowdrill had actually been fouled by Brooking, but the ref played advantage.											
7	H	NOTTS CO		1	W	3-0	1-0	Brooking 32, Goddard 60, Stewart 89p	Parkes	Stewart	Walford	Bonds	Martin	Devonshire	Goddard	Cottee	Swindlehurst	Brooking	Pike	
	24/9		20,613	*18*	18				*McDonough*	*Benjamin*	*Worthington*	*O'Neill*	*Kilcline*	*Hunt*	*McParland*	*Christie**	*McCulloch*	*Harkouk*	*Mair*	*Chiedozie*
								Ref: M James	Paul Goddard plays in midfield and scores the all-important second goal, lifting the ball over the keeper as he rushes off his line. Brooking had earned the first-half lead when chesting down Walford's centre. Stewart's penalty was the consequence of Benjamin shoving Tony Cottee.											
8	A	STOKE		1	L	1-3	0-1	Stewart *60p* *[Thomas 85]*	Parkes	Stewart	Walford	Bonds	Martin	Devonshire	Whitton	Goddard	Swindlehurst	Brooking	Pike	
	1/10		*13,852*	*18*	18			*McAughtrie 29, Chamberlain 70,*	*Fox*	*Berry*	*Hampton*	*James*	*Dyson*	*McAughtrie*	*Painter*	*McIlroy*	*O'Callaghan*	*Thomas*	*Chamberlain*	
								Ref: B Stevens	Stoke boss Ritchie Barker describes West Ham as 'fragile'. This angers Lyall, who felt his team looked stronger once Ray Stewart had levelled from the spot, Goddard having been felled. Tiny Ian Painter outjumped Bonds to set up Stoke's second goal. Mickey Thomas then broke away.											
9	H	LIVERPOOL		2	L	1-3	0-2	Devonshire 89	Parkes	Stewart	Walford	Bonds	Martin	Devonshire	Whitton	Goddard*	Swindlehurst	Brooking	Pike	Cottee
	15/10		**32,555**	*5*	18			*Robinson 15, 27, 75*	*Grobbelaar*	*Neal*	*Kennedy*	*Lawrenson*	*Johnston !*	*Hansen*	*Dalglish*	*Lee*	*Rush**	*Robinson*	*Souness*	*Hodgson*
								Ref: L Shapter	West Ham are toppled off the top by Michael Robinson's first league goals for Joe Fagan's European champions. Poor Bonds, on his 700th appearance, was partially responsible for all three. On the hour Craig Johnston was sent off for his second yellow card, having fouled Bonds.											
10	H	NORWICH		3	D	0-0	0-0		Parkes	Stewart	Walford	Bonds	Martin	Devonshire	Whitton*	Cottee	Swindlehurst	Brooking	Pike	Dickens
	22/10		18,958	*16*	19				*Woods*	*Haylock*	*Downs*	*Mendham*	*Hareide*	*Watson*	*Donowa*	*Channon*	*Devine*	*Bertschin*	*Bennett*	
								Ref: D Brazier	Liverpool join Man U above West Ham, who slip down to third. The Hammers were poor in the first half, when they tried to play through the middle, yet improved afterwards when using the long ball. One Billy Bonds' header brings a great save from Chris Woods; another goes wide.											

No	H/A, Date	Opponent, Att	Pos	Res, Pts	F-A	H-T	Scorers, Times, and Referees	1	2	3	4	5	6	7	8	9	10	11	12
11	A	WATFORD	4	D	0-0	0-0		Parkes	Stewart	Walford	Bonds	Martin	Devonshire	Allen	Cottee	Swindlehurst	Brooking	Orr	
	28/10	*14,559*	*19*	20				*Sherwood*	*Palmer*	*Sinnott*	*Jobson*	*Sims*	*Franklin*	*Callaghan*	*Richardson*	*Barnes*	*Bolton*	*Rostron*	
							Ref: B Hill	Had West Ham won this Friday match they would have gone back to the top. It was scheduled for TV, but was scrapped at the last moment, with *Carry On Girls* broadcast instead. It was a wise choice. According to *The Times*, West Ham were 'abysmal', rarely interested in scoring.											
12	H	IPSWICH	3	W	2-1	2-1	Swindlehurst 25, 41	Parkes	Stewart	Walford	Bonds*	Martin	Devonshire	Orr	Cottee	Swindlehurst	Dickens	Pike	Lampard
	5/11	20,682	*12*	23			*Osman 39*	*Cooper*	*Burley*	*McCall*	*Putney*	*Osman*	*Butcher*	*Wark*	*Gates*	*Mariner*	*Kinsella**	*O'Callaghan*	*Turner*
							Ref: T Bune	Bonds is the victim of a clash of heads that has him taken to hospital with impaired vision. Better news for David Swindlehurst, who celebrates the birth of twin sons by winning the match with twin headers. Both goals stemmed from free-kicks and both saw him outjump Russell Osman.											
13	A	WOLVES	2	W	3-0	1-0	Brooking 4, Swind'hurst 57, Cottee 89	Parkes	Stewart	Lampard	Walford	Martin	Devonshire	Orr	Cottee	Swindlehurst	Brooking	Pike	
	12/11	*12,062*	*22*	26				*Bradshaw*	*Humphrey*	*Bennett**	*Blair*	*Pender*	*Dodd*	*Hibbitt*	*Clarke*	*Cartwright*	*Mardenboro'*	*Crainie*	*Rudge*
							Ref: J Deakin	Devonshire is in such irrepressible form that he seems determined to add to his seven England caps. When he is fouled in the box by Dodd, Stewart's penalty is tipped over by Bradshaw, his second miss from the spot this season. Poor Wolves have now gone 18 games without a win.											
14	A	SUNDERLAND	2	W	1-0	0-0	Swindlehurst 85	Parkes	Stewart	Lampard	Walford	Martin	Devonshire	Whitton	Cottee	Swindlehurst	Brooking	Pike	
	19/11	*19,921*	*16*	29				*Turner*	*Venison*	*Pickering*	*Atkins*	*Chisholm*	*Hindmarch*	*Bracewell*	*Rowell*	*West*	*Proctor*	*James*	
							Ref: T Jones	Sunderland had lost just once in 10 games and looked set to extend that fine sequence until Swindlehurst continued his rich vein of goals with a late volley. Stewart had earlier hit the bar and Parkes had silenced the Roker Roar with a string of fine saves. Sunderland saw more of the ball.											
15	H	MANCHESTER U	2	D	1-1	0-0	Swindlehurst 58	Parkes	Stewart	Lampard	Walford	Martin	Devonshire	Whitton	Cottee	Swindlehurst	Brooking	Pike	
	27/11	23,355	*3*	30			*Wilkins 56*	*Bailey*	*Moses*	*Albiston*	*Wilkins*	*Duxbury*	*McQueen*	*Robson*	*Muhren**	*Stapleton*	*Crooks*	*Graham*	*Whiteside*
							Ref: C Thomas	A live TV audience saw Bryan Robson at his magnificent best, in a match which offered skill, entertainment and controversy. Wilkins turned inside Brooking for a rare goal, immediately cancelled out by Swindlehurst's header from Pike's corner. Norman Whiteside's header hit a post.											
16	A	ASTON VILLA	2	L	0-1	0-0		Parkes	Stewart	Lampard	Walford	Martin	Devonshire	Whitton	Orr*	Swindlehurst	Brooking	Pike	Cottee
	3/12	*21,297*	*7*	30			*Rideout 77*	*Spink*	*Williams*	*Gibson**	*Evans*	*Ormsby*	*Mortimer*	*Birch*	*Walters*	*Rideout*	*Walker*	*Morley*	*Deacy*
							Ref: N Glover	Two moments decided this match, both coming within seconds of one another. Brooking's shot was half-saved, the ball being whacked off the line by Williams. The ball was swept upfield and a cross from near the corner flag saw Rideout head in. Rideout later cleared off his own line.											
17	H	ARSENAL	2	W	3-1	1-0	Brooking 34, Whyte 70 (og), Pike 88	Parkes	Stewart	Lampard	Walford	Martin	Devonshire	Whitton	Orr	Swind'hurst!	Brooking	Pike	
	10/12	25,118	*16*	33			*Whyte 90*	*Jennings*	*Hill**	*Sansom*	*Kay !*	*Whyte*	*Caton*	*Madden*	*Davis*	*Woodcock*	*Nicholas*	*Allinson*	*Meade*
							Ref: E Read	Kay's late lunge on Swindlehurst and the latter's retaliation brought red cards for both players. West Ham were already in front through Trevor Brooking's diving header. When Whyte stuck out a boot to deflect man-of-the-match Devonshire's cross past Jennings, Arsenal's hopes faded.											
18	A	NOTT'M FOREST	3	L	0-3	0-1		Parkes	Stewart	Lampard	Walford	Martin	Devonshire	Whitton	Orr	Swindlehurst	Brooking	Pike*	Dickens
	17/12	*14,544*	*8*	33			*Hodge 27, Birtles 75, Walsh 85p*	*v Breukelen*	*Anderson*	*Swain*	*Fairclough*	*Hart**	*Bowyer*	*Wigley*	*Davenport*	*Birtles*	*Hodge*	*Walsh*	*Wallace*
							Ref: T Holbrook	Bad luck, the woodwork, and Van Breukelen's defiance combine to deny West Ham their first goal at the City Ground since 1969. Forest were flattered by the final score. Swain went past two Hammers defenders to tee up Gary Birtles for No 2 and Stewart fouled Wigley for the penalty.											
19	H	SOUTHAMPTON	5	L	0-1	0-0		Parkes	Stewart	Lampard*	Walford	Martin	Devonshire	Whitton	Orr	Cottee	Brooking	Dickens	**Donald**
	26/12	22,221	*4*	33			*Wallace 64*	*Shilton*	*Mills*	*Dennis*	*Armstrong K*	*Agboola*	*Williams*	*Holmes*	*Curtis**	*Worthington*	*Armstrong D*	*Wallace*	*Puckett*
							Ref: M Bodenham	Lawrie McMenemy's Saints climb above West Ham as a result of Wallace dancing round Orr, who had been switched to left-back in place of the subbed Lampard. Father Christmas handed out presents to the crowd at half-time, but snubbed West Ham when Cottee headed onto the bar.											
20	A	LUTON	4	W	1-0	0-0	Cottee 78	Parkes	Stewart	Brush	Walford	Martin	Devonshire	Whitton	Orr	Cottee	Brooking	Barnes	
	27/12	*16,343*	*5*	36				*Sealey*	*Stephens*	*Thomas*	*Horton*	*Elliott*	*Donaghy*	*Hill*	*Stein B*	*Walsh*	*Aylott**	*Daniel*	*Turner*
							Ref: K Baker	Luton saw most of the ball but succumbed to a volley by Cottee, who was only playing because Swindlehurst was suspended. The goal carried West Ham back above Luton, but the match saw more muscle than skill. Players were left black and blue, the same colour as the stormy sky.											
21	H	TOTTENHAM	3	W	4-1	1-1	Cottee 11, Martin 70, Stewart 72, [Brooking 76]	Parkes	Stewart	Brush	Walford	Martin	Devonshire	Whitton	Cottee	Swindlehurst	Brooking	Orr	
	31/12	30,939	*11*	39			*Stevens 30*	*Clemence*	*O'Reilly*	*Bowen*	*Webster*	*Stevens*	*Perryman*	*Ardiles*	*Archibald*	*Falco*	*Thomas*	*Dick*	
							Ref: T Spencer	Spurs have seven first-teamers injured or suspended and their depleted side assists Devonshire and Brooking in eclipsing Ardiles in midfield. Brooking set up the first goal for Cottee and the second through Martin's header. Brooking's bobbling shot for No 4 was the least he deserved.											

No	Date	Att	Pos	Pt	F-A	H-T	Scorers, Times, and Referees	1	2	3	4	5	6	7	8	9	10	11	12 sub used
22	A NOTTS CO		3	D	2-2	2-1	Stewart 20p, Swindlehurst 28	Parkes	Stewart	Brush	Walford	Martin	Devonshire	Whitton	Cottee	Swindlehurst	Brooking	Orr	
	2/1	*8,667*	*20*	40			*Christie 38, O'Neill 47*	*McDonough*	*Goodwin**	*Worthington*	*Richards*	*Hunt*	*Kilcline*	*O'Neill*	*Clarke*	*Christie*	*Harkouk*	*Chiedozie*	*McParland*
							Ref: G Courtney	In a gale-lashed match West Ham looked set to reclaim second spot above Man U. The ball hit Hunt's arm for the penalty. The ref waved play on until alerted by the linesman's waved flag. Swindlehurst began and ended the move for the second. Chiedozie inspired County's fight-back.											
23	A BIRMINGHAM		3	L	0-3	0-1		Parkes	Stewart	Brush	Walford	Martin	Barnes	Whitton	Cottee	Swindlehurst	Brooking	Orr	
	14/1	*10,334*	*19*	40			*Harford 30, Halsall 70, Hopkins 80*	*Coton*	*Stevenson*	*v d Hauwe*	*Blake*	*Wright*	*Broadhurst*	*Gayle*	*Kuhl*	*Harford*	*Halsall*	*Hopkins*	
							Ref: D Hedges	Ron Saunders' City had lost their last six home games. This is Phil Parkes' 600th league game but he is at fault for the first goal, bungling a clearance from Gayle's cross under pressure from Harford. Gayle had the beating of Brush and set up both of Birmingham's second-half goals.											
24	H WEST BROM		3	W	1-0	0-0	Cottee 81	Parkes	Stewart	Lampard	Walford	Orr	Brush	Barnes	Cottee	Swindlehurst	Brooking	Pike	
	21/1	17,213	*16*	43				*Barron*	*Whitehead*	*Cowdrill*	*Luke*	*McNaught*	*Robertson*	*Zondervan*	*Owen**	*Thompson*	*Regis*	*Morley*	*Jol*
							Ref: I Borrett	Alvin Martin has broken six ribs in a car crash. West Ham's desperate injury problem requires Stewart to play centre-back. Walford's through ball enabled Cottee to spring the offside trap for the only goal. A rough game saw more than 50 fouls. Sub Jol was booked within 90 seconds.											
25	H STOKE		3	W	3-0	2-0	Barnes 6, Cottee 35, Stewart 65p	Parkes	Stewart	Lampard	Walford	Orr	Brush	Barnes	Cottee	Swindlehurst	Allen	Dickens	
	4/2	18,775	*21*	46				*Fox*	*Bould*	*Maskery*	*James*	*Dyson*	*O'Callaghan*	*Painter*	*McIlroy*	*Maguire*	*Hudson*	*Chamberlain*	
							Ref: R Milford	West Ham's young mascot sported a broken nose and the ball burst after five minutes. Fortunately, woeful Stoke were not able to put up much opposition, other than Alan Hudson in midfield. West Ham scored two simple headers before O'Callaghan fouled Tony Cottee for the penalty.											
26	A QP RANGERS		3	D	1-1	1-1	Cottee 2	Parkes	Stewart	Lampard	Walford	Orr	Brush	Barnes	Cottee	Swindlehurst	Allen	Dickens	
	7/2	*20,102*	*5*	47			*Stainrod 15*	*Hucker*	*Neill*	*Dawes*	*Waddock*	*Wicks*	*Fenwick*	*Fillery**	*Stewart*	*Stainrod*	*Fereday*	*Gregory*	*Micklewhite*
							Ref: G Napthine	Loftus Road's notorious Omniturf pitch does not appear to discomfort West Ham, who are quickly in front as Swindlehurst's cross eludes Fenwick. Stainrod levelled when a high ball was missed by those in front of him. West Ham's nimble forwards always looked likely to score.											
27	A COVENTRY		3	W	2-1	1-0	Bamber 18 (og), Cottee 60	Parkes	Stewart	Lampard	Walford	Orr	Brush	Barnes	Cottee	Swindlehurst	Allen	Dickens	
	11/2	*13,271*	*10*	50			*Hunt 90*	*Avramovic*	*Roberts*	*Pearce*	*Daly*	*Peake*	*Allardyce*	*Bennett*	*Hunt*	*Bamber*	*Gibson*	*Grimes*	
							Ref: L Burden	Coventry paraded two mascots beforehand, but they could not ward off defeat by the only team still chasing the league and cup double. Tony Cottee's header from Allen's corner was goalbound before deflecting off Bamber's head. But Phil Parkes was by far the busier goalkeeper.											
28	H WATFORD		4	L	2-4	1-1	Swindlehurst 2, Barnes 60	Parkes	Stewart	Lampard	Bonds	Walford	**Hilton**	Barnes	Cottee	Swindlehurst	Allen	Dickens	
	21/2	19,241	*8*	50			*J'ston 45, Barnes 55, 75, Callaghan 79*	*Sherwood*	*Bardsley*	*Rostron*	*Sims*	*Franklin*	*Taylor*	*Jackett*	*Callaghan*	*Johnston*	*Barnes*	*Atkinson*	
							Ref: A Robinson	Watford's 20-year-old John Barnes steals the show. Playing in the middle alongside Mo Johnston, he terrorises Walford and Bonds. Barnes creates Watford's first goal, left-foots the second and heads their third. Play was held up in the second half when a glass smashed on the pitch.											
29	A NORWICH		4	L	0-1	0-0		Parkes	Stewart	Lampard	Bonds	Walford	Hilton	Barnes	Cottee	Swindlehurst	Allen	Dickens	
	25/2	*16,294*	*7*	50			*Deehan 65*	*Woods*	*Haylock*	*Downs*	*Mendham*	*Hareide*	*Watson*	*Devine*	*Channon*	*Deehan*	*Bertschin*	*Van Wyk*	
							Ref: J Ashworth	The Hammers' third defeat in a week leaves them with nothing to play for except a UEFA Cup place. They appeared to set out with nothing other than to achieve a goalless draw. Former Norwich player Steve Walford lost out in a scramble with John Deehan for the only goal.											
30	A IPSWICH		4	W	3-0	2-0	Hilton 4, Butcher 30 (og), Cottee 70	Parkes	Stewart	Lampard	Bonds	Walford	Hilton	Orr	Cottee	Swindlehurst	Brooking	Allen	
	3/3	*17,297*	*19*	53				*Cooper*	*Parkin*	*McCall*	*Putney*	*Osman*	*Butcher*	*Wark*	*Brennan**	*D'Avray*	*Sunderland*	*Gates*	*Dozzell*
							Ref: J Bray	The fact that Bonds and Brooking – 72 years between them – can stroll through this match shows what little fight Ipswich put up. Brooking laid on Paul Hilton's header, his first goal for the Hammers. Brooking's crafty cross then lured Terry Butcher to slice the ball into his own net.											
31	H WOLVES		3	D	1-1	1-1	Cottee 30	Parkes	Stewart	Lampard	Bonds	Walford	Orr	Barnes*	Cottee	Swindlehurst	Brooking	Allen	Dickens
	10/3	18,111	*21*	54			*McGarvey 22*	*Burridge*	*Buckland*	*Palmer*	*Rudge*	*Pender*	*Dodd*	*Towner*	*Clarke*	*Troughton*	*McGarvey*	*Crainie*	
							Ref: E Read	This surprise result enables Wolves to climb off the bottom. Stewart's error allowed Scott McGarvey, on loan from Man U, to volley past Phil Parkes. Trevor Brooking's sweet through ball set up Cottee's equaliser on a plate. Brooking is determined to retire at the end of this season.											

No	Venue / Date	Opponent / Att	Pos	Res / Pts	F-A	H-T	Scorers, Times, and Referees	1	2	3	4	5	6	7	8	9	10	11	12 sub used
32	A	LEICESTER	5	L	1-4	0-1	Stewart 89p	Parkes	Stewart	Lampard	Bonds	Walford	Orr*	Allen	Cottee	Swindlehurst	Brooking	Pike	Barnes
	17/3	*13,533*	*16*	54			*Hazell 42, Lynex 55p, 80p, Lineker 75*	*Wallington*	*Smith B*	*Wilson*	*MacDonald*	*Hazell*	*O'Neill*	*Lynex*	*Lineker*	*Smith A*	*Williams*	*Peake*	
							Ref: D Richardson	Yet more crowd trouble caused by a minority of West Ham fans. Man-of-the-match for Gordon Milne's Leicester was Steve Lynex, who was involved in all four goals. Lampard felled Lynex for the first penalty; Walford handled for the second. Pike had returned after stomach surgery.											
33	H	QP RANGERS	4	D	2-2	2-0	Pike 18, Cottee 45	Parkes	Stewart	Walford	Bonds	Martin	Orr	Allen P	Cottee	Swindlehurst	Brooking	Pike	
	31/3	21,099	*6*	55			*Allen C 76, 85*	*Hucker*	*Neill*	*Dawes*	*Waddock*	*Wicks*	*Fenwick*	*Micklewhite*	*Fillery*	*Allen C*	*Stainrod*	*Fereday**	*Burke*
							Ref: M Dimblebee	A match marred by capricious wind, slipshod passing and ill-timed tackles. Brooking's enterprise conjured two goals before the interval, but Clive Allen rescued a point for QPR single-handedly. He shrugged off Martin and Bonds to score a superb goal, then turned in Burke's corner.											
34	A	LIVERPOOL	6	L	**0-6**	0-4	*[Souness 61, 69]*	Parkes	Stewart	Walford	Bonds	Martin	Orr	Allen	Cottee	Whitton	Brooking	Pike	
	7/4	*38,359*	*1*	55			*Rush 5, 18, Dalglish 12, Whelan 29*	*Grobbelaar*	*Neal*	*Kennedy*	*Lawrenson*	*Whelan*	*Hansen*	*Dalglish*	*Lee*	*Rush*	*Wark*	*Souness*	
							Ref: D Hutchinson	How can a team lying fourth be thumped so comprehensively? Wingless Liverpool became arrogantly bored with West Ham's gutless showing and eased off. Parkes was to blame for two goals. Grobbelaar bantered with everyone. Joe Fagan sent a get-well letter to the flu-stricken Lyall.											
35	H	SUNDERLAND	6	L	0-1	0-0		Parkes	Stewart	Lampard	Bonds	Martin	Orr*	Allen	Cottee	Swindlehurst	Brooking	Pike	Barnes
	14/4	16,558	*18*	55			*Chisholm 71*	*Turner*	*Venison*	*Pickering*	*Atkins*	*Chisholm*	*Elliott*	*Bracewell*	*Robson*	*West*	*Hindmarch*	*James*	
							Ref: T Bune	A slow handclap resounds around Upton Park as Sunderland win their first away fixture in five months. Leighton James' free-kick was met by Chisholm but went in off Brooking. Biggest cheer of the night was to applaud the return of 38-year-old former Hammers idol Pop Robson.											
36	H	LUTON	6	W	3-1	2-0	Cottee 23, 81, Martin 37	Parkes	Stewart	Walford	Bonds	Martin	Barnes	Allen	Cottee	Swindlehurst	Brooking	Pike	
	17/4	**15,430**	*14*	58			*Walsh 65*	*Sealey*	*Stephens*	*Thomas*	*Horton*	*Elliott*	*Donaghy*	*Parker*	*Stein B*	*Walsh*	*Bunn**	*Moss*	*Goodyear*
							Ref: D Reeves	Luton had won just twice in 20 games, so hardly provided the most sterling opposition. Brooking chipped over the defence to Cottee for the first goal. Luton's Paul Walsh was being watched by representatives of four Italian clubs. He scored one, then missed a sitter when 1-2 down.											
37	A	SOUTHAMPTON	6	L	0-2	0-1		Parkes	Stewart	Walford	Bonds	Martin	Barnes*	Allen	Cottee	Swindlehurst	Brooking	Pike	Hilton
	21/4	*20,846*	*5*	58			*Holmes 34, Moran 77*	*Shilton*	*Mills*	*Golac*	*Curtis*	*Whitlock*	*Wright*	*Holmes*	*Moran*	*Worthington*	*Armstrong D*	*Wallace*	
							Ref: C Thomas	A sunny day, but the sun did not shine on West Ham, who seldom got within shooting range of Shilton's goal. Holmes netted the first, from Curtis's pass. The referee overruled the linesman's raised flag. Wallace hit the post before crossing for Moran, whose shot went in off Stewart.											
38	A	MANCHESTER U	7	D	0-0	0-0		Parkes	Stewart	Walford	Bonds	Martin	Hilton	Allen	Cottee	Orr	Brooking	Pike	
	28/4	***44,124***	*2*	59				*Bailey*	*Duxbury*	*Albiston*	*Wilkins*	*Moran*	*Hogg*	*McGrath**	*Moses*	*Stapleton*	*Hughes*	*Graham*	*Whiteside*
							Ref: K Hackett	West Ham line up with Cottee the sole forward and everyone else packing the defence. Cottee might have scored in the second minute, but that would have been hard on Man U, who imposed a siege around the visitors' goal. Parkes made save after save to keep the home team at bay.											
39	H	ASTON VILLA	9	L	0-1	0-1		Parkes	Stewart*	Walford	Bonds	Hilton	Orr	Allen	Cottee	Swindlehurst	Brooking	Pike	Goddard
	5/5	17,930	*8*	59			*Mortimer 19*	*Day*	*Williams*	*Deacy*	*Ormsby*	*Foster*	*Mortimer*	*Birch*	*Blair*	*Withe*	*McMahon*	*Walters**	*Walker*
							Ref: B Hill	West Ham needed to win to have any chance of pipping Arsenal and Spurs for a UEFA Cup place. But not even the return of Goddard, for his first game since October, could fashion a goal. Peter Withe's square pass from the left was thumped in by Mortimer from the edge of the box.											
40	A	ARSENAL	7	D	3-3	3-2	Whitton 4, 44, Hilton 35	Parkes	Stewart	Brush	Bonds	Walford	Hilton	Allen	Cottee	Orr	Brooking	Whitton	
	7/5	*33,347*	*6*	60			*Talbot 15, Woodcock 40, Mariner 75*	*Jennings*	*Hill*	*Sansom*	*Talbot*	*O'Leary*	*Caton*	*Robson*	*Nicholas*	*Mariner*	*Woodcock*	*Rix**	*Davis*
							Ref: R Lewis	An 11 am kick-off with five goals and a missed penalty by mid-day. It was Charlie Nicholas whose kick was saved, Orr having fouled Robson. Whitton made it 3-2 on half-time, when Allen's shot came back off the bar. Arsenal levelled yet again when Mariner stabbed in Robson's pass.											
41	H	NOTT'M FOREST	8	L	1-2	1-1	Stewart 19p	Parkes	Stewart	Brush*	Bonds	Walford	Hilton	Allen	Cottee	Orr	Brooking	Whitton	Pike
	12/5	18,468	*4*	60			*Birtles 22, Davenport 57*	*v Breukelen*	*Anderson*	*Swain*	*Fairclough*	*Hart*	*Bowyer*	*Wigley*	*Hodge*	*Birtles*	*Davenport*	*Walsh*	
							Ref: L Shapter	Brooking's six-year old son, Warren, is the secret mascot for dad's last Saturday game. Trevor had no idea. Brooking was fouled by Fairclough for the penalty – which looked like the referee's own parting gift. Birtles levelled from close range and Paul Brush's error led to the winner.											
42	H	EVERTON	9	L	0-1	0-1		Parkes	Stewart	Orr	Bonds	Walford	Donald	Allen	Cottee	Whitton	Brooking	Pike*	Swindlehurst
	14/5	25,452	*7*	60			*Richardson 14*	*Southall*	*Stevens*	*Harper*	*Ratcliffe*	*Mountfield*	*Reid*	*King*	*Richardson*	*Steven*	*Heath*	*Sharp*	
	Home	Away					Ref: M Taylor	Trevor Brooking's last match for West Ham, Warren Donald's first full 90 minutes. Everton have an appointment at Wembley in the FA Cup final, and Kevin Richardson's goal means they overtake West Ham in the league table. An angry Lyall locks his players in the dressing room.											
	Average 21,247	20,111																	

Milk Cup						F-A	H-T	Scorers, Times, and Referees	1	2	3	4	5	6	7	8	9	10	11	12 sub used
2:1	A	BURY		1	W	2-1	1-0	Goddard 16, Orr 82	Parkes	Stewart	Walford*	Bonds	Martin	Devonshire	Whitton	Goddard	Swindlehurst	Brooking	Pike	Orr
4/10			*8,050*	*4:5*				*Madden 61*	*Brown*	*Gardner*	*Pashley**	*Carrodus*	*Hilton*	*Bramhall*	*Potts*	*Madden*	*Spence*	*Jakub*	*Deacy*	*Coleman*
								Ref: M Heath	Torrential rain, a small pitch, and Bury's gutsy performance erased any obvious disparity between the teams. Brooking's reverse pass to Goddard was cancelled out by Madden at the far post. Bury were pressing hard when Alvin Martin's downfield clearance left Orr in the clear.											
2:2	H	BURY		3	W	10-0	5-0	Cot' 2,34,39,63, M'tin 17, S'wart 71p,	Parkes	Stewart	Walford	Bonds*	Martin	Devonshire	Allen	Cottee	Swindlehurst	Brooking	Pike	Orr
25/10			10,896	*4:8*				[Brooking 23, 83, Devonshire 67, 81]	*Brown*	*Gardner*	*Pashley*	*Coleman*	*Hilton*	*Bramhall*	*Potts*	*Entwhistle*	*Spence*	*Jakub*	*Deacy*	
								Ref: D Letts (Hammers win 12-1 on aggregate)	The crucial moment came in the fourth minute. Bonds fouled Entwistle, but Bramhall's penalty hit a post. Bury's spirit drained away. Stewart made it 8-0 on the night with a penalty after Coleman impeded Devonshire. Ironically, the ball went in off the same post Bramhall had struck.											
3	H	BRIGHTON		3	W	1-0	0-0	Swindlehurst 81	Parkes	Stewart	Lampard	Walford	Martin	Devonshire	Orr	Cottee	Swindlehurst	Brooking	Pike	
8/11			17,082	*2:12*					*Corrigan*	*Ramsey*	*Pearce*	*Grealish*	*Young E*	*Gatting*	*O'Reagan*	*Young A**	*Ryan*	*Connor*	*Howlett*	*Smith*
								Ref: M Scott	Brighton were happy to surrender midfield and give away corner-kicks by the dozen. Centre-half Eric Young and veteran England keeper Joe Corrigan held their defence together until Swindlehurst headed in Devonshire's cross. At one point Corrigan headed clear outside his area.											
4	H	EVERTON		2	D	2-2	1-1	Mountfield 35 (og), Pike 85	Parkes	Stewart	Lampard	Walford	Martin	Devonshire	Whitton	Cottee*	Swindlehurst	Brooking	Pike	Orr
30/11			19,702	*17*				*Reid 2, Sheedy 55*	*Southall*	*Stevens*	*Ratcliffe*	*Mountfield*	*Higgins*	*Reid*	*Irvine*	*Heath*	*Sharp*	*King*	*Sheedy*	
								Ref: A Gunn	West Ham enjoy the rub of the green against Howard Kendall's goal-shy Everton. Heath sold Martin an outrageous dummy for the first goal. Hammers equalised twice, first when Brooking's shot went in off Mountfield's knee, then when Pike squeezed the ball through a crowded box.											
4R	A	EVERTON		2	L	0-2	0-0		Parkes	Stewart	Lampard	Walford	Martin	Orr	Whitton	Cottee*	Swindlehurst	Brooking	Pike	Dickens
6/12			*21,609*	*16*		*aet*		*King 95, Sheedy 116*	*Southall*	*Stevens*	*Ratcliffe*	*Mountfield*	*Higgins*	*Reid*	*Irvine*	*Heath*	*Sharp*	*King*	*Sheedy*	
								Ref: T Mills	Alan Devonshire misses his first game of the season. West Ham look bereft of ideas without him, and their attacks are few and lack penetration. The breakthrough in extra-time came when Irvine's corner was headed on by Derek Mountfield. The ball came off the crossbar to King.											

FA Cup																				
3	H	WIGAN		3	W	1-0	1-0	Stewart 26p	Parkes	Stewart	Brush	Walford	Martin	Devonshire*	Whitton	Cottee	Swindlehurst	Brooking	Orr	Barnes
7/1			16,000	*3:17*					*Tunks*	*Cribley*	*Comstive*	*Butler*	*Walsh*	*Methven*	*Langley*	*Barrow*	*Lowe*	*Taylor*	*Bruce*	
								Ref: A Seville	Alan Devonshire's season is over after tearing ankle ligaments in the 15th minute. West Ham's penalty was fiercely contested. Brooking's shot struck Cribley on the hand, but it looked involuntary. Stewart drove the penalty into the centre of the goal. Keeper Tunks kept the score down.											
4	A	CRYS PALACE		3	D	1-1	0-1	Swindlehurst 80	Parkes	Stewart	Lampard	Walford	Orr	Brush*	Barnes	Cottee	Swindlehurst	Brooking	Pike	Allen
28/1			*27,590*	*2:18*				*McCulloch 29*	*Wood*	*Locke*	*Hughton*	*Stebbing*	*Cannon*	*Gilbert*	*Giles*	*Mabbutt*	*McCulloch*	*Nicholas*	*Hilaire*	
								Ref: J Hunting	A full-blooded cup-tie. Both goals were the result of goalmouth melees, with the ball finding the net at the third attempt. The ball hit the bar twice before McCulloch forced it in for Palace. Trevor Brooking's chip from the left paved the way for David Swindlehurst's late equaliser.											
4R	H	CRYS PALACE		3	W	2-0	1-0	Pike 22, Barnes 65	Parkes	Stewart	Lampard	Walford	Orr	Brush	Barnes	Cottee	Swindlehurst	Brooking	Pike*	Allen
31/1			27,127	*2:18*					*Wood*	*Locke*	*Hughton**	*Stebbing*	*Cannon*	*Gilbert*	*Giles*	*Mabbutt*	*McCulloch*	*Nicholas*	*Hilaire*	*Evans*
								Ref: J Hunting	Brooking looks head and shoulders better than anyone else, but is adamant that he will retire at the end of the season. Pike claimed West Ham's first goal, though Gilbert had turned his shot into his own net. Brush's centre was then missed by Cottee but converted by Bobby Barnes.											
5	A	BIRMINGHAM		3	L	0-3	0-2		Parkes	Stewart	Lampard	Walford	Orr	Brush*	Barnes	Cottee	Swindlehurst	Allen	Dickens	Bonds
18/2			*29,570*	*18*				*Hopkins 8, Rees 14, Wright 78p*	*Coton*	*McCarrick*	*v d Hauwe*	*Blake*	*Wright*	*Broadhurst*	*Rees*	*Kuhl*	*Harford*	*Stevenson*	*Hopkins*	
								Ref: G Courtney	Ron Saunders' City win before their biggest gate of the season. Two pitch invasions, instigated by West Ham fans after their team went 0-3 down, sparks an FA inquiry. Minus Brooking and Devonshire, West Ham lacked guile in midfield. Stewart fouled Rees to concede the penalty.											

	P	W	D	L	F	A	W	D	L	F	A	Pts
		Home					Away					
1 Liverpool	42	14	5	2	50	12	8	9	4	23	20	80
2 Southampton	42	15	4	2	44	17	7	7	7	22	21	77
3 Nott'm Forest	42	14	4	3	47	17	8	4	9	29	28	74
4 Manchester U	42	14	3	4	43	18	6	11	4	28	23	74
5 QP Rangers	42	14	4	3	37	12	8	3	10	30	25	73
6 Arsenal	42	10	5	6	41	29	8	4	9	33	31	63
7 Everton	42	9	9	3	21	12	7	5	9	23	30	62
8 Tottenham	42	11	4	6	31	24	6	6	9	33	41	61
9 WEST HAM	42	10	4	7	39	24	7	5	9	21	31	60
10 Aston Villa	42	14	3	4	34	22	3	6	12	25	39	60
11 Watford	42	9	7	5	36	31	7	2	12	32	46	57
12 Ipswich	42	11	4	6	34	23	4	4	13	21	34	53
13 Sunderland	42	8	9	4	26	18	5	4	12	16	35	52
14 Norwich	42	9	8	4	34	20	3	7	11	14	29	51
15 Leicester	42	11	5	5	40	30	2	7	12	25	38	51
16 Luton	42	7	5	9	30	33	7	4	10	23	33	51
17 West Brom	42	10	4	7	30	25	4	5	12	18	37	51
18 Stoke	42	11	4	6	30	23	2	7	12	14	40	50
19 Coventry	42	8	5	8	33	33	5	6	10	24	44	50
20 Birmingham	42	7	7	7	19	18	5	5	11	20	32	48
21 Notts Co	42	6	7	8	31	36	4	4	13	19	36	41
22 Wolves	42	4	8	9	15	28	2	3	16	12	52	29
	924	226	118	118	745	505	118	118	226	505	745	1268

Odds & ends

Double wins: (4) Spurs, Coventry, Ipswich, Luton.
Double losses (4) Liverpool, Aston Villa, Nott'm Forest, Southampton.

Won from behind: (2) Leicester (h), Coventry (h).
Lost from in front: (2) Watford (h), Nott'm Forest (h).

High spots: Winning the first five league games to top the league.
Six undefeated league games from 22 October, to stay 2nd.
Beating Bury 10-0 in the Milk Cup.

Low spots: Bad end to the season, failing to win any of the last six games.

Hammer of the Year Trevor Brooking.
Ever-presents: (2) Phil Parkes, Ray Stewart.
Hat-tricks: (2) David Swindlehurst (1), Tony Cottee (1).
Leading scorer: (19) Tony Cottee.

	Appearances						Goals			
	Lge	*Sub*	LC	*Sub*	FAC	*Sub*	**Lge**	LC	FAC	**Tot**
Allen, Paul	**19**		1		1	*2*				
Barnes, Bobby	**11**	*2*			3	*1*	**2**		1	**3**
Bonds, Billy	**27**		2			*1*				
Brooking, Trevor	**35**		5		3		**4**	3		**7**
Brush, Paul	**10**				4					
Cottee, Tony	**37**	*2*	4		4		**15**	4		**19**
Devonshire, Alan	**22**		4		1		**1**	2		**3**
Dickens, Alan	**7**	*3*		*1*	1					
Donald, Warren	**1**	*1*								
Goddard, Paul	**3**	*2*	1				**1**	1		**2**
Hilton, Paul	**7**	*1*					**2**			**2**
Lampard, Frank	**17**	*1*	3		3					
Martin, Alvin	**29**		5		1		**3**	1		**4**
Orr, Neil	**28**	*1*	2	*2*	4			1		**1**
Parkes, Phil	**42**		5		4					
Pike, Geoff	**27**	*1*	5		2		**2**	1		**3**
Stewart, Ray	**42**		5		4		**7**	1	1	**9**
Swindlehurst, Dave	**35**	*1*	5		4		**13**	1	1	**15**
Walford, Steve	**41**		5		4		**2**			**2**
Whitton, Steve	**22**		3		1		**5**			**5**
(own-goals)							**3**		1	**4**
20 players used	**462**	***15***	**55**	***3***	**44**	***4***	**60**	**15**	**4**	**79**

No	Date		Att	Pos	Pt	F-A	H-T	Scorers, Times, and Referees	1	2	3	4	5	6	7	8	9	10	11	12 sub used
1	H	IPSWICH			D	0-0	0-0		**McAlister**	Stewart	Walford	Allen	Martin	**Gale**	Whitton*	Cottee	Goddard	Dickens	Pike	Hilton
	25/8		19,032		1				*Cooper*	*Burley*	*McCall*	*Zondervan*	*Osman*	*Butcher*	*Putney*	*Brennan*	*D'Avray*	*Sunderland**	*Gates*	*O'Callaghan*
								Ref: H Taylor	A lacklustre opening to the new season. West Ham must do without the retired Brooking and the semi-retired Bonds, who declines to be named as substitute. So poorly do Lyall's youngsters – Alan Dickens, Tony Cottee, and Steve Whitton – play that all are dropped for the Anfield trip.											
2	A	LIVERPOOL			L	0-3	0-1		McAlister	Stewart	Walford	Allen	Martin	Gale	Barnes	Bonds	Goddard	Swindleh'rst*	Pike	Cottee
	27/8		*32,633*		1			*Walsh 1, Wark 75, 88*	*Grobbelaar*	*Neal*	*Kennedy*	*Lawrenson*	*Whelan*	*Hansen*	*Dalglish*	*Lee*	*Walsh*	*Wark*	*Molby*	
								Ref: G Tyson	Liverpool have won the European Cup for the fourth time, but Souness is gone and Rush injured. It takes his understudy, Paul Walsh, 14 seconds to put the skids under West Ham. Near the end Wark headed in Walsh's cross, then netted from 20 yards as defenders backed off.											
3	A	SOUTHAMPTON		12	W	3-2	2-0	Goddard 21, 44, Dickens 87	McAlister	Stewart	Walford	Allen	Martin	Gale	Barnes	Goddard*	Cottee	Dickens	Pike	Hilton
	1/9		*18,488*	*22*	4			*Armstrong 75, Jordan 88*	*Shilton*	*Mills*	*Golac**	*Williams*	*Agboola*	*Wright*	*Whitlock*	*Moran*	*Jordan*	*Armstrong*	*Wallace*	*Curtis*
								Ref: A Gunn	This was Paul Goddard's match. He had not scored in the league for almost a year and never in his career bagged two headers in one game. By the time a twisted ankle took him off he had done much to win the match. Barnes, Cottee and Goddard are the smallest attack in the league.											
4	H	COVENTRY		5	W	3-1	2-0	Stewart 24p, 65p, Cottee 32	McAlister	Stewart	Walford	Allen	Martin	Gale	Barnes*	**Campbell**	Cottee	Dickens	Pike	Bonds
	4/9		14,949	*10*	7			*Pearce 81*	*Ogrizovic*	*Stephens*	*Pearce*	*Jol*	*Kilcline*	*Peake*	*Bennett*	*Gynn*	*Latchford*	*Gibson*	*Platnauer*	
								Ref: A Robinson	A debut for former Portsmouth boss, Bobby Campbell's, son. West Ham's tiny strike force prove too nimble for plodding Coventry, for whom Hibbitt handled to concede the first penalty and Ogrizovic toppled Cottee for the second. This is Stuart Pearce's last season with Coventry.											
5	H	WATFORD		2	W	2-0	0-0	Sinnott 50 (og), Barnes 52	McAlister	Stewart	Walford	Allen	Martin	Gale	Barnes	Campbell*	Cottee	Dickens	Pike	Bonds
	8/9		20,377	*20*	10				*Sherwood*	*Bardsley*	*Sinnott*	*Terry*	*Jackett*	*Blissett*	*Callaghan*	*Johnston*	*Reilly**	*Barnes*	*Sterling*	*Porter*
								Ref: B Stevens	Seven former members of West Ham's youth team help take the team up to second, headed only by Arsenal. At 0-0 Stewart tripped Sterling, whose penalty was too close to McAlister. Paul Allen's low cross was turned into his own net by Sinnott, leaving boss Graham Taylor fuming.											
6	A	CHELSEA		6	L	0-3	0-1		McAlister	Stewart	Walford	Allen	Martin*	Gale	Barnes	Bonds	Cottee	Dickens	Pike	Goddard
	15/9		*32,411*	*12*	10			*Lee 14, Speedie 80, Nevin 84*	*Niedzwiecki*	*Lee*	*Rougvie*	*Pates*	*McLaughlin*	*Bumstead*	*Nevin*	*Spackman*	*Dixon*	*Speedie*	*Thomas*	
								Ref: T Spencer	Promoted Chelsea call upon 880 police to keep order. They make 100 arrests. Chelsea go 1-0 up from a penalty after McAlister felled Speedie. Lee's spot-kick was saved, but he volleyed in, only to have to retake it. Everything is repeated – side, save, volley – but this time it counted.											
7	H	NOTT'M FOREST		7	D	0-0	0-0		McAlister	Stewart	Walford	Allen	Bonds	Gale	Barnes	Goddard	Cottee	Dickens	Pike	
	22/9		17,434	*3*	11				*Sutton*	*Gunn*	*Swain*	*Fairclough*	*Smalley*	*Bowyer*	*Wigley*	*Metgod*	*Hodge*	*Davenport*	*Walsh*	
								Ref: J Martin	This draw knocks Forest off the top. In the first half West Ham did everything but score, stringing passes together with ease. The nearest they came was when Gale's header was pushed onto a post. After half-time Forest piled it on, and it was down to McAlister to keep the score blank.											
8	A	NEWCASTLE		8	D	1-1	0-1	Allen 55	McAlister	Stewart	Walford	Allen	Martin	Gale	Barnes	Goddard	Cottee	Bonds	Pike	
	29/9		*29,452*	*10*	12			*Beardsley 42*	*Carr*	*Brown*	*Saunders*	*Heard*	*Anderson*	*Roeder*	*McDonald*	*Wharton*	*Waddle*	*Beardsley*	*McCreery*	
								Ref: D Allison	Future England stars Chris Waddle and Peter Beardsley combine for the first goal, scored from outside the area. It was fitting that West Ham's equaliser was claimed by Paul Allen. He was the man of the match and netted his first goal for nearly two years with a blistering shot.											
9	H	LEICESTER		5	W	3-1	0-1	Stewart 68p, Bonds 75, Cottee 90	McAlister	Stewart	Walford	Allen	Martin	Gale	Barnes*	Goddard	Cottee	Bonds	Pike	Whitton
	6/10		15,306	*18*	15			*Lynex 28*	*Wallington*	*Ramsey*	*Smith R*	*MacDonald*	*Hazell*	*O'Neil*	*Lynex*	*Lineker*	*Smith A*	*Wilson*	*Peake**	*Bright*
								Ref: E Read	Lynex stuns Upton Park when capitalising on Tom McAlister's poor throw out. The Hammers rarely looked look like getting back into the game until Kevin MacDonald handled in the box. Billy Bonds' header, set up by Paul Goddard, was Bonzo's first league goal for 18 months.											
10	A	MANCHESTER U		8	L	1-5	0-2	Goddard 85 *[Moses 63, Hughes 76]*	McAlister	Stewart	Walford	Allen	Martin	Gale	Whitton	Goddard	Cottee	Bonds	Pike	
	13/10		***44,559***	*4*	15			*McQueen 26, Brazil 33, Strachan 50,*	*Bailey*	*Duxbury*	*Albiston*	*Moses*	*McQueen*	*Hogg*	*Robson*	*Strachan*	*Hughes*	*Brazil*	*Olsen*	
								Ref: T Holbrook	Ron Atkinson's United recover from a 0-3 defeat at Villa to give West Ham a thrashing. Olsen and Robson made the first goal for McQueen, playing his first game of the season. Alan Brazil's goal was a solo affair. Gale and Martin went AWOL when Strachan burst through for No 3.											

No	Date	Opponent	Pos	Res	F-A	H-T	Scorers, Times, Referees	1	2	3	4	5	6	7	8	9	10	11	12 sub used
11	A	STOKE	7	W	4-2	1-0	B'rry 34 (og), Cot' 56, G'ard 72, All'n 84	McAlister	Stewart	Walford	Allen	Martin	Gale	Whitton	Goddard	Cottee	Bonds	Pike*	Orr
	20/10	*9,945*	*22*	18			*Painter 80, Chamberlain 89*	*Fox*	*Bould*	*Hemming*	*Ebanks*	*Dyson*	*Berry*	*Painter*	*McIlroy**	*Heath*	*O'Callaghan*	*Chamberlain*	*Parkin*
							Ref: K Cooper	After the Old Trafford massacre, this is the perfect time to play dreadful Stoke. The score is deceptive, for former England winger Mark Chamberlain wasted two good chances at 0-0. George Berry headed an own-goal and Hemming nodded down to Cottee for Hammers' second.											
12	H	ARSENAL	5	W	3-1	2-1	Cottee 29, Goddard 36, Pike 49	McAlister	Stewart	Walford	Allen	Martin	Gale	Whitton	Goddard	Cottee	Bonds	Pike	
	27/10	**33,218**	*1*	21			*Allinson 44*	*Jennings*	*Anderson*	*Sansom*	*Talbot*	*O'Leary*	*Hill*	*Robson*	*Rix*	*Allinson*	*Davis*	*Nicholas*	
							Ref: A Seville	Greenwood returns to Upton Park to promote his autobiography. Bonds and Pike are the only players remaining from his time. Bonds set up the first two goals. Goddard's was the best. Arsenal had won their last five, and afterwards Don Howe locked his players in for a roasting.											
13	A	ASTON VILLA	5	D	0-0	0-0		McAlister	Stewart	Walford	Allen	Martin	Gale*	Whitton	Goddard	Cottee	Bonds	Pike	Orr
	3/11	*15,709*	*16*	22				*Day*	*Williams*	*Gibson*	*Evans*	*Ormsby*	*McMahon*	*Birch*	*Kerr*	*Withe*	*Cowans*	*Six*	
							Ref: T Jones	Both teams hit the wood. Villa in the first half, when Kerr's lob landed on top of the bar; West Ham after 87 minutes, when man-of-the-match Paul Allen rounded Mervyn Day but shot against the inside of a post. Pike blazed the rebound wide. An earlier shot had hit Ormsby in the face.											
14	H	EVERTON	6	L	0-1	0-0		McAlister	Stewart	Walford	Allen	Martin	Gale*	Whitton	Goddard	Cottee	Bonds	Pike	Dickens
	10/11	24,089	*1*	22			*Heath 78*	*Southall*	*Stevens*	*v d Hauwe*	*Ratcliffe*	*Mountfield*	*Reid*	*Steven*	*Heath*	*Sharp*	*Bracewell*	*Sheedy*	
							Ref: J Ashworth	Everton have surged up the table to the top. West Ham are headed in the opposite direction, largely because their strikers have lost their touch. Having received £1,000 from sponsors Canon for being top scorers in October, West Ham have netted just once in four games in November.											
15	H	SUNDERLAND	5	W	1-0	0-0	Cottee 52	McAlister	Stewart	Walford	Allen	Martin	Gale	Whitton	Goddard	Cottee	Bonds	Pike	
	17/11	15,204	*11*	25				*Turner*	*Venison*	*Pickering*	*Chisholm**	*Bennett*	*Elliott*	*Hodgson*	*Berry*	*West*	*Proctor*	*Walker*	*Gayle*
							Ref: D Letts	Having been booked just once in his career, Cottee gets another yellow card which might have been red after a contretemps with Shaun Elliott. The ref was lenient and Cottee stayed on to convert Whitlock's back-header. Dave Swindlehurst is fit again and challenging for Cottee's place.											
16	A	LUTON	5	D	2-2	1-1	Whitton 9, Martin 84	McAlister	Stewart	Walford*	Allen	Martin	Gale	Whitton	Goddard	Cottee	Bonds	Pike	Swindlehurst
	24/11	*10,789*	*21*	26			*Stein 36, Nwajiobi 48*	*Findlay*	*Breacker*	*Turner*	*North*	*Droy**	*Donaghy*	*Hill*	*Stein*	*Elliott*	*Bunn*	*Nwajiobi*	*Parker*
							Ref: K Barratt	David Pleat's Luton end a run of defeats and come within six minutes of a precious win. Whitton had opened the scoring from a free-kick but Luton took command when Walford's error let in Nigerian Nwajiobi. With Swindlehurst on for Walford, Martin headed the late equaliser.											
17	H	WEST BROM	8	L	0-2	0-0		McAlister	Stewart	Walford	Allen	Martin	Gale	Whitton	Goddard	Cottee	Bonds*	Pike	Swindlehurst
	1/12	15,572	*9*	26			*Hunt 49, Thompson 77*	*Godden*	*Nicholl*	*Statham*	*Hunt*	*Bennett*	*Robertson*	*Grealish*	*Thompson*	*Mackenzie*	*Cross D*	*Valentine*	
							Ref: L Burden	Bonds was on the touchline having his knee strapped – following a crushing tackle with Tony Grealish – when Hunt scored the first goal, and had been subbed by Swindlehurst when Thompson put WBA two up. In the first half both Stewart and Bonds had hit the Albion woodwork.											
18	A	NORWICH	12	L	0-1	0-1		McAlister	Stewart	Walford	Allen	Martin	Gale	Whitton	Goddard	Cottee	Dickens	Pike*	Hilton
	8/12	*13,908*	*11*	26			*Farrington 29*	*Woods*	*Haylock*	*Downs*	*Bruce*	*Mendham*	*Watson*	*Channon*	*Farrington*	*Goss*	*Hartford*	*Gordon*	
							Ref: D Hedges	West Ham are plunging down the table, and their passing game seems to have gone to pieces. Tony Cottee is initially at fault for Norwich's goal. His first touch lets him down, allowing 19-year-old Mark Farrington to pounce on the loose ball and score with a scorching cross-shot.											
19	H	SHEFFIELD WED	12	D	0-0	0-0		McAlister	Allen	Walford	Dickens	Martin	Gale	Whitton	Goddard	Swindlehurst	Cottee	Pike	
	15/12	14,896	*7*	27				*Hodge*	*Oliver*	*Shirtliff*	*Smith*	*Lyons*	*Worthington*	*Marwood*	*Blair*	*Varadi*	*Chapman*	*Shelton**	*Sterland*
							Ref: M James	Stewart's injury forces Paul Allen to play at right back. The Wednesday bench scream at their team to put him to the test, which he passes with flying colours. David Swindlehurst almost marked his first 90 minutes of the season with a late winner, but shot too close to Martin Hodge.											
20	H	SOUTHAMPTON	12	L	2-3	1-1	Cottee 6, 73	McAlister	Allen	Walford	Dickens*	Martin	Gale	Whitton	Goddard	Swindlehurst	Cottee	Pike	Orr
	22/12	14,221	*5*	27			*McAlister16(og), J'rdan 60, Wallace 71*	*Shilton*	*Mills*	*Dennis**	*Puckett*	*Whitlock*	*Wright*	*Holmes*	*Moran*	*Jordan*	*Armstrong*	*Wallace*	*Bond*
							Ref: I Borrett	England boss Bobby Robson runs his eye over Martin, comparing him with his main rival Mark Wright. Dickens manufactures a quick goal for Cottee, but Saints hit back thanks to a daft own-goal. Walford's back-pass is turned onto the post by McAlister, who fails to keep the ball out.											
21	A	TOTTENHAM	13	D	2-2	1-2	Cottee 43, Goddard 50	McAlister	Allen	Brush	Dickens	Martin	Gale	Orr	Hilton	Swind'hurst*	Cottee	Pike	Goddard
	26/12	*37,198*	*1*	28			*Mabbutt 17, Crooks 34*	*Clemence*	*Stevens*	*Hughton**	*Roberts*	*Miller*	*Perryman*	*Chiedozie*	*Falco*	*Galvin*	*Mabbutt*	*Crooks*	*Hazard*
							Ref: J Bray	Walford and Whitton have been dropped. Peter Shreeve's Spurs are the latest team to top the division, and are so impressed by Paul Allen's performance against them that they sign him in the summer. Galvin's corners brought both Spurs' goals. Paul Goddard's equaliser was special.											

No	Date		Att	Pos	Pt	F-A	H-T	Scorers, Times, and Referees	1	2	3	4	5	6	7	8	9	10	11	12 sub used
22	A	COVENTRY		12	W	2-1	0-0	Cottee 58, 87	McAlister	Allen	Brush	Dickens	Martin	Gale	Orr	Hilton*	Goddard	Cottee	Pike	Whitton
	29/12		*10,775*	*21*	31			*Stephens 62*	*Ogrizovic*	*Stephens*	*Pearce*	*Bowman*	*Kilcline*	*McGrath*	*Hibbitt*	*Gynn**	*Regis*	*Gibson*	*Barnes*	*Adams*
								Ref: N Ashley	Bobby Gould was sacked yesterday and Don Mackay takes temporary charge of the Sky Blues. Luck deserts them when Kilcline heads over an open goal and Pearce hits the bar. Stephens' effort, deflected by Orr, cancels out Cottee's first goal. But Goddard's dummy sets up his second.											
23	H	QP RANGERS		12	L	1-3	1-0	Brush 4	McAlister	**Potts**	Brush	Dickens	Martin	Gale*	Allen	Hilton	Goddard	Cottee	Orr	Whitton
	1/1		20,857	*14*	31			*Byrne 54, Bannister 71, Waddock 74*	*Hucker*	*James**	*Dawes*	*Waddock*	*Chivers*	*Fenwick*	*McDonald*	*Fillery*	*Bannister*	*Byrne*	*Gregory*	*Robinson*
								Ref: M Bodenham	Three players were stretchered off. First to go was QPR keeper Hucker, who collided with Dickens as Brush nodded in – his first West Ham goal. Gary Chivers took over until Hucker returned. Debut-boy Steve Potts headed off the line before QPR levelled from a quick free-kick.											
24	H	NEWCASTLE		13	D	1-1	1-0	Allen 16	McAlister	Stewart	Brush	Dickens	Martin	Walford	Allen	Barnes	Goddard	Cottee	Pike	
	2/2		17,723	*18*	32			*Waddle 64*	*Thomas*	*Brown*	*Wharton*	*Clarke*	*Roeder*	*Heard*	*McDonald*	*Megson*	*Waddle*	*Beardsley*	*McCreery*	
								Ref: J Ball	Time and again West Ham pumped up high balls to their midget strikers. John Lyall is being linked in the press with a job at managerless QPR, and he is conducting urgent negotiations with the West Ham board. Norwich manager Ken Brown is being tipped as Lyall's replacement.											
25	H	ASTON VILLA		15	L	1-2	0-0	Goddard 48	McAlister	Stewart	Brush	Walford	Martin	Dickens	Allen	Barnes*	Goddard	Cottee	Pike	Swindlehurst
	23/2		14,845	*10*	32			*Walford 59 (og), Ormsby 75*	*Spink*	*Williams*	*Dorigo*	*Evans*	*Ormsby*	*Gibson*	*Birch*	*Rideout*	*Withe*	*Cowans*	*Walters*	
								Ref: J Deakin	If only Geoff Pike's second-minute effort that hit the bar had gone in. Even when Goddard did score it was not enough to secure three points, because West Ham keep surrendering leads. Mark Walters pressured Steve Walford into an own-goal, and Ormsby's 40-yarder was deflected.											
26	A	ARSENAL		16	L	1-2	1-0	Cottee 28	McAlister	Stewart	Brush	Dickens	Martin	Walford	Allen	Orr	Goddard	Cottee	Pike	
	2/3		*25,818*	*6*	32			*Mariner 46, Robson 52*	*Lukic*	*Anderson*	*Sansom*	*Williams*	*O'Leary*	*Caton*	*Robson*	*Davis*	*Mariner*	*Woodcock*	*Nicholas*	
								Ref: K Baker	An 11.30 kick-off. Not a good game, but West Ham were superior except in front of goal. Cottee lobs in as Goddard and O'Leary miss a high ball. West Ham stood appealing for offside as Mariner equalised. Arsenal took the lead while Alvin Martin was being treated for a head injury.											
27	H	MANCHESTER U		13	D	2-2	1-1	Stewart 25p, Duxbury 51 (og)	McAlister	Stewart	Brush	Walford	Martin	Hilton	Allen	Orr	Goddard	Cottee	Dickens*	Swindlehurst
	15/3		16,674	*3*	33			*Stapleton 31, Robson 62*	*Bailey*	*Gidman*	*Albiston*	*Duxbury*	*McGrath*	*Hogg*	*Strachan*	*Whiteside**	*Hughes*	*Stapleton*	*Olsen*	*Robson*
								Ref: A Robinson / D Keen	Man U have just won in the FA Cup. TV cameras affect the gate, with Wogan on the other channel. Hogg's arm stops Allen's shot. Penalty, after consulting a linesman. Goddard's cross was turned in by Duxbury. Man U replied with two headers. Achilles problems affect the referee.											
28	A	LEICESTER		16	L	0-1	0-0		McAlister	Stewart	Brush	Walford	Martin	Gale	Allen	Orr	Goddard	Cottee	Dickens*	Swindlehurst
	23/3		*11,375*	*10*	33			*Lineker 83*	*Andrews*	*Feeley**	*Wilson*	*Smith R*	*Williams*	*O'Neil*	*Lynex*	*Lineker*	*Smith A*	*Ramsey*	*Banks*	*Bright*
								Ref: N Glover	Alan Devonshire has returned in the FA Cup, but flu denies him his first league game of the season. Alvin Martin is dispirited at being left out of Bobby Robson's England team to play the Republic of Ireland. Martin is caught out by Alan Smith's cross, which was turned in by Lineker.											
29	A	NOTT'M FOREST		16	W	2-1	1-0	Cottee 20, Goddard 75	McAlister	Stewart	Walford	Allen	Martin	Gale	Orr	Cottee	Goddard*	Pike	Barnes	Swindlehurst
	30/3		*13,560*	*7*	36			*Hodge 55*	*Segers*	*McInally*	*Swain*	*Fairclough*	*Hart**	*Bowyer*	*Wigley*	*Hodge*	*Riley*	*Davenport*	*Metgod*	*Campbell*
								Ref: G Tyson	When Tony Cottee slides in to convert Bobby Barnes' cross it brings West Ham's first goal at the City Ground since Geoff Hurst scored there back in 1969. Steve Wigley makes an equaliser for Steve Hodge, but Cottee's cross is turned in by Paul Goddard to secure a precious win.											
30	A	WATFORD		17	L	**0-5**	0-3	*[West 80]*	McAlister	Stewart	Orr	Walford	Martin	Gale	Allen	Barnes	Goddard	Cottee	Pike*	Swindlehurst
	2/4		*17,884*	*16*	36			*Taylor 3, Blissett 11, 16, Barnes 75,*	*Coton*	*Gibbs*	*Rostron*	*Taylor*	*Terry*	*McClelland*	*Callaghan*	*Blissett*	*West*	*Jackett*	*Barnes*	
								Ref: H King	Strangely, West Ham played well for an hour. But before and after they were ripped apart by Graham Taylor's fellow strugglers. Les Taylor's opener was mis-hit yet bobbled over McAlister's arms. John Barnes' gentle header was turned in by Luther Blissett for the second goal.											
31	H	TOTTENHAM		17	D	1-1	0-1	Dickens 84	McAlister	Stewart	Orr	Walford	Martin	Gale	Allen	Barnes*	Goddard	Cottee	Dickens	Swindlehurst
	6/4		24,435	*3*	37			*Ardiles 43*	*Clemence*	*Thomas*	*Bowen*	*Roberts*	*Miller*	*Perryman*	*Ardiles*	*Falco*	*Galvin**	*Hoddle*	*Crooks*	*Chiedozie*
								Ref: R Lewis	Home defeat by Everton has scuppered Spurs' championship hopes. Roberts' miscued pass falls perfectly for Ossie Ardiles to swivel and shoot past McAlister. West Ham's second-half enterprise was rewarded when Cottee robbed the injured Roberts, Orr crossed, and Dickens swept in.											

No	Ven / Date	Opponent	Att	Pos	Res / Pts	F-A	H-T	Scorers, Times, and Referees	1	2	3	4	5	6	7	8	9	10	11	12 sub used
32	A	QP RANGERS		17	L	2-4	1-1	Cottee 45, 84	McAlister*	Stewart	Orr	Walford	Martin	Gale	Allen	Swindlehurst	Goddard	Cottee	Dickens	Barnes
	8/4		*16,085*	*12*	37			*Byrne 1, Bann'ster 60, 65, F'nwick 69p*	*Hucker*	*Chivers*	*Dawes*	*Waddock*	*Wicks*	*Fenwick*	*McDonald*	*Fillery*	*Bannister*	*Byrne*	*Fereday**	*James*
								Ref: R Milford	The morning kick-off does not suit West Ham, who are behind in 38 seconds. Though Cottee turns in Walford's cross to equalise, Bannister finds space to beat the injured McAlister. Stewart takes his jersey but gives the ball to Bannister. Swindlehurst fouls McDonald for the penalty.											
33	H	CHELSEA		17	D	1-1	1-1	Cottee 23	Parkes	Stewart	Brush	Walford	Orr	Gale	Allen	Swindlehurst	Goddard	Cottee	Dickens	
	13/4		19,003	*9*	38			*Speedie 17*	*Francis*	*Jones J*	*Dublin*	*Pates*	*McLaughlin*	*Bumstead*	*Nevin*	*Spackman*	*Dixon*	*Speedie*	*Jasper*	
								Ref: N Midgley	Phil Parkes takes over from the injured McAlister. Bobby Robson watches Alvin Martin and Paul Allen. Cottee pierces the wall from a short free-kick to equalise, but the outcome hinges on Dickens' fine second-half 'goal', which was disallowed because Goddard had strayed offside.											
34	A	SUNDERLAND		17	W	1-0	1-0	Goddard 15	Parkes	Stewart	Brush	Orr	Martin	Gale	Allen	Swindlehurst	Goddard	Cottee	Dickens	
	20/4		*15,622*	*19*	41				*Turner*	*Venison*	*Pickering*	*Bennett*	*Chisholm*	*Agboola**	*Lemon*	*Wallace*	*Cummins*	*Berry*	*Walker*	*Hodgson*
								Ref: I Hendrick	A six-pointer. 'If West Ham were barely competent, Sunderland could only be described as abysmal,' said *The Times*. 'A bad match and a bad result,' lamented Sunderland boss Len Ashurst. Goddard's goal, converted at the second attempt, lifts West Ham above their relegation rivals.											
35	H	LUTON		17	D	0-0	0-0		Parkes	Stewart	Brush	Orr	Martin	Gale	Allen	Swind'hurst*	Goddard	Cottee	Dickens	Bonds
	27/4		17,303	*18*	42				*Sealey*	*Breacker*	*Thomas*	*Nicholas*	*Foster*	*Donaghy*	*Hill*	*Stein*	*Bunn**	*Nwajiobi*	*Preece*	*Parker*
								Ref: A Gunn	'A point is a point,' muses Luton's David Pleat afterwards. Though as West Ham have not won at home since November he might have felt more frustrated. Both sides marked two forwards with four defenders, stifling the life out of the game. But Les Sealey made several fine saves.											
36	A	WEST BROM		19	L	1-5	0-1	Stewart 54p *[Cross N 80]*	Parkes	Stewart	Brush	Bonds	Martin	Gale	Allen	Whitton	Goddard	Cottee	Dickens	
	4/5		***8,878***	*11*	42			*Hunt 24, Mack'nzie 56,58, Grealish 60,*	*Godden*	*Nicholl*	*Cowdrill*	*Hunt*	*Bennett*	*Robertson*	*Owen**	*Thompson*	*Mackenzie*	*Cross N*	*Valentine*	*Grealish*
								Ref: L Dilkes	Johnny Giles' Albion had been fifth at Christmas but have since collapsed. They had lost five of their last seven games, but find West Ham at their most charitable. Strange to say, when Ray Stewart levelled from the spot West Ham looked good for a point. Then the floodgates opened.											
37	H	NORWICH		19	W	1-0	0-0	Barnes 86	Parkes	Stewart	Brush	Orr	Martin	Gale	Allen	Bonds	Cottee	Goddard	Dickens*	Barnes
	6/5		16,233	*18*	45				*Woods*	*Haylock*	*Van Wyk*	*Bruce*	*Rosario*	*Watson*	*Spearing !*	*Channon**	*Deehan*	*Hartford*	*Donowa*	*Downs*
								Ref: L Shapter	Bobby Barnes, on for the injured Dickens, hooks a late goal that sees Alvin Martin sink to his knees with relief. But Barnes then fells Dave Watson in the box. Barnes admits it is a penalty but the ref says no. Spearing is sent off for dissent. The dropped point sends Norwich down.											
38	A	EVERTON		19	L	0-3	0-2		Parkes	Stewart	Brush	Orr	Martin	Gale	Allen	Bonds	Goddard	Cottee	Barnes	
	8/5		*32,657*	*1*	45			*Gray 11, Mountfield 42, 77*	*Southall*	*Stevens*	*v d Hauwe*	*Atkins*	*Mountfield*	*Reid*	*Steven*	*Sharp*	*Gray**	*Bracewell*	*Sheedy*	*Richardson*
								Ref: A Saunders	Everton are presented with the Canon championship trophy before kick-off. They extend their unbeaten run to 28 games against dismal West Ham, who get the Lyall riot act at the final whistle. Once Andy Gray had headed in Trevor Steven's corner, West Ham offered little resistance.											
39	A	SHEFFIELD WED		19	L	1-2	0-2	Cottee 77	Parkes	Stewart	Brush	Orr	Martin	Gale	Walford*	Bonds	Goddard	Cottee	Barnes	Whitton
	11/5		*24,314*	*8*	45			*Chapman 5, 32*	*Hodge*	*Sterland*	*Worthington*	*Smith*	*Lyons*	*Madden*	*Marwood*	*Blair*	*Varadi*	*Chapman*	*Shelton*	
								Ref: K Walmsley	This is the day of the Bradford City blaze that killed 56. Lyall sets out a defensive formation with Gale in midfield, but West Ham are so weak in the air that Chapman helps himself to two goals, the first from Blair's corner. Stewart had a penalty saved when Hodge floored Goddard.											
40	H	STOKE		17	W	**5-1**	3-0	Bonds 14, 89, Pike 32, Stewart 36p,	Parkes	Stewart	Brush	Gale	Martin	Pike	Orr*	Bonds	Barnes	Cottee	Goddard	Hilton
	14/5		**13,362**	*22*	48			*Painter 60p* [Hilton 90]	*Fox*	*Bould*	*Saunders*	*Dodd*	*Dyson*	*Maskrey*	*Painter*	*McIlroy*	*Hemming*	*Williams**	*Heath*	*Callaghan*
								Ref: J Martin	Awful conditions in which to face an awful team. Bonds scored two and won a penalty when fouled by Dyson. Stewart missed with his first kick but Saunders had encroached and the ref ordered a retake. When Brush fouled Saunders it brought Stoke's sixth away goal of the season.											
41	A	IPSWICH		16	W	1-0	1-0	Cottee 11	Parkes	Stewart	Brush	Walford	Martin	Hilton	Barnes	Bonds	Goddard	Cottee	Pike	
	17/5		*19,326*	*17*	51				*Cooper*	*Burley*	*Yallop*	*Zondervan*	*Osman*	*Steggles**	*Putney*	*Brennan*	*Dozzell*	*Wilson*	*Gates*	*Parkin*
								Ref: V Callow	West Ham looked safe beforehand, but Coventry will win their last three to survive yet again. Had West Ham lost at Portman Road they would have been relegated, but they win with something to spare against an injury-ravaged side. Paul Allen confirms he is leaving the Hammers.											
42	H	LIVERPOOL		16	L	0-3	0-2		Parkes	Stewart	Brush	**McPherson**	Martin	Lampard*	Barnes	**Parris**	Goddard	Walford	Pike	Gale
	20/5		22,408	*2*	51			*Walsh 27, 36, Beglin 56*	*Grobbelaar*	*Neal*	*Beglin*	*Molby**	*Nicol*	*Hansen*	*Dalglish*	*Whelan*	*Rush*	*Walsh*	*Wark*	*Lee*
		Home	Away					Ref: D Axcell	An early clash of heads between Molby and Hansen sees Molby led off with a broken nose and two missing teeth. When Walsh departed after 64 minutes Liverpool played on with 10 men, but still looked streets ahead of the Hammers. Lyall gave debuts to McPherson and Parris.											
Average		18,435	21,158																	

Milk Cup					F-A	H-T	Scorers, Times, and Referees	1	2	3	4	5	6	7	8	9	10	11	12 sub used
2:1	A	BRISTOL CITY	7	D	2-2	2-2	Cottee 28, Walford 37	McAlister	Stewart	Walford	Allen	Martin	Gale	Bonds	Goddard	Cottee	Dickens	Pike	
25/9		*15,894*	*3:7*				*Morgan 20, Walsh 33*	*Shaw*	*Stevens*	*Newman*	*P-Masters*	*Halliday*	*Walsh*	*Hirst*	*Crawford*	*Pritchard*	*Morgan*	*Riley*	
							Ref: V Callow	City led twice, first when Morgan broke clear to run on to Pritchard's overhead kick. Second when Walsh squeezed his shot underneath Tom McAlister's body. West Ham replied through Tony Cottee's right-foot volley and Steve Walford's 25-yarder from Paul Goddard's pass.											
2:2	H	BRISTOL CITY	5	W	6-1	1-1	Cottee 24, 70, Goddard 48, 57,	McAlister	Stewart	Walford	Allen	Martin	Gale	Whitton	Goddard	Cottee	Bonds*	Pike	Barnes
9/10		11,376	*3:9*				*Walsh 33p* [Whitton 67, Walford 79]	*Shaw*	*Stevens*	*Newman*	*Curle*	*Phil-Masters*	*Riley*	*Pritchard*	*Ritchie**	*Morgan*	*Walsh*	*Crawford*	*Smith*
							Ref: K Baker (Hammers win 8-3 on aggregate)	City boss Terry Cooper threatened to play himself, but does not. His players hold their own until half-time. They trailed to Cottee's hooked volley which went in off the bar, but levelled from the spot when Stewart fisted Walsh's header over the bar. Today Stewart would be sent off.											
3	A	MANCHESTER C	5	D	0-0	0-0		McAlister	Stewart	Walford	Allen	Martin	Gale	Whitton*	Barnes	Cottee	Bonds	Pike	Orr
31/10		*20,510*	*2:9*					*Williams*	*May*	*Power*	*Reid*	*McCarthy*	*Phillips*	*Smith**	*Baker*	*Cunningham*	*Wilson*	*Kinsey*	*Beckford*
							Ref: D Hutchinson	The critical moment came in the third minute, when Tom McAlister crashed into Baker without conceding a penalty-kick. McAlister enjoyed his let-off, knowing that fit-again Phil Parkes wants his place back, and defying Billy McNeill's City to the end. Goddard had a stomach virus.											
3R	H	MANCHESTER C	5	L	1-2	0-1	Whitton 65	McAlister	Stewart	Walford	Allen	Martin	Orr *	Whitton	Goddard	Cottee	Bonds	Pike	Dickens
6/11		17,461	*2:10*				*Cunningham 26, Kinsey 66*	*Williams*	*May*	*Power*	*Reid*	*McCarthy*	*Phillips*	*Smith*	*McNab*	*Cunningham*	*Wilson*	*Kinsey*	
							Ref: T Bune	Billy McNeill declared this to be his team's best performance since he arrived. West Ham were beaten fair and square. Whitton's 25-yarder was one of only a few efforts to trouble Alex Williams, but it was followed within seconds by Kinsey scoring off a post from Power's corner.											

FA Cup					F-A	H-T	Scorers, Times, and Referees	1	2	3	4	5	6	7	8	9	10	11	12 sub used
3	H	PORT VALE	12	W	4-1	2-0	Dickens 31, Goddard 33, 51, 80	McAlister	Allen	Brush	Dickens	Martin	Walford	Orr	Barnes	Goddard	Cottee	Pike	
5/1		11,452	*4:15*				*Griffiths 76*	*Siddall*	*Webb*	*Bromage*	*Hunter*	*Sproson*	*Cegielski*	*Williams*	*Earle*	*Brown*	*O'Keefe*	*Griffiths P*	
							Ref: E Read	Vale boss John Rudge misses the game with flu. Paul Goddard had never previously scored in the FA Cup for QPR or West Ham, now he gets three on a treacherously icy pitch. He secured his hat-trick when Cegielski was caught dithering four minutes after Vale had come back to 3-1.											
4	H	NORWICH	13	W	2-1	0-1	Pike 60, Stewart 61p	McAlister	Stewart	Brush	Dickens	Martin	Walford	Allen	Barnes	Goddard	Cottee	Pike	
4/2		20,098	*10*				*Donowa 27*	*Woods*	*Haylock*	*Van Wyk*	*Bruce*	*Mendham*	*Watson*	*Spearing*	*Channon*	*Deehan*	*Downs*	*Corrigan*	
							Ref: R Milford	Seven home-grown Hammers carry the team into Round 5. A fast and furious match was watched by Dave Bassett, whose Wimbledon await the winners. Two goals in a minute had the crowd roaring. The penalty was controversial and was given for Van Wyk's foul on Paul Allen.											
5	A	WIMBLEDON	16	D	1-1	0-0	Cottee 72	McAlister	Stewart	Brush	Walford	Martin	Devonshire	Allen	Orr	Goddard	Cottee	Pike	
4/3		*13,500*	*2:13*				*Evans 82*	*Beasant*	*Gage*	*Winterburn*	*Galliers*	*Morris*	*Smith*	*Evans*	*Fishenden*	*Cork*	*Sanchez*	*Hodges**	*Downes*
							Ref: K Hackett	Division 2 Dons maintain their record of scoring in every home match this season when Stewart Evans heads in a long-range cross. Cottee had earlier got in the way of Stewart's shot and scored himself. Alan Devonshire returns at last, distinguished as the hairiest player on the pitch.											
5R	H	WIMBLEDON	16	W	5-1	2-1	Cottee 5, 42, 85, Dickens 56, Allen 80	McAlister	Stewart	Brush	Hilton	Martin	Devonshire	Allen	Orr	Goddard*	Cottee	Dickens	Swindlehurst
6/3		20,258	*2:13*				*Fishenden 18*	*Beasant*	*Gage*	*Winterburn*	*Galliers*	*Morris*	*Smith*	*Evans*	*Fishenden*	*Cork*	*Sanchez*	*Downes**	*Martin*
							Ref: R Lewis	Devonshire's first home game for 14 months was marked by a dreadful back-pass to Paul Fishenden. With his hair in his eyes it was a wonder Devonshire could see at all. The win could have been even more emphatic. Goddard wasted three good second-half chances and failed to score.											
QF	A	MANCHESTER U	16	L	2-4	1-2	Hogg 29 (og), Allen 85	McAlister	Stewart	Brush	Walford	Martin	Dickens	Allen	Orr	Goddard	Cottee	Pike*	Hilton
9/3		*46,769*	*3*				*Hughes 20, Whiteside 38, 75, 88p*	*Bailey*	*Gidman*	*Albiston*	*Duxbury*	*McGrath*	*Hogg*	*Strachan*	*Whiteside*	*Hughes*	*Stapleton*	*Olsen*	
							Ref: T Mills	A flu epidemic delayed Lyall's selection and almost caused a postponement. Hughes controlled, turned, and scored in one movement. West Ham's equaliser flew in off Hogg's shin but was the least they deserved. Norman Whiteside's first ever hat-trick included his first ever penalty.											

		Home					Away					
	P	W	D	L	F	A	W	D	L	F	A	Pts
1 Everton	42	16	3	2	58	17	12	3	6	30	26	90
2 Liverpool	42	12	4	5	36	19	10	7	4	32	16	77
3 Tottenham	42	11	3	7	46	31	12	5	4	32	20	77
4 Manchester U	42	13	6	2	47	13	9	4	8	30	34	76
5 Southampton	42	13	4	4	29	18	6	7	8	27	29	68
6 Chelsea	42	13	3	5	38	20	5	9	7	25	28	66
7 Arsenal	42	14	5	2	37	14	5	4	12	24	35	66
8 Sheffield Wed	42	12	7	2	39	21	5	7	9	19	24	65
9 Nott'm Forest	42	13	4	4	35	18	6	3	12	21	30	64
10 Aston Villa	42	10	7	4	34	20	5	4	12	26	40	56
11 Watford	42	10	5	6	48	30	4	8	9	33	41	55
12 West Brom	42	11	4	6	36	23	5	3	13	22	39	55
13 Luton	42	12	5	4	40	22	3	4	14	17	39	54
14 Newcastle	42	11	4	6	33	26	2	9	10	22	44	52
15 Leicester	42	10	4	7	39	25	5	2	14	26	48	51
16 WEST HAM	42	7	8	6	27	23	6	4	11	24	45	51
17 Ipswich	42	8	7	6	27	20	5	4	12	19	37	50
18 Coventry	42	11	3	7	29	22	4	2	15	18	42	50
19 QP Rangers	42	11	6	4	41	30	2	5	14	12	42	50
20 Norwich	42	9	6	6	28	24	4	4	13	18	40	49
21 Sunderland	42	7	6	8	20	26	3	4	14	20	36	40
22 Stoke	42	3	3	15	18	41	0	5	16	6	50	17
	924	237	107	118	785	503	118	107	237	503	785	1279

Odds & ends

Double wins: (3) Coventry, Stoke, Sunderland.
Double losses: (4) Liverpool, Everton, WBA, QPR.

Won from behind: (2) Leicester (h), Norwich FAC (h).
Lost from in front: (4) Southampton (h), QPR (h), Villa (h), Arsenal (a).

High spots: Three consecutive league wins in September.

Low spots: Just one league win in 13 games from 24 November.
Losing all four league matches to the two Liverpool clubs.
Being knocked out of both cups by the two Manchester clubs.

Hammer of the Year: Paul Allen.
Ever-presents: (0).
Hat-tricks: (2) Paul Goddard (1), Tony Cottee (1).
Leading scorer: (24) Tony Cottee.

	Appearances						Goals			
	Lge	*Sub*	LC	*Sub*	FAC	*Sub*	Lge	LC	FAC	Tot
Allen, Paul	**38**		4		5		**3**		2	**5**
Barnes, Bobby	**18**	*2*	1	*1*	2		**2**			**2**
Bonds, Billy	**19**	*3*	4				**3**			**3**
Brush, Paul	**18**				5		**1**			**1**
Campbell, Greg	**2**									
Cottee, Tony	**40**	*1*	4		5		**17**	3	4	**24**
Dickens, Alan	**24**	*1*	1	*1*	4		**2**		2	**4**
Devonshire, Alan					2					
Gale, Tony	**36**	*1*	3		1					
Goddard, Paul	**38**	*2*	3		5		**9**	2	3	**14**
Hilton, Paul	**5**	*4*			1	*1*	**1**			**1**
Lampard, Frank	**1**									
McAlister, Tom	**32**		4		5					
McPherson, Keith	**1**									
Martin, Alvin	**40**		4		5		**1**			**1**
Orr, Neil	**17**	*3*	1	*1*	4					
Parkes, Phil	**10**									
Parris, George	**1**									
Pike, Geoff	**30**		4		4		**2**		1	**3**
Potts, Steve	**1**									
Stewart, Ray	**37**		4		4		**6**		1	**7**
Swindlehurst, Dave	**8**	*8*				*1*				
Walford, Steve	**33**		4		3			2		**2**
Whitton, Steve	**13**	*4*	3				**1**	2		**3**
(own-goals)							**3**		1	**4**
24 players used	**462**	***29***	**44**	***3***	**55**	***2***	**51**	**9**	**14**	**74**

No	Date		Att	Pos	Pt	F-A	H-T	Scorers, Times, and Referees	1	2	3	4	5	6	7	8	9	10	11	12 sub used
1	A	BIRMINGHAM			L	0-1	0-0		Parkes	Stewart	Walford	Gale	Martin	Devonshire	**Ward**	**McAvennie**	Goddard*	Cottee	Orr	Dickens
	17/8		*11,164*		0			*Hopkins 65*	*Seaman*	*Ranson*	*Roberts*	*Wright*	*Armstrong**	*Daly*	*Bremner*	*Clarke*	*Jones*	*Geddis*	*Hopkins*	*Kuhl*
								Ref: N Glover	After Heysel and Bradford City English football is in the dock. St Andrews also witnessed awful violence on the last day of last season. Today there is nothing to note, on or off the pitch. A Test Match is going on at Edgbaston. Hopkins scores from 20 yards in this morning kick-off.											
2	H	QP RANGERS			W	3-1	2-0	McAvennie 10, 66, Dickens 24	Parkes	Stewart	Walford	Gale	Martin	Devonshire	Ward	McAvennie	Dickens	Cottee	Orr	
	20/8		15,530		3			*Byrne 54*	*Hucker*	*Chivers*	*Dawes*	*Waddock*	*McDonald*	*Fenwick*	*Byrne*	*Robinson**	*Bannister*	*Fereday*	*Gregory*	*James*
								Ref: M James	Frank McAvennie, a £340,000 buy from St Mirren, scores twice on his home debut, turning in Cottee's low cross to round off the scoring. To many the transfer fee is too high. Dickens' stooping header had made it 2-0 before Bannister crossed to the far post for Byrne to pull one back.											
3	H	LUTON		14	L	0-1	0-0		Parkes	Stewart	Walford	Gale	Martin	Devonshire	Ward	McAvennie	Dickens	Cottee*	Orr	Campbell
	24/8		14,104	*7*	3			*Harford 48p*	*Dibble*	*Johnson*	*Thomas*	*Nicholas*	*Elliott*	*Donaghy*	*Parker*	*Stein B*	*Harford*	*Nwajiobi*	*Preece*	
								Ref: T Holbrook	Having reached the FA Cup semi-finals last season, David Pleat's Luton are on the up. Ray Stewart tripped Stein for the all-important penalty, after which shots went flying in from all angles. Welsh keeper Andy Dibble made a string of fine saves as West Ham sought to equalise.											
4	A	MANCHESTER U		17	L	0-2	0-0		Parkes	Stewart	Walford	Gale	Martin	Devonshire	Ward	McAvennie	Dickens	Cottee*	Orr	Campbell
	26/8		***50,773***	*1*	3			*Hughes 55, Strachan 75*	*Bailey*	*Duxbury*	*Albiston*	*Whiteside*	*McGrath*	*Hogg*	*Robson*	*Strachan*	*Hughes*	*Stapleton*	*Olsen*	
								Ref: R Bridges	West Ham strung 10 defenders outside their box to frustrate Man U. Gordon Strachan was determined to impress watching Scotland boss, Jock Stein, and his flicked pass to Hughes opened the scoring. Gale's woeful back-pass was responsible for No 2, when Strachan rounded Parkes.											
5	H	LIVERPOOL		17	D	2-2	1-0	McAvennie 21, 71	Parkes	Stewart	Walford	Gale	Martin	Devonshire	Ward	McAvennie	Dickens	Cottee	Orr	
	31/8		19,762	*8*	4			*Johnston 52, Whelan 83*	*Grobbelaar*	*Neal*	*Kennedy*	*Lawrenson*	*Whelan*	*Hansen*	*Johnston*	*Nicol*	*Rush*	*Molby*	*Lee*	
								Ref: B Hill	The TV cameras in evidence were not for a domestic audience but to beam this vibrant match to 35 countries around the world. Frank McAvennie nipped in front of Grobbelaar for both Hammers goals. Both Liverpool equalisers were headers following intricate build-ups.											
6	A	SOUTHAMPTON		17	D	1-1	0-0	McAvennie 81	Parkes	Stewart	Walford	Gale	Martin	Devonshire	Ward	McAvennie	Dickens	Campbell*	Orr	Cottee
	3/9		*14,477*	*19*	5			*Curtis 52*	*Shilton*	*Golac*	*Dennis*	*Case*	*Wright*	*Bond*	*Townsend*	*Curtis*	*Jordan**	*Armstrong*	*Wallace*	*Lawrence*
								Ref: J Deakin	Saints, under new boss Chris Nicholl, are still seeking their first win. They are fortunate when Wallace's shot deflects off a defender to play Curtis onside. Ward's shot from outside the box was helped past Shilton by McAvennie, who had earlier been denied by the England keeper.											
7	A	SHEFFIELD WED		17	D	2-2	1-1	McAvennie 9, Cottee 88	Parkes	Stewart	Walford	Gale	Martin	Parris	Ward	McAvennie*	Dickens	Cottee	Orr	Barnes
	7/9		*19,287*	*3*	6			*Chapman 18, Thompson 58*	*Hodge*	*Morris*	*Worthington*	*Smith*	*Lyons*	*Madden*	*Marwood*	*Thompson**	*Chapman*	*Jonsson*	*Shelton*	*Stainrod*
								Ref: N Midgley	In midweek the Owls lost their first match of the season, 1-5 at home to Everton. McAvennie had to hobble off with knee trouble, leaving Tony Cottee on his own. Cottee had been rested against Southampton, feeling jaded, now he scores his first goal of the season to rescue a point.											
8	H	LEICESTER		13	W	3-0	1-0	McAvennie 31, D'shire 46, Cottee 70	Parkes	Stewart	Walford	Gale	Martin	Devonshire	Ward	McAvennie	Dickens	Cottee	Orr	
	14/9		**12,125**	*21*	9				*Andrews*	*Williams*	*Smith R*	*Ramsey**	*Osman*	*O'Neill*	*Kelly*	*Bright*	*Smith A*	*Mauchlen*	*Banks*	*Jones*
								Ref: I Borrett	A terribly small crowd is attributed to the critical state of English football. Man-of-the-match Devonshire passed a late fitness test on a bruised shin. McAvennie is now Division 1's leading scorer, having netted all but four of West Ham's goals. Yet he arrived with a dubious reputation.											
9	A	MANCHESTER C		13	D	2-2	2-1	Cottee 7, McCarthy 41 (og)	Parkes	Stewart	Walford	Gale	Martin	Devonshire	Ward	McAvennie	Dickens	Cottee	Orr	
	21/9		*22,001*	*16*	10			*Lillis 10, Melrose 49*	*Nixon*	*May*	*Wilson*	*Clements*	*McCarthy*	*Phillips*	*Lillis*	*Power*	*Melrose*	*McIlroy*	*Simpson*	
								Ref: M Robinson	Billy McNeill's City have lost their last three and failed to score. A mistake by Tony Gale, caught dwelling on the ball, presented a quick equaliser to David Lillis. West Ham twice fail to protect a lead, though afterwards McNeill rails against his own team's defensive lapses.											
10	H	NOTT'M FOREST		13	W	4-2	3-0	Cottee 6, McAv'nie 12, 20, Dickens 59	Parkes	Stewart	Walford	Gale	Martin	Devonshire	Ward	McAvennie	Dickens	Cottee	Orr	
	28/9		14,540	*16*	13			*Metgod 61, Clough 70*	*Segers**	*Walker*	*Pearce*	*Butterworth*	*Metgod*	*Bowyer*	*Mills*	*Campbell*	*Clough*	*Davenport*	*Webb*	*Walsh*
								Ref: D Axcell	Forest have a ready-made excuse for going 0-4 down. Keeper Segers was hurt colliding with Dickens during West Ham's first goal and hashed a clearance that led to the second. He was replaced in goal by Neil Webb. Johnny Metgod was behind Forest's stirring second-half fight-back.											

11	A	NEWCASTLE		11	W	2-1	2-0	McAvennie 12, Cottee 25	Parkes	Stewart	Walford	Gale	Martin	Devonshire	Ward	McAvennie	Dickens	Cottee	Orr	
		5/10	*26,709*	*7*	16			*Reilly 84*	*Thomas*	*Haddock*	*Anderson*	*Davies*	*Clarke*	*Roeder*	*McDonald*	*McCreery*	*Reilly*	*Beardsley*	*Stewart*	
								Ref: D Scott	For the first time since 1968-69, when Martin Peters achieved it, a West Ham player reaches double figures in goals by the end of September. McAvennie's early strike, laid on by Mark Ward, gives him that distinction. Newcastle's first home defeat is largely due to Alvin Martin.											
12	H	ARSENAL		11	D	0-0	0-0		Parkes	Stewart	Walford	Gale	Martin	Devonshire	Ward	McAvennie	Dickens*	Cottee	Orr	Parris
		12/10	24,057	*4*	17				*Lukic*	*Anderson*	*Sansom*	*Davis*	*O'Leary**	*Caton*	*Whyte*	*Allinson*	*Nicholas*	*Woodcock*	*Rix*	*Rocastle*
								Ref: A Robinson	Attention focuses on two Scots, Arsenal's Charlie Nicholas, who has been left out of Jock Stein's plans, and McAvennie, who is anxious to take his place. Nicholas even looks on the way out of Don Howe's Arsenal, whereas the wholehearted McAvennie was denied by John Lukic.											
13	H	ASTON VILLA		7	W	4-1	2-1	McAvennie 23, 79, Cottee 34, 57	Parkes	Stewart	Walford	Gale	Martin	Devonshire	Ward	McAvennie	Parris	Cottee	Orr	
		19/10	15,034	*16*	20			*Stainrod 6*	*Spink*	*Williams**	*Dorigo*	*Evans*	*Ormsby*	*Walker*	*Birch*	*Stainrod*	*Gray*	*Hodge*	*Walters*	*Bradley*
								Ref: M Bodenham	Under the gaze of England boss Bobby Robson, Alvin Martin wages a stirring battle against Andy Gray. Pick of the goals were Cottee's 25-yard dipper to make it 3-1 and McAvennie's chip over Spink to conclude the scoring. Nine players were booked, six from naughty Villa.											
14	A	IPSWICH		7	W	1-0	1-0	Cottee 26	Parkes	Parris	Walford	Gale	Martin	Devonshire*	Ward	McAvennie	Dickens	Cottee	Orr	Potts
		26/10	*16,849*	*21*	23				*Cooper*	*Yallop*	*McCall*	*Zondervan*	*Cranson*	*Atkins*	*Gleghorn**	*Brennan*	*Wilson*	*Cole*	*Dozzell*	*D'Avray*
								Ref: M Scott	Woeful Ipswich have now managed just eight points and seven goals from 14 league games. Tony Cottee's poached effort was his 10th of the season, but afterwards Ipswich rallied strongly. Unfortunately for them, they have no eye for goal and no cutting edge. Ipswich will go down.											
15	H	EVERTON		6	W	2-1	0-0	McAvennie 74, 81	Parkes	Stewart	Walford*	Gale	Martin	Devonshire	Ward	McAvennie	Dickens	Cottee	Orr	Parris
		2/11	23,844	*7*	26			*Steven 60*	*Southall*	*Stevens*	*Harper*	*Ratcliffe*	*v d Hauwe*	*Heath*	*Steven*	*Lineker*	*Sharp*	*Bracewell*	*Sheedy*	
								Ref: A Seville	McAvennie is the talk of English football, yet he managed just 18 goals last season for St Mirren. After Steven turned in Lineker's low cross McAvennie showed why he is so regarded. He takes Parris's pass and feints Southall, then takes Cottee's cross on his chest to win the game.											
16	A	OXFORD		5	W	2-1	1-1	Cottee 38, Ward 68	Parkes	Stewart	Walford	Gale	Martin	Devonshire	Ward	McAvennie	Dickens	Cottee	Orr	
		9/11	*13,140*	*18*	29			*Aldridge 21*	*Hardwick*	*Langan*	*Slatter*	*Trewick*	*Briggs*	*Shotton*	*Houghton*	*Aldridge*	*Charles*	*Hebberd*	*R-Brown**	*Brock*
								Ref: J Ball	The headline is McAvennie did 'not' score. Oxford boss Maurice Evans tried to sign him when managing Reading. But this is Mark Ward's match. His 40-yard pass enabled Tony Cottee to cancel out John Aldridge's opener. Ward's 35-yard free-kick was his first Division 1 goal.											
17	H	WATFORD		4	W	2-1	1-0	McAvennie 27, Ward 56	Parkes	Stewart	Walford	Gale	Martin	Devonshire	Ward	McAvennie	Dickens	Cottee	Orr	
		16/11	21,490	*12*	32			*Sterling 66*	*Coton*	*Bardsley*	*Rostron*	*Talbot*	*Terry*	*Sinnott*	*Sterling*	*Allen*	*Barnes*	*Jackett*	*Porter**	*Smillie*
								Ref: H Taylor	McAvennie beats three defenders to reach Neil Orr's cross. Coton then allows Ward's free-kick to trickle through his hands and legs. At this point John Barnes took over, directing Watford's fight-back. Sterling's deflected goal was all they managed. Parkes saved well from Barnes.											
18	A	COVENTRY		4	W	1-0	0-0	McAvennie 55	Parkes	Stewart	Walford	Gale	Martin	Devonshire	Ward	McAvennie	Dickens	Cottee	Orr	
		23/11	***11,042***	*15*	35				*Ogrizovic*	*Borrows*	*Downs*	*Bowman*	*Rodger*	*Peake*	*Adams*	*McGrath*	*Evans**	*Gibson*	*Bennett*	*Turner*
								Ref: J Worrall	Frank McAvennie has made his Scottish debut, scoring in the World Cup-tie with Australia. His goal against Coventry was simplicity, when Dickens' low cross looped up off a defender. Thereafter West Ham had to defend stoutly. Neil Orr had one of his best games for West Ham.											
19	H	WEST BROM		3	W	4-0	2-0	Cottee 12, Parris 31, D'shire 47, Orr 66	Parkes	Stewart	Walford	Gale	Martin	Devonshire	Ward	Parris	Dickens	Cottee	Orr	
		30/11	16,325	*22*	38				*Bradshaw*	*Nicholl*	*Cowdrill*	*Hunt*	*Bennett*	*Robertson*	*Grealish*	*Whitehead**	*Varadi*	*Thomas*	*Crooks*	*MacKenzie*
								Ref: J Martin	Doomed Albion have earned just one win and seven points, yet played above themselves in the first half. With McAvennie in Australia on World Cup duty, Dickens partnered Cottee. Parris's goal was deflected in by Robertson. Devonshire ran though the Albion defence for No 3.											
20	A	QP RANGERS		3	W	1-0	0-0	McAvennie 73	Parkes	Stewart	Walford	Gale	Martin	Devonshire	Ward	McAvennie	Dickens	Cottee	Orr	
		7/12	*23,836*	12	*41*				*Barron*	*McDonald*	*Dawes*	*Robinson*	*Wicks*	*Fenwick*	*Allen*	*Fillery*	*Bannister**	*Byrne*	*Fereday*	*Rosenior*
								Ref: J Bray	West Ham's first win at Loftus Road since 1974 was partly due to two days intense training on the plastic pitch. Bobby Robson watches as Frank McAvennie, back from Australia yesterday, converts Martin's knock-down. QPR boss Jim Smith admits West Ham have 'added steel'.											
21	H	BIRMINGHAM		3	W	2-0	2-0	McAvennie 37, Stewart 40p	Parkes	Stewart	Walford*	Gale	Martin	Devonshire	Ward	McAvennie	Dickens	Cottee	Orr	Parris
		14/12	17,481	*20*	44				*Seaman*	*Ranson*	*Roberts*	*Hagan*	*Kuhl*	*Wright*	*Bremner*	*Dicks*	*Rees*	*Geddis*	*Platnauer*	
								Ref: L Shapter	McAvennie volleys over his shoulder past David Seaman. Stewart adds a second from the spot after Alan Dickens was fouled by Jim Hagan. West Ham's ninth successive league win, and 17th unbeaten game, leaves them behind second-placed Liverpool only on goal-difference.											

No	Date	Att	Pos	Pt	F-A	H-T	Scorers, Times, and Referees	1	2	3	4	5	6	7	8	9	10	11	12 sub used
22	A LUTON		3	D	0-0	0-0		Parkes	Stewart	Walford	Gale	Martin	Devonshire	Ward	McAvennie	Dickens	Cottee	Orr	
	21/12	*14,599*	*8*	45				*Sealey*	*Breacker*	*Thomas*	*Nicholas*	*Foster*	*Donaghy*	*Hill*	*Stein B*	*Harford*	*Daniel*	*Preece*	
							Ref: D Hedges	Luton gave away free programmes to everyone bar visiting supporters, whom they intend to ban completely from next season. Having endured a drab first half *The Times* described the second as 'like a pantomime'. Alan Devonshire was taken to hospital for treatment to a face injury.											
23	A TOTTENHAM		3	L	0-1	0-0		Parkes	Stewart	Walford	Gale	Martin	Devonshire	Ward	McAvennie	Dickens	Cottee	Orr	
	26/12	*33,835*	*9*	45			*Perryman 85*	*Clemence*	*Thomas*	*Hughton*	*Stevens G*	*Mabbutt*	*Perryman*	*Ardiles**	*Falco*	*Allen C*	*Hoddle*	*Waddle*	*Allen P*
							Ref: C Downey	Rain and gale-force winds. West Ham are five minutes from extending their unbeaten run to 19 games when Hoddle climaxes a 12-pass move by picking out Perryman at the near post. It is his first goal of the season and he has never scored twice in a season. West Ham created nothing.											
24	A LEICESTER		4	W	1-0	0-0	McAvennie 54	Parkes	Stewart	Walford	Gale	Martin	Devonshire	Ward	McAvennie	Dickens	Cottee	Parris	
	11/1	*11,359*	*17*	48				*Andrews*	*Feeley*	*Morgan*	*McAllister*	*Osman*	*O'Neil*	*Lynex*	*Bright**	*Smith A*	*Mauchlen*	*Banks*	*Smith R*
							Ref: A Robinson	Once again West Ham score first then spend the rest of the match hanging on grimly. McAvennie's looping header broke the deadlock. Parkes saved McAllister's penalty when Walford felled Lynex. Leicester missed other chances too. Martin said: 'We haven't played well for a month.'											
25	A LIVERPOOL		5	L	1-3	0-0	Dickens 82	Parkes	Stewart !	Walford	Gale	Martin	Devonshire	Ward	McAvennie	Dickens	Cottee	Parris	
	18/1	*41,056*	*3*	48			*Molby 58p, Rush 67, Walsh 70*	*Grobbelaar*	*Nicol*	*Gillespie*	*Lawrenson*	*Whelan*	*Hansen*	*Walsh*	*Johnston*	*Rush*	*Molby*	*Wark*	
							Ref: G Tyson	The team bus pulled up at Everton by mistake. West Ham were on top, enjoying the space Mark Ward was allowed by not having a full-back to mark. Martin shoved Walsh in the box and Stewart was sent off for dissent before Molby converted. Rush then netted his 100th league goal.											
26	H MANCHESTER U		5	W	2-1	0-1	Ward 62, Cottee 76	Parkes	Parris	Walford	Gale	Martin	Devonshire	Ward	McAvennie	Dickens	Cottee	Pike	
	2/2	22,642	*2*	51			*Robson 25*	*Bailey*	*Gidman*	*Albiston*	*Whiteside*	*McGrath*	*Moran*	*Robson**	*Olsen*	*Hughes*	*Stapleton*	*Gibson C*	*Gibson T*
							Ref: J Ball	Under the eyes of Bobby Robson, namesake Bryan lobs the first goal but limps off after 65 minutes with torn ankle ligaments. Ward's 25-yarder levels, and Whiteside's inattentive back-pass lets in Cottee for the winner. It is Man U's first defeat by any London side in 27 games.											
27	A ARSENAL		7	L	0-1	0-0		Parkes	Stewart	Parris	Gale	Martin !	Devonshire	Ward	McAvennie	Dickens	Cottee	Pike	
	15/3	*31,240*	*5*	51			*Woodcock 76*	*Lukic*	*Anderson*	*Sansom*	*Williams*	*O'Leary*	*Keown*	*Hayes*	*Rocastle*	*Nicholas*	*Woodcock*	*Rix*	
							Ref: I Borrett	It is six weeks since West Ham's last league fixture. This disgraceful match began with Williams being booked in the first minute and ended with Martin and O'Leary exchanging blows. Others joined in. Martin was expelled, O'Leary escaped. The only goal came from a corner-kick.											
28	A ASTON VILLA		7	L	1-2	1-1	Hunt 2 (og)	Parkes	Parris	Walford	Gale	Martin	Orr	Ward	McAvennie	Dickens	Cottee*	Pike	Goddard
	19/3	*11,579*	*20*	51			*Hodge 38, 78*	*Spink*	*Dorigo*	*Evans*	*Ormsby*	*Elliott*	*Hunt*	*Blair*	*Shaw*	*Gray*	*Hodge*	*Walters*	
							Ref: K Walmsley	Cottee played despite an ankle injury sustained at Highbury and misses three good chances. West Ham had a perfect start, Villa's new signing, Hunt, chesting the ball through Spink's legs. Pike, who had just become a father, hit a post. Steve Hodge struck twice for Villa from midfield.											
29	H SHEFFIELD WED		7	W	1-0	1-0	McAvennie 6	Parkes	Stewart	Parris	Gale	Martin	Orr	Ward	McAvennie	Dickens	Cottee*	Pike	Goddard
	22/3	16,604	*6*	54				*Hodge*	*Sterland*	*Morris*	*Hart*	*Shirtliff*	*Worthington*	*Marwood*	*Megson*	*Thompson*	*Shutt*	*Snodin*	
							Ref: K Barratt	Revenge for the FA Cup defeat is sweet. Chris Morris miscues a back-pass into the path of Frank McAvennie, who takes the ball round Martin Hodge. West Ham squandered chances to increase the lead. The result leaves them 12 points behind leaders Everton with four games in hand.											
30	A CHELSEA		6	W	4-0	1-0	D'shire 23, Cottee 55, 64, McAven' 68	Parkes	Stewart	Parris	Gale	Hilton	Devonshire*	Ward	McAvennie	Dickens	Cottee	Pike	Orr
	29/3	*29,955*	*4*	57				*Godden*	*Wood*	*Rougvie*	*Pates*	*McLaughlin*	*Bumstead**	*Nevin*	*Spackman*	*Lee*	*Speedie*	*McAllister*	*Hazard*
							Ref: R Lewis	The extraordinary result in this Easter fixture shows West Ham are back on the goal-trail. Chelsea, second at New Year, are chasing the title themselves, and are using their third keeper in a month. This will not be a fleeting blip for Chelsea; two days later they will lose 0-6 at QPR.											
31	H TOTTENHAM		5	W	2-1	2-1	Cottee 17, McAvennie 43	Parkes	Stewart	Parris	Gale	Hilton	Devonshire*	Ward	McAvennie	Dickens	Cottee	Pike	Orr
	31/3	27,497	*11*	60			*Ardiles 22*	*Clemence*	*Allen P*	*Thomas*	*Roberts*	*Miller*	*Stevens G*	*Mabbutt*	*Falco*	*Galvin*	*Ardiles**	*Waddle*	*Allen C*
							Ref: B Hill	Tempers frayed on both sides, but mercifully did not mar a fiercely contested match. Dickens on the halfway line flicked on for Cottee to score. Ardiles ducked to head in a near-post corner. The winner came from Ward's corner. Cottee's shot was charged out, straight to McAvennie.											

No		Date / Opponent	Att	Pos	Res	F-A	H-T	Scorers, Times, and Referees	1	2	3	4	5	6	7	8	9	10	11	subs used
32	A	NOTT'M FOREST		5	L	1-2	0-1	Cottee 69	Parkes	Stewart	Parris	Gale	Martin	Orr	Ward	McAvennie	Dickens	Cottee	Pike	
		2/4	*17,498*	*8*	60			*Metgod 39, Rice 88*	*Sutton*	*Fleming*	*Pearce*	*Walker*	*Metgod*	*Bowyer*	*Carr*	*Webb*	*Clough*	*Campbell*	*Rice*	
								Ref: L Dilkes	Forest's Brian Rice will remember this game for a long time. He misses an open goal at 0-0, but has the satisfaction of sinking West Ham with his late winner. Johnny Metgod earlier drove in a free-kick from 35 yards, and Stewart picked out Cottee, who wriggled clear to equalise.											
33	H	SOUTHAMPTON		4	W	1-0	1-0	Martin 26	Parkes	Stewart	Parris	Gale	Martin	Devonshire	Ward	McAvennie	Dickens	Cottee	Pike	
		8/4	22,459	*15*	63				*Shilton*	*Forrest*	*Dennis*	*Case*	*Townsend*	*Bond*	*Holmes*	*Cockerill*	*Jordan*	*Armstrong*	*Puckett**	*Whitlock*
								Ref: P Vanes	West Ham have a congested but comparatively easy run in. Saints have won away from home only once all season, and on Saturday lost an FA Cup semi-final to Spurs. Alvin Martin volleyed Gale's header past Shilton. Near the end Townsend's weak shot deceived Parkes and hit a post.											
34	H	OXFORD		5	W	3-1	0-1	Tr'wick 49 (og), McAv 65, St'wart 81p	Parkes	Stewart	Parris	Gale	Martin	Devonshire	Ward	McAvennie	Dickens	Cottee	Pike	
		12/4	23,956	*20*	66			*Houghton 13*	*Judge*	*Langan*	*Trewick*	*Phillips*	*Briggs*	*Shotton*	*Houghton*	*Aldridge*	*Hamilton**	*Hebberd*	*Perryman*	*Charles*
								Ref: N Butler	An exhilarating match, remembered for bad things as well as good. Ward was booked for flinging the ball at a linesman, and McAvennie might have been sent off had the ref seen his retaliation on Hebberd. Stewart scored one and missed one penalty, both given for fouls by Perryman.											
35	H	CHELSEA		5	L	1-2	0-0	Cottee 51	Parkes	Stewart	Parris	Gale*	Martin	Devonshire	Ward	McAvennie	Dickens	Cottee	Pike	Orr
		15/4	29,361	*4*	66			*Spackman 55, Nevin 78*	*Godden*	*Wood*	*Millar*	*Rougvie*	*McLaughlin*	*Bumstead**	*Nevin*	*Spackman*	*Dixon*	*Hazard*	*Murphy*	*McAllister*
								Ref: M Bodenham	Chelsea gain revenge for their 4-0 mauling two weeks earlier. After Dickens had set up Cottee's opener with a diagonal pass, Neil Orr fell over the ball to present a gift to Spackman. Pat Nevin's free header won a match that was interrupted by two minutes after a brief pitch invasion.											
36	A	WATFORD		5	W	2-0	0-0	Cottee 59, McAvennie 89	Parkes	Stewart	Parris	Gale	Martin	Devonshire	Ward	McAvennie	Dickens	Cottee	Orr	
		19/4	*16,651*	*12*	69				*Coton*	*Gibbs*	*Franklin**	*Talbot*	*Terry*	*McClelland*	*Sterling*	*Bardsley*	*West*	*Jackett*	*Barnes*	*Smillie*
								Ref: J Bray	Watford manager Graham Taylor pays West Ham the ultimate compliment, saying they are a better team than Everton. The double act of Cottee and McAvennie bagged a goal apiece and might have had more. Watford carved out just one chance, which West scooped over the bar.											
37	H	NEWCASTLE		3	W	**8-1**	4-0	Martin 3, 64p, 84, Stewart 11, Orr 35,	Parkes	Stewart	Parris	Gale	Martin	Devonshire	Ward	McAvennie	Dickens*	Cottee	Orr	Goddard
		21/4	24,735	*11*	72			*Whitehurst 76* [R'der 43 (og), G'ard 81,]	*Thomas**	*McDonald*	*Bailey*	*McCreery*	*Anderson*	*Roeder*	*Stephenson*	*Hedworth*	*Whitehurst*	*Beadsley*	*Cunningham*	*Stewart*
								Ref: T Hamer [McAvennie 83]	A game for the record books. West Ham's biggest win since October 1968 produced a hat-trick for Alvin Martin, each of whose goals was scored against a different keeper. Martin Thomas went off shell-shocked at half-time. Hedworth went in goal for a while, then Peter Beardsley.											
38	H	COVENTRY		4	W	1-0	0-0	Cottee 61	Parkes	Stewart	Parris	Gale	Martin	Devonshire	Ward	McAvennie	Dickens	Cottee	Orr	
		26/4	27,251	*18*	75				*Ogrizovic*	*Borrows*	*Downs*	*McGrath*	*Kilcline*	*Peake*	*Bennett*	*Brazil*	*Regis*	*Pickering*	*Adams*	
								Ref: I Hemley	West Ham suffer an understandable hangover after Newcastle. Coventry are desperate for points themselves and would have deserved one. They were denied it when, from Ward's throw-in, the ball reached Cottee for his 24th goal of the season. Bobby Robson watched the game.											
39	H	MANCHESTER C		3	W	1-0	1-0	Stewart 19p	Parkes	Stewart	Parris	Gale	Martin	Devonshire	Ward	McAvennie	Dickens	Cottee	Orr	
		28/4	27,153	*15*	78				*Siddall*	*Phillips*	*May*	*Reid*	*McCarthy*	*Wilson*	*Lillis*	*McIlroy*	*Davies*	*McNab*	*Simpson**	*Beckford*
								Ref: R Gifford	City have taken just three points from 11 games, yet they squander early chances against weary West Ham, who had created nothing when May tried to sell Cottee a dummy and fouled him. Stewart's penalty was his seventh in eight attempts. McCarthy and Phillips missed late chances.											
40	H	IPSWICH		2	W	2-1	0-0	Dickens 72, Stewart 86p	Parkes	Stewart	Parris	Gale	Martin	Devonshire	Ward	McAvennie	Dickens	Cottee	Orr*	Goddard
		30/4	**31,121**	*19*	81			*Wilson 63*	*Cooper*	*Atkins**	*McCall*	*Parkin*	*Cranson*	*Butcher*	*Gleghorn*	*Brennan*	*Dozzell*	*Wilson*	*Cole*	*Yallop*
								Ref: G Ashby	After three FA Cup-ties, another fiercely contested clash. The game exploded as a result of Stewart's late penalty, when Brennan and Gleghorn impeded Ward. Terry Butcher appeared to lash out at the ref after the final whistle. The point dropped will eventually send Ipswich down.											
41	A	WEST BROM		2	W	3-2	2-1	McAvennie 6, Cottee 24, Stewart 82p	Parkes	Stewart	Parris	Gale	Martin	Devonshire	Ward	McAvennie	Dickens	Cottee	Orr	
		3/5	*17,651*	*22*	84			*Madden 30, Reilly 64p*	*Naylor*	*Whitehead*	*Statham*	*Cowdrill*	*Dyson*	*Palmer*	*Dickinson*	*MacKenzie**	*Reilly*	*Madden*	*Bradley*	*Robson*
								Ref: A Robinson	WBA are sure to finish bottom but they put up sterling resistance before presenting West Ham with their sixth successive win. Stewart's third penalty in successive games earns three points after WBA had fought back from 0-2. But Liverpool's win at Chelsea has clinched the title.											
42	A	EVERTON		3	L	1-3	0-1	Cottee 89	Parkes	Stewart	Parris	Gale	Martin	Devonshire	Ward	McAvennie	Dickens*	Cottee	Orr	Goddard
		5/5	*40,073*	*2*	84			*Lineker 42, 47, Steven 72p*	*Mimms*	*Stevens*	*v d Hauwe*	*Mountford*	*Billing*	*Richardson*	*Steven*	*Lineker**	*Wilkinson*	*Heath*	*Sheedy*	*Aspinall*
		Home / Away Average 21,992 / 22,608						Ref: G Courtney	This is the battle for second place, which will be West Ham's if they draw. Sadly, they are outplayed, but win £15,000 from sponsors Canon. Cottee's 26th goal of the season is eclipsed by Lineker's 30th. At the final whistle players go to salute 6,000 supporters who had made the trip.											

Milk Cup					F-A	H-T	Scorers, Times, and Referees	1	2	3	4	5	6	7	8	9	10	11	12 sub used
2:1	H	SWANSEA	13	W	3-0	0-0	Cottee 48, McAven' 56, Stewart 90p	Parkes	Stewart	Walford	Gale	Martin	Devonshire	Ward	McAvennie	Dickens	Cottee	Orr	
24/9		9,282	*3:20*					*Rimmer*	*Lewis*	*Sullivan*	*Price*	*Stevenson*	*Marustik*	*Hutchison*	*Randell*	*Turner*	*Harrison*	*Pascoe*	
							Ref: A Gunn	Ex-Hammer, John Bond, is in charge of struggling Swansea. Tommy Hutchison looks dangerous during the 10 minutes that Devonshire is off receiving treatment. The breakthrough came when Dickens chipped to the near post for Cottee. Stevenson fouled Alvin Martin for the penalty.											
2:2	A	SWANSEA	11	W	3-2	3-2	Stewart 11p, 43p, Cottee 13	Parkes	Stewart	Walford	Gale	Martin	Devonshire	Ward	McAvennie*	Dickens	Cottee	Orr	Parris
8/10		*3,584*	*3:22*				*Waddle 6, Randell 23*	*Hughes*	*Sharpe*	*Sullivan*	*Price*	*McHale*	*Harrison*	*Hutchinson*	*Randell*	*Turner*	*Waddle**	*Pascoe*	*Stevenson*
							Ref: R Groves (Hammers win 6-2 on aggregate)	Swansea are facing a winding up order, and desperately need to cause an upset. They take the lead, then come back to 2-2, but are pegged back by two penalties, both conceded by John Sharpe. He hauls down McAvennie for the first and handles Cottee's shot on the line for the second.											
3	A	MANCHESTER U	7	L	0-1	0-0		Parkes	Stewart	Walford	Gale	Martin	Devonshire	Ward	McAvennie	Dickens*	Cottee	Orr	Parris
29/10		*32,057*	*1*				*Whiteside 77*	*Bailey*	*Duxbury**	*Albiston*	*Whiteside*	*Moran*	*Hogg*	*McGrath*	*Olsen*	*Hughes*	*Stapleton*	*Barnes*	*Brazil*
							Ref: F Roberts	The only goal came when Olsen cut inside and laid on a chance to Whiteside. Then Ward's indirect free-kick flew past the diving Gary Bailey. The ref consulted a linesman, agreed that Bailey had not got a touch, and ruled it out. Man U haven't lost to any London side for 27 games.											

FA Cup																			
3	A	CHARLTON	5	W	1-0	0-0	Cottee 88	Parkes	Stewart	Walford	Gale	Martin	Devonshire	Ward	McAvennie	Dickens	Cottee	Parris	
5/1		*13,037*	*2:3*					*Johns*	*Humphrey*	*Reid*	*Curbishley*	*Thompson*	*Pender*	*Gritt*	*Lee*	*Pearson*	*Aizlewood*	*Flanagan*	
							Ref: B Hill	Charlton play home matches at Selhurst Park. This televised Sunday cup-tie was rich in entertainment but short on goals. On a pitch so frozen that Crystal Palace's match on Saturday was called off, McAvennie seized on Humphrey's slice to lob Johns. Cottee got the finishing touch.											
4	H	IPSWICH	5	D	0-0	0-0		Parkes	Stewart	Walford*	Gale	Martin	Devonshire	Ward	McAvennie	Dickens	Cottee	Parris	Goddard
25/1		25,035	*19*					*Cooper*	*Yallop*	*McCall*	*Stockwell**	*Cranson*	*Butcher*	*Putney*	*Brennan*	*D'Avray*	*Wilson*	*Dozzell*	*Zondervan*
							Ref: J Martin	Lucky Hammers. In the second half they fell to pieces. Putney's downward header beat Parkes but reared up off the frozen surface to clear the crossbar. D'Avray and Dozzell also missed good chances for Ipswich. Terry Butcher kept Cottee and McAvennie in his pocket throughout.											
4R	A	IPSWICH	5	D	1-1	0-0	Cottee 106	Parkes	Parris	Walford*	Gale	Martin	Devonshire	Ward	McAvennie	Dickens	Cottee	Pike	Orr
4/2		*25,384*	*19*		*aet*		*Dozzell 93*	*Cooper*	*Yallop*	*McCall*	*Zondervan*	*Cranson*	*Butcher*	*Putney**	*Brennan*	*D'Avray*	*Wilson*	*Dozzell*	*Cole*
							Ref: J Martin	Ipswich are on a high after beating Liverpool three days earlier. Three hours without a goal sends this tie into extra-time. Jason Dozzell, whose earlier header had been brilliantly saved, shrugged off Dickens to put Ipswich in front. Tony Cottee levelled, putting away Parris's square pass.											
4 RR	A	IPSWICH	5	W	1-0	0-0	Cottee 111	Parkes	Stewart	Parris	Gale	Martin	Orr	Ward	McAvennie	Dickens	Cottee	Pike	
6/2		*14,515*	*19*		*aet*			*Cooper*	*Yallop*	*McCall*	*Zondervan*	*Cranson*	*Butcher*	*Putney**	*Brennan*	*D'Avray*	*Wilson*	*Dozzell*	*Baker*
							Ref: K Baker	Lyall lost the toss to decide the venue of this second replay. A red ball is used on an icy pitch. Once again extra-time is needed, and in the 321st minute of this protracted tie Cottee capitalised on Brennan's error. Cottee has now scored in each of his last five games at Portman Road.											
5	H	MANCHESTER U	5	D	1-1	1-0	McAvennie 25	Parkes	Stewart	Parris	Gale	Martin	Devonshire	Ward	McAvennie	Dickens	Cottee	Pike	
5/3		26,441	*2*				*Stapleton 73*	*Turner*	*Duxbury*	*Albiston*	*Whiteside*	*McGrath*	*Moran*	*Robson**	*Strachan*	*Hughes*	*Stapleton*	*Gibson C*	*Olsen*
							Ref: B Stevens	A month has been lost to the weather. After three minutes of this tempestuous tie Bryan Robson dislocates his shoulder when tackling Cottee. Cottee squared for McAvennie to net. Frank Stapleton's super header from Duxbury's cross earned a fourth recent cup-tie at Old Trafford.											
5R	A	MANCHESTER U	5	W	2-0	1-0	Pike 18, Stewart 54p	Parkes	Stewart	Parris	Gale	Martin	Devonshire	Ward	McAvennie	Dickens	Cottee	Pike	
9/3		*30,441*	*2*					*Turner*	*Duxbury*	*Albiston*	*Whiteside*	*McGrath*	*Higgins**	*Olsen*	*Strachan*	*Hughes*	*Stapleton*	*Gibson C*	*Blackmore*
							Ref: B Stevens	Two decisions determined the outcome of this televised Sunday replay and left Man U supporters wild with rage. West Ham were hanging on to Pike's header when Stapleton nudged Martin for a fiercely disputed penalty. Seconds later Stewart shoved Stapleton in the box. No penalty.											
QF	A	SHEFFIELD WED	5	L	1-2	0-2	Cottee 48	Parkes	Stewart	Parris	Gale	Martin	Devonshire	Ward	McAvennie	Dickens	Cottee	Pike	
12/3		*35,522*	*8*				*Worthington 16, Shutt 35*	*Hodge*	*Sterland*	*Morris*	*Smith*	*Shirtliff*	*Worthington*	*Marwood**	*Megson*	*Chapman*	*Shutt*	*Snodin*	*Chamberlain*
							Ref: J Worrall	Three days after beating Man U, West Ham get their come-uppance. Marwood's sixth corner in the first 16 minutes proves fatal. Shutt cuts inside Parris to set up Worthington. West Ham never recover. This is the Owls' first win in nine cup quarter-finals under Howard Wilkinson.											

		Home					Away					
	P	W	D	L	F	A	W	D	L	F	A	Pts
1 Liverpool	42	16	4	1	58	14	10	6	5	31	23	88
2 Everton	42	16	3	2	54	18	10	5	6	33	23	86
3 WEST HAM	42	17	2	2	48	16	9	4	8	26	24	84
4 Manchester U	42	12	5	4	35	12	10	5	6	35	24	76
5 Sheffield Wed	42	13	6	2	36	23	8	4	9	27	31	73
6 Chelsea	42	12	4	5	32	27	8	7	6	25	29	71
7 Arsenal	42	13	5	3	29	15	7	4	10	20	32	69
8 Nott'm Forest	42	11	5	5	38	25	8	6	7	31	28	68
9 Luton	42	12	6	3	37	15	6	6	9	24	29	66
10 Tottenham	42	12	2	7	47	25	7	6	8	27	27	65
11 Newcastle	42	12	5	4	46	31	5	7	9	21	41	63
12 Watford	42	11	6	4	40	22	5	5	11	29	40	59
13 QP Rangers	42	12	3	6	33	20	3	4	14	20	44	52
14 Southampton	42	10	6	5	32	18	2	4	15	19	44	46
15 Manchester C	42	7	7	7	25	26	4	5	12	18	31	45
16 Aston Villa	42	7	6	8	27	28	3	8	10	24	39	44
17 Coventry	42	6	5	10	31	35	5	5	11	17	36	43
18 Oxford	42	7	7	7	34	27	3	5	13	28	53	42
19 Leicester	42	7	8	6	35	35	3	4	14	19	41	42
20 Ipswich	42	8	5	8	20	24	3	3	15	12	31	41
21 Birmingham	42	5	2	14	13	25	3	3	15	17	48	29
22 West Brom	42	3	8	10	21	36	1	4	16	14	53	24
	924	229	110	123	771	517	123	110	229	517	771	1276

Odds & ends

Double wins: (8) QPR, Leicester, Newcastle, Ipswich, Oxford, Watford, Coventry, WBA.
Double losses: (0).

Won from behind: (7) Villa (h), Everton (h), Oxford (h&a), Man U (h), Ipswich (h), Swansea LC (a).
Lost from in front: (2) Villa (a), Chelsea (h).

High spots: Finishing 3rd, West Ham's highest ever position.
Winning nine successive league games from 19 October.

Low spots: Not clinching their first ever league championship.
Losing three of the first four league games.

West Ham faced Manchester U in both cups.
Nine of Ray Stewart's 10 goals were penalties.

Hammer of the Year: Tony Cottee.
Ever-presents: (3) Tony Gale, Phil Parkes, Mark Ward.
Hat-tricks: (1) Alvin Martin.
Leading scorer: (28) Frank McAvennie.

	Appearances						Goals			
	Lge	*Sub*	LC	*Sub*	FAC	*Sub*	**Lge**	LC	FAC	**Tot**
Barnes, Bobby		*1*								
Campbell, Greg	**1**	*2*								
Cottee, Tony	**41**	*1*	3		7		**20**	2	4	**26**
Devonshire, Alan	**38**		3		6		**3**			**3**
Dickens, Alan	**40**	*1*	3		7		**4**			**4**
Gale, Tony	**42**		3		7					
Goddard, Paul	**1**	*5*				*1*	**1**			**1**
Hilton, Paul	**2**									
McAvennie, Frank	**41**		3		7		**26**	1	1	**28**
Martin, Alvin	**40**		3		7		**4**			**4**
Orr, Neil	**33**	*3*	3		1	*1*	**2**			**2**
Parkes, Phil	**42**		3		7					
Parris, George	**23**	*3*		*2*	7		**1**			**1**
Pike, Geoff	**10**				5				1	**1**
Potts, Steve		*1*								
Stewart, Ray	**39**		3		6		**6**	3	1	**10**
Walford, Steve	**27**		3		3					
Ward, Mark	**42**		3		7		**3**			**3**
(own-goals)							**4**			**4**
(18 players used)	**462**	***17***	**33**	***2***	**77**	***2***	**74**	**6**	**7**	**87**

No	Date		Att	Pos	Pt	F-A	H-T	Scorers, Times, and Referees	1	2	3	4	5	6	7	8	9	10	11	12 sub used
1	H	COVENTRY			W	1-0	0-0	Gale 83	Parkes	Stewart	Parris	Gale	Martin	Devonshire	Ward	McAvennie	Dickens	Cottee	Orr	
	23/8		21,368		3				*Ogrizovic*	*Borrows*	*Downs*	*McGrath*	*Kilcline*	*Peake*	*Bennett**	*Phillips*	*Regis*	*Houchen*	*Pickering*	*Adams*
								Ref: L Shapter	Tony Gale, his eye bloodied from a collision with Coventry new boy, Keith Houchen, scores his first ever Hammers goal. Peake fouled Devonshire and Gale drove the free-kick past Ogrizovic. Coventry showed no interest in scoring until after they fell behind, and no ideas then.											
2	A	MANCHESTER U			W	3-2	2-1	McAvennie 1, 82, Devonshire 38	Parkes	Stewart	Parris	Hilton	Martin	Devonshire	Ward	McAvennie	Dickens	Cottee	Orr	
	25/8		***43,306***		6			*Stapleton 39, Davenport 46*	*Turner*	*Duxbury*	*Albiston*	*Whiteside*	*McGrath*	*Moran*	*Strachan*	*Blackmore*	*Stapleton*	*Davenport*	*Gibson**	*Olsen*
								Ref: G Tyson	After just 32 seconds Dickens chipped forward for McAvennie to net. Devonshire's lob, following a one-two with Parris, was quickly followed by Stapleton nodding in from Gibson. McAvennie's late header puts extra pressure on Ron Atkinson, whose Old Trafford days are numbered.											
3	A	OXFORD		3	D	0-0	0-0		Parkes	Stewart	Parris	Gale	Martin	Devonshire	Ward	McAvennie	Dickens	Cottee	Orr	
	30/8		*11,684*	*19*	7				*Judge*	*Langan*	*Trewick*	*Phillips*	*Briggs*	*Shotton*	*Houghton*	*Aldridge*	*Charles*	*Hebberd*	*Perryman*	
								Ref: H King	Trevor Hebberd plays a blinder as Oxford's sweeper, snuffing out whatever attacks West Ham muster. Oxford feel aggrieved at not bagging their first win of the season. Shotton's free-kick smashed against Parkes' left post, and Aldridge and Charles both missed gilt-edged chances.											
4	H	NOTT'M FOREST			L	1-2	1-0	McAvennie 19	Parkes	Stewart	Parris	Gale	Martin	Devonshire*	Ward	McAvennie	Dickens	Cottee	Orr	Goddard
	2/9		21,305		7			*Clough 62, Webb 64*	*Sutton*	*Fleming*	*Pearce*	*Walker*	*Metgod*	*Bowyer*	*Carr*	*Webb*	*Clough*	*Birtles*	*Campbell*	
								Ref: D Axcell	Dickens supplied McAvennie, who – angered by being left out of Roxburgh's Scottish squad – sprinted through to finish with a precise shot. In the space of three minutes Webb set up Nigel Clough's equaliser, then scored himself to transform the Boleyn into a ghostly, silent morgue.											
5	H	LIVERPOOL		12	L	2-5	1-1	Stewart 8p, Cottee 55 *[Rush 70]*	Parkes	Stewart	Parris	Gale	Martin	Pike*	Ward	McAvennie	Dickens	Cottee	Orr	**Keen**
	6/9		**29,807**	*2*	7			*Wh'lan 25, Johnst'n 50, D'glish 66, 90,*	*Hooper*	*Venison*	*Beglin*	*Gillespie*	*Whelan*	*Hansen**	*McDonald*	*Johnston*	*Rush*	*Lawrenson*	*McMahon*	*Dalglish*
								Ref: J Martin	The double winners see less of Dalglish on the pitch these days, but Hansen's torn hamstring brings him on early. West Ham's penalty came when Gillespie tripped Cottee. It was all-square after an hour. Dalglish's two goals were both deflected. He admitted: 'the margin flattered us'.											
6	A	QP RANGERS		6	W	3-2	2-0	Cottee 6, 10, 80	Parkes	Stewart	Parris	Gale	Martin	Walford	Keen	McAvennie	Dickens	Cottee	Orr	
	13/9		*19,257*	*7*	10			*James 70, Byrne 85*	*Seaman*	*Neill*	*Dawes*	*Allen*	*McDonald*	*Chivers*	*Lee*	*James*	*Rosenior*	*Byrne*	*Fereday**	*Robinson*
								Ref: B Stevens	Cottee has won his first England cap as a substitute in Sweden and celebrates with a hat-trick in this rain-drenched thriller, though two goals were deflected. His first goal was a free-kick; his second from McAvennie' cross. Byrne rounded Walford near the end to set nerves on edge.											
7	H	LUTON		4	W	2-0	1-0	Parris 41, Gale 57	Parkes	Stewart	Walford	Gale	Martin !	Parris	Keen	McAvennie	Dickens*	Cottee	Orr	Pike
	20/9		19,133	*13*	13				*Sealey*	*Johnston*	*Grimes*	*Nicholas*	*Foster*	*Donaghy*	*Hill*	*Stein B !*	*Newell**	*Wilson*	*Preece*	*Stein M*
								Ref: J Deakin	England boss Bobby Robson watches from the stand as Alvin Martin and Brian Stein swap punches 10 minutes from time and both are sent off. Martin fears for his England place, with an automatic two-match ban to come, and knowing that Mark Wright is coming back to fitness.											
8	A	SHEFFIELD WED		7	D	2-2	0-1	Martin 60, Orr 78	Parkes	Stewart	Parris	Gale	Martin	Walford	Ward	McAvennie	Dickens	Cottee	Orr	
	27/9		*25,715*	*8*	14			*Madden 18, Megson 89*	*Hodge*	*Sterland*	*Worthington*	*Madden*	*Knight*	*Chamberlain*	*Marwood*	*Megson*	*Chapman*	*Shutt*	*Shelton*	
								Ref: N Ashley	FA Chairman Bert Millichip stays in the same hotel as West Ham. He has publicly advised Bobby Robson to drop Alvin Martin for being sent off against Luton. Neil Orr, whose wife's baby is overdue, put West Ham 2-1 ahead in this fixture against Howard Wilkinson's Wednesday.											
9	A	WATFORD		8	D	2-2	2-1	Dickens 16, McAvennie 23	Parkes	Stewart	Parris	Gale	Hilton	Walford	Ward	McAvennie	Dickens	Cottee	Orr*	Keen
	4/10		*17,120*	*14*	15			*Callaghan 35, Blissett 70*	*Coton*	*Bardsley*	*Sinnott*	*Richardson*	*Terry*	*McClelland*	*Callaghan*	*Blissett*	*Roberts**	*Jackett*	*Barnes*	*Porter*
								Ref: B Hamer	For the fourth time this season West Ham fail to protect a lead. Luther Blissett rescues a point for Graham Taylor's Watford after a tactical switch pairs him up front with John Barnes. Lyall is furious that his team sat back to protect their lead rather than search for further goals.											
10	H	CHELSEA		4	W	5-3	2-1	McAvennie 32, Stewart 34p, 79p,	Parkes	Stewart	Parris	Gale	Hilton	Keen	Ward	McAvennie*	Dickens	Cottee	Orr	Bonds
	11/10		26,859	*19*	18			*Jones 24p, Dixon 58, Bumstead 62*	*Godden*	*Wood*	*Rougvie*	*Pates*	*Wicks*	*Bumstead*	*Nevin*	*Jones*	*Dixon*	*McAllister*	*McNaught*	
								Ref: M Reed [Cottee 85, 87]	John Hollins' Chelsea are in turmoil on and off the pitch. Both sides enjoy iffy penalties, Chelsea when Nevin fell over Gale's leg; West Ham when Godden collided with Keen. Chelsea led 3-2 after an hour, then collapsed. 'Pulsating' said Lyall. 'Backsides need kicking' said Hollins.											

No Date	Venue	Opponent Att	Pos	Res Pts	F-A	H-T	Scorers, Times, and Referees	1	2	3	4	5	6	7	8	9	10	11	12
11	A	NORWICH	5	D	1-1	0-0	Goddard 75	Parkes	Stewart	Parris	Gale	Hilton	Keen	Ward*	Goddard	Dickens	Cottee	Orr	Bonds
18/10		*22,884*	*2*	19			*Drinkell 58*	*Benstead*	*Culverhouse*	*Spearing*	*Bruce*	*Phelan*	*Elliott*	*Crook*	*Drinkell*	*Biggins*	*Barham*	*Gordon**	*Hedgson*
							Ref: A Seville	Ken Brown's enterprising Norwich are knocked off the top, conceding their first goal in six matches. The scorer was Paul Goddard, starting his first game in 14 months. He netted off Barham's shoulder, after the ball was headed on by Hilton. Biggins provided the equaliser for Drinkell.											
12	H	CHARLTON	8	L	1-3	1-2	Cottee 44	Parkes	Stewart	Parris	Gale	Hilton	Devonshire*	Ward	Goddard	Dickens	Cottee	Orr	Keen
25/10		24,141	*12*	19			*Melrose 1, Walsh 37, Pearson 76*	*Johns*	*Humphrey*	*Reid*	*Peake*	*Thompson*	*Shirtliff*	*Lee*	*Stuart*	*Melrose*	*Aizlewood*	*Walsh**	*Pearson*
							Ref: R Milford	Homeless Charlton win their fourth league game in a row, helped by a goal within nine seconds. Lee's through-ball enabled Melrose to chip over Parkes. At 0-2 Ward's deep cross was met by Tony Cottee's volley, but Pearson rounded Phil Parkes to eclipse hopes of a fight-back.											
13	H	EVERTON	8	W	1-0	0-0	Dickens 48	Parkes	Stewart	Parris	Gale	Hilton	Devonshire	Ward	Goddard	Dickens	Cottee	Orr	
2/11		19,094	*3*	22				*Southall*	*Harper*	*Power*	*Ratcliffe*	*Mountfield*	*Langley**	*Steven*	*Heath*	*Sharp*	*Wilkinson*	*Sheedy*	*Aspinall*
							Ref: P Vanes	This live Sunday match produced a TV thriller. Howard Kendall's Everton have now won just one out of six visits to London opponents. Alan Dickens' header from Devonshire's corner loops over Southall and under the bar, and West Ham somehow survive Everton's furious late rally.											
14	A	ARSENAL	7	D	0-0	0-0		Parkes	Stewart	Parris	Gale	Hilton	Devonshire	Ward	McAvennie	Dickens	Cottee	Walford	
8/11		*36,084*	*3*	23				*Lukic*	*Anderson*	*Sansom*	*Williams*	*O'Leary*	*Adams*	*Rocastle*	*Davis*	*Quinn*	*Groves*	*Hayes*	
							Ref: J Martin	Paul Goddard has been sold to Newcastle, but Cottee's partnership with McAvennie looks more penetrating than Arsenal's endless supply of high balls to Niall Quinn. West Ham might have had six, and had two efforts disallowed. Graham said: 'West Ham are much better than us'.											
15	A	WIMBLEDON	5	W	1-0	0-0	Cottee 55	Parkes	Stewart	Parris	Gale	Hilton	Devonshire*	Ward	McAvennie	Dickens	Cottee	Orr	Walford
15/11		*10,342*	*13*	26				*Beasant*	*Kay*	*Winterburn*	*Galliers**	*Gayle*	*Thorn*	*Clement*	*Cork*	*Fashanu*	*Downes*	*Fairweather*	*Gage*
							Ref: J Moules	Dave Bassett's promoted Wimbledon were top in September but are now spinning down the table. Bobby Robson looks on from Plough Lane's rickety stand as Cottee bags another all-important goal that maintains West Ham's unbeaten away record. Wimbledon were taught a lesson.											
16	H	ASTON VILLA	4	D	1-1	1-0	Cottee 9	Parkes	Walford	Parris	Gale	Hilton	Devonshire	Ward	McAvennie	Dickens	Cottee	Keen*	Bonds
22/11		21,959	*16*	27			*Thompson 63*	*Spink*	*Williams*	*Dorigo*	*Evans*	*Elliott*	*Keown*	*Norton*	*Kerr*	*Thompson*	*Hunt**	*Hodge*	*Daley*
							Ref: A Gunn	Villa boss Billy McNeill admits this was a great advert for football. Norton's wayward corner left all Villa's tall defenders at the wrong end of the pitch, leaving Cottee to waltz round Williams. Thompson's free header rescued a point for a Villa team that did not earn a single booking.											
17	A	NEWCASTLE	7	L	**0-4**	0-2	*[Jackson D 66]*	Parkes	Stewart	Parris	Gale	Hilton	Devonshire	Ward	McAvennie	Dickens*	Cottee	Orr	Ince
30/11		*22,077*	*22*	27			*McDonald 29, Thomas A 33, 80,*	*Thomas M*	*Anderson*	*Wharton*	*McCreery*	*Jackson P*	*Roeder*	*McDonald*	*Thomas A*	*Goddard**	*Beardsley*	*Stephenson*	*Jackson D*
							Ref: K Hackett	This Sunday TV match tore up West Ham's unbeaten away record and threw up an oddity. McDonald's opener was the first Newcastle goal seen on live TV since 1955. All four goals came from crosses pulled back from the byline. Willie McFaul's team pull out of the bottom three.											
18	H	SOUTHAMPTON	5	W	3-1	2-1	Ince 15, Devonshire 42, Cottee 61p	Parkes	Potts	Parris	Gale	Martin	Devonshire	Ward	McAvennie	Ince	Cottee	Orr	
6/12		18,111	*14*	30			*Clarke 19*	*Shilton*	*Forrest*	*Tankard*	*Case*	*Blake*	*Bond*	*Lawrence*	*Cockerill*	*Clarke*	*Hobson*	*Wallace*	
							Ref: M James	With Dickens injured, teenager Paul Ince steps in and plays a stormer. His uncompromising battle with veteran Jimmy Case in midfield made onlookers flinch. Ince opens the scoring with a diving header and later wins a penalty, when fouled by Blake, which is converted by Cottee.											
19	A	MANCHESTER C	6	L	1-3	0-1	Martin 46	Parkes	Potts	Parris	Gale	Martin	Devonshire	Ward	McAvennie	Ince	Cottee	Orr*	Dickens
13/12		*19,067*	*20*	30			*White 17, Varadi 59, 86*	*Suckling*	*Gidman*	*Wilson*	*Clements*	*McCarthy*	*Grealish**	*White*	*McNab*	*Varadi*	*Moulden*	*Simpson*	*Redmond*
							Ref: C Seel	Another bad defeat to a lowly northern team has Lyall complaining about slow build-ups. Jimmy Frizzell's City climb off the bottom thanks to sparkling displays from young wingers White and Simpson. Mick McCarthy easily snuffed out the combined threat of Cottee and McAvennie.											
20	H	QP RANGERS	7	D	1-1	1-0	Cottee 24p	Parkes	Potts	Parris	Gale	Martin	Devonshire	Ward	McAvennie	Dickens	Cottee	Orr	
20/12		17,290	*17*	31			*Fenwick 80p*	*Seaman*	*Neill*	*James*	*Allen*	*McDonald*	*Fenwick*	*Lee*	*Robinson*	*Bannister*	*Byrne**	*Peacock*	*Fillery*
							Ref: M Dimblebee	The offside tactics of Jim Smith's QPR don't endear the visitors to Upton Park. McDonald's duff challenge on Dickens brought the first penalty; Martin's foul on Gavin Peacock the second. Drained of confidence, Cottee spurns four great chances to add to his penalty-kick.											
21	A	TOTTENHAM	9	L	**0-4**	0-1		Parkes	Potts	Parris	Walford*	Martin	Devonshire	Ward	McAvennie	Dickens	Cottee	Orr	Hilton
26/12		*39,019*	5	31			*Allen C 13, 88, Hodge 53, Waddle 54*	*Clemence*	*Thomas D*	*Thomas M**	*Hodge*	*Gough*	*Mabbutt*	*Allen C*	*Allen P*	*Waddle*	*Hoddle*	*Galvin*	*Ardiles*
							Ref: R Lewis	Steve Hodge makes his Spurs debut in this rout, West Ham's heaviest defeat against Tottenham in 19 years. Hoddle made three goals for David Pleat's side. Cottee, McAvennie and Devonshire were invisible. Yet again Lyall locks the dressing room door behind his demoralised players.											

TODAY LEAGUE DIVISION 1

Manager: John Lyall

SEASON 1986-87

No	Date	Att	Pos	Pt	F-A	H-T	Scorers, Times, and Referees	1	2	3	4	5	6	7	8	9	10	11	12 sub used
22	H WIMBLEDON		12	L	2-3	2-2	Cottee 3, Hilton 35	Parkes	Potts	Parris	Hilton	Martin	Ince	Ward	McAvennie	Keen*	Cottee	Pike	Dickens
	27/12	19,122	*10*	31			*Fashanu 12, Sayer 37, Fairweather 64*	*Beasant*	*Kay*	*Winterburn*	*Sanchez*	*Gayle*	*Thorn*	*Fairweather*	*Sayer*	*Fashanu*	*Downes*	*Hodges*	
							Ref: B Hill	Lyall drops his entire midfield, but that cannot prevent the loss of seven goals in 24 hours. Only three teams in the division have now conceded fewer. Confidence has drained from the entire team, not least Phil Parkes, who makes a complete hash of saving Carlton Fairweather's winner.											
23	H LEICESTER		8	W	**4-1**	3-0	C'ttee 9, 20, Dickens 25, McAv'nie 90	Parkes	Walford	Parris	Hilton	Martin	Devonshire	Ward	McAvennie	Dickens	Cottee	Pike	
	1/1	16,625	*22*	34			*Moran 87*	*Andrews*	*Morgan*	*Venus*	*Feeley*	*O'Neill*	*McAllister*	*Lynex*	*Moran*	*Smith*	*Ramsey*	*Kelly**	*Alleyne*
							Ref: G Ashby	Bottom-placed Leicester are no match even for shell-shocked Hammers, whose first goal on a rain-soaked pitch is a thing of beauty. The ball was played rapidly from defence to attack, where Tony Cottee chests it down to score. Frank McAvennie's goal is his first for two months.											
24	A LIVERPOOL		10	L	0-1	0-0		Parkes	Walford	Parris	Hilton	Martin	Devonshire	Orr	McAvennie	Dickens*	Cottee	Pike	Ince
	3/1	*41,286*	*3*	34			*McMahon 84*	*Grobbelaar*	*Gillespie*	*Beglin*	*Lawrenson*	*Whelan*	*Hansen*	*Walsh*	*Johnston*	*Rush*	*Molby*	*McMahon*	
							Ref: M Peck	Liverpool press from the start, but never lose their patience in the face of resolute defending. Phil Parkes touched Molby's free-kick onto a post and then saved when Paul Walsh was put clear. With time running out Steve McMahon seized on Ian Rush's header to drive in the winner.											
25	A COVENTRY		9	W	3-1	2-0	Cottee 15, 45, 58	Parkes	Walford	Parris	Hilton	Martin	Devonshire	Ward	McAvennie	Dickens	Cottee	**Robson**	
	24/1	*14,191*	*8*	37			*Borrows 87p*	*Ogrizovic*	*Borrows*	*Downs*	*Emerson*	*Kilcline**	*Peake*	*McGrath*	*Houchen*	*Regis*	*Gynn*	*Phillips*	*Painter*
							Ref: D Allison	Cottee bags his third hat-trick of the season and Italian clubs are said to be queuing for his signature. West Ham have now done the double over Coventry for four seasons in a row. Cottee has helped himself to 10 goals. Stewart Robson, a £700,000 buy from Arsenal, has a fine debut.											
26	H OXFORD		9	L	0-1	0-1		Parkes	Stewart	Parris	Gale	Hilton	Devonshire	Ward	McAvennie	Dickens*	Cottee	Robson	Bonds
	7/2	15,220	*15*	37			*Leworthy 3*	*Hardwick*	*Langan*	*Dreyer*	*Trewick*	*Briggs*	*Caton*	*Houghton*	*Leworthy*	*Whitehurst*	*Hebberd*	*Brock*	
							Ref: K Baker	Maurice Evans' Oxford record their first away win in five months. Leworthy finds himself unopposed to score a quick goal, and thereafter much-maligned keeper Steve Hardwick – under even greater pressure now Peter Hucker has been signed from QPR – keeps Cottee at bay.											
27	A NOTT'M FOREST		9	D	1-1	0-1	Stewart 65p	Parkes	Stewart	Parris	Gale	Bonds	Walford	Ward	McAvennie	Pike	Cottee	Robson	
	14/2	*19,373*	*4*	38			*Birtles 42p*	*Sutton*	*Fleming*	*Williams*	*Walker*	*Fairclough*	*Bowyer*	*Carr*	*Webb*	*Clough*	*Birtles*	*Mills*	
							Ref: G Tyson	Forest extend their unbeaten run to seven, but their fans are fuming at the penalty which denied them a win. Fleming barely touched Parris, but the West Ham man went down and Ray Stewart levelled from the spot. Forest's own penalty – Robson fouling Webb – was no less dubious.											
28	A LUTON		13	L	1-2	1-1	Cottee 8	Parkes	Stewart	Walford*	Gale	Bonds	Dickens	Ward	McAvennie	Pike	Cottee	Robson	Ince
	28/2	*11,101*	*4*	38			*Nicholas 40, Grimes 70*	*Sealey*	*Johnston*	*Grimes*	*Nicholas*	*Foster*	*Donaghy*	*Hill*	*Stein B*	*Newell*	*Harford*	*Wilson*	
							Ref: B Hill	Luton are an unexpected fourth, five points behind leaders Everton. They have lost just once at home, and when Cottee turns in McAvennie's centre it is only the eighth goal conceded at Kenilworth Road. Luton turn the screw following Peter Nicholas's equaliser from 25 yards.											
29	A CHARLTON		14	L	1-2	0-1	Robson 68	Parkes	Stewart	Walford	Gale	Bonds	Dickens	Ward	McAvennie*	Pike	Cottee	Robson	Parris
	7/3	***10,100***	*18*	38			*Melrose 5, 47*	*Bolder*	*Humphrey*	*Reid*	*Peake*	*Thompson*	*Miller*	*Bennett**	*Lee*	*Melrose*	*Shipley*	*Walsh*	*Stuart*
							Ref: P Don	Charlton's first league win of 1987 is achieved against a West Ham defence which plays like strangers. Charlton were helped by an early goal, when Robert Lee eluded Walford to cross for Melrose's glancing header. Three Charlton players lined up for Melrose's cross for No 2.											
30	H NORWICH		14	L	0-2	0-1		Parkes	Stewart	Parris	Gale	Bonds	Dickens	**Brady**	Ince	Pike*	Cottee	Robson	Keen
	14/3	21,531	5	38			*Bruce 2, Drinkell 89*	*Gunn*	*Brown*	*Spearing*	*Bruce*	*Phelan*	*Butterworth*	*Crook*	*Drinkell*	*Rosario*	*Putney*	*Gordon*	
							Ref: M Bailey	31-year-old Liam Brady signs for West Ham instead of Celtic for a nominal fee. His arrival boosts the gate but is unable to prevent a fourth successive defeat. Norwich played slick football, in the mould of West Ham. Kevin Drinkell's neat right-footer sealed the points near the end.											
31	A CHELSEA		15	L	0-1	0-1		Parkes	Stewart	Parris	Gale	**Strodder**	Brady	Ward	McAvennie	Pike	Cottee	Robson	
	21/3	*25,386*	*20*	38			*Nevin 20*	*Godden*	*Clarke*	*Dublin*	*Wicks*	*McLaughlin*	*Wood*	*Nevin*	*Hazard*	*Durie*	*West*	*Jones**	*Dixon*
							Ref: J Key	Bottom of the table at Christmas, Chelsea have hauled themselves above West Ham. Hazard's rushed volley breaks kindly to Nevin. West Ham enjoyed much second-half possession, but threatened little. Cottee 'scored' through the side-netting, which was repaired by Chelsea's physio.											

No	H/A	Opponent / Date	Att	Pos	Res	Pts	F-A	H-T	Scorers, Times, and Referees	1	2	3	4	5	6	7	8	9	10	11	12
32	H	SHEFFIELD WED		15	L		0-2	0-1		Parkes	Stewart*	Parris	Gale	Strodder	Brady	Ward	McAvennie !	Dickens	Cottee	Robson	Keen
		24/3	**13,514**	*14*		38			*Chapman 6, Shutt 58*	*Hodge*	*Sterland*	*Snodin*	*Smith !*	*Madden*	*Worthington*	*Marwood*	*Megson*	*Chapman*	*Shutt**	*Shelton*	*Hirst*
									Ref: J Ashworth	Upton Park sees its lowest gate of the season as despondency sets in. The Hammers' sixth successive defeat was made worse by the expulsion of McAvennie for a reckless lunge at Smith, who retaliated and was also sent off. Lee Chapman found himself unmarked for the early goal.											
33	H	WATFORD		15	W		1-0	0-0	Parris 90	Parkes	Bonds	**McQueen**	Gale	Strodder	Brady	Ward	McAvennie	Parris	Cottee	Robson*	Dickens
		28/3	16,485	*10*		41				*Coton*	*Gibbs*	*Rostron*	*Richardson*	*Sims*	*McClelland*	*Bardsley*	*Blissett*	*Falco*	*Jackett*	*Porter*	
									Ref: I Borrett	Tommy McQueen is the third new boy, following the arrival of Brady and Strodder. Parris is shunted from left-back to midfield. He asks the referee how long is left, is told one minute, and lets fly. It brings West Ham's first win since 1 January and first clean sheet since November.											
34	H	ARSENAL		14	W		3-1	1-1	Cottee 4p, 56, Brady 79	McAlister	Bonds	McQueen	Gale	Strodder	Brady	Ward	Dickens	Parris	Cottee	Robson	
		8/4	26,174	*4*		44			*Hayes 12p*	*Wilmot*	*Anderson*	*Thomas*	*O'Leary*	*Adams*	*Williams*	*Rocastle*	*Davis*	*Groves*	*Nicholas*	*Hayes**	*Rix*
									Ref: D Hedges	Arsenal have won the Littlewoods Cup. Hayes' penalty was twice-taken, after Parris fouled Rocastle. The second half is delayed due to crowd trouble – the players led from the pitch. The trouble was exacerbated by Brady's inflammatory gesture following his goal. He was cautioned.											
35	A	EVERTON		14	L		**0-4**	0-4	*[Watson 39]*	McAlister	Bonds	McQueen	Gale*	Strodder	Brady	Pike	Dickens	Parris	Cottee	Robson	Orr
		11/4	*35,731*	*1*		44			*Clarke 20, Reid 25, Stevens 33,*	*Southall*	*Stevens*	*Power*	*Ratcliffe*	*Watson*	*Reid*	*Steven*	*Heath*	*Clarke*	*Harper*	*Sheedy*	
									Ref: D Hutchinson	West Ham's injury-ravaged team are no match for Kendall's champions-elect. The Hammers were growing in confidence, being on level terms after 20 minutes, but Wayne Clarke scores off a post and Reid bends a 20-yarder. Before they know it West Ham are 0-4 down by half-time.											
36	H	MANCHESTER U		14	D		0-0	0-0		McAlister	Parris	McQueen	Bonds	Strodder	Brady	Ward	McAvennie	Dickens	Cottee	Robson	
		14/4	23,486	*11*		45				*Walsh*	*Duxbury*	*Gibson C*	*Moses*	*McGrath*	*Moran*	*Robson**	*Strachan*	*Stapleton*	*Gibson T*	*Davenport*	*Albiston*
									Ref: J Martin	This was a frantic encounter for the first hour, but as it dawned on the players that no one was going to score it fizzled out. Four players were booked, including both Robsons – Bryan and Stewart. Bryan Robson eventually limped off, slowed by Dickens' crunching tackle early on.											
37	A	LEICESTER		14	L		0-2	0-0		McAlister	Bonds	McQueen	Gale	Strodder	Brady	Ward	McAvennie	Parris*	Cottee	Robson	Dickens
		18/4	*10,434*	*10*		45			*Smith 50, O'Neil 75*	*Andrews*	*Morgan*	*Venus*	*Osman*	*O'Neill*	*McAllister*	*Russell**	*Mauchlen*	*Smith*	*Ramsey*	*Wilson*	*Buckley*
									Ref: B Nixon	Leicester are one of those struggling teams desperate to drag West Ham further into the mire. Alan Smith's goals will later see him transferred to Arsenal, and his effort five minutes after half-time does wonders for Leicester's confidence. But they fail to win another match and go down.											
38	H	TOTTENHAM		14	W		2-1	1-0	McAvennie 43, Cottee 63p	McAlister	Bonds	McQueen	Gale	Strodder	Devonshire	Ward	McAvennie	Brady	Cottee	Robson	
		20/4	23,972	*3*		48			*Allen C 59*	*Clemence*	*Hughton*	*Thomas M*	*Hodge*	*Gough*	*Polston*	*Allen C*	*Allen P*	*Waddle*	*Hoddle*	*Galvin**	*Claesen*
									Ref: J Deakin	Spurs have thrashed West Ham twice this season, so revenge is sweet, especially as it ends Spurs' hopes of the championship. Not that the win was uncontested. Following Clive Allen's 47th goal of this extraordinary season Robson appeared to run straight into Richard Gough. Penalty!											
39	A	ASTON VILLA		14	L		**0-4**	0-2		McAlister	Bonds*	McQueen	Gale	Strodder	Devonshire	Ward	McAvennie	Brady	Cottee	Robson	Dickens
		25/4	*13,584*	*21*		48			*Hunt 15, Aspinall 35, 56, Stainrod 57*	*Poole*	*Williams*	*Dorigo*	*Keown*	*Elliott*	*Stainrod*	*Birch*	*Aspinall*	*Gray*	*Hunt*	*Daley**	*Walters*
									Ref: J Lloyd	Doomed Villa record their biggest win in two years. Robson should have scored at 0-0 but was dispossessed by Steve Hunt, who scored when Tom McAlister fumbled a corner. Warren Aspinall's goal was his first for Villa. West Ham have now conceded four or more goals six times.											
40	H	NEWCASTLE		15	D		1-1	0-1	Ward 84	McAlister	Potts	McQueen*	Bonds	Strodder	Ince	Ward	McAvennie	Dickens	Cottee	Robson	Keen
		2/5	17,844	*17*		49			*McDonald 7p*	*Thomas M*	*McDonald*	*Wharton*	*Jackson P*	*Roeder*	*McCreery*	*Jackson D*	*Gascoigne*	*Goddard*	*Cunningham*	*Anderson**	*Thomas A*
									Ref: M James	Newcastle were bottom in early March, but have now taken 25 points from 12 games. Paul Goddard can't stop scoring for the Magpies, though he fires blanks against his former club. Newcastle's winning run also coincided with the return of young Gascoigne, to link up with Beardsley.											
41	A	SOUTHAMPTON		16	L		0-1	0-0		McAlister	Bonds	McQueen	Potts	Strodder	Ince	Ward	McAvennie	Brady	Cottee	Robson	
		4/5	*16,810*	*13*		49			*Clarke 81*	*Flowers*	*Forrest*	*Armstrong*	*Case*	*Wright*	*Bond*	*Lawrence**	*Cockerill*	*Clarke*	*Hobson*	*Le Tissier*	*Maskell*
									Ref: M Reed	Yet another defeat, this time brought about by Northern Ireland's World Cup striker Colin Clarke, who headed his 22nd goal from David Armstrong's left-wing cross. Clarke had earlier hit a post from three yards out. At the death Cottee shrugged off Kevin Bond but shot wide.											
42	H	MANCHESTER C		15	W		2-0	1-0	Cottee 34, Brady 51	McAlister	Potts	Orr	Keen	Strodder	Brady	Ward*	McAvennie	Robson	Cottee	Ince	**Dolan**
		9/5	18,413	*21*		52				*Nixon*	*Clements*	*Wilson*	*Redmond*	*McCarthy**	*Langley*	*May*	*McNab*	*Moulden*	*Stewart*	*Simpson*	*White*
		Home	Away						Ref: B Stevens	Tony Cottee has handed in a transfer request. He deflects Ward's shot past Nixon for his 29th goal of the season. City would have been relegated even had they won, which did not look likely. Eamonn Dolan makes his debut as a sub, having scored 21 goals for the reserves.											
Average		20,545	22,121																		

Littlewoods Cup					F-A	H-T	Scorers, Times, and Referees	1	2	3	4	5	6	7	8	9	10	11	12 sub used
2:1	A	PRESTON	4	D	1-1	1-0	Ward 34	Parkes	Stewart	Parris	Gale	Martin	Walford	Ward	McAvennie	Pike	Cottee	Orr	
23/9		*13,153*	*4:2*				*Allardyce 62*	*Brown*	*Bulmer*	*McAteer*	*Atkins*	*Jones*	*Allardyce*	*Williams*	*Clark*	*Thomas*	*Hildersley*	*Brazil*	
							Ref: T Mills	Preston, from the soccer basement, dictated play from the start. Ward's breakaway goal, following an exchange of passes with McAvennie, prompted West Ham to fall back to protect their lead. Allardyce's header from Hildersley's cross was the least that Preston deserved.											
2:2	H	PRESTON	8	W	4-1	1-1	Cottee 12, 75, 84, Dickens 59	Parkes	Stewart	Parris	Keen	Hilton	Walford	Ward	McAvennie	Dickens*	Cottee	Orr	Bonds
7/10		12,742	*4:7*				*Williams 27*	*Kelly*	*McNeil*	*Bennett*	*Chapman**	*Jones*	*Atkins*	*Williams*	*McAteer*	*Thomas^*	*Hildersley*	*Brazil*	*Saunders/Allatt*
							Ref: V Callow (Hammers win 5-2 on aggregate)	The first goal of Cottee's hat-trick came when Kelly failed to hold Stewart's shot. Williams' equaliser looked ominous until Alan Dickens' header restored the lead, McAvennie nodding across goal. Five minutes from time Billy Bonds comes on, having been out for more than a year.											
3	A	WATFORD	8	W	3-2	1-0	Goddard 12, Dickens 52, Ward 61	Parkes	Stewart	Parris	Gale	Hilton*	Devonshire	Ward	Goddard	Dickens	Cottee	Orr	Walford
29/10		*17,523*	*17*				*Jackett 48p, Bardsley 83*	*Sherwood*	*Bardsley*	*Rostron*	*Richardson*	*Terry*	*McClelland*	*Sterling*	*Sinnott*	*Allen*	*Jackett*	*Barnes*	
							Ref: J Bray	A thrilling cup-tie. Paul Goddard's ferocious opener was neutralised from the spot when Tony Gale held down McClelland. Dickens restored the lead with a slow-motion shot. After Bardsley's diving header made it 3-2, John Barnes missed a glorious chance to earn Watford a replay.											
4	H	OXFORD	5	W	1-0	0-0	Cottee 81p	Parkes	Walford*	Parris	Gale	Hilton	Devonshire	Ward	McAvennie	Dickens	Cottee	Keen	Bonds
18/11		20,530	*11*					*Hardwick*	*Langan*	*Slatter*	*Phillips !*	*Briggs**	*Shotton*	*Houghton*	*Aldridge*	*Leworthy*	*Reck*	*Brock*	*Dreyer*
							Ref: H Taylor	The Milk Cup holders don't go out without a fight. Four Oxford players are booked and Phillips' second yellow card sees him sent off for dissent. Shotton felled McAvennie in the box for the crucial penalty, described by Maurice Evans as a 'total joke'. Brock hit Parkes' crossbar.											
QF	H	TOTTENHAM	9	D	1-1	0-1	Cottee 48	Parkes	Walford	Parris	Hilton	Martin	Devonshire	Ward	McAvennie	Dickens	Cottee	Robson	
27/1		29,477	*5*				*Allen C 39*	*Clemence*	*Thomas D*	*Thomas M*	*Ardiles*	*Gough*	*Mabbutt*	*Allen C*	*Allen P*	*Waddle*	*Hoddle*	*Galvin*	
							Ref: B Stevens	Spurs were no less superior than when winning 4-0 on Boxing Day. Clive Allen turned in cousin Paul Allen's cross, but missed a string of easier chances. West Ham's equaliser was unexpected and fluky. Danny Thomas blocked Dickens' run, but the ball flew in off Cottee's knee.											
QF R	A	TOTTENHAM	9	L	0-5	0-1		Parkes	Bonds	Parris*	Gale	Martin	Devonshire	Ward	McAvennie	Orr	Cottee	Robson	Hilton
2/2		*41,995*	*5*				*Cl'sen 5, Hoddle 71, Allen C 80,86p, 89*	*Clemence*	*Thomas D*	*Thomas M*	*Ardiles*	*Gough*	*Mabbutt*	*Allen C*	*Allen P*	*Waddle*	*Hoddle*	*Claesen*	
							Ref: V Callow	Billy Bonds' first start in 18 months cannot prevent another thrashing by David Pleat's Spurs. The nightmare began early, when Ardiles on the halfway line sent Claeson through. Clive Allen's late hat-trick included one penalty, when Martin felled Paul Allen. Spurs now meet Arsenal.											

FA Cup																			
3	A	ORIENT	10	D	1-1	1-0	Hilton 31	Parkes	Walford	Parris	Hilton	Martin	Devonshire	Ward	McAvennie	Ince	Cottee	Pike	
10/1		*19,225*	*4:21*				*Castle 90p*	*Wells*	*Cornwell*	*Dickenson*	*Foster*	*Hales**	*Cunningham*	*Castle*	*Brooks*	*Jones*	*Godfrey**	*John*	*Comfort*
							Ref: N Midgley	The Public Address System echoes to the *Eastenders* theme. Frank Clark's Orient are 79 league places below West Ham and have lost their last three home games. Hilton's header from Ward's free-kick looked to have brought victory, until Steve Castle converts his first ever penalty.											
3R	H	ORIENT	9	W	4-1	1-0	P'rris 27, Keen 79, McAv' 81, C'tee 90	Parkes	Walford*	Parris	Hilton	Gale	Keen	Dickens	McAvennie	Dickens	Cottee	Orr	Bonds
31/1		19,424	*4:19*				*Brooks 57*	*Wells*	*Cornwell*	*Dickenson*	*Foster*	*Hales*	*Cunningham**	*Castle*	*Brooks*	*Jones*	*Godfrey*	*John*	*Comfort*
							Ref: R Milford	Dickenson levelled for Orient, only for the referee to give them a free-kick instead, which Brooks blasts in from 25 yards. Parkes then makes a flying save from Jones. It took the arrival of Billy Bonds to turn the tie. Wells parried from Cottee and Kevin Keen turned in the loose ball.											
4	H	SHEFFIELD UTD	9	W	4-0	1-0	McAvennie 18, 54, Robson 52, Gale 67	Parkes	Bonds	Parris	Gale	Stewart	Devonshire*	Ward	McAvennie	Pike	Cottee	Robson	Keen
9/2		17,194	*2:13*					*Burridge*	*Wilder*	*Pike*	*Arnott*	*Stancliffe*	*Barnsley*	*Smith*	*Foley*	*Withe*	*Daws**	*Beagrie*	*Dempsey*
							Ref: D Hedges	The winners know they face Sheffield Wednesday in Round 5, which is a perfect incentive for the Blades. It was an untidy cup-tie. John Burridge entertained Upton Park with his warm-up routine, and entertained them again when spilling Cottee's cross for Robson to make it 2-0.											

No	Date	Venue	Opponent	Att	Pos	Res	F-A	H-T	Scorers, Times, and Referees	1	2	3	4	5	6	7	8	9	10	11	12 sub used
5		A	SHEFFIELD WED		9	D	1-1	1-1	McAvennie 10	Parkes	Stewart	Parris	Gale	Bonds	Walford	Ward	McAvennie	Pike	Cottee	Robson	
	21/2			*30,257*	*14*				*Shelton 40*	*Hodge*	*Sterland**	*Snodin*	*Smith*	*Madden*	*Worthington*	*Marwood*	*Megson*	*Bradshaw*	*Hirst^*	*Shelton*	*Morris/Shutt*
									Ref: H Taylor	Bonds was a pro before his opponent David Hirst was born. Wednesday preserve their 14-year unbeaten home record in the FA Cup through a four-man move finished by Shelton. Fortune had earlier smiled on West Ham. Cottee's shot turned into a cross which went in off McAvennie.											
5R		H	SHEFFIELD WED		9	L	0-2	0-2		Parkes	Stewart	Parris*	Gale	Bonds	Devonshire	Ward	McAvennie	Pike	Cottee	Robson	Dickens
	25/2			30,257	*14*				*Chapman 34, Bradshaw 43*	*Hodge*	*Sterland**	*Snodin*	*Smith*	*Madden*	*Worthington*	*Marwood*	*Megson*	*Chapman*	*Bradshaw^*	*Shelton*	*M'ris/Chamb'lain*
									Ref: H Taylor	Wednesday had won away from home only twice all season. Lee Chapman returns from suspension and turns the ball in from Marwood's corner. Gale and Bonds left the ball to each other, allowing Bradshaw to add a second. The Owls also beat West Ham in the FA Cup last year.											

		Home						Away					
		P	W	D	L	F	A	W	D	L	F	A	Pts
1	Everton	42	16	4	1	49	11	10	4	7	27	20	86
2	Liverpool	42	15	3	3	43	16	8	5	8	29	26	77
3	Tottenham	42	14	3	4	40	14	7	5	9	28	29	71
4	Arsenal	42	12	5	4	31	12	8	5	8	27	23	70
5	Norwich	42	9	10	2	27	20	8	7	6	26	31	68
6	Wimbledon	42	11	5	5	32	22	8	4	9	25	28	66
7	Luton	42	14	5	2	29	13	4	7	10	18	32	66
8	Nott'm Forest	42	12	8	1	36	14	6	3	12	28	37	65
9	Watford	42	12	5	4	38	20	6	4	11	29	34	63
10	Coventry	42	14	4	3	35	17	3	8	10	15	28	63
11	Manchester U	42	13	3	5	38	18	1	11	9	14	27	56
12	Southampton	42	11	5	5	44	24	3	5	13	25	44	52
13	Sheffield Wed	42	9	7	5	39	24	4	6	11	19	35	52
14	Chelsea	42	8	6	7	30	30	5	7	9	23	34	52
15	WEST HAM	42	10	4	7	33	28	4	6	11	19	39	52
16	QP Rangers	42	9	7	5	31	27	4	4	13	17	37	50
17	Newcastle	42	10	4	7	33	29	2	7	12	14	36	47
18	Oxford	42	8	8	5	30	25	3	5	13	14	44	46
19	Charlton*	42	7	7	7	26	22	4	4	13	19	33	44
20	Leicester	42	9	7	5	39	24	2	2	17	15	52	42
21	Manchester C	42	8	6	7	28	24	0	9	12	8	33	39
22	Aston Villa	42	7	7	7	25	25	1	5	15	20	54	36
		924	238	123	101	756	459	101	123	238	459	756	1263

* stay up after play-offs

Odds & ends

Double wins: (1) Coventry.
Double losses: (2) Liverpool, Charlton.

Won from behind: (1) Chelsea (h).
Lost from in front: (4) Forest (h), Liverpool (h), Wimbledon (h), Luton (a).

High spots: Winning the first two league games.
Six unbeaten league games from 13 September, up to 5th.

Low spots: Five successive league defeats from 28 February.
Anti-climactic season after finishing 3rd one year earlier.

Hammer of the Year: Billy Bonds.
Ever-presents: (1) Tony Cottee.
Hat-tricks: (3) Tony Cottee (3).
Leading scorer: (28) Tony Cottee.

	Appearances						Goals			
	Lge	*Sub*	LC	*Sub*	FAC	*Sub*	Lge	LC	FAC	Tot
Bonds, Billy	**13**	*4*	1	*2*	3	*1*				
Brady, Liam	**12**						**2**			**2**
Cottee, Tony	**42**		6		5		**22**	5	1	**28**
Devonshire, Alan	**20**		4		3		**2**			**2**
Dickens, Alan	**31**	*5*	4		2	*1*	**3**	2		**5**
Dolan, Eamonn		*1*								
Gale, Tony	**32**		4		4		**2**		1	**3**
Goddard, Paul	**3**	*1*	1				**1**	1		**2**
Hilton, Paul	**15**	*1*	4	*1*	2		**1**		1	**2**
Ince, Paul	**7**	*3*			1		**1**			**1**
Keen, Kevin	**7**	*6*	2		1	*1*			1	**1**
McAlister, Tom	**9**									
McAvennie, Frank	**36**		5		4		**7**		4	**11**
McQueen, Tom	**9**									
Martin, Alvin	**16**		3		1		**2**			**2**
Orr, Neil	**21**	*1*	4		1		**1**			**1**
Parkes, Phil	**33**		6		5					
Parris, George	**35**	*1*	6		5		**1**		1	**2**
Pike, Geoff	**10**	*1*	1		4					
Potts, Steve	**8**									
Robson, Stewart	**18**		2		3		**2**		1	**3**
Stewart, Ray	**23**		3		3		**4**			**4**
Strodder, Gary	**12**									
Walford, Steve	**13**	*1*	4	*1*	3					
Ward, Mark	**37**		6		5		**1**	2		**3**
25 players used	**462**	***25***	**66**	***4***	**55**	***3***	**52**	**10**	**10**	**72**

BARCLAYS LEAGUE DIVISION 1 Manager: John Lyall SEASON 1987-88

No	Date		Att	Pos	Pt	F-A	H-T	Scorers, Times, and Referees	1	2	3	4	5	6	7	8	9	10	11	subs used
1	H	QP RANGERS			L	0-3	0-3		McAlister	Stewart^	McQueen	Orr	Martin	Devonshire*	Ward	McAvennie	Brady	Cottee	Robson	Dickens/Strodder
	15/8		22,881		0			*St'wart 13(og), Bannister 38, Brock 44*	*Seaman*	*Fereday*	*Dennis*	*Parker*	*McDonald*	*Fenwick*	*Allen*	*Byrne*	*Coney*	*Bannister*	*Brock*	
								Ref: M Peck	QPR boss Jim Smith has spent £1 million of chairman David Bulstrode's money on four new players. Ray Stewart headed Fereday's cross into his own net. Fereday's cross provided No 2 and Brock's 25-yarder a third before half-time. Paul Parker tracked Tony Cottee wherever he went.											
2	A	LUTON		18	D	2-2	2-1	Brady 20, Stewart 30p	McAlister	Stewart	McQueen	Strodder	Martin	Brady	Ward	McAvennie	Ince	Cottee	Robson	
	22/8		*18,073*		1			*Harford 5, 51*	*Sealey*	*Breacker*	*Grimes*	*Hill*	*Foster*	*McDonough*	*Wilson D*	*Wilson R**	*Harford*	*Newell*	*Preece*	*Nwajiobi*
								Ref: J Martin	Both teams score their first goals and pick up their first point. Mick Harford headed in Tim Breacker's cross. Brady levelled on the volley after Sealey parried from McAvennie. McDonough whipped away Cottee's legs for the penalty. When Ricky Hill hit the bar, Harford made it 2-2.											
3	H	NORWICH		14	W	2-0	0-0	Cottee 51, 65	McAlister	Stewart	McQueen	Strodder	Martin	Brady	Ward	McAvennie	Ince	Cottee	Robson	
	29/8		16,394	*17*	4				*Gunn*	*Culverhouse*	*Spearing*	*Bruce*	*Phelan*	*Butterworth*	*Fox*	*Drinkell*	*Biggins*	*Crook*	*Bowen**	*Gordon*
								Ref: M Reed	West Ham are on song and Norwich take it on the chin. Cottee looked sharp throughout, prompting suggestions that England manager Bobby Robson must be considering him. Ward set up Cottee's first-time opener. Stewart's whipped cross was then met with a spectacular volley.											
4	A	PORTSMOUTH		14	L	1-2	1-1	Strodder 11	McAlister	Stewart*	McQueen	Strodder	Martin	Brady	Ward	McAvennie	Ince	Cottee	Robson	Parris
	31/8		*16,104*	*20*	4			*Dillon 15p, 69*	*Knight*	*Swain*	*Horne*	*Dillon*	*Shotton*	*Gilbert*	*Fillery*	*Kennedy*	*Baird*	*Mariner*	*Hilaire*	
								Ref: J Deakin	Winless Pompey have just been crushed 0-6 by Arsenal. Strodder heads his first goal for West Ham since his £100,000 transfer from Lincoln. McAlister felled Vince Hilaire for Pompey's equalising penalty. Dillon's second goal, from Fillery's cross, won the match for Portsmouth.											
5	H	LIVERPOOL		15	D	1-1	0-0	Cottee 73	McAlister	Stewart	McQueen*	Strodder	Martin	Brady	Ward	McAvennie	Ince	Cottee	Robson	Parris
	5/9		**29,865**	*9*	5			*Aldridge 51p*	*Grobbelaar*	*Gillespie*	*Venison*	*Nicol*	*Whelan*	*Hansen*	*Beardsley*	*Aldridge*	*Spackman*	*Barnes*	*McMahon*	
								Ref: A Gunn	A collapsed sewer at Anfield means Liverpool have yet to play at home. Dalglish has added Barnes and Beardsley to an already strong squad. Aldridge nets from the spot after Parris fells McMahon. Hansen's silly back-pass let in Cottee. Liverpool, on top throughout, hit the post twice.											
6	A	WIMBLEDON		16	D	1-1	0-1	Cottee 62	McAlister	Stewart	Parris	Strodder	Martin	Brady	Ward !	McAvennie	Ince	Cottee	Robson	
	12/9		*8,507*	*4*	6			*Wise 20*	*Beasant*	*Scales*	*Phelan*	*Ryan*	*Young**	*Thorn*	*Wise*	*Sayer^*	*Fashanu*	*Sanchez*	*Cork*	*Gayle/Gibson*
								Ref: A Buksh	10 minutes after scoring for the Dons, Dennis Wise gets involved with Mark Ward, who strikes Wise in the face and is shown the red card. 10-man West Ham should have had little chance to recover against obdurate opponents, but George Parris crosses for Cottee's headed equaliser.											
7	H	TOTTENHAM		18	L	0-1	0-1		McAlister	Stewart	Parris	Strodder*	Martin	Brady	Ward	McAvennie	Ince	Cottee	Robson	Hilton
	19/9		27,750	*2*	6			*Fairclough 38*	*Clemence*	*Stevens*	*Thomas*	*Gough*	*Fairclough*	*Moran^*	*Allen C**	*Allen P*	*Ardiles*	*Hodge*	*Claesen*	*Metgod/Samways*
								Ref: R Lewis	Spurs' boss David Pleat relishes the performance of 35-year-old Ardiles, who becomes so agitated that he is eventually booked. Fairclough's volley from Moran's cross is small reward for Spurs' first-half dominance. Fairclough's professional foul on Ince provoked a late free-for-all.											
8	A	ARSENAL		19	L	0-1	0-0		McAlister	Stewart	Parris	Strodder	Martin	Brady	Keen	McAvennie	Ince	Cottee	Robson	
	26/9		*40,127*	*7*	6			*Sansom 80*	*Lukic*	*Thomas*	*Sansom*	*Williams*	*O'Leary*	*Adams*	*Rocastle**	*Davis*	*Smith*	*Groves*	*Rix*	*Hayes*
								Ref: D Elleray	Liam Brady returns to Highbury for the first time since leaving for Italy seven years earlier. He is visibly choked and plays poorly. Afterwards he castigates George Graham's direct style, but admits it was effective. Full-back Sansom scores his first goal in two years, on his birthday.											
9	H	DERBY		17	D	1-1	1-0	Brady 24	McAlister	Stewart*	McQueen^	Strodder	Martin	Brady	Keen	Parris	Ince	Cottee	Robson	Hilton/**Slater**
	3/10		17,226	*12*	7			*Gee 63*	*Shilton*	*Sage*	*Forsyth*	*Williams*	*Wright*	*MacLaren*	*Callaghan*	*Gee*	*Davison*	*Gregory*	*Cross*	
								Ref: B Hill	Frank McAvennie has signed for Celtic for £800,000. West Ham deserved more for their first-half dominance than Liam Brady's blasted free-kick, touched to him by Robson. Phil Gee's simple equaliser left the Hammers hanging on desperately by the end. West Ham need a striker.											
10	H	CHARLTON		17	D	1-1	1-1	Ince 7	McAlister	Stewart	Parris	Keen	Martin	Brady	Ward	Dickens	Ince	Cottee	Robson	
	10/10		15,757	*21*	8			*Crooks 30*	*Bolder*	*Humphrey*	*Reid*	*Peake*	*Shirtliff*	*Thompson*	*Stuart*	*Lee*	*Jones*	*Campbell*	*Crooks*	
								Ref: R Groves	The search for a striker canvases the following names: Colin Clarke, Paul Walsh, Kerry Dixon, Mick Harford, Kevin Drinkell. Charlton are bottom, and looked up against it once Dickens made a quick goal for Ince. Steve Thompson's header was knocked over the line by Crooks.											

No Date	Venue	Opponent	Att	Pos	Res	F-A	H-T	Scorers, Times, and Referees	1	2	3	4	5	6	7	8	9	10	11	subs used
11	A	OXFORD		16	W	2-1	2-1	Caton 6 (og), Cottee 25	McAlister	Stewart	Parris	Dickens	Martin	Brady	Keen	Ward	Ince	Cottee	Robson	
17/10			9,092	10	11			*Saunders 34*	*Hucker*	*Bardsley*	*Dreyer*	*Shelton*	*Slatter*	*Caton*	*Houghton**	*Foyle^*	*Saunders*	*Phillips*	*Hebberd*	*Hill/Whitehurst*
								Ref: J Worrall	A great start, when Caton steers Mark Ward's cross into his own net. West Ham were helped again when Dreyer dives in rashly on Cottee, who cuts inside to score from a tight angle. But after Dean Saunders heads his first goal of the season it is all hands to the West Ham pump.											
12	H	MANCHESTER U		15	D	1-1	0-1	Stewart 68p	McAlister	Stewart	Parris	Keen	Martin	Brady	Ward	Dickens	Ince	Cottee	McQueen	
25/10			19,863	4	12			*Gibson 45*	*Walsh*	*Anderson*	*Gibson*	*McGrath*	*Moran*	*Duxbury*	*Robson*	*Strachan**	*McClair*	*Davenport*	*Olsen*	*Blackmore*
								Ref: B Stevens	This Sunday match failed to ignite, other than through Alex Ferguson's inflammatory post-match comments, suggesting that Stewart should have been sent off following a clash with Bryan Robson. Gibson's free-kick was deflected in. McGrath felled Ward for the disputed penalty.											
13	A	WATFORD		14	W	2-1	1-0	Dickens 15, Cottee 69	McAlister	Stewart	Parris	Keen	Martin	Brady	Ward	Dickens	Ince	Cottee	Robson	
31/10			14,427	20	15			*Allen 89*	*Coton*	*Gibbs*	*Rostron*	*Jackett*	*Morris*	*McClelland*	*Agana**	*Allen*	*Senior*	*Porter*	*Hodges*	*Sherwood*
								Ref: P Don	Dave Bassett's Watford slump to their fifth successive league defeat, though they had trounced Darlington 8-0 in the Littlewoods Cup. Dickens' header from Keen's centre went in off a post. Ince then set up Cottee. Allen's late reply was Watford's first league goal in six games.											
14	H	SHEFFIELD WED		15	L	0-1	0-1		McAlister	Stewart	Parris	Keen*	Martin	Brady	Ward	Dickens	Ince	Cottee	Robson	Dolan
7/11			16,277	16	15			*Bradshaw 22*	*Hodge*	*Jacobs*	*Worthington*	*Pearson*	*Madden*	*Proctor*	*Chamberl'n**	*Megson*	*West*	*Bradshaw^*	*Galvin*	*Owen/Fee*
								Ref: K Cooper	'A thousand apologies,' says Ron Atkinson afterwards, as the Owls win their fourth successive game with their one and only shot on target. McAlister parried Galvin's volley but Bradshaw tapped in. This is Wednesday's third win at Upton Park in a year, following wins in both cups.											
15	A	EVERTON		15	L	1-3	0-3	Hilton 81	McAlister	Bonds	Parris*	Hilton	Martin^	Brady	Ward	Dickens	Ince	Cottee	Robson	Strodder/Keen
14/11			29,405	5	15			*Watson 34, Reid 37, Sharp 45*	*Southall*	*Stevens*	*v d Hauwe*	*Ratcliffe*	*Watson*	*Reid*	*Steven**	*Heath*	*Sharp*	*Snodin*	*Sheedy^*	*Harper/Wilson*
								Ref: R Milford	Everton's Sharp is just the sort of target man Lyall covets, but of course he is unavailable. Colin Harvey's defending champions won as they pleased after Dave Watson headed Sheedy's free-kick in off a post. Bonds marked his first game of the season with a back-pass to Peter Reid.											
16	H	NOTT'M FOREST		13	W	3-2	1-1	Cottee 13, 52, Stewart 50p	McAlister	Bonds	Parris	Hilton	Stewart	Keen	Ward	Dickens	Ince	Cottee	Robson	
21/11			17,216	4	18			*Webb 32, Clough 70*	*Sutton*	*Chettle*	*Pearce*	*Walker*	*Foster*	*Wilson*	*Carr**	*Webb*	*Clough*	*Wilkinson^*	*Rice*	*Starbuck/Gaynor*
								Ref: G Courtney	Forest were unbeaten in the league in two months before this jewel of a match. Stewart's penalty had to be retaken as Sutton moved too soon. Cottee's second goal, a Brazilian-style scissors-kick volley, had the crowd in raptures. Referee Courtney said 'it was a pleasure to be involved.'											
17	A	COVENTRY		14	D	0-0	0-0		McAlister	Bonds	Parris	Hilton	Stewart	Keen	Ward	Dickens	Ince	Cottee	Robson	
28/11			16,740	15	19				*Ogrizovic*	*Borrows*	*Pickering*	*Emerson*	*Smith K*	*Downs*	*Bennett*	*Phillips*	*Houchen*	*Speedie*	*Gynn*	
								Ref: R Nixon	England manager Bobby Robson runs his eye over Tony Cottee, who had scored eight goals in five previous matches on this lucky ground. This time he was repeatedly denied by Ogrizovic. Stewart's professional foul on Houchen earned a yellow card. Today it would have been red.											
18	H	SOUTHAMPTON		11	W	2-1	1-1	Keen 13, Dickens 75	McAlister	Bonds	Parris	Strodder	Stewart	Keen	Ward !	Dickens	Ince	Cottee	Robson	
5/12			**14,975**	10	22			*Wallace D 42*	*Burridge*	*Forrest*	*Statham*	*Case*	*Moore*	*Bond*	*Townsend*	*Cockerill*	*Clarke*	*Baker G*	*Wallace D*	
								Ref: R Hamer	Mark Ward is sent off for the second time this season. His first yellow card was for dissent, his second in injury-time for not retreating 10 yards at a free-kick. West Ham won through Keen's first league goal and Dickens' neat effort, which erased memories of Robson's awful back-pass.											
19	A	CHELSEA		12	D	1-1	1-0	Parris 26	McAlister	Bonds	Parris	Strodder	Stewart	Keen	Ward	Dickens	Hilton	Cottee	Robson	
12/12			22,850	7	23			*Wilson K 83*	*Freestone*	*Clarke*	*Dorigo*	*Pates*	*McLaughlin*	*Wood*	*Nevin**	*Hazard*	*Dixon*	*Wilson K*	*Wilson C*	*Wegerle*
								Ref: D Hedges	Pre-match drama when Paul Ince collapses watching TV and is rushed to hospital. John Hollins' Chelsea maintain their unbeaten home record when Kevin Wilson – deputising for the injured Durie – scores his first ever Chelsea goal. West Ham have now lost just two out of 11 games.											
20	H	NEWCASTLE		10	W	2-1	0-0	Robson 47, Ince 82	McAlister	Bonds*	Parris	Strodder	Stewart	Keen	Brady	Dickens	Ince	Cottee	Robson	Hilton
19/12			18,679	14	26			*Mirandhina 78*	*Kelly*	*Anderson*	*Tinnion**	*McCreery*	*Jackson P^*	*Roeder*	*McDonald*	*Gascoigne*	*Goddard*	*Mirandhina*	*Cornwell*	*Jackson D*
								Ref: P Vanes	What a battle between 41-year-old Bonds and whipper-snapper Gascoigne, who says Bonds kept saying 'calm down'. Brady set up Robson's goal, which was cancelled out by the Brazilian Mirandhina's fifth goal in six games. Ince won the match with a 25-yarder into the top corner.											
21	H	WIMBLEDON		10	L	1-2	0-2	Stewart 58p	McAlister	Bonds	Parris*	Strodder	Stewart	Keen	Ward	Dickens^	Ince	Cottee	Robson	Hilton/Brady
26/12			18,605	7	26			*Sanchez 15, Fashanu 45*	*Beasant*	*Goodyear*	*Scales*	*Jones*	*Young*	*Thorn*	*Fairweather*	*Cork**	*Fashanu*	*Sanchez*	*Wise*	*Turner*
								Ref: A Gunn	Vinnie Jones is booked inside four seconds for a foul on Ince, but then shows his creative side by manufacturing both Dons' goals – Sanchez's side-footer and Fashanu's hook. When Wise and Robson tumbled in the box the ref gave a penalty but might have given a free-kick to Wise.											

No	Date		Att	Pos	Pt	F-A	H-T	Scorers, Times, and Referees	1	2	3	4	5	6	7	8	9	10	11	subs used
22	A	TOTTENHAM		13	L	1-2	0-1	Hilton 66	McAlister	Bonds	Parris	Hilton	Stewart	Keen	Ward*	Brady	Ince	Cottee	Robson	Strodder
	28/12		39,456	12	26			Waddle 31, Fairclough 70	Parks	Hughton	Thomas	Hodge	Fairclough	Stevens*	Moran^	Allen P	Waddle	Ardiles	Howells	Statham/Close
								Ref: J Martin	David Pleat has resigned. Spurs' second victory under new manager Terry Venables comes when Fairclough heads in Chris Waddle's cross. Earlier Waddle scored from a free-kick after Ray Stewart fouled Paul Moran, and Hilton levelled after a bout of head tennis with Tony Cottee.											
23	A	NORWICH		14	L	1-4	1-0	Cottee 27 [Rosario 85]	McAlister	Bonds	Parris	Hilton	Stewart	Keen^	Ward	Dickens	Ince*	Cottee	Robson	Gale/Dolan
	1/1		20,069	15	26			Gordon 47, Drinkell 67, Bowen 79,	Gunn	Culverhouse	Bowen	Putney	Phelan	Butterworth	Fox	Drinkell	Rosario	Gloss	Gordon	
								Ref: B Hill	The festive season continues to backfire as West Ham succumb to their third quick defeat and their heaviest of the season. Norwich started the season dreadfully, but despite selling Steve Bruce to Man U, have won all three holiday fixtures. They are poised to climb above West Ham.											
24	H	LUTON		14	D	1-1	0-0	Ince 60	McAlister	Bonds	Parris*	Strodder	Stewart	Potts	Ward	Gale	Hilton	Cottee	Robson	Ince
	2/1		16,716	8	27			Stein M 76	Sealey	Breacker	Johnson	McDonough	Foster	Donaghy	Wilson D	Stein B	Harford	Stein M	Allinson	
								Ref: P Foakes	The storm that burst before kick-off ruins the pitch. West Ham's dismal luck continues when they lose Parris with a broken ankle. Defender Hilton partners Cottee in attack and misses the chances that come his way. Ince's goal was half-saved. Harford headed down to Mark Stein.											
25	A	QP RANGERS		12	W	1-0	0-0	Dickens 75	McAlister	Stewart	McQueen	Bonds	Strodder	Gale	Ward	Brady	Dickens	Cottee	Robson	
	16/1		14,509	7	30				Johns	Dawes	Dennis	Parker	McDonald	Maguire	Allen	Falco	Bannister	Fereday*	Brock^	Byrne/Kerslake
								Ref: J Key	Potts and Ince were hurt in a car crash on their way to training at Basildon. West Ham won on the Omniturf pitch despite Falco hitting the underside of the bar and Bannister missing two sitters. Brady's precise pass let Dickens in on goal. The sides now meet again in the FA Cup.											
26	A	LIVERPOOL		14	D	0-0	0-0		McAlister	Stewart	Ince	Bonds	Strodder	Gale	Ward	Brady	Dickens*	Cottee	Robson	McQueen
	6/2		42,049	1	31				Grobbelaar	Ablett	Venison	Nicol	Spackman	Hansen	Beardsley	Aldridge*	Houghton	Barnes	McMahon	Johnston
								Ref: J McAulay	A 0-0 on the day that Luton beat Oxford 7-4 was never going to grab headlines, even though West Ham became the first team to avoid defeat at Anfield this season. McAlister was the star. Five players were booked, two from Liverpool, who had totted up only four cautions all season.											
27	H	PORTSMOUTH		13	D	1-1	0-0	Cottee 67	McAlister	Stewart	Ince	Bonds	Strodder	Gale	Ward	Brady	Dickens	Cottee	Robson	
	13/2		18,639	15	32			Connor 78	Knight	Whitehead	Hardyman	Dillon	Daish	Ball	Horne	Sandford*	Baird^	Connor	Hilaire	Kelly/Gilbert
								Ref: J Worrall	Alan Dickens sports two black eyes, donated by Liverpool players at Anfield. Cottee's 25-yarder, in off the bar, looked like earning three vital points. But McAlister left his goal-line to take Dillon's cross by the corner flag and the ball swerved behind him. It was touched in by Connor.											
28	A	DERBY		13	L	0-1	0-0		McAlister	Stewart	Ince	Bonds	Strodder	Gale	Ward	Brady*	Dickens^	Cottee	Robson	Keen/McQueen
	27/2		16,301	18	32			Callaghan 46	Shilton	Blades*	Forsyth	Williams	Wright	Hindmarch	McMinn^	Lewis	Gee	Gregory	Callaghan	MacLaren/Garner
								Ref: K Lupton	Only Brady stood out among the dross, but he caught his studs and was stretchered off after 39 minutes, his season over. Stodder fouled Gee in the box but McMinn's penalty hit a post. A headed goal gave Derby their first win since November. Lyall locks his team in the dressing room.											
29	H	OXFORD		13	D	1-1	0-0	Ward 71	McAlister	Stewart	McQueen	Bonds	Strodder	Gale	Ward	Keen	Ince*	Cottee	Robson	Dolan
	5/3		14,980	19	33			Phillips 69	Judge	Bardsley	Dreyer	Shelton	Briggs	Greenhall*	Whitehurst	Foyle	Saunders	Phillips	Hill	Rhoades-Brown
								Ref: R Milford	Lyall hopes to sign Kerry Dixon for £1.2 million, with Dickens going to Chelsea in part-exchange. Dickens is left out of the team. McAlister couldn't hold Phillips' effort, but West Ham levelled from Robson's long throw. Biggest cheer came when a fan thumped the ball into the net.											
30	A	CHARLTON		15	L	0-3	0-2		McAlister	Stewart	McQueen	Bonds	Strodder	Gale	Ward	Dickens*	Dolan	Cottee	Robson	Keen
	12/3		8,118	19	33			Crooks 29, 68, Stuart 31	Bolder	Humphrey	Reid	Mackenzie	Shirtliff	Miller	Stuart	Leaburn	Gritt	Lee	Crooks	
								Ref: J Martin	Dixon and Harford have both rejected moves to West Ham. Lowly Charlton won with embarrassing ease and Lyall wisely stays away from the press conference. Without injured Brady, West Ham were lacking in midfield. Charlton went 3-0 up when Crooks was left totally unmarked.											
31	H	WATFORD		15	W	1-0	0-0	Rosenior 61	McAlister	Stewart	Potts	Bonds	Strodder	Gale	Ward	Keen	**Rosenior**	Cottee	Robson*	Dickens
	19/3		16,051	21	36				Coton	Gibbs	Rostron	Sherwood	Terry	McClelland	Sterling	Allen*	Blissett	Porter	Jackett	Roberts
								Ref: R Lewis	Leroy Rosenior, who had rejected Watford, signs for £250,000 from Fulham and is an instant hit. He won his battle with Terry and also chased a long pass to score, earning West Ham their second win in 11 games. It might have been different had Watford taken any of their chances.											

No	Date	Opponent	Att	Pos	Res	F-A	H-T	Scorers, Times, and Referees	1	2	3	4	5	6	7	8	9	10	11	subs used
32	A	MANCHESTER U		15	L	1-3	0-0	Rosenior 81	McAlister	Stewart	Potts	Bonds	Strodder	Gale	Ward	Keen*	Rosenior	Cottee	Dickens	Parris
	26/3		*37,269*	*2*	36			*Strachan 58, Anderson 83, Robson 89*	*Turner*	*Anderson*	*Blackmore*	*Bruce*	*McGrath*	*Duxbury*	*Strachan*	*Robson**	*McClair*	*Davenport*	*Gibson*	*Olsen*
								Ref: G Ashby	Man U might be second, but Liverpool are so far out in front that the title is as good as theirs. Strachan orchestrated this win, scoring first by skipping round Stewart to net from 15 yards. West Ham's only grievance was the corner-kick which paved the way for Viv Anderson's goal.											
33	A	SHEFFIELD WED		15	L	1-2	0-1	Rosenior 65	McAlister	Stewart	**Dicks**	Bonds*	Strodder^	Gale	Ward	Parris	Rosenior	Cottee	Robson	Dickens/Potts
	2/4		*18,435*	*8*	36			*Hurst 37, Chamberlain 50*	*Pressman*	*Sterland*	*Worthington*	*Madden*	*Cranson*	*Proctor*	*Chamberl'n**	*Megson*	*Chapman*	*Hirst^*	*Jonsson*	*Bradshaw/Fee*
								Ref: B Hill	Julian Dicks makes his debut in this defeat, which saw Billy Bonds limp off at half-time with a wrenched knee. Leroy Rosenior scores his third goal in as many games, and late pressure almost earned West Ham a draw. Wednesday's third win in a row follows five straight defeats.											
34	H	EVERTON		17	D	0-0	0-0		McAlister	Stewart*	Dicks	Parris	Strodder	Gale	Ward	Dickens	Rosenior	Cottee	Robson	Ince
	4/4		21,195	*4*	37				*Southall*	*Stevens*	*Pointon*	*v d Hauwe*	*Mountfield*	*Reid*	*Steven*	*Clarke**	*Heath*	*Harper*	*Sheedy*	*Snodin*
								Ref: J Ashworth	Cottee sprinted out at Upton Park as if to endear himself to the club poised to sign him. West Ham were denied a win by the reflexes of Neville Southall, whose saves from Robson and Rosenior's header earned applause. Van den Hauwe's late back-header was disallowed for pushing.											
35	H	ARSENAL		17	L	0-1	0-0		Parkes	Potts*	Dicks	Bonds	Strodder	Gale	Ward	Parris	Rosenior	Cottee	Robson	Keen
	12/4		26,746	*6*	37			*Thomas 77*	*Lukic*	*Winterburn*	*Sansom*	*Thomas*	*Caesar*	*Adams*	*Rocastle*	*Davis*	*Smith*	*Merson*	*Richardson**	*Rix*
								Ref: R Gifford	Arsenal players are competing for places in the Littlewoods Cup final, and five bookings tells its own story. Mark Ward was the first, when he tried to kick Michael Thomas into the stand. Rocastle freed Thomas to score past Phil Parkes, who was playing his first game in over a year.											
36	A	NOTT'M FOREST		18	D	0-0	0-0		McAlister	Parris	Dicks	Bonds	Strodder	Gale	Ward	Dickens	Rosenior	Cottee	Robson	
	20/4		*15,775*	*5*	38				*Sutton*	*Fleming*	*Pearce*	*Chettle*	*Foster*	*Wilson*	*Crosby*	*Webb*	*Clough*	*Carr*	*Rice*	
								Ref: H King	Twice Cottee was clean through on Sutton, and twice he failed to capitalise. It is his ninth game without a goal, and West Ham could do with one. Forest exerted much pressure but created few chances. West Ham could have won it at the death, but Rosenior blazed over the crossbar.											
37	H	COVENTRY		16	D	1-1	0-0	Cottee 78	McAlister	Parris	Dicks	Keen^	Strodder	Gale	Ward	Dickens	Ince*	Cottee	Robson	Hilton/Slater
	23/4		17,733	*9*	39			*Regis 56*	*Ogrizovic*	*Borrows*	*Pickering*	*Sedgley*	*Kilcline*	*Peake*	*Emerson*	*Phillips*	*Regis*	*Speedie*	*Smith D*	
								Ref: M James	Lyall lost Bonds and Rosenior before kick-off. Ogrizovic's long punt sets up Regis's swivelling goal. Cottee's first goal in 10 games comes when Oggy and Peake get in a tizzy. Three super saves by McAlister earn a point that keeps West Ham one place above the play-off position.											
38	A	SOUTHAMPTON		18	L	1-2	0-0	Cottee 57	McAlister	Potts	Dicks	Bonds	Strodder	Gale	Ward	Dickens	Rosenior	Cottee	Parris	
	30/4		*15,652*	*11*	39			*Bond 72, 84*	*Burridge*	*Forrest*	*Statham*	*Case**	*Moore*	*Bond*	*Wallace R*	*Baker G*	*Clarke*	*Townsend*	*Shearer*	*Le Tissier*
								Ref: D Hedges	Saints end the season with a flourish, losing just once in their last eight games. West Ham could have done with less fired-up opponents, and lose to two late goals by central defender Kevin Bond, who had only scored once all season. Hammers now face a crisis match with Chelsea.											
39	H	CHELSEA		16	W	**4-1**	2-0	Rosenior 14, 36, Hilton 56, Cottee 89	McAlister	Parris	Dicks	Potts	Hilton	Gale	Ward	Dickens	Rosenior !	Cottee	Robson	
	2/5		28,521	*17*	42			*West 85*	*Digweed*	*Hall*	*Dorigo*	*Wicks*	*McLaughlin*	*Clarke*	*Nevin*	*Hazard**	*Dixon*	*Durie*	*Bumstead*	*West*
								Ref: D Scott	7th in December, Chelsea have collapsed with one win in 25 games. Two right-footed shots by Rosenior put West Ham in command, but he is later sent off for the first time ever for throttling Clarke. West Ham are safe as Chelsea must play Charlton. Both cannot overtake West Ham.											
40	A	NEWCASTLE		16	L	1-2	1-0	Robson 11	McAlister	Parris	Dicks	Potts	Hilton	Gale	Ward	Dickens	Rosenior	Cottee	Robson	
	7/5		*23,731*	*8*	42			*O'Neill 56, Dicks 67 (og)*	*Kelly*	*McDonald*	*Cornwell*	*McCreery*	*Anderson*	*Scott*	*Jackson D*	*Gascoigne*	*Goddard*	*O'Neill**	*Lormor*	*Bogie*
		Home	Away					Ref: K Walmsley	Nothing rides on this match, so Julian Dicks' embarrassment at scoring his first Hammers goal – at the wrong end – does not have tragic consequences. Chelsea's draw with Charlton means that all three clubs finish on 42 points. Chelsea lose the play-off final with Middlesbrough.											
Average		20,725	21,334																	

Littlewoods Cup					F-A	H-T	Scorers, Times, and Referees	1	2	3	4	5	6	7	8	9	10	11	subs used
2:1	A	BARNSLEY	18	D	0-0	0-0		McAlister	Potts*	Parris	Strodder	Martin	Brady	Ward	McAvennie	Ince	Cottee	Robson	McQueen
22/9			*10,330*	*2:4*				*Baker*	*Joyce*	*Cross*	*Thomas*	*Gray*	*Futcher*	*Wylde*	*Agnew*	*Lowndes*	*MacDonald*	*Clarke**	*Beresford*
							Ref: A Seville	Barnsley are just seven places below West Ham in the Football League, and there is no discernible gap in status. West Ham retreated for much of the time behind a five-man defence, with Ince sweeping up. Thomas hit McAllister's post. Manager Allan Clarke was booked for coaching.											
2:2	H	BARNSLEY	17	L	2-5	2-0	Keen 3, Robson 31 *[MacDonald 112]*	McAlister	Parris*	McQueen^	Strodder	Martin	Brady	Ward	Keen	Ince	Cottee	Robson	Dickens/Hilton
6/10			12,403	*2:13*	*aet*		*Ag'w 55p, 72, B'ford 102, L'ndes 104,*	*Baker*	*Joyce*	*Cross*	*Thomas*	*Gray*	*Futcher*	*Beresford*	*Agnew*	*Lowndes*	*MacDonald*	*Broddle*	
							Ref: K Morton (Hammers lose 2-5 on aggregate)	Fans call for Lyall's head. Barnsley had scored once in six games but hardly deserved to go 0-2 down when Cottee's penalty was pushed out to Robson. Martin's push on Gray and Agnew's bullet free-kick put Barnsley ahead on away goals. Beresford's free-kick in extra-time settled it.											

FA Cup					F-A	H-T	Scorers, Times, and Referees	1	2	3	4	5	6	7	8	9	10	11	subs used
3	H	CHARLTON	14	W	2-0	0-0	Brady 75, Cottee 87	McAlister	Potts	Stewart	Bonds	Strodder	Gale	Ward	Brady*	Hilton	Cottee	Robson	Ince
9/1			22,043	*20*				*Bolder*	*Humphrey*	*Reid*	*Mackenzie*	*Shirtliff*	*Thompson*	*Bennett*	*Campbell*	*Jones**	*Lee^*	*Mortimer*	*Williams/Crooks*
							Ref: V Callow	Billy Bonds, shortly to get his MBE, plays a blinder, and sets up the second, decisive goal for Cottee. The breakthrough had come when Shirtliff fouled Cottee, and Brady's free-kick flew into the net. Charlton never tested McAlister. West Ham will lose here 0-3 in the league.											
4	A	QP RANGERS	12	L	1-3	0-0	Cottee 51	McAlister	Stewart	McQueen*	Bonds	Strodder	Gale	Ward	Brady	Dickens	Cottee	Robson	Hilton
30/1			*23,651*	*1:7*			*Pizanti 49, Bannister 64, Allen 83*	*Johns*	*Dawes*	*Pizanti*	*Parker*	*McDonald*	*Maguire*	*Allen*	*Falco*	*Bannister*	*Fereday**	*Brock*	*Byrne*
							Ref: H King	West Ham have won on their three previous games on QPR's plastic pitch. Kick-off was delayed one hour after Hammers' fans spilled onto the touchlines. Cottee's close-range equaliser counted for nothing when Bannister, with his back to goal, restored the lead with a curling shot.											

		Home					Away					
	P	W	D	L	F	A	W	D	L	F	A	Pts
1 Liverpool	40	15	5	0	49	9	11	7	2	38	15	90
2 Manchester U	40	14	5	1	41	17	9	7	4	30	21	81
3 Nott'm Forest	40	11	7	2	40	17	9	6	5	27	22	73
4 Everton	40	14	4	2	34	11	5	9	6	19	16	70
5 QP Rangers	40	12	4	4	30	14	7	6	7	18	24	67
6 Arsenal	40	11	4	5	35	16	7	8	5	23	23	66
7 Wimbledon	40	8	9	3	32	20	6	6	8	26	27	57
8 Newcastle	40	9	6	5	32	23	5	8	7	23	30	56
9 Luton	40	11	6	3	40	21	3	5	12	17	37	53
10 Coventry	40	6	8	6	23	25	7	6	7	23	28	53
11 Sheffield Wed	40	10	2	8	27	30	5	6	9	25	36	53
12 Southampton	40	6	8	6	27	26	6	6	8	22	27	50
13 Tottenham	40	9	5	6	26	23	3	6	11	12	25	47
14 Norwich	40	7	5	8	26	26	5	4	11	14	26	45
15 Derby	40	6	7	7	18	17	4	6	10	17	28	43
16 WEST HAM	40	6	9	5	23	21	3	6	11	17	31	42
17 Charlton	40	7	7	6	23	21	2	8	10	15	31	42
18 Chelsea*	40	7	11	2	24	17	2	4	14	26	51	42
19 Portsmouth	40	4	8	8	21	27	3	6	11	15	39	35
20 Watford	40	4	5	11	15	24	3	6	11	12	27	32
21 Oxford	40	5	7	8	24	34	1	6	13	20	46	31
	840	182	132	106	610	439	106	132	182	439	610	1128

* relegated after play-offs

Odds & ends

Double wins: (1) Watford.
Double losses: (3) Spurs, Arsenal, Sheff Wed.

Won from behind: (0).
Lost from in front: (5) Portsmouth (a), Norwich (a), Southampton (a), Newcastle (a), Barnsley LC (h).

High spots: Five unbeaten games, winning three, from 16 November.
Five unbeaten games, winning two, from 3 October.

Low spots: Seven league games without a win from 26 March.
Catastrophic defeat by Second Division Barnsley in Littlewoods Cup.

Hammer of the Year: Stewart Robson.
Ever-presents: (1) Tony Cottee.
Hat-tricks: (0).
Leading scorer: (15) Tony Cottee.

	Appearances						Goals			
	Lge	*Sub*	LC	*Sub*	FAC	*Sub*	Lge	LC	FAC	Tot
Bonds, Billy	**22**				2					
Brady, Liam	**21**	*1*	2		2		**2**		1	**3**
Cottee, Tony	**40**		2		2		**13**		2	**15**
Devonshire, Alan	**1**									
Dickens, Alan	**25**	*3*		*1*	1		**3**			**3**
Dicks, Julian	**8**									
Dolan, Eamonn	**1**	*3*								
Gale, Tony	**17**	*1*			2					
Hilton, Paul	**9**	*5*		*1*	1	*1*	**3**			**3**
Ince, Paul	**26**	*2*	2			*1*	**3**			**3**
Keen, Kevin	**19**	*4*	1				**1**	1		**2**
McAlister, Tom	**39**		2		2					
McAvennie, Frank	**8**		1							
McQueen, Tom	**10**	*2*	1	*1*	1					
Martin, Alvin	**15**		2							
Orr, Neil	**1**									
Parkes, Phil	**1**									
Parris, George	**27**	*3*	2				**1**			**1**
Potts, Steve	**7**	*1*	1		1					
Robson, Stewart	**37**		2		2		**2**	1		**3**
Rosenior, Leroy	**9**						**5**			**5**
Slater, Stuart		*2*								
Stewart, Ray	**33**				2		**4**			**4**
Strodder, Gary	**27**	*3*	2		2		**1**			**1**
Ward, Mark	**37**		2		2		**1**			**1**
(own-goals)							**1**			**1**
25 players used	**440**	***30***	**22**	***3***	**22**	***2***	**40**	**2**	**3**	**45**

No	Date	Att	Pos	Pt	F-A	H-T	Scorers, Times, and Referees	1	2	3	4	5	6	7	8	9	10	11	subs used
1	A SOUTHAMPTON			L	0-4	0-2	*[Le Tissier 87]*	McAlister	Potts	Dicks	Gale*	Martin	Keen	Ward	Parris	Slater^	**Kelly**	Robson	Hilton/Dickens
	27/8	*18,407*		0			*Rideout 37, 60, Cockerill 44,*	*Burridge*	*Forrest*	*Statham*	*Case*	*Moore*	*Osman*	*Wallace Rod*	*Cockerill*	*Clarke*	*Rideout*	*Wallace D**	*Le Tissier*
							Ref: B Hill	Pre-season had gone well, but after this disaster John Lyall summons his players back for Bank Holiday punishment training. West Ham were not helped by losing Stuart Slater concussed in the first minute, or Gale, who limped off at half-time. £600,000 David Kelly had a tough debut.											
2	H CHARLTON		20	L	1-3	0-1	Keen 53p	McAlister	Potts*	Dicks	Dickens	Martin	Keen^	Ward	Parris	Slater	Kelly	Robson	Ince/Devonshire
	3/9	19,566	*10*	0			*Williams 23, 48, Robson 56 (og)*	*Bolder*	*Humphrey*	*Reid*	*MacKenzie*	*Shirtliff*	*Miller*	*Lee R*	*Williams*	*Gritt*	*Leaburn*	*Stuart*	
							Ref: D Axcell	A horror show against opponents West Ham expect to beat. Paul Williams capitalised on an almighty cock-up between Robson and McAlister for Charlton's first, and was unmarked to head the second. Kelly was impeded for the penalty, but Robson then headed into his own net.											
3	A WIMBLEDON		13	W	1-0	1-0	Ward 20	**McKnight**	Parris	Dicks	Hilton	Martin	Ince	Ward	Kelly*	Rosenior	Dickens	Robson	Devonshire
	10/9	*7,730*	*18*	3				*Green*	*Joseph*	*Phelan*	*Ryan**	*Young*	*Scales*	*Gibson*	*Fairweather*	*Fashanu*	*Cork*	*Wise*	*Brooke*
							Ref: R Lewis	Lyall, sober-suited and chain smoking, enjoys West Ham's first goal and first points. They also picked up four bookings against the FA Cup-holders, managed by Lyall's former player, Bobby Gould. Ward won the game with a curling free-kick. Five bookings in the last five minutes.											
4	H ASTON VILLA		13	D	2-2	0-2	Mountfield 63 (og), Kelly 66	McKnight	Parris	Dicks	Strodder*	Martin	Ince	Ward	Kelly	Rosenior	Dickens	Robson	Devonshire
	17/9	19,186	*10*	4			*McInally 31, 36*	*Spink*	*Price*	*Mountfield*	*Gray A*	*Evans**	*Keown*	*Daley*	*Platt*	*McInally*	*Cownas*	*Gray S*	*Gage*
							Ref: R Gifford	Alan McInally's two first-half goals appear to have ended the contest, but sub Alan Devonshire's arrival sparks West Ham into life. His lob hits a post but goes in off Mountfield. Allan Evans then fluffed a back-pass, which let in David Kelly for his first league goal for his new club.											
5	A MANCHESTER U		17	L	0-2	0-1		McKnight	Parris	Dicks	Strodder*	Hilton	Ince	Ward	Kelly	Rosenior	Dickens	Robson	Devonshire
	24/9	*39,941*	*5*	4			*Davenport 37, Hughes 69*	*Leighton*	*Blackmore*	*Sharpe**	*Bruce*	*Garton^*	*Duxbury*	*Robson*	*Strachan*	*McClair*	*Hughes*	*Davenport*	*Olsen/Beardsmore*
							Ref: G Tyson	This result was hard on West Ham. Alex Ferguson brought Mark Hughes back from Barcelona, and Hughes comes up with his first goal since his return. Peter Davenport had exchanged passes with McClair to score the opener. Dickens and Robson both missed good early openings.											
6	H ARSENAL		20	L	1-4	1-2	Dickens 30	McKnight	Parris*	Dicks	Hilton	Martin	Ince	Ward	Kelly	Rosenior^	Dickens	Robson	Strodder/Devonshire
	1/10	27,658	*7*	4			*Smith 17, 19, Thomas 82, Rocastle 90*	*Lukic*	*Dixon*	*Winterburn*	*Thomas*	*Bould*	*Adams*	*Rocastle*	*Davis*	*Smith*	*Groves**	*Marwood*	*Hayes*
							Ref: R Hamer	West Ham never recovered from presenting Alan Smith with two gift goals, taking his tally to nine from six games. Both were the result of crosses that should have been cleared. Dickens' goal flattered to deceive. Lyall raged at his players for an hour afterwards in the dressing room.											
7	A MIDDLESBROUGH		20	L	0-1	0-1		McKnight	Potts*	Dicks	Gale	Hilton	Devonshire	Ward	Kelly	Parris	Dickens	Ince	Keen
	8/10	*19,608*	*10*	4			*Pallister 40*	*Pears*	*Parkinson*	*Cooper*	*Mowbray*	*Hamilton*	*Pallister*	*Slaven*	*Brennan*	*Burke**	*Kerr^*	*Ripley*	*Glover/Kernaghan*
							Ref: K Breen	David Kelly plays alone up front, and keeps goalkeeper Steve Pears on his toes. But Kelly's cheeky dummy is cut out by Gary Pallister, who strides the length of the pitch and plays a one-two with Bernie Slaven to score a fine goal. Paul Ince gets his fourth yellow card of the season.											
8	A QP RANGERS		20	L	1-2	1-0	Kelly 30	McKnight	Potts	Dicks	Gale	Hilton	Devonshire*	Ward	Kelly	Rosenior	Dickens	Ince	Keen
	15/10	*14,566*	*9*	4			*Stein 55, Maddix 67*	*Johns*	*Barker*	*Allen*	*Parker*	*McDonald*	*Maddix*	*Falco*	*Francis*	*Fereday*	*Stein**	*Brock^*	*Coney/Kerslake*
							Ref: K Barratt	A super match that brought Loftus Road to its feet at the end. West Ham's first-half superiority was threatened after 34 minutes when Dicks brought down Stein, only for Trevor Francis to shoot wide from the spot. But Francis inspires QPR in the second half, crossing for both goals.											
9	H NEWCASTLE		18	W	2-0	0-0	Dickens 55, Stewart 81p	McKnight	Stewart	Dicks	Gale	Martin	Devonshire*	Ward	Kelly	Slater	Dickens	Ince	Keen
	22/10	17,765	*20*	7				*Beasant*	*Anderson*	*Tinnion*	*McCreery**	*Scott*	*Thorn^*	*Stephenson*	*Hendrie*	*Mirandinha*	*Jackson*	*O'Neill*	*Robertson/Bogie*
							Ref: A Gunn	The two bottom teams meet in this six-pointer. West Ham played above themselves at times. Dickens nets from Devonshire's quick free-kick, and Beasant flattens Slater for a late penalty. Drama at the end, when O'Neill is led from the pitch with a broken nose. No one saw nothing!											
10	H LIVERPOOL		18	L	0-2	0-0		McKnight	Stewart	Dicks	Gale	Martin	Devonshire	Ward	Kelly*	Slater	Dickens	Ince	Rosenior
	29/10	**30,188**	*4*	7			*Rush 69, Beardsley 80*	*Hooper*	*Ablett*	*Venison*	*Nicol*	*Whelan**	*Burrows*	*Beardsley*	*Aldridge*	*Rush*	*Barnes*	*Houghton*	*Spackman*
							Ref: R Milford	Liverpool always looked more likely, but it took a long time for them to stamp their authority. Rush broke the deadlock, killing the ball with his right foot and scoring with his left. 'There's only one Ian Rush,' sang Reds' fans. Burrows then enabled Beardsley to tuck away the second.											

No	Venue	Opponent	Pos	Res	F-A	H-T	Scorers, Times, and Referees	1	2	3	4	5	6	7	8	9	10	11	subs used
11	A	COVENTRY	18	D	1-1	1-0	Kelly 32	McKnight	Potts	Dicks	Gale	Martin	Keen	Ward	Kelly	Rosenior	Dickens	Ince	
5/11		14,651	7	8			Thompson 82	Ogrizovic	Borrows	Downs	Sedgley	Emerson*	Rodger	Clark	Speedie	Regis	Bannister^	Smith	Thompson/Houchen
							Ref: E Parker	Kelly nets the rebound after Alan Dickens' shot hits a post. Thereafter Allen McKnight pulls out the stops as injury-ravaged City pile forward. Time is running out when he turns aside Speedie's left-foot shot. But from the ensuing corner substitute Keith Thompson nets the equaliser.											
12	H	NOTT'M FOREST	17	D	3-3	2-3	Kelly 2, 42, Rosenior 57	McKnight	Potts	Dicks	Gale	Martin	Keen	Ward	Kelly*	Rosenior	Dickens	Ince^	Brady/Parris
12/11		21,583	9	9			Clough 7, 21, Hodge 41	Sutton	Chettle	Pearce*	Walker	Foster	Hodge	Starbuck	Wilson	Clough	Chapman^	Rice	Laws/Crosby
							Ref: I Hemsley	David Kelly sprained an ankle after scoring two goals and will miss Ireland's vital World Cup-tie in Spain. He was actually on the ground when scoring his second. After a thrill-a-minute first half, Leroy Rosenior earned a point for West Ham with a wonderful diving header.											
13	A	LUTON	19	L	1-4	0-3	Martin 63	McKnight	Potts	Dicks	Gale	Martin	Keen*	Ward	Brady	Rosenior	Dickens^	Ince	Parris/Hilton
19/11		9,308	16	9			Black 15, 38, Wegerle 19, Wilson 67	Sealey	Johnson R	Grimes	Preece	Foster	Johnson M	Wilson	Wegerle	Harford	Oldfield	Black	
							Ref: V Callow	West Ham are brought down by two athletic goals by Kingsley Black, the first of which arrived when Johnson's cross eluded the Hammers' defence. Goal of the match was Danny Wilson's belter from 20 yards. Paul Ince was one of the few Hammers to distinguish himself.											
14	H	EVERTON	19	L	0-1	0-0		McKnight	Potts	Dicks	Gale	Martin	Keen	Ward*	Brady	Rosenior	Dickens	Ince	Devonshire
26/11		22,176	10	9			Steven 53	Southall	Snodin	v d Hauwe	Ratcliffe	Watson	Reid	Steven	McCall	Sharp	Cottee	Wilson	
							Ref: P Durkin	Cottee was sold to Everton for £2 million in the summer and his first visit back provokes dreadful hostility. The crowd were further incensed by Colin Harvey's team's offside trap and constant passing back to Southall. Cottee almost scored in 30 seconds and set up Steven's winner.											
15	A	MILLWALL	19	W	1-0	1-0	Ince 17	McKnight	Potts	Dicks	Gale	Martin	Devonshire	Brady	Kelly	Rosenior	Dickens	Ince	
3/12		20,105	3	12				Horne	Stevens	Dawes	Hurlock	Wood	McLeary	Stephenson	Briley	Sheringham	Cascarino	O'Callaghan	
							Ref: R Wiseman	West Ham are on a high after their crushing cup win over Liverpool, and their achievement in ending the last undefeated home record in the division provokes an avalanche of coins. Dawes' misdirected back-pass presented Hammers with a gift goal. They endured a second-half siege.											
16	H	SHEFFIELD WED	19	D	0-0	0-0		McKnight	Potts	Parris	Gale	Martin	Devonshire	Brady	Kelly	Rosenior	Dickens	Ince	
10/12		16,676	12	13				Pressman	Sterland*	Worthington	Cranson	Pearson	Jonsson	Megson	Hirst	Hodgson	Harper	Proctor	Varadi
							Ref: L Shapter	A dreadful, tedious match that had supporters streaming for the exits long before the end. Brady hit the bar in the first minute; David Hodgson hit the wood for Wednesday. Parris, Martin and Kelly squandered half-chances near the end. Just one goal keeps West Ham off the bottom.											
17	H	TOTTENHAM	20	L	0-2	0-1		McKnight	Potts	Parris	Gale	Martin	Devonshire*	Brady	Kelly	Rosenior	Dickens	Ince	Keen
17/12		28,365	11	13			Mabbutt 23, Thomas 70	Mimms	Butters	Thomas	Fenwick	Fairclough	Mabbutt	Walsh*	Gascoigne^	Waddle	Stewart	Allen	Robson/Polston
							Ref: D Reeves	Gary Mabbutt starts and finishes the move that sends West Ham to the bottom. Gascoigne tormented the visitors through the first half, before retiring through injury. Mimms is barracked by Spurs fans, but he foils Dickens' 25-yarder. Mitchell Thomas's intended cross sails in for 0-2.											
18	A	NORWICH	20	L	1-2	0-0	Stewart 71p	McKnight	Potts	Parris	Gale	Martin*	Devonshire	Brady	Kelly	Rosenior	Dickens^	Ince	Stewart/Keen
27/12		17,491	1	13			Gordon 53, Townsend 61	Gunn	Culverhouse	Bowen	Crook	Linighan	Townsend*	Gordon	Fleck	Rosario	Phelan	Putney	Butterworth
							Ref: M Bailey	Norwich top the table, despite not winning at Carrow Road since October. In this televised match Gordon burst down the right to open the scoring. Fleck squares to Townsend for the second. Phelan barges over David Kelly for the penalty, but West Ham are now three points adrift.											
19	A	CHARLTON	20	D	0-0	0-0		McKnight	Potts	Dicks	Gale	Martin	Stewart	Brady*	Kelly	Rosenior	Dickens	Keen	Parris
31/12		11,084	18	14				Bolder	Humphrey	Reid	Shirtliff	Pates	Gritt*	Campbell	Mackenzie	Lee R	Leaburn^	Mortimer	Williams/Peake
							Ref: J Moules	The two bottom sides produce a predictable draw. Lennie Lawrence's team had not won in 11 games. Happiest man was keeper Bob Bolder: it was his 100th match. Liam Brady did his best, and when he was subbed after 83 minutes the crowd booed, not realising he had a groin injury.											
20	H	WIMBLEDON	20	L	1-2	1-1	Rosenior 39	McKnight	Potts	Dicks	Gale	Martin	Stewart	Brady	Kelly	Rosenior	Dickens	Keen	
2/1		18,346	17	14			Wise 14, 84	Segers	Scales	Phelan	Jones	Young	Curle	Fairweather	Gibson*	Fashanu	Sanchez	Wise^	Cork/Kruszynski
							Ref: R Milford	Uncompromising Dons are too tough for fragile Hammers. Dennis Wise featured in everything, blasting in Curle's centre and restoring the Dons' lead with a deflected free-kick. Wise was later carried off after a clash with Dicks. Rosenior's goal was his first since November.											
21	A	DERBY	19	W	2-1	2-1	Kelly 12, Brady 45	McKnight	Stewart*	Dicks	Gale	Potts	Devonshire	Brady^	Kelly	Rosenior	Dickens	Ince	Strodder/Keen
14/1		16,796	8	17			Saunders 1	Shilton	Blades	Forsyth	Williams	Wright	Hindmarch	McMinn*	Saunders	Gee^	Hebberd	Callaghan	Cross/Penney
							Ref: A Dawson	Dean Saunders' first-minute header was cancelled out by David Kelly's looping header. Kelly knew little about it, as Peter Shilton injured himself colliding with the goal-scorer. With half-time looming Liam Brady fired an exquisite 25-yarder in off the junction of post and bar.											

No	Date			Att	Pos	Pt	F-A	H-T	Scorers, Times, and Referees	1	2	3	4	5	6	7	8	9	10	11	subs used
22		H	MANCHESTER U		19	L	1-3	1-1	Brady 22p	McKnight	Potts	Dicks	Gale	Martin	Devonshire^	Brady	Kelly*	Rosenior	Ward	Ince	Strodder/Keen
	21/1			**29,822**	*6*	17			*Strachan 28, Martin 54, McClair 60*	*Leighton*	*Gill*	*Martin*	*Bruce*	*Blackmore*	*Donaghy*	*Robson*	*Strachan**	*McClair*	*Hughes*	*Milne*	*Sharpe*
									Ref: A Gunn	Man U's first win at Upton Park since winning the European Cup in 1968 looked unlikely when Kelly twice spurned one-on-one chances against Leighton. Bruce fouled Rosenior for Brady's penalty. Once McKnight failed to hold Robson's shot, to let in Strachan, the tide turned.											
23		A	ARSENAL		20	L	1-2	0-0	Dicks 84	McKnight	Potts	Dicks	Gale	Strodder	Devonshire*	Ward	Dickens	Rosenior	Brady	Ince	Kelly
	4/2			*40,139*	*1*	17			*Groves 58, Smith 61*	*Lukic*	*Dixon*	*Winterburn*	*Thomas*	*O'Leary**	*Adams*	*Rocastle*	*Richardson*	*Smith*	*Merson^*	*Groves*	*Bould/Hayes*
									Ref: J Worrall	Arsenal avenge their FA Cup defeat, though measured on chances created West Ham could consider themselves hard done by. McKnight's confidence is draining away. The keeper was at fault with both goals – Groves' looping header and a shot from Smith that squeezed under him.											
24		H	QP RANGERS		20	D	0-0	0-0		Parkes	Potts	Dicks	Gale	Martin	Devonshire	Ward	Dickens*	Slater	Brady	Ince	Parris
	25/2			17,371	*16*	18				*Seaman*	*Channing*	*Dennis**	*Reid*	*McDonald*	*Spackman*	*Barker*	*Gray*	*Falco^*	*Maddix*	*Stein*	*Pisanti/Coney*
									Ref: K Hackett	Both sets of supporters rise to acclaim Phil Parkes, who has served both clubs well. West Ham have not won at home for four months, while QPR have scored just once – a penalty – in their last six games. A goalless draw was therefore predictable, though Rangers had the edge.											
25		H	COVENTRY		20	D	1-1	0-1	Ince 81	Parkes	Potts	Dicks	Gale	Martin	Devonshire	Kelly	Dickens	Slater	Brady	Ince	
	11/3			15,205	*6*	19			*Kilcline 13p*	*Ogrizovic*	*Borrows*	*Dobson*	*Phillips*	*Kilcline*	*Peake*	*Bennett*	*Speedie*	*Regis**	*Bannister*	*Smith*	*Clark*
									Ref: B Stevens	Brady's dreadful back-pass, which led to Parkes bringing down Bennett, looked like costing West Ham the match until the inspirational Ince skirted Kilcline to equalise with a low drive. Three times Ogrizovic thwarted Dickens. At the death Oggy saved from Dicks in the top corner.											
26		A	ASTON VILLA		20	W	1-0	1-0	Ince 10	Parkes	Parris	Dicks	Gale	Hilton	Devonshire*	Ward	McAvennie	Slater	Brady	Ince	Dickens
	25/3			*22,471*	*14*	22				*Butler*	*Price*	*Gray S*	*Platt*	*Sims*	*Keown*	*Callaghan*	*Daley*	*McInally**	*Cownas^*	*Williams*	*Olney/Mountfield*
									Ref: D Scott	Frank McAvennie has re-signed from Celtic for £1.25 million, £400,000 more than Celtic paid for him 18 months previously. West Ham have just been knocked out of the FA Cup by Norwich, and Paul Ince's sensational goal – running 60 yards and scoring from 30 – was just the tonic.											
27		H	NORWICH		20	L	0-2	0-0		Parkes	Parris	Dicks	Gale	Hilton	Dickens	Ward	McAvennie	Slater	Brady*	Ince	Rosenior
	27/3			27,265	*2*	22			*Linighan 70, Allen 86*	*Gunn*	*Culverhouse*	*Bowen*	*Butterworth*	*Linighan*	*Townsend*	*Gordon*	*Fleck**	*Allen*	*Phelan^*	*Putney*	*Coney/Crook*
									Ref: J Deakin	Norwich's title hopes have been jolted by a home defeat by Newcastle, and they could have been 0-3 down to West Ham. The turning point was when Phelan pushed Ince in the box. The ref waved play on and Ince was booked for dissent. 10 minutes later Linighan had a free header.											
28		A	TOTTENHAM		20	L	0-3	0-1		Parkes	Parris	Dicks	Gale	Strodder*	Potts	Ward	McAvennie	Slater	Brady	Ince	Dickens
	1/4			*28,376*	*6*	22			*Nayim 41, Fenwick 82p, Stewart 88*	*Thorstvedt*	*Butters*	*Hughton*	*Fenwick*	*Nayim**	*Mabbutt*	*Walsh*	*Gascoigne*	*Waddle*	*Stewart*	*Allen*	*Howells*
									Ref: R Lewis	It is 20 years to the day since Parkes made his league debut with Walsall. Spurs were flattered by the score, and were indebted to Thorstvedt's 48th-minute save from McAvennie's header. When Parkes brought down Stewart, Fenwick scored twice from the spot after encroachment.											
29		H	DERBY		20	D	1-1	1-1	Rosenior 23	Parkes	Parris	Dicks	Gale*	Martin	Dickens	Ward	McAvennie	Rosenior	Brady^	Ince	Potts/Slater
	8/4			16,560	*9*	23			*Micklewhite 11*	*Shilton*	*Blades*	*Forsyth*	*Williams*	*Wright*	*Hindmarch*	*McMinn*	*Saunders*	*Goddard**	*Hebberd*	*Micklewhite*	*Cross*
									Ref: B Hill	Gary Micklewhite cannot believe his luck as he is allowed to saunter through a static Hammers defence to score with a feeble shot. Leroy Rosenior levelled with a far-post header, and Mark Ward missed the chance of securing a rare win when shooting into the side-netting.											
30		H	MIDDLESBROUGH		20	L	1-2	1-0	Keen 21	Parkes	Parris	Dicks	Potts	Hilton	Dickens	Ward	McAvennie	Rosenior	Brady	Keen	
	11/4			16,217	*15*	23			*Slaven 84, 86*	*Poole*	*Parkinson*	*Cooper*	*Mowbray*	*Proctor*	*Pallister*	*Slaven*	*Kernaghan*	*Ripley**	*Burke*	*Hamilton*	*Kerr*
									Ref: B Hamer	A killer defeat by a team which had not won in 11 games. Parris hit the bar from 30 yards before Keen exchanged passes with McAvennie to score. Bernie Slaven's late scrambled equaliser saw the scorer booked for excessive celebrations. Two minutes later Slaven headed the winner.											
31		H	SOUTHAMPTON		20	L	1-2	1-1	Brady 25p	Parkes	Parris	Keen	Potts	Hilton	Dickens^	Ward	McAvennie	Rosenior	Brady*	Ince	Slater/McQueen
	15/4			**14,766**	*16*	23			*Wallace Rod 1, Rideout 51*	*Burridge*	*Wallace Ray*	*Adams*	*Case*	*Moore*	*Osman*	*Wallace Rod*	*Cockerill*	*Rideout*	*Horne*	*Wallace D*	
									Ref: K Cooper	This was the day of the Hillsborough disaster. Chris Nichol's Saints ease their relegation fears with their second win in 24 games. Rod Wallace put away Cockerill's through ball in 33 seconds. Russell Osman needlessly handled for the penalty. Rideout headed in from Horne's cross.											

No	Venue	Opponent	Att	Pos	Res/Pts	F-A	H-T	Scorers, Times, and Referees	1	2	3	4	5	6	7	8	9	10	11	12 sub used
32	H	MILLWALL		20	W	**3-0**	3-0	Dicks 20, Dickens 23, Parris 43	Parkes	Parris	Dicks	Gale	Potts	Dickens	Ward	McAvennie	Slater	Keen	Ince*	McQueen
	22/4		16,603	*7*	26				*Horne*	*Stevens*	*Dawes*	*Carter**	*Wood*	*McLeary*	*Salman*	*Briley^*	*Horrix*	*Cascarino*	*O'Callaghan*	*Lawrence/Thompson*
								Ref: A Seville	The minute's silence for the victims of Hillsborough is sullied by obscenities that leaves Millwall chairman Reg Burr feeling ashamed. Horne fumbled Dicks' shot through a crowd of players. The goal of the match belonged to Parris, following a slick build-up with Ince and Slater.											
33	A	NEWCASTLE		20	W	2-1	1-1	Keen 7, Ward 79	Parkes	Parris	Dicks	Gale	Martin	Dickens	Ward	McAvennie^	Slater	Keen	Ince	Kelly
	3/5		*14,202*	*19*	29			*Lormer 1*	*Wright*	*Anderson**	*Sansom*	*McCreery*	*Scott*	*Roeder*	*Lormor*	*Sweeney*	*Thorn*	*Pinge^*	*Brock*	*Kristensen/McD'nald*
								Ref: J Key	Newcastle have played more games, so though they remain above West Ham this defeat relegates the Magpies. Gayle's error let in Lormor in the first minute. Slater's shot was then pushed out to Keen. Ward's angled winner provoked irate Geordies to menace the directors' box.											
34	H	LUTON		19	W	1-0	1-0	Dickens 17	Parkes	Parris	Dicks	Gale*	Martin	Dickens	Ward	Slater	Rosenior^	Keen	Ince	Potts/Kelly
	6/5		18,606	*17*	32				*Chamberlain*	*Breacker*	*Dreyer*	*Preece*	*Foster*	*Beaumont*	*Wilson*	*Wegerle*	*Harford*	*Hill*	*Black**	*Cooke*
								Ref: L Shapter	West Ham gain revenge over their Littlewoods Cup executioners with their third successive win. The Hammers are still six points from safety, but have played three games fewer than vanquished Luton. Their survival is now in their own hands, but all four remaining games are away.											
35	A	SHEFFIELD WED		19	W	2-0	0-0	Dickens 50, Rosenior 76	Parkes	Parris	Dicks	Gale*	Martin	Dickens	Ward	Slater	Rosenior	Keen	Ince	Potts^
	9/5		*19,905*	*18*	35				*Turner*	*Harper*	*Worthingt'n**	*Palmer*	*Pearson*	*Madden*	*Bennett^*	*Fee*	*Whitton*	*Hirst*	*Barrick*	*Galvin/Reeves*
								Ref: P Tyldesley	This is Ron Atkinson's Wednesday's first home match since the Hillsborough disaster. The Leppings Lane end is closed. With both teams in the drop zone, this is another critical six-pointer. Alan Dickens skipped between two defenders to lob a super goal. Rosenior headed a second.											
36	A	EVERTON		19	L	1-3	1-1	Slater 15	Parkes	Parris	Dicks	Gale	Martin	Dickens	Ward	Slater	Rosenior	Keen^	Ince*	Potts/Kelly
	13/5		*21,694*	*11*	*35*			*Sheedy 27, Watson 54, Bracewell 83*	*Southall*	*McDonald*	*Pointon*	*Ratcliffe*	*Watson*	*Bracewell*	*Nevin*	*Steven*	*Sharp*	*Cottee*	*Sheedy**	*Wilson*
								Ref: H Taylor	Everton have lost at home just twice, but when Slater capitalised on Pointon's error West Ham's fifth straight win looked on the cards. The bubble burst when Parkes carried the ball outside the box and Sheedy fired the free-kick into the top corner. Both Luton and Wednesday won.											
37	A	NOTT'M FOREST		19	W	2-1	2-1	Rosenior 1, 18	McKnight	Parris	Dicks	Gale	Martin	Dickens	Ward	Slater	Rosenior	Keen	Brady*	Potts
	18/5		*20,943*	*3*	38			*Chapman 31*	*Sutton*	*Laws*	*Pearce*	*Walker*	*Chettle*	*Hodge*	*Gaynor*	*Webb*	*Clough*	*Chapman*	*Parker*	
								Ref: D Phillips	Rosenior puts away Brady's cross in 19 seconds, the fastest goal of the season. West Ham's second goal is a duplicate of the first. But Lee Chapman heads in Tommy Gaynor's centre and Gaynor later hits the bar as the Hammers hang on defiantly to register five wins in six games.											
38	A	LIVERPOOL		19	L	**1-5**	1-1	Rosenior 29 *[Barnes 90]*	McKnight	Parris	Dicks	Gale	Martin	Dickens	Ward	Slater	Rosenior	Brady*	Ince^	McAvennie/Keen
	23/5		***41,855***	*1*	*38*			*Aldridge 20, Houghton 63,80, Rush 84,*	*Grobbelaar*	*Ablett*	*Venison*	*Nicol*	*Whelan*	*Hansen**	*Houghton*	*Aldridge ^*	*Rush*	*Barnes*	*McMahon*	*Burrows/Beardsley*
		Home	Away					Ref: S Lodge	Liverpool have already won the FA Cup and have won 16 out of their last 17 games. Aldridge's header from Barnes' cross is cancelled out by Rosenior's from Ward. Ray Houghton, once given away by West Ham, skirts Gale to make it 2-1. Liverpool will lose the decider to Arsenal.											
Average		20,743	21,014																	

Littlewoods Cup																				
2:1	A	SUNDERLAND		17	W	3-0	1-0	Kelly 6, 65, Rosenior 48	McKnight	Parris	Dicks	Hilton	Martin*	Ince	Ward	Kelly	Rosenior	Dickens	Robson	Potts
	27/9		*13,691*	*2:18*					*Hesford*	*Kay*	*Agboola*	*Bennett**	*MacPhail*	*Doyle*	*Owers*	*Armstrong*	*Gates*	*Gabbiadini*	*Pascoe*	*Gray*
								Ref: G Aplin	Sunderland have yet to win in Division 2 since promotion. They are so bad they make West Ham look good. Kelly was at the heart of all West Ham's best moments, scoring first with a chip and then converting Rosenior's cross to the far post. In between, his back-heel set up Rosenior.											
2:2	H	SUNDERLAND		20	W	2-1	1-0	Kelly 43, Dickens 59	McKnight	Potts	Dicks	Gale	Hilton	Devonshire*	Ward	Kelly	Parris	Dickens	Ince	Keen
	12/10		10,558	*2:16*				*Gabbiadini 74*	*Hesford*	*Gray*	*Agboola*	*Ord*	*MacPhail*	*Doyle**	*Owers*	*Armstrong*	*Gates*	*Gabbiadini*	*Pascoe^*	*Lemon/Ogilvie*
								Ref: A Seville (Hammers win 5-1 on aggregate)	A meaningless cup-tie played on a rain-sodden pitch before a paltry attendance. Sunderland face a reprimand for arriving late after their coach was held up. Midway through the first half, play was halted due to floodlight failure. Dickens' short pass to Kelly made it 4-0 before half-time.											
3	H	DERBY		18	W	5-0	1-0	Martin 44, 79, Stewart 53p, [Rosenior 69, Keen 89]	McKnight	Stewart	Dicks	Gale	Martin	Keen	Ward	Kelly*	Rosenior	Dickens	Ince	Brady
	1/11		14,226	*13*					*Shilton*	*Sage*	*Forsyth*	*Williams*	*Hindmarch*	*Blades*	*McMinn*	*Gee**	*Goddard*	*Hebberd*	*Callaghan^*	*Micklewhite/Cross*
								Ref: K Morton	Derby have the meanest defence, just five goals conceded in nine games. They miss cup-tied Saunders and suspended Wright. The second goal was odd. Ince headed in but the ref gave a penalty. Later Ward blasted the ball at the head of the prostrate Callaghan. No action was taken.											

Littlewoods Cup					F-A	H-T	Scorers, Times, and Referees	1	2	3	4	5	6	7	8	9	10	11	subs used
4	H	LIVERPOOL	19	W	4-1	2-1	Ince 21, 24, Staunton 56 (og), Gale 76	McKnight	Potts	Dicks	Gale	Martin	Devonshire	Brady	Kelly	Rosenior	Dickens	Ince	
	30/11	26,971	*4*				*Aldridge 34p*	*Hooper*	*Ablett*	*Venison*	*Nicol**	*Whelan*	*Spackman*	*Beardsley*	*Aldridge*	*Saunders*	*Houghton*	*McMahon^*	*Watson/Durnin*
							Ref: J Ashworth	This is heaviest defeat – on grass – of Dalglish's managerial career and Liverpool's heaviest cup defeat since before the War. Magnificent Ince threatens to win it on his own with a volley and a header. Pool's only bright moment came when Martin climbed all over Aldridge in the box.											
QF	H	ASTON VILLA	19	W	2-1	1-0	Ince 14, Kelly 85	McKnight	Potts	Dicks	Gale	Strodder	Devonshire	Brady	Kelly	Rosenior	Dickens*	Ince	Ward
	18/1	30,110	*12*				*Platt 90*	*Spink*	*Price*	*Gray S*	*Gage*	*Mountfield*	*Keown*	*Gray A*	*Platt*	*McInally*	*Cowans*	*Daley**	*Olney*
							Ref: J Martin	Gale is acting captain for this emphatic win, which is distorted by David Platt's late overhead-kick. After eight minutes Price toppled Rosenior, but Spink saved Brady's penalty. Ince scored when the ball spun off Mountfield. When Keown flattened Rosenior, Kelly fired in the free-kick.											
SF	H	LUTON	20	L	0-3	0-1		McKnight	Potts	Dicks	Gale	Martin	Devonshire	Ward	Dickens	Rosenior	Brady*	Ince	Kelly
1	12/2	24,602	*14*				*Harford 45, Wegerle 55, Wilson 75p*	*Sealey*	*Breacker*	*Grimes*	*Preece*	*Foster*	*Beaumont*	*Wilson*	*Wegerle*	*Harford*	*Hill*	*Black*	
							Ref: G Courtney	McKnight cements West Ham's elimination by gifting Luton their two first goals, which beat him at his near post. Dicks' upended Wegerle for the penalty that put the seal on West Ham's defeat. Poor McKnight was cheered whenever he held a back-pass; he now makes way for Parkes.											
SF	A	LUTON	20	L	0-2	0-1		Parkes	Potts	Dicks	Gale	Martin	Kelly	Ward	Parris	Slater	Brady	Ince	
2	1/3	*12,020*	*14*				*Harford 43, Wegerle 55*	*Sealey*	*Breacker*	*Grimes*	*Preece*	*Foster*	*Beaumont*	*Wilson*	*Wegerle*	*Harford*	*Hill*	*Black*	
							Ref: D Axcell (Hammers lose 0-5 on aggregate)	Without the injured Rosenior, West Ham never look like recouping the deficit, which means John Lyall tastes defeat for the first time in five semi-finals. Luton had not lost in 20 cup-ties played on their plastic pitch. Once Harford had been set up by Preece, everyone went to sleep.											

FA Cup																			
3	H	ARSENAL	20	D	2-2	2-1	Dickens 18, Bould 41 (og)	McKnight	Stewart	Dicks	Potts	Martin	Devonshire*	Brady	Kelly	Rosenior	Dickens	Ince	Keen
	8/1	22,017	*1*				*Merson 44, 65*	*Lukic*	*O'Leary*	*Winterburn*	*Thomas*	*Bould**	*Adams*	*Rocastle*	*Richardson*	*Smith*	*Merson*	*Marwood^*	*Davis/Groves*
							Ref: N Midgley	Top plays bottom, and bottom nearly wins. When Lukic and Bould get into a tizzy, trying to deal with Potts' high ball, West Ham lead 2-0. They need to hold out till half-time, but are pegged back when Merson beats McKnight with ease. A bout of head tennis precedes the equaliser.											
3R	A	ARSENAL	20	W	1-0	0-0	Rosenior 77	McKnight	Stewart	Dicks	Potts	Martin*	Devonshire	Brady^	Kelly	Rosenior	Dickens	Ince	Strodder/Keen
	11/1	*44,124*	*1*					*Lukic*	*Dixon*	*Winterburn*	*Thomas*	*O'Leary*	*Adams*	*Rocastle**	*Richardson*	*Smith*	*Merson*	*Marwood^*	*Davis/Groves*
							Ref: N Midgley	26 league points separate the sides. Arsenal are the division's top scorers. Smith, Merson and Marwood have bagged 36 between them, but fail to put McKnight under any pressure. Rosenior's header wins it. On three out of four previous Cup meetings, the victors have gone on to win it.											
4	A	SWINDON	19	D	0-0	0-0		McKnight	Potts	Dicks	Gale	Martin	Devonshire*	Ward	Kelly	Rosenior	Brady	Ince	Dickens
	28/1	*18,627*	*2:16*					*Digby*	*McLoughlin*	*Bodin*	*Jones*	*Calderwood*	*Gittens*	*Foley*	*Cornwell*	*Henry*	*MacLaren*	*Geddis**	*Hockaday*
							Ref: M Peck	An undistinguished cup-tie. After four minutes Rosenior fastened on to a poor back-pass but his effort was saved by Fraser Digby. After 48 minutes Digby saves from the same player. David Kelly hit the bar in the second half. Paul Ince had his name taken for excessive protests.											
4R	H	SWINDON	19	W	1-0	0-0	Rosenior 61	McKnight	Potts	Dicks	Gale	Martin*	Devonshire	Ward	Kelly^	Rosenior	Brady	Ince	Strodder/Dickens
	1/2	24,723	*2:16*					*Digby*	*McLoughlin*	*Bodin*	*Jones*	*Calderwood*	*Gittens*	*Foley*	*Cornwell*	*Hockaday**	*MacLaren*	*Geddis*	*Henry*
							Ref: M Peck	Lou Macari's Swindon are denied the victory their enterprise warranted, leaving West Ham to slink away unable to believe their luck. Dicks' cross was missed by Kelly and Ince, but not by Rosenior. Twice West Ham have won the Cup after beating Swindon. Macari has left his mark!											
5	A	CHARLTON	20	W	1-0	0-0	Slater 53	Parkes	Potts	Parris	Gale	Martin	Devonshire*	Ward !	Dickens	Slater	Brady	Ince	Keen
	18/2	*18,785*	*17*					*Bolder*	*Humphrey*	*Reid*	*Shirtliff*	*Pates*	*Peake**	*Lee R^*	*Mortimer*	*MacKenzie*	*Williams*	*Crooks*	*Leaburn/Campbell*
							Ref: J Ashworth	38-year-old Phil Parkes is recalled in goal, 10 years after he first signed for the Hammers. Charlton have not reached the last eight of the FA Cup for 42 years, but must have fancied their chances after Ward was sent off following a clash with Pates. Slater converts Devonshire's cross.											

QF	H	NORWICH	20	D	0-0	0-0		Parkes	Potts	Dicks	Gale	Strodder	Devonshire*	Kelly	Dickens	Slater	Brady	Ince	Keen
	18/3	29,119	*2*					*Gunn*	*Culverhouse*	*Bowen*	*Butterworth*	*Linighan*	*Townsend*	*Gordon*	*Rosario*	*Allen**	*Phelan*	*Putney*	*Fox*
							Ref: L Shapter	Norwich are still chasing the double. The tie was played in a cold wind. *The Times* wrote of West Ham's attack: 'Kelly and Slater were as effective as anaesthetised flies'. Strodder hit the post for West Ham and Gordon for Norwich. Twice Linighan wasted free headers at corners.											
QF	A	NORWICH	20	L	1-3	0-2	Ince 74	Parkes	Potts	Dicks	Gale	Strodder	Devonshire*	Kelly^	Dickens	Slater	Brady	Ince	Hilton/Keen
R	22/3	*25,785*	*2*				*Allen 25, 27, Gordon 85*	*Gunn*	*Culverhouse*	*Bowen*	*Butterworth*	*Linighan*	*Townsend**	*Gordon*	*Rosario*	*Allen*	*Phelan*	*Putney*	*Crook*
							Ref: L Shapter	Malcolm Allen bags two pickpocket goals for Norwich to leave West Ham chasing the improbable. They could never get a grip on City's 6ft 3in striker, Rosario, though they battled manfully to the end. There is nothing left in West Ham's season, other than near-inevitable relegation.											

		Home						Away					
	P	W	D	L	F	A		W	D	L	F	A	Pts
1 Arsenal	38	10	6	3	35	19		12	4	3	38	17	76
2 Liverpool	38	11	5	3	33	11		11	5	3	32	17	76
3 Nott'm Forest	38	8	7	4	31	16		9	6	4	33	27	64
4 Norwich	38	8	7	4	23	20		9	4	6	25	25	62
5 Derby	38	9	3	7	23	18		8	4	7	17	20	58
6 Tottenham	38	8	6	5	31	24		7	6	6	29	22	57
7 Coventry	38	9	4	6	28	23		5	9	5	19	19	55
8 Everton	38	10	7	2	33	18		4	5	10	17	27	54
9 QP Rangers	38	9	5	5	23	16		5	6	8	20	21	53
10 Millwall	38	10	3	6	27	21		4	8	7	20	31	53
11 Manchester U	38	10	5	4	27	13		3	7	9	18	22	51
12 Wimbledon	38	10	3	6	30	19		4	6	9	20	27	51
13 Southampton	38	6	7	6	25	26		4	8	7	27	40	45
14 Charlton	38	6	7	6	25	24		4	5	10	19	34	42
15 Sheffield Wed	38	6	6	7	21	25		4	6	9	13	26	42
16 Luton	38	8	6	5	32	21		2	5	12	10	31	41
17 Aston Villa	38	7	6	6	25	22		2	7	10	20	34	40
18 Middlesbro'	38	6	7	6	28	30		3	5	11	16	31	39
19 WEST HAM	38	3	6	10	19	30		7	2	10	18	32	38
20 Newcastle	38	3	6	10	19	28		4	4	11	13	35	31
	760	157	112	111	538	424		111	112	157	424	538	1028

Odds & ends

Double wins: (2) Newcastle, Millwall.
Double losses: (8) Southampton, Man U, Arsenal, Middlesbrough, Liverpool, Everton, Spurs, Norwich.

Won from behind: (2) Derby (h), Newcastle (a).
Lost from in front: (4) QPR (a), Man U (h), Middlesbrough (h), Everton (a).

High spots: Four successive league wins from 22 April to give a fighting chance of avoiding relegation.
Reaching semi-final of Littlewoods Cup.

Low spots: Relegation.
The anguish of having to wait several days after the last match to have relegation confirmed.

Hammer of the Year: Paul Ince.
Ever-presents: (0).
Hat-tricks: (0).
Leading scorer: (11) Leroy Rosenior.

	Appearances						Goals			
	Lge	*Sub*	LC	*Sub*	FAC	*Sub*	Lge	LC	FAC	Tot
Brady, Liam	21	*1*	4	*1*	7		3			3
Devonshire, Alan	14	*6*	4		7					
Dickens, Alan	34	*3*	6		5	*2*	5	1	1	7
Dicks, Julian	34		7		6		2			2
Gale, Tony	31		6		5			1		1
Hilton, Paul	9	*2*	2			*1*				
Ince, Paul	32	*1*	7		7		3	3	1	7
Keen, Kevin	16	*8*	1	*1*		*5*	3	1		4
Kelly, David	21	*4*	6	*1*	6		6	4		10
McAlister, Tom	2									
McAvennie, Frank	8	*1*								
McKnight, Allen	23		6		4					
McQueen, Tom		*2*								
Martin, Alvin	27		5		5		1	2		3
Parkes, Phil	13		1		3					
Parris, George	23	*4*	3		1		1			1
Potts, Steve	23	*5*	5	*1*	7					
Rosenior, Leroy	26	*2*	5		4		7	2	2	11
Robson, Stewart	6		1							
Slater, Stuart	16	*2*	1		3		1		1	2
Stewart, Ray	5	*1*	1		2		2	1		3
Strodder, Gary	4	*3*	1		2	*2*				
Ward, Mark	30		5	*1*	3		2			2
(own-goals)							1	1	1	3
23 players used	**418**	***45***	**77**	***5***	**77**	***10***	**37**	**16**	**6**	**59**

No	Date		Att	Pos	Pt	F-A	H-T	Scorers, Times, and Referees	1	2	3	4	5	6	7	8	9	10	11	subs used
1	A	STOKE			D	1-1	1-0	Keen 32	Parkes	Potts	Parris	Gale	Martin	Keen	Ward	McAvennie*	Slater	Brady	Ince	Kelly
	19/8		*16,058*		1			*Biggins 85*	*Fox*	*Butler*	*Statham*	*Kamara*	*Cranson*	*Beeston*	*Hackett*	*Scott**	*Bamber*	*Biggins*	*Beagrie*	*Saunders*
								Ref: G Aplin	Motorway roadworks delayed kick-off by 17 minutes. New boss Macari sees record buy Frank McAvennie break a leg in a 55th-minute clash with Chris Kamara. Hammers were ahead through Keen's goal, against the run of play. Beagrie's cross was glanced in by Wayne Biggins.											
2	H	BRADFORD C			W	2-0	2-0	Slater 32, 33	Parkes	Potts	Dicks	Gale	Martin	Keen	Ward	Kelly	Slater	Brady	Parris	
	23/8		19,914		4				*Tomlinson*	*Abbott*	*Tinnion*	*Aizlewood*	*Sinnott*	*Evans*	*Duxbury*	*Davies*	*Jewell*	*Quinn*	*Ellis**	*Chapman*
								Ref: B Hill	With Rosenior and McAvennie injured, Macari is short of strikers. Talk of Ince about to sign for Man U has the crowd chanting: 'We hate Paul Ince.' Slater's cheeky solo goal, when he skipped round Mark Aizlewood, was capped seconds later when he was unmarked for Ward's cross.											
3	H	PLYMOUTH		1	W	3-2	1-0	Kelly 20, Allen 50, Keen 75	Parkes	Potts	Dicks	Gale	Martin	Keen	Ward	Kelly	**Allen M**	Brady	Parris	
	26/8		20,231		7			*Stuart 54, 77*	*Wilmot*	*Brown*	*Brimcombe*	*Marker*	*Burrows*	*Smith*	*Byrne*	*McCarthy*	*Tynan*	*Thomas*	*Stuart*	
								Ref: T Holbrook	Martin Allen has signed from QPR for £675,000, having had a bust-up with Trevor Francis over attending the birth of his child. His header makes it 2-0. It was 3-1 when Ward's shot was blocked but Keen followed up. When Stuart fired inside the near post it set up a nervy climax.											
4	A	HULL		1	D	1-1	1-0	Ward 5	Parkes	Potts	Dicks	Gale	Martin	Keen	Ward	Kelly !	Allen	Brady*	Slater	Devonshire
	2/9		*9,235*		8			*Swan 64*	*Kelly*	*Murray**	*Jacobs*	*Swan*	*Terry*	*Jobson^*	*Askew*	*Roberts*	*Brown*	*McParland*	*Doyle !*	*de Mange/Jenkinson*
								Ref: J Ashworth	Kelly's cross is turned in by Mark Ward for the perfect start. Hull's makeshift striker Peter Swan levelled at the second attempt. Four minutes from time Dicks' free-kick cannons off the wall and a free-for-all ensues. Kelly and Doyle are sent off. Suspension will claim another striker.											
5	H	SWINDON		3	D	1-1	1-0	Allen 16	Parkes	Potts	Dicks	Gale	Martin	Keen	Ward	Kelly*	Allen	Brady^	Parris	Dolan/Devonshire
	9/9		21,469	*14*	9			*Gittens 53*	*Digby*	*Barnard*	*King*	*McLoughlin*	*Calderwood*	*Gittens*	*Jones*	*Close*	*White*	*MacLaren*	*Galvin**	*Cornwall*
								Ref: A Seville	Stuart Slater missed this match, having run into a goal-post in training. Ward combined with Liam Brady down the left for the first goal; John Gittens flicked over Parkes' head for the equaliser. Dicks and Galvin were booked for dissent in a match that at times threatened to boil over.											
6	A	BRIGHTON		8	L	**0-3**	0-3		Parkes	Potts	Dicks	Gale	Martin	Keen	Ward	Slater	Allen	Brady	Parris	
	16/9		*12,689*	*2*	9			*Bremner 4, Codner 15, Nelson 18*	*Keeley*	*Chivers*	*Chapman**	*Curbishley*	*Bissett*	*Gatting*	*Trusson*	*Wood*	*Bremner*	*Codner*	*Wilkins*	*Owers*
								Ref: R Wiseman	A cold wet day, and West Ham trail 0-3 after just 18 minutes. The crucial first goal was a deflected header. West Ham might have clawed their way back, but when Bissett felled Ward on 53 mins, Brady's penalty was saved. Macari kept his players behind locked doors for over an hour.											
7	H	WATFORD		5	W	1-0	1-0	Dicks 17p	Parkes	Potts	Dicks	Gale	Martin	Keen	Allen	Slater	Dolan*	**Foster**	Parris	Rosenior
	23/9		20,728	*9*	12				*Coton*	*Gibbins*	*Jackett*	*Richardson**	*Holdsworth*	*Roeder*	*Thomas*	*Wilkinson*	*Roberts^*	*Porter*	*Hodges*	*Henry/Falconer*
								Ref: K Morton	21-year-old Dicks is made skipper in place of Alvin Martin, who had held the honour for five years. When Gary Porter tugged Slater's shirt, Dicks obliged from the spot. Watford boss Steve Harrison complained that Potts twice handled in the box, but got away with it each time.											
8	A	PORTSMOUTH		2	W	1-0	0-0	Rosenior 89	Parkes	Potts	Dicks	Gale	Martin	Keen	Allen	Slater	Rosenior	Foster	Parris	
	26/9		*12,632*	*21*	15				*Knight*	*Maguire*	*Beresford*	*Fillery*	*Sandford*	*Ball*	*Wigley**	*Kuhl*	*Whittingham*	*Chamberlain*	*Black*	*Neill*
								Ref: D Hutchinson	Pompey are on a high following good results against Man U in the Littlewoods Cup and Middlesbrough in the league. Though still unfit, and having had two operations this year, Leroy Rosenior wants to play. He bags a precious late winner when George Parris cuts the ball back.											
9	H	WEST BROM		7	L	2-3	0-2	Dolan 68, Parris 70	Parkes	Potts	Dicks	Gale	Martin	Keen	Allen	Slater	Kelly*	Foster	Parris	Dolan
	30/9		19,842	*12*	15			*Ford 14, McNally 33, 73p*	*Naylor*	*Bradley*	*Burgess*	*Robson**	*Whyte*	*North*	*Ford*	*Goodman*	*Thomas*	*McNally*	*Anderson*	*Talbot*
								Ref: M Bodenham	George Parris made one goal and scored another – nutmegging Burgess and chipping Naylor – to haul West Ham back on level terms. Foster completed a wretched match by pushing Whyte for the decisive penalty. Foster had also been at fault when Goodman's cross made it 2-0.											
10	H	LEEDS		10	L	0-1	0-1		Parkes	Potts	Dicks	Gale*	Martin	Keen	Allen	Slater	Ward	Foster	Parris	Brady
	7/10		23,539	*3*	15			*Jones 22*	*Day*	*Sterland*	*Whitlow*	*Jones*	*Fairclough*	*Haddock*	*Strachan*	*Barry*	*Baird*	*Davison**	*Williams*	*Shutt*
								Ref: R Groves	An aimless match, settled by Vinnie Jones, who turned in Michael Whitlow's low cross. Stuart Slater was caught offside five times in the first seven minutes. Gale collided with Batty and went off with knee trouble. West Ham hardly ever threatened ex-Hammer Mervyn Day in goal.											
11	A	SHEFFIELD UTD		8	W	2-0	1-0	Ward 38, 71p	Parkes	Potts	Dicks	Strodder	Martin	Keen	Ward	Slater	Dolan	Foster	Parris	
	14/10		*20,822*	*1*	18				*Tracey*	*Hill**	*Rostron*	*Booker*	*Stancliffe*	*Morris*	*Bradshaw*	*Gannon*	*Agana*	*Deane*	*Bryson^*	*Todd/Francis*
								Ref: K Redfern	United lose their unbeaten record but retain their top position. Hammers' hero is Mark Ward, signed from Oldham for £250,000 in 1985, but unsettled at Upton Park. At 0-0 Tracey fouled Slater but Dicks' penalty hit the bar. When Jones felled Dolan, Ward took the kick himself.											

No	Venue	Opponent / Date	Att	Pos	Res	Pts	F-A	H-T	Scorers, Times, and Referees	1	2	3	4	5	6	7	8	9	10	11	subs used
12	H	SUNDERLAND		7	W		**5-0**	3-0	Allen 9, Slater 16, Keen 41, Dolan 85, 86	Parkes	Potts	Dicks*	Strodder	Martin	Keen	Ward	Slater	Dolan	Allen	Parris	Brady
		18/10	20,901	*8*		21				*Carter*	*Kay*	*Hardyman*	*Bennett*	*MacPhail*	*Owers*	*Bracewell*	*Armstrong*	*Gates**	*Gabbiadini*	*Pascoe^*	*Cullen/Hauser*
									Ref: J Martin	It takes Parris just 15 seconds to be booked and just nine minutes for Allen to curl the opening goal. When Slater chested down and volleyed No 2 you knew it wouldn't be Sunderland's day. Said boss Denis Smith: 'God knows what a full-strength Hammers would have done to us.'											
13	A	PORT VALE		4	D		2-2	1-0	Keen 43, Slater 64	Parkes	Potts	Dicks	Strodder	Martin	Keen	Ward	Slater	Dolan	Allen	Parris	
		21/10	*8,899*	*16*		22			*Martin 51 (og), Futcher 87*	*Grew*	*Webb*	*Hughes*	*Walker**	*Aspin*	*Glover*	*Miller^*	*Earle*	*Cross*	*Beckford*	*Mills*	*Jeffers/Futcher*
									Ref: J Hendrick	Wet and blustery, and motorway hold-ups delays the kick-off. Keen sprints from the halfway line to make it 1-0, only for Martin to head into his own net. Dolan's header hit a post before Slater restored the lead. Beckford headed down Webb's cross for Ron Futcher to make it 2-2.											
14	H	OXFORD		5	W		3-2	1-1	Parris 18, Slater 55, Dicks 69	Parkes	Potts	Dicks	Strodder	Martin	Keen	Brady	Slater	Dolan	Allen	Parris	
		28/10	19,177	*20*		25			*Stein 16, Mustoe 57*	*Judge*	*Smart*	*Phillips*	*Lewis*	*Foster*	*Greenall*	*Mustoe*	*Ford*	*Durin*	*Stein*	*Heath**	*Simpson*
									Ref: D Axcell	Liam Brady is the architect of this exciting win, which is remembered largely for two thunderbolts. George Parris's bullet from outside the area was a quick riposte to Marke Stein's opener. After Robbie Mustoe's equaliser Keen's short free-kick enabled Dicks' to fire a 30-yard screamer.											
15	A	BOURNEMOUTH		5	D		1-1	1-1	Strodder 33	Parkes	Potts	Dicks	Strodder	Martin	Keen*	Brady	Slater	Dolan	Allen	Parris	Ward
		1/11	*9,979*	*14*		26			*Blissett 21*	*Peyton*	*Bond*	*Coleman*	*Teale*	*Shearer*	*Peacock*	*O'Connor*	*Moulden*	*O'Driscoll*	*Brooks*	*Blissett*	
									Ref: H King	West Ham have never beaten the Cherries, but might have done had Keen's 71st-minute effort bounced in, rather than off the post. Ref Howard King gave Macari a lift home afterwards, and one wonders whether they discussed Luther Blisset's chipped goal, which looked to be offside.											
16	A	WOLVES		5	L		0-1	0-0		Parkes	Potts	Dicks	Strodder	Martin	Keen*	Brady	Slater	Dolan^	Allen	Parris	Ward/Foster
		4/11	*22,231*	*11*		26			*Bull 66*	*Kendall*	*Bennett*	*Venus*	*Bellamy*	*Westley*	*Downing*	*Thompson*	*Cook*	*Bull*	*Mutch*	*Dennison*	
									Ref: W Flood	West Ham managed just two shots on target – from Strodder and Allen – so they can have few complaints. Steve Bull had been sent off in midweek against Leicester. But now he took a delicate pass from Mutch, swept past Strodder, and scored coolly. Parkes was the busier keeper.											
17	H	NEWCASTLE		7	D		0-0	0-0		Parkes	Potts	Dicks	Strodder	Martin	Keen	Brady*	Slater	Dolan^	Ward	Parris	Devonshire/Kelly
		11/11	**25,892**	*3*		27				*Burridge*	*Ranson*	*Stimson*	*Dillon*	*Scott*	*Kristensen*	*Brazil**	*Brock^*	*Quinn*	*McGhee*	*O'Brien*	*Gallagher/Anderson*
									Ref: D Hedges	This was a no-holds-barred encounter that conjured up few memorable moments. Brady's 25-yard free-kick was turned aside by John Burridge, and sub David Kelly was off-target with a bicycle-kick. Jim Smith was the happier manager. Police had to go into the crowd to eject hooligans.											
18	H	MIDDLESBROUGH		5	W		2-0	1-0	Slater 8, Dicks 59p	Parkes	Potts	Dicks	Foster	Martin	Keen	Brady	Slater	Allen	Ward	Parris	
		18/11	18,720	*21*		30				*Poole*	*Parkinson*	*Mohan*	*Mowbray*	*Coleman*	*Putney*	*Slaven*	*Proctor*	*Burke**	*Brennan*	*Davenport*	*Kernaghan*
									Ref: K Cooper	Slater fears for his place now that Justin Fashanu has signed on loan, and scores with a low, angled shot. The lead was doubled when Parris was toppled by Simon Coleman in the box. The score looks comfortable but is deceptive. Slaven and Kernaghan both hit the wood late on.											
19	A	BLACKBURN		7	L		4-5	1-4	Brady 38, Dicks 47p, Slater 64, Ward 87	Parkes	Potts	Dicks	Strodder	Martin	Devonshire	Brady	Slater	Allen	Ward	**Fashanu**	
		25/11	*10,215*	*5*		30			*S'llars 4,9, G'rner 29, Stap' 34, J'hnrose 46*	*Collier*	*Atkins*	*Sulley*	*Reid*	*Hill*	*May*	*Irvine*	*Johnrose*	*Stapleton*	*Garner**	*Sellars*	*Kennedy*
									Ref: T Holbrook	The score sounds close until it is realised that West Ham were 0-4 down after 33 minutes and 1-5 after 46 minutes. Brady had pulled one back for West Ham when chesting down and turning to score. Keith Hill handled for Dicks' penalty. Devonshire plays his first game of the season.											
20	H	STOKE		7	D		0-0	0-0		Parkes	Potts	Dicks	Strodder	Martin	Devonshire*	Brady	Slater	Keen	Ward	Fashanu^	Kelly/Foster
		2/12	17,704	*23*		31				*Fox*	*Butler*	*Carr*	*Kamara*	*Higgins*	*Berry*	*Hackett*	*Beeston*	*Saunders*	*Biggins*	*Hilaire*	
									Ref: B Hill	Stoke's Chris Kamara was booed constantly for the tackle which broke McAvennie's leg on the opening day. Alan Ball's team relied on the offside trap, but should have lost when Butler tripped Ward after 55 mins. Dicks had already scored 7 penalties, but this one was saved by Fox.											
21	A	BRADFORD C		7	L		1-2	1-1	Ward 29	Parkes	Potts	McQueen	Strodder	Martin	Gale	Brady	Slater	Keen	Ward	Allen	
		9/12	*9,257*	*19*		31			*Leonard 15, Quinn 90*	*Tomlinson*	*Mitchell*	*Tinnion**	*Aizlewood*	*Oliver*	*Abbott*	*Megson*	*Evans*	*Leonard*	*Quinn*	*Campbell*	*Davies*
									Ref: A Wilkie	Hammers missed chances galore and cannot believe they lost. Brady had set up Ward's equaliser, after Leonard's header had put City in front. Thereafter there was only one team in it, but nearly three minutes into stoppage-time Jimmy Quinn was left unmarked on the edge of the box.											
22	H	OLDHAM		8	L		0-2	0-2		**Suckling**	Potts	Dicks	Strodder*	Martin	Gale	Brady	Slater	Foster^	Ward	Allen	Keen/Devonshire
		16/12	**14,960**	*4*		31			*Milligan 3, Ritchie 20*	*Rhodes*	*Irwin*	*Barlow*	*Henry*	*Barratt*	*Warhurst**	*Marshall*	*Ritchie*	*Bunn*	*Milligan*	*Holden R*	*Palmer*
									Ref: B Hamer	With Parkes having crocked knees and Miklosko's work permit being delayed, Perry Suckling is signed on loan from Palace. He is quickly beaten by Mike Milligan's header into the top corner. Irwin's cross was then turned in by Foster and Ritchie. Irwin's free-kick also hit the post.											
23	A	IPSWICH		10	L		0-1	0-1		Suckling	Potts	Dicks	Strodder	Martin	Gale	Brady*	Slater^	Keen	Ward	Allen	Parris/Kelly
		26/12	*24,365*	*5*		31			*Stockwell 40*	*Forrest*	*Stockwell*	*Thompson*	*Zondervan**	*Yallop*	*Linighan*	*Donowa*	*Dozzell*	*Wark*	*Kiwomya^*	*Milton*	*Humes/D'Avray*
									Ref: J Ashworth	West Ham have been beaten 3-4 by Chelsea in the Zenith-Data Cup. This Boxing Day fixture brings out Portman Road's biggest gate in four years. Louis Donowa's cross to Mick Stockwell earns three more points for John Duncan's young side. Bonds played Tony Gale in midfield.											

BARCLAYS LEAGUE DIVISION 2

Manager: Lou Macari ⇨ Billy Bonds

SEASON 1989-90

No	Date			Att	Pos	Pt	F-A	H-T	Scorers, Times, and Referees	1	2	3	4	5	6	7	8	9	10	11	subs used
24		A	LEICESTER		11	L	0-1	0-0		Suckling	Potts	Dicks	Strodder	Martin	Gale	Allen	**Bishop**	**Morley**	Kelly	Parris	
	30/12			*16,925*	*13*	31			*Mauchlen 88*	*Hodge*	*Mauchlen*	*Spearing**	*Mills*	*Walsh*	*Paris*	*Reid^*	*Moran*	*Campbell*	*McAllister*	*Wright*	*James/North*
									Ref: J Deakin	West Ham's dreadful run – one point from six games – continues, this time against David Pleat's resurgent Leicester. City were bottom of the league in October, but have now won five of their last six. Mauchlen's late strike is his first and last goal of the season. 1989 ends on a downer.											
25		H	BARNSLEY		11	W	4-2	3-0	Allen 4, Keen 23, 42, Dicks 50p	Suckling	Potts	Dicks	Parris	Martin	Gale	**Quinn**	Bishop	Keen*	Morley	Allen	Kelly
	1/1			18,391	*21*	34			*Dobbin 75, Archdeacon 88*	*Baker*	*Dobbin*	*Cross*	*Futcher*	*Sholton*	*Smith**	*Broddle^*	*Agnew*	*Foreman*	*Currie*	*Archdeacon*	*Cooper/Tiler*
									Ref: M James	Jimmy Quinn is the latest addition to West Ham's ranks. None of the three new buys gets on the scoresheet, but Trevor Morley comes closest – twice hitting the woodwork. Morley was also fouled for the penalty. Strangest goal was Keen's first, a cross which floated in off the far post.											
26		A	PLYMOUTH		10	D	1-1	0-1	Quinn 56	Suckling	Potts	Dicks	Gale	Martin	Devonshire*	Allen	Bishop	Keen^	Morley	Quinn	Brady/Parris
	13/1			*11,671*	*16*	35			*Tynan 2*	*Wilmot*	*Brown*	*Broddle*	*Marker*	*Burrows*	*Hodges*	*Summerfield*	*McCarthy**	*Tynan*	*Thomas*	*Robson*	*Campbell*
									Ref: M Reed	West Ham have been knocked out of the FA Cup by Torquay, and they are equally dreadful against these other west country opponents, who had not won at home in six attempts. Lou Macari refused to face the press afterwards over rumours of financial irregularities while at Swindon.											
27		H	HULL		11	L	1-2	1-1	Morley 17	Suckling	Potts*	McQueen	Strodder^	Martin	Gale	Brady	Bishop	Quinn	Morley	Keen	**Kelly P**/Kelly D
	20/1			16,847	*19*	35			*Buckley 34, Payton 60*	*Hesford*	*Brown*	*Jacobs*	*Jobson*	*Buckley*	*de Mange*	*Roberts*	*Payton**	*Whitehurst*	*Askew*	*Doyle*	*Agata*
									Ref: R Nixon	Paul Kelly makes his second-half debut but cannot prevent struggling Hull deepening Macari's wounds. West Ham looked punchless in attack, despite scoring first when Quinn's shot bounced off a defender to Morley. Buckley headed Hull level, then Payton converted de Mange's cross.											
28		H	BRIGHTON		11	W	3-1	0-1	Quinn 60, 84, Dicks 78	Parkes	Robson	Dicks	Parris*	Martin	Gale	Brady	Bishop	Kelly	Slater	Keen	Quinn
	10/2			19,101	*22*	38			*Nelson 14*	*Keeley*	*Chivers*	*Chapman*	*Curbishley*	*Gatting*	*Dublin*	*Nelson*	*Barham*	*Bissett*	*Codner*	*Wilkins*	
									Ref: P Danson	Quinn's half-time arrival transformed the match. Gary Nelson's close-range header had put lowly Brighton in front. Steve Gatting's comical lob over his own keeper set up the equaliser. Dicks then uncorked one of his 30-yard scorchers, before Quinn headed in Keen's free-kick.											
29		A	SWINDON		12	D	2-2	1-1	Quinn 29, 70	**Miklosko**	Robson	Dicks	Parris	Martin	Gale	Brady	Allen	Quinn	Slater*	Keen^	Bishop/Kelly
	18/2			*16,105*	*3*	39			*White 42, MacLaren 66*	*Digby*	*Kerslake*	*Bodin*	*McLoughlin*	*Calderwood*	*Gittens*	*Jones*	*Shearer*	*White*	*MacLaren*	*Foley*	
									Ref: V Callow	A Sunday match. Macari was absent, rather than face his ex-club, and Bonds takes charge. Not the most promising time for Miklosko to make his debut after his £300,000 transfer, but two saves from Tom Jones secures a point. Quinn's header equalised MacLaren's deflected free-kick.											
30		H	BLACKBURN		14	D	1-1	1-0	Quinn 23	Miklosko	Robson*	Dicks	Parris	Martin	Gale	Brady^	Allen	Quinn	Slater	Keen	Kelly/Bishop
	24/2			20,054	*6*	40			*Sellars 78*	*Gennoe*	*Atkins*	*Sulley*	*Reid*	*Moran*	*Mail*	*Kennedy*	*Millar*	*Stapleton*	*Garner**	*Sellars*	*Gayle*
									Ref: M Bodenham	Billy Bonds has been installed as manager, having played almost 800 games for the club, and he receives a rapturous welcome. Quinn's diving header is the least West Ham deserve for their first-half dominance, but Scott Sellars poached an equaliser from Howard Gayle's cross.											
31		A	MIDDLESBROUGH		10	W	1-0	0-0	Allen 86	Miklosko	Robson	Dicks	Parris	Martin	Gale	Brady*	Allen	Quinn^	Slater	Keen	Bishop/Morley
	3/3			*23,617*	*21*	43				*Pears*	*Parkinson*	*McGee*	*Kernaghan*	*Coleman*	*Proctor*	*Slaven*	*Kerr**	*Baird*	*Brennan*	*Ripley*	*Davenport*
									Ref: J Kirkby	Dicks announces: 'It is better now Lou Macari has gone.' Perhaps Dicks was on Cloud Nine after Pears failed to hold his shot and Martin Allen nips in for a late winner. It is Bonds' first win and Hammers' first away win since October. The less said about the rest of the match the better.											
32		H	PORTSMOUTH		10	W	2-1	1-0	Allen 32, Dicks 81p	Miklosko	Slater	Dicks	Parris	Foster	Gale	Brady*	Allen	Rosenior^	Keen	Kelly	Quinn/Bishop
	10/3			20,961	*17*	46			*Kuhl 63*	*Knight*	*Neill*	*Sevens*	*Fillery**	*Hogg*	*Ball*	*Wigley*	*Kuhl*	*Whittingham*	*Black*	*Chamberlain*	*Gilligan*
									Ref: D Axcell	West Ham did not perform, and Bonds admits Portsmouth were unlucky to lose to Kevin Ball's Maradona-style handball in his own box. Guy Whittingham had outjumped Foster – playing his first game since December – to draw level. A Dicks raid down the left brought the first goal.											
33		A	WATFORD		10	W	1-0	0-0	Morley 61	Miklosko	Slater	Dicks	Parris	Foster	Gale	Bishop	Allen	Quinn	Keen	Morley	
	13/3			*15,683*	*13*	49				*Coton*	*Williams*	*Drysdale*	*Richardson*	*Holdsworth*	*Roeder*	*Thomas*	*Allison**	*Pullan*	*Penrice*	*Ashby*	*Roberts*
									Ref: M Pierce	Watford started at a gallop, but once West Ham had weathered the storm they were always the more likely winners. Gale's free-kick led to Trevor Morley side-footing home at the far post. When Holdsworth felled Morley in the box, Dicks' penalty was turned aside by Tony Coton.											
34		A	LEEDS		10	L	2-3	0-2	Morley 51, Chapman 68 (og)	Miklosko	Slater	McQueen	Parris*	Foster	Gale	Bishop	Allen	Quinn	Keen	Morley	Brady
	17/3			***32,536***	*1*	49			*Chapman 18, 42, Strachan 64*	*Day*	*Sterland*	*Snodin*	*Jones*	*Fairclough*	*Haddock*	*Strachan*	*Speed*	*Chapman*	*Varadi**	*Hendrie*	*Shutt*
									Ref: K Redfern	Wilkinson's Leeds are unbeaten at home and heading for the championship. Gordon Strachan plays a blinder, setting up Lee Chapman's goals with a back-heel and a lob, before scoring himself. Chapman netted three times, but the third was at the wrong end, diverting Foster's header.											

No	Date	Opponent	Att	Pos	Res	F-A	H-T	Scorers, Times, and Referees	1	2	3	4	5	6	7	8	9	10	11	subs used
35	H	SHEFFIELD UTD		9	W	**5-0**	1-0	Morley 4, Quinn 53p, 57, 80, Allen 72	Miklosko	Slater	McQueen	Parris	Foster	Gale	Bishop	Allen	Quinn	Keen	Morley	
	21/3		21,629	*2*	52				*Tracey*	*Wilder*	*Rostron*	*Booker*	*Morris*	*Todd**	*Wood^*	*Gannon*	*Whitehurst*	*Deane*	*Bryson*	*Hill/Bradshaw*
								Ref: G Ashby	Blades' first league defeat since 1 January is a humiliating affair for manager Bassett. Man-of-the-match Slater pulled the strings, tormenting full-back Wilder and setting up goals for Morley and Quinn, who has scored six goals in five games. Tracey fouled Morley for the penalty.											
36	A	SUNDERLAND		10	L	3-4	1-1	Quinn 15, 58, Morley 80 *[Gabbiadini 77]*	Miklosko	Slater	McQueen	Parris	Strodder	Gale	Bishop	Allen	Quinn	Keen*	Morley	Brady
	24/3		*13,896*	*9*	52			*Brady 24, Hardyman 60p, Owers 70,*	*Norman*	*Kay*	*Hardyman**	*Heathcote*	*MacPhail*	*Owers*	*Bracewell*	*Armstrong*	*Brady*	*Gabbiadini*	*Pascoe*	*Agboola*
								Ref: T Mills	Dicks was eligible, but injured a thigh in training. With Martin out with tonsillitis, and Foster also injured, Bonds has little option choosing his defence. Pick of the goals was Kieron Brady's overhead kick. When Hardyman made it 2-2 from the spot, Sunderland began to take control.											
37	H	PORT VALE		10	D	2-2	0-0	Morley 53, Gale 58	Miklosko	Slater	Dicks	Parris	Foster	Gale	Bishop	Allen	Quinn*	Keen^	Morley	McAvennie/Brady
	31/3		20,507	*11*	53			*Beckford 54, Cross 75*	*Grew*	*Mills*	*Hughes*	*Walker*	*Parkin*	*Glover*	*Porter*	*Earle*	*Millar**	*Beckford*	*Jeffers*	*Cross*
								Ref: K Barratt	This match produced a rarity – two separate penalties saved by two different players. Mark Grew was Vale's hero, saving from Dicks at 0-0 and from Quinn at 2-1, after Gale's header had restored the lead. The misses proved costly when sub Nicky Cross equalised for the Valiants.											
38	A	WEST BROM		10	W	3-1	2-1	Quinn 6, Bishop 28, Keen 69	Miklosko	Slater	Dicks	Parris	Strodder	Gale	Bishop	Allen	Quinn	Keen	Morley	
	4/4		*11,556*	*16*	56			*Goodman 30*	*Naylor*	*Bradley*	*Harbey*	*Shakespeare*	*North*	*Whyte*	*Ford*	*Goodman*	*Bannister*	*Cartwright*	*Hackett**	*Foster*
								Ref: C Trussell	15 goals in five games sounds good, but West Ham have also let in 10, which is not so good. When Stacey North handled outside the box, Quinn's free-kick was deflected in. Quinn's far-post header made No 2 for Bishop. Goodman pulled one back after a corner was nodded on.											
39	A	OXFORD		8	W	2-0	0-0	Morley 69, Quinn 80	Miklosko	Slater	Dicks	Parris	Foster	Gale	Bishop	Allen	Quinn	Keen*	Morley	McQueen
	7/4		*8,371*	*14*	59				*Kee*	*Smart*	*Ford*	*Lewis*	*Foster*	*Evans*	*Heath**	*Mustoe*	*Durin*	*Stein*	*Simpson*	*Foyle*
								Ref: P Vanes	'We didn't play: it is as simple as that,' is Bonds' frank assessment of West Ham's flattering win over Brian Horton's Oxford. Goal No 1 came when Paul Kee failed to gather Bishop's corner. Quinn's 30-yard daisy-trimmer made the points safe but Miklosko played his best game so far.											
40	H	BOURNEMOUTH		8	W	4-1	2-1	Miller 20 (og), Bishop 21, Dicks 64p,	Miklosko	Slater	Dicks	Parris*	Foster	Gale	Bishop	Allen	Quinn	Keen	Morley^	Potts/McAvennie
	11/4		20,202	*19*	62			*Coleman 37* [Allen 74]	*Peyton*	*Slatter**	*Coleman*	*Shearer*	*Miller*	*Peacock*	*O'Driscoll*	*Redknapp*	*Aylott^*	*Holmes*	*Blissett*	*Mundee/Cadette*
								Ref: R Hamer	Cherries' manager Harry Redknapp has nothing but praise for the Hammers. This is the third game in a row in which Quinn scores a deflected goal, but this time the deviation is so great he cannot claim it. Miller's foul on Quinn earned the penalty. Quinn then nodded on for Allen.											
41	A	BARNSLEY		8	D	1-1	1-1	Morley 24	Miklosko	Slater	Dicks	Parris	Foster	Gale	Keen	Allen	Quinn	Morley	Brady	
	14/4		*10,344*	*18*	63			*Taggart 11*	*Baker*	*Fleming*	*Taggart*	*Tiler*	*Cross*	*Smith*	*McCord**	*Banks*	*Saville*	*Agnew*	*Cooper^*	*Lowndes/O'Connell*
								Ref: M Peck	This Easter fixture brought a rousing performance from West Ham, but the two dropped points suggest the play-offs may be beyond Billy Bonds' team. Barnsley's needs are of a different order. They are now unbeaten in six, and their late-season rally will stave off relegation.											
42	H	IPSWICH		7	W	2-0	2-0	Allen 27, Keen 36	Miklosko	Slater	Dicks	Parris	Foster	Gale	Brady^	Allen	Quinn	Keen	Morley*	McAvennie/Potts
	17/4		25,178	*10*	66				*Forrest*	*Yallop*	*Thompson*	*Zondervan*	*Gayle*	*Linighan*	*Kiwomya**	*Stuart*	*Wark*	*Dozzell*	*Milton^*	*Donowa/Humes*
								Ref: K Burge	Kevin Keen steals the show in this, his 100th senior appearance for the Hammers. His slide-rule pass makes the first goal for Martin Allen, and he scores the second with a thumping volley. John Duncan's Ipswich pressed hard, and Miklosko saved well from Linighan and Dozzell.											
43	A	OLDHAM		7	L	**0-3**	0-0		Miklosko	Slater	Dicks	Parris	Foster	Gale	Brady	Allen	Quinn	Keen	Morley*	McQueen
	21/4		*12,190*	*9*	66			*Ritchie 52p, Bunn 55, 85*	*Rhodes*	*Irwin*	*Barlow*	*Henry*	*Barrett*	*Warhurst*	*Redfearn*	*Ritchie*	*Bunn*	*Milligan*	*Holden R*	
								Ref: K Barratt	Oldham haunt West Ham's season, inflicting their heaviest cup and league defeats. West Ham were faring well until the 52nd minute when Miklosko brought down Redfearn, but insisted he had played the ball first. Once Ritchie had converted from the spot, West Ham fell apart.											
44	A	NEWCASTLE		7	L	1-2	1-0	Dicks 35p	Miklosko	Slater	Dicks	Potts	Foster	Gale	Robson	Allen	Quinn*	Keen	Morley^	McAvennie/Farris
	28/4		*31,496*	*3*	66			*Kristensen 52, Quinn 56*	*Burridge*	*Scott*	*Stimpson*	*Aitken*	*Anderson*	*Ranson*	*Brown*	*Dillon**	*Quinn*	*McGhee*	*Kristensen*	*O'Brien*
								Ref: V Callow	Dicks' penalty, when Martin Allen was knocked off the ball, was just reward for West Ham's first-half dominance. The Magpies took control after the break, taking all three points when Mick Quinn netted his 36th goal of the season. Frank McAvennie came on for the last 30 minutes.											
45	H	LEICESTER		7	W	3-1	2-0	Rosenior 28, Keen 36, Morley 48	Miklosko	Slater	Dicks	Potts	Foster	Gale	Robson	Allen	Rosenior	Keen*	Morley	Brady
	2/5		17,939	*12*	69			*Ramsey 61*	*Hodge*	*Mills*	*Linton**	*Ramsey*	*Oldfield^*	*James*	*Reid*	*North*	*Kelly*	*McAllister*	*Wright*	*Oakes/Smith*
								Ref: M Reed	Leroy Rosenior celebrates his surprise recall with a fine header from Dicks' cross. When Morley was tripped in the box, Dicks' penalty was saved by Martin Hodge, but Keen followed up. Leicester's Tommy Wright missed two late chances that might have turned the game around.											
46	H	WOLVES		7	W	4-0	2-0	Keen 18, Morley 39, Robson 47, Brady 88	Miklosko	Slater	Dicks	Potts	Foster	Gale	Robson	Allen	Rosenior	Keen*	Morley^	Brady/Quinn
	5/5		22,509	*10*	72				*Kendall*	*Bennett*	*Thompson*	*Venus*	*Westley*	*Bellamy*	*Cook**	*Downing^*	*Bull*	*Paskin*	*Dennison*	*Jones/McLoughlin*
		Home	Away					Ref: D Allison	Liam Brady bids farewell on a sun-kissed afternoon with a late goal that prompts the friendliest of pitch invasions. When play restarted, the ref let discretion rule and immediately blew for time. Fingers crossed that the FA will ban Swindon, and let West Ham take their play-off place.											
Average		20,278	15,686																	

Littlewoods Cup					F-A	H-T	Scorers, Times, and Referees	1	2	3	4	5	6	7	8	9	10	11	subs used
2:1	A	BIRMINGHAM	8	W	2-1	1-0	Allen 37, Slater 87	Parkes	Potts	Dicks	Gale	Martin	Keen	Ward*	Slater	Allen	Dolan	Parris	Brady
	19/9	*10,987*	*3:9*				*Sproson 86*	*Thomas*	*Ashley*	*Matthewson*	*Atkins*	*Sproson*	*Overson*	*Peer*	*Bailey*	*Gordon**	*Gleghorn*	*Hopkins*	*Sturridge*
							Ref: D Allison	The introduction of Brady for the hamstrung Ward on 27 minutes slowed the pace of the game and turned it West Ham's way. In a furious climax Hopkins' shot was charged down for Sproson. Almost from the kick-off Slater fired goalwards and Thomas failed to hold the shot.											
2:2	H	BIRMINGHAM	7	D	1-1	0-0	Dicks 53	Parkes	Potts	Dicks	Gale	Martin	Keen	Allen	Slater	Dolan*	Ward^	Parris	Kelly/Brady
	4/10	12,187	*3:4*				*Atkins 70*	*Thomas*	*Ashley*	*Matthewson*	*Atkins*	*Sproson*	*Overson*	*Tait**	*Bailey*	*Sturridge^*	*Gleghorn*	*Hopkins*	*Peer/Roberts*
							Ref: A Gunn (Hammers win 3-1 on aggregate)	The tie could have swung either way during an eventful first half, which might have finished 3-3. But Dicks' thunderbolt meant City needed to score twice. On another day Dennis Bailey might have grabbed a hat-trick, though Mark Ward's shot hit the Birmingham bar from 35 yards.											
3	A	ASTON VILLA	4	D	0-0	0-0		Parkes	Potts	Dicks	Strodder	Martin	Keen	Brady*	Slater	Dolan	Allen	Parris	Kelly
	25/10	*20,989*	*1:9*					*Spink*	*Price*	*Gage*	*Birch**	*Mountfield*	*Nielsen*	*Daley^*	*Platt*	*Olney*	*Cowans*	*Gray*	*Ormondroyd/Blake*
							Ref: G Courtney	West Ham beat Villa in the quarter-finals last season, and following this defiant draw are favourites to get past them again. Trouble is brewing off the pitch. Mark Ward arrives at the team bus but words are exchanged and he refuses to board it. His absence allowed a rare start for Brady.											
3R	H	ASTON VILLA	5	W	1-0	1-0	Dicks 31	Parkes	Potts	Dicks	Strodder	Martin	Keen	Brady	Slater	Dolan	Ward	Parris	
	8/11	23,833	*1:4*					*Spink*	*Price*	*Gage**	*McGrath*	*Mountfield*	*Nielsen*	*Daley^*	*Platt*	*Olney*	*Cowans*	*Ormondroyd*	*Comyn/Callaghan*
							Ref: D Hutchinson	Graham Taylor's Villa hit six past Everton last Sunday, but they have no answer to the inspirational Brady. The goal came when Paul McGrath fouled Slater. Kevin Keen rolled the free-kick to Dicks. England new boy David Platt had the ball in the net but it was scrubbed off for offside.											
4	H	WIMBLEDON	5	W	1-0	0-0	Allen 81	Parkes	Potts	Dicks !	Strodder	Martin	Keen*	Brady	Slater	Allen	Ward	Parris^	Fashanu/Devonshire
	22/11	24,746	*1:14*					*Segers*	*Joseph*	*Phelan*	*Ryan*	*Young*	*Curle*	*Fairweather*	*Miller**	*Cotterill*	*Sanchez^*	*Wise*	*Cork/Scales*
							Ref: A Buksh	A blood-curdling match, with five booked and Dicks sent off for a late tackle on Wise. Keen cleared Eric Young's header off the line as West Ham withstood early pressure. Ward's cross set up Martin Allen's sizzling volley, but there was still time for Alan Cork to miss an open goal.											
QF	H	DERBY	10	D	1-1	1-0	Dicks 37	Parkes	Potts	Dicks	Parris	Martin	Gale	Brady	Kelly	Rosenior*	Allen !	Keen	Slater
	17/1	25,035	*1:7*				*Saunders 78*	*Shilton*	*Sage*	*Forsyth*	*Williams*	*Wright*	*Hindmarch*	*Pickering*	*Saunders*	*Ramage**	*Hebberd*	*Cross^*	*Patterson/Francis*
							Ref: V Callow	When Hindmarch fouled Leroy Rosenior, Liam Brady touched the free-kick to Julian Dicks. Gayle's frightful back-pass let in Dean Saunders for the equaliser. Martin Allen was sent off for an airborne tackle on Mark Patterson, at which point 10-man Hammers shut up shop.											
QF	A	DERBY	11	D	0-0	0-0		Parkes	Strodder	McQueen	Parris	Martin	Gale	Brady*	Kelly	Slater	Robson^	Keen	**Milne**/Devonshire
R	24/1	*22,510*	*1:9*		*aet*			*Taylor*	*Sage*	*Forsyth*	*Williams*	*Wright*	*Hindmarch*	*Patterson*	*Saunders*	*Harford**	*Hebberd*	*McCord^*	*Francis/Briscoe*
							Ref: J Worrall	This cup-tie was all elbow grease and no skill. With Peter Shilton injured, Derby fielded rookie keeper Martin Taylor. Stewart Robson played his first West Ham match in 16 months. Liam Brady went down without earning a penalty, and a Kevin Keen effort was ruled out for offside.											
QF	H	DERBY	11	W	2-1	1-0	Slater 34, Keen 49	Parkes	Potts*	Dicks	Parris	Martin	Gale	Brady	Kelly	Slater	Robson	Keen	McQueen
RR	31/1	25,166	*1:9*				*Saunders 57*	*Taylor*	*Sage*	*Forsyth*	*Williams*	*Patterson*	*Davidson*	*Francis**	*Saunders*	*Harford*	*Hebberd*	*Briscoe*	*Ramage*
							Ref: K Barratt	Derby are missing the England pair Peter Shilton and Mark Wright, and in driving rain fall behind to Stuart Slater, who banged in Dicks' free-kick. After Keen's goal, Saunders' bullet made it 2-1. Brady cleared Forsyth's header off the line to send West Ham through after five hours.											
SF	A	OLDHAM	11	L	0-6	0-3	*[Holden 46, Palmer 69]*	Parkes	Robson	Dicks	Parris	Martin	Gale	Brady	Slater	Strodder*	Kelly	Keen	Devonshire
1	14/2	*19,263*	*4*				*Adams 11, Ritchie 19, 78, Barrett 33,*	*Hallworth*	*Irwin*	*Barlow*	*Henry*	*Marshall*	*Barrett*	*Adams*	*Ritchie*	*Palmer*	*Milligan*	*Holden R*	
							Ref: L Shapter	Lou Macari refuses to blame Oldham's plastic pitch for this nightmare defeat. He concedes that West Ham were 'outpaced, outworked, and outclassed'. Kick-off was delayed 15 minutes as trains were delayed. Hammers' only moment of ill-fortune came when Slater hit a post at 0-1.											
SF	H	OLDHAM	10	W	3-0	1-0	Martin 13, Dicks 46p, Kelly 65	Miklosko	Slater	Dicks	Parris	Martin	Gale	Brady*	Allen	Rosenior	Kelly	Keen	McQueen
2	7/3	15,431	*4*					*Hallworth*	*Irwin*	*Barlow*	*Henry*	*Barrett*	*Warhurst*	*Adams*	*Palmer*	*Marshall*	*Milligan*	*Holden R*	
							Ref: T Holbrook (Hammers lose 3-6 on aggregate)	It is all academic of course, though had the goals come earlier who knows what might have happened. Bonds uses this match to allow Rosenior his comeback. Hallworth hauled down Keen for Dicks' penalty. At 3-0 Dicks hit the bar. Had it gone in, Oldham's defence may have cracked.											

FA Cup

3	A	TORQUAY	11	L	0-1	0-0		Parkes	Potts	Dicks	Parris*	Martin	Gale	Quinn	Bishop	Keen	Morley	Allen	Rosenior
	6/1		*5,342 4:19*				*Hirons 77*	*Veysey*	*Holmes*	*Lloyd*	*Matthews*	*Elliott*	*Uzell*	*Smith P*	*Edwards*	*Taylor*	*Caldwell**	*Weston*	*Hirons*
							Ref: G Ashby												

Ex-Southend boss Dave Smith masterminds this humiliating defeat. On a quagmire pitch, Paul Smith crosses for 18-year-old sub Paul Hirons to score with his first touch. Coach Mick McGiven walked out on the Hammers 24 hours before the game, as the Swindon scandal deepens.

		Home						Away					
	P	W	D	L	F	A	W	D	L	F	A	Pts
1 Leeds	46	16	6	1	46	18	8	7	8	33	34	85
2 Sheffield Utd	46	14	5	4	43	27	10	8	5	35	31	85
3 Newcastle	46	17	4	2	51	26	5	10	8	29	29	80
4 Swindon †	46	12	6	5	49	29	8	8	7	30	30	74
5 Blackburn	46	10	9	4	43	30	9	8	6	31	29	74
6 Sunderland *	46	10	8	5	41	32	10	6	7	29	32	74
7 WEST HAM	46	14	5	4	50	22	6	7	10	30	35	72
8 Oldham	46	15	7	1	50	23	4	7	12	20	34	71
9 Ipswich	46	13	7	3	38	22	6	5	12	29	44	69
10 Wolves	46	12	5	6	37	20	6	8	9	30	40	67
11 Port Vale	46	11	9	3	37	20	4	7	12	25	37	61
12 Portsmouth	46	9	8	6	40	34	6	8	9	22	31	61
13 Leicester	46	10	8	5	34	29	5	6	12	33	50	59
14 Hull	46	7	8	8	27	31	7	8	8	31	34	58
15 Watford	46	11	6	6	41	28	3	9	11	17	32	57
16 Plymouth	46	9	8	6	30	23	5	5	13	28	40	55
17 Oxford	46	8	7	8	35	31	7	2	14	22	36	54
18 Brighton	46	10	6	7	28	27	5	3	15	28	45	54
19 Barnsley	46	7	9	7	22	23	6	6	11	27	48	54
20 West Brom	46	6	8	9	35	37	6	7	10	32	34	51
21 Middlesbro	46	10	3	10	33	29	3	8	12	19	34	50
22 Bournemouth	46	8	6	9	30	31	4	6	13	27	44	48
23 Bradford C	46	9	6	8	26	24	0	8	15	18	44	41
24 Stoke	46	4	11	8	20	24	2	8	13	15	39	37
	1104	252	165	135	886	640	135	165	252	640	886	1491

* promoted after play-offs
† promotion not accepted

Odds & ends

Double wins: (5) Watford, Portsmouth, Sheff U, Oxford, Middlesbrough.
Double losses: (2) Leeds, Oldham.

Won from behind: (2) Oxford (h), Brighton (h).
Lost from in front: (3) Hull (h), Sunderland (a), Newcastle (a).

High spots: Two unbeaten runs of six games, winning four, beginning 10 February and 31 March.
Reaching semi-final of Littlewoods Cup.

Low spots: Four successive league defeats in December that effectively put paid to hopes of promotion.
Being crushed 0-6 by Oldham in Littlewoods Cup semi-final.
Losing to Fourth Division Torquay in FA Cup.

Hammer of the Year Julian Dicks.
Ever-presents: (0).
Hat-tricks: (1) Jimmy Quinn.
Leading scorer: (13) Jimmy Quinn, Julian Dicks.

	Appearances						Goals			
	Lge	*Sub*	LC	*Sub*	FAC	*Sub*	Lge	LC	FAC	Tot
Allen, Martin	**39**		6		1		**9**	2		**11**
Bishop, Ian	**13**	*4*			1		**2**			**2**
Brady, Liam	**25**	*8*	8	*2*			**2**			**2**
Devonshire, Alan	**3**	*4*		*3*						
Dicks, Julian	**40**		9		1		**9**	4		**13**
Dolan, Eammon	**8**	*2*	4				**3**			**3**
Fashanu, Justin	**2**			*1*						
Foster, Colin	**20**	*2*								
Gale, Tony	**36**		7		1		**1**			**1**
Ince, Paul	**1**									
Keen, Kevin	**43**	*1*	10		1		**10**	1		**11**
Kelly, David	**8**	*8*	5	*2*			**1**	1		**2**
Kelly Paul		*1*								
McAvennie, Frank	**1**	*4*								
McQueen,Tom	**5**	*2*	1	*2*						
Martin, Alvin	**31**		10		1			1		**1**
Miklosko, Ludo	**18**		1							
Milne, Ralph				*1*						
Morley, Trevor	**18**	*1*			1		**10**			**10**
Parkes, Phil	**22**		9		1					
Parris, George	**35**	*3*	9		1		**2**			**2**
Potts, Steve	**30**	*2*	8		1					
Quinn, Jimmy	**18**	*3*			1		**13**			**13**
Rosenior, Leroy	**4**	*1*	2			*1*	**2**			**2**
Robson, Stewart	**7**		3				**1**			**1**
Slater, Stuart	**40**		9	*1*			**7**	2		**9**
Strodder, Gary	**16**		5				**1**			**1**
Suckling, Perry	**6**									
Ward, Mark	**17**	*2*	4				**5**			**5**
(own-goals)							**2**			**2**
29 players used	**506**	*48*	**110**	*12*	**11**	*1*	**80**	**11**		**91**

BARCLAYS LEAGUE DIVISION 2

Manager: Billy Bonds

SEASON 1990-91

No	Date		Att	Pos	Pt	F-A	H-T	Scorers, Times, and Referees	1	2	3	4	5	6	7	8	9	10	11	subs used
1	A	MIDDLESBROUGH			D	0-0	0-0		Miklosko	Potts	Dicks	Foster	Martin	Keen	Bishop	McAvennie	Slater	Allen	Morley	
	25/8		*20,680*		1				*Pears*	*Cooper*	*Phillips*	*Mowbray*	*Kernaghan*	*Wark*	*Slaven*	*Mustoe*	*Baird*	*Proctor*	*Hendrie*	
								Ref: J Worrall	Boro just escaped relegation in May, but would have got off to a winning start but for super saves from Miklosko, just back from the World Cup. Slaven was twice denied, first a 20-yard volley, then when Ludo dived at his feet. McAvennie returns after missing a year through injury.											
2	H	PORTSMOUTH		14	D	1-1	1-1	McAvennie 23	Miklosko	Potts	Dicks	Foster	Martin	Keen	Bishop	McAvennie	Slater	Allen	Morley	
	29/8		20,835	*13*	2			*Whittingham 20*	*Knight*	*Neill*	*Beresford*	*Finney*	*Kuhl*	*Maguire*	*Wigley*	*Stevens*	*Clarke*	*Whittingham*	*Chamberlain*	
								Ref:J Barratt	In an atmosphere of thunder and lightning, Frank McAvennie scores his first Hammers goal in three years. He swooped when Knight fumbled Morley's shot. Whittingham had put Pompey ahead from the edge of the box, after playing a one-two with Clarke. Pompey also hit the post.											
3	H	WATFORD		7	W	1-0	0-0	Dicks 83p	Miklosko	Potts	Dicks	Foster	Martin	Keen	Bishop	McAvennie	Slater	Allen^	Morley*	Quinn/Parris
	1/9		19,872	*22*	5				*James*	*Williams !*	*Dublin*	*Porter*	*McLaughlin*	*Holdsworth*	*Thomas*	*Wilkinson*	*Kennedy*	*Falconer*	*Bazeley**	*Drysdale*
								Ref: J Ashworth	West Ham's first win does not mean they played well. On the contrary, according to Bonds: 'We don't chase back when we lose the ball'. Williams was sent off in the second half for fouling Slater. With the game looking goalless, three Watford players seemed to drag down Keen.											
4	A	LEICESTER		4	W	2-1	1-0	James 38 (og), Morley 49	Miklosko	Potts	Dicks	Foster	Martin	Keen	Bishop	McAvennie*	Slater^	Allen	Morley	Quinn/Parris
	8/9		*14,605*	*20*	8			*Mills 63*	*Muggleton*	*Mills*	*Johnson*	*Mauchlen**	*Walsh*	*James*	*Hill^*	*North*	*Kitson*	*Davies*	*Kelly*	*Reid/Ramsey*
								Ref: R Milford	David Pleat's lightweight Leicester – spearheaded by former Hammer David Kelly – lose their third game in a row. They were not helped by losing Paul Kitson in the first half, following a collision with Slater. City's Tony James lobbed an intended back-pass over his own keeper.											
5	H	WOLVES		6	D	1-1	1-0	Martin 2	Miklosko	Potts	Dicks	Foster	Martin	Keen	Bishop	McAvennie	**Livett***	Allen	Morley	Parris
	15/9		23,241	*13*	9			*Bull 72*	*Stowell*	*Roberts**	*Venus*	*Bellamy*	*Hindmarch*	*Downing*	*Thompson*	*Cook*	*Bull*	*Mutch*	*Dennison^*	*Ashley/McLoughlin*
								Ref: P Danson	Wolves' Steve Bull played in the World Cup in Italy in the summer, but is kept at bay for 72 minutes, when he manages to shake off Foster to equalise. Alvin Martin had blasted a rare goal after just 90 seconds. Right at the end Trevor Morley crashed a shot against the crossbar.											
6	H	IPSWICH		3	W	3-1	0-1	Bishop 62, Quinn 81, Morley 90	Miklosko	Potts^	Dicks	Foster	Martin	Keen	Bishop	McAvennie*	Slater	Allen	Morley	Quinn/Parris
	19/9		18,764	*15*	12			*Milton 11*	*Forrest*	*Yallop*	*Hill*	*Stockwell*	*Gayle*	*Linighan**	*Gregory*	*Redford*	*Zondervan*	*Kiwomya*	*Milton*	*Thompson !*
								Ref: G Ashby	John Lyall, sacked by West Ham, makes a quick return to his former home. Inside 20 seconds Dicks clears off the line. Redford crosses for Milton to score; then Allen sets up Bishop. On 78 minutes Neil Thompson is sent off for toppling Morley, whereupon Quinn chips Forrest.											
7	A	NEWCASTLE		3	D	1-1	1-1	Morley 45	Miklosko	Potts	Dicks	Foster	Martin	Keen	Bishop	Quinn*	Slater^	Allen	Morley	McAvennie/Parris
	22/9		*25,462*	*7*	13			*McGhee 15*	*Burridge*	*Scott*	*Anderson**	*Aitken*	*Kristensen*	*Ranson*	*Dillon*	*Brock^*	*Quinn*	*McGhee*	*Fereday*	*Simpson/O'Brien*
								Ref: T Fitzharris	Jim Smith's Newcastle missed promotion via the play-offs and are now struggling. Billy Bonds disputed the goal that put the Magpies ahead, claiming that all the world saw skipper Roy Aitken handle during the build-up. Slater's cross to Morley maintained West Ham's unbeaten start.											
8	A	SHEFFIELD WED		4	D	1-1	0-1	Dicks 76	Miklosko	Potts	Dicks	Foster	Martin^	Keen	Bishop	Quinn*	Slater	Allen	Morley	McAvennie/Parris
	29/9		***28,786***	*2*	14			*Hirst 2*	*Pressman*	*Nilsson*	*King*	*Palmer*	*Shirtliff*	*Pearson*	*Wilson**	*Sheridan*	*Hirst*	*Williams*	*Worthington*	*Francis*
								Ref: E Parker	Two unbeaten teams, but West Ham were lucky. At half-time Bonds moaned: 'They outfought us, outran us, out-passed us.' Hirst had turned Martin to convert Sheridan's cross, after which Ludo kept the Owls at bay. Bishop squared a free-kick to Dicks, whose shot was deflected in.											
9	H	OXFORD		4	W	2-0	2-0	Foster 12, Morley 43	Miklosko	Potts	Dicks	Foster	Martin	Keen	Bishop	Quinn	Slater*	Allen	Morley	Parris
	3/10		**18,125**	*23*	17				*Walker*	*Robinson*	*Ford*	*Phillips*	*Jackson*	*Melville*	*Magilton*	*Lewis**	*Foyle*	*Stein*	*Simpson*	*Penney*
								Ref: K Morton	Two points from seven games for luckless Oxford, but Bonds is not deceived by this result. Miklosko made three fine saves from Martin Foyle, and Oxford also wasted a 34th-minute penalty when Martin bundled Foyle. Simpson shot wide. Quinn netted after Foster headed onto the bar.											
10	H	HULL		3	W	**7-1**	2-1	Quinn 8, 62, Potts 31, Dicks 46p, 81,	Miklosko	Potts	Dicks	Foster	Martin	Keen*	Bishop	Quinn^	Parris	Allen	Morley	McAvennie/**Rush**
	6/10		19,472	*17*	20			*Hockaday 30* [Parris 58, Morley 70]	*Hesford*	*Hockaday**	*Doyle*	*Mail^*	*Buckley*	*Wilcox*	*Thomas*	*Peyton*	*Swan*	*Palin*	*Finnigan*	*Ngata/McParland*
								Ref: B Stevens	Hull were unbeaten in seven. Men of the match were Parris and Potts, who restored Hammers' lead with his first ever goal, Hesford fumbling seconds after Hockaday had headed an equaliser. Mail brought down Morley for the penalty. Best goal was Quinn's second, a fierce volley.											
11	A	BRISTOL CITY		3	D	1-1	0-0	McAvennie 61	Miklosko	Potts	Dicks	Foster	Martin	Parris	Bishop	Quinn	Slater*	Allen	Morley	McAvennie
	13/10		*16,838*	*13*	21			*Morgan 64*	*Leaning*	*Llewellyn*	*Bailey*	*Aizlewood*	*Shelton*	*Rennie*	*May*	*Newman*	*Taylor*	*Morgan*	*Smith*	
								Ref: J Deakin	McAvennie, a £1.2 million signing, does not like being dropped in favour of Jimmy Quinn. He comes on for Slater and almost immediately puts away Morley's through-ball. Hammers' reject Nicky Morgan levelled with a far-post header. Dicks, promoted to captain, is booked again.											

No / Date	Venue	Opponent	Att	Pos	Res / Pts	F-A	H-T	Scorers, Times, and Referees	1	2	3	4	5	6	7	8	9	10	11	subs used
12	A	SWINDON		3	W	1-0	0-0	McAvennie 82	Miklosko	Potts	Dicks^	Foster	Martin	Parris	Bishop	Quinn*	Gale	Allen	Morley	McAvennie/Breacker
20/10			13,658	13	24				Digby	Kerslake	Bodin	Hazard*	Tanner	Gittens	Jones	Simpson	White	MacLaren	Foley	Close
								Ref: R Gifford	Swindon had the edge when McAvennie comes off the bench after 71 minutes. 11 minutes later Morley plays the ball into his path and the sub wins the game. McAvennie is so fed up with being sub that he is said to be signing for QPR for £400,000. Breacker comes on after 37 mins.											
13	H	BLACKBURN		3	W	1-0	1-0	Bishop 19	Miklosko	Breacker	Dicks^	Foster	Martin	Parris	Bishop	Quinn*	Gale	Allen	Morley	McAvennie/Slater
24/10			20,003	20	27				Grew	Duxbury*	Beglin	Reid	Dewhurst	Moran	Gayle	Millar	Stapleton	Garner	Atkins	Richardson
								Ref: J Martin	Pre-Dalglish, Rovers are managed by Don Mackay and playing badly. Bishop wins the ball off Moran in the centre circle, advances, and fires a right-footer from 20 yards. Morley later hit the underside of the bar with a floater. It's 15 without defeat, but Dicks faces surgery on his knee.											
14	H	CHARLTON		2	W	2-1	0-0	Allen 53, 70	Miklosko	Breacker	Keen	Foster	Martin	Parris	Bishop	McAvennie	Slater*	Allen	Morley	Rush
27/10			24,019	23	30			Dyer 81	Bolder	Pitcher	Reid	Peake	Webster	Balmer	Lee R	Mackenzie	Dyer	Watson	Minto	
								Ref: L Shapter	Relegated Charlton play their home matches at Selhurst Park, pending restoration of their Valley stadium. Lennie Lawrence's team played bright football, but are beaten by two thunderous strikes by Allen. Miklosko made some great saves before Alex Dyer scored from close range.											
15	A	NOTTS CO		2	W	1-0	0-0	Morley 57	Miklosko	Breacker	Parris	Foster	Martin	**Hughton**	Bishop	Keen	Rush	Allen	Morley	
3/11			10,871	8	33				Cherry	Palmer	Harding	Short, Craig	Yates	O'Riordan*	Thomas	Turner	Bartlett	Regis	Draper	Johnson
								Ref: J Watson	Fortune favours the Hammers as County miss chances galore. With both McAvennie and Quinn injured, Trevor Morley plays as a lone striker, spinning to volley the only goal over the keeper from 20 yards. Chris Hughton makes his first appearance, signed on loan from Tottenham.											
16	A	MILLWALL		2	D	1-1	0-0	McAvennie 73	Miklosko	Breacker	Parris	Foster	Martin	Hughton	Bishop	Keen	McAvennie	Allen*	Morley	Rush
10/11			20,591	6	34			Stephenson 47	Horne	Stevens	Dawes	Waddock	Wood	McLeary	Carter	Allen*	Sheringham	Rae	Stephenson	Goddard
								Ref: K Cooper	Bruce Rioch's Millwall play their part in this thrilling derby. Stephenson's rocket deserved to give Millwall the lead. Bishop then opens up the left side of the Lions' defence and Keen's cross eludes everyone except McAvennie. Bonds admits West Ham enjoyed a Houdini-like escape.											
17	H	BRIGHTON		2	W	2-1	0-1	Slater 56, Foster 72	Miklosko	Breacker	Parris	Foster	Martin	Hughton	Bishop	McAvennie	Rush*	Keen	Morley	Slater
17/11			23,082	9	37			Small 39	Digweed	Crumplin	Chapman	Wilkins	Gatting	Chivers	Barham	Byrne	Small	Codner	Walker	
								Ref: H King	So superior are Brighton that at half-time manager-of-the-month Bonds admits he would be delighted with a draw. Barham's cross had put the Seagulls ahead, but in rain and thunder Slater cuts in to fire into the top corner and Foster heads in Keen's corner. Oldham lose at Port Vale.											
18	A	PLYMOUTH		1	W	1-0	0-0	McAvennie 62	Miklosko	Breacker	Parris	Foster	Martin	Hughton	Bishop	McAvennie	Slater	Keen	Morley	
24/11			11,490	12	40				Wilmot	Brown	Morgan	Marker	Burrows	Salman	Barlow	Fiore	Robinson*	Ampadu^	Hodges	Morrison/Adcock
								Ref: R Hamer	Two goalkeeping moments determine this result, which sends West Ham top for the first time, unbeaten in 18 league games. Argyle's Wilmot cannot hold Morley's shot, which bounces out of his arms. In injury-time sub Morrison looked to have levelled, but Miklosko saves brilliantly.											
19	H	WEST BROM		1	W	3-1	2-0	Parris 20, Morley 24, McAvennie 59	Miklosko	Breacker	Parris	Foster	Martin	Hughton	Bishop	McAvennie	Slater	Keen*	Morley	Allen
1/12			24,753	17	43			Ford 60	Naylor	Robson	Harbey	Roberts	Bradley	Strodder	Ford	West	Bannister	Parkin	Anderson*	Goodman
								Ref: M Bailey	So fragile are the Hammers that even when 3-0 up they could easily have lost. Parris scores No 1 from 25 yards. Seconds after McAvennie's dipping volley, Ford nets at the far post. Miklosko pulled off save after save, and four minutes from time Colin West blazes wide from the spot.											
20	A	PORTSMOUTH		1	W	1-0	0-0	Morley 59	Miklosko	Breacker	Parris	Foster	Martin^	Hughton	Bishop	McAvennie*	Slater	Allen	Morley	Quinn/Gale
8/12			12,045	22	46				Knight	Neill	Beresford	Aspinall	Butters	Awford	Anderton*	Stevens	Clarke	Whittingham	Chamberlain	Wigley
								Ref: R Bigger	Miklosko saves the day and the points. On a cold windy day, Ludo pulls off a super save from Whittingham to keep yet another clean sheet. Pompey boss Frank Burrows is glad to see the back of West Ham for this season. With Oldham's match off, West Ham are five points clear.											
21	H	MIDDLESBROUGH		1	D	0-0	0-0		Miklosko	Breacker	Parris	Gale	Potts	Hughton	Keen	McAvennie	Slater	Allen	Morley*	Quinn
15/12			23,705	4	47				Pears	Cooper	McGee	Mowbray	Coleman	Wark	Slaven	Mustoe	Baird	Kerr	Hendrie*	Ripley
								Ref: A Gunn	The second 0-0 with Boro. For once it is West Ham who bemoan the run of the ball, as Stephen Pears in Boro's goal defies everything thrown at him. Both sides had penalty claims denied. With Breacker's arrival, Potts is switched to central defence, and the move may be permanent.											
22	A	BARNSLEY		2	L	0-1	0-1		Miklosko	Breacker	Parris	Gale	Potts	Hughton	Keen	McAvennie*	Slater	Allen	Morley	Quinn
22/12			10,348	8	47			Smith 20	Baker	Banks*	Taggart	Fleming	Smith	Tiler	O'Connell	Rammell^	Saville	Agnew	Archdeacon	Connolly/Deehan
								Ref: D Allison	Hammered 1-5 by Luton in midweek in the Zenith-Data Cup, West Ham now surrender their unbeaten league record. O'Connell's miskick fell to Smith for the only goal. Morley's 'goal' was controversially ruled offside. Arsenal now boast the only unbeaten record in all four divisions.											
23	H	OLDHAM		1	W	2-0	1-0	Morley 10, Slater 46	Miklosko	Breacker	Parris	Gale	Foster	Hughton	Keen	Quinn	Slater	Allen	Morley	
26/12			24,950	2	50				Hallworth	Warhurst	Barlow	Henry	Barrett	Jobson	Donachie*	Palmer	Marshall	Redfearn	Holden	Currie
								Ref: J Carter	A top of the table clash played in a blustery wind. Agony as Morley is toppled by Earl Barrett, but John Hallworth saves Quinn's penalty. All was put right when Foster flicked on for Morley to make it 1-0. West Ham go back to the top but have played one game more than Oldham.											

No	Date	Att	Pos	Pt	F-A	H-T	Scorers, Times, and Referees	1	2	3	4	5	6	7	8	9	10	11	subs used
24	H PORT VALE		1	D	0-0	0-0		Miklosko	Breacker	Parris	Gale	Foster	Hughton	Keen	Quinn	Slater	Allen*	Morley	Potts
	29/12	23,603	12	51				Wood	Aspin	Agboola	Walker	Parkin	Glover	Porter	Earle	Jepson	Beckford	Jeffers	
							Ref: G Singh	In treacherous wet conditions Vale looked stronger in the first half but were under the hammer afterwards. At the end Darren Beckford rounded Gale and Miklosko but fired into the side netting. Vale boss John Rudge said: 'I don't think West Ham have had a harder game all season'.											
25	A BRISTOL ROV		1	W	1-0	0-0	Quinn 48	Miklosko	Breacker	Parris	Gale	Foster	Hughton	Keen	Potts	Quinn	Slater	Morley	
	1/1	7,932	10	54				Parkin	Bloomer	Twentyman	Yates	Mehew*	Jones	Holloway	Reece	White	Saunders	Pounder	Nixon
							Ref: K Burge	Under Gerry Francis - once linked with West Ham - Rovers were unbeaten in nine games. That run comes to an end at tiny Twerton Park when Quinn finishes off Keen's cross with a mighty header. 20 minutes from time Breacker brought down Holloway, whose spot-kick was saved.											
26	A WATFORD		1	W	1-0	0-0	Morley 66	Miklosko	Breacker	Parris	Gale	Foster^	Hughton	Keen	Slater	Quinn*	Potts	Morley	**Clarke**/Robson
	12/1	17,172	22	57				James	Gibbs	Williams	Ashby	McLaughlin	Devonshire	Thomas*	Wilkinson	Penrice	Porter	Falconer	Gavin
							Ref: I Hemley	Jack Petchey bought Watford from Elton John in the summer, and under Steve Perryman they are unbeaten in eight. The goal stemmed from Miklosko's huge punt downfield. Watford's best player was former Hammers star Alan Devonshire. Stewart Robson returns after long injury.											
27	H LEICESTER		1	W	1-0	1-0	Parris 37	Miklosko	Breacker	Parris	Gale	Bishop	Hughton	Keen	Slater*	Quinn	Potts	Morley	McAvennie
	19/1	21,652	20	60				Muggleton	Mauchlen	Gibson	North	Madden	James	Peake*	Reid^	Oldfield	Mills	Kelly	Wright/Smith
							Ref: P Durkin	The only goal was down to Leicester's Ally Mauchlen, who was caught day-dreaming as Parris blasted past Muggleton. But this was no fluke: both Parris and Quinn hit the bar. The result keeps West Ham five points ahead of second-placed Oldham. David Pleat's Leicester will survive.											
28	A WOLVES		1	L	1-2	0-1	McAvennie 57	Miklosko	Breacker	Parris^	Gale	Bishop	Hughton	Keen	McAvennie	Slater*	Potts	Morley	Allen/Quinn
	2/2	19,454	8	60			Birch 44, Bull 48	Stowell	Bennett	Thompson	Hindmarch	Stancliffe	Blake	Birch	Cook	Bull	Mutch	Dennison*	Steele
							Ref: B Hill	Having beaten Luton 5-0 in the FA Cup, West Ham are rudely brought back to earth. Paul Birch scores on his Wolves' debut. Then Bishop's short pass is cut out, setting up a second. It is the first time Ludo has been beaten twice in the league all season. Oldham lose 1-5 at Oxford.											
29	H MILLWALL		1	W	3-1	1-1	McAvennie 16, 48, Morley 61	Miklosko	Breacker	Parris	Gale*	Bishop	Hughton	Keen	McAvennie	Slater	Potts	Morley	Allen
	24/2	20,503	7	63			Goodman 44	Horne	Cunningham	Dawes	Waddock*	Thompson	McLeary	Stephenson	Goodman	Sheringham	Rae	McGlashan	Allen
							Ref: M Peck	This Sunday match was sparked into life by McAvennie's far-post header, which was shortly cancelled out by John Goodman's snap-shot. The lead was restored when Horne saved at Slater's feet, but the ball fell to McAvennie. Gale broke his nose in a collision with Teddy Sheringham.											
30	A WEST BROM		1	D	0-0	0-0		Miklosko	Breacker	Parris	Gale	Bishop	Hughton	Keen*	McAvennie	Slater	Potts	Morley	Allen
	2/3	16,089	18	64				Rees	Hodson	Shakespeare	Roberts	Bradley	Burgess	Ford	Parkin	Bannister	Robson	Anderson	
							Ref: M Bodenham	Bobby Gould takes charge of his first game for Albion. Despite being at home he plays just one up front and packs his defence. West Ham's best chance came when Bradley cleared off the line from Morley. The Tannoy man gave the time as 17:10, then said 'that means 10 past 5.'											
31	H PLYMOUTH		1	D	2-2	1-0	Marker 18 (og), Breacker 77	Miklosko	Breacker	Parris	Foster	Bishop	Hughton*	Keen	McAvennie	Slater	Potts	Quinn	Allen
	5/3	18,933	17	65			Turner 50, 75	Wilmot	Brown	Morgan	Marker	Burrows	Salman	Barlow	Hodges	Turner	Clement	Fiore	
							Ref: A Gunn	Howard Kendall watches Everton's next FA Cup opponents. 6ft 4in Robbie Turner outjumped Foster to put Plymouth ahead, Breacker scores his first Hammers goal, and Wilmot saves Parris's penalty – the first he'd ever taken. Trevor Morley is in hospital after his wife stabbed him.											
32	A OXFORD		2	L	1-2	0-1	Quinn 54	Miklosko	Breacker*	Parris	Gale	Foster	Hughton	Bishop	McAvennie	**Carr**^	Potts	Quinn	Keen/Slater
	13/3	8,225	14	65			Simpson 10, Durnin 47	Veysey	Robinson	Ford	Foyle	Foster	Melville	Magilton	Phillips	Lewis	Durnin	Simpson	
							Ref: A Seville	It is just 48 hours since the famous win over Everton, and West Ham suffer a hangover. Franz Carr has signed on loan from Forest. Simpson, from a corner, and Durnin, after Foster's hesitancy, put Oxford two up. Quinn pounces after McAvennie hits a post. Oldham reclaim top spot.											
33	H SHEFFIELD WED		2	L	1-3	0-1	Quinn 51	Miklosko	Potts	Parris	Gale	Foster	Hughton*	Bishop	McAvennie	Slater	Keen	Quinn^	Allen/Carr
	16/3	26,182	3	65			Hirst 30, Williams 61, 81	Turner	Anderson	King	Palmer	Shirtliff	Pearson	Wilson*	Sheridan	Hirst^	Williams	McCall	MacKenzie/Francis
							Ref: K Redfearn	Ron Atkinson's Owls inflict Bonds' first home defeat since he took charge. It is the first time Ludo concedes three league goals, and the first time any of Big Ron's sides have won at Upton Park. It is Wednesday's 10th away win, but West Ham are still 10 points clear of the play-offs.											
34	H BRISTOL CITY		2	W	1-0	0-0	Gale 67	Miklosko	Potts	Parris	Gale	Foster	Hughton	Bishop	McAvennie !	Slater*	Keen	Quinn^	Allen/Rosenior
	20/3	22,951	7	68				Leaning	Llewellyn !	Scott	May	Bryant	Aizlewood	Shelton	Newman	Taylor	Morgan	Donowa*	Allison
							Ref: P Alcock	Tony Gale's Brazilian style free-kick won the points and brought West Ham back to winning ways, but the match ended two men short after McAvennie tussled with Andy Llewellyn and both were expelled. Leroy Rosenior returns from Fulham to play his first game of the season.											

No	Venue	Opponent	Att	Pos	Res	F-A	H-T	Scorers, Times, and Referees	1	2	3	4	5	6	7	8	9	10	11	subs used
35	A	HULL		2	D	0-0	0-0		Miklosko	Potts	Parris	Gale	Foster	Hughton	Bishop	McAvennie*	**Dowie**	Keen^	Allen	Carr/Rosenior
		23/3	*9,558*	23	69				*Butler*	*Norton*	*Thompson*	*Buckley*	*Mail*	*Shotton*	*Hockaday*	*Peyton*	*Swan*	*Atkinson*	*Warren**	*Jenkinson*
								Ref: J Kirkby	Hull lost 1-7 in October and have the most leaky defence in the division, so this result takes some explaining. Yet Hull beat leaders Oldham in midweek and have now conceded just two goals in six games. Iain Dowie makes his league debut after his £500,000 signing from Luton.											
36	A	OLDHAM		2	D	1-1	0-0	Bishop 58p	Miklosko	Potts	Parris	Gale	Foster	Hughton	Bishop	McAvennie	Dowie	Slater	Allen	
		29/3	*16,932*	*1*	70			*Ritchie 87p*	*Hallworth*	*Halle*	*Barlow*	*Henry*	*Barrett*	*Jobson*	*Adams*	*Ritchie*	*Palmer**	*Redfearn^*	*Holden*	*Currie/Warhurst*
								Ref: G Alpin	A Friday afternoon crunch game. Dowie had played for Northern Ireland in Yugoslavia on Wednesday and looked half fit. Oldham shaded the first half, but after Ritchie handled Dowie's header West Ham had the chances to clinch the win. Instead, Bishop pulled down Halle in the box.											
37	H	BARNSLEY		2	W	3-2	0-2	McAvennie 56, Dowie 83, Foster 88	Miklosko	Potts	Parris	Gale	Foster	Hughton*	Bishop	McAvennie	Dowie	Slater	Allen	Keen
		1/4	24,607	*9*	73			*Saville 13, O'Connell 31*	*Baker*	*Dobbin**	*Fleming*	*Robinson*	*Smith*	*Tiler*	*O'Connell*	*Rammell^*	*Saville*	*Agnew*	*Archdeacon*	*Rimmer/Deehan*
								Ref: P Vanes	Iain Dowie's home debut sees him wearing bicycle shorts to cover the dreadful burns suffered on Oldham's plastic pitch. Mel Machin's Barnsley are so close to completing the double, but substitute Keen supplies crosses for two of the three headers that turn the game around.											
38	A	PORT VALE		1	W	1-0	0-0	Bishop 71	Miklosko	Potts	Parris	Gale	Foster	Hughton	Bishop	Slater	Dowie	Keen	Allen	
		6/4	*9,658*	*15*	76				*Grew*	*Mills*	*Platnauer*	*Walker*	*Parkin*	*Glover*	*Kent*	*Earle*	*van der Laan*	*Beckford*	*Porter**	*Millar*
								Ref: K Cooper	Vale had lost just one of their previous six games. West Ham's 12th 1-0 win of the season is due to Bishop's thunderous drive from out of the blue. A swirling wind detracted from the match as a spectacle, but the result means West Ham are 13 points clear of the play-off positions.											
39	A	BRIGHTON		1	L	0-1	0-1		Miklosko	Potts	Parris	Stewart	Foster	Hughton^	Bishop	Keen	Dowie*	Morley	Slater	Allen/Quinn
		10/4	*11,904*	*6*	76			*Byrne 44*	*Digweed*	*Crumplin*	*Gatting*	*Wilkins*	*Pates*	*Chivers*	*Barham**	*Byrne*	*Small*	*Codner*	*Walker*	*Nelson*
								Ref: M Pierce	West Ham's smash and grab tactics on their travels were rudely copied by Brighton, who won despite taking a territorial hammering by West Ham for much of the game. John Byrne's cruel goal bounced over Ludo's head. Ray Stewart plays his first league game in 2½ years.											
40	A	IPSWICH		1	W	1-0	1-0	Morley 29	Miklosko	Potts	Parris	Gale	Foster^	Hughton	Bishop	Slater	Dowie*	Keen	Morley	McAvennie/Allen
		17/4	*20,290*	*16*	79				*Forrest*	*Humes**	*Thompson*	*Stockwell*	*Gayle*	*Linighan*	*Zondervan*	*Goddard*	*Houghton*	*Dozzell*	*Kiwomya^*	*Yallop/Milton*
								Ref: P Foakes	It is just three days since West Ham were thumped by Nottingham Forest in the FA Cup. They post a double over John Lyall's Ipswich, thanks to Trevor Morley's interception of Tony Hume's back-pass. But Foster goes off with hamstring trouble and will miss the next four games.											
41	H	SWINDON		1	W	2-0	1-0	Parris 21, Dowie 88	Miklosko	Potts	Parris	Gale	Stewart	Hughton	Bishop	Slater	Dowie	Keen*	Morley	Allen
		20/4	25,944	*19*	82				*Digby*	*Kerslake*	*Viveash*	*Hazard*	*Simpson*	*Calderwood*	*Jones*	*Shearer*	*Rideout**	*MacLaren*	*Foley*	*White*
								Ref: J Martin	This result guarantees promotion with five games still to play. West Ham enjoyed some luck, and Glenn Hoddle's Swindon dominated the second half. Many a Hammers supporters' finger nail was chewed down until Dowie's late strike settled the matter. Now for the championship.											
42	H	NEWCASTLE		1	D	1-1	0-1	Dowie 62	Miklosko	Potts	Parris	Gale	Stewart*	Hughton	Bishop	Slater	Dowie	Keen	Morley	Allen
		24/4	24,195	*12*	83			*Peacock 16*	*Srnicek*	*Watson*	*Elliott*	*O'Brien*	*Scott*	*Kristensen*	*Clark*	*Peacock*	*Quinn*	*Hunt*	*Brock*	
								Ref: R Milford	Ossie Ardiles' Newcastle, free from tension, run the show for the first half, when they had the chances to seal up the points. West Ham have no answer to their fluid tactic of playing on the ground through the middle. George Parris's cross on to Iain Dowie's head deflated the Magpies.											
43	A	BLACKBURN		1	L	**1-3**	1-3	Dowie 43	Miklosko	Potts	Parris	Gale	Stewart	Hughton	Bishop	Keen	Dowie	Slater*	Morley^	Allen/Quinn
		27/4	*10,808*	*17*	83			*Richardson 2, Atkins 4, Sellars 14*	*Mimms*	*Atkins*	*Sulley*	*Reid*	*Moran*	*Dobson*	*Irvine*	*Richardson*	*Livingstone*	*Stapleton*	*Sellars**	*Shepstone*
								Ref: J Key	This dreadful result was made worse by Oldham's win at Ipswich. Last season West Ham lost 4-5 at Ewood, and at half-time a repeat scoreline looked on the cards. Three rat-a-tat-tat Rovers goals looked to have killed off the contest until Keen's corner enabled Dowie to pull one back.											
44	A	CHARLTON		1	D	1-1	1-1	Allen 15	Miklosko	Potts	Parris	Breacker	Stewart	Hughton	Bishop	Allen	Dowie*	Slater	Morley	Quinn
		4/5	*16,137*	*14*	84			*Minto 32*	*Bolder*	*Pitcher*	*Reid*	*Peake*	*Webster**	*Balmer*	*Lee R*	*Dyer*	*Grant^*	*Mortimer*	*Minto*	*Curbishley/Leaburn*
								Ref: R Wiseman	Homeless Charlton are tenants at Selhurst Park, and this match entices their biggest home gate of the season. Tony Gale misses the rest of the season through suspension, and with Foster still out with hamstring problems, Billy Bonds has to send out a makeshift central defence.											
45	H	BRISTOL ROV		1	W	1-0	1-0	Slater 36	Miklosko	Breacker	Parris	Potts	Foster	Hughton	Bishop	Slater	Dowie*	Allen^	Morley	McAvennie/Keen
		8/5	23,054	*12*	87				*Parkin*	*Alexander*	*Twentyman*	*Yates*	*Boothroyd**	*Jones*	*Holloway*	*Reece*	*White*	*Saunders*	*Pounder*	*Hazel*
								Ref: T Holbrook	Gerry Francis' mid-table Rovers created nothing to threaten West Ham's defence, in which Foster returns after injury. The atmosphere is rather subdued, given the importance of the game, which brings the Hammers' 14th 1-0 win of the season. Everything is set up for the championship.											
46	H	NOTTS CO		2	L	1-2	0-2	Parris 77	Miklosko	Potts	Parris	Breacker	Foster	Hughton^	Bishop	Slater	Dowie*	Allen	Morley	McAvennie/Keen
		11/5	**26,551**	*4*	87			*Draper 17, 27*	*Cherry*	*Palmer*	*Paris*	*Short, Craig**	*Short, Chris*	*O'Riordan*	*Harding*	*Turner*	*Regis*	*Draper*	*Johnson*	*Davis*
	Home	Away						Ref: B Hill	Two Paris's play at No 3. West Ham need to match Oldham's result at home to third-place Sheffield Wednesday to seal the title. After an hour Oldham are losing 0-2 and Upton Park starts celebrating. But Oldham hit back, and Redfearn's injury-time winner shatters West Ham's dream.											
Average	22,565	15,193																		

Rumbelows Cup

Rd	Venue	Opponent	Att	Pos	Res	F-A	H-T	Scorers, Times, and Referees	1	2	3	4	5	6	7	8	9	10	11	subs used
2:1	H	STOKE		3	W	3-0	1-0	Dicks 43p, Keen 64, Quinn 86	Miklosko	Potts	Dicks	Foster	Martin	Keen	Bishop	Quinn	Slater	Allen*	Morley	Parris
		26/9	15,870 *3:7*						*Fox*	*Butler*	*Statham**	*Beeston*	*Blake*	*Sandford*	*Kennedy*	*Evans*	*Kelly^*	*Biggins*	*Ware*	*Fowler/Thomas*
								Ref: B Hill	Sandford brings down Morley in the box. Dicks blasts the penalty and foolish Fox almost gets his fingers cut off. Slater sets up Keen for No 2. Morley's cheeky backheel brought a third goal, for Quinn. Stoke boss Alan Ball knows his team can't score four goals at the Victoria Ground.											
2:2	A	STOKE		3	W	2-1	0-1	Allen 64, 79	Miklosko	Potts	Dicks	Foster	Martin	Keen*	Bishop	Parris	Quinn^	Allen	Morley	Gale/McAvennie
		10/10	*8,411* *3:4*					*Evans 37*	*Fox*	*Butler*	*Carr*	*Ware*	*Blake*	*Sandford*	*Scott*	*Ellis*	*Evans*	*Biggins*	*Kevan**	*Boughey*
								Ref: N Midgeley (Hammers win 5-1 on aggregate)	Tim Breacker has signed from Luton for £600,000, Bonds' first signing since taking over from Lou Macari in February 1990. But Bonds keeps faith with Potts and Breacker does not play. Dicks' dreadful back-header lets in Evans to lift Stoke's spirits. Allen's header settles the outcome.											
3	A	OXFORD		2	L	1-2	1-1	Morley 10	Miklosko	Rush	Keen	Foster	Martin	Parris	Bishop	Quinn	Slater	Allen	Morley	
		31/10	*7,528* *22*					*Foyle 18, Magilton 90*	*Kee*	*Robinson*	*Evans*	*Lewis*	*Foster*	*Melville*	*Magilton*	*Stein**	*Foyle*	*Nogan*	*Simpson*	*Penney*
								Ref: V Callow	A four-hour hold up on the M25 delays supporters. West Ham's first defeat in any competition comes when Paul Simpson sets up Magilton. Morley had driven in Keen's cross. When Foster brought down Stein, Simpson's penalty hit the post. He had also missed in the league fixture.											

FA Cup

Rd	Venue	Opponent	Att	Pos	Res	F-A	H-T	Scorers, Times, and Referees	1	2	3	4	5	6	7	8	9	10	11	subs used
3	A	ALDERSHOT		1	D	0-0	0-0		Miklosko	Breacker	Parris	Gale	Foster*	Hughton	Keen	Slater	Quinn	Potts	Morley	Livett
		5/1	*22,929* *4:19*						*Hucker*	*Brown*	*Cooper*	*Randall*	*Ogley*	*Flower*	*Burvill*	*Puckett*	*Williams*	*Henry*	*Stewart*	
								Ref: H King (At Upton Park)	The team-sheets handed out wrongly listed this as a Division 2 match, though it aptly summed up a shambles of a cup-tie. Aldershot had been drawn at home but switched the venue to reap the rewards. Morley came nearest to a goal, but was thwarted by Peter Hucker's double save.											
3R	H	ALDERSHOT		1	W	6-1	4-1	Morley 14, 82, Slater 28, Parris 35, [Bishop 39, Quinn 87]	Miklosko	Breacker	Parris	Gale	Robson*	Hughton	Keen	Slater	Quinn	Potts	Morley	Bishop
		16/1	21,484 *4:20*					*Randall 45*	*Hucker*	*Brown*	*Cooper*	*Randall*	*Ogley*	*Flower !*	*Burvill*	*Puckett**	*Williams*	*Henry*	*Stewart*	*Whitlock*
								Ref: H King	Aldershot manager Len Walker can at least count the reward of 44,000 spectators and the sale of TV rights to BSkyB. The leakiest defence in the division was not helped by having John Flower sent off for earning his second yellow card when fouling Slater. Parris fed Morley for No 1.											
4	A	LUTON		1	D	1-1	1-0	Parris 42	Miklosko	Breacker	Parris	Gale	Bishop	Hughton	Keen*	Slater	Allen	Potts	Morley	McAvennie
		26/1	*12,087* *1:16*					*Black 70*	*Chamberlain*	*James*	*Harvey*	*Williams*	*McDonough*	*Dreyer*	*Elstrup*	*Preece**	*Farrell^*	*Pembridge*	*Black*	*Rees/Dowie*
								Ref: R Groves	Having lost 1-5 here in the Zenith-Data Cup, West Ham lead until Keen fouls Preece on the edge of the box, and Williams' free-kick is turned in by Black. After the final whistle the teams hear that Crewe await the winners. The police normally need 10 days for a reply; not this time.											
4R	H	LUTON		1	W	5-0	1-0	Parris 45, Bishop 53, McAvennie 54, [Morley 68, 83]	Miklosko	Breacker	Parris	Gale	Bishop	Hughton	Keen	McAvennie	Slater	Potts	Morley	
		30/1	25,659 *1:16*						*Chamberlain*	*James**	*Harvey*	*Williams*	*McDonough*	*Dreyer*	*Elstrup^*	*Preece*	*Dowie*	*Pembridge*	*Black*	*Johnson/Farrell*
								Ref: R Groves	The loss of Lars Elstrup after 18 minutes disrupted Luton. They hold out till the stroke of half-time when George Parris - who might have had a first-half hat-trick - scores his fourth goal in four games. Morley's two goals make him Hammers' top scorer with 15. Now for lowly Crewe.											
5	H	CREWE		1	W	1-0	0-0	Quinn 75	Miklosko	Breacker	Parris	Gale	Bishop	Hughton	Keen	McAvennie*	Slater	Potts	Morley	Quinn
		16/2	25,298 *3:21*						*Edwards P*	*Swain*	*McKearney*	*Smart*	*Carr*	*Lennon*	*Jasper**	*Hignett^*	*Sussex*	*Gardiner*	*Doyle*	*Edwards R/Murphy*
								Ref: G Ashby	West Ham have never played Crewe before. Two minutes after coming off the bench Jimmy Quinn - who used to support Crewe as a boy - slips Keen's cross past Paul Edwards. Crewe's reserve keeper had done his best to improve upon the worst defensive record in Division 3.											
QF	H	EVERTON		1	W	2-1	1-0	Foster 33, Slater 59	Miklosko	Breacker	Parris	Gale	Foster	Hughton	Bishop	McAvennie	Slater	Potts	Quinn*	Keen
		11/3	28,161 *1:11*					*Watson 86*	*Southall*	*McDonald**	*Hinchcliffe*	*Ratcliffe*	*Watson*	*Keown*	*Nevin*	*McCall*	*Sharp*	*Milligan^*	*Ebbrell*	*Cottee/Newell*
								Ref: M Reed	A Monday night thriller. Everton line up with just Graeme Sharp up front. Foster finds himself upfield as a cross comes over. He ignores cries of 'leave it' and volleys past Southall. Ebbrell and Keown were booked for fouling Slater. Only when Cottee came on did Everton threaten.											
SF	N	NOTT'M FOREST		1	L	0-4	0-0	*[Charles 80]*	Miklosko	Potts	Parris	Gale !	Foster	Hughton	Bishop	Slater	Allen*	Keen	Morley^	Stewart/Quinn
		14/4	*40,041* *1:14*					*Crosby 49, Keane 58, Pearce 70,*	*Crossley*	*Charles*	*Pearce*	*Walker*	*Chettle*	*Parker*	*Crosby*	*Keane**	*Clough*	*Glover*	*Woan*	*Laws*
		(At Villa Park)						Ref: K Hackett	Who knows what might have happened had referee Hackett taken a different view of Gale's collision with Gary Crosby as both players chased a through ball. Gale was judged guilty of a professional foul and sent off for the first time in his career. In the second half Forest ran rampant.											

	P	W	D	L	F	A	W	D	L	F	A	Pts
		Home					Away					
1 Oldham	46	17	5	1	55	21	8	8	7	28	32	88
2 WEST HAM	46	15	6	2	41	18	9	9	5	19	16	87
3 Sheffield Wed	46	12	10	1	43	23	10	6	7	37	28	82
4 Notts Co*	46	14	4	5	45	28	9	7	7	31	27	80
5 Millwall	46	11	6	6	43	28	9	7	7	27	23	73
6 Brighton	46	12	4	7	37	31	9	3	11	26	38	70
7 Middlesbro	46	12	4	7	36	17	8	5	10	30	30	69
8 Barnsley	46	13	7	3	39	16	6	5	12	24	32	69
9 Bristol City	46	14	5	4	44	28	6	2	15	24	43	67
10 Oxford	46	10	9	4	41	29	4	10	9	28	37	61
11 Newcastle	46	8	10	5	24	22	6	7	10	25	34	59
12 Wolves	46	11	6	6	45	35	2	13	8	18	28	58
13 Bristol Rov	46	11	7	5	29	20	4	6	13	27	39	58
14 Ipswich	46	9	8	6	32	28	4	10	9	28	40	57
15 Port Vale	46	10	4	9	32	24	5	8	10	24	40	57
16 Charlton	46	8	7	8	27	25	5	10	8	30	36	56
17 Portsmouth	46	10	6	7	34	27	4	5	14	24	43	53
18 Plymouth	46	10	10	3	36	20	2	7	14	18	48	53
19 Blackburn	46	8	6	9	26	27	6	4	13	25	39	52
20 Watford	46	5	8	10	24	32	7	7	9	21	27	51
21 Swindon	46	8	6	9	31	30	4	8	11	34	43	50
22 Leicester	46	12	4	7	41	33	2	4	17	19	50	50
23 West Brom	46	7	11	5	26	21	3	7	13	26	40	48
24 Hull	46	6	10	7	35	32	4	5	14	22	53	45
	1104	253	163	136	866	615	136	163	253	615	866	1493

* promoted after play-offs

Odds & ends

Double wins: (5) Watford, Leicester, Ipswich, Swindon, Bristol Rov.
Double losses: (0).

Won from behind: (4) Ipswich (h), Brighton (h), Barnsley (h), Stoke RC (a).
Lost from in front: (1) Oxford RC (a).

High spots: Promotion.
Not losing until 22 December in the league, a run of 21 games.
Reaching semi-final of Rumbelows Cup.

Low spots: Four league games without a win from 2 March.
Losing so heavily in Rumbelows Cup semi-final.
Losing the Second Division championship on the final day of the season.

Hammer of the Year: Ludek Miklosko.
Ever-presents: (1) Ludek Miklosko.
Hat-tricks: (0).
Leading scorer: (17) Trevor Morley.

	Appearances						Goals			
	Lge	*Sub*	LC	*Sub*	FAC	*Sub*	Lge	LC	FAC	Tot
Allan, Martin	**28**	*12*	3		2		**3**	2		**5**
Bishop, Ian	**40**		3		5	*1*	**4**		2	**6**
Breacker, Tim	**23**	*1*			6		**1**			**1**
Carr, Franz	**1**	*2*								
Clarke, Simon		*1*								
Dicks, Julian	**13**		2				**4**	1		**5**
Dowie, Iain	**12**						**4**			**4**
Foster, Colin	**36**		3		3		**3**		1	**4**
Gale, Tony	**23**	*1*		*1*	7		**1**			**1**
Hughton, Chris	**32**				7					
Kevin, Kevin	**36**	*4*	3		6	*1*		1		**1**
Livett, Simon	**1**					*1*				
McAvennie, Frank	**24**	*10*		*1*	3	*1*	**10**		1	**11**
Martin, Alvin	**20**		3				**1**			**1**
Miklosko, Ludek	**46**		3		7					
Morley, Trevor	**38**		3		6		**12**	1	4	**17**
Parris, George	**37**	*7*	2	*1*	7		**5**		3	**8**
Potts, Steve	**36**	*1*	2		7		**1**			**1**
Quinn, Jimmy	**16**	*10*	3		3	*2*	**6**	1	2	**9**
Robson, Stewart		*1*			1					
Rosenior, Leroy		*2*								
Rush, Matthew	**2**	*3*	1							
Slater, Stuart	**37**	*3*	2		7		**3**		2	**5**
Stewart, Ray	**5**					*1*				
(own-goals)							**2**			**2**
24 players used	**506**	***58***	**33**	***3***	**77**	***7***	**60**	**6**	**15**	**81**

No	Date		Att	Pos	Pt	F-A	H-T	Scorers, Times, and Referees	1	2	3	4	5	6	7	8	9	10	11	subs used
1	H	LUTON			D	0-0	0-0		Miklosko	**Brown**	**Thomas**	Breacker	Foster	Parris	Bishop*	Slater	**Small**	Rosenior	Allen M	Keen
	17/8		25,079		1				*Chamberlain*	*Beaumont*	*Harvey*	*McDonough*	*Ridger*	*Dreyer*	*Farrell**	*Preece*	*Stein*	*Pembridge*	*Black*	*Gray*
								Ref: M Bodenham	Division 1 has been expanded from 20 teams to 22. West Ham are among the favourites for the drop, so manager David Pleat is happy with this opening day point. Bonds prefers Rosenior to Morley, and gives debuts to three players - Mike Small, Kenny Brown and Mitchell Thomas.											
2	A	SHEFFIELD UTD			D	1-1	0-0	Small 47	Miklosko	Brown	Thomas	Breacker	Foster	Parris	Bishop	Slater	Small	Rosenior*	Allen M^	Morley/Keen
	20/8		*21,463*		2			*Beesley 49*	*Tracey*	*Pemberton*	*Cowan*	*Jones*	*Beesley*	*Hill*	*Hoyland*	*Booker*	*Agana*	*Deane**	*Hodges^*	*Bryson/Whitehouse*
								Ref: I Hendrick	The Blades had a great run after Christmas. A grim match that produced seven bookings, just about par for Dave Bassett. The first half was extended by five minutes, not for injuries but for bookings. After Small swivelled to fire the opener, Beesley thundered an equaliser on the run.											
3	A	WIMBLEDON			L	0-2	0-1		Miklosko	Brown	Thomas	Breacker	Foster	Parris	Bishop	Slater^	Small	Rosenior	Allen M*	Morley/Rush
	24/8		***10,801***		2			*Earle 31, Fashanu 70*	*Segers*	*Joseph*	*Phelan*	*Barton*	*Scales*	*Fitzgerald*	*Clarke**	*Earle*	*Fashanu !*	*Ryan*	*Fairweath'r^*	*Cork/Elkins*
								Ref: I Wiseman	The match centred on Dons' new captain John Fashanu. First he broke Foster's nose, accusing the Hammer of racist abuse. Fashanu is booked, then booked again – and sent off – for clattering Miklosko with his foot up. Said Dons' boss Ray Harford: 'He showed a lack of intelligence.'											
4	H	ASTON VILLA			W	3-1	0-0	Small 66, Rosenior 68, Brown 87	Miklosko	Brown	Thomas	Breacker	Foster	Parris	Bishop	Slater	Small	Rosenior	Allen M*	Rush
	28/8		23,644	*9*	5			*Daley 50*	*Spink*	*Ehiogu*	*Price**	*Teale*	*McGrath*	*Richardson*	*Daley*	*Penrice*	*Regis*	*Cowans*	*Mortimer*	*Yorke*
								Ref: A Gunn	The pairing of Small and Rosenior – combined cost £700,000 – transformed this match to bring about Villa's first defeat. Daley's pacey opener was cancelled out when Small turned Ehiogu inside out. Thomas' flick set up Rosenior before Brown uncorked a spectacular 25-yarder.											
5	H	NOTTS CO		16	L	0-2	0-0		**Parks**	Brown	Thomas	Breacker	Foster	Parris	Bishop	Slater	Small	Rosenior*	Rush^	Morley/Hughton
	31/8		20,093		5			*Bartlett 64, 67*	*Cherry*	*Palmer*	*Paris*	*Short, Craig*	*Yates*	*Draper*	*Thomas*	*Dryden*	*Regis**	*Bartlett*	*Johnson*	*Turner*
								Ref: J Deakin	The last meeting of these sides saw West Ham robbed of the Division 2 Championship. Iain Dowie has gone to Southampton for a small profit. Miklosko is out with an injured ankle, making way for Tony Parks, on loan from Spurs. Lax defending brought two goals for Kevin Bartlett.											
6	A	QP RANGERS		13	D	0-0	0-0		Parks	Brown	Thomas	Breacker	Foster	Parris	Bishop	Slater	Small*	Potts	Morley^	Rush/Rosenior
	4/9		*16,616*	*21*	6				*Stejskal*	*Bardsley*	*Brevett*	*Holloway**	*Peacock*	*Maddix*	*Bailey*	*Barker*	*Thompson*	*Wegerle*	*Wilson*	*Ferdinand*
								Ref: P Don	Gerry Francis' team are still looking for their first win. Miklosko is on international duty with Czechoslovakia. This was an enterprising 0-0 draw that earned a standing ovation at the end. The better chances fell to QPR. Skipper Ian Bishop was booked after a clash with Thompson.											
7	H	CHELSEA		17	D	1-1	0-0	Small 48	Miklosko	Brown	Thomas	Breacker	Foster	Parris	Bishop	Slater	Small	Potts	Morley	
	7/9		18,875	*5*	7			*Dixon 56*	*Hitchcock*	*Clarke*	*Boyd*	*Jones*	*Elliott*	*Monkou*	*Le Saux*	*Townsend*	*Dixon*	*Wilson**	*Wise*	*Allon*
								Ref: J Carter	A vital Hammers win tossed away through bad luck, wasted chances and inspired goalkeeping by Hitchcock. West Ham hit the woodwork three times in the space of a few minutes. The third time, Small pounced to score. Le Saux crossed to the far post for Dixon's headed equaliser.											
8	A	NORWICH		18	L	1-2	1-2	Small 15	Miklosko	Brown	Thomas	Breacker	Foster	Parris*	Bishop	Slater	Small	Potts	Morley^	Rush/Rosenior
	14/9		*15,348*	*14*	7			*Fox 13, Gordon 39*	*Gunn*	*Culverhouse*	*Bowen*	*Butterworth*	*Blades*	*Crook*	*Gordon*	*Fleck*	*Newman*	*Fox*	*Ullathorne**	*Goss*
								Ref: T West	West Ham fans are growing restless. The sweeper system that looked effective against Chelsea back-fired, so the players reverted to 4-4-2 during the game. Kenny Brown returns to his former club. Gordon's winner was a fluke, the ball taking a deflection to wrong-foot Miklosko.											
9	A	CRYS PALACE		16	W	3-2	0-1	Thomas 52, Morley 56, Small 75	Miklosko	Brown	Parris	Thomas	Foster	Breacker	Bishop	Slater	Small	Potts	Morley	
	17/9		*21,363*	*15*	10			*Salako 12, Wright 61*	*Suckling*	*Humphrey*	*Sinton*	*Gray*	*Young*	*Thorn*	*McGoldrick**	*Pardew*	*Bright*	*Wright*	*Salako*	*Collymore*
								Ref: R Milford	Palace are besieged by the media following alleged racist remarks by chairman Ron Noades. Manager Steve Coppell said he felt punch-drunk by it all. West Ham's second goal was a fluke, Ludo's huge punt going in off Morley's heel. Small headed the winner from Breacker's cross.											
10	H	MANCHESTER C		18	L	1-2	0-0	Brown 83	Miklosko	Brown	Thomas	Breacker	Foster !	Parris	Bishop	Slater	Small	Potts	Morley*	Rosenior
	21/9		**25,558**	*6*	10			*Redmond 76p, Hendry 90*	*Coton*	*Hill*	*Pointon*	*Brightwell*	*Curle*	*Redmond*	*White*	*Heath*	*Quinn*	*Megson*	*Hughes**	*Hendry*
								Ref: K Barratt	After an awful first half things had to improve. Foster unintentionally handles Quinn's shot and is sent off. Redmond stumbles while taking the penalty but the ball still goes in. Slater's cross set up the equaliser, but at the death Coton's clearance bounced in the area for Hendry's winner.											

No	Venue / Date	Opponent / Att		Pos	Res / Pts	FT	HT	Scorers, Times, and Referees	1	2	3	4	5	6	7	8	9	10	11	subs used
11	A	NOTT'M FOREST		18	D	2-2	2-1	Small 16, 43	Miklosko	Breacker	Thomas	Gale	Foster	Parris	Bishop	Slater	Small*	Potts	Morley	Rosenior
	28/9		*25,613*	*14*	11			*Woan 4, Sheringham 77*	*Crossley*	*Charles*	*Pearce*	*Chettle*	*Tiler*	*Keane*	*Black*	*Parker*	*Gaynor**	*Sheringham*	*Woan*	*Walker*
								Ref: J Watson	Last season West Ham lost 0-4 to Forest in the FA Cup. Tony Gale plays his first full match of the season. Bishop plays a blinder. Hammers' first goal climaxed dazzling interplay between six players. Near the end Forest's centre-half Des Walker came on as a makeshift striker.											
12	H	COVENTRY		18	L	0-1	0-0		Miklosko	Breacker	Thomas*	Gale	Brown	Parris	Bishop	Slater	Small	Potts	Morley^	Allen M/Keen
	5/10		21,817	*5*	11			*Gallacher 78*	*Ogrizovic*	*Borrows*	*Billing*	*Robson*	*Pearce*	*Atherton*	*McGrath*	*Gynn*	*Furlong**	*Gallacher*	*Ndlovu^*	*Rosario/Emerson*
								Ref: P Foakes	Coventry are riding high and ex-Hammer Stewart Robson revels as their skipper. After 25 minutes Morley collides with keeper Ogrizovic and goes off shortly after with a gashed eye. West Ham looked the stronger team and came so close when Parris lobbed the keeper but hit a post.											
13	A	OLDHAM		18	D	2-2	1-2	Small 35, McAvennie 82	Miklosko	Breacker	Thomas	Gale	Potts	Parris	Bishop	Slater*	Small	Keen	Morley^	Allen M/McAvennie
	19/10		*14,365*	*16*	12			*McDonald 6, Breacker 40 (og)*	*Hallworth*	*Fleming*	*Barlow*	*Henry*	*Barrett*	*Jobson*	*McDonald*	*Marshall*	*Sharp*	*Milligan*	*Holden*	
								Ref: P Vanes	A meeting between the top two promoted clubs. Morley squandered two great chances before McAvennie came off the bench to replace him. Oldham boss Joe Royle complained about his defenders, even though two of them – Jobson and Barrett – were in last week's England squad.											
14	H	TOTTENHAM		17	W	2-1	2-1	Small 12, Thomas 28	Miklosko	Breacker	Thomas	Gale	Potts	Parris	Bishop	McAvennie	Small	Keen*	Slater	Allen M
	26/10		23,946	*13*	15			*Lineker 5*	*Thorstvedt*	*Edinburgh*	*v d Hauwe**	*Nayim^*	*Sedgley*	*Mabbutt*	*Stewart*	*Durie !*	*Samways*	*Lineker*	*Allen P*	*Bergsson/Houghton*
								Ref: D Elleray	The sting came in the tail. Breacker pushed Durie who claimed a penalty, not given. Durie took out his frustration on tiny Slater and provokes a brawl that even sucked in saintly Lineker. Durie was expelled. Small and McAvennie both hit a post, which denied West Ham an easier win.											
15	A	ARSENAL		14	W	1-0	0-0	Small 76	Miklosko	Breacker	Thomas	Gale	Potts	Parris	Bishop	McAvennie	Small	Keen	Slater	
	2/11		*33,539*	*5*	18				*Seaman*	*Dixon*	*Winterburn*	*Thomas**	*Pates*	*Linighan*	*Rocastle*	*Wright*	*Smith*	*Merson*	*Limpar*	*Groves*
								Ref: J Martin	Arsenal are distracted at the prospect of playing Benfica on Wednesday. They rest Tony Adams and look perfectly dreadful. Benfica spies dare not believe their eyes. West Ham hit Arsenal on the break with devastating effect. Mike Small's wonder strike had his team-mates in ecstasy.											
16	H	LIVERPOOL		15	D	0-0	0-0		Miklosko	Breacker	Thomas	Gale	Potts	Parris	Bishop	McAvennie	Small	Keen	Slater	
	17/11		23,569	*11*	19				*Grobbelaar*	*Jones*	*Burrows*	*Nicol*	*Molby*	*Tanner*	*McManam'n*	*Marsh*	*Rush*	*Walters*	*McMahon*	
								Ref: G Ashby	This Sunday match shown on TV was a wonderful advert for what is generally a dismal league. The result extends the Hammers' unbeaten run to seven games. Mike Small plays just 10 days after a cartilage operation. Ron Greenwood has returned to Upton Park as a 'consultant'.											
17	A	MANCHESTER U		16	L	1-2	0-2	McAvennie 76	Miklosko	Breacker	Thomas	Gale	Potts	Parris	Bishop	McAvennie	Small	Keen*	Slater	Allen M
	23/11		***47,185***	*1*	19			*Giggs 15, Robson 42*	*Schmeichel*	*Parker**	*Irwin*	*Bruce*	*Webb*	*Pallister*	*Robson*	*Kanchelskis*	*McClair*	*Hughes*	*Giggs*	*Blackmore*
								Ref: D Elleray	A ridiculous score, which greatly flattered the Hammers. Man U go back to the top with a wonder display. 'We could have had 10,' moaned Ferguson. Giggs scored with a super volley, and he and Kanchelskis were unstoppable, yet Schmeichel saved from McAvennie at the death.											
18	H	SHEFFIELD WED		17	L	1-2	0-1	Breacker 84	Miklosko	Breacker	Thomas	Gale	Potts	Parris	Bishop	McAvennie	Small	Keen*	Slater	Allen M
	30/11		24,116	*4*	19			*Harkes 24, Jemson 85*	*Woods*	*Harkes*	*King*	*Palmer**	*Warhurst*	*Pearson*	*B't-Williams*	*Sheridan*	*Hirst*	*Jemson*	*Worthington*	*Anderson*
								Ref: C Wilkes	Martin Allen comes off the bench and within seconds goes over the top on Carlton Palmer, who is stretchered off. Owls' boss Trevor Francis is angry that Allen isn't sent off. Friction between Francis and Allen dates from QPR, when Allen insisted on attending the birth of his first child.											
19	A	EVERTON		18	L	**0-4**	0-3	*[Johnston 53]*	Miklosko	Breacker !	Thomas	Gale	Potts	Parris*	Bishop	McAvennie	Small	Allen M	Slater	Keen
	7/12		*21,563*	*7*	19			*Cottee 8, Beagrie 10, Beardsley 37,*	*Southall*	*Jackson*	*Hinchcliffe*	*Ebbrell*	*Watson*	*Keown*	*Ward**	*Beardsley*	*Johnston*	*Cottee*	*Beagrie*	*Warzycha*
								Ref: A Wilkie	Everton were thrashed 1-4 by Leeds in the Rumbelows Cup in midweek, and West Ham feel the backlash. Breacker is booked for fouling Hinchcliffe and booked again for hacking Beagrie. So off he goes. Ian Bishop tried hard to impress Howard Kendall, who had twice sold him.											
20	H	SHEFFIELD UTD		18	D	1-1	0-0	Dicks 87p	Miklosko	Brown	Dicks	Gale	Potts	Foster	Bishop	McAvennie	Small*	Allen M	Slater	Keen
	21/12		19,287	*19*	20			*Deane 84*	*Tracey*	*Gage*	*Cowan*	*Gannon*	*Gayle !*	*Beesley*	*Bryson**	*Hoyland*	*Littlejohn*	*Deane*	*Whitehouse*	*Hodges*
								Ref: M Pierce	Julian Dicks makes his comeback after fourteen months out injured, but is to blame for the first goal when he fails to control the ball. West Ham revert to the sweeper system. After 70 minutes Gayle is sent off for swearing, which seems harsh. Dicks rescues a point with a vicious penalty.											
21	A	ASTON VILLA		19	L	1-3	0-2	McAvennie 64	Miklosko	Breacker	Dicks	Gale	Potts	Parris	Bishop	McAvennie	Small*	Keen	Slater	Morley
	26/12		*31,959*	*6*	20			*Yorke 34, Daley 35, Richardson 89*	*Sealey*	*Kubicki*	*Staunton*	*Teale*	*McGrath*	*Richardson*	*Daley*	*Blake*	*Regis*	*Parker*	*Yorke**	*Froggatt*
								Ref: L Dilkes	Villa enjoyed so much possession against lightweight West Ham that it was surprising they had to wait so long to seal this win. Yorke opened with a close-range header; Daley's shot went in off Potts; McAvennie headed in Dicks' chipped pass; Richardson turned in Yorke's cross.											

No	Date		Att	Pos	Pt	F-A	H-T	Scorers, Times, and Referees	1	2	3	4	5	6	7	8	9	10	11	subs used
22	A	NOTTS CO		21	L	0-3	0-0		Miklosko	Breacker	Dicks	Gale	Potts	Foster	Bishop	McAvennie	Small	Keen	Slater	
	28/12		*11,163*	*18*	20			*Turner 51, Harding 62, Agana 69*	*Cherry*	*Palmer*	*Paris*	*Short, Craig*	*Yates*	*Short, Chris*	*Thomas*	*Turner*	*Harding*	*Agana**	*Johnson^*	*Rideout/Slawson*
								Ref: J Worrall	West Ham are on a slippery slope now. They held their heads up through the first half, but once County took the lead the Hammers folded. Only skipper Ian Bishop acquitted himself adequately. With this result Luton climb above West Ham, who have taken just 2 points out of 21.											
23	H	LEEDS		21	L	1-3	1-2	Dicks 24p	Miklosko	Breacker	Dicks	Gale	Potts	Thomas	Bishop	McAvennie	Small*	Keen	Slater	Morley
	1/1		21,766	*1*	20			*Chapman 11, 85, McAllister 38*	*Lukic*	*Sterland*	*Dorigo*	*Batty*	*Fairclough*	*Whyte*	*Strachan*	*Wallace, Rod*	*Chapman*	*McAllister*	*Speed*	
								Ref: R Groves	From Farnborough to table-topping Leeds. West Ham's best moment came when Dorigo fouled Keen for the penalty which made it 1-1. But then luck deserted the Hammers. But for John Lukic's heroics Leeds might well have lost. David Batty admitted: 'We were lucky to hold out.'											
24	H	WIMBLEDON		21	D	1-1	0-0	Morley 89	Miklosko	Breacker	Dicks	Gale	Foster	Thomas*	Bishop	McAvennie	Brown	Keen^	Slater	Morley/Small
	11/1		18,485	*17*	21			*Sanchez 52*	*Segers*	*McGee*	*Phelan*	*Barton*	*Scales*	*Fitzgerald*	*Newhouse**	*Earle*	*Fashanu*	*Sanchez*	*Anthrobus*	*Clarke*
								Ref: R Gifford	The ill-fated debenture bond scheme for redeveloping Upton Park has enraged fans, who begin a series of demonstrations. Sanchez's powerful header gives the Dons a well-merited lead. Barton then fouled Bishop, Segers blocked Dicks' penalty, but Morley stooped to head into goal.											
25	A	LUTON		20	W	1-0	0-0	Small 69	Miklosko	Breacker	Dicks	Potts	Foster	Thomas	Bishop	McAvennie^	Brown	Morley	Slater*	Keen/Small
	18/1		*11,088*	*22*	24				*Sutton*	*James*	*Harvey*	*Kamara*	*Dreyer*	*Peake*	*Telfer**	*Stein*	*Nogan^*	*Pembridge*	*Preece*	*Campbell/Oakes*
								Ref: R Bigger	The two bottom teams swap places as a result of Mike Small's fortuitous goal. His shot deflected off Peake's right foot for the winner. Peake was lucky to be still on the pitch, having head-butted Morley in the first half. David Pleat admitted that Luton were never going to score.											
26	H	OLDHAM		20	W	1-0	1-0	Thomas 33	Parks	Breacker	Dicks	Potts	Foster	Thomas	Keen	McAvennie	Brown	Morley*	Slater	Small
	1/2		19,012	*16*	27				*Hallworth*	*Barrett*	*Barlow*	*Henry*	*Jobson*	*Marshall*	*Adams*	*Bernard*	*Sharp*	*Milligan**	*Holden^*	*Fleming/Palmer*
								Ref: K Cooper	Six points in two games and two clean sheets. But it was another dodgy goal that won this game. Mitchell Thomas, a £500,000 summer buy, sliced his shot badly, but the ball somehow beat Hallworth. Parks played instead of the calf-strained Miklosko, and saved well from Barlow.											
27	A	SHEFFIELD WED		21	L	1-2	1-0	Small 14	Parks	Breacker	Dicks	Potts	Foster	**Atteveld**	Bishop	Keen*	Small	Allen M	Slater	Brown
	22/2		*24,150*	*4*	27			*Palmer 80, Anderson 88*	*Woods*	*Nilsson*	*Worthington*	*Palmer*	*Anderson*	*Shirtliff*	*Wilson*	*Hyde**	*Hirst*	*Johnson^*	*Harkes*	*B'tWilliams/Williams*
								Ref: T Fitzharris	A grudge match, fuelled by memories of Martin Allen's crippling lunge at Palmer at Upton Park. Small heads in after the ball comes back off a post. The Owls force 17 second-half corners, but their winner comes from a disputed free-kick. Tony Parks was cautioned by police at the end.											
28	H	EVERTON		21	L	0-2	0-1		Parks	Breacker^	Dicks	Potts	Foster	Thomas	Bishop	Brown	Small	Allen M	Slater*	Morley/Rush
	29/2		20,976	*9*	27			*Johnston 6, Ablett 64*	*Southall*	*Jackson**	*Ablett*	*Ebbrell*	*Watson*	*Keown*	*Ward*	*Beardsley*	*Johnston*	*Cottee^*	*Hinchcliffe*	*Beagrie/Harper*
								Ref: A Smith	Out of the Cup, headed for the drop, and a pitch invasion to protest at the board. These are bad times for West Ham. Angry fans held up play by releasing thousands of balloons. One fan also planted the corner flag in the centre-circle. Martin Allen admitted later: 'we did not play well.'											
29	A	SOUTHAMPTON		22	L	0-1	0-0		Parks	Potts	Dicks	Gale^	Foster	Thomas*	Bishop	Brown	Small	Allen M	Slater	Morley/Rush
	3/3		*14,548*	*21*	27			*Dowie 62*	*Flowers*	*Dodd*	*Benali*	*Horne*	*Moore*	*Ruddock*	*Le Tissier*	*Cockerill*	*Shearer*	*Dowie*	*Hurlock*	
								Ref: R Lewis	The two bottom teams swap places, thanks to former Hammer Iain Dowie's header from Horne's deep cross. The game was dreadfully scrappy, ruled by fear, with highly promising Alan Shearer as anonymous as everyone else. Hammers find themselves bottom for the first time.											
30	A	LIVERPOOL		22	L	0-1	0-1		Miklosko	Brown	Dicks	Gale	Potts	Thomas*	Bishop	Keen	Small	Allen M	Slater	Rush
	11/3		*30,821*	*5*	27			*Saunders 3*	*Grobbelaar*	*Jones*	*Venison*	*Nicol*	*Redknapp*	*Wright*	*Saunders*	*Houghton**	*Thomas*	*Barnes^*	*McManam'n*	*Marsh/Rosenthal*
								Ref: J Rushton	Draws won't save West Ham, so Bonds instructs his players to go out to win. Jamie Redknapp's fierce 30-yarder took everyone by surprise and was spilled by Miklosko. That gave West Ham little option but to attack. Graeme Souness's tight-marking instructions stifled West Ham.											
31	H	ARSENAL		22	L	0-2	0-1		Miklosko	Brown	Dicks	Gale	Foster	Keen	Bishop	McAvennie*	Small	Allen M^	Slater	Morley/Parris
	14/3		22,640	*6*	27			*Wright 13, 51*	*Seaman*	*Dixon*	*Winterburn*	*Hillier*	*Bould*	*Adams*	*Rocastle*	*Wright*	*Smith**	*Merson*	*Groves^*	*Campbell/O'Leary*
								Ref: B Hill	Dicks spent the match kicking Perry Groves up in the air, in one spell committing five fouls on the winger in 11 minutes. The ref booked both players, Groves for over-protesting. Like West Ham, Arsenal fans are up in arms over redevelopment plans and release a barrage of balloons.											

No / Date	Venue	Opponent / Att			F-A	H-T	Scorers, Ref												
32	H	QP RANGERS	22	D	2-2	1-0	Small 28, Breacker 75	Miklosko	Brown	Dicks	Gale	Foster	Keen^	Bishop*	McAvennie	Small	Allen M	Slater	Thomas/Breacker
21/3		20,401	*9*	28			*Allen 50, 70*	*Stejskal*	*Bardsley*	*Wilson*	*Impey*	*Peacock*	*McDonald*	*Wilkins*	*Holloway*	*Ferdinand*	*Allen B**	*Sinton*	*Barker*
							Ref: D Allison	A tale of two Allens. Martin Allen's strike is disallowed, owing to Small being offside. West Ham could have been 2-0 up, but within seconds cousin Bradley Allen beat three defenders to equalise. After the game Dicks was called into Taylor's England squad to visit Czechoslovakia.											
33	A	LEEDS	22	D	0-0	0-0		Miklosko	Brown	Dicks	Breacker	Foster	Potts	Bishop	Thomas	Small	Allen M^	Slater*	McAvennie/Gale
28/3		*31,101*	*1*	29				*Lukic*	*Cantona*	*Dorigo*	*Batty*	*Fairclough*	*Newsome*	*Strachan*	*Wallace, Rd**	*Chapman*	*McAllister*	*Speed*	*Wetherall*
							Ref: K Barratt	Lee Chapman's unbelievable misses in this game threaten Leeds' championship hopes. The worst boob came after 20 minutes, when Cantona's wonderful reverse pass sent Batty clear down the right. Batty's cross was missed in front of the posts. Miklosko made some good saves too.											
34	A	TOTTENHAM	22	L	0-3	0-1		Miklosko	Brown*	Dicks	Gale	Foster	Breacker^	Bishop	Thomas	Small	Potts	Slater	McAvennie/Keen
1/4		*31,809*	*17*	29			*Lineker 16, 53, 60p*	*Walker*	*v d Hauwe**	*Edinburgh*	*Gray^*	*Dundy*	*Mabbutt*	*Stewart*	*Durie*	*Nayim*	*Lineker*	*Allen P*	*Sedgley/Walsh*
							Ref: D Gallagher	Three strikes from the right boot of Gary Lineker earn three points for the team with the worst home record in the division. Ex-Hammer Paul Allen rolled the ball into his path for 1-0. Breacker fouled Durie for the decisive penalty. At the end of the season Lineker will be off to Japan.											
35	A	CHELSEA	22	L	1-2	1-1	Allen C 27	Miklosko	Brown	Dicks	Gale	Foster	Potts	Bishop	McAvennie	Thomas	**Allen C**	Keen*	Morley
4/4		*20,684*	*9*	29			*Wise 26, Cascarino 48*	*Beasant*	*Clarke*	*Myers*	*Jones**	*Elliott*	*Monkou*	*Le Saux*	*Bailey*	*Stuart*	*Cascarino*	*Wise*	*Barnard*
							Ref: P Jones	Chelsea had won at home just once in 1992, and they too are immersed in off-pitch troubles over the future of their stadium. West Ham did not win their first corner till the 79th minute. Billy Bonds kept his players behind locked doors afterwards for an inquest into their lack of passion.											
36	H	NORWICH	22	W	**4-0**	2-0	Rush 14, 36, Dicks 71p, Bishop 79	Miklosko	Breacker	Dicks	Potts	Martin A	Thomas	Bishop	Rush	Small*	Allen C	Slater	Keen
11/4		**16,896**	*17*	32				*Walton*	*Bowen*	*Ullathorne*	*Butterworth*	*Polston*	*Goss*	*Fox*	*Power**	*Newman*	*Beckford*	*Smith*	*Sutton^/Sutch*
							Ref: P Foakes	John Major has just won the General Election. Bonds drops five players. Matthew Rush plays his first full 90 minutes, and is rewarded with two headers from Bishop corners. When Thomas was brought down for a penalty, Dicks had no intention of letting Rush claim his hat-trick.											
37	H	SOUTHAMPTON	22	L	0-1	0-0		Miklosko	Breacker	Gale	Hughton	Martin A	Morley	Bishop	Rush*	Small	Allen C	Slater	Keen
14/4		18,298	*17*	32			*Adams 88*	*Flowers*	*Kenna*	*Adams*	*Horne*	*Moore*	*Ruddock*	*Le Tissier*	*Cockerill*	*Shearer*	*Dowie**	*Benali*	*Widdrington*
							Ref: R Hamer	Two minutes from time Le Tissier crosses and Mickey Adams volleys in at the far post. This is Saints' seventh win in eight games, a superb run that hauls them out of the relegation mire. The Hammers crowd had threatened to walk out after 50 minutes in protest, but they stayed put.											
38	A	MANCHESTER C	22	L	0-2	0-1		Miklosko	Breacker	Dicks	Potts	Martin A	Keen	Bishop	Gale	Small*	Morley	Slater	Clarke
18/4		*25,601*	*5*	32			*Pointon 1, Clarke 77*	*Coton*	*Hill**	*Pointon*	*Brightwell*	*Curle*	*Vonk*	*White*	*Sheron*	*Hughes*	*Simpson*	*McMahon*	*Clarke*
							Ref: M Peck	In the first minute the ball rebounded into the path of City's Neil Pointon, who obliged with his first goal of the season. With West Ham having to press forward in a vain attempt to save the game, Wayne Clarke found himself with time and space to tuck the ball under Miklosko.											
39	H	CRYS PALACE	22	L	0-2	0-1		Miklosko	Breacker*	Dicks	Potts	Martin A	Thomas	Bishop	Keen	Morley	Allen C	Slater	Brown
20/4		17,710	*10*	32			*Bright 26, Coleman 53*	*Martyn*	*Humphrey*	*Sinnott*	*Southgate*	*Young*	*Thorn*	*Gordon**	*Thomas*	*Bright*	*Coleman*	*McGoldrick*	*Moralee*
							Ref: A Buksch	This is West Ham's first ever defeat by Palace, and it means only mathematical improbabilities can save them now. Tim Breacker's crazy back-pass set up Bright's 21st goal of the season. Palace's up-and-under tactics presented too many questions for West Ham to answer.											
40	H	MANCHESTER U	22	W	1-0	0-0	Brown 66	Miklosko	Potts	Dicks	Gale	Martin A	Thomas	Bishop	Keen	Small	Brown	Slater	
22/4		24,197	*2*	35				*Schmeichel*	*Irwin*	*Donaghy**	*Bruce*	*Phelan*	*Pallister*	*Giggs*	*Blackmore^*	*McClair*	*Hughes*	*Sharpe*	*Ferguson/Kanchel's*
							Ref: J Deakin	Having lost at home to Forest two days earlier, this is a crippling defeat for title chasing Man U. Ferguson's team played cautiously and with little rhythm, and managed no shots at all by half-time. Pallister inadvertently steered Slater's cross to Brown, whose father was in the stand.											
41	A	COVENTRY	22	L	0-1	0-1		Miklosko	Potts	Dicks	Gale	Martin A	Thomas	Bishop^	Keen	Small	Brown*	Slater	Morley/**Martin D**
25/4		*15,398*	*19*	35			*Gynn 44*	*Ogrizovic*	*McGrath*	*Sansom**	*Robson*	*Billing*	*Atherton*	*Flynn*	*Gynn*	*Ndlovu*	*Gallacher*	*Smith*	*Borrows*
							Ref: P Wright	This result sends West Ham down. Ironically, the only team they could in theory have overtaken was Don Howe's Coventry, who had failed to score in their last five games. Ludo made a hash of Kevin Gallacher's cross, and Gynn swept home. Dicks had West Ham's only shot on target.											
42	H	NOTT'M FOREST	22	W	3-0	0-0	McAvennie 60, 81, 85	Miklosko	Potts	Dicks	Gale	Martin A	Thomas*	Bishop	Allen M	Small	Martin D	Slater	McAvennie
2/5		20,629	*8*	38				*Crossley*	*Chettle*	*Williams*	*Walker*	*Crosby*	*Wilson**	*Black*	*Gemmill*	*Clough*	*Sheringham*	*Woan^*	*Stone/Glover*
	Home	Away					Ref: N Midgley	Frank McAvennie comes on as a second-half substitute and records a hat-trick in his farewell appearance in claret and blue. He was assisted by Brian Clough playing his son Nigel at centre-half. Alvin Martin set up Dean Martin to 'score' on his full debut, but the effort was disallowed.											
Average	21,285	22,641																	

Rumbelows Cup					F-A	H-T	Scorers, Times, and Referees	1	2	3	4	5	6	7	8	9	10	11	subs used
2:1	A	BRADFORD C	18	W	1-1	1-1	Small 12	Miklosko	Brown	Parris	Thomas	Foster	Breacker	Bishop	Slater	Small	Potts	Morley*	Gale
24/9		*7,034*	*3:10*				*Leonard 5*	*Tomlinson*	*Mitchell*	*Dowson*	*James*	*Leonard*	*Gardner*	*Babb*	*Duxbury*	*Torpey*	*Tinnion*	*Reid*	
							Ref: R Nixon	City have suffered only one defeat in eight and tackle the Hammers with gusto. Leonard scored off a post to put them in front, and had he paid proper attention Mitchell would have made it 2-0. Morley's cross drifted over the entire home defence for Small's downward header.											
2:2	H	BRADFORD C	18	W	4-0	2-0	Keen 9, Morley 36, Parris 56, Small 73	Miklosko	Breacker	Thomas	Gale	Foster	Parris	Bishop	Slater	Small*	Keen	Morley	McAvennie
9/10		17,232	*3:13*					*Tomlinson*	*Mitchell*	*Dowson*	*James*	*Oliver*	*Gardner*	*Babb*	*Duxbury*	*Torpey**	*Tinnion*	*Morgan^*	*Leonard/McCarthy*
							Ref: M James (Hammers win 5-1 on aggregate)	A huge ovation after 87 minutes greets Frank McAvennie's first appearance of the season, though the contest was over long before then. West Ham went in front when Slater's cross came off a defender for Keen. Morley and Small added headers, and Parris rounded keeper Tomlinson.											
3	A	SHEFFIELD UTD	17	W	2-0	1-0	McAvennie 44, Small 54p	Miklosko	Breacker	Thomas	Gale*	Potts	Parris	Bishop	McAvennie	Small	Keen	Slater	Allen M
29/10		*11,144*	*22*					*Kite*	*Pemberton*	*Cowan*	*Gannon*	*Gayle*	*Beesley*	*Bryson**	*Holroyd*	*Agana*	*Bradshaw^*	*Whitehouse*	*Mendonca/Lake*
							Ref: G Courtney	McAvennie's header from Slater's cross gives West Ham the edge they never surrender. The 4-4-2 system looks solid. When John Pemberton hacked down Slater in the box it extended West Ham's unbeaten run to five. The Blades didn't have the best of luck, hitting a post in each half.											
4	A	NORWICH	17	L	1-2	0-0	Small 73	Miklosko	Breacker	Thomas	Gale	Potts	Parris	Bishop	McAvennie	Small	Allen M	Slater	
4/12		*16,325*	*8*				*Fleck 65, 89p*	*Gunn*	*Phillips*	*Bowen*	*Sutton*	*Blades**	*Goss*	*Ullathorne*	*Fleck*	*Newman*	*Sherwood*	*Beckford^*	*Crook/Fox*
							Ref: K Morton	Robert Fleck sinks West Ham single handed. His first was a swivelling volley from 20 yards, his second – the late winner – a penalty when Thomas needlessly pushed Bowen in the area. McAvennie's flick on to Small had made it 1-1. Beckford missed numerous chances for City.											

FA Cup																			
3	A	FARNBOROUGH	21	D	1-1	0-0	Dicks 66	Miklosko	Breacker	Dicks	Gale	Potts*	Thomas	Bishop	McAvennie	Small	Keen	Slater	Morley
4/1		*23,449*					*Coney 86p*	*Power*	*Stemp*	*Baker**	*Broome*	*Bye*	*Wigmore*	*Doherty^*	*Holmes*	*Coney*	*Read*	*Fleming*	*Horton/Rogers*
							Ref: R Groves (At Upton Park)	Farnborough switch the tie to the Boleyn. New skipper Dicks plays a one-two with Small to put West Ham in front, but with time running out he handles in the box. Regular taker Mick Doherty had been subbed, so Dagenham-based Hammers' fan Dean Coney did the business instead.											
3R	H	FARNBOROUGH	21	W	1-0	0-0	Morley 88	Miklosko	Breacker	Dicks	Gale	Foster	Thomas	Bishop	McAvennie	Brown	Morley	Slater	
14/1		23,869						*Power*	*Stemp*	*Baker**	*Broome*	*Bye*	*Wigmore*	*Doherty*	*Holmes*	*Coney*	*Read*	*Fleming*	*Rogers*
							Ref: R Groves	West Ham look bewildered in the face of the GM Vauxhall Conference side's fluent play. Breacker's late cross set up the Hammers' totally ill-merited win. Power tried to fist clear, but the ball fell to Morley. Farnborough had had the best chance, but Ludo spread himself to deny Read.											
4	H	WREXHAM	20	D	2-2	1-0	Dicks 27, Morley 74	Miklosko	Breacker	Dicks	Potts	Foster	Thomas	Keen	McAvennie*	Brown	Morley	Slater	Small
25/1		24,712	*4:19*				*Phillips 60, Jones L 80*	*O'Keefe*	*Thackeray*	*Hardy*	*Taylor*	*Thomas*	*Sertori*	*Davies**	*Owen*	*Connolly*	*Watkin*	*Phillips*	*Jones L*
							Ref: C Trussell	Hammers fans stage a stand-up, sit-down demo before kick-off. Wrexham had beaten Arsenal in Round 3. Dicks and Morley both scored with headers from set pieces. Wrexham earned a replay when Miklosko could only get a faint touch to 18-year-old substitute, Lee Jones', effort.											
4R	A	WREXHAM	20	W	1-0	1-0	Foster 27	Parks	Breacker	Dicks	Potts	Foster	Thomas	Keen	McAvennie*	Brown	Small^	Slater	Martin D/Morley
4/2		*17,995*	*4:19*					*O'Keefe*	*Thackeray*	*Hardy*	*Taylor*	*Thomas*	*Seroti*	*Davies*	*Owen*	*Connolly*	*Watkin*	*Phillips**	*Jones L*
							Ref: C Trussell	Wrexham are near the foot of Division 4, and ex-Man U winger Mickey Thomas faces charges of counterfeiting. O'Keefe is stranded at Keen's corner: Foster's looping header is his first goal of the season. Breacker scythes Connolly, who has burst clear, but escapes with a yellow card.											
5	A	SUNDERLAND	20	D	1-1	0-0	Small 48	Parks	Breacker	Dicks	Potts	Foster	Atteveld	Keen	Brown	Small	Allen M	Slater	
15/2		*25,475*	*2:12*				*Byrne 64*	*Norman*	*Kay*	*Rogan*	*Bennett**	*Hardyman*	*Davenport*	*Bracewell*	*Ballk*	*Armstrong*	*Byrne*	*Atkinson*	*Pascoe*
							Ref: R Nixon	West Ham live to fight another day after a cup-tie played in an icy Roker wind, against a team with a caretaker manager – Malcolm Crosby. Martin Allen tried to claim Mike Small's goal. John Byrne miskicked Sunderland's equaliser. The winners will play Chelsea in the last eight.											
5R	H	SUNDERLAND	21	L	2-3	1-2	Allen 38, 56	Parks	Breacker	Dicks	Potts	Foster	Atteveld*	Bishop	Keen	Small	Allen M	Slater	Morley
26/2		25,830	*2:12*				*Byrne 6, 24, Rush 78*	*Norman*	*Kay*	*Rogan*	*Rush*	*Hardyman*	*Davenport**	*Bracewell*	*Ball*	*Armstrong*	*Byrne*	*Atkinson*	*Brady*
							Ref: R Nixon	Sunderland had not beaten a top division side in the FA Cup for 13 years. They were helped in this replay by on-loan Atteveld's ludicrous early back-pass from the halfway line. The result is West Ham's first home defeat under floodlights in three years. Sunderland will reach Wembley.											

		Home					Away					
	P	W	D	L	F	A	W	D	L	F	A	Pts
1 Leeds	42	13	8	0	38	13	9	8	4	36	24	82
2 Manchester U	42	12	7	2	34	13	9	8	4	29	20	78
3 Sheffield Wed	42	13	5	3	39	24	8	7	6	23	25	75
4 Arsenal	42	12	7	2	51	22	7	8	6	30	24	72
5 Manchester C	42	13	4	4	32	14	7	6	8	29	34	70
6 Liverpool	42	13	5	3	34	17	3	11	7	13	23	64
7 Aston Villa	42	13	3	5	31	16	4	6	11	17	28	60
8 Nott'm Forest	42	10	7	4	36	27	6	4	11	24	31	59
9 Sheffield Utd	42	9	6	6	29	23	7	3	11	36	40	57
10 Crys Palace	42	7	8	6	24	25	7	7	7	29	36	57
11 QP Rangers	42	6	10	5	25	21	6	8	7	23	26	54
12 Everton	42	8	8	5	28	19	5	6	10	24	32	53
13 Wimbledon	42	10	5	6	32	20	3	9	9	21	33	53
14 Chelsea	42	7	8	6	31	30	6	6	9	19	30	53
15 Tottenham	42	7	3	11	33	35	8	4	9	25	28	52
16 Southampton	42	7	5	9	17	28	7	5	9	22	27	52
17 Oldham	42	11	5	5	46	36	3	4	14	17	31	51
18 Norwich	42	8	6	7	29	28	3	6	12	18	35	45
19 Coventry	42	6	7	8	18	15	5	4	12	17	29	44
20 Luton	42	10	7	4	25	17	0	5	16	13	54	42
21 Notts Co	42	7	5	9	24	29	3	5	13	16	33	40
22 WEST HAM	42	6	6	9	22	24	3	5	13	15	35	38
	924	208	135	119	678	496	119	135	208	496	678	1251

Odds & ends

Double wins: (0).
Double losses: (6) Notts Co, Man C, Coventry, Sheff W, Everton, Southampton.

Won from behind: (3) Villa (h), Palace (a), Spurs (h).
Lost from in front: (1) Sheff W (a).

High spots: Four unbeaten league games from 18 October.

Low spots: Relegation, and the humiliation of finishing last.
Five successive league defeats from 22 February.

Hammer of the Year: Julian Dicks.
Ever-presents: (0).
Hat-tricks: (1) Frank McAvennie.
Leading scorer: (18) Mike Small.

	Appearances						Goals			
	Lge	*Sub*	LC	*Sub*	FAC	*Sub*	**Lge**	LC	FAC	**Tot**
Allen, Clive	**4**						1			**1**
Allen, Martin	**14**	*5*	1	*1*	2				2	**2**
Atteveld, Ray	**1**				2					
Bishop, Ian	**41**		4		3		1			**1**
Breacker, Tim	**33**	*1*	4		6		2			**2**
Brown, Kenny	**25**	*2*	1		4		3			**3**
Clarke, Simon		*1*								
Dicks, Julian	**23**				6		3		2	**5**
Foster, Colin	**24**		2		5				1	**1**
Gale, Tony	**24**	*1*	3	*1*	2					
Hughton, Chris		*1*								
Keen, Kevin	**20**	*9*	2		5			1		**1**
Martin, Alvin	**7**									
Martin, Dean	**1**	*1*				*1*				
Miklosko, Ludek	**36**		4		3					
McAvennie, Frank	**16**	*4*	2	*1*	4		6	1		**7**
Morley, Trevor	**13**	*11*	2		2	*3*	2	1	2	**5**
Parks, Tony	**6**				3					
Parris, George	**20**	*1*	4					1		**1**
Potts, Steve	**34**		3		5					
Rosenior, Leroy	**5**	*4*					1			**1**
Rush, Matthew	**3**	*7*					2			**2**
Slater, Stuart	**41**		4		6					
Small, Mike	**37**	*3*	4		4	*1*	13	4	1	**18**
Thomas, Mitchell	**34**	*1*	4		4		3			**3**
25 players used	**462**	***52***	**44**	***3***	**66**	***5***	**37**	**8**	**8**	**53**

No	Date		Att	Pos	Pt	F-A	H-T	Scorers, Times, and Referees	1	2	3	4	5	6	7	8	9	10	11	subs used
1	A	BARNSLEY			W	1-0	1-0	Allen C 21	Miklosko	Breacker	Dicks	Potts	Martin	Parris^	Bishop	**Butler**	Small !	Allen C*	Keen	Gale/**Robson**
	16/8		6,761		3				Butler	Robinson	Bishop	Fleming	Taggart	Archdeacon	Redfearn	Bullimore	Pearson	Currie	Rammell*	Liddell
								Ref: R Nixon	Supporters saddened by the sale of Stuart Slater to Celtic are cheered by this win, secured after Clive Allen played a one-two with Keen. West Ham hung on grimly after half-time and survived two strong penalty shouts. On 83 mins Small was expelled for foul language to a linesman.											
2	H	CHARLTON		17	L	0-1	0-1		Miklosko	Breacker	Dicks	Potts	Martin	Parris	Bishop*	Butler	Small	Allen C	Keen	Robson
	22/8		17,054	1	3			Pardew 31	Bolder	Pitcher*	Barness	Pardew	Webster	Gatting	Lee^	Bumstead	Dyer	Nelson	Walsh	Balmer/Grant
								Ref: P Durkin	Bonds had watched Robert Lee, whose cross set up a simple goal for Alan Pardew. Small hit a post, Keen's lob was disallowed, and Martin's header was cleared off the line. Mark Robson, a free-transfer from Spurs, comes off the bench. Alan Curbishley is co-manager of Charlton.											
3	A	NEWCASTLE		19	L	0-2	0-2		Miklosko	Breacker	Dicks !	Potts	Martin	**Holmes***	Bishop	Butler	Allen M	Allen C	Keen	Small
	29/8		**29,855**	4	3			Peacock 44, Kelly 45	Wright	Venison	Ranson	O'Brien	Scott	Howey	Carr	Peacock	Kelly	Clark	Sheedy	
								Ref: W Burns	The Keegan revival at St James' Park is under way. 15 minutes from time Dicks, already booked, was sent off for elbowing Franz Carr, who had played for Hammers on loan. New signing Matt Holmes also had to go off concussed. One Hammers goal in three games tells the story.											
4	H	WATFORD		13	W	2-1	0-0	Allen M 52, Allen C 84	Miklosko	Breacker	Dicks	Potts	Martin	Allen M	Robson*	Butler	Morley	Allen C	Keen	Parris
	5/9		11,921	8	6			Furlong 82	Suckling	Gibbs	Drysdale	Dublin	Holdsworth	Ashby	Hessenthaler	Nogan	Furlong	Butler*	Soloman^	Bazeley/Putney
								Ref: R Lewis	Watford boss Steve Perryman admitted: 'We didn't deserve a point.' But when Paul Furlong pushed Alvin Martin off the ball to score from a tight angle, it looked like they would get one. The new back-pass law saw a free-kick given against Ludo, after the ball spun to him off Dicks.											
5	A	PETERBOROUGH		7	W	3-1	3-1	Morley 25, Allen M 28, Keen 41	Miklosko	Breacker	Thomas	Potts	Martin	Allen M	Robson	Butler	Morley	Allen C*	Keen	Small
	12/9		10,657	17	9			Adcock 19	Bennett	Luke	Robinson	Halsall	Howarth	Welsh	Sterling	Ebdon	Adcock	Charlery	Barnes*	Costello
								Ref: J Rushton	The first ever competitive match with The Posh. Morley and Keen's goals were both aided by deflections. Martin Allen, who had missed badly earlier on, made amends by springing the offside trap to put West Ham 2-1 ahead. Bonds is rumoured to be about to enter the transfer market.											
6	A	BRISTOL CITY		5	W	5-1	3-0	Robson 6, Allen C 44, 85, Morley 27, 89	Miklosko	Breacker	Thomas	Potts	Martin	Allen M	Robson*	Butler	Morley	Allen C	Keen	Small
	15/9		14,130	9	12			Scott 54	Welch	Llewellyn	Scott	Thompson	Bryant	Edwards	Harrison	Dziek'owski*	Rosenior	Cole^	Shelton	Allison/Connor
								Ref: J Martin	Coach Harry Redknapp was interviewed by police for gestures allegedly aimed at the Ashton Gate crowd. The game looked over by half-time, but Scott's free-kick encouraged Andy Cole to spark a second-half onslaught. Clive Allen's second goal took the sting out of City's revival.											
7	H	DERBY		5	D	1-1	0-1	Morley 47	Miklosko	Breacker	Thomas	Potts	Martin	Allen M	Robson*	Butler	Morley	Allen C	Keen	Small
	20/9		11,493	24	13			Thomas 41 (og)	Taylor	Comyn	Forsyth	Short	Wassall	Pembridge	Johnson	Kitson	Gabbiadini*	Williams^	Simpson	Sturridge/Coleman
								Ref: I Hemsley	Rock-bottom Derby have equalled the British record transfer fee for a defender, signing Craig Short from Notts Co for £2.5 million. Morley, who has signed a new one-year contract, was marked by Short but escaped to equalise. Thomas' own-goal went in off Miklosko. Kitson plays.											
8	A	PORTSMOUTH		4	W	1-0	1-0	Allen C 45	Miklosko	Breacker	Dicks	Potts	Martin	Allen M	Robson*	Butler	Morley	Allen C	Keen	Holmes
	27/9		12,158	15	16				Knight	Awford	Daniel	McLoughlin	Symons	Aspinall	Neill*	Dolling	Clarke	Whittingham	Murray^	Walsh/Powell
								Ref: K Cooper	Dicks' suspension is over, but he was not immediately restored to the side. Friction with Bonds intensifies, though Dicks says: 'Me and Billy get on fine.' Morley is denied a goal by the inside of a post and by super saves from Knight. Bonds says: 'We played some great football.'											
9	A	WOLVES		7	D	0-0	0-0		Miklosko	Breacker	Dicks !	Potts	Martin	Allen M	Robson*	Butler	Morley	Allen C^	Keen	Holmes/Gale
	4/10		14,391	3	17				Stowell	Ashley	Edwards	Downing	Mountfield	Blades	Birch	Cook	Bull	Roberts*	Rankine	Mutch
								Ref: D Allison	Dicks is sent off yet again, this time for series of running clashes with Steve Bull. With both players having been booked, Dicks lunges at the England striker and gets his second yellow card. Bull was accused of feigning injury. A game which started brightly quickly degenerated.											
10	H	SUNDERLAND		5	W	**6-0**	3-0	Keen 25, Morley 28, Allen M 39,	Miklosko	Breacker	Dicks	Potts	Martin	Allen M	Robson	Butler	Morley	Allen C	Keen	
	11/10		**10,326**	15	20			[Martin 48, Robson 62, 89]	Carter	Kay	Rogan	Owers	Bennett	Ball	Cunningham*	Goodman	Davenport	Gray, Martin	Armstong^	Atkinson/Rush
								Ref: R Milford	Having lost to Crewe, this is a timely pick-me-up in front of a TV audience. The Hammers' record win, in 1968, was against Sunderland, when Geoff Hurst scored six. At 0-0 Don Goodman cleared the West Ham offside trap, but missed. The Boleyn's lowest league crowd for 30 years.											
11	A	BRISTOL ROV		2	W	4-0	3-0	Morley 17, Dicks 35p, Keen 41, Allen C 83	Miklosko	Breacker	Dicks	Potts	Martin	Allen M	Robson	Butler	Morley	Allen C	Keen	
	17/10		6,189	24	23				Kelly	Alexander	Clark	Yates	Hardyman	Skinner	Mehew	Reece	Taylor	Stewart	Cross	
								Ref: G Ashby	The Hammers started slowly but gradually upped the tempo. Morley held his nerve to put them in front. Dicks' thunderbolt penalty marked his temporary farewell, as he commences a five-match ban and is fined one week's wages. Clive Allen added No 4 when Butler's shot hit a post.											

12	H	SWINDON		3	L		0-1	0-0		Miklosko	Breacker	Parris !	Potts	Martin	Allen M	Robson	Butler	Morley	Allen C	Keen	
24/10			17,842	*2*		23			*Maskell 84*	*Hammond*	*Kerslake*	*Horlock*	*Hoddle*	*Calderwood*	*Taylor*	*Hazard*	*Moncur**	*Maskell*	*Ling*	*Mitchell*	*White*
									Ref: I Borrett	West Ham deserved better than this, losing to a disputed free-kick which led to a deflected goal. George Parris had brought down Martin Ling for which he was sent off. The healthy-sized crowd was a response to lowered ticket prices and the prospect of seeing Glenn Hoddle in action.											
13	A	CAMBRIDGE		4	L		1-2	0-1	Morley 50	Miklosko	Breacker	Parris	Potts	Martin	Allen M	Robson	Butler	Morley	Allen C	Keen	
31/10			*7,214*	*17*		23			*Norbury 36, White 72*	*Dennis*	*Fensome*	*Kimble*	*Raynor*	*Heathcote*	*O'Shea*	*Rowett*	*Norbury**	*White*	*Clayton*	*Philpott^*	*Ainsworth/Danzey*
									Ref: G Pooley	Managerless Cambridge, who reached last season's play-offs, are the arch-exponents of up-and-under football. At 1-1 Devon White capitalised when West Ham failed to clear their lines. So convinced were the Hammers that White was offside that Martin Allen was booked for dissent.											
14	A	GRIMSBY		4	D		1-1	0-0	Morley 74	Miklosko	Breacker	Parris	Potts	Martin	Allen M	Robson*	Butler	Morley	Allen C	Keen	Holmes
3/11			*9,119*	*13*		24			*Mendonca 54*	*Beasant*	*McDermott*	*Croft*	*Futcher*	*Lever*	*Dobbin*	*Watson*	*Gilbert*	*Groves*	*Mendonca*	*Rees**	*Smith*
									Ref: W Burns	West Ham are unchanged despite having lost their last two. Two super goals enlivened this match. Mendonca's 25-yard stunner was answered by Trevor Morley's drive, set up by Matt Holmes. For the second game in a row Clive Allen is one-on-one with the goalkeeper, and misses.											
15	H	NOTTS CO		4	W		2-0	1-0	Allen C 42, Morley 60	Miklosko	Breacker	Brown	Potts	Martin	Allen M	Robson	Butler	Morley	Allen C	Keen	
7/11			12,345	*21*		27				*Cherry*	*Short, Chris*	*Thomas*	*Palmer*	*Johnson*	*Williams*	*Devlin*	*Turner**	*Lund*	*Draper*	*Slawson*	*Bartlett*
									Ref: A Gunn	Upton Park is strangely subdued, perhaps by County's spoiling tactics. Mark Robson set Clive Allen away to curl the first goal. Trevor Morley added a second after Steve Potts' shot was parried. County manager Neil Warnock had the grace to say afterwards 'the score flattered us.'											
16	A	MILLWALL		5	L		1-2	0-1	Robson 77	Miklosko	Breacker	Brown	Potts	Martin	Parris	Robson	Holmes	Morley	Allen C	Keen*	Clarke
15/11			*12,445*	*4*		27			*Allen M 41p, Barber 55*	*Keller*	*Cunningham*	*Dawes*	*May*	*Cooper*	*Stevens*	*Rae*	*Moralee**	*Allen M^*	*Byrne*	*Barber*	*Dolby/Goodman*
									Ref: K Morton	Both teams have an M Allen, so it is as well for commentators that West Ham's 'Martin' is suspended. Millwall's 'Malcolm' scored from the spot after Robson felled Cunningham. At 2-0, Robson chipped Keller and Alvin Martin hit a post. Lions' Mick McCarthy was mighty relieved.											
17	H	OXFORD		4	W		5-3	3-1	Allen C 4, B'ker 38, Dicks 42, 50, M'ley 86	Miklosko	Breacker	Dicks	Potts	Martin	Parris	Robson	Holmes	Morley	Allen C	Keen*	Brown
21/11			11,842	*13*		30			*Durnin 1, Magilton 51, Melville 53*	*Reece*	*Smart*	*Ford*	*Lewis*	*Evans*	*Melville*	*Magilton*	*Beauchamp*	*Penney*	*Durnin**	*Allen C*	*Cusack*
									Ref: R Wiseman	A wonderful game, agreed Oxford boss Brian Horton, which earned a standing ovation at the end. Before kick-off Oxford boasted the meanest away defence in the division. A corner inside 45 seconds brought Durnin's goal. It was nip and tuck until Morley glanced in a late free-kick.											
18	H	BIRMINGHAM		3	W		3-1	1-1	Allen C 21, 86, Morley 85	Miklosko	Breacker	Dicks	Potts	Foster	Parris	Robson	Holmes	Morley	Allen C	Keen*	Bishop
28/11			15,004	*19*		33			*Rodgerson 12*	*Sealey*	*Holmes**	*Potter*	*Tait*	*Rogers*	*Matthewson*	*Rodgerson*	*Gayle*	*Speedie*	*Frain*	*Donowa*	*Sturridge*
									Ref: R Pawley	Trevor Morley was sent off in Reggiani in midweek in the Anglo-Italian Cup. With club captain Dicks suspended, and deputy Alvin Martin also missing, the armband passes to Steve Potts. Clive Allen equalised for the Hammers with a glancing header from Mark Robson's cross.											
19	A	TRANMERE		3	L		2-5	1-1	Morley 20, Allen C 79	Miklosko	Breacker	Dicks	Potts	Martin	Allen M^	Robson	Parris*	Morley	Allen C	Keen	Bishop/Foster
4/12			*11,782*	*2*		33			*Aldridge 17, 71, 89, Irons 48, Malkin 90*	*Nixon*	*Higgins*	*Brannan*	*Irons*	*Mungall*	*Vickers*	*Morrissey*	*Aldridge*	*Malkin*	*McNab**	*Nevin*	*Martindale*
									Ref: P Harrison	Tranmere stay on Newcastle's heels thanks to veteran John Aldridge's latest hat-trick. For his first he skipped round Miklosko; for his third he exploited Ludo's hashed clearance. Bonds: 'You could have driven a double decker bus through our defence.' Now off to Cozenza in Italy.											
20	H	SOUTHEND		3	W		2-0	1-0	Morley 37, Allen C 67	Miklosko	Breacker	Dicks	Potts	Martin	Parris*	Robson	Allen M	Morley	Allen C	Keen	Bishop
12/12			15,739	*24*		36				*Sansome*	*Edwards*	*Powell*	*Cornwall*	*Scully*	*Prior*	*Locke*	*Sussex*	*Brown*	*Collymore*	*Tilson*	
									Ref: W Burge	Hammers on half-throttle were still far too good for dreadful Southend, for whom only recent signing Stan Collymore made any impact. Keen and Robson out wide repeatedly opened up the visiting defence. Both goals were headers. Southend boss Colin Murphy had no poems to recite.											
21	A	BRENTFORD		3	D		0-0	0-0		Miklosko	Breacker	Dicks	Potts	Martin	Allen M	Robson*	Bishop	Morley	Allen C	Keen	**Bunbury**
20/12			*11,912*	*12*		37				*Benstead*	*Statham*	*Manuel*	*Millen*	*Westley*	*Ratcliffe*	*Bennett**	*Luscombe^*	*Allon*	*Blissett*	*Gayle*	*Smillie/Godfrey*
									Ref: M James	Trevor Morley won most of his aerial battles against a 6ft 4in centre-half. Keeper Graham Benstead did well to save from Clive Allen and Bishop, but West Ham might easily have lost at the death when substitute Neil Smillie was denied by Miklosko. Brentford's slide now begins.											
22	A	CHARLTON		3	D		1-1	1-0	Dicks 10	Miklosko	Breacker	Dicks	Potts	Martin	Allen M	Robson	Bishop*	Morley	Allen C	Keen	Bunbury
26/12			*8,337*	*11*		38			*Bumstead 79*	*Bolder*	*Pitcher*	*Minto*	*Bumstead*	*Webster*	*Balmer*	*Robinson*	*Power*	*Leaburn**	*Nelson*	*Walsh*	*Garland*
									Ref: I Hemley	The capacity of the restored Valley is so small that West Ham supporters are restricted to just 400 tickets. Julian Dicks' free-kick is deflected past Bob Bolder and the Hammers lead for over an hour, but when John Bumstead hits the post he is also quickest to pounce on the loose ball.											
23	H	LUTON		3	D		2-2	0-0	Dicks 52p, Breacker 67	Miklosko	Breacker	Dicks	Potts	Martin	Allen M	Robson	Butler	Morley	Allen C	Keen	
28/12			18,786	*20*		39			*Hughes 68, Dreyer 70*	*Chamberlain*	*Dreyer*	*James*	*Johnson*	*Hughes*	*Peake*	*Williams**	*Telfer*	*Rees^*	*Gray*	*Preece*	*Benjamin/Oakes*
									Ref: M Pierce	David Pleat thought his side were in control till half-time. When Robson was nudged off the ball by Hughes, Dicks obliged from the spot. Tim Breacker then scored from 25 yards against his former club. Hughes' instant reply was capped when a scrambled corner just crossed the line.											

No	Date			Att	Pos	Pt		F-A	H-T	Scorers, Times, and Referees	1	2	3	4	5	6	7	8	9	10	11	subs used
24	A	DERBY			2		W	2-0	2-0	Robson 9, Morley 15	Miklosko	Breacker	Dicks !	Potts	Martin^	Allen M	Robson*	Butler	Morley	Allen C	Keen	Foster/Parris
	10/1			*13,737*	*11*	42					*Sutton*	*Kavanagh*	*Forsyth*	*Short*	*Coleman*	*Pembridge*	*McMinn*	*Kuhl*	*Kitson*	*Johnson**	*Simpson*	*Gabbiadini*
										Ref: A Wilkie	Dicks is in the news again, this time for his late lunge at Ted McMinn which earned a second yellow card. It's his third dismissal of the season, and Bonds has no sympathy with him. Fortunately, West Ham were 2-0 up at the time, so Dicks' loss was not vital. Best Hammer was Morley.											
25	H	PORTSMOUTH			3		W	2-0	1-0	Morley 26, Foster 55	Miklosko	Breacker	Dicks	Potts	Foster	Allen M	Robson^	Butler	Morley	Allen C*	Keen	Holmes/Parris
	16/1			18,127	*6*	45					*Knight*	*Awford*	*Daniel*	*McLoughlin*	*Symons*	*Burns**	*Neill^*	*Chamberlain*	*Walsh*	*Whittingham*	*Aspinall*	*Powell/Maguire*
										Ref: R Gifford	Morley's brave flying header required treatment for a gashed lip. Foster's goal was also a header. Pompey boss Jim Smith said: 'West Ham are the best team we have played this season'. Pompey will shortly start their surge. Had they lost this game 0-1, they would have won promotion.											
26	H	BRISTOL CITY			2		W	2-0	0-0	Morley 66, Robson 73	Miklosko	Breacker	Brown	Potts	Gale	Allen M	Robson^	Butler	Morley	Bunbury*	Keen	Holmes/Parris
	27/1			12,118	*18*	48					*Welch*	*Atteveld**	*Scott*	*Aizlewood*	*Bryant*	*Osman*	*Shelton*	*Harrison*	*Allison*	*Cole*	*Gavin^*	*Rosenior/Dziek'owski*
										Ref: B Hill	Yet another 2-0 win. Russell Osman takes charge of City for the first time, and Canadian international Alex Bunbury starts a game for the first time. The break came when Welch failed to hold Keen's shot. Atteveld, formerly at Upton Park, escaped expulsion for a late foul on M Allen.											
27	A	LEICESTER			2		W	2-1	1-1	Robson 19, Gale 53	Miklosko	Breacker	Brown	Potts	Gale	Allen M	Robson*	Butler	Morley	Holmes	Keen^	Parris/**Jones**
	30/1			*18,838*	*6*	51				*Lowe 6*	*Hoult*	*Mills*	*Gibson*	*Smith*	*Walsh*	*Hill**	*Oldfield*	*Thompson*	*Joachim^*	*Lowe*	*Philpott*	*James/Gee*
										Ref: K Redfearn	Signed back in November, Billericay's Steve Jones makes his long-awaited debut. Mind you, he does not come on till the 88th minute. Gale's looping header was the transfer-listed player's first goal for two years. The result leaves third-placed Tranmere six points behind the Hammers.											
28	H	BARNSLEY			2		D	1-1	1-1	Jones 10	Miklosko	Breacker	Dicks	Potts	Gale	Allen M	Robson	Butler	Morley	Jones	Keen	
	6/2			14,101	*16*	52				*Rammell 42*	*Butler*	*Robinson*	*Taggart*	*Fleming*	*Bishop*	*Archdeacon*	*O'Connell*	*Redfearn*	*Pearson*	*Currie**	*Rammell*	*Liddell*
										Ref: S Dunn	Two weeks earlier Barnsley dumped West Ham from the FA Cup. Steve Jones starts his first game and scores his first goal, after Robson's shot fell to him. Martin Allen then hit a dipper against the bar. Rammell's equaliser came when a Barnsley corner was headed back across goal.											
29	H	PETERBOROUGH			2		W	2-1	2-1	Butler 4, Jones 13	Miklosko	Breacker	Dicks	Potts	Gale	Allen M	Robson	Butler	Morley	Jones	Keen*	Holmes
	9/2			12,537	*11*	55				*Ebdon 36*	*Bennett*	*Luke*	*Spearing*	*Halsall*	*Bradshaw*	*Welsh**	*Sterling*	*McGlashan*	*Adcock*	*Philliskirk*	*Curtis^*	*Howarth/Iorfa*
										Ref: G Pooley	Peter Butler scores his first Hammers goal, after Keen's header came back off a post. Steve Jones swivels to connect with Morley's header for his second goal in 72 hours. Ebdon made it 2-1 with a half-volley. Early in the second half Jones was fouled but Dicks' penalty was saved.											
30	A	WATFORD			2		W	2-1	1-0	Robson 21, Keen 68	Miklosko	Breacker	Dicks	Potts	Gale	Allen M	Robson*	Butler	Morley	Jones^	Keen	Holmes/Bishop
	13/2			*13,115*	*14*	58				*Charley 52*	*Suckling*	*Lavin**	*Drysdale*	*Dublin*	*Holdsworth*	*Willis*	*Hessenthaler*	*Nogan^*	*Furlong*	*Charlery*	*Soloman*	*Holdsworth/Porter*
										Ref: K Leach	Kevin Keen's father once managed, and was sacked by, Watford. Robson's diving header from Dicks' cross was cancelled out by Hessenthaler's low shot, turned in by Ken Charlery. Keen then fires a ballistic winner. This win leaves Hammers four points behind leaders Newcastle.											
31	H	NEWCASTLE			2		D	0-0	0-0		Miklosko	Brown	Dicks	Potts	Gale	Allen M	Robson	Butler	Morley	Bishop	Keen*	Jones
	21/2			24,159	*1*	59					*Srnicek*	*Venison*	*Beresford*	*O'Brien*	*Scott*	*Howey*	*Lee*	*Peacock*	*Kelly*	*Clark*	*Sheedy*	
										Ref: K Cooper	A Sunday TV stalemate. Keegan may be building a reputation for gung-ho football, but he knows the importance of not losing and packs his midfield. Bonds does the same, with the result that chances are few. Ex-Hammer David Kelly was rudely barracked on his return to Upton Pk.											
32	A	SUNDERLAND			2		D	0-0	0-0		Miklosko	Brown	Dicks	Potts	Gale	Bishop	Robson^	Butler	Morley	Bunbury*	Keen	Parris/Holmes
	27/2			*19,068*	*16*	60					*Norman*	*Kay*	*Ord*	*Atkinson*	*Butcher*	*Ball*	*Mooney**	*Goodman*	*Colquhoun*	*Gray, Michael*	*Armstrong*	*Davenport*
										Ref: J Worrall	Bobby Moore died in midweek and the football world is in mourning. Wreathes are laid by both sets of supporters and the minute's silence was scrupulously observed. With Martin Allen suspended, it falls to Ian Bishop to wear Moore's No 6 shirt. The game itself was forgettable.											
33	H	WOLVES			2		W	3-1	0-0	Morley 58, Dicks 61p, Holmes 87	Miklosko	Brown	Dicks	Potts	Gale	Bishop	Robson	Butler	Morley	Small	Keen^	Holmes
	6/3			24,679	*11*	63				*Bull 57*	*Stowell*	*Blades*	*Venus*	*Burke*	*Mountfield*	*Madden*	*Rankine**	*Cook*	*Bull*	*Thompson*	*Dennison*	*Mutch*
										Ref: R Bigger	Upton Park is awash with wreathes. Hurst and Peters place a floral No 6 in the centre-circle. Bishop wears No 12, not 6. Bull volleys in against the run of play. It is quickly levelled when Morley converts Robson's cross. Madden fouled Keen for the penalty, but it looked outside the box.											
34	H	GRIMSBY			2		W	2-1	2-0	Dicks 6, 11	Miklosko	Brown	Dicks	Potts	Gale	Allen M	Robson	Butler	Morley	Small*	Keen	Bishop
	9/3			13,170	*9*	66				*Groves 61*	*Wilmott*	*McDermott*	*Croft*	*Futcher*	*Lever*	*Jobling*	*Ford*	*Gilbert**	*Groves*	*Rees*	*Woods^*	*Mendonca/Agnew*
										Ref: A Gunn	Hammers' unbeaten league run is now 15 games. Dicks headed in Keen's corner, then blasted a second after a corner had been cleared. A post then denied him a hat-trick. But Dicks' hand also conceded a penalty, which Gilbert fired against the bar. Groves' goal was a fantastic volley.											

No	Venue	Opponent	Att	Pos	Res	Pts	F-A	H-T	Scorers, Times, and Referees	1	2	3	4	5	6	7	8	9	10	11	12
35	A	NOTTS CO		2	L		0-1	0-0		Miklosko	Brown	Dicks	Potts	Gale	Allen M	Robson*	Butler	Morley	Small	Keen	Bishop
	13/3		*10,272*	*17*		66			*Walker 70*	*Cherry*	*Short, Chris*	*Johnson*	*Thomas*	*Cox*	*Walker*	*Lund*	*Draper*	*Wilson*	*Williams**	*Smith*	*Devlin*
									Ref: I Cruickshanks	County have a plush new stadium and a new manager, Michael Walker. Richard Walker scores on his debut to inflict on West Ham their first league defeat since 4 December. Home keeper Steve Cherry was untroubled apart from Robson's cheeky back-heel. Dicks was booked again.											
36	H	TRANMERE		2	W		2-0	0-0	Dicks 54p, 82p	Miklosko	Brown	Dicks	Potts	Gale	Allen M	Robson*	Butler	**Speedie**	Morley	Keen	Holmes
	20/3		16,369	*7*		69				*Nixon*	*Higgins*	*Mungall*	*Irons*	*Proctor*	*Vickers*	*Morrissey*	*Coyne*	*Malkin**	*Nevin*	*Thomas*	*Branch*
									Ref: M Read	Dicks is rumoured to be about to sign for Chelsea. Perhaps they want his spot-kick expertise, for he blazed two penalties past Nixon, both for fouls against Morley. The first was questionable, as he and Vickers chased a through ball. Much-travelled David Speedie has arrived on loan.											
37	A	OXFORD		2	L		0-1	0-0		Miklosko	Brown	Dicks	Potts	Gale	Allen M	Holmes	Butler	Speedie	Morley	Keen*	Robson
	23/3		*9,506*	*15*		69			*Melville 85*	*Reece*	*Robinson*	*Ford*	*Lewis*	*Evans*	*Melville*	*Phillips*	*Beauchamp*	*Cusack*	*Durnin*	*Narbett*	
									Ref: K Burge	Oxford had taken just one point from their previous six games, so this is a mighty upset, watched by Oxford's biggest gate of the season. After half-time the home side were attacking at will down the Manor's slope. Near the end Cusack's cross was met by the unmarked Andy Melville.											
38	H	MILLWALL		2	D		2-2	2-1	Keen 12, Morley 13	Miklosko	Breacker	Brown	Potts	Gale	Bishop	Robson	Butler	Speedie	Morley	Keen	
	28/3		15,723	*5*		70			*Moralee 1, Stevens 77*	*Keller*	*Cunningham*	*Dawes*	*Roberts*	*Cooper*	*Stevens*	*Maguire**	*Bogie*	*Allen M^*	*Moralee*	*Barber*	*Kerr/Gaynor*
									Ref: M Bailey	A mid-day kick-off, after the clocks have been changed, seems to leave West Ham sluggish. Jamie Moralee's sensational start for Millwall was pegged back by Keen's flying volley and Morley's side-step. Stevens restored parity with a brave header, though Gale's free-kick hit a post.											
39	A	BIRMINGHAM		2	W		2-1	0-1	Brown 87, Bishop 89	Miklosko	Breacker	Brown	Potts	Gale	Bishop	Robson*	Butler	Speedie	Jones^	Keen	Holmes/Foster
	3/4		*19,053*	*21*		73			*Saville 12*	*Catlin*	*Clarkson*	*Frain*	*Parris*	*Dryden*	*Matthewson*	*Moulden**	*Rodgerson*	*Saville*	*Peer*	*Smith*	*Sturridge*
									Ref: M Peck	What a finish! Andy Saville had been playing for Hartlepool earlier in the season but his goal spelled gloom for Hammers until Kenny Brown's pile-driver and Ian Bishop's dipping winner sends the Boleyn into raptures. Colin Foster had come off the bench to play as a makeshift striker.											
40	A	SOUTHEND		3	L		0-1	0-1		Miklosko	Breacker	Dicks	Potts	Gale	Bishop	Robson	Butler	Speedie	Foster	Keen	
	7/4		*12,813*	*23*		73			*Angell 32*	*Royce*	*Edwards*	*Powell*	*Jones*	*Scully*	*Prior*	*Ansah*	*Smith*	*Tilson*	*Collymore*	*Angell*	
									Ref: I Borrett	Barry Fry has only been at Southend a few days but Roots Hall is a frenzy of excitement. West Ham played well, but the goal that beat them was a gem. Keith Jones freed Stan Collymore down the left. Potts was turned inside out and the cross was smashed in off the bar by Angell.											
41	H	LEICESTER		3	W		3-0	2-0	Speedie 10, 29, Keen 47	Miklosko	Breacker	Dicks	Potts	Gale	Bishop	Robson	Butler	Speedie	Morley	Keen	
	11/4		13,951			76				*Poole*	*Coatsworth**	*Mills*	*Smith*	*Walsh*	*Hill*	*Oldfield*	*Thompson*	*Joachim*	*Lowe*	*Philpott^*	*Whitlow/James*
									Ref: G Poll	33-year-old David Speedie has already played for four clubs this season. West Ham fans have not taken to him. He waits for this TV Sunday match to score his first Hammers goals. He bagged two but should have had five. Portsmouth's win the previous day keeps West Ham third.											
42	A	LUTON		3	L		0-2	0-0		Miklosko	Breacker	Dicks	Potts	Gale	Bishop	Allen M*	Butler	Speedie	Morley	Keen	Holmes
	13/4		*10,959*	*16*		76			*Gray 84p, Williams 88*	*Chamberlain*	*Dreyer*	*Telfer^*	*Johnson*	*James*	*Peake*	*Hughes**	*Kamara*	*Dixon*	*Gray*	*Preece*	*Oakes/Williams*
									Ref: G Singh	A calamitous defeat, which turned on a ferociously contested late penalty. Dicks was shoved off the ball by Kerry Dixon and in the subsequent melee handled the ball. Dicks should have been sent off. Phil Gray despatched the penalty. Williams then caught West Ham on the break.											
43	H	BRENTFORD		3	W		4-0	1-0	Butler 17, Keen 67, Morley 72, Allen M 89	Miklosko	Breacker	Dicks	Potts	Gale	Allen M	Robson	Butler	Speedie	Morley	Keen	
	17/4		16,522	*20*		79				*Peyton*	*Statham*	*Sansom*	*Westley*	*Evans*	*Manuel*	*Stephenson**	*Dickens*	*Gayle*	*Blissett*	*Bennett*	*Smillie*
									Ref: P Foakes	Peter Butler's son was born on the Monday and he celebrates with his second goal of the season – a glancing header from Dicks' cross. The Bees are on a dreadful slide and will go down. Speedie appeared to throw a punch but escaped. Portsmouth have won 10 out of their last 11.											
44	H	BRISTOL ROV		3	W		2-1	0-0	Dicks 55p, Speedie 58	Miklosko	Breacker	Dicks	Potts	Gale	Allen M	Robson*	Butler	Speedie	Morley	Keen	Bishop
	24/4		16,682	*24*		82			*Clark 49*	*Kelly*	*Maddison*	*Tillson*	*Yates*	*Clark*	*Mehew**	*Channing^*	*Evans*	*Taylor*	*Saunders*	*Waddock*	*Stewart/Reece*
									Ref: A Smith	Bottom-placed Rovers are already down, and Clark's goal is too much for some Hammers fans to stomach. Speedie is the butt of their abuse. But it is his cross which was handled for the penalty. His courageous headed winner, which left him semi-conscious, earned standing applause.											
45	A	SWINDON		2	W		3-1	1-0	Morley 42, Allen C 57, Brown 82	Miklosko	Breacker	Dicks	Potts	Gale	Bishop	Robson*	Butler	Speedie	Morley^	Keen	Allen C/Brown
	2/5		*17,004*	*5*		85			*Hazard 61*	*Digby*	*Summerbee*	*Viveash*	*Hoddle*	*Calderwood*	*Taylor*	*Hazard*	*MacLaren*	*Mitchell*	*Ling*	*White**	*Marwood*
									Ref: T Holbrook	This match was played on Sunday. On Saturday Portsmouth lost 1-4 at Sunderland, their first defeat in 12. Morley, recovered from flu, evades the offside trap for No 1. Clive Allen returns after three months out with a calf injury and adds No 2. Ludo then lets a shot go through his legs.											
46	H	CAMBRIDGE		2	W		2-0	0-0	Speedie 47, Allen C 90	Miklosko	Breacker	Dicks	Potts	Gale	Bishop	Robson*	Butler	Speedie^	Morley	Keen	Allen C/Allen M
	8/5		**27,399**	*23*		88				*Filan*	*Heathcote*	*Kimble**	*Raynor*	*Chapple*	*O'Shea*	*Sheffield^*	*Claridge*	*Butler*	*Clayton*	*Leadbitter*	*Fensome/Bartlett*
	Home		Away						Ref: D Elleray	Cambridge must win to stay up. Manager Ian Atkins has pinned up Bishop's quote: 'Cambridge ought to be a formality.' Portsmouth must beat Grimsby by more than West Ham beat Cambridge. Leadbitter's equaliser is disallowed for offside. Pompey lead 2-1 when Clive Allen seals it.											
Average	15,984		13,014																		

Coca-Cola Cup				F-A	H-T	Scorers, Times, and Referees	1	2	3	4	5	6	7	8	9	10	11	subs used
2:1 H CREWE	5	D		0-0	0-0		Miklosko	Breacker	Thomas	Potts	Martin	Allen M	Robson	Butler	Morley	Allen C	Keen*	Small
23/9	6,981	*3:4*					*Greygoose*	*McKearney*	*Whalley*	*Wilson*	*Carr*	*Macauley*	*Gardiner*	*Garvey*	*Clarkson**	*Harvey^*	*Walters*	*Naylor/Hughes*
						Ref: A Maile	A small crowd. Under Dario, Crewe are renowned for playing enterprising football, whoever the opposition. Using a sweeper, and spraying passes about, Crewe constantly frustrated the Hammers, though Greygoose saved well from Morley and Martin Allen. Bonds leaves out Dicks.											
2:2 A CREWE	7	L		0-2	0-0		Miklosko	Breacker	Dicks	Potts	Martin	Allen M	Robson	Butler	Morley	Allen C	Keen	
7/10	*5,427*	*3:4*				*Naylor 72, Hignett 79*	*Greygoose*	*McKearney*	*Whalley*	*Wilson*	*Carr*	*Macauley*	*Hignett*	*Naylor*	*Clarkson**	*Harvey^*	*Walters*	*Garvey/Gardiner*
						Ref: T Lunt (Hammers lose 0-2 on aggregate)	The unbeaten run comes to an abrupt end. Hammers blunted their swords against the inspired goalkeeping of Dean Greygoose – whose save from Dicks' volley was breathtaking – and were exposed to devastating counter-attacks. Crewe got behind West Ham's defence far too often.											

FA Cup				F-A	H-T	Scorers, Times, and Referees	1	2	3	4	5	6	7	8	9	10	11	subs used
3 A WEST BROM	3	W		2-0	2-0	Allen C 33, Robson 42	Miklosko	Breacker	Dicks	Potts	Martin	Allen M	Robson	Butler	Morley	Allen C	Keen	
2/1	*25,896*	*2:2*					*Naylor*	*Shakesp're**	*Lilwall*	*Bradley*	*Raven*	*Strodder*	*Garner*	*Hamilton*	*Taylor*	*McNally*	*Donovan^*	*Fereday/Hackett*
						Ref: A Gunn	Freezing weather and thickening fog, which did more to threaten West Ham's cup progress than could Ardiles' WBA. Martin Allen's through ball set up cousin Clive; and Dicks' dummy made No 2. Both Morley and Bradley hit the woodwork. Bobby Moore does radio commentary.											
4 A BARNSLEY	3	L		1-4	0-2	Morley 52p	Miklosko	Breacker	Brown	Potts	Foster	Allen M	Robson*	Butler	Morley	Holmes	Keen	Bunbury
24/1	*13,716*	*12*				*Rammell 32, 34, 77, Redfearn 71*	*Butler*	*Gridlet*	*Taggart*	*Fleming*	*Bishop*	*Archdeacon*	*Redfearn*	*O'Connell*	*Currie*	*Biggins**	*Rammell*	*Pearson*
						Ref: C Trussell	The squally wind was with West Ham in the first half but they could not capitalise. Instead Wayne Biggins made two goals for Andy Rammell. Hammers' only hope came when Fleming shoved Allen in the back. Penalty! Holmes later hit the bar. Rammell's hat-trick goal was deflected.											

		Home					Away					
	P	W	D	L	F	A	W	D	L	F	A	Pts
1 Newcastle	46	16	6	1	58	15	13	3	7	34	23	96
2 WEST HAM	46	16	5	2	50	17	10	5	8	31	24	88
3 Portsmouth	46	19	2	2	48	9	7	8	8	32	37	88
4 Tranmere	46	15	4	4	48	24	8	6	9	24	32	79
5 Swindon *	46	15	5	3	41	23	6	8	9	33	36	76
6 Leicester	46	14	5	4	43	24	8	5	10	28	40	76
7 Millwall	46	14	6	3	46	21	4	10	9	19	32	70
8 Derby	46	11	2	10	40	33	8	7	8	28	24	66
9 Grimsby	46	12	6	5	33	25	7	1	15	25	32	64
10 Peterborough	46	7	11	5	30	26	9	3	11	25	37	62
11 Wolves	46	11	6	6	37	26	5	7	11	20	30	61
12 Charlton	46	10	8	5	28	19	6	5	12	21	27	61
13 Barnsley	46	12	4	7	29	19	5	5	13	27	41	60
14 Oxford	46	8	7	8	29	21	6	7	10	24	35	56
15 Bristol City	46	10	7	6	29	25	4	7	12	20	42	56
16 Watford	46	8	7	8	27	30	6	6	11	30	41	55
17 Notts Co	46	10	7	6	33	21	2	9	12	22	49	52
18 Southend	46	9	8	6	33	22	4	5	14	21	42	52
19 Birmingham	46	10	4	9	30	32	3	8	12	20	40	51
20 Luton	46	6	13	4	26	26	4	8	11	22	36	51
21 Sunderland	46	9	6	8	34	28	4	5	14	16	36	50
22 Brentford	46	7	6	10	28	30	6	4	13	24	41	49
23 Cambridge	46	8	6	9	29	32	3	10	10	19	37	49
24 Bristol Rov	46	6	6	11	30	42	4	5	14	25	45	41
	1104	263	147	142	859	590	142	147	263	590	859	1509

* promoted after play-offs

Odds & ends

Double wins: (7) Watford, Peterborough, Bristol C, Portsmouth, Bristol R, Birmingham, Leicester.
Double losses: (0).

Won from behind: (7) Peterborough (a), Oxford (h), Birmingham (h&a), Leicester (a), Wolves (h), Bristol R (h).
Lost from in front: (0).

High spots: Promotion.
Four successive league wins in January and again in April-May.
Unbeaten run of 15 league games, from 20 December.

Low spots: Picking up just one point from three games beginning 24 October.
An embarrassing Coca-Cola Cup exit at Third Division Crewe.

Hammer of the Year: Steve Potts.
Ever-presents: (3) Ludek Miklosko, Steve Potts, Kevin Keen.
Hat-tricks: (0).
Leading scorer: (21) Trevor Morley.

	Appearances						Goals			
	Lge	*Sub*	LC	*Sub*	FAC	*Sub*	Lge	LC	FAC	Tot
Allen, Clive	**25**	*2*	2		1		**14**		1	**15**
Allen, Martin	**33**	*1*	2		2		**4**			**4**
Bishop, Ian	**15**	*7*					**1**			**1**
Breacker, Tim	**39**		2		2		**2**			**2**
Brown, Kenny	**13**	*2*			1		**2**			**2**
Bunbury, Alex	**2**	*2*				*1*				
Butler, Peter	**39**		2		2		**2**			**2**
Clarke, Simon		*1*								
Dicks, Julian	**34**		1		1		**11**			**11**
Foster, Colin	**3**	*3*			1		**1**			**1**
Gale, Tony	**21**	*2*					**1**			**1**
Holmes, Matt	**6**	*12*			1					
Jones, Steve	**4**	*2*					**2**			**2**
Keen, Kevin	**46**		2		2		**7**			**7**
Martin, Alvin	**23**		2		1		**1**			**1**
Miklosko, Ludek	**46**		2		2					
Morley, Trevor	**41**		2		2		**20**		1	**21**
Parris, George	**10**	*6*								
Potts, Steve	**46**		2		2					
Robson, Mark	**41**	*3*	2		2		**8**		1	**9**
Small, Mike	**5**	*4*		*1*						
Speedie, David	**11**						**4**			**4**
Thomas, Mitchell	**3**		1							
(own-goals)							**1**			**1**
23 players used	**506**	*47*	**22**	*1*	**22**	*1*	**81**		**3**	**84**

No	Date		Att	Pos	Pt	F-A	H-T	Scorers, Times, and Referees	SQUAD	NUMBERS	IN	USE								subs used
1	H	WIMBLEDON			L	0-2	0-0		Miklosko	Breacker	Dicks	Potts	Gale	Allen M	**Gordon**	Butler	Morley	Allen C	Holmes*	**Rowland**
	14/8		20,369		0			*Fashanu 63, Sanchez 72*	*Segers*	*Joseph*	*Kimble*	*Sanchez*	*Scales*	*Fitzgerald*	*Clarke^*	*Earle*	*Fashanu*	*Holdsworth*	*Fear**	*Blackwell/Barton*
								Ref: K Burge	Squad numbers are in, with Dons' Alan Kimble wearing shirt No 35. Upton Park resembles a building site for this first match back in the big time. Wimbledon cruise to a second-half victory, but Sam Hammam was reported to the FA for scrawling graffiti on the changing room walls.											
2	A	LEEDS			L	0-1	0-0		Miklosko	Breacker	Dicks	Potts^	Foster	Gale	Gordon	Butler	Morley	Allen C*	Allen M	Rowland/Robson
	17/8		*34,588*		0			*Speed 61*	*Lukic*	*Kelly*	*Dorigo*	*Batty*	*Fairclough*	*O'Leary*	*Strachan^*	*Whelan**	*Deane*	*McAllister*	*Speed*	*Wallace/Newsome*
								Ref: R Dilkes	Champions in 1992, Leeds barely survived the drop the following season. Nor are they firing on all cylinders this time, for this will be their only win in their first five games. Hammers are used to losing at Elland Road; once they fell behind they hadn't the firepower to fight back.											
3	A	COVENTRY		19	D	1-1	1-0	Gordon 45	Miklosko	Breacker	Dicks	Potts	Foster	Allen M	Gordon	Butler	Morley	Allen C	Rowland	
	21/8		*12,864*	*4*	1			*Wegerle 57*	*Gould*	*Sheridan^*	*Babb*	*Atherton*	*Rennie*	*Morgan*	*Williams**	*Ndlovu*	*Wegerle*	*Quinn*	*Flynn*	*Williams/Boland*
								Ref: S Lodge	Dale Gordon scores West Ham's first goal of 1993-94 at just the right moment, on the stroke of half-time, but not even that tonic can prompt a first victory. Off the field all the talk surrounds Julian Dicks, who Bonds seems set to sell to raise much-needed cash. But Dicks wants to stay.											
4	H	SHEFFIELD WED		15	W	2-0	0-0	Allen C 79, 84	Miklosko	Breacker	Dicks	Potts	Foster	Allen M	Gordon*	Butler	Morley	Allen C	Rowland	Holmes
	25/8		19,441	*21*	4				*Woods*	*Nilsson*	*Worthington*	*Palmer*	*Warhurst**	*Walker*	*Hyde*	*Waddle*	*Hirst^*	*Bt-Williams*	*Sinton*	*Bright/Pearson*
								Ref: J Worrall	Trevor Francis' Wednesday go into this game with no goals and just one point, so West Ham were looking to win this one. Upton Park is not impressed by Hammers' efforts, but Clive Allen then pops up with a double strike. They will stand as his only Hammers goals of the season.											
5	H	QP RANGERS		17	L	0-4	0-1	*[Penrice 53]*	Miklosko	Breacker	Dicks	Potts	Foster	Allen M	Robson	Butler	Morley	Allen C	Rowland	
	28/8		18,084	*13*	4			*Peacock 12, Ferdinand 47, 71,*	*Roberts*	*Bardsley*	*Wilson*	*Wilkins^*	*Peacock*	*McDonald*	*Impey*	*Sinclair*	*Ferdinand*	*Penrice**	*Barker*	*Allen/Ready*
								Ref: V Callow	Rangers have a defence like a sieve, and have conceded 10 goals in their first four games, so their first clean-sheet speaks volumes for West Ham's lack of enterprise. On the transfer front, Southampton boss Ian Branfoot has failed to sign the Hammers' Tim Breacker and Ian Bishop.											
6	A	MANCHESTER U		19	L	0-3	0-2		Miklosko	Breacker	Dicks	Potts	Foster	Allen M*	Gordon^	Holmes	Morley	Allen C	Rowland	Gale/Robson
	1/9		***44,613***	*1*	4			*Sharpe 17, Cantona 44p, Bruce 88*	*Schmeichel*	*Parker*	*Irwin*	*Bruce*	*Sharpe*	*Pallister*	*Cantona*	*Ince**	*Keane*	*Kanchelskis^*	*Giggs*	*McClair/Robson*
								Ref: R Milford	The defending champions will lead the table from August to May, and only Keegan's Newcastle have done so much as draw with them so far. Lee Sharpe is on fire, scoring his fourth goal in three games. Cantona's penalty just before half-time effectively settled the game's outcome.											
7	H	SWINDON		19	D	0-0	0-0		Miklosko	Breacker	Dicks	Potts	Gale	Bishop	Gordon*	Holmes	Morley	Jones	Rowland	Rush
	11/9		**15,777**	*22*	5				*Digby*	*Summerbee*	*Nijholt*	*Moncur*	*Whitbread*	*Taylor*	*Hazard*	*Mutch*	*Fjortoft**	*Ling*	*Horlock^*	*White/Fenwick*
								Ref: A Gunn	The play-offs brought promotion to Swindon, at which point Glenn Hoddle decamped to Chelsea. John Gorman's winless team have already been hit for five by Liverpool and Southampton, so this is yet another dismal result. Neither side looks good enough for the Premiership.											
8	A	BLACKBURN		18	W	2-0	1-0	Chapman 33, Morley 71	Miklosko	Rowland	**Burrows**	Potts	Gale	Bishop	Gordon	Holmes	**Chapman**	**Marsh***	Morley	Allen M
	18/9		*14,437*	*7*	8				*Mimms*	*May*	*Le Saux*	*Sherwood*	*Moran**	*Warhurst*	*Ripley*	*Berg*	*Newell*	*Gallacher*	*Wilcox^*	*Marker/Shearer*
								Ref: K Hackett	Rovers, unbeaten away, and victors at Anfield last time out, are proving vulnerable at Ewood. Dicks has gone to Liverpool, in exchange for Burrows and Marsh. Lee Chapman arrives from Portsmouth and scores with his one and only chance, after Mimms and Berg get in a dither.											
9	A	NEWCASTLE		18	L	0-2	0-0		Miklosko	Brown*	Burrows	Potts	Gale	Bishop	Gordon	Morley^	Chapman	Marsh	Holmes	Allen M/**Boere** !
	25/9		*34,179*	*11*	8			*Cole 51, 84*	*Hooper*	*Venison*	*Beresford*	*Bracewell*	*Scott*	*Watson*	*Lee*	*Beardsley*	*Cole*	*Clark*	*Allen*	
								Ref: M Reed	No one can stop Andy Cole scoring, least of all porous Hammers. Jeroen Boere signed from Go Ahead Eagles in midweek, comes on as sub after Cole's first goal and gets sent off after Cole's second for clashing with Kevin Scott and Barry Venison. Newcastle are unbeaten in eight.											
10	H	CHELSEA		17	W	1-0	1-0	Morley 41	Miklosko	Breacker	Burrows	Potts	Gale	Bishop	Butler	Morley	Chapman	Marsh*	Holmes	Allen M
	2/10		18,917	*14*	11				*Kharin*	*Clarke^*	*Sinclair*	*Kjeldbjerg*	*Dow**	*Donaghy*	*Hoddle*	*Newton*	*Shipperley*	*Peacock*	*Wise !*	*Spencer/Hall*
								Ref: R Hart	Rebuilding at Upton Park meant this match started at 2.15. Trevor Morley's neat goal did much to beat Chelsea, but so did Wise's dismissal for giving 12 studs to Burrows. Inspired by player-manager Hoddle, 10-man Chelsea pressed forward, leaving gaps that Chapman failed to exploit.											

No	Venue	Opponent	Att	Pos	Res/Pts	F-A	H-T	Scorers, Times, and Referees	1	2	3	4	5	6	7	8	9	10	11	subs used
11	H	ASTON VILLA		17	D	0-0	0-0		Miklosko	Breacker	Burrows	Potts	Gale	Bishop	Butler	Morley	Chapman	Marsh	Holmes	
	16/10		20,416	*7*	12				*Bosnich*	*Cox*	*Small*	*Teale*	*McGrath*	*Richardson*	*Houghton*	*Townsend*	*Saunders*	*Atkinson*	*Daley*	
								Ref: S Lodge	Atkinson's Villa preserve their unbeaten away record but maintain his own Boleyn jinx, where none of his teams have ever won. Ron is being talked of as the next England boss. The best chance in this physical clash fell to Chapman, when Bosnich tried and failed to dribble round him.											
12	A	NORWICH		17	D	0-0	0-0		Miklosko	Breacker	Burrows	Potts	Gale*	Bishop	Butler	Morley	Chapman	Marsh	Holmes	Rowland
	23/10		*20,175*	*2*	13				*Gunn*	*Culverhouse*	*Bowen*	*Butterworth*	*Newman*	*Goss*	*Crook*	*Megson*	*Sutch**	*Fox*	*Sutton*	*Eadie*
								Ref: J Worrall	These are heady times for Mike Walker's Norwich. They have beaten Inter Milan in the UEFA Cup, lie second in the league, and stretch their unbeaten run to seven with this draw. Their Achilles heel is their inability to score at home, just two goals in six games at Carrow Road.											
13	H	MANCHESTER C		14	W	3-1	2-0	Burrows 3, Chapman 29, Holmes 69	Miklosko	Breacker	Burrows	Potts	Martin	Bishop	Butler	Morley	Chapman	Marsh	Holmes*	Rowland
	1/11		16,605	*16*	16			*Curle 85p*	*Coton*	*Edghill*	*Phelan*	*McMahon*	*Curle*	*Kernaghan*	*White*	*Sheron^*	*Quinn*	*Flitcroft*	*Lomas**	*Vonk/Griffiths*
								Ref: K Morton	Beforehand West Ham boasted the feeblest Premier goal-tally. Brian Horton had been pulling City up the table, but they founder on the rock of Alvin Martin, who had a tooth extracted hours earlier. The third-minute breakthrough came when keeper Coton picked up Curle's back-pass.											
14	A	LIVERPOOL		15	L	0-2	0-0		Miklosko	Breacker	Burrows	Potts	Martin	Bishop	Butler	Morley	Chapman	Marsh	Holmes	
	6/11		*42,254*	*5*	16			*Clough 67, Martin 83 (og)*	*Grobbelaar*	*Jones**	*Harkness*	*Nicol^*	*Wright*	*Ruddock*	*Clough*	*Stewart*	*Rush*	*Matteo*	*Fowler*	*Redknapp/Bjornebye*
								Ref: K Barratt	It is 30 years since Hammers won at Anfield, but they were holding up against Souness's revamped team until Clough dribbled through. Martin then deflected Matteo's effort. Dicks was out of Liverpool's team with knee trouble, but Anfield applauded the return of Marsh and Burrows.											
15	H	OLDHAM		14	W	2-0	1-0	Martin 43, Morley 74	Miklosko	Breacker	Burrows	Potts	Martin	Bishop	Butler	Morley	Chapman	Marsh	Holmes	
	20/11		17,211	*21*	19				*Walsh*	*Fleming*	*Makin !*	*Brennan^*	*Jobson*	*Redmond*	*Halle*	*Olney**	*Sharp*	*Milligan*	*Bernard*	*Ritchie/Pointon*
								Ref: D Allison	Martin returns from Achilles injury to score his first goal in 14 months. Oldham's cause was not helped by the dismissal of Makin, booked for fouling Breacker in the first half, then repeating the offence in the second. Not to be outdone by Martin, Morley's own header was just as good.											
16	H	ARSENAL		14	D	0-0	0-0		Miklosko	Breacker	Burrows	Potts	Gale	Bishop	Butler	Morley	Chapman	Marsh	Holmes	
	24/11		20,279	*7*	20				*Seaman !*	*Dixon*	*Winterburn*	*Morrow*	*Linighan*	*Bould*	*Keown*	*Wright^*	*Smith*	*Merson*	*Limpar**	*Campbell/Miller*
								Ref: P Durkin	Arsenal have conceded two goals in eight away games. They would have lost a third in the 85th minute had not Seaman body-checked Morley, who was through on goal, for which he was sent off for the first time. A bad week for Seaman, beaten by an eight-second goal by San Marino.											
17	A	SOUTHAMPTON		10	W	2-0	2-0	Morley 30, Chapman 36	Miklosko	Breacker	Burrows	Potts	Gale	Bishop	Butler	Morley	Chapman	Allen M	Holmes	
	29/11		*13,258*	*20*	23				*Andrews*	*Kenna*	*Benali*	*Charlton**	*Wood*	*Monkou*	*Le Tissier*	*Cockerill^*	*Dowie*	*Maddison*	*Allen*	*Adams/Bennett*
								Ref: M Bodenham	West Ham's eighth clean sheet in 11 league games lifts them to 10th, their highest position for seven years. Holmes' crosses made both West Ham goals, a downward header by Morley and a deflected volley by Chapman. Saints looked to Le Tissier, but he fired nothing but blanks.											
18	A	WIMBLEDON		10	W	2-1	1-0	Chapman 44, 78	Miklosko	Breacker	Burrows	Potts	Gale	Bishop	Butler	Morley	Chapman	Allen M	Holmes	
	4/12		*10,903*	*15*	26			*Holdsworth 83*	*Segers*	*Barton*	*McAllister*	*Jones*	*Scales*	*Fitzgerald*	*Clarke*	*Earle*	*Berry**	*Holdsworth*	*Ardley*	*Talboys*
								Ref: D Gallagher	Dons leave out Fashanu, following the horrific injury to Spurs' Gary Mabbutt. Lee Chapman capitalises on Route 1 for his second goal, when Morley helped on Miklosko's long punt. Over the years Chapman has been a bogey-man to the Dons. Fashanu should have played centre-half.											
19	H	LEEDS		10	L	0-1	0-0		Miklosko	Breacker	Burrows	Potts	Gale	Bishop	Butler	Morley*	Chapman	Marsh	Holmes	Boere
	8/12		20,468	*2*	26			*Wallace Rod 84*	*Beaney*	*Kelly*	*Dorigo*	*Sharp*	*Fairclough*	*Wetherall*	*Strachan*	*Wallace Rod*	*Deane*	*McAllister*	*Speed**	*Pemberton*
								Ref: I Borrett	Leeds secure second place with their 14th unbeaten game. Dorigo's clever pass allowed Rod Wallace to sidefoot the winner, his seventh goal in seven matches. Had the Hammers won, they would have been just three points behind Leeds but Man U's lead at the top is a huge 12 points.											
20	H	COVENTRY		9	W	3-2	2-1	Breacker 11, Butler 40, Morley 59p	Miklosko	Breacker	Burrows	Potts	Gale	Bishop*	Butler	Morley	Chapman	Marsh	Holmes	Allen M
	11/12		17,243	*16*	29			*Darby 41, 77*	*Ogrizovic*	*Atherton*	*Morgan*	*Flynn*	*Babb*	*Rennie*	*Darby*	*Ndlovu*	*Wegerle**	*Quinn*	*Boland^*	*Williams/Marsden*
								Ref: K Cooper	West Ham climb to dizzy ninth, a mere 20 points behind Man U. Butler killed the ball to set up Breacker, then linked with Marsh and Morley for his first of the season. Ndlovu shoved Marsh for the penalty. Gale felled Williams but West Ham were lucky. It should have been a penalty.											
21	A	SHEFFIELD WED		11	L	**0-5**	0-1	*[Jemson 73, Palmer 88]*	Miklosko	Breacker	Burrows	Potts	Gale	Bishop*	Butler	Morley	Chapman	Marsh	Holmes^	Allen M/Boere
	18/12		*26,350*	*13*	29			*Marsh 35 (og), Bright 48, Waddle 51,*	*Pressman*	*Nilsson*	*Worthington*	*Palmer*	*Pearce*	*Walker*	*Jemson*	*Waddle*	*Bright*	*Hyde*	*Bt-Williams*	
								Ref: D Frampton	Until Mike Marsh, standing on the goal-line, helped in Pearce's header that had come down off the bar, there was little sign of this debacle to come. But 33-year-old, flu-stricken Chris Waddle was at his mesmerising best, scoring from 25 yards and engineering three Wednesday goals.											

No	Date		Att	Pos	Pt	F-A	H-T	Scorers, Times, and Referees	SQUAD	NUMBERS	IN	USE								subs used
22	A	IPSWICH		12	D	1-1	0-1	Chapman 77	Miklosko	Breacker	Burrows	Potts	Gale	Bishop	Butler	Morley	Chapman	Marsh	Holmes*	Rowland
	27/12		*20,988*	*11*	30			*Linighan 36*	*Forrest*	*Youds*	*Thompson*	*Stockwell*	*Wark**	*Linighan*	*Williams*	*Slater*	*Palmer*	*Whelan*	*Kiwomya*	*Marshall*
								Ref: G Poll	Ipswich are unbeaten in eight but needed to win before their season's biggest gate to leap-frog the Hammers. Linighan headed Ipswich in front from Thompson's free-kick, but Chapman headed an equaliser from Burrows' centre, which Forrest spilled when he should have gathered.											
23	H	TOTTENHAM		13	L	1-3	1-2	Holmes 11	Miklosko	Breacker	Burrows	Potts	Gale	Bishop	Butler	Morley	Chapman	Marsh	Holmes*	Jones
	28/12		20,787	*11*	30			*Dozzell 34, Hazard 42, Anderton 77*	*Thorstvedt*	*Kerslake*	*Edinburgh*	*Samways*	*Calderwood*	*Sedgley*	*Caskey*	*Barmby**	*Anderton*	*Dozzell*	*Hazard*	*Campbell*
								Ref: G Ashby	Both teams are unchanged after their exertions 24 hours earlier. Ardiles' Spurs are disrupted by the facial injury to Mabbutt, but show their mettle after falling behind to Holmes' cool finish. Best moment of the match came when Anderton lobbed onto the top netting from 45 yards.											
24	A	EVERTON		11	W	1-0	1-0	Breacker 5	Miklosko	Breacker	Burrows	Potts	Gale	Bishop	Butler	Morley	Chapman	Marsh	Holmes*	Rowland
	1/1		*19,602*	*16*	33				*Southall*	*Holmes*	*Snodin*	*Ebbrell*	*Jackson*	*Ablett*	*Ward^*	*Horne*	*Cottee**	*Rideout*	*Beagrie*	*Barlow/Stuart*
								Ref: J Lloyd	Howard Kendall's resignation has not stopped Everton plunging down the table; this is their sixth game without a goal. West Ham won with a neatly executed header during one of their few attacks. Tim Breacker threaded his way through the defence to meet Marsh's clipped pass.											
25	H	SHEFFIELD UTD		11	D	0-0	0-0		Miklosko	Breacker	Burrows	Potts	Gale	Bishop	Butler	Morley*	Chapman	Marsh	Rowland	Jones
	3/1		20,365	*18*	34				*Kelly*	*Bradshaw*	*Beesley*	*Kamara*	*Tuttle*	*Hoyland*	*Hodges*	*Ward*	*Flo*	*Davison**	*Whitehouse*	*Littlejohn*
								Ref: M Reed	The Blades hardly ever score, so their 'nil' was predictable. They wanted a point and in a swirling wind competed for each tackle as if Dave Bassett's life depended on it. The best of West Ham's few chances fell to Marsh, but his low shot was smothered. The crowd booed at the end.											
26	A	ASTON VILLA		12	L	1-3	1-2	Allen M 30	Miklosko	Breacker	Rowland	Potts	Gale	Bishop	Allen M	Morley*	Chapman	Marsh	Holmes	Jones
	15/1		*28,869*	*9*	34			*Richardson 15, Atkinson 43, 68*	*Bosnich*	*Barrett*	*Staunton**	*Teale*	*McGrath*	*Richardson*	*Houghton*	*Townsend*	*Saunders*	*Atkinson*	*Daley*	*Cox*
								Ref: S Lodge	Some sublime goals here. Richardson scores low and hard from 30 yards. Rowland's cross was perfectly headed in by Martin Allen to level. Dalian Atkinson's second goal was a contender for goal-of-the month when sprinting forward to fire a bullet high into the net past Miklosko.											
27	H	NORWICH		12	D	3-3	1-1	Sutton 37 (og), Jones 46, Morley 84	Miklosko	Breacker	Rowland	Potts	Gale^	Bishop	Allen M	Jones	Chapman*	Marsh	Holmes	Morley/Brown
	24/1		20,738	*7*	35			*Sutton 4, 57, Fox 78*	*Gunn*	*Culverhouse*	*Bowen*	*Butterworth*	*Woodthorpe*	*Megson**	*Crook*	*Newman*	*Sutton*	*Fox*	*Goss*	*Ekoku*
								Ref: J Worrall	Having lost manager Mike Walker to Everton, Norwich are bereft of leadership and will eventually sink from second into the bottom half. John Deehan had them playing beautifully in this match, and their intricate passing is a joy. Martin Allen tried to claim West Ham's first goal.											
28	A	MANCHESTER C		12	D	0-0	0-0		Miklosko	Breacker	Rowland	Potts	Brown	Bishop	Allen M	Marsh^	Chapman	Allen C*	Holmes	Morley/**Marquis**
	12/2		*29,118*	*19*	36				*Coton*	*Edghill*	*Phelan*	*McMahon*	*Curle**	*Vonk*	*Rocastle*	*Sheron*	*Griffiths*	*Flitcroft*	*Shutt^*	*Kernaghan/Lomas*
								Ref: V Callow	Francis Lee returns as Messiah to Maine Road, and manager Brian Horton will soon be shown the door. West Ham owe their point largely to Miklosko, who denied Shutt and Sheron with hands, feet, and body. Clive Allan started a game for Hammers for the first time in five months											
29	H	MANCHESTER U		12	D	2-2	0-1	Chapman 69, Morley 72	Miklosko	Breacker	Burrows	Potts	Martin	Bishop	Allen M	Morley	Chapman	Marsh	Holmes	
	26/2		**28,832**	*1*	37			*Hughes 6, Ince 87*	*Schmeichel*	*Parker*	*Irwin^*	*Bruce*	*Kanchelskis**	*Pallister*	*Cantona*	*Ince*	*McClair*	*Hughes*	*Keane*	*Dublin/Thornley*
								Ref: A Wilkie	Since moving to Old Trafford, Paul Ince has restricted his Upton Park appearances. He was cat-called and pelted with bananas before thumping home Keane's cross to level. Chapman's goal from Holmes' cross, followed by Pallister's lax back-pass, had set up a deserved Hammers win.											
30	A	SWINDON		13	D	1-1	0-0	Morley 47	Miklosko	Breacker	Burrows	Potts	Martin	Bishop	Allen M	Morley	Chapman	Marsh	Holmes*	Rowland
	5/3		*15,929*	*22*	38			*Fjortoft 88*	*Digby*	*Summerbee*	*Nijholt*	*Horlock*	*Whitbread*	*Taylor*	*Moncur*	*Mutch**	*Fjortoft*	*Ling*	*McAvennie^*	*Scott/Gooden*
								Ref: R Milford	Swindon will concede 100 league goals this season, which means each club averages five against them. West Ham manage just one, Morley putting away Chapman's header. Swindon include former Hammer Frank McAvennie, on loan from Celtic. Fjortoft heads in off a post for 1-1.											
31	H	NEWCASTLE		14	L	2-4	0-1	Breacker 56, Martin 81	Miklosko	Breacker	Rowland	Potts	Martin	Bishop	Butler	Morley*	Chapman	Marsh	Holmes	Boere
	19/3		23,132	*3*	38			*Lee 34, 73 , Cole 69, Mathie 90*	*Srnicek*	*Robinson*	*Beresford*	*Venison*	*Elliott*	*Watson^*	*Lee*	*Beardsley*	*Cole*	*Fox**	*Sellars*	*Mathie/Neilson*
								Ref: K Morton	This was one of those games that could have ended 10-10, wonderful for fans, awful for managers. Andy Cole seemed to score everywhere but in London, but he rectified that with his 35th of the season. For all Chapman's aerial dominance, both West Ham's goals came from defenders.											

32	A	CHELSEA	15	L	0-2	0-1		Miklosko	Breacker	Burrows^	Potts	Gale	Bishop	Allen M*	Butler	Chapman	Marsh	Rowland	Morley/Jones
	26/3	*19,545*	*14*	38			*Barnard 39, Hoddle 79*	*Kharin*	*Clarke*	*Barnard*	*Kjeldbjerg*	*Johnsen*	*Burley**	*Spencer*	*Newton*	*Shipperley^*	*Peacock*	*Wise*	*Hoddle/Donaghy*
							Ref: M Bodenham	Hours after Cambridge win the Boat Race, Chelsea keep the Thames celebrations in full voice. It was a game of firsts – Barnards's first goal of the season and Hoddle's first for Chelsea. Bonds, who let two strikers go on transfer deadline day, experimented with playing one up front.											
33	A	SHEFFIELD UTD	15	L	2-3	2-1	Bishop 7, Holmes 31	Miklosko	Breacker	Rowland	Potts	Gale	Bishop	Butler	Morley	Chapman	Marsh^	Holmes*	Allen M/Brown
	28/3	*13,646*	*20*	38			*Whitehouse 39, Gayle 47, Rogers 72*	*Kelly^*	*Bradshaw*	*Nilsen*	*Gannon**	*Tutte*	*Gayle*	*Carr*	*Rogers*	*Flo*	*Littlejohn*	*Whitehouse*	*Hodges/Tracey*
							Ref: P Durkin	Bassett's Blades will lose just two of their last 13, but will be relegated in the last minute of the last match. Three defeats in five days have left West Ham looking over their shoulder. Bishop had scored from 30 yards for the first goal; Miklosko fumbled one of many crosses for the fifth.											
34	H	IPSWICH	14	W	2-1	1-0	Rush 17, Morley 75	Miklosko	Breacker	Rowland	Potts	Gale	Bishop	Butler	Rush*	Morley	Marsh	Holmes	Brown
	2/4	18,307	*15*	41			*Mason 87*	*Baker*	*Stockwell*	*Johnson*	*Williams*	*Linighan*	*Whelan*	*Durrant^*	*Slater*	*Palmer*	*Guentchev*	*Kiwomya**	*Mason/Youds*
							Ref: D Elleray	Despite being leading scorer, Chapman is unpopular among the Upton Park faithfuls and is dropped. His replacement, the highly promising Matthew Rush, fired in a half-volley from 25 yards to set up this much-needed win. It was a foul on Rush that earned the free-kick for No 2.											
35	A	TOTTENHAM	13	W	4-1	1-0	Jones 37, Morley 60p, 72, Marsh 80	Miklosko	Breacker	Rowland	Potts	Gale	Bishop	Butler*	Rush	Morley	Marsh	Holmes	Jones
	4/4	***31,502***	*16*	44			*Sheringham 66p*	*Walker*	*Kerslake*	*Campbell*	*Samways*	*Scott*	*Mabbutt*	*Sedgley*	*Barmby*	*Anderton*	*Dozzell^*	*Rosenthal**	*Sheringham/Howells*
							Ref: P Don	As Spurs had won just three out of 18 games at home, the last of which was in October, this result is hardly a shock. Kevin Scott brought down Morley for the first penalty; Morley floored Mabbutt for the second. When Marsh angled West Ham's fourth, Spurs completely disintegrated.											
36	H	EVERTON	13	L	0-1	0-0		Miklosko	Breacker	Rowland*	Potts	Gale	Bishop	Jones	Rush	Morley	Marsh	Holmes	Martin
	9/4	20,243	*17*	44			*Cottee 72*	*Southall*	*Jackson*	*Snodin*	*Ebbrell*	*Watson*	*Abblett*	*Stuart*	*Horne*	*Cottee*	*Angell**	*Limpar*	*Rideout*
							Ref: P Foakes	Everton arrived with one point and one goal from six games, and a looming destiny with relegation. West Ham had all the play, most of the chances but lost when Cottee took the only chance to fall his way. Man of the match was undeniably Neville Southall for a succession of saves.											
37	A	OLDHAM	13	W	2-1	2-1	Allen M 1, Morley 29	Miklosko	Breacker	Burrows	Brown	Gale	Bishop	Allen M	Rush	Morley	Marsh	Holmes	
	16/4	*11,669*	*20*	47			*Holden 43p*	*Hallworth*	*Makin*	*Pointon**	*Henry*	*Jobson*	*Fleming*	*Bernard*	*Sharp*	*McCarthy*	*Milligan*	*Holden*	*Beckford*
							Ref: K Barratt	Oldham have just lost an FA Cup semi-final replay to Man U and their season comes crashing about their ears. Richard Jobson had just been called into the England squad by Venables, but was partially responsible for both Hammers' goals. Burrows shoved McCarthy for the penalty.											
38	H	LIVERPOOL	13	L	1-2	1-1	Allen M 1	Miklosko	Breacker	Burrows	Potts	Gale	Bishop*	Allen M	Rush	Morley	Marsh	Holmes	Chapman
	23/4	26,106	*7*	47			*Fowler 13, Rush 87*	*James*	*Harkness*	*Dicks*	*Hutchison*	*Nicol*	*Ruddock*	*Clough*	*Redknapp*	*Rush*	*Barnes*	*Fowler*	
							Ref: S Lodge	Julian Dicks returns to the Boleyn in Liverpool red and the stadium rises to acclaim him. Inside a minute Allen lobs David James from the edge of the box. Fowler pounces after John Barnes' shot comes back off a post. Tony Gale's miscued back-pass lets in Ian Rush for the late winner.											
39	H	BLACKBURN	13	L	1-2	0-1	Allen M 64	Miklosko	Breacker	Brown	Potts	Gale	Bishop	Allen M	Rush*	Morley	Marsh	Holmes^	Chapman/**Mitchell**
	27/4	22,186	*2*	47			*Berg 12, Pearce 75*	*Flowers*	*May*	*Le Saux*	*Sherwood*	*Hendry*	*Berg*	*Ripley^*	*Atkins*	*Shearer*	*Wright**	*Wilcox*	*Pearce/Morrison*
							Ref: T Holbrook	Rovers have hauled back Man U's lead to two points. Ian Pearce comes off the bench, controls Shearer's 40-yard pass with his first touch and scores with his second. It is their first win at Upton Park since 1964, when they won 8-2. Allen scored with a 25-yard deflected free-kick.											
40	A	ARSENAL	12	W	2-0	0-0	Morley 77, Allen M 88	Miklosko	Breacker	Burrows*	Potts	Gale	Bishop	Allen M	Rush	Morley	Marsh	Brown	**Williamson**
	30/4	*33,700*	*4*	50				*Miller*	*McGoldrick**	*Winterburn*	*Davis*	*Bould*	*Linighan*	*Parlour*	*Wright*	*Campbell*	*Merson^*	*Selley*	*Morrow/Dickov*
							Ref: R Milford	Arsenal play Parma in the final of the Cup-Winners' Cup on Wednesday. This, their first league defeat in 20 games, is the worst preparation. Graham rested Seaman and Adams. Miller did well before getting into a tangle with Linighan for the first goal. Allen hit a screamer for No 2.											
41	A	QP RANGERS	13	D	0-0	0-0		Miklosko	Breacker	Brown	Potts	Gale	Bishop	Allen M	Rush*	Morley	Marsh	Williamson	Chapman
	3/5	***10,850***	*9*	51				*Roberts*	*McCarthy*	*Wilson*	*Wilkins*	*Ready*	*Yates*	*Holloway^*	*Barker*	*Ferdinand*	*Penrice**	*Sinclair*	*Allen/Brevett*
							Ref: R Dilkes	Ray Wilkins' QPR, aided by a surprisingly muscular approach, will finish in the top half of the table. They have won just one of their last nine, but by avoiding defeat by the Hammers ensure that they will finish higher than their London rivals. QPR had won 4-0 at Upton Park in August.											
42	H	SOUTHAMPTON	13	D	3-3	1-1	Will'mson 11, Allen 62, Monkou 89 (og)	Miklosko	Breacker	Burrows	Potts	Gale	Bishop*	Allen M	Rush	Morley	Marsh	Williamson	Chapman
	7/5	26,952	*18*	52			*Le Tissier 45, 65p, Maddison 52*	*Beasant*	*Kenna*	*Benali*	*Charlton*	*Widdrington*	*Monkou*	*Le Tissier*	*Magilton*	*Dowie*	*Maddison*	*Allen*	
	Home	Away					Ref: G Ashby	Two dead-ball strikes takes Le Tissier's tally to 25. The first came when Potts rashly fouled Dowie 20 yards out. That equalised Williamson's 11th-minute goal on his home debut, shooting under Beasant. Player-of-the-Year Morley made it 2-2, before Gale felled Dowie in the box.											
Average	20,574	23,288																	

Coca-Cola Cup					F-A	H-T	Scorers, Times, and Referees	SQUAD	NUMBERS	IN	USE								subs used
2:1	H	CHESTERFIELD	18	W	5-1	3-0	Morley 6p, 69, Chapman 14, 65,	Miklosko	Rowland	Burrows	Potts	Gale	Bishop	Gordon	Morley	Chapman	Holmes	Marsh	
22/9		12,823 *3:16*					*Norris 55* [Burrows 33]	*Leonard*	*Hebberd*	*Carr C*	*Brien*	*Carr D*	*McGugan*	*Dyche*	*Norris*	*Jules**	*Cash^*	*Curtis*	*Davies/Knowles*
							Ref: I Borrett	John Duncan's Chesterfield are on a losing run in their own division, and their lack of confidence is all too obvious. Conceding a penalty after just six minutes drained away what little confidence they had to begin with. With a four-goal aggregate advantage, the second leg is pointless.											
2:2	A	CHESTERFIELD	17	W	2-0	0-0	Allen M 64, Boere 82	Miklosko	Breacker	Burrows	Potts	Gale	Bishop	Butler*	Morley	Chapman^	Marsh	Holmes	Allen M/Boere
5/10		*4,890 3:19*						*Marples*	*Hebberd*	*Carr C*	*Brien*	*Madden*	*Dennis*	*Dyche**	*Norris^*	*Davies*	*Curtis*	*Jules*	*Bettney/Taylor*
							Ref: G Singh (Hammers win 7-1 on aggregate)	The deficit is so big that even devoted Spirites are dispirited enough to stay away in droves. The longer the second leg went on without a home goal the more aimless the fixture became. All 22 players were looking forward to a bath by the time Martin Allen extinguished all worries.											
3	A	NOTT'M FOREST	17	L	1-2	0-1	Morley 82	Miklosko	Breacker	Burrows	Potts	Martin	Bishop	Butler*	Morley	Chapman	Marsh	Holmes	Allen M
27/10		*17,857 1:20*					*Black 28, Collymore 55*	*Wright*	*Laws*	*Pearce*	*Crosby*	*Chettle*	*Stone*	*Phillips*	*Gemmell*	*Glover**	*Collymore*	*Black*	*Webb*
							Ref: G Pooley	Forest fear relegation to Division 2. They also have the Indian sign over the Hammers in the League Cup, winning for the fourth time in four ties. Forest are unbeaten at home in this competition for 44 games, dating back to 1976. Super Stan Collymore headed in at the far post.											

FA Cup																			
3	H	WATFORD	11	W	2-1	0-1	Allen M 64, Marsh 84	Miklosko	Breacker	Burrows*	Potts	Gale	Bishop	Allen M	Morley^	Chapman	Marsh	Rowland	Brown/Jones
8/1		19,802 *1:21*					*Porter 27p*	*Sheppard*	*Lavin*	*Dublin*	*Hessenthaler*	*Holdsworth*	*Watson*	*Dyer*	*Johnston*	*Furlong*	*Porter*	*Nogan*	
							Ref: D Gallagher	Miklosko brings down Bruce Dyer for a hotly-argued penalty, whereupon the First Division side threaten to extend their lead. Martin Allen's header wiped away the blushes, but Watford still looked to be holding out comfortably. Mike Marsh, unmarked, won the tie at the far post.											
4	A	NOTTS CO	11	D	1-1	1-1	Jones 40	Miklosko	Breacker	Rowland	Potts	Brown	Bishop	Allen M	Jones	Chapman	Marsh	Holmes	
29/1		*14,952 1:14*					*Lund 38*	*Cherry*	*Palmer*	*Sherlock*	*Turner P*	*Murphy*	*Dijkstra*	*Devlin*	*Draper**	*Lund*	*Legg^*	*Agana*	*Cox/McSwegan*
							Ref: D Pierce	Gary Lund volleys the First Division side ahead, as Miklosko strays into no-man's land. The Hammers' former Billericay marksman and soap-factory worker, Steve Jones, hooks an immediate equaliser on the turn. It is his second goal in a week and his hustle and bustle look promising.											
4R	H	NOTTS CO	11	W	1-0	0-0	Chapman 110	Miklosko	Breacker	Rowland	Potts	Brown	Bishop	Allen M	Jones*	Chapman	Marsh	Holmes	Allen C
9/2		23,373 *1:14*			*aet*			*Cherry*	*Palmer*	*Sherlock*	*Turner P*	*Johnson*	*Dijkstra*	*Devlin*	*Draper*	*Lund**	*Legg*	*McSwegan*	*Matthews*
							Ref: D Pierce	Upton Park is in mean mood at Lee Chapman's uncoordinated display, when everything he tried went wrong, and urged Bonds to pull him off. Bonds resisted, and with County playing for a shoot-out in extra-time, had his faith vindicated when Chapman headed in Tim Breacker's cross.											
5	A	KIDDERMINSTER	11	W	1-0	0-0	Chapman 69	Miklosko	Breacker	Rowland	Potts	Martin	Bishop	Allen M	Marsh	Chapman	Allen C*	Holmes	Morley
19/2		*8,000 VC:1*						*Rose*	*Hodson*	*Bancroft*	*Weir*	*Brindley*	*Cartwright**	*Grainger*	*Forsyth*	*Humphreys*	*Davies*	*Purdie*	*Deakin*
							Ref: G Pooley	Kidderminster top the GM Vauxhall Conference. Having seen off Birmingham and Preston, many judges concur that the Harriers can cause an even bigger upset. But the sole remaining non-league team are well beaten. Keeper Rose missed a simple cross, giving Chapman a free header.											
QF	H	LUTON	13	D	0-0	0-0		Miklosko	Breacker	Burrows	Potts	Martin	Bishop	Allen M	Morley	Chapman*	Marsh	Holmes	Allen C
14/3		27,331 *1:15*						*Sommer*	*Linton*	*James*	*Harper*	*Greene*	*Dreyer*	*Telfer*	*Oakes**	*Dixon^*	*Hughes*	*Preece*	*Burke/Hartson*
							Ref: B Hill	This Monday night cup-tie gave West Ham the perfect opportunity to reach the semi-finals. David Pleat's Luton – two defeats in 17 games – beat Kevin Keegan's Newcastle in Round 4, after drawing at St James' Park, so are not at all overawed. West Ham will not relish the replay.											
QF R	A	LUTON	14	L	2-3	1-1	Allen M 30, Bishop 57	Miklosko	Breacker	Burrows	Potts	Martin	Bishop	Butler	Morley	Chapman	Marsh*	Allen M	Jones
23/3		*13,166 1:18*					*Oakes 34, 47, 74*	*Sommer*	*Linton*	*James*	*Harper*	*Peake*	*Dreyer*	*Telfer*	*Oakes*	*Dixon*	*Hughes*	*Preece*	
							Ref: B Hill	The name of Scott Oakes will haunt West Ham for years to come, after he single-handedly dumps them on their Premier backsides to win this thrilling cup replay. He had scored against Newcastle in Round 4, Cardiff in Round 5, and now pitches Luton into a semi-final with Chelsea.											

		Home					Away					
	P	W	D	L	F	A	W	D	L	F	A	Pts
1 Manchester U	42	14	6	1	39	13	13	5	3	41	25	92
2 Blackburn	42	14	5	2	31	11	11	4	6	32	25	84
3 Newcastle	42	14	4	3	51	14	9	4	8	31	27	77
4 Arsenal	42	10	8	3	25	15	8	9	4	28	13	71
5 Leeds	42	13	6	2	37	18	5	10	6	28	21	70
6 Wimbledon	42	12	5	4	35	21	6	6	9	21	32	65
7 Sheffield Wed	42	10	7	4	48	24	6	9	6	28	30	64
8 Liverpool	42	12	4	5	33	23	5	5	11	26	32	60
9 QP Rangers	42	8	7	6	32	29	8	5	8	30	32	60
10 Aston Villa	42	8	5	8	23	18	7	7	7	23	32	57
11 Coventry	42	9	7	5	23	17	5	7	9	20	28	56
12 Norwich	42	4	9	8	26	29	8	8	5	39	32	53
13 WEST HAM	42	6	7	8	26	31	7	6	8	21	27	52
14 Chelsea	42	11	5	5	31	20	2	7	12	18	33	51
15 Tottenham	42	4	8	9	29	33	7	4	10	25	26	45
16 Manchester C	42	6	10	5	24	22	3	8	10	14	27	45
17 Everton	42	8	4	9	26	30	4	4	13	16	33	44
18 Southampton	42	9	2	10	30	31	3	5	13	19	35	43
19 Ipswich	42	5	8	8	21	32	4	8	9	14	26	43
20 Sheffield Utd	42	6	10	5	24	23	2	8	11	18	37	42
21 Oldham	42	5	8	8	24	33	4	5	12	18	35	40
22 Swindon	42	4	7	10	25	45	1	8	12	22	55	30
	924	192	142	128	663	532	128	142	192	532	663	1244

Odds & ends

Double wins: (1) Oldham.
Double losses: (3) Leeds, Newcastle, Liverpool.

Won from behind: (1) Watford FAC (h).
Lost from in front: (4) Spurs (h), Sheff U (a), Liverpool (h), Luton FAC (a).

High spots: Nine league games with only one defeat from 2 October.

Low spots: Defeat in the FA Cup at First Division Luton.
Losing the first two league fixtures.
Nine league games without a win from 3 January.

Hammer of the Year: Trevor Morley.
Ever-presents: (1) Ludek Miklosko.
Hat-tricks: (0).
Leading scorer: (16) Trevor Morley.

	Appearances						Goals			
	Lge	*Sub*	LC	*Sub*	FAC	*Sub*	**Lge**	LC	FAC	**Tot**
Allen, Clive	7				1	*2*	**2**			**2**
Allen, Martin	20	*6*		*2*	6		**7**	1	2	**10**
Bishop, Ian	36		3		6		**1**		1	**2**
Boere, Jeroen		*4*		*1*				1		**1**
Breacker, Tim	40		2		6		**3**			**3**
Brown, Kenny	6	*3*			2	*1*				
Burrows, David	25		3		3		**1**	1		**2**
Butler, Peter	26		2		1		**1**			**1**
Chapman, Lee	26	*4*	3		6		**7**	2	2	**11**
Dicks, Julian	7									
Foster, Colin	5									
Gale, Tony	31	*1*	2		1					
Gordon, Dale	8		1				**1**			**1**
Holmes, Matt	33	*1*	3		4		**3**			**3**
Jones, Steve	3	*5*			2	*2*	**2**		1	**3**
Marquis, Paul		*1*								
Marsh, Mike	33		3		6		**1**		1	**2**
Martin, Alvin	6	*1*	1		3		**2**			**2**
Miklosko, Ludek	42		3		6					
Mitchell, Paul		*1*								
Morley, Trevor	39	*3*	3		3	*1*	**13**	3		**16**
Potts, Steve	41		3		6					
Rowland, Keith	16	*7*	1		4					
Robson, Marc	1	*2*								
Rush, Matthew	9	*1*					**1**			**1**
Williamson, Danny	2	*1*					**1**			**1**
(own-goals)							**1**			**1**
26 players used	**462**	***41***	**33**	***3***	**66**	***6***	**47**	**8**	**7**	**62**

No		Date	Att	Pos	Pt	F-A	H-T	Scorers, Times, and Referees	SQUAD	NUMBERS	IN	USE								subs used
1	H	LEEDS			D	0-0	0-0		Miklosko	Breacker	Burrows	Potts*	Martin	Allen	Bishop	Butler	Morley	Chapman	Holmes^	**Whitbread**/Marsh
		20/8	18,610		1				Lukic	Kelly	Worthington	White	Palmer	Wetherall	Strachan	Wallace R*	Deane	McAllister	Speed	Masinga
								Ref: K Burge	Harry Redknapp takes over from Billy Bonds on the eve of the season, and watches Howard Wilkinson's Leeds dominate this goalless draw. Brian Deane wasted most of Leeds' chances. The Hammers created just one opportunity, when Martin Allen's shot was saved by John Lukic.											
2	A	MANCHESTER C		17	L	**0-3**	0-2		Miklosko	Breacker	Burrows	Potts	Martin	Allen	Bishop	Butler^	Morley	Chapman*	Holmes	Marsh/Whitbread
		24/8	19,150	10	1			Walsh 14, Beagrie 42, Rosler 56	Coton	Phelan*	McMahon	Curle	Vonk	Summerbee	Walsh	Rosler^	Flitcroft	Beagrie	Brightwell I	Lomas/Quinn
								Ref: R Hart	Paul Walsh's header from Beagrie's cross knocked the stuffing out of West Ham. Beagrie cut in from the left to make it 2-0 from 20 yards. To suffer such a defeat against a team which barely escaped relegation, and lost their opening match 0-3 at Arsenal, augurs ill for the future.											
3	A	NORWICH		18	L	0-1	0-0		Miklosko	Breacker	Burrows	Potts	Martin	Allen	Bishop	Marsh^	**Moncur**	Jones	Rowland*	Chapman/Whitbread
		27/8	19,110	10	1			Robins 65	Gunn	Bradshaw	Bowen	Crook	Newsome	Polson	Ekoku*	Robins^	Goss	Ullathorne	Adams	Akinbiyi/Newman
								Ref: P Jones	Neither side had scored a goal beforehand, so this was always likely to be a low-scoring affair. John Moncur, signed from Swindon for £1 million, made an unspectacular debut. Sub Akinbiyi had been on just three minutes before crossing for Robins to score at the second attempt.											
4	H	NEWCASTLE		21	L	1-3	0-2	Hutchison 87p	Miklosko	Breacker	Burrows	Potts	Martin	Allen*	**Hutchison**	Marsh	Moncur	Butler	Holmes	Jones
		31/8	18,580	1	1			Potts 32 (og), Lee 35, Mathie 88	Srnicek	Venison	Beresford	Lee*	Hottiger	Peacock	Watson	Sellars	Albert	Cole	Mathie	Elliott
								Ref: B Hill	Keegan's Newcastle maintain their 100% record and take their tally to 15 goals in four games. Hammers hung on until Cole's angled shot went in off Potts. Don Hutchison, Hammers' £1.5 million record signing from Liverpool, opened the season's account after John Beresford handled.											
5	A	LIVERPOOL		19	D	0-0	0-0		Miklosko	Breacker	Rowland	Potts	Martin	Allen	Butler	Marsh	Moncur	Rush	Cottee !	
		10/9	30,907	4	2				James	Jones	Ruddock	Barnes	Scales	Molby	Redknapp	McManam'n	Bjornebye	Fowler	Rush	
								Ref: P Danson	Roy Evans' Liverpool relinquish their 100% record. Fowler hit the bar, John Barnes the post. Hammers nearly won it at the death when James saved from Moncur. Cottee returns after his six-year stay at Everton and gets sent off after 55 minutes for a two-footed lunge at Rob Jones.											
6	H	ASTON VILLA		17	W	1-0	0-0	Cottee 86	Miklosko	Breacker	Rowland	Potts	Martin	Allen	Butler*	Marsh	Moncur	Rush	Cottee	Chapman
		17/9	18,326	8	5				Bosnich	Staunton	Richardson	Houghton	Townsend	Ehiogu	Barrett	Teale	Yorke*	Saunders	Fashanu	Atkinson
								Ref: S Lodge	Hammers were without a win, Ron Atkinson's Villa without a defeat, so Cottee's late swivel put paid to both records. Villa looked tired, having played at Internazionale 48 hours earlier, but still had the chances to win. How West Ham reached half-time still level was a mystery.											
7	H	ARSENAL		19	L	0-2	0-1		Miklosko	Breacker	Rowland	Potts	Martin	Allen	Hutchison	Marsh	Moncur	Chapman	Holmes*	Rush
		25/9	18,498	14	5			Adams 18, Wright 54	Seaman	Dixon	Winterburn	Adams	Keown*	Merson	Schwarz	Davis	Selley	Wright	Smith	Linighan
								Ref: K Cooper	Both teams are locked on five points before start of play. Arsenal were still without an away league goal when Smith nodded Davis' free-kick on to Adams. Lee Chapman laboured alone up front for much of the game. Hutchison's two-footed lunge at Smith earned only a yellow card.											
8	A	CHELSEA		15	W	2-1	0-0	Allen 53, Moncur 66	Miklosko	Breacker	Rowland	Potts	Martin	Allen	Hutchison	Marsh	Moncur	Chapman	Rush	
		2/10	18,696	7	8			Furlong 62	Kharin	Clarke !	Kjeldbjerg	Johnsen	Sinclair	Rocastle^	Peacock	Newton	Barness*	Furlong	Spencer	Shipperley/Lee
								Ref: P Don	At last West Ham score twice in a game and win away. World Cup ref Philip Don gave 12 fouls in the first four minutes, booked seven players and sent off Steve Clarke for an 87th-minute lunge at Allen. Moncur's corner led to the first goal. His first Hammers goal then won the game.											
9	H	CRYS PALACE		13	W	1-0	0-0	Hutchison 72	Miklosko	Breacker	Rowland	Potts	Martin	Allen	Hutchison	Marsh	Moncur	Chapman*	Cottee	Rush
		8/10	16,959	18	11				Martyn	Patterson*	Gorden	Southgate	Shaw	Coleman	Bowey	Newman	Armstrong	Ndah^	Salako	Dyer/Launders
								Ref: G Poll	Three wins in a week for buoyant Hammers, inflicting a first away loss on struggling Palace. Three points had looked unlikely when Don Hutchison, pushed up front, stooped to head in Breacker's cross. The best chance for Alan Smith's side came when George Ndah hit a post.											
10	A	MANCHESTER U		14	L	0-1	0-1		Miklosko	Breacker	Rowland	Potts	Martin	Allen	Hutchison	Marsh	Moncur	Rush	Cottee	
		15/10	**43,795**	4	11			Cantona 45	Schmeichel	Bruce	Sharpe	Pallister	May	Ince	Cantona	Kanchelskis	Hughes*	Irwin	Keane	McClair
								Ref: R Gifford	Five home wins out of five for Man U, without the loss of a single goal. But this was a good time for West Ham to play them, with Barcelona due at Old Trafford on Wednesday. In first-half injury-time Giggs set up Cantona for the only goal, but West Ham wasted precious chances.											

No	Venue	Opponent	Pos	Res	F-A	H-T	Scorers, Times, and Referees	1	2	3	4	5	6	7	8	9	10	11	subs used
11	H	SOUTHAMPTON	12	W	2-0	0-0	Allen 49, Rush 61	Miklosko	Breacker	Dicks	Potts	Martin	Allen	Bishop	Marsh	Rush	Chapman	Cottee	
22/10		18,853	*10*	14				*Beasant*	*Kenna*	*Hall*	*Charlton**	*Allen*	*Magilton*	*Maddison^*	*Le Tissier*	*Monkou*	*Dowie*	*Ekelund*	*Benali/Hughes*
							Ref: J Worray	Inspired by the sight of a gorgeous rainbow, Julian Dicks returns from his unhappy time at Anfield to play a stormer and get booked. Matthew Rush is attracting admiring reviews at Upton Park, and having set up Allen's opener scores the second. Alan Ball bemoans Saints' defence.											
12	A	TOTTENHAM	13	L	1-3	1-1	Rush 42	Miklosko	Rowland	Dicks	Potts	Martin	Allen^	Bishop*	Marsh	Hutchison	Rush	Cottee	Whitbread/Chapman
29/10		*24,271*	*12*	14			*Klinsmann 18, Sheri'm 49, Barmby 63*	*Thorstvedt*	*Edinburgh**	*Popescu*	*Mabbutt*	*Barmby*	*Dumitrescu*	*Dozzell*	*Hazard^*	*Klinsmann*	*Kerslake*	*Campbell*	*Sheringham/Hill*
							Ref: K Morton	Spurs have now conceded 24 league goals, and have the threat of a 6-point deduction hanging over them. This is only Spurs' sixth home league win in 16 months under Ardiles. At 1-1 Cottee heads wide. Four minutes after coming on Sheringham turns the game by firing into the corner.											
13	A	EVERTON	13	L	0-1	0-0		Miklosko	Whitbread	Dicks	Potts	Martin	Rush	Bishop	Marsh	Hutchison	Chapman	Cottee	
1/11		*28,338*	*22*	14			*Ablett 54*	*Southall*	*Jackson*	*Watson*	*Ablett*	*Stuart**	*Parkinson*	*Burrows*	*Amokachi^*	*Durrant*	*Horne*	*Ferguson*	*Limpar/Rideout*
							Ref: K Bodenham	Without a win all season Mike Walker's Everton are in a terrible mess. After Ablett stooped to head them in front, Everton were forced on their heels. In a furious finale Martin's shot is cleared off the line and Chapman's volley hits the bar. Goodison exploded with relief at the end.											
14	H	LEICESTER	14	W	1-0	0-0	Dicks 77p	Miklosko	Whitbread	Dicks	Potts	Martin	Morley	Bishop	Moncur	Hutchison !	Rush	Cottee*	Brown
5/11		18,780	*21*	17				*Ward*	*Grayson*	*Whitlow*	*Mohan*	*Blake*	*Draper*	*Roberts*	*Philott*	*Lowe*	*Lewis*	*Carr*	
							Ref: R Dilkes	Having lost to the bottom team, West Ham dare not slip up against next-to-bottom Leicester. Things did not look bright until Mohan tripped Moncur and Dicks blasted the penalty. Don Hutchison's reputation is clouding his future. He kicked Lee Philpot twice and was expelled.											
15	A	SHEFFIELD WED	17	L	0-1	0-1		Miklosko	Brown	Dicks	Potts	Martin	Allen*	Bishop	Moncur	Morley	Rush	Cottee	Marsh
19/11		*25,300*	*16*	17			*Petrescu 29*	*Pressman*	*Petrescu**	*Nolan*	*Wacker*	*Atherton*	*Sinton*	*Sheridan*	*Bt-Williams^*	*Bright*	*Hyde*	*Pearce*	*Taylor/Watson*
							Ref: G Ashby	Trevor Francis' Wednesday are winning few friends, and nor to tell the truth are the Hammers. The goal that separated the two sides had an element of doubt about it. Chris Bart-Williams chipped the ball forward to Petrescu, who might have been offside. West Ham did not protest.											
16	H	COVENTRY	17	L	0-1	0-0		Miklosko	Brown	Dicks	Potts	Whitbread	Holmes	Bishop*	Marsh	Moncur	Morley	Cottee	Rush
26/11		17,251	*10*	17			*Busst 58*	*Ogrizovic*	*Burrows*	*Busst*	*Morgan*	*Darby*	*Flynn*	*Cook*	*Jones*	*Pressley*	*Ndlovu**	*Dublin*	*Jenkinson*
							Ref: M Reed	Cottee used to love playing Coventry, with 10 goals in six games against them before signing for Everton. Now he can't score against anyone, having a close-in header saved by Ogrizovic. Coventry's late arrival delayed the kick-off. David Busst's unmarked header wins the game.											
17	A	QP RANGERS	17	L	1-2	0-2	Boere 89	Miklosko	Brown	Dicks	Potts	Rowland	Rush	**Hughes**	Marsh	Moncur	Boere	Cottee	
4/12		*12,780*	*16*	17			*Ferdinand 2, Sinclair 37*	*Dykstra*	*Wilson*	*Yates*	*McDonald*	*Impey*	*Sinclair*	*Barker**	*Ferdinand*	*Gallen*	*Maddix*	*Hodge*	*Holloway*
							Ref: P Don	How West Ham envy QPR manager Ray Wilkins the talents of Les Ferdinand and Trevor Sinclair, who scored, respectively, with a prodigious leap and an astonishing burst of acceleration. QPR sat on their lead and were punished by Boere's header – West Ham's 10th goal in 17 games.											
18	A	LEEDS	19	D	2-2	1-2	Boere 45, 79	Miklosko	Brown	Dicks	Potts	**Rieper**	Rowland*	Bishop	Holmes	Rush	Boere	Cottee	Hughes
10/12		*28,987*	*7*	18			*Worthington 3, Deane 25*	*Lukic*	*Kelly*	*Worthingt'n**	*Palmer*	*Wetherall*	*Strachan*	*Deane*	*McAllister*	*Whelan*	*Tinkler*	*Dorigo*	*White*
							Ref: R Hart	Loan signings Rieper and Hughes are shaking things up. Leeds sliced open West Ham's defence twice by 25 minutes. Had it stayed 0-2 at half-time, when Ludo had stitches above an eye, West Ham may have been finished, but the first of Boere's two super headers revitalised the game.											
19	H	MANCHESTER C	17	W	**3-0**	2-0	Cottee 6, 9, 57	Miklosko	Breacker	Dicks	Potts	Martin	Holmes	Bishop	Hughes	Rush	Boere	Cottee	
17/12		17,286	*8*	21				*Dibble*	*Summerbee*	*Walsh*	*Rosler*	*Flitcroft*	*Brightwell I*	*Quinn*	*Lomas*	*Kerr**	*Brightw'll D^*	*Kernaghan*	*Vonk/Foster*
							Ref: T Holbrook	City present West Ham with their biggest win of the season and Cottee with his first Hammers hat-trick for eight years – the first with his left, the second with his right, the third a belter from 15 yards. City boss Brian Horton: 'No disrespect, we made them look better than they were.'											
20	H	IPSWICH	18	D	1-1	1-0	Cottee 16	Miklosko	Breacker	Dicks	Potts*	Martin	Holmes	Bishop	Hughes	Rush	Boere	Cottee	Rieper
26/12		20,562	*22*	22			*Thomson 71*	*Forrest*	*Yallop*	*Mason*	*Wark*	*Williams*	*Milton*	*Kiwomya*	*Sedgley**	*Thomsen*	*Vaughan*	*Whelan*	*Slater*
							Ref: P Durkin	Former Hammers are playing a major role in present-day Ipswich. John Lyall resigned three weeks ago, and caretaker boss Paul Goddard takes charge. Ipswich may be bottom, but Claus Thomsen's equalising header was deserved. Tony Cottee had earlier sprung Ipswich's offside trap.											
21	A	WIMBLEDON	18	L	0-1	0-0		Miklosko	Brown	Dicks	Potts	Martin	Rieper*	Bishop	Hughes	Holmes	Boere	Cottee	Rush
28/12		***11,212***	*12*	22			*Fear 55*	*Segers*	*Barton*	*Elkins**	*Jones^*	*Kimble*	*Perry*	*Thorn*	*Cunningham*	*Ekoku*	*Harford*	*Holdsworth*	*Clarke/Fear*
							Ref: P Don	A turgid match, settled by Peter Fear's right-footed half-volley. He had come on as a half-time substitute. 10 minutes later Tony Cottee blazed against the underside of the bar from close range. Redknapp appeared to become involved in an altercation with supporters at the final whistle.											

No	Date		Att	Pos	Pt	F-A	H-T	Scorers, Times, and Referees	SQUAD	NUMBERS	IN	USE								subs used
22	H	NOTT'M FOREST		16	W	3-1	3-0	Cottee 24, Bishop 26, Hughes 44	Miklosko	Breacker	Dicks	Potts	Martin	Holmes	Bishop	Hughes	Moncur^	Boere*	Cottee	Rush/Rieper
	31/12		20,644	*4*	25			*McGregor 89*	*Crossley*	*Lyttle*	*Chettle*	*Cooper**	*Pearce*	*Woan*	*Stone*	*Bohinen^*	*Haaland*	*Roy*	*Collymore*	*McGregor/Black*
								Ref: D Gallagher	The key battle was between evergreen Alvin Martin and Stan-the-Man Collymore, talked about as an England striker. The balding Martin won hands down. Other Hammers heroes were Moncur in midfield and Michael Hughes, who scored the goal of the game with a superb solo effort.											
23	A	BLACKBURN		16	L	2-4	1-1	Cottee 32, Dicks 58	Miklosko	Breacker	Dicks	Potts	Rieper	Holmes*	Bishop	Hughes	Moncur	Boere	Cottee	Rush
	2/1		*25,503*	*1*	25			*Shearer 14p, 75, 79p, Le Saux 61*	*Flowers*	*Berg*	*Gale*	*Hendry*	*Le Saux*	*Sherwood*	*Atkins**	*Ripley*	*Wilcox*	*Sutton*	*Shearer^*	*Warhurst/Newell*
								Ref: K Morton	Champions-elect Blackburn have won all but one match at Ewood, and go six points clear of Man U. West Ham led 2-1 after an hour, but were exposed by Le Saux's 25-yard free-kick. Alan Shearer's two penalties were conceded by Ludo Miklosko on Shearer, and Rieper on Wilcox.											
24	H	TOTTENHAM		19	L	1-2	1-0	Boere 10	Miklosko	Breacker	Brown	Potts	Martin	Holmes^	Bishop	Hughes*	Moncur	Boere	Cottee	Allen/Morley
	14/1		24,573	*6*	25			*Sheringham 58, Klinsmann 80*	*Walker*	*Austin*	*Calderwood*	*Mabbutt*	*Campbell**	*Popescu*	*Howells*	*Barmby*	*Anderton*	*Sheringham*	*Klinsmann*	*Edinburgh*
								Ref: B Hill	Gerry Francis has replaced Ardiles and masterminded Spurs' sixth successive clean sheet. Boere denied them a seventh, heading in Hughes' corner. Anderton then fouled Holmes inside the box, but the kick was given outside. Miklosko flapped at the free-kick which made it 1-1.											
25	H	SHEFFIELD WED		19	L	0-2	0-1		Miklosko	Breacker !	Brown	Potts	Martin !	Holmes^	Bishop	Hughes*	Moncur	Boere	Cottee	Rieper/Allen
	23/1		**14,554**	*7*	25			*Waddle 33, Bright 83*	*Pressman*	*Nolan*	*Wacker*	*Atherton*	*Bart-Williams*	*Bright*	*Hyde*	*Pearce*	*Ingesson*	*Waddle^*	*Whitt'gh'm**	*Watson/Petrescu*
								Ref: P Danson	Two red cards for the Irons, the first on 10 minutes when Martin stumbles across Mark Bright on the halfway line. It looked like a rugby tackle but is annulled. Waddle's exquisite angled chip deserved to win any game. Breacker went off on 73 mins, felling Hyde. That ended the contest.											
26	A	LEICESTER		20	W	2-1	2-1	Cottee 29, Dicks 43p	Miklosko	Breacker	Dicks	Potts	Martin	Allen	Moncur	Hughes	Hutchison*	Williamson	Cottee	Boere
	4/2		*20,375*	*22*	28			*Robins 45*	*Poole*	*Grayson*	*Smith**	*Hill*	*Mohan*	*Draper*	*Thompson*	*Roberts*	*Poole*	*Philott*	*Galloway*	*Lawrence*
								Ref: J Worray	Leicester are bottom and doomed, so three points are a must for West Ham. Dicks laid on Cottee's 100th Hammers goal, and when Cottee was fouled in the box Dicks smote home the penalty. Leicester's £1 million signing Mark Robins' goal on half-time ensured a nervy second period.											
27	H	EVERTON		20	D	2-2	1-1	Cottee 22, 60	Miklosko	Brown	Dicks	Potts	Martin	Allen	Moncur	Hughes*	Hutchison	Williamson	Cottee	Boere
	13/2		21,081	*17*	29			*Rideout 43, Limpar 79*	*Southall*	*Watson*	*Unsworth*	*Ablett**	*Stuart*	*Ebrell*	*Hinchcliffe*	*Barrett*	*Horne*	*Rideout*	*Ferguson*	*Limpar*
								Ref: M Reed	The classic six-pointer. Royle's Everton had scored only four goals in 13 away games, so when Cottee scored his second in the mud to make it 2-1, it should have been all over. Two swinging left-footed crosses from Hinchliffe brought two Everton goals, the second deflected by Potts.											
28	A	COVENTRY		20	L	0-2	0-1		Miklosko	Breacker	Dicks	Potts	Martin*	Allen	Holmes^	Moncur	Hutchison	Williamson	Cottee	Rieper/Boere
	18/2		*17,554*	*14*	29			*Ndlovu 25, Marsh 67*	*Ogrizovic*	*Burrows*	*Morgan*	*Rennie*	*Flynn*	*Cook*	*Pickering*	*Marsh*	*Richardson*	*Ndlovu*	*Dublin*	
								Ref: R Dilkes	Ron Atkinson has just taken charge at Highfield Road – his eighth club. The formidable Dion Dublin made both goals, the second for former-Hammer Mike Marsh. Redknapp complained that his team tried to play 'too much football'. Coventry are now five points ahead of West Ham.											
29	H	CHELSEA		20	L	1-2	1-0	Hutchison 11	Miklosko	Breacker	Dicks	Potts	Rieper	Allen	Bishop	Moncur	Hutchison	Morley	Cottee	
	25/2		21,500	*13*	29			*Burley 67, Stein 75*	*Kharin^*	*Clarke*	*Johnsen*	*Newton*	*Minto*	*Burley*	*Rocastle**	*Peacock*	*Spencer*	*Lee*	*Stein*	*Furlong/Hitchock*
								Ref: G Ashby	Chelsea have a date with FC Bruges and were there to be beaten. They should have been, too, as they fell behind to Hutchison's thumping half-volley. West Ham also bit bar and post. But Burley levelled, then set up Stein's terrific volley. Kharin had to be subbed 10 minutes from time.											
30	A	ARSENAL		19	W	1-0	1-0	Hutchison 20	Miklosko	Breacker	Dicks	Potts	Rieper	Allen	Bishop	Moncur	Hutchison	Morley*	Cottee	Rush
	5/3		*34,295*	*11*	32				*Bartram*	*Dixon*	*Winterburn*	*Linighan*	*Bould*	*Jensen**	*Merson*	*Schwarz*	*Parlour*	*Wright*	*Helder^*	*Morrow/Kiwomya*
								Ref: B Hill	George Graham has been 'bunged' into touch, and Stewart Houston is caretaker. Few could have expected this result, settled by Hutchison's sixth goal so far, as Winterburn fluffed a clearance. Seaman has a long-term injury. Moncur and Hutchison were booked as tension mounted.											
31	A	NEWCASTLE		19	L	0-2	0-1		Miklosko	Breacker	Dicks	Potts	Rieper	Allen	Bishop	Hughes	Hutchison	Rush*	Cottee	Morley
	8/3		*34,595*	*3*	32			*Clark 17, Kitson 52*	*Srnicek*	*Venison*	*Beresford*	*Fox*	*Howey^*	*Lee*	*Clark*	*Hottiger*	*Peacock*	*Gillespie*	*Kitson**	*Watson/Bracewell*
								Ref: T Holbrook	Newcastle are still unbeaten at St James', so this result is hardly unexpected, and leaves West Ham entrenched in the four relegation places. In truth, they got off lightly, and could have been 0-4 down instead of 0-1 at the break. £2.2 million Paul Kitson scored with a sweet left-footer.											

No	Venue	Opponent / Date	Att	Pos	Res	FT	HT	Scorers, Times, and Referees	1	2	3	4	5	6	7	8	9	10	11	subs used
32	H	NORWICH		18	D	2-2	0-1	Cottee 82, 88	Miklosko	Breacker	Dicks	Potts	Rieper	Williamson	Bishop	Moncur*	Hutchison	Morley	Cottee	Hughes
		11/3	21,464	*14*	33			*Eadie 22, Ullathorne 53*	*Marshall*	*Newman*	*Newsome*	*Polston*	*Ullathorne*	*Sutch*	*Eadie^*	*Johnson !*	*Prior*	*Cureton**	*Ward*	*Adams/Akinbiyi*
								Ref: A Wilkie / M Sims	Norwich are on a terrible slide. 7th at New Year, they have not won since. They even have the wrong player sent off – Johnson when it should have been Prior – for fouling Cottee. Substitute ref Sims had just replaced hamstrung Alan Wilkie. Cottee's goals extend Norwich's bad run.											
33	A	SOUTHAMPTON		19	D	1-1	1-0	Hutchison 39	Miklosko	Breacker	Dicks	Potts	Rieper	Rush*	Bishop	Moncur	Hutchison	Holmes	Cottee	Boere
		15/3	*15,178*	*18*	34			*Shipperley 48*	*Beasant*	*Hall*	*Widdrington*	*Benali*	*Magilton*	*Maddison^*	*Le Tissier*	*Heaney**	*Monkou*	*Dodd*	*Shipperley*	*Hughes/Ekelund*
								Ref: K Burge	Bruce Grobbelaar was arrested this morning on charges of match-fixing. Southampton's recent record is earning a fortune for someone – this is their ninth draw in 10 games. Hutchison's header, helped in by Widdrington, was cancelled out by Shipperley's first league goal for the Saints.											
34	A	ASTON VILLA		18	W	2-0	1-0	Moncur 11, Hutchison 49	Miklosko	Breacker	Dicks	Potts	Rieper	Allen	Bishop	Moncur	Hutchison^	Holmes*	Cottee	Rowland/Boere
		18/3	*28,682*	*15*	37				*Bosnich*	*Staunton*	*McGrath*	*Teale*	*Townsend*	*Taylor*	*Charles*	*Johnson**	*Saunders*	*Yorke^*	*Wright*	*Houghton/Ehiogu*
								Ref: M Bodenham	Villa have been reeling since losing a 4-1 lead over Leicester with 11 minutes left, and Brian Little's team are spiralling downwards. Moncur's 25-yarder drains Villa of what little confidence they have. Shaun Teale boobs for the second goal. Few away victories come as easy as this.											
35	A	NOTT'M FOREST		19	D	1-1	0-0	Dicks 65	Miklosko	Brown	Dicks	Potts	Rieper	Allen	Bishop	Hughes	Holmes*	Boere	Cottee	Whitbread
		8/4	*28,361*	*4*	38			*Collymore 78*	*Crossley*	*Lyttle*	*Chettle*	*Cooper*	*Pearce*	*Woan^*	*Stone*	*Phillips*	*Bohinen**	*Roy*	*Collymore*	*Lee/McGregor*
								Ref: G Poll	Three weeks without a fixture. Forest are going well, five wins on the trot, the last a 7-1 drubbing of Sheffield Wednesday at Hillsborough. But Dicks thumped in a free-kick. The equaliser was farcical. Potts and Ludo collided in mid-air, and Collymore rammed in the ensuing corner.											
36	H	WIMBLEDON		17	W	**3-0**	1-0	Dicks 41p, Boere 76, Cottee 78	Miklosko	Breacker	Dicks	Potts	Rieper	Allen	Bishop	Hughes	Holmes	Boere	Cottee	
		13/4	21,084	*9*	41				*Sullivan*	*Barton*	*Elkins*	*Jones*	*Reeves*	*Thorn*	*Cunningham*	*Leonhardsen*	*Gayle**	*Harford*	*Holdsworth*	*Clarke*
								Ref: M Reed	A rare Thursday night game. West Ham are unbeaten in five, beating the Dons at home in the league for the first time. The result also relegates Ipswich and Leicester. Barton fouled Holmes for the penalty, but West Ham were hanging on grimly until Boere's super header settled matters.											
37	A	IPSWICH		18	D	1-1	0-1	Boere 90	Miklosko	Breacker	Dicks	Potts	Rieper	Allen*	Bishop	Moncur	Holmes	Boere	Cottee	Hutchison
		17/4	*19,099*	*22*	42			*Thomson 11*	*Baker*	*Stockwell*	*Yallop*	*Wark*	*Williams*	*Milton**	*Marshall^*	*Mathie*	*Slater*	*Linighan*	*Thomsen*	*Mason/Chapman*
								Ref: M Bodenham	An unreal result. Ipswich had lost their last eight, scored just one goal, and suffered a 0-9 humiliation at Man U. West Ham might have had nine themselves. Instead they needed four minutes stoppage time to get a draw. Ipswich fans were singing 'We're s*** and we're beating you'.											
38	H	BLACKBURN		16	W	2-0	0-0	Rieper 50, Hutchison 83	Miklosko	Breacker	Dicks	Potts	Rieper	Allen	Bishop	Moncur	Hutchison^	Boere*	Holmes	Rush/**Webster**
		30/4	24,202	*1*	45				*Flowers*	*Berg*	*Hendry*	*Le Saux*	*Kenna*	*Sherwood*	*Batty*	*Ripley**	*Witschge*	*Sutton*	*Shearer*	*Newell*
								Ref: K Morton	Man U fans love West Ham as a result of this shock win. Shearer and Sutton, Rovers' 56-goal SAS, were well shackled by Potts and Rieper. Batty should have been expelled for a thigh-high lunge at Bishop. Rieper headed in Moncur's corner. Boere and Hutchison had broken noses.											
39	H	QP RANGERS		15	D	0-0	0-0		Miklosko	Breacker	Dicks	Potts	Rieper	Allen !	Bishop	Moncur	Hutchison^	Boere*	Holmes	Morley/Webster
		3/5	22,923	*8*	46				*Roberts*	*Bardsley*	*Wilson**	*McDonald*	*Impey*	*Holloway*	*Sinclair*	*Barker*	*Ferdinand*	*Penrice^*	*Maddix*	*Brevitt/Gallen*
								Ref: G Willard	Martin Allen was sent off on the hour, retaliating against a foul by Rufus Brevitt, who was one of seven Rangers booked. West Ham carved out few scoring chances and Ludo made a super double save to earn a point, but Palace's defeat at the Dell improves West Ham's survival chances.											
40	A	CRYS PALACE		16	L	0-1	0-0		Miklosko	Breacker	Dicks	Potts	Rieper	Allen^	Bishop	Moncur	Hutchison*	Boere	Holmes	Morley/Webster
		6/5	*18,224*	*19*	46			*Armstrong 50*	*Martyn*	*Humphrey*	*Gorden*	*Southgate*	*Shaw*	*Young*	*Pitcher*	*Houghton*	*Armstrong*	*Dowie*	*Salako*	
								Ref: S Lodge	Palace inflict West Ham's first defeat in nine games, to plunge them back in the mire. The first half was abject. The second had no sooner begun than Chris Armstrong finished off a fluid Palace move. Without the sprightly Cottee, West Ham seldom looked likely to salvage a point.											
41	H	LIVERPOOL		13	W	**3-0**	1-0	Holmes 29, Hutchison 60, 61	Miklosko	Breacker	Dicks*	Potts	Rieper	Moncur	Bishop	Hughes	Hutchison	Morley	Holmes	Webster
		10/5	22,446	*4*	49				*James*	*Babb*	*Scales*	*Matteo**	*Clough*	*Barnes*	*Redknapp*	*Thomas*	*McManam'n*	*Harkness*	*Fowler^*	*Kennedy/Walters*
								Ref: P Durkin	Two matches against Liverpool and Man U stand between West Ham and relegation. With Cottee and Boere out for the season, Hutchison is pushed up front and scores twice in a minute against his former club. Palace are four points behind with one game left, so West Ham are safe.											
42	H	MANCHESTER U		14	D	1-1	1-0	Hughes 31	Miklosko	Breacker	Rowland	Potts	Rieper	Moncur	Bishop	Hughes^	Hutchison*	Morley	Holmes	Allen/Webster
		14/5	**24,783**	*2*	50			*McClair 52*	*Schmeichel*	*Neville G*	*Bruce*	*Pallister*	*Irwin*	*Butt**	*Keane^*	*Ince*	*Sharpe*	*McClair*	*Cole*	*Hughes/Scholes*
		Home	Away					Ref: A Wilkie	Man U must win and Blackburn must lose. Had West Ham needed points themselves the tension would have been unbearable. Mark Hughes was left on the bench till the break, by which time the damage had been done. Two late saves by Miklosko from Cole send the title to Ewood.											
		Average 19,730	24020																	

Coca-Cola Cup				F-A	H-T	Scorers, Times, and Referees	SQUAD	NUMBERS	IN	USE								subs used
2:1 A	WALSALL	17	L	1-2	1-1	Ntamark 42 (og)	Miklosko	Breacker	Rowland	Potts	Martin	Allen^	Moncur	Marsh	Hutchison	Rush*	Cottee	Chapman/Whitbread
20/9	*5,994*	*2:11*				*Watkiss 25, Potts 74 (og)*	*Wood*	*Evans*	*Rogers*	*Watkiss*	*Marsh*	*Palmer**	*O'Connor*	*Peer*	*Lightbourne*	*Wilson*	*Ntamark^*	*Ryder/Mehew*
						Ref: P Harrison	Chris Nicholl takes charge of Walsall for the first time in this famous win. Watkiss headed in the far post for Walsall before Ntamark ran the ball inadvertently past his own keeper to make it 1-1. The second own-goal of the night came when Potts miscued a clearance past Miklosko.											
2:2 H	WALSALL	15	W	2-0	0-0	Hutchison 62, Moncur 94	Miklosko	Breacker	Rowland	Potts	Moncur*	Allen	Bishop	Marsh	Hutchison	Whitbread	Chapman	Brown
5/10	13,553	*2:7*		*aet*			*Woods*	*Rider*	*Rogers*	*Watkiss*	*Marsh**	*Palmer*	*O'Connor^*	*Peer*	*Lightbourne*	*Wilson*	*Mehew*	*Ntamark/Evans*
						Ref: J Holbrook (Hammers win 3-2 on aggregate)	With an hour gone West Ham were staring elimination in the face. Without the suspended Cottee, Hutchison played up front, scoring close in following Moncur and Allen's build-up. Mehew wasted the chance to win it for Walsall. In extra-time Moncur drove in a rebound off the post.											
3 H	CHELSEA	12	W	1-0	1-0	Hutchison 2	Miklosko	Breacker	Dicks	Potts	Martin	Allen	Bishop	Marsh	Hutchison	Rush	Cottee	
26/10	18,815	*7*					*Kharin*	*Kjeldberg*	*Johnsen*	*Spackman*	*Newton*	*Barness*	*Hall^*	*Rocastle*	*Peacock**	*Wise*	*Shipperley*	*Hopkin/Lee*
						Ref: K Cooper / J Norbury	Hutchison's sweet curler from 20 yards gave West Ham the perfect start. At half-time the ref's injured Achilles tendon forced a linesman to take over. Glenn Hoddle's injury-racked team made the running after the break, but two headers were kept out by super saves from Miklosko.											
4 H	BOLTON	17	L	1-3	0-1	Cottee 83	Miklosko	Brown	Dicks	Potts	Whitbread	Rush	Bishop	Holmes*	Moncur	Boere	Cottee	Morley
30/11	18,190	*1:4*				*McGinlay 16, 76p, Whitbread 53 (og)*	*Branagan*	*Green*	*Phillips*	*McAteer*	*Coleman*	*Stubbs*	*Lee**	*Sneakes*	*Paatelainen*	*McGinlay*	*Thompson*	*Patterson*
						Ref: P Durkin	First Division Bolton do to West Ham what they had done to Liverpool, Everton, Arsenal and Ipswich in the past two years – winning cup-ties away from home. West Ham's miserable night was sealed when Dicks needlessly handled Thompson's corner. The penalty made it 0-3.											

FA Cup																		
3 A	WYCOMBE WAN	16	W	2-0	0-0	Cottee 47, Brown 78	Miklosko	Breacker	Dicks	Potts	Martin	Moncur	Bishop	Hughes	Holmes*	Boere^	Cottee	Brown/Morley
7/1	*9,007*	*2:3*					*Hyde*	*Cousins*	*Brown*	*Crossley*	*Evans*	*Ryan*	*Carroll*	*Bell*	*Regis^*	*Garner*	*Thompson**	*Stapleton/Hemmings*
						Ref: G Willard	Wycombe – with FA Cup-winner Cyrille Regis in their ranks – had not lost at home since September, but could not contain Hughes' crosses. These led to both goals. Alan Hansen on *Match of the Day* had predicted an upset. Hammers fans sang 'There's only one Trevor Brooking'.											
4 A	QP RANGERS	19	L	0-1	0-1		Miklosko	Breacker	Dicks	Potts	Martin	Moncur	Bishop*	Hughes	Allen	Boere	Cottee	Hutchison
28/1	*17,694*	*17*				*Impey 20*	*Roberts*	*Bardsley*	*Yates*	*McDonald*	*Impey*	*Holloway*	*Sinclair*	*Barker*	*Gallen*	*Maddix*	*Dichio*	
						Ref: D Elleray	Ray Wilkins was not associated with robust play as a player, but his QPR side take no prisoners. Four Rangers are booked. Without the injured Ferdinand, Rangers had to find an alternative source of goals. Ian Holloway set up Andrew Impey. England boss Venables watched the game.											

		Home					Away					
	P	W	D	L	F	A	W	D	L	F	A	Pts
1 Blackburn	42	17	2	2	54	21	10	6	5	26	18	89
2 Manchester U	42	16	4	1	42	4	10	6	5	35	24	88
3 Nott'm Forest	42	12	6	3	36	18	10	5	6	36	25	77
4 Liverpool	42	13	5	3	38	13	8	6	7	27	24	74
5 Leeds	42	13	5	3	35	15	7	8	6	24	23	73
6 Newcastle	42	14	6	1	46	20	6	6	9	21	27	72
7 Tottenham	42	10	5	6	32	25	6	9	6	34	33	62
8 QP Rangers	42	11	3	7	36	26	6	6	9	25	33	60
9 Wimbledon	42	9	5	7	26	26	6	6	9	22	39	56
10 Southampton	42	8	9	4	33	27	4	9	8	28	36	54
11 Chelsea	42	7	7	7	25	22	6	8	7	25	33	54
12 Arsenal	42	6	9	6	27	21	7	3	11	25	28	51
13 Sheffield Wed	42	7	7	7	26	26	6	5	10	23	31	51
14 WEST HAM	42	9	6	6	28	19	4	5	12	16	29	50
15 Everton	42	8	9	4	31	23	3	8	10	13	28	50
16 Coventry	42	7	7	7	23	25	5	7	9	21	37	50
17 Manchester C	42	8	7	6	37	28	4	6	11	16	36	49
18 Aston Villa	42	6	9	6	27	24	5	6	10	24	32	48
19 Crys Palace	42	6	6	9	16	23	5	6	10	18	26	45
20 Norwich	42	8	8	5	27	21	2	5	14	10	33	43
21 Leicester	42	5	6	10	28	37	1	5	15	17	43	29
22 Ipswich	42	5	3	13	24	34	2	3	16	12	59	27
	924	205	134	123	697	498	123	134	205	498	697	1252

Odds & ends

Double wins: (2) Villa, Leicester.
Double losses: (4) Newcastle, Spurs, Sheff Wed, Coventry.

Won from behind: (0).
Lost from in front: (3) Blackburn (a), Spurs (h), Chelsea (h).

High spots: Undefeated run of eight league games from 11 March.

Low spots: Losing to First Division Bolton in Coca-Cola-Cup.
Terrible start to the league, just two points from first five games.
Five league defeats in six games from 29 October.

Hammer of the Year: Steve Potts.
Ever-presents: (2) Ludek Miklosko, Steve Potts.
Hat-tricks: (1) Tony Cottee.
Leading scorer: (15) Tony Cottee.

	Appearances						**Goals**			
	Lge	*Sub*	LC	*Sub*	FAC	*Sub*	**Lge**	LC	FAC	**Tot**
Allen, Martin	**26**	*3*	3		1		**2**			**2**
Bishop, Ian	**31**		3		2		**1**			**1**
Boere, Jeroen	**15**	*5*	1		2		**6**			**6**
Breacker, Tim	**33**		3		2					
Brown, Kenny	**8**	*1*	1	*1*		*1*			1	**1**
Burrows, David	**4**									
Butler, Peter	**5**									
Chapman, Lee	**7**	*3*	1	*1*						
Cottee, Tony	**31**		3		2		**13**	1	1	**15**
Dicks, Julian	**29**		2		2		**5**			**5**
Holmes, Matthew	**24**		1		1		**1**			**1**
Hughes, Michael	**15**	*2*			2		**2**			**2**
Hutchison, Don	**22**	*1*	3			*1*	**9**	2		**11**
Jones, Steve	**1**	*1*								
Marsh, Mike	**13**	*3*	3							
Martin, Alvin	**24**		2		2					
Miklosko, Ludek	**42**		4		2					
Moncur, John	**30**		3		2		**2**	1		**3**
Morley, Trevor	**10**	*4*		*1*		*1*				
Potts, Steve	**42**		4		2					
Rieper, Marc	**17**	*4*					**1**			**1**
Rowland, Keith	**11**	*1*	2							
Rush, Matthew	**15**	*8*	3				**2**			**2**
Webster, Simon		*5*								
Whitbread, Adrian	**3**	*5*	2	*1*						
Williamson, Danny	**4**									
(own-goals)								1		**1**
26 players used	**462**	*46*	**44**	*4*	**22**	*3*	**44**	**5**	**2**	**51**

No		Date	Att	Pos	Pt	F-A	H-T	Scorers, Times, and Referees	SQUAD	NUMBERS	IN	USE								subs used
1	H	LEEDS			L	1-2	1-0	Williamson 5	Miklosko	Breacker	Dicks	Potts	Rieper	Williamson*	Moncur	Bishop	Cottee	Hutchison	Rowland^	Martin/**Boogers**
		19/8	22,901		0			*Yeboah 48, 57*	*Lukic*	*Kelly*	*Dorigo^*	*Palmer"*	*Wetherall*	*Pemberton*	*Yeboah*	*Wallace**	*Deane*	*McAllister*	*Speed*	*Whelan/Worthington/*
								Ref: K Burge (Leeds' 3rd sub Beasley)	Tony Yeboah came to Leeds on loan from Eintracht Frankfurt. He has now signed permanently, and he sinks the Hammers with a fierce header and a ferocious volley. It had all started so brightly, Williamson tucking away Rowland's cross. Alvin Martin came on as substitute striker.											
2	A	MANCHESTER U		19	L	1-2	0-0	Bruce 56 (og)	Miklosko	Breacker	Dicks	Potts	Rieper	Allen	Moncur	Bishop	Cottee	Hutchison	Williamson*	Boogers !
		23/8	*31,966*	*10*	0			*Scholes 50, Keane 68*	*Schmeichel*	*Neville G*	*Irwin*	*Bruce*	*Sharpe*	*Pallister*	*Butt*	*Keane*	*McClair^*	*Scholes**	*Beckham*	*Cole/Thornley*
								Ref: D Gallagher	Rebuilding has turned Old Trafford into a three-sided ground. United lost their opening match 1-3 at Villa, and might have lost this one too. Hammers' cause was not helped by the dismissal of sub Marco Boogers for a nasty lunge at Gary Neville. 10 men could not rescue a point.											
3	A	NOTT'M FOREST		17	D	1-1	1-1	Allen 14	Miklosko	Breacker	Dicks	Potts	Rieper	Allen	Moncur	Bishop	Cottee*	Hutchison	Slater	Martin
		26/8	*26,645*	*2*	1			*Pearce 38p*	*Crossley*	*Lyttle*	*Pearce*	*Cooper*	*Chettle*	*Stone*	*Phillips*	*Roy**	*Bohinen^*	*Campbell*	*Woan*	*Lee/Gemmill*
								Ref: G Ashby	Three players took part in the corresponding fixture 10 years previously – Cottee, Martin, and Stuart Pearce. Hammers went in front when Dicks pumped a high ball onto Martin Allen's head. Tugging by Don Hutchison gave away the equaliser. Colin Cooper's header hit the bar.											
4	H	TOTTENHAM		17	D	1-1	1-0	Hutchison 24	Miklosko	Breacker	Dicks	Potts	Rieper	Allen	Moncur	Bishop	Cottee	Hutchison*	Slater	Boere
		30/8	23,516	*18*	2			*Rosenthal 54*	*Walker*	*Austin*	*Wilson*	*Howells*	*Calderwood*	*Mabbutt*	*McMahon**	*Dozzell*	*Armstrong*	*Sheringham*	*Rosenthal*	*Anderton*
								Ref: M Reed	Both sides are left still looking for their first win. Spurs are still mourning the departure of Klinsmann. Don Hutchison speared a 25-yard free-kick into the top corner, but that was cancelled out by Rosenthal, who turned Potts to level. Redknapp needs to find new strikers quickly.											
5	H	CHELSEA		19	L	1-3	0-2	Hutchison 73	Miklosko	Breacker	Dicks	Potts	Rieper	Bishop*	Moncur	Dowie	Cottee	Hutchison	Slater	**Lazaridis**
		11/9	19,228	*11*	2			*Wise 31, Spencer 33, 80*	*Kharine*	*Clarke*	*Minto*	*Gullit*	*Johnsen*	*Sinclair*	*Newton*	*Hughes*	*Spencer*	*Peacock**	*Wise*	*Lee*
								Ref: R Hart	Chelsea's John Spencer celebrates his 25th birthday with Julian Dicks' studs down his head. Dicks earns a yellow card, rather than red, but will face an FA disciplinary hearing. Iain Dowie re-signs after four years away. At 1-2 Miklosko saves Wise's penalty, following Breacker's foul.											
6	A	ARSENAL		19	L	0-1	0-0		Miklosko	Breacker	Dicks !	Potts	Rieper	Bishop	Moncur"	Dowie	Cottee*	Hutchison^	Slater	Martin/Laz/**Sealey**
		16/9	*38,065*	*5*	2			*Wright 75p*	*Seaman*	*Dixon*	*Winterburn*	*Parlour*	*Bould*	*Adams*	*Jensen*	*Wright*	*Merson*	*Bergkamp*	*Helder*	
								Ref: A Wilkie	One for the scrapbook. Dicks is booked for fouling Helder, concedes a penalty which Wright missed, and is sent off when fouling Wright once more. When Potts toppled Bergkamp, Wright's aim was more accurate. Hammers employed sub goalkeeper Les Sealey as a makeshift striker.											
7	H	EVERTON		17	W	2-1	2-1	Dicks 7p, 43p	Miklosko	Breacker	Dicks	Potts*	Martin	Bishop	Moncur	Dowie	Cottee^	Lazaridis	Slater	Rieper/Williamson
		23/9	21,085	*14*	5			*Samways 40*	*Southall*	*Barrett*	*Hinchcliffe*	*Parkinson*	*Watson*	*Short*	*Samways*	*Horne*	*Amokachi*	*Rideout^*	*Grant**	*Limpar/Stuart*
								Ref: P Durkin	An ugly match, settled by two nerveless penalties by Julian Dicks, who was at the heart of most that was good and bad. His strikes sandwiched a well-executed reply by Samways, and earned a belated first Hammers win. Alvin Martin creaked like an old tree at times, but did not break.											
8	A	SOUTHAMPTON		16	D	0-0	0-0		Miklosko	Breacker	Rowland	Potts	Martin	Bishop	Moncur	Lazaridis*	Dowie	Hutchison	Slater	Cottee
		2/10	*13,568*	*17*	6				*Beasant*	*Dodd*	*Benali*	*Magilton*	*Hall*	*Monkou*	*Charlton**	*Shipperley*	*Le Tissier*	*Maddison*	*Widdrington*	*Bennett*
								Ref: G Poll	Matt Le Tissier, dropped by England, fathers a daughter before this, his 300th league game for Saints. Dicks is suspended, following recent misdemeanours. In a game of few chances, Le Tissier fired wide, and Widdrington cleared off the line from Dowie, all on his own up front.											
9	A	WIMBLEDON		13	W	1-0	1-0	Cottee 18	Miklosko	Potts	Dicks	Rieper	Martin	Bishop	Moncur	Dowie	Cottee	Slater	Hughes	*[Fitzgerald]*
		16/10	***9,411***	*12*	9				*Heald*	*Cunningham*	*Perry*	*Jones*	*McAllister*	*Thorn"*	*Goodman*	*Earle*	*Skinner^*	*Holdsworth*	*Leonhard'n**	*Gayle/Clarke/*
								Ref: D Gallagher	Tony Cottee scores his first league goal for six months – also against Wimbledon – to defeat a Dons side plunging down the table. His sweet half-volley when the ball looped up off Paul Heald was threatened only by Andy Clarke's bicycle kick which hit the bar. Dicks had a stormer.											
10	H	BLACKBURN		13	D	1-1	1-0	Dowie 25	Miklosko	Potts	Dicks	Rieper	Martin	Bishop	Moncur	Dowie	Cottee	Slater*	Hughes	Hutchison
		21/10	21,776	*11*	10			*Shearer 89*	*Flowers*	*Berg*	*Kenna*	*Batty*	*Hendry*	*Pearce*	*Ripley*	*Sherwood^*	*Shearer*	*Sutton**	*Bohinen*	*Newell/McKinlay*
								Ref: S Lodge	The defending champions had lost all four previous away fixtures and were seconds away from losing this. Iain Dowie's first goal for the Hammers since his return – a sharp downward header – had looked to earn three deserved points, until Shearer headed in Bohinen's centre.											

No	Venue	Opponent / Date	Att	Pos	Pts	Result	H-T	Scorers, Times, and Referees	1	2	3	4	5	6	7	8	9	10	11	subs used
11	A	SHEFFIELD WED		12	W	1-0	1-0	Dowie 40	Miklosko	Potts	Dicks	Rieper	Martin	Bishop	Moncur*	Dowie	Cottee	Slater^	Hughes	Hutchison/**Harkes**
		28/10	*23,917*	*13*	13				*Pressman*	*Williams^*	*Nolan*	*Ingesson*	*Atherton*	*Hyde*	*Pembridge*	*Waddle*	*Hirst*	*Whitt'gh'm**	*Sinton*	*Bright/Degryse*
								Ref: K Cooper	Twice Wednesday hit the bar, and that made all the difference. The goal was too low for them. Dowie's conversion of Slater's cross – the ball being palmed in by Pressman – did not really reflect the balance of play. Fortified by the goal, Dowie almost scored another. He too hit the bar.											
12	H	ASTON VILLA		12	L	**1-4**	0-1	Dicks 85p	Miklosko	Potts	Dicks	Rieper	Martin	Bishop	Slater^	Dowie	Cottee	Hutchison*	Hughes	Boogers/Harkes
		4/11	23,637	*5*	13			*Milosevic 33,89, Johnson 49, Yorke 54*	*Bosnich*	*Charles*	*Wright*	*Southgate*	*McGrath*	*Ehiogu*	*Taylor*	*Draper*	*Milosevic*	*Townsend**	*Yorke*	*Johnson*
								Ref: P Jones	Hammers' heaviest home defeat follows on the heels of an unbeaten October. It was Villa's first win at the Boleyn for 10 years. West Ham had started brightly and twice hit the wood, but Villa missed easier chances than the four they scored. Dicks' fourth penalty makes him top scorer.											
13	A	BOLTON		11	W	**3-0**	0-0	Bishop 46, Cottee 68, Williamson 89	Miklosko	Potts	Rowland	Rieper	Martin	Bishop	Harkes	Dowie	Cottee	Williamson	Hughes	
		18/11	*19,047*	*18*	16				*Branagan*	*McAnespie^*	*Phillips*	*Curcic*	*Bergsson*	*Fairclough*	*Lee**	*Sneekes*	*Patterson !*	*McGinlay*	*Thompson*	*Green/Todd*
								Ref: P Durkin	Newcomers Bolton are heading back whence they came. Ian Bishop marked his 200th league game with a dipping 25-yarder. Bolton responded by collecting cards. Two yellows for skipper Mark Patterson and off he went. The Irons went for the kill. Bolton fans' frustration boiled over.											
14	H	LIVERPOOL		13	D	0-0	0-0		Miklosko	Potts	Rowland	Rieper	Martin	Bishop	Harkes	Dowie	Cottee	Williamson	Hughes	
		22/11	**24,324**	*6*	17				*James*	*Jones*	*Harkness*	*Babb*	*Wright*	*Ruddock*	*McManam'n*	*McAteer*	*Collymore*	*Barnes*	*Fowler*	
								Ref: J Winter	Liverpool had lost their last three and recall the sulking Collymore in place of the injured Ian Rush. Lack of goals did not mean lack of thrills. Potts had only scored once in 350 games, but nearly doubled his tally with a 30-yarder. Liverpool's best chances were wasted by Stan the Man.											
15	H	QP RANGERS		10	W	1-0	0-0	Cottee 84	Miklosko	Potts	Rowland*	Rieper	Martin	Bishop	Harkes^	Dowie	Cottee	Williamson	Hughes	Breacker/Slater
		25/11	21,504	*18*	20				*Sommer*	*Ready !*	*Brazier*	*Barker*	*Yeats*	*McDonald*	*Impey^*	*Holloway*	*Dichio*	*Gallen*	*Wilkins**	*Maddix/Charles*
								Ref: P Alcock	Boring for neutrals; ecstasy for Hammers as they poke their heads into the top half of the table. Cottee had twisted and turned to tuck away Potts' throw-in for the only goal. QPR's Karl Ready, five bookings in 10 games, body-checked Slater to earn his second yellow of the game.											
16	A	BLACKBURN		13	L	2-4	0-3	Dicks 75p, Slater 86	Miklosko	Breacker	Dicks	Potts	Rieper	Bishop*	Harkes^	Dowie	Cottee"	Williamson	Hughes	Hutch/Slat'r/Boogers
		2/12	*26,638*	*10*	20			*Shearer 3, 17, 65p, Newell 32*	*Flowers*	*Kenna*	*Le Saux*	*Batty*	*Hendry**	*Berg*	*Ripley*	*Sherwood*	*Shearer*	*Newell*	*Bohinen*	*Warhurst*
								Ref: K Burge	They love West Ham at Ewood. The Hammers always lose there, and they also defied Man U last May. Dicks returns from suspension. So careful is he not to get booked that Stuart Ripley enjoys more room than he could have expected, and is the source of all four Rovers goals.											
17	A	EVERTON		13	L	0-3	0-2		Miklosko !	Breacker	Dicks	Potts	Rieper	Bishop	Slater	Dowie	Cottee*	Williamson	Hughes	Rowland
		11/12	*31,778*	*11*	20			*Stuart 33, Unsworth 43p, Ebbrell 68*	*Southall*	*Jackson*	*Unsworth*	*Ebbrell*	*Watson*	*Short*	*Kanchelskis*	*Parkinson*	*Amokachi*	*Stuart*	*Limpar**	*Ferguson*
								Ref: M Reed	Miklosko is sent off for smashing Amokachi. Julian Dicks takes his jersey but can't save Unsworth's penalty. It was a day of returns. Cottee returned to the club for whom he scored 99 goals, and Duncan Ferguson returned to Everton from Barlinnie Prison. Dicks denied him a goal.											
18	H	SOUTHAMPTON		13	W	2-1	0-1	Cottee 80, Dowie 82	Miklosko	Potts	Dicks	Rieper	Martin*	Bishop	Moncur^	Dowie	Cottee	Williamson	Hughes	Breacker/Slater
		16/12	**18,501**	*15*	23			*Bishop 22 (og)*	*Beasant*	*Dodd*	*Benali*	*Magilton**	*Hall*	*Monkou*	*Le Tissier*	*Venison*	*Shipperley*	*Charlton*	*Oakley^*	*Maddison/Hughes*
								Ref: A Wilkie	It all seemed to be going wrong. Bishop had put through his own goal and Hammers still trailed with 10 minutes left. Foolish Saints had opted to protect their ill-gotten gains by surrendering possession outside their box. Dave Beasant kept out everything until the Hammers' final salvo.											
19	A	MIDDLESBROUGH		13	L	2-4	0-3	Cottee 80, Dicks 86 *[Hendrie 82]*	Miklosko	Breacker`	Dicks	Potts	Rieper	Bishop	Moncur*	Dowie	Cottee	Williamson	Hughes^	Rowland/Slater
		23/12	*28,640*	*5*	23			*Fjortoft 20, Cox 21, Morris 28,*	*Walsh*	*Cox*	*Morris*	*Vickers*	*Pearson*	*Whyte*	*Robson*	*Pollock*	*Fjortoft*	*Juninho*	*Hendrie*	
								Ref: S Dunn	High-flying Middlesbrough turn on the style and leave Hammers battered and demoralised. Juninho has set Teesside alight. The contest is over after half an hour, and Hammers are thankful Boro step off the gas. This is Boro's last win for three months, as they plummet down the league.											
20	A	MANCHESTER C		14	L	1-2	0-1	Dowie 74	**Finn**	Harkes	Dicks	Potts	Rieper	Bishop	Moncur	Slater	Dowie	Williamson*	Hughes	Hutchison
		1/1	*26,024*	*17*	23			*Quinn 21, 78*	*Immel*	*Summerbee*	*Brightwell*	*Curle*	*Symons*	*Brown*	*Lomas*	*Quinn*	*Rosler^*	*Flitcroft**	*Kinkladze*	*Ekelund/Phillips*
								Ref: M Reed	With Miklosko suspended and Sealey injured, Redknapp has to pitch in YTS signing Neil Finn, at 17 years and three days the Premiership's youngest ever player. Finn himself had hamstring trouble and was not to blame for City scoring twice in a match for the first time this season.											
21	A	LEEDS		14	L	0-2	0-1		Miklosko	Potts	Rowland*	Williamson	Rieper	Dicks	Moncur	Bishop	Cottee	Dowie	Hughes	Slater
		13/1	*30,472*	*9*	23			*Brolin 25, 62*	*Beaney*	*Kelly*	*Dorigo**	*Palmer*	*Wetherall*	*Ford*	*Brolin"*	*Wallace^*	*Chapman !*	*McAllister*	*Speed*	*Couzens/Gray/Harte*
								Ref: P Danson	Defeats are coming thick and fast, five from six games. A minute after disgruntled Tomas Brolin had put Leeds in front, Lee Chapman – back at Leeds after three years – clattered Rieper with his elbow and was expelled. Hammers last won at Leeds in 1978, on Alvin Martin's debut.											

No	Date		Att	Pos	Pt	F-A	H-T	Scorers, Times, and Referees	SQUAD	NUMBERS	IN	USE								subs used
22	H	MANCHESTER U		16	L	0-1	0-1		Miklosko	Brown	Dicks	Potts	Rieper	Bishop	Moncur	Dowie	Cottee	Williamson	Slater*	Rowland
	22/1		24,197	*2*	23			*Cantona 8*	*Schmeichel*	*Neville G*	*Irwin*	*Bruce*	*Sharpe*	*Neville P*	*Cantona*	*Keane*	*Cole**	*Butt !*	*Giggs*	*Beckham*
								Ref: S Lodge	In retrospect, this fiery match – with Nicky Butt expelled following a Dicks-Cole clash – enables United to reel in Newcastle. Alex Ferguson's team have won just twice in nine league games. Cantona's exquisite goal from an near-impossible angle sparks a six-game winning streak.											
23	H	COVENTRY		14	W	3-2	0-0	Rieper 46, Cottee 59, Dowie 85	Miklosko	Brown	Dicks	Potts	Rieper	Bishop	Moncur^	Dowie	Cottee*	Williamson	Hughes	Whitbread/**Lampard**
	31/1		18,884	*18*	26			*Dublin 62, Whelan 82*	*Ogrizovic*	*Pickering*	*Hall*	*Richardson**	*Shaw*	*Borrows*	*Telfer*	*Williams^*	*Dublin*	*Whelan*	*Salako*	*Ndlovu/Strachan*
								Ref: G Poll	The number of 'oohs' on the new video screen underlined a thrilling second half. Frank Lampard Jnr made his first appearance in Hammers' colours, and Gordon Strachan looked the best player on the pitch when he belatedly came on. Dowie won the game from Williamson's cross.											
24	H	NOTT'M FOREST		13	W	1-0	1-0	Slater 19	Miklosko	Brown	Dicks	Potts	Rieper	Bishop	Slater*	Dowie	Cottee^	Williamson	Hughes	Whitbread/**Dani**
	3/2		21,651	*9*	29				*Crossley*	*Lyttle*	*Phillips*	*Cooper*	*Chettle*	*B'rt-Williams*	*Campbell*	*Gemmill**	*Silenzi*	*Roy*	*Woan*	*Haaland*
								Ref: K Burge	Hectic end-to-end stuff that the purists hate but British fans love. The goal was as messy as the play. Williamson crossed, Cooper slashed and missed, and Slater shot past Crossley. Portuguese heart-throb Dani came on and tried to score from the halfway line. It was that kind of game.											
25	A	TOTTENHAM			W	1-0	1-0	Dani 4	Miklosko	Potts	Dicks	**Bilic**	Rieper	Bishop	Hughes^	Dowie	Dani*	Williamson	Rowland	Cottee/Harkes
	12/2		*29,781*		32				*Walker*	*Austin*	*Wilson*	*Campbell*	*Calderwood*	*Mabbutt*	*Fox*	*Dozzell*	*Armstrong*	*Sheringham*	*Rosenthal**	*Sinton*
								Ref: J Winter	Dean Austin needlessly concedes a corner from which Dani scores – a header from yards out. The chief puzzle was the dearth of goals, since both sides missed chances a-plenty. Dani will flatter to deceive, though Bilic was outstanding on his debut and will maintain his high standard.											
26	A	CHELSEA		12	W	2-1	0-1	Dicks 62, Williamson 72	Miklosko	Potts	Dicks	Bilic	Rieper	Bishop	Hughes	Dowie	Dani*	Williamson	Rowland	Cottee
	17/2		*25,252*	*10*	35			*Peacock 13*	*Hitchcock*	*Petrescu*	*Phelan*	*Duberry*	*Clarke*	*Lee*	*Gullit*	*Newton**	*Furlong*	*Peacock*	*Wise*	*Sinclair*
								Ref: G Willard	Julian Dicks is relishing his nice-boy image. He has not been booked for nine games and plays a stormer in central defence in Redknapp's revamped side. He even headed the equaliser. Chelsea's cause was not helped by losing Eddie Newton after five minutes with a broken leg.											
27	H	NEWCASTLE		13	W	2-0	1-0	Williamson 7, Cottee 82	Miklosko	Potts	Dicks	Bilic*	Rieper	Bishop	Hughes	Dowie	Cottee^	Williamson	Rowland	Harkes/Gordon
	21/2		23,843	*1*	38				*Srnicek*	*Barton*	*Beresford*	*Albert*	*Peacock*	*Howey*	*Asprilla*	*Beardsley*	*Ferdinand*	*Clark*	*Gillespie**	*Kitson*
								Ref: P Alcock	Newcastle start the match nine points clear of Man U, plus a game in hand. They have signed the Colombian Asprilla and he takes centre stage in this epic. He and Ferdinand hit a post, Newcastle dazzle throughout, but West Ham win their fifth game in a row with two fine breakaways.											
28	H	ARSENAL		11	L	0-1	0-1		Miklosko	Harkes*	Dicks	Potts	Rieper	Bishop	Hughes	Dowie	Cottee	Williamson	Rowland	Dani
	24/2		24,217	*6*	38			*Hartson 2*	*Seaman*	*Dixon*	*Winterburn*	*Hillier**	*Keown*	*Linighan*	*Parlour*	*Hartson*	*Merson*	*Bergkamp*	*Morrow*	*Platt*
								Ref: D Elleray	Hammers' winning run comes to a predictable end against Arsenal, who have a habit of winning at the Boleyn. John Harkes' errant back-pass fell to Merson, who set up John Hartson. Dicks then missed a penalty. Suffering from double-vision, his spot-kick lacked his usual venom.											
29	A	COVENTRY		11	D	2-2	2-2	Cottee 2, Rieper 22	Miklosko	Potts	Dicks	Bilic	Rieper	Bishop	Hughes	Dowie	Cottee*	Williamson	Rowland	Harkes
	2/3		*17,448*	*13*	39			*Salako 7, Whelan 15*	*Ogrizovic*	*Borrows*	*Burrows**	*Richardson*	*Shaw*	*Daish*	*Jess*	*Ndlovu*	*Dublin*	*Whelan*	*Salako*	*Williams*
								Ref: M Bodenham	Ron Atkinson has spent £13 million on his team. The game could have been 5-5 at half-time, and both managers made half-time changes to stem the haemorrhaging. Cottee's header was his 13th Hammers goal against Coventry. West Ham wasted three one-on-one opportunities.											
30	H	MIDDLESBROUGH		11	W	2-0	1-0	Dowie 2, Dicks 62p	Miklosko	Breacker	Dicks	Potts	Bilic	Bishop	Hughes	Dowie	Cottee*	Williamson	Rowland	**Dumitrescu**
	9/3		23,850	*13*	42				*Walsh*	*Morris"*	*Fleming*	*Cox*	*Pearson*	*Whyte*	*Hignett**	*Barmby*	*Fjortoft^*	*Mustoe*	*Kavanagh*	*Hendrie/Juninho/*
								Ref: M Reed (Boro's 3rd sub Branco)	Juninho was on the bench, jet-lagged from playing for Brazil. It took Dowie 67 seconds to tap in from six inches, after Gary Walsh botched a clearance. Cox inadvertently handled for a harsh penalty. Since beating West Ham on 23 December, Boro have taken one point from 11 games.											
31	A	NEWCASTLE		11	L	0-3	0-1		Miklosko	Potts	Dicks	Bilic	Rieper	Bishop*	Hughes	Dowie	Dumitrescu^	Williamson	Rowland	Breacker/Dani
	18/3		*36,331*	*1*	42			*Albert 21, Asprilla 55, Ferdinand 65*	*Srnicek*	*Barton**	*Beresford*	*Batty*	*Albert*	*Howie*	*Lee*	*Beardsey*	*Ferdinand*	*Ginola*	*Asprilla*	*Watson*
								Ref: S Lodge	Newcastle are irresistible, and Redknapp is brave and honest enough to admit it. But it is Keegan's first win in four games. Newcastle will lose their next two, and clearly they are there to be taken. West Ham are the only team not to score against Newcastle in this jittery six-game spell.											

No	Venue	Opponent	Att	Pos	Res/Pts	F-A	H-T	Scorers, Times, and Referees	1	2	3	4	5	6	7	8	9	10	11	subs used
32	H	MANCHESTER C		11	W	4-2	1-0	Dowie 21, 53, Dicks 83, Dani 84	Miklosko	Breacker	Dicks	Bilic	Rieper	Bishop	Hughes	Dowie	Dumitrescu*	Williamson	Rowland	Dani *[Mazzarelli]*
	23/3		24,017	*16*	45			*Quinn 76, 90*	*Immel*	*Summerbee"*	*Frontzeck^*	*Curle*	*Symons*	*Brightwell*	*Brown*	*Clough*	*Rosler**	*Lomas !*	*Kinkladze*	*Quinn/Hiley/*
								Ref: K Cooper	Both team-sheets were packed with foreigners, but the match was frenetically English. The match turned on 42 minutes, when Miklosko saved Curle's penalty. Dowie fired in two thumping headers from corners, Rosler missed open goals, and Lomas was sent off for two yellow cards.											
33	H	WIMBLEDON		11	D	1-1	1-1	Dicks 6	Miklosko	Breacker	Dicks	Bilic	Rieper	Bishop	Hughes	Dowie	Dani	Williamson	Rowland*	Slater
	6/4		20,462	*15*	46			*Jones 9*	*Sullivan*	*Ardley*	*Kimble*	*Jones*	*Blackwell*	*Perry*	*Gayle**	*Earle*	*Ekoku*	*Holdsworth*	*Clarke^*	*Goodman/Castledine*
								Ref: P Durkin	A power failure on the Underground delays kick-off. This is the first season since 1985-86 that West Ham will finish above Wimbledon in the league. Holdsworth forces two sharp shaves by Miklosko. Joe Kinnear summed up the game: 'West Ham's best player was 'wot's 'is name.'											
34	A	LIVERPOOL		11	L	0-2	0-2		Miklosko	Breacker	Dicks	Bilic	Rieper	Bishop	Hughes*	Dowie	Slater	Williamson	Rowland	Dani
	8/4		***40,326***	*3*	46			*Collymore 22, Barnes 38*	*James*	*McAteer*	*Bjornebye*	*Scales*	*Matteo*	*Thomas*	*McManam'n*	*Redknapp*	*Collymore*	*Barnes*	*Fowler*	
								Ref: P Alcock	Defeat at Coventry on Saturday has all but wrecked Liverpool's title chances, though that does not prevent the largest crowd to watch West Ham turning out. The previous Anfield game brought a 4-3 win over Newcastle, whose defeat at Blackburn tonight presents the title to Man U.											
35	H	BOLTON		11	W	1-0	1-0	Cottee 28	Miklosko	Breacker	Dicks	Bilic	Rieper	Bishop	Slater^	Dowie	Cottee	Williamson	Hughes*	Moncur/Rowland
	13/4		23,086	*20*	49				*Ward*	*Bergsson*	*Phillips*	*Curcic*	*Fairclough*	*Coleman*	*Sellars*	*Stubbs*	*Blake**	*McGinlay*	*Thompson*	*De Freitas*
								Ref: A Wilkie	Bolton have staged a late rally to avoid the drop, but this defeat makes it all but inevitable. They deserved better on the day. Bishop headed on to his own crossbar and Miklosko made two vital saves when strikers were clear. But Cottee's goal from Williamson's assist proved decisive.											
36	A	ASTON VILLA		11	D	1-1	0-1	Cottee 84	Miklosko	Breacker	Dicks	Potts*	Rieper	Bilic	Moncur	Dowie	Cottee	Williamson	Rowland	Dani
	17/4		*26,768*	*4*	50			*McGrath 27*	*Bosnich*	*Charles**	*Wright*	*Townsend*	*McGrath*	*Ehiogu*	*Taylor*	*Draper*	*Milosevic*	*Johnson*	*Yorke^*	*Scimeca/Joachim*
								Ref: S Dunn	Villa's Coca-Cola Cup win assure their place in Europe. West Ham have staved off the drop, so there was a lack of oomph in this match. Paul McGrath's superb volley was cancelled in the dying minutes when sub Dani's second touch set up Cottee. Villa's Gary Charles broke an ankle.											
37	A	QP RANGERS		11	L	0-3	0-0		Miklosko	Breacker	Dicks	Potts	Rieper	Bilic	Hughes	Moncur*	Cottee	Williamson	Rowland	**Watson**
	27/4		*18,828*	*19*	50			*Ready 60, Gallen 70, 79*	*Sommer*	*Ready*	*Brevett*	*Barker*	*Yeats*	*McDonald*	*Dichio*	*Wilkins*	*Hateley**	*Gallen*	*Sinclair*	*Charles*
								Ref: G Willard	Ray Wilkins' team had to win and hope other strugglers lost. Cottee wasted three early chances. Karl Ready's first league goal of the season opened the flood-gates but could not prevent QPR's relegation after 13 years in the top flight. Dani had failed to turn up for training and is out.											
38	H	SHEFFIELD WED		10	D	1-1	0-0	Dicks 72	Miklosko	Breacker	Dicks	Potts	Rieper	Bilic	Hughes	Dowie*	Cottee"	Williamson	Rowland^	Martin/L'pard/**Ferd'**
	5/5		23,790	*15*	51			*Newsome 89*	*Pressman*	*Atherton*	*Briscoe*	*Pembridge*	*Newsome*	*Walker*	*Degryse^*	*Blinker**	*Hirst*	*Hyde*	*Whittingham*	*Waddle/Humphreys*
	Home		Away					Ref: R Dilkes	Results elsewhere could still send Wednesday down unless they drew. Dicks' diving header was neutralised by Newsome's late header from Whittingham's cross, but it proved to be unnecessary. West Ham finish in the top half for the first time in 10 years. Alvin Martin's final match.											
	Average 22,340		26,449																	

Coca-Cola Cup

Match	Pos	Res	F-A	H-T	Scorers, Times, and Referees	SQUAD	NUMBERS	IN	USE								subs used
2:1 A BRISTOL ROV	19	W	1-0	1-0	Moncur 34	Miklosko	Breacker	Dicks	Potts	Martin	Bishop	Moncur	Dowie*	Cottee	Lazaridis	Slater^	Rieper/Williamson
20/9 *7,103*	*2:11*					*Parkin*	*Pritchard*	*Gurney*	*Browning*	*Wright*	*Tilson*	*Skinner*	*Miller*	*Stewart*	*Channing**	*Taylor*	*Wyatt*
					Ref: K Cooper	Rovers had lost two home games on the trot and showed little inner belief. Slater touched a short free-kick to Moncur, whose shot swerved into the top corner from 30 yards. Dicks – facing a disrepute charge – twice had headers cleared off the line. Still, the second leg looks comfortable.											
2:2 H BRISTOL ROV	16	W	3-0	0-0	Dicks 47p, Bishop 49, Cottee 75	Miklosko	Breacker	Dicks	Potts	Rieper	Bishop	Moncur	Dowie	Cottee	Slater	Hughes	
4/10 15,375	*2:11*					*Parkin*	*Pritchard*	*Gurney*	*Browning*	*Wright*	*Tilson*	*Sterling*	*Paul*	*Stewart*	*Skinner*	*Channing**	*Davis*
					Ref: R Gifford (Hammers win 4-0 on aggregate)	The longer this tie went on the less likelihood of Rovers springing an upset. Five minutes after half-time the outcome is effectively settled with two further Hammers goals. You can't keep Julian Dicks out of the news at the moment. He is either collecting cards or blasting penalties.											
3 A SOUTHAMPTON	13	L	1-2	1-1	Cottee 33	Miklosko	Potts	Dicks	Rieper	Martin	Bishop	Moncur	Dowie	Cottee	Slater	Hughes	
25/10 *11,059*	*17*				*Watson 4, Shipperley 79*	*Beasant*	*Dodd*	*Benali*	*Venison*	*Hall*	*Monkou*	*Le Tissier*	*Watson*	*Shipperley*	*Hughes*	*Heaney*	
					Ref: P Danson	Barry Venison has added steel to Dave Merrington's midfield. Four minutes into his Saints debut his wayward shot strikes Watson on the heel and wrong-foots Miklosko. Cottee spun to level from close in, but Neil Shipperley scuttled Hammers' hopes by heading in Jason Dodd's cross.											

FA Cup

Match	Pos	Res	F-A	H-T	Scorers, Times, and Referees	SQUAD	NUMBERS	IN	USE								subs used
3 H SOUTHEND	14	W	2-0	0-0	Moncur 58, Hughes 87	Miklosko	Harkes	Dicks	Potts	Rieper	Bishop	Moncur	Dowie	Cottee	Williamson	Hughes	
6/1 23,284	*1:7*					*Royce*	*Dublin*	*Powell*	*McNally*	*Bodley*	*Gridelet*	*Marsh*	*Byrne*	*Regis*	*Jones**	*Hails*	*Thomson*
					Ref: R Dilkes	Just 13 league places separated these teams, so well were Southend going in Div 1. But the Seasiders, with ex-Hammer Mike Marsh, created nothing and it was just a matter of time. Man of the match was young keeper Simon Royce. Dowie's effort was blocked and fell to Moncur.											
4 H GRIMSBY	10	D	1-1	1-1	Dowie 35	Miklosko	Potts	Dicks	Rieper	Whitbread	Bishop	Slater*	Dowie	Cottee	Williamson	Hughes	Lazaridis^/Rowland
7/2 22,030	*1:13*				*Laws 24*	*Crichton*	*McDermott*	*Croft*	*Laws*	*Lever*	*Groves*	*Childs*	*Shakespeare*	*Forrester*	*Woods**	*Bonetti^*	*Livingstone/Southall*
					Ref: G Willard	Grimsby, with just one win in 10, made a better fist of it than Southend. Former Italian star Ivano Bonetti set up player-manager Brian Laws for a breakaway goal. Dowie's header from Williamson's cross earned a replay, but fixture congestion is threatening West Ham's season.											
4R A GRIMSBY	10	L	0-3	0-1		Miklosko	Potts	Dicks	Rieper	Martin*	Bishop	Hughes	Dowie	Cottee	Williamson	Rowland^	Gordon/Harkes
14/2 *8,382*	*1:14*				*Childs 24, Woods 63, Forrester 89*	*Crichton*	*McDermott*	*Croft*	*Fickling*	*Lever*	*Groves*	*Childs**	*Shakespeare*	*Woods*	*Forrester*	*Southall*	*Livingstone*
					Ref: R Hart	Chelsea await the winners, but not even that prospect can fire the Hammers into life. Bonetti was out with a black eye from a plate flung at him by Brian Laws. At 0-2 Dale Gordon made his first appearance for two years. Grimsby's first home win over a top division team since 1936.											

		Home					Away					
	P	W	D	L	F	A	W	D	L	F	A	Pts
1 Manchester U	38	15	4	0	36	9	10	3	6	37	26	82
2 Newcastle	38	17	1	1	38	9	7	5	7	28	28	78
3 Liverpool	38	14	4	1	46	13	6	7	6	24	21	71
4 Aston Villa	38	11	5	3	32	15	7	4	8	20	20	63
5 Arsenal	38	10	7	2	30	16	7	5	7	19	16	63
6 Everton	38	10	5	4	35	19	7	5	7	29	25	61
7 Blackburn	38	14	2	3	44	19	4	5	10	17	28	61
8 Tottenham	38	9	5	5	26	19	7	8	4	24	19	61
9 Nott'm Forest	38	11	6	2	29	17	4	7	8	21	37	58
10 WEST HAM	38	9	5	5	25	21	5	4	10	18	31	51
11 Chelsea	38	7	7	5	30	22	5	7	7	16	22	50
12 Middlesbrough	38	8	3	8	27	27	3	7	9	8	23	43
13 Leeds	38	8	3	8	21	21	4	4	11	19	36	43
14 Wimbledon	38	5	6	8	27	33	5	5	9	28	37	41
15 Sheffield Wed	38	7	5	7	30	31	3	5	11	18	30	40
16 Coventry	38	6	7	6	21	23	2	7	10	21	37	38
17 Southampton	38	7	7	5	21	18	2	4	13	13	34	38
18 Manchester C	38	7	7	5	21	19	2	4	13	12	39	38
19 QP Rangers	38	6	5	8	25	26	3	1	15	13	31	33
20 Bolton	38	5	4	10	16	31	3	1	15	23	40	29
	760	186	98	96	580	408	96	98	186	408	580	1042

Odds & ends

Double wins: (1) Bolton.
Double losses: (3) Leeds, Manchester U, Arsenal.

Won from behind: (3) Leeds (h), Southampton (h), Chelsea (a).
Lost from in front: (0).

High spots: Five successive league wins from 31 January.
Just one defeat in nine league games from 23 September.

Low spots: Terrible start, no wins in the first six league games.
Six defeats out of seven league games from 2 December.
Losing at First Division Grimsby in FA Cup.

Hammer of the Year: Julian Dicks.
Ever-presents: (0).
Hat-tricks: (0).
Leading scorer: (12) Tony Cottee.

	Appearances						Goals			
	Lge	*Sub*	LC	*Sub*	FAC	*Sub*	Lge	LC	FAC	Tot
Allen, Martin	**3**						1			1
Bilic, Slaven	**13**									
Bishop, Ian	**35**		3		3		1	1		2
Boere, Jeroen		*1*								
Boogers, Marco		*4*								
Breacker, Tim	**19**	*3*	2							
Brown, Kenny	**3**									
Cottee, Tony	**30**	*3*	3		3		10	2		12
Dani	**3**	*6*					2			2
Dicks, Julian	**34**		3		3		10	1		11
Dowie, Iain	**33**		3		3		8		1	9
Dumitrescu, Ilie	**2**	*1*								
Ferdinand, Rio		*1*								
Finn, Neil	**1**									
Gordon, Dale		*1*				*1*				
Harkes, John	**6**	*5*			1	*1*				
Hughes, Michael	**28**		2		3				1	1
Hutchison, Don	**8**	*4*					2			2
Lampard, Frank		*2*								
Lazaridis, Stan	**2**	*2*	1			*1*				
Martin, Alvin	**10**	*4*	2		1					
Miklosko, Ludek	**36**		3		3					
Moncur, John	**19**	*1*	3		1			1	1	2
Potts, Steve	**34**		3		3					
Rieper, Marc	**35**	*1*	2	*1*	3		2			2
Rowland, Keith	**19**	*4*			1	*1*				
Sealey, Les	**1**	*1*								
Slater, Robbie	**16**	*6*	3		1		2			2
Watson, Mark		*1*								
Whitbread, Adrian		*2*			1					
Williamson, Danny	**28**	*1*		*1*	3		4			4
(own-goals)							1			1
31 players used	**418**	***54***	**33**	***2***	**33**	***4***	**43**	**5**	**3**	**51**

No	Date		Att	Pos	Pt	F-A	H-T	Scorers, Times, and Referees	SQUAD NUMBERS IN USE											subs used
1	A	ARSENAL			L	0-2	0-2		Miklosko	Breacker	Dicks	Rieper	Bilic*	Williamson	Hughes	Rowland^	Lampard"	Dowie	Jones	Ferdinand/Laz/Slater
	17/8		*38,056*		0			*Hartson 27, Bergkamp 40p*	*Seaman*	*Dixon*	*Winterburn*	*Bould*	*Merson*	*Bergkamp**	*Linighan*	*Keown*	*Parlour*	*Hartson^*	*Morrow*	*Wright/Dickov*
								Ref: P Durkin	Super weather; super pitch; tedious game. Bruce Rioch has left Highbury; Arsene Wenger is coming, and caretaker boss Stewart Houston enjoys a quick win. Rieper handled Dixon's cross for the penalty. Steve Jones, back from Bournemouth, squandered three second-half chances.											
2	H	COVENTRY			D	1-1	0-1	Rieper 74	Miklosko	Breacker*	Dicks	Rieper	Bilic	Williamson	Hughes	Lazaridis	Slater	Dowie	Jones^	**Futre/Bowen**
	21/8		21,680		1			*McAllister 12*	*Ogrizovic*	*Shaw*	*Burrows*	*Daish*	*Jess**	*McAllister*	*Salako*	*Telfer*	*Genaux^*	*Dublin*	*Ducros*	*Williams/Borrows*
								Ref: S Dunn	Paulo Futre made his long-awaited entrance after 53 minutes and lit the fuse for the Hammers' revival. Dicks' free-kick was half-cleared for Rieper to level. Earlier, Regis Genaux had crossed for £3 million Gary McAllister to head his first Coventry goal since signing from Leeds.											
3	H	SOUTHAMPTON		11	W	2-1	0-1	Hughes 73, Dicks 81p	Miklosko	Slater*	Dicks	Rieper^	Bilic	Williamson	Hughes	Lazaridis"	Futre	Dowie	Bowen	Braeck/**Radu/Dumit**
	24/8		21,227	*17*	4			*Heaney 19*	*Beasant*	*Dodd*	*Magilton*	*Le Tissier*	*Shipperley**	*Maddison^*	*Heaney"*	*Charlton*	*Neilson*	*Oakley*	*Dryden*	*Potter/B'nali!/Wats'n*
								Ref: D Elleray	Man of the match is referee David Elleray. First he gives the Hammers a penalty when Dryden topples Dumitrescu. Seconds later, he sends off Benali for mowing down Futre, who looked a class apart. Hammers had fallen behind when Bilic and Dicks got in a tizzy. A priceless first win.											
4	A	MIDDLESBROUGH		15	L	**1-4**	0-2	Hughes 57 *[Stamp 81]*	Miklosko	Breacker	Dicks	Potts*	Bilic	Williamson	Hughes	Lazaridis^	Futre	Raducioiu"	Bowen	Dowie/Dumit/L'pard
	4/9		*30,060*	*9*	4			*Emerson 12, Mustoe 28, Ravanelli 52,*	*Miller*	*Whyte*	*Vickers*	*Whelan*	*Cox*	*Emerson*	*Mustoe*	*Fleming*	*Juninho**	*Ravanelli*	*Barmby^*	*Stamp/Moore*
								Ref: P Jones	West Ham are overwhelmed at the Riverside by the dazzling talents of Emerson, Juninho and Fabrizio Ravanelli, who kept up his goal-a-match sequence since his arrival. But West Ham's goal was as good as any, Michael Hughes ramming the ball into the top corner from 25 yards.											
5	A	SUNDERLAND		16	D	0-0	0-0		Miklosko	Breacker	Dicks	Rieper	Bilic	Williamson	Hughes	Dumitrescu*	Futre^	Raducioiu"	Bowen	Rowland/Ferd/Jones
	8/9		*18,642*	*10*	5				*Coton*	*Kubicki*	*Ord*	*Melville*	*Scott*	*Agnew**	*Bracewell*	*Ball*	*Gray*	*Quinn*	*Stewart*	*Russell*
								Ref: G Poll	An apology of a Sunday football match, with Hammers mostly to blame. Redknapp knows who to blame, for he hauls off all three of his Latin forwards, none of whom showed appetite for a scrap. The only bonus was the point earned, following the hiding at the Riverside in midweek.											
6	H	WIMBLEDON		17	L	0-2	0-0		Miklosko	Breacker*	Dicks	Rieper	Bilic	Williamson	Hughes	Dumitrescu^	Futre"	Dowie	Bowen	Laz/Moncur/Cottee
	14/9		21,294	*8*	5			*Clarke 59, Ekoku 86*	*Sullivan*	*Cunningham*	*Perry*	*McAllister*	*Thatcher*	*Ardley*	*Jones*	*Earle*	*Gayle*	*Ekoku*	*Goodman**	*Clarke*
								Ref: R Dilkes	The Dons are on the march. Three losses are followed by three wins. This match opened Harry's eyes to the futility of fancy foreigners coming up against home-grown talents like Perry and Thatcher. 'I want my defenders to defend like they do,' he sighed. Clarke miscued the first goal.											
7	A	NOTT'M FOREST		13	W	2-0	1-0	Bowen 45, Hughes 54	**Mautone**	Bowen	Dicks	Rieper !	Bilic	Lazaridis	Hughes	Bishop*	Moncur	Dowie	Cottee	Lampard
	21/9		*23,352*	*16*	8				*Crossley*	*Lyttle*	*Pearce*	*Cooper*	*Phillips*	*Saunders*	*Woan*	*Jerkan**	*Allen*	*Haarland*	*Roy*	*Lee*
								Ref: G Willard	Before kick-off both teams had won just once. Mark Bowen heads in Lazaridis' cross at the far post. The game ignites early in the second half. Rieper goes off for a professional foul on Brian Roy. Within seconds Cottee – making his first start of the season – shoots and Hughes scores.											
8	H	LIVERPOOL		15	L	1-2	1-1	Bilic 15	Miklosko	Breacker	Dicks	Rieper	Bilic	Bowen*	Hughes	Bishop	Moncur	Dowie	Cottee^	Porfirio/Dumitrescu
	29/9		**25,064**	*1*	8			*Collymore 3, Thomas 55*	*James*	*Scales**	*Matteo*	*Babb*	*McAteer*	*McManam'n*	*Thomas*	*Barnes*	*Bjornebye*	*Berger^*	*Collymore"*	*R'uddock/Jones/*
								Ref: K Burge (Liverpool's 3rd sub Redknapp)	Unbeaten Liverpool stretch their winning sequence to seven, despite the absence of the injured Fowler and the withdrawal after 20 minutes of Collymore. He had turned Rieper to score after 135 seconds. Bilic headed in Hughes's corner. McAteer and Jamie Redknapp set up the winner.											
9	A	EVERTON		16	L	1-2	0-1	Dicks 86p	Miklosko	Bowen	Dicks	Potts*	Bilic	Rowland	Hughes	Bishop^	Moncur	Dowie	Porfirio	Raducioiu/Dumitres
	12/10		*36,571*	*9*	8			*Stuart 14, Speed 78*	*Southall*	*Barrett*	*Short*	*Unsworth*	*Hinchcliffe*	*Kanchelskis*	*Ebbrell**	*Parkinson^*	*Speed*	*Stuart*	*Branch*	*Hottiger/Grant*
								Ref: G Barber	Not a good advert for the Premiership. The first half offered little apart from Hinchcliffe's daisy-cutter and Stuart's conversion. Hammers only got to grips once they were two down. Hinchcliffe felled Porfirio for Dicks to smite a penalty. Afterwards, the gods kept Everton's goal intact.											
10	H	LEICESTER		13	W	1-0	0-0	Moncur 78	Miklosko	Bowen*	Dicks	Rieper	Bilic	Porfirio	Hughes	Bishop	Moncur	Dowie	Raducioiu^	Breacker/Lazaridis
	19/10		22,285	*14*	11				*Keller*	*Grayson*	*Whitlow*	*Watts*	*Walsh!*	*Izzet*	*Lennon*	*Taylor**	*Heskey*	*Prior*	*Marshall^*	*Parker/Claridge*
								Ref: M Riley	'I thought my team desperately unlucky' groaned Martin O'Neill. City had shown plenty of pluck. Walsh's 87th-minute dismissal (his 12th overall) for upending Miklosko, didn't help either. Porfirio's acceleration set up Moncur's side-footed winner. Cottee has gone to Malaysia.											

No		Date / Opponent	Att	Pos	Pts	F-A	H-T	Scorers, Times, and Referees	1	2	3	4	5	6	7	8	9	10	11	subs used
11	H	BLACKBURN		10	W	2-1	0-1	Porfirio 77, Berg 85 (og)	Miklosko	Bowen*	Dicks	Rieper	Bilic	Lazaridis	Hughes	Bishop	Moncur^	Dowie	Porfirio"	Braeck/Futre/L'pard
		26/10	23,947	*20*	14			*Berg 9*	*Flowers*	*Kenna*	*Sherwood*	*Le Saux**	*Wilcox*	*Marker*	*Fenton*	*McKinlay*	*Berg*	*Donis^*	*Flitcroft*	*Croft/Ripley*
								Ref: M Reed	Manager Ray Harford had quit in midweek, but Rovers welcomed back Le Saux after a long injury. They comfortably held their lead for over an hour. But then Futre came on to lift spirits. Dowie laid on the equaliser for Porfirio. Berg deflected Lazaridis' cross for a flattering winner.											
12	A	TOTTENHAM		12	L	0-1	0-0		Miklosko	Breacker	Dicks	Rieper	Bilic	Lazaridis	Hughes	Bishop	Moncur*	Dowie	Porfirio	Futre
		2/11	*32,999*	*8*	14			*Armstrong 67*	*Walker*	*Edinburgh*	*Howells*	*Calderwood*	*Nielsen*	*Sheringham*	*Armstrong*	*Wilson*	*Campbell*	*Carr*	*Allen**	*Rosenthal*
								Ref: J Winter	Spurs contrived just one chance throughout the 90 minutes, and with the unwitting intervention of Bilic – letting Neilsen's pass roll through his legs – they would have been denied that. Bilic nearly atoned, striking the post in the last minute. Redknapp: 'I don't know how we lost.'											
13	A	NEWCASTLE		13	D	1-1	1-0	Rowland 23	Miklosko	Breacker	Dicks	Potts	Bilic	Rowland	Hughes	Bishop	Moncur	Dowie	Raducioiu*	Futre
		16/11	*36,552*	*1*	15			*Beardsley 83*	*Srnicek*	*Elliott**	*Albert*	*Peacock*	*Gillespie^*	*Lee*	*Batty*	*Beardsley*	*Ginola*	*Ferdinand"*	*Asprilla*	*Beresford/Watson/*
								Ref: P Danson (Newcastle's 3rd sub Clark)	Newcastle lead the table, but consider two points were tossed away following Hammers' stubborn rearguard action. It could have been three. Breacker dispossessed Ginola to cross for Rowland at the far post. Beardsley shimmied past defenders before scoring his 200th league goal.											
14	H	DERBY		13	D	1-1	1-1	Bishop 17	Miklosko	Breacker	Dicks	Potts	Bilic	Lazaridis*	Hughes	Bishop	Moncur	Dowie	Porfirio	Futre
		23/11	24,576	*11*	16			*Sturridge 43*	*Hoult*	*Yates*	*McGrath*	*Rowett*	*Laursen**	*Flynn*	*Asanovic*	*Powell D*	*Powell C*	*Ward*	*Sturridge*	*Carsley*
								Ref: S Lodge	Two of the Premiership's lowest scoring teams were seldom likely to bust the net more than once apiece. More graft than skill on show, other than when Porfirio and Asanovic were in possession. Bishop made and scored a cracking opener, but Dean Sturridge's volley flew in off Potts.											
15	A	SHEFFIELD WED		14	D	0-0	0-0		Miklosko	Breacker	Dicks	Rieper	Bilic	Lampard	Hughes*	Bishop	Moncur	Dowie	Rowland	Lazaridis
		30/11	*22,321*	*10*	17				*Pressman*	*Nolan**	*Atherton*	*Walker*	*Briscoe^*	*Whittingham*	*Carbone*	*Pembridge*	*Hyde*	*Booth*	*Trustfull"*	*Oakes/Nicol/*
								Ref: P Durkin (Wednesday's 3rd sub Humphreys)	Hammers are still reeling from the Stockport debacle. Hammers supporters aren't too impressed by this dreary performance either. Yet with both Owls full-backs injured and subbed before half-time, West Ham might have chased a rare win. Hughes and Andy Booth each hit the bar.											
16	H	ASTON VILLA		15	L	0-2	0-1		Miklosko	Breacker*	Dicks	Rieper	Bilic	Rowland^	Hughes	Bishop	Moncur	Dowie	Raducioiu	Bowen/Lazaridis
		4/12	**19,105**	*5*	17			*Ehiogu 38, Yorke 74*	*Oakes*	*Ehiogu*	*Scimeca*	*Staunton*	*Nelson*	*Townsend*	*Taylor*	*Draper*	*Wright*	*Yorke*	*Milosevic*	
								Ref: M Riley	It was in the air that West Ham lost this match. Both Villa goals came from straightforward headers from corner-kicks, and Rieper and Bilic have no excuses. Dwight Yorke's was his eighth goal in nine games. Poor Dowie has not scored in 20 in the league, and was denied by Oakes.											
17	H	MANCHESTER U		14	D	2-2	0-0	Raducioiu 78, Dicks 80p	Miklosko	Bowen	Dicks	Rieper	Bilic*	Rowland^	Hughes	Bishop	Moncur	Dowie	Dumitrescu	Potts/Raducioiu
		8/12	25,045	*6*	18			*Solskjaer 54, Beckham 75*	*Schmeichel*	*Johnsen*	*May*	*Pallister*	*Irwin*	*Poborsky**	*Beckham*	*McClair*	*Giggs*	*Cantona*	*Solskjaer*	*Neville P*
								Ref: P Jones	United are on a high after midweek glory in Vienna. West Ham had fallen 0-2 behind to Beckham's delightful chip and Upton Park was getting restless. Then Raducioiu spun away from Johnsen to pull a goal back. Schmeichel then sent Hughes into orbit and Dicks' penalty was a blur.											
18	A	CHELSEA		15	L	1-3	1-3	Porfirio 11	Miklosko	Bowen	Dicks	Rieper	Bilic	Rowland*	Hughes	Bishop^	Moncur"	Porfirio	**Newell**	Radu/L'pard/W'mson
		21/12	*28,315*	*8*	18			*Hughes 6, 35, Zola 10*	*Grodas*	*Clarke*	*Gullit*	*Duberry*	*Petrescu*	*Burley**	*Newton*	*Di Matteo*	*Clement^*	*Zola*	*Hughes*	*Sinclair/Myers*
								Ref: A Wilkie	Not many players make Julian Dicks look foolish, but Zola's nutmeg *en route* to making it 0-2 did exactly that. Within seconds Porfirio halves the deficit, only for Mark Hughes to hammer No 3. Foolish or not, Dicks was West Ham's best player. His team-mates had nowhere to hide.											
19	H	SUNDERLAND		16	W	2-0	1-0	Bilic 37, Raducioiu 90	Miklosko	Bowen	Dicks	Rieper	Bilic	Williamson	Hughes	Bishop	Moncur*	Porfirio	Newell^	Lampard/Raducioiu
		28/12	24,077	*13*	21				*Perez*	*Hall*	*Melville*	*Ord*	*Kubicki*	*Rae*	*Bracewell*	*Agnew*	*Smith**	*Russell^*	*Kelly*	*Alston/Bridges*
								Ref: R Dilkes	Flu keeps Harry Redknapp in bed and denies him the pleasure of seeing West Ham's first win in two months. Bilic produced the game's two outstanding moments, diving to head the Hammers in front, and forcing the save of the game from Miklosko. Raducioiu scores a farewell goal.											
20	H	NOTT'M FOREST		16	L	0-1	0-1		Miklosko	Bowen*	Dicks	Rieper	Bilic	Williamson	Hughes	Bishop^	Porfirio	Raducioiu	Newell"	Potts/L'pard/Jones
		1/1	22,358	*19*	21			*Campbell 38*	*Crossley*	*Lyttle*	*Blath'rwick**	*Chettle*	*Pearce*	*Clough*	*Haaland*	*Cooper*	*Woan*	*Saunders*	*Campbell^*	*Phillips/Gemmill*
								Ref: P Durkin	Having dumped Forest twice this season, Hammers find themselves outplayed on an icy pitch. Half-time was shortened to 10 minutes. Stuart Pearce has taken over from Frank Clark and injected fizz into his team, who won more comfortably than the score suggests and climb to 19th.											
21	A	LIVERPOOL		17	D	0-0	0-0		Miklosko	Breacker	Dicks	Rieper	Bilic	Williamson*	Hughes	Bishop	Moncur	Porfirio^	Jones"	Potts/Newell/Laz'dis
		11/1	*40,102*	*1*	22				*James*	*Matteo*	*Ruddock**	*Babb^*	*McAteer*	*Thomas*	*Bjornebye*	*Barnes"*	*McManam'n*	*Fowler*	*Berger*	*Carragher/Collymore/*
								Ref: J Winter (Liverpool's 3rd sub Kennedy)	Liverpool still top the league, but injuries forced them to reshuffle. At one stage Michael Thomas played as centre-half. Though the game died on its feet before the finish, the first half saw the woodwork struck four times. Liverpool won that contest 3-1, Breacker the unlucky Hammer.											

No	Date	Att	Pos	Pt	F-A	H-T	Scorers, Times, and Referees	SQUAD	NUMBERS	IN	USE								subs used
22	H LEEDS		18	L	0-2	0-0		Miklosko	Breacker	Dicks	Rieper	Bilic	Williamson	Hughes	Bishop	Lazaridis*	Jones	Newell	Porfirio
	20/1	19,441	*11*	22			*Kelly 53, Bowyer 70*	*Martyn*	*Molenaar*	*Wetherall*	*Radebe*	*Kelly*	*Jackson*	*Palmer*	*Bowyer*	*Halle*	*Deane*	*Rush*	
							Ref: G Poll	Lee Bowyer was born three miles from Upton Park, but was snapped up by Charlton. He chested and volleyed Leeds' second, to add to Kelly's free-kick which flew down off the bar and in off Miklosko's head. Hammers seldom created anything, though Bilic hit the bar from 30 yards.											
23	H ARSENAL		18	L	1-2	0-1	Rose 63 (og)	Miklosko	Breacker	Dicks	Rieper	Bilic	Williamson	Hughes	Rowland*	Moncur^	Porfirio	Newell	Jones/Lampard
	29/1	24,382	*2*	22			*Parlour 8, Wright 67*	*Seaman*	*Dixon*	*Rose"*	*Adams*	*Bould*	*Winterburn*	*Parlour*	*Vieira*	*Hughes**	*Wright^*	*Merson*	*Morrow/Hartson/*
							Ref: M Bodenham (Arsenal's 3rd sub Marshall)	One win in 16 games. Afterwards demonstrators staged a sit-in against the board. West Ham had been overwhelmed, trailing to Parlour's low strike and needing the bar to keep out Merson's sweet chip. No sooner had Michael Rose turned in Bilic's header, than Merson set up Wright.											
24	A BLACKBURN		18	L	1-2	0-2	Ferdinand 64	Sealey	Breacker	Dicks	Rieper	Bilic	Williamson	Hughes	Bishop	Rowland*	Jones^	Newell	Lazaridis/Ferdinand
	1/2	*21,994*	*13*	22			*Gallacher 36, Sutton 39*	*Flowers*	*Kenna*	*Sherwood*	*Hendry*	*Le Saux*	*Gallacher*	*Sutton*	*Wilcox**	*McKinlay*	*Berg*	*Flitcroft*	*Donis*
							Ref: A Wilkie	The writing is on the wall and West Ham seem to be spiralling out of the Premiership. The score flattered the Hammers, Gallacher scoring from 25 yards and Sutton heading his 11th goal of the season. Rio Ferdinand, on at half-time, struck a beauty out of nothing to bring hope.											
25	A DERBY		18	L	0-1	0-0		Miklosko	Breacker	Dicks	Rieper*	Potts	Williamson	Rowland^	Bishop	Ferdinand	**Hartson**	**Kitson**	Porfirio/Lampard
	15/2	*18,057*	*13*	22			*Asanovic 53p*	*Hoult*	*Rowett*	*McGrath*	*Stimac*	*Carsley*	*van der Laan*	*Trollope*	*Powell C*	*Dailly*	*Sturridge*	*Asanovic*	
							Ref: G Ashby	Redknapp splashes out £6 million on a new strike force. The result? No goals and a booking for Hartson that brings a suspension. Ferdinand felled Asanovic for the penalty. West Ham were denied two themselves. At half-time a Derby fan proposed to his beloved in the centre circle.											
26	H TOTTENHAM		17	W	4-3	3-2	Dicks 21, 72p, Kitson 22, Hartson 38	Miklosko	Breacker	Dicks	Ferdinand	Potts	Bowen	Hughes	Bishop	Moncur	Hartson	Kitson*	Dowie
	24/2	23,998	*11*	25			*Sheringh'm 8, Anderton 29, Howells 53*	*Walker*	*Austin*	*Calderwood*	*Campbell*	*Carr*	*Anderton*	*Howells**	*Sinton^*	*Wilson*	*Sheringham*	*Iversen*	*Rosenthal/Nielsen*
							Ref: G Willard	Match of the season, played in howling wind and rain. On form, the two worst teams in the league. Both Hammers new boys leave their mark, as does never-say-die Dicks with the decisive penalty, which Walker wisely evades. Redknapp's verdict on the game: 'No, I did not enjoy it'.											
27	A LEEDS		18	L	0-1	0-0		Miklosko	Breacker*	Dicks	Ferdinand	Bilic	Bowen^	Hughes !	Bishop"	Moncur	Dowie	Kitson	**Omoy'**/R'land/L'pard
	1/3	*30,575*	*9*	25			*Sharpe 47*	*Martyn*	*Radebe*	*Halle*	*Wetherall*	*Molenaar*	*Bowyer**	*Rush*	*Sharpe*	*Harte*	*Yeboah*	*Deane*	*Palmer*
							Ref: P Jones	George Graham's team have stopped leaking daft goals, but Redknapp's have not. Dicks and Miklosko dither to present Lee Sharpe with the winner. Hughes is sent off after 78 minutes for kicking Radebe. Southampton and Forest both won away, dumping Hammers back in the mire.											
28	H CHELSEA		17	W	3-2	0-1	Dicks 55p, Kitson 68, 90	Miklosko	Breacker	Dicks	Ferdinand*	Bilic	Potts	Hughes	Bishop^	Moncur	Dowie	Kitson	W'son"/L'p'rd/P'rfirio
	12/3	24,502	*8*	28			*Vialli 26, Hughes 87*	*Colgan*	*Sinclair*	*Clarke*	*Johnsen*	*Petrescu**	*Burley*	*Wise*	*Hughes P*	*Minto*	*Zola*	*Vialli*	*Hughes M*
							Ref: K Burge	For 45 minutes West Ham were inept, with Gullit's Chelsea leading through Vialli's breakaway goal. An iffy penalty, when Sinclair tackled Porfirio, levels the scores. Super goals by Kitson and Mark Hughes make it 2-2. Then Kitson brushes Dowie's header past debutant Colgan.											
29	A ASTON VILLA		17	D	0-0	0-0		Miklosko	Breacker	Dicks	Potts	Bilic	Lampard*	Lazaridis	Bishop	Moncur	Hartson	Kitson	Ferdinand
	15/3	*35,992*	*6*	29				*Bosnich*	*Nelson*	*Wright*	*Southgate*	*Ehiogu*	*Hughes*	*Townsend*	*Taylor*	*Draper**	*Yorke*	*Joachim^*	*Hendrie/Johnson*
							Ref: D Elleray	Mark Bosnich is the main reason why the Hammers failed to score, denying both Hartson and Kitson. West Ham also thought they were denied a clear-cut penalty. Frank Lampard Jnr breaks a leg. Julian Dicks is booked for dissent and will miss the crunch match with Middlesbrough.											
30	A WIMBLEDON		16	D	1-1	0-1	Lazaridis 89	Miklosko	Breacker	Dicks	Rieper	Bilic	Potts*	Ferdinand	Bishop^	Moncur	Hartson	Kitson	Porfirio/Lazaridis
	18/3	*15,771*	*8*	30			*Harford 19*	*Sullivan*	*Cunningham*	*Kimble*	*Perry*	*Blackwell*	*Jones*	*Earle*	*Leonhardsen*	*Ekoku**	*Harford*	*Gayle*	*Holdsworth*
							Ref: J Winter	The new look Hammers are doing the business at home, but were seconds away from a fourth away blank when substitute Lazaridis fired back Gayle's headed clearance. Hartson and Leonhardsen both hit the woodwork, while Vinnie Jones missed a penalty when Breacker held Gayle.											
31	A COVENTRY		15	W	3-1	2-1	Hartson 27, 49, Ferdinand 34	Miklosko	Breacker*	Dicks	Rieper	Bilic	Potts	Ferdinand^	Bishop"	Moncur	Hartson	Kitson	R'land/Dowie/Porfirio
	22/3	*22,291*	*18*	33			*Rieper 9 (og)*	*Ogrizovic*	*Breen*	*Dublin*	*Shaw*	*Telfer*	*McAllister*	*Williams*	*Richardson*	*Hall**	*Whelan^*	*Huckerby*	*Ndlovu/Burrows*
							Ref: M Reed	Coventry began well, aided by Rieper's inadvertent header into the top corner. But then - to manager Strachan's chagrin - they stop playing the ball down the channels and West Ham wrestle the initiative. Hartson scores two neat goals. It is 11 points from six games. Championship form.											

No	Venue	Opponent	Pos	Res	F-A	H-T	Scorers, Times, and Referees	1	2	3	4	5	6	7	8	9	10	11	subs used
32	H	MIDDLESBROUGH	16	D	0-0	0-0		Miklosko	Potts	**Hall**	Rieper	Bilic	**Lomas**	Lazaridis*	Bishop	Hughes	Hartson	Kitson	Porfirio
	9/4	23,988	*18*	34				*Schwarzer**	*Fleming*	*Festa*	*Vickers*	*Kinder*	*Blackmore*	*Emerson*	*Mustoe*	*Moore^*	*Juninho*	*Ravanelli*	*Roberts/Beck*
							Ref: P Jones	Richard Hall and Steve Lomas play their first matches, while the suspended Dicks misses his first of the season. In spite of Boro's galaxy of stars the game splutters but never explodes. The Hammers fail to create a single worthwhile chance. Boro win on points, but not on goals.											
33	A	SOUTHAMPTON	17	L	0-2	0-2		Miklosko	Potts	Hall	Rieper*	Bilic	Lomas	Rowland^	Bishop"	Hughes	Hartson	Kitson	Dowie/Laz/Porfirio
	12/9	***15,244***	*16*	34			*Evans 13, Berkovic 36*	*Taylor*	*Dodd !*	*Lundekvam*	*Van Gobbel*	*Benali*	*Slater*	*Magilton*	*Berkovic**	*Evans*	*Oakley^*	*Ostenstad*	*Neilson/Dryden*
							Ref: S Dunn	First Roker, now the Dell. The press are scathing. The *Sunday Telegraph* says West Ham are disgraceful, contemptible, ignominious, pathetic. Magilton missed a penalty and Dodd was sent off on 44 minutes for a pro foul on Hartson. The result is Saints' first home win since December.											
34	H	EVERTON	18	D	2-2	2-0	Kitson 10, 32	Miklosko	Potts	Hall	Ferdinand	Bilic	Lomas	Porfirio*	Moncur^	Hughes	Hartson	Kitson	Rieper/Bishop
	19/4	24,525	*11*	35			*Branch 78, Ferguson 90*	*Southall*	*Barrett*	*Unsworth*	*Watson*	*Stuart*	*Speed*	*Thomsen*	*Ball**	*Dunne*	*Branch*	*Ferguson*	*Barmby*
							Ref: P Alcock	Crisis! Porfirio goes down, but Kitson refuses Hartson's offer to clinch his hat-trick from the spot. Hartson had been nominated. Kitson relents, but his shot is weak. At the death Miklosko misses Barmby's free-kick, Ferguson hooks in. Then a corner flies off a post into Southall's arms.											
35	A	LEICESTER	16	W	1-0	0-0	Moncur 75	Miklosko	Potts	Hall	Ferdinand	Rieper	Lomas	Porfirio*	Moncur	Hughes	Hartson	Kitson^	Rowland/Dowie
	23/4	*20,327*	*14*	38				*Keller*	*Grayson*	*Prior*	*Elliott*	*Walsh*	*Guppy**	*Lennon*	*Parker*	*Izzet^*	*Claridge*	*Heskey*	*Marshall/Campbell*
							Ref: R Dilkes / G Hegley	Little football was played, but that was hardly surprising. Nor were the 10 bookings. Dilkes dished out four in the first half, then collided with Moncur and was replaced. Moncur's goal, at the second attempt, was his second of the season, and his second winning goal against Leicester.											
36	H	SHEFFIELD WED	15	W	**5-1**	3-0	Kitson 5, 13, 89, Hartson 30, 67	Miklosko	Potts	Hall	Ferdinand	Bilic*	Lomas^	Porfirio	Moncur	Lazaridis"	Hartson	Kitson	Rieper/**Boylan**/Bishop
	3/5	24,960	*7*	41			*Carbone 82*	*Pressman*	*Nicol**	*Walker*	*Stefanovic*	*Nolan*	*Whitt'gh'm^*	*Atherton*	*Pembridge*	*Carbone*	*Booth*	*Hirst !*	*Oakes/Blinker*
							Ref: M Riley	No one was so full of praise for West Ham as Wednesday boss David Pleat. He managed Hartson at Luton and Kitson at Leicester. Hartson's power and Kitson's stealth overwhelm the Owls. On 58 minutes Hirst elbowed Ferdinand and was sent off. Rio got a yellow for retaliation.											
37	H	NEWCASTLE	12	D	0-0	0-0		Miklosko	Potts	Hall	Ferdinand	Bilic	Lomas	Porfirio*	Moncur^	Lazaridis	Hartson	Kitson	Hughes/Bishop
	6/5	24,617	*4*	42				*Srnicek*	*Watson*	*Peacock*	*Albert*	*Beresford*	*Barton*	*Clark*	*Batty*	*Elliott*	*Asprilla**	*Shearer*	*Gillespie*
							Ref: G Poll	Both teams need the points. Dalglish has put the clamps on Newcastle's defence and they are unrecognisable from Keegan's cavaliers. Both sides created one good chance. Hartson cut inside Peacock but shot wide. Then Shearer's header was wonderfully tipped over by Miklokso.											
38	A	MANCHESTER U	14	L	0-2	0-1		Miklosko*	Potts	Hall	Ferdinand^	Bilic	Lomas	Porfirio	Moncur	Lazaridis	Dowie	Kitson	Sealey/Hughes
	11/5	***55,249***	*1*	42			*Solskjaer 11, Cruyff 84*	*Schmeichel*	*Neville P*	*May*	*Johnsen*	*Irwin**	*Poborsky^*	*Beckham*	*Butt*	*Scholes"*	*Cantona*	*Solskjaer*	*Clegg/McClair/Cruyff*
	Home	Away					Ref: S Lodge	The fate of both sides had been determined days earlier, denying this fixture significance. Man U's first, second, third and fourth teams all won their respective leagues. Solskjaer netted after Scholes' effort came down off the bar, and Jordi Cruyff scored his first goal since August.											
Average	23,242	28,476																	

Coca-Cola Cup					F-A	H-T	Scorers, Times, and Referees	SQUAD	NUMBERS	IN	USE								subs used
2:1	A	BARNET	17	D	1-1	0-1	Cottee 77	Mautone	Breacker*	Dicks	Rieper	Bilic	Bowen	Hughes	Bishop	Moncur^	Dowie	Cottee	Lazaridis/Lampard
18/9		*3,849*	*3:17*				*Simpson 13*	*Taylor*	*Primus*	*Pardew*	*Howarth*	*McDonald*	*Wilson*	*Codner*	*Gale*	*Simpson**	*Rattray^*	*Devine*	*Tomlinson/Campbell*
							Ref: M Riley	Steve Mautone is recalled from his loan to Crewe, after Miklosko gets injured, but spills Shaun Gale's effort. Simpson capitalised. Hammers upped the pace kicking downhill after half-time. Cottee headed past lance-corporal Maik Taylor, who Barnet bought out of the Army for £600.											
2:2	H	BARNET	13	W	1-0	0-0	Bilic 48	Mautone	Breacker	Dicks	Rieper	Bilic	Moncur	Lazaridis*	Bishop	Dumitrescu	Dowie	Cottee^	Ferdinand/Jones
25/9		15,264	*3:13*				(Barnet's 3rd sub Tomlinson)	*Taylor*	*Gale**	*McDonald*	*Codner*	*Primus*	*Howarth*	*Rattray^*	*Hardyman"*	*Wilson*	*Devine*	*Pardew*	*Campbell/Hodges/*
							Ref: C Wilkes (Hammers win 2-1 on aggregate)	This had all the makings of a tricky tie. The longer the game went on the greater Barnet's hopes of a famous triumph, but they were sunk by Slaven Bilic's first ever goal for West Ham, heading in Lazaridis' corner. Bilic had been linked with Spurs, but agreed a new deal in midweek.											
3	H	NOTT'M FOREST	13	W	4-1	1-1	Dowie 16, 56, Porfirio 67, Dicks 73p	Miklosko	Bowen	Dicks	Rieper	Bilic	Lazaridis	Hughes	Bishop	Moncur	Dowie	Porfirio	
23/10		19,402	*18*				*Cooper 29*	*Crossley*	*Haarland*	*Cooper*	*Blatherwick*	*Phillips*	*Gemmell*	*Bart-Williams*	*Woan*	*Roy*	*Lee*	*Saunders*	
							Ref: D Elleray	Times are changing at Upton Park, for this team contains just three Englishmen. Hugo Porfirio, on loan from Sporting Lisbon, steals the show with a dazzling display. Forest's only moment to savour came when Cooper headed in Saunders' cross. No substitutes by either side. A rarity.											
4	H	STOCKPORT	13	D	1-1	1-0	Raducioiu 12	Miklosko	Breacker	Dicks	Potts	Bilic	Lazaridis*	Hughes	Bishop	Lampard	Dowie	Raducioiu	Dumitrescu
27/11		20,061	*2:11*				*Cavaco 51*	*Jones*	*Connelly*	*Gannon*	*Flynn*	*Todd*	*Durkan**	*Bennett*	*Marsden*	*Jeffers^*	*Armstrong*	*Angell*	*Dinning/Cavaco*
							Ref: M Bailey	Porfirio is out, leaving the only Portuguese player in Division 2 to grab the headlines. Luis Cavaco came on at half-time and punished Dicks' error. Raducioiu, at £2.6 million the Hammers then record signing, had notched his first goal. But by the end Upton Park was awash with jeers.											
4R	A	STOCKPORT	15	L	1-2	1-2	Dicks 22	Miklosko	Bowen	Dicks	Rieper	Bilic	Moncur	Hughes	Bishop	Dumitrescu	Dowie*	Porfirio	Williamson
18/12		*9,834*	*2:6*				*Dowie 23 (og), Angell 27*	*Jones*	*Connelly*	*Flynn*	*Gannon*	*Todd*	*Durkan*	*Bennett*	*Marsden*	*Cavaco**	*Armstrong*	*Angell*	*Dinning*
							Ref: U Rennie	Having accounted for Blackburn, Stockport claim another big scalp to reach the last eight for the first time. Heavy rain ruins the pitch. Dicks heads in a corner, only for Dowie to head into his own net and Angell to nod County ahead. Dowie breaks an ankle and Bishop hits the bar.											

FA Cup																			
3	A	WREXHAM	16	D	1-1	1-1	Porfirio 44	Miklosko	Breacker	Dicks	Rieper	Potts	Williamson	Hughes	Bishop	Moncur	Porfirio	Jones	
4/1		*9,747*	*2:10*				*Hughes 6*	*Marriott*	*McGregor*	*Carey*	*Humes*	*Hardy*	*Chalk*	*Hughes*	*Ward*	*Owen**	*Morris^*	*Watkin*	*Russell/Roberts*
							Ref: M Reed	Snow wipes out most of the Cup programme, but not here, much to Redknapp's displeasure, as the pitch is white and the ball orange. Bryan Hughes headed in Owen's early corner, but Porfirio's miscued lob (genius or fluke?) restored parity. It was his first sight of snow, he insisted.											
3R	H	WREXHAM	18	L	0-1	0-0		Miklosko	Breacker	Dicks	Ferdinand	Bilic	Williamson	Hughes	Bishop	Lampard	Lazaridis*	Jones	Porfirio
25/1		16,763	*2:10*				*Russell 90*	*Mariott*	*McGregor*	*Humes*	*Carey*	*Hardy*	*Chalk*	*Hughes*	*Owen**	*Ward*	*Connelly*	*Watkin*	*Russell*
							Ref: S Lodge	First Stockport, now Wrexham from Division 2 dump the Hammers from a cup. It is as bad as can be for Harry, whose foreign misfits have flown the nest leaving him without a goalscorer. The tie was seconds from extra-time when sub Kevin Russell leathered the ball from 20 yards.											

	P	W	D	L	F	A	W	D	L	F	A	Pts
		Home					Away					
1 Manchester U	38	12	5	2	38	17	9	7	3	38	27	75
2 Newcastle	38	13	3	3	54	20	6	8	5	19	20	68
3 Arsenal	38	10	5	4	36	18	9	6	4	26	14	68
4 Liverpool	38	10	6	3	38	19	9	5	5	24	18	68
5 Aston Villa	38	11	5	3	27	13	6	5	8	20	21	61
6 Chelsea	38	9	8	2	33	22	7	3	9	25	33	59
7 Sheffield Wed	38	8	10	1	25	16	6	5	8	25	35	57
8 Wimbledon	38	9	6	4	28	21	6	5	8	21	25	56
9 Leicester	38	7	5	7	22	26	5	6	8	24	28	47
10 Tottenham	38	8	4	7	19	17	5	3	11	25	34	46
11 Leeds	38	7	7	5	15	13	4	6	9	13	25	46
12 Derby	38	8	6	5	25	22	3	7	9	20	36	46
13 Blackburn	38	8	4	7	28	23	1	11	7	14	20	42
14 WEST HAM	38	7	6	6	27	25	3	6	10	12	23	42
15 Everton	38	7	4	8	24	22	3	8	8	20	35	42
16 Southampton	38	6	7	6	32	24	4	4	11	18	32	41
17 Coventry	38	4	8	7	19	23	5	6	8	19	31	41
18 Sunderland	38	7	6	6	20	18	3	4	12	15	35	40
19 Middlesbro*	38	8	5	6	34	25	2	7	10	17	35	39
20 Nott'm Forest	38	3	9	7	15	27	3	7	9	16	32	34
	760	162	119	99	559	411	99	119	162	411	559	1018

* deducted 3 points

Odds & ends

Double wins: (1) Leicester.
Double losses: (2) Arsenal, Leeds.

Won from behind: (5) Southampton (h), Blackburn (h), Spurs (h), Chelsea (h), Coventry (a).
Lost from in front: (1) Stockport LC (a).

High spots: The arrival of Hartson and Kitson, whose 13 league goals in the last 14 games staved off relegation.
One defeat in 10 games from 12 March.

Low spots: One point from six games prior to the arrival of Hartson and Kitson.
Going out of both cups to Second Division teams.
Calling upon 32 players in 38 league matches.

Hammer of the Year: Julian Dicks.
Ever-presents: (0).
Hat-tricks: (1) Paul Kitson.
Leading scorer: (8) Julian Dicks, Paul Kitson.

	Appearances						Goals			
	Lge	*Sub*	LC	*Sub*	FAC	*Sub*	Lge	LC	FAC	Tot
Bilic, Slaven	**35**		5		1		**2**	1		**3**
Bishop, Ian	**26**	*3*	5		2		**1**			**1**
Bowen, Mark	**15**	*2*	3				**1**			**1**
Boylan, Lee		*1*								
Breacker, Tim	**22**	*4*	3		2					
Cottee, Tony	**2**	*1*	2					1		**1**
Dicks, Julian	**31**		5		2		**6**	2		**8**
Dowie, Iain	**18**	*5*	5					2		**2**
Dumitrescu, Ilie	**3**	*4*	2	*1*						
Ferdinand, Rio	**11**	*4*		*1*	1		**2**			**2**
Futre, Paulo	**4**	*5*								
Hall, Richard	**7**									
Hartson, John	**11**						**5**			**5**
Hughes, Michael	**31**	*2*	4		2		**3**			**3**
Jones, Steve	**5**	*3*		*1*	2					
Kitson, Paul	**14**						**8**			**8**
Lampard, Frank	**3**	*10*	1	*1*	1					
Lazaridis, Stan	**13**	*9*	3	*1*	1		**1**			**1**
Lomas, Steve	**7**									
Mautone, Steve	**1**		2							
Miklosko, Ludek	**36**		3		2					
Moncur, John	**26**	*1*	4		1		**2**			**2**
Newell, Mike	**6**	*1*								
Omoyimni, Emmanuel		*1*								
Potts, Steve	**17**	*3*	1		1					
Porfirio, Hugo	**15**	*8*	2		1	*1*	**2**	1	1	**4**
Raducioiu, Florin	**6**	*5*	1				**2**	1		**3**
Rieper, Marc	**26**	*2*	4		1		**1**			**1**
Rowland, Keith	**11**	*4*					**1**			**1**
Sealey, Les	**1**	*1*								
Slater, Stuart	**2**	*1*								
Williamson, Danny	**13**	*2*		*1*	2					
(own-goals)							**2**			**2**
32 players used	**418**	***82***	**55**	***6***	**22**	***1***	**39**	**8**	**1**	**48**

No		Date	Att	Pos	Pt	F-A	H-T	Scorers, Times, and Referees	SQUAD	NUMBERS	IN	USE								subs used
1	A	BARNSLEY			W	2-1	0-1	Hartson 53, Lampard 76	Miklosko	Breacker*	Hughes	Potts	Ferdinand	Rieper	Moncur	**Berkovic**^	Kitson"	Hartson	Lomas	Lazaridis/Lampard/**Terrier**
	9/8		*18,667*		3			*Redfearn 9*	*Watson*	*Eaden*	*Barnard*	*Shirtliff**	*Moses*	*De Zeeuw*	*Hendrie*	*Redfearn*	*Wilkinson*^	*Bullock"*	*Tinkler*	*Marcelle/Hristov/Liddell*
								Ref: A Wilkie	On a blistering day, Danny Wilson's promoted Barnsley enjoy a quick goal – a header from their captain – against traditionally poor travellers, yet still lose. Hartson grabs a soft leveller, courtesy of the keeper's mistake, and 30 seconds after coming on Lampard fashions a super winner.											
2	H	TOTTENHAM			W	2-1	1-0	Hartson 4, Berkovic 70	Miklosko	Breacker	Lazaridis	Potts	Ferdinand	Rieper	Moncur^	Berkovic	Kitson*	Hartson"	Lomas	Hughes/Lampard/Dowie
	13/8		25,354		6			*Ferdinand 83*	*Walker*	*Carr*	*Edinburgh*	*Scales*	*Vega*	*Campbell**	*Ginola*	*Nielsen*^	*Iverson*	*Ferdinand*	*Howells*	*Sinton/Clemence*
								Ref: S Lodge	Hammers celebrate their best start in 11 years with the Hammerettes dancing troupe wiggling before kick-off. Gerry Francis' Spurs are dull but sparks fly from Rio Ferdinand's tussles with cousin Les. Berkovic, who snubbed an offer from Spurs last summer, nets from Lazaridis' pass.											
3	A	EVERTON		7	L	1-2	1-0	Watson 23 (og)	Miklosko	Breacker"	Lazaridis	**Unsworth**	Ferdinand	Rieper	Moncur*	Berkovic^	Kitson	Hartson	Lomas	Hughes/Lampard/Dowie
	23/8		*34,356*	*12*	6			*Speed 67, Stuart 83*	*Southall*	*Barrett*	*Phelan*	*Williams'n**	*Watson*	*Bilic*	*Stuart*	*Barmby*	*Ferguson*	*Farrelly*^	*Speed*	*Short/Oster*
								Ref: P Jones	For a while it looked like Hammers would win three out of three. Hartson's free-kick would have been saved had not Dave Watson diverted it wide of Southall. But Gary Speed headed in Barmby's corner and ex-Hammer Slaven Bilic was instrumental in giving Graham Stuart space.											
4	A	COVENTRY			D	1-1	0-1	Kitson 64	Miklosko	Breacker	Lazaridis	Unsworth	Ferdinand	Rieper	Moncur	Berkovic	Kitson*	Hartson	Lomas	Dowie
	27/8		*18,291*		7			*Huckerby 38*	*Ogrizovic*	*Telfer*	*Burrows*	*Williams*	*Shaw*	*Breen*	*Huckerby*^	*Soltvedt**	*Dublin*	*Richardson*	*Salako*	*Boland/Lightbourne*
								Ref: N Barry	Coventry dominate the first half. John Salako leads the attack and City are finally rewarded when Huckerby pounces on a loose ball. After the break it's a different story, as Trond Soltvedt misses a fine chance to clinch it. Hartson hits the bar but Kitson is there to nod the rebound home.											
5	H	WIMBLEDON		3	W	3-1	0-0	Hartson 48, Rieper 54, Berkovic 56	Miklosko	Breacker	Lazaridis	Unsworth	Ferdinand	Rieper	Moncur	Dowie	Hartson	Berkovic	Lomas	
	30/8		24,516	*20*	10			*Ekoku 81*	*Sullivan*	*Jupp*	*Kimble*	*McAllister"*	*Blackwell*	*Perry*	*Ardley*	*Earle*	*Euell*^	*Holdsw'rth**	*Cunningham*	*Ekoku/Gayle/Clarke*
								Ref: G Poll	Dons are bottom and winless after this, and West Ham third. Hartson swapped passes with Dowie to fire past Neil Sullivan, Rieper glanced in Berkovic's free-kick, and Breacker's lofted pass sent Berkovic free to beat Sullivan. Efan Ekoku's drive never looked like igniting the Dons.											
6	A	MANCHESTER U		6	L	1-2	1-1	Hartson 14	Miklosko	Breacker	Hughes	Potts	Ferdinand	Unsworth	Moncur*	Berkovic	Kitson	Hartson	Lomas	Lampard
	13/9		***55,068***	*1*	10			*Keane 21, Scholes 76*	*Schmeichel*	*Neville G*	*Neville P*	*Berg*	*Keane*	*Pallister*	*Beckham*	*Butt*	*Cole*^	*Scholes*	*Giggs**	*Poborsky/McClair*
								Ref: D Elleray	Man U had yet to concede a goal this season when Hartson pounced on Gary Pallister's short back-header. Keane's shot had no danger until it clipped Moncur. West Ham fans taunted Beckham in song about girlfriend Posh Spice, so Beckham supplied the cross for Scholes to head in.											
7	H	NEWCASTLE		6	L	0-1	0-1		Miklosko	Breacker*	Lazaridis	Unsworth	Ferdinand	**Pearce**	Lampard	Dowie	Hartson	Berkovic^	Lomas	Hughes/Potts
	20/9		25,884	*8*	10			*Barnes 44*	*Given*	*Watson*	*Beresford*	*Barton*	*Peacock*	*Albert*	*Lee*	*Batty*	*Asprilla*	*Barnes**	*Gillespie*	*Howey*
								Ref: S Dunn	Dalglish's Newcastle have just beaten Barcelona in the Champions League. Here they rode their luck until John Barnes netted his first Geordie goal, curling the ball into the top corner from an unpromising position. Upton Park had booed his every touch, expecting him to sign for them.											
8	A	ARSENAL			L	0-4	0-4	*[Wright 42p]*	Miklosko	Breacker	Lazaridis	Unsworth	Ferdinand*	Pearce	Lampard	Dowie	Hartson	Bishop	Lomas	Potts
	24/9		*38,012*		10			*Bergkamp 12, Overmars 39, 45,*	*Seaman*	*Dixon**	*Winterburn*^	*Vieira*	*Bould*	*Adams*	*Parlour*	*Wright"*	*Petit*	*Bergkamp*	*Overmars*	*Grimandi/Platt/Anelka*
								Ref: P Alcock	Bergkamp's eighth goal of the season is a contender for 'goal of the month': he outpaces Pearce and scores with the outside of his right foot. Lampard comes close to reviving Hammers' fortunes, but Wright's penalty, when Pearce handled, takes the Gunners to the top of the division.											
9	H	LIVERPOOL		7	W	2-1	1-0	Hartson 15, Berkovic 65	Miklosko	Breacker	**Impey**	Unsworth	Ferdinand	Pearce	Lampard	Dowie	Hartson	Berkovic	Lomas	
	27/9		**25,908**	*9*	13			*Fowler 52*	*James*	*Berger**	*Bjornebye*	*Kvarme"*	*Carragher*	*Babb*	*McMana'n*	*Ince*	*Fowler*	*Owen*	*Thomas*^	*Riedle/Murphy/McAteer*
								Ref: D Gallagher	Ince was booed throughout, naturally, and watching England boss Glenn Hoddle was disappointed with the display of McManaman, naturally. Berkovic hit the post and the ball came out to Hartson; Fowler volleyed back Unsworth's clearance; Berkovic uncorked a rocket past James.											
10	A	SOUTHAMPTON		10	L	0-3	0-0		Miklosko	Breacker	Impey	Unsworth	Ferdinand	Pearce	Bishop	Dowie*	Hartson	Berkovic	Lomas	**Moore**
	4/10		***15,212***	*19*	13			*Ostenstad 54, Davies 65, Dodd 68*	*Jones*	*Dodd*	*Charlton*^	*Richardson*	*Lundekvam*	*Monkou*	*Le Tissier*	*Palmer*	*Davies*	*Evans**	*Oakley"*	*Ostenstad/Benali/Slater*
								Ref: M Riley	Saints climb off the bottom, helped by Le Tissier's first full game of the season. Kevin Davies hit the underside of the bar at 0-0, so it could have been worse. The half-fit Ostenstad forced home the ball two minutes after coming on. Jason Dodd sealed the win with a 30-yard corker.											

No	Venue / Date	Opponent / Att	Pos	Res / Pts	F-A	H-T	Scorers, Times, and Referees	1	2	3	4	5	6	7	8	9	10	11	Subs used
11	H	BOLTON	8	W	3-0	0-0	Berkovic 67, Hartson 77, 90	**Forrest**	Potts	Rowland	Unsworth	Ferdinand	Lomas	Moncur	Dowie	Hartson	Berkovic	Lampard	
	18/10	24,864	*18*	16				*Branagan*	*Phillips*	*Whitlow*	*Frandsen*	*Taggart !*	*Bergsson*	*Pollock*	*Beardsley**	*Holdsworth*	*Sellars*	*Thompson^*	*McGinlay/Johansen*
							Ref: G Ashby	Promoted Bolton have only won once. Matters turned ugly when Gerry Taggart was sent off on 69 mins for a fracas with Forrest. Berkovic had just run the ball over the line from Hartson's nod across goal. Hartson volleyed the second goal and saw the third squirm past Keith Branagan.											
12	A	LEICESTER		L	1-2	0-1	Berkovic 58	Forrest	Potts	Rowland	Unsworth	Ferdinand	Lomas	Moncur	Dowie	Hartson	Berkovic	Lampard	
	27/10	*20,201*		16			*Heskey 16, Marshall 82*	*Arphexad*	*Kamark**	*Guppy*	*Elliott*	*Marshall*	*Prior*	*Lennon*	*Izzet*	*Claridge*	*Savage^*	*Heskey*	*Campbell/Parker*
							Ref: M Reed	Martin O'Neill's Leicester, who have not been out of the top six all season, need not have worried about ref Mike Reed, as Emile Heskey's low shot put them ahead. Reed was public enemy number one in Leicester last season for awarding Chelsea a controversial penalty in the FA Cup.											
13	A	CHELSEA	14	L	1-2	0-0	Hartson 85p	Forrest	Impey	Rowland	Unsworth*	Ferdinand	Pearce	Moncur^	Lampard	Hartson	Berkovic	Lomas	Potts/Abou
	9/11	*33,256*	*4*	16			*Ferdinand 57 (og), Zola 83*	*De Goey*	*Petrescu**	*Babayaro*	*Sinclair*	*Leboeuf^*	*Myers*	*Newton*	*Di Matteo*	*Zola*	*Hughes*	*Wise*	*Nicholls/Gullit*
							Ref: G Barber	Gullit's Chelsea avoid their habit of losing in the League following a European tie. Moncur and Berkovic had to be pulled apart, and Wise spat at a Hammers fan. As for the goals, Zola's cross-shot was turned in by Ferdinand, Zola curled in a free-kick, and Andy Myers felled sub Abou.											
14	A	LEEDS	15	L	1-3	0-0	Lampard 65	Miklosko	Breacker	Impey	Unsworth	Potts	Pearce	Lampard	Abou^	Hartson	Berkovic*	Lomas	Moncur/Dowie
	23/11	*29,447*	*4*	16			*Hasselbaink 76, 90, Haaland 88*	*Martyn*	*Halle*	*Robertson*	*Kelly*	*Radebe*	*Wetherall*	*Bowyer*	*Wallace*	*Hasselbaink*	*Ribeiro*	*Haaland*	
							Ref: G Ashby	George Graham's Leeds had to come from behind. Lampard outpaced Gunnar Halle to exploit John Hartson's knock-on, but when Potts fouled Hasselbaink the victim curled ball round the wall. Haaland headed home Ribeiro's corner and Hasselbaink nodded in David Robertson's cross.											
15	H	ASTON VILLA	12	W	2-1	1-0	Hartson 18, 48	Miklosko	Breacker	Rowland	Unsworth	Ferdinand	Pearce	Potts	Abou*	Hartson	Berkovic	Lomas	Alves
	29/11	24,976	*13*	19			*Yorke 46*	*Oakes*	*Charles*	*Wright*	*Scimeca**	*Ehiogu*	*Staunton*	*Nelson*	*Draper*	*Milosevic*	*Collymore*	*Yorke*	*Grayson*
							Ref: P Alcock	16-goal Hartson is the Premiership's hotshot, taking Unsworth's pass on his chest before nabbing the first and claiming No 2 as Villa congratulated themselves on Yorke's equaliser – exchanging passes with Milosevic. Collymore's boots cost £2,500 a pair, but Stan missed everything.											
16	H	CRYS PALACE		W	4-1	2-1	Hartson 31, Berkovic 45, Unsworth 48,	Forrest	Breacker	Lazaridis*	Unsworth	Ferdinand	Pearce	Moncur	Abou^	Hartson	Berkovic	Lomas	Rowland/Alves
	3/12	23,335		22			*Shipperley 42* [Lomas 71]	*Miller*	*Smith**	*Gordon*	*Edworthy*	*Hreidarsson*	*Linighan*	*Zohar*	*Warhurst*	*Shipperley*	*Emblen*	*Rodger*	*Padovano*
							Ref: D Elleray	Juventus' Vice Presidenr Roberto Bettega saw a great display from Hartson, who scored from Berkovic's pass. Shipperley's equaliser was his fifth goal in five games. Lazaridis, back from Australia's World Cup defeat by Iran, took a corner, headed on by Pearce and Unsworth netted.											
17	A	DERBY	11	L	0-2	0-1		Miklosko	Breacker*	Lazaridis^	Unsworth	Ferdinand	Pearce	Moncur	Lampard	Hartson	Berkovic	Lomas	Abou/Alves
	6/12	*29,300*	*7*	22			*Miklosko 10 (og), Sturridge 49*	*Poom*	*Kozluk*	*Powell C*	*Rowett*	*Stimac*	*Dailly*	*Eranio**	*Sturridge*	*Baiano^*	*Wanchope*	*Carsley*	*Hunt/Powell D*
							Ref: A Wilkie	Though Jim Smith's Derby were better, they needed two Miklosko gifts. Paulo Wanchope met Eranio's corner but, pressed by Dean Sturridge, Ludo fumbled it. And when Miklosko side-footed a goal-kick straight to Sturridge, that was that. At the other end, Hartson hardly had a kick.											
18	H	SHEFFIELD WED	10	W	1-0	0-0	Kitson 68	Forrest	Impey*	Rowland	Unsworth	Ferdinand	Pearce	Lampard	Berkovic	Kitson^	Hartson	Lomas	Breacker/Abou
	13/12	24,344	*13*	25				*Pressman*	*Nolan*	*Stefanovic*	*Rudi*	*Newsome*	*Walker*	*Whitt'gh'm^*	*Hyde**	*Booth"*	*Collins*	*Di Canio*	*P'bridge/Carbone/H'phreys*
							Ref: M Riley	Ron Atkinson is trying to keep Wednesday up, and with white-booted Di Canio illuminating their attack his team had their moments. Berkovic was man-of-the match but played no part in the goal. Lomas passed to Kitson, who swivelled and scored with a deflected shot past Pressman.											
19	A	BLACKBURN	10	L	0-3	0-1		Forrest	Impey	Rowland	Unsworth	Ferdinand	Pearce	Lampard	Berkovic	Kitson*	Hartson	Lomas !	Abou
	20/12	*21,653*	*2*	25			*Ripley 22, Duff 51, 72*	*Flowers*	*Kenna*	*Croft*	*Henchoz*	*Hendry*	*McKinlay*	*Ripley**	*Gallacher"*	*Duff^*	*Sherwood*	*Wilcox*	*Flitcroft/Bohinen/Beattie*
							Ref: G Ashby	This spineless defeat was lambasted in the press. Hammers played even worse after Lomas saw red for manhandling the ref, who had declined to give Kitson a penalty. Rovers boss Roy Hodgson praises young Damian Duff, whose goals capitalised on errors by Impey and Unsworth.											
20	H	COVENTRY	8	W	1-0	1-0	Kitson 17	Forrest	Impey	Lazaridis	Unsworth	Ferdinand	Pearce	Lampard	Berkovic*	Kitson	Hartson	Lomas	Potts
	26/12	**22,477**	*17*	28				*Hedman*	*Nilsson*	*Shilton*	*Dublin*	*Shaw*	*Hall*	*Telfer*	*Whelan*	*Huckerby*	*Boateng !*	*O'Neill**	*Lightbourne*
							Ref: G Poll	Ref Graham Poll was in the festive spirit as he gave four yellow cards and sent off Dutch midfielder George Boateng (55 minutes) for a second bookable offence. Gordon Strachan's Coventry, lacking attacking quality, fail to redress Kitson's goal, the result of a Berkovic through-ball.											
21	A	WIMBLEDON	8	W	2-1	1-0	Kimble 31 (og), Kitson 54	Forrest	Breacker	Lazaridis	Unsworth	Ferdinand	Pearce	Impey	Lampard	Kitson	Hartson	Lomas	
	28/12	*22,087*	*12*	31			*Solbakken 90*	*Sullivan*	*Cunningham*	*Kimble*	*Jones^*	*Blackwell*	*Thatcher !*	*Ardley*	*Earle*	*Gayle**	*Solbakken*	*Hughes*	*Clarke/Cort*
							Ref: P Durkin	'Win away: lose at home' Dons present West Ham with a first away win since the opening day. Only three minutes had passed when Thatcher saw red for elbowing Kitson. Alan Kimble beat Hartson to a through-ball for a fine own-goal. Cunningham then directed a weak back-header.											

No	Date		Att	Pos	Pt	F-A	H-T	Scorers, Times, and Referees	SQUAD	NUMBERS	IN	USE								subs used
22	H	BARNSLEY		8	W	**6-0**	2-0	Lampard 5, Abou 31,52, Moncur 57,	Forrest	Potts	Lazaridis	Unsworth	Ferdinand	Pearce	Impey*	Lampard	Hartson	Berkovic^	Abou	Moncur/Alves
	10/1		23,714	*20*	34			[Hartson 67, Lazaridis 90]	*Watson*	*Eaden*	*Barnard*	*Morgan*	*Appleby"*	*Krizan^*	*Sheridan*	*Redfearn*	*Hristov**	*Ward*	*Tinkler*	*Hendrie/Marcelle/Markstedt*
								Ref: N Barry	They painted the Upton Park mud 'green'. Biggest threat to Barnsley was Semassi Abou, who used inferior opponents to demonstrate his chief skill – flicking the ball with his right foot. His second goal was the pick of the six, putting the final touch to silky skills by Berkovic on the left.											
23	A	TOTTENHAM		8	L	0-1	0-1		Forrest	Potts	Lazaridis*	Unsworth	Ferdinand	Pearce	Moncur	Lampard	Hartson	Berkovic^	Abou !	Dowie/**Hodges**
	17/1		*30,284*	*18*	34			*Klinsmann 7*	*Baardsen*	*Carr*	*Wilson*	*Vega*	*Calderw'd**	*Campbell*	*Ginola^*	*Berti*	*Klinsmann*	*Fox"*	*Sinton*	*Howells/Dominguez/Brady*
								Ref: D Elleray	Jurgen Klinsmann's first goal since re-signing for Spurs – nudging in Ginola's near-post cross – settles this nasty affair and keeps Gross's team off the bottom. West Ham were a man short after 42 mins when Abou handled the ref and hell broke loose. Calderwood barged into Redknapp.											
24	H	EVERTON		8	D	2-2	1-1	Sinclair 10, 48	Forrest	Breacker	Lazaridis	Potts	Ferdinand	Pearce	Lomas	Lampard	Hartson	Berkovic	**Sinclair***	Hodges
	31/1		25,905	*14*	35			*Barmby 25, Madar 60*	*Myhre*	*Ward*	*O'Kane^*	*Ball*	*Watson*	*Bilic*	*Farrelly*	*Barmby*	*Ferguson*	*Grant*	*Madar**	*Cadamarteri/Allen*
								Ref: U Rennie	Trevor Sinclair marks his debut with a header from Lazaridis' corner and a neat finish from Berkovic's return pass. Howard Kendall's Everton hit back with Barmby's diving header and, a second time, when Ferdinand failed to clear Farrelly's cross, presenting a gift to Mikael Madar.											
25	A	NEWCASTLE		8	W	1-0	1-0	Lazaridis 16	Forrest	Breacker	Lazaridis	Lomas	Ferdinand	Pearce	Impey*	Moncur	Kitson^	Hartson	Sinclair	Potts/Berkovic
	7/2		*36,736*	*10*	38				*Given*	*Pistone*	*Griffin**	*Batty*	*Peacock*	*Pearce*	*Lee*	*Gillespie*	*Shearer*	*Andersson*	*Speed*	*Tomasson*
								Ref: P Jones	West Ham finally nail Dalglish's team's pretence to be title contenders, but they had much defending to do after Stan Lazaridis' ballistic shot. Andreas Andersson hit a post. Unsettled Newcastle keeper Shaka Hislop has refused to sign a new contract, which is good news for Hammers!											
26	A	BOLTON		9	D	1-1	0-0	Sinclair 65	Forrest	Impey	Lazaridis	Unsworth	Ferdinand	Pearce	Moncur	Lampard	Hartson !	Berkovic	Sinclair	
	21/2		*25,000*	*18*	39			*Blake 86*	*Branagan*	*Cox*	*Bergsson*	*Frandsen*	*Fairclough**	*Todd*	*Pollock*	*Johansen*	*Blake*	*Holdsworth*	*Thompson*	*Gunnlaugsson*
								Ref: P Alcock	Hartson is sent off after 56 mins for raising an arm to Per Frandsen. Berkovic's skill was capped by Sinclair's composure in scoring, and West Ham would have gone 2-0 had Berkovic not missed a gaping goal. His miss proved costly when Nathan Blake headed in from Gunnlaugsson.											
27	H	ARSENAL			D	0-0	0-0		**Lama**	Breacker*	Lazaridis	Lomas	Pearce	Unsworth	Impey	Lampard	Hartson	Berkovic	Sinclair	Potts
	2/3		25,717		40				*Manninger*	*Dixon*	*Upson**	*Vieira*	*Keown*	*Adams*	*Platt^*	*Anelka*	*Petit*	*Hughes*	*Overmars*	*Winterburn/Boa Morte*
								Ref: P Durkin	A fair result for this rehearsal for Sunday's FA Cup quarter-final, with both sides missing key players. Arsenal now trail leaders Man Utd by 11 points. Manninger's dive blocked Berkovic's shot and Sinclair missed a sitter. 'Neither side deserved to win', said Gunners boss Arsene Wenger.											
28	H	MANCHESTER U			D	1-1	1-0	Sinclair 6	Lama	Impey	Lazaridis	Potts	Ferdinand	Pearce	Lomas	Lampard	Abou	Berkovic	Sinclair	
	11/3		25,892		41			*Scholes 66*	*Schmeichel*	*Neville G*	*Irwin*	*May*	*McClair^*	*Berg*	*Beckham*	*Butt"*	*Cole**	*Sheringham*	*Scholes*	*Solskjaer/Thornley/Curtis*
								Ref: G Willard	Despite missing Hartson and Kitson, West Ham looked dangerous. Champions Man Utd were relieved to escape with a draw. Berkovic's mazy dribble and shot was blocked on the line by Sheringham, but Sinclair was there to ram in the rebound. Paul Scholes volleyed the equaliser.											
29	H	CHELSEA		8	W	2-1	0-0	Sinclair 69, Unsworth 75	Lama	Impey*	Lazaridis	Unsworth	Ferdinand	Pearce	Bishop	Lampard	Abou	Berkovic	Sinclair	Potts
	14/3		25,829	*4*	44			*Charvet 54*	*Kharine*	*Charvet*	*Granville*	*Duberry*	*Leboeuf*	*Myers*	*Newton*	*Di Matteo*	*Flo*	*Hughes*	*Morris**	*Zola*
								Ref: M Bodenham	Vialli's team are chasing two cups but have now lost four out of five in the League. Without Zola (dropped) and Wise (suspended), Chelsea go in front through Laurant Charvet's header, but are overhauled when Sinclair beat the keeper to Potts' pass, and then Unsworth at the far post.											
30	H	LEEDS			W	3-0	2-0	Hartson 8, Abou 23, Pearce 68	Lama	Potts	Lazaridis	Unsworth	Ferdinand	Pearce	Moncur	Berkovic*	Abou^	Hartson	Sinclair	**Mean**/Omoyimni
	30/3		24,107		47				*Martyn*	*Maybury**	*Harte*	*Kelly*	*Molenaar*	*Hiden*	*Haaland*	*Halle*	*Hasselbaink*	*Ribeiro*	*Bowyer^*	*Wetherall/Wallace*
								Ref: A Wilkie	Leeds boss George Graham blamed keeper Nigel Martyn for Hammers' first two goals. Pearce's move to right wing-back paid off as he scored his second goal of the season, a stunning left-footer. A collision between Hiden and Martyn enabled Abou to dribble the ball into an empty net.											
31	A	ASTON VILLA		7	L	0-2	0-0		Lama	Potts*	Lazaridis	Unsworth	Ferdinand	Pearce	Moncur	Lampard	Hartson	Lomas	Sinclair	Abou
	4/4		*39,372*	*9*	47			*Joachim 77, Milosevic 83*	*Bosnich*	*Charles**	*Wright*	*Southgate*	*Ehiogu*	*Staunton*	*Taylor*	*Draper^*	*Yorke*	*Hendrie*	*Joachim*	*Milosevic/Grayson*
								Ref: S Dunn	Since John Gregory replaced Brian Little, Villa have soared up the table. They are helped now by Redknapp resting two positive midfielders – Berkovic and Abou. Sub Milosevic upped the tempo. Joachim deflected Ian Taylor's shot and Milo pounced when Lama parried from Hendrie.											

32	H	DERBY		7	D	0-0	0-0		Lama	Impey"	Lazaridis	Unsworth	Ferdinand	Pearce*	Lomas	Lampard	Hartson !	Berkovic^	Sinclair	Potts/Moncur/Abou
	11/4		25,155	9	48				Poom	Delap	Powell C	Rowett	Stimac	Dailly	Eranio !	Bohinen	Sturridge^	Wanchope*	Carsley	Baiano/Burton
								Ref: G Barber	No goals, just two shots on target, two players sent off, and eight booked. Match of the Day reduced the highlights to 57 seconds. Hartson went for punching Igor Stimac (Redknapp called Hartson an 'idiot'), and Eranio followed for two yellows – 'ungentlemanly conduct' and 'dissent'.											
33	A	SHEFFIELD WED		8	D	1-1	1-0	Berkovic 7	Lama	Impey	Lazaridis	Unsworth	Ferdinand	Pearce	Lampard	Abou*	Hartson	Berkovic	Lomas	Omoyimni
	13/4		28,036	14	49			Magilton 59	Pressman	Barrett	Hinchcliffe	Stefanovic	Emerson	Walker	Rudi*	Magilton	Booth	Carbone	Di Canio	Pembridge
								Ref: N Barry	Jim Magilton's first goal for Wednesday since his £1.6 million move from Southampton dented Hammers European aspirations, and nudged the Owls closer to safety. His 20-yard drive levelled Berkovic's first goal since December. 'We're not safe yet,' warned boss Ron Atkinson.											
34	H	BLACKBURN		6	W	2-1	2-1	Hartson 7, 28	Lama	Impey	Lazaridis	Unsworth	Ferdinand	Pearce	Lomas	Lampard	Hartson	Berkovic*	Sinclair	Potts
	18/4		24,733	7	52			Wilcox 45	Fettis	Valery*	Kenna	Henchoz	Hendry	McKinlay	Ripley^	Gallacher	Sutton	Flitcroft	Wilcox	Sherwood/Dahlin
								Ref: P Durkin	Rovers have lost six of the last seven. A four-match ban means this is Hartson's last game of the season, but he signed off in style. Berkovic's reverse pass set up his first goal, and Hartson outjumped Colin Hendry for his second. Ian Pearce's hesitancy was responsible for Rovers' goal.											
35	H	SOUTHAMPTON		7	L	2-4	1-1	Sinclair 42, Lomas 82 [Palmer 80]	Lama	Impey	Lazaridis	Potts*	Ferdinand	Pearce	Lomas	Lampard	Abou	Berkovic	Sinclair	Kitson
	25/4		25,878	12	52			Le Tissier 40, Ostenstad 63, 86,	Jones	Dodd	Benali	Palmer	Lundekvam	Monkou	Le Tissier	Oakley	Hirst*	Ostenstad	Gibbens	Basham
								Ref: D Gallagher	Minus Hartson, Sinclair and Abou looked lightweight in attack. Le Tissier netted after his first attempt hit a post. Sinclair's pace brought his equaliser. When Egil Ostenstad headed in Carlton Palmer's cross, the match slipped away. Le Tissier sent Palmer clear for Saints' third goal.											
36	A	LIVERPOOL		10	L	0-5	0-4	[Leonhardsen 45, Ince 61]	Lama	Pearce	Lazaridis	Unsworth	Ferdinand	Lomas	Moncur"	Lampard	Kitson^	Berkovic*	Sinclair	Abou/Mean/Omoyimni
	2/5		44,414	3	52			Owen 4, McAteer 21, 25,	Friedel	Kvarme	Bjornbye	Babb	Harkness	Leonhards'n	McAteer	Ince	Owen	Riedle	Carragher	
								Ref: J Winter	West Ham have not won at Anfield since 1963 and have scored there only twice in 23 years. Michael Owen made England boss Hoddle eat his words after claiming he was not a natural scorer. A sloppy clearance gave him his 17th goal of the season. Jason McAteer's first was deflected.											
37	A	CRYS PALACE		9	D	3-3	1-1	Curcic 4 (og), Omoyimni 68, 89	Lama	Impey	Lazaridis	Unsworth !	Pearce	Lomas	Lampard	Abou*	Kitson	Berkovic	Sinclair	Omoyimni
	5/5		19,129	20	53			Bent 44, Rodger 48, Lombardo 63	Miller	Edworthy	Gordon	Ismael^	Hreidarsson	Warhurst	Lombardo	Bent	Shipperley	Rodger	Curcic*	Fullarton/Smith
								Ref: G Poll	Palace will finish bottom with just one home win, so this is an awful result for UEFA Cup-chasing Hammers. Without the suspended Hartson, Omoyimni notched his first goals for the club. Curcic own-goaled in tackling Lampard. Unsworth got two yellow cards for fouling Lombardo.											
38	H	LEICESTER		8	W	4-3	2-0	Lampard 15, Abou 31, 74, Sinclair 65	Lama	Omoyimni	Lazaridis	Unsworth	Ferdinand	Pearce	Lomas	Lampard	Abou	Berkovic*	Sinclair	Mean
	10/5		25,781	10	56			Cottee 59, 83, Heskey 66	Keller	Savage	Guppy	Elliott	Walsh*	Kamark	Lennon	Izzet	Marshall"	Zagorakis^	Heskey	Cottee/Parker/Wilson
		Home	Away					Ref: U Rennie	Without Hartson, West Ham have tailed away, missing out on Europe. Upton Park gave a great welcome to sub Cottee, who repaid the ovation by scoring twice. Abou stole the show, however, beating two defenders for his first goal and blasting a shot past Kasey Keller for his second.											
Average		24,967	29,406																	

Coca-Cola Cup			Att			F-A	H-T	Scorers, Times, and Referees												Subs used
2:1	A	HUDDERSFIELD		6	L	0-1	0-0		Miklosko	Breacker	Hughes	Unsworth	Ferdinand	Potts	Lampard	Berkovic	Kitson*	Hartson	Lomas	Dowie
	16/9		8,525	1:24				*Dyer 75*	*Francis*	*Jenkins*	*Martin**	*Dyson*	*Gray*	*Edmondson*	*Dalton^*	*Makel*	*Stewart*	*Dyer*	*Burnett*	*Baldry/Hurst*
								Ref: C Wilkes	West Ham have only themselves to blame for this defeat at the McAlpine Stadium, with Hartson and Kitson both wasting good opportunities. The night belonged to Alex Dyer, a lifelong West Ham supporter, who rose unmarked at the far post to head Town 1-0 up into the second leg.											
2:2	H	HUDDERSFIELD		7	W	3-0	2-0	Hartson 31, 45, 77	Miklosko	Breacker	Impey*	Unsworth	Ferdinand	Pearce	Lampard	Dowie	Hartson	Berkovic	Lomas	Potts
	29/9		16,137	1:24					*Francis*	*Jenkins*	*Edmondson*	*Collins*	*Morrison*	*Gray*	*Edwards**	*Makel^*	*Stewart*	*Payton*	*Dyer*	*Lawson/Burnett*
								Ref: M Bodenham (Hammers win 3-1 on aggregate)	Town, who have yet to win a league game, look fragile as they face a Hammers onslaught (27 goal attempts against Town's 4). Hartson nets his first hat-trick in club football. After missing many chances, he runs from the halfway line to make it 3-0, leaving three markers trailing behind.											
3	H	ASTON VILLA		10	W	3-0	2-0	Hartson 7, 80, Lampard 15	Forrest	Breacker*	Impey	Potts	Ferdinand	Unsworth	Lampard	Dowie^	Hartson	Berkovic	Lomas	Rowland/Bishop
	15/10		20,360	*9*					*Bosnich*	*Nelson**	*Wright*	*Southgate^*	*Ehiogu*	*Scimeca*	*Taylor*	*Draper*	*Milosevic"*	*Collymore*	*Yorke*	*Charles/Grayson/Curcic*
								Ref: S Lodge	West Ham, without half the team due to injury, lose Breacker (hamstring), Impey (toe), Dowie and Berkovic (both ankle) during the game. Stan Collymore, who cost more than double what Hammers paid for Hartson, misses many great chances. The fans chant 'What a waste of money'.											
4	H	WALSALL		14	W	4-1	2-1	Lampard 15, 72, 73, Hartson 16	Forrest	Breacker	Lomas	Unsworth	Ferdinand	Pearce	Moncur	Lampard	Hartson	Berkovic	Abou	
	19/11		17,463	*2:21*				*Watson 45*	*Walker*	*Evans*	*Marsh**	*Viveash*	*Mountfield*	*Peron*	*Boli*	*Keister^*	*Keates*	*Watson*	*Hodge*	*Ricketts/Porter*
								Ref: D Orr	Lampard follows his England U-21 debut last week with his first senior hat-trick. His first, a great shot from Berkovic's pass that beats keeper James Walker. Walsall, who beat Nott'm Forest in a previous round, pull a goal back from a corner. Rio Ferdinand makes his England debut.											
QF	H	ARSENAL		8	L	1-2	0-1	Abou 75	Forrest	Potts	Lazaridis	Unsworth	Ferdinand	Pearce*	Impey	Berkovic	Kitson^	Hartson	Lampard	Rowland/Abou
	6/1		24,770	*6*				*Wright 25, Overmars 52*	*Seaman*	*Grimaldi*	*Winterburn*	*Vieira*	*Bould*	*Keown*	*Parlour*	*Wright**	*Petit*	*Bergkamp*	*Overmars^*	*Wreh/Hughes*
								Ref: G Barber	West Ham should have led after 18 mins when Seaman sent Kitson flying, but Hartson scuffed the penalty on a treacherous pitch. Ian Wright's cracking goal ended his barren spell. The Gunners' tight defence is split apart when sub Abou sprints forward to net his first goal for Hammers.											

FA Cup			Att			F-A	H-T	Scorers, Times, and Referees												Subs used
3	H	EMLEY		8	W	2-1	1-0	Lampard 3, Hartson 80	Forrest	Breacker*	Lazaridis	Potts	Pearce	Unsworth	Lampard	Berkovic	Kitson	Hartson	Ferdinand	Abou
	3/1		18,629	*U:11*				*David 56*	*Marples*	*David*	*Lacey**	*Thompson*	*Jones*	*Calcutt"*	*Nicholson*	*Banks*	*Hurst*	*Graham*	*Reynolds*	*Wilson^/Woods/Tonks*
								Ref: J Winter	Part-time Emley are a small West Yorkshire village club from the Unibond League, who put out Lincoln City in the previous round. Berkovic set up Lampard with Lacey off the pitch injured. Paul David headed an equaliser from Banks' corner, before Hartson headed in from Lazaridis.											
4	A	MANCHESTER C		8	W	2-1	1-0	Berkovic 28, Lomas 76	Forrest	Potts	Lazaridis	Unsworth*	Ferdinand	Pearce	Lampard	Abou^	Hartson	Berkovic	Lomas	Breacker/Dowie
	25/1		*26,495*	*1:21*				*Kinkladze 59*	*Wright*	*Brightwell*	*Shelia*	*Brown*	*Symons*	*Edghill*	*Whitley,JF*	*Russell*	*Dickov*	*Kinkladze*	*Rosler*	
								Ref: D Gallagher	This televised Sunday match was lit up by Kinkladze's slalom goal for Frank Clark's City, which cancelled out Berkovic's opener. Uwe Rosler then shot over from the spot, after Potts had flattened Dickov. It was left to Lomas, sold to West Ham by Clark, to settle the tie from 20 yards.											
5	H	BLACKBURN		8	D	2-2	2-1	Kitson 25, Berkovic 43	Forrest	Breacker*	Lazaridis	Lomas	Ferdinand	Pearce	Lampard	Berkovic	Kitson^	Hartson	Impey	Potts/Hodges
	14/2		25,729	*4*				*Gallacher 3, Sutton 62*	*Flowers*	*Kenna*	*Croft**	*Henchoz*	*Hendry*	*McKinlay*	*Flitcroft*	*Gallacher !*	*Sutton*	*Sherwood*	*Wilcox*	*Duff*
								Ref: P Jones	Kevin Gallacher enjoyed good moments – putting away Chris Sutton's pass – and bad – sent off for elbowing Berkovic. Lazaridis's cross was tucked away by Kitson, and Berkovic got an unknowing touch to Hartson's shot. Hartson hit the bar, but Sutton then headed in from Wilcox.											
5R	A	BLACKBURN		9	D	1-1	0-0	Hartson 103	Forrest	Impey	Lazaridis	Unsworth	Ferdinand	Pearce	Moncur	Lampard	Hartson	Berkovic*	Lomas	Abou
	25/2		*21,972*	*5*				*Ripley 114*	*Fettis*	*Kenna*	*Croft**	*Henchoz*	*Hendry*	*McKinlay^*	*Ripley"*	*Gallacher*	*Sutton*	*Sherwood*	*Duff*	*Wilcox/Flitcroft/Dahlin*
								Ref: P Jones (Hammers win 5-4 on penalties)	A lacklustre affair, dominated by Blackburn, whose failure to convert many chances proved costly. Hartson netted from Abou's cross, Ripley's far-post header levelled matters. Hammers converted all 5 penalties. The crowd booed Berkovic for accusing Rovers players of anti-Semitism.											
QF	A	ARSENAL		9	D	1-1	1-1	Pearce 12	Lama	Impey	Lazaridis	Potts	Ferdinand	Pearce	Moncur	Lampard	Abou	Berkovic*	Lomas	Hodges
	8/3		*38,077*	*3*				*Bergkamp 26p*	*Manninger*	*Dixon*	*Winterburn*	*Vieira*	*Keown*	*Adams*	*Parlour*	*Anelka**	*Petit*	*Bergkamp*	*Overmars*	*Wreh*
								Ref:M Reed	Hartson is still suspended, and his presence was missed against Wenger's physical Arsenal. Lampard's corner flew low across the box and Ian Pearce drove it in. The tie turned when Berkovic mis-controlled the ball with the goal at his mercy. Pearce then brought down Martin Keown.											
QF R	H	ARSENAL		8	D	1-1	0-1	Hartson 83	Lama	Potts*	Lazaridis	Unsworth	Ferdinand	Pearce^	Lampard	Abou	Hartson	Berkovic	Lomas	Hodges/Moncur
	17/3		25,859	*2*				*Anelka 45*	*Manninger*	*Dixon*	*Winterburn*	*Vieira*	*Keown*	*Adams*	*Garde*	*Anelka**	*Petit^*	*Bergkamp !*	*Overmars"*	*Wreh/Boa Morte/Hughes*
								Ref: M Reed (Hammers lose 3-4 on penalties)	Arsenal kept their dreams of the double alive after a cruel penalty shoot-out. Anelka's beautiful strike put the Gunners ahead. Hartson beat Lee Dixon to equalise. Bergkamp walked (34 mins) for hitting Lomas. Hartson missed his second pen of the season. Arsenal will now face Wolves											

	P	W	D	L	F	A	W	D	L	F	A	Pts
		Home					Away					
1 Arsenal	38	15	2	2	43	10	8	7	4	25	23	78
2 Manchester U	38	13	4	2	42	9	10	4	5	31	17	77
3 Liverpool	38	13	2	4	42	16	5	9	5	26	26	65
4 Chelsea	38	13	2	4	37	14	7	1	11	34	29	63
5 Leeds	38	9	5	5	31	21	8	3	8	26	25	59
6 Blackburn	38	11	4	4	40	26	5	6	8	17	26	58
7 Aston Villa	38	9	3	7	26	24	8	3	8	23	24	57
8 WEST HAM	38	13	4	2	40	18	3	4	12	16	39	56
9 Derby	38	12	3	4	33	18	4	4	11	19	31	55
10 Leicester	38	6	10	3	21	15	7	4	8	30	26	53
11 Coventry	38	8	9	2	26	17	4	7	8	20	27	52
12 Southampton	38	10	1	8	28	23	4	5	10	22	32	48
13 Newcastle	38	8	5	6	22	20	3	6	10	13	24	44
14 Tottenham	38	7	8	4	23	22	4	3	12	21	34	44
15 Wimbledon	38	5	6	8	18	25	5	8	6	16	21	44
16 Sheffield Wed	38	9	5	5	30	26	3	3	13	22	41	44
17 Everton	38	7	5	7	25	27	2	8	9	16	29	40
18 Bolton	38	7	8	4	25	22	2	5	12	16	39	40
19 Barnsley	38	7	4	8	25	35	3	1	15	12	47	35
20 Crys Palace	38	2	5	12	15	39	6	4	9	22	32	33
	760	184	95	101	592	427	101	95	184	427	592	1045

Odds & ends

Double wins: (2) Barnsley, Wimbledon.
Double losses: (1) Southampton.

Won from behind: (2) Barnsley (a), Chelsea (h).
Lost from in front: (3) Everton (a), Manchester U (a), Leeds (a).

High spots: Reaching the quarter-finals in both cups.
Hammers' best start to a season in eleven years.
Hotshot Hartson.
6-0 win over Barnsley.

Low spots: Losing to Arsenal in both cups.
Hartson's four-match ban at the end of the season.
A run of eight away league defeats Spetember-December.

Hammer of the Year: Rio Ferdinand.
Ever-presents: (0).
Hat-tricks: (2) John Hartson, Frank Lampard.
Leading scorer: (24) John Hartson.

	Appearances						Goals			
	Lge	*Sub*	LC	*Sub*	FAC	*Sub*	**Lge**	LC	FAC	**Tot**
Abou, Samassi	**12**	*7*	1	*1*	3	*2*	**5**	1		**6**
Alves, Paolo		*4*								
Berkovic, Eyal	**34**	*1*	5		6		**7**		2	**9**
Bishop, Ian	**3**			*1*						
Breacker, Tim	**18**	*1*	4		2	*1*				
Dowie, Iain	**7**	*5*	2	*1*		*1*				
Ferdinand, Rio	**35**	*5*	5		6					
Forrest, Craig	**13**		3		4					
Hartson, John	**32**		5		5		**15**	6	3	**24**
Hodges, Lee		*2*				*3*				
Hughes, Michael	**2**	*3*	1							
Impey, Andrew	**19**		3		3					
Kitson, Paul	**12**	*1*	2		2		**4**		1	**5**
Lama, Bernard	**12**				2					
Lampard, Frank	**27**	*4*	5		6		**4**	4	1	**9**
Lazaridis, Stan	**27**	*1*	1		6		**2**			**2**
Lomas, Steve	**33**		4		5		**2**		1	**3**
Mean, Scott		*3*								
Miklosko, Ludek	**13**		2							
Moncur, John	**17**	*3*	1		2	*1*	**1**			**1**
Moore, Jason		*1*								
Omoyimni, Emmanuel	**1**	*4*					**2**			**2**
Pearce, Ian	**30**		3		6		**1**		1	**2**
Potts, Steve	**14**	*9*	3	*1*	4	*1*				
Rieper, Marc	**5**						**1**			**1**
Rowland, Keith	**6**	*1*		*2*						
Sinclair, Trevor	**14**						**7**			**7**
Terrier, David		*1*								
Unsworth, David	**32**		5		4		**2**			**2**
(own-goals)							**3**			**3**
29 players used	**418**	***56***	**55**	***6***	**66**	***9***	**56**	**11**	**9**	**76**

No	Date		Att	Pos	Pt	F-A	H-T	Scorers, Times, and Referees	SQUAD	NUMBERS	IN	USE								subs used
1	A	SHEFFIELD WED			W	1-0	0-0	Wright 84	**Hislop**	Impey	Lazaridis	Pearce	Ferdinand	**Ruddock**	Lampard	Berkovic*	Sinclair	**Wright**	Lomas	Moncur
	15/8		*30,236*		3				*Pressman*	*Cobian*	*Hinchcliffe*	*Atherton*	*Emerson*	*Walker*	*Jonk*	*Carbone*	*Booth*	*Rudi*	*Di Canio*	
								Ref: P Durkin	Danny Wilson's Premiership baptism at Barnsley was ruined by West Ham, and now at Wednesday too. The Owls were pressing and looked the more likely winners when nearly 35-year-old Ian Wright put away Sinclair's pass. 'Wrighty's ghetto-blaster lifts the dressing room spirits.'											
2	H	MANCHESTER U		7	D	0-0	0-0		Hislop	Impey	Lazaridis	Pearce	Ferdinand	Ruddock	Lampard	Berkovic*	Sinclair	Hartson	Lomas	Abou
	22/8		25,912	*11*	4				*Schmeichel*	*Neville G^*	*Irwin*	*Berg*	*Keane*	*Johnsen*	*Beckham*	*Butt*	*Cole**	*Yorke*	*Giggs*	*Sheringham/Neville P*
								Ref: P Jones	Yorke needs time to settle and Beckham is hounded over being sent off for England in the World Cup. Man U were so drab that Alex Ferguson declined to face the press afterwards. Ian Wright missed the game because of a dead-leg suffered in training. Ruddock handled early on unseen.											
3	A	COVENTRY		8	D	0-0	0-0		Hislop	Impey	Lazaridis	**Margas**	Ferdinand	Ruddock	Lampard	Berkovic	Hartson	Wright	Lomas*	Moncur
	29/8		*20,818*	*10*	5				*Hedman*	*Wallemme^*	*Burrows*	*Breen*	*Shaw*	*Boateng*	*Telfer*	*Soltvedt**	*Dublin*	*Whelan*	*Huckerby*	*Hall/Edworthy*
								Ref: N Barry	Magnus Hedman defied the Hammers, turning away Wright's fierce header and then blocking from the super Berkovic. Chilian Javier Margas (who needed four stitches in his lip) excelled with Ruddock. The frustrated Darren Huckerby was booked for faking a foul in the penalty area.											
4	H	WIMBLEDON		11	L	3-4	3-1	Hartson 7, Wright 14, 27	Hislop	Sinclair	Lazaridis	Pearce	Margas	Ruddock	Lampard	Berkovic*	Hartson	Wright	Moncur	Impey
	9/9		24,601	*4*	5			*Gayle 30, 77, Euell 64, Ekoku 81*	*Sullivan*	*Jupp*	*Kimble*	*Roberts*	*Cunningham*	*Perry*	*Gayle*	*Earle**	*Leaburn*	*Euell*	*Hughes M*	*Ekoku*
								Ref: G Barber	A standing ovation at half-time as Hammers tore the Dons apart down the flanks. Lazaridis squared for Wright – 3-0. Then the bombardment began. Margas let in Jason Euell, Hislop collided with Impey to free Gayle, and Euell crossed for Efan Ekoku. Wimbledon might have had ten.											
5	H	LIVERPOOL		8	W	2-1	1-0	Hartson 4, Berkovic 51	Hislop	Sinclair	Lazaridis	Potts	Pearce	Ruddock	Lampard	Berkovic*	Hartson^	Wright	Moncur	Breacker/**Keller**
	12/9		26,010	*2*	8			*Riedle 88*	*Friedel*	*Heggem^*	*Staunton"*	*Redknapp*	*Carragher*	*Babb*	*McMana'n*	*Ince*	*Berger*	*Owen*	*Harkness**	*Riedle/McAteer/Matteo*
								Ref: J Winter	Liverpool, jointly managed by Evans and Houllier, lose for the first time. Owen played up alone until Riedle joined him, but by then it was 2-0. Hartson's header went in off Carragher, and Berkovic played a one-two with Hartson. Riedle headed onto a post, then in off McAteer's cross.											
6	A	NOTT'M FOREST		8	D	0-0	0-0		Hislop	Sinclair	Impey	Potts	Ferdinand	Pearce	Lampard	Berkovic	Abou*	Wright	Keller	Omoyimni
	19/9		*26,463*	*11*	9				*Beasant*	*Lyttle"*	*Rogers*	*Stone*	*Chettle*	*Armstrong*	*Johnson*	*Quashie*	*Darcheville^*	*Harewood**	*Bonalair*	*Freedman/Gray/Louis-Jean*
								Ref: M Reed	The last time Forest beat West Ham at home was in 1986, courtesy of Metgod's free-kick. Wright could have won it at the end, but lost control of the ball. Dave Bassett's team, shorn of on-strike Van Hooijdonk, looked to sub Dougie Freedman for inspiration, but his lob sailed too far.											
7	H	SOUTHAMPTON		4	W	1-0	0-0	Wright 61	Hislop	Sinclair	Dicks	Pearce	Ferdinand	Ruddock	Lampard	Berkovic^	Hartson	Wright"	Keller*	Lazaridis/Moncur/Potts
	28/9		**23,153**	*20*	12				*Jones*	*Warner*	*Benali*	*Palmer*	*Lundekvam*	*Monkou*	*Le Tissier*	*Gibbens**	*Ostenstad*	*Hughes M*	*Bridge*	*Beattie*
								Ref: U Rennie	A poor match which David Jones' Saints thought they had saved, but Monkou's 'goal' was ruled out for a foul on Dicks – his first Premiership game for 18 months. Wright celebrated his fourth goal for Hammers by a party-piece with Ruddock, imitating Di Canio's push on ref Alcock.											
8	A	BLACKBURN		9	L	0-3	0-1		Hislop	Impey	Dicks	Potts*	Ferdinand^	Pearce	Lampard	Moncur	Hartson	Wright	Sinclair	Keller/Hodges
	3/10		*25,213*	*17*	12			*Flitcroft 10, 47, Davidson 68*	*Flowers*	*Dailly*	*Davidson*	*Sherwood*	*Peacock*	*Henchoz**	*McKinlay*	*Gallacher^*	*Duff"*	*Flitcroft*	*Wilcox*	*Kenna/Dahlin/Johnson*
								Ref: K Burge	Roy Hodgson is grateful for anything, especially Ferdinand's frailty at the back which cost his team the first two goals. First he deflected Garry Flitcroft's shot past Hislop, then hit a strong back-pass which Hislop tried to take on his chest, but the loose ball was hustled away to Flitcroft.											
9	H	ASTON VILLA		8	D	0-0	0-0		Hislop	Sinclair	Dicks	Pearce	Ferdinand	Ruddock*	Lampard	Berkovic	Hartson	Wright^	Lomas	Impey/Kitson
	17/10		26,002	*1*	13				*Oakes*	*Charles*	*Wright*	*Southgate*	*Ehiogu*	*Barry*	*Taylor*	*Hendrie*	*Collymore*	*Merson*	*Thompson*	
								Ref: P Alcock	John Gregory's unbeaten Villa are four points clear and have conceded just two goals. Off the pitch, Hartson is in trouble for kicking Berkovic in the head in training, and his days at Upton Park are numbered. The ref, Paul Alcock, was last seen shoved over by Wednesday's Di Canio.											
10	A	CHARLTON		14	L	2-4	2-1	Rufus 18 (og), Berkovic 41	Hislop	Sinclair	Dicks	Pearce	Ferdinand	Ruddock	Lampard	Berkovic*	Hartson	Wright^	Lomas	Moncur/Kitson
	24/10		*20,043*	*9*	13			*Tiler 30, Mills 73, Hunt 88, Redf'rn 90p*	*Petterson*	*Mills*	*Powell*	*Tiler^*	*Rufus*	*Youds*	*Kinsella*	*Redfearn*	*Hunt*	*Mendonca**	*Mortimer*	*Jones/Robinson*
								Ref: N Barry	Curbishley's Addicks are sliding down after a good start. The restored Julian Dicks was given the runaround by Danny Mills. Richard Rufus headed an own-goal from Lampard's corner and Berkovic put away Wright's cross. Hunt scored off a post and Ferdinand tripped Robinson.											

No	H/A	Opponent / Date	Att	Pos	Res / Pts	F-A	H-T	Scorers, Times, and Referees	1	2	3	4	5	6	7	8	9	10	11	subs used
11	A	NEWCASTLE		8	W	3-0	0-0	Wright 56, 90, Sinclair 76	Hislop	Sinclair	Impey^	Pearce	Ferdinand	Ruddock	Lampard	Keller	Kitson*	Wright	Lomas	Hartson/Potts
		31/10	*36,744*	*11*	16				*Given*	*Griffin*	*Pearce !*	*Dabizas*	*Charvet*	*Glass**	*Dalglish"*	*Batty*	*Shearer*	*Solano^*	*Speed*	*Pistone/Ketsbaia/Gillespie*
								Ref: G Poll	Stuart Pearce will soon join West Ham. Here he helps them by fouling Sinclair and being sent off on 48 minutes at 0-0. Wright netted from 20 yards as defenders backed off and Sinclair scored a carbon-copy. Ruud Gullit's Newcastle had two first-half penalty appeals turned down.											
12	H	CHELSEA		9	D	1-1	1-0	Ruddock 4	Hislop	Sinclair	Lomas	Pearce	Ferdinand	Ruddock	Lampard	Berkovic*	Kitson	Wright	Keller	Potts
		8/11	26,023	*5*	17			*Babayaro 76*	*De Goey*	*Ferrer*	*Le Saux*	*Babayaro*	*Lambourde*	*Desailly*	*Poyet*	*Di Matteo^*	*Zola"*	*Casiraghi**	*Wise*	*Flo/Petrescu/Nicholls*
								Ref: G Barber	A game marred by injury to Casiraghi, who collided with Hislop, crocking his right knee. Stretcher-bearers took so long to arrive that Le Saux did their job. Hammers were leading through Ruddock's free-kick, which sparked his unusual celebration. Babayaro headed in Wise's corner.											
13	H	LEICESTER		6	W	3-2	1-1	Kitson 37, Lomas 56, Lampard 76	Hislop	Sinclair	Dicks	Pearce	Ferdinand	Lomas	Lampard	Berkovic	Kitson*	Wright	Keller	Moncur
		14/11	25,642	*9*	20			*Izzet 28, Lampard 87 (og)*	*Keller*	*Savage*	*Guppy*	*Elliott*	*Walsh*	*Sinclair*	*Lennon*	*Izzet**	*Fenton^*	*Ullathorne*	*Parker"*	*Cottee/Wilson/Campbell*
								Ref: S Lodge	Heskey is called up by England and City lose for the first time in ten games. Ullathorne passed to Izzet, who scored, and Lampard contrived a bizarre own-goal. In between, Kitson scored his first of the season, Lomas' shot went in off Steve Walsh, and Lampard's free-kick off the wall.											
14	A	DERBY		6	W	2-0	1-0	Hartson 7, Keller 72	Hislop	Sinclair	Keller*	Pearce	Ferdinand	Ruddock	Lampard	Berkovic	Kitson	Hartson	Lomas	Potts
		22/11	*31,366*	*11*	23				*Poom*	*Delap*	*Dorigo*	*Laursen*	*Carbonari"*	*Prior*	*Powell^*	*Sturridge*	*Baiano**	*Wanchope*	*Bohinen*	*Carsley/Eranio/Harper*
								Ref: A Wilkie	Berkovic earned the man-of-the-match award. At 0-0 Rory Delap shot wide with only Hislop to beat. But then a Berkovic cross was put away by Hartson and another by Keller – his first for West Ham, which flew in off the bar. Redknapp is angry that Impey has been sold to Leicester.											
15	H	TOTTENHAM		2	W	2-1	1-0	Sinclair 39, 46	Hislop	Sinclair	Lazaridis	Pearce	Ferdinand	Ruddock	Lampard	Berkovic*	Kitson	Hartson	Lomas	Potts
		28/11	**26,044**	*12*	26			*Armstrong 72*	*Baardsen*	*Carr*	*Sinton*	*Clemence**	*Young*	*Campbell*	*Anderton*	*Nielsen*	*Armstrong*	*Iversen*	*Ginola*	*Fox*
								Ref: D Gallagher	A hammer and tongs match whose critical moment came on 79 mins when Spurs' debutant Luke Young hit the bar. Baardsen spilled a shot by Lampard (wanted by Spurs) to Sinclair, who was set up again by Kitson. The win puts West Ham second behind Villa, but have played more.											
16	A	LEEDS		5	L	0-4	0-1	*[Hasselbaink 79]*	Hislop	Sinclair	Lazaridis*	Pearce	Margas	Ruddock !	Lampard	Lomas	Hartson	Wright	Keller	Moncur
		5/12	*36,315*	*3*	26			*Bowyer 8, 61, Molenaar 68,*	*Robinson*	*Haaland*	*Harte*	*Woodgate*	*Radebe*	*Molenaar*	*Hopkin*	*Smith^*	*Hasselbaink*	*Kewell**	*Bowyer*	*Wijnhard/McPhail*
								Ref: J Winter	O'Leary's Leeds overtake Hammers in style. Architect of the win was Lee Bowyer, a confessed West Ham fan, who somehow slipped through the Eastender net to sign for Arsenal, then Charlton. Margas botched the first goal. Ruddock was expelled for a bad foul on Kewell on 70 mins.											
17	A	MIDDLESBROUGH		7	L	0-1	0-1		Hislop	Sinclair	Lazaridis^	Pearce	Ferdinand	Potts	Lampard	Keller*	Hartson	Wright	Lomas	Moncur/Omoyimni
		12/12	*34,623*	*4*	26			*Deane 40*	*Schwarzer*	*Stockdale^*	*Gordon*	*Vickers*	*Cooper*	*Pallister*	*Mustoe*	*Gascoigne*	*Ricard**	*Deane*	*Townsend*	*Beck/Stamp*
								Ref: K Burge	Bryan Robson's Boro are unbeaten at the Riverside. Gascoigne does not have many good matches, but he did here. Steve Vickers headed onto a post before Brian Deane's head met skipper Andy Townsend's corner. Hartson hit the junction, but a draw would have flattered West Ham.											
18	H	EVERTON		7	W	2-1	1-0	Keller 19, Sinclair 75	Hislop	Sinclair	Keller	Pearce	Ferdinand	Dicks	Lampard	Berkovic	Hartson	Wright	Lomas	
		19/12	25,998	*15*	29			*Cadamarteri 71*	*Myhre*	*Ward**	*Cleland*	*Bilic*	*Materazzi*	*Unsworth*	*Cad'marteri*	*Grant^*	*Madar"*	*Dacourt*	*Hutchison*	*Collins/Barmby/Branch*
									Walter Smith is turning things around for Everton on a principle of defence above all else. In ten home games, his team have scored just three goals, and overall had conceded only 15, bettered only by Arsenal. Cadamarteri is one of Everton's young hopefuls who will soon lose his way.											
19	A	ARSENAL		7	L	0-1	0-1		Hislop	Sinclair	Keller*	Pearce	Ferdinand	Potts	Lampard	Berkovic	Hartson	Wright	Lomas	Lazaridis
		26/12	*38,098*	*5*	29			*Overmars 7*	*Manninger*	*Dixon*	*Vivas*	*Vieira*	*Keown*	*Bould*	*Parlour*	*Anelka**	*Petit*	*Bergkamp*	*Overmars*	*Wreh^/Grimandi*
								Ref: P Jones	Driving sleet, numbing cold, yet Arsenal still mustered 30 shots between them. The same couldn't be said of Hammers, for whom Hartson was invisible and Wright – mysteriously named captain for the day – blew kisses to the crowd. Ray Parlour played Overmars into space to score.											
20	H	COVENTRY		6	W	2-0	1-0	Wright 7, Hartson 68	Hislop	Sinclair	Lazaridis	Pearce	Ferdinand	Dicks	Lampard	Berkovic*	Hartson	Wright^	Lomas	Potts/Omoyimni
		28/12	25,662	*17*	32				*Ogrizovic*	*Nilsson*	*Edworthy**	*Breen*	*Shaw*	*Boateng*	*Soltvedt*	*Whelan*	*Aloisi^*	*McAllister*	*Froggatt*	*Telfer/Huckerby*
								Ref: P Durkin	Coventry's seventh game without a win sees their fans turn against skipper Gary McAllister. Hartson's goal – only his second in three months – will be his last in claret and blue. Berkovic's dummy set up Wright's goal, and Wright's cross set up Hartson's, from close in at the far post.											
21	A	MANCHESTER U		8	L	1-4	0-2	Lampard 69	Hislop	Potts	Lazaridis	Pearce	Ferdinand	Ruddock	Lampard	Berkovic	Hartson	Sinclair*	Lomas	Cole
		10/1	***55,180***	*3*	32			*Yorke 10, Cole 40, 67, Solskjaer 80*	*Van der G'w*	*Brown**	*Irwin*	*Berg*	*Keane^*	*Stam*	*Blomqvist*	*Butt"*	*Cole*	*Yorke*	*Giggs*	*Johnsen/Cruyff/Solskjaer*
								Ref: M Reed	West Ham have no answer to the Cole-Yorke partnership, now extended to 13 goals each. The kick-off was delayed by 45 minutes for a power failure, but as one wag said 'only half the pitch was needed'. Another added that lumbering Hartson 'had put on weight during the 90 minutes'.											

No	Date	Opponent	Att	Pos	Pt	F-A	H-T	Scorers, Times, and Referees	SQUAD	NUMBERS	IN USE									Subs used
22	H	SHEFFIELD WED		8	L	0-4	0-2	*[Carbone 73p]*	Hislop	Keller	**Minto**	Pearce	Ferdinand	Ruddock^	Lampard	Berkovic*	Abou	Sinclair	Lomas	Kitson/Cole
	16/1		25,642	*13*	32			*Hinchcliffe 26, Rudi 31, Humphreys 68,*	*Srnicek*	*Atherton*	*Hinchcliffe**	*Jonk*	*Emerson*	*Walker*	*Alex'derss'n*	*Carbone*	*Humphreys*	*Rudi*	*Sonner*	*Briscoe*
								Ref: K Burge	The Owls' second away win caps a disastrous week for West Ham, mauled by Man U, knocked out of the FA Cup by Swansea, selling Hartson to Wimbledon, and now this! Benito Carbone is class, scoring from the spot when Pearce toppled him. Di Canio is serving a long suspension.											
23	A	WIMBLEDON		9	D	0-0	0-0		Hislop	Breacker	Minto	Ruddock	Ferdinand	Dicks	Moncur	Lampard	Kitson	Cole*	**Foe**	**Di Canio**
	30/1		*23,035*	*7*	33				*Sullivan*	*Cunningham*	*Kimble*	*Hughes C*	*Thatcher*	*Perry*	*Euell*	*Earle*	*Ekoku**	*Hartson*	*Hughes M^*	*Leaburn/Kennedy*
								Ref: P Durkin	A day of debuts, Foe and (for the last 20 mins) Di Canio for West Ham, while Joe Cole starts a match for the first time; Hartson for the Dons. Taunted by the Hammers fans, he did nothing, other than foul Lampard and get booked. Kinnear's team were dire, Redknapp's almost as bad.											
24	H	ARSENAL		9	L	0-4	0-2	*[Parlour 87]*	Hislop	Breacker*	Minto	Pearce	Ferdinand	Dicks	Sinclair	Lampard	Kitson	Di Canio	Foe	Berkovic
	6/2		26,042	*3*	33			*Bergkamp 35, Overmars 45, Anelka 83,*	*Seaman*	*Dixon*	*Winterburn*	*Vieira*	*Keown*	*Adams*	*Parlour*	*Anelka*	*Petit*	*Bergkamp*	*Overmars*	
								Ref: J Winter	Hoddle has been sacked as England boss, Man U hit Forest for eight, and West Ham lose successive home matches 0-4. Wenger's Arsenal are on a roll, and Bergkamp is at his imperious best, stroking a classic goal while Foe snaps at his heels (and is booked). Di Canio did nothing at all.											
25	H	NOTT'M FOREST		8	W	2-1	2-0	Pearce 35, Lampard 39	Hislop	Sinclair	Lazaridis^	Pearce	Ferdinand	Ruddock	Lampard	Berkovic*	Kitson	Di Canio	Lomas	Cole/Minto
	13/2		25,458	*20*	36			*Hjelde 84*	*Beasant*	*Harkes^*	*Stensaas**	*Hjelde*	*Palmer*	*Johnson*	*Stone*	*Gemmill"*	*Van H'ijdonk*	*Shipperley*	*Rogers*	*Chettle/Quashie/Porfirio*
								Ref: R Harris	Ron Atkinson's basement Forest try to recover from losing 1-8 at home to Man U, while West Ham hope to arrest a run of 0-4 home defeats. This was a poor match, dotted with errors. West Ham won through Pearce's header from Berkovic's cross, and Lampard's shot from Sinclair's.											
26	A	LIVERPOOL		8	D	2-2	1-2	Lampard 24p, Keller 74	Hislop	Lomas	Mint^	Pearce*	Ferdinand	Potts	Lampard	Berkovic	Cole"	Foe	Sinclair	Lazaridis/Keller/**Holligan**
	20/2		*44,511*	*6*	37			*Fowler 22, Owen 45*	*James*	*Heggem*	*Bjornebye**	*Babb*	*Song*	*Staunton*	*McMan'm"^*	*Carragher*	*Fowler*	*Owen*	*Redknapp*	*Riedle/Berger*
								Ref: N Barry	West Ham twice come from behind, and might have won had not Sinclair lifted a chance over the bar. This, on a ground where they had scored just twice in 16 previous visits. Heggem fouled Minto for the penalty. Owen's goal needed a deflection and Keller's was direct from a corner.											
27	H	BLACKBURN		6	W	2-0	2-0	Pearce 28, Di Canio 31	Hislop	Lomas	Keller	Pearce	Ferdinand	Potts	Lampard	Berkovic	Sinclair	Di Canio	Foe	
	27/2		25,529	*18*	40				*Filan*	*McAteer*	*Davidson*	*Dunn"*	*Peacock*	*Broomes*	*Jansen**	*Gillespie*	*Ward*	*Blake*	*Wilcox^*	*Davies/Duff/Croft*
								Ref: S Dunn	Brian Kidd's Rovers were so overwhelmed in the first half that he made three changes in the second that transformed the game. Di Canio had crossed for Pearce's far-post header and Di Canio netted his first for the club from close in, courtesy of Berkovic. Hislop made three fine saves.											
28	A	SOUTHAMPTON		7	L	0-1	0-1		Hislop	Lomas	Keller	Pearce	Ferdinand	Ruddock	Lampard	Berkovic	Sinclair	Di Canio	Foe*	Kitson
	6/3		***15,240***	*19*	40			*Kachloul 10*	*Jones*	*Hiley*	*Colleter*	*Marsden*	*Lundekvam*	*Benali*	*Kachloul*	*Oakley*	*Beattie*	*Hughes M*	*Le Tissier**	*Ripley*
								Ref: D Gallagher	Dave Jones' Saints are pulling clear. Their fifth home win out of the last six came from Moroccan Kachloul's shot, deflected by Rio Ferdinand. They were indebted to Paul Jones for defying a lively Hammers attack, and to Scott Hiley, who somehow cleared under the bar from Di Canio.											
29	A	CHELSEA		7	W	1-0	0-0	Kitson 75	Hislop	Sinclair	Mint	Pearce	Ferdinand	Ruddock	Lampard	Lomas	Kitson	Foe	Keller*	Potts
	13/3		*34,765*	*3*	43				*De Goey*	*Ferrer*	*Le Saux^*	*Goldbaek*	*Myers"*	*Desailly**	*Babayaro*	*Di Matteo*	*Flo*	*Zola*	*Wise*	*Duberry/Petrescu/Forssell*
								Ref: S Lodge	Chelsea went out of the FA Cup on Wednesday, and now lose at home for the first time this season. Their title chances have gone. A low-key match was settled by the recalled Kitson, the ball bobbling in off De Goey's legs after Foe had headed it down. Stamford Bridge went quiet.											
30	H	NEWCASTLE		5	W	2-0	1-0	Di Canio 17, Kitson 82	Hislop	Sinclair	Mint	Pearce	Ferdinand	Ruddock	Lampard	Foe	Kitson	Di Canio	Lomas	
	20/3		25,997	*12*	46				*Given*	*Griffin*	*Domi*	*Dabizas*	*Charvet*	*Solano*	*Maric^*	*Georgiadis**	*Shearer*	*Saha*	*Speed*	*Lee/Ketsbaia*
								Ref: P Durkin	Di Canio has come into his own, his white boots shimmering through Newcastle's defence. He netted with defenders appealing for offside, but one of them had played the ball. Back to goal, Kitson turned to fire No 2. Gullit's team were shapeless and lifeless, and Shearer looked bored.											
31	A	ASTON VILLA		5	D	0-0	0-0		Hislop	Sinclair	Mint	Pearce	Ferdinand*	Ruddock	Lampard	Lomas	Kitson	Di Canio	Foe	Potts
	2/4		*36,813*	*6*	47				*Bosnich*	*Watson*	*Wright*	*Southgate*	*Calderwood*	*Stone*	*Taylor*	*Draper*	*Dublin*	*Joachim*	*Thomps'n**	*Merson*
									John Gregory's Villa were top but are now on the slide. West Ham keep a third successive clean sheet and in the circumstances a goalless draw was always going to be the most likely result. West Ham might be fifth, but they are 10 points behind third-placed Leeds, so can go no higher.											

No					F-A	H-T	Scorers, Times, and Referees												
32	H	CHARLTON	5	L	0-1	0-0		Hislop	Sinclair	Minto	Lomas	Pearce	Ruddock	Lampard	Foe	Kitson*	Di Canio	Keller	Berkovic
	5/4	26,041	*16*	47			*Stuart 75*	*Ilic"*	*Mills*	*Powell*	*Robinson^*	*Rufus*	*Tiler*	*Kinsella*	*Pringle*	*Hunt**	*Barnes*	*Stuart*	*Jones/Bowen/Petterson*
							Ref: S Dunn	Charlton secure their first double of the season and move out of the bottom three. But the win has its price. Ilic and Robinson are stretchered off. John Barnes starts his first game for Charlton. The goal from £1m Graham Stuart, signed on the transfer deadline, exploited Minto's error.											
33	A	LEICESTER	6	D	0-0	0-0		Hislop	Sinclair	Minto	Potts	Pearce	Ruddock	Lampard	Berkovic	Kitson*	Di Canio^	Lomas	Wright/Moncur
	10/4	*20,402*	*13*	48				*Keller*	*Impey**	*Guppy*	*Elliott*	*Ullathorne*	*Sinclair*	*Lennon*	*Gunnl'gs'n^*	*Cottee*	*Savage*	*Heskey*	*Miller/Marshall*
							Ref: J Winter	When none of the original 22 players came close to scoring a goal, on comes Ian Wright for the final 18 minutes, following three months out following knee surgery. His awkward shovelled effort was kept out by Kasey Keller. This was Filbert Street's first goalless draw of the season.											
34	H	DERBY	6	W	**5-1**	2-0	Di Canio 19, Berkovic 28, Wright 55,	Hislop	Lomas^	Minto	Potts*	Pearce	Ruddock	Lampard	Berkovic	Sinclair	Di Canio	Foe	Wright/Cole
	17/4	25,485	*8*	51			*Wanchope 79* [Rudd'k 64, Sincl'r 68]	*Hoult*	*Schnoor*	*Dorigo**	*Laursen*	*Carbonari*	*Prior*	*Bohinen*	*Sturridge*	*Beck^*	*Wanchope*	*Powell*	*Harper/Murray*
							Ref: K Burge	The best goal of this peculiar match was scored by Paulo Wanchope from an angle so tight so it probably played a part in Redknapp's decision to buy him. Derby started the better, but were undone by Di Canio, whose 20-yard shot was deflected past Hoult. Injury-hit County collapsed.											
35	A	TOTTENHAM	6	W	2-1	1-0	Wright 5, Keller 66	Hislop	Sinclair	Minto	Moncur !	Ferdinand	Pearce	Lampard	Berkovic	Keller	Wright*	Lomas	Lazaridis
	24/4	*36,089*	*10*	54			*Ginola 73*	*Walker*	*Carr*	*Taricco*	*Freund*	*Young*	*Campbell*	*Anderton^*	*Sherwood*	*Iversen**	*Dominguez*	*Ginola*	*Armstrong/Nielsen*
							Ref: U Rennie	Spurs boss George Graham knows all about Ian Wright from their Arsenal days. But even Graham must have felt miffed by Wright's cheeky chip over Walker. Eyal Berkovic created that goal, and Keller's. Moncur was sent off in injury-time for a senseless lunge at Jose Dominguez.											
36	H	LEEDS	6	L	1-5	0-2	Di Canio 48 *[B'wyer 78, H'land 79]*	Hislop !	Sinclair*	Minto	Lomas !	Foe	Ruddock	Lampard	Berkovic	Di Canio^	Wright !	Moncur	Cole/**Coyne**/Forrest
	1/5	25,997	*4*	54			*Hasselbaink 1, Smith 45, Harte 62p*	*Martyn*	*Haaland*	*Harte*	*Woodgate*	*Radebe*	*Batty*	*McPhail*	*Smith^*	*Hasselb'nk**	*Kewell*	*Bowyer*	*Wijnhard/Ribeiro*
							Ref: R Harris	Leeds kept their heads and West Ham didn't. It all started in the first seconds, when Batty's lunge went unpunished and Hasselbaink cut in to score. Three Hammers were sent off, Wright for lunging at Ian Harte, Hislop for felling Hasselbaink (penalty), and Lomas for a foul on Harte.											
37	A	EVERTON	6	L	**0-6**	0-3	*[Hutchison 38, Jeffers 87]*	Hislop	Sinclair	Minto	Lomas	Ferdinand	Ruddock	Lampard	Berkovic	Di Canio	Wright*	Foe	Keller
	8/5	*40,029*	*14*	54			*Campbell 14, 52, 77, Ball 25p,*	*Myhre*	*Weir*	*Ball*	*Short*	*Watson*	*Unsworth*	*Gemmill*	*Jeffers*	*Campbell*	*Dacourt*	*Hutchison*	
							Ref: A Wilkie	Duncan Ferguson has gone to Newcastle but Kevin Campbell is filling his boots. Following his hat-trick he led Walter Smith's side on a lap of honour. Ian Wright had scored 15 goals in 17 games against Everton, but Unsworth kept him tied up. Lomas shoved Gemmill for the penalty.											
38	H	MIDDLESBROUGH	5	W	4-0	2-0	Lampard 4, Keller 26, Sinclair 75, 78	Forrest	Keller	Minto	Potts	Ferdinand	Ruddock	Lampard	Berkovic	Sinclair*	Di Canio	Foe	Keller
	16/5	25,902	*9*	57				*Schwarzer*	*Cummins*	*Gordon*	*Vickers*	*Townsend*	*Pallister*	*Mustoe*	*Summerbell*	*Ricard^*	*Deane**	*O'Neill"*	*C'pbell/Armstrong/Maddis'n*
	Home	Away					Ref: G Willard	This win lifts West Ham to fifth, the second highest placing in their history. Lampard's early rocket, following a short-corner routine, set the seal, as Redknapp shrugged off the loss of Wright, Lomas and Hislop, all suspended. Berkovic, in what would be his last match, was superb.											
Average	25,639	31,683																	

Worthington Cup		Att			F-A	H-T	Scorers, Times, and Referees	SQUAD	NUMBERS	IN	USE								subs used
2:1	A	NORTHAMPTON	8	L	0-2	0-0		Hislop	Sinlcair	Lazaridis	Potts	Pearce	Ruddock*	Lampard	Berkovic	Hartson	Wright	Moncur	Breacker
	15/9	*7254 2:19*					*Freestone 77, 85*	*Woodham*	*Gibb*	*Parrish*	*Sampson*	*Warburton*	*Peer*	*Hunter**	*Spedding*	*Freestone^*	*Corazzin"*	*Hill*	*Hunt/Heggs/Wilkinson*
							Ref: P Alcock	This is worse than it looks: in the League Ian Atkins' Cobblers won't win any of their first five games. New Sixfields Stadium erupted when Chris Freestone – £75,000 from Middlesbrough, pounced when Ali Gibbs' shot bounced off Pearce and a post. Roy Hunter crossed for No 2.											
2:2	H	NORTHAMPTON	8	W	1-0	0-0	Lampard 90	Hislop	Impey	Dicks	Potts	Ferdinand	Pearce	Keller	Lampard	Abou*	Wright	Sinclair	Omoyimni
	22/9	25,435 *2:20*						*Woodham*	*Gibb*	*Frain*	*Sampson*	*Warburton*	*Peer*	*Hunter**	*Wilkinson*	*Freestone"*	*Parrish*	*Hill*	*Spedding^/Dobson/Corazzin*
							Ref: D Gallagher (Hammers lose 1-2 on aggregate)	The stats say it all. West Ham mustered 27 shots to Northampton's three, and 16 corners to none. The match was in injury-time when Lampard put away Dicks' (18 months out) cross, but TV replays showed that Ian Wright had been onside when scoring earlier, but he was given offside.											

FA Cup																			
3	H	SWANSEA	6	D	1-1	0-0	Dicks 87	Hislop	Sinclair	Lazaridis*	Pearce	Ruddock	Dicks	Potts	Berkovic^	Hartson"	Wright	Lomas	Omoyimni/Cole/Abou
	2/1	26,039 *3:11*					*Smith 61*	*Freestone*	*Jones*	*Howard*	*Cusack*	*Smith*	*Bound*	*Coates*	*Thomas*	*Alsop*	*Watkin*	*Roberts*	
							Ref: S Lodge	It took Dicks' first goal in two years to deny John Hollins' Swans victory, the ball going under Freestone from 25 yards. Minus Redknapp (flu) and Ferdinand (back), West Ham were also handicapped by Swansea-born Hartson, who did nothing. Jason Smith headed in Robert's cross.											
3R	A	SWANSEA	8	L	0-1	0-1		Hislop	Breacker*	Lazaridis	Ruddock	Ferdinand	Dicks	Lampard	Omoyimni^	Hartson	Lomas	Sinclair	Hall/Berkovic
	13/1	*10,116 3:12*					*Thomas 29*	*Freestone*	*Jones S*	*Howard*	*Cusack*	*Smith*	*Bound*	*Coates*	*Thomas*	*Alsop*	*Watkin*	*Roberts*	
							Ref: S Lodge	This is the biggest Cup upset so far. Reasons are not hard to find. Swansea-born Hartson is invisible and within hours has signed for the Dons. Dicks is so crocked he was given the runaround and booked. Martin Thomas, given a free-transfer by Keegan's Fulham, netted from 20 yards.											

	P	Home W	D	L	F	A	Away W	D	L	F	A	Pts
1 Manchester U	38	14	4	1	45	18	8	9	2	35	19	79
2 Arsenal	38	14	5	0	34	5	8	7	4	25	12	78
3 Chelsea	38	12	6	1	29	13	8	9	2	28	17	75
4 Leeds	38	12	5	2	32	9	6	8	5	30	25	67
5 WEST HAM	38	11	3	5	32	26	5	6	8	14	27	57
6 Aston Villa	38	10	3	6	33	28	5	7	7	18	18	55
7 Liverpool	38	10	5	4	44	24	5	4	10	24	25	54
8 Derby	38	8	7	4	22	19	5	6	8	18	26	52
9 Middlesbro	38	7	9	3	25	18	5	6	8	23	36	51
10 Leicester	38	7	6	6	25	25	5	7	7	15	21	49
11 Tottenham	38	7	7	5	28	26	4	7	8	19	24	47
12 Sheffield Wed	38	7	5	7	20	15	6	2	11	21	27	46
13 Newcastle	38	7	6	6	26	25	4	7	8	22	29	46
14 Everton	38	6	8	5	22	12	5	2	12	20	35	43
15 Coventry	38	8	6	5	26	21	3	3	13	13	30	42
16 Wimbledon	38	7	7	5	22	21	3	5	11	18	42	42
17 Southampton	38	9	4	6	29	26	2	4	13	8	38	41
18 Charlton	38	4	7	8	20	20	4	5	10	21	36	36
19 Blackburn	38	6	5	8	21	24	1	9	9	17	28	35
20 Nott'm Forest	38	3	7	9	18	31	4	2	13	17	38	30
	760	169	115	96	553	406	96	115	169	406	553	1025

Odds & ends

Double wins: (3) Newcastle, Derby, Totttenham.
Double losses: (3) Charlton, Leeds, Arsenal.

Won from behind: (1) Leicester (h).
Lost from in front: (2) Wimbledon (h), Charlton (a).

High spots: Finishing fifth, the second highest position in West Ham's history.
Climbing to second in November, albeit having played more games.

Low spots: Humiliating defeats to lower division clubs in both cups.
Despite finishing fifth, a goal-difference of minus 7 was exceeded by only six other teams.
West Ham conceded four goals or more on *eight* occasions.
The fall of Hartson from scourge of defenders to overweight joke.
Losing 3-4 at home to Wimbledon after leading 3-0.

Hammer of the Year: Shaka Hislop
Ever-presents: Frank Lampard (League only).
Hat-tricks: (0).
Leading scorer: Ian Wright (9).

	Appearances Lge	*Sub*	LC	*Sub*	FAC	*Sub*	Goals Lge	LC	FAC	Tot
Abou, Samassi	**2**	*1*	1			*1*				
Berkovic, Eyal	**28**	*2*	1		1	*1*	**3**			**3**
Breacker, Tim	**2**	*1*		*1*	1					
Cole, Joe	**2**	*6*				*1*				
Coyne, Chris		*1*								
Di Canio, Paolo	**12**	*1*					**4**			**4**
Dicks, Julian	**9**		1		2			1		**1**
Ferdinand, Rio	**31**		1		1					
Foe, Marc Vivien	**13**									
Forrest, Craig	**1**	*1*								
Hall, Richard						*1*				
Hartson, John	**16**	*1*	1		2		**4**			**4**
Hislop, Shaka	**37**		2		2					
Hodges, Lee		*1*								
Holligan, Gavin		*1*								
Impey, Andrew	**6**	*2*	1							
Keller, Marc	**17**	*4*	1				**5**			**5**
Kitson, Paul	**13**	*4*					**3**			**3**
Lampard, Frank	**38**		2		1		**5**		1	**6**
Lazaridis, Stan	**11**	*4*	1		2					
Lomas, Steve	**30**				2					
Margas, Javier	**3**									
Minto, Scott	**14**	*1*								
Moncur, John	**6**	*8*	1							
Omoyimni, Emmanuel		*3*		*1*	1	*1*				
Pearce, Ian	**33**		2		1		**2**			**2**
Potts, Steve	**11**	*8*	2		1					
Ruddock, Neil	**27**		1		2		**2**			**2**
Sinclair, Trevor	**36**		2		2		**7**			**7**
Wright, Ian	**20**	*2*	2		1		**9**			**9**
(own-goals)							**1**			**1**
29 players used	**418**	***52***	**22**	***2***	**22**	***5***	**45**	**1**	**1**	**47**

No	Date		Att	Pos	Pt	F-A	H-T	Scorers, Times, and Referees	SQUAD	NUMBERS	IN	USE								subs used
1	H	TOTTENHAM			W	1-0	1-0	Lampard 45	Hislop	**Pearce S**	Ferdinand	Pearce I*	Potts	Foe	Di Canio^	Lampard	Minto	**Wanchope**	Sinclair	Keller/Cole
	8/8		26,010		3				*Walker*	*Carr*	*Campbell**	*Perry*	*Edinburgh*	*Anderton*	*Sherwood*	*Freund*	*Ginola^*	*Iversen*	*Dominguez"*	*Scales/Leon'sen/Ferdinand*
								Ref: P Durkin / D Elleray	Foe heads against the bar in the first minute, but West Ham keep their foot on the gas and Di Canio slips the ball through to Lampard. Injuries abound – ref Durkin and Campbell pull calf muscles, and Stuart Pearce crocks Ian's leg. Spurs pull off Ginola and Dominguez at half-time.											
2	A	ASTON VILLA		9	D	2-2	1-1	Southgate 7 (og), Sinclair 90	Hislop	Pearce S	Ferdinand	Minto	Potts	Foe	Di Canio*	Lampard	Moncur^	Wanchope	Sinclair	Kitson/Keller
	16/8		*26,250*	*2*	4			*Dublin 5, 52*	*James*	*Ehiogu*	*Southgate*	*Calderwood*	*Delaney*	*Boateng**	*Taylor*	*Thompson^*	*Wright*	*Joachim*	*Dublin*	*Hendrie/Stone*
								Ref: M Riley	These are the only two 100% teams in the Premiership. Dion Dublin easily skirts Ferdinand to score at the near post. Southgate turns Foe's wayward shot past James. Dublin belts his second when Wanchope fails to clear. But Wanchope deftly back-heels to Sinclair in injury-time.											
3	H	LEICESTER		7	W	2-1	1-1	Wanchope 29, Di Canio 53	Hislop	Pearce S	Ferdinand	Lomas	Potts	Foe	Di Canio	Lampard	Moncur	Wanchope	Sinclair	
	21/8		23,631	*15*	7			*Heskey 2*	*Flowers*	*Sinclair*	*Elliott*	*Taggart**	*Impey*	*Lennon*	*Izzet*	*Savage^*	*Guppy*	*Cottee*	*Heskey*	*Gilchrist/Marshall*
								Ref: A Wiley	Emile Heskey scores from an improbable angle past the embarrassed Ferdinand and Hislop. That silences Upton Park and Leicester appear untroubled for long spells. Wanchope turns in Lampard's wayward effort. Di Canio swivels to fire the winner. Both teams waste late chances.											
4	A	BRADFORD C		4	W	3-0	2-0	Di Canio 34, Sinclair 44, Wanchope 49	Hislop	Pearce S	Ferdinand*	Lomas	Potts	Keller	Di Canio	Lampard	Moncur	Wanchope	Sinclair	**Carrick**
	28/8		*17,926*	*18*	10				*Walsh*	*McCall*	*Wetherall*	*Whalley*	*Beagrie*	*O'Brien**	*Windass^*	*Halle*	*Dreyer*	*Jacobs*	*Saunders"*	*Mills/Redfearn/Blake*
								Ref: P Jones	This is Hammers' 10th match of the season, leaving them two games in hand over most Premiership opponents. West Ham withstood City's early onslaught, then Wanchope chests the ball into Di Canio's path. Sinclair then hit a belter. At 3-0, City hit the bar and Ferdinand limps off.											
5	H	WATFORD		3	W	1-0	0-0	Di Canio 48	Hislop	Pearce S*	**Stimac**	Lomas	Potts	Keller	Di Canio	Lampard	Moncur^	Wanchope	Sinclair	Margas/Carrick
	11/9		25,310	*15*	13				*Chamberlain*	*Lyttle*	*Kennedy*	*Page*	*Palmer*	*Robinson*	*Hyde*	*Mooney*	*Wright**	*Smart^*	*Williams*	*Gudmundsson/Ngonge*
								Ref: D Gallagher	Wanchope and Pearce strike the bar in the same attack, which ends with another Wanchope effort hacked off the line. Just before half-time Pearce breaks his leg in a tackle with Hyde, though Pearce tries to play on. Di Canio bends a free-kick in at the near post which no one expects.											
6	A	EVERTON		8	L	0-1	0-0		Hislop	Margas	Stimac	Lomas	Potts	Keller	Di Canio	Lampard	Moncur	Wanchope	Sinclair	
	19/9		*35,154*	*7*	13			*Jeffers 64*	*Gerrard*	*Dunne*	*Weir*	*Gough*	*Unsworth**	*Hutchison^*	*Xavier*	*Collins*	*Barmby*	*Jeffers"*	*Campbell*	*Gemmell/Ball/Cleland*
								Ref: S Bennett	Hammers' first defeat of the season sees Everton leapfrog above them, but the Toffees have played two games more. Young Francis Jeffers scored with a scuffed shot that slithered under Hislop, who was playing despite a thigh strain. Hutchison and Wanchope both missed chances.											
7	A	COVENTRY		9	L	0-1	0-1		Hislop	Lomas	Stimac	Foe	Potts	Keller*	Di Canio	Lampard	Moncur !	Wanchope	Sinclair	Newton
	25/9		*19,993*	*15*	13			*Hadji 36*	*Hedman*	*Hall*	*Shaw*	*Konjic*	*Edworthy*	*Chippo**	*Palmer*	*Telfer*	*McAllister^*	*Hadji*	*Keane*	*Williams/McSheffrey*
								Ref: D Elleray	Both teams are wrecked by injury. The season's second win for Coventry; second defeat for West Ham. Moroccan Hadji heads in McAllister's free-kick. Moncur gets a second yellow on 72 minutes for kicking McAllister, after which Hammers rule. Hedman saves Wanchope's effort.											
8	H	ARSENAL		9	W	2-1	1-0	Di Canio 29, 72	Hislop	Lomas	Stimac	Foe !	Potts	Ruddock	Di Canio	Lampard	Moncur*	Wanchope^	Sinclair	Margas/Kitson
	3/10		26,009	*5*	16			*Suker 77*	*Seaman*	*Luzhny**	*Adams*	*Keown*	*Silvinho*	*Ljungberg*	*Grimandi*	*Vieira !*	*Henry^*	*Bergkamp*	*Suker*	*Overmars/Kanu*
								Ref: M Reed	Hammers' first home win over Arsenal for 12 years is a thriller, fussily refereed by Mike Reed who flourishes 12 yellow cards, two apiece for Foe and Vieira, who gobs at Ruddock before departing. Di Canio scores two beauties, made by a dribble and a chip. Suker fluffs many chances.											
9	A	MIDDLESBROUGH		10	L	0-2	0-0		Hislop !	Lomas	Stimac	Ruddock	Ferdinand	Keller*	Di Canio	Lampard	Moncur^	Wanchope	Sinclair	Cole/Forrest
	17/10		*31,862*	*11*	16			*Deane 51, Armstrong 88*	*Schwarzer*	*Vickers*	*Pallister*	*Cooper*	*Fleming*	*Juninho*	*Ince*	*Ziege*	*O'Neill*	*Deane*	*Ricard**	*Armstrong*
								Ref: U Rennie	Di Canio's reputation for diving costs him a booking rather than the penalty he deserves when Pallister took his leg in the box. Hislop handles outside the box and walks before the ref can get the red card from his pocket. Deane capitalises when Ince's 25-yarder comes back off the bar.											
10	H	SUNDERLAND		11	D	1-1	0-1	Sinclair 89	Hislop	Lomas*	Stimac^	Margas	Ferdinand	Keller	Di Canio	Lampard	Cole	Wanchope"	Sinclair	Moncur/Ruddock/Kitson
	24/10		26,022	*3*	17			*Phillips 24*	*Sorensen*	*Makin*	*Butler*	*Bould !*	*Gray**	*Summerbee*	*McCann*	*Rae^*	*Schwarz*	*Phillips*	*Quinn"*	*Williams/Roy/Dichio*
								Ref: M Halsey	West Ham never play on Saturdays these days. Sunderland would have gone top had they held onto Kevin Phillips' 13th goal of the season. Bould goes for head-butting Wanchope on 19 mins and Hammers hit the woodwork three times before Sinclair tops a 50-yard run with a goal.											

No	Venue	Opponent / Date	Att	Pos	Res / Pts	F-A	H-T	Scorers, Times, and Referees	1	2	3	4	5	6	7	8	9	10	11	subs used
11	A	LIVERPOOL		12	L	0-1	0-1		Hislop	Potts	Ruddock	Ferdinand	Lomas	Keller	Lampard	Cole	Sinclair	Kitson	Wanchope	
		27/10	*44,012*	*9*	17			*Camara 43*	*Westerveld*	*Song*	*Henchoz*	*Hyypia*	*Matteo*	*Thompson**	*Redknapp*	*Carragher*	*Berger*	*Meijer*	*Camara^*	*Heggem/Smicer*
								Ref: S Lodge	Hammers are fading badly, and defeat at Anfield, where three teams have won so far this season, continues the trend. West Ham have only themselves to blame for the goal. Ferdinand made a hash of clearing Song's centre and Camara bundled the ball in. Di Canio is out, suspended.											
12	A	LEEDS		12	L	0-1	0-0		Hislop	Margas	Ruddock	Ferdinand	Lomas	Keller	Lampard	Moncur	Foe*	Kitson	Wanchope	Cole
		30/10	*40,190*	*1*	17			*Harte 57*	*Martyn*	*Kelly*	*Radebe*	*Woodgate*	*Harte*	*Bowyer*	*McPhail*	*Batty*	*Kewell*	*Smith**	*Bridges*	*Huckerby*
								Ref: G Poll	Five straight away league defeats without a goal send Hammers into the bottom half. Shock leaders Leeds control for 75 mins against defensive West Ham. Lomas's poor header out (shades of Arsenal) is whacked back by full-back Harte. Cole comes on too late to make any difference.											
13	A	CHELSEA		11	D	0-0	0-0		Forrest	Margas !	Stimac	Ferdinand	Lomas	Keller	Lampard	Cole*	Foe	Sinclair	Wanchope	Ruddock
		7/11	*34,935*	*9*	18				*De Goey*	*Ferrer*	*Leboeuf*	*Desailly*	*Babayaro*	*Petrescu*	*Morris*	*Deschamps*	*Poyet*	*Zola**	*Flo*	*Ambrosetti*
								Ref: M Riley	Chelsea can win in Europe but not in the league; West Ham can't win anywhere at the moment. They haven't scored an away league goal since August. In fact, neither side managed a serious shot for 44 mins. In the 87th minute Margas got his second yellow for elbowing Deschamps.											
14	H	SHEFFIELD WED		10	W	4-3	1-1	Wanchope 28, Di Canio 62p, Foe 70,	Hislop	Potts	Ruddock	Ferdinand	Foe	Sinclair	Lampard	Cole	Keller	Di Canio	Wanchope	
		22/11	23,015	*20*	21			*Rudi 38, Jonk 48, Booth 66* [Lamp' 76]	*Pressman*	*Nolan**	*Atherton*	*Walker*	*Hinchcliffe*	*Alex'ders'on*	*Sonner !*	*Jonk*	*Rudi^*	*De Bilde*	*Booth*	*Thorne/Cresswell*
								Ref: A Wilkie	A Sunday thriller, but the key decisions went against the Owls. They led 2-1 when Sinclair dived under Jonk's non-existent tackle to earn a penalty. Wednesday led 3-2 when Sonner clattered Di Canio twice within four minutes and earned two yellows. Lampard's screamer won it.											
15	H	LIVERPOOL		9	W	1-0	1-0	Sinclair 45	Hislop	Margas	Ruddock	Ferdinand	Lomas	Sinclair	Lampard	Cole	Keller	Di Canio	Wanchope*	Kitson
		28/11	26,043	*6*	24				*Westerfeld*	*Song**	*Henchoz*	*Hyypia*	*Matteo*	*Heggem*	*Gerrard*	*Hamann*	*Berger^*	*Murphy*	*Owen"*	*Meijer/Thompson/Staunton*
								Ref: G Barber	Yet again Hammers win a game that could have gone against them. Few condoned the out-of-form Owen for diving, for which he was booked, but the raised flag which denied Owen's header (the ball had gone out) looked harsh. Sinclair pounced after Westerfeld parried from Di Canio.											
16	A	TOTTENHAM		8	D	0-0	0-0		Hislop	Margas*	Ruddock	Ferdinand	Lomas !	Foe	Lampard	Cole	Sinclair	Di Canio^	Kitson"	Potts/Wanchope/Minto
		6/12	*36,233*	*7*	25				*Walker*	*Young*	*Campbell*	*Perry*	*Taricco*	*Leonhards'n*	*Freund*	*Sherwood**	*Dominguez^*	*Ginola*	*Iversen*	*Nielsen/Armstrong*
								Ref: P Jones	Two things of note in this forgettable 100th league derby with Spurs. First it extends Hammers' goalless run on their league travels to 11 hours, 11 minutes, since scoring 3 at Bradford in August. Second, Lomas was sent off for two debatable yellows on Dominguez late in the first half.											
17	H	MANCHESTER U		9	L	2-4	1-3	Di Canio 23, 52	Hislop	Lomas	Ruddock	Ferdinand	Minto	Foe	Lampard	Keller	Sinclair	Di Canio	Wanchope	
		18/12	26,037	*1*	25			*Yorke 9, 62, Giggs 13, 19*	*V d Gouw*	*Neville G*	*Stam*	*Silvestre*	*Irwin**	*Beckham^*	*Scholes*	*Keane*	*Giggs*	*Sheringham*	*Yorke*	*Neville P/Butt*
								Ref: U Rennie	Astonishing! Stunned by the Villa cup fiasco, Hammers are hit by three quick goals. Each is a mixture of Man U's skill and Ruddock's frailty. Di Canio, a one-man team, hauls the Hammers back. But he fails when one-on-one with the keeper. Yorke's killer goes through Hislop's legs.											
18	A	WIMBLEDON		11	D	2-2	0-1	Sinclair 45, Lampard 81	Hislop	Margas	Ruddock	Ferdinand	Minto	Foe	Lampard	Cole	Sinclair	Di Canio	Wanchope	
		26/12	*21,180*	*14*	26			*Hreidarsson 33, Ardley 85*	*Sullivan*	*Cunningh'm*	*Andersen*	*Hreidarss'n*	*Kimble*	*Badir*	*Earle*	*Euell*	*Ardley*	*Leaburn**	*Gayle*	*Hughes*
								Ref: S Dunn	The Dons' 10th Premiership draw, achieved without the injured Hartson. Hreidarsson headed his first goal since signing from Brentford, but Sinclair headed in one Di Canio's cross and Lampard another. West Ham thought they had won until Hislop spilled Kimble's corner to Ardley.											
19	H	DERBY		10	D	1-1	1-1	Di Canio 21	Hislop	Potts	Margas	Ferdinand	Minto*	Foe	Lampard	Cole	Sinclair	Di Canio	Wanchope	Keller
		28/12	24,998	*18*	27			*Sturridge 4*	*Poom*	*Prior*	*Carboni*	*Elliott*	*Laursen*	*Burley*	*Bohinen*	*Powell*	*Johnson*	*Robinson**	*Sturrock*	*Beck*
								Ref: A Wiley	A wretched December for Hammers, who fail to win in the league, are knocked out of FA Cup by Tranmere, and have to replay their League Cup-tie with Villa. Lowly Derby scored early when the ball broke to Sturridge, but local hero Di Canio beat two men to shoot in off the bar.											
20	A	NEWCASTLE		11	D	2-2	0-1	Lampard 84, Stimac 88	Hislop	Potts	Stimac	Ferdinand	Minto	Foe	Lampard	Cole	Sinclair	Keller*	Carrick	Byrne
		3/1	*36,314*	*15*	28			*Dabizas 18, Speed 65*	*Harper*	*Barton*	*Marcelino*	*Dabizas*	*Pistone*	*Solano*	*Lee**	*Speed*	*Gallacher^*	*Shearer*	*Ferguson"*	*Fumaca/Glass/Ketsbaia*
								Ref: R Harris	Newcastle have yet to lose at home under Bobby Robson and fielded their first unchanged team for 68 games. Without their regular strikeforce Hammers looked set to lose, but Lampard scored off a post and then Stimac headed his first goal for the Hammers from Sinclair's free-kick.											
21	H	ASTON VILLA		11	D	1-1	0-1	Di Canio 78	Hislop	Stimac	Margas	Ferdinand	Keller	Lomas	Lampard	Cole	Sinclair	Di Canio	Wanchope	
		15/1	24,237	*10*	29			*Taylor 24*	*James*	*Ehiogu*	*Southgate*	*Barry*	*Stone*	*Boateng**	*Taylor*	*Merson*	*Wright*	*Carbone^*	*Joachim*	*Calderwood/Vassell*
								Ref: G Poll	These two teams are sick of each other, not least Wanchope, whose scoop over the bar from five yards counts as miss of the season. Ian Taylor, scourge of the replayed quarter-final puts away a low cross. David James drops the ball to Di Canio who levels. Wanchope heads onto the bar.											

No	Date		Att	Pos	Pt	F-A	H-T	Scorers, Times, and Referees	SQUAD	NUMBERS	IN	USE								subs used
22	A	LEICESTER		8	W	3-1	2-1	Wanchope 13, 45, Di Canio 60	Hislop*	Ruddock	Ferdinand	Margas	Lomas^	Cole	Lampard	Sinclair	Keller"	Di Canio	Wanchope	Forrest/Carrick/Minto
	22/1		19,019	10	32			Heskey 24	Arphexad	Sinclair	Gilchrist	Elliott	Goodwin	Eadie	Campbell	Zagorakis*	Gun'l'g'son^	Heskey	Fenton	Stewart/Thomas
								Ref: D Elleray	Neither team had won in the league since November. Perhaps it was the rumour that Stan Collymore would sign that make Wanchope notch his first goals for ages. Hislop's hamstring almost took him off during the warm-up. He lasted only till Heskey beat him from outside the area.											
23	A	SOUTHAMPTON		10	L	1-2	0-0	Lampard 65	Forrest	Margas*	Ferdinand	Stimac	**Charles**	Lomas	Lampard	Cole	Minto	Sinclair	Wanchope	Moncur
	5/2		15,257	16	32			Pahars 54, Charles 86 (og)	Jones	Dodd	Richards	Benali	Colleter*	Tessem	Marsden	Oakley	Pahars^	Davies	Boa Morte"	Bridge/Soltvedt/Hughes
								Ref: B Knight	The appointment of Glenn Hoddle as Saints' boss – with Dave Jones facing sex charges – overshadows this match, which kicked-off 30 mins late because of traffic problems. The teams took to the field to 'We will rock you' and left it after Charles whacked Tessem's cross into his net.											
24	H	BRADFORD C		9	W	5-4	2-2	S'r 35, M'r 43, Di C' 65p, Cole 70, L'd 83	Hislop*	Ferdinand	Stimac	Minto	Charles^	Lomas	Lampard	Moncur	Cole	Di Canio	Sinclair	**Bywater**/Kitson
	12/2		25,417	18	35			Wind's 30, Beagrie 45p, Lawr' 47, 51	Davison	Halle	Wetherall	O'Brien	Jacobs	Lawrence	McCall	Whalley	Beagrie	Saunders	Windass	
								Ref: N Barry	Hammers trailed 0-1 and 2-4 when Dean Saunders hit the post. That would surely have sealed the outcome in this crazy game. Saunders broke Hislop's leg after two mins. Debutant Bywater fumbled everything. Di Canio demanded to be subbed, then snatched the ball to take a penalty.											
25	H	EVERTON		11	L	0-4	0-1		**Ilic**	Ferdinand	Stimac	Pearce S	Lomas	Sinclair	Moncur	Cole	Keller	Kitson	Wanchope	
	26/2		26,025	7	35			Barmby 8, 64, 67, Moore 71	Myrne	Weir	Gough	Unsworth	Xavier	Barmby*	Collins	Pembridge	Ball	Campbell	Moore	Ward
								Ref: P Alcock	West Ham concede four at home yet again, but with Lampard suspended, Di Canio hamstrung, and Ilic on loan. Ilic gifts two goals, Barmby doubles his season's tally, then sets up Joe Max Moore when a fourth awaited. Redknapp makes no subs and blasts Joe Cole for not passing.											
26	A	WATFORD		10	W	2-1	2-0	Lomas 3, Wanchope 35	Forrest	Ferdinand	Stimac	Pearce S	Lomas	Sinclair	Moncur	Foe	Minto	Lampard	Wanchope	
	4/3		18,619	20	38			Helguson 61	Chamberlain	Kennedy	Page	Gibbs*	Palmer	Hyde	Smart	Wooter	Bonnot^	Williams"	Helguson	Robinson/Johnson/Cox
								Ref: M Reed	Cole is dropped. A fine goal for Lomas, finishing off a sweeping move involving Wanchope and Lampard. Kennedy headed against the bar and Watford's confidence drained away. Wanchope hooked a second goal and desperate Graham Taylor made three substitutions at half-time.											
27	H	SOUTHAMPTON		6	W	2-0	1-0	Wanchope 18, Sinclair 48	Forrest	Lomas	Ferdinand	Stimac	Pearce S*	Lampard	Cole^	Foe	Moncur	Wanchope	Sinclair	Minto/Di Canio
	8/3		23,484	15	41				Jones	Dodd	Lundekvam	Benali	Bridge	Tessem	Marsden	Oakley	Pahars	Kachloul*	Davies	Soltvedt
								Ref: S Lodge	Stuart Pearce breaks the same leg he broke in September, going in hard on Kevin Davies. Wanchope's angled finish to a fine move, and man-of-the-match Sinclair's shot under Paul Jones's body, earned the win. At 1-0 Davies hit Forrest's bar. The ball came out, deciding the outcome.											
28	A	SHEFFIELD WED		10	L	1-3	1-0	Lampard 10	Forrest	Lomas	Ferdinand	Stimac	Ruddock	Lampard	Moncur*	Foe	Sinclair	Di Canio	Wanchope	Cole
	11/3		21,147	19	41			Cresswell 55, Hinch' 63, Alex'son 66	Srnicek	Atherton	Jonk*	Walker	Hinchcliffe	Sibon^	Alexan'son	Nolan	Haslam	De Bilde	Quinn	Sonner/Cresswell
								Ref: P Jones	Di Canio was booed on his return to Hillsborough. Wilson's Owls snatch this surprise win, despite Srnicek slapping at Moncur's cross, which fell to Lampard. Ferdinand was punished for trying to dribble clear, Hinchcliffe blasted in from 30 yards, but the third goal trickled pitifully in.											
29	H	CHELSEA		9	D	0-0	0-0		Forrest	Lomas	Ferdinand	Stimac !	Minto	Lampard	Moncur*	Foe	Sinclair	Di Canio	Wanchope^	Cole/Kitson"/Ruddock
	18/3		26,041	4	42				De Goey	Ferrer	Leboeuf	Desailly	Babayaro	Petrescu*	Wise	Deschamps	Morris^	Zola	Flo"	Poyet/Di Matteo/Sutton
								Ref: S Dunn	West Ham would have gone sixth had they won, but that looked unlikely after Di Canio's mesmeric run and tame shot, De Goey's slap against the bar and catching the rebound, and the expulsion of Stimac for fouling Wise, after he had been wrongly booked earlier (mistaken identity).											
30	H	WIMBLEDON		8	W	2-1	1-0	Di Canio 9, Kanoute 59	Forrest	Lomas	Ferdinand	Stimac	Minto	Lampard	Moncur*	Foe	Sinclair	Di Canio	**Kanoute**	Keller
	26/3		**22,438**	18	45			Hughes 75	Sullivan	Cunningham	Andersen	Willmott*	Kimble	Hughes	Ardley^	Earle"	Euell	Lund	Gayle	Blackwell/Leaburn/Francis
								Ref: R Harris	West Ham had beaten the Dons at home just twice in ten. Di Canio's airborne far-post volley had the crowd roaring, and Kanoute headed onto the bar before netting when Sullivan raced from his line. Hughes volleyed from 25 yards, but the ref could have given three pens to Hammers.											
31	A	MANCHESTER U		8	L	**1-7**	1-3	Wanchope 11 [Beck'm 66, Solsk' 73]	Forrest	Lomas	Ferdinand	Potts	Minto	Lampard	Moncur	Foe	Sinclair	Wanchope	Kanoute	
	1/1		**61,611**	1	45			Scholes 24, 51, 62p, Irwin 26, Cole 45,	Bosnich	Neville G	Stam	Silvestre	Irwin	Beckham	Keane*	Scholes^	Fortune	Yorke	Cole"	Butt/Solskjaer/Shering'm
								Ref: M Riley	Forrest conceded 9 at Old Trafford with Ipswich. Wanchope's weak angled shot merely sparks a volcano. Scholes back-heels a saucy goal and Beckham flights a super free-kick. Potts fouls Keane for the first pen (Irwin nets at second attempt), Solskjaer trips himself up for the second.											

No	V	Opponent / Date	Att	Pos	Pts	Res	F-A	H-T	Scorers, Times, and Referees	1	2	3	4	5	6	7	8	9	10	11	Subs used
32	H	NEWCASTLE		8	W	2-1	0-0		Wanchope 60, 89	Forrest	Ferdinand	Stimac*	Ruddock^	Minto	Keller"	Foe	Cole	Lampard	Di Canio	Kanoute	Margas/Charles/Wanchope
		12/4	25,817	*10*	48				*Speed 48*	*Given*	*Barton*	*Dabizas**	*Goma*	*Solano*	*Lee*	*Speed*	*Domi*	*Hughes*	*Shearer*	*Dyer"*	*Howey/Ketsbaia*
									Ref: P Alcock	Bobby Robson's Geordies have just lost an FA Cup semi-final to Chelsea. They are equally unlucky here, twice hitting the bar in the first half. Gary Speed's left-footer was overturned first by sub Wanchope's back-header, then at the death by his drag-back, turn and shot from six yards.											
33	A	DERBY		8	W	2-1	2-0		Wanchope 15, 32	**Feuer**	Ferdinand	Stimac*	Margas	Minto	Sinclair	Foe	Cole^	Lampard	Di Canio	Wanchope	Charles/Carrick
		15/4	*31,202*	*16*	51				*Sturridge 84*	*Poom*	*Laursen*	*Elliott*	*Schnoor**	*Delap*	*Dorigo^*	*Powell*	*Burley*	*Johnson*	*Sturridge*	*Strupar*	*Christie/Robinson*
									Ref: M Halsey	Wanchope returns to his former club, nets both goals – a header from Minto's cross and a volley – to take his tally to four in four games and 15 overall. Dean Sturridge forced home an attempted clearance late on. Joe Cole was harshly treated and hobbled off. Stimac was stretchered off.											
34	H	COVENTRY		8	W	**5-0**	2-0		Carrick 7, Margas 14, Di Canio 48, 67, [Kanoute 83]	Feuer	Ferdinand	Stimac	Margas	Minto*	Sinclair	Lampard	Carrick	Kanoute	Di Canio	Wanchope	Newton
		22/4	24,729	*14*	54					*Hedman*	*Telfer*	*Breen*	*Hendry**	*Burrows*	*Quinn^*	*Eustace*	*McAllister*	*Normann"*	*Whelan*	*Keane*	*Shaw/Betts/Roussel*
									Ref: A D'Urso	Coventry have not won away for a year, and against Di Canio's inspired showing they had no hope. Di Canio is now ranked among Hammers' all-time greats. He had a part in all five goals, two of which he netted himself – the first went in off both posts, the second from a tight angle.											
35	H	MIDDLESBROUGH		8	L	0-1	0-0			Feuer	Ferdinand	Stimac	Margas	Keller	Sinclair	Lampard	Foe	Kanoute	Di Canio	Wanchope	
		29/4	25,472	*13*	54				*Deane 60p*	*Schwarzer*	*Stamp*	*Vickers*	*Festa*	*Cooper*	*Fleming*	*Juninho**	*Ince*	*Summerbell*	*Deane*	*Campbell^*	*Ricard/Mustoe*
									Ref: B Knight	From the sublime (v Coventry) to the ridiculous. Bryan Robson's Boro do their homework and shackle Di Canio. Even with three strikers, the Hammers fail to create anything. Feuer plays despite a leg strain, and brings down Andy Campbell, yet strangely receives only a yellow card.											
36	A	ARSENAL		8	L	1-2	1-0		Di Canio 40	Bywater	Potts	Stimac	Foe	Keller	Sinclair !	Carrick	Moncur	Kanoute	Di Canio	Wanchope	
		2/5	*38,093*	*2*	54				*Overmars 69, Petit 90*	*Seaman*	*Dixon**	*Luzhny*	*Adams*	*Silvinho*	*Parlour*	*Grimandi*	*Vieira*	*Overmars*	*Kanu*	*Bergkamp*	*Petit*
									Ref: P Durkin	Mayhem as Petit handles and fires a late winner via Stimac's head. Durkin allows the goal, then books Sinclair twice in the remaining seconds. All told, nine yellows were dished out to under-strength West Ham. Overmars slipped Foe, playing in defence, to level Di Canio's 17th goal.											
37	A	SUNDERLAND		9	L	0-1	0-1			Bywater	Ferdinand	Stimac	Foe	Potts	Sinclair	Carrick	Moncur	Kanoute	Di Canio	Wanchope	
		6/5	*41,684*	*7*	54				*Phillips 14*	*Sorensen*	*Makin*	*Craddock*	*Butler P*	*Gray*	*Summerbee*	*Roy**	*Thirlwell*	*Oster^*	*Phillips*	*Quinn"*	*Butler T/Holloway/Dichio*
									Ref: N Barry	A game for the stats buffs. Sunderland have their best season for 45 years and Kevin Phillips' 30th Premiership goal has been achieved only by Andy Cole and Alan Shearer. Ferdinand might blame himself for Phillips' header, but Leo was brushed aside by big Niall Quinn far too often.											
38	H	LEEDS		9	D	0-0	0-0			Bywater	Ferdinand	Stimac	Margas	Potts	Sinclair	Foe !	Moncur	Kanoute	Di Canio	Wanchope	
		14/5	**26,044**	*3*	55					*Martin*	*Kelly*	*Woodgate*	*Radebe*	*Mills*	*Jones*	*McPhail*	*Bakke**	*Wilcox^*	*Bridges"*	*Kewell*	*Bowyer/Huckerby/Smith*
		Home	Away						Ref: B Barber	Leeds needed a better result than Liverpool to secure 3rd place, and achieved it. Both teams tried but the game never took off until injury-time, when Foe kicked the prostrate Matthew Jones. It is rumoured that Foe is leaving Upton Park. A miserable end of season for the Hammers.											
Average		25,093	31,088																		

InterToto Cup

No	V	Opponent / Date	Att		Res	F-A	H-T	Scorers, Times, and Referees	1	2	3	4	5	6	7	8	9	10	11	Subs used
1:1	H	JOKERIT (Finland)			W	1-0	1-0	Kitson 18	Forrest	Potts*	Ferdinand	Ruddock	Minto	Lampard	Lomas	Cole	Sinclair^	Kitson	Di Canio	Wright/Keller
		17/7	11,908						*Laaksonen*	*Rasanen*	*Hyrylainien*	*Holmegren*	*Tuunainen**	*Nenonen*	*Koskela^*	*Roiko"*	*Viren*	*Helin*	*Sumiala*	*Paavola/Pylkas/Rantanen*
								Ref: M Liba (Czech Republic)	It is the close-season in England but mid-season in Finland. Eyal Berkovic has gone to Celtic and 17-year-old Joe Cole is groomed to replace him. Kitson heads in Di Canio's cross, Sinclair hits the inside of a post, and in the second half everyone runs out of steam and goes to sleep.											
1:2	A	JOKERIT			D	1-1	0-1	Lampard 71	Hislop	Jones*	Ferdinand	Ruddock	Mint	Sinclair	Lampard	Lomas	Keller^	Di Canio"	Kitson	Potts/Lazaridis/Carrick
		24/7	*5,000*					*Koskela 33*	*Laaksonen*	*Viren*	*Jossila*	*Hyrylainen**	*Rolko*	*Nenonen*	*Holmegren*	*Rantanen*	*Koskela !*	*Ristila^*	*Sumiala*	*Rasanen/Lehthoen*
								(Hammers win 2-1 on aggregate)	West Ham know they have a game on when Jokerit midfielder Koskela levels the overall scores. His joy is short-lived, as he is then sent off for his second yellow when fouling Di Canio, who is doubtful for the league curtain raiser. Lampard saves Hammers' blushes with a free-kick.											
2:1	H	HEEREN' (Holland)			W	1-0	1-0	Lampard 7	Hislop	Potts	Ferdinand	Ruddock*	Keller^	Lomas	Lampard	Sinclair	Minto	Di Canio"	Wanchope	Pearce/Moncur/Kitson
		29/7	7,485						*Vonk*	*Venema*	*Hansma*	*De Nooijer*	*Mitrita*	*Nurmela**	*Talan*	*Radomski*	*Huizinghzic*	*Samardzic*	*Pahlplatz^*	*Jensen/Jepsen*
								Ref: E Steinborn (Germany)	Shoot-on-sight Lampard runs 20 yards before hitting a rising shot that goes in off a post. Thereafter, though the Dutch side swamp midfield, West Ham create a dozen chances and Wanchope, Kitson and Lampard all strike the woodwork. Ruddock goes off with a hamstring injury.											
2:2	A	HEERENVEEN			W	1-0	1-0	Wanchope 26	Hislop	Lomas	Ferdinand	Pearce	Mint	Sinclair	Lampard	Moncur*	Foe	Wanchope	Di Canio^	Cole/Kitson
		4/8	*13,500*						*Vonk*	*Venema*	*Hansma*	*De Nooijer*	*Mitrita*	*Nurmela*	*Talan**	*Denneb'm**	*Huizinghzic*	*Samardzic*	*Pahlplatz*	*Hakansson/Lurlinglatz*
								Ref: P Garibian (France) (Hammers win 2-0 on aggregate)	Wanchope nets his first competitive goal since his £3.25 million transfer from Derby. It stemmed from a short corner, and Wanchope pounced when Vonk spilled Lampard's ensuing drive. Thereafter Di Canio, Sinclair and Cole had chances to make the tie safe, though Hislop was busy.											

InterToto Cup (cont.)	Att		F-A	H-T	Scorers, Times, and Referees	SQUAD	NUMBERS	IN	USE								subs used
3:1 H METZ (France)		L	0-1	0-1		Hislop	Lomas	Potts	Ferdinand	Mint	Moncur	Lampard	Foe*	Di Canio	Wanchope	Sinclair	Kitson
10/8	25,372				*Saha 13*	*Letizi*	*Schemmel**	*Pierre*	*Kastend'ch*	*Gailliot*	*Bastien^*	*Proment*	*Meyrieu*	*Boffin*	*Gousse*	*Saha*	*Marchal/Toyes*
					Ref: M Diaz Vega (Spain)	It might have been better, it might have been worse, when Saha wasted a last-minute chance to make it 0-2. Boffin's hopeful ball passes over Ferdinand for Saha to head past Hislop. When Proment dragged back Di Canio, Lampard's soft penalty was saved by man-of-the-match Letizi.											
3:2 A METZ		W	3-1	2-0	Sinclair 23, Lampard 43, Wanchope 78	Hislop	Lomas	Ferdinand	Potts	Sinclair	Lampard	Foe	Moncur	Keller	Di Canio*	Wanchope	Cole
24/8	*19,599*				*Jestrovic 68*	*Letizi*	*Pierre**	*Marchal*	*Kastendch*	*Schemmel*	*Boffin*	*Meyrieu*	*Toyes*	*Gailliot*	*Saha*	*Gousse^*	*Asuar/Jestrovic*
					Ref: M Krug (Germany) (Hammers win 3-2 on aggregate)	The rowdier elements of Hammers' travelling support attempt to pull down a fence, but their actions cannot mar this superb result. Sinclair's goal from Di Canio's lay-back and Lampard's half-volley put Hammers ahead. Metz hit the bar, then level, only for Wanchope to round Letizi.											

UEFA Cup																	
1:1 H NK OSIJEK (Croatia)		W	3-0	1-0	Wanch' 39, Di Canio 48, Lampard 58	Hislop	Lomas	Margas	Potts	Stimac	Lampard	Sinclair	Moncur*	Keller	Di Canio^	Wanchope	Foe/Kitson
16/9	25,331					*Galinovic*	*Zebec*	*Beljan*	*Vuica*	*Gaspar*	*Ergovic*	*Babic*	*Prisc**	*Besirevic^*	*Vranjes*	*Bubalo"*	*Mitu/Balatinic/Turkovic*
					Ref: G Paraty Silva (Portugal)	Other than the Inter-Toto, West Ham have waited 18 years for the taste of Europe. Even though the Croatian side are let down by two goalie howlers, Hammer turn on the style. Di Canio contributed to all three goals, best of which was Lampard's. Margas dyed his hair claret and blue.											
1:2 A NK OSIJEK		W	3-1	1-0	Kitson 27, Ruddock 83, Foe 90	Hislop	Lomas	Ferdinand*	Potts	Stimac	Lampard	Sinclair^	Foe	Keller	Di Canio"	Kitson	Rudd'ck/Newt'n/Wanch'pe
30/9	*15,000*				*Bubalo 70*	*Malovan*	*Zebec*	*Beljan*	*Vuica*	*Dumitru*	*Ergovic*	*Babic*	*Prisc**	*Besirevic*	*Vranjes^*	*Bubalo"*	*Jukic/Zrilic/Turkovic*
					Ref: J van Hulten (Holland) (Hammers win 6-1 on aggregate)	Stimac returns to his homeland. With progress assured, and with Arsenal looming, Redknapp gives a game to Ferdinand, Ruddock and Kitson. When no coach arrived to fetch the players from their hotel, the press's coach was commandeered. Kitson's header meant Osijek needed five.											
2:1 A STEAUA (Romania)		L	0-2	0-1		Hislop	Ruddock	Ferrdinand	Potts*	Lomas	Lampard	Sinclair	Foe	Moncur	Di Canio^	Wanchope	Margas/Cole
21/10	12,500				*Rosu 39, Ilie 56*	*Ritli*	*Reghecampf*	*Baclu*	*Miu*	*Bordeanu*	*Lincar*	*Duro*	*Danc'lescu**	*Rosu*	*Ciocoiu^*	*Ilie"*	*Lutu/Ogararu/Luca*
					Ref: C Larsen (Denmark)	Dallas's JR Ewing greets the players on a wet and murky night. West Ham try to attack and are exposed when Rosu runs through a deserted defence. The ref apparently warned Redknapp that Di Canio was likely to get sent off, so Harry subbed him. Potts' slip let in Ilie for the second.											
2:2 H STEAUA BUCHAR'		D	0-0	0-0		Hislop	Ruddock	Ferdinand	Margas	Lomas	Lampard	Sinclair	Keller*	Cole	Di Canio	Wanchope	Kitson
4/11	24,514					*Ritli*	*Duro*	*Baciu*	*Miu*	*Bordeanu*	*Reghecampf*	*Lincar**	*Danc'lescu^*	*Rosu*	*Ciocoiu"*	*Liie*	*Lacatus/Trica/Lutu*
					L Pucek (Czech Republic) (Hammers lose 0-2 on aggregate)	It is hard to know which bears the greatest responsibility for Hammers' exit – a forward line that missed chances galore, a keeper who thwarted them – or a referee who refused to send off Duro, who committed half-a-dozen bookable offences. Ruddock butted him but stayed on the pitch.											

Worthington Cup																	
3 H BOURNEMOUTH 9		W	2-0	0-0	Keller 62, Lampard 77	Hislop	Ferdinand	Stimac	Ruddock	Sinclair	Lampard	Foe	Cole	Keller	Wanchope*	Di Canio	Kitson
13/10	22,067 *2:7*					*Ovendale*	*Warren**	*Cox*	*Howe*	*Young*	*Mean*	*Broadhurst*	*Jorgenson^*	*Robinson*	*Fletcher S*	*Stein*	*Huck/O'Neill*
					Ref: R Harris	Europe means West Ham enjoy a bye into Round 3. Mel Machin's Bournemouth have plenty of Hammers connections and play their part in a keen cup-tie. Keller makes space for a belter that flies in off a post. Mean's free-kick bounces off the angle before Lampard hooks number two.											
4 A BIRMINGHAM 9		W	3-2	1-2	Lomas 21, Kitson 87, Cole 89	Hislop	Charles*	Margas^	Ruddock	Ferdinand	Keller	Lampard	Foe	Lomas	Di Canio	Wanchope"	Cole/Sinclair/Kitson
30/11	*17,728* *1:7*				*Hyde 8, Grainger 44*	*Poole*	*Bass*	*Rowett*	*Holdsworth*	*Johnson*	*Grainger*	*Hyde**	*Holland*	*O'Connor*	*Purse*	*Johnston*	*Hughes*
					Ref: G Poll	Lucky Hammers. Trevor Francis' Brum have 11 first-teamers out injured and he fields a stopper and a winger as his strike-force. Lomas' long-range strike took a deflection before Grainger's super free-kick appeared to win the tie. Kitson's leveller creeps in before Cole's first ever goal.											
QF H ASTON VILLA		W	2-2	0-1	Lampard 72, Di Canio 90	Hislop	Ferdinand	Ruddock	Margas	Sinclair	Lampard	Lomas	Keller	Cole*	Di Canio	Wanchope^	Kitson/Omoyinmi
15/12	23,974		*aet*		*Taylor 4, Dublin 89*	*James*	*Ehiogu*	*Southgate*	*Barry*	*Watson*	*Taylor*	*Merson**	*Boateng*	*Wright*	*Dublin*	*Joachim^*	*Stone/Vassell*
(result expunged from records)					Ref: A Lodge (Hammers win 5-4 on penalties)	Hammers are seconds from being k.o'd from two cups in five days. Dublin's super hook looks like taking Villa through. Moments later Kitson falls under Wright's non-existent challenge and Di Canio strokes the equaliser. Sad Southgate, villain of Euro 96, sees his kick saved yet again.											
QF H ASTON VILLA 11		L	1-3	0-0	Lampard 47	Hislop	Ferdinand	Potts*	Stimac	Minto	Lomas	Lampard	Foe	Cole	Di Canio	Sinclair^	Ruddock/Keller
11/1	25,592 *10*		*aet*		*Taylor 80, 118, Joachim 93*	*James*	*Watson*	*Ehiogu*	*Southgate*	*Barry*	*Wright*	*Stone*	*Taylor*	*Boateng*	*Joachim*	*Merson**	*Vassell*
					Ref: J Winter	Omoyinmi's cup-tied appearance forces this replay. Doug Ellis wears a 'Santa supports Villa' hat. All seems well when Lampard chips James – Joachim having already hit the post. But Southgate's knock-down is blasted in by Ian Taylor, and in extra-time Ehiogu heads on for Joachim.											

FA Cup

			Att	Pos	Res	F-A	H-T	Scorers, Times, and Referees												
3	A	TRANMERE		8	L	0-1	0-1		Hislop	Lomas	Potts*	Ruddock	Ferdinand	Minto	Cole	Lampard	Foe	Sinclair	Di Canio^	Ki:son/Wanchope
11/12			13,629 2:13					*Henry 21*	*Murphy*	*Morgan*	*Challinor*	*Hazell*	*Roberts*	*Parkinson*	*Henry*	*Mahon*	*Jones*	*Kelly**	*Allison*	*Taylor*
								Ref: D Gallagher												

John Aldridge's Tranmere follow the example of Swansea and Wrexham as lower division clubs to knock Hammers out of the Cup. Nor was it a fluke as West Ham's goal was under frequent siege. Nick Henry's 20-yard left-footer flew past Hislop. Murphy saved well from Lampard.

		Home					Away					
	P	W	D	L	F	A	W	D	L	F	A	Pts
1 Manchester U	38	15	4	0	59	16	13	3	3	38	29	91
2 Arsenal	38	14	3	2	42	17	8	4	7	31	26	73
3 Leeds	38	12	2	5	29	18	9	4	6	29	25	69
4 Liverpool	38	11	4	4	28	13	8	6	5	23	17	67
5 Chelsea	38	12	5	2	35	12	6	6	7	18	22	65
6 Aston Villa	38	8	8	3	23	12	7	5	7	23	23	58
7 Sunderland	38	10	6	3	28	17	6	4	9	29	39	58
8 Leicester	38	10	3	6	31	24	6	4	9	24	31	55
9 WEST HAM	38	11	5	3	32	23	4	5	10	20	30	55
10 Tottenham	38	10	3	6	40	26	5	5	9	17	23	53
11 Newcastle	38	10	5	4	42	20	4	5	10	21	34	52
12 Middlesbro	38	8	5	6	23	26	6	5	8	23	26	52
13 Everton	38	7	9	3	36	21	5	5	9	23	28	50
14 Coventry	38	12	1	6	38	22	0	7	12	9	32	44
15 Southampton	38	8	4	7	26	22	4	4	11	19	40	44
16 Derby	38	6	3	10	22	25	3	8	8	22	32	38
17 Bradford C	38	6	8	5	26	29	3	1	15	12	39	36
18 Wimbledon	38	6	7	6	30	28	1	5	13	16	46	33
19 Sheffield Wed	38	6	3	10	21	23	2	4	13	17	47	31
20 Watford	38	5	4	10	24	31	1	2	16	11	46	24
	760	187	92	101	635	425	101	92	187	425	635	1048

Odds & ends

Double wins: (3) Leicester, Bradford C, Watford.
Double losses: (3) Everton, Middlesbrough, Manchester U.

Won from behind: (5) Leicester (h), Sheffield Wed (h), Bradford C (h), Newcastle (h), Birmingham LC (a).
Lost from in front: (4) Sheffield Wed (a), Manchester U (a), Arsenal (a), Aston Villa LC (h).

High spots: The form and personality of Paolo Di Canio.
Di Canio's BBC 'goal of the season' v Wimbledon.
Climbing to third after five games.
Beating Bradford City 5-4 after being 2-4 down.
Finishing in the top 9 for the third successive season.
Qualifying for the UEFA Cup via the Inter-Toto Cup.

Low spots: Going out of the FA Cup at lower division Tranmere.
Not winning a single match in the League throughout December.
Losing Stuart Pearce and Ian Pearce to leg-breaks early on.
Stuart Pearce breaking the same leg twice!
The agony of having to replay the Worthington Cup quarter-final after fielding an ineligible player v Villa.
Getting smashed 1-7 at Old Trafford.

Hammer of the Year: Paolo Di Canio.
Ever-presents: 0.
Hat-tricks: 0.
Leading scorer: (17) Paolo Di Canio.

	Appearances								Goals				
	Lge	*Sub*	LC	*Sub*	FAC	*Sub*	Eur	*Sub*	Lge	LC	FAC	Eur	Tot
Byrne, Shaun		*1*											
Bywater, Stephen	3	*1*											
Carrick, Michael	4	*4*						*1*	1				1
Charles, Gary	2	*2*	1										
Cole, Joe	17	*5*	2	*1*	1		2	*3*	1	1			2
Di Canio, Paolo	29	*1*	3		1		10		16			1	17
Ferdinand, Rio	33		3		1		9						
Feuer, Ian	3												
Foe, Marc-Vivien	25		3		1		5	*1*	1			1	2
Forrest, Craig	9	*2*					1						
Hislop, Shaka	22		3		1		9						
Ilic, Sasa	1												
Kanoute, Frederic	8								2				2
Keller, Marc	19	*4*	2	*1*			6	*1*		1			1
Kitson, Paul	4	*6*		*2*		*1*	3	*5*		1		2	3
Jones, Rob							1						
Lampard, Frank	34		3		1		10		7	2		4	13
Lomas, Steve	25		2		1		10		1	1			2
Margas, Javier	15	*3*	1				2	*1*	1				1
Minto, Scott	15	*3*	1		1		5						
Moncur, John	20	*2*					5	*1*	1				1
Newton, Adam		*2*						*1*					
Pearce, Ian	1						1	*1*					
Pearce, Stuart	8												
Potts, Steve	16	*1*	1		1		7	*1*					
Ruddock, Neil	12	*3*	2	*1*	1		5	*1*				1	1
Sinclair, Trevor	36		2	*1*	1		10		7			1	8
Stimac, Igor	24		2				2		1				1
Wanchope, Paulo	33	*2*	2			*1*	7	*1*	12			3	15
Wright, Ian								*1*					
(own-goals)									1				1
29 players used	418	*42*	33	*6*	11	*2*	110	*19*	52	6		13	71

No	Date		Att	Pos	Pt	F-A	H-T	Scorers, Times, and Referees	SQUAD	NUMBERS	IN	USE								subs used
1	A	CHELSEA			L	2-4	0-1	Di Canio 48, Kanoute 85	Hislop	Lomas	**Winterb'rn**	Margas	Stimac	Pearce S	Lampard	Kanoute	**Suker**	Di Canio	Carrick*	Cole
	19/8		*34,914*		0			*Has'baink 31p, Zola 59, Stanic 78, 90*	*De Goey*	*Melchiot*	*Babayaro**	*Stanic*	*Panucci*	*Desailly*	*Poyet^*	*Di Matteo*	*Hasselbaink*	*Zola"*	*Wise*	*Le Saux/Morris/Flo*
								Ref: G Barber	Plenty of goals, but this was still a scratchy win for Chelsea boss Gianluca Vialli. Suker and Kanoute missed chances to reverse the outcome, and Hasselbaink's penalty was iffy, but there was no disputing Croatian Stanic's likely goal of the season, a juggle and thump from 30 yards.											
2	H	LEICESTER		20	L	0-1	0-0		Hislop	Ferdinand	Winterburn	Margas*	Stimac !	Pearce S	Lomas	Kanoute^	Suker"	Di Canio	Carrick	Cole/Kitson/Charles
	23/8		*25,195*	*4*	0			*Eadie 54*	*Flowers*	*Impey*	*Guppy*	*Elliott*	*Rowett*	*Taggart*	*Lennon*	*Izzet*	*Akinbiyi*	*Eadie**	*Savage*	*Cottee*
								Ref: R Styles	Peter Taylor's Foxes go joint top after this win, which leaves West Ham propping up the table. The game hinged on Stimac's second yellow card, just on half-time, for a nothing challenge on arch-provocateur Robbie Savage. Eadie headed his first goal since signing from Norwich.											
3	H	MANCHESTER U		20	D	2-2	0-1	Di Canio 86p, Suker 89	Hislop	Ferdinand^	Winterburn	Margas*	Stimac	Pearce S	Lomas	Cole	Suker	Di Canio	Carrick	Kitson/**Bassila**
	26/8		25,998	*16*	1			*Beckham 6, Cole 49*	*Barthez*	*Neville G*	*Neville P*	*Silvestre*	*Keane*	*Stam**	*Beckham*	*Scholes*	*Cole A*	*Sheringham*	*Giggs*	*Berg*
								Ref: D Gallagher	On the face of it, a stunning Hammers come-back. Beckham's free-kick and 60-yard pass to Andy Cole seemed to settle matters. But Henning Berg nudged Di Canio in the box, and Suker netted with a close-in header. There was still time for Man U to race upfield and hit the bar twice.											
4	A	SUNDERLAND		20	D	1-1	1-1	Suker 32	Hislop	Sinclair	Winterburn	Lomas	Stimac	Pearce S	Lampard	Cole	Suker*	Di Canio	Carrick	Moncur
	5/9		*46,605*		2			*Arca 25*	*Macho*	*Makin*	*Gray*	*Holloway*	*Craddock*	*Emerson*	*Hutchison*	*Arca*	*Quinn*	*Phillips*	*Kilbane*	
								Ref: P Jones	On Saturday, England drew 1-1 in France in a friendly. Now, on the Tuesday, West Ham were pegged back by Argentine Julio Arca's glancing header on his debut, but recovered when Jurgen Macho conceded an unnecessary corner-kick, which was turned in at the far post by Suker.											
5	A	TOTTENHAM		20	L	0-1	0-0		Hislop	Sinclair	Winterburn	Lomas	Ferdinand	Pearce S	Lampard	Cole	Kanoute	Di Canio	Carrick	
	11/9		*33,282*	*5*	2			*Campbell 67*	*Sullivan*	*Carr*	*Taricco**	*Freund*	*Campbell*	*Young^*	*Sherwood*	*Iversen*	*Rebrov*	*Ferdinand*	*Leonhard'n*	*Thatcher/Vega*
								Ref: S Dunn	A messy game, settled for George Graham's Spurs by Sol Campbell's first goal in over a year – heading Leonhardsen's corner in off the bar. The defeat confirms West Ham's worst start since relegation in 1992, but defiant Redknapp claims this is the best Hammers team for 20 years.											
6	H	LIVERPOOL		20	D	1-1	0-1	Di Canio 69p	Hislop	Sinclair	Winterburn	Stimac	Ferdinand	Pearce S	Lomas	Cole	Kanoute	Di Canio	Carrick	
	17/9		*25,998*	*4*	3			*Gerrard 12*	*Westerveld*	*Song*	*Traore*	*Hamann*	*Henchoz*	*Babbel*	*Gerrard^*	*Barmby*	*Heskey*	*Murphy**	*Carragher*	*Ziege/Heggem*
								Ref: D Elleray	Gerard Houllier's Reds return from European action in Romania without the injured Owen. Winterburn and Stuart Pearce show their age, as when Gerrard volleyed in at the far post, but parity was restored when Henchoz uprooted Di Canio. Chelsea are rumoured to covet the Italian.											
7	A	COVENTRY		18	W	3-0	2-0	Di Canio 38, Cole 40, Lampard 69	Hislop	Sinclair^	Winterburn	Stimac	Ferdinand*	Pearce S	Lampard	Cole	Kanoute"	Di Canio	Lomas	Carrick/Potts/**Diawara**
	23/9		*20,020*	*17*	6				*Hedman*	*Edworthy*	*Hall**	*Williams*	*Shaw*	*Chippo*	*Thompson^*	*Palmer*	*Bellamy*	*Hadji*	*Zuniga"*	*Breen/Eustace/Aloisi*
								Ref: N Barry	Britain is winning plenty of golds at the Sydney Olympics, and West Ham win their first game. Strachan's Coventry have yet to win at home, and they were destroyed by Di Canio's sorcery. First he skipped round Richard Shaw. Next he tee'd up Cole at the far post. Hadji hit a post.											
8	H	BRADFORD C		18	D	1-1	1-0	Cole 26	Hislop	Sinclair	Winterburn	Stimac	Ferdinand	Pearce S	Lomas	Cole	Kanoute	Di Canio	Carrick	
	30/9		25,407	*19*	7			*Petrescu 90*	*Clarke*	*Lawrence*	*Jacobs**	*McCall*	*Wetherall*	*Atherton*	*Petrescu*	*Windass*	*Ward*	*Carbone*	*Whalley^*	*Beagrie/Halle"/Sharpe*
								Ref: M Dean	City boss Chris Hutchings hardly expected any reward, as his team were outclassed from start to finish. Yet all West ham had to show was a strong header by Joe Cole. But at the death Stimac conceded a free-kick, Carbone lobbed the ball over the wall, and Dan Petrescu headed in.											
9	A	IPSWICH		18	D	1-1	0-1	Di Canio 72	Hislop	Sinclair	Winterb'rn*	Stimac^	Ferdinand	Pearce S	Lampard	Cole	Kanoute	Di Canio	Lomas	Moncur/Potts
	14/10		*22,243*	*8*	8			*Stewart 5*	*Wright*	*Wilnis*	*Clapham*	*Venus*	*Hreidarsson*	*McGreal*	*Holland*	*Magilton*	*Stewart^*	*Naylor**	*Wright*	*Johnson/Scowcroft*
								Ref: N Barry	George Burley's Ipswich are going well and should have been home and dry after Marcus Stewart headed in Fabian Wilnis's cross. But then the chances went begging, allowing Di Canio to equalise from Sinclair's centre. Stimac collided with Hislop and had to be stretchered off.											
10	H	ARSENAL		18	L	1-2	0-2	Pearce S 56	Hislop	Sinclair	Winterburn	Lomas	Ferdinand	Pearce S	Lampard	Cole	Kanoute	Di Canio	Moncur*	Suker
	21/10		26,034	*2*	8			*Pires 12, Ferdinand 21 (og)*	*Seaman*	*Luzhny*	*Silvinho*	*Vieira*	*Keown*	*Grimaldi*	*Lauren*	*Ljungberg**	*Wiltord"*	*Bergkamp^*	*Pires*	*Parlour/Kanu/Henry*
								Ref: D Gallagher	Patrick Vieira dominated a match which saw Thierry Henry start on the bench. Arsenal were gifted early goals by Sinclair and Ferdinand and thereafter seemed to relax after their midweek Champions League trip to Rome. Stuart Pearce replied with a free-kick, dummied by Di Canio.											

No/Date	H/A	Opponent/Att	Pos	Res/Pts	F-A	H-T	Scorers, Times, Referees	1	2	3	4	5	6	7	8	9	10	11	Subs used
11	H	NEWCASTLE	15	W	1-0	0-0	Kanoute 73	Hislop	Sinclair	Winterb'rn"	Pearce I	Ferdinand	Pearce S	Lampard	Cole^	Kanoute*	Di Canio	Carrick	Moncur/Suker/Potts
28/10		26,044	8	11				Given	Griffin	Solano	Goma	Hughes	Lee^	Dyer	Acuna	Shearer	Lua-Lua*	Speed	Cordone/Glass
							Ref: M Riley	West Ham's first home win takes them out of the bottom three. Di Canio, captain for the day with Lomas injured, had a quiet time. Not so 38-year-old Stuart Pearce, who plays a blinder to keep Bobby Robson's team at bay. Newcastle have gone 20 games in London without winning.											
12	A	DERBY	15	D	0-0	0-0		Hislop	Lomas	Sinclair	Pearce I	Ferdinand	Pearce S	Lampard	Kanoute*	Suker^	Di Canio	Carrick	Moncur/Diawara
6/11		24,621	20	12				Poom	Martin^	Johnson	Riggott	Carbonari	Schnoor	Burley	Delap	Christie"	Kinkladze	Powell*	Valakari/Morris/Burton
							Ref: P Durkin	What a reversal of fortunes! Jim Smith's winless Derby have slipped to the bottom, and are still six points behind reviving West Ham. But after four losses this was County's first clean sheet of the season. A Monday monsoon left much of Derby flooded, but Pride Park was playable.											
13	H	MANCHESTER C	13	W	4-1	0-1	Lomas 53, Sinclair 58, Pearce I 67	Hislop	Sinclair	Winterburn	Pearce I	Ferdinand	Pearce S	Lampard	Lomas	Kanoute	Di Canio*	Carrick	Potts
11/11		26,022	16	15			Prior 32 [Di Canio 90p]	Weaver	Charvet	Ritchie*	Wiekens	Howey	Prior	Kennedy	Haaland	Wanchope^	Whitley	Wr'-Phillips	Dunne/Allsopp
							Ref: J Winter	Joe Royle's City looked bright in the first half, dreadful in the second. Their misery was capped in the last minute with Di Canio's insulting penalty chipped down the middle. It sealed West Ham's 100th Premiership win, in what was Shaun Wright-Phillips' full Premiership debut.											
14	A	LEEDS	12	W	1-0	1-0	Winterburn 45	Hislop	Sinclair	Winterburn	Pearce I*	Ferdinand	Pearce S	Lampard	Kanoute	Diawara	Lomas	Carrick	Potts
18/11		40,005	11	18				Robinson	Kelly	Harte	Mills	Radebe	Bakke*	Dacourt	Bowyer	Smith	Viduka	Matteo	Huckerby
							Ref: P Taylor	David O'Leary's Leeds await Real Madrid in midweek, so this is the worst possible preparation. The last time West Ham won here was against Everton in the 1980 FA Cup semi-final, when Frank Lampard Snr danced around the corner flag. Winterburn heads his first Hammers goal.											
15	A	SOUTHAMPTON	11	W	3-2	2-1	Kanoute 41, Pearce S 43, Sinclair 69	Hislop	Lomas	Winterburn	Lampard*	Stimac	Pearce S	Sinclair	Kanoute	Diawara	Di Canio	Carrick	Moncur
25/11		15,232	15	21			Oakley 20, Beattie 53	Jones	Dodd	Bridge	El Khalej	Lund'kv'm^	Richards	Tessem*	Oakley	Beattie	Pahars	Kachloul	Rosler/Draper
							Ref: S Bennett	West Ham have sold Ferdinand to Leeds for £18m, and now jump into the top half by winning at The Dell for only the second time in 14 years. Each of the game's five goals had a touch of class, not least Oakley's volley. Saints' boss Glenn Hoddle admitted his team played poorly.											
16	H	MIDDLESBROUGH	7	W	1-0	1-0	Di Canio 42	Hislop	Sinclair	Winterburn	Song	Stimac*	Pearce S	Lampard^	Kanoute	Diawara	Di Canio	Carrick	Potts/Moncur
2/12		25,459	19	24				Schwarzer	Festa	Fleming	Vickers	Ehiogu !	Cooper*	Stamp	Mustoe	Whelan	Deane^	Ince	Karembeu/Job
							Ref: A D'Urso	While West Ham jet up to sixth, Bryan Robson's Boro are plunging down and playing with fear. Ferdinand's replacement, Rigobert Song from Liverpool, was hardly tested on his debut. Di Canio won the game, darting inside to drive in. Ehiogu's second yellow came for fouling Paolo.											
17	H	ASTON VILLA	7	D	1-1	1-1	Carrick 15	Hislop	Sinclair	Potts	Pearce I	Song	Pearce S	Lomas	Kanoute	Diawara*	Di Canio	Carrick	Moncur
9/12		25,888	8	25			Hendrie 37	James	Stone	Wright	Southgate	Alpay	Barry	Merson	Boateng	Dublin	Hendrie	Ginola	
							Ref: M Riley	Song spent the game tracking David Ginola. Carrick's goal, in off a post, should have won it for West Ham, but John Gregory's Villa earned their third 1-1 draw in a row when Lee Hendrie's effort went in off both posts. Villa keeper David James was booed for a spat with Di Canio.											
18	A	EVERTON	8	D	1-1	0-0	Kanoute 83	Hislop	Sinclair	Winterburn	Pearce I	Song	Pearce S	Lampard	Lomas	Kanoute	Di Canio	Carrick	
16/12		31,260	14	26			Cadamarteri 75	Gerrard^	Watson	Naysmith	Gravesen*	Weir	Ball	Gemmill	Cadamart'ri	Campbell	Pembridge	Hughes	Alexandersson/Simonsen
							Ref: C Wilkes	This was the game which saw Di Canio praised for his sportsmanship, or blasted for his unprofessionalism, depending on your point of view. In the dying moments he might have tried to volley Sinclair's cross, but with home keeper Gerrard lying injured, Paolo caught the ball instead.											
19	A	LEICESTER	10	L	1-2	1-1	Kanoute 8	Hislop	Sinclair	Winterburn	Pearce I*	Song	Pearce S	Lampard	Camara	Kanoute	Lomas	Carrick	Cole
23/12		21,524	3	26			Izzet 26, Savage 63	Flowers	Impey	Sinclair	Elliott^	Rowett	Taggart	Savage	Izzet"	Akinbiyi*	Jones	Oakes	Eadie/Guppy/Benjamin
							Ref: G Poll	West Ham's first defeat in nine gives the Foxes the double and takes them joint-second. 'We missed enough chances to have won two games,' moaned Redknapp. Di Canio was absent, 'tackled' by Sinclair in training. Debutant Camara had not started a game for Liverpool all season.											
20	H	CHARLTON	8	W	5-0	3-0	Rufus 13 (og), Kanoute 18, 84,	Hislop	Lomas	Winterburn	Sinclair^	Song	Pearce S	Lampard	Camara*	Kanoute	Di Canio"	Carrick	Cole/Moncur/Tihinen
26/12		26,046	13	29			[Lampard 45, Sinclair 71]	Kiely	Kishinev^	Powell	Stuart	Rufus	Brown	Kinsella	Jensen	Svensson"	Johansson	Robinson*	Konchesky/Parker/Pringle
							Ref: S Dunn	A Boxing Day pounding for Curbishley's men: 'We were inept.' The mood was set by Di Canio's impudent back-heel, the ball going in off Rufus. Charlton's sixth straight away defeat was confirmed by Sinclair's 25-yard volley and Carrick's through-pass into the path of Kanoute.											
21	A	MANCHESTER U	10	L	1-3	0-2	Kanoute 72	Hislop	Lomas	Winterburn	Camara^	Song	Pearce S	Sinclair	Lampard	Kanoute	Moncur*	Carrick	Cole/Tihinen
1/1		67,603	1	29			Solskjaer 3, Pearce 33(og), Yorke 58	Barthez	Neville P	Silvestre	Brown	Keane*	Neville G	Beckham	Scholes^	Solskjaer	Yorke	Giggs"	Wellwork/Butt/Greening
							Ref: P Jones	Man U moved 11 points clear of Arsenal with this easy win. It was so one-sided that Barthez wandered to the centre-circle to view the carnage at the other end. England's latest captain, Beckham, robbed Song inside the Hammers box to set up the opener. Hislop kept the score down.											

No		Date		Att	Pos	Pt	F-A	H-T	Scorers, Times, and Referees	SQUAD	NUMBERS	IN	USE								subs used
22	H		SUNDERLAND		11	L	0-2	0-1		Hislop^	Sinclair	Winterburn	Tihinen*	Song	Pearce S	Lampard	Cole	Kanoute	Di Canio	Lomas	Camara/Forrest
		13/1		26,014	*2*	29			*Varga 22, Hutchison 68*	*Sorensen*	*Williams*	*Gray*	*Varga*	*Emerson*	*McCann*	*Rae*	*Schwarz*	*Quinn**	*Phillips*	*Hutchison*	*Kilbane*
									Ref: M Massias	Peter Reid's 'functional' team climb to second on a cold, grey day with their eighth win in ten games. Both goals stemmed from free-kicks, but the Roker men were dependent on Sorensen for keeping West Ham at bay. England's boss Eriksson was impressed by 19-year-old Joe Cole.											
23	A		CHARLTON		12	D	1-1	0-1	Di Canio 74	Forrest	**Schemmel**	Winterburn	Tihinen	Song	**Dailly**	Lampard	Cole*	Kanoute	Di Canio	Carrick	Moncur
		22/1		*20,043*	*8*	30			*Bartlett 7*	*Kiely*	*Kishinev*	*Konch'sky**	*Todd*	*Rufus*	*Fish*	*Stuart*	*Jensen"*	*Bartlett*	*Svensson^*	*Parker*	*Powell/Lisbie/Salako*
									Ref: D Gallagher	Eriksson casts his eye over his English talent, but must have drooled over that of Di Canio, who he coveted at Lazio. Konchesky set up Bartlett to fire past Forrest, playing instead of the injured Hislop. West Ham's defence are all newcomers and they are grateful for Paolo's bullet shot.											
24	H		TOTTENHAM		13	D	0-0	0-0		Hislop	Schemmel	Winterburn	Tihinen	Dailly	Pearce S	Lampard	Cole	Kanoute	Di Canio	Carrick	
		31/1		**26,048**	*10*	31				*Walker*	*Anderton*	*Clemence**	*Doherty*	*Campbell*	*Perry*	*Leonhard'n*	*Freund*	*Rebrov^*	*Booth*	*King*	*Young/McEwen*
									Ref: N Barry	This was the first 0-0 between these clubs at Upton Park since 1924. West Ham had won one in seven in the Premiership, and Spurs one in 10, and the Hammers still seemed to be celebrating their FA Cup win at Old Trafford. Booth and Kanoute both had efforts disallowed for offside.											
25	A		LIVERPOOL		14	L	**0-3**	0-2		Forrest	Schemmel*	Winterburn	Tihinen	Dailly	Pearce S	Lampard	Cole^	Kanoute"	Camara	Carrick	Song/**Soma/Todorov**
		3/2		*44,045*	*3*	31			*Smicer 20, Fowler 45, 57*	*Westerveld*	*Babbel"*	*Vignal*	*Hamann*	*Henchoz*	*Hyppia*	*Gerrard*	*Smicer*	*Heskey*	*Fowler*	*Biscan**	*Barmby^/Ziege/Wright*
									Ref: S Bennett	Liverpool prepare for a trip to Roma in the UEFA Cup by dismissing West Ham in disdainful manner. The match was settled in midfield where West Ham's prodigies chased Gerrard's shadow. Smicer fired in from 25 yards then set up Fowler for the third. Di Canio was missing with flu.											
26	H		COVENTRY		14	D	1-1	0-0	Cole 83	Forrest	Schemmel	Winterburn	Tihinen	Dailly	Pearce S	Lampard	Cole	Kanoute	Di Canio	Carrick	
		12/2		**22,586**	*19*	32			*Dailly 90 (og)*	*Hedman*	*Quinn"*	*Hall*	*Breen*	*Shaw*	*Carsley**	*Thompson*	*Hartson*	*Bellamy^*	*Hadji*	*Eustace*	*Chippo/Edw'rthy/B'throyd*
									Ref: D Gallagher	This was the only Upton Park game not to be a sell-out this season. An insipid game appeared to turn West Ham's way when Cole converted Winterburn's cross at the far post. Former Hammer John Hartson was warmly received. Dailly headed Thompson's free-kick past Forrest.											
27	A		BRADFORD C		13	W	2-1	1-0	Lampard 18, 75	Bywater	Schemmel^	Winterburn	Dailly	Stimac	Pearce S	Lampard	Cole	Camara*	Di Canio	Carrick	Suker/Pearce I
		24/2		*20,469*	*20*	35			*Jess 62*	*Walsh*	*Lawrence*	*Jacobs"*	*Myers*	*Molenaar^*	*Wetherall*	*Locke**	*O'Brien*	*Ward*	*Carbone*	*Jess*	*McCall/Hopkin/Blake*
									Ref: S Lodge	Jim Jefferies' City escaped the drop on the last day last season. They won't this time, even though Jess's goal is their first since New Year's Day. Star man was Frank Lampard who scored with a low shot from the edge of the box, and again when the ball broke to him off Joe Cole.											
28	A		ARSENAL		13	L	**0-3**	0-3		Hislop	Schemmel	Winterburn	Song	Stimac*	Pearce S^	Lampard	Soma	Suker	Diawara"	Dailly	Pearce I/Tihinen/Todorov
		3/3		*38,076*	*2*	35			*Wiltord 6, 13, 39*	*Seaman*	*Dixon*	*Cole^*	*Vieira*	*Grimaldi*	*Adams*	*Pires"*	*Lauren*	*Wiltord**	*Bergkamp*	*Ljungberg*	*Henry/Vivas/Edu*
									Ref: M Riley	Last week Man U beat Arsenal 6-1, but Wenger's Gunners return to winning ways. Silvain Wiltord secured his first hat-trick since signing for £13m in August. Winterburn was made captain on his return to Highbury, but Hammers minds are now focussed on the FA Cup quarter-final.											
29	H		CHELSEA		13	L	0-2	0-2		Hislop	Song	Soma	Pearce I	Dailly	Pearce S*	Lampard	Cole	Suker"	Di Canio	Potts	Schem^/Diawara/Bassila
		7/3		26,016	*10*	35			*Gudjohnsen 32, Hasselbaink 38*	*Cudicini*	*Ferrer*	*Le Saux"*	*Stanic**	*Leboeuf*	*Desailly*	*Wise*	*Jokanovic^*	*Hasselbaink*	*Gudjohnsen*	*Gronkjaer*	*Poyet/Dalla Bona/Terry*
									Ref: A Wiley	West Ham's season hinges on Sunday's FA Cup quarter-final with Spurs. This was Chelsea's first away win in 11months, but it might have been different had Joe Cole's strike against the bar from six yards gone in. Gronkjaer set up Gudjohnsen, and Hasselbaink looped a second.											
30	H		IPSWICH		14	L	0-1	0-0		Hislop	Schemmel*	Winterburn	Pearce I	Song	Pearce S	Lampard	Cole^	Kanoute	Di Canio	Carrick	Moncur/Todorov
		17/3		26,046	*3*	35			*Reuser 60*	*Wright*	*Wilnis*	*Makin*	*Reuser**	*Hreidarsson*	*McGreal*	*Holland*	*Magilton*	*Stewart^*	*Armstrong*	*Wright*	*Clapham/Burchill*
									Ref: M Dean	Ipswich are chasing a Champions League place. This was a 1-0 'thrashing', so one-sided was the contest, but it was Town's first away points in over three months. The goal came when Stuart Pearce fouled Stewart inside the box. The ref gave a free-kick outside, which Reuser curled in.											
31	H		EVERTON		14	L	0-2	0-1		Hislop	Song	Winterburn	Stimac	**Foxe**	Pearce S !	Lampard	Cole	Kanoute	Di Canio	Carrick	
		31/3		26,044	*15*	35			*Unsworth 45p, Alexandersson 71*	*Gerrard*	*Hibbert*	*Unsworth*	*Watson*	*Weir*	*Ball*	*Nyarko*	*Gravesen**	*Ferguson*	*Alex'ders'n*	*Gemmill*	*Jeffers*
									Ref: A D'Urso	Four successive goalless league defeats are leaving West Ham looking anxiously below them. They were booed off for the second home game in a row. The Hammers were under the cosh before Stuart Pearce felled Hibbert inside the box, got sent off, and Unsworth netted from the spot.											

No	Venue	Opponent	Att	Pos	Res	F-A	H-T	Scorers, Times, and Referees	1	2	3	4	5	6	7	8	9	10	11	subs used
32	A	ASTON VILLA		15	D	2-2	0-0	Kanoute 46, Lampard 87	Hislop	Schemmel*	Winterburn	Song	Stimac	Pearce S	Lampard	Moncur	Kanoute	Di Canio^	Carrick	Cole/Soma
	7/4		*31,432*	*8*	36			*Ginola 71, Hendrie 78*	*James*	*Delaney*	*Staunton**	*Southgate*	*Barry*	*Taylor*	*Stone^*	*Merson*	*Joachim*	*Hendrie*	*Ginola*	*Wright/Vassell*
								Ref: R Harris	A 'sad' first half was followed by a 'hot' second, according to Villa boss Gregory. 28 seconds into the second half Kanoute completed a slick Hammers goal, their first in yonks. Ginola's free-kick and Hendrie's tap in turned the tables, but Lampard pounced after a rebound off a post.											
33	H	DERBY		13	W	3-1	3-0	Kanoute 5, Lampard 7, Cole 45	Hislop	Song	Winterburn	Lampard	Stimac	Pearce I	Moncur	Cole	Kanoute	Di Canio	Carrick	
	14/4		25,319	*17*	39			*Gudjonsson 83*	*Poom*	*Delap*	*Higginb'm"*	*Riggott*	*Carbonari*	*West*	*Eranio**	*Kinkladze^*	*Burton*	*Johnson*	*Powell*	*Christie/Gudj'n'son/Morris*
								Ref: R Styles	Bottom in September, up to 6th, down to 15th. This was the result that effectively secured West Ham's Premiership status in this yo-yo season. Eriksson sees Kanoute score the Hammers' first home goal in four matches – off his shin! Two minutes later Lampard's fierce drive seals it.											
34	A	NEWCASTLE		14	L	1-2	0-1	Lampard 78p	Hislop	Song	Winterburn	Schemmel^	Stimac	Pearce I	Lampard	Cole	Kanoute"	Moncur*	Carrick	Diawara/Dailly/Todorov
	16/4		*51,107*	*13*	39			*Cort 32, Solano 56p*	*Given*	*Barton**	*Quinn*	*O'Brien*	*Dabizas*	*Solano*	*Lee^*	*Bassedas*	*Gallacher"*	*Cort*	*Speed*	*Caldwell/Acuna/Lua-Lua*
								Ref: P Durkin	This is Bobby Robson's team's first win in seven, enabling them to leapfrog West Ham. Lampard's late penalty denied Newcastle their first clean sheet in 28 league and cup games. Cort's volley and Solano's spot-kick, after Winterburn handled, had put the home team in command.											
35	H	LEEDS		14	L	0-2	0-1		Hislop	Dailly*	Winterburn	Lampard	Stimac	Pearce I	Moncur"	Cole	Kanoute^	Di Canio	Carrick	Diawara/Todorov/Foxe
	21/4		26,041	*4*	39			*Keane 8, Ferdinand 47*	*Martyn*	*Mills*	*Harte*	*Batty !*	*Ferdinand*	*Matteo*	*Dacourt*	*Bowyer*	*Keane**	*Kewell^*	*Bakke*	*Kelly/Wilcox*
								Ref: G Poll	David O'Leary fielded nine of the players who played in midweek against La Coruna, but they still look fresher than did comatose West Ham. Batty was sent off for elbowing Cole. Rio Ferdinand returned to Upton Park for the first time, scored with an easy header, and looked ashamed.											
36	A	MANCHESTER C		15	L	0-1	0-1		Hislop	Dailly	Winterb'rn^	Stimac	Song	Pearce S	Pearce I"	Cole	Diawara*	Di Canio	Carrick	Suker/Todorov/Foxe
	28/4		*33,737*	*18*	39			*Pearce I 23 (og)*	*Nash*	*Haaland"*	*Granville*	*Wiekens*	*Howey*	*Dunne*	*Kennedy*	*Whitley*	*Dickov**	*Goater^*	*Tiatto*	*Wanch'pe/Huck'by/Charv'*
								Ref: P Jones	City must win all three of their last games to stand any chance of avoiding the drop. They accomplished the first task thanks to Shaun Goater's deflected effort, and the second-half defiance of keeper Nash and assorted clearances off the goal-line. 'We were lucky,' admitted Joe Royle.											
37	H	SOUTHAMPTON		14	W	3-0	0-0	Cole 59, Di Canio 70, Kanoute 90	Hislop	Foxe	Dailly	Stimac^	Song	Pearce S	Todorov*	Cole	Kanoute	Di Canio	Carrick	Schemmel/Bassila
	5/5		26,041	*13*	42				*Jones*	*Dodd*	*Bridge*	*Marsden*	*Lundekvam*	*Richards*	*Davies*	*Oakley*	*Beattie*	*Pahars"*	*Kachloul**	*Rosler^/Tess'm/Le Tissier*
								Ref: C Wilkes	At last West Ham are mathematically safe, thanks to their first clean sheet in 12 games against opponents who have also collapsed, since Glenn Hoddle's walk-out six weeks earlier. New Saints boss Stuart Gray saw his team start brightly, but fall apart after Joe Cole fired in on the hour.											
38	A	MIDDLESBROUGH		15	L	1-2	1-2	Todorov 31	Hislop	Schemmel	Minto*	Foxe	Song	Pearce S	Dailly	Cole	Kanoute	Todorov^	Carrick	**McCann/Defoe**
	19/5		33,057	*14*	42			*Job 21, Karembeu 45*	*Schwarzer*	*Gavin*	*Cooper*	*Vickers*	*Ehiogu*	*Okon*	*Karembeu^*	*Windass*	*Marinelli**	*Job*	*Ince*	*Deane/Hudson*
		Home	Away					Ref: P Durkin	Terry Venables has saved Boro from relegation, pushing Bryan Robson into the wilderness, and at Upton Park Harry Redknapp has gone too, to be 'temporarily' replaced by Glenn Roeder. Job rounded Hislop for the opener, Todorov side-footed the leveller, but Karembeu broke clear.											
Average		25,697	33,048																	

Worthington Cup			Att			F-A	H-T	Scorers, Times, and Referees	SQUAD	NUMBERS	IN USE									subs used
2:1	A	WALSALL		20	W	1-0	0-0	Defoe 84	Hislop	Potts	Winterburn	Stimac	Ferdinand	Pearce S	Lomas	Cole	Sinclair	Carrick	Keller*	Defoe
	19/9		*5,435*	*2:1*					*Walker*	*Brightwell*	*Aranalde*	*Tillson*	*Barras*	*Bukran*	*Hall**	*Keates*	*Leitao*	*Byfield*	*Matias*	*Angell*
								Ref: S Lodge	Bottom of the Premiership meets top of Division 2 in a rain-drenched stadium. 17-year-old Jermain Defoe, controversially signed from Charlton, came on with 13 minutes left and pounced when Ferdinand's shot came back off the bar. Otherwise it was a game of few chances.											
2:2	H	WALSALL		18	D	1-1	1-1	Lomas 2	Hislop	Margas	Winterburn	Stimac	Lampard*	Pearce S	Lomas	Cole	Di Canio	Carrick	Kanoute	Potts
	27/9		11,963	*2:1*				*Leitao 8*	*Walker*	*Brightwell*	*Aranalde*	*Tillson*	*Barras**	*Bukran*	*Hall^*	*Bennett*	*Leitao*	*Angell"*	*Matias*	*Roper/Wright/Byfield*
								Ref: A D'Urso (Hammers win 2-1 on aggregate)	Lomas's quick-fire goal seemed to have settled this tie but, when Jorge Leitao equalised, Ray Graydon's table-toppers seized the ascendancy and considered themselves unfortunate not to force extra-time. Walsall created enough chances to do so, but failed to take any more of them.											
3	H	BLACKBURN		15	W	2-0	0-0	Suker 67, Di Canio 84	Hislop	Potts	Pearce I	Sinclair	Ferdinand	Pearce S	Lampard	Di Canio	Suker	Carrick	Kanoute*	Moncur
	31/10		21,863	*1:8*					*Kelly*	*Kenna*	*Curtis*	*Taylor**	*Dailly*	*Carsley*	*McAteer*	*Dunning*	*Ostenstad*	*Richards^*	*Johnson"*	*Flitcroft/Dunn/Douglas*
								Ref: A Wiley	West Ham made heavy weather of beating Division 1 opponents, who had the effrontery to 'rest' most of their better players to concentrate on promotion. At last Kanoute nodded Di Canio's corner to Suker. The second goal came from a twice-taken penalty given for a foul by Dunning.											
4	H	SHEFFIELD WED		11	L	1-2	0-1	Lampard 72	Hislop	Song*	Winterburn	Stimac	Ferdinand	Pearce S	Lampard	Di Canio	Sinclair	Carrick	Kanoute	Suker
	29/11		25,853	*1:17*				*Morrison 30, Westwood 49*	*Pressman*	*Haslam*	*Geary*	*Lescott*	*Westwood*	*Walker*	*Crane*	*Sibon**	*Ekoku*	*Morrison*	*Quinn*	*Booth*
								Ref: P Danson	Rigobert Song is thrown into the fray after signing for £2.5 million from Liverpool. Lampard's first-minute miss set the scene for what was to come, as chances went begging. Song was out of position for Paul Jewell's Owls' first goal. Westwood headed in Morrison's corner for No 2.											

FA Cup																				
3	A	WALSALL		11	W	3-2	1-1	Lampard 6, Kanoute 57, 81	Hislop	Song	Winterburn	Tihinen	Carrick	Pearce S	Lampard	Cole	Sinclair	Camara*	Kanoute	Bassila
	6/1		*9,402*	*2:3*				*Wrack 33, Angell 87*	*Walker*	*Brightwell**	*Aranalde*	*Tillson*	*Barras*	*Bukran*	*Hall^*	*Bennett*	*Leitao"*	*Angell*	*Wrack*	*Marsh/Keates/Byfield*
								Ref: A D'Urso	Having disposed of Walsall in the Worthington Cup, West Ham are now paired with them again. Walsall no longer top Division 2, while West Ham are in mid-table. Although the teams traded goals in the first half, Kanoute's header and ferocious strike put the game beyond Walsall.											
4	A	MANCHESTER U		13	W	1-0	0-0	Di Canio 76	Hislop	Schemmel	Winterburn	Tihinen	Dailly	Pearce S	Lampard	Cole*	Carrick	Di Canio^	Kanoute	Pearce I/Soma
	28/1		*67,029*	*1*					*Barthez*	*Irwin**	*Silvestre*	*Neville G*	*Keane*	*Stam*	*Beckham*	*Butt^*	*Cole*	*Sheringham*	*Giggs*	*Solskjaer/Yorke*
								Ref: P Durkin	One of the shocks of the round, especially as West Ham conceded ten on their last two visits. Man U should have won this by half-time on a pitch ruined by the Rugby League World Cup final. They were undone by Di Canio who beat the offside trap then Barthez who played possum.											
5	A	SUNDERLAND		13	W	1-0	0-0	Kanoute 76	Hislop	Schemmel	Winterburn	Stimac	Dailly	Pearce S	Lampard	Cole	Carrick	Di Canio	Kanoute	
	17/2		*36,005*	*4*					*Sorensen*	*Williams*	*Makin*	*McCann*	*Varga**	*Emerson*	*Schwarz*	*Arca*	*Quinn*	*Phillips*	*Oster*	*McCartney^/Dichio*
								Ref: A Wiley	A noon kick-off. The high-flying hosts, beaten just once at home, are stricken by injuries and suspensions, and offered nothing more than high balls aimed at Niall Quinn. Kanoute had spurned enough chances by the time he rolled a pass from Lampard past Sorensen. That was enough.											
QF	H	TOTTENHAM		14	L	2-3	1-1	Pearce S 43, Todorov 72	Hislop	Schemmel*	Winterburn	Stimac	Dailly	Pearce S	Lampard	Cole	Carrick	Di Canio	Kanoute	Todorov
	11/3		*26,048*	*11*				*Rebrov 31, 57, Doherty 62*	*Sullivan*	*Young*	*Clemence*	*Doherty*	*Campbell*	*Perry*	*Freund*	*Iversen*	*Rebrov*	*Ferdinand**	*King*	*Korsten*
								Ref: A D'Urso	West Ham's first home tie is played in a deluge. Rebrov's volley was cancelled out by Pearce's hard free-kick. Rebrov fired a second, Doherty headed in a corner, and Todorov came off the bench to ignite a barnstorming finish. The semi-final draw was actually made during the game!											

	P	Home W	D	L	F	A	Away W	D	L	F	A	Pts
1 Manchester U	38	15	2	2	49	12	9	6	4	30	19	80
2 Arsenal	38	15	3	1	45	13	5	7	7	18	25	70
3 Liverpool	38	13	4	2	40	14	7	5	7	31	25	69
4 Leeds	38	11	3	5	36	21	9	5	5	28	22	68
5 Ipswich	38	11	5	3	31	15	9	1	9	26	27	66
6 Chelsea	38	13	3	3	44	20	4	7	8	24	25	61
7 Sunderland	38	9	7	3	24	16	6	5	8	22	25	57
8 Aston Villa	38	8	8	3	27	20	5	7	7	19	23	54
9 Charlton	38	11	5	3	31	19	3	5	11	19	38	52
10 Southampton	38	11	2	6	27	22	3	8	8	13	26	52
11 Newcastle	38	10	4	5	26	17	4	5	10	18	33	51
12 Tottenham	38	11	6	2	31	16	2	4	13	16	38	49
13 Leicester	38	10	4	5	28	23	4	2	13	11	28	48
14 Middlesbro'	38	4	7	8	18	23	5	8	6	26	21	42
15 WEST HAM	38	6	6	7	24	20	4	6	9	21	30	42
16 Everton	38	6	8	5	29	27	5	1	13	16	32	42
17 Derby	38	8	7	4	23	24	2	5	12	14	35	42
18 Manchester C	38	4	3	12	20	31	4	7	8	21	34	34
19 Coventry	38	4	7	8	14	23	4	3	12	22	40	34
20 Bradford C	38	4	7	8	20	29	1	4	14	10	41	26
	760	184	101	95	587	405	95	101	184	405	587	1039

Odds & ends

Double wins: (1) Southampton.
Double losses: (3) Chelsea, Leicester, Arsenal.

Won from behind: (2) Manchester City (h), Southampton (a).
Lost from in front: (1) Leicester (a).

High spots: Climbing from the foot of the table to sixth and chasing a UEFA Cup place.
Winning at Old Trafford in the FA Cup with Di Canio's impudent goal.
Reaching the quarter-finals of the FA Cup.
Receiving £18 million for the sale of Rio Ferdinand to Leeds.
Beating Charlton 5-0 on Boxing Day.

Low spots: The worst league start for a decade.
The grim end to the league season, which could not end quickly enough.
Losing Rio Ferdinand, despite the huge fee received.
Losing to Tottenham in the quarter-finals of the FA Cup.

Hammer of the Year: Stuart Pearce.
Ever-presents: (0).
Hat-tricks: (0).
Leading scorer: (14) Frederic Kanoute.

	Appearances Lge	*Sub*	LC	*Sub*	FAC	*Sub*	Goals Lge	LC	FAC	Tot
Bassila, Christian		*3*				*1*				
Bywater, Stephen	**1**									
Camara, Titi	**5**	*1*			1					
Carrick, Michael	**32**	*1*	4		4		1			1
Charles, Gary		*1*								
Cole, Joe	**24**	*6*	2		4		5			5
Dailly, Christian	**11**	*1*			3					
Defoe, Jermain		*1*		*1*				1		1
Diawara, Kaba	**6**	*5*								
Di Canio, Paolo	**31**		3		3		9	1	1	11
Ferdinand, Rio	**12**		3							
Forrest, Craig	**3**	*1*								
Foxe, Hayden	**3**	*2*								
Hislop, Shaka	**34**		4		4					
Kanoute, Frederic	**32**		3		4		11		3	14
Keller, Marc			1							
Kitson, Paul		*2*								
Lampard, Frank	**30**		3		4		7	1	1	9
Lomas, Steve	**20**		2				1	1		2
McCann, Grant		*1*								
Margas, Javier	**3**		1							
Minto, Scott	**1**									
Moncur, John	**6**	*10*		*1*						
Pearce, Ian	**13**	*2*	1			*1*	1			1
Pearce, Stuart	**34**		4		4		2		1	3
Potts, Steve	**2**	*6*	2	*1*						
Schemmel, Sebastian	**10**	*2*			3					
Sinclair, Trevor	**19**		3		1		3			3
Soma, Ragnvald	**2**	*2*				*1*				
Song, Rigobert	**18**	*1*	1		1					
Stimac, Igor	**19**		3		2					
Suker, Davor	**7**	*4*	1	*1*			2	1		3
Tihinen, Hannu	**5**	*3*			2					
Todorov, Svetoslav	**2**	*6*				*1*	1		1	2
Winterburn, Nigel	**33**		3		4		1			1
(own-goals)							1			1
35 players used	**418**	***61***	**44**	***4***	**44**	***4***	**45**	**5**	**7**	**57**

No	Date		Att	Pos	Pt	F-A	H-T	Scorers, Times, and Referees	SQUAD	NUMBERS	IN	USE								subs used
1	A	LIVERPOOL			L	1-2	1-1	Di Canio 30p	Hislop	Schemmel	Winterburn	Moncur*	Song	Dailly	Sinclair	Cole^	Todorov"	Di Canio	Carrick	McCann/**Courtois**/Defoe
	18/8		43,935		0			Owen 18, 77	Arphexad	Babbel*	Carragher	Hamann	Henchoz	Hyppia	Murphy^	Litmanen	Owen	McAllister	Biscan"	Riise/Redknapp/Barmby
								Ref: J Winter	Liverpool were patchy, apart from Michael Owen, who took his tally to 15 in eight games. West Ham played positively under new boss Glenn Roeder, helped by Henchoz's trip on Todorov. Owen had earlier converted McAllisters's flick and now he carves out space to drill past Hislop.											
2	H	LEEDS		17	D	0-0	0-0		Hislop	Schemmel	Winterburn	Moncur^	Song	Dailly	Sinclair	Cole	Todorov*	Di Canio	Carrick	Defoe//McCann
	25/8		24,517	2	1				Martyn	Mills	Harte*	Batty	Ferdinand	Matteo	Dacourt^	Keane	Viduka	Kewell	Bowyer	Woodgate/Maybury
								Ref: P Durkin	Upton Park looks like a builders' yard and the Dr Martens Stand a bomb site. Leeds arrived from having had two men sent off at Highbury, and failure to qualify for the Champions League hits them hard. Di Canio was behind West Ham's best moments, turning Danny Mills inside out.											
3	A	DERBY		17	D	0-0	0-0		Hislop	Schemmel	Winterburn	**Hutchison**	Song	Dailly	Sinclair	Cole*	Kanoute^	Di Canio"	Carrick	Moncur/Todorov/Defoe
	8/9		27,802	12	2				Oakes	Mawene	Boertien	Riggott	Hi'ginbot'm	Johnson	Burley	Kinkladze	Burton*	Ravanelli	Powell	Morris
								Ref: C Wilkes	This was one of those games where West Ham exuded any class on show, but Jim Smith's Derby enjoyed – and wasted – the better openings. Hislop also stood tall, capitalising on David James' injury. Defoe missed West Ham's best chances at the death, scooping Todorov's pass wide.											
4	A	MIDDLESBROUGH		20	L	0-2	0-2		Hislop	Schemmel	Winterb'rn"	Song^	**Repka !**	Dailly	Moncur*	Cole	Sinclair	Hutchison	Carrick	Todorov/Defoe/Soma
	15/9		24,455	19	2			Deane 31, Johnston 41	Schwarzer	Fleming	Cooper^	Southgate	Ehiogu	Mustoe	Greening	Windass	Deane	Johnston*	Ince	Wilson/Gavin
								Ref: M Riley	Boro had lost their first four games, but now overtake West Ham, who drop to bottom. Hate-figure Paul Ince controlled Boro's midfield, while Hammers debutant, Repka, from Fiorentina, received his second yellow ten minutes from time. Hislop and Song blundered for Boro's goals.											
5	H	NEWCASTLE		15	W	3-0	1-0	Hutch' 18, Di Canio 53, Kanoute 82	Hislop	Schemmel	Winterburn	Hutchison	Repka	Dailly	Sinclair	Courtois*	Kanoute^	Di Canio	Carrick	Moncur/Defoe
	23/9		24,810	9	5				Given	Barton^	Elliott	Dabizas	O'Brien	Solano*	Lee	Acuna	Shearer	Bellamy	Robert	Ameobi/Distin
								Ref: P Jones	West Ham climb five places, extended Bobby Robson's Geordies' winless run in London to 26, while inflicting their first defeat in 13 since the end of last season. Don Hutchison, bought to replace Lampard, has his best game so far. Trevor Sinclair is thought to be headed to Sunderland.											
6	A	EVERTON		18	L	0-5	0-1	[Gravesen 56, Watson 75, Radz' 79]	Hislop	Schemmel	Winterb'rn*	Hutchison	Song	Dailly	Sinclair	Courtois^	Kanoute"	Di Canio	Carrick	Soma/Byrne/Kitson
	29/9		32,049	10	5			Campbell 45, Hutchison 52 (og),	Gerrard	Watson	Naysmith	Xavier	Weir	Pistone	Alexand's'n	Gascoigne*	Campbell	Radzinski"	Gravesen	Pembridge^/Hibbert/Moore
								Ref: P Durkin	Under-pressure Everton boss Walter Smith was smiling at the end, unlike Paul Gascoigne who limped off after eight minutes. Di Canio missed two openings for West Ham before Campbell headed in. After Hislop collided with Hutchison and the ball bounced in, the floodgates opened.											
7	A	BLACKBURN		19	L	1-7	1-3	Carrick 39 [Tug' 80,Jan' 82,Hig' 90]	Hislop	Schemmel	Soma	Moncur*	Repka !	Dailly^	Sinclair	Hutchison	Kanoute	Di Canio	Carrick	McCann/Foxe
	14/10		22,712	11	5			Flit' 18,Dunn 27,J'son 28,McC' 63(og),	Friedel	Neill	Bjornebye	Johansson	Berg*	Tugay	Johnson"	Flitcroft	Grabbi^	Jansen	Dunn	Short/Hughes/Hignett
								Ref: A D'Urso	12 goals shipped in two games should bring relegation and dismissal of the manager. Graeme Souness's Rovers were grateful to Sinclair's bad miss and to Repka's second dismissal in four games. Not until McCann turned an off-target shot past Hislop, making it 4-1, did the rout begin.											
8	H	SOUTHAMPTON		16	W	2-0	0-0	Kanoute 53, 81	Hislop	Schemmel	Winterburn	Courtois*	Repka	Dailly	Sinclair	Hutchison	Kanoute	Di Canio	Carrick	Moncur
	20/10		25,842	19	8				Jones	Dodd	Bridge	Marsden	Lundekvam	El Khalej	Delap	Draper	Beattie	Pahars^	Davies*	Svensson/Ripley
								Ref: N Barry	One sensed that whichever manager lost this game would lose his job. Saints' Stuart Gray was the unlucky man, with Gordon Strachan named almost immediately. Edgy Hammers saw Di Canio and Winterburn square up to one another just before Kanoute settled the nerves by scoring.											
9	H	CHELSEA		14	W	2-1	2-1	Carrick 5, Kanoute 13	Hislop	Schemmel	Winterburn	Courtois*	Repka	Dailly	Sinclair	Hutchison	Kanoute^	Di Canio	Carrick	Defoe/Kitson
	24/10		26,520	7	11			Hasselbaink 22	Bosnich	Melchiot	Le Saux	Petit"	Terry	Gallas	Jokanovic	Lampard^	Hasselbaink	Zola	Gudjo'son*	Zenden/Fors'ell/DallaBona
								Ref: D Gallagher	A thriller sees Claudio Ranieri's Blues lose their unbeaten record and enables Roeder to shrug off predecessor Redknapp's criticisms of him. Di Canio set up Carrick's early opener, Sinclair sparked Kanoute's glorious second, but Hasselbaink replied with his ninth goal in nine games.											
10	A	IPSWICH		11	W	3-2	1-0	Di Canio 22, Kanoute 72, Defoe 90	Hislop	Schemmel	Winterburn	Minto	Foxe	Dailly	Sinclair	Hutchison	Kanoute	Di Canio*	Carrick	Defoe
	28/10		22,826	17	14			Hreidarsson 63, Holland 90	Sereni	Makin	Clapham"	Venus	Gaardsoe	Hreidarsson	Reuser	Holland	Stewart	Armstr'ng^	Wright*	Magilton/Counago/Peralta
								Ref: S Dunn	West Ham reacted to two thrashings by winning their next three. This was their first away from home since February. Roeder adopted 3-5-2. Burley's Ipswich, however, fifth last season, are going down. Defoe made it 3-1 in injury-time, whereupon Holland drove in from 25 yards.											

11	H	FULHAM		14	L	0-2	0-1		Hislop	Schemmel	Winterburn	Courtois*	Foxe	Dailly	Sinclair	Hutchison	Kanoute	Di Canio	Carrick	Defoe
3/11			26,217	*12*	14			*Legwinski 44, Malbranque 65*	*Van d Saar*	*Finnan*	*Brevett*	*Melville*	*Goma*	*Malbr'que"*	*Legwinski*	*Collins^*	*Saha**	*Hayles*	*Boa Morte*	*Davies/Goldbaek/Stolcers*
								Ref: G Barber	Australian Foxe did well, deputising for the suspended Repka, but West Ham had no answer to Steed Malbranque's scheming behind Fulham's front two. Di Canio was partially responsible for the second goal, falling under a feeble challenge and staying down as Fulham broke upfield.											
12	A	CHARLTON			D	4-4	2-2	Kitson 3, 30, 64, Defoe 84	Hislop	Schemmel	Minto"	Foxe	Repka	Dailly	Sinclair	Hutchison*	Kitson^	Di Canio	Carrick	Cole/Defoe/Lomas
19/11			*23,198*		15			*Euell 21, 28, Johansson 51, 90*	*Kiely*	*Young^*	*Powell*	*Konchesky*	*Brown*	*Fish*	*Kinsella*	*Jensen*	*Euell*	*Johansson*	*Parker**	*Bartlett/Robinson*
								Ref: A Wiley	Kitson hadn't started for West Ham for 21 months. He was subbed after his hat-trick, only the Premiership's second hat-trick of the season. All the goals were scored by Addicks past or present. West Ham have shipped 22 goals in 7 away games. Johansson's overhead kick denied them.											
13	H	TOTTENHAM		15	L	0-1	0-0		**James**	Schemmel	Minto	Lomas*	Repka	Dailly	Sinclair	Hutchison	Kitson	Cole	Defoe	Moncur
24/11			32,780	*24*	15			*Ferdinand 50*	*Sullivan*	*Anderton*	*Ziege*	*King*	*Perry*	*Richards*	*Freund*	*Davies*	*Ferdinand*	*Sheringham*	*Poyet**	*Leonhardsen*
								Ref: D Elleray	Spurs were far better but had only Les Ferdinand's first Premiership away goal in two years to show. This was Defoe's first start but he learned much from watching Sheringham and Ferdinand. Injury had delayed James' debut. He pushed Poyet's header onto a post. Ferdinand pounced.											
14	A	SUNDERLAND		16	L	0-1	0-0		James	Schemmel	Minto^	Hutchison	Repka	Dailly	Sinclair	Cole*	Kitson	Defoe	Carrick	Moncur/Todorov
1/12			*47,537*	*13*	15			*Phillips 85*	*Sorensen*	*Haas*	*Gray*	*McCann*	*Williams*	*Emerson*	*McAteer^*	*Arca*	*Quinn**	*Phillips*	*Thirlwell*	*Laslandes/Butler*
								Ref: P Jones	Sunderland deserved nothing after being outplayed. Thomas Sorensen kept lively West Ham at bay until Kevin Phillips flicked his eighth goal of the season from Arca's cross. 'They were really unlucky,' admitted Peter Reid. Biggest culprit in front of goal was young Jermain Defoe.											
15	H	ASTON VILLA			D	1-1	0-1	Defoe 90	James	Schemmel	Winterburn	Hutchison	Repka	Dailly	Sinclair	Cole	Defoe	Di Canio	Carrick	
5/12			28,377		16			*Dublin 1*	*Enckelman*	*Delaney^*	*Wright*	*Mellberg*	*Staunton*	*Boateng*	*Stone*	*Hendrie*	*Dublin*	*Merson**	*Barry*	*Vassell/Samuel*
								Ref: M Dean	West Ham were heading for defeat after Dublin captalised on James's scuffed clearance in the first minute. Di Canio's penalty was saved after Defoe was felled by Mellberg, but Defoe put away Cole's late through ball. This was the seventh consecutive league draw between the sides.											
16	A	MANCHESTER U		16	W	1-0	0-0	Defoe 64	James	Schemmel	Winterburn	Hutchison	Repka	Dailly	Sinclair	Cole	Defoe*	Di Canio	Carrick	Camara
8/12			**67,582**	*9*	19				*Barthez*	*Neville G*	*Neville P*	*O'Shea*	*Keane*	*Silvestre*	*Chadwick**	*Butt^*	*Solskjaer*	*Yorke"*	*Scholes*	*Beckham/Cole/Fortune*
								Ref: P Durkin	This result ends Man U's run of one win and one draw in seven games. They win their next eight! Perhaps they were put off by James' yellow hair. The goal was a classic, an eight-man move topped by Defoe's header. It brought a second win at Old Trafford, following the FA Cup win.											
17	H	ARSENAL		14	D	1-1	1-1	Kanoute 36	James	Schemmel	Winterburn	Hutchison	Repka	Dailly	Sinclair	Cole	Kanoute*	Di Canio	Carrick	Defoe
15/12			34,523	*2*	20			*Cole 39*	*Taylor*	*Lauren*	*Cole*	*Vieira*	*Campbell*	*Keown*	*Grimaldi*	*Wiltord^*	*Henry*	*Bergkamp*	*Pires**	*Kanu/Edu*
								Ref: A Wiley	As at Old Trafford, Cole and Carrick play in the centre of a four-man midfield, and it seems to be working. Kanoute converted Schemmel's cross, but Thierry Henry quickly set up Ashley Cole for his first goal of the season. Arsenal's Grimandi and Bergkamp both hit the goal-frame.											
18	A	LEICESTER		15	D	1-1	0-1	Di Canio 74p	James	Schemmel	Winterburn	Hutchison	Repka	Dailly	Sinclair	Cole	Defoe	Di Canio	Carrick	Kitson
22/12			*20,131*	*19*	21			*Izzet 43*	*Walker*	*Marshall*	*Stewart*	*Elliott !*	*Sinclair*	*Savage*	*Impey"*	*Izzet*	*Deane**	*Scowcroft*	*Oakes^*	*Akinbiyi/Wise/Rogers*
								Ref: E Wolstenholme	A spiteful match in biting cold. A needless corner conceded by James was met by Muzzy Izzet's deflected half-volley. City might have hung on, but Matt Elliott fouled Cole from behind, sparking an ugly brawl before and after he was sent off. Di Canio's penalty was a cheeky chip.											
19	H	DERBY		11	W	4-0	1-0	Schem'l 5, Di Canio 73, Sinclair 86, [Defoe 90]	James	Schemmel	Winterburn	Hutchison	Repka	Dailly	Sinclair	Cole	Kanoute^	Di Canio*	Carrick	Moncur/Defoe
26/12			31,397	*18*	24				*Poom*	*Grenet*	*Boertien*	*Riggott^*	*Hig'inbot'm*	*Mawene*	*Ducrocq**	*Powell*	*Carbone !*	*Ravanelli*	*Zavagno*	*Kinkladze/Bolder*
								Ref: G Poll	Derby's Benito Carbone was booked twice in five minutes (diving, then fouling Repka) and was off in the 54th minute, escorted by Di Canio. Depleted opposition enabled West Ham to strike three more goals, the best of which was Sinclair's first of the season, a brilliant scissors kick.											
20	H	LIVERPOOL		11	D	1-1	1-0	Sinclair 39	James	Schemmel	Winterburn	Hutchison	Repka	Dailly	Sinclair	Cole	Kanoute	Defoe	Carrick	
29/12			35,103	*4*	25			*Owen 88*	*Dudek*	*Carragher*	*Riise*	*McAllister"*	*Henchoz*	*Hyppia*	*Murphy^*	*Smicer**	*Heskey*	*Anelka*	*Berger*	*Litmanen/Owen/Gerrard*
								Ref: R Styles	Eriksson took in this lively match, in which West Ham were largely in control. Sinclair's crisp low shot from the edge of the box looked like winning the game, but Gerrard and Owen came off the bench. The European Footballer of the Year netted his 21st goal from Heskey's lay-off.											
21	A	LEEDS		11	L	0-3	0-2		James	Schemmel	Winterburn	Hutchison	Repka	Dailly	Sinclair	Cole	Kanoute^	Defoe*	Moncur	Todorov/**Garcia**
1/1			*39,322*	*1*	25			*Viduka 4, 7, Fowler 50*	*Martyn*	*Mills*	*Harte*	*Batty*	*Ferdinand*	*Woodgate*	*Kelly*	*Smith*	*Viduka*	*Fowler*	*Bowyer**	*Wilcox*
								Ref: S Dunn	History shows this result was crucial to Leeds, for David O'Leary's side won't win any of their next seven, beginning the spiral that would lead to relegation. For the moment they go top for the first time in eight weeks, spurred by Mark Viduka's volley and header inside seven minutes.											

FA BARCLAYCARD PREMIERSHIP

Manager: Glenn Roeder

SEASON 2001-02

No	Date		Att	Pos	Pt	F-A	H-T	Scorers, Times, and Referees	SQUAD	NUMBERS	IN	USE								subs used
22	H	LEICESTER		11	W	1-0	1-0	Di Canio 36	James	Schemmel	Winterburn	Hutchison	Repka	Dailly	Sinclair	Cole	Kanoute*	Di Canio	Moncur^	Defoe/Foxe
	12/1		34,698	*20*	28				*Walker*	*Impey*	*Rogers**	*Lauren*	*Sinclair*	*Davidson*	*Savage*	*Akinbiyi^*	*Deane*	*Scowcroft*	*Wise*	*Marshall/Stevenson*
								Ref: D Gallagher	Man U have apparently been keen to sign Di Canio, but each offer from Old Trafford for the 33-year-old is rejected. Is each Hammers goal his last? He prods in Schemmel's cross and celebrates by breaking the corner flag with a kick. City never threatened until keeper Walker came up.											
23	A	CHELSEA		12	L	1-5	0-1	Defoe 88 *[Forssell 90]*	James	Schemmel	Winterburn	Hutchison	Repka	Dailly	Sinclair*	Cole	Kanoute^	Di Canio !	Carrick	Courtois/Defoe
	20/1		*40,054*	*6*	28			*Hasselbaink 45, 60, Gudj'sen 51,87,*	*Cudicini*	*Melchiot*	*Gallas*	*Petit^*	*Terry*	*Desailly*	*Stanic*	*Lampard*	*Hasselb'nk"*	*Gudjohnsen*	*Zola**	*Zenden/Morris/Forssell*
								Ref: A D'Urso	Ranieri's Chelsea are chasing the league and two cups. Two players – Terry and Morris – are in trouble after a nightclub fight. West Ham were better in the first half, but Hasselbaink took his tally to 19 and Gudjohnsen to 16. Di Canio was sent off at 0-3 for stamping on Morris' tummy.											
24	A	SOUTHAMPTON		14	L	0-2	0-1		James	Schemmel	**Labant**	Lomas	Repka	Dailly	Hutchison^	Cole	Kanoute	Di Canio	Carrick*	Moncur/Defoe
	30/1		*31,879*	*13*	28			*Davies 43, Fernandes 66*	*Jones*	*Dodd*	*Bridge*	*Oakley**	*Lundekvam*	*Williams*	*Telfer*	*Fernandes"*	*Davies^*	*Pahars*	*Svensson*	*Tessem/LeTissier/Bleidelis*
								Ref: P Dowd	Saints are climbing under Gordon Strachan, and even rise above West Ham, who started brightly. Kanoute headed over and Cole's effort was easily saved before Kevin Davies bundled in Fernandes' free-kick, possibly with the use of his arm. Fernandes then fired in another free-kick.											
25	H	BLACKBURN		11	W	2-0	1-0	Sinclair 17, Kanoute 56	James	Schemmel	Winterburn	Lomas	Repka	Dailly	Hutchison"	Cole	Kanoute^	Di Canio	Sinclair*	Moncur/Defoe/Labant
	2/2		35,307	*17*	31				*Friedel*	*Neill*	*Bjornebye**	*Tugay*	*Tay'-Martin*	*Johansson*	*Hignett*	*Flitcroft^*	*Cole A*	*Jansen*	*Duff*	*Gillespie/Mahon*
								Ref: P Jones	Ironically, West Ham have conceded the fewest home goals in the Premiership and the most away. The nearest they got to shipping their eighth home goal came when James pushed Jansen's flick onto a post. Sinclair had rounded Friedel for the first goal. Di Canio then set up Kanoute.											
26	A	BOLTON		12	L	0-1	0-1		James	Schemmel	Minto	Lomas	Foxe	Dailly	Garcia*	Cole	Kanoute	Defoe	Labant	Kitson
	9/2		*24,342*	*17*	31			*Gardner 38*	*Jaaskelain'*	*N'Gotty*	*Charlton*	*Warhurst^*	*Bergsson*	*Whitlow*	*Nolan*	*Tofting*	*Bobic**	*Ricketts"*	*Gardner*	*Hansen/South'l/Holdsw'th*
								Ref: D Pugh	Ricardo Gardner's ferocious strike even had Roeder applauding. It earned Bolton their first home win since August and lifted them out of the bottom three. West Ham pressed after half-time, creating nothing but half-chances, except when the unmarked Dailly headed a corner too high.											
27	H	MIDDLESBROUGH		11	W	1-0	0-0	Kanoute 76	James	Pearce	Winterburn	Moncur	Repka	Dailly	Hutchison"	Cole	Kanoute	Defoe	Lomas^	Labant/Garcia
	23/2		35,420	*12*	34				*Schwarzer*	*Stockdale*	*Queudrue*	*Southgate*	*Ehiogu !*	*Mustoe**	*Greening^*	*Carbone*	*Boksic*	*Whelan"*	*Ince*	*Windass/Nemeth/Murphy*
								Ref: C Foy	Paul Ince was booed 'Judas' every time he touched the ball, though his departure was 12 years ago. Ince's 66th-minute shot was the nearest Boro came. Mark Schwarzer grabbed the ball but threw it to Labant who set up Kanoute for the goal. Ehiogu's second yellow was near the end.											
28	A	ASTON VILLA		13	L	1-2	1-1	Di Canio 13p	James	Schemmel	Winterburn	Pearce	Repka	Dailly	Sinclair	Cole	Defoe	Di Canio	Garcia*	Labant
	2/3		*37,341*	*7*	34			*Angel 23, Vassell 90*	*Schmeichel*	*Delaney*	*Samuel*	*Mellberg*	*Staunton*	*Boateng*	*Hadji**	*Hitzlsperger*	*Angel*	*Vassell*	*Barry*	*Merson*
								Ref: G Barber	New England call-up Darius Vassell won the game by sweeping in a cross by J Lloyd Samuel. West Ham had gone in front from the penalty spot when Defoe was toppled by Olof Mellberg, but Angel headed in a centre from Gareth Barry. This latest defeat was harsh on the Hammers.											
29	H	EVERTON			W	1-0	0-0	Sinclair 59	James	Schemmel^	Winterburn	Pearce	Repka	Dailly	Sinclair	Cole	Kanoute*	Di Canio	Labant	Defoe/Garcia
	6/3		29,883		37				*Simonsen*	*Pistone*	*Unsworth*	*Stubbs*	*Weir*	*Carsley"*	*Alexand'n**	*Gemmill*	*Campbell^*	*Radzinski*	*Blomqvist*	*Gravesen/Ginola/Linderoth*
								Ref: B Knight	The 0-5 debacle at Goodison seems light years away. Everton have won only won of their last 13 and the trap-door looms ever nearer. Typical of their recent luck, they were beaten by a deflected goal. Cole cut inside, shot, and the ball was deflected by Sinclair's head past Simonsen.											
30	H	MANCHESTER U		10	L	3-5	2-2	Lomas 8, Kanoute 20, Defoe 78	James	Schemmel	Winterb'rn*	Lomas	Repka	Dailly	Carrick	Cole	Kanoute	Di Canio	Labant	Defoe
	16/3		35,281	*1*	37			*Bec' 17,89p,Butt 22,Sch' 55,Sol' 64*	*Barthez*	*Neville G*	*Silvestre*	*Johnsen*	*Keane*	*Blanc*	*Beckham*	*Butt*	*V Nistelr'y**	*Solskjaer^*	*Scholes*	*Fortune/Forlan*
								Ref: M Halsey	Man U were at their best, climbing back to the top (temporarily, they'll finish third). They recovered from Lomas's leaping header to equalise through Beckham's exquisite chip on the run. West Ham had previously conceded just seven goals in 14 home games, which gives some idea.											
31	H	IPSWICH		10	W	3-1	1-0	Lomas 36, Di Canio, 74, Defoe 86	James	Schemmel	Winterburn	Lomas	Repka	Dailly	Sinclair	Cole	Kanoute^	Di Canio*	Carrick	Moncur/Defoe
	30/3		33,871	*18*	40			*Bent 71*	*Sereni*	*Wilnis*	*Clapham*	*Venus*	*McGreal*	*Hreidarsson*	*Peralta**	*Holland*	*Stewart*	*Bent*	*Wright^*	*George/Miller*
								Ref: A Wiley	Ipswich won seven out of eight at the turn of the year, but are losing again. Lomas headed in Di Canio's cross, although Marcus Bent cancelled it out in a goalmouth melee. Three minutes later Di Canio beat Sereni at the second attempt, and Defoe had acres of space to score the third.											

No	Venue	Opponent	Pos	Res	FT	HT	Scorers, Times, and Referees	1	2	3	4	5	6	7	8	9	10	11	subs used
32	A	FULHAM	8	W	1-0	1-0	Kanoute 45	James	Schemmel	Labant"	Lomas	Repka	Dailly	Sinclair	Cole	Kanoute^	Di Canio*	Carrick	Moncur/Defoe/Pearce
	1/4	***19,416***	*15*	43				*Van d Sar*	*Finnan*	*Brevett*	*Melville*	*Goma*	*Davis**	*Legwinski*	*Collins"*	*Saha^*	*Hayles*	*Malbranque*	*Harley/Boa Morte/Marlet*
							Ref: M Halsey	West Ham are up to eighth, their latest victims being Jean Tigana's Fulham, who are deep in the mire with one win in ten. Kanoute headed the only goal, from Lomas's cross, on half-time. The crowd hooted Fulham's weak efforts to level. Goalkeeper Van der Sar even ventured upfield.											
33	H	CHARLTON	7	W	2-0	2-0	Di Canio 23p, Kanoute 34	James	Schemmel	Winterburn	Lomas	Repka	Dailly	Sinclair	Cole*	Kanoute	Di Canio^	Carrick	Moncur/Defoe
	6/4	32,389	*12*	46				*Kiely*	*Young*	*Fortune*	*Stuart*	*Rufus*	*Costa*	*Konchesky*	*Kinsella*	*Euell*	*Johansson*	*Parker*	
							Ref: M Riley	Roeder's team climb to seventh, with a hint of Europe, helped by Di Canio's 100th appearance for the club. He lured Rufus into a clumsy challenge, then converted the penalty himself. Paolo was also part of West Ham's superb second goal, from James to Kanoute and into the net.											
34	A	TOTTENHAM	7	D	1-1	0-0	Pearce 89	James	Schemmel	Labant*	Pearce	Repka	Dailly	Sinclair	Lomas	Kanoute	Defoe	Carrick	Winterburn
	13/4	*36,083*	*8*	47			*Sheringham 53*	*Keller*	*Davies*	*Ziege**	*Gardner*	*Thatcher*	*Perry*	*Anderton*	*Sherwood*	*Rebrov^*	*Sheringham*	*Poyet*	*Doherty/Iversen*
							Ref: N Barry	Sheringham scored his 12th goal of the season, reacting quickest when James saved from Iversen. At 36 Sheringham is playing well enough to get picked for the World Cup finals. Ian Pearce levelled at the death with a half-volley to celebrate his 100th appearance for the Hammers.											
35	H	SUNDERLAND	7	W	3-0	1-0	Sinclair 28, Lomas 52, Defoe 77	James	Schemmel*	Winterburn	Pearce	Repka	Dailly	Sinclair	Cole	Defoe^	Lomas	Carrick	Labant/Garcia
	20/4	33,319	*17*	50				*Sorensen*	*Williams*	*McCartney*	*McCann*	*Craddock*	*Bjorklund*	*Thirlwell"*	*Reyna*	*Quinn^*	*Phillips**	*Kilbane*	*Schwarz/Kyle/Butler*
							Ref: S Bennett	Cole performed well as a second-half sub against Paraguay in a World Cup friendly, and his star is rising. He was the star against Sunderland. He made two of the goals, and might have scored his first Premiership goal of the season at 0-0, but for a raised flag. A one-sided match.											
36	A	ARSENAL	7	L	0-2	0-0		James	Schemmel^	Winterburn	Pearce	Repka	Dailly	Sinclair	Cole	Kanoute*	Lomas	Carrick	Defoe/Labant
	24/4	*38,038*	*1*	50			*Ljungberg 77, Kanu 80*	*Seaman*	*Lauren*	*Cole*	*Vieira*	*Keown*	*Adams*	*Parlour*	*Edu^*	*Henry*	*Bergkamp**	*Ljungberg"*	*Grimaldi/Kanu/Dixon*
							Ref: S Dunn	Arsenal are pulling clear of Liverpool and Man U, and this was their 10th straight win in the Premiership. The turning point was Kanoute's effort which crossed the line before Ashley Cole cleared. Bergkamp then set up Ljungberg. Eriksson sat with girlfriend Nancy up in the stand.											
37	A	NEWCASTLE	8	L	1-3	1-1	Defoe 20	James	Pearce	Labant^	Lomas	Repka	Dailly	Sinclair*	Cole	Kanoute	Defoe	Carrick	Winterburn/Garcia
	27/4	*52,127*	*4*	50			*Shearer 41, Lua-Lua 53, Robert 66*	*Givan*	*Hughes*	*Bernard*	*Dabizas*	*O'Brien**	*Solano*	*Dyer^*	*Speed*	*Shearer*	*Lua-Lua"*	*Robert*	*Distin/Jenas/Cort*
							Ref: P Durkin	Top at Christmas, Newcastle will finish fourth. Bobby Robson saw his team being torn and stretched for most of the first half. Defoe, Lomas and Kanoute should have added to Defoe's opener. James headed a ball clear in the second half from inside the box, leading to Lua-Lua's goal.											
38	H	BOLTON	7	W	2-1	1-0	Lomas 45, Pearce 89	James	Pearce	Winterburn	Lomas	Repka	Dailly	Sinclair	Cole	Kanoute^	Defoe	Carrick*	Moncur/Garcia
	11/5	**35,546**	*16*	53			*Djorkaeff 67*	*Jaaskelain'*	*Barness*	*Charlton*	*Frandsen*	*Bergsson*	*Konstant's"*	*Farrelly*	*Tofting**	*Bobic*	*Ricketts^*	*Djorkaeff*	*Nolan/Holdsworth/Smith*
	Home	Away					Ref: M Dean	West Ham and Spurs are vying for seventh spot. Spurs lose at Leicester and give it to the Hammers, a fine success for manager Glenn Roeder. Lomas half-volleyed in after Defoe's shot was parried; Djorkaeff's deflected free-kick went through James' hands; Pearce nodded the winner.											
Average	31,359	34,190																	

Worthington Cup

Rd	Venue	Opponent / Date	Att	Pos	Res	F-A	H-T	Scorers, Times, and Referees	SQUAD	NUMBERS	IN	USE								subs used
2	A	READING		17	W	0-0	0-0		Hislop	Schemmel	Minto	Hutchison	Song	Dailly	Moncur*	Todorov^	Sinclair	Defoe	Carrick	Courtois/Garcia
		11/9	*21,173*	*2:7*		*aet*		Ref: W Jordan (Hammers lost 5-6 on penalties)	*Whitehead*	*Murty*	*Robinson*	*Whitbread*	*Williams^*	*Parkinson*	*Igoe*	*Harper*	*Cureton**	*Butler"*	*Smith*	*Hend'son/Viveash/Rougier*

The League Cup is now one-legged, not two. Ex-Royals keeper Shaka Hislop was beaten by Adrian Viveash's penalty in the shoot-out, to give future Hammers boss Alan Pardew a moment to savour. Hislop had earlier saved from James Harper only for Defoe to hit the outside of a post.

FA Cup

Rd	Venue	Opponent / Date	Att	Pos	Res	F-A	H-T	Scorers, Times, and Referees	SQUAD	NUMBERS	IN	USE								subs used
3	A	MACCLESFIELD		11	W	3-0	1-0	Defoe 45, 72, Cole 85	James	Schemmel	Winterburn	Hutchison*	Repka	Dailly	Sinclair	Cole	Kitson	Defoe	Moncur !	Foxe
		6/1	*5,706*	*3:20*				Ref: J Winter	*Wilson*	*Hitchen*	*Adams*	*Byrne*	*Tinson*	*Macauley*	*Tracey**	*Priest^*	*Lambert*	*Glover*	*Keen*	*McAvoy/Ridler*

John Moncur does not start many games for West Ham these days, and after being sent off for skirmishing with Chris Byrne, one can see why. The deadlock was broken on half-time when Defoe turned in Schemmel's cross. Macclesfield had former Hammer Kevin Keen in their ranks.

Rd	Venue	Opponent / Date	Att	Pos	Res	F-A	H-T	Scorers, Times, and Referees	SQUAD	NUMBERS	IN	USE								subs used
4	A	CHELSEA		12	D	1-1	0-1	Kanoute 83	James	Schemmel	Winterb'rn*	Soma^	Repka	Dailly	Hutchison"	Cole	Kanoute	Di Canio	Carrick	Labant/Defoe/Lomas
		26/1	*33,443*	*6*				*Hasselbaink 21* Ref: D Elleray	*Cudicini*	*Ferrer*	*Melchiot*	*Petit**	*Terry*	*Desailly*	*Lampard*	*Forssell^*	*Has'lbaink"*	*Zola*	*Le Saux*	*Jokanovic/Gudj'/D Bona*

West Ham conceded five at Stamford Bridge last week, so this was some improvement on a sodden surface. Chelsea have just lost 1-5 to Spurs in the Worthington Cup semi-final, and celebrate Hasselbaink's superb shot into the top corner. Kanoute dedicated his equaliser to his new son.

Rd	Venue	Opponent / Date	Att	Pos	Res	F-A	H-T	Scorers, Times, and Referees	SQUAD	NUMBERS	IN	USE								subs used
4R	H	CHELSEA		11	L	2-3	1-1	Defoe 38, 50	James	Schemmel	Winterburn	Hutchison*	Repka	Dailly	Sinclair	Cole	Kitson^	Defoe	Lomas	Labant/Todorov
		6/2	27,272	*5*				*Ha'selbaink 43, Fors'ell 65, Terry 90* Ref: G Poll	*Cudicini*	*Ferrer*	*Le Saux*	*Petit*	*Terry*	*Desailly*	*Stanic*	*Lampard*	*Hasselbaink*	*Gudj'nsen**	*DallaBona^*	*Forssell/Zola*

If West Ham won, they would meet Preston in a re-run of the 1964 final. They led twice, helped by Terry's deflection for the first and Cudicini spilling Hutchison's low centre for the second. Hutchison's errant back-header led to 2-2, and Terry headed the winner from Le Saux's corner.

		Home					Away					
	P	W	D	L	F	A	W	D	L	F	A	Pts
1 Arsenal	38	12	4	3	42	25	14	5	0	37	11	87
2 Liverpool	38	12	5	2	33	14	12	3	4	34	16	80
3 Manchester U	38	11	2	6	40	17	13	3	3	47	28	77
4 Newcastle	38	12	3	4	40	23	9	5	5	34	29	71
5 Leeds	38	9	6	4	31	21	9	6	4	22	16	66
6 Chelsea	38	11	4	4	43	21	6	9	4	23	17	64
7 WEST HAM	38	12	4	3	32	14	3	4	12	16	43	53
8 Aston Villa	38	8	7	4	22	17	4	7	8	24	30	50
9 Tottenham	38	10	4	5	32	24	4	4	11	17	29	50
10 Blackburn	38	8	6	5	33	20	4	4	11	22	31	46
11 Southampton	38	7	5	7	23	22	5	4	10	23	32	45
12 Middlesbro'	38	7	5	7	23	26	5	4	10	12	21	45
13 Fulham	38	7	7	5	21	16	3	7	9	15	28	44
14 Charlton	38	5	6	8	23	30	5	8	6	15	19	44
15 Everton	38	8	4	7	26	23	3	6	10	19	34	43
16 Bolton	38	5	7	7	20	31	4	6	9	24	31	40
17 Sunderland	38	7	7	5	18	16	3	3	13	11	35	40
18 Ipswich	38	6	4	9	20	24	3	5	11	21	40	36
19 Derby	38	5	4	10	20	26	3	2	14	13	37	30
20 Leicester	38	3	7	9	15	34	2	6	11	15	30	28
	760	165	101	114	557	444	114	101	165	444	557	1039

Odds & ends

Double wins: (1) Ipswich.
Double losses: (0).

Won from behind: (0).
Lost from in front: (4) Aston Villa (a), Manchester U (h), Newcastle (a), Chelsea FAC (h).

High spots: Finishing 7th, unimaginable after losing 1-7 at Blackburn.
Joint best home defence in Premiership (14). It would have been even better but for losing 3-5 to Man U.
Winning at Old Trafford for two seasons in a row (FA Cup and league).
Signing England's international goalkeeper, David James.
Emergence of midfield of real class – Cole, Carrick, Sinclair.

Low spots: Losing to Reading on penalties in Worthington Cup.
Bad away record and dreadful away defence. Six times West Ham conceded three or more goals on their travels.
As West Ham won and lost the same number of games (15), but let in 9 more goals than they scored, finishing 7th flattered them.

Hammer of the Year: Sebastian Schemmel.
Ever-presents: (1) Christian Dailly.
Hat-tricks: (0).
Leading scorer: (14) Jermain Defoe.

	Appearances						Goals			
	Lge	*Sub*	LC	*Sub*	FAC	*Sub*	**Lge**	LC	FAC	**Tot**
Byrne, Shaun		*1*								
Camara, Titi		*1*								
Carrick, Michael	**30**		1		1		**2**			**2**
Cole, Joe	**29**	*1*			3				1	**1**
Courtois, Laurent	**5**	*2*		*1*						
Dailly, Christian	**38**		1		3					
Defoe, Jermain	**14**	*21*	1		2	*1*	**10**		4	**14**
Di Canio, Paolo	**26**				1		**9**			**9**
Foxe, Hayden	**4**	*2*				*1*				
Garcia, Richard	**2**	*6*		*1*						
Hislop, Shaka	**12**		1							
Hutchison, Don	**24**		1		3		**1**			**1**
James, David	**26**				3					
Kanoute, Frederic	**27**				1		**11**		1	**12**
Kitson, Paul	**3**	*4*			2		**3**			**3**
Labant, Vladimir	**7**	*5*				*2*				
Lomas, Steve	**14**	*1*			1	*1*	**4**			**4**
McGann,Grant		*3*								
Minto, Scott	**5**		1							
Moncur, John	**7**	*12*	1		1					
Pearce, Ian	**8**	*1*					**2**			**2**
Repka, Tomas	**31**				3					
Schemmel, Sebastian	**35**		1		3		**1**			**1**
Sinclair, Trevor	**34**		1		2		**5**			**5**
Soma, Ragnvald	**1**	*2*			1					
Song, Rigobert	**5**		1							
Todorov, Svetoslav	**2**	*4*	1			*1*				
Winterburn, Nigel	**29**	*2*			3					
28 players used	**418**	***68***	**11**	***2***	**33**	***6***	**48**		**6**	**54**

No	Date		Att	Pos	Pt	F-A	H-T	Scorers, Times, and Referees	SQUAD	NUMBERS	IN	USE								subs used
1	A	NEWCASTLE			L	0-4	0-0		James	Pearce	Winterburn	Schemmel*	Repka	Dailly	Sinclair	**Cisse**^	Defoe	Cole	Carrick	Labant/Moncur
	19/8		*51,072*		0			*Lua-Lua 61, 72, Shearer 76, Solano 86*	*Given*	*Hughes*	*Barnard*	*Dabizas*	*Bramble*	*Solano**	*Dyer*	*Jenas*	*Shearer*	*Lua-Lua*^	*Viana"*	*McClen/Ameobi/Elliott*
								Ref: P Durkin	Sir Bobby Robson was indebted to Lomana Lua-Lua from Congo, who supported West Ham as a lad, but who sparks the rout by volleying in Jenas's flick-on, then sends a bullet header that James pushed onto the bar and in. Roeder had spent six years at St James', and this result hurts.											
2	H	ARSENAL		16	D	2-2	1-0	Cole 44, Kanoute 53	James	Schemmel	Winterb'rn*	Cisse	Repka	Dailly	Sinclair	Cole^	Kanoute	Defoe	Carrick	**Breen**/Moncur
	24/8		35,048	*4*	1			*Henry 65, Wiltord 88*	*Seaman*	*Lauren**	*Cole*	*Vieira*	*Campbell*	*Keown*	*Parlour*^	*Edu*	*Henry*	*Bergkamp"*	*Wiltord*	*Toure/Pennant/Kanu*
								Ref: N Barry	A match to please the gods but even now fans blame Kanoute's dire 75th-min penalty at 2-1 as the cause of relegation. It would have clinched a first win – over the Double winners, unbeaten in 23 games. Instead, Wiltord poached an equaliser, and it would be a long wait for a first win.											
3	H	CHARLTON		20	L	0-2	0-2		James	Schemmel	Winterb'rn*	Cisse^	Repka	Dailly	Sinclair	Cole	Kanoute	Defoe	Carrick	Camara/Lomas
	31/8		32,424	*6*	1			*Jensen 4, Fortune 44*	*Kiely*	*Young*	*Powell*	*B't-Williams*	*Rufus*	*Fortune*	*Kishishev*	*Jensen*	*Euell*	*Svensson*^	*Robinson**	*Johansson/Bartlett*
								Ref: J Winter	Charlton played in black, and Cole was in the mood to beat four men, lose to the fifth, and get booked for petulance. West Ham's defence stood and stared as Jensen scored, and weren't much more convincing when Jon Fortune doubled it. A streaker came on, trousers at his ankles.											
4	H	WEST BROM		20	L	0-1	0-1		James	Schemmel	Winterb'rn*	Cisse	Repka	Breen	Sinclair	Cole	Kanoute	Di Canio^	Carrick"	Dailly/Defoe/Lomas
	11/9		34,927	*14*	1			*Roberts 28*	*Hoult*	*Balis*	*Clement*	*Gregan*	*Moore*	*Gilchrist*	*Koumas**	*Wallwork*	*Hughes*^	*Roberts"*	*Johnson*	*Sigurds'n/Dobie/Chambers*
								Ref: A D'Urso	Having lost their first three, Gary Megson's Albion will win their next three. For West Ham this is the third season in a row in which they have been adrift in September. New-boy Breen was constantly tormented by Jason Roberts who eased past the Irishman to convert Wallwork's pass.											
5	A	TOTTENHAM		20	L	2-3	0-0	Kanoute 66, Sinclair 77	James	Pearce !	Lomas	Breen	Repka*	Dailly	Sinclair	Cole	Kanoute^	Di Canio"	Cisse	Winterburn/Defoe/Carrick
	15/9		*36,005*	*2*	1			*Davies 62, Sher'm 71p, Gardner 89*	*Keller*	*Taricco*^	*Ziege*	*Gardner*	*Perry"*	*Bunjevcevic*	*Davies*	*Redknapp*	*Keane*	*Sheringham*	*Etheringt'**	*Iversen/Thatcher/Doherty*
								Ref: U Rennie	A sad first half sparked five goals in the second. Twice West Ham levelled, but had no time to do so a third time after Gardner finished a long run by firing in off Breen. West Ham's goals came from Kanoute, converting Dailly's nod across goal, and Sinclair from Di Canio's free-kick.											
6	H	MANCHESTER C		20	D	0-0	0-0		James	Schemmel	Minto	Lomas	Repka	Breen	Sinclair	Cole*	Kanoute	Di Canio^	Cisse"	Pearce/Defoe/Carrick
	21/9		**35,050**	*14*	2				*Schmeichel*	*W't-Phillips*	*Jensen*	*Jihai*	*Howey*	*Distin*	*Benarbia**	*Berkovic*	*Anelka*	*Horlock*	*Foe*	*Huckerby*
								Ref: G Barber	Two points from six games makes this West Ham's worst ever start. They carved out two early chances, crosses from Schemmel and Di Canio, but both fell to Cole and fizzled out. The Hammers' first clean sheet was threatened only once, when James saved with his feet from Anelka.											
7	A	CHELSEA		20	W	3-2	1-1	Defoe 40, Di Canio 48, 84	James	Schemmel	Minto	Lomas	Repka	Breen	Sinclair	Cole	Kanoute^	Di Canio*	Carrick	Cisse/Defoe
	28/9		*38,929*	*5*	5			*Hasselbaink 21p, Zola 74*	*Cudicini*	*Melchiot*	*Stanic*	*Morris*	*Gallas*	*Huth*	*Gronkjaer*	*Lampard*	*Hasselbaink*	*Gudjohnsen*	*Zenden**	*Zola*
								Ref: M Dean	Hammers' first win was also Ranieri's Chelsea's first loss. Defoe's close-in effort cancelled out Hasselbaink's penalty before Di Canio juggled the ball on his knee and volleyed home from 25 yards. Zola's neat free-kick restored parity but Di Canio exploited Melchiot and Gallas's error.											
8	H	BIRMINGHAM		20	L	1-2	1-2	Cole 17	James	Schemmel*	Minto	Lomas	Repka	Breen	Sinclair	Cole^	Defoe	Di Canio	Carrick	Pearce/Camara
	5/10		35,010	*12*	5			*John 4, 43*	*Vaesen*	*Kenna*	*Johnson*	*Cunningh'm*	*Purse*	*Cisse*	*Devlin*	*Savage*	*Morrison*	*John**	*Lazaridis*^	*Horsfield/Powell*
								Ref: P Dowd	Steve Bruce's promoted Brum snatch their first away win through Trinidadian Stern John. West Ham looked classy at times going forward but fragile at all times going backwards. After half-time City's midfield protected their defence in a way that under-fire Roeder could only envy.											
9	A	SUNDERLAND		17	W	1-0	1-0	Sinclair 23	James	Dailly	Minto	Lomas	Repka	Pearce*	Sinclair^	Cole	Defoe	Di Canio	Carrick	Breen/Cisse
	19/10		*44,352*	*19*	8				*Macho*	*Wright*	*Gray*	*McCann*	*Babb*	*Craddock*	*Piper"*	*Reyna*^	*Stewart**	*Phillips*	*Kilbane*	*Quinn/Thirlwell/Bellion*
								Ref: G Barber	Howard Wilkinson's side look even worse than West Ham. Mind you, Sinclair's goal deserved to win any game. Di Canio's 50-yard crossfield pass, over the head of Gray, received the super finish it deserved. Wilkinson's appointment was unpopular on Wearside, and he won't last long.											
10	A	FULHAM		14	W	1-0	1-0	Di Canio 90p	James	Dailly	Minto	Pearce	Repka	Cisse	Sinclair	Cole	Defoe	Di Canio	Carrick	
	23/10		***15,858***	*9*	11				*Van d Sar*	*Finnan*	*Wome*	*Melville*	*Knight !*	*Malbranque*	*Legwinksi*	*Inamoto**	*Marlet*	*Hayles*	*BoaMorte*^	*Djetou/Stolcers*
								Ref: R Styles	Crisis, what crisis? West Ham soar to 14th after spurning a galaxy of chances before Zat Knight lunged at Defoe. The defender was sent off. Di Canio netted from the spot to inflict on Jean Tigana's Fulham their first home defeat in 13, since West Ham last beat them the previous Easter.											

11	H	EVERTON		15	L	0-1	0-0		James	Dailly	Minto^	Lomas*	Repka	Pearce	Sinclair	Cole	Defoe	Di Canio	Carrick	Cisse/Camara
		27/10	34,117	*8*	11			*Carsley 70*	*Wright*	*Hibbert*	*Unsworth*	*Stubbs*	*Yobo*	*Linderoth*	*Carsley*	*Li Tie^*	*Campbell*	*Radzinski**	*Pembridge*	*Rooney/Pistone*
								Ref: A Wiley	Three straight away wins had lifted West Ham to lower mid-table, a launch-pad for better things. Instead, all talk is of David Moyes' prodigy Wayne Rooney, who blasted Arsenal to defeat the previous week. Rooney's mere presence seemed to distract everyone as Carsley headed in.											
12	A	LIVERPOOL		17	L	0-2	0-1		James	Dailly	Minto	Lomas	Repka	Pearce	Cisse	Cole	Defoe*	Sinclair	Carrick	Camara
		2/11	*44,048*	*1*	11			*Owen 28, 55*	*Dudek*	*Carragher*	*Riise*	*Hamann*	*Traore*	*Hyypia*	*Murphy*	*Diao*	*Smicer**	*Owen*	*Heskey*	*Gerrard*
								Ref: E Wolstenholme	Michael Owen is red hot, ten goals from seven games now. His first against West Ham saw him dance round Lomas, Dailly and Repka before scoring. For his second, he took the ball round James from Smicer's pass, and rolled it almost too softly into goal on the sodden Anfield pitch.											
13	H	LEEDS		18	L	3-4	1-4	Di Canio 21, 50p, Sinclair 74	James	Dailly	Winterburn	Lomas^	Repka*	Pearce	Sinclair	Cole	Defoe	Di Canio	Carrick	Schemmel/Cisse
		10/11	33,297	*10*	11			*Barmby 11, Kewell 28, 41, Viduka 45*	*Robinson*	*Kelly*	*Harte*	*Bakke*	*Radebe*	*Lucic*	*Barmby*	*Bowyer*	*Viduka^*	*Kewell**	*Wilcox"*	*McPhail/Bridges/Milner*
								Ref: S Dunn	Dire defending hands Terry Venables' Leeds four first-half goals, at which point Roeder drags off Repka before he is sent off. Gary Kelly then fouled Di Canio in the box – 2-4. Sinclair, masked because of a fractured cheekbone, headed in Schemmel's corner – 3-4. Pearce headed wide.											
14	H	MANCHESTER U		19	D	1-1	0-1	Defoe 86	James	Schemmel	Winterburn	Pearce	Dailly	Cisse	Sinclair	Cole	Defoe	Di Canio	Carrick	
		17/11	35,049	*5*	12			*Van Nistelrooy 38*	*Barthez*	*O'Shea*	*Silvestre*	*Brown*	*Fortune*	*Blanc*	*Scholes*	*Veron*	*V Nistelr'y*	*Solskjaer*	*Giggs*	
								Ref: M Halsey	For once fortune smiles on West Ham. Defoe was offside as he rolled the ball past Fabien Barthez. Defoe, who earlier hit the bar, looked across for a raised flag, but there wasn't one. Earlier, Van Nistelrooy, trotting back from offside, raced forward to flick Solskjaer's cross over James.											
15	A	ASTON VILLA		20	L	1-4	0-1	Di Canio 70 *[Vassell 80]*	James	Schemmel	Winterburn	Pearce	Dailly	Cisse	Sinclair	Cole	Defoe	Di Canio	Carrick	
		23/11	*33,279*	*11*	12			*Hendrie 29, Leonhard' 59, Dublin 72,*	*Enckelman*	*Samuel*	*Barry*	*Mellberg*	*Staunton*	*Taylor*	*Leonh'dsen*	*Hitzlsperger*	*Dublin"*	*Vassell^*	*Hendrie**	*Kinsella/Allback/Angel*
								Ref: C Foy	West Ham are back on the bottom again. This was a pleasant game for neutrals, which could have gone either way before Dion Dublin headed his 100th Premiership goal from Hendrie's free-kick to make it 3-1. While James was dropping balls, his ex-understudy, Enckelman, did well.											
16	H	SOUTHAMPTON		20	L	0-1	0-0		James	Schemmel	Winterburn	Cole	Repka	Dailly	Sinclair	Pearce	Defoe	Di Canio*	Carrick	Moncur
		2/12	**28,344**	*9*	12			*Beattie 90*	*Niemi*	*Dodd*	*Bridge*	*Marsden*	*Lundekvam*	*Svensson*	*Fernandes^*	*Delap*	*Beattie*	*Delgado**	*Oakley"*	*Svensson/Telfer/Ormerod*
								Ref: M Riley	For an hour West Ham had Southampton – arriving late because of traffic – on the rack. Pearce was forced into being an emergency striker, but he was no more culpable than those around him. Though West Ham ran out of steam they didn't deserve Beattie putting away Ormerod's cross.											
17	A	MIDDLESBROUGH		20	D	2-2	0-0	Cole 46, Pearce 76	James	Schemmel	Winterburn	Cole	Repka	Dailly	Sinclair	Cisse*	Defoe	Pearce^	Carrick	Moncur/Breen
		7/12	*28,283*	*9*	13			*Nemeth 58, Ehiogu 88*	*Schwarzer*	*Parnaby*	*Queuedrue*	*Southgate*	*Ehiogu*	*Vidmar^*	*Geremi*	*Boateng*	*Boksic**	*Mac'arone"*	*Greening*	*Whelan/Nemeth/Wilkshire*
								Ref: G Poll	A freezing wind announces West Ham's new captain – Joe Cole. Boro remain unbeaten at the Riverside, despite trailing twice, first to Cole, then to an effort from stand-in striker Pearce. Ugo Ehiogu's late header means West Ham stay last. Had they won, they would have been 17th.											
18	A	MANCHESTER U		20	L	0-3	0-2		James	Schemmel	Minto^	Lomas*	Repka	Dailly	Sinclair	Cole	Defoe	Pearce	Carrick	Moncur/Breen
		14/12	***67,555***	*2*	13			*Solskj'r 15, Veron 17, Schem' 61(og)*	*Barthez*	*Neville G*	*O'Shea^*	*Brown*	*Neville P*	*Silvestre*	*Solskjaer**	*Veron*	*V Nistelr'y*	*Scholes"*	*Giggs*	*Beckham/Blanc/Forlan*
								Ref: R Styles	Solskjaer headed in Gary Neville's cross, and two minutes later, after Repka was booked for flattening Ruud van Nistelrooy, Veron directed a free-kick into the far corner. Schemmel turned in Gary Neville's cross. No excuses, but Defoe thought he should have had a penalty at 0-0.											
19	H	BOLTON		20	D	1-1	1-0	Pearce 17	James	Schemmel	Winterburn	Lomas	Repka	Dailly	Sinclair	Cole	Defoe	Pearce*	Carrick	Hutchison
		21/12	34,892	*19*	14			*Ricketts 65*	*Jaaskelain'*	*Barness*	*Charlton*	*Frandsen*	*Berggson*	*N'Gotty^*	*Okocha*	*Nolan*	*Pedersen*	*Djorkaeff**	*Gardner*	*Ricketts/Whitlow*
								Ref: S Bennett	A six-pointer between the bottom two. Makeshift forward Pearce scored with his right foot, and things looked bright when Per Frandsen hit a post. Sam Allardyce's team were level when Repka played Ricketts onside. West Ham could still have won it, only for Sinclair to head wide.											
20	H	FULHAM		20	D	1-1	0-0	Sinclair 65p	James	Schemmel	Winterburn	Lomas^	Repka !	Dailly	Sinclair	Cole	Kanoute*	Defoe	Carrick	Pearce/Hutchison
		26/12	35,025	*15*	15			*Sava 49*	*Taylor*	*Finnan*	*Brevett*	*Melville*	*Goma*	*Davis*	*Malbr'que^*	*Legwinski**	*Marlet*	*Sava"*	*Wome*	*Djetou/Goldb'k/Hammond*
								Ref: D Gallagher	Previously no Premiership club bottom at Christmas has survived. West Ham wanted six points from struggling Bolton and Fulham, and got only two. Sava netted from Finnan's cross, but Sinclair levelled when Legwinski handled. Repka was red-carded in the last minute for dissent.											
21	A	BLACKBURN		20	D	2-2	1-1	Taylor-Martin 24 (og), Defoe 86	James	Schemmel	Winterb'rn"	Lomas*	Breen	Dailly	Sinclair	Cisse^	Pearce	Cole	Carrick	Defoe/Moncur/Minto
		28/12	*24,998*	*11*	16			*Duff 4, Cole 78*	*Friedel*	*Curtis^*	*Johansson*	*Short"*	*Tay'-Martin*	*Tugay*	*Thompson*	*Flitcroft*	*Cole*	*Ostenstad*	*Duff**	*Gillespie/Yorke/Todd*
								Ref: A Wiley	It was 1-7 last season, so this was a welcome point. Graeme Souness admitted his team were bad but they were twice in front, first when James fluffed Duff's shot, then when diving early at the feet of Andy Cole. West Ham replied with Lomas' deflected cross and Defoe's late toe-poke.											

No	Date		Att	Pos	Pt	F-A	H-T	Scorers, Times, and Referees	SQUAD NUMBERS IN USE											subs used
22	H	NEWCASTLE		20	D	2-2	2-1	Cole 14, Defoe 45	James	Lomas	Winterb'rn^	Cisse"	Breen	Dailly	**Bowyer**	Cole	Defoe	Sinclair*	Carrick	Pearce/Minto/Hutchison
	11/1		35,048	*4*	17			*Bellamy 9, Jenas 81*	*Given*	*Griffin*	*Bernard*	*Acuna**	*Caldwell*	*Hughes*	*Dyer*	*Jenas*	*Ameobi^*	*Bellamy*	*Robert*	*Lua-Lua/Cort*
								Ref: J Winter	Bad-boy Lee Bowyer has a quiet debut, but West Ham deserved more than a draw after recovering from Craig Bellamy evading Lomas to put Bobby Robson's team ahead. Cole beat Given from close range, Defoe netted with an angled drive, but Jenas replied with a 25-yard rocket.											
23	A	ARSENAL		20	L	1-3	1-1	Defoe 40	James	Lomas !	Winterb'rn^	Pearce	Breen	Dailly	Sinclair	Cisse*	Defoe	Cole	Bowyer	Moncur/Minto
	19/1		*38,053*	*1*	17			*Henry 14p, 71, 86*	*Seaman*	*Lauren*	*V Bronckh't*	*Silva*	*Campbell*	*Keown*	*Wiltord"*	*Edu**	*Henry*	*Bergkamp^*	*Pires*	*Parlour/Luzhny/Jeffers*
								Ref: M Dean	Arsenal are five points clear, yet will be overhauled by Man U. They showed two sides of their character, magical skills mixed with Bergkamp elbowing Bowyer in the face as he crossed for the second goal, and Pires diving theatrically to win an earlier penalty and get Lomas sent off.											
24	A	CHARLTON		20	L	2-4	1-2	Rufus 19 (og), Fish 62 (og)	James	Lomas	Minto*	Cisse^	Breen	Dailly	Sinclair	Bowyer	Defoe	**Ferdinand**	Carrick	Winterburn/**Johnson**
	22/1		*26,340*	*11*	17			*Jensen 42, Parker 45, 52, Kish'v 90*	*Kiely*	*Kishishev*	*Powell*	*Fortune*	*Rufus*	*Fish*	*Jensen^*	*Euell*	*Lisbie"*	*Bartlett**	*Parker*	*Johans'n/Svens'n/Konch'*
								Ref: E Wolstenholme	It's 14 without a win now, and West Ham were not saved by the gift of two own-goals. This is the sixth time they have failed to win after being ahead. The game was rescheduled from Christmas, when the pitch was waterlogged. Most damage was done by Scott Parker's two neat goals.											
25	H	BLACKBURN		18	W	2-1	0-1	Di Canio 58p, Defoe 89	James	Johnson	Winterb'rn*	Pearce	Repka	Lomas	Bowyer	Cole	Ferdinand"	Di Canio^	Carrick	Defoe/Sinclair/Kanoute
	29/1		34,743	*11*	20			*Yorke 38*	*Friedel*	*Neill*	*McEveley"*	*Todd*	*Tay-Martin*	*Tugay*	*Gillespie**	*Flitcroft*	*Cole*	*Yorke^*	*Thompson*	*Johans'n/Ost'stad/Jansen*
								Ref: A Wiley	At the 13th attempt, West Ham win at home. Things looked bleak when Graeme Souness's men went in front – Dwight Yorke scoring at the second attempt. Di Canio netted from the spot after luring Andy Todd into the foul. With six minutes left, on came Defoe to fire a late winner.											
26	H	LIVERPOOL		19	L	0-3	0-2		James	Johnson	Winterb'rn"	Cole	Repka	Dailly	Sinclair*	Bowyer	Ferdinand^	Di Canio	Carrick	Defoe/Kanoute/**Brevett**
	2/2		35,033	*6*	20			*Baros 7, Gerrard 9, Heskey 67*	*Dudek*	*Carragher*	*Riise*	*Gerrard*	*Henchoz*	*Hyypia*	*Murphy**	*Diouf*	*Heskey*	*Baros^*	*Smicer"*	*Hamann/Owen/Cheyrou*
								Ref: M Messias	'Those were cheap goals,' complained Roeder after the latest James-Repka horror show. There was no escape after being 0-2 down after nine minutes, James being rooted at Riise's corner and Repka static as Baros headed the first. West Ham managed just one shot on target all game.											
27	A	LEEDS		19	L	0-1	0-1		James	Johnson	Brevett*	Lomas	Repka	Pearce	Bowyer	Cole	Kanoute !	Di Canio^	Carrick"	Sinclair/Defoe/Hutchison
	8/2		*40,126*	*13*	20			*Johnson 20*	*Robinson*	*Mills*	*Bravo*	*Johnson*	*Duberry*	*Matteo^*	*Kelly*	*Okon*	*Milner*	*Bakke**	*Wilcox*	*McMaster/Kilgallon*
								Ref: D Gallagher	West Ham have two new full-backs, Johnson and Brevett, but the real weakness is in the centre. Luck was against them when Cole hit a post. They weren't helped by Kanoute's 70-min dismissal for retaliation. Seth Johnson's first Leeds goal earned their first Premiership win in five.											
28	A	WEST BROM		18	W	2-1	1-0	Sinclair 45, 67	James	Johnson	Brevett	Lomas	Repka	Pearce	Sinclair	Bowyer^	Ferdinand"	Di Canio*	Carrick	Defoe/Breen/Hutchison
	23/2		*27,042*	*19*	23			*Dichio 50*	*Hoult*	*Chambers*	*Udeze*	*Gregan*	*Moore*	*Gilchrist*	*Wallwork**	*McInnes^*	*Dichio*	*Hughes*	*Koumas*	*Sigurdsson/Dobie*
								Ref: M Dean	Ten games left and Bolton (17th) are three points ahead. Hammers survived Repka squaring up to James and Di Canio finger-jabbing at Roeder after being subbed to climb above Gary Megson's Albion. Sinclair slid in the first and headed the second. Dichio headed through James' hands.											
29	H	TOTTENHAM		18	W	2-0	1-0	Ferdinand 31, Carrick 47	James	Johnson	Brevett	Cole	Repka	Pearce	Sinclair	Bowyer	Ferdinand*	Defoe	Carrick	Hutchison
	1/3		35,049	*9*	26				*Keller*	*Carr*	*Taricco*	*King*	*Richards*	*Bunjevce'**	*Davies*	*Etheringt'^*	*Doherty"*	*Sheringham*	*Anderton*	*Thatcher/Acimovic/Freund*
								Ref: N Barry	Glenn Hoddle's Spurs were humbled, not least in midfield where Cole and Carrick reigned. Ex-Spur Les Ferdinand grabbed his first West Ham goal by scoring a softie from Defoe's pass. When Carrick's cross was cleared back to him, he netted his first Premiership goal in 49 games.											
30	A	EVERTON		18	D	0-0	0-0		James	Johnson	Brevett	Lomas	Repka	Pearce	Sinclair	Cole*	Ferdinand^	Defoe	Carrick	Cisse/Dailly
	15/3		*40,158*	*5*	27				*Wright*	*Hibbert*	*Unsworth*	*Stubbs*	*Weir*	*Gravesen*	*Watson*	*Gemmill**	*McBride^*	*Radzinski*	*Naysmith"*	*Li Tie/Rooney/Campbell*
								Ref: M Halsey	Everton have only lost once at home, but David Moyes celebrates his first 12 months at Goodison with a stifling draw. Even West Ham's back line looked stubborn. West Ham's best opportunity came when Alan Stubbs nearly diverted Glen Johnson's cross past Wright into his own net.											
31	H	SUNDERLAND		17	W	2-0	1-0	Defoe 24, Kanoute 65	James	Johnson	Brevett	Lomas"	Repka	Pearce	Sinclair	Cole*	Ferdinand^	Defoe	Carrick	Cisse/Kanoute/Hutchison
	22/3		35,033	*20*	30				*Sorensen*	*Williams*	*McCartn'y"*	*Butler**	*El Khark'ri*	*Bjorklund*	*Kilbane*	*Thornton*	*Flo^*	*Phillips*	*Gray*	*Stewart/Kyle/Proctor*
								Ref: R Styles	West Ham are out of the bottom three, but only because Bolton play (and win) on Monday. For Sunderland's new boss, Mick McCarthy, this was his team's eighth straight loss. Once West Ham went two up, Kanoute capitalising on Carrick's through ball, Cole started to show-boat.											

No	Date	Opponent	Att	Pos	Res	F-A	H-T	Scorers, Times, and Referees	1	2	3	4	5	6	7	8	9	10	11	subs used
32	A	SOUTHAMPTON		18	D	1-1	0-1	Defoe 83	James	Johnson	Brevett	Lomas*	Repka	Pearce	Bowyer	Cole	Ferdinand^	Defoe	Sinclair	Cisse/Kanoute
	5/4		*31,941*	*11*	31			*Beattie 44*	*Niemi*	*Telfer*	*Bridge*	*Marsden*	*Lundekvam*	*Svensson*	*Fernandes**	*Oakley*	*Beattie*	*Ormerod^*	*Prutton*	*Svensson/Davies*
								Ref: M Messias	Only Man U and Liverpool have won at St Mary's, but what should have been a good result was offset by Bolton's earlier win. West Ham are four points below the cut-off line. It might have been worse, but for Defoe hooking a late equaliser. Saints prepare for their FA Cup semi-final.											
33	H	ASTON VILLA		18	D	2-2	1-1	Sinclair 15, Kanoute 65	James	Johnson	Brevett	Lomas	Repka	Pearce	Bowyer^	Cole	Kanoute*	Defoe	Sinclair	Hutchison/Ferdinand
	12/4		35,029	*14*	32			*Vassell 36p, Leonhardsen 53*	*Enckelman*	*Edwards*	*Samuel*	*Mellberg*	*Staunton*	*Barry*	*Hadji**	*Hitzlsperger*	*Allback^*	*Vassell*	*Hendrie"*	*Leonh'n/Taylor/Gudjons'n*
								Ref: M Dean	With hindsight, this was the result which sent the Hammers down. Villa arrive with two points from six games but level Sinclair's opener when Repka shoved Allback in the back. Leonhardsen headed in Barry's cross. Kanoute side-stepped Staunton but West Ham wasted chances to win.											
34	A	BOLTON		18	L	0-1	0-1		James	Johnson	Brevett	Lomas	Repka	Pearce !	Cisse*	Cole	Kanoute	Defoe	Sinclair	Ferdinand
	19/4		*27,160*	*17*	32			*Okocha 38*	*Jaaskelain'*	*N'Gotty*	*Charlton*	*Campo*	*Berggson*	*Laville*	*Mendy*	*Frandsen*	*Pedersen*	*Djorkaeff**	*Okocha^*	*Nolan/Andre*
								Ref: U Rennie	Another six-pointer, which leaves Hammers six points behind and seemingly doomed. It was settled by Jay-Jay Okocha's exquisite run from his own half and chip over James, which was better than anything West Ham tried. Pearce was sent off for fouling Andre. Fisticuffs at the end.											
35	H	MIDDLESBROUGH		18	W	1-0	0-0	Sinclair 77	James	Johnson	Brevett	Lomas	Repka	Pearce	Sinclair	Cole	Ferdinand	Defoe	Cisse	
	21/4		35,019	*11*	35				*Schwarzer*	*Cooper*	*Queuedrue**	*Southgate*	*Ehiogu*	*Wilkshire*	*Boateng*	*Juninho^*	*Christie"*	*Maccarone*	*Greening*	*Stockdale/Job/Ricketts*
								Ref: A Wiley	Roeder was booed beforehand and hospitalised afterwards with what turned out to be a stroke. The win was earned when Glen Johnson crossed for Sinclair to shoot past Schwarzer. At half-time 1980s' hero van der Elst raised a laugh by wishing that West Ham 'stay in the first division'.											
36	A	MANCHESTER C		18	W	1-0	0-0	Kanoute 81	James	Johnson	Brevett	Lomas	Repka	Pearce*	Sinclair	Cisse^	Ferdinand"	Defoe	Cole	Dailly/Kanoute/Hutchison
	27/4		*34,815*	*11*	38				*Schmeichel*	*Dunne*	*Jensen**	*Sommeil*	*Distin*	*Barton*	*Benarbia^*	*Foe*	*Anelka*	*Fowler"*	*W't-Phillips*	*Goater/Belmadi/Macken*
								Ref: R Styles	Trevor Brooking oversees West Ham's last three games. This precious win was partially undone by Bolton recovering from 0-2 to draw with Arsenal. City were better for long stretches. At half-time Brooking sent on Kanoute, who netted after Schmeichel pushed the ball onto a post.											
37	H	CHELSEA		18	W	1-0	0-0	Di Cano 71	James	Johnson	Brevett	Lomas	Repka	Dailly	Sinclair	Defoe	Ferdinand*	Kanoute	Cole	Di Canio
	3/5		35,042	*4*	41				*Cudicini*	*Melchiot*	*Babayaro*	*Petit*	*Gallas*	*Desailly*	*Morris^*	*Lampard*	*Gudj'nsen**	*Zola"*	*Le Saux*	*Hasselbaink/Zenden/Cole*
								Ref: A D'Urso	Di Canio comes off the bench to score his 50th West Ham goal and perhaps the most vital. Chelsea failed to clear Sinclair's centre for Paolo to belt the ball in. If only results elsewhere were kind. Bolton drew at Southampton to stay above West Ham. On Sunday, Leeds won at Arsenal.											
38	A	BIRMINGHAM		18	D	2-2	0-0	Ferdinand 66, Di Canio 89	James	Johnson	Brevett*	Lomas	Repka	Dailly	Sinclair	Defoe	Ferdinand	Kanoute	Cole^	Di Canio/Hutchison
	11/5		29,505	*13*	42			*Horsfield 80, John 88*	*Bennett*	*Kenna"*	*Clapham*	*Purse*	*Upson*	*Clemence*	*Johnson*	*Savage*	*Horsfield*	*Dugarry**	*Lazaridis^*	*John/Hughes/Devlin*
		Home	Away					Ref: G Poll	Bolton's two early goals against Middlesbrough effectively settles things. West Ham's 22 points from the last 11 games was matched by 22 from 11 by Birmingham, and 19 from 11 by Bolton. The only hope came when Boro pulled one back and Ferdinand headed West Ham ahead.											
Average		34,404	35,744																	

Worthington Cup			Att			F-A	H-T	Scorers, Times, and Referees	SQUAD	NUMBERS	IN	USE								subs used
2	A	CHESTERFIELD		20	D	1-1	1-0	Defoe 13	James	Schemmel	Minto	Lomas	Repka	Breen	Sinclair	Cole	Defoe	Di Canio	Carrick	
	1/10		*7,102*	*2:5*				*Brandon 52*	*Muggleton*	*Davies*	*Rushbury**	*Dawson*	*Blath'rwick*	*Howson*	*Booty^*	*Hudson*	*Allott*	*Reeves"*	*Ebdon*	*Edwards/Brandon/Burt*
								Ref: A Hall (Hammers won 5-4 on penalties)	Roeder sent out his strongest team, including seven internationals. When Defoe put away Schemmel's long pass, it was the first goal put past Chesterfield in 589 mins. Free-transfer Chris Brandon was sent away by Mark Allott to level. In the shoot-out, Allott was the only one to miss.											
3	H	OLDHAM		17	L	0-1	0-1		James	Dailly	Minto*	Lomas	Pearce	Breen^	Camara	Cole	Defoe	Cisse"	Carrick	Schem'l/Wint'burn/Garcia
	6/11		21,919	*2:2*				*Corazzin 42*	*Pogliacomi*	*Low*	*Eyres*	*Beharall*	*Hall*	*Hill*	*Murray*	*Armstrong*	*Andrews**	*Corazzin*	*Eyre*	*Killen*
								Ref: U Rennie	Ex-Hammer Iain Dowie's Oldham are second in Division 2, and win the tie through Carlo Corazzin's free header from David Eyres' corner. West Ham were without Sinclair, Di Canio and Kanoute, which weakened their attack. Defoe wasted chances and was then booked for diving.											

FA Cup																				
3	H	NOTT'M FOREST		20	W	3-2	1-1	Defoe 26, 83, Cole 61	James	Schemmel	Winterb'rn*	Cisse	Breen	Dailly	Sinclair	Cole	Defoe	Pearce^	Carrick	Repka/Camara
	4/1		29,612	*1:4*				*Harewood 17, Reid 50*	*Ward*	*Louis-Jean*	*Brennan*	*Thompson*	*Dawson*	*Doig*	*Prutton*	*Scimea*	*Johnson*	*Harewood*	*Reid*	
								Ref: P Durkin	Hammers' first win of the season comes against Paul Hart's Forest's promotion chasers but they needed a penalty miss (by David Johnson) and a disallowed 'goal' to secure it. Defoe's winner was also a deflection. James had another nightmare. Marlon Harewood will later be a Hammer.											
4	A	MANCHESTER U		20	L	0-6	0-2	*[Neville P 50, Solskjaer 69]*	James	Lomas	Minto	Pearce	Breen*	Cisse^	Sinclair"	Bowyer	Defoe	Cole	Carrick	Dailly/Garcia/Johnson
	25/1		*67,181*	*2*				*Giggs 8, 29, Van Nistelrooy 49, 58,*	*Barthez*	*Neville G*	*Neville P*	*O'Shea*	*Keane*	*Ferdinand*	*Beckham**	*Veron^*	*V Nistelr'oy*	*Scholes"*	*Giggs*	*Solksjaer/Butt/Forlan*
								Ref: S Bennett	Roeder emerged from the changing room an hour after final whistle to admit to an 'excruciating' performance. Man U were queuing up to put away the first goal, by Giggs, who then added a second with a shot that spun in off Breen. 0-6 after 69 minutes, Roeder must have feared ten.											

		Home					Away					
	P	W	D	L	F	A	W	D	L	F	A	Pts
1 Manchester U	38	16	2	1	42	12	9	6	4	32	22	83
2 Arsenal	38	15	2	2	47	20	8	7	4	38	22	78
3 Newcastle	38	15	2	2	36	17	6	4	9	27	31	69
4 Chelsea	38	12	5	2	41	15	7	5	7	27	23	67
5 Liverpool	38	9	8	2	30	16	9	2	8	31	25	64
6 Blackburn	38	9	7	3	24	15	7	5	7	28	28	60
7 Everton	38	11	5	3	28	19	6	3	10	20	30	59
8 Southampton	38	9	8	2	25	16	4	5	10	18	30	52
9 Manchester C	38	9	2	8	28	26	6	4	9	19	28	51
10 Tottenham	38	9	4	6	30	29	5	4	10	21	33	50
11 Middlesbro'	38	10	7	2	36	21	3	3	13	12	23	49
12 Charlton	38	8	3	8	26	30	6	4	9	19	26	49
13 Birmingham	38	8	5	6	25	23	5	4	10	16	26	48
14 Fulham	38	11	3	5	26	18	2	6	11	15	32	48
15 Leeds	38	7	3	9	25	26	7	2	10	33	31	47
16 Aston Villa	38	11	2	6	25	14	1	7	11	17	33	45
17 Bolton	38	7	8	4	27	24	3	6	10	14	27	44
18 WEST HAM	38	5	7	7	21	24	5	5	9	21	35	42
19 West Brom	38	3	5	11	17	34	3	3	13	12	31	26
20 Sunderland	38	3	2	14	11	31	1	5	13	10	34	19
	760	187	90	103	570	430	103	90	187	430	570	1050

Odds & ends

Double wins: (2) Chelsea, Sunderland.
Double losses: (3) Charlton, Liverpool, Leeds.

Won from behind: (3) Chelsea (a), Blackburn (h), Nott'm Forest (h) FAC.
Lost from in front: (1) Charlton (a).

High points: Beating Chelsea – who reach the Champions League – twice.
Three successive away wins lift the team to 14th in October.
22 points from the last 11 games almost brings safety.

Low points: Dreadful home record, failing to win in first 12 games.
Failing to beat relegation rivals at home in that dreadful opening spell.
Relegation on 42 pts, though they would also have gone down on 44.
0-6 hammering at Man U in the FA Cup.
Woeful defending during the first half of the season.
Frequently taking the lead but failing to hang on to win.
Health scare to manager Glenn Roeder.

Hammer of the Year: Joe Cole.
Ever-presents: (1) David James.
Hat-tricks: (0).
Leading scorer: (11) Jermain Defoe.

	Appearances						Goals			
	Lge	*Sub*	LC	*Sub*	FAC	*Sub*	**Lge**	LC	FAC	**Tot**
Bowyer, Lee	**10**				1					
Breen, Gary	**9**	*5*	2		2					
Brevett, Rufus	**12**	*1*								
Camara, Titi		*4*	1			*1*				
Carrick, Michael	**28**	*2*	2		2		**1**			**1**
Cisse, Edouard	**18**	*7*	1		2					
Cole, Joe	**36**		2		2		**4**		1	**5**
Dailly, Christian	**23**	*3*	1		1	*1*				
Defoe, Jermain	**29**	*9*	2		2		**8**	1	2	**11**
Di Canio, Paolo	**16**	*2*	1				**9**			**9**
Ferdinand, Les	**12**	*2*					**2**			**2**
Garcia, Richard				*1*		*1*				
Hutchison, Don		*10*								
James, David	**38**		2		2					
Johnson, Glen	**14**	*1*				*1*				
Kanoute, Frederic	**12**	*5*					**5**			**5**
Labant, Vladimir		*1*								
Lomas, Steve	**27**	*2*	2		1					
Minto, Scott	**9**	*3*	2		1					
Moncur, John		*7*								
Pearce, Ian	**26**	*4*	1		2		**2**			**2**
Repka, Tomas	**32**		1							
Schemmel, Sebastian	**15**	*1*	1	*1*	1					
Sinclair, Trevor	**36**	*2*	1		2		**8**			**8**
Winterburn, Nigel	**16**	*2*		*1*	1					
(own-goals)							**3**			**3**
25 players used	**418**	*73*					**42**			**46**

No	Date		Att	Pos	Pt	F-A	H-T	Scorers, Times, and Referees	SQUAD	NUMBERS	IN	USE								subs used
1	A	PRESTON			W	2-1	1-1	Defoe 5, Connolly 69	James	**Ferdinand**	Brevett	Hutchison	Repka	Dailly	Garcia*	Lee	**Mellor^**	Defoe	**Etherington**	**Sofiane/Connolly**
	9/8		*18,246*		3			*Lewis 2*	*Gould*	*Alexander*	*Edwards*	*O'Neil*	*Lucketti*	*Jac' Michael*	*Etuhu**	*Healy*	*Cresswell*	*Fuller*	*Lewis*	*Skora*
								Ref: P Danson	Conceding a goal within 94 seconds of the new season was the stuff of nightmares. Although Defoe quickly equalised, and Connolly came off the bench to bag the winner, Craig Brown's Preston created more chances. Repka conceded a clear penalty against Fuller, which wasn't given.											
2	H	SHEFFIELD UTD		8	D	0-0	0-0		James	Dailly	Brevett*	Hutchison	Repka	Pearce	Lee"	**Horlock**	Connolly	Defoe	Etherington	Garcia^/Mellor/**Noble**
	16/8		28,972	*14*	4				*Kenny*	*Kozluk*	*Jagielka*	*McCall*	*Page*	*Morgan*	*Ndlovu*	*Montgomery*	*Lester*	*Ward*	*Tonge*	
								Ref: K Hill	Off the field, the arrival of Abramovich's millions at Chelsea has saved West Ham from Administration. He has paid handsomely for Cole and Johnson. On it, only James and Defoe (and injured Carrick) remain. Neil Warnock's Blades got a point in this dreary, lifeless, goalless draw.											
3	A	ROTHERHAM		12	L	0-1	0-1		James	Ferdinand*	Pearce	Hutchison"	Repka	Dailly	Horlock	Lee	Connolly^	Defoe	Etherington	Garcia/Mellor/Carrick
	23/8		*8,739*	*15*	4			*Byfield 14*	*Pollitt*	*Barker*	*Minto*	*Sedgwick*	*Swailes*	*McIntosh*	*Monkhouse*	*Talbot*	*Barker*	*Byfield*	*Mullin*	
								Ref: M Pike	This result brings the sacking of Glenn Roeder and the season is only three games old. Darren Byfield hooked in Talbot's cross and then forced a fine save from James. Defoe's free-kick, turned onto a post, was the nearest West Ham came. The team changed in a hotel, not at Millmoor.											
4	H	BRADFORD C			W	1-0	1-0	Defoe 32	James	Lee*	Horlock	Pearce	Repka	Dailly	Carrick	Connolly	Mellor	Defoe	Etherington	Hutchison
	26/8		30,370		7				*Paston*	*Edds*	*Jacobs*	*Evans*	*Wetherall*	*Gavin*	*Francis*	*Windass^*	*Branch**	*Gray*	*Heck'gbot'm*	*Wolleaston/Standing*
								Ref: R Beeby	Brooking takes charge as the search for a new man continues. City's team were entirely free-transfers. In the first half Paston turned efforts by Defoe and Connolly against post and bar, while Edds missed badly at the other end. Fortunately, Defoe beat three men to score a humdinger.											
5	A	IPSWICH		6	W	2-1	1-0	Defoe 21, Connolly 47	James	Repka	**Kilgallon**	Horlock	Dailly	Pearce	Carrick	Connolly	Mellor*	Defoe	Etherington	Hutchison
	30/8		***29,679***	*22*	10			*Wright 65*	*Davis*	*Wilnis*	*Makin^*	*Naylor*	*Diallo*	*Santos"*	*Magilton*	*Miller*	*Counago*	*Armstrong*	*Westlake**	*Bent D/Richards/Wright*
								Ref: A Hall	Defoe's spinning opener was topped by Connolly's waist-high volley to put West Ham in command. It got nervy after Jermaine Wright was sent on by Joe Royle and whacked a goal, and David James spent the closing minutes saving with his arms, body and legs to keep Ipswich out.											
6	H	READING		3	W	1-0	1-0	Dailly 17	James	Ferdinand^	**Quinn**	Pearce	Repka	Dailly	Lee	Connolly	Mellor*	Defoe	Horlock	Etherington/**Alexanders'n**
	13/9		32,634	*7*	13				*Hahnemann*	*Murty*	*Shorey*	*Brown*	*Williams*	*Harper**	*Murray^*	*Sidwell*	*Goater*	*Forster*	*Hughes*	*Watson/Tyson*
								Ref: D Gallagher	Alan Pardew walked out of Reading after they refused him permission to talk to West Ham. He stayed away from his match, leaving Kevin Dillon in charge of the Royals. Five minutes after Defoe hit a post he sent over a corner which Dailly headed in to record Brooking's third win.											
7	A	CREWE		2	W	3-0	3-0	Connolly 18, 21, Etherington 25	James	Repka	Quinn"	Horlock	Dailly	Pearce	Lee	Alex'ders'n^	Connolly	Defoe	Etherington*	Ferdinand/Noble/Kilgallon
	16/9		*9,575*	*11*	16				*Ince*	*Wright*	*Tonkin*	*Brammer*	*Foster*	*Walker*	*Lunt*	*Cochrane**	*Ashton*	*Jones^*	*Rix*	*Sorvel/Edwards*
								Ref: A Butler	Four straight wins for Brooking. This was the first ever league meeting with Crewe, whose dreadful defending gifted early goals to Connolly, robbing Foster, and then pouncing when Ince failed to hold Horlock's free-kick. Etherington's rocket shot, however, brooked no argument.											
8	A	GILLINGHAM		4	L	0-2	0-0		James	Repka	Quinn	Horlock^	Dailly	Pearce	Lee	Alex'ders'n*	Connolly	Defoe !	Etherington	Ferdinand/Noble
	20/9		*11,418*	*13*	16			*King 57, Benjamin 82*	*Brown J*	*Nosworthy*	*Brown W*	*Hope*	*Saunders*	*Cox*	*Spiller*	*Hes'nthaler**	*Sidibe"*	*King*	*Shaw^*	*Perpetuini/Smith/Benjamin*
								Ref: P Armstrong	Indiscipline costs Brooking his first defeat. Repka fouled Spiller, gave him the finger, and was booked. From the advanced free-kick, King scored with his right foot. Ten minutes from time Defoe gave a linesman the verbals and was red-carded. Benjamin's shot went in off Repka.											
9	H	MILLWALL		5	D	1-1	1-0	Connolly 24	James	Repka	Quinn	Horlock	Dailly	Pearce*	Lee	Connolly	Mellor^	Defoe	Etherington	Ferdinand/Alexandersson
	28/9		31,626	*8*	17			*Cahill 74*	*Warner*	*Dunne^*	*Craig*	*Cahill*	*Nethercott*	*Ward*	*Wise*	*Livermore*	*Peeters*	*Ifill*	*Roberts**	*Harris/Lawrence*
								Ref: M Halsey	The first meeting for ten years passed without incident, on and off the pitch. Mark McGhee's Lions were on top when Connolly's jinking run broke the deadlock. Etherington hit the bar. James turned Ifill's effort against the bar at the other end. Cahill levelled with a downward header.											
10	H	CRYSTAL PALACE		4	W	3-0	2-0	Defoe 19, Mellor 32, 56	James	Repka	Quinn^	Horlock	Dailly	Pearce	Lee*	Connolly	Mellor"	Defoe	Etherington	Ferdinand/Kilgallon/Alex'son
	1/10		31,861	*16*	20				*Berthelin*	*Butterfield*	*Smith^*	*Mullins*	*Powell"*	*Riihilahti*	*Derry*	*Johnson*	*Freedman*	*Shipperley**	*Hughes*	*Routl'ge/Borr'wdale/Fleming*
								Ref: M Jones	Steve Kember's Eagles arrive with two points from seven games. Defoe did a Pele and dummied the keeper, but whereas Pele missed (against Uruguay in the 1970 World Cup), Defoe did not. Mellor headed a second from Etherington's cross and tapped in a third from Quinn's centre.											
11	A	DERBY		3	W	1-0	0-0	Hutchison 90	James	Repka	Quinn	Horlock	Dailly	Pearce	Alexanders'n	Carrick^	Mellor*	Connolly	Etherington	Hutchison/Lee
	4/10		*22,810*	*20*	23				*Oakes*	*Caldwell*	*Zavagno*	*Huddlestone*	*Mills*	*Johnson*	*Costa*	*Taylor*	*Morris^*	*Svensson**	*Holmes*	*Valakari/Tudgay*
								Ref: M Fletcher	This win continues Brooking's Midas touch, leaving West Ham just two points off the top. But it took a last-minute corner from Quinn to bring the only goal. Defoe was missing, suspended. George Burley's Derby lose their first match in six. Injuries mean playing Ian Taylor up front.											

No	Venue	Opponent	Att	Pos	Res	Pts	F-A	H-T	Scorers, Times, and Referees	1	2	3	4	5	6	7	8	9	10	11	subs used
12	H	NORWICH		4	D		1-1	1-0	Edworthy 6 (og)	James	Repka	Quinn	Horlock"	Dailly	Pearce	Alexanders'n	Carrick	Mellor	Garcia^	Etherington*	Ferdinand/Hutchison/Lee
	15/10		31,308	7		24			Crouch 63	Green	Edworthy	Drury	Fleming	MacKay	Holt	Harper^	Francis	Huckerby*	Crouch"	McVeigh	Rivers/Mulryne/Roberts
									Ref: S Tomlin	With Defoe and Connolly suspended, West Ham were always going to be lightweight. Mellor had three clear headers, but put all of them over the bar. Fortunately, Edworthy had already turned Mellor's low cross into his own net. Crouch headed in, and Damien Francis hit James' post.											
13	H	BURNLEY		5	D		2-2	1-1	Connolly 20, Hutchison 86	James	Repka	Quinn^	Lee	Dailly	Pearce	Alex'ders'n*	Carrick	Connolly	Defoe	Etherington	Hutchison/Mellor
	18/10		31,474	13		25			Facey 38, Moore 82	Jensen	West	Camara	Chaplow	Branch	Gnohere	Weller*	Blake^	Moore I	Facey	Chadwick	Grant/Farrelly
									Ref: I Williamson	Pardew takes charge after this game though he was introduced to the crowd before. Brooking's last act was to send on Hutchison, who volleyed a late equaliser. Brooking's ten games in charge this season earned 21 points. Pardew orders modern cardiac and fitness tests for the squad.											
14	H	NOTT'M FOREST		5	D		1-1	0-1	Defoe 56	James	Repka	Quinn	Hutchison	Dailly	**Mullins**	Lee*	Carrick	Connolly^	Defoe	Etherington	Ferdinand/Mellor
	22/10		29,544	9		26			Reid 5	Ward	Louis-Jean	Morgan	Williams	Dawson	Walker	Jess^	Stewart*	Taylor	Harewood	Reid	Gunnarsson/Sonner
									Ref: A Bates	Pardew's six weeks gardening leave is over. He signs Mullins, who immediately slips to let Reid score from 25 yards. Although Defoe finally headed in one of Etherington's crosses, it could have gone either way. Defoe and Reid hit the woodwork at either end, and Reid missed a sitter.											
15	A	CARDIFF		5	D		0-0	0-0		James	**Stockdale**	Quinn	Repka	Dailly	Mullins*	Hutchison	Carrick	Connolly^	Defoe	Etherington	Lee/Mellor"/Ferdinand
	25/10		19,202	12		27				Alexander	Croft	Barker	Bonner	Gabbidon	Vidmar	Langley	Kavanagh	Earnshaw	Gordon*	Robinson	Collins
									Ref: M Ryan	City's biggest crowd for 23 years don't get a repeat of the Carling Cup thriller. Cardiff set off at a gallop, though James was untroubled until the 23rd minute when he saved from Robinson with his feet. James was beaten only once, but Langley's 66th-minute shot bounced off a post.											
16	A	COVENTRY		6	D		1-1	1-1	Defoe 15	James	Repka	Quinn	Horlock	Dailly	Pearce	Lee*	Mullins	**Deane**	Defoe	Etherington	Garcia
	1/11		19,126	14		28			Barrett 38	Arphexad	Whing	Warnock	McAllister	Konjic	Shaw	Barrett*	Safri	Suffo	Morrell	Doyle	Pead
									Ref: G Salisbury	Five straight draws means ten points lost. Defoe had poached the ball off City's player-manager Gary McAllister for the opener, only for West Ham's defence to be shredded as Graham Barrett turned in Doyle's cross. Patrick Suffo shot wide at the end when he should have done better.											
17	H	WEST BROM		6	L		3-4	3-2	Defoe 1, Deane 10, 18	James	Repka	Quinn*	Mullins	Dailly	Pearce	Hutchison	Carrick	Deane	Defoe !	Etherington	Lee
	8/11		30,359	1		28			Hulse 25,40, Deane 66(og), Hughes 77	Hoult	Haas	Robinson*	Gregan	Gaardsoe	Gilchrist	O'Connor^	Johnson	Hulse	Dobie"	Koumas	Clement/Sakiri/Hughes
									Ref: M Dean	Deane's tap-in and header, on top of Defoe's opener, has Albion boss Gary Megson fuming. Dailly dithered to let in Rob Hulse, who then let fly from 25 yards. Defoe was sent off for lunging at Gregan before half-time. Deane volleyed an own-goal and James punched out to Hughes.											
18	A	WATFORD		9	D		0-0	0-0		James	Repka	Quinn	Horlock	Dailly	Pearce	Mullins	Hutchison	Connolly	Deane*	Carrick	Garcia
	22/11		20,950	15		29				Pidgeley	Smith	Brown	Cox	Gayle	Vernazza	Ardley	Hyde	Webber	Fitzgerald	Devlin	
									Ref: P Prosser	After conceding four at home to WBA, a clean sheet on the road is cause for some satisfaction. With Defoe suspended, Pardew also lost Lee and Etherington in fitness tests. A churned pitch helped neither side, though Ray Lewington's team have now lost just twice in twelve games.											
19	A	WIMBLEDON		8	D		1-1	0-0	Deane 51	James	Repka	Quinn	Horlock	Dailly	Pearce	Mullins	Connolly	**Harewood**	Deane*	Carrick	Hutchison
	25/11		**8,118**	24		30			McAnuff 63	Banks	Darlington	Lewington	Chorley	Herzig	Leigertwood	McAnuff	Small"	Agyemang^	Nowland	Reo-Coker*	Holloway/Holdsworth/Gray
									Ref: B Knight	A sell-out for Stuart Murdoch's Dons at Milton Keynes, but this will be the smallest audience to watch West Ham this season. Harewood, a rushed signing from Forest for £500,000, saw a point-blank effort saved. Deane scored from Connolly's assist, but Nowland then fed McAnuff.											
20	H	WIGAN		7	W		4-0	2-0	Horlock 4, Jarrett 17 (og), [Harewood 55p, 75]	James	Repka*	Quinn	Horlock^	Dailly	Pearce	Mullins	Connolly"	Harewood	Deane	Carrick	Ferdinand/Garcia/Hutchison
	29/11		34,375	5		33				Filan	Eaden	Baines*	Jarrett	Breckin	Jackson !	Liddell"	Bullard	Ellington	Horsfield^	McCulloch !	De Vos/Roberts N/Lawrence
									Ref: F Stretton	Pardew's first win in eight. Paul Jewell's team had Matt Jackson sent off for a two-footed lunge at Mullins, and McCulloch for two yellows. Harewood netted against Wigan last week for Forest; he now scores two more. He won a penalty, chipped a second, crossed for the own-goal.											
21	A	WEST BROM		8	D		1-1	0-0	Deane 68	James	Stockdale*	Quinn	Repka	Dailly	Pearce	Mullins	Connolly	Harewood	Deane^	Carrick	Horlock/Hutchison
	6/12		26,194	1		34			Mullins 80 (og)	Hoult	Haas	Clement	Gregan	Gaardsoe	Gilchrist*	O'Connor	Johnson	Hulse	Dichio^	Koumas"	Robinson/Dobie/Sakiri
									Ref: M Clattenburg	Deane's fourth goal in six games looks to have avenged that 3-4 freak against the table-toppers, but Mullins then heads a spectacular own-goal. West Ham have taken just one point from Albion when they should have had all six. Pardew is bullish at the end about his team's prospects.											
22	H	STOKE			L		0-1	0-1		James	Stockdale	Quinn	Repka*	Dailly	Pearce	Mullins	Connolly	Harewood	Deane^	Carrick	Horlock/Hutchison
	9/12		**24,365**			34			Richardson 33	De Goey	Thomas	Clarke	Eustace	Hall	Taggart	Russell	Richardson	Akinbiyi*	N'I-Williams^	Halls	Asaba/Johnson
									Ref: B Curson	Bitter temperatures and a bitter result. Tony Pulis's Stoke arrive with a dreadful away record, but they were good value for the win that lifted them out of the bottom three. The game turned when Connolly's free-kick hit a post. De Goey's goal-kick led straight to Richardson's goal.											
23	H	SUNDERLAND		6	W		3-2	0-2	Defoe 55, 61, Pearce 80	James	Repka	Quinn*	Horlock	Dailly	Pearce	Mullins	Connolly	Harewood^	Defoe	Etherington"	Hutchison/Deane/**Cohen**
	13/12		30,329	10		37			McAteer 4, Oster 30	Poom	Wright	Arca	Thirlwell	Bjorklund	McCartney	McAteer*	Whitley	Smith^	Stewart	Oster	Kyle/Butler
									Ref: P Joslin	At half-time the fans were in uproar and the defence imploding. Had Whitley's strike onto the bar on 53 mins made it 0-3, one feared the result. But sub Deane nodded down for Defoe, who added another from Etherington's cross. Pearce netted when Horlock's free-kick came off a post.											

No		Date	Att	Pos	Pt	F-A	H-T	Scorers, Times, and Referees	SQUAD	NUMBERS	IN	USE								subs used
24	A	WALSALL		6	D	1-1	1-0	Harewood 10	James	Repka	Quinn	Horlock	Mullins	Pearce	Carrick	Connolly*	Harewood^	Defoe !	Etherington	Hutchison/Deane
		20/12	9,272	*14*	38			*Leitao 69*	*Walker*	*Bazeley*	*Aranalde*	*Osborn^*	*Roper*	*Ritchie*	*Wrack*	*Merson*	*Leitao**	*Birch*	*Samways*	*Emblen/Dinning*
								Ref: S Mathieson	Defoe gets his third red card of the season on six minutes for swinging a boot at Ian Roper. He had hoped to put himself in the shop-window. Harewood hit a belter, then West Ham sat back to protect their lead. Jorge Leitao levelled it from close in, but otherwise West Ham stood firm.											
25	H	IPSWICH		8	L	1-2	0-0	Defoe 49	James	Repka	Quinn*	Horlock"	Mullins	Pearce	Carrick	Connolly^	Harewood	Defoe	Etherington	Mellor/Hutchison/Stockdale
		26/12	**35,021**	*4*	38			*Counago 70p, 79*	*Davis*	*Wilnis*	*Richards*	*B't-Williams*	*McGreal**	*Naylor*	*Magilton*	*Miller^*	*Bent D"*	*Kuqi*	*Wright*	*Santos/Counago/Reuser*
								Ref: B Knight	Ipswich arrive having lost the local derby to Norwich. They might have lost here, too, when Harewood bulldozed into the box to set up Defoe. Pablo Counago tumbled under Horlock and sent James the wrong way from the spot. The Spaniard then glanced in Reuser's long-range shot.											
26	A	NOTT'M FOREST		7	W	2-0	1-0	Harewood 7, Defoe 84	James	Repka	Quinn	Stockdale*	Mullins	Pearce	Carrick	Connolly^	Harewood	Defoe	Etherington	Ferdinand/Horlock
		28/12	27,491	*20*	41				*Ward*	*Louis-Jean*	*Thompson*	*Williams*	*Dawson*	*Doig*	*Stewart**	*Gardner*	*Taylor*	*King*	*Reid*	*Jess*
								Ref: R Beeby	Harewood pushes Paul Hart's Forest closer to the brink, converting Defoe's cushioned header. Defoe clinched the points by sprinting on to Repka's belted clearance that sailed over Michael Dawson's head. It will be Defoe's last goal in his last game before he signs for Tottenham.											
27	H	PRESTON		8	L	1-2	1-0	Connolly 19	James	Stockdale*	Quinn^	Mullins	Dailly	Pearce	Carrick	Hutchison"	Harewood	Connolly	Etherington	Mellor/Ferdinand/Deane
		10/1	28,777	*5*	41			*Fuller 64, Healy 67*	*Gould*	*Alexander*	*Keane^*	*Davis**	*Lucketti*	*Mears*	*O'Neil*	*McKenna*	*Cresswell*	*Fuller*	*Healy*	*Jac'Michael/Koumantarakis*
								Ref: M Warren	Four defeats in six home games is hard to take. Connolly had superbly converted Etherington's pass. Harewood was booked for not retreating, the ball was moved on, and Fuller headed his 15th of the season. Healy fired through a crowded box, whereupon Cresswell twice hit the frame.											
28	A	SHEFFIELD UTD		8	D	3-3	3-1	Carrick 19, Harley 22, Harewood 37	Bywater	Ferdinand	**Harley**	Mullins	Dailly	**Melville**	Carrick	Horlock"	Harewood^	Connolly	Etherington*	Mellor/Stockdale/Deane
		17/1	*22,787*	*3*	42			*Peschisolido 5, Shaw 72, Jagielka 90*	*Kenny*	*Kozluk*	*Morgan*	*McCall*	*Jagielka*	*Page**	*Montgomery*	*Allison*	*Lester^*	*Peschisolido*	*Tonge*	*Sturridge/Shaw*
								Ref: P Durkin	James and Pearce have gone. An attacking orgy from both teams, but West Ham looked home and dry. Debutant Harley's 20-yarder was the pick of the first-half goals. Another debutant netted, Shaw from Gillingham. Bywater's first game in three years saw him save Tonge's penalty.											
29	H	ROTHERHAM		7	W	2-1	1-1	Deane 15, Dailly 59	Bywater	Repka	Harley	Mullins	Dailly	**Reo-Coker**	Carrick	Connolly	Harewood^	Deane*	Etherington	Melville/**Nowland**
		31/1	34,483	*18*	45			*Repka 23 (og)*	*Pollitt*	*Barker*	*Minto*	*Garner*	*Swailes*	*Baudet*	*Sedgwick*	*Mullin*	*Barker*	*Byfield**	*Hurst^*	*Warne/Monkhouse*
								Ref: G Hegley	It was defeat at Millmoor which got Roeder the sack. Reo-Coker from Wimbledon enjoys a stirring debut, acting as captain in spite of Dailly's armband. Deane's sixth goal for West Ham was undone by Rekpa's own-goal. Dailly restored the lead by heading in Etherington's corner.											
30	A	BRADFORD C		5	W	2-1	0-1	Zamora 65, Harewood 78	Bywater	Mullins	Harley	Repka	Dailly	Reo-Coker	Carrick	Connolly*	Harewood	Deane^	**McAnuff"**	Melville/**Zamora**/Nowland
		7/2	*13,078*	*23*	48			*Atherton 35*	*Combe*	*Francis*	*Heck'gbot'm*	*Atherton*	*Wetherall*	*Gavin*	*Summ'rbee**	*Wallwork*	*Armstrong^*	*Gray*	*Farrelly*	*Windass/Branch*
								Ref: M Halsey	Bryan Robson's City are going down, so Peter Atherton's crisp drive was a shock. Armstrong was twice denied by Bywater. At half-time West Ham sent on debutant Zamora who headed in Dailly's cross. City were under the cosh. Nowland and Connolly set up Harewood for the winner.											
31	A	NORWICH		5	D	1-1	0-0	Harewood 61	Bywater	Mullins	Harley	Reo-Coker	Repka	Dailly	Carrick	Connolly^	Harewood	Zamora*	Etheringt'n !	Deane/Nowland
		21/2	*23,940*	*1*	49			*Huckerby 76*	*Green*	*Edworthy*	*Drury*	*Fleming*	*MacKay*	*Holt*	*Francis*	*Brennan*	*Roberts**	*Huckerby*	*McVeigh*	*Svensson*
								Ref: R Olivier	Norwich celebrate the opening of their new stand by a display of green and yellow cards. Etherington also received two yellows, the second for time-wasting when placing the ball at a corner. Harewoods' superb goal had been cancelled out Repka's back-header which let in Huckerby.											
32	H	CARDIFF		6	W	1-0	0-0	Zamora 73	Bywater	Mullins	Harley	Reo-Coker	Repka	Dailly	Carrick	Connolly*	Harewood^	Zamora"	Etherington	Deane/Nowland/McAnuff
		28/2	31,858	*11*	52				*Margetson*	*Weston**	*Barker*	*Boland*	*Gabbidon*	*Vidmar*	*Langley^*	*Kavanagh*	*Earnshaw*	*Lee*	*Parry"*	*Prior/Robinson/Campbell*
								Ref: G Cain	West Ham dominated and missed multiple chances. They might not have done so had Repka earned the red card he deserved for stealing yards at a free-kick then giving the referee an earful. The card was yellow. Goalscorer Zamora is enjoying life, netting the winner on his home debut.											
33	A	BURNLEY		5	D	1-1	1-1	Connolly 36p	Bywater	Mullins	Harley	Reo-Coker	Repka	Dailly	Carrick	Connolly*	Harewood"	Zamora	Etheringt'n^	Deane/Nowland/McAnuff
		2/3	*12,440*	*18*	53			*Branch 31*	*Jensen*	*Roche**	*Camara*	*Grant*	*May*	*McGregor*	*Little*	*Blake*	*Moore I*	*Branch*	*Chadwick^*	*West/Moore A*
								Ref: P Dowd	Stan Ternant's 300th game as Burnley boss was spoiled when Mullins shoved David May in the box, unseen by the referee. That was all he had to moan about for West Ham ruled the game before Branch netted from close range. McGregor's foul on Zamora produced Connolly's penalty.											
34	H	WALSALL		5	D	0-0	0-0		Bywater	Mullins^	Harley	Reo-Coker	Repka	Dailly	Carrick	Connolly*	Harewood	Zamora	Nowland"	Deane/Melville/McAnuff
		6/3	33,177	*21*	54				*Walker*	*Bazeley*	*Aranalde*	*Osborn*	*Roper*	*Emblen*	*Matias*	*Taylor*	*Leitao*	*Birch^*	*Samways**	*Wales/Fryatt*
								Ref: G Laws	'Kids for a quid' might put thousands on the gate, but it reflects a need for bums on seats. Walsall boss Colin Lee has sent Paul Merson to a re-hab clinic in Arizona. West Ham made just four goal-attempts on target and have now become the draw-specialists of the four top divisions.											

No	Venue	Opponent / Date	Att	Pos	Res / Pts	F-A	H-T	Scorers, Times, and Referees	1	2	3	4	5	6	7	8	9	10	11	Subs used
35	H	WIMBLEDON		3	W	**5-0**	2-0	Etherington 37, 49, 70, Zamora 39, [Reo-Coker 62]	Bywater	Repka	Harley*	Reo-Coker	Melville	Dailly	Carrick^	Connolly	Harewood	Zamora"	Etherington	Ferdin'd/Nowland/McAnuff
		9/3	29,818	*24*	57				*Banks*	*Darlington*	*Hawkins*	*Williams*	*Herzig*	*Gier*	*Harding*	*Barton^*	*Gray**	*Kamara*	*Chorley*	*Gordon/Jarrett*
								Ref: E Evans	Stuart Murdoch's wooden-spoonists took the field to face four former players. The rout didn't look on until Etherington scored at the near post from Harewood's cross. Zamora belted one from 25 yards and the party began. Etherington's hat-trick goal was a delicate shot into the corner.											
36	A	SUNDERLAND		5	L	0-2	0-0		Bywater	Repka	Harley	Reo-Coker	Melville	Dailly	Carrick	McAnuff*	Harewood"	Zamora	Etheringt'n^	Deane/Horlock/Nowland
		13/3	*29,533*	*7*	57			*Kyle 61, Whitley 76*	*Poom*	*Wright*	*McCartney*	*Thirlwell*	*Breen*	*Babb*	*Oster**	*Whitley*	*Kyle*	*Smith"*	*Thornton^*	*Piper/Williams/Byfield*
								Ref: R Beeby	These two relegated teams hope to bounce straight back, but this was an eyesore of a match. The first goal was in keeping, the ball cannoning off players before being steered in by Kyle. Early injury to Etherington meant West Ham's tactics were simply hoofing the ball up to Deane.											
37	H	CREWE		3	W	4-2	4-0	Harew'd 6, 20, R-Coker 35, McAnuff 41	Bywater	Repka	Harley	Reo-Coker^	Melville	Dailly	Carrick	Horlock	Harewood	Zamora*	McAnuff"	Deane/Cohen/**Carole**
		17/3	31,158	*15*	60			*Jones 61, 72*	*Ince**	*Jones^*	*Vaughan*	*Lunt*	*Foster*	*Walker*	*Hignett"*	*Cochrane*	*Ashton*	*Jones*	*Sorvel*	*Tomlins'a/Tonkin/McCready*
								Ref: D Crick	It sounds quite close, but for an hour it was as one-sided as could be. Harewood headed in from a corner, then belted in a second, whereupon the goals came quick and fast. But at 4-0 Steve Jones snatched a 'consolation', and shortly rounded Bywater to add a second 'consolation'.											
38	A	MILLWALL		5	L	**1-4**	0-1	Harewood 49p	Bywater !	Repka	Harley	Reo-Coker	Melville	Dailly	Carrick	Horlock*	Harewood^	Zamora	Etherington"	Deane/McAnuff/**Srnicek**
		21/3	*14,055*	*7*	60			*Dailly 34(og), Cahill 46, 56, Chadwick 80*	*Marshall*	*Muscat*	*Ryan*	*Cahill*	*Lawrence*	*Ward*	*Ifill*	*Livermore*	*Harris*	*Dichio**	*Roberts*	*Chadwick*
								Ref: J Winter	West Ham's biggest defeat might have been worse: Millwall missed two penalties. 1,000 police were on hand in case of trouble. Bywater was sent off (at 1-3). Dennis Wise's Lions are into the FA Cup semi-finals. Horlock hit the bar at 0-0. Dailly then swept the ball into his own goal.											
39	H	GILLINGHAM		4	W	2-1	1-1	Zamora 3, Etherington 76	Bywater	Repka	Harley	Reo-Coker*	Melville	Dailly	Carrick	Connolly^	Harewood	Zamora	Etherington	Deane/Nowland
		27/3	34,551	*21*	63			*Spiller 32*	*Banks*	*Southall*	*Rose*	*Johnson*	*Hope*	*Smith^*	*Hess'nthaler*	*Pouton*	*Sidibe"*	*Agyemang*	*Spiller**	*Jarvis/Crofts/Wales*
								Ref: A Penn	Etherington destroys Andy Hessenthaler's struggling Gills, but Connolly looks out of touch. Dailly was booed even before kick-off. Zamora netted from Harewood's flick but Spiller crashed an equaliser from Hope's nod on. Etherington's one-two with Nowland settled the outcome.											
40	A	READING		4	L	0-2	0-1		Bywater	Repka	Harley	Reo-Coker	Melville^	Dailly	Carrick	Connolly*	Harewood"	Zamora	Etherington	Deane/Hutchison/Nowland
		3/4	*21,718*	*7*	63			*Kitson 35, 52*	*Ashdown*	*Murty*	*Hughes*	*Ingimarsson*	*Newman*	*Harper*	*Brooker*	*Sidwell**	*Kitson*	*Morgan^*	*Salako*	*Watson/Owusu*
								Ref: P Joslin	A third successive away defeat for a manager jeered on his return. Steve Coppell's men won through two goals by Dave Kitson, signed from Cambridge United on Boxing Day. Kitson's first came when Melville dithered, his second via a free-kick which he converted off the crossbar.											
41	H	DERBY		5	D	0-0	0-0		Srnicek	Repka	Harley	Lomas	Mullins	Dailly	Carrick	Connolly	Harewood"	Zamora*	Cohen^	Deane/Reo-Coker/McAnuff
		10/4	28,207	*22*	64				*Grant*	*Jackson*	*Vincent*	*Huddlestone*	*Mawene*	*Kenna*	*Osman*	*Taylor*	*Tudgay*	*Pesc'solido^*	*Holmes**	*Bolder/Manel*
								Ref: J Robinson	This apology for a football match was partly down to the 'dead' pitch, said Pardew. Most of the entertainment came when Repka threw three throw-ins to Derby players. Lomas wrenched the ball away before a fourth throw. At the death Manel 'scored', but it was wrongly disallowed.											
42	A	CRYSTAL PALACE		8	L	0-1	0-0		Srnicek	Ferdinand	Harley"	Reo-Coker*	Repka	Dailly	Mullins	McAnuff^	Harewood	Connolly !	Horlock	Deane/Zamora/Cohen
		12/4	*23,977*	*9*	64			*Freedman 66*	*Vaesen*	*Butterfield*	*Granville*	*Hudson*	*Popovic*	*Riihilahti**	*Routledge*	*Gray*	*Johnson^*	*Freedman"*	*Hughes*	*Derry/Soares/Leigertwood*
								Ref: A Bates	Dowie's Eagles are on the march. West Ham were handicapped by the dismissal of Connolly on 36 minutes for two yellows for late challenges. The goal came when Srnicek saved from Gray at the expense of a corner. Andy Johnson flicked it on and Freedman buried it from a yard out.											
43	H	COVENTRY		6	W	2-0	1-0	Zamora 37, Connolly 71p	Bywater	Ferdinand	Horlock	Lomas	Melville	Dailly	Mullins	Connolly	Harewood^	Zamora*	Nowland"	Deane/McAnuff/Cohen
		17/4	27,890	*13*	67				*Shearer*	*Deloumeaux*	*Staunton*	*Gudjonsson**	*Konjic*	*Davenport*	*Doyle*	*Safri"*	*McSheffrey*	*Joachim^*	*Warnock*	*Barrett/Morrell/Kerr*
								Ref: H Webb	West Ham had gone 321 goalless minutes when Zamora – offside – shot under Shearer. The game turned on 54 minutes when Joachim missed from three yards. A linesman gave a penalty for Staunton's tug on Zamora. A fourth defeat in five ends play-off hopes for Eric Black's team.											
44	A	STOKE		5	W	2-0	1-0	Connolly 39, Harewood 59	Bywater	Ferdinand	Lomas	Mullins	Melville	Dailly	Carrick	Connolly*	Harewood	Zamora	Etheringt'n^	Hutchison/Cohen
		24/4	*18,227*	*13*	70				*Cutler*	*Halls*	*Hall"*	*Thomas*	*Taggart*	*Henry*	*Hoekstra^*	*Commons*	*Russell**	*N'l-Williams*	*Clarke*	*Gunnarsson/Svard/Palmer*
								Ref: N Barry	West Ham's discipline eventually overwhelmed Stoke. They took the points through Connolly's first goal from open play in three months. It came with the assistance of Zamora losing possession. Harewood's 23rd goal of the season was a header from Etherington's clipped shot.											
45	H	WATFORD		3	W	4-0	2-0	Hutchison 17, 44, Harewood 63p, 90	Bywater	Ferdinand	Lomas	Mullins	Melville	Dailly	Carrick	Hutchison	Harewood	Zamora^	Etherington*	Cohen/McAnuff
		1/5	34,685	*17*	73				*Chamberlain*	*Baird*	*Mayo*	*Blizzard*	*Cox*	*Mahon*	*Devlin*	*Hyde**	*Bouazza^*	*Dyer*	*Cook"*	*Fitzger'd/Helguson/Vernazza*
								Ref: M Jones	Watford were slaughtered, which bodes well for the play-offs. Elijah Wood – star of Lord of the Rings – came on to make the half-time draw. Hutchison had drilled a free-kick and then converted a flicked-on corner. Harewood's first was a twice-taken penalty after Zamora was fouled.											
46	A	WIGAN		4	D	1-1	0-1	Deane 90	Bywater	Ferdinand	Lomas	Mullins	Melville	Dailly	Carrick	Hutchison*	Harewood	Zamora^	Etherington"	Connolly/Deane/Reo-Coker
		9/5	*20,069*	*7*	74			*Roberts 34*	*Filan*	*Eaden*	*Baines*	*Bullard*	*Breckin*	*De Vos*	*Teale*	*Farrelly**	*Ellington*	*Roberts N^*	*Mahon"*	*Jarrett/Liddell/McMillan*
		Home	Away					Ref: R Pearson	West Ham must avoid a three-goal defeat. Wigan seemed sure of the win they needed to send both sides through until 49 seconds from the end, when Deane headed in Carrick's free-kick, given for Teale's push on Reo-Coker. The goal meant Wigan dropped out, to be replaced by Palace.											
		Average 31,167	18,724																	

Play-Offs			Att			F-A	H-T	Scorers, Times, and Referees	1	2	3	4	5	6	7	8	9	10	11	subs used
1:1	A	IPSWICH		4	L	0-1	0-0		Bywater	Repka	Lomas	Mullins	Melville	Dailly	Carrick	Connolly	Harewood*	Zamora^	Etherington"	Deane/McAnuff/Reo-Coker
15/5			*28,435*	*5*				*Bent 57*	*Davis*	*Wilnis*	*Richards*	*Miller*	*McGreal**	*Elliott*	*Magilton^*	*Wright*	*Naylor*	*Bent D"*	*Westlake*	*Kuqi/B't-Williams/Bowditch*
								Ref: M Clattenberg	West Ham wasted first-half chances, but by the end were grateful to be only one goal down. It came from Richard Naylor's shot which crashed off the bar and deflected off Repka into the path of Darren Bent. Rather than hit back, West Ham lost their way, happy to hear the final whistle.											
1:2	H	IPSWICH		4	W	2-0	0-0	Etherington 50, Dailly 71	Bywater	Repka	Lomas	Mullins	Melville	Dailly	Carrick	Connolly*	Harewood	Zamora^	Etherington	Reo-Coker/Deane
18/5			34,002	*4*					*Davis*	*Wilnis*	*Richards*	*Miller*	*Naylor*	*Elliott*	*Magilton**	*Wright*	*Bent*	*Kuqi^*	*Westlake*	*Reuser/Armstrong*
								Ref: N Barry (Hammers win 2-1 on aggregate)	A euphoric night at Upton Park. Etherington's opener had the crowd on its feet, blasting in from the edge of the box after Carrick had rolled the ball to him. Dailly was almost hero turned villain. He netted the second, but then tugged Matt Elliott in the box. It should have been a penalty.											
F	N	CRYSTAL PALACE		4	L	0-1	0-0		Bywater	Repka	Lomas	Mullins	Melville	Dailly	Carrick	Connolly*	Harewood^	Zamora"	Etherington	Hutchison/Reo-Coker/Deane
29/5			*72,523*	*6*				*Shipperley 62*	*Vaesen*	*Butterfield**	*Granville*	*Leigertwood*	*Popovic*	*Riihilahti*	*Routledge*	*Derry*	*Johnson*	*Shipperley*	*Hughes*	*Powell*
		(at Millennium Stadium, Cardiff)						Ref: G Poll	Palace feared relegation when ex-Hammer Ian Dowie arrived in December. Apart from Zamora's low shot, easily saved, and a possible penalty when Carrick was tackled by Leigertwood, West Ham offered little. Johnson shot between Repka's legs, Bywater parried, Shipperley pounced.											

Carling Cup																				
1	H	RUSHDEN & DIAM'			W	3-1	2-1	Defoe 9, Connolly 14, 78	James	Ferdinand*	Brevett	Sofiane^	Repka	Dailly	Noble	Lee	Connolly	Defoe	Etherington	Garcia/Byrne
13/8			13,715					*Lowe 34*	*Turley*	*Bignot*	*Underwood*	*Bell*	*Hunter**	*Edwards*	*Hall*	*Mills^*	*Jack"*	*Lowe*	*Burgess*	*Dempster/Gray/Darby*
								Ref: M Cowburn	'Sack the board' chanted fans outside, following this turgid win. It all started brightly, Defoe tapping in from close range after Connolly's lob was turned againt the bar. After Connolly doubled the lead, Onandi Lowe fired a free-kick into the top corner, leaving West Ham ragged.											
2	A	CARDIFF		7	W	3-2	1-2	Defoe 45p, 64, 88	James	Ferdinand	Quinn	Pearce	Repka	Dailly	Horlock	Mellor*	Connolly	Defoe	Etherington	Garcia
23/9			*10,724*	*2:14*				*Earnshaw 12, 25*	*Margetson*	*Weston*	*Barker*	*Boland*	*Gabbidon*	*Vidmar*	*Bowen**	*Kavanagh*	*Earnshaw*	*Thorne^*	*Bonner*	*Campbell/Gordon*
								Ref: A D'Urso	Lennie Lawrence sees his men lose a two-goal lead, established by Earnshaw's close and long-range finishes. Vidmar's foul on Connolly let West Ham back in. It was 2-2 when Defoe's shot was deflected in off Gabbidon. Defoe's hat-trick goal was a slick left-footer from 18 yards.											
3	A	TOTTENHAM		6	L	0-1	0-0		James	Stockdale*	Quinn	Horlock^	Kilgallon	Dailly	Carrick	Lee"	Hutchison	Defoe	Etherington	Ferdinand/Mellor/Garcia
29/10			*36,053*	*P:12*		*aet*		*Zamora 91*	*Keller*	*Carr*	*Ziege**	*Gardner*	*Doherty*	*King*	*Konchesky*	*Dalmat^*	*Keane*	*Zamora*	*Ricketts"*	*Blondel/Mabizela/Postiga*
								Ref: G Barber	Zamora's first goal since his £1.5 million signing from Brighton on his eighth Spurs appearance denied West Ham the victory they deserved. Lee and Defoe missed chances to have won the tie in normal time. Zamora turned Anton Ferdinand and drilled in a low shot with his left foot.											

FA Cup																				
3	A	WIGAN		8	W	2-1	0-0	Mullins 80, Connolly 85	James	Stockdale	Quinn	Mullins	Repka*	Pearce	Carrick	Horlock^	Harewood"	Connolly	Etherington	Dailly/Hutchison/Mellor
3/1			*11,793*	*7*				*Quinn 90 (og)*	*Filan*	*Eaden*	*Baines**	*Mitchell*	*Breckin*	*De Vos*	*Teale*	*Bullard*	*Ellington*	*Roberts*	*McCulloch*	*Jackson*
								Ref: H Webb	The Cup might not matter much this season, but West Ham soaked up Wigan pressure with ease before going for the jugular. Connolly hit the bar before half-time, contributed to Mullins' goal, then added a solo second. Quinn's hooked own-goal came too late to affect the outcome.											
4	A	WOLVERHAMPTON		8	W	3-1	3-1	Deane 4, Harewood 21, Connolly 32	Bywater	Ferdinand*	Harley	Mullins	Dailly	Horlock	Carrick	Connolly	Harewood	Deane	Etherington	Quinn
24/1			*24,413*	*P:19*				*Ganea 23*	*Oakes*	*Luzhny**	*Naylor*	*Ince*	*Clyde*	*Butler*	*Silas^*	*Cameron*	*Ganea*	*Miller"*	*Kennedy*	*Craddock/Gudjons'n/Clarke*
								Ref: M Halsey	Doomed Wolves looked bad, even though Dave Jones rested key players for Premiership survival. Horlock squared for Deane, and Harewood hooked a second. Although Miller crossed for Ganea to reply, Connolly's ferocious shot restored the two-goal cushion. Alex Rae struck a post.											
5	A	FULHAM		5	D	0-0	0-0		Bywater	Ferdinand	Horlock	Mullins	Dailly	Repka	Carrick	Connolly*	Harewood	Deane^	Etherington	Lomas/Mellor
14/2			*14,705*	*P:9*					*Van der Sar*	*Volz*	*Bocanegra*	*Knight*	*Goma*	*Davis*	*Legwinski*	*Malbranque*	*McBride*	*Hayles*	*Boa Morte**	*Petra*
								Ref: G Poll	Fulham were lucky to survive and Chris Coleman blasted his team afterwards in public. Harewood missed a great opening after 18 seconds and Fulham's best moment came when Malbranque's lob hit the bar. West Ham had five players ineligible, but Van der Sar was the busier keeper.											
5R	H	FULHAM		5	L	0-3	0-0		Bywater	Ferdinand	Horlock*	Mullins	Dailly^	Quinn	Carrick	Connolly	Harewood	Deane"	Etherington	Lee/Mellor/Lomas
24/2			27,934	*P:9*				*McBride 76, Hayles 79, Boa Morte 90*	*Van der Sar*	*Volz*	*Bocanegra*	*Djetou**	*Goma*	*Davis^*	*Legwinski*	*Malbranque*	*McBride*	*Petta"*	*Boa Morte*	*Knight/Pembridge/Hayles*
								Ref: M Riley	The winners are drawn to play Manchester United at Old Trafford. West Ham were as dominant as they had been at Loftus Road. Bocanegra found Brian McBride with a long pass and the ball was volleyed in from 18 yards. Hammers then ran out of steam and conceded two more.											

		Home					Away					
	P	W	D	L	F	A	W	D	L	F	A	Pts
1 Norwich	46	18	3	2	44	15	10	7	6	35	24	94
2 West Brom	46	14	5	4	34	16	11	6	6	30	26	86
3 Sunderland	46	13	8	2	33	15	9	5	9	29	30	79
4 WEST HAM	46	12	7	4	42	20	7	10	6	25	25	74
5 Ipswich	46	12	3	8	49	36	9	7	7	35	36	73
6 Crys Palace *	46	10	8	5	34	25	11	2	10	38	36	73
7 Wigan	46	11	8	4	29	16	7	9	7	31	29	71
8 Sheffield Utd	46	11	6	6	37	25	9	5	9	28	31	71
9 Reading	46	11	6	6	29	25	9	4	10	26	32	70
10 Millwall	46	11	8	4	28	15	7	7	9	27	33	69
11 Stoke	46	11	7	5	35	24	7	5	11	23	31	66
12 Coventry	46	9	9	5	34	22	8	5	10	33	32	65
13 Cardiff	46	10	6	7	40	25	7	8	8	28	33	65
14 Nott'm For	46	8	9	6	33	25	7	6	10	28	33	60
15 Preston	46	11	7	5	43	29	4	7	12	26	42	59
16 Watford	46	9	8	6	31	28	6	4	13	23	40	57
17 Rotherham	46	8	8	7	31	27	5	7	11	22	34	54
18 Crewe	46	11	3	9	33	26	3	8	12	24	40	53
19 Burnley	46	9	6	8	37	32	4	8	11	23	45	53
20 Derby	46	11	5	7	39	33	2	8	13	14	34	52
21 Gillingham	46	10	1	12	28	34	4	8	11	20	33	51
22 Walsall	46	8	7	8	29	31	5	5	13	16	34	51
23 Bradford C	46	6	3	14	23	35	4	3	16	15	34	36
24 Wimbledon	46	3	4	16	21	40	5	1	17	20	49	29
	1104	247	145	160	816	619	160	145	247	619	816	1511

* promoted after play-offs

Odds & ends

Double wins: (2) Bradford C, Crewe.
Double losses: (0).

Won from behind: (4) Preston (a), Sunderland (h), Bradford C (a), Cardiff LC (a).
Lost from in front: (3) West Brom (h), Ipswich (h), Preston (h).

High spots: Reaching the Play-Offs immediately after relegation.
Beating Sunderland after trailing 0-2.
Beating Ipswich at home in the Play-Offs, on a night of high drama.

Low spots: The sale of an entire team of Premiership quality.
The dismissal of Glenn Roeder and his health scare.
Losing at home to West Brom after leading 3-0.
Freezing at the Millennium Stadium in the Play-Off final with Palace.
Losing to Premiership Tottenham and Fulham in the cups, which suggests West Ham were short of Premiership quality.
West Ham lost at home four times. In three of those games they led.

Hammer of the Year: Matthew Etherington.
Ever-presents: (0).
Hat-tricks: (2) Matthew Etherington (plus Jermain Defoe, Carling Cup).
Leading scorer: (15) Jermain Defoe.

	Appearances								Goals				
	Lge	*Sub*	LC	*Sub*	FAC	*Sub*	PO	*Sub*	Lge	LC	FAC	PO	Tot
Alexandersson, Niclas	5	*3*											
Brevett, Rufus	2		1										
Byrne, Shaun				*1*									
Bywater, Stephen	17				3		3						
Carole, Sebastien		*1*											
Carrick, Michael	34	*1*	1		4		3		1				1
Cohen, Chris	1	*6*											
Connolly, David	37	*2*	2		4		3		10	2	2		14
Dailly, Christian	43		3		3	*1*	3		2			1	3
Deane, Brian	9	*17*			3			*3*	6		1		7
Defoe, Jermain	19		3						11	4			15
Etherington, Matthew	34	*1*	3		4		3		5			1	6
Ferdinand, Anton	9	*11*	2	*1*	3								
Garcia, Richard	2	*5*		*3*									
Harewood, Marlon	28				4		3		13		1		14
Harley, Jon	15				1				1				1
Horlock, Kevin	23	*4*	2		4				1				1
Hutchison, Don	10	*14*	1			*1*		*1*	4				4
James, David	27		3		1								
Kilgallon, Matthew	1	*2*	1										
Lee, Robert	12	*4*	2			*1*							
Lomas, Steve	5					*2*	3						
McAnuff, Jobi	4	*8*						*1*	1				1
Mellor, Neil	8	*8*	1	*1*		*3*			2				2
Melville, Andy	11	*3*					3						
Mullins, Hayden	27				4		3				1		1
Noble, David		*3*	1										
Nowland, Adam	2	*9*											
Pearce, Ian	24		1		1				1				1
Quinn, Wayne	22		2		2	*1*							
Reo-Coker, Nigel	13	*2*						*3*	2				2
Repka, Tomas	40		2		2		3						
Sofiane, Youssef		*1*	1										
Srnicek, Pavel	2	*1*											
Stockdale, Robbie	5	*2*	1		1								
Zamora, Bobby	15	*2*					3		5				5
(own-goals)									2				2
36 players used	**506**	***110***	**33**	***6***	**44**	***9***	**33**	***8***	**67**	**6**	**5**	**2**	**80**

No		Date	Att	Pos	Pt	F-A	H-T	Scorers, Times, and Referees	SQUAD NUMBERS IN USE											subs used
1	A	LEICESTER			D	0-0	0-0		Bywater	Repka	Brevett !	Mullins	Melville	Dailly	Rebrov^	Reo-Coker	Harewood*	Sheringham"	Etherington	Zamora/McAnuff/Cohen
		7/8	30,231		1				Walker	Makin	Dabizas	Heath*	Wilcox^	Scowcroft	Williams	Nalis	Stewart	Connolly	Dublin !	Keown/Blake
								Ref: M Ryan	The new season is 17 minutes old when Dion Dublin lashes out at Brevett and is dismissed. That meant ex-Hammer Connolly playing as a lone striker, but he still posed a considerable threat. Brevett himself earned a second yellow card six minutes from time for fouling Scowcroft.											
2	H	READING			W	1-0	0-0	Sheringham 82	Bywater	Repka	Cohen	Mullins	Melville*	Dailly	Rebrov"	Reo-Coker	Harewood^	Sheringham	Etherington	Ferdin'nd/Zamora/Chadwick
		10/8	26,242		4				Hahnemann	Murty	Williams	Ingimarsson	Shorey	Little*	Harper	Sidwell	Hughes^	Foster	Kitson	Convey/Goater
								Ref: P Taylor	Sheringham marked his 800th senior appearance in English soccer with West Ham's first goal of the season. He turned in Luke Chadwick's cross. The result was hard on Pardew's successor, Steve Coppell. Reading's counter-attacks produced a series of chances. None were taken.											
3	H	WIGAN		14	L	1-3	0-2	Zamora 69	Bywater	Ferdinand	Brevett"	Mullins	Melville	Repka	Rebrov*	Reo-Coker	Harewood^	Sheringham	Etherington	Chadwick/Zamora/Cohen
		15/8	23,271	1	4			Ellington 5, 58, Roberts 45	Filan	Wright	Jackson	Breckin	Baines	Teale	Frandsen	Bullard	McCulloch*	Roberts^	Ellington	Eaden/Graham
								Ref: A D'Urso	Paul Jewell's team have no fondness for West Ham, who 'unnecessarily' denied them a play-off spot. Nathan Ellington planted two headers past Bywater. The second (Wigan's third) saw Teale's ball to the far post headed in with great power. The game was lost before Zamora struck.											
4	A	CREWE		7	W	3-2	3-1	Sheringham 16, 22, Brevett 30	Bywater	Ferdinand	Brevett	Mullins*	Repka	Nowland	Chadwick	Reo-Coker	Harewood	Sheringham	Etheringt'n^	McClenahan/Cohen
		21/8	7,857	22	7			Ashton 31, 82	Williams	Briggs^	Walker	Foster	Jones B	Lunt	Cochrane*	Sorvel	Vaughan	Rivers"	Ashton	Jones S/Tonkin/Higdon
								Ref: A Kaye	West Ham have taken a liking to Crewe, and so has Sheringham who bossed this game and scored twice – a shot from 18 yards and a glancing header. Brevett's deflected third was soon countered by Dean Ashton, soon to move to Norwich. Ashton's second raised his fee another notch.											
5	H	BURNLEY		6	W	1-0	0-0	Nowland 62	Bywater	Brevett	Repka	Ferdinand	Mullins	Nowland	Chadwick*	Reo-Coker	Harewood	Shering'm^	Etherington	Lomas/Cohen !
		28/8	22,119	11	10				Coyne	Duff	McGreal	Sinclair	Camara	Chaplow	Branch*	Grant	Moore	Hyde	Blake	Roche
								Ref: J Robinson	Kelly Holmes wins her second gold and 20 players at Upton Park indulge in an old-fashioned bargy. 'Like WWF wrestling,' said Burnley boss Chris Cotterell. Cohen was sent off for a two-footed tackle on Grant. Nowland's first Hammers goal – a downward volley – silenced the jeers.											
6	A	COVENTRY		7	L	1-2	1-1	Sheringham 42	Bywater	Brevett"	Repka	Ferdinand	Mullins	Nowland*	Rebrov^	Reo-Coker	Harewood	Sheringham	Etherington	Lomas !/Chadwick/Garcia
		30/8	17,404	5	10			Doyle 45, Morrell 76	Shearer	Carey	Shaw	Davenport	Staunton	Doyle	Sherwood	Hughes	Wood*	Morrell"	Johnson^	Barrett/Suffo/Gudjonsson
								Ref: C Webster	Peter Reid's City are on the point of financial collapse. They have sold Calum Davenport to Spurs but he plays against West Ham. Sheringham put the Hammers ahead, but that was cancelled out by Mick Doyle's curling free-kick. Andy Morrell's winner was a classic scissors kick.											
7	A	SHEFFIELD UTD		5	W	2-1	1-0	Harewood 9, Sheringham 85	Bywater	Mullins"	Brevett	**Davenport**	Repka	Chadwick*	**Fletcher**	Reo-Coker	Harewood^	Sheringham	Etherington	Nowland/Rebrov/MacKay
		11/9	21,058	7	13			Quinn 65	Kenny	Bromby^	Morgan	Jagielka	Wright	Quinn	Thirlwell	Tonge*	Harley	Gray	Ward	Lester/Forte
								Ref: A Wiley	A batch of newcomers for West Ham, and some special goals too. Harewood's was a treat, as was Alan Quinn's dipping free-kick to restore parity. West Ham should have been out of sight by then, but all ended happily when Sheringham's free-kick was grazed in by Carl Fletcher.											
8	H	ROTHERHAM		4	W	1-0	0-0	Etherington 68	Bywater	Repka	**Powell C**	**MacKay**	Davenport	Fletcher	Chadwick*	Reo-Coker	Harewood	Sheringham	Etheringt'n^	Rebrov/Mullins
		14/9	26,233	24	16				Pollitt	Stockdale	Gilchrist	Swailes	Minto	Sedgwick	Vernazza^	Mullin	Garner	Shaw*	Barker"	Hurst/Warne/Proctor
								Ref: M Jones	Ronnie Moore's Rotherham arrive winless and bottom. They leave the same way, but in the first 68 minutes West Ham showed few ideas. Then a free-kick, which enraged the visitors, but Etherington curled it sweetly round the wall. Four West Ham players made their home debuts.											
9	H	IPSWICH		5	D	1-1	1-0	MacKay 11	Bywater	Repka	Powell C	MacKay	Davenport	Fletcher	Chadwick*	Reo-Coker	Harewood	Shering'm^	Etherington	Mullins/Rebrov
		18/9	28,812	4	17			Counago 57	Davis	Diallo	De Vos	Naylor	Wilnis	Horlock	Miller	Magilton*	Westlake	Bent	Counago^	Dinning/Kuqi
								Ref: R Styles	West Ham looked better in the first half, helped by MacKay heading in Chadwick's cross. The game might have been beyond Joe Royle's Ipswich had not Sheringham fired wide from the spot after Davis took Fletcher's legs. Pablo Counago connected with Magilton's corner-kick.											
10	A	NOTT'M FOREST		6	L	1-2	0-0	Harewood 58	Bywater	Repka	Powell C	MacKay	Davenport	Fletcher	Chadwick*	Reo-Coker	Harewood	Sheringham	Etherington	Lomas
		26/9	25,615	21	17			Evans 84, King 90	Gerrard	Perch	Morgan	Hjelde	Rogers	Impey*	Jess^	Evans	Reid	Taylor	Johnson	King/Bopp
								Ref: M Massias	The City Ground is a shrine to Brian Clough. Joe Kinnear's Forest win their first game of the season, yet trailed with six minutes left. Paul Evans levelled from 25 yards and Marlon King curled a winner two minutes into added time. Harewood had netted from Etherington's cross.											
11	A	DERBY		6	D	1-1	1-1	Etherington 11	Bywater	Repka	Powell C	Mullins	Davenport	Fletcher	Chadwick	Reo-Coker	Harewood	Shering'm*	Etherington	Zamora
		29/9	23,112	13	18			Johnson 6	Camp	Kenna	Konjic	Johnson	Talbot	Bolder	Huddlestone	Idiakez^	Reich*	Smith	Rasiak	Peschisolido/Taylor
								Ref: G Poll	A tetchy encounter with George Burley's County, who have now failed to beat West Ham in twelve attempts. Loanee Davenport was pressured into giving away a corner, headed in by Johnson. Five minutes later Chadwick's cross wasn't cleared and Etherington's shot was deflected in.											

12	H	WOLVERHAMPTON	5	W	1-0	0-0	Sheringham 75	Bywater	Repka	Powell C	Mullins	Davenport	Fletcher	Chadwick^	Reo-Coker	Harewood	Zamora"	Etherington*	Lomas/Rebrov/Sheringham
	2/10	29,585	19	21				*Oakes*	*Clyde*	*Craddock*	*Lescott*	*Naylor^*	*Newton*	*Olofinjana"*	*Ince*	*Seol Ki-H'n**	*Cort*	*Miller*	*Cameron/Clarke/Andrews*
							Ref: B Knight	Sheringham comes off the bench to score the only goal – a peach from 25 yards with his right foot. 'Judas' Ince saw his first-half volley fly too high. While 38-year-old Teddy continues to be a hero, Ince – almost 37 – will continue to be a villain. But is this his last visit to Upton Park?											
13	A	QP RANGERS	6	L	0-1	0-1		Bywater	Mullins	Powell C	Lomas	Repka	Ferdinand	Chadwick*	Reo-Coker	Harewood	Zamora^	Rebrov	Cohen/Hutchison
	16/10	18,363	7	21			*Rose 22*	*Day*	*Bignott*	*Shittu"*	*Santos*	*Rose*	*Rowland*	*Bircham^*	*Gallen*	*Cook*	*Furlong*	*Cureton**	*McLeod/Branco/Padula*
							Ref: P Taylor	The last time these rivals met was in the Premiership eight seasons earlier. Paul Furlong played then and now. Ian Holloway's team secured their seventh straight win when Cureton squared the ball for Matthew Rose to side-foot past Bywater. In the last seconds Harewood shot over.											
14	H	STOKE	5	W	2-0	1-0	Harewood 30, Sheringham 59	Bywater	Mullins	Brevett	Lomas	Repka	MacKay	Chadwick*	Reo-Coker	Harewood	Zamora^	Etherington"	Sheringham/Fletcher/Rebrov
	19/10	29,808	9	24				*De Goey*	*Halls*	*Clarke*	*Thomas*	*Hill*	*Duberry*	*Russell*	*Henry**	*Akinbiyi*	*N'I-Williams*	*Hall^*	*Brammer/Asaba*
							Ref: L Probert	Pardew has been at Upton Park a year, and he celebrates with a comfortable win over a Stoke side who will muster just 36 goals all season. Sub Sheringham settled the points with a delightful back-heel. With Sunderland being held to a 1-1 draw at Watford, West Ham climb up to fifth.											
15	H	GILLINGHAM	4	W	3-1	3-1	Zamora 18, Harewood 25, Mullins 39	Bywater	Mullins	Brevett	Lomas	MacKay	Repka	Rebrov	Reo-Coker*	Harewood	Zamora"	Etherington*	Fletcher/Cohen/Chadwick
	23/10	25,247	23	27			*Byfield 45*	*Brown*	*Nosworthy*	*Hope*	*Cox*	*Rose*	*Spiller*	*Southall"*	*Crofts*	*Hes'enthaler*	*Agyemang**	*Sidibe^*	*Byfield/Henderson/Jarvis*
							Ref: E Evans	Judging by their body language, Gillingham – seven straight defeats – were happy to lose so lightly. Judging by his, Zamora enjoyed himself. His name had provoked boos when announced, but he shot cleanly inside the left post and was instrumental in West Ham's second and third.											
16	A	PLYMOUTH	6	D	1-1	1-0	Lomas 43	Bywater	Mullins	Brevett	Lomas	Davenport	Repka	Fletcher	Reo-Coker	Harewood	Zamora*	Etherington	Hutchison
	30/10	20,220	12	28			*Wotton 76*	*Larrieu*	*Worrell*	*Coughlan*	*Doumbe*	*Gilbert*	*Norris*	*Makel*	*Hodges**	*Friio*	*Crawford^*	*Evans*	*Wotton/Milne*
							Ref: A Penn	Bobby Williamson's Argyle are slipping after a fine start. They might have slipped even more when Harewood put away Etherington's cross, only to be given offside. Lomas then headed in a cross by Zamora. Argyle replied when sub Wotton's free-kick went through Bywater's hands.											
17	A	CARDIFF	6	L	1-4	0-2	Harewood 60p	Bywater	Mullins"	Brevett^	Lomas	Davenport	Repka	Chadwick*	Fletcher	Harewood	Zamora	Etherington	Hutchison/Powell C/Rebrov
	2/11	14,222	18	28			*Lee 1, Ledley 16, Parry 53, McAnuff 77*	*Warner*	*Williams*	*Gabbidon*	*Collins*	*Barker*	*McAnuff*	*Kavanagh*	*O'Neil^*	*Ledley*	*Parry**	*Lee*	*Jerome/Boland*
							Ref: R Beeby	Cardiff's pace and power might have brought them a bigger win. Ex-Hammer McAnuff produced a neat dummy, allowing Alan Lee to score the first. McAnuff side-footed Cardiff's fourth, after Harewood's penalty – when tripped by O'Neil – had suggested a West Ham fight-back.											
18	H	QP RANGERS	5	W	2-1	1-0	Harewood 36p, 84	Bywater	Mullins	Powell C	Lomas	Davenport	Repka	Chadwick*	Fletcher	Harewood	Hutchison^	Etherington	Zamora/Ferdinand
	6/11	31,365	6	31			*McLeod 72*	*Day*	*Simek"*	*Santos*	*Shittu*	*Rose*	*Cureton*	*Bircham*	*Gallen*	*Cook^*	*Thorpe**	*Furlong*	*Ainsworth/McLeod/Padula*
							Ref: M Atkinson	Hutchison was about to be loaned to Leeds when Rebrov was injured and he was reinstated. The deadlock was broken when Chadwick went down easily under Shittu's challenge. McLeod's equaliser helped to right QPR's injustice, but Harewood unleashed a corker to win the game.											
19	H	BRIGHTON	6	L	0-1	0-0		Bywater	Mullins !	Powell C	Lomas	Davenport	Repka	Chadwick*	Hutchison"	Harewood	Fletcher	Etheringt'n^	Zamora/Reo-Coker/Rebrov
	13/11	29,514	18	31			*Butters 68*	*Kuipers*	*Reid*	*Hinshelwood*	*Cullip*	*Butters*	*Harding*	*Nicolas*	*Oatway*	*Carpenter*	*Virgo !*	*Claridge**	*Currie*
							Ref: P Armstrong	Seagulls' boss Mark McGhee wants a draw, and gives a debut to 38-year-old Steve Claridge. They were only going to score from a set-piece, and duly did so when Guy Butters outjumped everyone. West Ham missed plenty of chances. Mullins and Virgo were sent off for wrestling.											
20	A	MILLWALL	6	L	0-1	0-0		Bywater	**Taricco***	Powell C	Lomas	**Powell D**	Repka	Chadwick^	Reo-Coker	Harewood !	Fletcher	Etherington	Ferdinand/Zamora
	21/11	15,025	9	31			*Dichio 78*	*Stack*	*Muscat*	*Phillips*	*Lawrence**	*Ward*	*Simpson*	*Tessem^*	*Wise"*	*Livermore*	*Dobie*	*Hayles*	*Ifill/Dichio/Elliott*
							Ref: P Walton	A Hammer is sent off at the New Den for the second successive season. Harewood thought he had won a penalty under Ward's challenge, but the ref viewed it as simulation and issued a second yellow. Shortly afterwards sub Danny Dichio headed in Muscat's cross at the far post.											
21	H	WATFORD	6	W	3-2	2-2	Reo-Coker 28, Powell D 30, Rebrov 58	Bywater	Repka	Powell C	Lomas	Powell D	Fletcher	Chadwick	Reo-Coker	Rebrov	Zamora	Etherington*	Ferdinand
	27/11	24,541	12	34			*Gunnarsson 5, Dyer 21*	*Lee*	*Darlington"*	*Cox*	*Dyche*	*Doyley*	*Ardley^*	*Gunnar'son**	*Mahon*	*Chambers*	*Dyer*	*Helguson*	*Young/Devlin/Gayle*
							Ref: K Wright	Ukrainian politics impinge on this match: Rebrov wears an orange wristband in sympathy with the Orange Revolution. Bad defending gifted Watford two goals. Then Rebrov's free-kick was parried out to Reo-Coker. Darren Powell's header was followed by Rebrov's at the far post.											
22	A	SUNDERLAND	5	W	2-0	0-0	Harewood 59, Sheringham 90	Bywater	Repka	Powell C	Lomas	Powell D	Ferdinand	Chadwick^	Fletcher	Harewood	Rebrov*	Etherington	Sheringham/Zamora
	4/12	29,510	3	37				*Myhre*	*Wright*	*Breen*	*Caldwell !*	*Collins*	*Lawrence*	*Whitehead*	*Carter*	*McCartney*	*Stewart^*	*Elliott**	*Brown/Bridges*
							Ref: G Salisbury	This marked a high point for Pardew, masterminding a first home defeat of the season for Mick McCarthy's champions-elect. It was made easier by Steve Caldwell's 41st-minute dismissal for stamping on Chadwick. Chadwick had hit a post before crossing for Harewood to convert.											
23	H	LEEDS	5	D	1-1	0-0	Chadwick 49	Bywater	Repka	Powell C	Lomas	Powell D	Ferdinand	Chadwick^	Fletcher	Harewood	Rebrov*	Etherington	Sheringham/Reo-Coker
	10/12	30,684	19	38			*Healy 90*	*Sullivan*	*Kelly*	*Butler*	*Kilgallon*	*Richardson*	*Wright"*	*Pugh*	*Gregan*	*Healy*	*Deane**	*Oster^*	*Joachim/McMaster/Walton*
							Ref: M Pike	This Friday night game had an explosive climax. Kevin Blackwell's Leeds arrived with two wins from 11. They fell behind when a cross from Etherington reached Chadwick, who scored from close in. In the 93rd minute Northern Ireland's David Healy flung himself to steal a penalty.											

No	Date		Att	Pos	Pt	F-A	H-T	Scorers, Times, and Referees	SQUAD	NUMBERS	IN	USE								subs used
24	A	PRESTON		6	L	1-2	0-2	Reo-Coker 50	Bywater	Repka	Powell C	Lomas	Powell D^	Ferdinand	Chadwick*	Fletcher	Harewood	Sheringham	Etherington	Reo-Coker/Rebrov
	18/12		*13,451*	*14*	38			*Lewis 9, O'Neil 45*	*Lonergan*	*Mawene*	*Lucketti*	*Davis*	*Davidson*	*Sedgwick"*	*McKenna*	*O'Neil**	*Lewis*	*Cresswell*	*Agyemang^*	*Etuhu/Oliveira/Alexander*
								Ref: A Kaye	Billy Davies' Preston are beginning their surge that will culminate at the Millennium Stadium, and two long-range belters were enough to beat West Ham. Sub Reo-Coker turned in Repka's low cross and Harewood shot across the goalmouth near the end, but Lewis also struck the bar.											
25	H	NOTT'M FOREST		6	W	3-2	2-0	Etherington 17, Sheringham 39, 82	Bywater	Repka	Powell C	Lomas	MacKay	Ferdinand*	Chadwick^	Reo-Coker	Harewood	Sheringham	Etherington	Mullins/Williams
	26/12		32,270	*22*	41			*Johnson 65, 68*	*Gerrard*	*Impey**	*Robertson*	*Bopp*	*Dawson*	*Morgan*	*Thompson^*	*Derry*	*Johnson*	*Harris*	*Rogers*	*Commons/Westcarr*
								Ref: A Marriner	Mick Harford's clueless Forest snatch two quick goals. 'Are you Roeder in disguise?' rains down. Gerrard had hit the ball into Etherington's back for the first goal. Sheringham side-footed a second before Forest hit back. Chris Powell's late cross went in off Sheringham's shoulder.											
26	A	ROTHERHAM		7	D	2-2	0-2	Sheringham 71p, Harewood 76p	Bywater	Repka	Powell C	Mullins	MacKay	Lomas*	**Williams**	Reo-Coker	Harewood	Sheringh'm^	Etherington	Chadwick/Zamora
	28/12		*7,769*	*24*	42			*Butler 13, McIntosh 37*	*Pollitt*	*Scott*	*Swailes*	*McIntosh*	*Hurst*	*Monkhouse**	*Barker*	*McLaren*	*Camp'l-Ryce*	*Butler*	*Junior^*	*Hoskins/Proctor*
								Ref: I Williamson	Two down and booed off at half-time, West Ham need two iffy penalties to nick a point. Harewood sprung the offside trap (or did he?), took Sheringham's pass but was felled by Pollitt. Sheringham converted, then fell under McIntosh's challenge. This time Harewood took the kick.											
27	A	IPSWICH		5	W	2-0	1-0	Harewood 1, Etherington 89	Bywater	Mullins	Powell C	Repka	MacKay	Fletcher	Williams	Reo-Coker^	Harewood	Zamora*	Etherington"	Rebrov/Ferdinand/McClen'n
	1/1		*30,003*	*1*	45				*Davis*	*Wilnis*	*De Vos*	*Naylor*	*Richards*	*Miller*	*Magilton*	*Westlake*	*Currie*	*Kuqi*	*Bent**	*Bowditch*
								Ref: P Taylor	Ipswich had scored in every home match in the past 13 months. West Ham lined up with six men in midfield and within seconds a goal came. Davis and Naylor got in a tizzy and Harewood darted in. Ipswich's first chance came in the 85th minute, but Bywater blocked Westlake's shot.											
28	H	SHEFFIELD UTD		6	L	0-2	0-1		Bywater	Mullins	Powell C	Repka	MacKay"	Fletcher	Williams	Reo-Coker	Harewood	Zamora^	Etherington*	Chadwick/Rebrov/Cohen
	3/1		27,424	*5*	45			*Repka 40 (og), Bromby 60*	*Kenny*	*Geary*	*Cullip*	*Bromby*	*Morgan*	*Jagielka*	*Tonge**	*Quinn*	*Liddell^*	*Harley*	*Gray"*	*Wright/Montgom'y/Cad'teri*
								Ref: T Kettle	Neil Warnock played five at the back, with Andy Gray as a lone forward, and it worked. Geary's cross was turned past Bywater by Repka. Liddell's free-kick from the right was charged down and Leigh Bromby pounced. Jon Harley was hit by something thrown from the crowd.											
29	A	WOLVERHAMPTON		7	L	2-4	1-1	Zamora 36, 57	**Walker**	Repka	Powell C	Mullins	MacKay	Ferdinand	Chadwick^	Noble*	Harewood	Zamora	Rebrov	Williams/Cohen
	15/1		*28,411*	*18*	45			*Miller 29, 54, Ince 72, Cort 75*	*Murray*	*Clyde*	*Craddock*	*Lescott*	*Naylor*	*Ince*	*Olofinjana**	*Kennedy*	*Seol Ki-Hy'n*	*Miller*	*Cort*	*Cameron*
								Ref: C Penton	Glenn Hoddle's Wolves are steadily climbing the table. This enthralling match, played on a wretched surface, saw Kenny Miller and Zamora trade two goals apiece before Paul Ince struck to help Wolves pull away. The result means that West Ham drop out of the play-off places.											
30	H	DERBY		9	L	1-2	1-1	Fletcher 26	Walker	Mullins	Powell C	Repka	MacKay	Fletcher	Williams*	Reo-Coker	Harewood	Rebrov^	Chadwick	Noble/Sheringham
	23/1		30,347	*8*	45			*Rasiak 10, 63*	*Camp*	*Kenna*	*Huddlestone*	*Mills*	*Jackson*	*Idiakez*	*Bisgaard**	*Bolder*	*Taylor*	*Smith^*	*Rasiak"*	*Tudgay/Reich/Junior*
								Ref: L Mason	George Burley's Derby record a fourth straight away win to leapfrog West Ham who drop to their lowest position since relegation. The ref did not send off Derby's keeper for bodychecking Harewood. Fletcher's first Hammers goal preceded Rasiak's winner hooked in from close range.											
31	H	CARDIFF		7	W	1-0	0-0	Fletcher 89	Bywater	Mullins	Powell C	Ferdinand	MacKay	Fletcher	Harewood	Reo-Coker	Sheringham	Zamora*	Noble^	Chadwick/Rebrov
	6/2		23,716	*19*	48				*Alexander*	*Weston**	*Collins*	*Gabbidon*	*Barker*	*Langley*	*Inamoto^*	*Kavanagh*	*McAnuff*	*Thorne*	*Lee*	*Vidmar/Ledley*
								Ref: K Stroud	Lennie Lawrence's Cardiff were looking for their seventh unbeaten game when Fletcher headed in Chris Powell's cross for a last-gasp winner. Moments earlier Lee's raking shot had missed Bywater's goal by inches. City fans were singing '[Pardew] You'll get the sack in the morning.'											
32	H	PLYMOUTH		6	W	**5-0**	3-0	Harewood 10p, McCormick 23 (og), [MacKay 40, Sheringham 76, 84p]	Bywater	Repka	Powell C	Mullins^	MacKay	Ferdinand	Rebrov*	Noble"	Harewood	Sheringham	Fletcher	Reo-Coker/Lomas/Zamora
	19/2		25,490	*21*	51				*McCormick*	*Worrell*	*Doumbe !*	*Coughlan*	*Aljofree*	*Buzsaky*	*Gudjonsson**	*Lasley^*	*Adams*	*Blackstock*	*Chadwick*	*Capaldi/Norris*
								Ref: K Friend	Out of the Cup, the reprieved Pardew oversees this massacre. When Coughlan fisted a corner, Harewood – who missed in the Cup – scored. McCormick then fumbled Rebrov's corner. MacKay beat the offside trap, Sheringham headed a fourth, then netted with a twice-taken penalty.											
33	A	GILLINGHAM		5	W	1-0	1-0	Harewood 13	Bywater	Repka	Powell C	Lomas	MacKay	Ferdinand	Fletcher	Reo-Coker"	Harewood	Zamora^	Etherington*	Sheringham/Cohen/Williams
	22/2		*9,510*	*22*	54				*Banks*	*Nosworthy*	*Ashby*	*Cox*	*Southall*	*Smith*	*Flynn^*	*Crofts"*	*Henderson*	*Byfield**	*Jarvis*	*Hills/Pouton/Spiller*
								Ref: P Crossley	Three straight wins, secured by a messy goal from Harewood, lifts West Ham to fifth. They would have been fourth had Sheringham's free-kick gone in instead of hitting the bar. Only Etherington and Repka played in the corresponding game last season, which inflicted a first defeat.											
34	A	LEEDS		6	L	1-2	0-0	Williams 68	Bywater	Repka	Powell C"	Lomas	MacKay	Ferdinand*	Williams	Fletcher	Harewood	Sheringham	Etheringt'n^	Mullins/Cohen/Zamora
	26/2		*34,115*	*10*	54			*Hulse 51, Derry 86*	*Sullivan*	*Kelly*	*Butler*	*Kilgallon*	*Gray*	*Lennon^*	*Derry*	*Gregan*	*Walton**	*Healy*	*Hulse*	*Pugh/Carlisle*
								Ref: A Hall	Rob Hulse's volley at the near post was cancelled out by Williams' deflected lob. But a point was snatched from West Ham by Shaun Derry – part of the Palace team who beat them at the Millennium Stadium. He admitted afterwards: 'Another day that would have gone for a throw-in.'											

No		Opponent	Att	Pos	Res	Pts	FT	HT	Scorers, Times, Referees	1	2	3	4	5	6	7	8	9	10	11	Subs used
35	H	PRESTON		7	L		1-2	0-1	Zamora 87	Bywater	Mullins	Powell C	Lomas	MacKay^	Repka !	Williams	Fletcher	Harewood	Sheringh'm*	Etherington	Zamora/Reo-Coker
	5/3		26,442	*5*		54			*Nugent 17, Agyemang 81*	*Day*	*Alexander*	*Mawene*	*Lucketti*	*Hill*	*Sedgwick*	*McKenna*	*O'Neil"*	*Lewis**	*Nugent^*	*Cresswell*	*Davis/Agyemang/Etuhu*
									Ref: S Tanner	A nasty match sees Preston earn the double. Repka was sent off before half-time for butting O'Neil. David Nugent had exploited Bywater's poor kick, and sub Agyemang's first contribution was his killer goal. Police were on hand to prevent trouble at the players' tunnel afterwards.											
36	A	READING		7	L		1-3	0-2	Sheringham 82	Bywater	**Newton**	Powell C	Lomas	MacKay	Mullins"	Fletcher*	Noble	Harewood	Zamora^	Etherington	Chadwick/Shering'm/**Ward**
	12/3		*22,268*	*6*		54			*Kitson 13, 27, 57*	*Hahnemann*	*Murty*	*Sonko*	*Ingimarsson*	*Shorey*	*Little**	*Sidwell*	*Newman^*	*Hughes*	*Morgan"*	*Kitson*	*Brooker/Harper/Owusu*
									Ref: P Joslin	Pardew admits to wrongly selecting a team shorn of Repka, suspended, and Dailly and Ferdinand, both injured. He should not have switched Mullins to defence, rather he should have given a debut to Elliott Ward. Reading's first win since Boxing Day takes them above West Ham.											
37	H	CREWE		7	D		1-1	0-0	Sheringham 76	Bywater	Newton	Powell C	Fletcher	Ward	Ferdinand	Williams^	Noble	Harewood	Sheringh'm"	Etherington*	Chadwick/Zamora/Mullins
	15/3		26,593	*17*		55			*Jones 90*	*Williams*	*McCready*	*Walker*	*Murdock*	*Tonkin*	*Bell"*	*Lunt*	*Sorvel*	*Roberts**	*Rivers^*	*Varney*	*White/Jones/Cochrane*
									Ref: M Thorpe	Three points were badly needed to recover from three defeats. Sheringham's curling free-kick seemed to have secured them. West Ham then spurned a clutch of chances before Steve Jones headed in McCready's cross. It was Crewe's first point against West Ham in four attempts.											
38	H	LEICESTER		8	D		2-2	1-2	Sheringham 28, 62	Bywater	Newton	Powell C	Fletcher	Ward	Ferdinand	Chadwick*	Reo-Coker	Harewood	Sheringham	Noble	Rebrov^Zamora
	18/3		**22,031**	*16*		56			*Connolly 25p, Gillespie 44*	*Walker*	*Kenton*	*Dabizas !*	*McCarthy*	*Maybury*	*Gillespie*	*Gudjonsson*	*Hughes*	*Tiatto**	*Dublin^*	*Connolly"*	*Williams/de Vries/Stewart*
									Ref: A Marriner	City have no wins in eight. West Ham perform well but are never in front. Bywater fouled Hughes for ex-Hammer Connolly to score. A header by Sheringham was followed by Gillespie's volley. At 2-2 Dabizas was sent off for handling Noble's shot. Walker saved Harewood's penalty.											
39	A	WIGAN		7	W		2-1	0-0	Sheringham 55, Harewood 67	Walker	Repka	Powell C	Newton*	Ward	Ferdinand	Mullins	Reo-Coker	Harewood	Sheringham	Noble	Fletcher
	2/4		*12,993*	*2*		59			*Roberts 51*	*Filan*	*Eaden*	*Wright*	*Breckin*	*Baines^*	*Teale*	*Bullard*	*Kavanagh*	*McCulloch**	*Ellington*	*Roberts*	*Ormerod/Mahon*
									Ref: B Curson	Sheringham celebrates his 39th birthday by equalising Jason Roberts' goal. Harewood then outsprints Eaden to score the winner. Ironically, West Ham have now won at the top three – Sunderland, Wigan, Ipswich – having gone into this match with just two points from five games.											
40	A	BURNLEY		7	W		1-0	0-0	Sheringham 83	Walker	Repka	Powell C	Newton	Ward	Ferdinand	Mullins*	Reo-Coker	Harewood^	Sheringham	Noble"	Fletcher/Zamora/Etheringt'n
	5/4		*12,209*	*14*		62				*Coyne*	*Sinclair^*	*Camara*	*Hyde*	*McGreal*	*Cahill*	*Oster"*	*O'Connor*	*Bowditch*	*Akinbiyi*	*Branch**	*Duff/Grant/Valois*
									Ref: K Friend	All the teams around West Ham also won, so their relative position is unchanged. Preston beat Brighton, Reading stole a late win over Millwall and Derby triumphed at Crewe. Sheringham's worth to West Ham is immense, no less for his 20th goal of the season, which saw off Burnley.											
41	H	COVENTRY		7	W		3-0	0-0	Shaw 76 (og), Sher'ham 89p, Zamora 90	Walker	Repka	Powell C	Mullins*	Ward	Ferdinand	Newton	Reo-Coker	Harewood^	Sheringham	Noble	Etherington/Zamora
	9/4		26,839	*16*		65				*Steele*	*Duffy*	*Page*	*Shaw*	*Hall*	*McSheffrey*	*Doyle*	*Osbourne**	*Dyer*	*Goater^*	*Adebola"*	*Staunton/John/Morrell*
									Ref: I Williamson	Nine points in eight days has revitalised West Ham's play-off hopes. The tannoy man had deflated the crowd by telling them beforehand that rivals Reading had won at Sunderland. On the pitch, West Ham left it late, Shaw deflecting super Etherington's hard cross into his own goal.											
42	H	MILLWALL		7	D		1-1	1-1	Harewood 35	Walker	Repka	Powell C	Noble	Ward	Ferdinand	Newton*	Reo-Coker	Harewood	Sheringham	Etherington	Zamora
	16/4		28,2221	*11*		66			*Hayles 12*	*Marshall*	*Phillips*	*Lawrence*	*Ward*	*Muscat*	*Sweeney*	*Elliott*	*Morris^*	*Livermore*	*Hayles**	*Dichio*	*Ifill/Simpson*
									Ref: U Rennie	This noon kick-off leaves West Ham four points adrift of the play-off places. It might have been worse when Muscat set up Hayles to score from a tight angle. Sheringham chested the ball to Harewood for 1-1, and in the last minute Sheringham chipped to Zamora, who shot over.											
43	A	STOKE		7	W		1-0	0-0	Zamora 78	Walker	Repka^	Powell C	Mullins*	Ward	Ferdinand	Newton	Reo-Coker	Harewood"	Sheringham	Etherington	Fletcher/Zamora/Chadwick
	19/4		*14,534*			69				*Simonsen*	*Buxton**	*Duberry*	*Taggart*	*Hill*	*Greenacre^*	*Brammer*	*Russell*	*Clarke*	*N'l-Williams*	*Jones"*	*Henry/Neal/Ricketts*
									Ref: G Laws	Stoke boss Tony Pulis tried to sign Zamora for £800,000 in January. He comes off the bench, goes on a run and his shot glances off the angle. That was his first contribution. His second was to score. West Ham survived Ferdinand's 'foul' on Noel-Williams and a late disallowed 'goal'.											
44	A	BRIGHTON		6	D		2-2	1-0	Reo-Coker 8, Harewood 55	Walker	Repka	Powell C	Mullins	Ward	Ferdinand	Newton	Reo-Coker	Harewood	Sheringh'm*	Etheringt'n^	Zamora/Fletcher
	23/4		***6,819***	*22*		70			*Hammond 54, 90*	*Blayney*	*El Abd**	*Virgo*	*Butters*	*Harding*	*Reid*	*Carpenter*	*Oatway^*	*Hammond*	*McPhee*	*Knight*	*Hart/Robinson*
									Ref: A Penn	This result leaves Brighton in the drop-zone and West Ham in the play-offs, but only because of Reading's defeat at Cardiff. Sheringham had been instrumental in both goals before limping off with hamstring trouble. Brighton countered with two terrific headers from Dean Hammond.											
45	H	SUNDERLAND		6	L		1-2	1-0	Harewood 43	Walker	Repka	Powell C	Mullins	Ferdinand	Ward	Newton^	Reo-Coker	Harewood	Zamora	Etherington*	Noble/Rebrov
	29/4		**33,482**	*1*		70			*Arca 52, Elliott 87*	*Alnwick*	*Wright*	*Caldwell*	*Breen**	*McCartney*	*Lawrence*	*Whitehead*	*Robinson*	*Arca*	*Stewart^*	*Brown"*	*Collins/Elliott/Deane*
									Ref: R Beeby	Both clubs went down together, but now Sunderland bounce back as champions. The champagne was put on ice when Harewood scuffed a shot in off a post. Repka contributed to the equaliser, poking the ball past Walker for Arca to pounce. Elliott dashed clear to break Hammers' hearts.											
46	A	WATFORD		6	W		2-1	1-0	Ferdinand 42, Harewood 70p	Walker	Repka	Powell C	Mullins	Ferdinand	Ward	Newton^	Reo-Coker"	Harewood	Zamora	Etherington*	Noble/Rebrov/Dailly
	8/5		*19,673*	*17*		73			*Helguson 89p*	*Chamberlain*	*Doyley*	*Cullip*	*DeMerit*	*Chambers*	*Blizzard*	*Bangura*	*Young*	*McNamee*	*Bouazza**	*Helguson*	*Osborne*
		Home	Away						Ref: A D'Urso	West Ham must equal Reading's score at Wigan. Reading are soon 0-2 down, so this potential nerve-shredder turned out to be a stroll in the sun. Ferdinand volleyed in Ward's cross for his first ever goal. Chambers handled in the box at one end; Repka fouled Helguson at the other.											
Average		27,403	18,886																		

Play-Offs	Att			F-A	H-T	Scorers, Times, and Referees	SQUAD	NUMBERS	IN	USE								subs used
1:1 H IPSWICH		6	D	2-2	2-1	Harewood 7, Zamora 13	Walker	Repka	Ferdinand	Ward	Powell C	Newton^	Reo-Coker	Mullins	Etherington	Zamora*	Harewood	Noble/Rebrov
14/5	33,723	*3*				*Walker 45 (og), Kuqi 74*	*Davis*	*Diallo**	*De Vos*	*Naylor*	*Wilnis*	*Miller*	*Magilton*	*Horlock^*	*Westlake*	*Bent*	*Kuqi*	*Richards/Currie*
						Ref: U Rennie	The same opponents as last year. West Ham finished 12 points behind but were soon two up. Etherington was offside for Harewood's goal. An advanced free-kick by Miller was deflected against a post, the ball going in off Walker. Walker and Ferdinand collided, giving a gift to Kuqi.											
1:2 A IPSWICH		6	W	2-0	0-0	Zamora 61, 72	Walker	Repka*	Ferdinand	Ward	Powell C	Mullins	Fletcher	Reo-Coker	Etherington"	Harewood	Zamora^	Dailly/Newton/Noble
18/5	*30,010*	*3*					*Davis*	*Wilnis*	*De Vos*	*Naylor*	*Richards*	*Currie*	*Magilton**	*Miller*	*Westlake*	*Bent*	*Kuqi*	*Bowditch*
						Ref: S Dunn (Hammers win 4-2 on aggregate)	Ipswich's sixth play-off defeat in seven attempts. Pardew changed his tactics from the first leg, employing a midfield diamond with Reo-Coker and Etherington on the flanks. Harewood crossed for Zamora to convert from two yards, and the same pair later delivered the coup de grace.											
F N PRESTON		6	W	1-0	0-0	Zamora 57	Walker"	Repka	Ferdinand	Ward	Powell C	Newton^	Mullins	Reo-Coker	Etherington	Harewood	Zamora*	Dailly/Noble/Bywater
30/5	*70,275*	*5*					*Nash*	*Davis*	*Mawene"*	*Luckett*	*Hill*	*Sedgwick**	*O'Neil^*	*McKenna*	*Lewis*	*Nugent*	*Cresswell*	*Agyemang/Etuhu/Alexander*
(at Millennium Stadium, Cardiff)						Ref: M Riley	Preston had done the double, but freeze as West Ham had done last year. Repka hit a post, Carlo Nash kept out Etherington and Harewood, but when Zamora swept in Etherington's cross the outcome was clear. Had West Ham lost, would Pardew have been sacked? Quite probably, yes.											

Carling Cup																		
1 H SOUTHEND		7	W	2-0	1-0	Harewood 11, 90	Walker	McClenahan	Repka	Ward	Brevett	Chadwick*	Nowland	Reo-Coker	Cohen	Harewood	Rebrov^	Noble/Sheringham
24/8	16,910	*2:24*					*Griemink*	*Jupp*	*Barrett*	*Edwards*	*Nicolau*	*Pettefer*	*Maher*	*Bentley*	*Gower*	*Broughton**	*Dudfield^*	*Bramble/Gray*
						Ref: P Armstrong	Promotion awaits both clubs via the play-offs. Reo-Coker slipped the ball into the path of Harewood, but Steve Tilson's side surged forward after half-time. Ward blocked a goal-bound effort by Bentley, who had another shot deflected. When McClenahan handled, the ref didn't see it.											
2 H NOTTS CO		5	W	3-2	1-1	Zamora 1, 54, Rebrov 62	Walker	Mullins	Brevett	Lomas	MacKay	Repka*	Rebrov	Reo-Coker	Harewood	Zamora	Etheringt'n^	Melville/Cohen
21/9	11,111	*2:24*				*Wilson 13, Richardson 57*	*Deeney*	*Wilson*	*Ullathorne**	*Richardson*	*Whitlow*	*Edwards^*	*Pipe*	*Bolland*	*Scully*	*Hurst*	*Gill*	*Oakes/Williams*
						Ref: I Williamson	Almost an entirely different team from the one which beat Southend in the previous round. Zamora's two goals were each cancelled out, first by Kevin Wilson and then by Ian Richardson, but Rebrov settled the matter. Two home draws against basement clubs is a recipe for progress.											
3 A CHELSEA		4	L	0-1	0-0		Walker	Mullins	Repka	Ferdinand	Brevett	Etherington"	Lomas	Nowland*	Reo-Coker	Zamora^	Harewood	Noble/Hutchison/Rebrov
27/10	*41,774*	*P:2*				*Kezman 57*	*Cudicini*	*Ferreira*	*Gallas*	*Carvalho*	*Babayaro*	*Parker^*	*Cole**	*Geremi*	*Tiago*	*Robben"*	*Kezman*	*Duff/Lampard/Gudjohnsen*
						Ref: A D'Urso	Chelsea have spent £200 million on players; West Ham have sold £32 million. Cole's pass set up Mateja Kezman to score off a post – his first Chelsea goal. He received a cut eye from a missile for his pains. In the 79th minute Repka felled Robben but sub Lampard's penalty was saved.											

FA Cup																		
3 H NORWICH		6	W	1-0	0-0	Harewood 81	Walker	Repka	MacKay	Ferdinand	Powell C	Chadwick*	Mullins	Fletcher	Noble	Harewood	Rebrov	Cohen
8/1	23,389	*P:18*					*Green*	*Edworthy*	*Fleming*	*Doherty*	*Charlton*	*Bentley**	*Helveg^*	*Francis*	*Brennan*	*Huckerby*	*Jonson*	*Mulryne/Jarvis*
						Ref: U Rennie	This is West Ham's first cup win (and first goal) over Premiership opponents in two seasons, having lost to Tottenham, Fulham and Chelsea. Bentley headed over from close in and Huckerby, one on one with Walker, hit a post. Then Chadwick pulled the ball back for Harewood. Goal.											
4 H SHEFFIELD UTD		9	D	1-1	1-0	Harewood 39	Bywater	Repka	Ferdinand	MacKay	Powell C	Noble	Fletcher	Mullins^	Chadwick*	Sheringham	Harewood	Reo-Coker/Rebrov
29/1	19,444					*Jagielka 57*	*Kenny*	*Morgan*	*Bromby*	*Cullip*	*Geary*	*Jagielka*	*Liddell**	*Montgomery*	*Harley*	*Gray*	*Tonge*	*Forte*
						Ref: D Gallagher	Tempers frayed after Sheringham neatly passed to Harewood to notch his 11th of the season. Bywater almost saved Jagielka's header from Liddell's centre, but the ball inched over the line. The Blades ratcheted up the physical, but West Ham picked up three of the four bookings.											
4R A SHEFFIELD UTD		7	D	1-1	0-1	Sheringham 63p	Bywater	Repka	Powell C	Ferdinand	MacKay	Fletcher	Chadwick*	Reo-Coker	Harewood	Sheringham	Noble	Mullins
13/2	*15,067*			*aet*		*Liddell 8*	*Kenny*	*Bromby*	*Cullip*	*Morgan !*	*Harley*	*Liddell*	*Jagielka*	*Montgomery*	*Tonge*	*Shaw**	*Gray*	*Geary*
						Ref: M Clattenburg (Hammers lose 1-3 on penalties)	Arsenal at Highbury await the winners. Liddell fired the Blades ahead with a curling free-kick. Morgan up-ended Harewood from behind and was sent off as Sheringham levelled. In the shoot-out, Kenny saved from Sheringham and Harewood, Fletcher missed, and Liddell sealed it.											

		Home					Away					
	P	W	D	L	F	A	W	D	L	F	A	Pts
1 Sunderland	46	16	4	3	45	21	13	3	7	31	20	94
2 Wigan	46	13	5	5	42	15	12	7	4	37	20	87
3 Ipswich	46	17	3	3	53	26	7	10	6	32	30	85
4 Derby	46	10	7	6	38	30	12	3	8	33	30	76
5 Preston	46	14	7	2	44	22	7	5	11	23	36	75
6 WEST HAM *	46	12	5	6	36	24	9	5	9	30	32	73
7 Reading	46	13	7	3	33	15	6	6	11	18	29	70
8 Sheffield Utd	46	9	7	7	28	23	9	6	8	29	33	67
9 Wolves	46	9	11	3	40	26	6	10	7	32	33	66
10 Millwall	46	12	5	6	33	22	6	7	10	18	23	66
11 QP Rangers	46	10	7	6	32	26	7	4	12	22	32	62
12 Stoke	46	11	2	10	22	18	6	8	9	14	20	61
13 Burnley	46	10	7	6	26	19	5	8	10	12	20	60
14 Leeds	46	7	10	6	28	26	7	8	8	21	26	60
15 Leicester	46	8	8	7	24	20	4	13	6	25	26	57
16 Cardiff	46	10	4	9	24	19	3	11	9	24	32	54
17 Plymouth	46	9	8	6	31	23	5	3	15	21	41	53
18 Watford	46	5	10	8	25	25	7	6	10	27	34	52
19 Coventry	46	8	7	8	32	28	5	6	12	29	45	52
20 Brighton	46	7	7	9	24	29	6	5	12	16	36	51
21 Crewe	46	6	8	9	37	38	6	6	11	29	48	50
22 Gillingham	46	10	6	7	22	23	2	8	13	23	43	50
23 Nott'm For	46	7	10	6	26	28	2	7	14	16	38	44
24 Rotherham	46	2	7	14	17	34	3	7	13	18	35	29
	1104	235	162	155	762	580	155	162	235	580	762	1494

* promoted after play-offs

Odds & ends

Double wins: (4) Burnley, Gillingham, Stoke, Watford.
Double losses: (1) Preston.

Won from behind: (2) Watford (h), Wigan (a).
Lost from in front: (3) Coventry (a), Nott'm Forest (a), Sunderland (h).

High spots: Promotion after two seasons out of the Premiership.
Three straight wins in February.
One defeat in the last 10, to secure a play-off spot on the last day.

Departure of the under-rated Michael Carrick.
Dreadful run of three defeats and two draws in February and March.

Hammer of the Year: Teddy Sheringham.
Ever-presents: (0).
Hat-tricks: (0).
Leading scorer: (22) Marlon Harewood.

	Appearances								Goals				
	Lge	*Sub*	LC	*Sub*	FAC	*Sub*	PO	*Sub*	Lge	LC	FAC	PO	Tot
Brevett, Rufus	10		3						1				1
Bywater, Stephen	36				2			*1*					
Chadwick, Luke	22	*10*	1		3				1				1
Cohen, Chris	1	*10*	1	*1*		*1*							
Dailly, Christian	2	*1*						*2*					
Davenport, Calum	10												
Etherington, Matthew	37	*2*	2				3		4				4
Ferdinand, Anton	24	*5*	1		3		3		1				1
Fletcher, Carl	26	*6*			3		1		2				2
Garcia, Richard		*1*											
Harewood, Marlon	45		3		3		3		17	2	2	1	22
Hutchison, Don	2	*3*		*1*									
Lomas, Steve	18	*5*	2						1				1
MacKay, Malky	17	*1*	1		3				2				2
McAnuff, Jobi		*1*											
McClenahan, Trent		*2*	1										
Melville, Andy	3			*1*									
Mullins, Hayden	32	*5*	2		2	*1*	3		1				1
Newton, Shaun	11						2	*1*					
Noble, Mark	10	*3*		*2*	3			*3*					
Nowland, Adam	3	*1*	2						1				1
Powell, Chris	35	*1*			3		3						
Powell, Darren	5								1				1
Rebrov, Sergei	12	*14*	2	*1*	1	*1*		*1*	1	1			2
Reo-Coker, Nigel	34	*5*	3		1	*1*	3		3				3
Repka, Tomas	42		3		3		3						
Sheringham, Teddy	26	*7*		*1*	2				20		1		21
Taricco, Mauricio	1												
Walker, James	10		3		1		3						
Ward, Elliott	10	*1*	1				3						
Williams, Gavin	7	*3*							1				1
Zamora, Bobby	15	*19*	2				3		7	2		4	13
(own-goals)									2				2
32 players used	**506**	***105***	**33**	***7***	**33**	***4***	**33**	***8***	**66**	**5**	**3**	**5**	**79**

No	Date		Att	Pos	Pt	F-A	H-T	Scorers, Times, and Referees	SQUAD	NUMBERS	IN	USE								subs used
1	H	BLACKBURN			W	3-1	0-1	Sheringham 46, Reo-Coker 62	**Carroll**	Dailly	**Konchesky**	**Gabbidon**	Ferdinand	Mullins*	**Benayoun**	Reo-Coker	Harewood	Shering'm^	Etherington	Noble/Newton
	13/8		33,305		3			*Todd 18* [Etherington 80]	*Friedel*	*Neill*	*Matteo*	*Savage*	*Todd*	*Mokoena**	*Emerton*	*Reid*	*Bellamy*	*Kuqi^*	*Pedersen*	*Dickov !/Gresco*
								Ref: A Wiley	Winning by two goals puts the Hammers top of the table. Todd had capitalised on a bad clearance from a corner but debutant Benayoun created two goals. In between, Reo-Coker put with West Ham ahead with a belter. Rovers' sub Dickov saw red for a two-footed lunge at Konchesky.											
2	A	NEWCASTLE		5	D	0-0	0-0		Carroll	Repka	Konchesky	!Gabbidon	Ferdinand	Mullins	Benayoun*	Reo-Coker	Harewoo"	Shering'm^	Etherington	Dailly/Newton/Zamora
	20/8		*51,620*	*17*	4				*Given*	*Carr*	*Babayaro*	*Parker*	*Taylor*	*Boumsong*	*Milner*	*Jenas*	*Shearer*	*Bowyer*	*N'Zogbia**	*Clark*
								Ref: D Gallagher	Toonside jeered boss Graeme Souness after this abject match. Benayoun and Sheringham looked sharp, but Hammers had their backs to the wall after Konchesky was sent off for fouling Jenas, despite claiming to have won the ball. Pardew is hunting Dean Ashton of Norwich City.											
3	H	BOLTON		8	L	1-2	0-0	Sheringham 90p	Carroll	Repka	Konchesky	Gabbidon^	Ferdinand	Mullins	Benayoun	Reo-Coker	Harewood*	Sheringham	Ethering'n"	Zamora/Ward/**Aliadiere**
	27/8		31,629	*5*	4			*Nolan 59, Campo 85*	*Jaaskelain' Hunt*		*Pedersen*	*Speed*	*Ben Haim*	*N'Gotty*	*Okocha"*	*Nolan*	*Diouf**	*Davies^*	*Giannakop'*	*Campo/Diag'-Faye/Borgetti*
								Ref: P Dowd	West Ham were getting on top when Bolton sub Campo came on, thumped the bar from 35 yards, and turned the tide. Following Nolan's opener, Campo played a one-two with Okocha for the decisive second. Harewood and Zamora were off the pace, but Sheringham hit the bar.											
4	H	ASTON VILLA		7	W	**4-0**	2-0	Harewood 25, 29, 50, Benayoun 89	Carroll	Repka	Konchesky	Gabbidon	Ferdinand	Mullins*	Benayoun	Reo-Coker	Harewood^	Sheringham	Ethering'n"	Dailly/Zamora/Newton
	12/9		**29,582**	*14*	7				*Sorensen*	*Hughes*	*Bouma*	*Davis*	*Mellberg*	*Ridgewell*	*Milner*	*McCann"*	*Baros*	*Phillips**	*Barry^*	*Angel/Berger/Hendrie*
								Ref: R Styles	Pardew's 100th game in charge brings what will be their biggest win of the season. Harewood's last goal in the top division was back in 1998. His hat-trick was bread and butter stuff, leaving the best goal for Benayoun – his first for the club. Villa's David O'Leary moans at his players.											
5	A	FULHAM		6	W	2-1	0-0	Harewood 46, Warner 52 (og)	Carroll	Repka	Konchesky	Gabbidon	Ferdinand	Mullins	Benayoun*	Reo-Coker	Harewood"	Zamora^	Etherington	Shering'/Newton/Aliadiere
	17/9		*21,907*	*16*	10			*Boa Morte 66*	*Warner*	*Volz*	*Jensen*	*Diop*	*Knight ^*	*Bocanegra*	*Malbranque*	*Jensen*	*McBride*	*Radzinski**	*Boa Morte*	*John/Christanval*
								Ref: G Poll	West Ham rode their luck before Harewood – apparently the team's dressing-room 'music master'– dumped Zak Knight on his backside before opening the scoring, then fired against a post and saw the ball bounce in off keeper Warner's head. Boa Morte's curler led to an anxious finish.											
6	H	ARSENAL		4	D	0-0	0-0		Carroll	Repka	Konchesky	Gabbidon	Ferdinand	Mullins	Benayoun	Reo-Coker	Harewood	Shering'm*	Ethering'n^	Zamora/Newton
	24/9		34,742	*7*	11				*Lehmann*	*Lauren*	*Cole*	*Silva**	*Toure*	*Campbell*	*Ljungberg*	*Fabregas*	*Reyes"*	*VanPersie^*	*Hleb*	*Flamini/Clichy/Owusu/*
								Ref: M Dean	Arsenal's first away point in three games should have been cause for Hammers' dismay rather than congratulations. West Ham were grateful that Henry was out, injured, but this match showed more heat than light. West Ham registered no shots on target at all, Arsenal merely two.											
7	A	SUNDERLAND		9	D	1-1	0-1	Benayoun 72	Carroll	Repka*	Konchesky	Gabbidon	Ferdinand	Mullins	Benayoun	Reo-Coker	Harewood	Shering'm^	Ethering'n"	Dailly/Zamora/Newton
	1/10		*31,212*	*17*	12			*Miller 45*	*Davis*	*Nosworthy*	*Hoyte*	*Bassila**	*Breen*	*Caldwell*	*Whitehead*	*Miller*	*Elliott*	*Gray*	*Welsh^*	*Lawrence/Murphy*
								Ref: M Atkinson	McCarthy's promoted Sunderland pick up their second home point in four games and perhaps deserved all three. Tommy Miller's crisp goal on half-time looked likely to be decisive until Benayoun broke forward to equalise. West Ham become just one of five teams not to win up here.											
8	A	MANCHESTER C		9	L	1-2	0-1	Zamora 90	Carroll	Repka*	Konchesky	Gabbidon	Ferdinand	Mullins	Benayoun	Reo-Coker	Harewood	Shering'm^	Ethering'n"	Dailly/Zamora/Newton
	16/10		*43,647*	*4*	12			*Cole 18, 56*	*James*	*Mills*	*Jordan*	*Onuoha*	*Distin*	*Barton*	*Ireland**	*Reyna*	*Cole*	*Vassell*	*Musampa^*	*Croft/Jihai*
								Ref: M Clattenburg	Stuart Pearce has lifted City up to fourth, helped by two strikes by the rejuvenated Andrew Cole, as West Ham sink to their first away defeat. Cole's neat exchange with Vassell threatened a rout. It might have ended 6-0 rather than 2-1, when Zamora rounded ex-Hammer David James.											
9	H	MIDDLESBROUGH		9	W	2-1	0-0	Sheringham 66, Riggott 74 (og)	Hislop	Repka	Konchesky	Gabbidon	Ferdinand	Mullins	Benayoun*	Reo-Coker	Harewood	Zamora^	Ethering'n"	Dailly/Sheringh'm/Newton
	23/10		34,612	*12*	15			*Queudrue 87*	*Schwarzer*	*Bates*	*Pogatetz*	*Doriva"*	*Riggott*	*Southgate**	*Mendieta*	*Boateng*	*Yakubu*	*Mac'arone^*	*Roch'back*	*Queudrue/Hasselb'k/Viduka*
								Ref: S Bennett	West Ham will enjoy an amazing seven own-goals this season and go 2-0 up when Riggott diverts Konchesky's free-kick 'over' the line before Schwarzer grabbed it. McLaren's fury and Pardew's wry smile told of a phantom goal. Boro looked fatigued by their midweek UEFA Cup-tie.											
10	A	LIVERPOOL		9	L	0-2	0-1		Hislop	Repka"	Konchesky	Gabbidon	Ferdinand	Mullins	Benayoun	Reo-Coker	Harewood	**Bellion**^	Ethering'n*	Shering'm/Aliadiere/Collins
	29/10		*44,537*	*13*	15			*Xabi Alonso 18, Zenden 82*	*Reina*	*Finnan*	*Riise*	*Xabi Alonso*	*Carragher*	*Hyppia*	*Sissoko*	*Gerrard*	*Cisse**	*Morientes^*	*Luis Garcia*	*Zenden/Crouch*
								Ref: U Rennie	Benitez's job is on the line. Liverpool are in the bottom half, and this is only their third win in nine. West Ham had few complaints after Xabi Alonso smacked the opening goal through a packed penalty area. West Ham's record of two shots on target explains their lack of penetration.											

No	Venue	Opponent	Att	Pos	Res	Pts	FT	HT	Scorers, Times, and Referees	1	2	3	4	5	6	7	8	9	10	11	Subs used
11	H	WEST BROM		9	W		1-0	0-0	Sheringham 57	Hislop"	Repka	Konchesky	Gabbidon	Ferdinand	Mullins	Benayoun^	Reo-Coker*	Harewood	Sheringham	Etherington	Dailly/Newton/Bywater
	5/11		34,325	18		18				Kuszczak	Watson	Albrechtsen	Wallwork	Davies	Clement	Kamara	Inamoto	Kanu*	Earnshaw^	Greening	Campbell/Horsfield
									Ref: P Walton	West Brom's one goal in six away games explains why Bryan Robson's team failed to score. Hammers created and missed so many chances that Pardew ordered that the huge screens stop replaying them. After Sheringham broke through, it was Albion's turn to miss good chances.											
12	A	TOTTENHAM		8	D		1-1	0-1	Ferdinand 90	Hislop	Repka"	Konchesky	Gabbidon	Ferdinand	Mullins	Benayoun	Noble	Harewood*	Sheringham	Ethering'n^	Zamora/Bellion/Newton
	20/11		36,154	6		19			Mido 16	Robinson	Staltieri	Lee	King	Dawson	Tainio^	Jenas	Carrick	Mido	Keane*	Davids	Defoe/Lennon
									Ref: A Wiley	Six players faced their former clubs, all 'Judas's' with a point to prove. In the past two matches between these sides Sheringham had netted for Spurs and Carrick for West Ham. Mido's looping header was cancelled out by Anton Ferdinand, helped by Hislop coming upfield for a corner.											
13	H	MANCHESTER U		9	L		1-2	1-0	Harewood 1	Carroll	Repka	Konchesky	Gabbidon	Ferdinand	Mullins^	Benayoun	Noble	Harewood	Shering'm*	Ethering'n"	Dailly/Zamora/Newton
	27/11		34,755	2		19			Rooney 47, O'Shea 56	Van der Sar	Brown	O'Shea	Smith	Ferdinand	Silvestre*	Fletcher	Scholes	V Nistelr'y^	Rooney	Park	Neville G/Richardson
									Ref: S Bennett	Harewood's 52-second goal, set up by Etherington, is only the third first-half Hammers goal all season. Man U always win when Rooney nets, so his strike, set up by Park Ji Sung, set a predictable tone. Man of the match Rooney might have had three before O'Shea's winning header.											
14	A	BIRMINGHAM		9	W		2-1	2-1	Zamora 36, Harewood 45	Carroll	Repka	Konchesky	Gabbidon	Ferdinand	Mullins	Benayoun^	Noble*	Harewood	Zamora"	Etherington	Dailly/Newton/Bellion
	5/12		24,010	19		22			Heskey 11	Vaesen	Melchiot^	Cunningh'm	Izzet*	Upson	Taylor"	Pennant	Johnson	Heskey	Dunn	Gray	Butt/Lazaridis/Kilkenny
									Ref: M Atkinson	Steve Bruce's City have now taken just one point from seven home games, yet ex-England Heskey marked his 350th League appearance by ghosting past Carroll. Zamora equalised by scoring through Vaesen's legs, and Etherington's cross somehow arrived at the feet of Harewood.											
15	A	BLACKBURN		9	L		2-3	1-0	Zamora 45, Harewood 63	Carroll	Repka	Konchesky	Gabbidon*	Ferdinand	Mullins	Benayoun	Noble^	Harewood	Zamora"	Etherington	Dailly/Bellion/Aliadiere
	10/12		20,370	12		22			Dickov 56p 57, Kuqi 76	Friedel	Neill	Gray	Savage	Khizanish'	Tugay*	Emerton^	Reid	Dickov	Bentley"	Pedersen	Mokoena/Kuqi/Jansen
									Ref: M Riley	After Gabbidon badly gashed his knee, Zamora scored from West Ham's first goal-attempt. Repka's handball was innocent, insisted Pardew, and Dickov poached another seconds later. Harewood's header made West Ham the likely winners, but they lost when Kuqi muscled through.											
16	A	EVERTON		7	W		2-1	1-1	Weir 19 (og), Zamora 67	Carroll	Repka	Konchesky	Collins	Ferdinand	Mullins	Benayoun	Fletcher	Harewood	Zamora^	Ethering'n*	Dailly/Newton
	14/12		35,704	15		25			Beattie 9	Wright	Hibbert*	NunoValente	Yobo	Weir	Neville	Osman	Davies	Beattie	McFadden"	Kilbane^	Arteta/Ferguson/Bent
									Ref: P Walton	Three away games in a row sees West Ham rack up six points. As at Birmingham, they recovered from falling behind – to Beattie's first-time left-footer. Home skipper David Weir then sliced Repka's cross over his keeper's head, and Zamora pounced after Wright's failure to clear.											
17	H	NEWCASTLE		9	L		2-4	1-2	Solano 20 (og), Harewood 73p	Carroll	Repka*	Konchesky	Collins	Ferdinand	Mullins	Benayoun^	Fletcher	Harewood	Zamora	Etherington	Aliadiere/Bellion
	17/12		34,836	10		25			Owen 5, 43, 90, Shearer 66	Given	Ramage	Elliott	Faye	Bramble	Boumsong	Solano*	Parker	Shearer	Owen	Ameobi	Bowyer
									Ref: P Dowd	Alan Shearer's 199th Newcastle goal was eclipsed by Michael Owen's hat-trick. Such a pairing was far too savvy for the raw Ferdinand and Collins. Hammers enjoyed Bramble driving the ball against Solano for an own-goal, and Ameobi's handball for the penalty, but not much else.											
18	A	PORTSMOUTH		9	D		1-1	0-1	Collins 56	Carroll	Repka*	Konchesky	Collins	Ferdinand	Mullins"	Newton	Reo-Coker	Harewood	Zamora	Etherington	Gabbidon^/Dailly/Fletcher
	26/12		20,168	18		26			O'Neil 17	Ashdown	Primus^	Griffin	Hughes	O'Brien	Stefanovic	Taylor	O'Neil	DarioSilva*	Lua-Lua	Robert !	Viafara/Priske
									Ref: A Wiley	Pardew has to use all three subs in the first half, as Mullins (illness), Repka (hamstring) and Gabbidon (gashed knee) all had to depart. Dario Silva's step-over enabled O'Neil to fire Pompey ahead. They might have had more and paid for it when Collins fired in Ferdinand's knock-on.											
19	H	WIGAN		9	L		0-2	0-2		Carroll	Dailly	Konchesky	Collins	Ferdinand	Mullins	Bellion*	Reo-Coker	Harewood"	Fletcher^	Etherington	Newton/Zamora/Aliadiere
	28/12		34,131	5		26			Roberts 43, Camara 45	Pollitt	Chimbonda	Baines	Kavanagh	Jackson	De Zeeuw	Teale*	Bullard	Camara^	Roberts	McCulloch	Francis/Connolly
									Ref: S Bennett	Newcomers Wigan are going well, particularly away from home. Roberts and Camara both notched their fifth goal in three games to settle the outcome late in the first half. Roberts bullied his way past Collins and Camara danced round Carroll. Zamora missed a sitter; Dailly was booed.											
20	A	CHARLTON		10	L		0-2	0-1		Carroll	Dailly*	Konchesky	Collins	Ferdinand	Mullins	Newton	Reo-Coker	Harewood	Aliadiere^	Etherington	Benayoun/Bellion
	31/12		25,952	12		26			Bartlett 21, Bent 63	Myhre	Young	Powell	Holland	Fortune	Hreidarsson	Kishishev	Rommedahl	Bent D	Bartlett*	Hughes	Lisbie
									Ref: G Poll	Darren Bent made and scored the goals that sank West Ham, crossing for Shaun Bartlett, then sealing things with a neat header. Curbishley's Addicks arrest their slide following a fine start to the season. This is only their third home win in ten games, as West Ham ran out of ideas.											
21	H	CHELSEA		10	L		1-3	0-1	Harewood 46	Carroll	Dailly	Konchesky	Collins	Ferdinand	Mullins*	Benayoun	Reo-Coker	Harewood	Fletcher	Ethering'n^	Zamora/Bellion
	2/1		34,758	1		26			Lampard 25, Crespo 61, Drogba 80	Cech	Geremi	Del Horno	Makelele	Terry	Carvalho	Duff*	Lampard	Drogba	Essien"	Robben	Crespo^/W-Phillips/Gudj'n
									Ref: H Webb	Chelsea go 14 points clear at the top. Mourinho rages at Reo-Coker's foul on Essien that will put the Ghanain out of the African Nations Cup. Lampard's volley – his first goal against Hammers – was met with 'You're just a fat Paul Ince'. Crespo nets within 30 seconds of coming on.											

No	Date		Att	Pos	Pt	F-A	H-T	Scorers, Times, and Referees	SQUAD	NUMBERS	IN	USE								subs used
22	A	ASTON VILLA		10	W	2-1	0-1	Zamora 51, Harewood 60p	Carroll	Repka	Konchesky	Gabbidon	Ferdinand	Mullins	Newton^	Reo-Coker	Harewood	Zamora"	Ethering'n*	Dailly/Benayoun/**Katan**
	14/1		*36,700*	*15*	29			*Hendrie 27*	*Sorensen*	*Hughes*	*Samuel*	*Davis*	*Mellberg*	*Delaney*	*Milner*	*McCann*	*Baros*	*Moore**	*Bakke^*	*Angel/Hendrie*
								Ref: P Dowd	Villa are rumoured to have Sven Goran-Eriksson as their new manager. Sub Hendrie heads his first goal for a year, from Jlloyd Samuel's cross. Zamora, who specialises in away goals, headed in Konchesky's free-kick, and Mark Delaney handled Mullins' shot for the decisive penalty.											
23	H	FULHAM		9	W	2-1	2-0	Ferdinand 17, Benayoun 28	Carroll	Repka	Konchesky	Gabbidon	Ferdinand	Mullins	Benayoun"	Reo-Coker	Harewood	Zamora*	Ethering'^	Dailly/Newton/Katan
	23/1		29,812	*13*	32			*Helguson 52*	*Niemi*	*Rosenior*	*Bridge*	*Elliott*	*Knight*	*Bocanegra*	*Legwinski*	*Malbr'que**	*McBride^*	*Helguson*	*Boa Morte*	*Radzinski/John*
								Ref: U Rennie	Anton's volley from Niemi's fist-out is candidate for Goal of the Season and sets West Ham up after four straight home defeats. Benayoun bamboozled Wayne Bridge – his on-loan debut for Fulham – before chipping Niemi. Repka's farewell after getting 55 yellow and 5 red cards.											
24	A	ARSENAL		9	W	3-2	2-1	Reo-Cok' 25, Zamora 32, Ether'n 80	Hislop	Clarke^	Konchesky	Gabbidon	Ferdinand	Mullins	Benayoun*	Reo-Coker	Harewood	Zamora"	Etherington	Newton/Fletcher/**Ashton**
	1/2		*38,216*	*6*	35			*Henry 45, Pires 89*	*Lehmann*	*Gilbert^*	*Senderos*	*Silva*	*Djourou*	*Campbell"*	*Ljungberg*	*Diaby**	*Van Persie*	*Henry*	*Pires*	*Bergkamp/Flamini/Larsson*
								Ref: M Halsey	Arsenal's last season at Highbury, where they will only lose twice. This match centred on Sol Campbell – out-paced by Reo-Coker for the first goal, muscled off the ball by Zamora for the second – who vanishes into the night at half-time. Henry's 151st League goal passes Cliff Bastin.											
25	H	SUNDERLAND		8	W	2-0	0-0	Ashton 81, Konchesky 87	Hislop	**Scaloni**	Konchesky	Gabbidon	Ferdinand	Mullins^	Benayoun	Reo-Coker	Ashton*	Zamora"	Etherington	Dailly/Harewood/Shering'
	4/2		34,745	*20*	38				*Davis*	*Wright !*	*McCartney*	*Lawrence**	*Breen*	*Caldwell*	*Whitehead*	*Bassila*	*Kyle*	*Le Tallac^*	*Arca"*	*Stead/Nosworthy/Woods*
								Ref: R Styles	Sunderland will create a new low-points record, but it was still 0-0 after 80 minutes, despite Wright's expulsion on 24 minutes for two yellows. This win was West Ham's sixth in a row in all competitions, a feat not achieved for 20 years. Davis parried Harewood's shot out to Ashton.											
26	H	BIRMINGHAM		6	W	3-0	1-0	Harewood 11, 63, Ashton 65	Hislop	Scaloni	Konchesky	Gabbidon	Ferdinand	Mullins*	Benayoun	Reo-Coker	Harewood	Ashton^	Ethering'n"	Dailly/Zamora/Katan
	13/2		31,294	*18*	41				*Taylor Maik*	*Melchiot*	*Gray*	*Clemence*	*Latka**	*Cunningh'm*	*Pennant*	*Bruce*	*Sutton*	*Forssell"*	*Jarosik^*	*Clapham/Painter/Campbell*
								Ref: D Gallagher	West Ham's seventh successive win lifts them to sixth, within sight of the UEFA Cup, yet they are only the fourth best team in London! Ron Greenwood has died. Reo-Coker's shot ricocheted to Harewood. Latka then handled: Harewood's kick was saved but he poached the rebound.											
27	H	EVERTON		8	D	2-2	2-1	Harewood 10, Ashton 23	Hislop	Scaloni	Konchesky	Gabbidon	Ferdinand	Mullins	Benayoun^	Reo-Coker	Harewood	Ashton*	Ethering'n"	Shering'/Zamora/Newton
	4/3		34,866	*12*	42			*Osman 18, Beattie 71*	*Westerveld*	*Hibbert*	*NunoValente*	*Stubbs*	*Weir*	*Arteta^*	*Osman*	*Neville*	*Beattie*	*Cahill*	*McFadden**	*Davies/Kilbane*
								Ref: M Riley	Sven Goran-Eriksson watches Everton's man of the match, Phil Neville, but won't pick him. Best of the goals were both Everton's equalisers. Ashton had restored West Ham's lead from a tight angle, Beattie's delicate chip made it 2-2, and Everton might have nicked it at the death.											
28	A	BOLTON		9	L	**1-4**	0-3	Sheringham 79	Hislop	Scaloni	Konchesky	Gabbidon	Ferdinand	Ward*	Newton^	Mullins	Zamora	Sheringham	Etherington	Dailly/Benayoun
	11/3		*24,461*	*6*	42			*Gianna' 12, 23, Speed 45, Pedersen 81*	*Jaaskelain'*	*O'Brien**	*Gardner*	*Speed*	*Ben Haim*	*Jaidi*	*Okocha"*	*Vaz Te*	*Nolan*	*Davies*	*Giannakop^*	*Hunt/Pedersen/Nakata*
								Ref: M Dean	Hammers' biggest defeat of the season, having drawn 0-0 in the Cup three weeks earlier. The replay is in four days' time. Pardew's team had eight English starts, but quickly trailed by two goals from Giannakopoulos, a tap-in and a diversion. Bolton are unbeaten at home in 20 games.											
29	H	PORTSMOUTH		10	L	2-4	0-3	Shering' 69, Benay'n 90 *[Todorov 77]*	Walker	Scaloni	Konchesky	Gabbidon	Ferdinand"	Dailly	Katan^	Reo-Coker	Zamora	Sheringham	Clarke*	Benay'n/Harew'd/Fletcher
	18/3		34,837	*19*	42			*Lua-Lua 19, Davis 25, Mendes 42,*	*Kiely*	*Priske*	*Taylor*	*Davis*	*O'Brien*	*Primus*	*O'Neil*	*P Mendes*	*Mwar'wari**	*Lua-Lua*	*D'Alessand'*	*Todorov/*
								Ref: A Wiley	On his first return to Upton Park, Redknapp's Pompey – next to bottom and looking doomed – exploit Hammers' Cup distractions, the quarter-final is two days away. Taylor set up Lua-Lua, Priske centred for Davis, and Petro Mendes unleashed one of his specials – 0-3 after 42 minutes.											
30	A	WIGAN		9	W	2-1	0-1	Harewood 52, Reo-Coker 90	Hislop	Scaloni	Konchesky	Gabbidon	Collins	Mullins	Benayoun^	Reo-Coker	Harewood	Ashton*	Ethering'n"	Shering'/Newton/Zamora
	25/3		***18,736***	*8*	45			*McCulloch 45*	*Filan"*	*Chimbonda*	*Baines*	*Kavanagh^*	*Scharner*	*De Zeeuw*	*Teale**	*Bullard*	*Camara*	*Roberts*	*McCulloch*	*Thompson/Ziegler/Pollitt*
								Ref: D Gallagher	McCulloch's eighteen-yard drive put Paul Jewell's side ahead. Harewood put the ball into an empty net after sub keeper Pollitt and Scharner got into a tizzy. 'Superman' Sheringham then comes off the bench to swap passes with Harewood and cross for Reo-Coker to net from close in.											
31	A	MANCHESTER U		9	L	0-1	0-1		Hislop	Scaloni*	Konchesky	Gabbidon	Collins	Mullins	Benayoun	Reo-Coker	Harewood	Ashton^	Ethering'n"	Ferdin'd/Shering'/Zamora
	29/3		***69,522***	*2*	45			*Van Nistelrooy 45*	*Van der Sar*	*O'Shea*	*Evra**	*Pique*	*Ferdinand*	*Vidic*	*Ronaldo"*	*Fletcher^*	*V Nistelro'y*	*Rooney*	*Park*	*Silvestre/Giggs/Saha*
								Ref: G Poll /M Atkinson	Van Nistelrooy returns, as captain, after six weeks cast out by Fergie and scores the only goal – his 149th for Man U – for their seventh straight win. Hammers fans sang 'Fortune's Always Hiding'. It might have been worse: Vidic hit the post, Rooney the bar. Ref Poll pulled a hamstring.											

No	Venue / Date	Opponent / Attendance	Pos	Res / Pts	FT	HT	Scorers, Times, and Referees	1	2	3	4	5	6	7	8	9	10	11	subs used
32	H	CHARLTON	8	D	0-0	0-0		Hislop	Ferdinand	Konchesky	Gabbidon	Collins	Mullins	Benayoun	Reo-Coker^	Harewood"	Ashton*	Etherington	Sheringh'm/Zamora/Katan
	2/4	34,753	*11*	46				*Myhre*	*Young^*	*Powell*	*Holland*	*Perry*	*Hreidarsson*	*Kishishev*	*Hughes*	*Bent D*	*Bent M"*	*Rom'edahl**	*Thomas/Spector/Bothroyd*
							Ref: R Styles	Sheringham's 40th birthday failed to produce a goal. This somnolent game reminded us of Scaloni's claim to have slept in a Hammers' replica shirt when hearing that they wanted to sign him. Both clubs are still alive in the FA Cup, perhaps that is why this was such a shapeless contest.											
33	A	CHELSEA	9	L	**1-4**	1-2	Collins 10 *[Gallas 69]*	Hislop	Scaloni	Konchesky	Gabbidon	Collins	Mullins	Benayoun*	Reo-Coker	Harewood	Ashton^	Etherington	Sheringham/Zamora
	9/4	*41,919*	*1*	46			*Drogba 28, Crespo 31, Terry 54,*	*Cech*	*Geremi*	*Del Horno*	*Makelele*	*Terry*	*Gallas*	*Maniche !*	*Lampard*	*Drogba**	*Crespo^*	*Essien"*	*Cole/Robben/Carvalho*
							Ref: C Foy	Chelsea only registered five shots on target, but scored from four. West Ham were a goal and a man to the good – Collins heading in before on-loan Maniche went over-the-top on Scaloni – but Didier Drogba scored at the second attempt, then crossed for Crespo's tap in before half-time.											
34	H	MANCHESTER C	7	W	1-0	1-0	Newton 7	Walker	Scaloni	Konchesky	Gabbidon	Collins	Mullins	Benayoun	Reo-Coker	Zamora*	Ashton^	Newton"	Harew'd/Shering'/Fletcher
	15/4	34,305	*13*	49				*James*	*Richards*	*Thatcher^*	*Dunne*	*Distin*	*Reyna"*	*Sinclair*	*Musampa*	*Samaras**	*Vassell*	*Riera*	*Sibierski/Sommeil/Flood*
							Ref: S Bennett	Zamora turned and passed for Newton to fire West Ham ahead. City boss Stuart Pearce was aggrieved twice, when 'goals' from ex-Hammer Sinclair and Vassell were ruled out by linesman's flags. West Ham's attention now switches to two successive matches against Middlesbrough.											
35	A	MIDDLESBROUGH	9	L	0-2	0-1		Hislop	Scaloni^	Konchesky	Gabbidon	Collins	Mullins	Newton	Reo-Coker	Harewood"	Sheringham	Katan*	Zamora/Fletcher/Ashton
	17/4	*27,658*	*13*	49			*Hasselbaink 41, Maccarone 57p*	*Schwarzer*	*Bates*	*Queudrue*	*Wheater*	*Riggott*	*Doriva*	*Maccarone*	*Parlour*	*Hasselb'k**	*Viduka"*	*Johnson^*	*Kenneay/Taylor/Christie*
							Ref: M Atkinson	Six days later these teams meet in the FA Cup semi-final. In between Boro face Steaua Bucharest in the UEFA Cup semis in the biggest week in their history. Their win makes their survival mathematically sure, but late chances by Sheringham and sub Ashton almost rescued a point.											
36	H	LIVERPOOL	10	L	1-2	0-1	Reo-Coker 46	Walker	Scaloni	Ward	Collins^	Ferdinand	Mullins !	Benayoun*	Reo-Coker	Zamora	Sheringham	Etherington	Harewood/Fletcher
	26/4	34,852	*3*	49			*Cisse 19, 54*	*Dudek*	*Finnan**	*Traore*	*Hamann*	*Carragher*	*Kromkamp*	*Sissoko*	*Cisse*	*Fowler^*	*Morientes"*	*Warnock*	*Hyppia/Luis Garcia !/Riise*
							Ref: H Webb	West Ham lost to Bolton and Boro in the League just prior to beating them in the Cup, so losing to Liverpool might have a silver lining. And it almost did. Luis Garcia clashed with Mullins near the end, both saw red, and miss the final. Cisse's goals gave Liverpool a ninth straight win.											
37	A	WEST BROM	9	W	1-0	1-0	Reo-Coker 42	Hislop	Scaloni	Dailly*	Gabbidon	Ward	Fletcher	Newton	Reo-Coker	Zamora^	Ashton"	**Reid**	Konch'ky/Harew'd/Shering'
	1/5	*24,462*	*19*	52				*Kuszczak*	*Albrechtsen*	*Robinson*	*Wallwork*	*Davies*	*Watson*	*Clement*	*Quashie*	*Ellington*	*Kanu*	*Greening*	
							Ref: G Poll	Bryan Robson's Albion become the only side this season not to use any subs against West Ham. They are already relegated and Robson was greeted with chants of 'Taxi for Robbo'. Ellington might have had a hat-trick, Albion might have had two penalties, Ashton goes off injured.											
38	H	TOTTENHAM	9	W	2-1	1-1	Fletcher 10, Benayoun 80	Hislop	Scaloni	Konchesky	Gabbidon	Ferdinand	Fletcher	Newton	Reo-Coker	Zamora	Shering'm*	Benayoun^	Harewood/Reid
	7/5	**34,970**	*5*	55			*Defoe 35*	*Robinson*	*Kelly*	*Lee"*	*Gardner*	*Dawson*	*Lennon*	*Tainio^*	*Carrick**	*Keane*	*Defoe*	*Davids*	*Reid/Davenport/Bernard*
	Home	Away					Ref: C Foy	Spurs are down with food-poisoning and want the game off. In fact it was a bug spread internally. West Ham's win knocks Spurs out of the Champions League placings in favour of Arsenal. Robinson saved Sheringham's penalty at 1-1 but Benayoun eluded Dawson for the winner.											
Average	33,743	33,524																	

Carling Cup			Att			F-A	H-T	Scorers, Times, and Referees	SQUAD	NUMBERS	IN	USE								subs used
2	A	SHEFFIELD WED		6	W	4-2	1-0	Zamora 2, 63, Dailly 54, Bellion 84	Hislop	Repka*	Collins	Williams^	Cohen	Ward	Newton	Dailly	Harewood"	Zamora	Noble	**Stokes/Ephraim**/Bellion
		20/9	14,976	C:24				Coughlan 76, Graham 77	Lucas	Ross	Bullen	Whelan*	Coughlan	Wood	McGovern^	Rocastle	Graham	Corr"	Brunt	O'Brien/Hills/Peacock
								Ref: S Tanner	Paul Sturrock's Owls are bottom of the Championship and fall behind after 75 seconds. Dailly's bullet header and Zamora's lazy half-volley from 25 yards appear to settle the tie, but stopper Coughlan powers in a header and Graham smacks in another seconds later to make it 2-3.											
3	A	BOLTON		9	L	0-1	0-0		Hislop	Repka	Collins	Konchesky	Bellion	Ward	Mullins	Dailly	Harewood*	Shering'm^	Clarke"	Fletcher/Aliadiere/Newton
		26/10	10,927	7				Borgetti 64	Walker	O'Brien	Gardner	Diag'-Faye*	Ben Haim	Jaidi	Fernandes^	Nolan	Borgetti	Fadiga	Giannakop"	Djetou/N'Gotty/Pedersen
								Ref: A Marriner	These teams will meet in both cups this season. First blood to Allardyce's Bolton, courtesy of Mexican striker Jared Borgetti, who follows two UEFA Cup goals by squeezing past Collins for the crucial far-post header. West Ham had created and wasted most of the chances of a poor tie.											

FA Cup																				
3	A	NORWICH		10	W	2-1	1-0	Mullins 6, Zamora 57	Hislop	Repka	Konchesky	Collins	Gabbidon	Mullins*	Newton	Reo-Coker	Harewood	Zamora^	Ethering'n"	Fletcher/Katan/Dailly
		7/1	23,968	C:11				McVeigh 72p	Green*	Jarrett^	Drury	Fleming	Doherty	Charlton	Henderson	Jarvis Ros"	McVeigh	Thorne	Etuhu	Ward/Spillane/Cave-Brown
								Ref: M Riley	Future Hammers Green and Ashton are in the wars. The keeper collided with Harewood's knee: the striker was absent through a groin strain to prevent being Cup-tied in the transfer window. Zamora set up Mullins, then headed a second. 'We want to go to the final and win it' – Pardew.											
4	H	BLACKBURN		10	W	4-2	2-1	Shering' 33p, Ethering' 37, Khiz' 59(og)	Hislop	Dailly	Konchesky	Gabbidon	Ferdinand	Mullins	Benayoun*	Reo-Coker	Zamora^	Shering'm"	Etherington	Fletcher/Katan/Harewood
		28/1	23,700	8				Bentley 1, Neill 65 [Zamora 73]	Friedel	Neill	Gray	Mokoena*	Todd	Khizanish'	Reid	Savage	Bentley^	Kuqi"	Pedersen	Tugay/Johnson/Emerton
								Ref: M Atkinson	Repka has joined Sparta Prague, Dailly filled in at right-back and got booed for his pains. Dean Ashton, £7.25 million, watched Sheringham's cheeky penalty for handball cancel out Rovers' 27-seconed opener. The floodlights went off at 3-2, but came on again for Zamora to clinch it.											
5	A	BOLTON		6	D	0-0	0-0		Hislop	Scaloni	Konchesky	Gabbidon	Ferdinand	Mullins	Benayoun*	Reo-Coker	Harewood^	Ashton"	Etherington	Dailly/Zamora/Sheringham
		18/2	17,120	9					Jaaskelain'	O'Brien	Gardner	Speed	Ben Haim	Jaidi	Okacha	Nakata	Nolan	Davies*	Giannakop^	Borgetti/Vaz Te
								Ref: C Foy	Hammers' winning run comes to an end in this turgid Cup-tie but it could have been worse. Scaloni's tug on Giannakopoulos's shoulder would have merited a penalty but for the Greek spinning in the air as if shot. Hammers' best chance was headed wide by Ashton in the second half.											
5R	H	BOLTON		9	W	2-1	1-1	Jaaskelainen 10 (og), Harewood 96	Hislop	Scaloni	Konchesky	Gabbidon	Ferdinand	Mullins	Benayoun	Reo-Coker*	Harewood	Ashton^	Ethering'n"	Dailly/Sheringham/Zamora
		15/3	24,685	7		aet		Davies 31	Jaaskelain'	Hunt*	Gardner	Diag'-Faye^	Ben Haim	Jaidi	Okocha	Speed"	Nolan	Davies	Giannakop'	Borgetti/Pedersen/Vaz Te
								Ref: R Styles	At 1-1 in extra-time Bolton's Pedersen heads over by inches. Seconds later Harewood clipped in Benayoun's cross for the winner. Earlier when Hunt's clearance went in off the keeper it was the first Cup goal Bolton had conceded. Davies' 25-yard leveller should not have beaten Hislop.											
QF	A	MANCHESTER C		10	W	2-1	1-0	Ashton 41, 69	Hislop	Dailly*	Konchesky	Gabbidon	Collins	Mullins	Benayoun	Reo-Coker^	Harewood	Ashton"	Etherington	Scaloni/Fletcher/Zamora
		20/3	39,357	11				Musampa 85	James	Richards	Jordan*	Dunne	Distin	Barton^	Jihai !	Musampa	Wr-Phillips"	Vassell	Riera	Sommeil/Ireland/Croft
								Ref: H Webb	Five days after beating Bolton, West Ham triumph at Eastlands on a bitter night. Ashton's quick feet carved out a classic first goal. Sun Jihai's red card on 55 minutes for 'slapping' Etherington looked harsh. With Dailly writhing on the turf, West Ham burst upfield for Ashton's second.											
SF	N	MIDDLESBROUGH		7	W	1-0	0-0	Harewood 78	Hislop	Ferdinand	Konchesky	Gabbidon	Collins	Mullins	Benayoun	Reo-Coker	Harewood	Ashton*	Ethering'n^	Zamora/Newton
		23/4	39,148	14					Schwarz'r*	Parnaby	Queudrue	Boeteng	Riggott	Southgate	Taylor^	Roch'back"	Hasselbaink	Yakubu	Downing	Jones/Maccarone/Parlour
		(at Villa Park)						Ref: M Riley	Lucky West Ham avoid Chelsea (1st) and Liverpool (3rd). John Lyall's death saw a minute's silence. Boro – this was their 24th cup-tie of the season – edged the first half but couldn't score. Ashton broke Schwarzer's cheek in the first half and nodded down to Harewood in the second.											
F	N	LIVERPOOL		9	L	3-3	2-1	Carragh' 21(og), Ashton 28, Konch' 64	Hislop	Scaloni	Konchesky	Gabbidon	Ferdinand	Fletcher*	Benayoun	Reo-Coker	Harewood	Ashton^	Ethering'n"	Dailly/Zamora/Sheringham
		13/5	74,000	3				Cisse 32, Gerrard 54, 90	Reina	Finnan	Riise	XabiAlonso*	Carragher	Hyppia	Sissoko	Gerrard	Crouch^	Cisse	Kewell"	Kromk'/Hamman/Morientes
		(at Millennium Stadium, Cardiff)						Ref: A Wiley (Hammers lose 1-3 on penalties)	West Ham score two freak goals, Gerrard hits two belters, and it adds up to a classic final. In injury-time Scaloni's weak clearance at last fell to Gerrard who blasts home from 35 yards. Zamora, Konchesky, and Ferdinand's penalties are saved. Only Sheringham nets. Hyppia also missed.											

		Home					Away					
	P	W	D	L	F	A	W	D	L	F	A	Pts
1 Chelsea	38	18	1	0	47	9	11	3	5	25	13	91
2 Manchester U	38	13	5	1	37	8	12	3	4	35	26	83
3 Liverpool	38	15	3	1	32	8	10	4	5	25	17	82
4 Arsenal	38	14	3	2	48	13	6	4	9	20	18	67
5 Tottenham	38	12	5	2	31	16	6	6	7	22	22	65
6 Blackburn	38	13	3	3	31	17	6	3	10	20	25	63
7 Newcastle	38	11	5	3	28	15	6	2	11	19	27	58
8 Bolton	38	11	5	3	29	13	4	6	9	20	28	56
9 WEST HAM	38	9	3	7	30	25	7	4	8	22	30	55
10 Wigan	38	7	3	9	24	26	8	3	8	21	26	51
11 Everton	38	8	4	7	22	22	6	4	9	12	27	50
12 Fulham	38	13	2	4	31	21	1	4	14	17	37	48
13 Charlton	38	8	4	7	22	21	5	4	10	19	34	47
14 Middlesbro'	38	7	5	7	28	30	5	4	10	20	28	45
15 Manchester C	38	9	2	8	26	20	4	2	13	17	28	43
16 Aston Villa	38	6	6	7	20	20	4	6	9	22	35	42
17 Portsmouth	38	5	7	7	17	24	5	1	13	20	38	38
18 Birmingham	38	6	5	8	19	20	2	5	12	9	30	34
19 West Brom	38	6	2	11	21	24	1	7	11	10	34	30
20 Sunderland	38	1	4	14	12	37	2	2	15	14	32	15
	760	192	77	111	555	389	111	77	192	389	555	1063

Odds & ends

Double wins: (4) Aston Villa, Fulham, West Brom, Birmingham.
Double losses: (4) Bolton, Chelsea, Manchester U, Liverpool.

Won from behind: (4) Blackburn (h), Birmingham (a), Everton (a), Aston Villa (a).
Lost from in front: (3) Manchester U (h), Blackburn (a), Chelsea (a).

High spots: Being seconds from winning the FA Cup.
Finishing in the top half when everyone expected a League struggle.
The sixteen goals of Marlon Harewood.
The form of defender Gabbidon and midfielder Benayoun.
High hopes for 2006-07, strangely misplaced.

Low spots: Gerrard's superb equaliser to take the final to extra-time.
Losing four successive home League games from November to January.

Hammer of the Year: Danny Gabbidon.
Ever-presents: (0).
Hat-tricks: (0).
Leading scorer: (16) Marlon Harewood.

	Appearances						Goals			
	Lge	*Sub*	LC	*Sub*	FAC	*Sub*	Lge	LC	FAC	Tot
Aliadiere, Jeremie	**1**	*6*		*1*						
Ashton, Dean	**9**	*2*			5		**3**		3	**6**
Bellion, David	**2**	*6*	1	*1*				1		**1**
Benayoun, Yossi	**30**	*4*			6		**5**			**5**
Bywater, Stephen		*1*								
Carroll, Roy	**19**									
Clarke, Clive	**2**		1							
Collins, James	**13**	*1*	2		3		**2**			**2**
Cohen, Chris			1							
Dailly, Christian	**6**	*16*	2		2	*4*		1		**1**
Ephraim, Hogan				*1*						
Etherington, Matthew	**33**				7		**2**		1	**3**
Ferdinand, Anton	**32**	*1*			5		**2**			**2**
Fletcher, Carl	**6**	*6*		*1*	1	*3*	**1**			**1**
Gabbidon, Daniel	**31**	*1*			7					
Harewood, Marlon	**31**	*6*	2		6	*1*	**14**		2	**16**
Hislop, Shaka	**16**		2		7					
Katan, Yaniv	**2**	*4*				*2*				
Konchesky, Paul	**36**	*1*	1		7		**1**		1	**2**
Mullins, Hayden	**35**		1		6				1	**1**
Newton, Shean	**8**	*18*	1	*1*	1	*1*	**1**			**1**
Noble, Mark	**4**	*1*	1							
Reid, Kyel	**1**	*1*								
Reo-Coker, Nigel	**31**				7		**5**			**5**
Repka, Tomas	**19**		2		1					
Scaloni, Lionel	**13**				3	*1*				
Sheringham, Teddy	**15**	*11*	1		1	*3*	**6**		1	**7**
Stokes, Tony				*1*						
Walker, James	**3**									
Ward, Elliott	**3**	*1*	2							
Williams, Gavin			1							
Zamora, Bobby	**17**	*17*	1		2	*5*	**6**	2	2	**10**
(own-goals)							**4**		3	**7**
(32 players used)	**418**	***104***	**22**	***6***	**77**	***20***	**52**	**4**	**14**	**70**

No Date	Att	Pos	Pt	F-A	H-T	Scorers, Times, and Referees	SQUAD	NUMBERS	IN	USE								subs used
1 H CHARLTON			W	3-1	0-1	Zamora 52, 66, Cole 90	Carroll	**Mears***	Konchesky	Ferdinand	Gabbidon	Mullins	Reo-Coker	Bowyer	Benayoun	Harewood"	Zamora^	**Paintsil**/Sheringh'm/**Cole**
19/8	34,937		3			*Bent D 15p*	*Carson*	*Young*	*El Karkouri*	*Hreidarsson*	*Traore !*	*Ambrose**	*Holland*	*Faye*	*Hughes^*	*Hasselb'nk"*	*Bent D*	*Sorondo/Reid/Bent M*
						Ref: H Webb	Three years after his previous incarnation as a Hammer, Lee Bowyer took the eye, hit a post, made goals for Zamora and Cole, and was pivotal to the 27th-minute expulsion of Traore – for blocking a free-kick. Gabbidon's handball cost a penalty but Charlton boss Dowie wanted him off.											
2 A WATFORD		1	D	1-1	0-0	Zamora 64	Carroll	Paintsil	Konchesky	Ferdinand	Gabbidon*	Mullins	Reo-Coker	Bowyer	Collins	Harewood^	Zamora"	Benayoun/Shering'm/Cole
22/8	*18,344*	*13*	4			*King 62*	*Foster*	*Doyley*	*DeMerit*	*Shittu*	*Powell*	*Francis**	*Mahon*	*Bouazza^*	*Young*	*King*	*Henderson*	*Spring/Preskin*
						Ref: M Atkinson	A Tuesday point takes West Ham top! Little do they know! Watford were streets better, despite Pardew playing with three centre-backs. King hit the post before belting into the top corner from 25 yards. Under the gaze of England's McClaren, Zamora hit his third goal in two games.											
3 A LIVERPOOL		4	L	1-2	1-2	Zamora 12	Carroll	Paintsil	Konchesky^	Ferdinand	Gabbidon	Mullins	Reo-Coker"	Bowyer	Benayoun	Harewood*	Zamora	Cole/Mears/Sheringham
26/8	*43,965*	*6*	4			*Agger 42, Crouch 45*	*Reina*	*Finnan*	*Hyppia*	*Agger*	*Aurelio*	*Pennant"*	*Xabi Alonso*	*Gerrard*	*LuisGarcia^*	*Bellamy*	*Crouch**	*Kuyt/Gonzales/Zenden*
						Ref: A Wiley	Reo-Coker is linked with Arsenal and Manchester United and his form slips. Reina palms Zamora's cross into his own net, but Agger scores from 30 yards and Crouch rounds Carroll, all before half-time. Gerrard was man of the match and West Ham conceded just six fouls all match.											
4 H ASTON VILLA		8	D	1-1	0-1	Zamora 52	Carroll	Mears	Konchesky	Ferdinand	Gabbidon	Mullins	Reo-Coker	Bowyer^	Benayoun	Harewood*	Zamora"	**Tevez**/Etherington/Cole
10/9	34,576	*5*	5			*Ridgewell 4*	*Sorensen*	*Barry*	*Laursen*	*Mellberg*	*Ridgewell*	*Petrov*	*McCann*	*Davis*	*Moore*	*Agbonlahor*	*Angel**	*Baros*
						Ref: S Bennett	For the third match out of four, Hammers come from behind to salvage something. Ridgewell pounced after Carroll blocked from Agbonlahor. Angel headed against the bar before Zamora notched his fifth goal of the season, from Konchesky's nod back from a corner. Tevez debuts.											
5 H NEWCASTLE		11	L	0-2	0-0		Carroll	Mears^	Konchesky	Ferdinand	Gabbidon	**Masche'o"**	Reo-Coker	Bowyer	Tevez*	Zamora	Etherington	Harew'd/Mullins/Benay'un
17/9	34,938	*9*	5			*Duff 50, Martins 75*	*Given^*	*Babayaro*	*Carr*	*Ramage*	*Moore*	*Parker*	*Emre"*	*Duff*	*Milner*	*Martins*	*Ameobi**	*Sibierski/Harper/Butt*
						Ref: R Styles	West Ham were booed off, except Tevez and Masch, who had already been subbed! Newcastle get their first away League win and goals since April, and Duff and Martins record their first goals since signing. A triumphant return for Glenn Roeder, but Given hospitalised after collision.											
6 A MANCHESTER C		15	L	0-2	0-0		Carroll	Dailly	Konchesky	Ferdinand*	Gabbidon	Mascher'no	Reo-Coker	Benayoun	Harewood^	Zamora"	Etherington	Mullins/Cole/Tevez
23/9	*41,073*	*12*	5			*Samaras 50, 63*	*Weaver*	*Richards*	*Dunne*	*Distin*	*Jordan*	*Sinclair*	*Barton*	*Hamann*	*Miller^*	*Corradi**	*Samaras"*	*Dickov/Reyna/Ireland*
						Ref: C Foy	Both managers – Pearce and Pardew – are under pressure already. City's £6m Greek international Georgios Samaras settled the match with a volley and a lob. Of West Ham's Argentinian imports, Tevez was on the bench and Mascherano invisible. West Ham had no shots on target!											
7 H READING		16	L	0-1	0-1		Carroll	**Spector**	Konchesky	Gabbidon	Mullins	Reo-Coker"	Dailly	Benayoun	Tevez*	Cole^	Etherington	Shering'/Zamora/Harew'd
1/10	34,872	*7*	5			*Seol 2*	*Hahnemann*	*Ingimars'on*	*De la Cruz*	*Sonko*	*Shorey*	*Sidwell*	*Harper*	*Doyle*	*Lita**	*Convey^*	*Seol"*	*Long/Gunnarsson/Hunt*
						Ref: U Rennie	For once, West Ham can claim they were hard done by, pressing hard after Reading's 78-second goal from a short free-kick 25 yard out. Amid thunder and lightning West Ham hit back. In injury-time Benayoun lobbed Hahnemann but Sidwell, racing back, nodded the ball over the bar.											
8 A PORTSMOUTH		18	L	0-2	0-1		Carroll	Spector	Konchesky	Ferdinand	Gabbidon	Mullins	Reo-Coker	Benayoun"	Shering'm*	Zamora^	Etherington	Harew'd/Cole/Mascher'no
14/10	*20,142*	*4*	5			*Kanu 24, Cole 82*	*James*	*Primus*	*Campbell*	*Johnson*	*Stefanovic*	*Fernandes*	*P Mendes*	*O'Neil*	*Taylor*	*Mwar'w'ri^*	*Kanu**	*Lua-Lua/Cole*
						Ref: G Poll	Redknapp's revitalised Pompey show the value of veteran strikers – Kanu is 30 and Andrew Cole 35. Fratton Park's evacuation siren was tried before kick-off, a good time for Hammers fans to depart, for their team was dire. Pardew replied: 'I didn't think the performance was that bad.'											
9 A TOTTENHAM		19	L	0-1	0-1		**Green**	Paintsil	Konchesky	Ferdinand	Gabbidon	Mullins	Reo-Coker	Benayoun^	Mascher'o*	Harewood"	Zamora	Tevez/Cole/Dailly
22/10	*36,162*	*13*	5			*Mido 45*	*Robinson*	*Dawson*	*King*	*Chimbonda*	*Assou-Ekot'*	*Jenas*	*Huddlest'ne*	*Lennon**	*Davids*	*Mido*	*Defoe^*	*Keane/Ghaly*
						Ref: S Bennett	West Ham's seventh successive defeat without scoring. Runs come no worse than that, but attention falls on ex-Hammer Defoe who allegedly bites Mascherano's arm. Aaron Lennon's first start for two months was instrumental in Spurs' win. Mido flicked the ball up and volleyed in.											
10 H BLACKBURN		16	W	2-1	1-0	Sheringham 21, Mulllins 80	Green	Spector	McCartn'y"	Ferdinand	Gabbidon	Mullins	Reo-Coker	Benayoun^	Shering'm*	Zamora	Etherington	Harewood/Bowyer/Dailly
29/10	33,833	*11*	8			*Bentley 90*	*Friedel*	*Ooijer*	*Neill*	*Khizan'hvili*	*Peter*	*Tugay*	*Bentley*	*McCarthy*	*Roberts**	*Mokoena^*	*Gray"*	*Jeffers/Gallag'r/McEveley*
						Ref: A Wiley	Hammers' first League goal not scored by Zamora or Cole and a first win after eight straight losses. Sheringham, 40, heads his first goal since March. With Tevez injured and Masch an unused sub, West Ham win. Is that a lesson? Mullins bundles in Etherington's corner to settle nerves.											

No		Opponent / Date	Att	Pos	Res / Pts	F-A	H-T	Scorers, Times, and Referees												Subs
11	H	ARSENAL		15	W	1-0	0-0	Harewood 89	Green	Spector	Konchesky	Ferdinand*	Gabbidon	Mullins	Reo-Coker	Bowyer^	Benayoun	Zamora"	Etherington	McCart'y/Shering'/Harew'd
		5/11	34,969	*5*	11				*Lehmann*	*Toure*	*Gallas*	*Hoyte"*	*Fabregas*	*Gilberto*	*Rosicky*	*Clichy*	*Hleb^*	*Henry*	*Van Persie**	*Adebayor/Eboue/Flamini*
								Ref: R Styles	Only two Gunners shots on target. West Ham's first clean sheet. Van Persie spent the game winding up the Hammers and was struck by a coin. Etherington's cross was fired in by Harewood, who removed his shirt and was booked. Pardew and Wenger get physical in the technical areas.											
12	A	MIDDLESBROUGH		16	L	0-1	0-0		Green	Spector	Konchesky	Collins	Gabbidon	Mullins	Reo-Coker	Benayoun^	Sheringham	Harewood*	Etherington	Tevez/Cole
		11/11	*25,898*	*13*	11			*Maccarone 74*	*Schwarzer*	*Woodgate*	*Pogatetz*	*Davies*	*Taylor*	*Cattermole*	*Boateng*	*Rochemb'k**	*Morrison*	*Aiyegbeni*	*Downing^*	*Maccarone/Huth*
								Ref: M Halsey	Gareth Southgate is three months in charge of Boro. When a player at Palace he once cleaned Pardew's boots. This game was pretty negative before Maccarone came on and fired the winner from a tight angle. Reo-Coker had a stinker, and West Ham only came to life with Tevez on.											
13	A	CHELSEA		16	L	0-1	0-1		Green	Spector	Konchesky	Ferdinand	Gabbidon	Mullins	Reo-Coker	Bowyer"	Tevez	Zamora*	Ethering'n^	Harew'd/McCart'y/Shering'
		18/11	*41,916*	*2*	11			*Geremi 22*	*Cudicini*	*Carvalho**	*Terry*	*Geremi*	*Makelele*	*Cole A*	*Essien*	*Lampard*	*Shevch'ko^*	*Drogba*	*Robben"*	*Boulahrouz/Cole J/Mikel*
								Ref: M Dean	Chelsea are second behind Man U and will stay there. They beat West Ham – through Geremi's curled free-kick – without ever getting out of second gear. Hammers played with one up front and created not a single shot on target. Mascherano couldn't even get a place on the bench.											
14	H	SHEFFIELD UTD		15	W	1-0	1-0	Mullins 36	Green	Spector	Konchesky	Ferdinand	Gabbidon*	Mullins	Reo-Coker	Bowyer	Tevez^	Zamora"	Etherington	McCart'y/Shering'/Harew'd
		25/11	34,454	*18*	14				*Kenny*	*Jagielka*	*Davis*	*Geary*	*Montgom'y^*	*Leigertwo'd*	*Kozluk*	*Gillespie"*	*Quinn**	*Law*	*Hulse*	*Nade/Kabba/Kazim Rich's*
								Ref: M Riley	West Ham have a new owner, the Egg Man. Tevez gets subbed, storms out of the ground and Pardew can't wait to be rid of his two Argentines. Mullins is keeping Mascherano out, and he scores neatly from Ferdinand's near-post flick. Kozluk's legit 'equaliser' was harshly disallowed.											
15	A	EVERTON		17	L	0-2	0-0		Green	Spector"	Konchesky	Ferdinand	Collins	Mullins	Reo-Coker	Bowyer^	Tevez	Zamora*	Etherington	Shering'/Harew'd/Masch'
		3/12	*32,968*	*7*	14			*Osman 51, Vaughan 90*	*Howard*	*Stubbs*	*Lescott*	*Yobo*	*Carsley*	*Osman^*	*Valente*	*V d Meyde**	*Beattie"*	*Johnson*	*McFadden*	*Vaughan/Weir/Hughes*
								Ref: M Atkinson	West Ham forced ten first-half corners but never threatened from any of them. Everton's on-loan keeper Tim Howard saved from Bowyer and Tevez, but Everton were spluttering until Leon Osman chested down and fired home for his first goal of the season on his 100th appearance.											
16	H	WIGAN		18	L	0-2	0-0		Green	Spector	Konchesky	Ferdinand*	Collins	Mullins	Reo-Coker	Benayoun^	Tevez	Harewood	Ethering'n"	McCart'y/Shering'/Bowyer
		6/12	**33,805**	*11*	14			*Cottrill 51, Spector 58 (og)*	*Kirkland*	*Wright*	*Hall*	*Boyce*	*Baines*	*Cottrill^*	*Scharner*	*Skoko**	*Kilbane*	*Heskey*	*McCulloch*	*Landzaat/Camara*
								Ref: A Wiley	The Icemen are introduced to Upton Park. Wigan hit the post in the first minute, and Tevez did the same just after half-time. Then Cottrill cuts inside to drive into the far corner, whereupon Spector diverts Baines' shot past Green. Scharner nodded in a third but was harshly ruled offside.											
17	A	BOLTON		18	L	0-4	0-1		Green	Spector^	Konchesky	McCartney	Collins	Mullins	Reo-Coker	Dailly	Tevez*	Harewood	Etherington	Sheringham/Paintsil
		9/12	*22,283*	*5*	14			*Davies 17, 52, Diouf 77, Anelka 78*	*Jasskelain'*	*Meite*	*Faye*	*Hunt*	*Campo*	*Pedersen*	*Diouf**	*Nolan*	*Speed"*	*Davies^*	*Anelka*	*Tal/Vaz Te/Gardner*
								Ref: H Webb	West Ham's 10th successive away defeat, eight in the League. Egg Man slides lower in his seat as the goals fly in. Ferdinand and Gabbidon were missing and Bolton capitalised for their second win in eight. Davies scored twice from close in. Gary Speed's 500th Premiership game.											
18	H	MANCHESTER U		18	W	1-0	0-0	Reo-Coker 75	Green	Spector	Konchesky	Ferdinand	Collins	Mullins^	Reo-Coker	Bowyer	Harewood	Zamora*	Ethering'n"	Shering'/Benay'/McCart'y
		17/12	34,966	*1*	17				*Van der Sar*	*Neville*	*Ferdinand*	*Vidic*	*Heinze"*	*Ronaldo*	*Carrick^*	*Scholes*	*Giggs**	*Rooney*	*Saha*	*Solskjaer/O'Shea/Park*
								Ref: P Dowd	Curbs takes over and sees Man U have 9 shots on target; Hammers 2. Reo-Coker's conversion of Harewood's cut-back proved decisive. That Green was man of the match speaks volumes. Curbs never beat Man U in 15 years as Charlton's boss. He starts by leaving Tevez on the bench.											
19	A	FULHAM		18	D	0-0	0-0		Green	Spector	Konchesky!	Ferdinand	Dailly	Mullins	Reo-Coker	Bowyer*	Harewood"	Zamora^	Etherington	Benay'n/Shering'/McCart'y
		23/12	*22,452*	*12*	18				*Niemi*	*Rosenior*	*Bocanegra*	*Christanval*	*Queudrue*	*Radzinski*	*Brown*	*Volz*	*Routledge*	*Helguson*	*McBride*	
								Ref: C Foy	On 85 minutes Konchesky was sent off for a foul on Routledge. Hammers end a run of ten away winless games but extend their away run in the Premiership without a goal to 13 hours. They hit the wood twice: Etherington's header scraped the bar, Harewood volleyed against a post.											
20	H	PORTSMOUTH		18	L	1-2	0-2	Sheringham 81	Green	Spector"	Konchesky	Ferdinand	Gabbidon	Mullins	Reo-Coker	Benayoun	Harewood*	Zamora	Ethering'n^	Sheringham/Tevez/Dailly
		26/12	34,913	*5*	18			*Primus 17, 38*	*James*	*Johnson*	*Primus*	*Campbell*	*Pamarot*	*O'Neil*	*Davis*	*Fernandes*	*P Mendes*	*Taylor*	*Kanu**	*Cole*
								Ref: M Atkinson	Linvoy Primus's last goal was also on Boxing Day – at Palace two years earlier. His two first-half headers sank West Ham. Curbs had released him 12 years earlier from Charlton. David James was untroubled until he parried Campbell's miscued clearance and Sheringham chipped in.											
21	H	MANCHESTER C		18	L	0-1	0-0		Green	Spector	Dailly	Ferdinand	Gabbidon"	Mullins	Bowyer	Benayoun	Shering'm"	Harewood	Ethering'n*	Tevez/Cole/Mears
		30/12	34,574	*10*	18			*Beasley 83*	*Weaver*	*Onuoha*	*Dunne*	*Distin*	*Jordan*	*Trabelsi*	*Ireland**	*Dabo*	*Richards*	*Vassell"*	*Corradi^*	*Beasley/Samaras/Miller*
								Ref: S Bennett	The last time City won at Upton Park, in 1991, Hammers went down. The fans called for sub Tevez to come on, Curbs bowed and Tevez bull-dozed into the City defence. But it was Stuart Pearce's American sub DeMarcus Beasley who barged past Ferdinand and Spector to hammer in.											

No	Date		Att	Pos	Pt	F-A	H-T	Scorers, Times, and Referees	SQUAD	NUMBERS	IN	USE								subs used
22	A	READING		18	L	**0-6**	0-4	[Doyle 36, 78, Lita 53]	Green	Dailly	Konchesky	Ferdinand	Gabbidon	Mullins	Reo-Coker	Bowyer*	Benayoun"	Harewood^	Zamora	Newton/Spector/Cole
	1/1		24,073	9	18			Gun'son 12, Hunt 15, Ferdinand 30(og),	Hahnemann	Ingimars'on	Sonko*	Shorey	Hunt	Gunnarsson	Sidwell	Little^	Harper"	Doyle	Lita	Bikey/Oster/Seol
								Ref: L Mason	A 0-4 loss at Bolton put paid to Pardew, so what now, after Reading's first win in six? Headers by Gunnarsson and Hunt – his first goal in the Premiership – opened the floodgates. Curbs aims for containment after half-time, and then lambasts the Baby-Bentley culture of his players.											
23	H	FULHAM		18	D	3-3	1-1	Zamora 28, Benayoun 46, 64	Carroll	Dailly	McCartney	Collins*	Gabbidon"	**Quashie**	Reo-Coker	Benayoun	Tevez^	Cole	**Boa Morte**	Spector/Zamora !/Newton
	13/1		**34,977**	13	19			Radz'ski 26, McBride 59, Christ'val 90	Lastuvka	Christianval	Bocanegra	Rosenior	Volz	Brown	Queudrue	Routledge	McBride	Helguson*	Radzinski	Montella
								Ref: G Poll	West Ham have two players sent off this season, both against Fulham – sub Zamora stupidly so. Tevez went off with a calf strain. Benayoun's lovely chip to make it 2-1 suggested it was West Ham's day but Christianval's late goal was his first since with Barcelona five years earlier.											
24	A	NEWCASTLE		18	D	2-2	2-1	Cole 18, Harewood 22	Carroll	Dailly	McCartney	Ferdinand^	**Davenport**	Quashie	Reo-Coker	Benayoun	Boa Morte	Cole*	Harewood	Etherington/Spector
	20/1		52,095	12	20			Milner 45, Solano 53p	Given^	Solano	Ramage*	Huntington	Carr	Milner	Parker	Butt	O'Brien	Dyer	Martins	Edgar/Harper
								Ref: U Rennie	Newcastle have just lost 1-5 at home to Championship Birmingham in the FA Cup. Cole's goal was West Ham's first in the Premiership away from home for 905 minutes. Newcastle's first should have been disallowed as Parker stood in front of Carroll. Boa Morte needlessly handled.											
25	H	LIVERPOOL		18	L	1-2	0-0	Blanco 77	Carroll	Spector	McCartney	Dailly	Davenport	Quashie	Reo-Coker	Benayoun	Boa Morte	Cole*	Harewood^	Zamora/**Blanco**
	30/1		34,966	3	20			Kuyt 46, Crouch 53	Reina	Carragher	Hyppia	Agger	Finnan	Gerrard	Alonso	Riise	Crouch*	Bellamy^	Kuyt"	Pennant/Gonzales/Fowler
								Ref: M Atkinson	Kepa Blanco's goal on his debut gave him something to cheer. The crowd sang 'We want our money back'. Liverpool sign Mascherano, who will play in the Champions League final but could not make the bench for West Ham. Kuyt netted from 25 yards, Crouch swept in from 16 yds.											
26	A	ASTON VILLA		18	L	0-1	0-1		Carroll	Spector	McCartney	**Upson***	Davenport	Quashie	Reo-Coker	Benayoun	Boa Morte"	Blanco^	Zamora	Dailly/Harew'd/Ethering'n
	3/2		41,202	13	20			Carew 36	Sorensen	Mellberg	Cahill	Bardsley	Petrov	McCann	Bouma	Agbonlahor	Barry	Carew*	Young^	Berger/Ridgewell
								Ref: C Foy	Martin O'Neill's Villa have been on the slide, but he bought Watford's Ashley Young, who rejected West Ham, and now torments them by playing a one-two for Carew's winning goal. Not until the dying seconds did West Ham threaten, when Davenport and Etherington went close.											
27	H	WATFORD		18	L	0-1	0-1		Green	**Neill***	McCartney	Ferdinand	Davenport	Quashie"	Reo-Coker	Benayoun	Harewood	Zamora^	Etherington	Spector/Tevez/Boa Morte
	10/2		34,625	20	20			Henderson 12p	Foster	DeMerit	Mackay	Mariappa	Mahon	Francis	Stewart	Smith	Cavalli*	Henderson"	Kabba^	Bangura/Ashikodi/Shittu
								Ref: A Wiley	Doomed Watford have won only twice away all season – Upton Park in League and Cup. Lucas Neill limped off after 32 minutes of his debut. Henderson was shoved by Ferdinand and netted his first goal in 29 games. Harewood missed from the spot after Mahon fouled Reo-Coker.											
28	A	CHARLTON		19	L	0-4	0-3	[Bent D 41]	Green	Dailly	Konchesky	Ferdinand	Davenport	Quashie	Mullins"	Benayoun	Tevez	Cole^	Ethering'n*	Harewood/Blanco/Newton
	24/2		27,111	18	20			Ambrose 24, Thomas 34, 80,	Carson	El Karkouri	Diawara	Young	Thatcher	Ambrose	Holland	Song"	Thomas	Bent M*	Bent D^	Hasselbaink/Zheng/Faye
								Ref: R Styles	The two 'Alans' have swapped clubs, and Pardew's Addicks thrash Curbs' Hammers. The Valley chants 'thank you for Pardew', and there is talk of Curbs throwing in the towel. Ambrose volleyed the first, Davenport backed off to allow Thomas the second, and then West Ham folded.											
29	H	TOTTENHAM		20	L	3-4	2-0	Noble 16, Tevez 41, Zamora 85	Green	Neill	Konchesky	Ferdinand	Upson*	Quashie^	Noble	Bowyer	Tevez	Harewood	Ethering'n"	Davenport/Blanco/Zamora
	4/3		34,966	8	20			Def' 51p, Tain' 63, Berb'v 89, Stalt' 90	Robinson	Dawson	Gardner	Chimb'nda"	Lee Y'g-pyo	Jenas^	Tainio	Ghaly*	Defoe	Berbatov	Lennon	Hudd'stone/Stalteri/Taarabt
								Ref: M Dean	West Ham go bottom, yet Noble's half-volley and Tevez's free-kick – his first goal – had put them in charge. Then Bowyer hacked Lennon and all changed. Sub Zamora headed in, 3-2, but Berbatov replied with a free-kick, and Stalteri followed up after Defoe's shot was blocked.											
30	A	BLACKBURN		19	W	2-1	0-0	Tevez 71p, Zamora 75	Green	Neill	McCartney	Ferdinand	Collins	Noble*	Reo-Coker	Bowyer	Tevez"	Harewood^	Etherington	Mullins/Zamora/Boa Morte
	17/3		18,591	10	23			Samba 47	Friedel	Samba	Khizanishv'i	Emerton	Tugay^	Warnock	Bentley	Dunn	Pedersen	McCarthy	Derbyshire*	Roberts/Peter
								Ref: H Webb	The revival starts with a joke penalty and a phantom goal. Samba's header looked to send Hammers to another loss. Emerton 'fouled' Tevez in the box. Tevez accidentally cleared Zamora's poke off the line, but the linesman said the ball was over. Off the bottom with a first away win.											
31	H	MIDDLESBROUGH		19	W	2-0	2-0	Zamora 2, Tevez 45	Green	Neill	McCartney	Ferdinand	Collins	Noble	Reo-Coker*	Bowyer	Tevez"	Zamora^	Etherington	Mullins/Blanco/Boa Morte
	31/3		**34,977**	12	26				Schwarzer	Woodgate	Pogatetz^	Xavier	Boateng	Rochemb'k"	Taylor	Parnaby*	Viduka	Ayegbeni	Downing	Johnson/Huth/Euell
								Ref: M Halsey	Tevez failed to score in his first 19 Hammers outings, but it is three in three games now, netting after Taylor pushed the ball into his path six yards out. Earlier his cross had deflected into the path of Zamora. Southgate's Boro looked resigned to defeat from the first minute to the last.											

No		Opponent	Att	Pos	Res	F-A	H-T	Scorers, Times, and Referees	1	2	3	4	5	6	7	8	9	10	11	subs used
32	A	ARSENAL		19	W	1-0	1-0	Zamora 45	Green	Neill	McCartn'y*	Ferdinand	Collins	Noble	Reo-Coker	Bowyer	Tevez"	Zamora^	Etherington	Spector/Boa Morte/Blanco
	7/4		*60,098*	*4*	29				*Lehmann*	*Eboue*	*Toure*	*Gallas*	*Clichy*	*Rosicky*	*Febregas*	*Gilberto"*	*Hleb**	*Ljungberg^*	*Adebayor*	*Aliadiere/Baptista/Diaby*
								Ref: G Poll	Revival? Hammers were lucky at Rovers and Fortress Emirates. Arsenal peppered 25 shots at Green's goal and forced 14 corners against one. Fed by Neill, Zamora chipped Lehmann on half-time. Fabregas hit the bar, Gilberto the post. 'We should have scored ten,' moaned Wenger.											
33	A	SHEFFIELD UTD		19	L	0-3	0-1		Green	Neill	McCartney	Ferdinand	Collins	Noble"	Reo-Coker*	Bowyer	Tevez	Zamora	Ethering'n^	Mullins/Boa Morte/Blanco
	14/4		*31,593*	*17*	29			*Tonge 39, Jagielka 68, Stead 78*	*Kenny*	*Jagielka*	*Davis**	*Geary*	*Montgom'y*	*Tonge*	*Armstrong*	*Gillespie*	*Nade^*	*Stead*	*Kazim-R"*	*Morgan/Quinn/Webber*
								Ref: S Bennett	A six-pointer which goes Warnock's way. Curbs banned his players from talking to the media afterwards. Not surprising, as they were woeful. Man-of-the match Tonge belted in a 20-yard free-kick. Jagielka headed the second, and Stead settled it with a good run and shot. Chelsea next.											
34	H	CHELSEA		19	L	1-4	1-2	Tevez 35 *[Drogba 62]*	Green	Neill	McCartney	Spector	Collins	Noble	Reo-Coker^	Boa Morte	Tevez"	Zamora*	Benayoun	Cole/Mullins/Blanco
	18/4		34,966	*2*	29			*Wright-Phillips 31, 36, Kalou 52,*	*Cech*	*Diarra**	*Carvalho*	*Terry*	*Bridge*	*Essien*	*Wr-Phillips*	*Lampard"*	*Mikel*	*Drogba^*	*Kalou*	*Ferreira/Cole J/Ballack*
								Ref: M Dean	Shaun Wright-Phillips hadn't scored for Chelsea in two years before his slalom run, followed by an athletic volley. In between came Tevez's fabulous strike, the first Premiership goal Cech had conceded for 13 hours, 46 minutes. Wright-Phillips also broke Ashton's foot pre-season.											
35	H	EVERTON		19	W	1-0	1-0	Zamora 13	Green	Neill	McCartney	Ferdinand	Collins	Noble	Reo-Coker	Benayoun	Tevez	Zamora*	Ethering'n^	Cole/Boa Morte
	21/4		34,945	*5*	32				*Howard*	*Yobo*	*Stubbs*	*Hibbert*	*Neville^*	*Carsley*	*Lescott*	*Osman*	*Johnson**	*Beattie*	*Arteta*	*McFadden/Fernandes*
								Ref: M Clattenburg	Andrew Johnson soon hobbled off with an ankle injury. Zamora had missed training because of tendonitis in a knee, but his curling left-footer inflicted Moyes' Everton's first defeat in eight, although six minutes stoppage time was almost unbearable. Fears of points-deductions loom.											
36	A	WIGAN		18	W	**3-0**	1-0	Boa Morte 30, Benayoun 57 [Harewood 82]	Green	Neill	McCartney	Ferdinand	Collins	Noble	Reo-Coker"	Benayoun	Tevez^	Zamora*	Boa Morte	Harew'd/Spector/Mullins
	28/4		*24,726*	*17*	35				*Filan*	*Boyce*	*Jackson*	*De Zeeuw**	*Baines*	*Kilbane"*	*Landzaat^*	*Skoko*	*McCulloch*	*Heskey*	*Camara*	*Unsw'th/Scharner/Ag'howa*
								Ref: G Poll	At last the Great Escape looks possible. 24 hours previously West Ham were find £5.5 million but not deducted points for covering up Tevez and Mascherano's contracts. Filan dashed from his goal-line to allow Boa Morte to lift the ball over him. Green hardly had a shot to save.											
37	H	BOLTON		17	W	3-1	3-0	Tevez 10, 21, Noble 29	Green	Neill	McCartney	Ferdinand	Collins	Noble	Reo-Coker"	Benayoun	Tevez	Zamora*	Boa Morte^	Harew'd/Spector/Mullins
	5/5		34,404	*6*	38			*Speed 67*	*Jaaskelain'*	*Campo*	*Meite*	*Michalik*	*Gardner"*	*Thompson**	*Speed*	*Teymou'n^*	*Nolan*	*Davies*	*Anelka*	*Sinclair/Vaz Te/Giannak's*
								Ref: M Riley	San Allardyce stuns Bolton by quitting. Sammy Lee takes over, so this is the perfect time to play them. Tevez has won the Hammer of the Year vote with 84% of the vote. He bends in a free-kick for the first, slides in the second from Boa Morte's cross, then watched Noble's hard volley.											
38	A	MANCHESTER U		15	W	1-0	1-0	Tevez 45	Green	Neill	McCartn'y*	Ferdinand	Collins	Noble	Reo-Coker	Benayoun	Tevez"	Zamora^	Boa Morte	Spector/Harew'd/Mullins
	13/5		**75,927**	*1*	41				*Van der Sar*	*O'Shea*	*Brown*	*Heinze*	*Evra**	*Solskjaer*	*Carrick^*	*Fletcher*	*Richardson*	*Rooney*	*Smith"*	*Giggs/Scholes/Ronaldo*
		Home	Away					Ref: M Atkinson	More good luck, for Man U are already champions and Ferguson rests key players for the Cup final. Wes Brown's half-hearted challenge lets Tevez finish from an angle. West Ham have beaten Arsenal and Man U twice. The Egg Man hugs everyone within reach in the directors box.											
Average		34,716	34,769																	

UEFA CUP			Att			F-A	H-T	Scorers, Times, and Referees	SQUAD	NUMBERS	IN	USE								subs used
1:1	H	PALERMO (Italy)		8	L	0-1	0-1		Carroll	Mears	Konchesky	Ferdinand	Gabbidon	Mascher'no	Reo-Coker	Bowyer*	Benayoun	Tevez"	Zamora^	Etherington/Cole/Harew'd
	14/9		32,222					*Caracciolo 45*	*Fontana*	*Cassani*	*Zaccardo*	*Barzagli*	*Pisano*	*Diana*	*Simplicio*	*Parravicini**	*Bresciano"*	*Di Michele^*	*Caracciolo*	*Guana/Capuano/Biava*
								Ref: S Johannesson (Sweden)	Back in Europe, but not for long, after Caracciolo nicks a vital away goal from Diana's cross. Palermo get their first booking after 54 seconds, after Cassini chopped Tevez. Harewood, dropped for Tevez, comes off the bench to hit a post. Both Argentines start the game – a distraction.											
1:2	A	PALERMO		15	L	0-3	0-1		Carroll	Spector	Konchesky	Collins	Gabbidon	Masch'no^	Reo-Coker	Bowyer	Tevez	Cole*	Harewood"	Zamora/Benay'n/Shering'
	28/9		*19,284*					*Simplicio 35 , 62, Di Michele 68*	*Fontana*	*Cassani*	*Zaccardo*	*Barzagli*	*Pisano*	*Diana"*	*Simplicio*	*Corini**	*Bresciano*	*Di Michele^*	*Caracciolo*	*Guana/Brienza/Dellafiore*
								Ref: G Kasnaferis (Greece) (Hammers lose 0-4 on aggregate)	Pardew drops Benayoun and leading scorer Zamora. Simplicio hit the first from a quickly taken free-kick, and any chances West Ham had of salvaging the tie disappeared when Cole headed against a post and injured himself. Trouble with Hammers fans in Palermo before the game.											

Carling Cup																				
3	A	CHESTERFIELD		19	L	1-2	1-0	Harewood 4	Green	Paintsil	McCartn'y"	Ferdinand	Gabbidon	Mullins	Reo-Coker	Reid^	Dailly	Harewood*	Zamora	Shering'/Ethering'/Konch'
	24/10		*7,787 1:15*					*Larkin 50, Folan 87*	*Roche*	*Bailey**	*Hazell*	*Downes*	*O'Hare*	*Hall*	*Niven*	*Allott*	*Hurst*	*Larkin^*	*Folan*	*Lowry/Allison*
								Ref: L Probert	Roy MacFarland's Spireites had already accounted for Manchester City. Harewood's half-volley was West Ham's first goal in 672 minutes but it was cancelled out after Green turned Folan's shot against a post. Zamora's late miss proved expensive when Folan was first to a loose ball.											

FA Cup																				
3	H	BRIGHTON		18	W	3-0	0-0	Noble 49, Cole 58 Mullins 90	Carroll	Dailly	McCartney	Ferdinand*	Gabbidon	Mullins	Noble	Boa Morte"	Benayoun	Cole^	Tevez	Spector/Zamora/Newton
	6/1		32,874 *1:15*						*Henderson*	*O'Cearuill*	*Lynch*	*Butters*	*Mayo*	*Fraser**	*El-Abd*	*Hammond*	*Frutos^*	*Revell"*	*Robinson*	*Hart/Rents/Gatting*
								Ref: M Halsey	Following the 0-6 crash at Reading, Curbs makes six changes, including dropping the ever-present Reo-Coker. Boa Morte's crosses led to two welcome goals, though Fraser and Revell missed chances for Brighton. Curbs rails against journalists afterwards and refuses to take questions.											
4	H	WATFORD		18	L	0-1	0-1		Carroll	Neill*	Spector	Dailly	McCartney	Newton^	Reo-Coker	Quashie	Boa Morte"	Zamora	Cole	Paintsil/Shering'/Ethering'n
	27/1		31,168 *20*					*McNamee 42*	*Foster*	*Mariappa*	*Mackay*	*DeMerit*	*Stewart*	*McNamee**	*Bangura*	*Francis*	*Bouazza*	*Smith*	*Henderson*	*Powell*
								Ref: H Webb	The Cup final last year, dumped at home by the bottom club this year. McNamee's hook shot, coupled with Carroll's error, was enough. This was almost an entirely different side from that fielded by Pardew in his last game at Bolton, but Curbs looks rudderless and on borrowed time.											

		Home					Away					
	P	W	D	L	F	A	W	D	L	F	A	Pts
1 Manchester U	38	15	2	2	46	12	13	3	3	37	15	89
2 Chelsea	38	12	7	0	37	11	12	4	3	27	13	83
3 Liverpool	38	14	4	1	39	7	6	4	9	18	20	68
4 Arsenal	38	12	6	1	43	16	7	5	7	20	19	68
5 Tottenham	38	12	3	4	34	22	5	6	8	23	32	60
6 Everton	38	11	4	4	33	17	4	9	6	19	19	58
7 Bolton	38	9	5	5	26	20	7	3	9	21	32	56
8 Reading	38	11	2	6	29	20	5	5	9	23	27	55
9 Portsmouth	38	11	5	3	28	15	3	7	9	17	27	54
10 Blackburn	38	9	3	7	31	25	6	4	9	21	29	52
11 Aston Villa	38	7	8	4	20	14	4	9	6	23	27	50
12 Middlesbro'	38	10	3	6	31	24	2	7	10	13	25	46
13 Newcastle	38	7	7	5	23	20	4	3	12	15	27	43
14 Manchester C	38	5	6	8	10	16	6	3	10	19	28	42
15 WEST HAM	38	8	2	9	24	26	4	3	12	11	33	41
16 Fulham	38	7	7	5	18	18	1	8	10	20	42	39
17 Wigan	38	5	4	10	18	30	5	4	10	19	29	38
18 Sheffield Utd	38	7	6	6	24	21	3	2	14	8	34	38
19 Charlton	38	7	5	7	19	20	1	5	13	15	40	34
20 Watford	38	3	9	7	19	25	2	4	13	10	34	28
	760	182	98	100	552	379	100	98	182	379	552	1042

Odds & ends

Double wins: (3) Blackburn, Arsenal, Manchester United.
Double losses: (6) Liverpool, Manchester City, Chelsea, Reading, Portsmouth, Tottenham.

Won from behind: (2) Charlton (h), Blackburn (a).
Lost from in front: (2) Liverpool (h), Tottenham (h).

High spots: Surviving relegation on the last day of the season.
The extraordinary form of chief saviour, Carlos Tevez.
Achieving a League double over Arsenal and Manchester United.
Fantastic luck with referees against Sheffield United and at Blackburn, and playing Bolton with a change of manager and Man U after they had secured the championship.

Low spots: Losing 0-4 at Bolton and 0-6 at Reading.
Elimination by Chesterfield in the League Cup.
Knocked out by Palermo at the first hurdle of the UEFA Cup.
Reaching the FA Cup final last season, but now knocked out at once.
Javier Mascherano is good enough for the Champions League final with Liverpool but can't get a game with West Ham.
(Temporary) loss of form of key players Reo-Coker and Harewood.

No own-goals this season, after seven own-goals in 2005-06.

Hammer of the Year: Carlos Tevez.
Ever-presents: (0).
Hat-tricks: (0).
Leading scorer: (11) Bobby Zamora.

	Appearances							Goals					
	Lge	*Sub*	LC	*Sub*	FAC	*Sub*	Eur	*Sub*	**Lge**	LC	FAC	Eur	**Tot**
Benayoun, Yossi	**25**	*4*			1		1	*1*	**3**				**3**
Blanco, Kepa	**1**	*7*							**1**				**1**
Boa Morte, Luis	**8**	*6*			2				**1**				**1**
Bowyer, Lee	**18**	*2*					2						
Carroll, Roy	**12**				2		2						
Cole, Carlton	**5**	*12*			2		1	*1*	**2**		1		**3**
Collins, James	**16**						1						
Dailly, Christian	**10**	*4*	1		2								
Davenport, Calum	**5**	*1*											
Etherington, Matthew	**24**	*3*		*1*		*1*		*1*					
Ferdinand, Anton	**31**		1		1		1						
Gabbidon, Daniel	**18**		1		1		2						
Green, Robert	**26**		1										
Harewood, Marlon	**19**	*13*	1				1	*1*	**3**	1			**4**
Konchesky, Paul	**22**			*1*			2						
Mascherano, Javier	**3**	*2*					2						
McCartney, George	**16**	*6*	1		2								
Mears, Tyrone	**3**	*2*					1						
Mullins, Hayden	**21**	*9*	1		1				**2**		1		**3**
Neill, Lucas	**11**				1								
Newton, Shaun		*3*			1	*1*							
Noble, Mark	**10**				1				**2**		1		**3**
Paintsil, John	**3**	*2*	1			*1*							
Quashie, Nigel	**7**				1								
Reid, Kyel			1										
Reo-Coker, Nigel	**35**		1		1		2		**1**				**1**
Sheringham, Teddy	**4**	*13*		*1*		*1*		*1*	**2**				**2**
Spector, Jonathan	**17**	*8*			1	*1*	1						
Tevez, Carlos	**19**	*7*			1		2		**7**				**7**
Upson, Matthew	**2**												
Zamora, Bobby	**27**	*5*	1		1	*1*	1	*1*	**11**				**11**
(31 players used)	**418**	***109***	**11**	***3***	**22**	***6***	**22**	***6***	**35**	**1**	**3**		**39**

Some say it is better to win the play-off trophy than the divisional championship
West Ham United 2004-05